Is it in F
2002

A guide to the commencement of statutes
passed since 1st January 1977
(incorporating Statutes Not Yet In Force)

Editors
JULIA GOLDING, LLB
AMANAT ALI YOUSAF, LLB

Revising Editors
ELEANOR HAYMAN, LLB
JOHN SNELL, LLB

Production Editor
GAVIN WILLIAMS, BA

Butterworths
LexisNexis™

Members of the LexisNexis Group worldwide

United Kingdom	LexisNexis Butterworths Tolley, a Division of Reed Elsevier (UK) Ltd, Halsbury House, 35 Chancery Lane, LONDON, WC2A 1EL, and 4 Hill Street, EDINBURGH EH2 3JZ
Argentina	LexisNexis Argentina, BUENOS AIRES
Australia	LexisNexis Butterworths, CHATSWOOD, New South Wales
Austria	LexisNexis Verlag ARD Orac GmbH & Co KG, VIENNA
Canada	LexisNexis Butterworths, MARKHAM, Ontario
Chile	LexisNexis Chile Ltda, SANTIAGO DE CHILE
Czech Republic	Nakladatelství Orac sro, PRAGUE
France	Editions du Juris-Classeur SA, PARIS
Hong Kong	LexisNexis Butterworths, HONG KONG
Hungary	HVG-Orac, BUDAPEST
India	LexisNexis Butterworths, NEW DELHI
Ireland	Butterworths (Ireland) Ltd, DUBLIN
Italy	Giuffrè Editore, MILAN
Malaysia	Malayan Law Journal Sdn Bhd, KUALA LUMPUR
New Zealand	Butterworths of New Zealand, WELLINGTON
Poland	Wydawnictwo Prawnicze LexisNexis, WARSAW
Singapore	LexisNexis Butterworths, SINGAPORE
South Africa	Butterworths SA, DURBAN
Switzerland	Stämpfli Verlag AG, BERNE
USA	LexisNexis, DAYTON, Ohio

A CIP Catalogue record for this book is available from the British Library

ISBN 0 406 947 104

ISBN 0 406 957 10X (Scottish edition)

Printed by The Bath Press, Bath, Avon
Visit Butterworths LexisNexis *direct* at www.butterworths.com

Preface

Is it in Force? contains the information you need to establish the exact commencement dates of Acts of general application in England, Wales and Scotland and General Synod Measures passed between 1 January 1977 and 31 December 2001.

1 What's in *Is it in Force?*

The short title and chapter number of every Act is given, and unless an Act is of limited or local application only, or has been repealed, the following details are provided:

(a) the date on which the Act received the royal assent;

(b) a list of provisions which deal with the commencement of an Act or any part of an Act (including any commencement orders which have been made);

(c) in limited circumstances (see para 2 below), information on whether the commencement of provisions has been superseded by their repeal/substitution etc;

(d) any date or dates which have been appointed for the provisions of the Act to come into force;

(e) an indication where any provision is not in force (and note also para 5 below).

2 How to use *Is it in Force?*

Acts passed during each calendar year are arranged alphabetically, and the years are dealt with in chronological order.

Each Act is dealt with according to its commencement provisions. Thus, an Act is treated as a single unit if the whole Act was brought into force on one date. An Act will only be treated on a section by section or subsection by subsection basis where the complexity of its commencement provisions demands this. It therefore follows that, whereas the repeal of a whole Act will always be noted, *partial* repeals, substitutions etc of many Acts (which are not otherwise broken down into parts) will not.

It should also be noted that saving and transitional provisions, non-textual amendments (eg extensions or applications) and textual amendments *within* sections, subsections etc, are not in general noted to any Act in this book. **For information about repeals, amendments, savings etc, reference should be made to the volumes of Halsbury's Statutes, and to the Cumulative Supplement and the Noter-up to that work**.

Where a provision of an Act applying both to England and Wales and to Scotland is brought into force on the same date by different provisions, it is noted thus:

11 Apr 1983 (SI 1982/1857; SI 1983/24)

Where such a provision is brought into force on different dates, it is noted thus:

1 Jul 1978 (E, W) (SI 1977/2164)
1 Sep 1978 (S) (1978/816)

Where a provision of an Act which applies both to England and Wales and to Scotland is repealed, substituted etc in relation to one jurisdiction only, it is noted thus:

30 Dec 1986 (E, W) (SI 1986/2145)
Repealed (S)

3 Finance Acts

Finance Acts are not dealt with in detail, as the dates from which their provisions take effect are usually stated clearly and unambiguously in the text of the Act, and charging provisions will normally state for which year or years of assessment they are to have effect.

The following information may be of use to readers when considering the effect of taxing provisions in Finance Acts which are expressed to have effect from a date prior to that on which the Act received royal assent:

(a) Income tax and corporation tax are annual taxes which have to be reimposed by Parliament for each year of assessment (Income and Corporation Taxes Act 1988, ss 1, 6).

(b) Under the rules of procedure of the House of Commons a ways and means resolution is a necessary preliminary to the imposition, increase or extension of income tax (but not for its alleviation).

(c) From 1998, the Chancellor of the Exchequer will normally open his budget in March (usually on a Tuesday) and at the conclusion of his speech move a set of ways and means resolutions which embody his proposals.

(d) The Provisional Collection of Taxes Act 1968, s 1, makes provision, subject to certain conditions, for statutory effect to be given to those resolutions in so far as they relate to income tax for a period ending on 5 May in the next calendar year (in the case of a resolution passed in November or December) and for a period ending with 5 August in the same calendar year in the case of a resolution passed in February or March in any year (or at the end of 4 months after the date on which the resolution takes effect if the resolution is passed at any other time).

(e) If statutory effect is lost, or expires without an Act coming into operation to renew or vary the tax, or the provisions in the resolution are modified by the Act renewing or varying the tax, any money paid or overpaid must be repaid or made good (Provisional Collection of Taxes Act 1968, s 1(6), (7)).

(f) It may be desirable that some motions should have immediate effect without waiting for the conclusion of the Budget debate. The House of Commons may therefore resolve that *provisional* statutory effect shall be given to one or more motions which, if passed, would be resolutions to which statutory effect could be given under s 1 of the 1968 Act. Upon the House so resolving, the motions have statutory effect immediately, subject to that motion or a similar motion being agreed to by a confirmatory resolution of the House within the next 10 sitting days; the provisions of s 1 then apply. If not confirmed, the motion is of no effect and any money paid or overpaid must be repaid or made good; there is similar adjustment if the confirmatory resolution differs from the original motion (Provisional Collection of Taxes Act 1968, s 5).

4 General principles governing commencement of statutes

(a) 'Commencement' means the time when the Act comes into force (Interpretation Act 1978, s 5, Sch 1).

(b) Where no provision is made for the coming into force of an Act, it comes into force at the beginning of the day on which it receives the Royal Assent (Interpretation Act 1978, s 4(b)).

(c) Where provision is made for an Act to come into force on a particular day, it comes into force at the beginning of that day (Interpretation Act 1978, s 4(a)).

(d) Where an Act does not come into force immediately on its passing, and it confers power to make subordinate legislation, or to make appointments, give notices, prescribe forms or do any other thing for the purposes of the Act, then, unless the contrary intention appears, the power may be exercised, and any instrument made under it may be made so as to come into force, at any time after the passing of the Act so far as may be necessary or expedient for the purpose of (i) bringing the Act or any provision of the Act into force, or (ii) giving full effect to the Act or any such provision at or after the time when it comes into force (Interpretation Act 1978, s 13).

(e) There is a general presumption that an enactment is not intended to have retrospective effect. Parliament undoubtedly has power to enact with retrospective effect, so the general presumption applies unless the contrary is clearly stated.

5 Statutes Not Yet In Force

Statutes Not Yet In Force lists provisions of Acts, arranged alphabetically, for which no commencement dates have yet been appointed. The list includes provisions prospectively inserted or repealed; orders made under the relevant amending Act bringing those prospective amendments into force will be noted to that Act in the service to this work. It also includes information on whether the commencement of provisions has been superseded by their repeal/substitution etc. To establish the commencement date or dates appointed for the provisions not listed in this part of this book, and for details of any commencement orders, reference should be made to Is it in Force?

Updating and the Is it in Force? Telephone Helpline

Is it in Force? is an annual publication. Each subsequent edition incorporates the most recent year's statutes and in addition deals with new commencement orders, repeals and amendments affecting material already published.

Interim updating is provided for subscribers to Halsbury's Statutes as part of their Service in the form of looseleaf pages filed following the guide card 'Is it in Force?' in the Noter-up Service binder.

Where a provision has not been noted as having been brought into force in either this volume or the current service issue, subscribers to Halsbury's Statutes are invited to call the **Is it in Force?** telephone helpline on **0207 400 2518** or email **hsieb@butterworths.com** for the latest available information.

In addition, the latest information is available online, updated on a daily basis. To see the online version, visit **Legislation Direct** at **www.butterworths.com**.

Queries on the content or scope of this work should be directed to the Publishing Manager, Halsbury's Statutes, at Halsbury House, 35 Chancery Lane, London, WC2A 1EL.

BUTTERWORTHS

This book includes the effect of commencement orders published up to 14 March 2002.

Contents

1977

Administration of Justice Act 1977 (c 38)

RA: 29 Jul 1977

Commencement provisions: s 32(5)–(7); Administration of Justice Act 1977 (Commencement No 1) Order 1977, SI 1977/1405; Administration of Justice Act 1977 (Commencement No 2) Order 1977, SI 1977/1490; Administration of Justice Act 1977 (Commencement No 3) Order 1977, SI 1977/1589; Administration of Justice Act 1977 (Commencement No 4) Order 1977, SI 1977/2202; Administration of Justice Act 1977 (Commencement No 5) Order 1978, SI 1978/810; Administration of Justice Act 1977 (Commencement No 6) Order 1979, SI 1979/972; Administration of Justice Act 1977 (Commencement No 7) Order 1980, SI 1980/1981

Section

1		Spent (E, W)
		Repealed (S)
2		29 Aug 1977 (s 32(5))
3		See Sch 3 below
4, 5		29 Aug 1977 (s 32(5))
6		Repealed
7		29 Aug 1977 (s 32(5))
8–10		Repealed
11		29 Aug 1977 (s 32(5)); prospectively repealed by Administration of Justice Act 1982, s 75, Sch 9, Pt I[1] and spent
12		Spent
13–18		Repealed
19	(1)	Repealed
	(2)	Spent
	(3), (4)	Repealed
	(5)	3 Jul 1978 (SI 1978/810)
20, 21		Repealed
22		29 Aug 1977 (s 32(5))
23		17 Oct 1977 (SI 1977/1589)
24		29 Aug 1977 (s 32(5))
25		Repealed
26		29 Aug 1977 (s 32(5))
27		Repealed
28		15 Sep 1977 (SI 1977/1490)
29		29 Aug 1977 (s 32(5))
30		Repealed
31, 32		29 Jul 1977 (RA)

1

Administration of Justice Act 1977 (c 38)—*contd*

Schedule

1		Repealed
2		29 Aug 1977 (s 32(5))
3, para	1–10	1 Jan 1981 (SI 1980/1981)
	11, 12	1 Sep 1977 (SI 1977/1405)
4		17 Oct 1977 (SI 1977/1589)
5, Pt	I–IV	29 Aug 1977 (s 32(5))
	V	17 Oct 1977 (SI 1977/1589)
	VI	29 Jul 1977 (s 32(6))

[1]   Orders made under Administration of Justice Act 1982, s 76, bringing the prospective repeal into force will be noted to that Act

Agricultural Holdings (Notices to Quit) Act 1977 (c 12)

Whole Act repealed

Aircraft and Shipbuilding Industries Act 1977 (c 3)

RA: 17 Mar 1977

17 Mar 1977 (RA)

Note: under ss 19, 56, the vesting date for the aircraft industry was 29 Apr 1977 (under Aircraft and Shipbuilding Industries (Aircraft Industry Vesting Date) Order 1977, SI 1977/539) and for the shipbuilding industry was 1 Jul 1977 (under Aircraft and Shipbuilding Industries (Shipbuilding Industry Vesting Date) Order 1977, SI 1977/540)

Appropriation Act 1977 (c 35)

Whole Act repealed

British Airways Board Act 1977 (c 13)

Whole Act repealed

Coal Industry Act 1977 (c 39)

RA: 29 Jul 1977

Commencement provisions: s 16(2)

29 Aug 1977 (s 16(2))

Whole Act repealed (in part prospectively) as follows: ss 1, 7, 9–16, Schs 1, 3, Sch 4, paras 1–3, Sch 5 repealed by Coal Industry Act 1994, s 67(8), Sch 11, Pts II–IV (prospectively in the case of ss 1, 7, 9(5) (part), 10, 11(1)–(6), (8), 12–16, Schs 1, 3, Sch 4, paras 1(1)–(4), (6), (7), 2, 3, Sch 5)[1]; ss 2, 3 repealed by Coal Industry Act 1983, ss 2(3), 6(3), Schedule; ss 4, 5, 8 repealed by Coal Industry Act 1980, ss 5, 11(2); s 6, Sch 2, Sch 4, para 5 repealed by Coal Industry Act 1987, ss 4(1), 10(3), Sch 3, Pt I; Sch 4, para 4 repealed by Overseas Development and Co-operation Act 1980, s 18(1), Sch 2, Pt I

[1]   Orders made under Coal Industry Act 1994 bringing the prospective repeals into force will be noted to that Act

Consolidated Fund Act 1977 (c 1)

Whole Act repealed

Consolidated Fund (No 2) Act 1977 (c 52)

Whole Act repealed

Control of Food Premises (Scotland) Act 1977 (c 28)

Whole Act repealed

Control of Office Development Act 1977 (c 40)

Whole Act repealed

Covent Garden Market (Financial Provisions) Act 1977 (c 2)

Limited application only

Criminal Law Act 1977 (c 45)

RA: 29 Jul 1977

Commencement provisions: s 65(7); Criminal Law Act 1977 (Commencement No 1) Order 1977, SI 1977/1365; Criminal Law Act 1977 (Commencement No 2) Order 1977, SI 1977/1426; Criminal Law Act 1977 (Commencement No 3) Order 1977, SI 1977/1682; Criminal Law Act 1977 (Commencement No 4) (Scotland) Order 1977, SI 1977/1744; Criminal Law Act 1977 (Commencement No 5) Order 1978, SI 1978/712; Criminal Law Act 1977 (Commencement No 6) (Scotland) Order 1978, SI 1978/900; Criminal Law Act 1977 (Commencement No 7) Order 1980, SI 1980/487; Criminal Law Act 1977 (Commencement No 8) (Scotland) Order 1980, SI 1980/587; Criminal Law Act 1977 (Commencement No 9) Order 1980, SI 1980/1632; Criminal Law Act 1977 (Commencement No 10) (Scotland) Order 1980, SI 1980/1701; Criminal Law Act 1977 (Commencement No 11) Order 1982, SI 1982/243; Criminal Law Act 1977 (Commencement No 12) Order 1985, SI 1985/579

Section

1	(1)	1 Dec 1977 (SI 1977/1682); substituted by Criminal Attempts Act 1981, s 5, except as to agreements entered into before 27 Aug 1981 (ie date of commencement of 1981 Act) when the conspiracy continued to exist after that date
	(1A), (1B)	Repealed
	(2)	1 Dec 1977 (SI 1977/1682)
	(3)	Repealed
	(4)	1 Dec 1977 (SI 1977/1682)
	(5), (6)	Repealed

Criminal Law Act 1977 (c 45)—*contd*

Section

1A			Inserted by Criminal Justice (Terrorism and Conspiracy) Act 1998, s 5(1) (qv)
2–4			1 Dec 1977 (SI 1977/1682)
5	(1)–(9)		1 Dec 1977 (SI 1977/1682)
	(10)	(a)	1 Dec 1977 (SI 1977/1682)
		(b)	8 Sep 1977 (SI 1977/1365)
	(11)		Repealed
6	(1)		1 Dec 1977 (SI 1977/1682)
	(1A)		Inserted by Criminal Justice and Public Order Act 1994, s 72(1), (2) (qv)
	(2)		1 Dec 1977 (SI 1977/1682)
	(3)		Repealed
	(4)–(7)		1 Dec 1977 (SI 1977/1682)
7			Substituted by Criminal Justice and Public Order Act 1994, s 73 (qv)
8–10			1 Dec 1977 (SI 1977/1682)
11			Repealed
12			1 Dec 1977 (SI 1977/1682)
12A			Inserted by Criminal Justice and Public Order Act 1994, s 74 (qv)
13			1 Dec 1977 (SI 1977/1682)
14			Repealed
15	(1)		17 Jul 1978 (SI 1978/712)
	(2), (3)		Repealed
	(4)		17 Jul 1978 (SI 1978/712; SI 1978/900)
	(5)		17 Jul 1978 (SI 1978/712)
16–27			Repealed
28			17 Jul 1978 (SI 1978/712)
29			Repealed
30	(1), (2)		17 Jul 1978 (SI 1978/712)
	(3)		17 Jul 1978 (SI 1978/712; SI 1978/900)
	(4)		Repealed
31	(1)		8 Sep 1977 (SI 1977/1365)
	(2)–(6)		17 Jul 1978 (SI 1978/712)
	(7)		Repealed
	(8), (9)		17 Jul 1978 (SI 1978/712)
	(10)		17 Jul 1978 (SI 1978/712; SI 1978/900)
	(11)		17 Jul 1978 (SI 1978/712)
32	(1)		17 Jul 1978 (SI 1978/712)
	(2)		Repealed
	(3)		17 Jul 1978 (SI 1978/712; SI 1978/900)
33			8 Sep 1977 (SI 1977/1365)
34, 35			Repealed

Criminal Law Act 1977 (c 45)—*contd*

Section

36		Repealed or spent
37		17 Jul 1978 (SI 1978/712)
38		Repealed
38A		Inserted by Criminal Justice (Scotland) Act 1980, s 51 (qv)
38B		Inserted by Criminal Justice Act 1982, s 52 (qv)
39		12 May 1980 (SI 1980/487; SI 1980/587)
40		1 Dec 1980 (SI 1980/1632; SI 1980/1701)
41–46		Repealed
47		Repealed
48		20 May 1985 (SI 1985/579)
49, 50		Repealed
51, 52		8 Sep 1977 (SI 1977/1365)
53		1 Dec 1977 (SI 1977/1682)
54		8 Sep 1977 (SI 1977/1365)
55–57		Repealed
58		Repealed or spent
59–62		Repealed
63	(1)	8 Sep 1977 (SI 1977/1365)
	(2)	8 Sep 1977 (so far as relates to ss 33, 51, 52, 55, 65, Schs 12 (part), 13 (part), 14) (SI 1977/1365)
		1 Dec 1977 (so far as relates to s 50, Schs 12 (part), 13 (part)) (SI 1977/1744)
		17 Jul 1978 (so far as relates to ss 15(2)–(4), 30(3), 31(10), 32(3), Schs 9, para 3(3), 12 (part), 13 (part)) (SI 1978/900)
		12 May 1980 (so far as relates to ss 38, 39, Sch 13 (part)) (SI 1980/587)
		1 Dec 1980 (so far as relates to s 40, Schs 7, 12 (part), 13 (part)) (SI 1980/1701)
64		17 Jul 1978 (SI 1978/712)
65		8 Sep 1977 (SI 1977/1365)

Schedule

1	17 Jul 1978 (SI 1978/712)
2–4	Repealed
5	17 Jul 1978 (SI 1978/712)
6	8 Sep 1977 (SI 1977/1365); repealed in part and superseded by Criminal Justice Act 1982
7, 8	Repealed
9	Spent
10, 11	Repealed

Criminal Law Act 1977 (c 45)—*contd*
Schedule
12

8 Sep 1977 (so far as relates to
Offences Against the Person
Act 1861; Explosive Substances
Act 1883; Sexual Offences Act 1956,
Sch 2, Pt II, paras 14, 15; Housing
(Scotland) Act 1966; Children and
Young Persons Act 1969, s 13(3);
Powers of Criminal Courts
Act 1973, ss 15(2), 17(3); Adoption
Act 1976; Bail Act 1976, ss 3(8), 5)
(SI 1977/1365)

1 Dec 1977 (so far as relates to
Metropolitan Police Courts
Act 1839; Public Stores Act 1875;
Obscene Publications Act 1959;
Criminal Justice Act 1961;
Criminal Justice Act 1967, ss 60, 91;
Theft Act 1968; Finance Act 1972;
Criminal Justice Act 1972;
Administration of Justice Act 1973;
Powers of Criminal Courts
Act 1973, ss 1, 2(5); Legal Aid
Act 1974 (repealed); Juries Act 1974;
Bail Act 1976, s 7(4)) (E, W)
(SI 1977/1682)

1 Dec 1977 (so far as relates to Public
Stores Act 1875; Prison Act 1952
(in its application to persons for the
time being in Scotland); Criminal
Justice Act 1961, ss 26, 28, 29,
39(1); Criminal Justice Act 1967,
s 60; Road Traffic Act 1972, s 179)
(S) (SI 1977/1744)

1 Jan 1978 (so far as relates to
Coroners Act 1887; Births and
Deaths Registration Act 1953; Bail
Act 1976, s 2(2)) (SI 1977/1682)

17 Jul 1978 (so far as relates to Night
Poaching Act 1828; Accessories and
Abettors Act 1861; Sexual Offences
Act 1956, Sch 2, Pt II, paras 17, 18;
Criminal Law Act 1967; Firearms
Act 1968; Children and Young
Persons Act 1969, ss 15, 16; Powers
of Criminal Courts Act 1973,
s 9(1); Health and Safety at Work
etc Act 1974; Rehabilitation of
Offenders Act 1974) (E, W)
(SI 1978/712)

Criminal Law Act 1977 (c 45)—*contd*
Schedule

12—*contd*

> 17 Jul 1978 (so far as relates to Night Poaching Act 1828; Health and Safety at Work etc Act 1974; Rehabilitation of Offenders Act 1974) (S) (SI 1978/900)
> Repealed or spent (remainder)

13

> 8 Sep 1977 (repeals of or in Criminal Justice Act 1848, s 19(3); Criminal Justice Act 1967, Sch 3, Pt I; Children and Young Persons Act 1969, s 13(3); Powers of Criminal Courts Act 1973, Sch 3, para 9; Bail Act 1976, Sch 2, para 38) (SI 1977/1365)
> 8 Sep 1977 (repeals of or in Exchange Control Act 1947, Sch 5, Pt II, para 3(1); Customs and Excise Act 1952, s 285(1); Magistrates' Courts Act 1952, Sch 3, para 3; Land Commission Act 1967, s 82(5); Criminal Justice Act 1967, s 93) (SI 1977/1426)
> 1 Dec 1977 (repeals of or in Forcible Entry Act 1381; Statutes concerning forcible entries and riots confirmed; Forcible Entry Acts, 1429, 1588, 1623; Metropolitan Police Courts Act 1839, s 24; Offences against the Person Act 1861, s 4; Public Stores Act 1875, ss 7, 9, 10; Conspiracy and Protection of Property Act 1875, s 3; Justices of the Peace Act 1949, s 43(3); Obscene Publications Act 1959, s 1(3); Criminal Justice Act 1961, ss 26(6), 28(2); Licensing Act 1964, s 30(5); Road Traffic Regulation Act 1967, ss 43(2), 80(5), (11); Criminal Justice Act 1967, ss 60(6)(a), (8)(d), 91(5); Transport Act 1968, s 131(2); Road Traffic Act 1972, Sch 4, Pt I; Criminal Justice Act 1972, s 34(1); Powers of Criminal Courts Act 1973, ss 2(8)(a), 49(1)–(3), 50(1)–(3), 51, 57(1), Sch 1, para 3(2)(b), Sch 3, paras 11, 12, 18(1)(b); Road Traffic Act 1974, Sch 5, Pts II, III) (SI 1977/1682; SI 1977/1744)

Criminal Law Act 1977 (c 45)—*contd*

Schedule

13—*contd*

1 Jan 1978 (repeals of or in
Prosecution of Offences Act 1879,
s 5; Coroners Act 1887, ss 4(2),
(3), 5, 9, 10, 16, 18(4), (5), 20;
City of London Fire Inquests
Act 1888; Interpretation Act 1889,
s 27; Indictments Act 1915, s 8(3);
Coroners (Amendment) Act 1926,
ss 13(2)(a), (d), 25; Suicide Act
1961, Sch 1; Criminal Justice
Act 1967, s 22(4); Administration
of Justice Act 1970, Sch 9, Pt I,
para 4; Courts Act 1971, s 57(2);
and Bail Act 1976, ss 2(2), 10, Sch 2,
paras 4, 37(4)) (SI 1977/1682)

17 Jul 1978 (repeals of or in Night
Poaching Act 1828, ss 4, 11; Truck
Act 1831, s 10; Conspiracy and
Protection of Property Act 1875,
ss 5, 7, 9, 19(1), (2); Cruelty to
Animals Act 1876, ss 15, 17;
Newspaper Libel and Registration
Act 1881, s 5; Truck Amendment
Act 1887, s 13(1), (3); Witnesses
(Public Inquiries) Protection
Act 1892, ss 3, 6, para 2; Criminal
Justice Act 1925, s 28(3); Water
Act 1945, Sch 3, s 71(1); Exchange
Control Act 1947, Sch 5, Pt II,
para 2(3); Children Act 1948,
s 29(5); Customs and Excise
Act 1952, s 283(2)(a); Magistrates'
Courts Act 1952, ss 18, 19, 24, 25,
32, 104, 125, 127(2), Sch 1, Sch 2,
para 8; Protection of Animals
(Amendment) Act 1954, s 3;
Sexual Offences Act 1956, Sch 2,
Pt II, Sch 3; Police, Fire and
Probation Officers Remuneration
Act 1956; Magistrates' Courts
Act 1957, s 1(1)(a); Prevention of
Fraud (Investments) Act 1958,
s 13(2); Obscene Publications
Act 1959, s 2(2), (3); Films Act 1960,
s 45(3); Criminal Justice Act 1961,
ss 8(1), 11(2); Criminal Justice
Administration Act 1962, ss 12(3),
13, Sch 3, Sch 4, Pt II; Penalties
for Drunkenness Act 1962,

Criminal Law Act 1977 (c 45)—*contd*
Schedule
13—*contd*

s 1(2)(a), (b); Public Order
Act 1963, s 1(1); Building Control
Act 1966, s 1(8); Industrial
Development Act 1966, s 8(10);
Veterinary Surgeons Act 1966,
ss 19(2), 20(6); Finance Act 1967,
Sch 7, para 4; Criminal Law
Act 1967, ss 4(5), 5(4); Sexual
Offences Act 1967, ss 4(2), 5(2),
7(2)(b), 9; Road Traffic
Regulation Act 1967, s 91;
Criminal Justice Act 1967, ss 27,
35, 43, 92(8), 106(2)(f), Sch 3, Pt II;
Firearms Act 1968, s 57(4); Theft
Act 1968, s 29(2), Sch 2, Pt III;
Transport Act 1968, Sch 8, para 8;
Decimal Currency Act 1969, Sch
2, para 21; Development of
Tourism Act 1969, Sch 2, para
3(2), (4); Children and Young
Persons Act 1969, ss 3(1)(b), (6),
6(1), (2), 12(2)(a), (3)(b)–(e), 15(1),
34(5), Sch 5, para 56; Auctions
(Bidding Agreements) Act 1969,
s 1(2), (4); Administration of Justice
Act 1970, s 51(1); Courts Act
1971, Sch 8, paras 15(1), 16, 20,
34(1); Misuse of Drugs Act 1971,
s 26(4); Road Traffic Act 1972,
Sch 5, Pt IV, para 3; Gas Act 1972,
s 43(2)(b); Industry Act 1972, Sch 1,
para 4(2), (5); Criminal Justice
Act 1972, s 47; Costs in Criminal
Cases Act 1973, s 20(3); Hallmarking
Act 1973, Sch 3, para 2(2), (5);
Powers of Criminal Courts
Act 1973, s 30(1), (2); Control of
Pollution Act 1974, s 87(3);
Housing Act 1974, Sch 13, para 2;
Road Traffic Act 1974, Sch 5, Pt IV,
para 4(1)–(3), (4)(a); Trade Union
and Labour Relations Act 1974,
s 29(7); District Courts (Scotland)
Act 1975, ss 3(3), 27(1), Sch 1,
para 26; Criminal Procedure
(Scotland) Act 1975, s 403(4);
Protection of Birds (Amendment)
Act 1976) (SI 1978/712;
SI 1978/900)

Criminal Law Act 1977 (c 45)—*contd*

Schedule	
13—*contd*	12 May 1980 (repeals of or in Magistrates' Courts Act 1952, s 102(3); Criminal Procedure (Scotland) Act 1975, ss 17, 325, 463(1)(a), (b)) (SI 1980/487; SI 1980/587)
	1 Dec 1980 (repeals of or in Criminal Justice (Scotland) Act 1963, ss 26, 53(1), Sch 3, Pt II; Criminal Justice Act 1967, s 106(2)(f), Sch 6, paras 14–16, 21; Administration of Justice Act 1970, s 41(6)(a); Courts Act 1971, s 59(5)(e), Sch 8, paras 34(3), 48(a); Powers of Criminal Courts Act 1973, ss 33, 58(a), Sch 5, paras 6, 8; Criminal Procedure (Scotland) Act 1975, ss 403(1), (5), 463(1); District Courts (Scotland) Act 1975, Sch 1, para 26) (SI 1980/1632; SI 1980/1701)
	29 Mar 1982 (repeals of or in Criminal Procedure (Scotland) Act 1975, Sch 9, paras 15, 35) (SI 1982/243)
14	8 Sep 1977 (SI 1977/1365)

Farriers (Registration) (Amendment) Act 1977 (c 31)

RA: 22 Jul 1977

Commencement provisions: s 2(2), (3)

Section		
1, 2		22 Oct 1977 (s 2(2))
Schedule		
para	1–4	22 Oct 1977 (s 2(2))
	5	22 Jan 1978 (s 2(3))
	6, 7	22 Oct 1977 (s 2(2))

Finance Act 1977 (c 36)

Budget Day: 29 Mar 1977

RA: 29 Jul 1977

Details of the commencement of Finance Acts are not set out in this work

---

Finance (Income Tax Reliefs) Act 1977 (c 53)

Whole Act repealed

General Rate (Public Utilities) Act 1977 (c 11)

RA: 30 Mar 1977

30 Mar 1977 (RA)

Whole Act repealed, with savings, by Local Government Finance (Repeals, Savings and Consequential Amendments) Order 1990, SI 1990/776, art 3, Sch 1

Housing (Homeless Persons) Act 1977 (c 48)

Whole Act repealed

Incumbents (Vacation of Benefices) Measure 1977 (No 1)

RA: 30 Jun 1977

Commencement provisions: s 21(3)
Section

1	Inserted by Incumbents (Vacation of Benefices) (Amendment) Measure 1993, s 1 (qv)
1A	30 Dec 1977 (s 21(3)); original s 1 renumbered s 1A by Incumbents (Vacation of Benefices) (Amendment) Measure 1993, s 1 (qv)
2–4	30 Dec 1977 (s 21(3))
5	Substituted by Incumbents (Vacation of Benefices) (Amendment) Measure 1993, s 14(1), Sch 3, para 3 (qv)
6, 7	30 Dec 1977 (s 21(3))
7A	Inserted by Incumbents (Vacation of Benefices) (Amendment) Measure 1993, s 5 (qv)
8, 9	30 Dec 1988 (s 21(3))
9A	Inserted by Incumbents (Vacation of Benefices) (Amendment) Measure 1993, s 6 (qv)
10–12	30 Dec 1977 (s 21(3))
13	Substituted by Incumbents (Vacation of Benefices) (Amendment) Measure 1993, s 8 (qv)
14	30 Dec 1977 (s 21(3))
15	Repealed
16, 17	30 Dec 1977 (s 21(3))
18	Substituted by Incumbents (Vacation of Benefices) (Amendment) Measure 1993, s 9 (qv)
19	30 Dec 1997 (s 21(3))

Incumbents (Vacation of Benefices) Measure 1977 (No 1)—*contd*
Section
19A   Inserted by Incumbents (Vacation
                                                   of Benefices (Amendment)
                                                   Measure 1993, s 10 (qv)
20, 21   30 Dec 1977 (s 21(3))
Schedule
1   Original Schedule renumbered
                                                   as Sch 1 and substituted
                                                   by Incumbents (Vacation
                                                   of Benefices) (Amendment)
                                                   Measure 1993, s 12, Sch 1
                                                   (qv)
2   Added by Incumbents (Vacation
                                                   of Benefices) (Amendment)
                                                   Measure 1993, s 13, Sch 2
                                                   (qv)

Insurance Brokers (Registration) Act 1977 (c 46)

Whole Act repealed

International Finance, Trade and Aid Act 1977 (c 6)

Whole Act repealed

Job Release Act 1977 (c 8)

RA: 30 Mar 1977

30 Mar 1977 (RA)

Note: s 1(4) of the Act stated that it would have effect for a period of eighteen months from
    Royal Assent unless further extended by order made by the Secretary of State; the last
    such order extended the Act to 29 Sep 1988 (SI 1987/1339)

Licensing (Amendment) Act 1977 (c 26)

RA: 22 Jul 1977

Commencement provisions: s 2(2)

22 Aug 1977 (s 2(2))

Local Authorities (Restoration of Works Powers) Act 1977 (c 47)

RA: 29 Jul 1977

29 Jul 1977 (RA)

Marriage (Scotland) Act 1977 (c 15)

RA: 26 May 1977

Commencement provisions: s 29(2)
Section

1–23	1 Jan 1978 (s 29(2))
23A	Inserted (retrospectively) by Law Reform (Miscellaneous Provisions) (Scotland) Act 1980, s 22(1)(d) (qv)
24–28	1 Jan 1978 (s 29(2))
29	26 May 1977 (RA)
Schedule	
1–3	1 Jan 1978 (s 29(2))

Merchant Shipping (Safety Convention) Act 1977 (c 24)

Whole Act repealed

Minibus Act 1977 (c 25)

Whole Act repealed

National Health Service Act 1977 (c 49)

RA: 29 Jul 1977

Commencement provisions: s 130(5)

29 Aug 1977 (s 130(5))

New Towns Act 1977 (c 23)

Whole Act repealed

New Towns (Scotland) Act 1977 (c 16)

RA: 26 May 1977

26 May 1977 (RA)

Northern Ireland (Emergency Provisions) (Amendment) Act 1977 (c 34)

Whole Act repealed

Nuclear Industry (Finance) Act 1977 (c 7)

RA: 30 Mar 1977

30 Mar 1977 (RA)

Passenger Vehicles (Experimental Areas) Act 1977 (c 21)

Whole Act repealed

Patents Act 1977 (c 37)

RA: 29 Jul 1977

Commencement provisions: s 132(5); Patents Act 1977 (Commencement No 1) Order 1977, SI 1977/2090; Patents Act 1977 (Commencement No 2) Order 1978, SI 1978/586; Patents (Amendment) Rules 1987, SI 1987/288, r 4 (made for the purposes of ss 77(9), 78(8))

Section		
1–28		1 Jun 1978 (SI 1978/586)
28A		Inserted by Copyright, Designs and Patents Act 1988, s 295, Sch 5, para 7 (qv)
29–31		1 Jun 1978 (SI 1978/586)
32		Substituted by Patents, Designs and Marks Act 1986, s 1, Sch 1, para 4 (qv)
33, 34		1 Jun 1978 (SI 1978/586)
35		Repealed
36–43		1 Jun 1978 (SI 1978/586)
44, 45		Repealed
46, 47		1 Jun 1978 (SI 1978/586)
48		Substituted (29 Jul 1999) by Patents and Trade Marks (World Trade Organisation) Regulations 1999, SI 1999/1899, regs 3, 8, subject to transitional provisions
48A, 48B		Inserted (29 Jul 1999) by Patents and Trade Marks (World Trade Organisation) Regulations 1999, SI 1999/1899, regs 4, 5, 8, subject to transitional provisions
49, 50		1 Jun 1978 (SI 1978/586)
51		Substituted by Copyright, Designs and Patents Act 1988, s 295, Sch 5, para 14 (qv)
52		Substituted (29 Jul 1999) by Patents and Trade Marks (World Trade Organisation) Regulations 1999, SI 1999/1899, regs 6, 8, subject to transitional provisions
53	(1)	*Not in force*
	(2)–(5)	1 Jun 1978 (SI 1978/586)
54–57		1 Jun 1978 (SI 1978/586)
57A		Inserted by Copyright, Designs and Patents Act 1988, s 295, Sch 5, para 16(1) (qv)

Patents Act 1977 (c 37)—*contd*

Section

58, 59		1 Jun 1978 (SI 1978/586)
60	(1)–(3)	1 Jun 1978 (SI 1978/586)
	(4)	*Not in force*
	(5), (6)	1 Jun 1978 (SI 1978/586)
	(6A)–(6C)	Inserted (28 Jul 2000) by Patents Regulations 2000, SI 2000/2037, reg 4, in relation to applications for patents, and to patents granted in pursuance of such applications, made on or after 28 Jul 2000
	(7)	1 Jun 1978 (SI 1978/586)
61–63		1 Jun 1978 (SI 1978/586)
64		Substituted by Copyright, Designs and Patents Act 1988, s 295, Sch 5, para 17 (qv)
65–75		1 Jun 1978 (SI 1978/586)
76		Substituted by Copyright, Designs and Patents Act 1988, s 295, Sch 5, para 20 (qv)
76A		Inserted (28 Jul 2000) by Patents Regulations 2000, SI 2000/2037, reg 5, in relation to applications for patents, and to patents granted in pursuance of such applications, made on or after 28 Jul 2000
77	(1), (2)	1 Jun 1978 (SI 1978/586)
	(3)	Substituted by Copyright, Designs and Patents Act 1988, s 295, Sch 5, para 21 (1), (2) (qv)
	(4), (4A)	Substituted for original sub-s (4) by Copyright, Designs and Patents Act 1988, s 295, Sch 5, para 21(1), (3) (qv)
	(5)	1 Jun 1978 (SI 1978/586)
	(6)	1 Sep 1987 (SI 1987/288)
	(7)	29 Jul 1977 (RA)
	(8)	1 Jun 1978 (SI 1978/586)
	(9)	29 Jul 1977 (RA)
78	(1)–(4)	1 Jun 1978 (SI 1978/586)
	(5), (5A)	Substituted for original sub-s (5) by Copyright, Designs and Patents Act 1988, s 295, Sch 5, para 22 (qv)
	(6)	1 Jun 1978 (SI 1978/586)
	(7)	1 Sep 1987 (SI 1987/288)
	(8)	29 Jul 1977 (RA)
79–83		1 Jun 1978 (SI 1978/586)
84, 85		Repealed
86, 87		*Not in force*

Patents Act 1977 (c 37)—*contd*

Section

88		Repealed (*never in force*)
89–89B		Substituted for original s 89 by Copyright, Designs and Patents Act 1988, s 295, Sch 5, para 25 (qv)
90–95		1 Jun 1978 (SI 1978/586)
96		Repealed
97–99		1 Jun 1978 (SI 1978/586)
99A, 99B		Inserted by Copyright, Designs and Patents Act 1988, s 295, Sch 5, para 26 (qv)
100, 101		1 Jun 1978 (SI 1978/586)
102, 102A		Substituted for original s 102 by Copyright, Designs and Patents Act 1988, s 295, Sch 5, para 27 (qv)
103		1 Jun 1978 (SI 1978/586)
104		Repealed
105–113		1 Jun 1978 (SI 1978/586)
114, 115		Repealed
116–125		1 Jun 1978 (SI 1978/586)
125A		Inserted by Copyright, Designs and Patents Act 1988, s 295, Sch 5, para 30 (qv)
126		Repealed
127	(1)–(4)	1 Jun 1978 (SI 1978/586)
	(5)	See Sch 3 below
	(6), (7)	1 Jun 1978 (SI 1978/586)
128, 129		1 Jun 1978 (SI 1978/586)
130		31 Dec 1977 (SI 1977/2090)
131		1 Jun 1978 (SI 1978/586)
132	(1)–(4)	1 Jun 1978 (SI 1978/586)
	(5)	29 Jul 1977 (RA)
	(6)	1 Jun 1978 (SI 1978/586)
	(7)	See Sch 6 below

Schedule

A1, A2	Inserted (28 Jul 2000) by Patents Regulations 2000, SI 2000/2037, reg 8, Schs 1, 2, in relation to applications for patents, and to patents granted in pursuance of such applications, made on or after 28 Jul 2000
1, 2	1 Jun 1978 (SI 1978/586)
3	29 Jul 1977 (repeal of Patents Act 1949, s 41) (RA) 1 Jun 1978 (otherwise) (SI 1978/586)
4, 5	1 Jun 1978 (SI 1978/586)

Patents Act 1977 (c 37)—*contd*
Schedule
6 | 29 Jul 1977 (repeal of Patents Act 1949, s 41) (RA)
31 Dec 1977 (repeal of Patents Act 1949, s 88) (SI 1977/2090)
1 Jun 1978 (otherwise) (SI 1978/586)

Pensioners Payments Act 1977 (c 51)

Whole Act repealed

Post Office Act 1977 (c 44)

Whole Act repealed

Presumption of Death (Scotland) Act 1977 (c 27)

RA: 22 Jul 1977

Commencement provisions: s 20(2); Presumption of Death (Scotland) Act 1977 (Commencement) Order 1978, SI 1978/159
Section
1–19 | 1 Mar 1978 (SI 1978/159)
20 | 22 Jul 1977 (RA)
Schedule
1, 2 | 1 Mar 1978 (SI 1978/159)

Price Commission Act 1977 (c 33)

RA: 22 Jul 1977

Commencement provisions: s 24(2) (repealed)

Whole Act repealed, except ss 16, 17, by Competition Act 1980, s 33(4), Sch 2 (the repeal of s 15(4) and Sch 2, para 4(b), (d) being as from 1 Jan 2011). S 17 repealed by Statute Law (Repeals) Act 1989, s 1(1), Sch 1, Pt II. S 16 came into force on 1 Aug 1977 (s 24(2))

Protection from Eviction Act 1977 (c 43)

RA: 29 Jul 1977

Commencement provisions: s 13(2)

29 Aug 1977 (s 13(2))

Redundancy Rebates Act 1977 (c 22)

Whole Act repealed

Rent Act 1977 (c 42)

RA: 29 Jul 1977

Commencement provisions: s 156(2)

29 Aug 1977 (s 156(2))

Rent (Agriculture) Amendment Act 1977 (c 17)

RA: 26 May 1977

Commencement provisions: s 2(2)

9 Jun 1977 (s 2(2))

Rentcharges Act 1977 (c 30)

RA: 22 Jul 1977

Commencement provisions: s 18(2); Rentcharges Act 1977 (Commencement) Order 1978, SI 1978/15

Section		
1–3		22 Aug 1977 (s 18(2))
4–11		1 Feb 1978 (SI 1978/15)
12–15		22 Aug 1977 (s 18(2))
16		1 Feb 1978 (SI 1978/15)
17	(1)	22 Aug 1977 (in relation to Sch 1, para 2) (s 18(2))
		1 Feb 1978 (otherwise) (SI 1978/15)
	(2)	See Sch 2 below
	(3)	22 Aug 1977 (s 18(2))
	(4), (5)	1 Feb 1978 (SI 1978/15)
	(6)	22 Aug 1977 (s 18(2))
18		22 Aug 1977 (s 18(2))
Schedule		
1, para	1	1 Feb 1978 (SI 1978/15)
	2	22 Aug 1977 (s 18(2))
	3, 4	1 Feb 1978 (SI 1978/15)
2		22 Aug 1977 (except repeals of Inclosure Act 1854, s 10; Law of Property Act 1925, s 191) (s 18(2))
		1 Feb 1978 (exceptions noted above) (SI 1978/15)

Representation of the People Act 1977 (c 9)

Whole Act repealed

Restrictive Trade Practices Act 1977 (c 19)

Whole Act repealed

Returning Officers (Scotland) Act 1977 (c 14)

Whole Act repealed

Roe Deer (Close Seasons) Act 1977 (c 4)

Whole Act repealed

Social Security (Miscellaneous Provisions) Act 1977 (c 5)

RA: 30 Mar 1977

Commencement provisions: s 25(2), (3), (4); Social Security (Miscellaneous Provisions) Act 1977 (Commencement No 1) Order 1977, SI 1977/617; Social Security (Miscellaneous Provisions) Act 1977 (Commencement No 2) Order 1977, SI 1977/618

Section

1–11		Repealed
12		25 Apr 1977 (SI 1977/618)
13		Repealed
14		Repealed or spent
15–21		Repealed
22		Repealed or spent
23		25 Apr 1977 (SI 1977/618)
24	(1)	30 Mar 1977 (RA)
	(2)	Repealed
	(3)	30 Mar 1977 (RA)
	(4)	Repealed
	(5)	30 Mar 1977 (RA)
	(6)	See Sch 2 below
25		30 Mar 1977 (RA)

Schedule

1	Repealed
2	30 Mar 1977 (repeals of or in Social Security Act 1975, ss 30(2), 45(4), 66(5), 124(1)(d)) (RA)
	6 Apr 1977 (repeals of Employment Protection Act 1975, s 113; Supplementary Benefits Act 1976, Sch 7, para 41) (SI 1977/617)
	25 Apr 1977 (repeals of or in Tribunals and Inquiries Act 1971; Social Security Act 1975, ss 1(5), 129(3); Social Security (Northern Ireland) Act 1975; Social Security Pensions Act 1975; Employment Protection Act 1975, s 40(3); Supplementary Benefits Act 1976, s 29) (SI 1977/618)

Social Security (Miscellaneous Provisions) Act 1977 (c 5)—*contd*

Schedule

2—*contd*   27 Jun 1977 (repeals of Social
                                              Security Act 1975, Sch 20)
                                              (SI 1977/618)
                                              1 Jul 1977 (repeals in Industrial
                                              Injuries and Diseases (Old Cases)
                                              Act 1975) (SI 1977/618)

Statute Law (Repeals) Act 1977 (c 18)

RA: 16 Jun 1977

16 Jun 1977 (RA)

Torts (Interference with Goods) Act 1977 (c 32)

RA: 22 Jul 1977

Commencement provisions: s 17(2); Torts (Interference with Goods) Act 1977
(Commencement No 1) Order 1977, SI 1977/1910; Torts (Interference with
Goods) Act 1977 (Commencement No 2) Order 1978, SI 1978/627; Torts
(Interference with Goods) Act 1977 (Commencement No 3) Order 1980,
SI 1980/2024[1]

Section

1–11   1 Jun 1978 (SI 1978/627)
12–16   1 Jan 1978 (SI 1977/1910)
17   (1), (2)   1 Jan 1978 (SI 1977/1910)
             (3)   1 Jun 1978 (SI 1978/627)

Schedule

1   1 Jan 1978 (SI 1977/1910)
2   1 Jun 1978 (SI 1978/627)

[1]   Note that Torts (Interference with Goods) Act 1977 (Commencement No 3) Order 1980,
       SI 1980/2024, brought this Act into force, so far as not already in force by virtue of SI 1977/1910,
       in Northern Ireland on 1 Jan 1981 (SI 1978/627 applied to England and Wales only)

Town and Country Planning (Amendment) Act 1977 (c 29)

Whole Act repealed

Town and Country Planning (Scotland) Act 1977 (c 10)

Whole Act repealed

Transport (Financial Provisions) Act 1977 (c 20)

Whole Act repealed

Unfair Contract Terms Act 1977 (c 50)

RA: 26 Oct 1977

Commencement provisions: s 31(1)

1 Feb 1978 (s 31(1); note that this Act does not apply to contracts before this date but applies to liability for loss or damage suffered on or after that date (s 31(2)))

Water Charges Equalisation Act 1977 (c 41)

Whole Act repealed

1978

Adoption (Scotland) Act 1978 (c 28)

RA: 20 Jul 1978

Commencement provisions: s 67(2); Adoption (Scotland) Act 1978 Commencement
Order 1984, SI 1984/1050

Section	
1, 2	1 Feb 1985 (SI 1984/1050)
3–5	1 Sep 1984 (SI 1984/1050)
6	Substituted by Children (Scotland) Act 1995, s 95 (qv)
6A	Inserted by Children (Scotland) Act 1995, s 96 (qv)
7	1 Sep 1984 (SI 1984/1050)
8	Repealed
9	1 Sep 1984 (SI 1984/1050)
10	Repealed
11–16	1 Sep 1984 (subject to transitional provisions) (SI 1984/1050)
17	1 Sep 1984 (subject to transitional provisions) (SI 1984/1050); prospectively substituted by Adoption (Intercountry Aspects) Act 1999, s 3[1]
18–20	1 Sep 1984 (subject to transitional provisions) (SI 1984/1050)
21	Substituted by Children Act 1989, s 88, Sch 10, para 37 (qv)
22	1 Sep 1984 (subject to transitional provisions) (SI 1984/1050)
22A	Inserted by Children (Scotland) Act 1995, s 98(1), Sch 2, paras 1, 15 (qv)
23–25	1 Sep 1984 (subject to transitional provisions) (SI 1984/1050)
25A	Inserted by Children (Scotland) Act 1995, s 98(1), Sch 2, paras 1, 18 (qv)
26	Repealed
27–31	1 Sep 1984 (subject to transitional provisions) (SI 1984/1050)
32–37	Repealed

Adoption (Scotland) Act 1978 (c 28)—*contd*

Section

38, 39	1 Sep 1984 (subject to transitional provisions) (SI 1984/1050)
40	Repealed
41–50	1 Sep 1984 (subject to transitional provisions) (SI 1984/1050)
50A	Prospectively inserted by Adoption (Intercountry Aspects) Act 1999, s 14[1]
51	1 Sep 1984 (subject to transitional provisions) (SI 1984/1050)
51A, 51B	Inserted by Children (Scotland) Act 1995, s 98(1), Sch 2, paras 1, 25 (qv)
52–62	1 Sep 1984 (subject to transitional provisions) (SI 1984/1050)
63	1 Sep 1984 (subject to transitional provisions) (SI 1984/1050); prospectively repealed by Adoption (Intercountry Aspects) Act 1999, s 15, Sch 2, para 4(7), Sch 3[1]
64–67	1 Sep 1984 (subject to transitional provisions) (SI 1984/1050)

Schedule

1–4	1 Sep 1984 (SI 1984/1050)

[1]   Orders made under Adoption (Intercountry Aspects) Act 1999, s 18(3), bringing the prospective amendments into force will be noted to that Act

---

Appropriation Act 1978 (c 57)

Whole Act repealed

Chronically Sick and Disabled Persons (Northern Ireland) Act 1978 (c 53)

Applies to Northern Ireland only

Church of England (Miscellaneous Provisions) Measure 1978 (No 3)

RA: 30 Jun 1978

Commencement provisions: s 13(4)

30 Jul 1978 (s 13(4))

Civil Aviation Act 1978 (c 8)

Whole Act repealed

Civil Liability (Contribution) Act 1978 (c 47)

RA: 31 Jul 1978

Commencement provisions: s 10(2)

1 Jan 1979 (s 10(2))

Commonwealth Development Corporation Act 1978 (c 2)

RA: 23 Mar 1978

Commencement provisions: s 19(2)

Whole Act repealed, subject to savings in Commonwealth Development Corporation Act 1999, ss 7, 8, except ss 1(1), 19, Sch 2, which came into force on 23 Apr 1978

Community Service by Offenders (Scotland) Act 1978 (c 49)

RA: 31 Jul 1978

Commencement provisions: s 15(2); Community Service by Offenders (Scotland) Act 1978 (Commencement No 1) Order 1978, SI 1978/1944; Community Service by Offenders (Scotland) Act 1978 (Commencement No 2) Order 1980, SI 1980/268

Section	
1–8	Repealed
9	1 Feb 1979 (SI 1978/1944)
10–13	Repealed
14	1 Feb 1979 (SI 1978/1944)
15	Repealed
Schedule	
1	Repealed
2	1 Feb 1979 (SI 1978/1944)

Consolidated Fund Act 1978 (c 7)

Whole Act repealed

Consolidated Fund (No 2) Act 1978 (c 59)

Whole Act repealed

Consumer Safety Act 1978 (c 38)

Whole Act repealed

Co-operative Development Agency Act 1978 (c 21)

Whole Act repealed

Dioceses Measure 1978 (No 1)

RA: 2 Feb 1978

Commencement provisions: s 25(2)

2 May 1978 (s 25(2))

Dividends Act 1978 (c 54)

Whole Act repealed

Domestic Proceedings and Magistrates' Courts Act 1978 (c 22)

RA: 30 Jun 1978

Commencement provisions: s 89(3); Domestic Proceedings and Magistrates' Courts Act 1978 (Commencement No 1) Order 1978, SI 1978/997; Domestic Proceedings and Magistrates' Courts Act 1978 (Commencement No 2) Order 1978, SI 1978/1489; Domestic Proceedings and Magistrates' Courts Act 1978 (Commencement No 1) (Scotland) Order 1978, SI 1978/1490; Domestic Proceedings and Magistrates' Courts Act 1978 (Commencement No 3) Order 1979, SI 1979/731; Domestic Proceedings and Magistrates' Courts Act 1978 (Commencement No 4) Order 1980, SI 1980/1478; Domestic Proceedings and Magistrates' Courts Act 1978 (Commencement No 2) (Scotland) Order 1980, SI 1980/2036; Children Act 1975 and the Domestic Proceedings and Magistrates' Courts Act 1978 (Commencement) Order 1985, SI 1985/779

Section	
1, 2	1 Feb 1981 (SI 1980/1478)
3	Substituted by Matrimonial and Family Proceedings Act 1984, s 9 (qv)
4, 5	1 Feb 1981 (SI 1980/1478)
6	Substituted by Matrimonial and Family Proceedings Act 1984, s 10 (qv)
7	1 Feb 1981 (SI 1980/1478)
8	Substituted by Children Act 1989, s 108(5), Sch 13, para 36 (qv)
9–15	Repealed
16–18	Repealed
19, 20	1 Feb 1981 (SI 1980/1478)
20ZA	Inserted by Maintenance Enforcement Act 1991, s 5 (qv)
20A	Inserted by Family Law Reform Act 1987, s 33(1), Sch 2, para 69; substituted by Children Act 1989, s 108(5), Sch 15, para 39(1) (qv)
21	Repealed
22, 23	1 Feb 1981 (SI 1980/1478)
24	Repealed
25–27	1 Feb 1981 (SI 1980/1478)

Domestic Proceedings and Magistrates' Courts Act 1978 (c 22)—*contd*

Section

28			1 Nov 1979 (SI 1979/731)
29	(1), (2)		1 Nov 1979 (SI 1979/731)
	(3)		1 Feb 1981 (SI 1980/1478)
	(4)		Repealed
	(5)		1 Nov 1979 (SI 1979/731)
30			1 Nov 1979 (SI 1979/731)
31, 32			1 Feb 1981 (SI 1980/1478)
33, 34			Repealed
35			1 Feb 1981 (SI 1980/1478)
36–53			Repealed
54			1 Feb 1981 (SI 1980/1478)
55			23 Oct 1978 (SI 1978/1490)
56			1 Feb 1981 (SI 1980/1478)
57, 58			Repealed
59			Spent
60			1 Feb 1981 (SI 1980/1478)
61			23 Oct 1978 (SI 1978/1490)
62, 63			1 Feb 1981 (SI 1980/1478)
64–72			Repealed
73			20 Nov 1978 (SI 1978/1489)
74			20 Nov 1978 (E, W) (SI 1978/1489)
			Repealed (S)
75–86			Repealed
87			23 Oct 1978 (S) (SI 1978/1490)
			20 Nov 1978 (E, W) (SI 1978/1489)
88	(1)–(4)		1 Nov 1979 (SI 1979/731)
	(5)		18 Jul 1978 (SI 1978/997)
89	(1)		18 Jul 1978 (SI 1978/997)
	(2)	(a)	23 Oct 1978 (S) (so far as brings Sch 2, paras 17, 18 into force) (SI 1978/1490)
			29 Nov 1978 (E, W) (SI 1978/1489)
			1 Feb 1981 (S) (otherwise) (SI 1980/2036)
		(b)	18 Jul 1978 (SI 1978/997)
	(3)–(6)		18 Jul 1978 (SI 1978/997)
90			18 Jul 1978 (SI 1978/997)

Schedule

1			18 Jul 1978 (SI 1978/997)
2, para	1, 2		1 Feb 1981 (SI 1980/1478)
	3–5		Repealed
	6		1 Feb 1981 (SI 1980/1478)
	7		Spent
	8		Repealed
	9		1 Feb 1981 (SI 1980/1478)
	10, 11		Spent
	12		1 Nov 1979 (SI 1979/731)
	13, 14		1 Feb 1981 (SI 1980/1478)
	15–25		Repealed or spent

Domestic Proceedings and Magistrates' Courts Act 1978 (c 22)—*contd*

Schedule

2, para	26	1 Feb 1981 (SI 1980/1478)
	27	Repealed
	28	1 Feb 1981 (SI 1980/1478)
	29–31	Repealed
	32	1 Feb 1981 (SI 1980/1478)
	33	Spent
	34–36	Repealed
	37	1 Feb 1981 (SI 1980/1478)
	38	1 Nov 1979 (SI 1979/731); prospectively repealed by Family Law Act 1996, s 66(3), Sch 10[1]
	39	1 Nov 1979 (SI 1979/731)
	40	Spent
	41–54	Repealed or spent
3		18 Jul 1978 (repeal in Administration of Justice Act 1964, s 2) (SI 1978/997)
		20 Nov 1978 (repeals of or in Adoption (Hague Convention) Act (Northern Ireland) 1969, s 7(2); Children Act 1975, Sch 3, para 26; Adoption Act 1976, Sch 1, para 6) (SI 1978/1489)
		1 Nov 1979 (repeals of or in National Assistance Act 1948, s 43(7); Magistrates' Courts Act 1952, ss 57(4), 60(1), (2)(a), 61, 62, 121(2); Matrimonial Proceedings (Magistrates' Courts) Act 1960, s 8(3); Criminal Justice Act 1961, Sch 4; Maintenance Orders (Reciprocal Enforcement) Act 1972, s 17(1)–(3), Schedule, para 1; Affiliation Proceedings (Amendment) Act 1972, s 3(1), (2); Children Act 1975, s 21(3), Sch 3, para 12; Adoption Act 1976, s 64(c), Sch 3, para 4; Supplementary Benefits Act 1976, s 18(7), Sch 7) (SI 1979/731)
		1 Feb 1981 (repeals of or in Maintenance Orders Act 1950, s 2(3); Magistrates' Courts Act 1952, s 59; Affiliation Proceedings Act 1957, s 7(1)–(3); Matrimonial Proceedings (Magistrates' Courts) Act 1960 except s 8(3) (repealed as above); Administration of Justice Act 1964, Sch 3, para 27; Matrimonial Causes Act 1965,

Domestic Proceedings and Magistrates' Courts Act 1978 (c 22)—*contd*

Schedule

3—*contd*

s 42; Criminal Justice Act 1967, Sch 3 (entry relating to Matrimonial Proceedings (Magistrates' Courts) Act 1960); Family Law Reform Act 1969, s 5(2); Local Authority Social Services Act 1970, Sch 1 (entry relating to Matrimonial Proceedings (Magistrates' Courts) Act 1960); Matrimonial Proceedings and Property Act 1970, ss 30(1), 31–33; Guardianship of Minors Act 1971, ss 9(3), 14(4); Misuse of Drugs Act 1971, s 34; Maintenance Orders (Reciprocal Enforcement) Act 1972, s 27(3); Local Government Act 1972, Sch 23, para 10; Matrimonial Causes Act 1973, s 27(8); Guardianship Act 1973, ss 2(5), 3(2), 8, Sch 2, para 1(2); Legal Aid Act 1974, Sch 1, para 3(a); Children Act 1975, ss 17(1), 91; Adoption Act 1976, s 26(1)) (SI 1980/1478)

[1] Orders made under Family Law Act 1996, s 67, bringing the prospective repeal into force will be noted to that Act

---

Education (Northern Ireland) Act 1978 (c 13)

Whole Act repealed

Employment (Continental Shelf) Act 1978 (c 46)

RA: 31 Jul 1978

31 Jul 1978 (RA)

Whole Act prospectively repealed by Oil and Gas (Enterprise) Act 1982, s 37, Sch 4 and Petroleum Act 1998, s 51(1), Sch 5, Pt I; orders made under the 1982 Act, s 38(2), and the 1998 Act, s 52(5), bringing the prospective repeals into force will be noted to those Acts

---

Employment Protection (Consolidation) Act 1978 (c 44)

RA: 31 Jul 1978

Commencement provisions: s 160(2)

Whole Act repealed (ss 1, 2, 2A, 4, 5, 5A, 6 repealed subject to savings in their application to certain employees)

Employment Subsidies Act 1978 (c 6)

Whole Act lapsed (31 Dec 1991) in accordance with terms of s 3(4)

European Parliamentary Elections Act 1978 (c 10)

RA: 5 May 1980

5 May 1980 (RA)

Export Guarantees and Overseas Investment Act 1978 (c 18)

Whole Act repealed

Finance Act 1978 (c 42)

Budget Day: 11 Apr 1978

RA: 31 Jul 1978

Details of the commencement of Finance Acts are not set out in this work

Gun Barrel Proof Act 1978 (c 9)

RA: 5 May 1978

Commencement provisions: s 9(3); Gun Barrel Proof Act 1978 (Commencement No 1) Order 1978, SI 1978/1587; Gun Barrel Proof Act 1978 (Commencement No 2) Order 1980, SI 1980/640

Section			
1			5 Jun 1980 (SI 1980/640)
2–7			1 Dec 1978 (SI 1978/1587)
8	(1)		1 Dec 1978 (so far as relates to Sch 3) (SI 1978/1587)
			5 Jun 1980 (otherwise) (SI 1980/640)
	(2)		1 Dec 1978 (SI 1978/1587)
	(3)		5 Jun 1980 (SI 1980/640)
9			1 Dec 1978 (SI 1978/1587)
Schedule			
1, 2			5 Jun 1980 (SI 1980/640)
3, para	1	(a)	5 Jun 1980 (SI 1980/640)
		(b)	1 Dec 1978 (except definition 'convention proof mark') (SI 1978/1587)
			5 Jun 1980 (exception noted above) (SI 1980/640)
	2–9		1 Dec 1978 (SI 1978/1587)
	10	(1)	1 Dec 1978 (SI 1978/1587)
		(2)	5 Jun 1980 (SI 1980/640)
	11–14		1 Dec 1978 (SI 1978/1587)
	15	(1), (2)	1 Dec 1978 (SI 1978/1587)
		(3)	5 Jun 1980 (SI 1980/640)

Gun Barrel Proof Act 1978 (c 9)—*contd*

Schedule

3, para	16	1 Dec 1978 (except words 'or which is or at any time was a convention proof mark') (SI 1978/1587)
		5 Jun 1980 (exception noted above) (SI 1980/640)
	17–19	1 Dec 1978 (SI 1978/1587)
	20	Repealed
4		1 Dec 1978 (SI 1978/1587)

Home Purchase Assistance and Housing Corporation Guarantee Act 1978 (c 27)

Whole Act repealed

Homes Insulation Act 1978 (c 48)

Whole Act repealed

House of Commons (Administration) Act 1978 (c 36)

RA: 20 Jul 1978

Commencement provisions: s 5(5)

Section

1		20 Jul 1978 (RA)
2		1 Jan 1979 (s 5(5))
3		Substituted by Government Resources and Accounts Act 2000, s 29(1), Sch 1, para 17 (qv)
4, 5		20 Jul 1978 (RA)

Schedule

1		20 Jul 1978 (RA)
2, para	1, 2	20 Jul 1978 (RA)
	3	1 Jan 1979 (s 5(5))
	4, 5	Repealed
3		1 Jan 1979 (s 5(5))

Housing (Financial Provisions) (Scotland) Act 1978 (c 14)

RA: 25 May 1978

Commencement provisions: s 19(2), (3) (repealed)

Whole Act repealed, except for Sch 2, paras 12–14, 39, which came into force on 25 Jun 1978 (s 19(2))

Import of Live Fish (Scotland) Act 1978 (c 35)

RA: 20 Jul 1978

20 Jul 1978 (RA)

Independent Broadcasting Authority Act 1978 (c 43)

Whole Act repealed

Industrial and Provident Societies Act 1978 (c 34)

RA: 20 Jul 1978

Commencement provisions: s 3(3)

20 Aug 1978 (s 3(3))

Inner Urban Areas Act 1978 (c 50)

RA: 31 Jul 1978

31 Jul 1978 (RA)

Internationally Protected Persons Act 1978 (c 17)

RA: 30 Jun 1978

Commencement provisions: s 5(5); Internationally Protected Persons Act 1978 (Commencement) Order 1979, SI 1979/455

24 May 1979 (SI 1979/455)

Interpretation Act 1978 (c 30)

RA: 20 Jul 1978

Commencement provisions: s 26

1 Jan 1979 (s 26)

Iron and Steel (Amendment) Act 1978 (c 41)

Whole Act repealed

Judicature (Northern Ireland) Act 1978 (c 23)

RA: 30 Jun 1978

Commencement provisions: s 123(2); Judicature (Northern Ireland) Act 1978 (Commencement No 1) Order 1978, SI 1978/1101; Judicature (Northern Ireland) Act 1978 (Commencement No 2) Order 1978, SI 1978/1829; Judicature (Northern Ireland) Act 1978 (Commencement No 3) Order 1979, SI 1979/124; Judicature (Northern Ireland) Act 1978 (Commencement No 4) Order 1979, SI 1979/422

Judicature (Northern Ireland) Act 1978 (c 23)—*contd*

Section

1–26	18 Apr 1979 (SI 1979/422)
27, 28	Repealed
29–33	18 Apr 1979 (SI 1979/422)
33A	Inserted by Administration of Justice Act 1982, s 69(1), Sch 7, Pt I (qv)
34–38	18 Apr 1979 (SI 1979/422)
39, 40	Repealed
41–51	18 Apr 1979 (SI 1979/422)
51A–51H	Inserted by Criminal Procedure and Investigations Act 1996, ss 66(1), (4), (5), 79(4), Sch 4, paras 1–3, 28 (qv)
52, 53	21 Aug 1978 (SI 1978/1101)
54–56	2 Jan 1979 (SI 1978/1829) (Note that ss 54(2)–(4), (6), 55(3), 56(1)–(3) came into force on 21 Aug 1978 so far as they apply to the Crown Court Rules Committee and Crown Court Rules (SI 1978/1101))
57–72	18 Apr 1979 (SI 1979/422)
73	Substituted (1 Nov 1982) by Supreme Court (Departments and Officers) (Northern Ireland) Order 1982, SR 1982/300, art 5(1)
74	18 Apr 1979 (SI 1979/422)
75	Substituted (1 Nov 1982) by Supreme Court (Departments and Officers) (Northern Ireland) Order 1982, 1982/300, art 4
76–82	18 Apr 1979 (SI 1979/422)
83	Repealed
84–94	18 Apr 1979 (SI 1979/422)
94A	Inserted by Administration of Justice Act 1982, s 70, Sch 8, para 11 (qv)
95, 96	Repealed
97, 98	18 Apr 1979 (SI 1979/422)
99	21 Aug 1978 (SI 1978/1101)
100	18 Apr 1979 (SI 1979/422)
101	Repealed
102–106	18 Apr 1979 (SI 1979/422)
107	21 Aug 1978 (SI 1978/1101)
108–115	18 Apr 1979 (SI 1979/422)
116	21 Aug 1978 (SI 1978/1101)
117	18 Apr 1979 (SI 1979/422)
117A	Inserted by Administration of Justice Act 1982, s 70, Sch 8, para 12 (qv)
118–121	21 Aug 1978 (SI 1978/1101)
122	See Schs 5–7 below
123	21 Aug 1978 (SI 1978/1101)

Judicature (Northern Ireland) Act 1978 (c 23)—*contd*

Schedule

1–4			18 Apr 1979 (SI 1979/422)
5, Pt	I, para	1, 2	18 Apr 1979 (SI 1979/422)
		3, 4	2 Jan 1979 (SI 1978/1829)
	II		21 Aug 1978 (amendments to Bills of Sale (Ireland) Act 1879; Deeds of Arrangement Act 1887; Deeds of Arrangement Amendment Act 1890) (SI 1978/1101)
			2 Jan 1979 (amendments to Probates and Letters of Administration Act (Ireland) 1857; Juries Act (Ireland) 1871, s 18; Bankruptcy (Ireland) Amendment Act 1872, ss 57, 124; Bills of Sale (Ireland) Act 1879, s 4; Land Law (Ireland) Act 1887; Foreign Judgments (Reciprocal Enforcement) Act 1933; Trade Marks Act 1938; Exchange Control Act 1947; Representation of the People Act 1949, s 163; Arbitration Act 1950; Arbitration (International Investment Disputes) Act 1966; Criminal Appeal (Northern Ireland) Act 1968, ss 49, 50 (definition 'rules of court'); Administration of Justice Act 1969, ss 20(5), 21(4); Social Security (Northern Ireland) Act 1975) (SI 1978/1829)
			18 Apr 1979 (all other amendments to Acts of UK Parliament) (SI 1979/422)
			21 Aug 1978, 2 Jan 1979, 21 Feb 1979, 18 Apr 1979 and 1 Sep 1979 (Acts of Irish Parliament and Parliament of Northern Ireland; Orders in Council)
6			18 Apr 1979 (SI 1979/422); except para 3, and para 10 so far as it relates to para 3, which came into force on 2 Jan 1979 (SI 1978/1829); and except para 7 and, para 10 so far as it relates to para 7, which came into force on 21 Aug 1978 (SI 1978/1101)
7, Pt	I		21 Aug 1978 (repeal of Supreme Court of Judicature Act (Ireland) 1877) (SI 1978/1101)

Judicature (Northern Ireland) Act 1978 (c 23)—*contd*

Schedule

7, Pt	I—*contd*	2 Jan 1979 (repeals of or in Law of Property Amendment Act 1860, s 10; Settled Estates Act 1877, s 42; Bills of Sale (Ireland) Act 1879, s 21; Conveyancing Act 1881, ss 48(5), 72(5); Deeds of Arrangement Act 1887, s 18; Deeds of Arrangement Amendment Act 1890, s 3; Administration of Justice Act 1920, ss 11, 12(2); Representation of the People Act 1949, s 160; Arbitration Act 1950, s 42(4); Administration of Justice Act 1960, s 9(2); Northern Ireland Act 1962, ss 7–9, Sch 1; Criminal Appeal (Northern Ireland) Act 1968, s 49) (SI 1978/1829)
		18 Apr 1979 (all other repeals to Acts of UK Parliament) (SI 1979/422)
	II, III	21 Aug 1978, 2 Jan 1979 and 18 Apr 1979 (Acts of Irish Parliament and Parliament of Northern Ireland; Orders in Council)

Local Government Act 1978 (c 39)

RA: 20 Jul 1978

20 Jul 1978 (RA)

Local Government (Scotland) Act 1978 (c 4)

RA: 23 Mar 1978

Commencement provisions: s 8(3)

23 Mar 1978 (RA), except Schedule, para 2 (repealed)

Medical Act 1978 (c 12)

Whole Act repealed

National Health Service (Scotland) Act 1978 (c 29)

RA: 20 Jul 1978

Commencement provisions: s 110(4)

1 Jan 1979 (s 110(4))

Northern Ireland (Emergency Provisions) Act 1978 (c 5)

Whole Act repealed

Nuclear Safeguards and Electricity (Finance) Act 1978 (c 25)

RA: 30 Jun 1978

30 Jun 1978 (RA)

Oaths Act 1978 (c 19)

RA: 30 Jun 1978

Commencement provisions: s 8(5)

1 Aug 1978 (s 8(5))

Parliamentary Pensions Act 1978 (c 56)

Whole Act repealed

Parochial Registers and Records Measure 1978 (No 2)

RA: 2 Feb 1978

Commencement provisions: s 27(2)

1 Jan 1979 (day appointed by the Archbishops of Canterbury and York under s 27(2))

Participation Agreements Act 1978 (c 1)

Whole Act repealed

Pensioners Payments Act 1978 (c 58)

Whole Act repealed

Protection of Children Act 1978 (c 37)

RA: 20 Jul 1978

Commencement provisions: s 9(3)

Section	
1–7	20 Aug 1978 (s 9(3))
8, 9	20 Jul 1978 (s 9(3))

Rating (Disabled Persons) Act 1978 (c 40)

RA: 20 Jul 1978

Commencement provisions: s 9(4)

1 Apr 1979 (s 9(4))

Rating (Disabled Persons) Act 1978 (c 40)—*contd*

Whole Act repealed (E, W) except s 9, Sch 2 (by Local Government Finance (Repeals, Savings and Consequential Amendments) Order 1990, SI 1990/776, art 3(1), Sch 1, as from 1 Apr 1990)

Refuse Disposal (Amenity) Act 1978 (c 3)

RA: 23 Mar 1978

Commencement provisions: s 13(2)

23 Apr 1978 (s 13(2))

Representation of the People Act 1978 (c 32)

Whole Act repealed

Scotland Act 1978 (c 51)

Whole Act repealed

Shipbuilding (Redundancy Payments) Act 1978 (c 11)

Whole Act repealed

Solomon Islands Act 1978 (c 15)

RA: 25 May 1978

Independence Day: 7 Jul 1978

State Immunity Act 1978 (c 33)

RA: 20 Jul 1978

Commencement provisions: s 23(5); State Immunity Act 1978 (Commencement) Order 1978, SI 1978/1572

22 Nov 1978 (SI 1978/1572; note that Pts I, II of this Act do not apply to proceedings in respect of matters that occurred before 22 Nov 1978 (s 23(3), (4)))

Statute Law (Repeals) Act 1978 (c 45)

RA: 31 Jul 1978

Whole Act repealed, except ss 1(2), 3(1), 4, Sch 2, which came into force on 31 July 1978

Suppression of Terrorism Act 1978 (c 26)

RA: 30 Jun 1978

Commencement provisions: s 9(3); Suppression of Terrorism Act 1978 (Commencement) Order 1978, SI 1978/1063

21 Aug 1978 (SI 1978/1063)

Theatres Trust (Scotland) Act 1978 (c 24)

RA: 30 Jun 1978

30 Jun 1978 (RA)

Theft Act 1978 (c 31)

RA: 20 Jul 1978

Commencement provisions: s 7(2)

20 Oct 1978 (s 7(2))

Transport Act 1978 (c 55)

RA: 2 Aug 1978

Commencement provisions: s 24(1); Transport Act 1978 (Commencement No 1) Order 1978, SI 1978/1150; Transport Act 1978 (Commencement No 2) Order 1978, SI 1978/1187; Transport Act 1978 (Commencement No 3) Order 1978, SI 1978/1289

Section			
1–8			Repealed
9			1 Nov 1978 (SI 1978/1187)
10			1 Sep 1978 (SI 1978/1187)
11, 12			Repealed
13			1 Sep 1978 (SI 1978/1187)
14			Repealed
15			4 Aug 1978 (SI 1978/1150)
16, 17			Repealed
18			4 Aug 1978 (SI 1978/1150)
19, 20			Repealed
21			4 Aug 1978 (SI 1978/1150)
22			Spent
23			4 Aug 1978 (SI 1978/1150)
24	(1)–(3)		4 Aug 1978 (SI 1978/1150)
	(4)		See Sch 4 below
25			*Not in force*[1]
Schedule			
1, 2			Repealed
3, Pt	A		Repealed
	B		1 Nov 1978 (SI 1978/1187)
4			4 Aug 1978 (repeal in Transport Act 1968, Sch 2, para 3) (SI 1978/1150)
			1 Sep 1978 (repeals except in Transport Act 1968, Sch 2, para 3; Road Traffic Act 1972, s 57(7)) (SI 1978/1187)
			1 Nov 1978 (repeal in Road Traffic Act 1972, s 57(7)) (SI 1978/1187)

---

[1]   The fact that s 25 has not been brought into force appears to be due to an oversight

Trustee Savings Banks Act 1978 (c 16)

Whole Act repealed

Tuvalu Act 1978 (c 20)

RA: 30 Jun 1978

Independence Day: 1 Oct 1978

Wales Act 1978 (c 52)

Whole Act repealed

1979

Administration of Justice (Emergency Provisions) (Scotland) Act 1979 (c 19)

Whole Act repealed

Agricultural Statistics Act 1979 (c 13)

RA: 4 Apr 1979

Commencement provisions: s 8(2)

22 Apr 1979 (s 8(2))

Alcoholic Liquor Duties Act 1979 (c 4)

RA: 22 Feb 1979

Commencement provisions: s 93(2)

1 Apr 1979 (s 93(2))

Ancient Monuments and Archaeological Areas Act 1979 (c 46)

RA: 4 Apr 1979

Commencement provisions: s 65(2); Ancient Monuments and Archaeological Areas Act 1979 (Commencement No 1) Order 1979, SI 1979/786; Ancient Monuments and Archaeological Areas Act 1979 (Commencement No 2) Order 1981, SI 1981/1300; Ancient Monuments and Archaeological Areas Act 1979 (Commencement No 3) Order 1981, SI 1981/1466; Ancient Monuments and Archaeological Areas Act 1979 (Commencement No 4) Order 1982, SI 1982/362

Section	
1	9 Oct 1981 (E, W) (SI 1981/1300)
	30 Nov 1971 (S) (SI 1981/1466)
1A	Inserted by National Heritage Act 1983, s 33, Sch 4, para 26 (qv)
2–6	9 Oct 1981 (E, W) (SI 1981/1300)
	30 Nov 1981 (S) (SI 1981/1466)
6A	Inserted by National Heritage Act 1983, s 33, Sch 4, para 32 (qv)
7–32	9 Oct 1981 (E, W) (SI 1981/1300)
	30 Nov 1981 (S) (SI 1981/1466)
33–41	14 Apr 1982 (E, W) (SI 1982/362)
	Not in force (S)

41

Ancient Monuments and Archaeological Areas Act 1979 (c 46)—*contd*

Section

42–47	9 Oct 1981 (except so far as relate to Pt II) (E, W) (SI 1981/1300)
	30 Nov 1981 (S) (SI 1981/1466)
	14 Apr 1982 (so far as relate to Pt II) (E, W) (SI 1982/362)
48, 49	16 Jul 1979 (E, W) (SI 1979/786)
	30 Nov 1981 (S) (SI 1981/1466)
50–52	9 Oct 1981 (except so far as relate to Pt II) (E, W) (SI 1981/1300)
	30 Nov 1981 (S) (SI 1981/1466)
	14 Apr 1982 (so far as relate to Pt II) (E, W) (SI 1982/362)
52A	Inserted (E, W) by Norfolk and Suffolk Broads Act 1988, s 2(5), Sch 3, Pt I, para 30(1) (qv)
53–62	9 Oct 1981 (except so far as relate to Pt II) (E, W) (SI 1981/1300)
	30 Nov 1981 (S) (SI 1981/1466)
	14 Apr 1982 (so far as relate to Pt II) (E, W) (SI 1982/362)
63	Repealed
64	9 Oct 1981 (except so far as relates to Pt II) (E, W) (SI 1981/1300)
	30 Nov 1981 (S) (SI 1981/1466)
	14 Apr 1982 (so far as relates to Pt II) (E, W) (SI 1982/362)
65	4 Apr 1979 (RA)
Schedule	
1	9 Oct 1981 (E, W) (SI 1981/1300)
	30 Nov 1981 (S) (SI 1981/1466)
2	14 Apr 1982 (E, W) (SI 1982/362)
	Not in force (S)
3–5	9 Oct 1981 (except so far as relate to Pt II) (E, W) (SI 1981/1300)
	30 Nov 1981 (S) (SI 1981/1466)
	14 Apr 1982 (so far as relate to Pt II) (E, W) (SI 1982/362)

Appropriation Act 1979 (c 24)

Whole Act repealed

Appropriation (No 2) Act 1979 (c 51)

Whole Act repealed

Arbitration Act 1979 (c 42)

Whole Act repealed

Banking Act 1979 (c 37)

RA: 4 Apr 1979

Commencement provisions: s 52(3), (4); Banking Act 1979 (Commencement No 1) Order 1979, SI 1979/938; Banking Act 1979 (Commencement No 2) Order 1982, SI 1982/188; Banking Act 1979 (Commencement No 3) Order 1985, SI 1985/797

Section		
1–37		Repealed
38		1 Oct 1979 (SI 1979/938)
39–46		Repealed
47		1 Oct 1979 (SI 1979/938)
48–50		Repealed
51	(1)	See Sch 6 below
	(2)	Spent
52		1 Oct 1979 (SI 1979/938)
Schedule		
1–5		Repealed
6, para	1–3	19 Feb 1982 (SI 1982/188)
	4–8	Repealed
	9	1 Jul 1985 (SI 1985/797)
	10–12	Repealed
	13–15	19 Feb 1982 (SI 1982/188)
	16–18	Repealed
	19	19 Feb 1982 (SI 1982/188)
7		Repealed

Capital Gains Tax Act 1979 (c 14)

Whole Act repealed

Carriage by Air and Road Act 1979 (c 28)

RA: 4 Apr 1979

Commencement provisions: ss 2(2), 7(2); Carriage by Air and Road Act 1979 (Commencement No 1) Order 1980, SI 1980/1966; Carriage by Air and Road Act 1979 (Commencement No 2) Order 1997, SI 1997/2565; Carriage by Air and Road Act 1979 (Commencement No 3) Order 1998, SI 1998/2562; Carriage by Air and Road Act 1979 (Commencement No 4) Order 2000, SI 2000/2768

Section		
1		*Not in force*
2		4 Apr 1979 (does not apply to loss which occurred before that date) (s 2(2))
3	(1)	22 Oct 1998 (SI 1998/2562)
	(2)	12 Oct 2000 (SI 2000/2768)
	(3)	28 Dec 1980 (SI 1980/1966)
	(4)	*Not in force*

Carriage by Air and Road Act 1979 (c 28)—*contd*

Section

4	(1)		1 Dec 1997 (SI 1997/2565)
	(2)		28 Dec 1980 (SI 1980/1966)
	(3)		*Not in force*
	(4)		28 Dec 1980 (so far as relates to amendment of Carriage of Goods by Road Act 1965 by s 4(2)) (SI 1980/1966)
			1 Dec 1997 (so far as relates to amendment of Carriage by Air Act 1961 by s 4(1)) (SI 1997/2565)
			Not in force (otherwise)
5			28 Dec 1980 (so far as relates to amendment of Carriage of Goods by Road Act 1965 by s 4(2)) (SI 1980/1966)
			1 Dec 1997 (so far as relates to amendment of Carriage by Air Act 1961 by s 4(1)) (SI 1997/2565)
			Not in force (otherwise)
6	(1)	(a)	1 Dec 1997 (so far as relates to Carriage by Air Act 1961, ss 9, 10) (SI 1997/2565)
			12 Oct 2000 (otherwise) (SI 2000/2768)
		(b)	28 Dec 1980 (SI 1980/1966)
		(c)	*Not in force*
	(2)		*Not in force*
	(3)		1 Dec 1997 (so far as relates to the provisions specified in SI 1997/2565, Schedule) (SI 1997/2565)
			12 Oct 2000 (so far as relates to the provisions specified in SI 2000/2768, Schedule) (SI 2000/2768)
	(4)		*Not in force*
7			4 Apr 1979 (RA)
Schedule			
1, 2			*Not in force*

Charging Orders Act 1979 (c 53)

RA: 6 Dec 1979

Commencement provisions: s 8(2); Charging Orders Act 1979 (Commencement) Order 1980, SI 1980/627

3 Jun 1980 (SI 1980/627)

Confirmation to Small Estates (Scotland) Act 1979 (c 22)

RA: 29 Mar 1979

Commencement provisions: s 3(2); Confirmation to Small Estates (Scotland) Act 1979 (Commencement) Order 1980, SI 1980/734

Section	
1, 2	1 Jul 1980 (SI 1980/734)
3	29 Mar 1979 (RA)
Schedule	1 Jul 1980 (SI 1980/734)

Consolidated Fund Act 1979 (c 20)

Whole Act repealed

Consolidated Fund (No 2) Act 1979 (c 56)

Whole Act repealed

Credit Unions Act 1979 (c 34)

RA: 4 Apr 1979

Commencement provisions: s 33(2); Credit Unions Act 1979 (Commencement No 1) Order 1979, SI 1979/936; Credit Unions Act 1979 (Commencement No 2) Order 1980, SI 1980/481

Section		
1, 2		20 Aug 1979 (SI 1979/936)
3	(1)	20 Aug 1979 (SI 1979/936)
	(2), (3)	*Not in force*
	(4)	20 Aug 1979 (SI 1979/936)
4–11		20 Aug 1979 (SI 1979/936)
11A		Inserted (1 Sep 1996) by Deregulation (Credit Unions) Order 1996, SI 1996/1189, arts 5(1), 7
11B–11D		Inserted (1 Sep 1996) by Deregulation (Credit Unions) Order 1996, SI 1996/1189, arts 5(1), 7; repealed by Financial Services and Markets Act 2000, ss 338(4), 432(3), Sch 18, Pt V, para 23, Sch 22, as from 2 July 2002 (SI 2001/3538, art 2(5)(a))
12–14		20 Aug 1979 (SI 1979/936)
15		1 Oct 1980 (SI 1980/481)
16–24		20 Aug 1979 (SI 1979/936)
25		Repealed
26–28		20 Aug 1979 (SI 1979/936)

Credit Unions Act 1979 (c 34)—*contd*

Section

29   Substituted (1 Dec 2001) by
                                                  Financial Services and Markets
                                                  Act 2000 (Mutual Societies)
                                                  Order 2001, SI 2001/2617,
                                                  art 13(1), Sch 3, Pt IV,
                                                  paras 264, 287

30   Repealed
31   20 Aug 1979 (SI 1979/936)
32, 33   4 Apr 1979 (s 33(2))

Schedule

1, 2   20 Aug 1979 (SI 1979/936)
3   Repealed

Criminal Evidence Act 1979 (c 16)

RA: 22 Mar 1979

Commencement provisions: s 2(2)

22 Apr 1979 (s 2(2))

Crown Agents Act 1979 (c 43)

RA: 4 Apr 1979

4 Apr 1979 (RA; but note that most of the provisions of the Act became effective
    from 1 Jan 1980, the day appointed by the Crown Agents Act 1979 (Appointed
    Day) Order 1979, SI 1979/1672, made under s 1(1)).

Ss 1(7), 2–24, 27(2), 28, 31(2), (3), Sch 1, paras 8, 9, 11, 13–15, Schs 2–4, Sch 6, Pt II
are repealed by the Crown Agents Act 1995, s 13(2), Sch 2, Pt I (ie from the
appointed day under s 1(1) of the 1995 Act), and further repeals will come into
force from the day on which the Crown Agents are dissolved in accordance with
s 8(4) of the 1995 Act.

Customs and Excise Duties (General Reliefs) Act 1979 (c 3)

RA: 22 Feb 1979

Commencement provisions: ss 20(2), 59(7), 62(2)

1 Apr 1979 (s 20(2))

Customs and Excise Management Act 1979 (c 2)

RA: 22 Feb 1979

Commencement provisions: ss 59(7), 62(2), 178(3)

1 Apr 1979 (s 178(3)) except ss 59, 62(2) which are *not in force*

Education Act 1979 (c 49)

Whole Act repealed

Electricity (Scotland) Act 1979 (c 11)

RA: 22 Mar 1979

Commencement provisions: s 47(4)

Whole Act repealed by Electricity Act 1989, s 112(4), Sch 18 (the repeal being
brought into force on 31 Mar 1990 by Electricity Act 1989 (Commencement
No 2) Order 1990, SI 1990/117), except repeals of or in s 1, Sch 1, paras 2–6
which came into force on 22 Apr 1979 (s 47(4)); orders made under Electricity
Act 1989, s 113(2), bringing the prospective repeal of the excepted provisions
into force will be noted to that Act in the service to this work

---

Estate Agents Act 1979 (c 38)

RA: 4 Apr 1979

Commencement provisions: s 36(2); Estate Agents Act 1979 (Commencement No 1)
Order 1981, SI 1981/1517

Section	
1–15	3 May 1982 (SI 1981/1517)
16, 17	*Not in force*
18	3 May 1982 (SI 1981/1517)
19	*Not in force*
20, 21	3 May 1982 (SI 1981/1517)
22	*Not in force*
23–34	3 May 1982 (SI 1981/1517)
35	Repealed
36	3 May 1982 (SI 1981/1517)
Schedule	
1, 2	3 May 1982 (SI 1981/1517)

European Communities (Greek Accession) Act 1979 (c 57)

RA: 20 Dec 1979

20 Dec 1979 (RA; but note that the accession of Greece to the European
Communities did not take effect until 1 Jan 1981)

European Parliament (Pay and Pensions) Act 1979 (c 50)

RA: 26 Jul 1979

26 Jul 1979 (RA)

Exchange Equalisation Account Act 1979 (c 30)

RA: 4 Apr 1979

Commencement provisions: s 5(3)

5 May 1979 (s 5(3))

Excise Duties (Surcharges or Rebates) Act 1979 (c 8)

RA: 22 Feb 1979

Commencement provisions: s 5(2)

1 Apr 1979 (s 5(2))

Films Act 1979 (c 9)

Whole Act repealed

Finance Act 1979 (c 25)

Whole Act repealed

Finance (No 2) Act 1979 (c 47)

Budget Day: 12 Jun 1979

RA: 26 Jul 1979

Details of the commencement of Finance Acts are not set out in this work

---

Forestry Act 1979 (c 21)

RA: 29 Mar 1979

Commencement provisions: s 3(3)

30 May 1979 (s 3(3))

House of Commons (Redistribution of Seats) Act 1979 (c 15)

Whole Act repealed

Hydrocarbon Oil Duties Act 1979 (c 5)

RA: 22 Feb 1979

Commencement provisions: s 29(2)

1 Apr 1979 (s 29(2))

Independent Broadcasting Authority Act 1979 (c 35)

Whole Act repealed

Industry Act 1979 (c 32)

RA: 4 Apr 1979

4 Apr 1979 (RA)

International Monetary Fund Act 1979 (c 29)

RA: 4 Apr 1979

Commencement provisions: s 7(2)

5 May 1979 (s 7(2))

Isle of Man Act 1979 (c 58)

RA: 20 Dec 1979

Commencement provisions: s 14(6), (7)

Section	
1–5	1 Apr 1980 (s 14(6))
6, 7	20 Dec 1979 (subject to the proviso that no Order in Council and no provision by virtue of s 6(5) or 7(5) be made by or under an Act of Tynwald so as to come into force before 1 Apr 1980) (s 14(7))
8, 9	1 Apr 1980 (s 14(6))
10	20 Dec 1979 (s 14(7))
11	20 Dec 1979 (subject to the proviso that no Order in Council be made under this section so as to come into force before 1 Apr 1980) (s 14(7))
12–14	1 Apr 1980 (s 14(6))
Schedule	
1, 2	1 Apr 1980 (s 14(6))

Justices of the Peace Act 1979 (c 55)

Whole Act repealed

Kiribati Act 1979 (c 27)

RA: 19 Jun 1979

Independence Day: 12 Jul 1979

Land Registration (Scotland) Act 1979 (c 33)

RA: 4 Apr 1979

Commencement provisions: s 30(2); Land Registration (Scotland) Act 1979 (Commencement No 1) Order 1980, SI 1980/1412; Land Registration (Scotland) Act 1979 (Commencement No 2) Order 1982, SI 1982/520; Land Registration (Scotland) Act 1979 (Commencement No 3) Order 1983, SI 1983/745; Land Registration (Scotland) Act 1979 (Commencement No 4) Order 1985, SI 1985/501; Land Registration (Scotland) Act 1979 (Commencement No 5) Order 1992, SI 1992/815; Land Registration (Scotland) Act 1979 (Commencement No 6) Order 1992, SI 1992/2060; Land Registration (Scotland) Act 1979 (Commencement No 7) Order 1993, SI 1993/922; Land Registration (Scotland) Act 1979 (Commencement No 8) Order 1994, SI 1994/2588; Land Registration (Scotland) Act 1979 (Commencement No 9) Order 1995, SI 1995/2547; Land Registration (Scotland) Act 1979 (Commencement No 10) Order 1996, SI 1996/2490; Land Registration (Scotland) Act 1979 (Commencement No 11) Order 1998, SI 1998/1810; Land Registration (Scotland) Act 1979 (Commencement No 12) Order 1998, SI 1998/2980; Land Registration (Scotland) Act 1979 (Commencement No 13) Order 1999, SSI 1999/111; Land Registration (Scotland) Act 1979 (Commencement No 14) Order 2000, SSI 2000/338; Land Registration (Scotland) Act 1979 (Commencement No 15) Order 2001, SSI 2001/309

Section

1		4 Apr 1979 (s 30(2))
2	(1), (2)	6 Apr 1981 (in the area, for the purpose of registration of writs, of the County of Renfrew) (SI 1980/1412)
		4 Oct 1982 (in the area, for the purpose of registration of writs, of the County of Dunbarton) (SI 1982/520)
		3 Jan 1984 (in the area, for the purpose of registration of writs, of the County of Lanark) (SI 1983/745)
		30 Sep 1985 (in the area, for the purpose of registration of writs, of the Barony and Regality of Glasgow) (SI 1985/501)
		1 Oct 1992 (in the area, for the purpose of registration of writs, of the County of Clackmannan) (SI 1992/815)
		1 Apr 1993 (in the area, for the purpose of registration of writs, of the County of Stirling) (SI 1992/2060)
		1 Oct 1993 (in the area, for the purpose of registration of writs, of the County of West Lothian) (SI 1993/922)

Land Registration (Scotland) Act 1979 (c 33)—*contd*

Section

2	(1), (2)—*contd*	1 Apr 1995 (in the area, for the purpose of registration of writs, of the County of Fife) (SI 1994/2588)
		1 Apr 1996 (in the areas, for the purpose of registration of writs, of the Counties of Aberdeen and Kincardine) (SI 1995/2547)
		1 Apr 1997 (in the areas, for the purpose of registration of writs, of the Counties of Ayr, Dumfries, Stewartry of Kirkcudbright and Wigtown) (SI 1996/2490)
		1 Apr 1999 (in the areas, for the purpose of registration of writs, of the Counties of Perth, Angus and Kinross) (SI 1998/1810)
		1 Oct 1999 (in the areas, for the purpose of registration of writs, of the Counties of Berwick, East Lothian, Roxburgh, Selkirk and Peebles) (SI 1998/2980)
		1 Apr 2000 (in the areas, for the purpose of registration of writs, of the Counties of Argyll and Bute) (SSI 1999/111)
		1 Apr 2001 (in the area, for the purpose of registration of writs, of the County of Midlothian) (SSI 2000/338)
		1 Apr 2002 (in the areas, for the purpose of registration of writs, of the Counties of Inverness and Nairn) (SSI 2001/309)
		Not in force (otherwise)
	(3)–(6)	6 Apr 1981 (SI 1980/1412)
3	(1), (2)	6 Apr 1981 (SI 1980/1412)
	(3)	6 Apr 1981 (in the area, for the purpose of registration of writs, of the County of Renfrew) (SI 1980/1412)
		4 Oct 1982 (in the area for the purpose of registration of writs, of the County of Dunbarton) (SI 1982/520)
		3 Jan 1984 (in the area, for the purpose of registration of writs, of the County of Lanark) (SI 1983/745)

Enquiry Bureau 020 7400 2518

Land Registration (Scotland) Act 1979 (c 33)—*contd*

Section

3	(3)—*contd*	30 Sep 1985 (in the area, for the purpose of registration of writs, of the Barony and Regality of Glasgow) (SI 1985/501)

1 Oct 1992 (in the area, for the purpose of registration of writs, of the County of Clackmannan) (SI 1992/815)

1 Apr 1993 (in the area, for the purpose of registration of writs, of the County of Stirling) (SI 1992/2060)

1 Oct 1993 (in the area, for the purpose of registration of writs, of the County of West Lothian) (SI 1993/922)

1 Apr 1995 (in the area, for the purpose of registration of writs, of the County of Fife) (SI 1994/2588)

1 Apr 1996 (in the areas, for the purpose of registration of writs, of the Counties of Aberdeen and Kincardine) (SI 1995/2547)

1 Apr 1997 (in the areas, for the purpose of registration of writs, of the Counties of Ayr, Dumfries, Stewartry of Kirkcudbright and Wigtown) (SI 1996/2490)

1 Apr 1999 (in the areas, for the purpose of registration of writs, of the Counties of Perth, Angus and Kinross) (SI 1998/1810)

1 Oct 1999 (in the areas, for the purpose of registration of writs, of the Counties of Berwick, East Lothian, Roxburgh, Selkirk and Peebles) (SI 1998/2980)

1 Apr 2000 (in the areas, for the purpose of registration of writs, of the Counties of Argyll and Bute) (SSI 1999/111)

1 Apr 2001 (in the area, for the purpose of registration of writs, of the County of Midlothian) (SSI 2000/338)

1 Apr 2002 (in the areas, for the purpose of registration of writs, of the Counties of Inverness and Nairn) (SSI 2001/309)

Not in force (otherwise)

Land Registration (Scotland) Act 1979 (c 33)—*contd*

Section

3	(4)–(7)	6 Apr 1981 (SI 1980/1412)
4–15		6 Apr 1981 (SI 1980/1412)
16–22		4 Apr 1979 (s 30(2))
22A		Inserted by Law Reform (Miscellaneous Provisions) Act 1985, s 2 (qv)
23		4 Apr 1979 (s 30(2))
24–29		4 Apr 1979 (so far as relate to ss 1, 16–23, 30) (s 30(2)) 6 Apr 1981 (otherwise) (SI 1980/1412)
30		4 Apr 1979 (s 30(2))
Schedule		
1		4 Apr 1979 (s 30(2))
2–4		4 Apr 1979 (so far as relate to ss 1, 16–23, 30) (s 30(2)) 6 Apr 1981 (otherwise) (SI 1980/1412)

Leasehold Reform Act 1979 (c 44)

RA: 4 Apr 1979

4 Apr 1979 (RA)

Legal Aid Act 1979 (c 26)

Whole Act repealed

Matches and Mechanical Lighters Duties Act 1979 (c 6)

Whole Act repealed

Merchant Shipping Act 1979 (c 39)

Whole Act repealed; note however s 47, which was repealed with savings by Merchant Shipping (Registration, etc) Act 1993, s 8(4), Sch 5, Pt II, as from 1 May 1994, but instruments made under s 47 and in force on that date remained in force until superseded by an instrument made under Sch 4, para 4 to the 1993 Act (Merchant Shipping (Registration, etc) Act 1993 (Commencement No 1 and Transitional Provisions) Order 1993, SI 1993/3137, art 7(1), Sch 3). Sch 4, para 4 to the 1993 Act was repealed by Merchant Shipping Act 1995, s 314(1), Sch 12, and by virtue of Interpretation Act 1978, s 17(2)(b), such instruments remain in force until superseded by an instrument made under s 315 of the 1995 Act

Nurses, Midwives and Health Visitors Act 1979 (c 36)

RA: 4 Apr 1979

Commencement provisions: s 24(2); Nurses, Midwives and Health Visitors Act 1979 (Commencement No 1) Order 1980, SI 1980/893; Nurses, Midwives and Health Visitors Act 1979 (Commencement No 2) Order 1982, SI 1982/963; Nurses, Midwives and Health Visitors Act 1979 (Commencement No 3) Order 1982, SI 1982/1565; Nurses, Midwives and Health Visitors Act 1979 (Commencement No 4) Order 1983, SI 1983/668

Section		
1–22B		Repealed
23	(1)–(3)	Repealed
	(4)	1 Jul 1983 (SI 1983/668)
	(5)	Repealed
24		4 Apr 1979 (s 24(2))
Schedule		
1–6		Repealed
7		1 Jul 1983 (SI 1983/668)
8		Repealed

Pensioners' Payments and Social Security Act 1979 (c 48)

Whole Act repealed

Pneumoconiosis etc (Workers' Compensation) Act 1979 (c 41)

RA: 4 Apr 1979

Commencement provisions: s 10(3)

4 Jul 1979 (s 10(3))

Price Commission (Amendment) Act 1979 (c 1)

Whole Act repealed

Prosecution of Offences Act 1979 (c 31)

Whole Act repealed

Public Health Laboratory Service Act 1979 (c 23)

RA: 29 Mar 1979

29 Mar 1979 (RA)

Public Lending Right Act 1979 (c 10)

RA: 22 Mar 1979

Commencement provisions: s 5(3); Public Lending Right Act 1979 (Commencement) Order 1980, SI 1980/83

1 Mar 1980 (SI 1980/83)

Representation of the People Act 1979 (c 40)

Whole Act repealed

Sale of Goods Act 1979 (c 54)

RA: 6 Dec 1979

Commencement provisions: s 64(2)

1 Jan 1980 (s 64(2))

Shipbuilding Act 1979 (c 59)

RA: 20 Dec 1979

20 Dec 1979 (RA)

Social Security Act 1979 (c 18)

RA: 22 Mar 1979

Commencement provisions: s 21(2), (3); Social Security Act 1979 (Commencement No 1) Order 1979, SI 1979/369; Social Security Act 1979 (Commencement No 2) Order 1979, SI 1979/1031; Social Security Act 1986, s 72 (repealed)

Section		
1		22 Mar 1979 (RA)
2–10		Repealed
11		6 Apr 1979 (s 21(3))
12–15		Repealed
16		22 Mar 1979 (S) (RA)
		Repealed (E, W)
17–19		Repealed
20, 21		22 Mar 1979 (RA)
Schedule		
1, 2		Repealed
3, para	1–11	Repealed
	12, 13	Spent
	14–16	Repealed
	17	Spent
	18	Repealed
	19	Spent
	20	6 Apr 1979 (s 21(3))
	21	22 Mar 1979 (RA)
	22	6 Apr 1979 (s 21(3))
	23–29	Repealed
	30	Repealed or spent
	31, 32	Repealed

Southern Rhodesia Act 1979 (c 52)

RA: 14 Nov 1979

Appointed Day: 18 Apr 1980

Tobacco Products Duty Act 1979 (c 7)

RA: 22 Feb 1979

Commencement provisions: s 12(2)

1 Apr 1979 (s 12(2))

_____

Vaccine Damage Payments Act 1979 (c 17)

RA: 22 Feb 1979

22 Feb 1979 (RA)

_____

Wages Councils Act 1979 (c 12)

Whole Act repealed

_____

Weights and Measures Act 1979 (c 45)

Whole Act repealed

_____

Zimbabwe Act 1979 (c 60)

RA: 20 Dec 1979

Independence Day: 18 Apr 1980

_____

1980

Anguilla Act 1980 (c 67)

RA: 16 Dec 1980

16 Dec 1980 (RA; but note the Anguilla (Appointed Day) Order 1980, SI 1980/1953, appointing 19 Dec 1980 for the purposes of s 1(1) (repealed))

Appropriation Act 1980 (c 54)

Whole Act repealed

Bail etc (Scotland) Act 1980 (c 4)

Whole Act repealed

Bees Act 1980 (c 12)

RA: 20 Mar 1980

Commencement provisions: s 5(2); Bees Act 1980 (Commencement) Order 1980, SI 1980/791

10 Jun 1980 (SI 1980/791)

Betting, Gaming and Lotteries (Amendment) Act 1980 (c 18)

Whole Act repealed

British Aerospace Act 1980 (c 26)

RA: 1 May 1980

1 May 1980 (RA; but note Act largely took effect on 1 Jan 1981, the day appointed under s 14(1))

Broadcasting Act 1980 (c 64)

Whole Act repealed

Child Care Act 1980 (c 5)

Whole Act repealed

Civil Aviation Act 1980 (c 60)

RA: 13 Nov 1980

Commencement provisions: ss 10(1), 12 (repealed); Civil Aviation Act 1980 (Commencement) Order 1981, SI 1981/671; Civil Aviation Act 1980 (Appointed Day) Order 1983, SI 1983/1940

Section	
1	13 Nov 1980 (RA), but not effective until 1 Apr 1984, the day appointed under s 10(1) by SI 1983/1940
2	Spent
3–10	13 Nov 1980 (RA), but not effective until 1 Apr 1984, the day appointed under s 10(1) by SI 1983/1940
11–19	Repealed
20	13 Nov 1980 (RA)
21–26	Repealed
27	Spent
28	See Sch 3 below
29–31	13 Nov 1980 (RA)
Schedule	
1, 2	13 Nov 1980 (RA)
3	13 Nov 1980 (except repeal of Civil Aviation Act 1971, s 24(2)) (RA)
	22 May 1981 (exception noted above) (SI 1981/671)

Coal Industry Act 1980 (c 50)

RA: 8 Aug 1980

8 Aug 1980 (RA)

Whole Act repealed (in part prospectively) as follows: ss 1, 2, 7–11 prospectively repealed by Coal Industry Act 1994, s 67(8), Sch 11, Pts III, IV[1]; s 3 repealed by Coal Industry Act 1985, s 5(2); ss 4, 5 repealed by Coal Industry Act 1983, ss 2(3), 6(3), Schedule; s 6 repealed by Coal Industry Act 1987, s 10(3), Sch 3, Pt I

---

[1]   Orders made under Coal Industry Act 1994 bringing these prospective repeals into force will be noted to that Act

---

Companies Act 1980 (c 22)

Whole Act repealed

Competition Act 1980 (c 21)

RA: 3 Apr 1980

Commencement provisions: s 33(5); Competition Act 1980 (Commencement No 1) Order 1980, SI 1980/497; Competition Act 1980 (Commencement No 2) Order 1980, SI 1980/978

Section

1–10			Repealed (the repeal of ss 4, 9 are subject to savings and transitional provisions in Competition Act 1998, s 74(2), Sch 13)
11	(1), (2)		4 Apr 1980 (SI 1980/497)
	(3)	(a)	4 Apr 1980 (SI 1980/497)
		(aa)	Inserted by Railways Act 1993, s 152(1), Sch 12, para 12(1) (qv)
		(b)	Substituted by Transport Act 1985, s 114(1) (qv)
		(bb)	Inserted by London Regional Transport Act 1984, s 71(3)(a), Sch 6, para 15 (qv)
		(c)	Substituted by Water Act 1989, s 190(1), Sch 25, para 59(1) (qv)
		(cc)	Inserted (S) by Local Government etc (Scotland) Act 1994, s 72 (qv)
		(d), (e)	4 Apr 1980 (SI 1980/497)
		(f)	4 Apr 1980 (except so far as relates to s 11(3)(b)) (SI 1980/497) 12 Aug 1980 (exception noted above) (SI 1980/978)
	(4), (5)		12 Aug 1980 (SI 1980/978)
	(6), (7)		4 Apr 1980 (SI 1980/497)
	(8)	(a)	4 Apr 1980 (SI 1980/497)
		(b)	Repealed (subject to savings and transitional provisions in Competition Act 1998, s 74(2), Sch 13)
	(9)		Substituted for new sub-ss (9), (9A) by Competition Act 1998, s 74(1), Sch 12, para 4(1), (3) (qv)
	(9A)		Inserted as noted to sub-s (9) above
	(10), (11)		4 Apr 1980 (SI 1980/497)
12, 13			1 May 1980 (SI 1980/497)
14			Repealed
15	(1)		1 May 1980 (SI 1980/497)
	(2)	(a), (b)	Repealed
		(c)	4 Apr 1980 (for purposes of s 11) (SI 1980/497) 12 Aug 1980 (otherwise) (SI 1980/978)
	(3), (4)		Repealed

Competition Act 1980 (c 21)—*contd*

Competition Act 1980 (c 21)—*contd*

Schedule

1   Repealed
2   4 Apr 1980 (except as noted below)
                                       (SI 1980/457)
                                     1 Jan 2011 (repeals of Counter-
                                       Inflation Act 1973, ss 17(6), (8),
                                       (9), 18(4), (5), 19, 20(4), (5)(i),
                                       (iii), (7), 23(2), Sch 4, para 4
                                       (except sub-para (2)(b)); Price
                                       Commission Act 1977, s 15(4),
                                       Sch 2, para 4(b), (d)) (SI 1980/497)

Concessionary Travel for Handicapped Persons (Scotland) Act 1980 (c 29)

RA: 23 May 1980

23 May 1980 (RA)

Consolidated Fund Act 1980 (c 14)

Whole Act repealed

Consolidated Fund (No 2) Act 1980 (c 68)

Whole Act repealed

Consular Fees Act 1980 (c 23)

RA: 1 May 1980

1 May 1980 (RA)

Coroners Act 1980 (c 38)

Whole Act repealed

Criminal Appeal (Northern Ireland) Act 1980 (c 47)

RA: 1 Aug 1980

Commencement provisions: s 52(2)

1 Sep 1980 (s 52(2))

Criminal Justice (Scotland) Act 1980 (c 62)

RA: 13 Mar 1980

Commencement provisions: s 84(2); Criminal Justice (Scotland) Act 1980 (Commencement No 1) Order 1981, SI 1981/50; Criminal Justice (Scotland) Act 1980 (Commencement No 2) Order 1981, SI 1981/444; Criminal Justice (Scotland) Act 1980 (Commencement No 3) Order 1981, SI 1981/766; Criminal Justice (Scotland) Act 1980 (Commencement No 4) Order 1981, SI 1981/1751; Criminal Justice (Scotland) Act 1980 (Commencement No 5) Order 1983, SI 1983/1580

Criminal Justice (Scotland) Act 1980 (c 62)—*contd*

Section

1–3		Repealed
3A–3D		Inserted by Law Reform (Miscellaneous Provisions) (Scotland) Act 1985, s 35 (qv); prospectively repealed by Terrorism Act 2000, s 125, Sch 16, Pt I[2]
4–44		Repealed
45		15 Nov 1983 (SI 1983/1580)
46–50		Repealed
51		1 Jun 1981 (SI 1981/766)
52–55		Repealed
56, 57		1 Feb 1981 (SI 1981/50)
58–78		Repealed
79		1 Feb 1981 (SI 1981/50)
80		Repealed
81, 82		1 Feb 1981 (SI 1981/50)
83		See Schs 6–8 below
84	(1)–(4)	1 Feb 1981 (SI 1981/50)
	(5)	1 Feb 1981 (for purposes of extending to England and Wales ss 22, 84(1)–(5), Sch 6, paras 2, 8, Sch 7, paras 8, 9, 11(a), 24(c), 58, 79, Sch 8 (so far as repeals Criminal Procedure (Scotland) Act 1975, s 365)) (SI 1981/50)
		1 Apr 1981 (for purposes of extending to England and Wales s 66, Sch 6, para 9) (SI 1981/444)
		1 Jun 1981 (for purposes of extending to England and Wales s 51, Sch 6, para 10) (SI 1981/766)
		15 Nov 1983 (for purposes of extending to England and Wales Sch 7, paras 6(a), 10, 24(a), (b)(i), (ii), (d)(i), (ii), Sch 8 (so far as repeals Criminal Justice Act 1961, s 32(2)(b) and words in ss 32(2)(f), 38(3)(a))) (SI 1983/1580)
	(6)	1 Feb 1981 (for purposes of extending to Northern Ireland ss 22, 84(1)–(4), (6), Sch 6, paras 2, 8, Sch 7, paras 8, 9, 11(a), 77) (SI 1981/50)
		1 Apr 1981 (for purposes of extending to Northern Ireland s 66, Sch 6, para 9) (SI 1981/444)
		1 Jun 1981 (for purposes of extending to Northern Ireland s 51, Sch 6, para 10) (SI 1981/766)

Criminal Justice (Scotland) Act 1980 (c 62)—*contd*

Section

84	(6)—*contd*			15 Nov 1983 (for purposes of extending to Northern Ireland Sch 7, paras 6(a), 10, Sch 8 (so far as repeals Criminal Justice Act 1961, s 32(2)(b) and words in ss 32(2)(f), 38(3)(a))) (SI 1983/1580)
	(7)			15 Nov 1983 (for purposes of extending to Channel Islands and Isle of Man s 84(1)–(4), (7), Sch 7, paras 6(a), 10(a), Sch 8 (so far as repeals Criminal Justice Act 1961, s 32(2)(b))) (SI 1983/1580)

Schedule

1–5				Repealed
6, para	1–8			1 Feb 1981 (SI 1981/50)
	9			1 Apr 1981 (SI 1981/444)
	10			1 Jun 1981 (SI 1981/766)
7, para	1–7			Repealed
	8, 9			1 Feb 1981 (SI 1981/50)
	10			15 Nov 1983 (SI 1983/1580)
	11	(a)		1 Feb 1981 (SI 1981/50)
		(b)		Spent
	12			Repealed
	13			1 Feb 1981 (SI 1981/50)
	14, 15			Repealed
	16			1 Feb 1981 (SI 1981/50)
	17–21			Repealed
	22			1 Feb 1981 (SI 1981/50); prospectively repealed by Transport Act 1981, s 40(4), Sch 12, Pt III[1]
	23			Repealed
	24	(a)		1 Apr 1981 (SI 1981/444)
		(b)	(i)	1 Apr 1981 (SI 1981/444)
			(ii)	15 Nov 1983 (SI 1983/1580)
		(c)		1 Feb 1981 (SI 1981/50)
		(d)	(i)	15 Nov 1983 (SI 1983/1580)
			(ii)	1 Apr 1981 (SI 1981/444)
	25–78			Repealed
	79			1 Feb 1981 (SI 1981/50)
8				1 Feb 1981 (repeals of or in Treason Act 1708, s 7; Treason Act 1800; Conspiracy and Protection of Property Act 1875, s 11; Burgh Police (Scotland) Act 1892, s 382; Children and Young Persons Act 1933, s 26(5); Treason Act 1945; Criminal Justice (Scotland) Act 1949, ss 21, 75(3)(e); Prisons (Scotland)

Criminal Justice (Scotland) Act 1980 (c 62)—*contd*
Schedule
8—*contd*

Act 1952, ss 7(4), 19, 31(4), 35(5)(a);
Road Traffic Act 1960, s 246;
Penalties for Drunkenness Act 1962,
s 1(2)(a), (b); Road Traffic
Regulation Act 1967, s 93;
Criminal Justice Act 1961, s 70(1);
Firearms Act 1968, Sch 6, Pt II,
para 1; Road Traffic Act 1972,
Sch 4, Pt IV, para 3; Social Security
Act 1975, s 147(6); Criminal
Procedure (Scotland) Act 1975,
ss 141, 191(1), 193(2), 195, 197–
202, 228, 285, 289D(3)(c), 296(5),
310, 314(3), 337(e), 346, 365,
392(1), 399(1), 405, 410, 411(2),
417, 434(3), 460(5), (6), Schs 4,
7B, para 1; Child Benefit Act 1975,
s 11(8); Licensing (Scotland)
Act 1976, s 128(2); Sexual
Offences (Scotland) Act 1976, ss 7,
16; Supplementary Benefits
Act 1976, s 26(5); Criminal Law
Act 1977, Sch 11, paras 11–13;
Customs and Excise Management
Act 1979, s 149(2)) (SI 1981/50)

1 Apr 1981 (repeals of or in Railways
Clauses Consolidation (Scotland)
Act 1845, s 144; Protection of
Animals (Scotland) Act 1912, s 4;
Criminal Justice Act 1967, s 60(6),
(8); Immigration Act 1971, s 6(5);
Criminal Procedure (Scotland)
Act 1975, ss 229, 232, 234(1), (3),
236, 240, 245(3), 247, 253(2), 257,
263(1), 265(3), 272, 274(1), 277,
444(6), 445, 447(2), 448(9), 454(2),
Sch 9, para 40) (SI 1981/444)

1 Jan 1982 (repeals of or in Criminal
Procedure (Scotland) Act 1887,
Schs F, G; Criminal Procedure
(Scotland) Act 1975, ss 68(3),
74(3), 105–107, 120–122)
(SI 1981/1751)

15 Nov 1983 (repeals of or in Prisons
(Scotland) Act 1952, ss 32, 33,
37(2); Criminal Justice Act 1961,
ss 32(2)(b), (f), 38(3)(a); Criminal
Justice (Scotland) Act 1963, ss 2, 4,
5, 9(1), (2), 11, 50(1);

Criminal Justice (Scotland) Act 1980 (c 62)—*contd*
Schedule
8—*contd*

Rehabilitation of Offenders
Act 1975, s 5(2); Criminal
Procedure (Scotland) Act 1975,
ss 204, 208–11, 218, 414, 416,
418–420) (SI 1983/1580)
Remainder repealed or spent

1   Orders made under Transport Act 1981, s 40(4), bringing this prospective repeals into force will be noted to that Act

2   Orders made under Terrorism Act 2000, s 128, bringing the prospective repeal into force will be noted to that Act in the service to this work

---

Deaconesses and Lay Workers (Pensions) Measure 1980 (No 1)

RA: 20 Mar 1980

20 Mar 1980 (RA)

Deer Act 1980 (c 49)

Whole Act repealed

Diocese in Europe Measure 1980 (No 2)

RA: 30 Jun 1980

Commencement provisions: s 7(2)

2 Jul 1980 (s 7(2) (following establishment of Diocese in Europe))

Education Act 1980 (c 20)

RA: 3 Apr 1980

Commencement provisions: s 37(2) (repealed); Education Act 1980 (Commencement No 1) Order 1980, SI 1980/489; Education Act 1980 (Commencement No 2) Order 1980, SI 1980/959; Education Act 1980 (Commencement No 3) Order 1981, SI 1981/789; Education Act 1980 (Commencement No 4) Order 1981, SI 1981/1064

Section		
1–19		Repealed
20		5 May 1980 (SI 1980/489); repealed (S)
21–35		Repealed
36		14 Apr 1980 (SI 1980/489)
37		Repealed
38	(1)	14 Apr 1980 (SI 1980/489)
	(2)	Repealed
	(3)	Substituted by Education Act 1996, s 582(1), Sch 37, Pt I, para 47 (qv)

Education Act 1980 (c 20)—*contd*

Section

38	(4)–(6)	Repealed
	(7)	14 Apr 1980 (SI 1980/489)
		Section repealed (S)

Schedule

| 1–7 | | Repealed |

Education (Scotland) Act 1980 (c 44)

RA: 1 Aug 1980

Commencement provisions: s 137(2)–(4); Education (Scotland) Act 1980 (Commencement) Order 1980, SI 1980/1287[1]

Section

1	(1)	1 Sep 1980 (s 137(2))
	(1A)–(1C)	Prospectively inserted by Standards in Scotland's Schools etc Act 2000 (asp 6), s 32(3)[3]
	(2)	1 Sep 1980 (s 137(2)); prospectively repealed by Standards in Scotland's Schools etc Act 2000 (asp 6), s 32(4)[3]
	(2A)	Inserted by Further and Higher Education (Scotland) Act 1992, s 2 (qv)
	(3)	1 Sep 1980 (s 137(2), (3))[2]
	(4)	1 Sep 1980 (s 137(2))
	(4A), (4B)	Prospectively inserted by Standards in Scotland's Schools etc Act 2000 (asp 6), s 32(5)[3]
	(5)	1 Sep 1980 (s 137(2))
2		1 Sep 1980 (s 137(2))
2A		Inserted by Education (Scotland) Act 1996, s 32 (qv)
3, 4		1 Sep 1980 (s 137(2))
5		Repealed
6–9		1 Sep 1980 (s 137(2))
10, 11		1 Sep 1980 (s 137(2), (3))[2]
12, 13		1 Sep 1980 (s 137(2))
14		1 Sep 1980 (s 137(2)); prospectively substituted by Standards in Scotland's Schools etc Act 2000 (asp 6), s 40[3]
14ZA		Inserted by Further and Higher Education (Scotland) Act 1992, s 62(2), Sch 9, para 7(1), (2) (qv)
14A		Inserted by Education (Scotland) Act 1981, s 12 (qv)
15–19		1 Sep 1980 (s 137(2))
19A		Inserted by Education (Amendment) (Scotland) Act 1984, s 1 (qv)

Education (Scotland) Act 1980 (c 44)—*contd*

Section

20–22			1 Sep 1980 (s 137(2))
22A–22D			Inserted by Education (Scotland) Act 1981, s 6 (qv)
23	(1)		1 Sep 1980 (s 137(2), (3))[2]
	(1A)–(1C)		Inserted by Local Government etc (Scotland) Act 1994, s 32(1), (2) (qv)
	(2), (3)		1 Sep 1980 (s 137(2), (3))[2]
	(3A)		Inserted by Local Government etc (Scotland) Act 1994, s 32(1), (3) (qv)
	(4)		1 Sep 1980 (s 137(2), (3))[2]
	(5)–(7)		Repealed
24–28			1 Sep 1980 (s 137(2))
28A–28H			Inserted by Education (Scotland) Act 1981, s 1(1) (qv)
28I–28K			Inserted by Education (Schools) Act 1992, s 17 (qv)
29			Repealed
30–44			1 Sep 1980 (s 137(2))
45–48			Repealed
48A			Inserted by Education (No 2) Act 1986, s 48 (qv); prospectively repealed by Standards in Scotland's Schools etc Act 2000 (asp 6), s 16(6)[3]
49			1 Sep 1980 (s 137(2))
50	(1)	(a), (b)	1 Sep 1980 (s 137(2), (3))[2]
		(c)	Repealed
	(1A)		Inserted by Self-Governing Schools etc (Scotland) Act 1989, s 82(1), Sch 10, para 8(10)(b) (qv)
	(2)		1 Sep 1980 (s 137(2), (3))[2]
	(3), (4)		Inserted by Education (Scotland) Act 1981, s 2(2)(b) (qv)
51			1 Sep 1980 (s 137(2))
52			1 Sep 1980 (s 137(2), (3))[2]
53–56			1 Sep 1980 (s 137(2))
57, 58			1 Sep 1980 (s 137(2), (3))[2]
59			Repealed
60–65F			Substituted for ss 60–65 by Education (Scotland) Act 1981, s 4(1), Sch 8 (qv)
65G			Inserted by Self-Governing Schools etc (Scotland) Act 1989, s 71(2) (qv)
66			1 Sep 1980 (s 137(2), (3))[2]
66A			Inserted by Standards in Scotland's Schools etc Act 2000 (asp 6), s 12
67			1 Sep 1980 (s 137(2))

Education (Scotland) Act 1980 (c 44)—*contd*

Section

68		1 Sep 1980 (s 137(2), (3))[2]
69–71		1 Sep 1980 (s 137(2))
72	(1)	1 Sep 1980 (s 137(2))
	(2)	1 Sep 1980 (s 137(2), (3))[2]
73		1 Sep 1980 (s 137(2))
73A–73D		Inserted by Teaching and Higher Education Act 1998, s 29(2) (qv)
73E		Inserted by Teaching and Higher Education Act 1998, s 30 (qv)
74, 75		1 Sep 1980 (s 137(2))
75A, 75B		Inserted by Education (Scotland) Act 1981, s 5(1) (qv)
76		1 Sep 1980 (s 137(2))
77, 78		Repealed
79–85		1 Sep 1980 (s 137(2))
86, 87		1 Sep 1980 (s 137(2), (3))[2]
87A, 87B		Inserted by Self-Governing Schools etc (Scotland) Act 1989, s 74 (qv)
88		Repealed
89, 90		1 Sep 1980 (s 137(2))
91–93		Substituted by Education (Scotland) Act 1981, s 14(1), Sch 8 (qv)
94–97		Repealed
97A–97D		Inserted by Education (Scotland) Act 1981, s 14(1), Sch 8 (qv)
98		1 Sep 1980 (s 137(2))
98A		Inserted by Standards in Scotland's Schools etc Act 2000 (asp 6), s 24(2)
99–107		1 Sep 1980 (s 137(2))
108	(1)	1 Sep 1980 (s 137(2))
	(2)	1 Sep 1980 (s 137(2)); renumbered s 108A by Education (Scotland) Act 1981, Sch 6, para 7(b) (qv)
108A		See s 108(2) above
109–112		1 Sep 1980 (s 137(2))
113		Repealed
114		1 Sep 1980 (s 137(2))
115, 116		Repealed
117		1 Sep 1980 (s 137(2))
118		Substituted by Education (Scotland) Act 1981, Sch 6, para 16, Sch 8 (qv)
118A		Inserted by Education (Scotland) Act 1981, Sch 6, para 17 (qv)
119–123		1 Sep 1980 (s 137(2))
124		Repealed
125		1 Sep 1980 (s 137(2))
125A		Inserted by Children (Scotland) Act 1995, s 35 (qv)

Education (Scotland) Act 1980 (c 44)—*contd*

Section		
126		1 Sep 1980 (s 137(2))
127	(1), (2)	1 Sep 1980 (s 137(2))
	(3), (4)	*Not in force*
	(5)	Repealed
	(6)	1 Sep 1980 (s 137(2))
128		1 Sep 1980 (s 137(2))
129		Repealed
130, 131		1 Sep 1980 (s 137(2))
131A		Inserted by Standards in Scotland's Schools etc Act 2000 (asp 6), s 57
132–137		1 Sep 1980 (s 137(2))
Schedule		
A1		Inserted by Education (Scotland) Act 1981, s 1(2), Sch 1 (qv)
A2		Inserted by Education (Scotland) Act 1981, s 4(3), Schs 3, 8 (qv)
1		1 Sep 1980 (s 137(2))
1A		Repealed
1B		Inserted by Education (Scotland) Act 1981, s 14(2), Sch 5 (qv)
2–5		1 Sep 1980 (s 137(2))
6, para	1–15	Repealed
	16	Inserted (retrospectively) by Local Government (Miscellaneous Provisions) (Scotland) Act 1981, s 38 (qv)

[1] This order, made under s 137(4), (5), appointed 1 Sep 1980 for the coming into force of s 23(5)–(7) (now repealed) of this Act

[2] So far as relating to junior colleges (or, in the case of s 1(3), as originally enacted, so far as relating to compulsory further education and junior colleges), the commencement of the provision(s) was postponed under paras 1–15 (now repealed) of Sch 6, until a day appointed under s 137(3); no day was appointed before the Self-Governing Schools etc (Scotland) Act 1989 removed references to junior colleges in the provision(s)

[3] Orders made under Standards in Scotland's Schools ect Act 2000, s 61(2), bringing the prospective amendments into force will be noted to that Act

---

Employment Act 1980 (c 42)

Whole Act repealed

Films Act 1980 (c 41)

Whole Act repealed

Finance Act 1980 (c 48)

Budget Day: 26 Mar 1980

RA: 1 Aug 1980

Details of the commencement of Finance Acts are not set out in this work

---

Foster Children Act 1980 (c 6)

Whole Act repealed

Gaming (Amendment) Act 1980 (c 8)

RA: 20 Mar 1980

20 Mar 1980 (RA)

Gas Act 1980 (c 37)

Whole Act repealed

Health Services Act 1980 (c 53)

RA: 8 Aug 1980

Commencement provisions: s 26(2), (3); Health Services Act 1980 (Commencement No 1) Order 1980, SI 1980/1257; Health Services Act 1980 (Commencement No 2) Order 1981, SI 1981/306; Health Services Act 1980 (Commencement No 3) Order 1981, SI 1981/884; Health Services Act 1980 (Commencement No 4) Order 1983, SI 1983/303

Section		
1		8 Aug 1980 (RA)
2		Repealed
3		8 Aug 1980 (RA)
4		Repealed
5–9		8 Aug 1980 (RA)
10–15		Repealed
16		1 Aug 1981 (SI 1981/884)
17–19		Repealed
20		8 Aug 1980 (RA)
21		1 Apr 1983 (SI 1983/303)
22		Repealed
23, 24		8 Aug 1980 (RA)
25	(1)	8 Aug 1980 (RA)
	(2)	1 Apr 1981 (SI 1981/306)
	(3)	8 Aug 1980 (RA)
	(4)	See Sch 7 below
26		8 Aug 1980 (RA)
Schedule		
1, 2		8 Aug 1980 (RA)
3		Repealed
4		1 Aug 1981 (SI 1981/884)
5		1 Apr 1981 (SI 1981/306)
6		8 Aug 1980 (RA)
7		8 Aug 1980 (except repeals in Nursing Homes Registration (Scotland) Act 1938; Nursing Homes Act 1975; Nurses, Midwives and Health Visitors Act 1979) (RA)

Health Services Act 1980 (c 53)—*contd*

Schedule

7—*contd*   1 Aug 1981 (exceptions noted above)
                                             (SI 1981/884)

Highlands and Islands Air Services (Scotland) Act 1980 (c 19)

RA: 3 Apr 1980

Commencement provisions: s 5(2)

15 Dec 1980 (s 5(2))

Highways Act 1980 (c 66)

RA: 13 Nov 1980

Commencement provisions: s 345(2)

1 Jan 1981 (s 345(2))

Housing Act 1980 (c 51)

RA: 8 Aug 1980

Whole Act repealed (S)

Commencement provisions: s 153; Housing Act 1980 (Commencement No 1) Order 1980,
    SI 1980/1406; Housing Act 1980 (Commencement No 2) Order 1980,
    SI 1980/1466; Housing Act 1980 (Commencement No 3) Order 1980,
    SI 1980/1557; Housing Act 1980 (Commencement No 4) Order 1980,
    SI 1980/1693; Housing Act 1980 (Commencement No 5) Order 1980,
    SI 1980/1706; Housing Act 1980 (Commencement No 6) Order 1980,
    SI 1980/1781; Housing Act 1980 (Commencement No 7) Order 1981,
    SI 1981/119; Housing Act 1980 (Commencement No 8) Order 1981,
    SI 1981/296; Rent Rebates and Rent Allowances (England and Wales)
    (Appointed Day) Order 1981, SI 1981/297

Section

1–50	Repealed
51	28 Nov 1980 (SI 1980/1706)
52	28 Nov 1980 (SI 1980/1706); repealed, subject to saving, by Housing Act 1988, s 140(2), Sch 18, Note 2 (qv)
53–55	28 Nov 1980 (SI 1980/1706)
56–58	6 Oct 1980 (SI 1980/1706); ss 56–58 (including ss 56A–56D which were inserted by Housing and Planning Act 1986, s 12(2)) repealed, subject to saving, by Housing Act 1988, s 140(2), Sch 18, Note 3 (qv)
59 (1)	Repealed
(2)	28 Nov 1980 (SI 1980/1706)
(3)	See Sch 6 below

Housing Act 1980 (c 51)—*contd*

Section

60		Repealed
61–77		28 Nov 1980 (SI 1980/1706)
78, 79		20 Oct 1980 (SI 1980/1557)
80		Repealed
81–86		3 Oct 1980 (SI 1980/1406)
87		Repealed
88, 89		3 Oct 1980 (SI 1980/1406)
90–137		Repealed
138		8 Aug 1980 (s 153(3))
139		Repealed
140		8 Aug 1980 (s 153(3)); repealed, subject to saving, by Housing and Planning Act 1986, ss 18, 24(3), Sch 4, paras 7, 11(2), Sch 12, Pt I (qv)
141		3 Oct 1980 (except in relation to Sch 21, para 7) (SI 1980/1406)
		Not in force (exception noted above)
142		31 Mar 1981 (SI 1981/119)
143		3 Oct 1980 (SI 1980/1406)
144–147		Repealed
148		3 Oct 1980 (SI 1980/1406)
149		Repealed
150, 151		8 Aug 1980 (s 153(3))
152	(1)	See Sch 25 below
	(2)	8 Aug 1980 (s 153(3))
	(3)	See Sch 26 below
153		8 Aug 1980 (RA)
154, 155		8 Aug 1980 (s 153(3))
Schedule		
1–4A		Repealed
5		6 Oct 1980 (SI 1980/1466)
6		*Not in force*—it has been stated that amendments made by this Schedule will not be brought into operation (Regulated Tenancies (Procedure) Regulations 1980, SI 1980/1696 (made under Rent Act 1977, s 74))
7–10		28 Nov 1980 (SI 1980/1706)
11–20		Repealed
21, para	1, 2	3 Oct 1980 (SI 1980/1406)
	3	Repealed
	4–6	3 Oct 1980 (SI 1980/1706)
	7	*Not in force*
	8	3 Oct 1980 (SI 1980/1406)
22		31 Mar 1981 (SI 1981/119)
23, 24		Repealed
25, para	1–3	28 Nov 1980 (SI 1980/1706)

Housing Act 1980 (c 51)—*contd*

Schedule

25, para	4–6	Spent
	7–31	Repealed
	32, 33	28 Nov 1980 (SI 1980/1706)
	34	Repealed
	35	28 Nov 1980 (SI 1980/1706)
	36	Repealed
	37–45	28 Nov 1980 (SI 1980/1706)
	46	Repealed
	47–60	28 Nov 1980 (SI 1980/1706)
	61	3 Oct 1980 (SI 1980/1406)
	62, 63	Repealed
	64–68	8 Aug 1980 (s 153(3))
	69	Repealed
	70	Spent
	71	Repealed
	72, 73	Spent
	74	Repealed
	75	8 Aug 1980 (s 153(3))
	76	Repealed
	77, 78	8 Aug 1980 (s 153(3))
26		3 Oct 1980 (repeals of or in Housing Act 1957, ss 5, 43(4), 113(5), 119(3); Housing (Financial Provisions) Act 1958, s 43(1); Housing Act 1961, s 20; Housing Act 1964, ss 65(1A), 66; Housing Subsidies Act 1967, ss 24(5), 26A; Leasehold Reform Act 1967, Sch 1; Housing Act 1969, s 61(6); Housing Finance Act 1972, ss 90–91A; Local Government Act 1972; Housing Act 1974, ss 5(3), 13(4), (5)(a), 14, 19(1), 30(5), 31, 32(1), (4), (8), 33(6), 104, 114; Criminal Law Act 1977, Schs 6, 12) (SI 1980/1406)
		27 Oct 1980 (repeals of or in Housing Act 1961 (so far as not already repealed); Housing Act 1969, s 60; Housing Act 1974, ss 56(1)(d), 57(6), 62(3), 64(7), 67, 84) (SI 1980/1557)
		28 Mar 1980 (repeals of or in Landlord and Tenant Act 1927; Reserve and Auxiliary Forces (Protection of Civil Interests) Act 1951; Landlord and Tenant Act 1954; Housing Act 1964 (so far as not already repealed); Tribunals and Inquiries Act 1971;

Housing Act 1980 (c 51)—*contd*
Schedule
26—*contd*

Rent (Agriculture) Act 1976; Rent
Act 1977 except repeals in Sch 12,
paras 4, 9) (SI 1980/1706)

15 Dec 1980 (repeals of or in Housing
Act 1957, s 96(e); Housing
(Financial Provisions) Act 1958,
ss 14, 15; Housing Act 1969 (so
far as not already repealed);
Chronically Sick and Disabled
Persons Act 1970; Local
Employment Act 1972; Housing
(Amendment) Act 1973; Housing
Act 1974, ss 38(2)(a), 42, 50,
52–55, 56(2)(d), 71(3)(a), Sch 5,
Pt I, Pt II, para 4; Housing Rents
and Subsidies Act 1975, Schs 1, 5;
Remuneration, Charges and
Grants Act 1975; Local Land
Charges Act 1975) (SI 1980/1781)

31 Mar 1981 (repeal of Leasehold
Reform Act 1967 (so far as not
already repealed)) (SI 1981/119)

1 Apr 1981 (repeals of Housing
Finance Act 1972, ss 8, 20(5), (7),
24(5), 26(1), Sch 3, Pt II, Sch 4,
paras 1(3)(a), 16, 17) (SI 1981/296)

Not in force (repeals of or in Housing
Act 1957, ss 91, 105, 106; Housing
(Financial Provisions) Act 1958,
s 45; New Towns Act 1959, s 4;
Housing Subsidies Act 1967,
ss 24(2)–(4), (5A), 24B, 26, 28A;
Town and Country Planning
Act 1968, s 39; Housing Finance
Act 1972, Sch 4, para 14; Housing
Act 1974, s 79, Schs 8, 11; Housing
Rents and Subsidies Act 1975, ss 1,
2, 4; New Towns (Amendment)
Act 1976, s 9; Supplementary
Benefits Act 1976, Sch 7, para 28;
Development of Rural Wales
Act 1976, ss 18, 22, Sch 5; Rent
Act 1977, Sch 12, paras 4, 9)

Import of Live Fish (England and Wales) Act 1980 (c 27)

RA: 15 May 1980

15 May 1980 (RA)

Imprisonment (Temporary Provisions) Act 1980 (c 57)

RA: 29 Oct 1980

29 Oct 1980 (RA)

Industry Act 1980 (c 33)

RA: 30 Jun 1980

30 Jun 1980 (RA)

Insurance Companies Act 1980 (c 25)

RA: 1 May 1980

Commencement provisions: s 5(2); Insurance Companies Act 1980 (Commencement) Order 1980, SI 1980/678

Whole Act repealed, except ss 4(1), 5, Sch 3, paras 9, 15(b), 17, 18, 20 which came into force on 1 Jun 1980 (SI 1980/678); ss 4(1), 5, Sch 3, para 9 prospectively repealed by Policyholders Protection Act 1997, s 22, Sch 5; orders made under the 1997 Act, s 23(3), bringing the prospective repeal into force will be noted to that Act

---

Iran (Temporary Powers) Act 1980 (c 28)

Whole Act repealed

Law Reform (Miscellaneous Provisions) (Scotland) Act 1980 (c 55)

RA: 29 Oct 1980

Commencement provisions: s 29(2); Law Reform (Miscellaneous Provisions) (Scotland) Act 1980 (Commencement) Order 1980, SI 1980/1726

Section	
1–11	22 Dec 1980 (SI 1980/1726)
12	Repealed
13, 14	22 Dec 1980 (SI 1980/1726)
15	Repealed
16–25	22 Dec 1980 (SI 1980/1726)
26	Repealed
27, 28	22 Dec 1980 (SI 1980/1726)
29	29 Oct 1980 (RA)
Schedule	
1, 2	22 Dec 1980 (SI 1980/1726)
3	Repealed

Licensed Premises (Exclusion of Certain Persons) Act 1980 (c 32)

RA: 30 Jun 1980

30 Jun 1980 (RA)

Licensing (Amendment) Act 1980 (c 40)

RA: 17 Jul 1980

Commencement provisions: s 4(2); Licensing (Amendment) Act 1980 (Commencement) Order 1982, SI 1982/1383

Section

1	17 Jul 1980 (RA)
2, 3	1 Oct 1982 (SI 1982/1383)
4	17 Jul 1980 (RA)

Limitation Act 1980 (c 58)

RA: 13 Nov 1980

Commencement provisions: s 41(2), (3); Limitation Act 1980 (Commencement) Order 1981, SI 1981/588

1 May 1981 (s 41(2); note that s 35 also came into force on that date by virtue of SI 1981/588)

Limitation Amendment Act 1980 (c 24)

RA: 1 May 1980

Whole Act repealed, except ss 10, 14(1), (5) which came into force on 1 Aug 1980 (s 14(3) (repealed))

Local Government, Planning and Land Act 1980 (c 65)

RA: 13 Nov 1980

Commencement provisions: ss 23(3), 47, 68(8), 85, 86(8)–(11), 178; Local Government, Planning and Land Act 1980 (Commencement No 1) Order 1980, SI 1980/1871; Local Government, Planning and Land Act 1980 (Commencement No 2) Order 1980, SI 1980/1893; Local Government, Planning and Land Act 1980 (Commencement No 3) Order 1980, SI 1980/2014; Local Government, Planning and Land Act 1980 (Commencement No 4) Order 1981, SI 1981/194; Local Government, Planning and Land Act 1980 (Commencement No 5) Order 1981, SI 1981/341; Local Government, Planning and Land Act 1980 (Commencement No 6) Order 1981, SI 1981/1251; Local Government, Planning and Land Act 1980 (Commencement No 7) Order 1981, SI 1981/1618; Local Government, Planning and Land Act 1980 (Commencement No 8) (Scotland) Order 1982, SI 1982/317[1]; Local Government, Planning and Land Act 1980 (Commencement No 8) Order 1983, SI 1983/94; Community Land Act 1975 (Appointed Day for Repeal) Order 1983, SI 1983/673; Local Government, Planning and Land Act 1980 (Commencement No 9) Order 1984, SI 1984/1493

Section

1–4	13 Nov 1980 (RA)
5–23	Repealed
24–27	13 Nov 1980 (RA)

Local Government, Planning and Land Act 1980 (c 65)—*contd*
Section

28–31   13 Nov 1980 (s 47(7)); repealed, with
                                                 savings, by Local Government
                                                 Finance (Repeals, Savings and
                                                 Consequential Amendments)
                                                 Order 1990, SI 1990/776, art 3,
                                                 Sch 1[2]

32   13 Nov 1980 (s 47(7))

33, 34   13 Nov 1980, but only to have effect
                                                 for any rate passed beginning after
                                                 31 Mar 1981 (s 47(1), (7);
                                                 SI 1980/2014); repealed, with savings,
                                                 by Local Government Finance
                                                 (Repeals, Savings and Consequential
                                                 Amendments) Order 1990,
                                                 SI 1990/776, art 3, Sch 1[2]

35, 36   13 Nov 1980 (s 47(7)); repealed, with
                                                 savings, by Local Government
                                                 Finance (Repeals, Savings and
                                                 Consequential Amendments)
                                                 Order 1990, SI 1990/776, art 3,
                                                 Sch 1[2]

37   13 Nov 1980, but only to have effect
                                                 for any rate period beginning after
                                                 31 Mar 1981 (s 47(1), (7);
                                                 SI 1980/2014); repealed, with savings,
                                                 by Local Government Finance
                                                 (Repeals, Savings and Consequential
                                                 Amendments) Order 1990,
                                                 SI 1990/776, art 3, Sch 1[2]

38–40   13 Dec 1980 (s 47(3)); repealed, with
                                                 savings, by Local Government
                                                 Finance (Repeals, Savings and
                                                 Consequential Amendments)
                                                 Order 1990, SI 1990/776, art 3,
                                                 Sch 1[2]

41–43   13 Nov 1980 (s 47(7)); repealed, with
                                                 savings, by Local Government
                                                 Finance (Repeals, Savings and
                                                 Consequential Amendments)
                                                 Order 1990, SI 1990/776, art 3,
                                                 Sch 1[2]

44   13 Nov 1980, but only to have effect
                                                 for rate periods beginning after
                                                 31 Mar 1981 (s 47(1), (7);
                                                 SI 1980/2014); repealed, with savings,
                                                 by Local Government Finance
                                                 (Repeals, Savings and Consequential
                                                 Amendments) Order 1990,
                                                 SI 1990/776, art 3, Sch 1[2]

Local Government, Planning and Land Act 1980 (c 65)—*contd*

Section

45, 46		Repealed
47		13 Nov 1980 (RA)
48–61		13 Nov 1980 (RA) but the commencing year for purposes of Pt VI of this Act was that beginning 1 Apr 1981 (SI 1980/1893)
62		Repealed
63		13 Nov 1980 (RA); commencing year began 1 Apr 1981 (SI 1980/1893)
63A		Inserted by Local Government Act 1985, s 83(2) (qv)
64		Repealed
65		Substituted by Local Government Finance Act 1987, s 11(1), Sch 4, para 4 (with effect as noted in para 12(3) of that Schedule) (qv)
66, 67		13 Nov 1980 (RA); commencing year began 1 Apr 1981 (SI 1980/1893)
68	(1)	13 Nov 1980 (RA); commencing year began 1 Apr 1981 (SI 1980/1893)
	(2)	11 Dec 1980 (s 68(8); SI 1980/1893)
	(3)–(6)	Repealed
	(7)–(9)	13 Nov 1980 (RA)
69		13 Nov 1980 (RA)
70		13 Nov 1980 (RA); repealed (E, W), with a saving, by Criminal Justice and Public Order Act 1994, s 80(5) (qv)
71–85		Repealed
86	(1)–(7)	Repealed
	(8)–(11)	13 Jan 1981 (s 86(8), (11))
87–90		Repealed
91, 92		13 Nov 1980 (RA)
93–96		Brought into force, together with ss 98, 99, 100 of this Act, area by area on different dates as follows: 31 Dec 1980 (Birmingham, Bradford, Bristol, Coventry, Dudley, Ealing, Gateshead, Leeds, Liverpool, Manchester, Middlesborough, Newcastle-under-Lyme, Newcastle-upon-Tyne, Preston, Salford, Sefton, Stockport, Stoke, Trafford, Wandsworth, Wirral) (SI 1980/1871)

Local Government, Planning and Land Act 1980 (c 65)—*contd*
Section

93–96—*contd*	19 Mar 1981 (Derby, Leicester, Newham, North Bedfordshire, Nottingham, Portsmouth, Sandwell, Sheffield, South Staffordshire, Southwark, Tower Hamlets, Walsall) (SI 1981/194)
	2 Oct 1981 (Knowsley, St Helens) (SI 1981/1251)
	11 Dec 1981 (areas of all other councils of districts in England, all other London boroughs and the City of London) (SI 1981/1618)
	3 Mar 1983 (Alyn and Deeside, Cardiff, Newport, Swansea, Vale of Glamorgan, Wrexham, Maelor) (SI 1983/94)
	24 Oct 1984 (areas of all other district councils in Wales) (SI 1984/1493)
96A	Prospectively inserted by Local Government Act 1988, s 31, Sch 5, para 2(1) (qv)[3]
97	Substituted by Local Government Act 1988, s 31, Sch 5, para 3 (qv)
98, 99	See ss 93–96 above
99A	Inserted by Local Government Act 1988, s 31, Sch 5, para 6 (qv)
100	See ss 93–96 above
101	See Sch 17 below
102–111	Repealed
112–116	13 Nov 1980 (RA)
117	Repealed
118	13 Nov 1980 (RA)
119	Repealed
120	13 Nov 1980 (RA); repealed in part as it applies to E, W and now applies to S only
121	13 Nov 1980 (RA) but effective from 12 Dec 1975 (s 121(1))
122	13 Nov 1980 (RA)
123	13 Nov 1980 (RA) but effective from 12 Dec 1975 (s 123(1))
124, 125	13 Nov 1980 (RA)
126–130	Repealed
131–146	13 Nov 1980 (RA)
147	Repealed
148, 149	13 Nov 1980 (RA)
150	Repealed

Local Government, Planning and Land Act 1980 (c 65)—*contd*

Section

151–153		13 Nov 1980 (RA)
154		Substituted by Social Security and Housing Benefits Act 1982, s 48(5), Sch 4, para 36 (qv)
155, 156		13 Nov 1980 (RA)
157, 157A, 157B		Substituted for original s 157 by Leasehold Reform, Housing and Urban Development Act 1993, s 178 (qv)
158		Repealed
159–165		13 Nov 1980 (RA)
165A		Inserted by Leasehold Reform, Housing and Urban Development Act 1993, s 180(2) (qv)
165B		Inserted by Housing Grants, Construction and Regeneration Act 1996, s 143(1) (qv)
166–172		13 Nov 1980 (RA)
173	(a)	13 Dec 1980 (s 178(3))
	(b)	13 Dec 1981 (s 178(2))
174		13 Feb 1981 (s 178(1))
175–178		13 Dec 1980 (s 178(3))
179, 180		13 Nov 1980 (RA)
181, 182		Repealed
183–186		13 Nov 1980 (RA)
187–190		Repealed
191–197		13 Nov 1980 (RA)

Schedule

1–10		13 Nov 1980 (RA)
11–15		Repealed
16		13 Nov 1980 (RA)
17, Pt	I	13 Nov 1980 (RA)
	II	13 Nov 1980 (repeals of Community Land Act 1975, except as noted below) (RA)
		1 Jun 1983 (repeals of Community Land Act 1975, ss 1, 2, 6(1) (part), (6), 7, 26, 40, 43, 44 (except part of sub-s (3)), 51–58, Sch 2) (SI 1983/673)
	III, IV	13 Nov 1980 (RA)
18–22		Repealed
23, 24		13 Nov 1980 (RA)
25, Pt	I	Repealed
	II–IV	13 Nov 1980 (RA)
26–32		13 Nov 1980 (RA)
33, para	1–3	13 Nov 1980 (RA)

Local Government, Planning and Land Act 1980 (c 65)—*contd*

Schedule

33, para	4	Effective from 25 Mar 1981 when power to prescribe appropriate multiplier first exercised (s 47(5), (6)); Landlord and Tenant Act 1954 (Appropriate Multiplier) Regulations 1981, SI 1981/69)
	5	13 Nov 1980 (RA)
	6	Repealed
	7	13 Nov 1980 (RA)
	8	Repealed
	9	13 Nov 1980 (RA); repealed, with savings, by Local Government Finance (Repeals, Savings and Consequential Amendments) Order 1990, SI 1990/776, art 3, Sch 1[2]
	10	13 Nov 1980, but not to have effect for rate periods beginning before first date after 13 Nov 1980, on which new valuation lists were to come into force[4] (s 47(4), (7)); repealed, with savings, by Local Government Finance (Repeals, Savings and Consequential Amendments) Order 1990, SI 1990/776, art 3, Sch 1[2]
	11	13 Nov 1980 (RA); repealed, with savings, by Local Government Finance (Repeals, Savings and Consequential Amendments) Order 1990, SI 1990/776, art 3, Sch 1[2]
	12	Repealed
	13	13 Nov 1980 (RA) but note para 13(2) only effective for applications after 12 Dec 1975
	14	Effective when power to prescribe multipliers is exercised (s 47(5), (6)) (It is thought that the coming into force of Landlord and Tenant Act 1954 (Appropriate Multiplier) Regulations 1981, SI 1981/69, brought this paragraph into effect on 25 Mar 1981)
34, Pt	I–VIII	13 Nov 1980 (RA)
	IX	Rate periods beginning after 31 Mar 1981 (repeals of General Rate Act 1967, ss 4(2), 5(1)(g), 48(4),

Local Government, Planning and Land Act 1980 (c 65)—*contd*

Schedule

34, Pt	IX—*contd*	50(2), Sch 10; Decimal Currency Act 1969; GLC (General Powers) Act 1973; Local Government Act 1974) (s 47(1); SI 1980/2014)
		Rate periods beginning after first date after 13 Nov 1980 on which new valuation lists in force (repeals of General Rate Act 1967, ss 19, 30) (s 47(4)(d))
		13 Nov 1980 (repeals of General Rate Act 1967, s 20, Schs 1, 2; General Rate Act 1975; Rating (Caravan Sites) Act 1976) (RA)
	X	13 Nov 1980 (RA)
	XI	13 Nov 1980 (RA) but note Sch 17 above in relation to repeal of Community Land Act 1975
	XII–XVI	13 Nov 1980 (RA)

1   No commencement orders under this Act, which affect Scotland, were made prior to this order; certain provisions of this Act, not subject to commencement order, were already in force in Scotland

2   This Order, made consequent upon (inter alia) Local Government Finance Act 1988 (which established new systems of community charges and non-domestic rates to replace the rating system) came into force on 1 Apr 1990

3   An order made under Local Government Act 1988, s 31(3) bringing the prospective insertion into force will be noted to that Act

4   The New Valuation Lists Order 1987, SI 1987/921 (made under General Rate Act 1967, s 68(1) (repealed), as substituted by s 28 of this Act), specified 1 Apr 1990 as the date on which new valuation lists were to come into force; that Order was revoked by SI 1988/2146, made under Local Government Finance Act 1988; SI 1988/2146 was itself revoked and replaced by SI 1992/1643, made under Sch 6, para 2(3)(b) to 1988 Act. Accordingly, SI 1987/921 was ineffective to bring s 29(1)–(3) of, and Sch 33, para 10(1) to, this Act into force

---

Magistrates' Courts Act 1980 (c 43)

RA: 1 Aug 1980

Commencement provisions: s 155(7)

6 Jul 1981 (s 155(7))

Married Women's Policies of Assurance (Scotland) (Amendment) Act 1980 (c 56)

RA: 29 Oct 1980

29 Oct 1980 (RA)

National Health Service (Invalid Direction) Act 1980 (c 15)

Whole Act repealed

National Heritage Act 1980 (c 17)

RA: 31 Mar 1980

31 Mar 1980 (RA)

New Hebrides Act 1980 (c 16)

RA: 20 Mar 1980

Commencement provisions: s 4(2); New Hebrides Order 1980, SI 1980/1079
Section

1	Repealed
2	30 Jul 1980 (SI 1980/1079)
3	Repealed
4	20 Mar 1980 (RA)
Schedule	
1, 2	30 Jul 1980 (SI 1980/1079)

New Towns Act 1980 (c 36)

Whole Act repealed

Overseas Development and Co-operation Act 1980 (c 63)

RA: 13 Nov 1980

Commencement provisions: s 19(2)

14 Dec 1980 (s 19(2))

Papua New Guinea, Western Samoa and Nauru (Miscellaneous Provisions) Act 1980 (c 2)

RA: 31 Jan 1980

Commencement provisions: s 3(3)
Section

1	(1)	Repealed
	(2)	31 Jan 1980 (RA)
	(3)	Repealed
2		Repealed
3	(1)	See Schedule below
	(2)	Repealed
	(3)	See Schedule below
4		31 Jan 1980 (RA)
Schedule		
para	1	16 Sep 1975 (retrospective; s 3(3))
	2	Repealed
	3	16 Sep 1975 (retrospective; s 3(3))
	4, 5	Repealed
	6–14	31 Jan 1980 (RA)

Petroleum Revenue Tax Act 1980 (c 1)

RA: 31 Jan 1980

Commencement provisions: s 3(3)
Section

1		Effective for chargeable periods ending on or after 31 Dec 1979 (s 3(3))
2	(1), (2)	Effective for chargeable periods ending on or after 31 Dec 1979 (s 3(3))
	(3)	Repealed
3		31 Jan 1980 (RA); repealed in relation to chargeable periods beginning on or after 18 Aug 1989
Schedule		Effective for chargeable periods ending on or after 31 Dec 1979 (s 3(3))

Note: Petroleum Revenue Tax abolished for new oil and gas fields ('non-taxable fields') with effect from 16 Mar 1993, by Finance Act 1993, s 185

Police Negotiating Board Act 1980 (c 10)

Whole Act repealed

Port of London (Financial Assistance) Act 1980 (c 31)

Whole Act repealed

Protection of Trading Interests Act 1980 (c 11)

RA: 20 Mar 1980

20 Mar 1980 (RA)

Representation of the People Act 1980 (c 3)

Whole Act repealed

Reserve Forces Act 1980 (c 9)

RA: 20 Mar 1980

Commencement provisions: s 158(4)

20 Apr 1980 (s 158(4))

Residential Homes Act 1980 (c 7)

Whole Act repealed

Sea Fish Industry Act 1980 (c 35)

Whole Act repealed

Slaughter of Animals (Scotland) Act 1980 (c 13)

RA: 20 Mar 1980

20 Mar 1980 (RA)

Social Security Act 1980 (c 30)

RA: 23 May 1980

Commencement provisions: s 21(5); Social Security Act 1980 (Commencement No 1) Order 1980, SI 1980/729; Social Security Act 1980 (Commencement No 2) Order 1981, SI 1981/1438; Social Security Act 1980 (Commencement No 3) Order 1983, SI 1983/1002; Social Security Act 1980 (Commencement No 4) Order 1984, SI 1984/1492

Section			
1–3			Repealed
4	(1)		Spent
	(2)		23 May 1980 (s 21(5))
	(3)–(6)		Repealed
5			Repealed
6	(1)		24 Nov 1980 (SI 1980/729)
	(2)		Repealed
	(3)		24 Nov 1980 (SI 1980/729)
	(4)		Repealed
7			Repealed
8			23 May 1980 (SI 1980/729)
9	(1)–(5)		Repealed
	(6)		24 Nov 1980 (SI 1980/729)
	(7)		Repealed
10, 11			Repealed
12			23 May 1980 (s 21(5))
13–15			Repealed
16			23 May 1980 (s 21(5))
17, 18			Repealed
19–21			23 May 1980 (s 21(5))
Schedule			
1			Repealed
2, Pt	I, para	1–30	Repealed
		31	Repealed or spent
		32	24 Nov 1980 (SI 1980/729)
	II		24 Nov 1980 (SI 1980/729)
3			Repealed
4, para	1, 2		24 Nov 1980 (SI 1980/729)
	3		Spent
	4		Repealed
	5–7		24 Nov 1980 (SI 1980/729)
	8		Spent

Social Security Act 1980 (c 30)—*contd*

Schedule

4, para	9, 10	Repealed
	11	24 Nov 1980 (SI 1980/729)
	12	Spent
	13, 14	Repealed
5, Pt	I	23 May 1980 (s 21(5))
	II	14 Jul 1980 (repeals of or in Social Security Act 1975, ss 44(5)(b), 47(2)(b), Sch 4, Pt IV; Social Security (Miscellaneous Provisions) Act 1977, s 8(3)) (SI 1980/729)
		24 Nov 1980 (repeals of or in Polish Resettlement Act 1947; National Assistance Act 1948; Legal Aid (Scotland) Act 1967; Social Work (Scotland) Act 1968; Merchant Shipping Act 1970; Family Income Supplements Act 1970, ss 7(2), 10(2)(h); Housing (Financial Provisions) (Scotland) Act 1972; Housing Finance Act 1972; Legal Aid Act 1974; Social Security Act 1975, ss 138, 139, 142(5), 168(4), Sch 15; Social Security (Consequential Provisions) Act 1975; House of Commons Disqualification Act 1975; Northern Ireland Assembly Disqualification Act 1975; Social Security Pensions Act 1975; Child Benefit Act 1975; Supplementary Benefits Act 1976; National Insurance Surcharge Act 1976; Social Security (Miscellaneous Provisions) Act 1977, ss 14(1)–(4), (7)–(10), 15, 24(4); Employment Protection (Consolidation) Act 1978; Social Security Act 1979; Legal Aid Act 1979; Reserve Forces Act 1980) (SI 1980/729)
		23 Nov 1981 (repeals of or in Social Security Act 1975, ss 44(3)(b), (6), 47 (so far as not already repealed), 66(1)(c), (8)) (SI 1981/1438)
		21 Nov 1983 (repeals of Social Security Act 1975, ss 44(5) (so far as not already repealed), 66(1)(b), Sch 20; Family Income Supplements Act 1970, s 17(1)) (SI 1983/1002)

Social Security Act 1980 (c 30)—*contd*
Schedule

5, Pt II—*contd*	26 Nov 1984 (repeal of Social Security Act 1975, ss 41(1), 65(4), 158, Sch 19) (SI 1984/1492)

Social Security (No 2) Act 1980 (c 39)

Whole Act repealed

Solicitors (Scotland) Act 1980 (c 46)

RA: 1 Aug 1980

Commencement provisions: s 67(3)

1 Sep 1980 (s 67(3))

Statute Law Revision (Northern Ireland) Act 1980 (c 59)

Whole Act repealed

Tenants' Rights, Etc (Scotland) Act 1980 (c 52)

RA: 8 Aug 1980

Commencement provisions: s 86(4); Tenants' Rights, etc (Scotland) Act 1980 (Commencement) Order 1980, SI 1980/1387

Section	
1–32	Repealed
33	1 Dec 1980 (SI 1980/1387)
34–36	Repealed
37	1 Dec 1980 (SI 1980/1387)
38	Repealed
39	1 Dec 1980 (SI 1980/1387)
40	Repealed
41	1 Dec 1980 (SI 1980/1387)
42–45	Repealed
46	1 Dec 1980 (SI 1980/1387)
47, 48	Repealed
49	1 Dec 1980 (SI 1980/1387)
50–63	Repealed
64, 65	1 Dec 1980 (SI 1980/1387)
66–73	Repealed
74	3 Oct 1980 (SI 1980/1387)
75–85	Repealed
86	3 Oct 1980 (SI 1980/1387)
Schedule	
A1, 1–4	Repealed

Tenants' Rights, Etc (Scotland) Act 1980 (c 52)—*contd*

Schedule

5   3 Oct 1980 (except repeals of or in Reserve and Auxiliary Forces (Protection of Civil Interests) Act 1951, ss 16(1), (2)(c), (4)(b), 17(2)(a), (b), 18(2)(a), (b), 19(5); Rent (Scotland) Act 1971, ss 4(1), 5(4), (5), 7(1), (2), 9(1), 24, 25(1), 29, 30, 36, Pt V, ss 70–76, 80(2), 81, 82, 84, 85, 97(2), 100, 106(8), 110(1)(b), (2), 111(1), 113–115, 122(1)(b), 123(2), (3), 125(2), 129(2), 133, 135(1), Sch 2, Sch 3, Case 5, Case 6, Case 9, Schs 8, 10–12, 14, 16, 17, 19, paras 9, 10, 14(1) (c), 19(1); Fire Precautions Act 1971, Sch, Pt III, paras 1(1), (2)(a), (6), (7), 4; Housing (Financial Provisions) (Scotland) Act 1972, ss 61(3), 62(2), (4), 64, 65, Sch 7, paras 1–7; Local Government (Scotland) Act 1973, Sch 13, paras 4, 5, 7; Housing Act 1974, s 18(2), (5); Rent Act 1974, s 1(3); Criminal Procedure (Scotland) Act 1975, Sch 7C; Housing Rents and Subsidies (Scotland) Act 1975, ss 7–11, Schs 2, 3, para 5) (SI 1980/1387)

                                1 Dec 1980 (exceptions noted above) (SI 1980/1387)

Tenants' Rights, Etc (Scotland) (Amendment) Act 1980 (c 61)

Whole Act repealed

Transport Act 1980 (c 34)

RA: 30 Jun 1980

Commencement provisions: s 70; Transport Act 1980 (Commencement No 1) Order 1980, SI 1980/913; Transport Act 1980 (Commencement No 2) Order 1980, SI 1980/1353; Transport Act 1980 (Commencement No 3) Order 1980, SI 1980/1424; Transport Act 1980 (Commencement No 4) Order 1981, SI 1981/256

Section

1–31		Repealed
32	(1)–(4)	Repealed
	(5)	6 Oct 1980 (SI 1980/1353)
33		Repealed

Transport Act 1980 (c 34)—*contd*

Section

34		Spent
35–41		Repealed
42		Repealed except for sub-ss (1), (2)(b)(iii), which came into force on 6 Oct 1980 (SI 1980/1353)
43	(1)	See Sch 5, Pt II below
	(2)	Repealed
44		Repealed
45–50		30 Jun 1980 (s 70(3), but generally of no effect until 1 Oct 1980, the day appointed under s 45(2) by SI 1980/1380)
51	(1)	30 Jun 1980 (s 70(3))
	(2)	1 Oct 1980 (appointed day under SI 1980/1380)
52		30 Jun 1980 (s 70(3))
52A–52D		Inserted by Railways Act 1993, s 134(1), Sch 11, para 9(2), (3) (qv)
53–60		30 Jun 1980 (s 70(3))
61		Repealed
62		6 Oct 1980 (SI 1980/1353)
63		Repealed
64		31 Jul 1980 (SI 1980/913)
65		6 Oct 1980 (SI 1980/913)
66–68		30 Jun 1980 (s 70(3))
69		See Sch 9 below
70		30 Jun 1980 (s 70(3))

Schedule

1–3		Repealed
4		6 Oct 1980 (SI 1980/913)
5, Pt	I	Repealed
	II	6 Oct 1980 (amendments of Local Government (Miscellaneous Provisions) Act 1953; Transport Act 1962; Road Traffic Act 1972; Road Traffic (Foreign Vehicles) Act 1972 (paras 1(b), 2 only); Local Government (Miscellaneous Provisions) Act 1976 (para 2 only); Energy Act 1976 (sub-paras (a), (c) only)) (SI 1980/913)
		1 Apr 1981 (amendments of Road Traffic (Foreign Vehicles) Act 1972 (paras 1(a), 3); Road Traffic Act 1974; Local Government (Miscellaneous Provisions) Act 1976 (para 1); Energy Act 1976 (sub-para (b))) (SI 1981/256)
		Remainder repealed

Transport Act 1980 (c 34)—*contd*
Schedule

6	30 Jun 1980 (s 70(3); but not generally effective until 1 Oct 1980, the date appointed under s 45(2) by SI 1980/1380)
7	1 Oct 1980 (appointed day under SI 1980/1380)
8	30 Jun 1980 (s 70(3))
9, Pt I	31 Jul 1980 (repeals of Road Traffic Act 1960, ss 144, 145(1), 147(1)(d), 154, 155, 158, 160(1)(f), 163(1); Transport (London) Act 1969, s 24(2), (3); Local Government (Scotland) Act 1973, Sch 18, para 30; Road Traffic Act 1974, Sch 6, para 2; Energy Act 1976, Sch 1, para 2) (SI 1980/913)

6 Oct 1980 (repeals of Education (Miscellaneous Provisions) Act 1953, s 12; Transport Charges &c (Miscellaneous Provisions) Act 1954, s 2, Sch 1; Public Service Vehicles (Travel Concessions) Act 1955, s 1(7); Local Government (Omnibus Shelters and Queue Barriers) (Scotland) Act 1958, s 7(1); Road Traffic Act 1960, ss 117, 118, 119(3)(a), 128(2), 134–139, 139A, 140, 143(1)–(3), (4), (9) (in so far as relate to road service licences), 149, 156(1), 160 (repeals in heads (a) and (c)), 234, 240, 247(2), 257(1), (definition 'road service licence'), 258, Schs 12, 17; Transport Act 1962, Sch 2, Pt I; London Government Act 1963, ss 9(6)(b), 14(6)(d), Sch 5, Pt I, para 25; Finance Act 1965, s 92(8); Road Traffic Regulation Act 1967, s 1(3), Sch 6; Transport Act 1968, ss 21(1), 30, 138(1)(a), (3)(a), 145(1), 159(1); Transport (London) Act 1969, ss 23(6), (7), 24(4)(b), (d), Sch 3, paras 8, 11; Tribunals and Inquiries Act 1971, s13(5), (6)(a), Sch 1, para 30(a) (in so far as relate to road service licences); European Communities Act 1972, Sch 4, para 10; Local

Transport Act 1980 (c 34)—*contd*
Schedule

9, Pt	I—*contd*	Government Act 1972, s 186(3); Local Government (Scotland) Act 1973, Sch 18, paras 26, 31–35; Road Traffic Act 1974, Sch 5, Pt I (except entries relating to Road Traffic Act 1960, ss 127, 128(3), 132(3), 148(2), 239), Sch 6, para 1, Sch 7; Transport Act 1978, ss 6, 7(1), (2), 8, Schs 1, 2) (SI 1980/1353)
		1 Apr 1981 (repeal of Road Traffic Act 1960, ss 127, 129, 130(2), 132, 133, 133A, 143 (so far as unrepealed), 153(2), 257(1) (definition 'owner'); Transport Act 1968, s 35(1), (2), (3)(a); Tribunals and Inquiries Act 1971, s 13(5), (6)(a), Sch 1, para 30(a) (so far as unrepealed); Road Traffic Act 1972, s 44(4); Road Traffic Act 1974, Sch 2, paras 1, 3–5, Sch 5, Pt I (entries relating to Road Traffic Act 1960, ss 127, 128(3), 132(2)); Transport Act 1978, s 5(10)) (SI 1981/256)
	II	30 Jun 1980 (s 70(3))
	III	1 Oct 1980 (date appointed by SI 1980/1380)
	IV	1 Apr 1981 (SI 1981/256)

Water (Scotland) Act 1980 (c 45)

RA: 1 Aug 1980

1 Aug 1980 (RA)

1981

Acquisition of Land Act 1981 (c 67)

RA: 30 Oct 1981

Commencement provisions: s 35(2)

30 Jan 1982 (s 35(2))

Animal Health Act 1981 (c 22)

RA: 11 Jun 1981

Commencement provisions: s 97(3)

11 Jul 1981 (s 97(3))

Appropriation Act 1981 (c 51)

Whole Act repealed

Armed Forces Act 1981 (c 55)

RA: 28 Jul 1981

Commencement provisions: ss 1(5), 29(1)–(3), (5), Sch 5, Pt II, para 1; Armed Forces Act 1981 (Commencement No 1) Order 1981, SI 1981/1503; Armed Forces Act 1981 (Commencement No 2) Order 1982, SI 1982/497

Section	
1	Repealed
2–5	1 May 1982 (SI 1982/497)
6	1 Nov 1981 (SI 1981/1503)
7	28 Jul 1981 (s 29(4))
8	1 May 1982 (SI 1982/497)
9	Repealed
10–13	1 May 1982 (SI 1982/497)
14	Repealed
15–17	28 Jul 1981 (s 29(4))
18	1 May 1982 (SI 1982/497)
19–22	28 Jul 1981 (s 29(4))
23, 24	1 May 1982 (SI 1982/497)
25–27	28 Jul 1981 (s 29(4))

Armed Forces Act 1981 (c 55)—*contd*

Section

28	(1)	1 May 1982 (SI 1982/497)
	(2)	28 Jul 1981 (s 29(4))
29, 30		28 Jul 1981 (s 29(4))

Schedule

1, 2		1 May 1982 (SI 1982/497)
3		28 Jul 1981 (s 29(4))
4		1 May 1982 (SI 1982/497)
5, Pt	I	28 Jul 1982 (s 29(5), Sch 5, para 2)
	II	28 Jul 1982 (repeals of or in Naval Agency and Distribution Act 1864, s 17; Naval and Marine Pay and Pensions Act 1865, s 12; Army Pensions Act 1914; Naval Discipline Act 1957, s 93; Armed Forces Act 1976, Sch 9) (s 29(5), Sch 5, para 1)
		1 Sep 1981 (repeal of Armed Forces Act 1976, s 1) (s 29(5), Sch 5, para 2)
		1 May 1982 (repeals of or in Greenwich Hospital Act 1885, s 4; Colonial Naval Defence Act 1931, s 2(1); Colonial Naval Defence Act 1949, s 1(4); Army Act 1955, ss 82(2)(b), 99(2), 131(2), 153(3), 209(3), Sch 7, para 6; Air Force Act 1955, ss 82(2)(b), 99(2), 131(2), 153(3), 209(3); Naval Discipline Act 1957, ss 51(1), (2), 101(2); Army and Air Force Act 1961, s 26(3); Criminal Justice (Scotland) Act 1963, s 9(3), (4); Armed Forces Act 1976, Sch 9, para 12) (s 29(1); SI 1982/497)

Atomic Energy (Miscellaneous Provisions) Act 1981 (c 48)

RA: 27 Jul 1981

27 Jul 1981 (RA)

Belize Act 1981 (c 52)

RA: 28 Jul 1981

Commencement provisions: s 6(2); Belize Independence Order 1981, SI 1981/1107

Independence Day: 21 Sep 1981

Betting and Gaming Duties Act 1981 (c 63)

RA: 30 Oct 1981

30 Oct 1981 (RA)

British Nationality Act 1981 (c 61)

RA: 30 Oct 1981

Commencement provisions: s 53(2), (3); British Nationality Act 1981 (Commencement) Order 1982, SI 1982/933

Section	
1–48	1 Jan 1983 (SI 1982/933)
49	Repealed
50–52	1 Jan 1983 (SI 1982/933)
53	30 Oct 1981 (s 53(3))
Schedule	
1–9	1 Jan 1983 (SI 1982/933)

British Telecommunications Act 1981 (c 38)

RA: 27 Jul 1981

27 Jul 1981 (RA; note, however, that many provisions of the Act did not come into force until 1 Oct 1981, the date appointed by British Telecommunications Act 1981 (Appointed Day) Order 1981, SI 1981/1274, made under s 1(2) (repealed))

Broadcasting Act 1981 (c 68)

Whole Act repealed

Companies Act 1981 (c 62)

Whole Act repealed

Compulsory Purchase (Vesting Declarations) Act 1981 (c 66)

RA: 30 Oct 1981

Commencement provisions: s 17(2)

30 Jan 1982 (s 17(2))

Consolidated Fund Act 1981 (c 4)

Whole Act repealed

Consolidated Fund (No 2) Act 1981 (c 70)

Whole Act repealed

Contempt of Court Act 1981 (c 49)

RA: 27 Jul 1981

Commencement provisions: s 21(2), (3)

27 Aug 1981 (s 21(3) with the exception of the provisions relating to legal aid (namely, s 13, Sch 2, Pts I, II) which, in relation to E, W, S, were *not in force* and are now repealed)

Countryside (Scotland) Act 1981 (c 44)

RA: 27 Jul 1981

Commencement provisions: s 18(2); Countryside (Scotland) Act 1981 (Commencement) Order 1981, SI 1981/1614

Section	
1	1 Apr 1982 (SI 1981/1614)
2–4	5 Nov 1981 (SI 1981/1614)
5	Repealed
6–14	5 Nov 1981 (SI 1981/1614)
15	See Sch 2 below
16–18	5 Nov 1981 (SI 1981/1614)
Schedule	
1	5 Nov 1981 (SI 1981/1614)
2	5 Nov 1981 (except repeal of Countryside (Scotland) Act 1967, ss 67, 68) (SI 1981/1614)
	1 Apr 1982 (exception noted above) (SI 1981/1614)

Criminal Attempts Act 1981 (c 47)

RA: 27 Jul 1981

Commencement provisions: s 11(1)

27 Aug 1981 (s 11(1))

Criminal Justice (Amendment) Act 1981 (c 27)

RA: 2 Jul 1981

Commencement provisions: s 2(2)

2 Oct 1981 (s 2(2))

Deep Sea Mining (Temporary Provisions) Act 1981 (c 53)

RA: 28 Jul 1981

Commencement provisions: s 18(2); Deep Sea Mining (Temporary Provisions) Act 1981 (Appointed Day) Order 1982, SI 1982/52

25 Jan 1982 (SI 1982/52)

Disabled Persons Act 1981 (c 43)

RA: 27 Jul 1981

Commencement provisions: ss 6(6), 9(2)
Section
1	27 Oct 1981 (s 9(2))
2, 3	Repealed
4, 5	27 Oct 1981 (s 9(2))
6	*Not in force*
7–9	27 Oct 1981 (s 9(2))

Disused Burial Grounds (Amendment) Act 1981 (c 18)

RA: 21 May 1981

21 May 1981 (RA)

Education Act 1981 (c 60)

Whole Act repealed

Education (Scotland) Act 1981 (c 58)

RA: 30 Oct 1981

Commencement provisions: s 22(2), (3); Education (Scotland) Act 1981 (Commencement No 1) Order 1981, SI 1981/1557; Education (Scotland) Act 1981 (Commencement No 2) Order 1982, SI 1982/951; Education (Scotland) Act 1981 (Commencement No 3) Order 1982, SI 1982/1737; Education (Scotland) Act 1981 (Commencement No 4) Order 1983, SI 1983/371
Section
1	(1)	15 Feb 1982 (so far as inserts Education (Scotland) Act 1980, ss 28A, 28B (except s 28B(1)(d)), and s 28G so far as relates to those sections) (SI 1981/1557)
		15 Mar 1982 (so far as inserts Education (Scotland) Act 1980, ss 28C, 28D, 28E (except ss 28E(2)), 28F and s 28G so far as relates to those sections) (SI 1981/1557)
		1 Jan 1983 (so far as inserts Education (Scotland) Act 1980, ss 28B(1)(d), 28E(2)) (SI 1982/951)
		9 Mar 1983 (so far as inserts Education (Scotland) Act 1980, s 28G so far as relates to ss 28B(1)(d), 28E(2) and Sch A1) (SI 1983/371)

Education (Scotland) Act 1981 (c 58)—*contd*

Section

1	(1)—*contd*	5 Apr 1983 (so far as inserts Education (Scotland) Act 1980, s 28H) (SI 1982/1737)
	(2)	15 Mar 1982 (SI 1981/1557)
	(3), (4)	15 Feb 1982 (SI 1981/1557)
2		15 Feb 1982 (SI 1981/1557)
3, 4		1 Jan 1983 (SI 1982/951)
5		16 Aug 1982 (SI 1982/951)
6–8		1 Dec 1981 (SI 1981/1557)
9–12		30 Oct 1981 (SI 1981/1557)
13	(1)–(7)	1 Jan 1982 (SI 1981/1557)
	(8)	16 Aug 1982 (SI 1982/951)
14		1 Jan 1982 (SI 1981/1557); prospectively repealed by Standards in Scotland's Schools etc Act 2000 (asp 6), s 60(2), Sch 3[1]
15		10 Nov 1981 (SI 1981/1557)
16		1 Jan 1983 (SI 1982/1737)
17–20		30 Oct 1981 (SI 1981/1557)
21	(1)	See Sch 7 below
	(2)	See Sch 8 below
	(3)	See Sch 9 below
22		30 Oct 1981 (SI 1981/1557)

Schedule

1		15 Mar 1982 (SI 1981/1557)
2, 3		1 Jan 1983 (SI 1982/951)
4		16 Aug 1982 (SI 1982/951)
5		1 Jan 1982 (SI 1981/1557); prospectively repealed by Standards in Scotland's Schools etc Act 2000 (asp 6), s 60(2), Sch 3[1]
6		10 Nov 1981 (SI 1981/1557)
7, para	1–3	30 Oct 1981 (SI 1981/1557)
	4	1 Dec 1981 (SI 1981/1557)
	5	30 Oct 1981 (SI 1981/1557)
	6	15 Feb 1982 (so far as relates to Education (Scotland) Act 1980, ss 50, 51) (SI 1981/1557) 1 Jan 1983 (so far as relates to Education (Scotland) Act 1980, ss 1(5)(c), (d), 28A(1) (as it has effect under the 1980 Act, Sch A2), 60–65F) (SI 1982/951)
	7	15 Feb 1982 (SI 1981/1557)
8, para	1	1 Jan 1983 (SI 1982/951)
	2	15 Feb 1982 (SI 1981/1557)
	3	15 Mar 1982 (SI 1981/1557)
	4	1 Jan 1983 (SI 1982/951)
	5	30 Oct 1981 (SI 1981/1557)

Education (Scotland) Act 1981 (c 58)—*contd*

Schedule

8, para	6	1 Jan 1982 (SI 1981/1557)
	7	30 Oct 1981 (SI 1981/1557)
9		30 Oct 1981 (repeals of or in Education (Scotland) Act 1980, ss 98(1), 132(1), Sch 2, paras 1, 3, 4) (SI 1981/1557)
		10 Nov 1981 (repeals of or in Education (Scotland) Act 1980, ss 104(2), 105(5), 108(2), 110(3), 111(1), (2), (3), (4), (5), 112(6), 113, 114(1), 115, 116, 117 (proviso), 121(b)) (SI 1981/1557)
		1 Dec 1981 (repeals of or in Education (Scotland) Act 1980, ss 7(1)(c), (8), 17(1), 22(1), (4), proviso (ii), 29) (SI 1981/1557)
		1 Jan 1982 (repeals in Education (Scotland) Act 1980, s 129(3), (4)(e), (5)) (SI 1981/1557)
		15 Feb 1982 (repeals of or in Education (Scotland) Act 1980, ss 23(2), proviso, 28(2)) (SI 1981/1557)
		16 Aug 1982 (repeal of Education (Scotland) Act 1980, s 129(6)) (SI 1982/951)
		1 Jan 1983 (repeals of or in Education (Scotland) Act 1980, ss 4(b), (c), 5, 59, 135(1)) (SI 1982/951)
		1 Jan 1983 (repeal of Education (Scotland) Act 1980, s 66(2)) (SI 1982/1737)

[1] Orders made under Standards in Scotland's Schools ect Act 2000, s 61(2), bringing the prospective amendments into force will be noted to that Act

---

Employment and Training Act 1981 (c 57)

RA: 31 Jul 1981

Commencement provisions: s 11(3); Employment and Training Act 1981 (Commencement) Order 1982, SI 1982/126

Section	
1–8	Repealed
9–11	31 Jul 1981 (RA)
Schedule	
1	Repealed
2	31 Jul 1981 (RA)
3	31 Jul 1981 (except entry relating to Industrial Training Act 1964, Schedule) (RA)

Employment and Training Act 1981 (c 57)—*contd*
Schedule
3—*contd*   1 Apr 1982 (entry relating to
                                                        Industrial Training Act 1964,
                                                        Schedule, except for the purposes
                                                        of specified industrial training
                                                        boards, but note whole of 1964
                                                        Act except s 16 was repealed as
                                                        from 29 Jun 1982, except as
                                                        applied to agricultural training
                                                        boards) (SI 1982/126)

Energy Conservation Act 1981 (c 17)

RA: 21 May 1981

21 May 1981 (RA)

English Industrial Estates Corporation Act 1981 (c 13)

Whole Act repealed

European Parliamentary Elections Act 1981 (c 8)

Whole Act repealed

Film Levy Finance Act 1981 (c 16)

Whole Act repealed

Finance Act 1981 (c 35)

Budget Day: 10 Mar 1981

RA: 27 Jul 1981

Details of the commencement of Finance Acts are not set out in this work

---

Fisheries Act 1981 (c 29)

RA: 2 Jul 1981

Commencement provisions: s 46(3), (4); Fisheries Act 1981 (Commencement No 1)
    Order 1981, SI 1981/1357; Fisheries Act 1981 (Commencement No 2)
    Order 1981, SI 1981/1640
Section
1–9   1 Oct 1981 (SI 1981/1357)
10   Substituted by Trustee Act 2000,
                                                        s 40(1), Sch 2, Pt II, para 41
11–14   1 Oct 1981 (SI 1981/1357)

Fisheries Act 1981 (c 29)—*contd*

Section

15–18	2 Aug 1981 (s 46(3))
18A	Inserted (S) 1 Jul 1999 by Scotland Act 1998 (Consequential Modifications) (No 2) Order 1999, SI 1999/1820, art 4, Sch 2, Pt I, para 68(1), (4)
19–30	2 Aug 1981 (s 46(3))
31	18 Nov 1981 (SI 1981/1640)
32–45	2 Aug 1981 (s 46(3))
46	2 Aug 1981 (except as noted below) (s 46(3))
	1 Oct 1981 (for the purposes of Sch 5, Pt I) (SI 1981/1357)

Schedule

1–3	1 Oct 1981 (SI 1981/1357)
4	2 Aug 1981 (s 46(3))
5, Pt I	1 Oct 1981 (SI 1981/1357)
II	2 Aug 1981 (s 46(3))

Food and Drugs (Amendment) Act 1981 (c 26)

Whole Act repealed

Forestry Act 1981 (c 39)

RA: 27 Jul 1981

27 Jul 1981 (RA)

Forgery and Counterfeiting Act 1981 (c 45)

RA: 27 Jul 1981

Commencement provisions: s 33

27 Oct 1981 (s 33)

Friendly Societies Act 1981 (c 50)

Whole Act repealed

Gas Levy Act 1981 (c 3)

RA: 19 Mar 1981

19 Mar 1981 (RA); whole Act repealed by Finance Act 1998, s 165, Sch 27, Pt V(3), except in relation to gas levy for the year 1997–98 or any previous year

Horserace Betting Levy Act 1981 (c 30)

RA: 2 Jul 1981

2 Jul 1981 (RA)

House of Commons Members' Fund and Parliamentary Pensions Act 1981 (c 7)

RA: 19 Mar 1981

19 Mar 1981 (RA)

Housing (Amendment) (Scotland) Act 1981 (c 72)

Whole Act repealed

Indecent Displays (Control) Act 1981 (c 42)

RA: 27 Jul 1981

Commencement provisions: s 5(5)

27 Oct 1981 (s 5(5))

Industrial Diseases (Notification) Act 1981 (c 25)

RA: 2 Jul 1981

2 Jul 1981 (RA)

Industry Act 1981 (c 6)

RA: 19 Mar 1981

Commencement provisions: s 7(2)

Section		
1		Repealed
2	(1)–(3)	Repealed
	(4)	19 Mar 1981 (RA)
3, 4		19 Mar 1981 (RA)
5, 6		Repealed
7		19 Mar 1981 (RA)
Schedule		19 Mar 1981 (RA)

Insurance Companies Act 1981 (c 31)

RA: 2 Jul 1981

Commencement provisions: s 37(1) (repealed); Insurance Companies Act 1981 (Commencement) Order 1981, SI 1981/1657

1 Jan 1982 (SI 1981/1657)

Whole Act repealed, except ss 36(1), 38, Sch 4, Pt II (which make minor and consequential amendments)

International Organisations Act 1981 (c 9)

RA: 15 Apr 1981

15 Apr 1981 (RA)

Iron and Steel Act 1981 (c 46)

Whole Act repealed

Iron and Steel (Borrowing Powers) Act 1981 (c 2)

Whole Act repealed

Judicial Pensions Act 1981 (c 20)

RA: 21 May 1981

Commencement provisions: s 37(2)

21 Jun 1981 (s 37(2))

Licensing (Alcohol Education and Research) Act 1981 (c 28)

RA: 2 Jul 1981

Commencement provisions: s 13(3); Licensing (Alcohol Education and Research) Act 1981 (Commencement) Order 1981, SI 1981/1324

1 Oct 1981 (SI 1981/1324)

Licensing (Amendment) Act 1981 (c 40)

RA: 27 Jul 1981

Commencement provisions: s 3(2); Licensing (Amendment) Act 1981 (Commencement) Order 1982, SI 1982/1383

1 Oct 1982 (SI 1982/1383)

Local Government and Planning (Amendment) Act 1981 (c 41)

Whole Act repealed

Local Government (Miscellaneous Provisions) (Scotland) Act 1981 (c 23)

RA: 11 Jun 1981

Commencement provisions: s 43(2)–(4); Local Government (Miscellaneous Provisions) (Scotland) Act 1981 (Commencement No 1) Order 1981, SI 1981/1402

Section	
1	11 Jun 1981 (RA)
2–4	Repealed

**Local Government (Miscellaneous Provisions) (Scotland) Act 1981
(c 23)**—*contd*

Section

5	1 Apr 1982 (s 43(3))
6	Repealed
7, 8	1 Apr 1982 (s 43(3))
9–11	Repealed
12, 13	11 Jun 1981 (RA)
14–23	Repealed
24–26	11 Jun 1981 (RA)
27	11 Jun 1981 (RA); prospectively repealed by Local Government etc (Scotland) Act 1994, s 180(2), Sch 14[1]
28	11 Jun 1981 (RA)
29	1 Oct 1981 (SI 1981/1402)
30–33	11 Jun 1981 (RA)
34–36	Repealed
37	*Not in force*
38–40	11 Jun 1981 (RA)
41	See Sch 4 below
42, 43	11 Jun 1981 (RA)

Schedule

1–3	11 Jun 1981 (RA)
4	11 Jun 1981 (except repeals of Local Government (Financial Provisions etc) (Scotland) Act 1962, s 4(2); Social Work (Scotland) Act 1968, s 7) (RA)
	1 Oct 1981 (repeal of Social Work (Scotland) Act 1968, s 7) (SI 1981/1402)
	1 Apr 1982 (repeal of Local Government (Financial Provisions etc) (Scotland) Act 1962, s 4(2)) (s 43(3))

---

[1]   Orders made under Local Government etc (Scotland) Act 1994, s 184(2), (3), bringing the prospective repeal into force will be noted to that Act

---

Matrimonial Homes and Property Act 1981 (c 24)

RA: 2 Jul 1981

Commencement provisions: s 9; Matrimonial Homes and Property Act 1981 (Commencement No 1) Order 1981, SI 1981/1275; Matrimonial Homes and Property Act 1981 (Commencement No 2) Order 1983, SI 1983/50

Section

1–3		Repealed
4	(1)	14 Feb 1983 (SI 1983/50)
	(2)–(4)	Repealed
5, 6		Repealed

Matrimonial Homes and Property Act 1981 (c 24)—*contd*

Section

7–9		1 Oct 1981 (SI 1981/1275)
10	(1)	1 Oct 1981 (SI 1981/1275)
	(2)	14 Feb 1983 (SI 1983/50)
	(3)	1 Oct 1981 (SI 1981/1275)

Schedule

1, 2	Repealed
3	14 Feb (SI 1983/50)

Matrimonial Homes (Family Protection) (Scotland) Act 1981 (c 59)

RA: 30 Oct 1981

Commencement provisions: s 23(3); Matrimonial Homes (Family Protection) (Scotland) Act 1981 (Commencement) Order 1982, SI 1982/972

Section

1–9	1 Sep 1982 (SI 1982/972)
10	Repealed
11–22	1 Sep 1982 (SI 1982/972)
23	30 Oct 1981 (RA)

Merchant Shipping Act 1981 (c 10)

Whole Act repealed

National Film Finance Corporation Act 1981 (c 15)

Whole Act repealed

New Towns Act 1981 (c 64)

RA: 30 Oct 1981

Commencement provisions: s 82(4)

30 Nov 1981 (s 82(4))

Nuclear Industry (Finance) Act 1981 (c 71)

Whole Act repealed

Parliamentary Commissioner (Consular Complaints) Act 1981 (c 11)

RA: 15 Apr 1981

15 Apr 1981 (RA)

Ports (Financial Assistance) Act 1981 (c 21)

RA: 11 Jun 1981

11 Jun 1981 (RA)

Public Passenger Vehicles Act 1981 (c 14)

RA: 15 Apr 1981

Commencement provisions: s 89(2); Public Passenger Vehicles Act 1981 (Commencement)
    Order 1981, SI 1981/1387

Public Passenger Vehicles Act 1981 (c 14)—*contd*
Section

64–66	30 Oct 1981 (s 89(2); SI 1981/1387)
66A	Prospectively inserted by Transport Act 1982, s 24(4)[1]
67–89	30 Oct 1981 (s 89(2); SI 1981/1387)

Schedule

1	30 Oct 1981 (s 89(2); SI 1981/1387)
2	Substituted by Transport Act 1985, s 3(3), Sch 2, Pt I (qv)
3	30 Oct 1981 (s 89(2); SI 1981/1387)
4, 5	Repealed
6–8	30 Oct 1981 (s 89(2); SI 1981/1387)

[1]   Orders made under Transport Act 1982, s 76(2), bringing the prospective insertion into force will be noted to that Act

---

Redundancy Fund Act 1981 (c 5)

Whole Act repealed

Representation of the People Act 1981 (c 34)

RA: 2 Jul 1981

2 Jul 1981 (RA)

Social Security Act 1981 (c 33)

RA: 2 Jul 1981

Commencement provisions: s 8(3); Social Security Act 1981 Commencement Order 1981, SI 1981/953

Section

1–6		Repealed or spent
7		10 Aug 1981 (SI 1981/953)
8	(1)	2 Jul 1981 (RA)
	(2)	Repealed
	(3)	2 Jul 1981 (RA)
	(4)	10 Aug 1981 (SI 1981/953)
	(5)	Repealed
	(6)	2 Jul 1981 (RA)

Schedule

1, 2	Repealed

Social Security (Contributions) Act 1981 (c 1)

Whole Act repealed

Statute Law (Repeals) Act 1981 (c 19)

RA: 21 May 1981

21 May 1981 (RA)

Supreme Court Act 1981 (c 54)

RA: 28 Jul 1981

Commencement provisions: s 153(2), (3)
Section

1–28	1 Jan 1982 (s 153(2))
28A	Inserted by Statute Law (Repeals) Act 1993, s 1(2), Sch 2, para 9 (qv); substituted by Access to Justice Act 1999, s 61 (qv)
29–32	1 Jan 1982 (s 153(2))
32A	Inserted by Administration of Justice Act 1982, s 6(1) (qv)
33–35	1 Jan 1982 (s 153(2)); repealed so far as apply to county courts
35A	Inserted by Administration of Justice Act 1982, s 15(1), Sch 1, Pt I (qv)
36–40	1 Jan 1982 (s 153(2))
40A	Inserted by Administration of Justice Act 1982, s 55(1), Sch 4, Pt I (qv)
41–43	1 Jan 1982 (s 153(2))
43ZA	Inserted by Access to Justice Act 1999, s 62 (qv)
43A	Inserted by Courts and Legal Services Act 1990, s 100 (qv)
44–46	1 Jan 1982 (s 153(2))
46A	Inserted by Merchant Shipping Act 1995, s 314(2), Sch 13, para 59(1), (4) (qv)
47	Repealed
48–50	1 Jan 1982 (s 153(2))
51	Substituted by Courts and Legal Services Act 1990, s 4(1) (qv)
52–56	1 Jan 1982 (s 153(2))
56A, 56B	Inserted by Criminal Justice and Public Order Act 1994, s 52(6), (8), (9) (qv)
57	1 Jan 1982 (s 153(2))
58	Substituted by Access to Justice Act 1999, s 60 (qv)
59–71	1 Jan 1982 (s 153(2))
72	28 Jul 1981 (s 153(3))
73–82	1 Jan 1982 (s 153(2))
83	Repealed
84	1 Jan 1982 (s 153(2))

Supreme Court Act 1981 (c 54)—*contd*

Section

85		Repealed
86–93		1 Jan 1982 (s 153(2))
94		Repealed
95–102		1 Jan 1982 (s 153(2))
103		Repealed
104–125		1 Jan 1982 (s 153(2))
126		1 Jan 1982 (s 153(2)); prospectively repealed by Administration of Justice Act 1982, s 75, Sch 9, Pt I[1]
127–138		1 Jan 1982 (s 153(2))
138A, 138B		Inserted by Statute Law (Repeals) Act 1989, s 1(2), Sch 2, Pt I, para 4 (qv)
139–142		1 Jan 1982 (s 153(2))
143, 144		Repealed
145–147		1 Jan 1982 (s 153(2))
148, 149		Repealed
150, 151		1 Jan 1982 (s 153(2))
152	(1)	1 Jan 1982 (s 153(2))
	(2)	Spent
	(3)–(5)	1 Jan 1982 (s 153(2))
153		28 Jul 1981 (s 153(3))

Schedule

1		1 Jan 1982 (s 153(2))
2		Substituted by Courts and Legal Services Act 1990, s 71(2), Sch 10, para 49 (qv)
3		Repealed
4–7		1 Jan 1982 (s 153(2))

[1] Orders made under Administration of Justice Act 1982, s 76(5), (6), bringing the prospective repeal into force will be noted to that Act

---

Town and Country Planning (Minerals) Act 1981 (c 36)

Whole Act repealed or spent

Transport Act 1962 (Amendment) Act 1981 (c 32)

Whole Act repealed

Transport Act 1981 (c 56)

RA: 31 Jul 1981

Commencement provisions: ss 5, 15(1), (2), 18(3), 31 (repealed), 32(2), 35(5), 40(4); Transport Act 1981 (Commencement No 1) Order 1981, SI 1981/1331; Transport Act 1981 (Dissolution of National Ports Council) (Appointed Day) Order 1981, SI 1981/1364; Transport Act 1981 (Commencement No 2) Order 1981, SI 1981/1617; Transport Act 1981 (Dissolution of National Ports

Transport Act 1981 (c 56)—*contd*
    Council) (Final) Order 1981, SI 1981/1665; Transport Act 1981 (Commencement
    No 3) Order 1982, SI 1982/300; Transport Act 1981 (Commencement No 4)
    Order 1982, SI 1982/310; Transport Act 1981 (Commencement No 5)
    Order 1982, SI 1982/866; Transport Act 1981 (Commencement No 6)
    Order 1982, SI 1982/1341; Transport Act 1981 (Commencement No 7)
    Order 1982, SI 1982/1451; Transport Act 1981 (Commencement No 8)
    Order 1982, SI 1982/1803; Transport Act 1981 (Commencement No 9)
    Order 1983, SI 1983/576; Transport Act 1981 (Commencement No 10)
    Order 1983, SI 1983/930; Transport Act 1981 (Commencement No 11)
    Order 1983, SI 1983/1089; Transport Act 1981 (Commencement No 12)
    Order 1988, SI 1988/1037; Transport Act 1981 (Commencement No 13)
    Order 1988, SI 1988/1170

Section		
1–4		Repealed
5		31 Jul 1981 (RA)
		31 Dec 1982 (appointed day for reconstitution of the British Transport Docks Board (s 5; SI 1982/1887)
6–15		31 Jul 1981 (RA)
		1 Oct 1981 (date on which the functions of the National Ports Council were determined) (s 15(1); SI 1981/1364)
		1 Dec 1981 (date on which the National Ports Council was dissolved) (s 15(2); SI 1981/1665)
16, 17		31 Jul 1981 (RA)
18		See Sch 6 below
19–31		Repealed
32		25 Aug 1983 (E, W) (s 32(2); SI 1983/1089)
		Repealed (S)
33, 34		Repealed
35	(1), (2)	Repealed
	(3)	12 Oct 1981 (s 35(5); SI 1981/1331)
	(3A)	Inserted by Local Government (Wales) Act 1994, s 22(1), Sch 7, Pt II, para 37 (qv)
	(4), (5)	12 Oct 1981 (s 35(5); SI 1981/1331)
36		Repealed
37–43		31 Jul 1981 (RA)
Schedule		
1		Repealed
2–5		31 Jul 1981 (RA)
6, para	1–9	1 Oct 1981 (s 18(2); SI 1981/1364)
	10	2 Aug 1983 (s 18(3); SI 1983/930)
	11–15	1 Oct 1981 (s 18(2); SI 1981/1364)
7–9		Repealed

Transport Act 1981 (c 56)—*contd*
Schedule

10		25 Aug 1983 (E, W) (s 32(2); SI 1983/1089)
		Repealed (S)
11		Repealed
12, Pt	I	31 Dec 1982 (ss 5(4), 40(2))
	II	1 Oct 1981 (except repeal of entry for National Ports Council in House of Commons Disqualification Act 1975, Sch 1, Pt II) (ss 5(3), 15(1))
		1 Dec 1981 (exception noted above) (s 15(1))
	III	31 Jul 1981 (repeals of or in Railway Fires Act (1905) Amendment Act 1923; Public Passenger Vehicles Act 1981) (s 40(4))
		12 Oct 1981 (repeal of Town Police Clauses Act 1847, s 39) (s 40(4); SI 1981/1331)
		1 Apr 1982 (repeal in Metropolitan Public Carriage Act 1869) (s 40(4); SI 1982/310)
		1 Nov 1982 (repeals of or in Road Traffic Act 1972, ss 93(3), (5), 177(2)) (s 40(4); SI 1982/1451)
		6 May 1983 (repeals of or in Road Traffic Act 1972, ss 89, 90, 189, Sch 4, Pt V, para 1) (s 40(4); SI 1983/576)
		25 Aug 1983 (repeal of entry relating to Road Traffic Act 1974, s 17) (E, W) (s 40(4); SI 1983/1089)
		Not in force (repeals of or in Road Traffic Act 1974, Sch 3; British Railways (No 2) Act 1975, s 21; London Transport Act 1977, s 13(1); British Railways Act 1977, s 14(1); Criminal Justice (Scotland) Act 1980, Sch 7, para 22)

Trustee Savings Banks Act 1981 (c 65)

Whole Act repealed

Water Act 1981 (c 12)

RA: 15 Apr 1981

Commencement provisions: ss 2(5), 6(8); Water Act 1981 (Commencement No 1) Order 1981, SI 1981/1755

Water Act 1981 (c 12)—*contd*
Section
1	15 Apr 1981 (RA)
2–6	Repealed
7	15 Apr 1981 (RA)

Wildlife and Countryside Act 1981 (c 69)

RA: 30 Oct 1981

Commencement provisions: s 74(2), (3); Wildlife and Countryside Act 1981 (Commencement No 1) Order 1982, SI 1982/44; Wildlife and Countryside Act 1981 (Commencement No 2) Order 1982, SI 1982/327; Wildlife and Countryside Act 1981 (Commencement No 3) Order 1982, SI 1982/990; Wildlife and Countryside Act 1981 (Commencement No 4) Order 1982, SI 1982/1136; Wildlife and Countryside Act 1981 (Commencement No 5) Order 1982, SI 1982/1217; Wildlife and Countryside Act 1981 (Commencement No 6) Order 1983, SI 1983/20; Wildlife and Countryside Act 1981 (Commencement No 7) Order 1983, SI 1983/87

Section
1–11	28 Sep 1982 (SI 1982/1217)
12	16 Feb 1982 (SI 1982/44)
13–19	28 Sep 1982 (SI 1982/1217)
19ZA, 19ZB	Inserted by Countryside and Rights of Way Act 2000, s 81(1), Sch 12, para 8
19A	Inserted (S) by Prisoners and Criminal Proceedings (Scotland) Act 1993, s 36 (qv)
20–27	28 Sep 1982 (SI 1982/1217)
27A	Inserted by Environmental Protection Act 1990, s 132, Sch 9, para 11(8) (qv)
28–28R	Substituted for original s 28 by Countryside and Rights of Way Act 2000, s 75(1), Sch 9, para 1 (subject to transitional provisions; see ss 75(2), 76(2) of, and Sch 11 to, the 2000 Act)
29	Repealed (Subject to transitional provisions; see s 76(2) of, and Sch 11, paras 15–18 to, the 2000 Act)
30	Repealed (Subject to savings; see s 76(2) of, and Sch 11, para 19(1) to, the 2000 Act)
31	6 Sep 1982 (SI 1982/1136)
32	28 Feb 1983 (SI 1983/87)
33–37	30 Nov 1981 (s 74(2))
37A	Inserted by Countryside and Rights of Way Act 2000, s 77

Wildlife and Countryside Act 1981 (c 69)—*contd*
Section

38		Repealed
39, 40		30 Nov 1981 (s 74(2))
41		28 Feb 1983 (SI 1983/87)
42–45		30 Nov 1981 (s 74(2))
46		Repealed
47		1 Apr 1982 (SI 1982/327)
48		Repealed
49–52		30 Nov 1981 (s 74(2))
53		28 Feb 1983 (SI 1983/20)
53A, 53B		Prospectively inserted by Countryside and Rights of Way Act 2000, s 51, Sch 5, Pt I, para 2[1]
54		28 Feb 1983 (SI 1983/20); prospectively repealed by Countryside and Rights of Way Act 2000, ss 47(1), 102, Sch 16, Pt II[1]
55–57		28 Feb 1983 (SI 1983/20)
57A		Prospectively inserted by Countryside and Rights of Way Act 2000, s 51, Sch 5, Pt I, para 8[1]
58, 59		28 Feb 1983 (SI 1983/20)
60, 61		Repealed
62–66		28 Feb 1983 (SI 1983/20)
67–70		30 Nov 1981 (s 74(2))
70A		Inserted by Wildlife and Countryside (Service of Notices) Act 1985 s 1(1) (qv)
71		30 Nov 1981 (s 74(2))
72	(1)	Repealed
	(2), (3)	30 Nov 1981 (s 74(2))
	(4)	28 Sep 1982 (SI 1982/1217)
	(5)	30 Nov 1981 (s 74(2))
	(6)	28 Sep 1982 (SI 1982/1217)
	(7)–(9)	30 Nov 1981 (s 74(2))
	(10)	Repealed
	(11)–(13)	30 Nov 1981 (s 74(2))
	(14)	28 Sep 1982 (SI 1982/1217)
73	(1)	See Sch 17
	(2), (3)	30 Nov 1981 (s 74(2))
	(4)	Repealed
74		30 Nov 1981 (s 74(2))

Schedule

1–6	28 Sep 1982 (SI 1982/1217)
7	16 Feb 1982 (SI 1982/44)
8–10	28 Sep 1982 (SI 1982/1217)
10A	Inserted by Countryside and Rights of Way Act 2000, s 75(1), Sch 9, para 7

Wildlife and Countryside Act 1981 (c 69)—*contd*
Schedule

11		30 Nov 1981 (so far as relates to orders under s 34) (s 74(2))
		6 Sep 1982 (so far as relates to orders under s 29) (SI 1982/1136)
12		30 Nov 1981 (s 74(2))
13		1 Apr 1982 (SI 1982/327)
14–16		28 Feb 1983 (SI 1983/20)
17, Pt	I	30 Nov 1981 (s 74(2))
	II	16 Feb 1982 (repeals of or in Deer Act 1963, Sch 2; Conservation of Seals Act 1970, s 10(1); Badgers Act 1973, ss 6, 7, 8(2)(c), 11) (SI 1982/44)

1 Apr 1982 (repeals of or in National Parks and Access to the Countryside Act 1949, ss 2, 4, 95; Countryside Act 1968, s 3) (SI 1982/327)

28 Sep 1982 (repeals of or in Protection of Animals (Scotland) Act 1912, s 9; Protection of Birds Act 1954 (Amendment) Act 1964; Protection of Birds Act 1967; Countryside Act 1968, s 1; Local Government Act 1972, Sch 29, para 37; Water Act 1973, Sch 8, para 67; Nature Conservancy Council Act 1973, s 5(3), Sch 1, paras 3, 5, 7, 12; Local Government (Scotland) Act 1973, Sch 27, Pt II, paras 115, 168; Criminal Procedure (Scotland) Act 1975, Sch 7C; Conservation of Wild Creatures and Wild Plants Act 1975; Statute Law (Repeals) Act 1976, Sch 2, Pt II; Endangered Species (Import and Export) Act 1976, s 13(6); Criminal Law Act 1977, Sch 6; Customs and Excise Management Act 1979, Sch 4, para 12; Animal Health Act 1981, Sch 5, para 1; Zoo Licensing Act 1981, s 4(5)) (SI 1982/1217)

28 Feb 1983 (repeals of or in National Parks and Access to the Countryside Act 1949, ss 27–35, 38; London Government Act 1963, s 60(1)–(4); Countryside Act 1968, Sch 3; Courts Act 1971, Sch 8,

Wildlife and Countryside Act 1981 (c 69)—*contd*
Schedule

17, Pt	II	para 31, Sch 9, Pt II; Town and Country Planning Act 1971, Sch 20; Local Government Act 1972, Sch 17; Highways Act 1980, ss 31(10), 340(2)(d)) (SI 1983/20)

[1]   Orders made under Countryside and Rights of Way Act 2000, s 103(3), bringing the prospective insertion into force will be noted to that Act

Zoo Licensing Act 1981 (c 37)

RA: 27 Jul 1981

Commencement provisions: s 23(2); Zoo Licensing Act 1981 (Commencement) Order 1984, SI 1984/423

30 Apr 1984 (SI 1984/423)

1982

Administration of Justice Act 1982 (c 53)

RA: 28 Oct 1982

Commencement provisions: s 76; Administration of Justice Act 1982 (Commencement No 1) Order 1983, SI 1983/236; Administration of Justice Act 1982 (Commencement No 2) Order 1984, SI 1984/1142; Administration of Justice Act 1982 (Commencement No 3) Order 1984, SI 1984/1287; Administration of Justice Act 1982 (Commencement No 4) Order 1985, SI 1985/858; Administration of Justice Act 1982 (Commencement No 5) Order 1986, SI 1986/2259; Administration of Justice Act 1982 (Commencement No 6) Order 1991, SI 1991/1245; Administration of Justice Act 1982 (Commencement No 7) Order 1991, SI 1991/1786

Section

1–5		1 Jan 1983 (s 76(11))
6		1 Jul 1985 (SI 1985/858)
7–11		1 Jan 1983 (s 76(11))
12		1 Sep 1984 (SI 1984/1287)
13		1 Jan 1983 (s 76(11))
14	(1)	1 Jan 1983 (s 76(11))
	(2)	1 Sep 1984 (SI 1984/1287)
	(3), (4)	1 Jan 1983 (s 76(11))
15		1 Apr 1983 (SI 1983/236)
16		1 Apr 1983 (SI 1983/236); prospectively repealed by Family Law Act 1996, s 66(3), Sch 10[1]
17–22		1 Jan 1983 (s 76(11))
23–25		*Not in force*
26		1 Jan 1983 (s 76(11))
27, 28		*Not in force*
29–33		Repealed
34		1 Sep 1984 (SI 1984/1142)
35		Spent
36		Repealed
37		1 Jan 1983 (s 76(11))
38–47		2 Jan 1987 (SI 1986/2259)
48		*Not in force*
49–51		1 Jan 1983 (s 76(11))
52		28 Oct 1982 (s 76(9), (10))
53		1 Jan 1983 (s 76(11))
54		1 Apr 1983 (SI 1983/236)
55, 56		1 Jan 1983 (s 76(11))

Administration of Justice Act 1982 (c 53)—*contd*

Section

57		1 Apr 1983 (SI 1983/236)
58, 59		1 Jan 1983 (s 76(11))
60		Repealed
61		1 Jan 1983 (s 76(11))
62		Repealed
63		1 Jan 1983 (s 76(11))
64		28 Oct 1982 (s 76(9), (10))
65		Repealed
66, 67		1 Jan 1983 (s 76(11))
68		See Sch 6 below
69		1 Jun 1983 (SI 1983/236)
70		See Sch 8 below
71		Repealed
72		1 Jan 1983 (s 76(11))
73	(1)–(7)	1 Jan 1983 (s 76(11))
	(8)	Spent
	(9)	1 Jan 1983 (s 76(11))
74		Repealed
75		See Sch 9 below
76–78		28 Oct 1982 (s 76(9), (10))

Schedule

1, Pt	I	1 Apr 1983 (SI 1983/236)
	II	Repealed
	III	1 Apr 1983 (SI 1983/236)
	IV	Repealed
2		*Not in force*
3–5		1 Jan 1983 (s 76(11))
6, para	1–9	1 Jan 1983 (s 76(11))
	10	1 Sep 1991 (SI 1991/1786)
7		1 Jun 1983 (SI 1983/236)
8, para	1–5	1 Jan 1983 (s 76(11))
	6–8	13 Jun 1991 (SI 1991/1245)
	9–12	1 Jan 1983 (s 76(11))
9, Pt	I	1 Jan 1983 (except repeals noted below) (s 76(11))
		1 Apr 1983 (repeal in Judicial Trustees Act 1896) (SI 1983/236)
		1 Jun 1983 (repeal of Law Reform (Miscellaneous Provisions) Act (Northern Ireland) 1937, s 17) (SI 1983/236)
		1 Sep 1984 (repeal in County Courts Act 1959, s 148) (SI 1984/1142)
		1 Sep 1984 (repeal in Damages (Scotland) Act 1976) (SI 1984/1287)
		2 Jan 1987 (repeal of County Courts Act 1959, ss 99(3), 168–174A, 176) (SI 1986/2259)

Administration of Justice Act 1982 (c 53)—*contd*

Schedule

9	I—*contd*	13 Jun 1991 (repeals of Administration of Justice Act 1965, ss 1–16; Judicature (Northern Ireland) Act 1978, s 83) (SI 1991/1245)
		Not in force (repeals of or in Prevention of Fraud (Investments) Act 1958; Administration of Justice Act 1977; Supreme Court Act 1981, s 126)
	II	1 Jan 1983 (revocation of or in SI 1967/761; SI 1977/1251) (s 76(11))
		Not in force (revocation in SI 1979/1575)

1   Orders made under Family Law Act 1996, s 67(3), bringing the prospective repeal into force will be noted to that Act

---

Agricultural Training Board Act 1982 (c 9)

RA: 29 Mar 1982

Commencement provisions: s 12(3)

29 Jun 1982 (s 12(3))

Appropriation Act 1982 (c 40)

Whole Act repealed

Aviation Security Act 1982 (c 36)

RA: 23 Jul 1982

Commencement provisions: s 41(2)

23 Oct 1982 (s 41(2))

Canada Act 1982 (c 11)

RA: 29 Mar 1982

29 Mar 1982 (RA)

Children's Homes Act 1982 (c 20)

Whole Act repealed

Cinematograph (Amendment) Act 1982 (c 33)

Whole Act repealed

Civic Government (Scotland) Act 1982 (c 45)

RA: 28 Oct 1982

Commencement provisions: s 137(2)–(4); Civic Government (Scotland) Act 1982 (Commencement) Order 1983, SI 1983/201 (as amended by SI 1984/573, SI 1984/774)

Section	
1–8	1 Apr 1983 (for purpose only of enabling preliminary arrangements to be made for when provisions fully effective in operation) (SI 1983/201)
	1 Jul 1984 (otherwise) (SI 1983/201)
9–23	1 Apr 1983 (for purpose only of enabling preliminary arrangements to be made for when provisions fully effective in operation) (SI 1983/201)
	1 Jul 1984 (otherwise, except in relation to areas of local authorities noted below) (SI 1983/201, as amended by SI 1984/744)
	2 Aug 1984 (as respects the area of Lochaber District Council) (SI 1984/744)
	20 Aug 1984 (as respects the area of the City of Glasgow District Council) (SI 1984/744)
	20 Sep 1984 (as respects the area of Wigtown District Council) (SI 1984/744)
	1 Nov 1984 (as respects the area of Cunninghame District Council) (SI 1984/744)
24–27	As noted to ss 9–23 above, and in addition:
	1 Jan 1985 (as respects the area of Monklands District Council) (SI 1984/744)
28–37	1 Apr 1983 (for purpose only of enabling preliminary arrangements to be made for when provisions fully effective in operation) (SI 1983/201)
	1 Jul 1984 (otherwise) (SI 1983/201)
38–41	As noted to ss 9–23, 24–27 above

Civic Government (Scotland) Act 1982 (c 45)—*contd*

Section

41A		Inserted by Fire Safety and Safety of Places of Sport Act 1987, s 44 (qv)
42–44		As noted to ss 9–23, 24–27 above
45–52		1 Apr 1983 (SI 1983/201)
52A		Inserted by Criminal Justice Act 1988, s 161 (qv)
53–61		1 Apr 1983 (SI 1983/201)
62–66		1 Apr 1983 (for purpose only of enabling preliminary arrangements to be made for when provisions fully effective in operation) (SI 1983/201)
		1 Jul 1984 (otherwise) (SI 1983/201)
67–86		1 Apr 1983 (SI 1983/201)
86A–86J		Inserted by Police (Property) Act 1997, s 6(4) (qv)
87–109		1 Apr 1983 (SI 1983/201)
110	(1)	1 Apr 1983 (so far as relates to s 110(2)) (SI 1983/201)
		1 Jul 1984 (otherwise) (SI 1983/201)
	(2)	1 Apr 1983 (SI 1983/201)
	(3)	1 Jul 1984 (SI 1983/201)
111–118		1 Apr 1983 (SI 1983/201)
119		18 Apr 1984 (for purpose only of enabling preliminary arrangements to be made for when provisions fully effective in operation) (SI 1983/201, as amended by SI 1984/573)
		1 Jul 1984 (otherwise) (SI 1983/201)
120–123		1 Apr 1983 (SI 1983/201)
124, 125		1 Apr 1983 (SI 1983/201); repealed (1 Apr 1992) subject to transitional and saving provisions by Environmental Protection Act 1990, s 162(1), (2), Sch 16, Pt II
126	(1)	Repealed
	(2)	1 Apr 1983 (SI 1983/201)
	(3)	Repealed
127		1 Apr (SI 1983/201)
128	(1)	Repealed
	(2), (3)	1 Apr 1983 (SI 1983/201)
129–133		1 Apr 1983 (SI 1983/201)
134–136		28 Oct 1982 (s 137(2))
137	(1)–(6)	28 Oct 1982 (s 137(2))
	(7)	See Sch 3 below
	(8)	See Sch 4 below
	(9)	28 Oct 1982 (s 137(2))

Civic Government (Scotland) Act 1982 (c 45)—*contd*
Schedule

1		1 Apr 1983 (for purpose only of enabling preliminary arrangements to be made for when provisions fully effective in operation) (SI 1983/201)
		1 Jul 1984 (otherwise) (SI 1983/201)
2		1 Apr 1983 (SI 1983/201)
2A		Inserted by Crime and Disorder Act 1998, s 24(4), Sch 1 (qv)
3, para	1	Repealed
	2, 3	1 Apr 1983 (SI 1983/201)
	4	Repealed
	5	1 Jul 1984 (SI 1983/201)
4		1 Apr 1983 (repeals of or in Vagrancy Act 1824, s 4; Prevention of Crime Act 1871, ss 7, 15; Licensing (Scotland) Act 1903; Dogs Act 1906, s 3(6), (7); Countryside (Scotland) Act 1967, ss 56, 57(1), (2); Theatres Act 1968, s 2(4)(c); Sexual Offences (Scotland) Act 1976, s 13(3)) (SI 1983/201)
		1 Jul 1984 (otherwise) (SI 1983/201)

Civil Aviation Act 1982 (c 16)

RA: 27 May 1982

Commencement provisions: s 110(2)

27 Aug 1982 (s 110(2))

Civil Aviation (Amendment) Act 1982 (c 1)

RA: 2 Feb 1982

2 Feb 1982 (RA)

Civil Jurisdiction and Judgments Act 1982 (c 27)

RA: 13 Jul 1982

Commencement provisions: s 53(1), Sch 13, Pt I; Civil Jurisdiction and Judgments Act 1982 (Commencement No 1) Order 1984, SI 1984/1553; Civil Jurisdiction and Judgments Act 1982 (Commencement No 2) Order 1986, SI 1986/1781; Civil Jurisdiction and Judgments Act 1982 (Commencement No 3) Order 1986, SI 1986/2044

Section

1–3	1 Jan 1987 (SI 1986/2044)
3A, 3B	Inserted by Civil Jurisdiction and Judgments Act 1991, s 1(1) (qv)

Civil Jurisdiction and Judgments Act 1982 (c 27)—*contd*

Section

4–23			1 Jan 1987 (SI 1986/2044)
24	(1)	(a)	24 Aug 1982 (s 53(1), Sch 13, Pt I)
		(b)	1 Jan 1987 (SI 1986/2044)
	(2)	(a)	24 Aug 1982 (s 53(1), Sch 13, Pt I)
		(b)	1 Jan 1987 (SI 1986/2044)
	(3)		24 Aug 1982 (s 53(1), Sch 13, Pt I)
25			1 Jan 1987 (SI 1986/2044)
26			1 Nov 1984 (SI 1984/1553)
27, 28			1 Jan 1987 (SI 1986/2044)
29–34			24 Aug 1982 (s 53(1), Sch 13, Pt I)
35	(1)		14 Nov 1986 (SI 1986/1781)
	(2)		1 Jan 1987 (SI 1986/2044)
	(3)		24 Aug 1982 (s 53(1), Sch 13, Pt I)
36, 37			1 Jan 1987 (SI 1986/2044)
38			24 Aug 1982 (s 52(1), Sch 13, Pt I)
39			1 Jan 1987 (SI 1986/2044)
40			24 Aug 1982 (s 53(1), Sch 13, Pt I)
41–48			1 Jan 1987 (SI 1986/2044)
49–52			24 Aug 1982 (s 53(1), Sch 13, Pt I)
53	(1)		13 Jul 1982 (s 53(1), Sch 13, Pt I)
	(2)		24 Aug 1982 (so far as relates to Sch 13, Pt II, paras 7–10) (s 53(1), Sch 13, Pt I)
			1 Nov 1984 (so far as relates to Sch 13, Pt II, para 6) (SI 1984/1553)
			1 Jan 1987 (otherwise) (SI 1986/2044)
54			24 Aug 1982 (so far as relates to repeal in Foreign Judgments (Reciprocal Enforcement) Act 1933, s 4) (s 53(1), Sch 13, Pt I)
			1 Jan 1987 (otherwise) (SI 1986/2044)
55			13 Jul 1982 (s 53(1), Sch 13, Pt I)

Schedule

1, 2		Substituted (1 Dec 1991) by Civil Jurisdiction and Judgments Act 1982 (Amendment) Order 1990, SI 1990/2591, art 12(1)–(3), Schs 1–3; further substituted by Civil Jurisdiction and Judgments Act 1982 (Amendment) Order 2000, SI 2000/1824, art 8, Schs 1, 2[1]
3		Substituted (1 Dec 1991) by Civil Jurisdiction and Judgments Act 1982 (Amendment) Order 1990, SI 1990/2591, art 12(1)–(3), Schs 1–3

Civil Jurisdiction and Judgments Act 1982 (c 27)—*contd*
Schedule

3A			Inserted (1 Oct 1989) by Civil Jurisdiction and Judgments Act 1982 (Amendment) Order 1989, SI 1989/1346, art 9(3), Sch 3
3B			Inserted (1 Dec 1991) by Civil Jurisdiction and Judgments Act 1982 (Amendment) Order 1990, SI 1990/2591, art 12(4), Sch 4
3BB			Inserted by Civil Jurisdiction and Judgments Act 1982 (Amendment) Order 2000, SI 2000/1824, art 8, Sch 3[1]
3C			Inserted by Civil Jurisdiction and Judgments Act 1991, s 1(3), Sch 1 (qv)
4			Substituted (1 Mar 2002) by Civil Jurisdiction and Judgments Order 2001, SI 2001/3929, art 4, Sch 2, Pt II, para 4
5–9			1 Jan 1987 (SI 1986/2044)
10			14 Nov 1986 (SI 1986/1781)
11, 12			1 Jan 1987 (SI 1986/2044)
13, Pt	I		13 Jul 1982 (s 53(1), Sch 13, Pt I, para 2)
	II, para	1–5	1 Jan 1987 (SI 1986/2044)
		6	1 Nov 1984 (SI 1984/1553)
		7–10	24 Aug 1982 (s 53(1), Sch 13, Pt I, para 2)
14			24 Aug 1982 (repeals in Foreign Judgments (Reciprocal Enforcement) Act 1933, s 4) (s 53(1), Sch 13, Pt I) 1 Jan 1987 (otherwise) (SI 1986/2044)

[1] That order comes into force on the date on which the Convention on the accession of the Republic of Austria, the Republic of Finland and the Kingdom of Sweden to the 1968 Convention on Jurisdiction and the Enforcement of Judgments in Civil and Commercial Matters and to the 1971 Protocol on the Interpretation of the Convention by the Court of Justice of the European Communities enters into force in respect of the United Kingdom, both of which dates shall be notified in the *London Gazette*

Clergy Pensions (Amendment) Measure 1982 (No 2)

RA: 23 Jul 1982

23 Jul 1982 (RA)

Coal Industry Act 1982 (c 15)

RA: 7 Apr 1982

7 Apr 1982 (RA)

Whole Act repealed (in part prospectively) as follows: ss 1, 2, 4 repealed by Coal Industry Act 1983, s 6(3), Schedule; ss 3, 5, 6 prospectively repealed by Coal Industry Act 1994, s 67(8), Sch 11, Pt III[1]

---

[1]   Orders made under Coal Industry Act 1994, s 68(4), (5), bringing the prospective repeals into force will be noted to that Act

---

Commonwealth Development Corporation Act 1982 (c 54)

Whole Act repealed

Consolidated Fund Act 1982 (c 8)

Whole Act repealed

Copyright Act 1956 (Amendment) Act 1982 (c 35)

Whole Act repealed

Criminal Justice Act 1982 (c 48)

RA: 28 Oct 1982

Commencement provisions: s 80; Criminal Justice Act 1982 (Commencement No 1) Order 1982, SI 1982/1857; Criminal Justice Act 1982 (Scotland) (Commencement No 1) Order 1983, SI 1983/24; Criminal Justice Act 1982 (Commencement No 2) Order 1983, SI 1983/182; Criminal Justice Act 1982 (Scotland) (Commencement No 2) Order 1983, SI 1983/758

Section		
1		24 May 1983 (SI 1983/182)
1A–9		Repealed
10, 11		24 May 1983 (SI 1983/182)
12–27		Repealed
28		Spent
29		24 May 1983 (SI 1983/182)
30, 31		31 Jan 1983 (SI 1982/1857)
32		28 Oct 1982 (s 80(1))
33, 34		Repealed
35–40		11 Apr 1983 (SI 1982/1857)
41, 42		11 Apr 1983 (SI 1982/1857; SI 1983/24)
43–45		Repealed
46		11 Apr 1983 (SI 1982/1857)
47	(1)	11 Apr 1983 (SI 1982/1857)
	(2)	11 Apr 1983 (SI 1982/1857; SI 1983/24)

Criminal Justice Act 1982 (c 48)—*contd*

Section

48		11 Apr 1983 (SI 1982/1857)
49		Repealed
50		11 Apr 1983 (SI 1982/1857; SI 1983/24)
51		24 May 1983 (SI 1983/182)
52		31 Jan 1983 (SI 1982/1857)
53–56		Repealed
57	(1)	28 Oct 1982 (s 80(1))
	(2)	Repealed
58		24 May 1983 (SI 1983/182; SI 1983/758)
59–61		24 May 1983 (SI 1983/182)
62, 63		Repealed
64		31 Jan 1983 (SI 1982/1857; SI 1983/24)
65		Repealed
66		31 Jan 1983 (SI 1982/1857)
67		Repealed
68	(1)	24 May 1983 (SI 1983/182)
	(2)	24 May 1983 (SI 1983/182; SI 1983/758)
69		24 May 1983 (SI 1983/182)
70, 71		31 Jan 1983 (SI 1982/1857)
72		24 May 1983 (SI 1983/182)
73		31 Jan 1983 (SI 1983/24)
74, 75		28 Oct 1982 (s 80(1)); repealed (except in relation to Channel Islands and Isle of Man) by Criminal Justice Act 1988, s 170(2), Sch 16
76		28 Oct 1982 (s 80(1))
77		See Schs 14, 15 below
78		See Sch 16 below
79		See Sch 17 below
80, 81		28 Oct 1982 (s 80(1))

Schedule

1		28 Oct 1982 (s 80(1))
2–4		11 Apr 1983 (SI 1982/1857)
5–7		Repealed
8		24 May 1983 (SI 1983/182; SI 1983/758)
9		24 May 1983 (SI 1983/182)
10		31 Jan 1983 (SI 1982/1857; SI 1983/24))
11		Repealed
12		24 May 1983 (SI 1983/182)
13		24 May 1983 (SI 1983/182; SI 1983/758)
14, para	1	31 Jan 1983 (SI 1982/1857)
	2	Repealed

Criminal Justice Act 1982 (c 48)—*contd*

Schedule

14, para	3		31 Jan 1983 (SI 1983/24)
	4		Repealed
	5		31 Jan 1983 (SI 1982/1857)
	6, 7		24 May 1983 (SI 1983/182)
	8, 9		Repealed
	10	(a)	31 Jan 1983 (SI 1982/1857)
		(b)	24 May 1983 (SI 1983/182)
	11–13		24 May 1983 (SI 1983/182; SI 1983/758)
	14		24 May 1983 (SI 1983/182)
	15–17		24 May 1983 (SI 1983/182; SI 1983/758)
	18	(a)	24 May 1983 (SI 1983/182; SI 1983/758); repealed (S)
		(b)	31 Jan 1983 (SI 1982/1857; SI 1983/24); repealed (S)
		(c)	24 May 1983 (SI 1983/182; SI 1983/758); repealed (S)
	19		24 May 1983 (SI 1983/182; SI 1983/758); repealed (S)
	20		28 Oct 1982 (s 80(1)); repealed (S)
	21		31 Jan 1983 (SI 1982/1857; SI 1983/24); repealed (S)
	22		31 Jan 1983 (SI 1982/1857)
	23		24 May 1983 (SI 1983/182)
	24		24 May 1983 (SI 1983/182; SI 1983/758)
	25		Repealed
	26		24 May 1983 (SI 1983/182)
	27		Spent
	28		Repealed
	29		24 May 1983 (SI 1983/182; SI 1983/758)
	30		24 May 1983 (SI 1983/182)
	31		31 Jan 1983 (SI 1982/1857; SI 1983/24)
	32, 33		Repealed
	34		24 May 1983 (SI 1983/182)
	35		Spent
	36, 37		24 May 1983 (SI 1983/182; SI 1983/758)
	38		24 May 1983 (SI 1983/182)
	39		24 May 1983 (SI 1983/182; SI 1983/758)
	40, 41		31 Jan 1983 (SI 1982/1857)
	42, 43		31 Jan 1983 (SI 1982/1857; SI 1983/24)
	44		Spent
	45, 46		Repealed

Criminal Justice Act 1982 (c 48)—*contd*

Schedule

14, para	47	24 May 1983 (SI 1983/182)
	48	Repealed
	49, 50	24 May 1983 (SI 1983/182)
	51	Repealed
	52–56	24 May 1983 (SI 1983/182)
	57	Spent
	58–60	24 May 1983 (SI 1983/182)
15, para	1	11 Apr 1983 (SI 1983/24)
	2–5	Repealed
	6, 7	11 Apr 1983 (SI 1983/24); prospectively repealed by Environment Act 1995, s 120(3), Sch 24[1]
	8–13	11 Apr 1983 (SI 1983/24)
	14	Repealed
	15	31 Jan 1983 (SI 1983/24)
	16	Repealed
	17	11 Apr 1983 (SI 1983/24)
	18, 19	31 Jan 1983 (SI 1983/24)
	20, 21	11 Apr 1983 (SI 1983/24)
	22	Repealed
	23–29	11 Apr 1983 (SI 1983/24)
	30	31 Jan 1983 (SI 1983/24)
16		28 Oct 1982 (repeal of Imprisonment (Temporary Provisions) Act 1980) (s 80(1))
		31 Jan 1983 (repeals of or in Merchant Shipping Act 1894, s 680(1); Prison Act 1952, s 55(3); Criminal Justice Act 1967, s 95(1); Immigration Act 1971, s 6(5); Powers of Criminal Courts Act 1973, ss 2, 4, 23(1), 47(d), 48–51, 57(1), Sch 1, para 7, Sch 3; Criminal Procedure (Scotland) Act 1975, s 421(1); Criminal Law Act 1977, Sch 9, para 10, Sch 12 (repeals in the entry relating to Powers of Criminal Courts Act 1973 only); Customs and Excise Management Act 1979, ss 147(5), 156(3); Criminal Justice (Scotland) Act 1980, s 55; Magistrates' Courts Act 1980, s 108(3)(a); Animal Health Act 1981, s 70) (SI 1982/1857; SI 1983/24)
		11 Apr 1983 (repeals of or in Sea Fisheries (Scotland) Amendment Act 1885, s 4; Electric Lighting

Criminal Justice Act 1982 (c 48)—*contd*
Schedule

16—*contd*		(Clauses) Act 1899, Sch; Housing (Scotland) Act 1966, s 185(2); Criminal Procedure (Scotland) Act 1975, ss 8(2), 289D(2), (3A), 291(1); Criminal Law Act 1977, s 31; National Health Service (Scotland) Act 1978, Sch 9, para 1(1), Sch 10, para 7(2)(b); Electricity (Scotland) Act 1979, s 41(1)(b); Merchant Shipping Act 1979, s 43; Water (Scotland) Act 1980, Sch 4, para 10(3); Criminal Justice (Scotland) Act 1980, ss 7(3), 8, 46(1), Sch 7, para 50) (SI 1982/1857; SI 1983/24)
		24 May 1983 (otherwise, except as noted below) (SI 1983/182; SI 1983/758)
		Not in force (repeal of Criminal Justice Act 1961, s 38(5)(c), (d))
17, para	1–14	24 May 1983 (SI 1983/182)
	15	28 Oct 1982 (s 80(1))
	16, 17	Repealed
	18	31 Jan 1983 (SI 1983/24)

[1]   Orders made under Environment Act 1995, s 125(3), bringing the prospective repeal into force will be noted to that Act

---

Currency Act 1982 (c 3)

RA: 2 Feb 1982

2 Feb 1982 (RA)

Deer Amendment (Scotland) Act 1982 (c 19)

Whole Act repealed

Derelict Land Act 1982 (c 42)

RA: 30 Jul 1982

Commencement provisions: s 5(3)

30 Aug 1982 (s 5(3))

Duchy of Cornwall Management Act 1982 (c 47)

Local application only

Electricity (Financial Provisions) (Scotland) Act 1982 (c 56)

Whole Act repealed

Employment Act 1982 (c 46)

RA: 28 Oct 1982

Commencement provisions: s 22; Employment Act 1982 (Commencement) Order 1982, SI 1982/1656

Whole Act repealed, except ss 21(2), 22, Sch 3, paras 14, 31 which came into force on 1 Dec 1982 (SI 1982/1656)

Finance Act 1982 (c 39)

Budget Day: 9 Mar 1982

RA: 30 Jul 1982

Details of the commencement of Finance Acts are not set out in this work

---

Fire Service College Board (Abolition) Act 1982 (c 13)

Whole Act repealed

Firearms Act 1982 (c 31)

RA: 13 Jul 1982

Commencement provisions: s 4(3); Firearms Act 1982 (Commencement) Order 1983, SI 1983/1440

1 Nov 1983 (SI 1983/1440)

Food and Drugs (Amendment) Act 1982 (c 26)

Whole Act repealed

Forfeiture Act 1982 (c 34)

RA: 13 Jul 1982

Commencement provisions: s 7(2); Forfeiture Act 1982 Commencement Order 1982, SI 1982/1731

Section	
1–3	13 Oct 1982 (s 7(2))
4	31 Dec 1982 (SI 1982/1731)
5	13 Oct 1982 (s 7(2))
6, 7	13 Jul 1982 (RA)

Gaming (Amendment) Act 1982 (c 22)

RA: 28 Jan 1982

Commencement provisions: s 3(2)

28 Aug 1982 (s 3(2))

Harbours (Scotland) Act 1982 (c 17)

RA: 27 May 1982

27 May 1982 (RA)

Hops Marketing Act 1982 (c 5)

RA: 25 Feb 1982

25 Feb 1982 (RA); note that for practical purposes the majority of the Act came into effect on 1 Apr 1982, the day appointed for the revocation of the Hops Marketing Scheme under s 1(2)

Industrial Development Act 1982 (c 52)

RA: 28 Oct 1982

Commencement provisions: s 20(2)

28 Jan 1983 (s 20(2))

Industrial Training Act 1982 (c 10)

RA: 29 Mar 1982

Commencement provisions: s 21(3)

29 Jun 1982 (s 21(3))

Industry Act 1982 (c 18)

Whole Act repealed

Insurance Companies Act 1982 (c 50)

Whole Act repealed

Iron and Steel Act 1982 (c 25)

RA: 13 Jul 1982

Commencement provisions: s 39(2)

13 Oct 1982 (39(2))

Whole Act repealed, partly prospectively (s 1, Sch 1), except ss 33 (part), 34 (part), by British Steel Act 1988, s 16(3), Sch 2[1]

[1]   The repeals of s 1, Sch 1, by British Steel Act 1988, s 16(3), Sch 2, Pt II, come into force on a day to be appointed by order under s 10 of that Act for the dissolution of the British Steel Corporation (s 17(4)); any such order will be noted to that Act

Lands Valuation Amendment (Scotland) Act 1982 (c 57)

RA: 22 Dec 1982

22 Dec 1982 (RA)

Legal Aid Act 1982 (c 44)

Whole Act repealed

Local Government and Planning (Scotland) Act 1982 (c 43)

RA: 30 Jul 1982

Commencement provisions: s 69(2); Local Government and Planning (Scotland) Act 1982 (Commencement No 1) Order 1982, SI 1982/1137; Local Government and Planning (Scotland) Act 1982 (Commencement No 2) Order 1982, SI 1982/1397; Local Government and Planning (Scotland) Act 1982 (Commencement No 3) Order 1984, SI 1984/239

Section		
1–4		Repealed
5		1 Sep 1982 (SI 1982/1137)
6, 7		Repealed
8		1 Sep 1982 (SI 1982/1137)
9		Substituted by Local Government etc (Scotland) Act 1994, s 180(1), Sch 13, para 128(1), (2) (qv)
10–13		1 Apr 1983 (SI 1982/1397)
14	(1), (2)	1 Apr 1983 (SI 1982/1397)
	(3)	Inserted by Local Government etc (Scotland) Act 1994, s 180(1), Sch 13, para 128(1), (3)(c) (qv)
15, 16		1 Apr 1983 (SI 1982/1397)
17		Substituted by Local Government etc (Scotland) Act 1994, s 180(1), Sch 13, para 128(1), (6) (qv)
18–28		1 Apr 1983 (SI 1982/1397)
29		1 Nov 1982 (SI 1982/1397)
30, 31		1 Apr 1983 (SI 1982/1397)

Local Government and Planning (Scotland) Act 1982 (c 43)—*contd*

Section			
32			1 Nov 1982 (SI 1982/1397)
33, 34			Repealed
35			1 Sep 1982 (SI 1982/1137)
36–48			Repealed
49, 50			1 Sep 1982 (SI 1982/1137)
51–56			Repealed
57			1 Apr 1983 (SI 1982/1397)
58–60			1 Nov 1982 (SI 1982/1397)
61–65			1 Sep 1982 (SI 1982/1137)
66	(1)		See Sch 3 below
	(2)		See Sch 4 below
67, 68			1 Sep 1982 (SI 1982/1137)
69			30 Jul 1982 (RA)
Schedule			
1, Pt	I		Repealed
	II		1 Apr 1983 (SI 1982/1397)
2			Repealed
3, para	1, 2		1 Apr 1983 (SI 1982/1397)
	3	(a)	1 Sep 1982 (SI 1982/1137)
		(b)	1 Apr 1983 (SI 1982/1397)
	4		1 Nov 1982 (SI 1982/1397)
	5–7		Repealed
	8–11		1 Nov 1982 (SI 1982/1397)
	12		1 Apr 1983 (SI 1982/1397)
	13		1 Nov 1982 (SI 1982/1397)
	14		1 Nov 1982 (SI 1982/1397); prospectively repealed (S) by Ethical Standards in Public Life etc (Scotland) Act 2000 (asp 7), s 36, Sch 4[1]
	15		1 Nov 1982 (SI 1982/1397)
	16		Repealed
	17		1 Sep 1982 (SI 1982/1137)
	18–20		Repealed
	21		1 Apr 1983 (SI 1982/1397)
	22, 23		1 Nov 1982 (SI 1982/1397)
	24		14 May 1984 (SI 1984/239)
	25–28		1 Nov 1982 (SI 1982/1397)
	29–33		Repealed
	34		1 Nov 1982 (SI 1982/1397)
	35, 36		Repealed
	37, 38		1 Apr 1983 (SI 1982/1397)
	39, 40		Repealed
	41		1 Apr 1983 (SI 1982/1397)
	42		1 Sep 1982 (SI 1982/1137)
	43		Repealed
4			1 Sep 1982 (repeals of or in Local Government (Scotland) Act 1966, s 5(1), Sch 1, Pt II, paras 2, 3;

Local Government and Planning (Scotland) Act 1982 (c 43)—*contd*
Schedule
4—*contd*

Local Government (Scotland)
Act 1973, ss 216(2)–(5), 218, 221,
224(1)–(4), (6); Local Government
(Scotland) Act 1975, Sch 1, paras 2,
2A, 3, 4, 4A; Electricity (Scotland)
Act 1979, Sch 4, paras 1, 3, 5, 6;
Tenants' Rights, Etc (Scotland)
Act 1980, ss 1(1), 4(3))
(SI 1982/1137)

1 Nov 1982 (repeals of or in
Requisitioned Land and War
Works Act 1945, s 52; Civic
Restaurants Act 1947;
Requisitioned Land and War
Works Act 1948, Sch, para 10;
Highlands and Islands
Development (Scotland) Act 1965,
s 10(1), (3); Countryside (Scotland)
Act 1967, ss 14(5), 34(5), 35A,
Sch 3, paras 1(2), 2(1)–(3), 4;
Social Work (Scotland) Act 1968,
s 6(1)(d); Town and Country
Planning (Scotland) Act 1972,
ss 12(1), (2), 37(1), 54(2), 61(7),
84(6), 85(8), 92(1), 93(5)(b),
154(2), 164(6), 167C(2)(b), 215(1),
231(1)(b), (3)(f), 262(2), (3),
262A(3), (4), 262B(3), Sch 10,
para 11(1); Local Government
(Scotland) Act 1973, ss 49(2)(a),
164, Sch 22, Pt II, para 5, 8, 9;
Safety of Sports Grounds Act 1975,
s 11; Scottish Development
Agency Act 1975, s 10(1); Refuse
Disposal (Amenity) Act 1978,
s 8(1); Water (Scotland) Act 1980,
Sch 3, para 7(5), Sch 4, para 23;
Countryside (Scotland) Act 1981,
s 5) (SI 1982/1397)

1 Apr 1983 (repeals of or in Public
Parks (Scotland) Act 1878; Burgh
Police (Scotland) Act 1892, ss 107,
110, 112, 116, 277, 288, 307, 308;
Public Health (Scotland) Act 1897,
ss 29, 39; Burgh Police (Scotland)
Act 1903, s 44; Physical Training
and Recreation Act 1937, ss 4(1)–
(4), 5, 7, 10(4)–(7), (11); Food and
Drugs (Scotland) Act 1956, s 26(3);

Local Government and Planning (Scotland) Act 1982 (c 43)—*contd*
Schedule
4—*contd*

Physical Training and Recreation
Act 1958; Caravan Sites and
Control of Development Act 1960,
s 32(1)(h)(iii); Social Work
(Scotland) Act 1968, s 85;
Agriculture Act 1970, ss 95, 96;
Local Government (Scotland)
Act 1973, ss 55, 91, 137(2), 139,
158, 162, 178, 219, 220, Sch 23,
para 2(a); Control of Pollution
Act 1974, ss 22, 23, Sch 4;
Education (Scotland) Act 1980,
s 1(3)(b), (5)(b)(iii); Local
Government, Planning and Land
Act 1980, s 70(4))
(SI 1982/1397)
14 May 1984 (otherwise) (SI 1984/239)

[1]   Orders made under Ethical Standards in Public Life etc (Scotland) Act 2000, s 37(2), bringing the
       prospective repeal into force will be noted to that Act

---

Local Government Finance Act 1982 (c 32)

RA: 13 Jul 1982

Commencement provisions: See notes to individual provisions below
Section
1

13 Jul 1982 (RA, but only effective
for financial years 1 Apr 1982
onwards); repealed (1 Apr 1990),
with savings, by Local
Government Finance (Repeals,
Savings and Consequential
Amendments) Order 1990,
SI 1990/776, art 3, Sch 1

2–4

13 Jul 1982 (RA; but only effective
for financial years 1 Apr 1982
onwards)

5

13 Jul 1982 (RA; but only effective
for financial years 1 Apr 1982
onwards); sub-s (1) repealed by
Local Government and Housing
Act 1989, s 194(2), Sch 12, Pt I
(qv), except in relation to any
bodies which have not been
prescribed by regulations under s
39(3) of that Act; sub-ss (2), (3)
repealed by Local Government
Act 1985, s 102(2), Sch 17 (qv)

Local Government Finance Act 1982 (c 32)—*contd*

Section

6	13 Jul 1982 (RA; but only effective for financial years 1 Apr 1982 onwards); repealed (1 Apr 1990), with savings, by Local Government Finance (Repeals, Savings and Consequential Amendments) Order 1990, SI 1990/776, art 3, Sch 1
7	13 Jul 1982 (RA)
8–10	13 Jul 1982 (RA; s 8 only effective in relation to block grant for years 1 Apr 1982 onwards, except s 8(2) so far as relates to consultation; s 8(4A) effective in relation to years 1 Apr 1987 onwards; s 8(8) which only applies to years 1 Apr 1983 onwards; s 10 (and Sch 2) only effective for years 1 Apr 1983 onwards)
11–36	Repealed
37–39	13 Jul 1982 (RA)

Schedule

1		13 Jul 1982 (RA; but only effective for financial years 1 Apr 1982 onwards)
2		See ss 8–10 above
3–5		Repealed
6, Pt	I	Effective for financial years 1 Apr 1982 onwards (s 38(2))
	II	Effective for financial years 1 Apr 1981 onwards (s 38(3))
	III	Effective for financial years 1 Apr 1983 onwards (s 38(4))
	IV	Repealed

Local Government (Miscellaneous Provisions) Act 1982 (c 30)

RA: 13 Jul 1982

Commencement provisions: ss 1(12), 7(3), 25(3), 40(10), 47(3), Sch 3, para 30(1); Local Government (Miscellaneous Provisions) Act 1982 (Commencement No 1) Order 1982, SI 1982/1119; Local Government (Miscellaneous Provisions) Act 1982 (Commencement No 2) Order 1982, SI 1982/1160

Note: certain provisions of this Act must be adopted by local authority resolution to have effect in particular areas

Section

1		1 Jan 1983 (s 1(12))
2–6		13 Jul 1982 (RA)
7	(1), (2)	13 Oct 1982 (s 7(3))

Local Government (Miscellaneous Provisions) Act 1982 (c 30)—*contd*

Section

7	(3), (4)	13 Jul 1982 (RA)
8–17		13 Jul 1982 (RA)
18, 19		Repealed
20–23		13 Jul 1982 (RA)
24–26		Repealed
27		13 Jul 1982 (RA)
28		Repealed
29–34		13 Jul 1982 (RA)
35, 36		Repealed
37–39		13 Jul 1982 (RA)
40		13 Sep 1982 (s 40(10))
41		13 Jul 1982 (RA)
42		Repealed
43–46		13 Jul 1982 (RA)
47	(1)	13 Jul 1982 (RA)
	(2), (3)	See Sch 7 below
	(4)	13 Jul 1982 (RA)
48, 49		13 Jul 1982 (RA)

Schedule

1, 2		1 Jan 1983 (s 1(12))
3		13 Jul 1982 (except in relation to sex cinemas) (RA)
		13 Oct 1982 (exception noted above) (SI 1982/1119)
4–6		13 Jul 1982 (RA)
7, Pt	I, II	1 Jan 1983 (s 47(3))
	III–XV	13 Jul 1982 (RA)
	XVI	13 Jul 1982 (except as noted below) (RA)
		1 Sep 1982 (repeal of Health and Safety at Work etc Act 1974, s 63) (SI 1982/1160)

Mental Health (Amendment) Act 1982 (c 51)

RA: 28 Oct 1982

Commencement provisions: s 69

Section

1–33		Repealed
34		30 Sep 1983 (s 69(1))
35–63		Repealed
64		30 Sep 1983 (s 69(1))
65	(1)	See Sch 3 below
	(2)	See Sch 4 below
66		Repealed
67–70		30 Sep 1983 (s 69(1))

Schedule

1, 2		Repealed

Mental Health (Amendment) Act 1982 (c 51)—*contd*

Schedule

3, Pt	I	30 Sep 1983 (s 69(1))
	II	Repealed
4, Pt	I	30 Sep 1983 (s 69(1))
	II	28 Oct 1984 (s 69(4))
5, para	1	30 Sep 1983 (s 69(1))
	2–15	Repealed

Merchant Shipping (Liner Conferences) Act 1982 (c 37)

RA: 23 Jul 1982

Commencement provisions: s 15(2); Merchant Shipping (Liner Conferences) Act 1982 (Commencement) Order 1985, SI 1985/182

14 Mar 1985 (SI 1985/182)

National Insurance Surcharge Act 1982 (c 55)

Whole Act repealed (with respect to earnings paid on or after 6 April 1985)

New Towns Act 1982 (c 7)

RA: 25 Feb 1982

25 Feb 1982 (RA)

Whole Act repealed (E, W)

Northern Ireland Act 1982 (c 38)

Whole Act repealed

Oil and Gas (Enterprise) Act 1982 (c 23)

RA: 28 Jun 1982

Commencement provisions: s 38(2); Oil and Gas (Enterprise) Act 1982 (Commencement No 1) Order 1982, SI 1982/895; Oil and Gas (Enterprise) Act 1982 (Commencement No 2) Order 1982, SI 1982/1059; Oil and Gas (Enterprise) Act 1982 (Commencement No 3) Order 1982, SI 1982/1431; Oil and Gas (Enterprise) Act 1982 (Commencement No 4) Order 1987, SI 1987/2272

Section

1–23	Repealed
24	1 Nov 1982 (SI 1982/1431)
25	Repealed
26	1 Nov 1982 (SI 1982/1431)
27–30	Repealed
31	1 Oct 1982 (SI 1982/1059)
32–36	Repealed
37	See Schs 3, 4 below
38	2 Jul 1982 (SI 1982/895)

Oil and Gas (Enterprise) Act 1982 (c 23)—*contd*

Schedule

1, 2		Repealed
3, para	1	1 Oct 1982 (SI 1982/1059)
	2	Repealed
	3	1 Feb 1988 (SI 1987/2272)
	4	1 Oct 1982 (SI 1982/1059)
	5–7	Repealed
	8	1 Nov 1982 (SI 1982/1431)
	9, 10	Repealed
	11	1 Nov 1982 (SI 1982/1431)
	12–33	Repealed (para 24 never in force)
	34	1 Feb 1988 (SI 1987/2272)
	35, 36	Repealed (*Never in force*)
	37	18 Aug 1982 (SI 1982/1059)
	38	Repealed (*Never in force*)
	39	31 Dec 1982 (SI 1982/1431)
	40–46	Repealed
4		18 Aug 1982 (repeals in Petroleum (Production) Act 1934; Gas Act 1972 (except repeal in s 7(2)); Oil Taxation Act 1975; Energy Act 1976; Gas Act 1980) (SI 1982/1059)
		1 Oct 1982 (repeals in Continental Shelf Act 1964, s 2; Mineral Workings (Offshore Installations) Act 1971, s 10 (except in relation to offences within sub-s (1)(a)); Petroleum and Submarine Pipe-lines Act 1975, ss 22, 26, 41; Customs and Excise Management Act 1979) (SI 1982/1059)
		1 Nov 1982 (repeals of or in Mineral Workings (Offshore Installations) Act 1971, ss 6(2), 12(1); Petroleum and Submarine Pipe-lines Act 1975, ss 1(3)(c), 3(3), 44(1)–(4), 45(3)) (SI 1982/1431)
		31 Dec 1982 (repeals of or in Petroleum and Submarine Pipe-lines Act 1975, ss 2(4)(d), 7(2), 14(4)(b), 40(2)(a), (c), (3)(a), (c)) (SI 1982/1431)
		1 Apr 1983 (repeals of Petroleum and Submarine Pipe-lines Act 1975, s 40(1), (4), 40(3) (so far as not brought into force on 31 Dec 1982)) (SI 1982/1431)

Oil and Gas (Enterprise) Act 1982 (c 23)—*contd*

Schedule

4—*contd*   1 Feb 1988 (repeals of Continental
                                                Shelf Act 1964, ss 3, 11(3);
                                                Mineral Workings (Offshore
                                                Installations) Act 1971, ss 8, 9(5),
                                                10 (so far as not already repealed))
                                                (SI 1987/2272)
                                                Not in force (otherwise)

Pastoral (Amendment) Measure 1982 (No 1)

Whole Measure repealed

Planning Inquiries (Attendance of Public) Act 1982 (c 21)

Whole Act repealed

Reserve Forces Act 1982 (c 14)

Whole Act repealed

Shipbuilding Act 1982 (c 4)

Whole Act repealed

Social Security and Housing Benefits Act 1982 (c 24)

RA: 28 Jun 1982

Commencement provisions: s 48(3); Social Security and Housing Benefits Act 1982
     (Commencement No 1) Order 1982, SI 1982/893; Social Security and Housing
     Benefits Act 1982 (Commencement No 2) Order 1982, SI 1982/906

Section

1–9		Repealed
10		6 Apr 1983 (SI 1982/893)
11–38		Repealed
39		6 Apr 1983 (SI 1982/893)
40, 41		Repealed
42		28 Jun 1982 (s 48(3))
43		30 Aug 1982 (SI 1982/893)
44		Repealed
45–47		28 Jun 1982 (s 48(3))
48	(1)	28 Jun 1982 (s 48(3))
	(2)	Repealed
	(3), (4)	28 Jun 1982 (s 48(3))
	(5), (6)	See Schs 4, 5 below
	(7)	28 Jun 1982 (s 48(3))
Schedule		
1–3		Repealed

Social Security and Housing Benefits Act 1982 (c 24)—*contd*

Schedule

4, para	1–35	Repealed or spent
	36	4 Apr 1983 (SI 1982/906)
	37	28 Jun 1982 (RA)
	38, 39	Repealed
5		30 Jun 1982 (repeals of or in Social Security Act 1975, s 4(2), Sch 11, para 2) (SI 1982/893)
		6 Apr 1983 (remaining repeals in Social Security Act 1975, except words in s 65(4); repeals of or in Child Benefit Act 1975, Sch 4, para 39; Social Security Act 1980, Sch 1; Social Security (No 2) Act 1980, s 3(2)) (SI 1982/893)
		4 Apr 1983 (otherwise except repeals in Social Security Act 1975, s 65(4); Social Security Pensions Act 1975, Sch 4, para 22) (SI 1982/906)

Note: it is unclear why the outstanding repeals were not brought into force; the whole of Social Security Act 1975 was repealed (1 Jul 1992) by Social Security (Consequential Provisions) Act 1992, s 3, Sch 1; Social Security Pensions Act 1975, Sch 4, para 22 amended Housing Finance Act 1972, Sch 3, which was repealed (4 Apr 1983) by Sch 5 to this Act

Social Security (Contributions) Act 1982 (c 2)

Whole Act repealed

Stock Transfer Act 1982 (c 41)

RA: 30 Jul 1982

Commencement provisions: s 6(2); Stock Transfer Act 1982 (Commencement) Order 1985, SI 1985/1137

Section

1–3		23 Jul 1985 (SI 1985/1137)
4		Repealed
5	(1)	Repealed
	(2)	30 Oct 1982 (s 6(2)); prospectively repealed by Local Government etc (Scotland) Act 1994, s 180(2), Sch 14[1]
6		30 Oct 1982 (s 6(2))
Schedule		
1, 2		23 Jul 1985 (SI 1985/1137)

[1] Orders made under Local Government etc (Scotland) Act 1994, s 184(2), bringing the prospective repeal into force will be noted to that Act

Supply of Goods and Services Act 1982 (c 29)

RA: 13 Jul 1982

Commencement provisions: s 20(3); Supply of Goods and Services Act 1982 (Commencement) Order 1982, SI 1982/1770

Section	
1–5	4 Jan 1983 (s 20(3))
5A	Inserted by Sale and Supply of Goods Act 1994, s 7(1), Sch 2, para 6(1), (5) (qv)
6–10	4 Jan 1983 (s 20(3))
10A	Inserted by Sale and Supply of Goods Act 1994, s 7(1), Sch 2, para 6(1), (9) (qv)
11	4 Jan 1983 (s 20(3))
11A–11L	Inserted (S) by Sale and Supply of Goods Act 1994, s 6, Sch 1, para 1 (qv)
12–16	4 Jul 1983 (SI 1982/1770)
17	4 Jan 1983 (s 20(3))
18, 19	4 Jan 1983 (so far as relate to ss 1–11) (s 20(3))
	4 Jul 1983 (so far as relate to ss 12–16) (SI 1982/1770)
20	13 Jul 1982 (RA)
Schedule	Spent

Taking of Hostages Act 1982 (c 28)

RA: 13 Jul 1982

Commencement provisions: s 6; Taking of Hostages Act 1982 (Commencement) Order 1982, SI 1982/1532

26 Nov 1982 (SI 1982/1532)

Transport Act 1982 (c 49)

RA: 28 Oct 1982

Commencement provisions: s 76; Transport Act 1982 (Commencement No 1) Order 1982, SI 1982/1561; Transport Act 1982 (Commencement No 2) Order 1982, SI 1982/1804; Transport Act 1982 (Commencement No 3) Order 1983, SI 1983/276; Transport Act 1982 (Commencement No 4) Order 1983, SI 1983/577; Transport Act 1982 (Scotland) (Commencement No 1) Order 1983, SI 1983/650; Transport Act 1982 (Commencement No 5) Order 1984, SI 1984/175; Transport Act 1982 (Commencement No 6) Order 1986, SI 1986/1326; Transport Act 1982 (Scotland) (Commencement No 2) Order 1986, SI 1986/1874; Transport Act 1982 (Commencement No 7 and Transitional Provisions) Order 1996, SI 1996/1943

Section	
1–7	Repealed
8–15	*Not in force*
16	Repealed

Transport Act 1982 (c 49)—*contd*

Section

17		*Not in force*
18		1 Aug 1996 (SI 1996/1943)
19		Repealed
20		Substituted by Road Traffic Act 1991, s 48, Sch 4, para 20 (qv)
21–26		*Not in force*
27–64		Repealed
65		11 Apr 1983 (SI 1983/276)
66		*Not in force*
67		20 Dec 1982 (SI 1982/1804)
68		1 Nov 1982 (SI 1982/1561)
69		Repealed
70		1 Nov 1982 (SI 1982/1561)
71		20 Dec 1982 (SI 1982/1804)
72	(a)	*Not in force*
	(b)	Repealed
73		30 Jun 1983 (S) (SI 1983/650)
		1 Oct 1986 (E, W) (SI 1986/1326)
74		See Schs 5, 6 below
75, 76		30 Jun 1983 (S) (SI 1983/650)
		1 Oct 1986 (E, W) (SI 1986/1326)

Schedule

1–4		Repealed
5, para	1–4	Repealed
	5	*Not in force*
	6–16	Repealed
	17	*Not in force*
	18, 19	Repealed
	20	*Not in force*
	21	Repealed
	22–24	*Not in force*
	25, 26	Repealed
6		1 Nov 1982 (repeal of Road Traffic Regulation Act 1967, s 72(2), (4)) (SI 1982/1561)
		1 Jun 1984 (repeals in Transport Act 1968) (SI 1984/175)
		Not in force (otherwise, although most remaining repeals by Sch 6 have been superseded)

Transport (Finance) Act 1982 (c 6)

RA: 25 Feb 1982

25 Feb 1982 (RA)

Travel Concessions (London) Act 1982 (c 12)

Whole Act repealed

1983

Agricultural Holdings (Amendment) (Scotland) Act 1983 (c 46)

Whole Act repealed

Agricultural Marketing Act 1983 (c 3)

RA: 1 Mar 1983

Commencement provisions: s 9(3); Agricultural Marketing Act 1983 (Commencement) Order 1983, SI 1983/366

23 Mar 1983 (SI 1983/366)

Appropriation Act 1983 (c 27)

Whole Act repealed

Appropriation (No 2) Act 1983 (c 48)

Whole Act repealed

British Fishing Boats Act 1983 (c 8)

RA: 28 Mar 1983

28 Mar 1983 (RA)

British Nationality (Falkland Islands) Act 1983 (c 6)

RA: 28 Mar 1983

Commencement provisions: s 5(2)

1 Jan 1983 (retrospective: s 5(2))

British Shipbuilders Act 1983 (c 15)

RA: 9 May 1983

Commencement provisions: s 3(4)

9 Jul 1983 (s 3(4))

British Shipbuilders (Borrowing Powers) Act 1983 (c 58)

RA: 21 Dec 1983

21 Dec 1983 (RA)

Car Tax Act 1983 (c 53)

RA: 26 Jul 1983

Commencement provisions: s 11(2)

26 Oct 1983 (s 11(2))

Note: car tax abolished with effect from 13 Nov 1992 by Car Tax (Abolition) Act 1992, but
1983 Act has not been repealed)

Church of England (Miscellaneous Provisions) Measure 1983 (No 2)

RA: 9 May 1983

Commencement provisions: s 13(3)

9 Jun 1983 (s 13(3))

Civil Aviation (Eurocontrol) Act 1983 (c 11)

RA: 11 Apr 1983

Commencement provisions: s 4(2); Civil Aviation (Eurocontrol) Act 1983
(Commencement No 1) Order 1983, SI 1983/1886; Civil Aviation
(Eurocontrol) Act 1983 (Commencement No 2) Order 1985, SI 1985/1915

Section		
1, 2		1 Jan 1986 (SI 1985/1915)
3	(1)	1 Jan 1986 (SI 1985/1915)
	(2)	Repealed
4		1 Jan 1984 (s 4(2); SI 1983/1886)

Coal Industry Act 1983 (c 60)

RA: 21 Dec 1983

21 Dec 1983 (RA)

Whole Act repealed (in part prospectively) as follows: ss 1, 2, 4–6 and Schedule
prospectively repealed by Coal Industry Act 1994, s 67(8), Sch 11, Pt III[1]; s 3
repealed by Coal Industry Act 1987, s 10(3), Sch 3, Pt I

[1]   Orders made under Coal Industry Act 1994, s 68(4), (5), bringing the prospective repeals into force
        will be noted to that Act

Companies (Beneficial Interests) Act 1983 (c 50)

Whole Act repealed

Consolidated Fund Act 1983 (c 1)

Whole Act repealed

Consolidated Fund (No 2) Act 1983 (c 5)

Whole Act repealed

Consolidated Fund (No 3) Act 1983 (c 57)

Whole Act repealed

Conwy Tunnel (Supplementary Powers) Act 1983 (c 7)

Local application only

Copyright (Amendment) Act 1983 (c 42)

Whole Act repealed

Coroners' Juries Act 1983 (c 31)

Whole Act repealed

County Courts (Penalties for Contempt) Act 1983 (c 45)

RA: 13 May 1983

13 May 1983 (RA)

Currency Act 1983 (c 9)

RA: 28 Mar 1983

28 Mar 1983 (RA)

Dentists Act 1983 (c 38)

Whole Act repealed

Diseases of Fish Act 1983 (c 30)

RA: 13 May 1983

Commencement provisions: s 11(2); Diseases of Fish Act 1983 (Commencement) Order 1984, SI 1984/302

Section	
1–10	1 Apr 1984 (SI 1984/302)
11	13 May 1983 (RA)
Schedule	1 Apr 1984 (SI 1984/302)

Divorce Jurisdiction, Court Fees and Legal Aid (Scotland) Act 1983 (c 12)

RA: 11 Apr 1983

Commencement provisions: s 7(2), (3); Divorce Jurisdiction, Court Fees and Legal Aid (Scotland) Act 1983 (Commencement) Order 1984, SI 1984/253

Section			
1			1 May 1984 (SI 1984/253)
2, 3			Repealed
4, 5			1 Apr 1984 (SI 1984/253)
6	(1)		See Sch 1 below
	(2)		See Sch 2 below
7			11 Jun 1983 (s 7(2))
Schedule			
1, para	1		1 May 1984 (SI 1984/253)
	2–5		Repealed
	6		1 Apr 1984 (certain purposes) (SI 1984/253)
			1 May 1984 (otherwise) (SI 1984/253)
	7, 8		Repealed
	9, 10		1 Apr 1984 (SI 1984/253)
	11		Repealed
	12		1 May 1984 (SI 1984/253)
	13–17		Repealed
	18–20		1 May 1984 (SI 1984/253)
	21		Repealed
	22		1 May 1984 (SI 1984/253)
	23		Repealed
	24		1 May 1984 (SI 1984/253)
2			1 Apr 1984 (repeals of or in Court of Session Act 1821, s 31; Sheriff Courts (Scotland) Act 1907, s 40; Church of Scotland (Property and Endowments) Act 1925, s 1(3); Juries Act 1949, s 26(1); Legal Aid (Scotland) Act 1967, s 16(1)(b)(i), (2), (4); Legal Advice and Assistance Act 1972, ss 3(3), 5(6)) (SI 1984/253)
			1 May 1984 (otherwise) (SI 1984/253)

Education (Fees and Awards) Act 1983 (c 40)

RA: 13 May 1983

13 May 1983 (RA)

Energy Act 1983 (c 25)

RA: 9 May 1983

Commencement provisions: s 37(1); Energy Act 1983 (Commencement No 1) Order 1983, SI 1983/790; Energy Act 1983 (Commencement No 2) Order 1988, SI 1988/1587

Energy Act 1983 (c 25)—*contd*

Section

1–26		Repealed
27–34		1 Sep 1983 (SI 1983/790)
35	(a)	1 Jun 1983 (SI 1983/790)
	(b)	1 Sep 1983 (SI 1983/790)
36		See Sch 4 below
37	(1), (2)	1 Jun 1983 (SI 1983/790)
	(3)	1 Sep 1983 (SI 1983/790)
38		1 Jun 1983 (SI 1983/790)

Schedule

1–3		Repealed
4, Pt	I	1 Jun 1983 (repeals of or in Electric Lighting (Clauses) Act 1899, Schedule, ss 2, 52, 54(2); Electric Lighting Act 1909, s 23; Electricity (Supply) Act 1919, ss 11, 36; Electricity (Supply) Act 1922, s 23; Electricity Supply (Meters) Act 1936, s 1(1), (3); Acquisition of Land (Authorisation Procedure) Act 1946, Sch 4; Electricity Act 1947 (except for s 60, in Sch 4, Pt I, the entry relating to Electricity (Supply) Act 1946, s 24, and in Sch 4, Pt III, the entry relating to Electric Lighting (Clauses) Act 1899, Schedule, s 60); South of Scotland Electricity Order Confirmation Act 1956, s 40; Electricity Act 1957 (except in Sch 4, Pt I, the entry relating to Electricity Act 1947, s 60); North of Scotland Electricity Order Confirmation Act 1958, s 27; Post Office Act 1969, Sch 4, para 11; Energy Act 1976, s 14(6)(b); Electricity (Scotland) Act 1979 (except reference to Electricity Act 1947, s 60 in Sch 10, para 13); Acquisition of Land Act 1981, Sch 4, para 1) (SI 1983/790)
		1 Oct 1988 (repeals of or in Electric Lighting (Clauses) Act 1899, Schedule, ss 10, 38, 60, 69(1), (2); Electricity Act 1947, s 60, in Sch 4, Pt III, the entry relating to Electric Lighting (Clauses) Act 1899, Schedule, s 60; Electricity Act 1957, in Sch 4, Pt I, the entry relating to Electricity Act 1947, s 60;

Energy Act 1983 (c 25)—*contd*
Schedule

4, Pt	I—*contd*	Post Office Act 1969, Sch 4, para 8(c), (g); Electricity (Scotland) Act 1979, in Sch 10, para 13, the reference to Electricity Act 1947, s 60) (SI 1988/1587)
		Spent (otherwise)
	II	1 Sep 1983 (SI 1983/790)

Finance Act 1983 (c 28)

Budget Day: 15 Mar 1983

RA: 13 May 1983

Details of the commencement of Finance Acts are not set out in this work

---

Finance (No 2) Act 1983 (c 49)

RA: 26 Jul 1983

Details of the commencement of Finance Acts are not set out in this work

---

Health and Social Services and Social Security Adjudications Act 1983 (c 41)

RA: 13 May 1983

Commencement provisions: s 32(1), (2); Health and Social Services and Social Security Adjudications Act 1983 (Commencement No 1) Order 1983, SI 1983/974; Health and Social Services and Social Security Adjudications Act 1983 (Commencement No 2) Order 1983, SI 1983/1862; Health and Social Services and Social Security Adjudications Act 1983 (Commencement No 3) Order 1984, SI 1984/216; Health and Social Services and Social Security Adjudications Act 1983 (Commencement No 4) Order 1984, SI 1984/957; Health and Social Services and Social Security Adjudications Act 1984 (Commencement No 5) Order 1984, SI 1984/1347; Health and Social Services and Social Security Adjudications Act 1983 (Scotland) (Commencement No 1) Order 1985, SI 1985/704; Health and Social Services and Social Security Adjudications Act 1983 (Commencement No 6) Order 1992, SI 1992/2974

Section

1	15 Aug 1983 (so far as relates to (i) National Health Service Act 1977, s 28A(2)(a)–(d), but only for the purpose of giving effect to s 28B(1)(a) of that Act, and (ii) s 28B of the 1977 Act) (SI 1983/974)
	1 Apr 1984 (so far as relates to new s 28A of the 1977 Act) (SI 1984/216)
2	1 May 1985 (SI 1985/704)
3	15 Aug 1983 (SI 1983/974)

**Health and Social Services and Social Security Adjudications Act 1983
(c 41)**—*contd*

Section

4		1 Jan 1984 (SI 1983/974)
5–7		Repealed
8		30 Jan 1984 (SI 1983/1862)
9		See Sch 2 below
10		1 Apr 1984 (SI 1983/974)
11		1 Oct 1984 (so far as relates to Sch 4, para 24 (repealed)) (SI 1984/957) 1 Jan 1985 (otherwise) (SI 1984/1347))
12		See Sch 5 below
13, 14		15 Aug 1983 (SI 1983/974)
15, 16		1 Oct 1984 (SI 1983/974)
17, 18		1 Jan 1984 (SI 1983/974)
19		Repealed
20		15 Aug 1983 (SI 1983/974)
21–24		12 Apr 1993 (SI 1992/2974)
25		See Sch 8 below
26–28		15 Aug 1983 (SI 1983/974)
29	(1)	See Sch 9, Pt I below
	(2)	See Sch 9, Pt II below
30	(1)	See Sch 10, Pt I below
	(2)	See Sch 10, Pt II below
	(3)	Repealed
31		15 Aug 1983 (SI 1983/974)
32–34		13 May 1983 (s 32(1))

Schedule

1		Repealed
2, para	1–6	Repealed
	7	15 Aug 1983 (SI 1983/974)
	8–14	Repealed
	15, 16	15 Aug 1983 (SI 1983/974)
	17, 18	1 Jan 1984 (SI 1983/974)
	19	15 Aug 1983 (SI 1983/974)
	20–24	Repealed
	25, 26	Spent
	27, 28	Repealed
	29	15 Aug 1983 (SI 1983/974); prospectively repealed by Care Standards Act 2000, s 117(2), Sch 6[2]
	30–33	15 Aug 1983 (SI 1983/974)
	34	Repealed
	35, 36	15 Aug 1983 (SI 1983/974)
	37	Repealed
	38–45	15 Aug 1983 (SI 1983/974)
	46–62	Repealed
3		1 Apr 1984 (SI 1983/974)
4		Repealed
5, para	1	15 Aug 1983 (SI 1983/974)
	2	1 Apr 1984 (SI 1984/216)

**Health and Social Services and Social Security Adjudications Act 1983
(c 41)**—*contd*

Schedule

5, para	3		15 Aug 1983 (SI 1983/974)
6, 7			15 Aug 1983 (SI 1983/974)
8			Repealed (except paras 1(3)(a), 29, which came into force on 23 Apr 1984 (SI 1984/216)); prospectively repealed by Social Security Act 1998, s 86(2), Sch 8[1]
9, Pt	I, para	1	Repealed
		2	15 Aug 1983 (SI 1983/974)
		3	1 Apr 1984 (SI 1983/974)
		4–7	Repealed
		8	15 Aug 1983 (SI 1983/974)
		9–17	Repealed
		18	23 Apr 1984 (SI 1984/216)
		19	1 Jan 1985 (SI 1984/1347)
		20	Repealed
		21	15 Aug 1983 (SI 1983/974)
		22	1 Jan 1984 (SI 1983/974)
		23	1 Apr 1984 (SI 1983/974)
		24	15 Aug 1983 (SI 1983/974)
		25, 26	Repealed
		27	1 Jan 1985 (SI 1984/1347)
		28	Repealed
	II		1 Jan 1984 (SI 1983/974)
10, Pt	I		15 Aug 1983 (repeals of or in Public Health Act 1936; Food and Drugs Act 1955; Health Services and Public Health Act 1968, ss 48(2), 64 (so far as relates to Scotland); Social Work (Scotland) Act 1968, s 31(2); Radiological Protection Act 1970; Powers of Criminal Courts Act 1973; Children Act 1975, s 109(3); Adoption Act 1976; Criminal Law Act 1977; National Health Service Act 1977, ss 8(1A), 9, 100(2), 128(1), Sch 5; Adoption (Scotland) Act 1978; Employment Protection (Consolidation) Act 1978; Child Care Act 1980, ss 71, 79(5)(h); Health Services Act 1980, ss 1, 4(1) (but only for the purpose of giving effect to new s 28B(1)(a) of National Health Service Act 1977), Sch 1; Overseas Development and Co-operation Act 1980) (SI 1983/974, as partly revoked by SI 1983/1862)

**Health and Social Services and Social Security Adjudications Act 1983
(c 41)**—*contd*
Schedule
10, Pt   I—*contd*

1 Jan 1984 (repeals of or in National
    Assistance Act 1948; Local
    Government Act 1966; Health
    Services and Public Health Act 1968,
    s 45(2); Social Work (Scotland)
    Act 1968, ss 14(2), 78(1)(b);
    Children and Young Persons
    Act 1969; Local Government
    Act 1972; National Health Service
    Act 1977, Sch 8; Domestic
    Proceedings and Magistrates'
    Courts Act 1978; Child Care
    Act 1980, ss 10(2), 36(1), 39(2),
    43(3), 44(5), 45(1)(ii), 87(1),
    Schs 1, 5; Residential Homes
    Act 1980 (but only for the
    purposes of the repeal of s 8 of that
    Act); Criminal Justice Act 1982)
    (SI 1983/974, as partly revoked by
    SI 1983/1862)
30 Jan 1984 (repeals of or in Social
    Work (Scotland) Act 1968, s 59A(1),
    (3); Children Act 1975, s 72)
    (SI 1983/1862)
1 Apr 1984 (repeals of or in Health
    Visiting and Social Work
    (Training) Act 1962; Local
    Authority Social Services Act 1970;
    National Health Service Act 1977,
    Sch 15; Nurses, Midwives and
    Health Visitors Act 1979)
    (SI 1983/974, as partly revoked by
    SI 1983/1862)
1 Apr 1984 (repeal of Health Services
    Act 1980, s 4(1) for remaining
    purposes) (SI 1984/216)
23 Apr 1984 (repeals of or in Family
    Income Supplements Act 1970;
    Tribunals and Inquiries Act 1971;
    Social Security Act 1975; House
    of Commons Disqualification
    Act 1975; Child Benefit
    Act 1975; Supplementary
    Benefits Act 1976; Social
    Security (Miscellaneous
    Provisions) Act 1977; Social
    Security and Housing Benefits
    Act 1982) (SI 1984/216)

Health and Social Services and Social Security Adjudications Act 1983 (c 41)—*contd*

Schedule

10, Pt	I—*contd*	1 Jan 1985 (repeals of or in Nursing Homes Act 1975; Child Care Act 1980, s 58, Sch 3; Residential Homes Act 1980 (except s 8, repealed on 1 Jan 1984); Children's Homes Act 1982) (SI 1984/1347, as amended by SI 1984/1767)
		1 May 1985 (repeal of Health Services Act 1980, s 4(2)) (SI 1985/704)
	II	15 Aug 1983 (SI 1983/974)

[1]   Orders made under Social Security Act 1998, s 87, bringing the prospective repeals into force will be noted to that Act

[2]   Orders made under Care Standards Act 2000, s 122, bringing the prospective repeals into force will be noted to that Act

Importation of Milk Act 1983 (c 37)

Whole Act repealed

International Monetary Arrangements Act 1983 (c 51)

RA: 26 Jul 1983

Commencement provisions: s 3(2); International Monetary Arrangements Act 1983 (Commencement) Order 1983, SI 1983/1643

Section

1	14 Nov 1983 (SI 1983/1643)
2, 3	26 Jul 1983 (RA)

International Transport Conventions Act 1983 (c 14)

RA: 11 Apr 1983

Commencement provisions: s 11(3); International Transport Convention Act 1983 (Certification of Commencement of Convention) Order 1985, SI 1985/612

Section

1	1 May 1985 (SI 1985/612)
2–10	11 Apr 1983 (RA)
11	11 Apr 1983 (RA; sub-s (2) effective from 1 May 1985, the day on which the Convention comes into force as regards the United Kingdom) (s 11(3); SI 1985/612)

Schedule

1, 2	11 Apr 1983 (RA)
3	1 May 1985 (SI 1985/612)

Level Crossings Act 1983 (c 16)

RA: 9 May 1983

Commencement provisions: s 2(2)

9 Aug 1983 (s 2(2))

Licensing (Occasional Permissions) Act 1983 (c 24)

RA: 9 May 1983

Commencement provisions: s 5(2)

9 Aug 1983 (s 5(2))

Litter Act 1983 (c 35)

RA: 13 May 1983

Commencement provisions: s 13(2), (3)

Section		
1, 2		Repealed
3		13 Aug 1983 (s 13(3))
4		*Not in force*
5–11		13 Aug 1983 (s 13(3))
12	(1)	Repealed
	(2)	13 Aug 1983 (s 13(3))
	(3)	See Sch 2 below
13		13 Aug 1983 (s 13(3))
Schedule		
1		13 Aug 1983 (s 13(3))
2		13 Aug 1983 (except repeal of Control of Pollution Act 1974, s 24(1)–(3)) (s 13(2))
		Not in force (exception noted above)

Local Authorities (Expenditure Powers) Act 1983 (c 52)

RA: 26 Jul 1983

26 Jul 1983 (RA)

Whole Act repealed (E, W)

Marriage Act 1983 (c 32)

RA: 13 May 1983

Commencement provisions: s 12(5); Marriage Act 1983 (Commencement) Order 1984, SI 1984/413

1 May 1984 (SI 1984/413)

Matrimonial Homes Act 1983 (c 19)

Whole Act repealed

Medical Act 1983 (c 54)

RA: 26 Jul 1983

Commencement provisions: s 57(2)

26 Oct 1983 (s 57(2))

Mental Health Act 1983 (c 20)

RA: 9 May 1983

Commencement provisions: s 149(2), (3); Mental Health Act 1983 Commencement
Order 1984, SI 1984/1357

Section		
1–20		30 Sep 1983 (s 149(2))
21, 21A, 21B		Substituted (for s 21) by Mental Health (Patients in the Community) Act 1995, s 2(2) (qv)
22–25		30 Sep 1983 (s 149(2))
25A–25J		Inserted by Mental Health (Patients in the Community) Act 1995, s 1(1) (qv)
26		30 Sep 1983 (s 149(2))
27		Substituted by Children Act 1989, s 108(5), Sch 13, para 48 (qv)
28–34		30 Sep 1983 (s 149(2))
35, 36		1 Oct 1984 (SI 1984/1357)
37		30 Sep 1983 (s 149(2))
38		1 Oct 1984 (SI 1984/1357)
39		30 Sep 1983 (s 149(2))
39A		Inserted by Criminal Justice Act 1991, s 27(1) (qv)
40	(1), (2)	30 Sep 1983 (s 149(2))
	(3)	1 Oct 1984 (SI 1984/1357)
	(4), (5)	30 Sep 1983 (s 149(2))
	(6)	Inserted by Mental Health (Patients in the Community) Act 1995, s 2(4) (qv)
41–45		30 Sep 1983 (s 149(2))
45A, 45B		Inserted by Crime (Sentences) Act 1997, s 46 (qv)
46		30 Sep 1983 (s 149(2)); prospectively repealed by Armed Forces Act 1996, s 35(2), Sch 7, Pt III[1]
47–54		30 Sep 1983 (s 149(2))
54A		Inserted by Criminal Justice Act 1991, s 27(2) (qv)

Mental Health Act 1983 (c 20)—*contd*

Section

55–80	30 Sep 1983 (s 149(2))
80A	Inserted by Crime (Sentences) Act 1997, s 48, Sch 3, Pt I, para 1 (qv)
81	30 Sep 1983 (s 149(2))
81A	Inserted by Crime (Sentences) Act 1997, s 48, Sch 3, Pt I, para 2 (qv)
82	30 Sep 1983 (s 149(2))
82A	Inserted by Crime (Sentences) Act 1997, s 48, Sch 3, Pt I, para 3 (qv)
83	30 Sep 1983 (s 149(2))
83A	Inserted by Crime (Sentences) Act 1997, s 48, Sch 3, Pt I, para 4 (qv)
84, 85	30 Sep 1983 (s 149(2))
85A	Inserted by Crime (Sentences) Act 1997, s 48, Sch 3, Pt I, para 5 (qv)
86–123	30 Sep 1983 (s 149(2))
124	Repealed
125–149	30 Sep 1983 (s 149(2))
Schedule	
1–6	30 Sep 1983 (s 149(2))

[1] Orders made under Armed Forces Act 1996, s 36(2), bringing the prospective repeal into force will be noted to that Act

---

Mental Health (Amendment) (Scotland) Act 1983 (c 39)

Whole Act repealed

Merchant Shipping Act 1983 (c 13)

Whole Act repealed

Miscellaneous Financial Provisions Act 1983 (c 29)

RA: 13 May 1983

Commencement provisions: s 9(1), (2); Miscellaneous Financial Provisions Act 1983 (Commencement of Provisions) Order 1983, SI 1983/1338

Section

1	1 Apr 1984 (SI 1983/1338)
2	13 Jul 1983 (s 9(2))
3	Repealed
4–7	13 Jul 1983 (s 9(2))
8	1 Apr 1984 (SI 1983/1338)
9–11	13 Jul 1983 (s 9(2))

Miscellaneous Financial Provisions Act 1983 (c 29)—*contd*
Schedule

1	Repealed
2	13 Jul 1983 (s 9(2))
3	1 Apr 1984 (SI 1983/1338)

Mobile Homes Act 1983 (c 34)

RA: 13 May 1983

Commencement provisions: s 6(3)

20 May 1983 (s 6(3))

National Audit Act 1983 (c 44)

RA: 13 May 1983

Commencement provisions: s 15(2), (3)
Section

1–15	1 Jan 1984 (s 15(2))

Schedule

1–4	1 Jan 1984 (s 15(2))
5	1 Jan 1984 (repeal of Exchequer and Audit Departments Act 1866, s 24; Exchequer and Audit Departments Act 1921, in s 1(2), the proviso, ss 3(3), (4), 8(1)) (s 15(2))
	1 Oct 1984 (repeal of Exchequer and Audit Departments Act 1921, s 8(2)) (s 15(3))

National Heritage Act 1983 (c 47)

RA: 13 May 1983

Commencement provisions: s 41(1)–(3); National Heritage Act 1983 (Commencement No 1) Order 1983, SI 1983/1062; National Heritage Act 1983 (Commencement No 2) Order 1983, SI 1983/1183; National Heritage Act 1983 (Commencement No 3) Order 1983, SI 1983/1437; National Heritage Act 1983 (Commencement No 4) Order 1984, SI 1984/208, National Heritage Act 1983 (Commencement No 5) Order 1984, SI 1984/217; National Heritage Act 1983 (Commencement No 6) Order 1984, SI 1984/225

Section

1	(1)	30 Sep 1983 (SI 1983/1062)
	(2)	See Sch 1, Pt I below
2, 3		1 Apr 1984 (SI 1984/225)
4	(1)–(4)	1 Apr 1984 (SI 1984/225)
	(5)	13 Jul 1983 (s 41(3))
	(6)	1 Apr 1984 (SI 1984/225)
	(7)	13 Jul 1983 (s 41(3))

National Heritage Act 1983 (c 47)—*contd*

Section

4	(8)		1 Apr 1984 (SI 1984/225)
5–7			1 Apr 1984 (SI 1984/225)
8			Repealed
9	(1)		30 Sep 1983 (SI 1983/1062)
	(2)		See Sch 1, Pt II below
10, 11			1 Apr 1984 (SI 1984/225)
12	(1)–(4)		1 Apr 1984 (SI 1984/225)
	(5), (6)		13 Jul 1983 (s 41(3))
	(7)		1 Apr 1984 (SI 1984/225)
13–15			1 Apr 1984 (SI 1984/225)
16			Repealed
17			1 Oct 1983 (SI 1983/1437)
18			1 Apr 1984 (SI 1984/208)
18A			Inserted by Museums and Galleries Act 1992, s 11(2), Sch 8, Pt II, para 13(4) (qv)
19	(1)–(3)		1 Apr 1984 (SI 1984/208)
	(4), (5)		13 Jul 1983 (s 41(3))
	(6)		1 Apr 1984 (SI 1984/208)
20, 21			1 Apr 1984 (SI 1984/208)
22			1 Oct 1983 (SI 1983/1437)
23			8 Aug 1983 (SI 1983/1183)
24–28			1 Apr 1984 (SI 1984/217)
29			8 Aug 1983 (SI 1983/1183)
30, 31			13 Jul 1983 (s 41(3))
31A			Inserted by Armed Forces Act 1996, s 31 (qv)
32			1 Oct 1983 (SI 1983/1437)
33	(1), (2)		1 Apr 1984 (SI 1984/208)
	(2A)		Inserted by Planning and Compensation Act 1991, s 29(1) (qv)
	(2B)		Inserted by Leasehold Reform, Housing and Urban Development Act 1993, s 187(1), Sch 21, para 9 (qv)
	(2C)		Inserted by Housing Act 1996, s 118(6) (qv)
	(3), (4)		1 Apr 1984 (SI 1984/208)
	(5)		1 Oct 1983 (SI 1983/1437)
	(6)–(8)		1 Apr 1984 (SI 1984/208)
34			1 Apr 1984 (SI 1984/208)
35			1 Oct 1983 (SI 1983/1437)
36, 37			1 Apr 1984 (SI 1984/208)
38			1 Oct 1983 (SI 1983/1437)
39			1 Apr 1984 (SI 1984/208)
40	(1)		See Sch 5 below
	(2)		See Sch 6 below
41–43			13 Jul 1983 (s 41(3))

Schedule

1, Pt	I, para	1–8	30 Sep 1983 (SI 1983/1062)

National Heritage Act 1983 (c 47)—*contd*

Schedule

1, Pt	I, para	9	Repealed
		10	30 Sep 1983 (SI 1983/1062)
	II	11–18	30 Sep 1983 (SI 1983/1062)
		19	Repealed
		20	30 Sep 1983 (SI 1983/1062)
	III	21–30	1 Oct 1983 (SI 1983/1437)
	IV	31–40	8 Aug 1983 (SI 1983/1183)
2			13 Jul 1983 (s 41(3))
3			1 Oct 1983 (SI 1983/1437)
4, para	1–11		1 Apr 1984 (SI 1984/208)
	12		Spent
	13, 14		Repealed
	15–17		Spent
	18		Repealed
	19–24		Spent
	25–71		1 Apr 1984 (SI 1984/208)
5, para	1, 2		Repealed
	3		8 Aug 1983 (so far as relates to Royal Botanic Gardens, Kew) (SI 1983/1183)
			30 Sep 1983 (so far as relates to Science Museum and Victoria and Albert Museum) (SI 1983/1062)
			1 Oct 1983 (so far as relates to Armouries, the Historic Buildings and Monuments Commission for England and Board of Trustees of the Armouries) (SI 1983/1437)
	4–7		Repealed
6			3 Aug 1983 (repeal in National Gallery and Tate Gallery Act 1954, s 4(2)) (SI 1983/1062)
			1 Apr 1984 (repeals in Historic Buildings and Ancient Monuments Act 1953; Town and Country Planning (Amendment) Act 1972; Ancient Monuments and Archaeological Areas Act 1979) (SI 1984/208)
			1 Apr 1984 (repeals in Patents and Designs Act 1907, s 47(1); Public Records Act 1958, Sch 1, para 3 (entries in Pt I of the Table relating to Victoria and Albert Museum and Science Museum) (SI 1984/225)

Nuclear Material (Offences) Act 1983 (c 18)

RA: 9 May 1983

Commencement provisions: s 8(2); Nuclear Material (Offences) Act 1983 (Commencement) Order 1991, SI 1991/1716

Section		
1–4		2 Oct 1991 (SI 1991/1716)
5		Repealed
6		2 Oct 1991 (SI 1991/1716)
7	(1)	Repealed
	(2)	24 Jul 1991 (in relation to any Order in Council) (SI 1991/1716)
		2 Oct 1991 (otherwise) (SI 1991/1716)
8		2 Oct 1991 (SI 1991/1716)
Schedule		2 Oct 1991 (SI 1991/1716)

Oil Taxation Act 1983 (c 56)

RA: 1 Dec 1983

1 Dec 1983 (RA) (though largely effective from 1 Jul 1982)

Pastoral Measure 1983 (No 1)

RA: 9 May 1983

Commencement provisions: s 94(4)

1 Nov 1983 (s 94(4))

Pet Animals Act 1951 (Amendment) Act 1983 (c 26)

RA: 9 May 1983

Commencement provisions: s 2(2)

9 Nov 1983 (s 2(2))

Petroleum Royalties (Relief) Act 1983 (c 59)

RA: 21 Dec 1983

Commencement provisions: s 2(2)

21 Feb 1984 (s 2(2))

Pig Industry Levy Act 1983 (c 4)

RA: 1 Mar 1983

1 Mar 1983 (RA)

Pilotage Act 1983 (c 21)

Whole Act repealed

Plant Varieties Act 1983 (c 17)

Whole Act repealed

Ports (Reduction of Debt) Act 1983 (c 22)

RA: 9 May 1983

9 May 1983 (RA)

Representation of the People Act 1983 (c 2)

RA: 8 Feb 1983

Commencement provisions: s 207(2); Representation of the People Act 1983 (Commencement) Order 1983, SI 1983/153

15 Mar 1983 (SI 1983/153)

Road Traffic (Driving Licences) Act 1983 (c 43)

Whole Act repealed

Social Security and Housing Benefits Act 1983 (c 36)

Whole Act repealed

Solvent Abuse (Scotland) Act 1983 (c 33)

Whole Act repealed

Transport Act 1983 (c 10)

RA: 28 Mar 1983

Commencement provisions: s 10(1)(a)–(c)

This Act came into force on Royal Assent, subject to certain provisions of Pt I taking effect; see the relevant provisions as noted below:

Section		
1		28 Mar 1983 (s 10(1))
2		Effective in relation to any accounting period of an Executive ending after 31 Mar 1983 (s 10(1)(a))
3–5		Repealed
6	(1), (2)	1 Apr 1983 (s 10(1)(b)); prospectively repealed by Transport Act 2000, 274, Sch 31, Pt II (W)[1]
		Repealed (E)
	(3), (4)	Repealed
	(5), (6)	1 Apr 1983 (s 10(1)(b)); prospectively repealed by Transport Act 2000, 274, Sch 31, Pt II (W)[1]
		Repealed (E)

Transport Act 1983 (c 10)—*contd*

Section

6	(7)	Effective in relation to any accounting period of an Executive ending after 31 Mar 1983 (s 10(1)(a))
7, 8		28 Mar 1983 (s 10(1))
9	(1)	See Schedule below
	(2)	Repealed
	(3)	Effective in relation to any accounting period of an Executive ending after 31 Mar 1983 (s 10(1)(a))
	(4), (5)	Repealed
10		28 Mar 1983 (s 10(1))
11, 12		28 Mar 1983 (RA)
Schedule		31 Mar 1983 (repeals in Transport (London) Act 1969, ss 5, 7) (s 10(1)(a))
		1 Apr 1983 (repeals in Transport (London) Act 1969, s 11) (s 10(1)(b))

[1]   Orders made under Transport Act 2000, s 275, bringing the prospective repeal into force will be noted to that Act

Value Added Tax Act 1983 (c 55)

Whole Act repealed (for transitional provisions and savings, see Value Added Tax Act 1994, Sch 13)

Water Act 1983 (c 23)

RA: 9 May 1983

Commencement provisions: ss 3(1), 9(2), 11(4), (5); Water Act 1983 (Commencement No 1) Order 1983, SI 1983/1173; Water Act 1983 (Water Space Amenity Commission Appointed Day) Order 1983, SI 1983/1174; Water Act 1983 (Commencement No 2) Order 1983, SI 1983/1234; Water Act 1983 (National Water Council Appointed Day) Order 1983, SI 1983/1235; Water Act 1983 (Dissolution of the National Water Council) Order 1983, SI 1983/1927; Water Act 1983 (Representation of Consumers' Interests) (Appointed Date) Order 1984, SI 1984/71

Section

1	(1)	Repealed
	(2)	1 Oct 1983 (SI 1983/1234); prospectively repealed by Water Act 1989, s 190(3), Sch 27, Pt II[1]
	(3)	Repealed
2		Repealed
3, 4		9 May 1983 (s 11(4))
5–7		Repealed
8		10 Aug 1983 (SI 1983/1173)
9, 10		9 May 1983 (s 11(4))
11	(1)	9 May 1983 (s 11(4))

Water Act 1983 (c 23)—*contd*

Section

11	(2), (3)	See Schs 4, 5 below
	(4)–(7)	9 May 1983 (s 11(4))

Schedule

1		Repealed
2		9 May 1983 (s 11(4))
3		Repealed
4, para	1–6	Repealed
	7	1 Oct 1983 (SI 1983/1234)
	8, 9	9 May 1983 (s 11(4))
5, Pt	I	10 Aug 1983 (repeals of or in Development of Rural Wales Act 1976, Sch 7, para 11; Water Charges Equalisation Act 1977; Local Government Planning and Land Act 1980, s 158(1), (2); New Towns Act 1981, Sch 12, para 12) (SI 1983/1173)

1 Oct 1983 (repeals of or in Water Act 1973, ss 23, 24(12)(a), 25(5)(a), Sch 3, para 40, sub-para (1)(b) and word 'and' immediately preceding it, and sub-para (5)) (SI 1983/1174)

1 Oct 1983 (repeals of or in Public Bodies (Admission to Meetings) Act 1960; Local Government Act 1972; Water Act 1973, ss 6, 17(5); House of Commons Disqualification Act 1975, Sch 1, Pt III; Local Government, Planning and Land Act 1980, s 25(4)) (SI 1983/1234)

1 Oct 1983 (repeals of or in Public Health Act 1961, s 9(3); Water Act 1973, ss 4, 5(3), 26(2)–(4), 29(2), 30(6), 38(1), Sch 3, Sch 8, para 90; House of Commons Disqualification Act 1975, Sch 1, Pt III; Land Drainage Act 1976, Sch 5, para 8(1); Water (Scotland) Act 1980, Sch 10) (SI 1983/1235)

Not in force (repeal of Local Government (Scotland) Act 1973, Sch 17, para 64)

	II	9 May 1983 (revocation of SI 1982/944) (s 11(4))
		1 Oct 1983 (otherwise) (SI 1983/1234)

[1]   Orders made under Water Act 1989, s 194(4), (5), bringing the prospective repeal into force will be noted to that Act

1984

Agricultural Holdings Act 1984 (c 41)

Whole Act repealed

Agriculture (Amendment) Act 1984 (c 20)

RA: 24 May 1984

Commencement provisions: s 3(2)

24 Jul 1984 (s 3(2))

Anatomy Act 1984 (c 14)

RA: 24 May 1984

Commencement provisions: s 13(3); Anatomy Act 1984 (Commencement) Order 1988, SI 1988/81

14 Feb 1988 (SI 1988/81)

Animal Health and Welfare Act 1984 (c 40)

RA: 12 Jul 1984

Commencement provisions: s 17(2)–(4); Animal Health and Welfare Act 1984 (Commencement No 1) Order 1985, SI 1985/1267

Section		
1–4		12 Sep 1984 (s 17(2))
5		Repealed
6–12		12 Sep 1984 (s 17(2))
13		16 Aug 1985 (SI 1985/1267)
14–17		12 Sep 1984 (s 17(2))
Schedule		
1, para	1	12 Sep 1984 (s 17(2))
	2	Repealed
	3	16 Aug 1985 (SI 1985/1267)
	4	12 Sep 1984 (s 17(2))
2		12 Sep 1984 (except repeals in Medicines Act 1968) (s 17(2))
		16 Aug 1985 (exception noted above) (SI 1985/1267)

Appropriation Act 1984 (c 44)

Whole Act repealed

Betting, Gaming and Lotteries (Amendment) Act 1984 (c 25)

RA: 26 Jun 1984

Commencement provisions: s 4(2); Betting, Gaming and Lotteries (Amendment) Act 1984
   (Commencement) Order 1986, SI 1986/102

Section

1	26 Aug 1984 (s 4(2))
2	10 Mar 1986 (SI 1986/102)
3	26 Aug 1984 (s 4(2))
4	26 Jun 1984 (RA)

Building Act 1984 (c 55)

RA: 31 Oct 1984

Commencement provisions: s 134; Building Act 1984 (Commencement No 1) Order 1985,
   SI 1985/1602; Building Act 1984 (Appointed Day and Repeal) Order 1985,
   SI 1985/1603; Building Act 1984 (Commencement No 2) Order 1998,
   SI 1998/1836

Section

1–11		1 Dec 1984 (s 134(2))
12, 13		1 Dec 1984 (so far as enable regulations to be made) (s 134(1)(a))
		Not in force (otherwise)
14, 15		1 Dec 1984 (s 134(2))
16		1 Dec 1984 (11 Nov 1985 being the appointed day under sub-s (13)) (SI 1985/1603)
17		1 Dec 1984 (s 134(2))
18		Repealed
19		1 Dec 1984 (s 134(2)); prospectively repealed by sub-s (9) on the entry into force of s 20 of this Act
20		*Not in force*
21–25		1 Dec 1984 (s 134(2))
26–30		Repealed
31		1 Dec 1984 (so far as enables regulations to be made) (s 134(1)(a))
		Not in force (otherwise)
32		1 Dec 1984 (s 134(2))
33		*Not in force*
34–37		1 Dec 1984 (s 134(2))
38		1 Dec 1984 (so far as enables regulations to be made) (s 134(1)(a))
		Not in force (otherwise)
39–41		1 Dec 1984 (s 134(2))
42	(1)–(3)	*Not in force*

Building Act 1984 (c 55)—*contd*
Section

42	(4)–(6)	1 Dec 1984 (so far as enable regulations to be made) (s 134(1)(a))
		Not in force (otherwise)
	(7)	1 Dec 1984 (but no day appointed)
43	(1), (2)	*Not in force*
	(3)	1 Dec 1984 (so far as enables regulations to be made) (s 134(1)(a))
		Not in force (otherwise)
44, 45		*Not in force*
46–49		1 Dec 1984 (s 134(2))
50	(1)	1 Dec 1984 (s 134(2))
	(2), (3)	11 Nov 1985 (SI 1985/1602)
	(4)–(8)	1 Dec 1984 (s 134(2))
51		1 Dec 1984 (s 134(2))
51A–51C		Inserted (14 Oct 1996) by Deregulation (Building) (Initial Notices and Final Certificates) Order 1996, SI 1996/1905, art 2
52–68		1 Dec 1984 (s 134(2))
69		Repealed (for savings see Water Act 1989, s 190(2), Sch 26, Pt II, para 20(2))
70–108		1 Dec 1984 (s 134(2))
109		Repealed
110–132		1 Dec 1984 (s 134(2))
133	(1)	1 Dec 1984 (s 134(2))
	(2)	1 Dec 1984 (except so far as relates to Town and Country Planning Act 1947 (repealed); Atomic Energy Authority Act 1954) (s 134(2))
		Not in force (exceptions noted above) (s 134(1)(c))
134		1 Dec 1984 (s 134(2))
135		1 Dec 1984 (s 134(2))
Schedule		
1, para	1–8	1 Dec 1984 (s 134(2))
	9	7 Aug 1998 (SI 1998/1836)
	10, 11	1 Dec 1984 (s 134(2))
2–6		1 Dec 1984 (s 134(2))
7		1 Dec 1984 (except repeals of or in Town and Country Planning Act 1947 (repealed); Atomic Energy Authority Act 1954) (s 134(2))
		Not in force (exceptions noted above) (s 134(1)(c))

Cable and Broadcasting Act 1984 (c 46)

Whole Act repealed

Capital Transfer Tax Act 1984 (c 51)

RA: 31 Jul 1984

Commencement provisions: s 274(1)

1 Jan 1985 (s 274(1))

Note: this Act does not apply to transfers of value made before 1985 or to other events
   before then on which tax is or would be chargeable. Note also s 275 of, and Sch 7 to,
   the Act in relation to continuity and construction of references to old and new law

Note: on and after 25 Jul 1986 the tax charged under this Act is known as inheritance tax
   and this Act may be cited as Inheritance Tax Act 1984 (Finance Act 1986, s 100)

Child Abduction Act 1984 (c 37)

RA: 12 Jul 1984

Commencement provisions: s 13(2)

12 Oct 1984 (s 13(2))

Consolidated Fund Act 1984 (c 1)

Whole Act repealed

Consolidated Fund (No 2) Act 1984 (c 61)

Whole Act repealed

Co-operative Development Agency and Industrial Development Act 1984 (c 57)

RA: 31 Oct 1984

Commencement provisions: s 7(1); Co-operative Development Agency and Industrial
   Development Act 1984 (Commencement) Order 1984, SI 1984/1845

Section		
1, 2		Repealed
3		31 Oct 1984 (s 7(1))
4, 5		29 Nov 1984 (SI 1984/1845)
6		See Sch 2 below
7, 8		31 Oct 1984 (s 7(1))
Schedule		
1		29 Nov 1984 (SI 1984/1845)
2, Pt	I	31 Oct 1984 (s 7(1))
	II	31 Dec 1990 (see note below)
	III	29 Nov 1984 (SI 1984/1845)

Note: the days appointed for the winding up and dissolution of the Co-operative
   Development Agency were 30 Sep 1990 and 31 Dec 1990, by Co-operative
   Development Agency (Winding up and Dissolution) Order 1990 (SI 1990/279)

County Courts Act 1984 (c 28)

RA: 26 Jun 1984

Commencement provisions: s 150

1 Aug 1984 (s 150)

Cycle Tracks Act 1984 (c 38)

RA: 12 Jul 1984

Commencement provisions: s 9(2)

12 Sep 1984 (s 9(2))

Data Protection Act 1984 (c 35)

Whole Act repealed, subject to transitional provisions and savings in Data Protection Act 1998, s 73, Sch 14

Dentists Act 1984 (c 24)

RA: 26 Jun 1984

Commencement provisions: s 55(1)–(3); Dentists Act 1984 (Commencement) Order 1984, SI 1984/1815

Section		
1		1 Oct 1984 (s 55(1))
2	(1), (2)	1 Oct 1984 (s 55(1))
	(3)	1 Oct 1984 (s 55(1)); prospectively repealed by Dentists Act 1984 (Amendment) Order 2001, SI 2001/3926, arts 2, 6(a) as from date to be notified in *London Gazette*
	(4)	1 Jan 1985 (SI 1984/1815)
	(4A)	Prospectively inserted by Dentists Act 1984 (Amendment) Order 2001, SI 2001/3926, arts 2, 6(c) as from date to be notified in *London Gazette*
	(5)	1 Jan 1985 (SI 1984/1815); prospectively repealed by Dentists Act 1984 (Amendment) Order 2001, SI 2001/3926, arts 2, 6(a) as from date to be notified in *London Gazette*
	(6)–(8)	Prospectively inserted by Dentists Act 1984 (Amendment) Order 2001, SI 2001/3926, arts 2, 6(d) as from date to be notified in *London Gazette*

Dentists Act 1984 (c 24)—*contd*
Section

3–12		1 Oct 1984 (s 55(1))
13		1 Oct 1984 (s 55(1)); prospectively repealed by Dentists Act 1984 (Amendment) Order 2001, SI 2001/3926, arts 2, 5(2)(b) as from date to be notified in *London Gazette*
14–21		1 Oct 1984 (s 55(1))
21A		Inserted (14 Apr 1998) by European Primary and Specialist Dental Qualifications Regulations 1998, SI 1998/811, reg 21(1)
22–27		1 Oct 1984 (s 55(1))
28		1 Jan 1985 (SI 1984/1815)
29, 30		1 Oct 1984 (except so far as relates to proceedings before Health Committee or any direction or order given or made by that Committee) (s 55(1)) 1 Jan 1985 (otherwise) (SI 1984/1815)
31		1 Jan 1985 (SI 1984/1815)
32		1 Oct 1984 (s 55(1))
33		As noted to ss 29, 30 above
34		1 Oct 1984 (s 55(1))
34A	(1)	Inserted (21 Dec 2001) by Dentists Act 1984 (Amendment) Order 2001, SI 2001/3926, arts 2, 8
	(2)–(5)	Prospectively inserted by Dentists Act 1984 (Amendment) Order 2001, SI 2001/3926, arts 2, 8 as from date to be notified in *London Gazette*
	(6)	Inserted (28 Dec 2001) by Dentists Act 1984 (Amendment) Order 2001, SI 2001/3926, arts 2, 8
	(7), (8)	Prospectively inserted by Dentists Act 1984 (Amendment) Order 2001, SI 2001/3926, arts 2, 8 as from date to be notified in *London Gazette*
34B		Prospectively inserted by Dentists Act 1984 (Amendment) Order 2001, SI 2001/3926, arts 2, 8 as from date to be notified in *London Gazette*
35–48		1 Oct 1984 (s 55(1))
49		26 Jul 1984 (s 55(2))
50–53		1 Oct 1984 (s 55(1))
54	(1)	See Sch 5 below
54	(2)	See Sch 6, Pt I below

Dentists Act 1984 (c 24)—*contd*

Section

54	(3)		See Sch 6, Pt II below
55, 56			1 Oct 1984 (s 55(1))

Schedule

1, para	1–5		1 Oct 1984 (s 55(1)); prospectively substituted by Dentists Act 1984 (Amendment) Order 2001, SI 2001/3926, arts 2, 4(1), (2) as from date to be notified in *London Gazette*
	6, 7		1 Oct 1984 (s 55(1))
	8	(1)	1 Oct 1984 (s 55(1))
		(2)	1 Jan 1985 (SI 1984/1815); prospectively substituted by Dentists Act 1984 (Amendment) Order 2001, SI 2001/3926, arts 2, 7(1), (4)(b) as from date to be notified in *London Gazette*
		(2A)	Prospectively inserted by Dentists Act 1984 (Amendment) Order 2001, SI 2001/3926, arts 2, 7(1), (4)(c) as from date to be notified in *London Gazette*
		(3)–(12)	1 Oct 1984 (s 55(1))
	9–12		1 Oct 1984 (s 55(1)); prospectively repealed by Dentists Act 1984 (Amendment) Order 2001, SI 2001/3926, arts 2, 7(1), (5) as from date to be notified in *London Gazette*
2			1 Oct 1984 (s 55(1))
3, para	1, 2		As noted to ss 29, 30 above
	3		1 Jan 1985 (SI 1984/1815)
	3A		Prospectively inserted by Dentists Act 1984 (Amendment) Order 2001, SI 2001/3926, arts 2, 10(6) as from date to be notified in *London Gazette*
	4, 5		As noted to ss 29, 30 above
	6		1 Jan 1985 (SI 1984/1815)
	7, 8		As noted to ss 29, 30 above
	9		Repealed
3A			Prospectively inserted by Dentists Act 1984 (Amendment) Order 2001, SI 2001/3926, arts 2, 9 as from date to be notified in *London Gazette*
4, 5			1 Oct 1984 (s 55(1))
6, Pt	I		26 Jul 1984 (repeal of Dentists Act 1983, s 29) (s 55(2))

Dentists Act 1984 (c 24)—*contd*
Schedule

6, Pt	I—*contd*	1 Oct 1984 (otherwise) (s 55(1))
	II	1 Oct 1984 (s 55(1))
7		1 Oct 1984 (s 55(1))

Education (Amendment) (Scotland) Act 1984 (c 6)

RA: 13 Mar 1984

Commencement provisions: s 2

13 May 1984 (s 2)

Education (Grants and Awards) Act 1984 (c 11)

Whole Act repealed

Finance Act 1984 (c 43)

Budget Day: 13 Mar 1984

RA: 26 Jul 1984

Details of the commencement of Finance Acts are not set out in this work

Food Act 1984 (c 30)

RA: 26 Jun 1984

Commencement provisions: s 136(4)

26 Sep 1984 (s 136(4))

Foreign Limitation Periods Act 1984 (c 16)

RA: 24 May 1984

Commencement provisions: s 7(2); Foreign Limitation Periods Act 1984 (Commencement)
    Order 1985, SI 1985/1276

1 Oct 1985 (SI 1985/1276)

Fosdyke Bridge Act 1984 (c 17)

Local application only

Foster Children (Scotland) Act 1984 (c 56)

RA: 31 Oct 1984

Commencement provisions: s 23(2)

31 Jan 1985 (s 23(2))

Friendly Societies Act 1984 (c 62)

RA: 20 Dec 1984

20 Dec 1984 (RA)

Health and Social Security Act 1984 (c 48)

RA: 26 Jul 1984

Commencement provisions: s 27; Health and Social Security Act 1984 (Commencement No 1) Order 1984, SI 1984/1302; Health and Social Security Act 1984 (Commencement No 1) Amendment Order 1984, SI 1984/1467; Health and Social Security Act 1984 (Commencement No 2) Order 1986, SI 1986/974

Section			
1	(1), (2)		Repealed
	(3)		1 Jul 1986 (SI 1986/974)
	(4)		1 Apr 1985 (SI 1984/1302)
	(5)	(a)	1 Jul 1986 (SI 1986/974)
		(b)	1 Apr 1985 (SI 1984/1302)
	(6), (7)		1 Jul 1986 (SI 1986/974)
2–4			Repealed
5	(1)		Repealed
	(2)		1 Apr 1985 (SI 1984/1302)
	(3)		Repealed
	(4)		See Sch 3 below
	(5), (6)		Repealed
	(7), (8)		26 Sep 1984 (SI 1984/1302)
6	(1)		Repealed
	(2)		1 Apr 1985 (SI 1984/1302)
	(3)		26 Sep 1984 (SI 1984/1302)
	(4)		26 Jul 1984 (s 27(2))
7	(1)–(3)		*Not in force*
	(4)		26 Jul 1984 (s 27(2))
8			Repealed
9, 10			26 Jul 1984 (s 27(2))
11–14			Repealed
15			26 Jul 1984 (s 27(2))
16–20			Repealed
21			See Sch 7 below
22			Repealed
23			26 Jul 1984 (s 27(2))
24			See Sch 8 below
25–29			26 Jul 1984 (s 27(2))
Schedule			
1			1 Jul 1986 (SI 1986/974)
2			Repealed
3, para	1		26 Sep 1984 (SI 1984/1302)
	2		Repealed
	3–6		1 Apr 1985 (SI 1984/1302)
	7		Repealed
	8		1 Apr 1985 (SI 1984/1302)

Health and Social Security Act 1984 (c 48)—*contd*

Schedule

3, para	9–11	Repealed
	12	26 Sep 1984 (SI 1984/1302); prospectively repealed by National Health Service and Community Care Act 1990, s 66(2), Sch 10[1]
	13, 14	Repealed
	15	1 Apr 1985 (SI 1984/1302)
	16, 17	Repealed
4–6		Repealed
7, para	1–8	Repealed
	9	Spent
8		26 Sep 1984 (repeal in Social Security Pensions Act 1975, s 38(3)) (s 27(3))
		26 Sep 1984 (repeals of or in National Health Service Act 1977, ss 45(2), (3), 97(1)(a), (c), (2); National Health Service (Scotland) Act 1978, s 85(1); Health Services Act 1980, s 18, Sch 1, paras 30, 79, 88, 99; Social Security Act 1980, s 3(5)) (SI 1984/1302)
		1 Nov 1984 (repeal in Opticians Act 1958, s 13(3)) (spent) (SI 1984/1302)
		26 Nov 1984 (repeals of or in Social Security Act 1975, ss 12(1)(d), 41(2)(d), (3), Sch 4, Pt IV, para 3) (SI 1984/1302)
		28 Nov 1984 (repeal of Child Benefit Act 1975, Sch 4, para 25) (SI 1984/1302)
		29 Nov 1984 (repeals of or in Social Security Act 1975, s 57(2), Sch 4, Pt IV, para 1(a), (c); Social Security (Miscellaneous Provisions) Act 1977, s 22(2); Social Security and Housing Benefits Act 1982, Sch 4, para 18(4)) (SI 1984/1302)
		1 Apr 1985 (repeals of or in Tribunals and Inquiries Act 1971, Sch 1 (repealed); National Health Service Act 1977, ss 12(b), 15(1), (2), 39(c), 98(2), Sch 5, paras 9(1)–(3), 10; National Health Service (Scotland) Act 1978, s 26(2)(c); Health Services Act 1980, ss 1(6), 2, Sch 1, paras 35, 37, 56, 57, 69, 77(b), 82(2), (3), 87, 89–98) (SI 1984/1302)

Health and Social Security Act 1984 (c 48)—*contd*
Schedule
8—*contd*   6 Apr 1985 (repeal in Social Security
                                                  Pensions Act 1975, s 4(1))
                                                  (SI 1984/1302)
                                                  1 Jul 1986 (repeals of or in National
                                                  Health Service Act 1977, ss 44, 46,
                                                  72, 81–83, Sch 5, paras 1, 2,
                                                  6(3)(e), (5)(iv), Sch 12; National
                                                  Health Service (Scotland) Act 1978,
                                                  ss 26 (except sub-s (2)(c)), 29, 64,
                                                  73–75, Schs 8, 11; Health Services
                                                  Act 1980, Sch 5) (SI 1986/974)
                                                  Not in force (otherwise)

1   Orders made under National Health Service and Community Care Act 1990 bringing the
    prospective repeal into force will be noted to that Act

Housing and Building Control Act 1984 (c 29)

RA: 26 Jun 1984

Commencement provisions: s 66(3) (repealed)

Whole Act repealed, except ss 60(1), (2)(a), (c), 62(1), 64(1), (4), which came into
force on 26 Aug 1984 (s 66(3))

Housing Defects Act 1984 (c 50)

Whole Act repealed

Inheritance Tax Act 1984 (c 51)

See entry for Capital Transfer Tax Act 1984 ante

Inshore Fishing (Scotland) Act 1984 (c 26)

RA: 26 Jun 1984

Commencement provisions: s 11(2); Inshore Fishing (Scotland) Act 1984 (Commencement)
    Order 1985, SI 1985/961

26 Jul 1985 (SI 1985/961)

Juries (Disqualification) Act 1984 (c 34)

RA: 12 Jul 1984

Commencement provisions: s 2(3); Juries (Disqualification) Act 1984 (Commencement)
    Order 1984, SI 1984/1599

1 Dec 1984 (SI 1984/1599)

Law Reform (Husband and Wife) (Scotland) Act 1984 (c 15)

RA: 24 May 1984

Commencement provisions: s 10(2)

24 Jul 1984 (s 10(2))

Local Government (Interim Provisions) Act 1984 (c 53)

RA: 31 Jul 1984

Commencement provisions: s 1(1) (repealed); Local Government (Interim Provisions) Act 1984 (Appointed Day) Order 1985, SI 1985/2 (appointed 1 Feb 1985 for the coming into force of Pt II (ss 2, 3 (now repealed)) of this Act)

Whole Act repealed, except ss 4, 6(3), 10, 11 and 13, which came into force on 31 Jul 1984 (RA)

London Regional Transport Act 1984 (c 32)

RA: 26 Jun 1984

Commencement provisions: s 72(2)–(6); London Regional Transport (Appointed Day) Order 1984, SI 1984/877

Whole Act prospectively repealed by Greater London Authority Act 1999, s 423, Sch 34, Pt II[1]

Section	
1–6	29 Jun 1984 (SI 1984/877)
7	29 Jun 1984 (SI 1984/877); repealed (3 Jul 2000) by London Regional Transport (Transitional Modifications) Order 2000, SI 2000/1504, art 3(2), Schedule[2]
8–12	29 Jun 1984 (SI 1984/877)
13, 14	Repealed by Local Government Finance Act 1988, s 149, Sch 13, Pt III, in accordance with s 127 of that Act (qv) and subject to any regulations made under that section
15–28	29 Jun 1984 (SI 1984/877)
29	29 Jun 1984 (SI 1984/877); repealed (3 Jul 2000) by London Regional Transport (Transitional Modifications) Order 2000, SI 2000/1504, art 3(2), Schedule[2]
30, 31	29 Jun 1984 (SI 1984/877)
31A	Inserted by Railways Act 1993, s 152(1), Sch 12, para 17 (qv)
31B	Inserted by London Regional Transport Act 1996, s 3 (qv)
32–34	29 Jun 1984 (SI 1984/877)

London Regional Transport Act 1984 (c 32)—*contd*

Section

35		29 Jun 1984 (SI 1984/877); repealed (3 Jul 2000) by London Regional Transport (Transitional Modifications) Order 2000, SI 2000/1504, art 3(2), Schedule[2]
36–41		Repealed
41A		Inserted by Greater London Authority Act 1999, s 200(3) (qv)
42	(1), (2)	29 Jun 1984 (SI 1984/877)
	(3)–(5)	Repealed
	(6)	29 Jun 1984 (SI 1984/877)
43–45		Repealed
46–49		29 Jun 1984 (SI 1984/877)
50–53		29 Jun 1984 (SI 1984/877); repealed, in relation to any accounting year beginning after 31 Mar 2001, by London Regional Transport (Transitional Modifications) Order 2000, SI 2000/1504, art 3(2), Schedule[2]
54–58		Repealed
59		29 Jun 1984 (SI 1984/877); repealed (3 Jul 2000) by London Regional Transport (Transitional Modifications) Order 2000, SI 2000/1504, art 3(2), Schedule[2]
60		26 Jun 1984 (s 72(3))
61–63		29 Jun 1984 (SI 1984/877)
64	(1)–(6)	Repealed
	(7)	29 Jun 1984 (SI 1984/877)
	(7A)	Inserted by Greater London Authority Act 1999, s 418(3) (qv)
	(8)	Repealed
65–67		29 Jun 1984 (SI 1984/877)
68, 69		26 Jun 1984 (s 72(3))
70		29 Jun 1984 (SI 1984/877)
71	(1)	29 Jun 1984 (SI 1984/877)
	(2)	See Sch 5 below
	(3)	See Schs 6, 7 below
	(4)–(7)	29 Jun 1984 (SI 1984/877)
72		26 Jun 1984 (s 72(3))

Schedule

1, 2		29 Jun 1984 (SI 1984/877)
3		26 Jun 1984 (s 72(4)); repealed (3 Jul 2000) by London Regional Transport (Transitional Modifications) Order 2000, SI 2000/1504, art 3(2), Schedule[2]
4		29 Jun 1984 (SI 1984/877)

London Regional Transport Act 1984 (c 32)—*contd*

Schedule

5, para	1–6			29 Jun 1984 (SI 1984/877)
	7			26 Jun 1984 (s 72(3))
	8	(1)–(5)		26 Jun 1984 (s 72(3))
		(6)–(8)		29 Jun 1984 (SI 1984/877)
		(9)		26 Jun 1984 (s 72(3))
		(10)	(a)	26 Jun 1984 (s 72(3))
			(b)	29 Jun 1984 (SI 1984/877)
	9–19			29 Jun 1984 (SI 1984/877)
6				29 Jun 1984 (SI 1984/877)
7				29 Jun 1984 (repeals of or in London Government Act 1963, Sch 2; Local Government, Planning and Land Act 1980, Sch 13, para 9) (SI 1984/877) 1 Apr 1985 (otherwise) (s 72(6))

[1] Orders made under Greater London Authority Act 1999, s 425, bringing the prospective amendments into force will be noted to that Act

[2] The amendments made by London Regional Transport (Transitional Modifications) Order 2000, SI 2000/1504, are in force for a transitional period only, beginning with 3 July 2000 and ending with the day on which London Regional Transport ceases to provide or secure the provision of public passenger transport services

---

Lotteries (Amendment) Act 1984 (c 9)

RA: 12 Apr 1984

Commencement provisions: s 2(2)

12 Jun 1984 (s 2(2))

Matrimonial and Family Proceedings Act 1984 (c 42)

RA: 12 Jul 1984

Commencement provisions: s 47; Matrimonial and Family Proceedings Act 1984 (Commencement No 1) Order 1984, SI 1984/1589; Matrimonial and Family Proceedings Act 1984 (Commencement No 2) Order 1985, SI 1985/1316; Matrimonial and Family Proceedings Act 1984 (Commencement No 3) Order 1986, SI 1986/635; Matrimonial and Family Proceedings Act 1984 (Commencement No 4) Order 1986, SI 1986/1049; Matrimonial and Family Proceedings Act 1984 (Commencement No 3) (Scotland) Order 1986, SI 1986/1226; Matrimonial and Family Proceedings Act 1984 (Commencement No 5) Order 1991, SI 1991/1211

Section

1	12 Oct 1984 (s 47(1)); prospectively repealed by Family Law Act 1996, s 66(3), Sch 10[1]
2–9	12 Oct 1984 (s 47(1))
10	1 Oct 1986 (SI 1986/1049)
11	12 Oct 1984 (s 47(1))

Matrimonial and Family Proceedings Act 1984 (c 42)—*contd*

Section

12–20			16 Sep 1985 (SI 1985/1316)
21			16 Sep 1985 (SI 1985/1316); renumbered sub-s (1) and sub-ss (2)–(5) added by Welfare Reform and Pensions Act 1999, s 22(4), (5) (qv)
22			Substituted (subject to a transitional provision) by Family Law Act 1996, s 66(1), Sch 8, Pt III, para 52 (qv)
23–25			16 Sep 1985 (SI 1985/1316)
26			Repealed
27			16 Sep 1985 (SI 1985/1316)
28, 29			1 Sep 1986 (SI 1986/1226)
29A			Inserted (S) by Family Law (Scotland) Act 1985, Sch 1, para 12 (qv)
30, 31			1 Sep 1986 (SI 1986/1226)
32–39			28 Apr 1986 (SI 1986/635)
40, 41			14 Oct 1991 (SI 1991/1211)
42, 43			28 Apr 1986 (SI 1986/635)
44			12 Oct 1984 (SI 1984/1589)
45			Repealed
46			See Schs 1–3 below
47, 48			12 Jul 1984 (s 47(1))

Schedule

1, para	1	(a)	16 Sep 1985 (SI 1985/1316)
		(b)	1 Sep 1986 (SI 1986/1226)
	2		12 Oct 1984 (SI 1984/1589)
	3		28 Apr 1986 (SI 1986/635)
	4		12 Oct 1984 (SI 1984/1589)
	5		16 Sep 1985 (SI 1985/1316)
	6, 7		1 Sep 1986 (SI 1986/1226)
	8		16 Sep 1985 (SI 1985/1316)
	9		Repealed
	10		12 Oct 1984 (SI 1984/1589); prospectively repealed by Family Law Act 1996, s 66(3), Sch 10[1]
	11–13		12 Oct 1984 (SI 1984/1589)
	14		Repealed
	15		16 Sep 1985 (SI 1985/1316)
	16, 17		28 Apr 1986 (SI 1986/635)
	18, 19		Repealed
	20	(a)	*Not in force*
		(b)	28 Apr 1986 (SI 1986/635)
	21		1 Oct 1986 (SI 1986/1049)
	22		12 Oct 1984 (SI 1984/1589)
	23		Repealed
	24–26		1 Oct 1986 (SI 1986/1049)
	27		12 Oct 1984 (SI 1984/1589)

Matrimonial and Family Proceedings Act 1984 (c 42)—*contd*

Schedule

1, para	28	1 Sep 1986 (SI 1986/1226)
	29	Repealed
	30	28 Apr 1986 (SI 1986/635)
	31	Repealed
2, para	1, 2	12 Oct 1984 (s 47(1))
	3	*Not in force*
3		12 Oct 1984 (repeal of Matrimonial Causes Act 1973, ss 43(9), 44(6)) (SI 1984/1589)
		28 Apr 1986 (repeals of or in Matrimonial Causes Act 1967; Guardianship of Minors Act 1971; Courts Act 1971; Matrimonial Causes Act 1973, s 45, Sch 2; Domicile and Matrimonial Proceedings Act 1973; Children Act 1975; Adoption Act 1976; Domestic Proceedings and Magistrates' Courts Act 1978; Matrimonial Homes and Property Act 1981; Matrimonial Homes Act 1983; County Courts Act 1984) (SI 1986/635)
		14 Oct 1991 (otherwise) (SI 1991/1211)

[1]   Orders made under Family Law Act 1996, s 67(3), bringing the prospective repeals into force will be noted to that Act

---

Mental Health (Scotland) Act 1984 (c 36)

RA: 12 Jul 1984

Commencement provisions: s 130

30 Sep 1984 (s 130)

Merchant Shipping Act 1984 (c 5)

Whole Act repealed: s 13 was repealed with savings by Merchant Shipping (Registration, etc) Act 1993, s 8(4), Sch 5, Pt II, as from 1 May 1994, but instruments made under that section and in force on that date remained in force until superseded by an instrument made under Sch 4, para 4 to the 1993 Act (Merchant Shipping (Registration, etc) Act 1993 (Commencement No 1 and Transitional Provisions) Order 1993, SI 1993/3137, art 7(1), Sch 3). Sch 4, para 4 to the 1993 Act was repealed by Merchant Shipping Act 1995, s 314(1), Sch 12, and by virtue of Interpretation Act 1978, s 17(2)(b), such instruments remain in force until superseded by an instrument made under s 315 of the 1995 Act

Occupiers' Liability Act 1984 (c 3)

RA: 13 Mar 1984

Commencement provisions: s 4(2)

13 May 1984 (s 4(2))

Ordnance Factories and Military Services Act 1984 (c 59)

RA: 31 Oct 1984

31 Oct 1984 (RA)

Parliamentary Pensions etc Act 1984 (c 52)

RA: 31 Jul 1984

Commencement provisions: ss 1(5), 2(8), 4(5), 5(6) (repealed)
Section
1–11	Repealed[1]
12	31 Jul 1984 (RA)
13	Repealed
14, 15	31 Jul 1984 (RA)[1]
16	Repealed[1]
17	31 Jul 1984 (RA)
Schedule	Repealed[1]

[1]   Ss 1–11, 15(2)(a), 16 and the Schedule repealed by Parliamentary and other Pensions Act 1987,
s 6(2), Sch 4 (qv), but by s 2(a) of, and Sch 2 to, that Act, ss 3(4)–(6), 4(3)–(6), 5(1), (2) and 6 of
this Act continued to have effect as if contained in regulations made under and in accordance with
s 2 of the 1987 Act. The Parliamentary Pensions (Consolidation and Amendment) Regulations 1993,
SI 1993/3253 (made under s 2 of the 1987 Act, and in force from 21 Jan 1994), revoked and
replaced (with savings), ss 3(4)–(6), 4(3)–(6), 5(1), (2) and 6 of this Act

---

Pensions Commutation Act 1984 (c 7)

RA: 13 Mar 1984

Commencement provisions: s 3(2); Pensions Commutation Act 1984 (Commencement)
     Order 1984, SI 1984/1140

20 Aug 1984 (SI 1984/1140)

Police and Criminal Evidence Act 1984 (c 60)

RA: 31 Oct 1984

Commencement provisions: s 121; Police and Criminal Evidence Act 1984
     (Commencement No 1) Order 1984, SI 1984/2002; Police and Criminal
     Evidence Act 1984 (Commencement No 2) Order 1984, SI 1985/623; Police
     and Criminal Evidence Act 1984 (Commencement No 3) Order 1985/1934;
     Police and Criminal Evidence Act 1984 (Commencement No 4) Order 1991,
     SI 1991/2686; Police and Criminal Evidence Act 1984 (Commencement No 5)
     Order 1992, SI 1992/2802

Police and Criminal Evidence Act 1984 (c 60)—*contd*

Section

1			1 Jan 1985 (so far as relates to search for stolen articles in localities in which, on 31 Dec 1984, an enactment (other than one contained in a public general Act or one relating to statutory undertakers) applies conferring power on a constable to search for stolen or unlawfully obtained goods) (SI 1984/2002)
			1 Jan 1986 (otherwise) (SI 1985/1934)
2–6			1 Jan 1986 (SI 1985/1934)
7	(1)		1 Jan 1986 (SI 1985/1934)
	(2)	(a)	1 Jan 1986 (SI 1985/1934)
		(b)	1 Jan 1985 (SI 1984/2002)
	(3)		1 Jan 1985 (SI 1984/2002)
8–22			1 Jan 1986 (SI 1985/1934)
23			1 Jan 1985 (SI 1984/2002)
24–32			1 Jan 1986 (SI 1985/1934)
33			Repealed
34–36			1 Jan 1986 (SI 1985/1934)
37	(1)–(10)		1 Jan 1986 (SI 1985/1934)
	(11)–(14)		Repealed
	(15)		1 Jan 1986 (SI 1985/1934)
38–40			1 Jan 1986 (SI 1985/1934)
40A			Prospectively inserted by Criminal Justice and Police Act 2001, s 73(1), (2)[2]
41–45			1 Jan 1986 (SI 1985/1934)
45A			Prospectively inserted by Criminal Justice and Police Act 2001, s 73(1), (3)[2]
46			1 Jan 1986 (SI 1985/1934)
46A			Inserted by Criminal Justice and Public Order Act 1994, s 29(1), (2), (5) (qv)
47	(1)		1 Jan 1986 (SI 1985/1934)
	(1A)		Inserted by Criminal Justice and Public Order Act 1994, s 27(1)(b) (qv)
	(2)–(4)		1 Jan 1986 (SI 1985/1934)
	(5)		Repealed
	(6)–(8)		1 Jan 1986 (SI 1985/1934)
47A			Inserted by Crime and Disorder Act 1998, s 119, Sch 8, para 62 (qv)
48–51			1 Jan 1986 (SI 1985/1934)
52			Repealed
53, 54			1 Jan 1986 (SI 1985/1934)
54A			Inserted by Anti-terrorism, Crime and Security Act 2001, s 90(1) (qv)

Police and Criminal Evidence Act 1984 (c 60)—*contd*
Section

55–58			1 Jan 1986 (SI 1985/1934)
59			Repealed
60	(1)	(a)	1 Jan 1986 (SI 1985/1934)
		(b)	29 Nov 1991 (in the following police areas: Avon and Somerset, Bedfordshire, Cambridgeshire, Cheshire, City of London, Cleveland, Cumbria, Derbyshire, Devon and Cornwall, Dorset, Durham, Dyfed-Powys, Essex, Gloucestershire, Greater Manchester, Gwent, Hampshire, Hertfordshire, Humberside, Kent, Lancashire, Leicestershire, Lincolnshire, Merseyside, Metropolitan Police District, Norfolk, Northamptonshire, Northumbria, North Wales, North Yorkshire, Nottinghamshire, South Wales, South Yorkshire, Staffordshire, Suffolk, Surrey, Sussex, Warwickshire, West Mercia, West Midlands, West Yorkshire, Wiltshire) (SI 1991/2686) 9 Nov 1992 (in the Thames Valley police area) (SI 1992/2802)
	(2)		29 Nov 1991 (SI 1991/2686)
60A			Inserted by Criminal Justice and Police Act 2001, s 76(1) (qv)
61	(1)–(3)		1 Jan 1986 (SI 1985/1934)
	(3A)		Prospectively inserted by Criminal Justice and Police Act 2001, s 78(3)[2]
	(4)		1 Jan 1986 (SI 1985/1934)
	(4A), (4B)		Prospectively inserted by Criminal Justice and Police Act 2001, s 78(4)[2]
	(5)–(7)		1 Jan 1986 (SI 1985/1934)
	(7A)		Inserted by Criminal Justice and Public Order Act 1994, s 168(2), Sch 10, para 56(a) (qv)
	(8)		1 Jan 1986 (SI 1985/1934)
	(8A)		Prospectively inserted by Criminal Justice and Police Act 2001, s 78(7)[2]
	(9)		1 Jan 1986 (SI 1985/1934)
62	(1)		1 Jan 1986 (SI 1985/1934)
	(1A)		Inserted by Criminal Justice and Public Order Act 1994, s 54(1), (2) (qv)
	(2)–(7)		1 Jan 1986 (SI 1985/1934)

Police and Criminal Evidence Act 1984 (c 60)—*contd*

Section

62	(7A)	Inserted by Criminal Justice and Public Order Act 1994, s 168(2), Sch 10, para 57(a) (qv)
	(8)–(11)	1 Jan 1986 (SI 1985/1934)
	(12)	Substituted by Terrorism Act 2000, s 125, Sch 15, para 5(8) (qv)
63	(1)–(3)	1 Jan 1986 (SI 1985/1934)
	(3A), (3B)	Inserted by Criminal Justice and Public Order Act 1994, s 55(1), (2) (qv)
	(3C)	Inserted by Criminal Evidence (Amendment) Act 1997, s 2(2) (qv), with effect for the purposes referred to in s 2(3), (4) of that Act
	(4)–(5)	1 Jan 1986 (SI 1985/1934)
	(5A)	Prospectively inserted by Criminal Justice and Police Act 2001, s 80(3)[2]
	(6)–(8)	1 Jan 1986 (SI 1985/1934)
	(8A)	Inserted by Criminal Justice and Public Order Act 1994, s 55(1), (4) (qv)
	(8B)	Inserted by Criminal Justice and Public Order Act 1994, s 168(2), Sch 10, para 59(a) (qv)
	(9)	1 Jan 1986 (SI 1985/1934)
	(9A)	See note to first sub-s (10) below A second sub-s (9A) is prospectively inserted by Criminal Justice and Police Act 2001, s 80(4)[2]
	(10)	Substituted by Terrorism Act 2000, s 125, Sch 15, para 5(9) (qv)
	(10)	Substituted by Terrorism Act 2000, s 125, Sch 15, para 5(9) (qv)
63A		Inserted by Criminal Justice and Public Order Act 1994, s 56 (qv)
63B, 63C		Prospectively inserted by Criminal Justice and Court Services Act 2000, s 57(1), (2)[2]
64	(1A), (1B)	Substituted for original sub-ss (1), (2) by Criminal Justice and Police Act 2001, s 82(1), (2) (qv)
	(3)	1 Jan 1986 (SI 1985/1934)
	(3AA)–(3AD)	Substituted for original sub-ss (3A), (3B) by Criminal Justice and Police Act 2001, s 82(1), (4) (qv)
	(4)	Repealed
	(5)	Substituted by Criminal Justice Act 1988, s 148 (qv)
	(6)	1 Jan 1986 (SI 1985/1934)

Police and Criminal Evidence Act 1984 (c 60)—*contd*
Section

64	(6A), (6B)	Inserted by Criminal Justice Act 1988, s 148 (qv)
	(7)	1 Jan 1986 (SI 1985/1934)
64A		Inserted by Anti-terrorism, Crime and Security Act 2001, s 92 (qv)
65		1 Jan 1986 (SI 1985/1934)
66, 67		1 Jan 1985 (SI 1984/2002)
68–70		Repealed
71–80		1 Jan 1986 (SI 1985/1934)
80A		Prospectively inserted by Youth Justice and Criminal Evidence Act 1999, s 67, Sch 4, para 14[1]
81, 82		1 Jan 1986 (SI 1985/1934)
83–106		Repealed
107		1 Jan 1986 (SI 1985/1934)
108	(1)	1 Mar 1985 (SI 1984/2002)
	(2), (3)	Repealed
	(4)–(6)	1 Mar 1985 (SI 1984/2002)
109		Repealed
110, 111		1 Mar 1985 (SI 1984/2002)
112		Repealed
113	(1), (2)	1 Jan 1986 (SI 1985/1934)
	(3)–(13)	1 Jan 1985 (SI 1984/2002)
114		1 Jan 1986 (SI 1985/1934)
114A		Inserted by Criminal Justice and Police Act 2001, s 85 (qv)
115		1 Jan 1985 (SI 1984/2002)
116		29 Apr 1985 (SI 1985/623)
117		1 Jan 1986 (SI 1985/1934)
118		1 Jan 1985 (SI 1984/2002)
119		See Schs 6, 7 below
120–122		31 Oct 1984 (RA)
Schedule		
1, 2		1 Jan 1986 (SI 1985/1934)
3, 4		Repealed
5		29 Apr 1985 (SI 1985/623)
6, para	1–12	1 Jan 1986 (SI 1985/1934)
	13–16	Repealed
	17–21	1 Jan 1986 (SI 1985/1934)
	22, 23	Repealed
	24–26	1 Jan 1986 (SI 1985/1934)
	27	Repealed
	28, 29	1 Jan 1986 (SI 1985/1934)
	30–33	1 Mar 1985 (SI 1984/2002)
	34	Repealed
	35	29 Apr 1985 (SI 1985/623)
	36	Repealed
	37–40	1 Jan 1986 (SI 1985/1934)
	41	Repealed

Police and Criminal Evidence Act 1984 (c 60)—*contd*

Schedule

7   1 Mar 1985 (repeals in Police (Scotland)
                                     Act 1967) (SI 1984/2002, as
                                     amended by SI 1985/623)
                                     29 Apr 1985 (repeals of or in Police
                                     Act 1964; Superannuation Act 1972;
                                     House of Commons
                                     Disqualification Act 1975;
                                     Northern Ireland Assembly
                                     Disqualification Act 1975;
                                     Police Act 1976) (SI 1985/623)
                                     1 Jan 1986 (otherwise) (SI 1985/1934)

[1]   Orders made under Youth Justice and Criminal Evidence Act 1999, s 68(3), bringing the prospective insertion and repeals into force will be noted to that Act

[2]   Orders made under Criminal Justice and Court Services Act 2000, s 80, bringing the prospective insertions into force will be noted to that Act

---

Prescription and Limitation (Scotland) Act 1984 (c 45)

RA: 26 Jul 1984

Commencement provisions: s 7(2)

26 Sep 1984 (s 7(2))

Prevention of Terrorism (Temporary Provisions) Act 1984 (c 8)

Whole Act repealed

Public Health (Control of Disease) Act 1984 (c 22)

RA: 26 Jun 1984

Commencement provisions: s 79(2)

26 Sep 1984 (s 79(2))

Rates Act 1984 (c 33)

RA: 26 Jun 1984

Commencement provisions: s 18
Section

1–8   26 Jun 1984 (RA) (but maximum rate
                                     or precept may only be prescribed
                                     from financial year 1 Apr 1985
                                     onwards (s 18(1)))

9   26 Jun 1984 (RA)
10, 11   *Not in force*
12   26 Jun 1984 (RA)
13   Repealed

Rates Act 1984 (c 33)—*contd*

Section

14		26 Jun 1984 (RA)
15		Repealed, with savings, by Local Government Finance (Repeals, Savings and Consequential Amendments) Order 1990, SI 1990/776, art 3, Sch 1
16	(1)	See Sch 1 below
	(2)	See Sch 2 below
	(3)	26 Jun 1984 (RA)
17–19		26 Jun 1984 (RA)

Schedule

1, para	1	26 Jun 1984 (RA)
	2–22	Repealed, with savings, by Local Government Finance (Repeals, Savings and Consequential Amendments) Order 1990, SI 1990/776, art 3, Sch 1
	23	Effective for any financial year from 1 Apr 1983 (para 23(2))
	24	Effective for any financial year from 1 Apr 1984 (para 24(2))
2		Repealed, with savings, by Local Government Finance (Repeals, Savings and Consequential Amendments) Order 1990, SI 1990/776, art 3, Sch 1

Rating and Valuation (Amendment) (Scotland) Act 1984 (c 31)

RA: 26 Jun 1984

Commencement provisions: s 23(1)

Section

1–4		Repealed
5		26 Aug 1984 (s 23(1)(c))
6–8		Repealed
9–13		1 Apr 1985 (s 23(1)(b))
14		26 Aug 1984 (s 23(1)(c))
15		Repealed
16		26 Aug 1984 (s 23(1)(c))
17–19		1 Apr 1985 (s 23(1)(b))
20		26 Aug 1984 (s 23(1)(c))
21	(1)	See Sch 2 below
	(2)	Repealed
22		26 Aug 1984 (s 23(1)(c))
23		26 Jun 1984 (s 23(1)(a))

Schedule

1		Repealed
2, para	1	26 Aug 1984 (s 23(1)(c))

Rating and Valuation (Amendment) (Scotland) Act 1984 (c 31)—*contd*

Schedule

2, para	2–5	Repealed
	6	26 Aug 1984 (s 23(1)(c))
	7, 8	Repealed
	9	1 Apr 1985 (s 23(1)(b))
	10	Repealed
	11	26 Aug 1984 (s 23(1)(c))
	12	Repealed
	13–15	1 Apr 1985 (s 23(1)(b))
	16	Repealed
	17	1 Apr 1985 (s 23(1)(b))
	18	Repealed
3		Repealed

Registered Homes Act 1984 (c 23)

RA: 26 Jun 1984

Commencement provisions: s 59(2); Registered Homes Act 1984 (Commencement) Order 1984, SI 1984/1348

1 Jan 1985 (except s 1 so far as relates to an establishment which is a school referred to in s 1(5)(f), for which the date is 1 Jan 1986) (SI 1984/1348)

Whole Act prospectively repealed by Care Standards Act 2000, s 117(2), Sch 6; orders made under the 2000 Act, s 122, bringing the prospective repeal into force will be noted to that Act in the service to this work

---

Rent (Scotland) Act 1984 (c 58)

RA: 31 Oct 1984

Commencement provisions: s 118(2)

31 Jan 1985 (s 118(2))

Repatriation of Prisoners Act 1984 (c 47)

RA: 26 Jul 1984

Commencement provisions: s 9(2); Repatriation of Prisoners (Commencement) Order 1985, SI 1985/550

15 Apr 1985 (SI 1985/550)

Restrictive Trade Practices (Stock Exchange) Act 1984 (c 2)

Whole Act repealed

Road Traffic (Driving Instruction) Act 1984 (c 13)

Whole Act repealed

Road Traffic Regulation Act 1984 (c 27)

RA: 26 Jun 1984

Commencement provisions: s 145(1), (2); Road Traffic Regulation Act 1984 (Commencement No 1) Order 1986, SI 1986/1147

Section		
1–11		26 Sep 1984 (s 145(1))
12, 13		Repealed
13A		Inserted by Road Traffic Act 1991, s 81, Sch 7, para 4 (qv)
14, 15		Substituted by Road Traffic (Temporary Restrictions) Act 1991, s 1(1), Sch 1 (qv)
16	(1)	26 Sep 1984 (s 145(1))
	(2), (2A)	Substituted for original sub-s (2) by Road Traffic (Temporary Restrictions) Act 1991, s 1(2) (qv)
	(3), (4)	Repealed
16A–16C		Inserted by Road Traffic Regulation (Special Events) Act 1994, s 1(1) (qv)
17	(1)	Substituted by New Roads and Street Works Act 1991, s 168(1), Sch 8, Pt II, para 28(1), (2) (qv)
	(2)–(4)	26 Sep 1984 (s 145(1))
	(5)	Substituted by New Roads and Street Works Act 1991, s 168(1), Sch 8, Pt II, para 28(1), (4) (qv)
	(6)	26 Sep 1984 (s 145(1))
17A		Inserted by New Roads and Street Works Act 1991, s 168(1), Sch 8, Pt II, para 29 (qv)
18–22		26 Sep 1984 (s 145(1))
22A		Inserted by Countryside and Rights of Way Act 2000, s 66(4) (qv)
23–26		26 Sep 1984 (s 145(1))
27		Repealed
28		26 Sep 1984 (s 145(1))
29		Substituted for original ss 29, 30 by New Roads and Street Works Act 1991, s 168(1), Sch 8, Pt II, para 37 (qv)
30		See note to s 29 above
31–35		26 Sep 1984 (s 145(1))
35A, 35B		Inserted by Parking Act 1989, ss 2, 3 (qv)
35C		Inserted by Road Traffic Act 1991, s 41 (qv)
36–46		26 Sep 1984 (s 145(1))
46A		Inserted by Road Traffic Act 1991, s 42 (qv)

Road Traffic Regulation Act 1984 (c 27)—*contd*

Section

47–49	26 Sep 1984 (s 145(1))
50	Repealed
51	Substituted by Road Traffic Regulation (Parking) Act 1986, s 2(1) (qv)
52, 53	26 Sep 1984 (s 145(1))
54	Repealed
55–63	26 Sep 1984 (s 145(1))
63A	Inserted by Road Traffic Act 1991, s 44(1) (qv)
64–74	26 Sep 1984 (s 145(1))
74A	Inserted by Greater London Authority Act 1999, s 276 (qv)
74B	Inserted by Greater London Authority Act 1999, s 277 (qv)
74C	Inserted by Greater London Authority Act 1999, s 278 (qv)
75	26 Sep 1984 (s 145(1))
76	Repealed
77	26 Sep 1984 (s 145(1))
78	Repealed
79–89	26 Sep 1984 (s 145(1))
90, 91	Repealed
92, 93	26 Sep 1984 (s 145(1))
94	Substituted by Local Government Act 1985, s 8, Sch 5, para 4 (qv)
95–97	26 Sep 1984 (s 145(1))
98	Repealed
99–106	26 Sep 1984 (s 145(1))
106A	Inserted by Road Traffic Act 1991, s 75 (qv)
107–112	26 Sep 1984 (s 145(1))
113, 114	Repealed
115–117	26 Sep 1984 (s 145(1))
118	Repealed
119	26 Sep 1984 (s 145(1))
120, 121	Repealed
121A	Inserted by New Roads and Street Works Act 1991, s 168(1), Sch 8, Pt II, para 70 (qv)
121B	Inserted by Greater London Authority Act 1999, s 291 (qv)
121C	Inserted by Greater London Authority Act 1999, s 292(2) (qv)
122	26 Sep 1984 (s 145(1))
122A	Inserted by New Roads and Street Works Act 1991, ss 24 (E, W), 44 (S) (qv)
123	Repealed

Road Traffic Regulation Act 1984 (c 27)—*contd*
Section

124	26 Sep 1984 (s 145(1))
124A	Inserted by Greater London Authority Act 1999, s 272 (qv)
124B, 124C	Inserted (1 Oct 2000) by Road Traffic Regulation Act 1984 (GLA Side Roads Amendment) Order 2000, SI 2000/2237, art 2(4), Schedule
125–132	26 Sep 1984 (s 145(1))
132AA	Inserted by Greater London Authority Act 1999, s 293 (qv)
132A	Inserted (S) by Roads (Scotland) Act 1984, s 127 (repealed)
133–140	26 Sep 1984 (s 145(1))
141	Repealed
141A	Inserted by Road Traffic Act 1991, s 46(1) (qv)
142–147	26 Sep 1984 (s 145(1))

Schedule

1, 2		26 Sep 1984 (s 145(1))
3		Repealed
4–6		26 Sep 1984 (s 145(1))
7		Repealed
8, para	1, 2	26 Sep 1984 (s 145(1))
	3	*Not in force*
	4–6	26 Sep 1984 (s 145(1))
9–11		26 Sep 1984 (s 145(1))
12		Repealed
13, 14		26 Sep 1984 (s 145(1))

Roads (Scotland) Act 1984 (c 54)

RA: 31 Oct 1984

Commencement provisions: s 157(2), (3); Roads (Scotland) Act 1984 (Commencement No 1) Order 1985, SI 1985/1953; Roads (Scotland) Act 1984 (Commencement No 2) Order 1989, SI 1989/1094; Roads (Scotland) Act 1984 (Commencement No 3) Order 1990, SI 1990/2622

Section

1–12	1 Jan 1985 (s 157(2))
12A–12F	Inserted by Local Government etc (Scotland) Act 1994, s 38(1), (2) (qv)
13–20	1 Jan 1985 (s 157(2))
20A	Inserted (15 Jul 1988) by Environmental Assessment (Scotland) Regulations 1988, SI 1988/1221, regs 69, 70; substituted (1 Aug 1999) for new

Roads (Scotland) Act 1984 (c 54)—*contd*

Section

20A—*contd*		ss 20A, 20B by Environmental Impact Assessment (Scotland) Regulations 1999, SSI 1999/1, reg 49, subject to a saving
20B		Inserted as noted to s 20A above
21–35		1 Jan 1985 (s 157(2))
36–39		1 Aug 1989 (so far as relates to areas of Tayside and Lothian Regional Councils) (SI 1989/1084)
		8 Jan 1991 (otherwise) (SI 1990/2622)
39A–39C		Inserted by Traffic Calming Act 1992, s 2(1), Sch 2 (qv)
40		1 Aug 1989 (so far as relates to areas of Tayside and Lothian Regional Councils) (SI 1989/1084)
		8 Jan 1991 (otherwise) (SI 1990/2622)
41–55		1 Jan 1985 (s 157(2))
55A		Inserted (15 Jul 1988) by Environmental Assessment (Scotland) Regulations 1988, SI 1988/1221, regs 69, 71; substituted (1 Aug 1999) for new ss 55A, 55B by Environmental Impact Assessment (Scotland) Regulations 1999, SSI 1999/1, reg 50, subject to a saving
55B		Inserted as noted to s 55A above
56–61		1 Jan 1985 (s 157(2))
61A		Inserted by New Roads and Street Works Act 1991, s 168(1), Sch 8, Pt III, para 88 (qv)
62–81		1 Jan 1985 (s 157(2))
81A		Inserted by Local Government etc (Scotland) Act 1994, s 39 (qv)
82–113		1 Jan 1985 (s 157(2))
113A		Inserted by Local Government etc (Scotland) Act 1994, s 147 (qv)
114–125		1 Jan 1985 (s 157(2))
126		1 Jan 1986 (SI 1985/1953)
127		Repealed
128–132		1 Jan 1985 (s 157(2))
133		Repealed
134–155		1 Jan 1985 (s 157(2))
156	(1), (2)	1 Jan 1985 (s 157(2))
	(3)	See Sch 11 below
157		31 Oct 1984 (RA)
Schedule		
1–6		1 Jan 1985 (s 157(2))
7		1 Jan 1986 (SI 1985/1953))

Roads (Scotland) Act 1984 (c 54)—*contd*
Schedule

8–10	1 Jan 1985 (s 157(2))
11	1 Jan 1985 (except repeal of Road Traffic Regulation Act 1984, Sch 10, paras 14–16) (s 157(2)) 1 Jan 1986 (exception noted above) (SI 1985/1953)

Somerset House Act 1984 (c 21)

Local application only

Telecommunications Act 1984 (c 12)

RA: 12 Apr 1984

Commencement provisions: ss 60(1), 69(2), 110(2)–(5); Telecommunications Act 1984 (Appointed Day) (No 1) Order 1984, SI 1984/749; Telecommunications Act 1984 (Appointed Day) (No 2) Order 1984, SI 1984/876; British Telecommunications (Dissolution) Order 1994, SI 1994/2162

Section

1	18 Jun 1984 (SI 1984/749)
2–7	5 Aug 1984 (SI 1984/876)
7A	Inserted (31 Dec 1997) by Telecommunications (Licensing) Regulations 1997, SI 1997/2930, reg 3(7)
8–12	5 Aug 1984 (SI 1984/876)
12A	Inserted by Electronic Communications Act 2000, s 11(4) (qv)
13–21	5 Aug 1984 (SI 1984/876)
22	5 Aug 1984 (SI 1984/876); repealed in relation to applicable terminal equipment by Telecommunications Terminal Equipment Regulations 1992, SI 1992/2423, reg 2(1), as from 6 Nov 1992
23–27	5 Aug 1984 (SI 1984/876)
27A, 27B	Inserted by Competition and Service (Utilities) Act 1992, s 1 (qv)
27C	Inserted by Competition and Service (Utilities) Act 1992, s 2 (qv)
27D	Inserted by Competition and Service (Utilities) Act 1992, s 3 (qv)
27E	Inserted by Competition and Service (Utilities) Act 1992, s 4 (qv)
27F	Inserted by Competition and Service (Utilities) Act 1992, s 5(1) (qv)

Telecommunications Act 1984 (c 12)—*contd*

Section

27G	Inserted (prospectively in the case of sub-s (8)) by Competition and Service (Utilities) Act 1992, s 6(1) (qv)[1]
27H	Inserted (prospectively in the case of sub-s (4)) by Competition and Service (Utilities) Act 1992, s 7 (qv)[1]
27I	Inserted by Competition and Service (Utilities) Act 1992, s 7 (qv)
27J	Inserted by Competition and Service (Utilities) Act 1992, s 8 (qv)
27K	Inserted by Competition and Service (Utilities) Act 1992, s 9 (qv)
27L	Inserted by Competition and Service (Utilities) Act 1992, s 10 (qv)
28–30	5 Aug 1984 (SI 1984/876)
31	Repealed, with savings, by Local Government Finance (Repeals, Savings and Consequential Amendments) Order 1990, SI 1990/776, art 3, Sch 1
32	5 Aug 1984 (SI 1984/876)
33	Repealed
34–42	5 Aug 1984 (SI 1984/876)
42A	Inserted by Telecommunications (Fraud) Act 1997, s 1 (qv)
43, 44	5 Aug 1984 (SI 1984/876)
45	Substituted by Interception of Communications Act 1985, s 11(1), Sch 2 (qv)
46	5 Aug 1984 (SI 1984/876)
46A	Inserted by Competition and Service (Utilities) Act 1992, s 49 (qv)
46B	Inserted (20 Dec 1999) by Telecommunications (Appeals) Regulations 1999, SI 1999/3180, reg 3(3)
47–55	5 Aug 1984 (SI 1984/876)
56–59	Repealed
60–73	6 Aug 1984 (SI 1984/876)
74	Repealed
75	16 Jul 1984 (SI 1984/876)
76	Repealed
77	16 Jul 1984 (SI 1984/876)
78	Repealed
79–83	16 Jul 1984 (SI 1984/876)

Telecommunications Act 1984 (c 12)—*contd*

Section

84		16 Jul 1984 (SI 1984/876); repealed in relation to applicable terminal equipment by Telecommunications Terminal Equipment Regulations 1992, SI 1992/2423, reg 2(1), as from 6 Nov 1992
85–92		16 Jul 1984 (SI 1984/876)
93–95		5 Aug 1984 (SI 1984/876)
96		*Not in force*
97, 98		5 Aug 1984 (SI 1984/876)
99, 100		Repealed
101–107		5 Aug 1984 (SI 1984/876)
108		18 Jun 1984 (SI 1984/749)
109	(1)–(3)	5 Aug 1984 (SI 1984/876)
	(4)	See Sch 5 below
	(5)	5 Aug 1984 (SI 1984/876)
	(6)	See Sch 7 below
	(7)	5 Aug 1984 (SI 1984/876)
110		18 Jun 1984 (SI 1984/749)
Schedule		
1		18 Jun 1984 (SI 1984/749)
2		5 Aug 1984 (SI 1984/876)
3		16 Jul 1984 (SI 1984/876)
4		5 Aug 1984 (SI 1984/876)
5, Pt	I	5 Aug 1984 (SI 1984/876)
	II	6 Aug 1984 (SI 1984/876)
6		6 Aug 1984 (SI 1984/876)
7, Pt	I	5 Aug 1984 (SI 1984/876)
	II	6 Aug 1984 (SI 1984/876)
	III	6 Sep 1994 (SI 1994/2162)
	IV	16 Jul 1984 (SI 1984/876)

[1] Orders made under Competition and Service (Utilities) Act 1992, s 56(2), bringing the prospective insertion into force will be noted to that Act

---

Tenant's Rights, Etc (Scotland) Amendment Act 1984 (c 18)

Whole Act repealed

Tourism (Overseas Promotion) (Scotland) Act 1984 (c 4)

RA: 13 Mar 1984

Commencement provisions: s 3

13 May 1984 (s 3)

Town and Country Planning Act 1984 (c 10)

Whole Act repealed

Trade Marks (Amendment) Act 1984 (c 19)

Whole Act repealed

Trade Union Act 1984 (c 49)

Whole Act repealed

Video Recordings Act 1984 (c 39)

RA: 12 Jul 1984

Commencement provisions: s 23(2); Video Recordings Act 1984 (Commencement No 1) Order 1985, SI 1985/883; Video Recordings Act 1984 (Scotland) (Commencement No 1) Order 1985, SI 1985/904; Video Recordings Act 1984 (Commencement No 2) Order 1985, SI 1985/1264; Video Recordings Act 1984 (Scotland) (Commencement No 2) Order 1985, SI 1985/1265; Video Recordings Act 1984 (Commencement No 3) Order 1986, SI 1986/1125; Video Recordings Act 1984 (Scotland) (Commencement No 3) Order 1986, SI 1986/1182; Video Recordings Act 1984 (Commencement No 4) Order 1987, SI 1987/123; Video Recordings Act 1984 (Scotland) (Commencement No 4) Order 1987, SI 1987/160; Video Recordings Act 1984 (Commencement No 5) Order 1987, SI 1987/1142; Video Recordings Act 1984 (Scotland) (Commencement No 5) Order 1987, SI 1987/1249; Video Recordings Act 1984 (Commencement No 6) Order 1987, SI 1987/2155; Video Recordings Act 1984 (Scotland) (Commencement No 6) Order 1987, SI 1987/2273; Video Recordings Act 1984 (Commencement No 7) Order 1988, SI 1988/1018; Video Recordings Act 1984 (Scotland) (Commencement No 7) Order 1988, SI 1988/1079

Section	
1	10 Jun 1985 (SI 1985/883; SI 1985/904)
2, 3	1 Sep 1985 (SI 1985/1264; SI 1985/1265)
4	10 Jun 1985 (SI 1985/883; SI 1985/904)
4A, 4B	Inserted by Criminal Justice and Public Order Act 1994, s 90 (qv)
5	10 Jun 1985 (SI 1985/883; SI 1985/904)
6	1 Sep 1985 (SI 1985/1264; SI 1985/1265)
7, 8	10 Jun 1985 (SI 1985/883; SI 1985/904)
9, 10[1]	1 Sep 1985 (for the purpose of prohibiting the supply, the offer to supply or the possession for the purpose of supply of a video recording containing a video work where—

Video Recordings Act 1984 (c 39)—*contd*

Section

9, 10[1]—*contd*

(a) a video recording containing such video work has not been sold, let on hire or offered for sale or hire in the United Kingdom to the public before 1 Sep 1985; and

(b) no classification certificate in respect of such video work has been issued) (SI 1985/1264; SI 1985/1265)

1 Sep 1986 (for the purpose of prohibiting the supply, the offer to supply or the possession for the purpose of supply of a video recording which has been sold, let on hire or offered for sale in the UK to the public in video form before 1 Sep 1985 where—

(a) its visual images, when shown as a moving picture, are not substantially the same as the moving picture produced on showing a film registered, or deemed to have been registered, under Films Act 1960, Pt II, on or after 1 Jan 1940;

(b) its visual images are accompanied by sound which comprises or includes words predominantly in the English language; and

(c) no classification certificate has been issued in respect of it.

Where such a video recording also contains another video work which does not satisfy the above requirements these sections are only brought into force for the above purpose in respect of the video work which does satisfy the requirements) (SI 1986/1125; SI 1986/1182)

1 Mar 1987 (for the purpose of prohibiting the supply, the offer to supply, or the possession for the purpose of supply of a video recording which has been sold, let on hire or offered for sale in the UK to the public in video form before 1 Sep 1985 where—

Video Recordings Act 1984 (c 39)—*contd*

(a) its visual images, when shown as a moving picture, are substantially the same as the moving picture produced on showing a film registered, or deemed to have been registered, under Pt II of Films Act 1960 on or after 1 Jan 1980;

(b) its visual images are accompanied by sound which comprises or includes words predominantly in the English language; and

(c) no classification certificate has been issued in respect of it.

Where such a video recording also contains another video work which does not satisfy the above requirements these sections are only brought into force for the above purpose in respect of the video work which does satisfy the requirements) (SI 1987/123; SI 1987/160)

1 Sep 1987 (for the purpose of prohibiting the supply, the offer to supply or the possession for the purpose of supply of a video recording which has been sold, let on hire or offered for sale in the UK to the public in video form before 1 Sep 1985 where—

(a) its visual images, when shown as a moving picture, are substantially the same as the moving picture produced on showing a film registered, or deemed to have been registered, under Pt II of Films Act 1960 on or after 1 Jan 1975;

(b) its visual images are accompanied by sound which comprises or includes words predominantly in the English language; and

(c) no classification certificate has been issued in respect of it.

Where such a video recording also contains another video work which does not satisfy the above requirements these sections are only brought into force for the

Video Recordings Act 1984 (c 39)—*contd*
Section

9, 10[1]—*contd*		above purposes in respect of the video work which does satisfy the requirements) (SI 1987/1142; SI 1987/1249)
		1 Mar 1988 (for the purpose of prohibiting the supply, the offer to supply or the possession for the purpose of supply of a video recording which has been sold, let on hire or offered for sale in the UK to the public in video form before 1 Sep 1985 where—
		(a) its visual images, when shown as a moving picture, are substantially the same as the moving picture produced on showing a film registered under Pt II of Films Act 1960 on or after 1 Jan 1970;
		(b) its visual images are accompanied by sound which comprises or includes words predominantly in the English language; and
		(c) no classification certificate has been issued in respect of it.
		Where such a video recording also contains another video work which does not satisfy the above requirements these sections are only brought into force for the above purposes in respect of the video work which does satisfy the requirements) (SI 1987/2155; SI 1987/2273)
		1 Sep 1988 (otherwise) (SI 1988/1018; SI 1988/1079)
11	(1), (2)	1 Sep 1985 (SI 1985/1264; SI 1985/1265)
	(3)	Added by Criminal Justice and Public Order Act 1994, s 88(1), (4) (qv)
12	(1)–(4)	1 Sep 1985 (SI 1985/1264; SI 1985/1265)
	(4A)	Inserted by Criminal Justice and Public Order Act 1994, s 88(1), (5) (qv)
	(5), (6)	1 Sep 1985 (SI 1985/1264; SI 1985/1265)
13	(1), (2)	1 Sep 1985 (SI 1985/1264; SI 1985/1265)

Video Recordings Act 1984 (c 39)—*contd*
Section

---

[1]   Ie ss 9(1), (2), 10(1), (2); ss 9(3), 10(3) added by Criminal Justice and Public Order Act 1994, s 88(1)–(3) (qv)

1985

Administration of Justice Act 1985 (c 61)

RA: 30 Oct 1985

Commencement provisions: s 69(2)–(4); Administration of Justice Act 1985 (Commencement No 1) Order 1986, SI 1986/364; Administration of Justice Act 1985 (Commencement No 2) Order 1986, SI 1986/1503; Administration of Justice Act 1985 (Commencement No 3) Order 1986, SI 1986/2260; Administration of Justice Act 1985 (Commencement No 4) Order 1987, SI 1987/787; Administration of Justice Act 1985 (Commencement No 5) Order 1988, SI 1988/1341; Administration of Justice Act 1985 (Commencement No 6) Order 1989, SI 1989/287; Administration of Justice Act 1985 (Commencement No 7) Order 1991, SI 1991/2683

Section		
1		Repealed
2		12 Mar 1986 (except so far as relates to the investigation of any complaint made to the Law Society relating to the quality of any professional services provided by a solicitor) (SI 1986/364)
		1 Jan 1987 (exception noted above) (SI 1986/2260)
3		Repealed
4, 5		12 Mar 1986 (SI 1986/364)
6	(1)–(3)	11 May 1987 (SI 1987/787)
	(4)	1 Dec 1987 (SI 1987/787)
	(5)	11 May 1987 (SI 1987/787)
7, 8		12 Mar 1986 (SI 1986/364)
9, 10		1 Jan 1992 (SI 1991/2683)
11		11 May 1987 (SI 1987/787)
12		12 Mar 1986 (SI 1986/364)
13		1 Oct 1986 (SI 1986/1503)
14–21		11 May 1987 (SI 1987/787)
22, 23		1 Oct 1986 (SI 1986/1503)
24–33		11 May 1987 (SI 1987/787)
34	(1), (2)	11 May 1987 (SI 1987/787)
	(3)	*Not in force*
35–37		11 May 1987 (SI 1987/787)
38		1 Oct 1986 (SI 1986/1503)
39		11 May 1987 (SI 1987/787)

Administration of Justice Act 1985 (c 61)—*contd*

Section		
40		1 Apr 1989 (SI 1989/287)
41, 42		Substituted by Legal Aid Act 1988, s 33 (qv)
43, 44		1 Apr 1989 (SI 1989/287)
45, 46		Repealed
47		1 Oct 1986 (SI 1986/1503)
48		1 Jan 1987 (SI 1986/2260)
49		30 Dec 1985 (s 69(4))
50		28 Apr 1986 (SI 1986/364)
51		1 Oct 1986 (SI 1986/1503)
52		30 Dec 1985 (s 69(4))
53		1 Oct 1988 (SI 1988/1341)
54		30 Dec 1985 (s 69(4))
55		1 Oct 1986 (SI 1986/1503)
56		30 Dec 1985 (s 69(4))
57, 58		Repealed
59		30 Dec 1985 (s 69(4))
60		Repealed
61		30 Dec 1985 (s 69(4)); prospectively repealed by Access to Justice Act 1999, s 106, Sch 15, Pt V(2)[1]
62		30 Dec 1985 (s 69(4))
63		Repealed
64		30 Dec 1985 (s 69(4))
65, 66		Repealed
67	(1)	See Sch 7 below
	(2)	See Sch 8 below
68, 69		30 Oct 1985 (s 69(3))
Schedule		
1		12 Mar 1986 (SI 1986/364)
2		1 Jan 1992 (SI 1991/2683)
3		12 Mar 1986 (SI 1986/364)
4–6		11 May 1987 (SI 1987/787)
7, para	1–5	Repealed
	6	*Not in force*
	7	1 Oct 1986 (SI 1986/1503)
	8	30 Dec 1985 (s 69(4))
8, Pt	I	30 Oct 1985 (s 69(3))
	II	30 Dec 1985 (s 69(4))
	III	12 Mar 1986 (repeals in Solicitors Act 1974) (SI 1986/364)
		1 Oct 1986 (repeals in Supreme Court Act 1981; County Courts Act 1984) (SI 1986/1503)
		Not in force (otherwise)
9		30 Oct 1985 (s 69(3))

---

[1]   Orders made under Access to Justice Act 1999, s 108(1) bringing the prospective repeal into force will be noted to that Act

---

Agricultural Training Board Act 1985 (c 36)

RA: 16 Jul 1985

Commencement provisions: s 4(2)

16 Sep 1985 (s 4(2))

Appropriation Act 1985 (c 55)

Whole Act repealed

Bankruptcy (Scotland) Act 1985 (c 66)

RA: 30 Oct 1985

Commencement provisions: s 78(2); Bankruptcy (Scotland) Act 1985 (Commencement) Order 1985, SI 1985/1924; Bankruptcy (Scotland) Act 1985 (Commencement No 2) Order 1986, SI 1986/1913

Section		
1		Substituted for original s 1 by Bankruptcy (Scotland) Act 1993, s 1 (qv); further substituted by Scotland Act 1998, s 125(1), Sch 8, para 22 (qv)
1A–1C		Substituted for original s 1 by Bankruptcy (Scotland) Act 1993, s 1 (qv)
2		Substituted by Bankruptcy (Scotland) Act 1993, s 2 (qv)
3	(1)–(4)	1 Apr 1986 (SI 1985/1924)
	(5)–(7)	Inserted by Bankruptcy (Scotland) Act 1993, s 11, Sch 1, para 1 (qv)
4		1 Apr 1986 (SI 1985/1924)
5	(1)	1 Apr 1986 (SI 1985/1924)
	(2)–(2C)	Substituted for original sub-s (2) by Bankruptcy (Scotland) Act 1993, s 3(1), (2) (qv)
	(3), (4)	1 Apr 1986 (SI 1985/1924)
	(4A)	Inserted by Bankruptcy (Scotland) Act 1993, s 3(1), (4) (qv)
	(5), (6)	1 Apr 1986 (SI 1985/1924)
	(6A)	Inserted by Bankruptcy (Scotland) Act 1993, s 3(1), (6) (qv)
	(7), (8)	1 Apr 1986 (SI 1985/1924)
	(9), (10)	Inserted by Bankruptcy (Scotland) Act 1993, s 3(1), (7) (qv)
6–11		1 Apr 1986 (SI 1985/1924)
12	(1)	Substituted by Bankruptcy (Scotland) Act 1993, s 4(1), (2) (qv)
	(1A)	Inserted by Bankruptcy (Scotland) Act 1993, s 4(1), (3) (qv)

Bankruptcy (Scotland) Act 1985 (c 66)—*contd*

Bankruptcy (Scotland) Act 1985 (c 66)—*contd*
Section

25	(1), (2)	1 Apr 1986 (SI 1985/1924)
	(2A)	Inserted by Bankruptcy (Scotland) Act 1993, s 11, Sch 1, para 13(1), (2) (qv)
	(3)–(6)	1 Apr 1988 (SI 1985/1924)
25A		Inserted by Bankruptcy (Scotland) Act 1993, s 7 (qv)
26	(1)–(5)	1 Apr 1986 (SI 1985/1924)
	(5A)	Inserted by Bankruptcy (Scotland) Act 1993, s 11, Sch 1, para 14(1), (4) (qv)
26A		Inserted by Bankruptcy (Scotland) Act 1993, s 11, Sch 1, para 15 (qv)
27	(1)–(4)	1 Apr 1986 (SI 1985/1924)
	(4A)	Inserted by Bankruptcy (Scotland) Act 1993, s 11, Sch 1, para 16(1), (2) (qv)
	(5)–(7)	1 Apr 1986 (SI 1985/1924)
	(7A)	Inserted by Bankruptcy (Scotland) Act 1993, s 11, Sch 1, para 16(1), (3) (qv)
28	(1), (1A)	Substituted for original sub-s (1) by Bankruptcy (Scotland) Act 1993, s 11, Sch 1, para 17(1), (2) (qv)
	(2)–(4)	1 Apr 1986 (SI 1985/1924)
	(5)	Substituted by Bankruptcy (Scotland) Act 1993, s 11, Sch 1, para 17(1), (4) (qv)
	(6), (7)	1 Apr 1986 (SI 1985/1924)
	(8)	Inserted by Bankruptcy (Scotland) Act 1993, s 11, Sch 1, para 17(1), (5) (qv)
29–36		1 Apr 1986 (SI 1985/1924)
36A–36C		Prospectively inserted by Pensions Act 1995, s 95(2) (repealed); substituted by Welfare Reform and Pensions Act 1999, s 16 (qv)
36D–36F		Inserted by Welfare Reform and Pensions Act 1999, s 84, Sch 12, para 69 (qv)
37–50		1 Apr 1986 (SI 1985/1924)
51	(1)	1 Apr 1986 (SI 1985/1924)
	(2)	29 Dec 1986 (SI 1986/1913)
	(3)–(7)	1 Apr 1986 (SI 1985/1924)
52	(1), (2), (2A)	Substituted for original sub-ss (1), (2) by Bankruptcy (Scotland) Act 1993, s 11, Sch 1, para 21 (qv)
	(3)–(5)	1 Apr 1986 (SI 1985/1924)
	(6)	Repealed

Bankruptcy (Scotland) Act 1985 (c 66)—*contd*

Section		
52	(7)–(9)	1 Apr 1986 (SI 1985/1924)
53	(1)	1 Apr 1986 (SI 1985/1924)
	(2), (2A)	Substituted for original sub-s (2) by Bankruptcy (Scotland) Act 1993, s 11, Sch 1, para 22(1), (2) (qv)
	(3)–(10)	1 Apr 1986 (SI 1985/1924)
54		1 Apr 1986 (SI 1985/1924)
55	(1), (2)	1 Apr 1986 (SI 1985/1924)
	(3)	Inserted (retrospectively) by Bankruptcy (Scotland) Act 1993, s 11, Sch 1, para 23(1), (3), (4)
56		1 Apr 1986 (SI 1985/1924)
57	(1)–(4)	1 Apr 1986 (SI 1985/1924)
	(4A)	Inserted by Bankruptcy (Scotland) Act 1993, s 11, Sch 1, para 24(1), (2) (qv)
	(5)–(7)	1 Apr 1986 (SI 1985/1924)
	(8)	Inserted by Bankruptcy (Scotland) Act 1993, s 11, Sch 1, para 24(1), (3) (qv)
58		1 Apr 1986 (SI 1985/1924)
58A		Inserted by Bankruptcy (Scotland) Act 1993, s 11, Sch 1, para 26 (qv)
59–69		1 Apr 1986 (SI 1985/1924)
69A		Inserted by Bankruptcy (Scotland) Act 1993, s 8 (qv)
70, 71		1 Apr 1986 (SI 1985/1924)
72		1 Feb 1986 (SI 1985/1924)
72A		Inserted by Bankruptcy (Scotland) Act 1993, s 11, Sch 1, para 28 (qv)
73	(1)	1 Feb 1986 (except definition 'preferred debt') (SI 1985/1924) 29 Dec 1986 (exception noted above) (SI 1986/1913)
	(2)–(5)	1 Feb 1986 (SI 1985/1924)
	(6)	Added by Bankruptcy (Scotland) Act 1993, s 11, Sch 1, para 29 (qv)
74, 75		1 Apr 1986 (SI 1985/1924)
76		1 Feb 1986 (SI 1985/1924)
77		1 Apr 1986 (SI 1985/1924)
78		30 Oct 1985 (RA)
Schedule		
1		1 Apr 1986 (SI 1985/1924)
2, para	1	1 Apr 1986 (SI 1985/1924)
	2, 2A	Substituted for original para 2 by Bankruptcy (Scotland) Act 1993, s 11, Sch 1, para 30(1), (3) (qv)

Bankruptcy (Scotland) Act 1985 (c 66)—*contd*
Schedule

2, para	3, 4	Substituted by Bankruptcy (Scotland) Act 1993, s 11, Sch 1, para 30(1), (4), (5) (qv)
	5–7	1 Apr 1986 (SI 1985/1924)
	7A	Inserted by Bankruptcy (Scotland) Act 1993, s 11, Sch 1, para 30(1), (8) (qv)
	8	1 Apr 1986 (SI 1985/1924)
	9	Substituted by Bankruptcy (Scotland) Act 1993, s 11, Sch 1, para 30(1), (10) (qv)
2A		Inserted by Bankruptcy (Scotland) Act 1993, s 6(2) (qv)
3		29 Dec 1986 (SI 1986/1913)
4–6		1 Apr 1986 (SI 1985/1924)
7, para	1	1 Apr 1986 (SI 1985/1924)
	2	Repealed
	3–6	1 Apr 1986 (SI 1985/1924)
	7	Repealed
	8, 9	1 Apr 1986 (SI 1985/1924)
	10	Repealed
	11, 12	1 Apr 1986 (SI 1985/1924)
	13, 14	Repealed
	15–18	1 Apr 1986 (SI 1985/1924)
	19–22	Repealed
	23–25	1 Apr 1986 (SI 1985/1924)
8		1 Apr 1986 (repeals of or in Bankruptcy Act 1621; Bankruptcy Act 1696; Titles to Land Consolidation (Scotland) Act 1868; Married Women's Property (Scotland) Act 1881; Judicial Factors (Scotland) Act 1889; Merchant Shipping Act 1894; Bankruptcy (Scotland) Act 1913 (except repeal of s 118); Married Women's Property (Scotland) Act 1920; Conveyancing (Scotland) Act 1924; Third Parties (Rights Against Insurers) Act 1930; Industrial Assurance and Friendly Societies Act 1948; Post Office Act 1969; Road Traffic Act 1972; Insolvency Act 1976; Banking Act 1979; Sale of Goods Act 1979; Law Reform (Miscellaneous Provisions) (Scotland) Act 1980; Matrimonial

Bankruptcy (Scotland) Act 1985 (c 66)—*contd*
Schedule
8—*contd*   Homes (Family Protection)
                                                 (Scotland) Act 1981; Companies
                                                 Act 1985) (SI 1985/1924)
                                                 29 Dec 1986 (otherwise)
                                                 (SI 1986/1913)

Betting, Gaming and Lotteries (Amendment) Act 1985 (c 18)

RA: 9 May 1985

Commencement provisions: s 3(2), (3); Betting, Gaming and Lotteries (Amendment)
   Act 1985 (Commencement) Order 1985, SI 1985/1475
Section
1   9 Jul 1985 (s 3(2))
2   (1)   9 Jul 1985 (s 3(2))
                (2)   Repealed
                (3), (4)   28 Oct 1985 (SI 1985/1475)
                (5)   9 Jul 1985 (s 3(2))
                (6)   Repealed
3   9 Jul 1985 (s 3(2))
Schedule   9 Jul 1985 (s 3(2))

Brunei and Maldives Act 1985 (c 3)

RA: 11 Mar 1985

11 Mar 1985 (RA)

Business Names Act 1985 (c 7)

RA: 11 Mar 1985

Commencement provisions: s 10

1 Jul 1985 (s 10)

Charities Act 1985 (c 20)

Whole Act repealed

Charter Trustees Act 1985 (c 45)

RA: 16 Jul 1985

16 Jul 1985 (RA)

Child Abduction and Custody Act 1985 (c 60)

RA: 25 Jul 1985

Commencement provisions: s 29(2); Child Abduction and Custody Act 1985 (Commencement) Order 1986, SI 1986/1048

1 Aug 1986 (SI 1986/1048)

Cinemas Act 1985 (c 13)

RA: 27 Mar 1985

Commencement provisions: s 25(2)

27 Jun 1985 (s 25(2))

Coal Industry Act 1985 (c 27)

RA: 13 Jun 1985

13 Jun 1985 (RA)

Whole Act repealed (in part prospectively) as follows: s 1 repealed by Coal Industry Act 1994, s 67(8), Sch 11, Pt II; s 2 repealed by Coal Industry Act 1987, s 10(3), Sch 3, Pt I; ss 3–5 prospectively repealed by Coal Industry Act 1994, s 67(8), Sch 11, Pt III; orders made under the 1994 Act, s 68, bringing the prospective repeals into force will be noted to that Act

Companies Act 1985 (c 6)

RA: 11 Mar 1985

Commencement provisions: ss 243(6), 746

1 Jul 1985 (s 746), except s 243(3), (4) (which provision has now been replaced)

Companies Consolidation (Consequential Provisions) Act 1985 (c 9)

RA: 11 Mar 1985

Commencement provisions: s 34

1 Jul 1985 (s 34)

Company Securities (Insider Dealing) Act 1985 (c 8)

Whole Act repealed

Consolidated Fund Act 1985 (c 1)

Whole Act repealed

Consolidated Fund (No 2) Act 1985 (c 11)

Whole Act repealed

Consolidated Fund (No 3) Act 1985 (c 74)

Whole Act repealed

Controlled Drugs (Penalties) Act 1985 (c 39)

RA: 16 Jul 1985

Commencement provisions: s 2(1)

16 Sep 1985 (s 2(1))

Copyright (Computer Software) Amendment Act 1985 (c 41)

Whole Act repealed

Dangerous Vessels Act 1985 (c 22)

RA: 23 May 1985

Commencement provisions: s 8(2)

23 Jul 1985 (s 8(2))

Elections (Northern Ireland) Act 1985 (c 2)

RA: 24 Jan 1985

Commencement provisions: s 7(2), (3); Elections (Northern Ireland) Act 1985 (Commencement) Order 1985, SI 1985/1221

Section		
1–3		24 Jan 1985 (so far as gives effect to s 5(1)) (s 7(3))
		6 Aug 1985 (otherwise) (SI 1985/1221)
4		6 Aug 1985 (SI 1985/1221)
5	(1)	24 Jan 1985 (s 7(3))
	(2), (3)	6 Aug 1985 (SI 1985/1221)
6, 7		24 Jan 1985 (s 7(3))

Enduring Powers of Attorney Act 1985 (c 29)

RA: 26 Jun 1985

Commencement provisions: s 14(2); Enduring Powers of Attorney Act 1985 (Commencement) Order 1986, SI 1986/125

10 Mar 1986 (SI 1986/125)

European Communities (Finance) Act 1985 (c 64)

Whole Act repealed

European Communities (Spanish and Portuguese Accession) Act 1985 (c 75)

RA: 19 Dec 1985

19 Dec 1985 (RA); but note that the accession of Spain and Portugal to the European Communities did not take effect until 1 Jan 1986

Family Law (Scotland) Act 1985 (c 37)

RA: 16 Jul 1985

Commencement provisions: s 29(2), (3); Family Law (Scotland) Act 1985 (Commencement No 1) Order 1986, SI 1986/1237; Family Law (Scotland) Act 1985 (Commencement No 2) Order 1988, SI 1988/1887

Section	
1–8	1 Sep 1986 (SI 1986/1237)
8A	Inserted by Welfare Reform and Pensions Act 1999, s 84, Sch 12, para 7 (qv)
9–12	1 Sep 1986 (SI 1986/1237)
12A	Inserted by Pensions Act 1995, s 167(3) (qv)
13–24	1 Sep 1986 (SI 1986/1237)
25	30 Nov 1988 (SI 1988/1887)
26–29	1 Sep 1986 (SI 1986/1237)
Schedule	
1, 2	1 Sep 1986 (SI 1986/1237)

Films Act 1985 (c 21)

RA: 23 May 1985

Commencement provisions: s 8(2)

Section		
1		23 May 1985 (RA)
2		Repealed
3		23 May 1985 (RA)
4		Repealed
5		23 May 1985 (RA)
6		23 Jul 1985 (s 8(2))
7	(1)	See Sch 2 below
	(2)	Repealed
	(3), (4)	23 May 1985 (RA)
	(5), (6)	Repealed
	(7)	23 May 1985 (RA)
8		23 May 1985 (RA)

Films Act 1985 (c 21)—*contd*
Schedule

1	23 Jul 1985 (s 8(2))
2	23 May 1985 (except repeals noted below) (RA)
	23 Jul 1985 (repeals in Finance Act 1982; Finance Act 1984) (s 8(2))

Finance Act 1985 (c 54)

Budget Day: 19 Mar 1985

RA: 25 Jul 1985

Details of the commencement of Finance Acts are not set out in this work

---

Food and Environment Protection Act 1985 (c 48)

RA: 16 Jul 1985

Commencement provisions: s 27; Food and Environment Protection Act 1985 (Commencement No 1) Order 1985, SI 1985/1390; Food and Environment Protection Act 1985 (Commencement No 2) Order 1985, SI 1985/1698

Section

1–4	16 Jul 1985 (s 27(2))
5–7	1 Jan 1986 (SI 1985/1698)
7A	Inserted by Petroleum Act 1998, s 50, Sch 4, para 20 (qv)
8–13	1 Jan 1986 (SI 1985/1698)
14	Substituted by Environmental Protection Act 1990, s 147 (qv)
15	1 Jan 1986 (SI 1985/1698)
16, 17	5 Sep 1985 (SI 1985/1390)
18	Substituted by Pesticides (Fees and Enforcement) Act 1989, s 1(2) (qv)
19	5 Sep 1985 (SI 1985/1390)
20–26	16 Jul 1985 (so far as relate to Pt I (ss 1–4)) (s 27(2))
	1 Jan 1986 (otherwise) (SI 1985/1698)
27, 28	16 Jul 1985 (s 27(2))
Schedule	
1	16 Jul 1985 (s 27(2))
2	16 Jul 1985 (so far as relates to Pt I (ss 1–4)) (s 27(2))
	5 Sep 1985 (so far as relates to Pt III (ss 16–19)) (SI 1985/1390)
	1 Jan 1986 (otherwise) (SI 1985/1698)
3	1 Jan 1986 (SI 1985/1698)

Food and Environment Protection Act 1985 (c 48)—*contd*
Schedule

4	1 Jan 1986 (SI 1985/1698); prospectively repealed by Environmental Protection Act 1990, s 162(2), Sch 16, Pt VIII[1]
5	5 Sep 1985 (SI 1985/1390)

[1]   Orders made under Environmental Protection 1990, s 164, bringing the prospective repeal into force will be noted to that Act

Further Education Act 1985 (c 47)

RA: 16 Jul 1985

Commencement provisions: s 7; Further Education Act 1985 (Commencement) (No 1) Order 1985, SI 1985/1429; Further Education Act 1985 (Commencement No 2) (Scotland) Order 1987, SI 1987/1335
Section

1–3	16 Sep 1985 (s 7(3))
4	16 Sep 1985 (E, W) (SI 1985/1429)
	17 Aug 1987 (S) (SI 1987/1335)
5–8	16 Jul 1985 (s 7(2))

Gaming (Bingo) Act 1985 (c 35)

RA: 16 Jul 1985

Commencement provisions: s 5(2); Gaming (Bingo) Act 1985 (Commencement) Order 1986, SI 1986/832

9 Jun 1986 (SI 1986/832)

Hill Farming Act 1985 (c 32)

RA: 26 Jun 1985

Commencement provisions: s 2(3)

26 Aug 1985 (s 2(3))

Hong Kong Act 1985 (c 15)

RA: 11 Mar 1985

11 Mar 1985 (RA)

Hospital Complaints Procedure Act 1985 (c 42)

RA: 16 Jul 1985

Commencement provisions: s 2(2); Hospital Complaints Procedure Act 1985 (Commencement) Order 1989, SI 1989/1191

11 Jul 1989 (SI 1989/1191)

Housing Act 1985 (c 68)

RA: 30 Oct 1985

Commencement provisions: s 625(2)

1 Apr 1986 (s 625(2))

Housing Associations Act 1985 (c 69)

RA: 30 Oct 1985

Commencement provisions: s 107(2)

1 Apr 1986 (s 107(2))

Housing (Consequential Provisions) Act 1985 (c 71)

RA: 30 Oct 1985

Commencement provisions: s 6(2)

1 Apr 1986 (s 6(2))

Industrial Development Act 1985 (c 25)

RA: 13 Jun 1985

Commencement provisions: s 6(4)

Section	
1, 2	13 Aug 1985 (s 6(4)); prospectively repealed by Leasehold Reform, Housing and Urban Development Act 1993, s 187(2), Sch 22[1]
3	1 Apr 1986 (s 6(4)); prospectively repealed by Leasehold Reform, Housing and Urban Development Act 1993, s 187(2), Sch 22[1]
4	13 Aug 1985 (s 6(4)); prospectively repealed by Leasehold Reform, Housing and Urban Development Act 1993, s 187(2), Sch 22[1]
5, 6	13 Aug 1985 (s 6(4))
Schedule	13 Aug 1985 (s 6(4))

[1] Orders made under Leasehold Reform, Housing and Urban Development Act 1993, s 188(2), (3), bringing the prospective repeals into force will be noted to that Act

Insolvency Act 1985 (c 65)

RA: 30 Oct 1985

Commencement provisions: s 236(2); Insolvency Act 1985 (Commencement No 1) Order 1986, SI 1986/6; Insolvency Act 1985 (Commencement No 2) Order 1986, SI 1986/185; Insolvency Act 1985 (Commencement No 3) Order 1986, SI 1986/463; Insolvency Act 1985 (Commencement No 4) Order 1986, SI 1986/840; Insolvency Act 1985 (Commencement No 5) Order 1986, SI 1986/1924

Section

1–216		Repealed
217	(1)–(3)	Repealed
	(4)	29 Dec 1986 (SI 1986/1924)
218		Repealed
219		Spent
220		29 Dec 1986 (SI 1986/1924)
221–234		Repealed
235	(1)	1 Mar 1986 (SI 1986/185)
	(2)–(5)	Repealed
236	(1), (2)	1 Feb 1986 (SI 1986/6)
	(3)–(5)	Repealed

Schedule

1, para	1–5	Repealed
	6	1 Jul 1986 (SI 1986/840)
2–5		Repealed
6, para	1, 2	Repealed
	3, 4	28 Apr 1986 (SI 1986/463)
	5–7	Repealed
	8	29 Dec 1986 (SI 1986/1924); now superseded
	9	Repealed
	10–13	29 Dec 1986 (SI 1986/1924)
	14–17	Repealed
	18, 19	29 Dec 1986 (SI 1986/1924)
	20–23	Repealed
	24	1 Mar 1986 (so far as relates to the making of rules under s 106 in relation to England and Wales) (SI 1986/185) 29 Dec 1986 (otherwise) (SI 1986/1924)
	25–45	Repealed
	46, 47	29 Dec 1986 (SI 1986/1924)
	48–52	Repealed
7		Repealed
8, para	1–7	29 Dec 1986 (SI 1986/1924)
	8, 9	Repealed
	10	Spent
	11–13	29 Dec 1986 (SI 1986/1924)
	14	Spent
	15	29 Dec 1986 (SI 1986/1924)

Insolvency Act 1985 (c 65)—*contd*
Schedule

8	16		Repealed
	17		Spent
	18, 19		29 Dec 1986 (SI 1986/1924)
	20		Spent
	21–23		29 Dec 1986 (SI 1986/1924)
	24		Repealed
	25		29 Dec 1986 (SI 1986/1924)
	26		Repealed
	27		1 Apr 1986 (so far as relates to the awarding by a court in Scotland of the sequestration of an individual's estate) (SI 1986/463)
			29 Dec 1986 (otherwise) (SI 1986/1924)
	28–31		Repealed
	32		Spent
	33–35		29 Dec 1986 (SI 1986/1924)
	36		1 Apr 1986 (SI 1986/185)
	37	(1)–(3)	29 Dec 1986 (SI 1986/1924)
		(4)	1 Mar 1986 (so far as relates to the making of rules under s 106 in relation to England and Wales) (SI 1986/185)
			29 Dec 1986 (otherwise) (SI 1986/1924)
	38–40		29 Dec 1986 (SI 1986/1924)
9, 10			Repealed

Insurance (Fees) Act 1985 (c 46)

RA: 16 Jul 1985

16 Jul 1985 (RA)

Interception of Communications Act 1985 (c 56)

RA: 25 Jul 1985

Whole Act repealed

Intoxicating Substances (Supply) Act 1985 (c 26)

RA: 13 Jun 1985

Commencement provisions: s 2(2)

13 Aug 1985 (s 2(2))

Landlord and Tenant Act 1985 (c 70)

RA: 30 Oct 1985

Commencement provisions: s 40(2)

1 Apr 1986 (s 40(2))

Law Reform (Miscellaneous Provisions) (Scotland) Act 1985 (c 73)

RA: 30 Oct 1985

Commencement provisions: s 60(3), (4); Law Reform (Miscellaneous Provisions) (Scotland) Act 1985 (Commencement No 1) Order 1985, SI 1985/1908; Law Reform (Miscellaneous Provisions) (Scotland) Act 1985 (Commencement No 2) Order 1985, SI 1985/2055; Law Reform (Miscellaneous Provisions) (Scotland) Act 1985 (Commencement No 3) Order 1986, SI 1986/1945; Law Reform (Miscellaneous Provisions) (Scotland) Act 1985 (Commencement No 4) Order 1988, SI 1988/1819

Section		
1–13		30 Dec 1985 (s 60(3))
14, 15		8 Dec 1986 (SI 1986/1945)
16		Repealed
17		30 Dec 1985 (s 60(3))
18		30 Nov 1988 (SI 1988/1819)
19		8 Dec 1986 (SI 1986/1945)
20		30 Dec 1985 (s 60(3))
21		Repealed
22–25		30 Dec 1985 (s 60(3))
26–29		30 Oct 1985 (s 60(3))
30–32		Repealed
33, 34		30 Dec 1985 (s 60(3))
35		Repealed
36–40		Repealed
41		30 Dec 1985 (s 60(3))
42–45		Repealed
46–49		30 Dec 1985 (s 60(3))
50		1 Feb 1986 (SI 1985/1908)
51–53		30 Dec 1985 (s 60(3))
54		30 Oct 1985 (s 60(3))
55–58		30 Dec 1985 (s 60(3))
59	(1)	See Sch 2 below
	(2)	30 Dec 1985 (s 60(3))
60		30 Oct 1985 (s 60(3))
Schedule		
1		30 Dec 1985 (s 60(3))
2, para	1–7	30 Dec 1985 (s 60(3))
	8	Repealed
	9–11	30 Dec 1985 (s 60(3))
	12, 13	8 Dec 1986 (SI 1986/1945)
	14, 15	30 Dec 1985 (s 60(3))
	16–20	Repealed
	21, 22	30 Dec 1985 (s 60(3))

Law Reform (Miscellaneous Provisions) (Scotland) Act 1985 (c 73)—*contd*

Schedule

2, para	23	Repealed
	24	8 Dec 1986 (SI 1986/1945)
	25	30 Dec 1985 (s 60(3))
	26, 27	Repealed
	28–30	30 Oct 1985 (s 60(3))
	31	30 Dec 1985 (s 60(3))
	32	30 Oct 1985 (s 60(3))
3		30 Oct 1985 (s 60(3))
4		30 Dec 1985 (s 60(3))

Licensing (Amendment) Act 1985 (c 40)

RA: 16 Jul 1985

16 Jul 1985 (RA)

Local Government Act 1985 (c 51)

RA: 16 Jul 1985

This Act largely came into force on the date of Royal Assent, but the effective date of operation for many of its provisions (except as otherwise provided) is 1 Apr 1986 (the date of abolition of the Greater London Council and the metropolitan county councils). In addition certain provisions come into force in different areas on dates appointed by order before and after 1 Apr 1986

Local Government (Access to Information) Act 1985 (c 43)

RA: 16 Jul 1985

Commencement provisions: s 5

1 Apr 1986 (s 5)

London Regional Transport (Amendment) Act 1985 (c 10)

RA: 11 Mar 1985

11 Mar 1985 (RA)

Milk (Cessation of Production) Act 1985 (c 4)

RA: 11 Mar 1985

Commencement provisions: s 7(2)

Section

1–5	11 May 1985 (s 7(2))
6	11 Mar 1985 (RA)
7	11 May 1985 (s 7(2))

Mineral Workings Act 1985 (c 12)

RA: 27 Mar 1985

Commencement provisions: s 11(2)–(4)

Section	
1	1 Apr 1985 (s 11(2))
2	Repealed
3–6	1 Apr 1985 (s 11(2))
7, 8	27 May 1985 (s 11(3))
9, 10	1 Apr 1985 (s 11(2))
11	27 Mar 1985 (s 11(4))
Schedule	
1, 2	1 Apr 1985 (s 11(2))

Motor-Cycle Crash-Helmets (Restriction of Liability) Act 1985 (c 28)

Whole Act repealed

National Heritage (Scotland) Act 1985 (c 16)

RA: 4 Apr 1985

Commencement provisions: s 25(1); National Heritage (Scotland) Act 1985 Commencement Order 1985, SI 1985/851

Section				
1				4 Jun 1985 (SI 1985/851)
2–5				1 Oct 1985 (SI 1985/851)
6	(1)–(4)			1 Oct 1985 (SI 1985/851)
	(5)–(7)			4 Jun 1985 (SI 1985/851)
7–9				1 Oct 1985 (SI 1985/851)
10				4 Jun 1985 (SI 1985/851)
11–15				1 Apr 1986 (SI 1985/851)
16				4 Jun 1985 (SI 1985/851)
17				4 Jun 1985 (so far as adds paras 1–7, 9 of Schedule to National Galleries of Scotland Act 1906) (SI 1985/851)
				1 Apr 1986 (so far as adds para 8 of that Schedule) (SI 1985/851)
18	(1)–(5)			4 Jun 1985 (SI 1985/851)
	(6)			1 Apr 1986 (SI 1985/851)
19	(1)			1 Oct 1985 (SI 1985/851)
	(2), (3)			4 Jun 1985 (SI 1985/851)
20				Repealed, subject to a transitional provision in SI 1998/2329
21–23				4 Jun 1985 (SI 1985/851)
24				See Sch 2 below
25				4 Apr 1985 (RA)
Schedule				
1, Pt	I, para	1–3		4 Jun 1985 (SI 1985/851)
		4	(1)–(5)	4 Jun 1985 (SI 1985/851)
			(6)	1 Oct 1985 (SI 1985/851)
		5–7		4 Jun 1985 (SI 1985/851)

National Heritage (Scotland) Act 1985 (c 16)—*contd*

Schedule

1, Pt	I, para	8	Repealed
		9, 10	4 Jun 1985 (SI 1985/851)
	II, para	11–18	4 Jun 1985 (SI 1985/851)
		19	Repealed
		20, 21	4 Jun 1985 (SI 1985/851)
2, Pt	I, para	1	1 Apr 1986 (SI 1985/851)
		2	Repealed
		3, 4	1 Oct 1985 (SI 1985/851)
	II		4 Jun 1985 (repeal of words in National Library of Scotland Act 1925, s 2(f)) (SI 1985/851)
			1 Oct 1985 (repeal of or in National Museum of Antiquities of Scotland Act 1954; National Gallery and Tate Gallery Act 1954, Sch 1) (SI 1985/851)
			1 Apr 1986 (repeal of National Library of Scotland Act 1925, s 10) (SI 1985/851)

New Towns and Urban Development Corporations Act 1985 (c 5)

RA: 11 Mar 1985

Commencement provisions: s 15(2)

Section

1, 2	11 May 1985 (s 15(2))
3, 4	11 May 1985 (s 15(2)); prospectively repealed by Local Government and Housing Act 1989, s 194(4), Sch 12, Pt II[1]
5	11 Mar 1985 (RA)
6–10	11 May 1985 (s 15(2))
11	Repealed[2]
12	Repealed
13–15	11 May 1985 (s 15(2))

Schedule

1, 2		11 May 1985 (s 15(2))
3, para	1–6	11 May 1985 (s 15(2))
	7	11 Mar 1985 (RA); prospectively repealed by Local Government and Housing Act 1989, s 194(4), Sch 12, Pt II[1]
	8–16	11 May 1985 (s 15(2))

[1] Orders made under Local Government and Housing Act 1989, s 195(2), bringing the prospective repeal into force will be noted to that Act

[2] The repeal of s 11 of this Act by Government of Wales Act 1998, s 152, Sch 18, Pt IV, does not affect the validity of anything done by, or in relation to, the Development Board for Rural Wales before its functions ceased to exist; see s 131(1) of the 1998 Act

Northern Ireland (Loans) Act 1985 (c 76)

RA: 19 Dec 1985

19 Dec 1985 (RA)

Oil and Pipelines Act 1985 (c 62)

RA: 30 Oct 1985

Commencement provisions: s 8(2), (3); Oil and Pipelines Act 1985 (Commencement) Order 1985, SI 1985/1748; Oil and Pipelines Act 1985 (Appointed Day) Order 1985, SI 1985/1749; British National Oil Corporation (Dissolution) Order 1986, SI 1986/585

Section		
1, 2		1 Dec 1985 (SI 1985/1748)
3		1 Dec 1985 (SI 1985/1749)
4–8		1 Dec 1985 (SI 1985/1748)
Schedule		
1		1 Dec 1985 (SI 1985/1748)
2		1 Dec 1985 (SI 1985/1749)
3		1 Dec 1985 (SI 1985/1748)
4, Pt	I	1 Dec 1985 (SI 1985/1749)
	II	27 Mar 1986 (SI 1986/585)

Ports (Finance) Act 1985 (c 30)

RA: 26 Jun 1985

Commencement provisions: s 7(2); Ports (Finance) Act 1985 (Commencement) Order 1985, SI 1985/1153

Section	
1	Repealed
2	5 Aug 1985 (SI 1985/1153)
3–5	1 Jan 1986 (SI 1985/1153)
6, 7	5 Aug 1985 (SI 1985/1153)
Schedule	5 Aug 1985 (SI 1985/1153)

Prohibition of Female Circumcision Act 1985 (c 38)

RA: 16 Jul 1985

Commencement provisions: s 4(2)

16 Sep 1985 (s 4(2))

Prosecution of Offences Act 1985 (c 23)

RA: 23 May 1985

Commencement provisions: s 31(2); Prosecution of Offences Act 1985 (Commencement No 1) Order 1985, SI 1985/1849; Prosecution of Offences Act 1985 (Commencement No 2) Order 1986, SI 1986/1029; Prosecution of Offences Act 1985 (Commencement No 3) Order 1986, SI 1986/1334

Prosecution of Offences Act 1985 (c 23)—*contd*
Section

1, 2	1 Apr 1986 (in the counties of Durham, Greater Manchester, Merseyside, Northumberland, South Yorkshire, Tyne and Wear, West Midlands and West Yorkshire only) (SI 1985/1849) 1 Oct 1986 (otherwise) (SI 1986/1029)
3	1 Apr 1986 (in the counties noted to ss 1, 2 above only; but s 3(2) (a), (c), (d) does not apply in relation to proceedings transferred (whether on appeal or otherwise) to an area where those provisions are in force from an area where they are not) (SI 1985/1849) 1 Oct 1986 (otherwise) (SI 1986/1029)
4–7	1 Apr 1986 (in the counties noted to ss 1, 2 above only) (SI 1985/1849) 1 Oct 1986 (otherwise) (SI 1986/1029)
7A	Inserted by Courts and Legal Services Act 1990, s 114 (qv); substituted by Crime and Disorder Act 1998, s 53 (qv)
8	1 Apr 1986 (in the counties noted to ss 1, 2 above only) (SI 1985/1849) 1 Oct 1986 (otherwise) (SI 1986/1029)
9	5 Apr 1987 (SI 1986/1029)
10	1 Apr 1986 (in the counties noted to ss 1, 2 above only) (SI 1985/1849) 1 Oct 1986 (otherwise) (SI 1986/1029)
11–13	23 May 1985 (s 31(2))
14	1 Apr 1986 (in the counties noted to ss 1, 2 above only) (SI 1985/1849) 1 Oct 1986 (otherwise) (SI 1986/1029)
15	23 May 1985 (so far as applies in relation to ss 11–13) (s 31(2)) 1 Oct 1986 (otherwise) (SI 1986/1029)
16–19	1 Oct 1986 (SI 1986/1334)
19A	Inserted by Courts and Legal Services Act 1990, s 111 (qv)
20, 21	1 Oct 1986 (SI 1986/1334)
22	1 Oct 1986 (SI 1986/1029)
22A	Inserted by Crime and Disorder Act 1998, s 44 (qv)
22B	Inserted by Crime and Disorder Act 1998, s 45 (qv)
23	1 Apr 1986 (in the counties noted to ss 1, 2 above only) (SI 1985/1849) 1 Oct 1986 (otherwise) (SI 1986/1029)

Prosecution of Offences Act 1985 (c 23)—*contd*

Section

23A		Inserted, partly prospectively, by Crime and Disorder Act 1998, s 119, Sch 8, para 64[1]
24		1 Apr 1986 (SI 1985/1849)
25, 26		1 Apr 1986 (in the counties noted to ss 1, 2 above only) (SI 1985/1849)
		1 Oct 1986 (otherwise) (SI 1986/1029)
27		Repealed
28		1 Apr 1986 (SI 1985/1849)
29, 30		23 May 1985 (s 31(2))
31	(1)–(4)	23 May 1985 (s 31(2))
	(5), (6)	1 Apr 1986 (SI 1985/1849)
	(7)	23 May 1985 (s 31(2))

Schedule

1, para	1	Repealed
	2, 3	1 Apr 1986 (in the counties noted to ss 1, 2 above only) (SI 1985/1849)
		1 Oct 1986 (otherwise) (SI 1986/1029)
	4, 5	1 Apr 1986 (SI 1985/1849)
	6–10	1 Oct 1986 (otherwise) (SI 1986/1334)
	11	*Not in force*
2		1 Apr 1986 (repeals of or in Perjury Act 1911; Administration of Justice (Miscellaneous Provisions) Act 1933; Industrial Development Act 1966; Transport Act 1968; European Communities Act 1972; Bail Act 1976; Representation of the People Act 1983) (SI 1985/1849)
		1 Apr 1986 (in the counties noted to ss 1, 2 above only) (repeals of or in Prosecution of Offences Act 1979; Magistrates' Courts Act 1980, s 25) (SI 1985/1849)
		1 Oct 1986 (in counties other than those noted above) (repeals of or in Prosecution of Offences Act 1979; Magistrates' Courts Act 1980, s 25) (SI 1986/1029)
		1 Oct 1986 (repeals of or in Indictments Act 1915; Criminal Justice Act 1967; Criminal Appeal Act 1968; Administration of Justice Act 1970; Costs in Criminal Cases Act 1973; Administration of Justice Act 1973; Magistrates' Courts Act 1980, s 30(3); Legal Aid Act 1982) (SI 1986/1334)

Prosecution of Offences Act 1985 (c 23)—*contd*
Schedule
2—*contd*   *Not in force* (repeal in Supreme Court
                                             Act 1981, s 77)

---

1   Orders made under Crime and Disorder Act 1998, s 121(2), bringing the prospective insertion into force will be noted to that Act

---

Rating (Revaluation Rebates) (Scotland) Act 1985 (c 33)

RA: 26 Jun 1985

Commencement provisions: s 3(1)

26 Aug 1985 (s 3(1))

Rent (Amendment) Act 1985 (c 24)

RA: 23 May 1985

23 May 1985 (RA)

Representation of the People Act 1985 (c 50)

RA: 16 Jul 1985

Commencement provisions: s 29(2), (3); Representation of the People Act 1985 (Commencement No 1) Order 1985, SI 1985/1185; Representation of the People Act 1985 (Commencement No 2) Order 1986, SI 1986/639; Representation of the People Act 1985 (Commencement No 3) Order 1986, SI 1986/1080; Representation of the People Act 1985 (Commencement No 4) Order 1987, SI 1987/207

Section

1		11 Jul 1986 (SI 1986/1080); substituted by Representation of the People Act 2000, s 8, Sch 2, paras 1, 2 (qv)
2		11 Jul 1986 (SI 1986/1080); substituted by Representation of the People Act 2000, s 8, Sch 2, paras 1, 3 (qv)
3		11 Jul 1986 (SI 1986/1080); substituted by Representation of the People Act 2000, s 8, Sch 2, paras 1, 4 (qv)
4		11 Jul 1986 (SI 1986/1080)
5–9		Repealed (E, W, S) 16 Feb 1987 (SI 1986/1080) (NI)
10, 11		16 Feb 1987 (SI 1986/1080)
12	(1), (2)	11 Jul 1986 (SI 1986/1080)
	(3)	16 Feb 1987 (SI 1986/1080)

Representation of the People Act 1985 (c 50)—*contd*

Section

12	(4)		11 Jul 1986 (SI 1986/1080)
13, 14			1 Oct 1985 (SI 1985/1185)
15, 16			16 Feb 1987 (SI 1986/1080)
17			1 Sep 1985 (SI 1985/1185)
18			1 Oct 1985 (SI 1985/1185)
19	(1)–(5)		16 Feb 1987 (SI 1986/1080)
	(6)	(a)	1 Oct 1985 (SI 1985/1185)
		(b), (c)	16 Feb 1987 (SI 1986/1080)
20			1 Oct 1985 (SI 1985/1185)
21			16 Feb 1987 (SI 1986/1080)
22			Substituted by Welsh Language Act 1993, s 35(5) (qv)
23, 24			1 Oct 1985 (SI 1985/1185)
25	(1)		16 Jul 1985 (s 29(3))
	(2)		1 Oct 1985 (SI 1985/1185)
26			1 Oct 1985 (SI 1985/1185)
27	(1)		16 Jul 1985 (s 29(3))
	(2), (3)		1 Oct 1985 (SI 1985/1185)
28			1 Oct 1985 (SI 1985/1185)
29			16 Jul 1985 (s 29(3))

Schedule

1			*Not in force*
2			16 Feb 1987 (SI 1986/1080)
3			1 Oct 1985 (SI 1985/1185)
4, para	1		1 Oct 1985 (SI 1985/1185)
	2, 3		Repealed
	4–6		1 Oct 1985 (SI 1985/1185)
	7		16 Feb 1987 (SI 1986/1080)
	8		1 Oct 1985 (SI 1985/1185)
	9		16 Feb 1987 (SI 1986/1080)
	10–16		1 Oct 1985 (SI 1985/1185)
	17, 18		Repealed
	19–33		1 Oct 1985 (SI 1985/1185)
	34		30 Mar 1987 (except for the purposes of an election, notice of which is published before that date) (SI 1987/207)
	35		Repealed
	36–68		1 Oct 1985 (SI 1985/1185)
	69		21 Apr 1986 (SI 1986/639)
	70–72		1 Oct 1985 (SI 1985/1185)
	73		16 Feb 1987 (SI 1986/1080)
	74–77		1 Oct 1985 (SI 1985/1185)
	78		Repealed
	79, 80		16 Feb 1987 (SI 1986/1080)
	81–83		1 Oct 1985 (SI 1985/1185)
	84–86		16 Feb 1987 (SI 1986/1080)
	87–89		1 Oct 1985 (SI 1985/1185)
	90		Repealed

Representation of the People Act 1985 (c 50)—*contd*
Schedule
5   16 Jul 1985 (repeals in Police and
                                                              Criminal Evidence Act 1984)
                                                              (s 29(3))
                                                              1 Oct 1985 (repeals of or in Meeting
                                                              of Parliament Act 1797, ss 3–5;
                                                              Representation of the People
                                                              Act 1918; Local Government Act
                                                              1972, s 243(3); Representation of
                                                              the People Act 1983, ss 18(2)(b),
                                                              (6)(b), 39(8), 49(1)(d), (2)(c), 51,
                                                              52(2), 53(2), 55, 56(1)(c), (6),
                                                              76(3), 103(2), 104(b), 106(4), 108(3),
                                                              (4), 124(a), (b), 125(a), 126(3),
                                                              136(4), (5), (7), 140(5), (7), 141(3),
                                                              (4), 142, 148(4)(a), 156(2)–(4),
                                                              161, 162, 163(1)(b), 168(5), (6),
                                                              169, 171, 172, 173(a), 176(1), (3),
                                                              181(3), (6), 187(1), 190, 191(1)(a),
                                                              192, 196, 199, 202(1), 203(4)(a),
                                                              Sch 1, rule 5, para (1), rule 23,
                                                              para (2)(c), (3), Appendix of
                                                              Forms, Sch 2, para 9, Sch 7,
                                                              paras 8, 9) (SI 1985/1185)
                                                              16 Feb 1987 (repeals of or in City of
                                                              London (Various Powers) Act 1957;
                                                              Representation of the People
                                                              Act 1983, ss 19–22, 32–34, 38,
                                                              40(1), 43(2)(b), 44, 49(3), 61,
                                                              Sch 1, rr 2(3), 27, 40(1)(b), Sch 2,
                                                              para 5(4), Sch 8) (SI 1986/1080)
                                                              Not in force (otherwise)

Reserve Forces (Safeguard of Employment) Act 1985 (c 17)

RA: 9 May 1985

Commencement provisions: s 23(3)

9 Aug 1985 (s 23(3))

Road Traffic (Production of Documents) Act 1985 (c 34)

Whole Act repealed

Sexual Offences Act 1985 (c 44)

RA: 16 Jul 1985

Commencement provisions: s 5(4)

16 Sep 1985 (s 5(4))

Shipbuilding Act 1985 (c 14)

Whole Act repealed

Social Security Act 1985 (c 53)

RA: 22 Jul 1985

Commencement provisions: s 32; Social Security Act 1985 (Commencement No 1) Order 1985, SI 1985/1125; Social Security Act 1985 (Commencement No 2) Order 1985, SI 1985/1364

Section		
1–7		Repealed
8	(1)	Repealed
	(2), (3)	22 Jul 1985 (s 32(2))
9–20		Repealed
21		See Sch 4 below
22		Repealed
23–25		22 Jul 1985 (s 32(2))
26		Repealed, subject to a saving, by Pension Schemes Act 1993, s 188(1), Sch 5 (qv)
27		Repealed
28	(1)	22 Jul 1985 (s 32(2))
	(2)	Repealed
29	(1)	See Sch 5 below
	(2)	See Sch 6 below
30		Repealed
31–33		22 Jul 1985 (s 32(2))

Schedule		
1–3		Repealed
4, para	1	16 Sep 1985 (SI 1985/1125)
	2–7	Repealed
5, para	1–5	Repealed
	6	6 Oct 1985 (SI 1985/1125); repealed (prospectively in the case of para (b)) by Social Security Act 1986, s 86(2), Sch 11[1]
	7–15	Repealed
	16	6 Oct 1985 (SI 1985/1125); prospectively repealed by Social Security Act 1986, s 86(2), Sch 11[1]
	17–32	Repealed
	33	6 Oct 1985 (SI 1985/1364)
	34–38	Repealed
	39	6 Oct 1985 (SI 1985/1125)
	40	6 Oct 1985 (SI 1985/1364)
6		22 Jul 1985 (repeals of or in Social Security Pensions Act 1975, s 41D; Social Security (Miscellaneous Provisions) Act 1977, s 22(7); Social Security Act 1981; Health and Social Security Act 1984) (s 32(2))

Social Security Act 1985 (c 53)—*contd*
Schedule

23 Jul 1985 (repeals of or in Social
Security Act 1975, s 28(2); Social
Security Act 1979, Sch 1, para 11)
(SI 1985/1125)

5 Aug 1985 (repeals of or in Social
Security Act 1975, ss 79, 82, 90)
(s 32(3))

16 Sep 1985 (repeals of or in Social
Security Act 1975, ss 5(3), (4),
125(1), 126A(1); Social Security
(Miscellaneous Provisions) Act 1977,
s 5(1); Social Security and Housing
Benefits Act 1982, s 24, Sch 2,
paras 7–11) (SI 1985/1125;
SI 1985/1364)

6 Oct 1985 (repeals of or in Social
Security Pensions Act 1975,
ss 41B(4), 59(5)(b), Sch 4,
para 36(b); Social Security
(Contributions) Act 1982, s 1(5),
Sch 1, para 1(3)) (SI 1985/1125;
SI 1985/1364)

25 Nov 1985 (repeals of or in Social
Security Act 1975, s 39(2), Sch 4,
Pt III, para 5) (SI 1985/1125)

1 Jan 1986 (repeals of or in Social
Security Act 1973, Sch 16,
para 6(1)(a); Social Security
Pensions Act 1975, ss 26(2), 34(4),
41A(4)(i), 66; Social Security
(Miscellaneous Provisions) Act 1977,
s 22(9)–(11); Social Security
Act 1980, s 3(6), (7))
(SI 1985/1364)

6 Apr 1986 (remaining repeals in
Social Security and Housing
Benefits Act 1982) (SI 1985/1125)

[1]   Orders made under Social Security Act 1986, s 88, bringing the prospective repeals into force will
be noted to that Act; but note para 1 of the Report of the Law Commission and the Scottish Law
Commission on the Consolidation of the Legislation relating to Social Security (Law Com No 203;
Scot Law Com No 132; Cm 1726), in relation to the repeal of Sch 5, para 6(b); the prospective
nature of the repeal of Sch 5, para 16 is preserved by Social Security (Consequential Provisions)
Act 1992, s 6, Sch 4, paras 1–3

Sporting Events (Control of Alcohol etc) Act 1985 (c 57)

RA: 25 Jul 1985

25 Jul 1985 (RA)

Surrogacy Arrangements Act 1985 (c 49)

RA: 16 Jul 1985

16 Jul 1985 (RA)

Town and Country Planning (Amendment) Act 1985 (c 52)

Whole Act repealed

Town and Country Planning (Compensation) Act 1985 (c 19)

Whole Act repealed

Transport Act 1985 (c 67)

RA: 30 Oct 1985

Commencement provisions: s 140(2); Transport Act 1985 (Commencement No 1) Order 1985, SI 1985/1887; Transport Act 1985 (Commencement No 2) Order 1986, SI 1986/80; Transport Act 1985 (Commencement No 3) Order 1986, SI 1986/414; Transport Act 1985 (Commencement No 4) Order 1986, SI 1986/1088; Transport Act 1985 (Commencement No 5) Order 1986, SI 1986/1450; Transport Act 1985 (Commencement No 6) Order 1986, SI 1986/1794 (as amended by SI 1988/2294); Transport Act 1985 (Commencement No 7) Order 1987, SI 1987/1228

Section

1	(1), (2)	26 Oct 1986 (SI 1986/1794)
	(3)	See Sch 1 below
2, 3		6 Jan 1986 (SI 1985/1887)
4		6 Jan 1986 (to extent necessary to replace Public Passenger Vehicles Act 1981, s 54 with sub-ss (1), (2) only of the new s 54) (SI 1985/1887)
		26 Oct 1986 (otherwise) (SI 1986/1794)
5		6 Jan 1986 (SI 1985/1887)
6		26 Oct 1986 (SI 1986/1794)
7–9		14 Jul 1986 (SI 1986/1088)
10, 11		1 Aug 1986 (SI 1986/1088)
12	(1), (2)	6 Jan 1986 (SI 1985/1887)
	(3)	Repealed
	(4)–(13)	6 Jan 1986 (SI 1985/1887)
13		6 Jan 1986 (to the extent that supplements s 12 of this Act) (SI 1985/1887)
		1 Aug 1986 (otherwise) (SI 1986/1088)
14, 15		1 Jan 1987 (SI 1986/1794)
16		6 Jan 1986 (SI 1985/1887)
17		1 Aug 1986 (SI 1986/1088)

Transport Act 1985 (c 67)—*contd*
Section

18		1 Aug 1986 (so far as relates to the use of any vehicle under a permit granted under s 22 or the driving of any vehicle so used) (SI 1986/1088) 13 Aug 1987 (otherwise) (SI 1987/1228)
19–21		13 Aug 1987 (SI 1987/1228)
22, 23		1 Aug 1986 (SI 1986/1088)
24	(1)	26 Oct 1986 (SI 1986/1794)
	(2)	Repealed
25–27		26 Oct 1986 (SI 1986/1794)
28	(1), (2)	26 Oct 1986 (SI 1986/1794)
	(2A)	Inserted by Deregulation and Contracting Out Act 1994, s 67 (qv)
	(3)–(6)	26 Oct 1986 (SI 1986/1794)
	(6A)	Inserted by Deregulation and Contracting Out Act 1994, s 67 (qv)
	(7)	26 Oct 1986 (SI 1986/1794)
29, 30		6 Jan 1986 (SI 1985/1887)
31		15 Sep 1986 (SI 1986/1450)
32		6 Jan 1986 (to the extent that applies to Public Passenger Vehicles Act 1981, s 28) (SI 1985/1887) 26 Oct 1986 (otherwise) (SI 1986/1794)
33		1 Aug 1986 (SI 1986/1088)
34		6 Jan 1986 (SI 1985/1887); prospectively repealed by Greater London Authority Act 1999, s 423, Sch 34, Pt II[1]
35–46		26 Oct 1986 (SI 1986/1794); prospectively repealed by Greater London Authority Act 1999, s 423, Sch 34, Pt II[1]
47–53		Repealed
54–56		6 Jan 1986 (SI 1985/1887)
57	(1)–(5)	6 Jan 1986 (SI 1985/1887)
	(6)	See Sch 3 below
58		30 Oct 1985 (s 140(2))
59–80		6 Jan 1986 (SI 1985/1887)
81	(1), (2)	6 Jan 1986 (SI 1985/1887)
	(2A)	Inserted by Local Government (Wales) Act 1994, s 22(1), Sch 7, Pt II, para 39 (qv)
	(3)–(5)	6 Jan 1986 (SI 1985/1887)
	(5A)	Inserted by Local Government (Wales) Act 1994, s 22(1), Sch 7, Pt II, para 39 (qv)

Transport Act 1985 (c 67)—*contd*

Section

81	(6), (7)		6 Jan 1986 (SI 1985/1887)
82–84			6 Jan 1986 (SI 1985/1887)
85, 86			13 Aug 1987 (SI 1987/1228)
87–92			6 Jan 1986 (SI 1985/1887)
93	(1)–(7)		14 Feb 1986 (SI 1986/80)
	(8)	(a)	14 Feb 1986 (SI 1986/80)
		(b)	1 Apr 1986 (SI 1986/414)
	(9), (10)		14 Feb 1986 (SI 1986/80)
94–101			14 Feb 1986 (SI 1986/80)
102			1 Apr 1986 (SI 1986/414)
103			14 Feb 1986 (SI 1986/80)
104			15 Sep 1986 (SI 1986/1450)
105	(1), (2)		14 Feb 1986 (SI 1986/80)
	(2A)		Inserted by Local Government (Wales) Act 1994, s 22(1), Sch 7, Pt II, para 39 (qv)
	(3)		14 Feb 1986 (SI 1986/80)
106			6 Jan 1986 (SI 1985/1887)
106A			Inserted by Local Government and Rating Act 1997, s 27 (qv)
107			1 Apr 1986 (SI 1985/1887); prospectively repealed by Greater London Authority Act 1999, s 423, Sch 34, Pt II[1]
108			1 Apr 1986 (SI 1986/414)
109			Repealed
110			6 Jan 1986 (SI 1985/1887); prospectively repealed by Transport Act 2000, s 274, Sch 31, Pt II[2]
111			26 Oct 1986 (SI 1986/1794); prospectively repealed in relation to England and Wales by Transport Act 2000, ss 154(6), 274, Sch 31, Pt II and in relation to Scotland by Transport (Scotland) Act 2001, s 38(6)[2]
112, 113			6 Jan 1986 (SI 1985/1887)
114			26 Jul 1986 (SI 1986/1088)
115, 116			Repealed
117			15 Sep 1986 (SI 1986/1450)
118–124			6 Jan 1986 (SI 1985/1887); prospectively repealed by Transport Act 2000, s 274, Sch 31, Pt IV[2]
125			6 Jan 1986 (SI 1985/1887)
126	(1), (2)		1 Aug 1986 (so far as relate to fees chargeable in respect of applications for, and the grant of, permits under s 22) (SI 1986/1088)

Transport Act 1985 (c 67)—*contd*
Section

126	(1), (2)—*contd*		26 Oct 1986 (otherwise, except so far as sub-s (1) relates to applications for and the grant of permits under s 19) (SI 1986/1794)
			13 Aug 1987 (otherwise) (SI 1987/1228)
	(3)	(a)	26 Oct 1986 (SI 1986/1794)
		(b)	14 Jul 1986 (SI 1986/1088)
		(c)	26 Oct 1986 (SI 1986/1794)
127	(1), (2)		1 Aug 1986 (SI 1986/1088)
	(3)		6 Jan 1986 (SI 1985/1887)
	(4)		6 Jan 1986 (so far as relates to s 30(2)) (SI 1985/1887)
			1 Aug 1986 (so far as relates to s 23(5)) (SI 1986/1088)
			26 Oct 1986 (otherwise) (SI 1986/1794)
	(5)–(7)		6 Jan 1986 (SI 1985/1887)
128–130			6 Jan 1986 (SI 1985/1887)
131	(1)–(5)		Repealed
	(6), (7)		6 Jan 1986 (SI 1985/1887)
132–136			6 Jan 1986 (SI 1985/1887)
137	(1), (2)		6 Jan 1986 (SI 1985/1887)
	(2A)		Inserted by Local Government (Wales) Act 1994, s 22(1), Sch 7, Pt II, para 39 (qv)
	(3)–(8)		6 Jan 1986 (SI 1985/1887)
138			6 Jan 1986 (SI 1985/1887)
139	(1)–(3)		See Schs 6–8 below
	(4), (5)		6 Jan 1986 (SI 1985/1887)
140			30 Oct 1985 (s 140(2))

Schedule

1, para	1, 2		6 Jan 1986 (SI 1985/1887)
	3	(1), (2)	6 Jan 1986 (SI 1985/1887)
		(3)	26 Oct 1986 (SI 1986/1794)
		(4)	6 Jan 1986 (except omission of words 'or Part III') (SI 1985/1887)
			26 Oct 1986 (exception noted above) (SI 1986/1794)
		(5)	6 Jan 1986 (SI 1985/1887)
	4		6 Jan 1986 (SI 1985/1887)
	5		Repealed
	6		6 Jan 1986 (SI 1985/1887)
	7–11		26 Oct 1986 (SI 1986/1794)
	12		6 Jan 1986 (SI 1985/1887)
	13		6 Jan 1986 (except omission of definitions 'excursion or tour', 'road service licence', 'trial area') (SI 1985/1887)

Transport Act 1985 (c 67)—*contd*

Schedule

1, para	13—*contd*		26 Oct 1986 (exceptions noted above) (SI 1986/1794)
	14		6 Jan 1986 (SI 1985/1887)
	15	(1)	6 Jan 1986 (SI 1985/1887)
		(2), (3)	26 Oct 1986 (SI 1986/1794)
		(4), (5)	6 Jan 1986 (SI 1985/1887)
	16		6 Jan 1986 (SI 1985/1887)
2			6 Jan 1986 (SI 1985/1887)
3, para	1–7		6 Jan 1986 (SI 1985/1887)
	8		Repealed
	9–21		6 Jan 1986 (SI 1985/1887)
	22		Repealed
	23		6 Jan 1986 (SI 1985/1887)
	24		6 Jan 1986 (to the extent that it relates to Local Government Act 1972, s 202(1), (4)–(7)) (SI 1985/1887)
			1 Apr 1986 (otherwise) (SI 1986/414)
	25		6 Jan 1986 (SI 1985/1887)
	26		1 Apr 1986 (SI 1986/414)
	27, 28		6 Jan 1986 (SI 1985/1887)
	29		Repealed
	30–33		6 Jan 1986 (SI 1985/1887)
4			15 Sep 1986 (SI 1986/1450)
5			6 Jan 1986 (SI 1985/1887)
6, para	1–5		Spent
	6–11		6 Jan 1986 (SI 1985/1887)
	12		30 Oct 1985 (s 140(2))
	13		6 Jan 1986 (SI 1985/1887)
	14		26 Oct 1986 (SI 1986/1794)
	15		6 Jan 1986 (SI 1985/1887)
	16–18		26 Oct 1986 (SI 1986/1794)
	19		6 Jan 1986 (SI 1985/1887)
	20		Spent
	21		6 Jan 1986 (SI 1985/1887)
	22, 23		14 Feb 1986 (SI 1986/80) (also purportedly brought into force, to the extent that not already in force, by SI 1986/414)
	24, 25		15 Sep 1986 (SI 1986/1450)
	26		6 Jan 1986 (SI 1985/1887)
7, para	1		6 Jan 1986 (SI 1985/1887)
	2		1 Aug 1986 (SI 1986/1088)
	3		1 Apr 1986 (SI 1986/414)
	4		6 Jan 1986 (SI 1985/1887)
	5		26 Oct 1986 (SI 1986/1794)
	6		6 Jan 1986 (SI 1985/1887); prospectively repealed by Transport Act 2000, s 274, Sch 31, Pt IV[2]

Transport Act 1985 (c 67)—*contd*
Schedule

7, para	7, 8		15 Sep 1986 (SI 1986/1450)
	9		1 Apr 1986 (SI 1986/414)
	10–12		6 Jan 1986 (SI 1985/1887)
	13		Repealed
	14		6 Jan 1986 (SI 1985/1887)
	15		Repealed
	16		26 Oct 1986 (SI 1986/1794)
	17		1 Apr 1986 (SI 1986/414)
	18		6 Jan 1986 (SI 1985/1887)
	19		1 Apr 1986 (SI 1986/414)
	20		6 Jan 1986 (SI 1985/1887)
	21	(1)	6 Jan 1986 (SI 1985/1887)
		(2), (3)	Repealed
		(4)	6 Jan 1986 (except words 'sub-section (1A) below and') (SI 1985/1887) 26 Oct 1986 (exception noted above) (SI 1986/1794)
		(5)	26 Oct 1986 (SI 1986/1794)
		(6)	6 Jan 1986 (SI 1985/1887)
		(7)	Repealed
		(8)	6 Jan 1986 (SI 1985/1887)
		(9)	26 Oct 1986 (SI 1986/1794)
		(10)	26 Oct 1986 (SI 1986/1794); prospectively repealed by Transport Act 2000, s 274, Sch 31, Pt V[2]
		(11)	15 Sep 1986 (SI 1986/1450)
		(12)	6 Jan 1986 (SI 1985/1887)
	22		Repealed
	23		6 Jan 1986 (SI 1985/1887)
	24		1 Apr 1986 (SI 1986/414)
	25, 26		26 Oct 1986 (SI 1986/1794)
8			6 Jan 1986 (repeals of or in Road Traffic Act 1930; Transport Act 1962, ss 4, 92; Finance Act 1965; Transport Act 1968, ss 9, 10(2), 11(1), 12(3)(d), 14(3), 15, 15(A)(1), 16(2), 17–19, 20, 21, 22, 24(3), 29(4), 34, 36, 54, 59(3), 90, 103(1), 159(1), Sch 5; Post Office Act 1969; Local Government Act 1972, ss 80(4), 202, Sch 24, Pt II; Local Government Act 1974; Energy Act 1976, Sch 1, para 1(2); Transport Act 1978; Transport Act 1980; Public Passenger Vehicles Act 1981, ss 1, 2, 28, 46, 53(1) (word 'the' before words 'traffic commissioners'), 56, 60, 61(2), 62,

Transport Act 1985 (c 67)—*contd*
Schedule
8—*contd*

81(2), 82(1) (definitions 'contract carriage', 'express carriage', 'express carriage service', 'stage carriage' and 'stage carriage service'), 83, Sch 1, paras 3, 4; Transport Act 1982, s 73(4); Transport Act 1983, s 9(2); Road Traffic Regulation Act 1984, Sch 13, para 49; London Regional Transport Act 1984, s 28, Sch 6, paras 3, 6) (SI 1985/1887)

1 Apr 1986 (repeals of or in Finance Act 1970; Local Government Act 1972, s 202(2), (3); Local Government (Scotland) Act 1973, s 150; Transport Act 1983, s 3; Local Government Act 1985) (SI 1986/414)

26 Jul 1986 (repeal of London Regional Transport Act 1984, Sch 6, para 15(1)(a)) (SI 1986/1088)

15 Sep 1986 (repeals of or in Transport Act 1962, s 57, Sch 10; Transport Act 1968, s 88, Sch 10) (SI 1986/1450)

26 Oct 1986 (otherwise except those of or in Town Police Clauses Act 1847 (which entry is now itself repealed); Public Passenger Vehicles Act 1981, ss 42–44, 52, 67, 76 (words 'except sections 42 to 44' and word 'thereof')) (SI 1986/1794)

13 Aug 1987 (otherwise except repeal of words 'such number of' and 'as they think fit' in Town Police Clauses Act 1847, s 37 (which repeal entry is now itself repealed)) (SI 1987/1228)

---

[1]   Orders made under Greater London Authority Act 1999, s 425, bringing the prospective repeals into force will be noted to that Act

[2]   Orders made under Transport Act 2000, s 275, and Transport (Scotland) Act 2001, s 84, bringing the prospective repeals into force will be noted to the respective Acts

Trustee Savings Banks Act 1985 (c 58)

RA: 25 Jul 1985

Commencement provisions: ss 1(4), 2(4), 4(3)–(5), 7(2), Sch 1, Pt III, para 13; Trustee
 Savings Banks Act 1985 (Appointed Day) (No 1) Order 1985, SI 1986/1219;
 Trustee Savings Banks Act 1985 (Appointed Day) (No 2) Order 1986,
 SI 1986/1220; Trustee Savings Banks Act 1985 (Appointed Day) (No 3)
 Order 1986, SI 1986/1222; Trustee Savings Banks Act 1985 (Appointed Day)
 (No 4) Order 1986, SI 1986/1223; Trustee Savings Banks Act 1985 (Appointed
 Day) (No 6) Order 1988, SI 1988/1168; Trustee Savings Banks Act 1985
 (Appointed Day) (No 7) Order 1990, SI 1990/1982 (*Note:* No (Appointed Day)
 (No 5) Order was made)

Section

1–5		25 Sep 1985 (s 7(2)) (but note 21 Jul 1986 was the vesting day appointed under s 1(4) (SI 1986/1222); 31 Oct 1990 was the day appointed under s 2(4) on which the Trustee Savings Bank Central Board ceased to exist (SI 1990/1982))
6		Repealed
7		25 Sep 1985 (s 7(2))
Schedule		
1, para	1–7	25 Sep 1985 (s 7(2))
	8, 9	Repealed
	10, 11	25 Sep 1985 (s 7(2))
	12	25 Sep 1985 (s 7(2)); but this paragraph never had any effect
	13	20 Jul 1986 (SI 1986/1219)
2		25 Sep 1985 (s 7(2))
3		Repealed
4		20 Jul 1986 (repeals of or in Finance Act 1921; Finance Act 1946; Finance Act 1969; National Savings Bank Act 1971; Trustee Savings Banks Act 1981, Sch 7, para 10, para 12(a) (words '4 to 7')) (SI 1986/1220)
		21 Jul 1986 (repeals of or in Bankers' Books Evidence Act 1879; Consolidated Fund (Permanent Charges Redemption) Act 1883; Savings Banks Act 1887; Bankruptcy Act 1914; Agricultural Credits Act 1928; Agricultural Credits (Scotland) Act 1929; Government Annuities Act 1929; Payment of Wages Act 1960; Companies Act (Northern

Trustee Savings Banks Act 1985 (c 58)—*contd*
Schedule
4—*contd*

Ireland) 1960; Trustee
Investments Act 1961; Clergy
Pensions Measure 1961; Building
Societies Act 1962; Administration
of Estates (Small Payments)
Act 1965; Building Societies Act
(Northern Ireland) 1967; Payment
of Wages Act (Northern Ireland)
1970; Friendly Societies Act
(Northern Ireland) 1970; Northern
Ireland Constitution Act 1973;
Pensions (Increase) Act 1974;
Friendly Societies Act 1974;
Solicitors Act 1974; Financial
Provisions (Northern Ireland)
Order 1976; Home Purchase
Assistance and Housing
Corporation Guarantee Act 1978;
Credit Unions Act 1979, s 31(1)(b)
in definition 'authorised bank';
Banking Act 1979; Solicitors
(Scotland) Act 1980; British
Telecommunications
Act 1981; Trustee Savings Banks
Act 1981, ss 1, 2, 3(1), (2), 4, 5,
6(1), 7(3), (5), (6), 8–11, 13
(words 'to the Central Board and'
and ', and shall furnish such
particulars of that person as the
Central Board may direct'), 14,
15(1)–(8), (11), 16(1), (3), (4), 17,
18, 19(1)–(4), 20–22, 25(1) (the
words 'to the Central Board and'),
(2), 26–50, 52, 55(1), (3), Schs 1,
2, paras 1(a), (c), (3), (4), 4, 11,
13–16, Schs 4, 6, Sch 7, para 5–8,
9(1), 11, 12, (so far as unrepealed),
13–15, Sch 8; Housing (Northern
Ireland) Order 1981; Companies
(Northern Ireland) Order 1982;
Companies Act 1985)
(SI 1986/1223)

5 Jul 1988 (repeal of Trustee
Savings Banks Act 1981, ss 12, 13
(so far as unrepealed), 23, 24, 25
(so far as unrepealed), 51, 53,
Schs 3, 5, Sch 7, para 9(2);
Insolvency Act 1986, s 220(3))
(SI 1988/1168)

Trustee Savings Banks Act 1985 (c 58)—*contd*
Schedule
4—*contd*   31 Oct 1990 (repeal of Trustee
                                              Savings Banks Act 1981, ss 3(3),
                                              6(2), 7(1), (2), (4), 15(9), (10),
                                              16(2), 19(5), 54, 55(2), (4), 56, 57,
                                              Sch 2 (so far as unrepealed), Sch 7,
                                              paras 1–4) (SI 1990/1982)

Water (Fluoridation) Act 1985 (c 63)

RA: 30 Oct 1985

30 Oct 1985 (RA)

Whole Act repealed (E, W)

Weights and Measures Act 1985 (c 72)

RA: 30 Oct 1985

Commencement provisions: ss 43(2) (repealed), 99(2); Weights and Measures Act 1985
    (Commencement) Order 1992, SI 1992/770 (revoked); Weights and Measures
    Act 1985 (Revocation) Order 1993, SI 1993/2698 (revoked Weights and
    Measures Act 1985 (Commencement) Order 1992, SI 1992/770, which
    appointed 1 Apr 1994 as the date on which s 43 (now repealed) was to come
    into force)
Section
1–11   30 Jan 1986 (s 99(2))
11A   Inserted (29 Mar 1999) by
                                              Deregulation (Weights and
                                              Measures) Order 1999,
                                              SI 1999/503, art 2(7)
11B   Inserted (29 Mar 1999) by
                                              Deregulation (Weights and
                                              Measures) Order 1999,
                                              SI 1999/503, art 3
12–15   30 Jan 1986 (s 99(2))
15A   Inserted (29 Mar 1999) by
                                              Deregulation (Weights and
                                              Measures) Order 1999,
                                              SI 1999/503, art 4(1)
16–42   30 Jan 1986 (s 99(2))
43   Repealed (*never in force*)
44–59   30 Jan 1986 (s 99(2))
60, 61   Repealed
62–99   30 Jan 1986 (s 99(2))
Schedule
1–3   30 Jan 1986 (s 99(2))

Weights and Measures Act 1985 (c 72)—*contd*

Schedule

3A	Inserted (29 Mar 1999) by Deregulation (Weights and Measures) Order 1999, SI 1999/503, art 2(15)
4–8	30 Jan 1986 (s 99(2))
9	Repealed
10–13	30 Jan 1986 (s 99(2))

Wildlife and Countryside (Amendment) Act 1985 (c 31)

RA: 26 Jun 1985

Commencement provisions: s 5(3)

26 Aug 1985 (s 5(3))

Wildlife and Countryside (Service of Notices) Act 1985 (c 59)

RA: 25 Jul 1985

25 Jul 1985 (RA)

1986

Advance Petroleum Revenue Tax Act 1986 (c 68)

RA: 18 Dec 1986

18 Dec 1986 (RA)

Note: Petroleum Revenue Tax (levied in accordance with Oil Taxation Act 1975, Pt I (ss 1–12, Schs 1–8)) abolished for new oil and gas fields ("non-taxable fields") with effect from 16 Mar 1993, by Finance Act 1993, s 185

Agricultural Holdings Act 1986 (c 5)

RA: 18 Mar 1986

Commencement provisions: s 102(2)

18 Jun 1986 (s 102(2))

Note: by virtue of Agricultural Tenancies Act 1995, s 4, this Act does not apply in relation to any tenancy beginning on or after 1 Sep 1995, with the exception of specified tenancies of an agricultural holding

---

Agriculture Act 1986 (c 49)

RA: 25 Jul 1986

Commencement provisions: s 24(2), (3); Agriculture Act 1986 (Commencement) (No 1) Order 1986, SI 1986/1484; Agriculture Act 1986 (Commencement) (No 2) (Scotland) Order 1986, SI 1986/1485; Agriculture Act 1986 (Commencement No 3) Order 1986, SI 1986/1596; Agriculture Act 1986 (Commencement No 4) Order 1986, SI 1986/2301; Agriculture Act 1986 (Commencement No 5) Order 1991, SI 1991/2635; Agriculture Act 1986 (Commencement No 6) Order 1998, SI 1998/879

Section		
1–7		25 Sep 1986 (s 24(2))
8	(1)	*Not in force*
	(2)	8 Sep 1986 (SI 1986/1596)
	(3)	*Not in force*
	(4)–(6)	1 Apr 1998 (SI 1998/879)
9		25 Sep 1986 (s 24(2))
10		31 Dec 1986 (SI 1986/2301)
11		25 Sep 1986 (s 24(2))
12		25 Jul 1986 (RA)
13		25 Sep 1986 (SI 1986/1484)

Agriculture Act 1986 (c 49)—*contd*

Section

14		25 Sep 1986 (SI 1986/1485)
15		25 Sep 1986 (SI 1986/1484)
16		25 Sep 1986 (SI 1986/1485)
17		25 Sep 1986 (s 24(2))
18	(1)–(4)	25 Sep 1986 (s 24(2))
	(4A)	Inserted (1 Jul 1997) by Agriculture Act 1986 (Amendment) Regulations 1997, SI 1997/1457, reg 2
	(5)–(12)	25 Sep 1986 (s 24(2))
	(13)	25 Jul 1986 (RA)
19, 20		25 Sep 1986 (s 24(2))
21, 22		Repealed
23		25 Sep 1986 (s 24(2))
23A		Inserted (S) by Agricultural Holdings (Scotland) Act 1991, s 88(1), Sch 11, para 45 (qv)
24		25 Sep 1986 (s 24(2))

Schedule

1	25 Sep 1986 (SI 1986/1484)
2	25 Sep 1986 (SI 1986/1485)
3	25 Sep 1986 (s 24(2))
4	25 Sep 1986 (except repeals consequential on ss 8–10) (s 24(2))
	31 Dec 1986 (repeals consequential on ss 9, 10) (SI 1986/2301)
	21 Nov 1991 (repeals in House of Commons Disqualification Act 1975; Northern Ireland Assembly Disqualification Act 1975) (SI 1991/2635)
	Not in force (repeals consequential on s 8)

Airports Act 1986 (c 31)

RA: 8 Jul 1986

Commencement provisions: s 85(2)–(6); Airports Act 1986 (Commencement No 1 and Appointed Day) Order 1986, SI 1986/1228; Airports Act 1986 (Commencement No 2) Order 1986, SI 1986/1487

Section

1	Spent
2	1 Aug 1986 (SI 1986/1228)
3	8 Jul 1986 (s 85(2))
4–9	1 Aug 1986 (SI 1986/1228)
10	1 Aug 1986 (SI 1986/1228); prospectively repealed by Financial Services Act 1986, s 212(3), Sch 17, Pt I[1]

Airports Act 1986 (c 31)—*contd*

Section

11		1 Aug 1986 (SI 1986/1228)
12–35		8 Sep 1986 (s 85(4))
36–56		1 Oct 1986 (SI 1986/1487)
57–62		31 Jul 1986 (SI 1986/1228)
63–66		1 Apr 1986 (SI 1986/1228)
67		1 Oct 1986 (SI 1986/1487)
68		8 Sep 1986 (SI 1986/1228)
69		1 Oct 1986 (SI 1986/1487)
70, 71		Repealed
72		8 Sep 1986 (s 85(4))
73, 74		1 Oct 1986 (SI 1986/1487)
75		8 Jul 1986 (s 85(2))
76	(1), (2)	Repealed
	(3), (4)	8 Jul 1986 (s 85(2))
	(5)	Repealed
77	(1), (2)	1 Aug 1986 (SI 1986/1228)
	(3)	Substituted by Finance Act 1996, s 104, Sch 14, para 3 (qv)
	(4)	1 Aug 1986 (SI 1986/1228)
	(5), (6)	8 Jul 1986 (s 85(2))
78		8 Sep 1986 (s 85(4))
79–82		8 Jul 1986 (s 85(2))
83	(1)	See Sch 4 below
	(2)	1 Aug 1986 (SI 1986/1228)
	(3)	1 Oct 1986 (SI 1986/1487)
	(4)	1 Aug 1986 (SI 1986/1228)
	(5)	See Sch 6 below
84		8 Sep 1986 (s 85(4))
85		8 Jul 1986 (s 85(2))

Schedule

1		1 Oct 1986 (SI 1986/1487)
2		31 Jul 1986 (SI 1986/1228)
3		1 Aug 1986 (SI 1986/1228)
4, para	1, 2	Repealed
	3–8	1 Oct 1986 (SI 1986/1487)
	9	1 Aug 1986 (SI 1986/1228)
	10	1 Aug 1986 (except the expression '60(3)(o)') (SI 1986/1228) 1 Apr 1987 (exception noted above) (SI 1986/1487)
5		1 Aug 1986 (SI 1986/1228)
6, Pt	I	1 Aug 1986 (SI 1986/1228)
	II	1 Aug 1986 (repeals of or in Civil Aviation Act 1982, ss 27, 29, 32, 33, 37, 40, 58, 99, Sch 5, Sch 13, Pt II (entries relating to ss 32(5), 33(1), 37, 40(2)), Sch 14; Criminal Justice Act 1982) (SI 1986/1228)

Airports Act 1986 (c 31)—*contd*

Schedule

6, Pt	II—*contd*	1 Oct 1986 (repeal in Fair Trading Act 1973) (SI 1986/1487) 1 Apr 1987 (repeals of or in Local Government, Planning and Land Act 1980; Civil Aviation Act 1982, s 38, Sch 13, Pt II, entry relating to s 61(6)) (SI 1986/1487)

---

[1] Orders made under Financial Services Act 1986, s 211, bringing the prospective repeal into force will be noted to that Act

---

Animals (Scientific Procedures) Act 1986 (c 14)

RA: 20 May 1986

Commencement provisions: s 30(3); Animals (Scientific Procedures) Act (Commencement) Order 1986, SI 1986/2088; Animals (Scientific Procedures) (1986 Act) (Commencement No 1) Order (Northern Ireland) 1986, SR 1986/364 (NI); Animals (Scientific Procedures) Act (Commencement No 2) Order 1989, SI 1989/2306; Animals (Scientific Procedures) (1986 Act) (Commencement No 2) Order (Northern Ireland) 1989, SR 1989/496 (NI)

Section

1–6		1 Jan 1987 (SI 1986/2088)
7		1 Jan 1990 (SI 1989/2306; SR 1989/496)
8, 9		1 Jan 1987 (SI 1986/2088)
10	(1), (2)	1 Jan 1987 (SI 1986/2088)
	(2A)	Inserted (5 Sep 1998) by Animals (Scientific Procedures) Act 1986 (Amendment) Regulations 1998, SI 1998/1974, reg 2, Schedule, paras 1, 4(1), (2)
	(3)	1 Jan 1990 (SI 1989/2306; SR 1989/496)
	(3A)	Inserted (1 Oct 1993) by Animals (Scientific Procedures) Act 1986 (Amendment) Regulations 1993, SI 1993/2102, reg 2(1), (3)
	(3B)–(3D)	Inserted (5 Sep 1998) by Animals (Scientific Procedures) Act 1986 (Amendment) Regulations 1998, SI 1998/1974, reg 2, Schedule, paras 1, 4(1), (4)
	(4), (5)	1 Jan 1987 (SI 1986/2088)
	(5A)	Inserted (5 Sep 1998) by Animals (Scientific Procedures) Act 1986 (Amendment) Regulations 1998, SI 1998/1974, reg 2, Schedule, paras 1, 4(1), (5)
	(6)	1 Jan 1987 (SI 1986/2088)

Animals (Scientific Procedures) Act 1986 (c 14)—*contd*
Section

10	(6A)–(6D)	Inserted (5 Sep 1998) by Animals (Scientific Procedures) Act 1986 (Amendment) Regulations 1998, SI 1998/1974, reg 2, Schedule, paras 1, 4(1), (6)
	(7)	1 Jan 1987 (SI 1986/2088)
11–13		1 Jan 1987 (SI 1986/2088)
14		Substituted (5 Sep 1998) by Animals (Scientific Procedures) Act 1986 (Amendment) Regulations 1998, SI 1998/1974, reg 2, Schedule, paras 1, 5
15–28		1 Jan 1987 (SI 1986/2088)
29		1 Jan 1987 (NI) (SR 1986/364)
30		1 Jan 1987 (SI 1986/2088)

Schedule

1	Substituted (1 Mar 1997) by Animals (Scientific Procedures) Act 1986 (Appropriate Methods of Humane Killing) Order 1996, SI 1996/3278, art 2, Schedule
2	1 Jan 1990 (SI 1989/2306; SR 1989/496)
2A	Inserted (5 Sep 1998) by Animals (Scientific Procedures) Act 1986 (Amendment) Regulations 1998, SI 1998/1974, reg 2, Schedule, paras 1, 6
3, 4	1 Jan 1987 (SI 1986/2088)

Appropriation Act 1986 (c 42)

Whole Act repealed

Armed Forces Act 1986 (c 21)

RA: 26 Jun 1986

Commencement provisions: s 17(2), (3); Armed Forces Act 1986 (Commencement No 1) Order 1986, SI 1986/2071; Armed Forces Act 1986 (Commencement No 2) Order 1986, SI 1986/2124; Armed Forces Act 1986 (Commencement No 3) Order 1987, SI 1987/1998

Section

1	Repealed
2	1 Jan 1987 (SI 1986/2124)
3	1 Jan 1987 (SI 1986/2124)
	Repealed (E, W)
4–8	1 Jan 1987 (SI 1986/2124)

Armed Forces Act 1986 (c 21)—*contd*
Section
9		31 Dec 1987 (SI 1987/1998)
10–12		1 Jan 1987 (SI 1986/2124)
13		Repealed
14		30 Dec 1986 (SI 1986/2071)
15		26 Jun 1986 (RA)
16	(1)	1 Jan 1987 (SI 1986/2124)
	(2)	See Sch 2 below
	(3)	1 Jan 1987 (SI 1986/2124)
17		26 Jun 1986 (RA)

Schedule
1	1 Jan 1987 (SI 1986/2124)
2	1 Sep 1986 (repeal of Armed Forces Act 1981, s 1) (s 17(3))
	30 Dec 1986 (repeal of Army Act 1955, s 213(a)) (SI 1986/2071)
	1 Jan 1987 (otherwise) (SI 1986/2124)

Atomic Energy Authority Act 1986 (c 3)

RA: 19 Feb 1986

Commencement provisions: s 10(2)

1 Apr 1986 (s 10(2))

Australia Act 1986 (c 2)

RA: 17 Feb 1986

Commencement provisions: s 17(2); Australia Act 1986 (Commencement) Order 1986, SI 1986/319

3 Mar 1986 (at 5 am GMT) (SI 1986/319)

Bishops (Retirement) Measure 1986 (No 1)

RA: 18 Mar 1986

Commencement provisions: s 13(3)

1 Jun 1986 (the day appointed by the Archbishops of Canterbury and York under s 13(3))

British Council and Commonwealth Institute Superannuation Act 1986 (c 51)

RA: 25 Jul 1986

Commencement provisions: s 3(2); British Council and Commonwealth Institute Superannuation Act 1986 (Commencement No 1) Order 1986, SI 1986/1860; British Council and Commonwealth Institute Superannuation Act 1986 (Commencement No 2) Order 1987, SI 1987/588

10 Nov 1986 (in relation to British Council) (SI 1986/1860)

1 Apr 1987 (in relation to Commonwealth Institute) (SI 1987/588)

British Shipbuilders (Borrowing Powers) Act 1986 (c 19)

Whole Act repealed

Building Societies Act 1986 (c 53)

RA: 25 Jul 1986

Commencement provisions: s 126(2)–(4); Building Societies Act 1986 (Commencement No 1) Order 1986, SI 1986/1560; Building Societies Act 1986 (Commencement No 2) Order 1989, SI 1989/1083

Section

1–4	Substituted (1 Dec 2001) by Financial Services and Markets Act 2000 (Mutual Societies) Order 2001, SI 2001/2617, art 13(1), Sch 3, Pt II, paras 131, 132
5	1 Jan 1987 (SI 1986/1560)
6	Substituted by Building Societies Act 1997, s 4 (qv)
6A	Inserted by Building Societies Act 1997, s 5 (qv)
6B	Inserted by Building Societies Act 1997, s 6, subject to transitional provisions (qv)
6C	Inserted by Building Societies Act 1997, s 7(1) (qv)
7	Substituted by Building Societies Act 1997, s 8 (qv)
8	Substituted by Building Societies Act 1997, s 9, subject to savings (qv)
9	Repealed
9A	Inserted by Building Societies Act 1997, s 10 (qv)
9B	Inserted by Building Societies Act 1997, s 11(qv)
10–31	Repealed
32	1 Jan 1987 (SI 1986/1560)
33, 34	Repealed
35	Repealed (*never in force*)
36	Substituted by Building Societies Act 1997, s 13(1) (qv)
36A	Inserted by Building Societies Act 1997, s 14 (qv)
37	Substituted by Building Societies Act 1997, s 15 (qv)
38–42A	Repealed
42B	Inserted by Building Societies Act 1997, s 17 (qv)
42C	Inserted by Building Societies Act 1997, s 18 (qv)

Building Societies Act 1986 (c 53)—*contd*

Building Societies Act 1986 (c 53)—*contd*

Section

102B–102D		Inserted by Building Societies (Distributions) Act 1997, s 1(1) (qv), with effect in relation to a transfer of business of a building society in any case where the decision of the board of directors of the society to enter into the transfer in question is made public after 22 Jan 1997
103	(1)	1 Jan 1987 (so far as relates to societies dissolved by ss 93(5) or 94(10)) (SI 1986/1560)
		1 Jan 1988 (otherwise) (SI 1986/1560)
	(2)–(9)	1 Jan 1987 (SI 1986/1560)
104		1 Jan 1987 (SI 1986/1560)
104A		Inserted by Building Societies Act 1997, s 42 (qv)
105		Repealed
106, 107		1 Jan 1987 (SI 1986/1560)
108		Repealed
109	(1)	25 Sep 1986 (so far as it relates to the exemption from stamp duties of any instrument referred to in s 109(1)(e) and required or authorised to be given, issued, signed, made or produced in pursuance of this Act) (SI 1986/1560)
		1 Jan 1987 (otherwise) (SI 1986/1560)
		(Formerly s 109, renumbered (29 Jul 1988) as s 109(1) by Finance Act 1988, s 145, Sch 12, para 8)
	(2)	Added (29 Jul 1988) by Finance Act 1988, s 145, Sch 12, para 8
110, 111		1 Jan 1987 (SI 1986/1560)
112	(1)	25 Sep 1986 (SI 1986/1560)
	(2)	Repealed
	(3), (4)	25 Sep 1986 (SI 1986/1560)
113		25 Sep 1986 (so far as relates to a memorandum or rules agreed upon under Sch 20, para 2) (SI 1986/1560)
		1 Jan 1987 (otherwise) (SI 1986/1560)
114		1 Jan 1987 (SI 1986/1560)
115		25 Sep 1986 (SI 1986/1560)
116		Substituted (1 Dec 2001) by Financial Services and Markets Act 2000 (Mutual Societies) Order 2001, SI 2001/2617, art 13(1), Sch 3, Pt II, paras 131, 195

Building Societies Act 1986 (c 53)—*contd*

Building Societies Act 1986 (c 53)—*contd*
Schedule

14		1 Jan 1987 (SI 1986/1560)
15, para	1–33	1 Jan 1988 (SI 1986/1560)
	34–55E	Substituted (1 Oct 1991) for original paras 34–55 by Insolvency (Northern Ireland) Order 1989, SI 1989/2405 (NI 19), art 381, Sch 9, Pt II(1), para 45(c)
	56, 57	1 Jan 1988 (SI 1986/1560)
	58, 59	1 Jan 1987 (SI 1986/1560)
15A		Inserted by Building Societies Act 1997, s 39(2), Sch 6 (qv)
16		1 Jan 1987 (SI 1986/1560)
17		1 Jan 1988 (SI 1986/1560)
18		1 Jan 1987 (SI 1986/1560)
19, Pt	I	1 Jan 1987 (except repeals of or in Building Societies Act 1874; Building Societies Act 1894; Building Societies Act 1960, Sch 5; Building Societies Act 1962, ss 28–31, Pt VII) (SI 1986/1560)
		1 Jan 1988 (otherwise, except repeal of 1962 Act, ss 28–31) (SI 1986/1560)
		17 Jul 1989 (repeal of 1962 Act, ss 28–31) (SI 1989/1083)
	II	1 Jan 1987 (SI 1986/1560)
	III	1 Jan 1987 (except repeal of Building Societies Act (Northern Ireland) 1967, ss 28–31, Pt VII) (SI 1986/1560)
		1 Jan 1988 (repeal of 1967 Act, Pt VII) (SI 1986/1560)
		17 Jul 1989 (repeal of 1967 Act, ss 28–31) (SI 1989/1083)
20, para	1	25 Sep 1986 (SI 1986/1560)
	2–4	Repealed
	5, 6	1 Jan 1987 (SI 1986/1560)
	7–15	Repealed
	16	1 Jan 1987 (SI 1986/1560)
	17, 18	Repealed
21		*Not in force*; prospectively repealed by virtue of Courts and Legal Services Act 1990, s 125(7), Sch 20[1]

[1] Orders made under Courts and Legal Services Act 1990, s 124(3), bringing the prospective repeal into force will be noted to that Act

Children and Young Persons (Amendment) Act 1986 (c 28)

Whole Act repealed

Civil Protection in Peacetime Act 1986 (c 22)

RA: 26 Jun 1986

Commencement provisions: s 3(2)

26 Aug 1986 (s 3(2))

Commonwealth Development Corporation Act 1986 (c 25)

Whole Act repealed

Company Directors Disqualification Act 1986 (c 46)

RA: 25 Jul 1986

Commencement provisions: s 25

29 Dec 1986 (s 25)

Consolidated Fund Act 1986 (c 4)

Whole Act repealed

Consolidated Fund (No 2) Act 1986 (c 67)

Whole Act repealed

Consumer Safety (Amendment) Act 1986 (c 29)

Whole Act repealed

Corneal Tissue Act 1986 (c 18)

RA: 26 Jun 1986

Commencement provisions: s 2(2)

26 Aug 1986 (s 2(2))

Crown Agents (Amendment) Act 1986 (c 43)

Whole Act repealed

Deacons (Ordination of Women) Measure 1986 (No 4)

RA: 7 Nov 1986

Commencement provisions: s 5(2)

16 Feb 1987 (the day appointed by the Archbishops of Canterbury and York under s 5(2))

Disabled Persons (Services, Consultation and Representation) Act 1986 (c 33)

RA: 8 Jul 1986

Commencement provisions: s 18(2); Disabled Persons (Services, Consultation and Representation) Act 1986 (Commencement No 1) Order 1987, SI 1987/564; Disabled Persons (Services, Consultation and Representation) Act 1986 (Commencement No 2) Order 1987, SI 1987/729; Disabled Persons (Services, Consultation and Representation) Act 1986 (Commencement No 3) (Scotland) Order 1987, SI 1987/911; Disabled Persons (Services, Consultation and Representation) Act 1986 (Commencement No 4) Order 1988, SI 1988/51; Disabled Persons (Services, Consultation and Representation) Act 1986 (Commencement No 5) (Scotland) Order 1988, SI 1988/94; Disabled Persons (Services, Consultation and Representation) Act 1986 (Commencement No 5) Order 1989, SI 1989/2425

Section		
1–3		*Not in force*
4	(a)	1 Apr 1987 (E, W) (SI 1987/564)
		1 Oct 1987 (S) (SI 1987/911)
	(b)	*Not in force*
	(c)	1 Apr 1987 (E, W) (SI 1987/564)
		1 Oct 1987 (S) (SI 1987/911)
5	(1), (2)	1 Feb 1988 (SI 1988/51)
	(3), (3A)–(3C), (4)	Substituted for original sub-ss (3), (4) by Further and Higher Education Act 1992, s 93(1), Sch 8, Pt II, para 91(1), (2) (qv)
	(5)–(10)	1 Feb 1988 (SI 1988/51)
6	(1)	Substituted by Further and Higher Education Act 1992, s 93(1), Sch 8, Pt II, para 92 (qv)
	(2)	1 Feb 1988 (SI 1988/51)
7		*Not in force*
8	(1)	1 Apr 1987 (E, W) (SI 1987/564)
		1 Oct 1987 (S) (SI 1987/911)
	(2), (3)	*Not in force*
9, 10		1 Apr 1987 (E, W) (SI 1987/564)
		1 Jun 1987 (S) (SI 1987/911)
11		1 Jun 1987 (S) (SI 1987/911)
		18 Dec 1989 (E, W) (SI 1989/2425)
12		1 Jun 1987 (SI 1987/911)
13		1 Feb 1988 (SI 1988/94)
14		1 Jun 1987 (SI 1987/911)
15		Repealed (*never in force*)
16–18		17 Apr 1987 (E, W) (SI 1987/729)
		1 Jun 1987 (S) (SI 1987/911)

Dockyard Services Act 1986 (c 52)

RA: 25 Jul 1986

Commencement provisions: s 5(2)

25 Sep 1986 (s 5(2))

Drainage Rates (Disabled Persons) Act 1986 (c 17)

Whole Act repealed

Drug Trafficking Offences Act 1986 (c 32)

RA: 8 Jul 1986

Commencement provisions: s 40(2) (repealed); Drug Trafficking Offences Act 1986 (Commencement No 1) Order 1986, SI 1986/1488; Drug Trafficking Offences Act 1986 (Commencement No 2) (Scotland) Order 1986, SI 1986/1546; Drug Trafficking Offences Act 1986 (Commencement No 3) Order 1986, SI 1986/2145; Drug Trafficking Offences Act 1986 (Commencement No 4) (Scotland) Order 1986, SI 1986/2266

Whole Act repealed, except ss 24(6), 32, 34, 40(1), (3), (4) (now substituted), (5), which came into force as follows: s 24(6) on 30 Sep 1986 (SI 1986/1488); s 32 on 12 Jan 1987 (SI 1986/2145); s 34 on 30 Sep 1986 (SI 1986/1488; SI 1986/1546); s 40(1), (3) on 30 Sep 1986 (SI 1986/1488; SI 1986/1546); s 40(4) substituted (3 Feb 1995) by Drug Trafficking Act 1994, s 65(1), Sch 1, para 11; s 40(5) on 30 Sep 1986 (SI 1986/1488; SI 1986/1546)

Ecclesiastical Fees Measure 1986 (No 2)

RA: 18 Mar 1986

Commencement provisions: s 12(3)

1 Sep 1986 (the day appointed by the Archbishops of Canterbury and York under s 12(3))

Education Act 1986 (c 40)

RA: 18 Jul 1986

Commencement provisions: s 6(2)
Section
1	18 Sep 1986 (s 6(2))
2–6	18 Jul 1986 (RA)

Education (Amendment) Act 1986 (c 1)

Whole Act repealed or spent

Education (No 2) Act 1986 (c 61)

RA: 7 Nov 1986

Commencement provisions: s 66(1)–(4); Education (No 2) Act 1986 (Commencement No 1) Order 1986, SI 1986/2203; Education (No 2) Act 1986 (Commencement No 2) Order 1987, SI 1987/344; Education (No 2) Act 1986 (Commencement No 3) Order 1987, SI 1987/1159

Education (No 2) Act 1986 (c 61)—*contd*

Section

1–42		Repealed
43		1 Sep 1987 (SI 1987/344)
44–47		Repealed
48		15 Aug 1987 (SI 1987/344)
49		7 Jan 1987 (s 66(2))
50		7 Jan 1987 (SI 1986/2203)
51–60		Repealed
61, 62		1 Sep 1987 (SI 1987/344)
63–66		7 Nov 1986 (s 66(1))
67	(1)	7 Nov 1986 (s 66(1))
	(2)	Repealed
	(3)	7 Nov 1986 (s 66(1))
	(4)	See Sch 4 below
	(5), (6)	Repealed
	(7)	7 Nov 1986 (s 66(1))

Schedule

1–3		Repealed
4, para	1, 2	Repealed
	3	1 Sep 1987 (SI 1987/344)
	4–7	Repealed
5, 6		Repealed

European Communities (Amendment) Act 1986 (c 58)

RA: 7 Nov 1986

7 Nov 1986 (RA; but note that the repeals and revocations in the Schedule took effect on 1 Jul 1987, the day on which the Single European Act came into force; see Art 33(2) thereof, Cmnd 9758)

Family Law Act 1986 (c 55)

RA: 7 Nov 1986

Commencement provisions: s 69(2), (3); Family Law Act 1986 (Commencement No 1) Order 1988, SI 1988/375

Section

1	4 Apr 1988 (SI 1988/375)
2, 2A	Substituted for original s 2 by Children Act 1989, s 108(5), Sch 13, para 64 (qv)
3	4 Apr 1988 (SI 1988/375)
4	Repealed
5, 6	4 Apr 1988 (SI 1988/375)
7	Substituted by Children Act 1989, s 108(5), Sch 13, para 67 (qv)
8–18	4 Apr 1988 (SI 1988/375)
19, 19A	Substituted (4 Nov 1996) for original s 19 by Children (Northern Ireland) Order 1995, SI 1995/755 (NI 2), art 185(1), Sch 9, para 124

Family Law Act 1986 (c 55)—*contd*

Section

20	4 Apr 1988 (SI 1988/375)
21	Repealed
22, 23	4 Apr 1988 (SI 1988/375)
24	Substituted (4 Nov 1996) by Children (Northern Ireland) Order 1995, SI 1995/755 (NI 2), art 185(1), Sch 9, para 127
25	4 Apr 1988 (SI 1988/375)
26	Substituted by Children (Scotland) Act 1995, s 105(4), Sch 4, para 41(1), (6) (qv)
27–55	4 Apr 1988 (SI 1988/375)
55A	Inserted by Child Support, Pensions and Social Security Act 2000, s 83(1), (2) (qv)
56	Substituted by Family Law Reform Act 1987, s 22 (qv)
57–62	4 Apr 1988 (SI 1988/375)
63, 64	Repealed
65	7 Jan 1987 (s 69(2))
66	Repealed
67	7 Jan 1987 (s 69(2))
68, 69	4 Apr 1988 (SI 1988/375)

Schedule

1, para	1, 2	Repealed
	3–9	4 Apr 1988 (SI 1988/375)
	10, 11	Repealed
	12	4 Apr 1988 (SI 1988/375)
	13	Repealed
	14, 15	4 Apr 1988 (SI 1988/375)
	16, 17	Repealed
	18, 19	Spent
	20	Repealed
	21, 22	4 Apr 1988 (SI 1988/375)
	23	Repealed
	24–26	4 Apr 1988 (SI 1988/375)
	27	4 Apr 1988 (SI 1988/375); prospectively repealed by Family Law Act 1996, s 66(3), Sch 10[1]
	28–31	4 Apr 1988 (SI 1988/375)
	32, 33	Repealed
	34	4 Apr 1988 (SI 1988/375)
2		4 Apr 1988 (SI 1988/375)

---

[1]   Orders made under Family Law Act 1996, s 67, bringing the prospective repeal into force will be noted to that Act

Finance Act 1986 (c 41)

Budget Day: 18 Mar 1986

RA: 25 Jul 1986

Details of the commencement of Finance Acts are not set out in this work

Financial Services Act 1986 (c 60)

Whole Act repealed

Forestry Act 1986 (c 30)

RA: 8 Jul 1986

Commencement provisions: s 2(1)

8 Sep 1986 (s 2(1))

Gaming (Amendment) Act 1986 (c 11)

RA: 2 May 1986

Commencement provisions: s 3(3); Gaming (Amendment) Act 1986 (Commencement) Order 1988, SI 1988/1250

19 Sep 1988 (SI 1988/1250)

Gas Act 1986 (c 44)

RA: 25 Jul 1986

Commencement provisions: ss 3, 49(1), 57(2), 68(2)–(5); Gas Act 1986 (Commencement No 1) Order 1986, SI 1986/1315; Gas Act 1986 (Appointed Day) Order 1986, SI 1986/1316; Gas Act 1986 (Transfer Date) Order 1986, SI 1986/1318; Gas Act 1986 (Commencement No 2) Order 1986, SI 1986/1809; British Gas Corporation (Dissolution) Order 1990, SI 1990/147

Section	
1–3	Repealed
4	Substituted by Utilities Act 2000, s 9 (qv)
4A	Substituted by Utilities Act 2000, s 11 (qv)
4AA, 4AB	Inserted by Utilities Act 2000, ss 9, 10 (qv)
4B	Inserted by Utilities Act 2000, s 12 (qv)
5	Substituted by Gas Act 1995, s 3(1), subject to savings and transitional provisions (qv)
6	Repealed
6A	Inserted by Gas (Exempt Supplies) Act 1993, s 2 (repealed); substituted by Gas Act 1995, s 4, subject to savings and transitional provisions (qv)

Gas Act 1986 (c 44)—*contd*
Section

7	Substituted by Gas Act 1995, s 5, subject to savings and transitional provisions (qv)
7A, 7B	Inserted by Gas Act 1995, ss 6(1), 7, subject to savings and transitional provisions (qv)
8	Substituted by Gas Act 1995, s 8(1) (qv)
8A	Inserted by Competition and Service (Utilities) Act 1992, s 37 (qv)
8AA	Substituted by Utilities Act 2000, s 85 (qv)
8B	Inserted by Gas Act 1995, s 9(1) (qv)
9, 10	Substituted by Gas Act 1995, s 10(1), Sch 3, paras 3–7 (qv)
10A	Inserted by Utilities Act 2000, s 77(1) (qv)
11–13	Substituted by Gas Act 1995, s 10(1), Sch 3, paras 3–7 (qv)
14, 14A, 15	Repealed
15A	Prospectively inserted by Competition and Service (Utilities) Act 1992, s 17[1]
15B	Repealed
16	Repealed; new s 16 inserted by Utilities Act 2000, s 101 (qv)
17	Substituted by Gas Act 1995, s 10(1), Sch 3, para 13, subject to savings and transitional provisions (qv)
18	23 Aug 1986 (s 68(2); SI 1986/1316)
18A	Inserted by Gas Act 1995, s 10(1), Sch 3, para 15 (qv)
19	Substituted by Gas Act 1995, s 10(1), Sch 3, para 16 (qv)
19A–19E	Inserted (10 Aug 2000) by Gas (Third Party Access and Accounts) Regulations 2000, SI 2000/1937, reg 2(2), Sch 2, para 1
20	Repealed
21, 22	23 Aug 1986 (s 68(2); SI 1986/1316)
22A	Inserted by Gas Act 1995, s 10(1), Sch 3, para 20 (qv)
23	Substituted by Gas Act 1995, s 10(1), Sch 3, para 21 (qv)
24–26	23 Aug 1986 (s 68(2); SI 1986/1316)
26A	Inserted by Utilities Act 2000, s 83(4) (qv)
27	Substituted by Gas Act 1995, s 10(1), Sch 3, para 25 (qv)
27A	Inserted by Gas Act 1995, s 10(1), Sch 3, para 26 (qv)
28–30	23 Aug 1986 (s 68(2); SI 1986/1316)

Gas Act 1986 (c 44)—*contd*

Section

30A–30F		Inserted by Utilities Act 2000, s 95(2) (qv)
31		Repealed
32		Substituted by Utilities Act 2000, s 22(1) (qv)
32A		Repealed
33		Substituted by Utilities Act 2000, s 23(1) (qv)
33A		Repealed
33AA, 33AB		Inserted by Utilities Act 2000, s 90(2) (qv)
33B		Repealed
33BA, 33BAA		Inserted by Utilities Act 2000, ss 91, 92 (qv)
33BB		Repealed
33BC		Inserted by Utilities Act 2000, s 99 (qv)
33C, 33D		Repealed
33DA		Inserted by Utilities Act 2000, s 20(5) (qv)
33E		Repealed
33F		Inserted by Utilities Act 2000, s 97 (qv)
34		23 Aug 1986 (s 68(2); SI 1986/1316)
35		Substituted by Utilities Act 2000, s 6(1) (qv)
36		23 Aug 1986 (s 68(2); SI 1986/1316)
36A, 36B		Inserted by Gas Act 1995, s 10(1), Sch 3, paras 43, 44 (qv)
37		Substituted by Gas Act 1995, s 10(1), Sch 3, para 45 (qv)
38		23 Aug 1986 (s 68(2); SI 1986/1316)
38A		Substituted by Utilities Act 2000, s 87 (qv)
39–41		Repealed
41A–41I		Inserted by Utilities Act 2000, ss 18(5), 88, 98 (qv)
42		Repealed
43–48		23 Aug 1986 (s 68(2); SI 1986/1316)
49–57		24 Aug 1986 (s 68(3); SI 1986/1318)
58		Repealed
59–61		24 Aug 1986 (s 68(3); SI 1986/1318)
62		14 Nov 1986 (SI 1986/1809); repealed (1 Mar 2005) by Competition Act 1998 (Transitional, Consequential and Supplemental Provisions) Order 2000, SI 2000/311, art 18
63		Repealed
64		23 Aug 1986 (SI 1986/1315)
65		18 Aug 1986 (SI 1986/1315)
66		23 Aug 1986 (s 68(2); SI 1986/1316)
67	(1), (2)	23 Aug 1986 (s 68(2); SI 1986/1316)
	(3)	See Sch 8 below
	(4)	See Sch 9 below
68		18 Aug 1986 (SI 1986/1315)

Gas Act 1986 (c 44)—*contd*
Schedule

1, 2		Repealed
2A		Inserted by Gas Act 1995, s 3(2), Sch 1 (qv); prospectively repealed by Utilities Act 2000, s 108, Sch 8[2]
2B		Inserted by Gas Act 1995, s 9(2), Sch 2 (qv)
3, 4		23 Aug 1986 (s 68(2); SI 1986/1316)
5, 6		Repealed
7		23 Aug 1986 (s 68(2); SI 1986/1316)
8, Pt	I	23 Aug 1986 (s 68(3); SI 1986/1316)
	II	24 Aug 1986 (s 68(3); SI 1986/1318)
9, Pt	I	23 Aug 1986 (s 68(2); SI 1986/1316)
	II	24 Aug 1986 (s 68(3); SI 1986/1318)
	III	28 Feb 1990 (SI 1990/147)

[1] Orders made under Competition and Service (Utilities) Act 1992, s 56(2), bringing the prospective insertion into force will be noted to that Act

[2] Orders made under Utilities Act 2000, s 110(2), bringing the prospective amendments into force will be noted to that Act

---

Health Service Joint Consultative Committee (Access to Information) Act 1986 (c 24)

Whole Act repealed

Highways (Amendment) Act 1986 (c 13)

RA: 2 May 1986

Commencement provisions: s 2(2)

2 Jul 1986 (s 2(2))

Horticultural Produce Act 1986 (c 20)

RA: 26 Jun 1986

Commencement provisions: s 7(3)

26 Aug 1986 (s 7(3))

Housing and Planning Act 1986 (c 63)

RA: 7 Nov 1986

Commencement provisions: s 57(1), (2); Housing and Planning Act 1986 (Commencement No 1) Order 1986, SI 1986/2262; Housing and Planning Act 1986 (Commencement No 2) Order 1987, SI 1987/178 (revoked); Housing and Planning Act 1986 (Commencement No 3) Order 1987, SI 1987/304; Housing and Planning Act 1986 (Commencement No 4) Order 1987, SI 1987/348; Housing and Planning Act 1986 (Commencement No 5) Order 1987, SI 1987/754; Housing and Planning Act 1986 (Commencement No 6) Order 1987,

Housing and Planning Act 1986 (c 63)—*contd*
SI 1987/1554 (revoked); Housing and Planning Act 1986 (Commencement No 7) (Scotland) Order 1987, SI 1987/1607; Housing and Planning Act 1986 (Commencement No 8) Order 1987, SI 1987/1759; Housing and Planning Act 1986 (Commencement No 9) Order 1987, SI 1987/1939; Housing and Planning Act 1986 (Commencement No 10) Order 1987, SI 1987/2277; Housing and Planning Act 1986 (Commencement No 11) Order 1988, SI 1988/283; Housing and Planning Act 1986 (Commencement No 12) Order 1988, SI 1988/1787; Housing and Planning Act 1986 (Commencement No 13) Order 1989, SI 1989/430; Housing and Planning Act 1986 (Commencement No 14) Order 1990, SI 1990/511; Housing and Planning Act 1986 (Commencement No 15) Order 1990, SI 1990/614; Housing and Planning Act 1986 (Commencement No 16) Order 1990, SI 1990/797 (bringing into force enabling provision in relation to Sch 11, paras 39, 40 only); Housing and Planning Act 1986 (Commencement No 17 and Transitional Provisions) Order 1992, SI 1992/1753; Housing and Planning Act 1986 (Commencement No 18 and Transitional Provisions) (Scotland) Order 1993, SI 1993/273; Housing and Planning Act 1986 (Commencement No 19) (Scotland) Order 1996, SI 1996/1276

Section

1	Repealed
2	7 Jan 1987 (SI 1986/2262)
3	Repealed
4	7 Jan 1987 (SI 1986/2262)
5	13 Jul 1992 (SI 1992/1753)
6	11 Mar 1988 (SI 1988/283)
7	Repealed
8	5 Apr 1989 (SI 1989/430)
9	13 May 1987 (SI 1987/754)
10	7 Jan 1987 (SI 1986/2262)
11	Spent
12	Repealed
13	7 Jan 1987 (SI 1986/2262)
14	Repealed, except in relation to an applicant whose application for accommodation or assistance in obtaining accommodation was made before 20 Jan 1997
15	17 Feb 1988 (SI 1987/2277); prospectively repealed by Local Government and Housing Act 1989, s 194, Sch 12, Pt II[1]
16, 17	7 Jan 1987 (SI 1986/2262)
18	See Sch 4 below
19	Repealed
20	7 Jan 1987 (SI 1986/2262); prospectively repealed by Local Government and Housing Act 1989, s 194, Sch 12, Pt II[1]
21	7 Nov 1986 (s 57(1))
22, 23	7 Jan 1987 (SI 1986/2262)

Housing and Planning Act 1986 (c 63)—*contd*

Section

24	(1), (2)	See Sch 5 below (note sub-s (1)(j) came into force on 7 Nov 1986) (s 57(1))
	(3)	See Sch 12, Pt I below
25–29		Repealed
30–34		Repealed (*never in force*)
35–38		Repealed
39		11 Dec 1987 (SI 1987/1939)
40		1 Apr 1987 (SI 1987/348)
41		Repealed
42		17 Nov 1988 (SI 1988/1787)
43		31 Mar 1990 (SI 1990/614)
44–46		Repealed
47, 48		7 Jan 1987 (SI 1986/2262)
49	(1)	See Sch 11, Pt I below
	(2)	See Sch 12, Pt III below
50, 51		Repealed
52		7 Nov 1986 (s 57(1))
53	(1)	See Sch 11, Pt II below
	(2)	See Sch 12, Pt IV below
54, 55		7 Jan 1987 (SI 1986/2262)
56–59		7 Nov 1986 (s 57(1))

Schedule

1		11 Mar 1988 (SI 1988/283)
2		5 Apr 1989 (SI 1989/430)
3		17 Feb 1988 (SI 1988/2277); prospectively repealed by Local Government and Housing Act 1989, s 194, Sch 12, Pt II[1]
4, para	1–9	11 Dec 1987 (SI 1987/1939)
	10	Repealed
	11	11 Dec 1987 (SI 1987/1939)
5, para	1–4	7 Jan 1987 (SI 1986/2262)
	5	Repealed
	6, 7	7 Jan 1987 (SI 1986/2262)
	8	Repealed
	9	17 Feb 1988 (SI 1987/2277)
	10–12	7 Nov 1986 (s 57(1))
	13, 14	Repealed
	15	7 Jan 1987 (SI 1986/2262)
	16	*Not in force*
	17	Repealed
	18, 19	17 Aug 1992 (SI 1992/1753)
	20	Repealed
	21–26	7 Jan 1987 (SI 1986/2262)
	27	17 Aug 1992 (so far as relates to definitions 'consent' and 'management agreement and manager') (SI 1992/1753)

Housing and Planning Act 1986 (c 63)—*contd*

Schedule

5, para	27—*contd*		*Not in force* (otherwise)
	28		7 Jan 1987 (SI 1986/2262)
	29		17 Aug 1992 (subject to transitional provisions) (SI 1992/1753)
	30		7 Jan 1987 (SI 1986/2262)
	31		17 Aug 1992 (SI 1992/1753)
	32, 33		7 Jan 1987 (SI 1986/2262)
	34–38		17 Aug 1992 (subject to transitional provisions) (SI 1992/1753)
	39		7 Jan 1987 (SI 1986/2262)
	40		17 Aug 1992 (subject to transitional provisions) (SI 1992/1753)
	41, 42		7 Jan 1987 (SI 1986/2262)
6, 7			Repealed
8			11 Dec 1987 (SI 1987/1939)
9, Pt	I, para	1–5	Repealed
		6	1 Apr 1987 (SI 1987/348)
		7–12	Repealed
	II		Repealed
10			Repealed
11, Pt	I, para	1–24	Repealed
		25	7 Jan 1987 (SI 1986/2262)
		26, 27	Repealed
	II, para	28–60	Repealed
		61	7 Jan 1987 (SI 1986/2262)
		62	Repealed
12, Pt	I		7 Nov 1986 (repeals in Housing (Consequential Provisions) Act 1985 specified in first part of Sch 12, Pt I) (s 57(1))
			7 Jan 1987 (repeals of or in Housing Rents and Subsidies (Scotland) Act 1975; Rent Act 1977, s 70; Housing Act 1980, s 56; New Towns Act 1981; Housing Act 1985, ss 30, 46, 127, Schs 4, 6; Housing (Consequential Provisions) Act 1985, Sch 2, paras 27, 35(3), 45(2)) (SI 1986/2262)
			11 Dec 1987 (repeals of or in Housing Act 1980, s 140; Local Government Planning and Land Act 1980, s 156(3); Local Government Act 1985, Sch 13, para 14(d), Sch 14, para 58(e)) (SI 1987/1939)
			Not in force (otherwise)
	II		11 Dec 1987 (SI 1987/1939)

Housing and Planning Act 1986 (c 63)—*contd*
Schedule

12, Pt	III	7 Jan 1987 (repeals of or in Electric Lighting (Clauses) Act 1899; Electricity (Supply) Act 1926; Requisitioned Land and War Works Act 1945; Town and Country Planning Act 1947; Electricity Act 1947; Requisitioned Land and War Works Act 1948; Electricity Act 1957; Town and Country Planning Act 1971, ss 29A, 29B, 66–86, 88B, 105, 147, 151, 165, 169, 180, 185, 191, 237, 250–252, 260, 287(4), (5), (7), 290, Schs 12, 13, 21, 24; Town and Country Planning (Amendment) Act 1972; Local Government Act 1972, s 182; Local Government Act 1974; Town and Country Amenities Act 1974, s 3; Control of Office Development Act 1977; Local Government, Planning and Land Act 1980 (except s 88); Industrial Development Act 1982; Local Government Act 1985, s 3) (SI 1986/2262)
		1 Apr 1987 (repeals of or in Town and Country Planning Act 1971, s 55(4); Town and Country Amenities Act 1974, s 5; National Heritage Act 1983; Local Government Act 1985, Sch 2, para 1(8)) (SI 1987/348)
		2 Nov 1987 (repeals of or in Local Government Act 1972, s 183(2), Sch 16, paras 1–3; Local Government, Planning and Land Act 1980, s 88; Local Government (Miscellaneous Provisions) Act 1982, Sch 6, para 7(b)) (SI 1987/1759)
		17 Nov 1988 (repeals of or in Public Expenditure and Receipts Act 1968; Local Government Act 1972, s 250(4); Land Drainage Act 1976; Road Traffic Regulation Act 1984) (SI 1988/1787)
		31 Mar 1990 (repeal in Acquisition of Land Act 1981, Sch 4, para 1) (SI 1990/614)
		Not in force (otherwise)

Housing and Planning Act 1986 (c 63)—*contd*

Schedule

12, Pt	IV	7 Jan 1987 (repeals of or in Town and Country Planning (Scotland) Act 1972, ss 29, 63, 64–83, 85, 136, 140, 154, 164, 174, 180, 226, 231, 233, 237–239, 247, 273 (4), (5), (7), (8), 275, Schs 19, 22; Local Government Planning and Land Act 1980; Industrial Development Act 1982) (SI 1986/2262)
		1 Jun 1996 (repeals of or in Public Expenditure and Receipts Act 1968; Town and Country Planning (Scotland) Act 1972, ss 53(2), 53(4); Town and Country Amenities Act 1974; Road Traffic Regulation Act 1984) (SI 1996/1276)
		Not in force (otherwise)

[1] Orders made under Local Government and Housing Act 1989, s 195(2), bringing the prospective repeal into force will be noted to that Act

---

Housing (Scotland) Act 1986 (c 65)

RA: 7 Nov 1986

Commencement provisions: s 26(2); Housing (Scotland) Act 1986 (Commencement) Order 1986, SI 1986/2137

Section

1–12		Repealed
13		7 Jan 1987 (SI 1986/2137)
14–16		Repealed
17		7 Jan 1987 (SI 1986/2137)
18		Repealed
19, 20		7 Jan 1987 (SI 1986/2137)
21		Repealed
22–25		7 Jan 1987 (SI 1986/2137)
26		7 Nov 1986 (RA)

Schedule

1		Repealed
2, para	1	7 Jan 1987 (SI 1986/2137)
	2	Repealed
	3, 4	7 Jan 1987 (SI 1986/2137)
3		7 Jan 1987 (SI 1986/2137)

Incest and Related Offences (Scotland) Act 1986 (c 36)

RA: 18 Jul 1986

Commencement provisions: s 3(2); Incest and Related Offences (Scotland) Act 1986 (Commencement) Order 1986, SI 1986/1803

1 Nov 1986 (SI 1986/1803)

Industrial Training Act 1986 (c 15)

RA: 20 May 1986

Commencement provisions: s 2(2)

20 Jul 1986 (s 2(2))

Insolvency Act 1986 (c 45)

RA: 25 Jul 1986

Commencement provisions: s 443; Insolvency Act 1985 (Commencement No 5) Order 1986, SI 1986/1924

29 Dec 1986 (s 443; SI 1986/1924)

Land Registration Act 1986 (c 26)

RA: 26 Jun 1986

Commencement provisions: s 6(4); Land Registration Act 1986 (Commencement) Order 1986, SI 1986/2117

1 Jan 1987 (SI 1986/2117)

Latent Damage Act 1986 (c 37)

RA: 18 Jul 1986

Commencement provisions: s 5(3)

18 Sep 1986 (s 5(3))

Law Reform (Parent and Child) (Scotland) Act 1986 (c 9)

RA: 26 Mar 1986

Commencement provisions: s 11(2); Law Reform (Parent and Child) (Scotland) Act 1986 (Commencement) Order 1986, SI 1986/1983

8 Dec 1986 (SI 1986/1983)

Legal Aid (Scotland) Act 1986 (c 47)

RA: 25 Jul 1986

Commencement provisions: s 46(2); Legal Aid (Scotland) Act 1986 (Commencement No 1) Order 1986, SI 1986/1617; Legal Aid (Scotland) Act 1986 (Commencement No 2) Order 1987, SI 1987/289; Legal Aid (Scotland) Act 1986 (Commencement No 3) Order 1992, SI 1992/1226; Legal Aid (Scotland) Act 1986 (Commencement No 4) Order 2001, SSI 2001/393

Section		
1	(1)	1 Oct 1986 (SI 1986/1617)
	(2)	1 Apr 1987 (SI 1987/289)

Legal Aid (Scotland) Act 1986 (c 47)—*contd*
Section

1	(3)–(6)		1 Oct 1986 (SI 1986/1617)
2	(1)		1 Apr 1987 (SI 1987/289)
	(2), (3)		1 Oct 1986 (SI 1986/1617)
3	(1), (2)		1 Oct 1986 (SI 1986/1617)
	(3)		1 Apr 1987 (SI 1987/289)
	(4)–(6)		1 Oct 1986 (SI 1986/1617)
4–25			1 Apr 1987 (SI 1987/289)
25AA			Inserted by Crime and Punishment (Scotland) Act 1997, s 62(1), Sch 1, para 12(7) (qv)
25A–25F			Inserted by Crime and Punishment (Scotland) Act 1997, s 49 (qv)
26–28			2 Nov 2001 (SSI 2001/393)
28A			Inserted by Crime and Punishment (Scotland) Act 1997, s 50 (qv)
29			Substituted by Children (Scotland) Act 1995, s 92 (qv)
30			1 Jul 1992 (SI 1992/1226)
31–33			1 Apr 1987 (SI 1987/289)
33A			Inserted by Crime and Punishment (Scotland) Act 1997, s 52 (qv)
34, 35			1 Apr 1987 (SI 1987/289)
35A–35C			Inserted by Crime and Punishment (Scotland) Act 1997, s 53 (qv)
36–39			1 Apr 1987 (SI 1987/289)
40	(1)	(a)	1 Apr 1987 (SI 1987/289)
		(b)	1 Oct 1986 (SI 1986/1617)
	(2)	(a)	1 Apr 1987 (SI 1987/289)
		(b)	1 Oct 1986 (SI 1986/1617)
	(3), (4)		1 Apr 1987 (SI 1987/289)
41			1 Oct 1986 (SI 1986/1617)
41A			Inserted by Crime and Punishment (Scotland) Act 1997, s 54 (qv)
42, 43			1 Apr 1987 (SI 1987/289)
43A			Inserted by Law Reform (Miscellaneous Provisions) (Scotland) Act 1990, s 38 (qv)
44			1 Apr 1987 (SI 1987/289)
45	(1)		See Sch 3 below
	(2), (3)		1 Apr 1987 (SI 1987/289)
46			25 Jul 1986 (RA)
Schedule			
1			1 Oct 1986 (SI 1986/1617)
2			1 Apr 1987 (SI 1987/289)
3, para	1, 2		1 Apr 1987 (SI 1987/289)
	3, 4		1 Oct 1986 (SI 1986/1617)
	5–9		1 Apr 1987 (SI 1987/289)
4, 5			1 Apr 1987 (SI 1987/289)

Local Government Act 1986 (c 10)

RA: 26 Mar 1986

Commencement provisions: s 12(2); Local Government Act 1986 (Commencement)
   Order 1987, SI 1987/2003

Section	
1	26 Mar 1986 (s 12(2)); repealed by Local Government Finance Act 1988, s 149, Sch 13, Pt I (qv), with effect for financial years beginning in or after 1990
2	1 Apr 1986 (s 12(2))
2A	Inserted by Local Government Act 1988, s 28 (qv); repealed (S) by Ethical Standards in Public Life etc (Scotland) Act 2000 (asp 7), s 34
3, 4	1 Apr 1986 (s 12(2))
5	1 Apr 1988 (SI 1987/2003)
6	1 Apr 1986 (s 12(2))
7	26 Mar 1986 (s 12(2))
8	Repealed
9, 10	26 Mar 1986 (s 12(2))
11	Repealed
12	26 Mar 1986 (s 12(2))

Marriage (Prohibited Degrees of Relationship) Act 1986 (c 16)

RA: 20 May 1986

Commencement provisions: s 6(5); Marriage (Prohibited Degrees of Relationship) Act 1986
   (Commencement) Order 1986, SI 1986/1343

1 Nov 1986 (SI 1986/1343)

Marriage (Wales) Act 1986 (c 7)

RA: 18 Mar 1986

18 Mar 1986 (RA)

Museum of London Act 1986 (c 8)

RA: 26 Mar 1986

Commencement provisions: s 7(2)

1 Apr 1986 (RA)

National Health Service (Amendment) Act 1986 (c 66)

RA: 7 Nov 1986

Commencement provisions: s 8(4), (5); National Health Service (Amendment) Act 1986 (Commencement No 1) Order 1987, SI 1987/399

Section	
1, 2	Repealed
3	1 Apr 1987 (SI 1987/399)
4	7 Nov 1986 (RA)
5	7 Nov 1986 (except so far as inserts National Health Service (Scotland) Act 1978, s 13B) (RA)
	Not in force (exception noted above)
6–8	7 Nov 1986 (RA)

Outer Space Act 1986 (c 38)

RA: 18 Jul 1986

Commencement provisions: s 15(2); Outer Space Act 1986 (Commencement) Order 1989, SI 1989/1097

31 Jul 1989 (SI 1989/1097)

Parliamentary Constituencies Act 1986 (c 56)

RA: 7 Nov 1986

Commencement provisions: s 9(2)

7 Feb 1986 (s 9(2))

Patents, Designs and Marks Act 1986 (c 39)

RA: 18 Jul 1986

Commencement provisions: s 4(6), (7); Patents, Designs and Marks Act 1986 (Commencement No 1) Order 1986, SI 1986/1274; Patents, Designs and Marks Act 1986 (Commencement No 2) Order 1988, SI 1988/1824

Section		
1		See Sch 1 below
2		Repealed
3		See Sch 3 below
4	(1)–(3)	18 Jul 1986 (RA)
	(4)	Repealed
	(5)–(7)	18 Jul 1986 (RA)
Schedule		
1, para	1, 2	Repealed
	3, 4	1 Jan 1989 (SI 1988/1824)
2		Repealed
3, Pt	I	1 Oct 1986 (repeals in Trade Marks Act 1938) (SI 1986/1274)

Patents, Designs and Marks Act 1986 (c 39)—*contd*

Schedule

3, Pt	I—*contd*	1 Jan 1989 (repeals of Registered Designs Act 1949, s 24; Patents Act 1977, s 35) (SI 1988/1824)
	II	1 Oct 1986 (s 4(7))

Patronage (Benefices) Measure 1986 (No 3)

RA: 18 Jul 1986

Commencement provisions: s 42(3)

The provisions of this Measure were brought into force on the following dates by an instrument made by the Archbishops of Canterbury and York and dated 31 Dec 1986 (made under s 42(3))

Section

1, 2		1 Oct 1987
3–5		1 Jan 1989
6		1 Oct 1987
7–25		1 Jan 1989
26, 27		1 Jan 1987
28–34		1 Jan 1989
35	(1)–(3)	1 Oct 1987
	(4)–(9)	1 Jan 1989
36, 37		1 Oct 1987
38, 39		1 Jan 1987
40		1 Oct 1987
41		1 Jan 1989
42		1 Jan 1987
Schedule		
1		1 Oct 1987
2		1 Jan 1989
3		1 Jan 1987
4		1 Jan 1989
5		1 Jan 1987 (repeal of Benefices (Diocesan Boards of Patronage) Measure 1932)
		1 Jan 1989 (otherwise)

Prevention of Oil Pollution Act 1986 (c 6)

Whole Act repealed

Protection of Children (Tobacco) Act 1986 (c 34)

RA: 8 Jul 1986

Commencement provisions: s 3(3)

8 Oct 1986 (s 3(3))

Protection of Military Remains Act 1986 (c 35)

RA: 8 Jul 1986

Commencement provisions: s 10(2)

8 Sep 1986 (s 10(2))

Public Order Act 1986 (c 64)

RA: 7 Nov 1986

Commencement provisions: s 41(1); Public Order Act 1986 (Commencement No 1) Order 1986, SI 1986/2041; Public Order Act 1986 (Commencement No 2) Order 1987, SI 1987/198; Public Order Act 1986 (Commencement No 3) Order 1987, SI 1987/852

Section			
1–4			1 Apr 1987 (SI 1987/198)
4A			Inserted by Criminal Justice and Public Order Act 1994, s 154 (qv)
5–10			1 Apr 1987 (SI 1987/198)
11			1 Jan 1987 (SI 1986/2041)
12–14			1 Apr 1987 (SI 1987/198)
14A, 14B			Inserted by Criminal Justice and Public Order Act 1994, s 70 (qv)
14C			Inserted by Criminal Justice and Public Order Act 1994, s 71 (qv)
15			1 Apr 1987 (SI 1987/198)
16			1 Jan 1987 (SI 1986/2041)
17–29			1 Apr 1987 (SI 1987/198)
30–34			Repealed
35			1 Aug 1987 (SI 1987/852); prospectively repealed (with savings) by Football Spectators Act 1989, s 27(5)[1]
36			Repealed
37			1 Aug 1987 (SI 1987/852); prospectively repealed (with savings) by Football Spectators Act 1989, s 27(5)[1]
39			Repealed
40	(1)		See Sch 1 below
	(2)		See Sch 2 below
	(3)		See Sch 3 below
	(4), (5)		1 Apr 1987 (SI 1987/198)
41–43			1 Jan 1987 (SI 1986/2041)
Schedule			
1			1 Jan 1987 (SI 1986/2041)
2, para	1		Repealed
	2		1 Apr 1987 (SI 1987/198)
	3	(1), (2)	1 Jan 1987 (SI 1986/2041)
		(3)–(6)	1 Apr 1987 (SI 1987/198)

Public Order Act 1986 (c 64)—*contd*
Schedule

2, para	4	1 Apr 1987 (SI 1987/198)
	5, 6	Repealed
	7	1 Apr 1987 (SI 1987/198)
3		1 Jan 1987 (repeals in Erith Tramways and Improvement Act 1903; Middlesex County Council Act 1944; County of South Glamorgan Act 1976; County of Merseyside Act 1980; West Midlands County Council Act 1980; Cheshire County Council Act 1980; Isle of Wight Act 1980; Greater Manchester Act 1981; East Sussex Act 1981; Civic Government (Scotland) Act 1982, s 62; Sporting Events (Control of Alcohol etc) Act 1985) (SI 1986/2041) 1 Apr 1987 (otherwise) (SI 1987/198)

[1]   Orders made under Football Spectators Act 1989, s 27(2), for the commencement of s 2 of that Act, bringing the prospective repeal in force will be noted to that Act

Public Trustee and Administration of Funds Act 1986 (c 57)

RA: 7 Nov 1986

Commencement provisions: s 6(2); Public Trustee and Administration of Funds Act 1986 Commencement Order 1986, SI 1986/2261

2 Jan 1987 (SI 1986/2261)

Rate Support Grants Act 1986 (c 54)

RA: 21 Oct 1986

21 Oct 1986 (RA)

Road Traffic Regulation (Parking) Act 1986 (c 27)

RA: 8 Jul 1986

Commencement provisions: s 3(3)

8 Sep 1986 (s 3(3))

Safety at Sea Act 1986 (c 23)

Whole Act repealed

Salmon Act 1986 (c 62)

RA: 7 Nov 1986

Commencement provisions: s 43(1), (2); Salmon Act 1986 (Commencement and Transitional Provisions) Order 1992, SI 1992/1973

Section	
1–3	7 Jan 1987 (s 43(1))
4	Repealed
5–20	7 Jan 1987 (s 43(1))
21	1 Jan 1993 (subject to transitional provisions) (SI 1992/1973)
22–43	7 Jan 1987 (s 43(1))
Schedule	
1–5	7 Jan 1987 (s 43(1))

Sex Discrimination Act 1986 (c 59)

RA: 7 Nov 1986

Commencement provisions: s 10(2)–(4); Sex Discrimination Act (Commencement) Order 1986, SI 1986/2313; Sex Discrimination Act 1986 (Commencement No 2) Order 1988, SI 1988/99

Section		
1		7 Feb 1987 (s 10(2))
2		7 Nov 1987 (s 10(4))
3		Repealed
4, 5		7 Nov 1986 (RA)
6	(1)–(4)	7 Feb 1987 (s 10(2))
	(4A)–(4D)	Inserted by Trade Union Reform and Employment Rights Act 1993, s 32 (qv)
	(5)–(7)	7 Feb 1987 (s 10(2))
7		Repealed
8		27 Feb 1987 (SI 1986/2313)
9	(1)	7 Feb 1987 (s 10(2))
	(2)	7 Nov 1986 (RA)
	(3)	7 Feb 1987 (s 10(2))
10		7 Nov 1986 (RA)
Schedule		
Pt	I	7 Nov 1986 (RA)
	II	7 Feb 1987 (s 10(2))
	III	27 Feb 1987 (repeals of or in Baking Industry (Hours of Work) Act 1954; Mines and Quarries Act 1954, ss 125, 126, 128, 131; Factories Act 1961; Civil Evidence Act 1968; Health and Safety at Work etc Act 1974; Sex Discrimination Act 1975; Companies Consolidation (Consequential Provisions) Act 1985) (SI 1986/2313)

Sex Discrimination Act 1986 (c 59)—*contd*

Schedule

Pt	III—*contd*	26 Feb 1988 (repeals in Hours of Employment (Conventions) Act 1936; Mines and Quarries Act 1954, Sch 4) (SI 1988/99)

Social Security Act 1986 (c 50)

RA: 25 Jul 1986

Commencement provisions: s 88; Social Security Act 1986 (Commencement No 1) Order 1986, SI 1986/1609; Social Security Act 1986 (Commencement No 2) Order 1986, SI 1986/1719; Social Security Act (Commencement No 3) Order 1986, SI 1986/1958; Social Security Act 1986 (Commencement No 4) Order 1986, SI 1986/1959 (as amended by SI 1987/354); Social Security Act 1986 (Commencement No 5) Order 1987, SI 1987/354 (also amending SI 1986/1959); Social Security Act 1986 (Commencement No 6) Order 1987, SI 1987/543; Social Security Act 1986 (Commencement No 7) Order 1987, SI 1987/1096 (as amended by SI 1987/1853); Social Security Act 1986 (Commencement No 8) Order 1987, SI 1987/1853 (also amending SI 1987/1096); Social Security Act 1986 (Commencement No 9) Order 1988, SI 1988/567 (also amending SI 1987/1096)

Section

1–8		Repealed
9	(1)–(7)	Repealed
	(8), (9)	6 Apr 1988 (SI 1987/543)
10–29		Repealed
30	(1)–(9)	Repealed
	(10)	25 Jul 1986 (s 88(5))
	(11)	Repealed
31–36		Repealed
37	(1)	Repealed
	(2)	25 Jul 1986 (s 88(5))
38		Repealed
39		See Sch 3 below
40–53		Repealed or spent
54	(1)	6 Apr 1987 (SI 1986/1958)
	(2)	Repealed
55		Repealed
56, 57		6 Apr 1987 (SI 1986/1959)
58–69		Repealed
70	(1)	Repealed
	(2)	25 Jul 1986 (s 88(5))
71–75		Repealed
76		25 Jul 1986 (s 88(5))
77		11 Apr 1988 (SI 1987/1853)
78–81		Repealed
82		6 Apr 1987 (SI 1987/1853)
83	(1)	25 Jul 1986 (s 88(5))
	(2), (3)	Repealed
	(4)	Substituted by Social Security Act 1990, s 21(1), Sch 6, para 8(9) (qv)

Social Security Act 1986 (c 50)—*contd*

Section

83	(5), (6)	25 Jul 1986 (s 88(5))
84	(1)	25 Jul 1986 (s 88(5))
	(2), (3)	Repealed
	(4)	25 Jul 1986 (s 88(5))
85	(1), (2)	25 Jul 1986 (s 88(5))
	(3), (4)	Repealed
	(5), (6)	25 Jul 1986 (s 88(5))
	(7)–(12)	Repealed
	(13)	25 Jul 1986 (s 88(5))
86	(1)	See Sch 10 below
	(2)	See Sch 11 below
87–90		25 Jul 1986 (s 88(5))

Schedule

1, 2		Repealed
3, para	1–16	Repealed
	17	1 Oct 1986 (SI 1986/1609)
4–8		Repealed
9		6 Apr 1987 (SI 1986/1958)
10, para	1	Spent
	2–10	Repealed
	11	Spent
	12–31	Repealed
	32, 33	Repealed or spent
	34	Repealed
	35, 36	11 Apr 1988 (SI 1987/1853)
	37	Repealed
	38, 39	11 Apr 1988 (SI 1987/1853)
	40	Repealed
	41–43	11 Apr 1988 (SI 1987/1853)
	44	1 Apr 1988 (so far as relates to housing benefit in a case where rent is payable at intervals of one month or any other interval which is not a week or a multiple thereof or in a case where payments by way of rates are not made together with payments of rent at weekly intervals or multiples thereof) (SI 1987/1853) 4 Apr 1988 (otherwise) (SI 1987/1853)
	45–48	Repealed
	49	1 Apr 1988 (so far as relates to housing benefit in a case where rent is payable at intervals of one month or any other interval which is not a week or a multiple thereof or in a case where payments by way of rates are not made together with payments of rent at weekly intervals or multiples thereof) (SI 1987/1853)

Social Security Act 1986 (c 50)—*contd*

Schedule

10, para	49—*contd*		4 Apr 1988 (otherwise) (SI 1987/1853)
			Spent (E, W)
	50, 51		Repealed
	52		1 Apr 1988 (so far as relates to housing benefit in a case where rent is payable at intervals of one month or any other interval which is not a week or a multiple thereof or in a case where payments by way of rates are not made together with payments of rent at weekly intervals or multiples thereof) (SI 1987/1853)
			4 Apr 1988 (otherwise) (SI 1987/1853)
	53		Spent
	54		Repealed
	55		11 Apr 1988 (SI 1987/1853)
	56		Repealed
	57		11 Apr 1988 (SI 1987/1853)
	58		Spent
	59, 60		1 Apr 1988 (so far as relates to housing benefit in a case where rent is payable at intervals of one month or any other interval which is not a week or a multiple thereof or in a case where payments by way of rates are not made together with payments of rent at weekly intervals or multiples thereof) (SI 1987/1853)
			4 Apr 1988 (otherwise) (SI 1987/1853)
	61		11 Apr 1988 (SI 1987/1853)
	62–78		Repealed
	79, 80		6 Apr 1987 (SI 1986/1959)
	81–92		Repealed
	93		1 Oct 1986 (SI 1986/1609); now superseded
	94	(a)	25 Jul 1986 (s 88(5))
		(b)	26 Jun 1987 (SI 1987/1096)
	95–101		Repealed
	102		26 Jun 1987 (SI 1987/1096)
	103	(a), (b)	Repealed
		(c)	Spent
	104–107		Repealed
	108	(a)	Repealed
		(b)	11 Apr 1988 (except so far as substitutes words for reference in Forfeiture Act 1982, s 4(5), to Family Income Supplements Act 1970 and Supplementary Benefits Act 1976) (SI 1987/1096)

Social Security Act 1986 (c 50)—*contd*
Schedule

10, para	108	(b)—*contd*	11 Apr 1988 (exception noted above) (SI 1987/1853)
11			25 Jul 1986 (repeals of or in Social Security Act 1975, ss 37, 141; Social Security Pensions Act 1975, s 52D, Sch 1A; Social Security (Miscellaneous Provisions) Act 1977, s 22(2) (reference to Social Security Act 1975, s 37(3)(b)); Social Security Act 1980, s 10; Social Security and Housing Benefits Act 1982, s 29) (s 88(5))
			1 Oct 1986 (repeals of or in Statute Law Revision (Consequential Repeals) Act 1965; Social Security Act 1975, ss 12(3), 28, 34, 37A, 57, 60, 124–126A, Schs 14, 20 (definition 'Up–rating Order'); Social Security Pensions Act 1975, ss 22, 23; Child Benefit Act 1975, ss 5, 17(3), (4); Social Security Act 1979, s 13, Social Security Act 1980, s 1; Social Security (No 2) Act 1980, ss 1, 2; Social Security Act 1981, s 1; Social Security and Housing Benefits Act 1982, ss 7, 42; Social Security and Housing Benefits Act 1983; Social Security Act 1985, ss 15, 16, Sch 5, para 10) (SI 1986/1609)
			1 Nov 1986 (repeals of or in Social Security Act 1973, s 99; Social Security Pensions Act 1975, ss 30, 32–34, 36, 37, 39, 41, 44A, 46, 49, 66, Schs 2, 4, paras 31, 32(a); Social Security Act 1985, Sch 5, paras 19, 28) (SI 1986/1719)
			6 Apr 1987 (repeals of or in Supplementary Benefit Act 1966; Social Work (Scotland) Act 1968; Income and Corporation Taxes Act 1970; Family Income Supplements Act 1970, ss 8(5), (6), 12; Local Government Act 1972; Social Security Act 1973, s 92, Sch 23; National Insurance Act 1974, s 6(1) (the words 'or the Social Security and Housing Benefits Act 1982'); Social Security

Social Security Act 1986 (c 50)—*contd*
Schedule
11—*contd*

Act 1975, ss 13(1), 21, 32, 92, 95,
100, 104, 106, 107, 110, 114,
119(1)–(2A), (5), (6), 135(2)(g),
136, 144, 145, 146(3)(c), (5), 147,
164, Sch 3, Pt I, para 7, Pt II,
paras 8(3), 12, Sch 4, Pt II, Sch 8,
Sch 16, para 4; Industrial Injuries
and Diseases (Old Cases) Act 1975,
ss 9, 10; Social Security
(Consequential Provisions) Act 1975,
Sch 2, paras 5, 35; Social Security
Pensions Act 1975, s 19, Sch 4,
para 17; Child Benefit Act 1975,
ss 9–11, 24, Sch 4, paras 11, 31;
Adoption Act 1976;
Supplementary Benefits Act 1976,
s 20(1), (2), (5)–(7); Social Security
(Miscellaneous Provisions) Act 1977,
s 19; Social Security Act 1979, ss 6,
8; Child Care Act 1980; Social
Security Act 1980, ss 5, 14, 15, 17,
20, Sch 1, paras 9, 10, Sch 2,
paras 19(a), (b), (d), 21, Sch 3, Pt II,
paras 16–18; Social Security
Act 1981, Sch 1, paras 1–5; Social
Security and Housing Benefits
Act 1982, ss 8, 9, 11–16, 19–21,
25, 41, Schs 2, 3, Sch 4, paras 26,
38; Health and Social Services and
Social Security Adjudications
Act 1983, Sch 8, paras 18, 31, Sch 9;
Public Health (Control of Disease)
Act 1984; Health and Social
Security Act 1984, Sch 4, para 12;
Social Security Act 1985, s 17,
Sch 4, Sch 5, paras 37, 38;
Insolvency Act 1985; Bankruptcy
(Scotland) Act 1985) (SI 1986/1959,
as amended by SI 1987/354)

6 Apr 1987 (repeals of or in Social
Security Act 1975, ss 1(1)(b),
122(4), 134(5)(b); Employment
Protection Act 1975, s 40(2), (4);
Supplementary Benefits Act 1976,
s 26; Social Security (Miscellaneous
Provisions) Act 1977, s 18(1)(c),
(2)(a), (b); Employment Protection
(Consolidation) Act 1978 (except
ss 123(5), 127(3), 132(6)); Social

Social Security Act 1986 (c 50)—*contd*
Schedule
11—*contd*

Security Act 1979, ss 3(2), 12, Sch 3,
para 16; Social Security Act 1985,
Sch 5, para 7) (SI 1987/354)

7 Apr 1987 (repeals of or in Family
Income Supplement Act 1970,
s 8(3), (4); Social Security Act 1975,
ss 86, 119(3), (4)(b)–(d); Social
Security (Consequential Provisions)
Act 1975, Sch 2, para 41; Social
Security Pensions Act 1975,
Sch 4, para 13; Child Benefit
Act 1975, ss 7, 8 (except in relation
to Social Security Act 1975,
ss 82(3)), 17(5), (6), Sch 4, paras 5,
29, 33; Supplementary Benefits
Act 1979, s 7, Sch 3, para 9; Social
Security Act 1980, s 4, Sch 1,
para 12, Sch 2, paras 11, 19(c);
Social Security and Housing
Benefits Act 1982; Sch 4, para 22;
Health and Social Services and
Social Security Adjudications
Act 1983, Sch 8, para 17)
(SI 1986/1959)

26 Jun 1987 (repeals of or in
Attachment of Earnings Act 1971;
Social Security (Consequential
Provisions) Act 1975, Sch 2,
para 44; Social Security and
Housing Benefits Act 1982,
s 45(2)(a)) (SI 1987/1096)

4 Jan 1988 (repeals of or in Social
Security Act 1975, ss 146(1),
151(1), 152(8); Employment
Protection (Consolidation)
Act 1978, ss 123(5), 127(3))
(SI 1987/543)

1 Apr 1988 or 4 Apr 1988 (repeals of
or in Social Security Act 1980,
Sch 3, Pt II, para 15B; Social
Security and Housing Benefits
Act 1982, Pt II, ss 45(1), (2)(b),
(c), (3), 47, Sch 4, paras 5, 19,
27, 28, 35(1), (2); Social
Security Act 1985, ss 22, 32(2))
(SI 1987/1853)

6 Apr 1988 (repeal of or in Social
Security Pensions Act 1975, s 6(2))
(SI 1987/543)

Social Security Act 1986 (c 50)—*contd*
Schedule
11—*contd*

11 Apr 1988 (repeals of or in
Pensioners and Family Income
Supplement Payments Act 1972
(except s 3 and s 4 so far as it refers
to expenses attributable to s 3);
Pensioners' Payments and National
Insurance Contributions Act 1972;
Pensioners' Payments and National
Insurance Act 1973 (except s 7 and
the Schedule); Pensioners'
Payments Act 1974; Social Security
Act 1975, ss 12(1)(h), (2), 13(1)
(entry relating to widow's
allowance), (5)(a), 25(3), 26(3),
41(2)(e), (2C), 50(2), 79–81, 82,
84(3), 88(a), 90, 101(3), Sch 3,
Pt II, paras 8(2), 9, 10, Sch 4, Pt I,
para 5, Pt IV, para 4, Pt V, paras 6,
11, Sch 20 (definitions 'Relative',
'Short-term benefit'); Industrial
Injuries and Diseases (Old Cases)
Act 1975, s 4(4); Social Security
Pensions Act 1975, s 56K(4), Sch 4,
para 51; Child Benefit Act 1975,
ss 6, 8 (so far as not already in
force), 15(1), Sch 4, paras 3, 4, 6,
27; Social Security (Miscellaneous
Provisions) Act 1977, ss 9, 17(2),
22(2), (reference to Social Security
Act 1975, s 24(2)); Pensioners'
Payments Act 1977; Pensioners'
Payments Act 1978; Pensioners'
Payments and Social Security
Act 1979; Social Security (No 2)
Act 1980, s 4(2); Social Security
and Housing Benefits Act 1982,
s 44(1)(f), Sch 4, para 14; Health
and Social Security Act 1984,
ss 22, 27(2), Sch 4, paras 3, 14,
Sch 5, paras 5, 6; Social Security
Act 1985, ss 27, 32(2) ('section 15'),
Sch 5, para 6(a)) (SI 1987/1096)
11 Apr 1988 (repeals of or in National
Assistance Act 1948; Family
Income Supplements Act 1970 (so
far as it is not already repealed);
Pensioners and Family Income
Supplement Payments Act 1972
(so far as it is not already repealed);

Social Security Act 1986 (c 50)—*contd*
Schedule
11—*contd*

National Insurance Act 1974, s 6(1);
Social Security Act 1975, ss 67(2)(b),
143(1); Supplementary Benefits
Act 1976, ss 1–11, 13–19, 21, 24,
25, 27, 31–34, Sch 1, Sch 5, para
1(2), Sch 7, paras 1(b), (d), 3(a), 5,
19, 21, 23, 24, 31, 33, 37; Social
Security (Miscellaneous Provisions)
Act 1977, s 18(1); Employment
Protection (Consolidation)
Act 1978, s 132(6); Social Security
Act 1979, Sch 3, paras 1, 2, 24–27;
Social Security Act 1980, ss 7, 8(1),
9(7), 18(1), Sch 2, paras 1–10,
12–18, 22–30, Sch 3, Pt II, paras 11,
15; Social Security (No 2) Act 1980,
s 6; Social Security Act 1981, s 4,
Sch 1, paras 8, 9; Social Security
and Housing Benefits Act 1982,
ss 38, 44(1)(a), Sch 4, paras 2, 4,
23–25; Health and Social Services
and Social Security Adjudications
Act 1983, s 19(2), Sch 8, Pts III,
IV (so far as not already repealed);
Law Reform (Parent and Child)
(Scotland) Act 1986)
(SI 1987/1853)

11 Apr 1988 (repeals of or in Social
Security Act 1975, ss 67, 68, 70–75,
117(4), (5)) (SI 1988/567)

Not in force (repeals of or in Social
Security Act 1975, ss 13(5A),
50(5), 91(2), 135(6), Sch 16,
para 3 and Social Security
Pensions Act 1975, s 6(5), Sch 4,
paras 41, 42 and Social Security
(Consequential Provisions)
Act 1975, Sch 3, para 18, all of
which provisions have now been
repealed by Social Security
(Consequential Provisions)
Act 1992, s 3, Sch 1, as from
1 Jul 1992; also repeals of
Pensioners' Payments and
National Insurance Act 1973, s 7,
Schedule; Social Security Act 1985,
Sch 5, paras 6(b), 16, as to which
see note 1 to that Act ante)

Statute Law (Repeals) Act 1986 (c 12)

RA: 2 May 1986

2 May 1986 (RA)

Wages Act 1986 (c 48)

Whole Act repealed

1987

Abolition of Domestic Rates etc (Scotland) Act 1987 (c 47)

Whole Act repealed

Access to Personal Files Act 1987 (c 37)

Whole Act repealed, subject to transitional provisions and savings in Data Protection Act 1998, s 73, Sch 14

Agricultural Training Board Act 1987 (c 29)

RA: 15 May 1987

Commencement provisions: s 2(2)

15 Jul 1987 (s 2(2))

AIDS (Control) Act 1987 (c 33)

RA: 15 May 1987

15 May 1987 (RA)

Animals (Scotland) Act 1987 (c 9)

RA: 9 Apr 1987

Commencement provisions: s 9(2)

9 Jun 1987 (s 9(2))

Appropriation Act 1987 (c 17)

Whole Act repealed

Appropriation (No 2) Act 1987 (c 50)

Whole Act repealed

Banking Act 1987 (c 22)

Whole Act repealed

Billiards (Abolition of Restrictions) Act 1987 (c 19)

Whole Act repealed

British Shipbuilders (Borrowing Powers) Act 1987 (c 52)

RA: 23 Jul 1987

23 Jul 1987 (RA)

Broadcasting Act 1987 (c 10)

Whole Act repealed

Channel Tunnel Act 1987 (c 53)

Local application only

Chevening Estate Act 1987 (c 20)

Local application only

Coal Industry Act 1987 (c 3)

RA: 5 Mar 1987

Commencement provisions: s 10(2)
Section

1[1]	5 Mar 1987 (RA)
2	Repealed
3, 4	5 Mar 1987 (RA); prospectively repealed by Coal Industry Act 1994, s 67(8), Sch 11, Pt III[2]
5	5 Mar 1987 (RA)
6	5 May 1987 (s 10(2)); prospectively repealed, subject to transitional provisions, by Coal Industry Act 1994, s 67(8), Sch 11, Pt III[2]
7, 8	5 May 1987 (s 10(2)); prospectively repealed by Coal Industry Act 1994, s 67(8), Sch 11, Pt III[2]
9	5 Mar 1987 (RA); prospectively repealed by Coal Industry Act 1994, s 67(8), Sch 11, Pt III[2]
10	5 Mar 1987 (RA)
Schedule	
1[1]	5 Mar 1987 (RA)
2, 3	5 Mar 1987 (RA); prospectively repealed by Coal Industry Act 1994, s 67(8), Sch 11, Pt III[2]

Coal Industry Act 1987 (c 3)—*contd*

1   S 1 and Sch 1, so far as previously unrepealed and except insofar as amend Housing Act 1985, are prospectively repealed by Coal Industry Act 1994, s 67(8), Sch 11, Pt IV; orders made under s 68 of that Act bringing these prospective repeals into force will be noted to that Act

2   Orders made under Coal Industry Act 1994, s 68, bringing the prospective repeals into force will be noted to that Act

Consolidated Fund Act 1987 (c 8)

Whole Act repealed

Consolidated Fund (No 2) Act 1987 (c 54)

Whole Act repealed

Consolidated Fund (No 3) Act 1987 (c 55)

Whole Act repealed

Consumer Protection Act 1987 (c 43)

RA: 15 May 1987

Commencement provisions: s 50(2), (4), (5); Consumer Protection Act 1987 (Commencement No 1) Order 1987, SI 1987/1680; Consumer Protection Act 1987 (Commencement No 2) Order 1988, SI 1988/2041; Consumer Protection Act 1987 (Commencement No 3) Order 1988, SI 1988/2076

Section		
1–9		1 Mar 1988 (SI 1987/1680)
10–19		1 Oct 1987 (SI 1987/1680)
20–26		1 Mar 1989 (subject to transitional provisions in relation to s 20(1), (2)) (SI 1988/2076)
27–35		1 Oct 1987 (for purposes of or in relation to Pt II) (SI 1987/1680)
		1 Mar 1989 (otherwise) (SI 1988/2076)
36		1 Mar 1988 (SI 1987/1680)
37–40		1 Oct 1987 (for purposes of or in relation to Pt II) (SI 1987/1680)
		1 Mar 1989 (otherwise) (SI 1988/2076)
41	(1)	1 Oct 1987 (for purposes of or in relation to Pt II) (SI 1987/1680)
		1 Mar 1989 (otherwise) (SI 1988/2076)
	(2)	1 Oct 1987 (for purposes of or in relation to Pt II) (SI 1987/1680)
		1 Mar 1988 (for purposes of or in relation to Pt I) (SI 1987/1680)
		1 Mar 1989 (otherwise) (SI 1988/2076)
	(3)–(5)	1 Oct 1987 (for purposes of or in relation to Pt II) (SI 1987/1680)
		1 Mar 1989 (otherwise) (SI 1988/2076)
	(6)	1 Oct 1987 (for purposes of or in relation to Pt II) (SI 1987/1680)

Consumer Protection Act 1987 (c 43)—*contd*
Section

41	(6)—*contd*		1 Mar 1988 (for purposes of or in relation to Pt I) (SI 1987/1680)
			1 Mar 1989 (otherwise) (SI 1988/2076)
42–44			1 Oct 1987 (so far as have effect for purposes of or in relation to Pt II) (SI 1987/1680)
			1 Mar 1989 (otherwise) (SI 1988/2076)
45, 46			1 Oct 1987 (so far as have effect for purposes of or in relation to Pt II) (SI 1987/1680)
			1 Mar 1988 (so far as have effect for purposes of or in relation to Pt I) (SI 1987/1680)
			1 Mar 1989 (otherwise) (SI 1988/2076)
47			1 Oct 1987 (for purposes of or in relation to Pt II) (SI 1987/1680)
			1 Mar 1989 (otherwise) (SI 1988/2076)
48	(1)		See Sch 4 below
	(2)	(a)	31 Dec 1988 (SI 1988/2041)
		(b)	1 Oct 1987 (SI 1987/1680)
	(3)		See Sch 5 below
49, 50			1 Oct 1987 (SI 1987/1680)
Schedule			
1			1 Mar 1988 (SI 1987/1680)
2			1 Oct 1987 (SI 1987/1680)
3			1 Mar 1988 (SI 1987/1680)
4, para	1, 2		1 Oct 1987 (SI 1987/1680)
	3		1 Mar 1989 (SI 1988/2076)
	4		1 Oct 1987 (SI 1987/1680)
	5		1 Mar 1988 (SI 1987/1680)
	6, 7		1 Oct 1987 (SI 1987/1680)
	8		Repealed
	9–11		1 Oct 1987 (SI 1987/1680)
	12		1 Mar 1988 (SI 1987/1680)
	13		1 Oct 1987 (SI 1987/1680)
5			1 Oct 1987 (repeals of or in Fabrics (Misdescription) Act 1913; Criminal Justice Act 1967; Fines Act (Northern Ireland) 1967; Local Government Act 1972; Local Government (Scotland) Act 1973; Explosives (Age of Purchase etc) Act 1976; Consumer Safety Act 1978; Magistrates' Courts Act 1980; Telecommunications Act 1984; Food Act 1984; Consumer Safety (Amendment) Act 1986; Airports Act 1986; Gas Act 1986) (SI 1987/1680)

Consumer Protection Act 1987 (c 43)—*contd*
Schedule

5—*contd*	1 Mar 1988 (repeals of or in Prescription and Limitation (Scotland) Act 1973; Health and Safety at Work etc Act 1974) (SI 1987/1680)
	31 Dec 1988 (repeal of Trade Descriptions Act 1972) (SI 1988/2041)
	1 Mar 1989 (repeal of Trade Descriptions Act 1968, s 11) (SI 1988/2076)

Criminal Justice Act 1987 (c 38)

RA: 15 May 1987

Commencement provisions: s 16; Criminal Justice Act 1987 (Commencement No 1) Order 1987, SI 1987/1061; Criminal Justice Act 1987 (Commencement No 2) Order 1988, SI 1988/397; Criminal Justice Act 1987 (Commencement No 3) Order 1988, SI 1988/1564

Section

1	20 Jul 1987 (for purposes of appointment of person to be Director of the Serious Fraud Office, staff for Office and doing of such other things necessary or expedient for establishment of Office) (SI 1987/1061)
	6 Apr 1988 (otherwise) (SI 1988/397)
2, 3	6 Apr 1988 (SI 1988/397)
4, 5	31 Oct 1988 (SI 1988/1564)
6	Substituted by Criminal Justice Act 1988, s 144(1), (5) (qv)
7–9	31 Oct 1988 (SI 1988/1564)
9A	Inserted by Criminal Procedure and Investigations Act 1996, s 72, Sch 3, paras 1, 4 (qv)
10	Substituted by Criminal Procedure and Investigations Act 1996, s 72, Sch 3, paras 1, 5 (qv)
11, 11A	Substituted for original s 11 by Criminal Procedure and Investigations Act 1996, s 72, Sch 3, paras 1, 6 (qv)
12	20 Jul 1987 (except in relation to things done before that date) SI 1987/1061)
13	15 May 1987 (s 16(3))
14	20 Jul 1987 (SI 1987/1061)

Criminal Justice Act 1987 (c 38)—*contd*

Section

15		See Sch 2 below
16–18		15 May 1987 (s 16(3))
Schedule		
1		See s 1 above
2, para	1	31 Oct 1988 (SI 1988/1564)
	2	Repealed
	3–5	31 Oct 1988 (SI 1988/1564)
	6	6 Apr 1988 (SI 1988/397)
	7, 8	Repealed
	9–12	31 Oct 1988 (SI 1988/1564)
	13	6 Apr 1988 (SI 1988/397)
	14–16	31 Oct 1988 (SI 1988/1564)

Criminal Justice (Scotland) Act 1987 (c 41)

RA: 15 May 1987

Commencement provisions: s 72(2); Criminal Justice (Scotland) Act 1987 (Commencement No 1) Order 1987, SI 1987/1468; Criminal Justice (Scotland) Act 1987 (Commencement No 2) Order 1987, SI 1987/1594; Criminal Justice (Scotland) Act 1987 (Commencement No 3) Order 1987, SI 1987/2119; Criminal Justice (Scotland) Act 1987 (Commencement No 4) Order 1988, SI 1988/483; Criminal Justice (Scotland) Act 1987 (Commencement No 5) Order 1988, SI 1988/482; Criminal Justice (Scotland) Act 1987 (Commencement No 6) Order 1988, SI 1988/1710

Section

1–47		Repealed
48, 49		1 Oct 1987 (SI 1987/1594)
50		1 Apr 1988 (SI 1988/482)
51–55		1 Jan 1988 (SI 1987/2119)
56–68		Repealed
69		1 Oct 1987 (SI 1987/1594)
70		See Schs 1, 2 below
71		1 Apr 1988 (SI 1988/482)
72		15 May 1987 (s 72(2))
Schedule		
1, para	1, 2	1 Sep 1987 (SI 1987/1468)
	3–19	Repealed
2		1 Sep 1987 (repeals of or in Circuit Courts (Scotland) Act 1709; Heritable Jurisdiction (Scotland) Act 1746; Circuit Courts (Scotland) Act 1828; Justiciary (Scotland) Act 1848; Circuit Clerks (Scotland) Act 1898; Criminal Procedure (Scotland) Act 1975, ss 5(1), 87, 88, 113, 115–119) (SI 1987/1468)

Criminal Justice (Scotland) Act 1987 (c 41)—*contd*
Schedule

2—*contd*	1 Oct 1987 (repeals of or in Road Traffic Act 1974, Sch 3, para 10(4); Criminal Procedure (Scotland) Act 1975, s 263(2)) (SI 1987/1594)
	1 Jan 1988 (repeals of or in Road Traffic Act 1972; Criminal Procedure (Scotland) Act 1976, s 300(5); Sexual Offences (Scotland) Act 1976; Community Service by Offenders (Scotland) Act 1978) (SI 1987/2119)
	1 Apr 1988 (repeals of or in Children and Young Persons (Scotland) Act 1937; Social Work (Scotland) Act 1968; Criminal Procedure (Scotland) Act 1975, s 193B; Law Reform (Miscellaneous Provisions) (Scotland) Act 1985; Drug Trafficking Offences Act 1986) (SI 1988/482)
	12 Oct 1988 (repeals of or in Criminal Procedure (Scotland) Act 1975, ss 289B(3), (4), 289D(1A), (2)–(4)) (SI 1988/1710)

Crossbows Act 1987 (c 32)

RA: 15 May 1987

Commencement provisions: s 8(2)
Section

1–6	15 Jul 1987 (s 8(2))
7, 8	15 May 1987 (RA)

Crown Proceedings (Armed Forces) Act 1987 (c 25)

RA: 15 May 1987

15 May 1987 (RA)

Debtors (Scotland) Act 1987 (c 18)

RA: 15 May 1987

Commencement provisions: s 109(2); Debtors (Scotland) Act 1987 (Commencement No 1) Order 1987, SI 1987/1838; Debtors (Scotland) Act 1987 (Commencement No 2) Order 1988, SI 1988/1818
Section

1–15	30 Nov 1988 (SI 1988/1818)

Debtors (Scotland) Act 1987 (c 18)—*contd*
Section

16–45	30 Nov 1988 (SI 1988/1818); prospectively repealed as from 31 Dec 2002 or such earlier date as may be appointed by Abolition of Poindings and Warrant Sales (Scotland) Act 2001, s 3(2), Sch, Pt 1
46–67	30 Nov 1988 (SI 1988/1818)
68	Repealed
69–74	30 Nov 1988 (SI 1988/1818)
75, 76	2 Nov 1987 (SI 1987/1838)
77–96	30 Nov 1988 (SI 1988/1818)
97	2 Nov 1987 (SI 1987/1838)
98–108	30 Nov 1988 (SI 1988/1818)
109	15 May 1987 (RA)

Schedule

1	30 Nov 1988 (SI 1988/1818); prospectively repealed as from 31 Dec 2002 or such earlier date as may be appointed by Abolition of Poindings and Warrant Sales (Scotland) Act 2001, s 3(2), Sch, Pt 1
2–4	30 Nov 1988 (SI 1988/1818)
5	30 Nov 1988 (SI 1988/1818); prospectively repealed as from 31 Dec 2002 or such earlier date as may be appointed by Abolition of Poindings and Warrant Sales (Scotland) Act 2001, s 3(2), Sch, Pt 1
6–8	30 Nov 1988 (SI 1988/1818)

Deer Act 1987 (c 28)

Whole Act repealed

Diplomatic and Consular Premises Act 1987 (c 46)

RA: 15 May 1987

Commencement provisions: s 9(2); Diplomatic and Consular Premises Act 1987 (Commencement No 1) Order 1987, SI 1987/1022; Diplomatic and Consular Premises Act 1987 (Commencement No 2) Order 1987, SI 1987/2248; Diplomatic and Consular Premises Act 1987 (Commencement No 3) Order 1987, SI 1988/106

Section

1–5	1 Jan 1988 (SI 1987/2248)
6, 7	11 Jun 1987 (SI 1987/1022)
8	1 Jan 1988 (SI 1987/2248)
9	3 Feb 1988 (SI 1988/106)

Schedule

1	1 Jan 1988 (SI 1987/2248)
2	11 Jun 1987 (SI 1987/1022)

Family Law Reform Act 1987 (c 42)

RA: 15 May 1987

Commencement provisions: s 34(2); Family Law Reform Act 1987 (Commencement No 1) Order 1988, SI 1988/425; Family Law Reform Act 1987 (Commencement No 2) Order 1989, SI 1989/382; Family Law Reform Act 1987 (Commencement No 3) Order 2001, SI 2001/777

Section			
1			4 Apr 1988 (SI 1988/425)
2			1 Apr 1989 (SI 1989/382)
3–7			Repealed
8			1 Apr 1989 (SI 1989/382)
9–16			Repealed
17			1 Apr 1989 (SI 1989/382)
18–22			4 Apr 1988 (SI 1988/425)
23			1 Apr 2001 (SI 2001/777)
24, 25			1 Apr 1989 (SI 1989/382)
26–29			4 Apr 1988 (SI 1988/425)
30			1 Apr 1989 (SI 1989/382)
31			4 Apr 1988 (SI 1988/425)
32			*Not in force*[1]
33			See Schs 2–4 below
34			4 Apr 1988 (SI 1988/425)
Schedule			
1			Spent
2, para	1		1 Apr 1989 (SI 1989/382)
	2–4		4 Apr 1988 (SI 1988/425)
	5–8		1 Apr 1989 (SI 1989/382)
	9, 10		4 Apr 1988 (SI 1988/425)
	11		Repealed
	12, 13		1 Apr 1989 (SI 1989/382)
	14		Repealed
	15		1 Apr 1989 (SI 1989/382)
	16	(a), (b)	1 Apr 1989 (SI 1989/382)
		(c)	4 Apr 1988 (SI 1988/425)
	17, 18		1 Apr 1989 (SI 1989/382)
	19		4 Apr 1988 (SI 1988/425)
	20		Repealed
	21–25		1 Apr 2001 (SI 2001/777)
	26		Repealed
	27		1 Apr 1989 (SI 1989/382)
	28–43		Spent
	44, 45		1 Apr 1989 (SI 1989/382)
	46		Repealed
	47–50		1 Apr 1989 (SI 1989/382)
	51		Repealed
	52		1 Apr 1989 (SI 1989/382)
	53–58		Spent
	59		Repealed
	60–66		Spent
	67, 68		Repealed

Family Law Reform Act 1987 (c 42)—*contd*

Schedule

2, para	69–72		1 Apr 1989 (SI 1989/382)
	73, 74		4 Apr 1988 (SI 1988/425)
	75–79		Spent
	80–90		1 Apr 1989 (SI 1989/382)
	91–95		Repealed
	96		4 Apr 1988 (SI 1988/425)
3, para	1		4 Apr 1988 (SI 1988/425)
	2–7		1 Apr 1988 (SI 1989/382)
	8–10		4 Apr 1988 (SI 1988/425)
	11, 12		Repealed
4			4 Apr 1988 (repeals of or in Domestic and Appellate Proceedings (Restriction of Publicity) Act 1968, s 2(1); Family Law Reform Act 1969, ss 14, 15, 17; Interpretation Act 1978, Sch 2, para 4) (SI 1988/425) 1 Apr 1989 (otherwise) (SI 1989/382)

[1]   Provision not brought into force consequent on errors in Sch 1

Finance Act 1987 (c 16)

Budget Day:17 Mar 1987

RA: 15 May 1987

Details of the commencement of Finance Acts are not set out in this work

---

Finance (No 2) Act 1987 (c 51)

RA: 23 Jul 1987

Details of the commencement of Finance Acts are not set out in this work

---

Fire Safety and Safety of Places of Sport Act 1987 (c 27)

RA: 15 May 1987

Commencement provisions: s 50(2); Fire Safety and Safety of Places of Sport Act 1987 (Commencement No 1) Order 1987, SI 1987/1762; Fire Safety and Safety of Places of Sport Act 1987 (Commencement No 2) Order 1988, SI 1988/485; Fire Safety and Safety of Places of Sport Act 1987 (Commencement No 3) (Scotland) Order 1988, SI 1988/626; Fire Safety and Safety of Places of Sport Act 1987 (Commencement No 4) Order 1988, SI 1988/1806; Fire Safety and Safety of Places of Sport Act 1987 (Commencement No 5) Order 1989, SI 1989/75; Fire Safety and Safety of Places of Sport Act 1987 (Commencement No 6) Order 1990, SI 1990/1984; Fire Safety and Safety of Places of Sport Act 1987 (Commencement No 7) Order 1993, SI 1993/1411

Section

1, 2	1 Apr 1989 (SI 1989/75)
3, 4	1 Jan 1988 (SI 1987/1762)
5–7	1 Apr 1989 (SI 1989/75)

Fire Safety and Safety of Places of Sport Act 1987 (c 27)—*contd*

Section

8, 9		1 Jan 1988 (SI 1987/1762)
10		*Not in force*
11–14		1 Jan 1988 (SI 1987/1762)
15		1 Aug 1993 (SI 1993/1411)
16	(1)	1 Jan 1988 (SI 1987/1762)
	(2)	See Sch 1 below
	(3)	1 Jan 1988 (SI 1987/1762)
17		1 Jan 1988 (SI 1987/1762)
18	(1)	See s 18(2)–(4) below
	(2)	1 Jan 1988 (so far as it amends Fire Precautions Act 1971, s 40(1)(a), by insertion of a reference to '5(2A)') (SI 1987/1762)
		1 Apr 1989 (otherwise) (SI 1989/75)
	(3)	1 Jan 1988 (so far as amends Fire Precautions Act 1971, s 40(1)(b), by insertion of references to '8B' and '10B') (SI 1987/1762)
		1 Apr 1989 (otherwise) (SI 1989/75)
	(4)	1 Apr 1989 (SI 1989/75)
19–25		1 Jan 1988 (SI 1987/1762)
26–41		1 Jan 1989 (SI 1988/1806)
42, 43		1 Jun 1988 (SI 1988/485)
44		1 Jun 1988 (SI 1988/626)
45		1 Jun 1988 (SI 1988/485)
46		1 Jan 1988 (SI 1987/1762)
47		31 Dec 1990 (SI 1990/1984)
48		1 Jun 1988 (SI 1988/626)
49		See Schs 4, 5 below
50	(1)–(3)	1 Jan 1988 (SI 1987/1762)
	(4)–(7)	1 Jan 1988 (so far as have effect in relation to Pt II of this Act) (SI 1987/1762)
		1 Jan 1989 (otherwise) (SI 1988/1806)

Schedule

1	1 Jan 1988 (so far as gives effect to Fire Precautions Act 1971, Sch 2, Pt I, Pt II, para 3(1), (2), (3) (so far as para 3(3) has effect in relation to references to the occupier in ss 5(2A), 7(3A), 7(4), 8B(1) of 1971 Act)) (SI 1987/1762)
	1 Apr 1989 (otherwise) (SI 1989/75)
2	1 Jan 1988 (SI 1987/1762)
3	1 Jun 1988 (SI 1988/485)
4	1 Jan 1988 (repeals of or in Fire Precautions Act 1971, ss 2, 12(1), 43(1), (2); Safety of Sports Grounds Act 1975) (SI 1987/1762)

Fire Safety and Safety of Places of Sport Act 1987 (c 27)—*contd*
Schedule

4—*contd*		1 Jun 1988 (repeals in London Government Act 1963, Sch 12) (SI 1988/485)
		1 Apr 1989 (repeal of Health and Safety at Work etc Act 1974, s 78(4)) (SI 1989/75)
		1 Aug 1993 (repeals in Fire Precautions Act 1971, ss 5(3)(c), 6(1)(d)) (SI 1993/1411)
5, para	1	1 Jan 1988 (SI 1987/1762)
	2	1 Apr 1989 (SI 1989/75)
	3–7	1 Jan 1988 (SI 1987/1762)
	8	1 Jun 1988 (SI 1988/485)
	9	1 Jan 1988 (SI 1987/1762)
	10	1 Jun 1988 (SI 1988/485)

Gaming (Amendment) Act 1987 (c 11)

RA: 9 Apr 1987

Commencement provisions: s 2(2); Gaming (Amendment) Act 1987 (Commencement) Order 1987, SI 1987/1200

1 Aug 1987 (SI 1987/1200)

Housing (Scotland) Act 1987 (c 26)

RA: 15 May 1987

Commencement provisions: s 340(2)

15 Aug 1987 (s 340(2))

Immigration (Carriers' Liability) Act 1987 (c 24)

RA: 15 May 1987

Commencement provisions: s 2(4)

Act has effect in relation to persons arriving in UK after 4 Mar 1987 except persons arriving by voyage or flight for which they embarked before that date (s 2(4)); *whole Act prospectively repealed* by Immigration and Asylum Act 1999, s 169(3), Sch 16; orders made under s 170 of that Act bringing the prospective repeal into force will be noted to that Act

Irish Sailors and Soldiers Land Trust Act 1987 (c 48)

RA: 15 May 1987

Commencement provisions: s 3(2); Irish Sailors and Soldiers Land Trust Act 1987 (Commencement) Order 1987, SI 1987/1909

4 Nov 1987 (SI 1987/1909)

Landlord and Tenant Act 1987 (c 31)

RA: 15 May 1987

Commencement provisions: s 62(2); Landlord and Tenant Act 1987 (Commencement No 1) Order 1987, SI 1987/2177; Landlord and Tenant Act 1987 (Commencement No 2) Order 1988, SI 1988/480; Landlord and Tenant Act 1987 (Commencement No 3) Order 1988, SI 1988/1283

Section		
1–4		1 Feb 1988 (SI 1987/2177)
4A		Inserted by Housing Act 1996, s 89(1) (qv)
5, 5A–5E, 6–8, 8A–8E, 9A, 9B, 10		Substituted for original ss 6–10 by Housing Act 1996, s 92(1), Sch 6, Pt I (qv)
10A		Inserted by Housing Act 1996, s 91 (qv)
11, 11A, 12A–12D, 13, 14		Substituted for original ss 11–15 by Housing Act 1996, s 92(1), Sch 6, Pt II (qv)
15		See ss 11, 11A, 12A–12D, 13, 14 above
16, 17		Substituted by Housing Act 1996, s 92(1), Sch 6, Pt III (qv)
18		1 Feb 1988 (SI 1987/2177)
18A		Inserted by Housing Act 1996, s 92(1), Sch 6, Pt IV, para 2 (qv)
19, 20		1 Feb 1988 (SI 1987/2177)
21–24		18 Apr 1988 (SI 1988/480)
24A, 24B		Inserted by Housing Act 1996, s 86(1), (5) (qv)
25–40		18 Apr 1988 (SI 1988/480)
41		1 Sep 1988 (SI 1988/1283)
42		1 Apr 1989 (SI 1988/1283)
43, 44		1 Sep 1988 (SI 1988/1283)
45		Repealed
46–50		1 Feb 1988 (SI 1987/2177)
51		Repealed
52		1 Feb 1988 (so far as relate to ss 1–20, 45–51) (SI 1987/2177)
		18 Apr 1988 (so far as relate to ss 21–40) (SI 1988/480)
		1 Sep 1988 (otherwise) (SI 1988/1283)
52A		Inserted by Housing Act 1996, s 92(1), Sch 6, Pt IV, para 7 (qv)
53–60		1 Feb 1988 (so far as relate to ss 1–20, 45–51) (SI 1987/2177)
		18 Apr 1988 (so far as relate to ss 21–40) (SI 1988/480)
		1 Sep 1988 (otherwise) (SI 1988/1283)
61	(1)	See Sch 4 below
	(2)	See Sch 5 below
62		1 Feb 1988 (SI 1987/2177)

Landlord and Tenant Act 1987 (c 31)—*contd*

Schedule

1, Pt	I		1 Feb 1988 (SI 1987/2177)
	II		18 Apr 1988 (SI 1988/480)
2, 3			1 Sep 1988 (SI 1988/1283)
4, para	1, 2		18 Apr 1988 (SI 1988/480)
	3	(a)	1 Sep 1988 (SI 1988/1283)
		(b)	1 Feb 1988 (SI 1987/2177)
	4–6		1 Sep 1988 (SI 1988/1283)
	7		Repealed
5			1 Sep 1988 (SI 1988/1283)

Licensing (Restaurant Meals) Act 1987 (c 2)

Whole Act repealed

Local Government Act 1987 (c 44)

RA: 15 May 1987

Commencement provisions: ss 1, 2(3), (4), 3(7)
Section

1, 2	Repealed
3	15 Jul 1987 (s 3(7))
4	15 May 1987 (RA)
Schedule	Repealed

Local Government Finance Act 1987 (c 6)

RA: 12 Mar 1987

12 Mar 1987 (RA)

Ministry of Defence Police Act 1987 (c 4)

RA: 5 Mar 1987

Commencement provisions: s 8(2)

5 May 1987 (s 8(2))

Minors' Contracts Act 1987 (c 13)

RA: 9 Apr 1987

Commencement provisions: s 5(2)

9 Jun 1987 (s 5(2))

Motor Cycle Noise Act 1987 (c 34)

RA: 15 May 1987

Commencement provisions: s 2(3); Motor Cycle Noise Act 1987 (Commencement) Order 1995, SI 1995/2367

1 Aug 1996 (SI 1995/2367)

Northern Ireland (Emergency Provisions) Act 1987 (c 30)

Whole Act repealed

Parliamentary and Health Service Commissioners Act 1987 (c 39)

RA: 15 May 1987

Commencement provisions: s 10(3)

15 Jul 1987 (s 10(3))

Parliamentary and other Pensions Act 1987 (c 45)

RA: 15 May 1987

Commencement provisions: s 7(2); Parliamentary and other Pensions Act 1987 (Commencement No 1) Order 1987, SI 1987/1311; Parliamentary and other Pensions Act 1987 (Commencement No 2) Order 1989, SI 1989/892

Section		
1–3		24 May 1989 (SI 1989/892)
4	(1)	23 Jul 1987 (SI 1987/1311)
	(2)	24 May 1989 (SI 1989/892)
	(3)	23 Jul 1987 (SI 1987/1311)
5–7		24 May 1989 (SI 1989/892)
Schedule		
1–4		24 May 1989 (SI 1989/892)

Petroleum Act 1987 (c 12)

RA: 9 Apr 1987

Commencement provisions: s 31(1), (2); Petroleum Act 1987 (Commencement No 1) Order 1987, SI 1987/820; Petroleum Act 1987 (Commencement No 2) Order 1987, SI 1987/1330

Section	
1–20	Repealed
21–24	1 Sep 1987 (SI 1987/1330)
25–27	9 Jun 1987 (s 31(1))
28	Repealed
29–32	9 Jun 1987 (s 31(1))
Schedule	
1, 2	Repealed

Petroleum Act 1987 (c 12)—*contd*
Schedule
3   9 Jun 1987 (except repeals of or in
                                                              Oil and Gas (Enterprise) Act 1982,
                                                              ss 21, 27) (s 31(1))
                                                            1 Sep 1987 (exception noted above)
                                                              (SI 1987/1330)

Pilotage Act 1987 (c 21)

RA: 15 May 1987

Commencement provisions: s 33(2), (3); Pilotage Act 1987 (Commencement No 1)
    Order 1987, SI 1987/1306; Pilotage Act 1987 (Commencement No 2)
    Order 1987, SI 1987/2138; Pilotage Act 1987 (Commencement No 3)
    Order 1988, SI 1988/1137; Pilotage Act 1987 (Commencement No 4)
    Order 1991, SI 1991/1029

Section		
1–23		1 Oct 1988 (SI 1988/1137)
24, 25		1 Sep 1987 (SI 1987/1306)
26		1 Oct 1988 (SI 1988/1137)
27		Repealed
28		1 Sep 1987 (SI 1987/1306)
29		1 Aug 1988 (SI 1988/1137)
30, 31		1 Sep 1987 (SI 1987/1306)
32	(1)–(3)	1 Sep 1987 (SI 1987/1306)
	(4)	1 Oct 1988 (SI 1988/1137)
	(5)	See Sch 3 below
33		1 Sep 1987 (SI 1987/1306)
Schedule		
1, para	1–4	1 Sep 1987 (SI 1987/1306)
	5, 6	1 Oct 1988 (SI 1988/1137)
2		1 Oct 1988 (SI 1988/1137)
3		1 Feb 1988 (repeal of Pilotage
		Act 1983, s 15(1)(i)) (SI 1987/2138)
		1 Oct 1988 (otherwise, except repeal
		of Pilotage Act 1983, ss 1(1), 2, 4,
		5(4), 8, Sch 1) (SI 1988/1137)
		30 Apr 1991 (exception noted above)
		(SI 1991/1029)

Prescription (Scotland) Act 1987 (c 36)

RA: 15 May 1987

15 May 1987 (RA)

Protection of Animals (Penalties) Act 1987 (c 35)

RA: 15 May 1987

Commencement provisions: s 2(3)

15 Jul 1987 (s 2(3))

Rate Support Grants Act 1987 (c 5)

RA: 12 Mar 1987

12 Mar 1987 (RA)

Recognition of Trusts Act 1987 (c 14)

RA: 9 Apr 1987

Commencement provisions: s 3(2); Recognition of Trusts Act 1987 (Commencement) Order 1987, SI 1987/1177

1 Aug 1987 (SI 1987/1177)

Register of Sasines (Scotland) Act 1987 (c 23)

RA: 15 May 1987

Commencement provisions: s 3(1)

15 Jul 1987 (s 3(1))

Registered Establishments (Scotland) Act 1987 (c 40)

RA: 15 May 1987

Commencement provisions: s 8(2); commencement order dated 26 Sep 1988 (not a statutory instrument)

17 Oct 1988 (commencement order dated 26 Sep 1988)

Reverter of Sites Act 1987 (c 15)

RA: 9 Apr 1987

Commencement provisions: s 9(2); Reverter of Sites (Commencement) Order 1987, SI 1987/1260

17 Aug 1987 (SI 1987/1260)

Scottish Development Agency Act 1987 (c 56)

Whole Act repealed

Social Fund (Maternity and Funeral Expenses) Act 1987 (c 7)

Whole Act repealed

Teachers' Pay and Conditions Act 1987 (c 1)

Whole Act repealed

Territorial Sea Act 1987 (c 49)

RA: 15 May 1987

Commencement provisions: s 4(2); Territorial Sea Act 1987 (Commencement) Order 1987,
SI 1987/1270

1 Oct 1987 (SI 1987/1270)

Urban Development Corporations (Financial Limits) Act 1987 (c 57)

RA: 17 Dec 1987

Commencement provisions: s 2(2)

17 Feb 1988 (s 2(2))

1988

Access to Medical Reports Act 1988 (c 28)

RA: 29 Jul 1988

Commencement provisions: s 10(2)

1 Jan 1989 (s 10(2))

Appropriation Act 1988 (c 38)

Whole Act repealed

Arms Control and Disarmament (Privileges and Immunities) Act 1988 (c 2)

RA: 9 Feb 1988

9 Feb 1988 (RA)

British Steel Act 1988 (c 35)

RA: 29 Jul 1988

Commencement provisions: ss 1(1), 10(2), 17(2)–(4); British Steel Act 1988 (Appointed Day) Order 1988, SI 1988/1375

Section		
1		5 Sep 1988 (SI 1988/1375)
2		29 Jul 1988 (s 17(2))
3–14		5 Sep 1988 (SI 1988/1375)
15	(1)	29 Jul 1988 (s 17(2))
	(2)	5 Sep 1988 (SI 1988/1375)
16	(1), (2)	5 Sep 1988 (SI 1988/1375)
	(3)	See Sch 2 below
	(4)	5 Sep 1988 (SI 1988/1375)
17		29 Jul 1988 (s 17(2))
Schedule		
1		5 Sep 1988 (SI 1988/1375)
2, Pt	I	5 Sep 1988 (SI 1988/1375)
	II	*Not in force*
3		5 Sep 1988 (SI 1988/1375)

Church Commissioners (Assistance for Priority Areas) Measure 1988 (No 2)

RA: 3 May 1988

Commencement provisions: s 4(3)

4 May 1988 (the day appointed by the Archbishops of Canterbury and York under
  s 4(3))

Church of England (Ecumenical Relations) Measure 1988 (No 3)

RA: 29 Jul 1988

Commencement provisions: s 9(3)

1 Nov 1988 (the day appointed by the Archbishops of Canterbury and York under
  s 9(3))

Church of England (Legal Aid and Miscellaneous Provisions) Measure 1988 (No 1)

RA: 9 Feb 1988

Commencement provisions: s 15(2)

The provisions of this Measure were brought into force on the following dates
  by an instrument made by the Archbishops of Canterbury and York and dated
  19 Apr 1988 (made under s 15(2))

Part		
I (ss 1–4)		Repealed
II, III (ss 5–15)		1 May 1988
Schedule		
1		Repealed
2, para	1, 2	1 Aug 1988
	3	1 May 1988
	4	1 Aug 1988
3		1 May 1988 (repeals of or in Pluralities Act 1838, ss 97, 98; Parochial Church Councils (Powers) Measure 1956, s 7; Clergy (Ordination and Miscellaneous Provisions) Measure 1964, ss 10, 12)
		1 Aug 1988 (otherwise)

Church of England (Pensions) Measure 1988 (No 4)

RA: 27 Oct 1988

Commencement provisions: s 19(2)

The provisions of this Measure were brought into force on the following dates
  by an instrument made by the Archbishops of Canterbury and York and dated
  31 Oct 1988 (made under s 19(2))

Section	
1–4	Repealed
5	1 Dec 1988
6	Repealed

Church of England (Pensions) Measure 1988 (No 4)—*contd*
Section

7–14	1 Dec 1988
15	Repealed
16	1 Nov 1988
17	Repealed
18, 19	1 Dec 1988

Schedule

1	Repealed
2, 3	1 Dec 1988

Civil Evidence (Scotland) Act 1988 (c 32)

RA: 29 Jul 1988

Commencement provisions: s 11(2); Civil Evidence (Scotland) Act 1988 (Commencement) Order 1989, SI 1989/556

3 Apr 1989 (SI 1989/556)

Community Health Councils (Access to Information) Act 1988 (c 24)

RA: 29 Jul 1988

Commencement provisions: s 3(2)

1 Apr 1989 (s 3(2))

Consolidated Fund Act 1988 (c 6)

Whole Act repealed

Consolidated Fund (No 2) Act 1988 (c 55)

Whole Act repealed

Consumer Arbitration Agreements Act 1988 (c 21)

Whole Act repealed

Copyright, Designs and Patents Act 1988 (c 48)

RA: 15 Nov 1988

Commencement provisions: s 305; Copyright, Designs and Patents Act 1988 (Commencement No 1) Order 1989, SI 1989/816 (as amended by SI 1989/1303); Copyright, Designs and Patents Act 1988 (Commencement No 2) Order 1989, SI 1989/955 (as amended by SI 1989/1032); Copyright, Designs and Patents Act 1988 (Commencement No 3) Order 1989, SI 1989/1032 (amends SI 1989/955); Copyright, Designs and Patents Act 1988 (Commencement No 4) Order 1989, SI 1989/1303 (amends SI 1989/816); Copyright, Designs and Patents Act 1988 (Commencement No 5) Order 1990, SI 1990/1400; Copyright, Designs and Patents Act 1988 (Commencement No 6) Order 1990, SI 1990/2168

Copyright, Designs and Patents Act 1988 (c 48)—*contd*

Section

1–3	1 Aug 1989 (SI 1989/816)
3A	Inserted (1 Jan 1998) by Copyright and Rights in Databases Regulations 1997, SI 1997/3032, reg 6, subject to transitional provisions and savings
4	1 Aug 1989 (SI 1989/816)
5	See ss 5A, 5B below
5A, 5B	Substituted (1 Jan 1996) for original s 5 by Duration of Copyright and Rights in Performances Regulations 1995, SI 1995/3297, reg 9(1), subject to transitional provisions and savings
6	1 Aug 1989 (SI 1989/816)
6A	Inserted (1 Dec 1996) by Copyright and Related Rights Regulations 1996, SI 1996/2967, regs 4, 6(2), subject to transitional provisions and savings
7–11	1 Aug 1989 (SI 1989/816)
12	Substituted (1 Jan 1996) by Duration of Copyright and Rights in Performances Regulations 1995, SI 1995/3297, regs 5(1), subject to transitional provisions and savings
13	See ss 13A, 13B below
13A, 13B	Substituted (1 Jan 1996) for original s 13 by Duration of Copyright and Rights in Performances Regulations 1995, SI 1995/3297, regs 6(1), subject to transitional provisions and savings
14	Substituted (1 Jan 1996) by Duration of Copyright and Rights in Performances Regulations 1995, SI 1995/3297, regs 7(1), subject to transitional provisions and savings
15	1 Aug 1989 (SI 1989/816)
15A	Inserted (1 Jan 1996) by Duration of Copyright and Rights in Performances Regulations 1995, SI 1995/3297, regs 8(1), subject to transitional provisions and savings

Copyright, Designs and Patents Act 1988 (c 48)—*contd*
Section

16–18	1 Aug 1989 (SI 1989/816)
18A	Inserted (1 Dec 1996) by Copyright and Related Rights Regulations 1996, SI 1996/2967, regs 4, 10(2), subject to transitional provisions and savings
19–36	1 Aug 1989 (SI 1989/816)
36A	Inserted (1 Dec 1996) by Copyright and Related Rights Regulations 1996, SI 1996/2967, regs 4, 11(1), subject to transitional provisions and savings
37–40	9 Jun 1989 (for purposes of making regulations) (SI 1989/955; SI 1989/1032)
	1 Aug 1989 (otherwise) (SI 1989/816)
40A	Inserted (1 Dec 1996) by Copyright and Related Rights Regulations 1996, SI 1996/2967, regs 4, 11(2), subject to transitional provisions and savings
41–43	9 Jun 1989 (for purposes of making regulations) (SI 1989/955; SI 1989/1032)
	1 Aug 1989 (otherwise) (SI 1989/816)
44–46	1 Aug 1989 (SI 1989/816)
47	9 Jun 1989 (for purposes of making orders) (SI 1989/955; SI 1989/1032)
	1 Aug 1989 (otherwise) (SI 1989/816)
48–50	1 Aug 1990 (SI 1989/816)
50A–50C	Inserted in relation to agreements entered into on or after 1 Jan 1993 by Copyright (Computer Programs) Regulations 1992, SI 1992/3233, regs 2, 8, 12(2)
50D	Inserted (1 Jan 1998) by Copyright and Rights in Databases Regulations 1997, SI 1997/3032, reg 9, subject to transitional provisions and savings
51	1 Aug 1990 (SI 1989/816)
52	9 Jun 1989 (for purposes of making orders) (SI 1989/955; SI 1989/1032)
	1 Aug 1989 (otherwise) (SI 1989/816)
53–60	1 Aug 1989 (SI 1989/816)
61	9 Jun 1989 (for purposes of making orders) (SI 1989/955; SI 1989/1032)
	1 Aug 1989 (otherwise) (SI 1989/816)
62–65	1 Aug 1989 (SI 1989/816)

Copyright, Designs and Patents Act 1988 (c 48)—*contd*
Section

66	Substituted (1 Dec 1996) by Copyright and Related Rights Regulations 1996, SI 1996/2967, regs 4, 11(3), subject to transitional provisions and savings
66A	Inserted (1 Jan 1996) by Duration of Copyright and Rights in Performances Regulations 1995, SI 1995/3297, reg 6(2), subject to transitional provisions and savings
67–72	1 Aug 1989 (SI 1989/816)
73, 73A	Substituted for original s 73 by Broadcasting Act 1996, s 138, Sch 9, para 1 (qv)
74, 75	9 Jun 1989 (for purposes of making orders) (SI 1989/955; SI 1989/1032) 1 Aug 1989 (otherwise) (SI 1989/816)
76–93	1 Aug 1989 (SI 1989/816)
93A–93C	Inserted (1 Dec 1996) by Copyright and Related Rights Regulations 1996, SI 1996/2967, regs 4, 12, 14(1), subject to transitional provisions and savings
94–99	1 Aug 1989 (SI 1989/816)
100	9 Jun 1989 (for purposes of making orders) (SI 1989/955; SI 1989/1032) 1 Aug 1989 (otherwise) (SI 1989/816)
101–107	1 Aug 1989 (SI 1989/816)
107A	Prospectively inserted by Criminal Justice and Public Order Act 1994, s 165(1), (2)[1]
108–111	1 Aug 1989 (SI 1989/816)
112	9 Jun 1989 (for purposes of making regulations) (SI 1989/955; SI 1989/1032) 1 Aug 1989 (otherwise) (SI 1989/816)
113–116	1 Aug 1989 (SI 1989/816)
117	Substituted (1 Dec 1996) by Copyright and Related Rights Regulations 1996, SI 1996/2967, regs 4, 15(1), (2), subject to transitional provisions and savings
118–123	1 Aug 1989 (SI 1989/816)
124	Substituted (1 Dec 1996) by Copyright and Related Rights Regulations 1996, SI 1996/2967, regs 4, 15(1), (3), subject to transitional provisions and savings
125–135	1 Aug 1989 (SI 1989/816)

Copyright, Designs and Patents Act 1988 (c 48)—*contd*
Section

135A–135G	Inserted by Broadcasting Act 1990, s 175 (qv)
135H	Inserted by Broadcasting Act 1996, s 139(1) (qv)
136–141	1 Apr 1989 (SI 1989/816)
142	Substituted (1 Dec 1996) by Copyright and Related Rights Regulations 1996, SI 1996/2967, regs 4, 13(2), subject to transitional provisions and savings
143, 144	1 Aug 1989 (SI 1989/816)
144A	Inserted (1 Dec 1996) by Copyright and Related Rights Regulations 1996, SI 1996/2967, regs 4, 7, subject to transitional provisions and savings
145–149	1 Aug 1989 (SI 1989/816)
150	9 Jun 1989 (for purposes of making rules) (SI 1989/955; SI 1989/1032) 1 Aug 1989 (otherwise) (SI 1989/816)
151	1 Aug 1989 (SI 1989/816)
151A	Inserted by Broadcasting Act 1996, s 139(2), (3), subject to a saving (qv)
152	9 Jun 1989 (for purposes of making rules) (SI 1989/955; SI 1989/1032) 1 Aug 1989 (otherwise) (SI 1989/816)
153–158	1 Aug 1989 (SI 1989/816)
159	9 Jun 1989 (for purposes of making orders) (SI 1989/955; SI 1989/1032) 1 Aug 1989 (otherwise) (SI 1989/816)
160–166	1 Aug 1989 (SI 1989/816)
166A	Inserted by Scotland Act 1998, s 125(1), Sch 8, para 25(1), (6) (qv)
166B	Inserted by Northern Ireland Act 1998, s 99, Sch 13, para 8(1), (6) (qv)
167	1 Aug 1989 (SI 1989/816)
168	9 Jun 1989 (for purposes of making orders) (SI 1989/955; SI 1989/1032) 1 Aug 1989 (otherwise) (SI 1989/816)
169	1 Aug 1989 (SI 1989/816)
170	See Sch 1 below
171, 172	1 Aug 1989 (SI 1989/816)
172A	Inserted (1 Jan 1996) by Duration of Copyright and Rights in Performances Regulations 1995, SI 1995/3297, reg 11(1), subject to transitional provisions and savings

Copyright, Designs and Patents Act 1988 (c 48)—*contd*

Section

173	1 Aug 1989 (SI 1989/816)
174	9 Jun 1989 (for purposes of making orders) (SI 1989/955; SI 1989/1032)
	1 Aug 1989 (otherwise) (SI 1989/816)
175–181	1 Aug 1989 (SI 1989/816)
182	Substituted (1 Dec 1996) by Copyright and Related Rights Regulations 1996, SI 1996/2967, regs 4, 20(1), subject to transitional provisions and savings
182A–182D	Inserted (1 Dec 1996) by Copyright and Related Rights Regulations 1996, SI 1996/2967, regs 4, 20(2), subject to transitional provisions and savings
183–188	1 Aug 1989 (SI 1989/816)
189	See Sch 2 below
190	1 Aug 1989 (SI 1989/816)
191	Substituted (1 Jan 1996) by Duration of Copyright and Rights in Performances Regulations 1995, SI 1995/3297, reg 10, subject to transitional provisions and savings
191A–191M	Inserted (1 Dec 1996) by Copyright and Related Rights Regulations 1996, SI 1996/2967, regs 4, 21(1), subject to transitional provisions and savings
192	See ss 192A, 192B below
192A, 192B	Substituted (1 Dec 1996) for original s 192 by Copyright and Related Rights Regulations 1996, SI 1996/2967, regs 4, 21(2), subject to transitional provisions and savings
193–195	1 Aug 1989 (SI 1989/816)
196	9 Jun 1989 (for purposes of making orders) (SI 1989/955; SI 1989/1032)
	1 Aug 1989 (otherwise) (SI 1989/816)
197, 198	1 Aug 1989 (SI 1989/816)
198A	Prospectively inserted by Criminal Justice and Public Order Act 1994, s 165(1), (3)[1]
199–205	1 Aug 1989 (SI 1989/816)
205A, 205B	Inserted (1 Dec 1996) by Copyright and Related Rights Regulations 1996, SI 1996/2967, regs 4, 22(1), 24(1), subject to transitional provisions and savings

Copyright, Designs and Patents Act 1988 (c 48)—*contd*
Section

206, 207		1 Aug 1989 (SI 1989/816)
208		9 Jun 1989 (for purposes of making orders) (SI 1989/955; SI 1989/1032)
		1 Aug 1989 (otherwise) (SI 1989/816)
209–249		1 Aug 1989 (SI 1989/816)
250		9 Jun 1989 (for purposes of making rules) (SI 1989/955; SI 1989/1032)
		1 Aug 1989 (otherwise) (SI 1989/816)
251–255		1 Aug 1989 (SI 1989/816)
256		9 Jun 1989 (for purposes of making orders) (SI 1989/955; SI 1989/1032)
		1 Aug 1989 (otherwise) (SI 1989/816)
257–264		1 Aug 1989 (SI 1989/816)
265		Repealed
266, 267		1 Aug 1989 (SI 1989/816)
268		Repealed
269–271		1 Aug 1989 (SI 1989/816)
272		See Sch 3 below
273		See Sch 4 below
274–281		10 Jul 1990 (for purpose of making rules expressed to come into force on or after 13 Aug 1990) (SI 1990/1400)
		13 Aug 1990 (otherwise) (SI 1990/1400)
282–284		Repealed (with savings) by Trade Marks Act 1994, ss 105, 106(2), Sch 3, para 22(1), Sch 5 (qv)
285, 286		10 Jul 1990 (for purpose of making rules expressed to come into force on or after 13 Aug 1990) (SI 1990/1400)
		13 Aug 1990 (otherwise) (SI 1990/1400)
287–289		1 Aug 1989 (SI 1989/816)
290		1 Aug 1989 (SI 1989/816); prospectively repealed by Courts and Legal Services Act 1990, s 125(7), Sch 20[2]
291, 292		1 Aug 1989 (SI 1989/816)
293, 294		15 Jan 1989 (s 305(2))
295		See Sch 5 below
296	(1), (2)	1 Aug 1989 (SI 1989/816)
	(2A)	Inserted in relation to agreements entered into on or after 1 Jan 1993 by Copyright (Computer Programs) Regulations 1992, SI 1992/3233, regs 2, 10, 12(2)
	(3)–(6)	1 Aug 1989 (SI 1989/816)

Copyright, Designs and Patents Act 1988 (c 48)—*contd*
Section

296A		Inserted in relation to agreements entered into on or after 1 Jan 1993 by Copyright (Computer Programs) Regulations 1992, SI 1992/3233, regs 2, 11, 12(2)
296B		Inserted (1 Jan 1998) by Copyright and Rights in Databases Regulations 1997, SI 1997/3032, reg 10, subject to transitional provisions and savings
297		1 Aug 1989 (SI 1989/816)
297A		Inserted by Broadcasting Act 1990, s 179 (qv); substituted (28 May 2000) by Conditional Access (Unauthorised Decoders) Regulations 2000, SI 2000/1175, reg 2(1), (2)
298		Substituted (28 May 2000) by Conditional Access (Unauthorised Decoders) Regulations 2000, SI 2000/1175, reg 2(1), (3)
299		1 Aug 1989 (SI 1989/816)
300		Repealed
301		See Sch 6 below
302		1 Aug 1989 (SI 1989/816)
303	(1)	See Sch 7 below
	(2)	See Sch 8 below
304	(1)–(3)	1 Aug 1989 (SI 1989/816)
	(4)	28 Jul 1989 (SI 1989/816; SI 1989/1303)
	(5)	1 Aug 1989 (SI 1989/816)
	(6)	28 Jul 1989 (SI 1989/816; SI 1989/1303)
305		15 Nov 1988 (RA)
306		1 Aug 1989 (SI 1989/816)
Schedule		
1, para	1–33	1 Aug 1989 (SI 1989/816)
	34	9 Jun 1989 (for purposes of making rules) (SI 1989/955; SI 1989/1032) 1 Aug 1989 (otherwise) (SI 1989/816)
	35–46	1 Aug 1989 (SI 1989/816)
2		1 Aug 1989 (SI 1989/816)
2A		Inserted (1 Dec 1996) by Copyright and Related Rights Regulations 1996, SI 1996/2967, regs 4, 22(2), subject to transitional provisions and savings
3, para	1, 2	Repealed
	3	1 Aug 1989 (SI 1989/816)

Copyright, Designs and Patents Act 1988 (c 48)—*contd*

Schedule

3, para	4		Repealed
	5		1 Aug 1989 (SI 1989/816)
	6		Repealed
	7, 8		1 Aug 1989 (SI 1989/816)
	9		Repealed
	10–20		1 Aug 1989 (SI 1989/816)
	21		13 Aug 1990 (SI 1990/1400)
	22–38		1 Aug 1989 (SI 1989/816)
4			13 Aug 1990 (SI 1990/1400)
5, para	1–11		1 Nov 1990 (for purposes of making rules) (SI 1990/2168)
			7 Jan 1991 (otherwise) (SI 1990/2168)
	12–16		1 Aug 1989 (SI 1989/816)
	17–23		1 Nov 1990 (for purposes of making rules) (SI 1990/2168)
			7 Jan 1991 (otherwise) (SI 1990/2168)
	24		Repealed
	25, 26		1 Nov 1990 (for purposes of making rules) (SI 1990/2168)
			7 Jan 1991 (otherwise) (SI 1990/2168)
	27		13 Aug 1990 (SI 1990/1400)
	28		1 Nov 1990 (for purposes of making rules) (SI 1990/2168)
			7 Jan 1991 (otherwise) (SI 1990/2168)
	29		15 Nov 1988 (s 305(1))
	30		1 Nov 1990 (for purposes of making rules) (SI 1990/2168)
			7 Jan 1991 (otherwise) (SI 1990/2168)
6			15 Nov 1988 (s 305(1))
7, para	1–5		1 Aug 1989 (SI 1989/816)
	6		1 Aug 1989 (SI 1989/816); repealed (1 Dec 1996) by Copyright and Related Rights Regulations 1996, SI 1996/2967, regs 11(7), subject to transitional provisions and savings
	7		1 Aug 1989 (SI 1989/816)
	8		1 Aug 1989 (SI 1989/816); repealed (1 Dec 1996) by Copyright and Related Rights Regulations 1996, SI 1996/2967, regs 11(7), subject to transitional provisions and savings
	9–13		1 Aug 1989 (SI 1989/816)
	14		Repealed
	15		13 Aug 1990 (SI 1990/1400)
	16, 17		1 Aug 1989 (SI 1989/816)
	18	(1)	1 Aug 1989 (SI 1989/1400)
		(2)	13 Aug 1990 (SI 1990/1400)

Copyright, Designs and Patents Act 1988 (c 48)—*contd*
Schedule

7, para	18	(3)	1 Aug 1989 (SI 1989/816)
	19, 20		1 Aug 1989 (SI 1989/816)
	21		13 Aug 1990 (SI 1990/1400)
	22–25		1 Aug 1989 (SI 1989/816)
	26		Repealed
	27, 28		1 Aug 1989 (SI 1989/816)
	29, 30		Repealed
	31		1 Aug 1989 (SI 1989/816); prospectively repealed by Companies Act 1989, s 212, Sch 24[3]
	32, 33		1 Aug 1989 (SI 1989/816)
	34		1 Aug 1989 (SI 1989/816); repealed (1 Dec 1996) by Copyright and Related Rights Regulations 1996, SI 1996/2967, regs 11(7), subject to transitional provisions and savings
	35		Repealed
	36		1 Aug 1989 (SI 1989/816)
8			1 Aug 1989 (except repeals of or in of Registered Designs Act 1949, s 32; Patents Act 1977 (other than s 49(3), Sch 5, para 1, 3)) (SI 1989/816)
			13 Aug 1990 (repeals of or in Registered Design Act 1949, s 32; Patents Act 1977, ss 84, 85, 104, 105, 114, 115, 123(2)(k), 130(1)) (SI 1990/1400)
			7 Jan 1991 (repeals of or in Patents Act 1977 (so far as not already in force)) (SI 1990/2168)

[1] Orders made under Criminal Justice and Public Order Act 1994, s 172, bringing the prospective insertion into force will be noted to that Act

[2] Orders made under Courts and Legal Services Act 1990, s 124(3), bringing the prospective repeal into force will be noted to that Act

[3] Orders made under Companies Act 1989, s 215, bringing the prospective repeal into force will be noted to that Act

---

Coroners Act 1988 (c 13)

RA: 10 May 1988

Commencement provisions: s 37(2)

10 Jul 1988 (s 37(2))

Court of Session Act 1988 (c 36)

RA: 29 Jul 1988

Commencement provisions: s 53(2)

29 Sep 1988 (s 53(2))

Criminal Justice Act 1988 (c 33)

RA: 29 Jul 1988

Commencement provisions: ss 166(4), 171; Land Registration Act 1988, s 3(2); Extradition Act 1989, s 38(4)[1]; Criminal Justice Act 1988 (Commencement No 1) Order 1988, SI 1988/1408; Criminal Justice Act 1988 (Commencement No 2) Order 1988, SI 1988/1676; Criminal Justice Act 1988 (Commencement No 3) Order 1988, SI 1988/1817; Criminal Justice Act 1988 (Commencement No 4) Order 1988, SI 1988/2073; Criminal Justice Act 1988 (Commencement No 5) Order 1989, SI 1989/1; Criminal Justice Act 1988 (Commencement No 6) Order 1989, SI 1989/50; Criminal Justice Act 1988 (Commencement No 7) Order 1989, SI 1989/264; Criminal Justice Act 1988 (Commencement No 8) Order 1989, SI 1989/1085; Criminal Justice Act 1988 (Commencement No 9) Order 1989, SI 1989/1595; Criminal Justice Act 1988 (Commencement No 10) Order 1990, SI 1990/220; Criminal Justice Act 1988 (Commencement No 11) Order 1990, SI 1990/1145; Land Registration Act 1988 (Commencement) Order 1990, SI 1990/1359; Criminal Justice Act 1988 (Commencement No 12) Order 1990, SI 1990/2084; Criminal Justice Act 1988 (Commencement No 13) Order 1999, SI 1999/3425

Section			
1–21			Repealed
22			5 Jun 1990 (SI 1990/1145)
23–28			3 Apr 1989 (except in relation to a trial, or proceedings before a magistrates' court acting as examining justices, which began before that date) (SI 1989/264)
29			Repealed
30, 31			3 Apr 1989 (except in relation to a trial, or proceedings before a magistrates' court acting as examining justices, which began before that date) (SI 1989/264)
32	(1)	(a)	26 Nov 1990 (in relation only to proceedings for murder, manslaughter or any other offence of killing any person; proceedings being conducted by the Director of the Serious Fraud Office under Criminal Justice Act 1987, s 1(5); and proceedings for serious and complex fraud where there has been given a notice of transfer under s 4 of that Act) (subject to transitional provisions set out in SI 1990/2084, art 3) (SI 1990/2084)

Criminal Justice Act 1988 (c 33)—*contd*
Section

32	(1)	(a)—*contd*	*Not in force* (otherwise)
		(b)	Substituted by Criminal Justice Act 1991, s 55(2) (qv); prospectively repealed by Youth Justice and Criminal Evidence Act 1999, s 67(3), Sch 6[2]
	(1A)		Inserted by Criminal Justice Act 1991, s 55(3) (qv)
	(2)		5 Jan 1989 (SI 1988/2073); prospectively repealed by Youth Justice and Criminal Evidence Act 1999, s 67, Sch 6[2]
	(3)		26 Nov 1990 (in relation only to proceedings for murder, manslaughter or any other offence of killing any person; proceedings being conducted by the Director of the Serious Fraud Office under Criminal Justice Act 1987, s 1(5); and proceedings for serious and complex fraud where there has been given a notice of transfer under s 4 of that Act) (subject to transitional provisions set out in SI 1990/2084, art 3) (SI 1990/2084)
			Not in force (otherwise)
	(3A), (3B)		Inserted by Criminal Justice Act 1991, s 55(4) (qv); prospectively repealed by Youth Justice and Criminal Evidence Act 1999, s 67, Sch 6[2]
	(3C)–(3E)		Inserted by Criminal Procedure and Investigations Act 1996, s 62(1), (3), where the leave concerned is given on or after a day to be appointed under s 62(4) of the 1996 Act[4]; prospectively repealed by Youth Justice and Criminal Evidence Act 1999, s 67, Sch 6[2]
	(4), (5)		5 Jan 1989 (SI 1988/2073)
	(6)		Inserted Criminal Justice Act 1991, s 55(6) (qv); prospectively repealed by Youth Justice and Criminal Evidence Act 1999, s 67, Sch 6[2]
32A			Inserted by Criminal Justice Act 1991, s 54 (qv); prospectively repealed by Youth Justice and Criminal Evidence Act 1999, s 67, Sch 6[2]
33			12 Oct 1988 (SI 1988/1676)

Criminal Justice Act 1988 (c 33)—*contd*

Section

33A	Inserted by Criminal Justice Act 1991, s 52(1) (qv); prospectively repealed by Youth Justice and Criminal Evidence Act 1999, s 67, Sch 6[2]
34	12 Oct 1988 (SI 1988/1676)
34A	Repealed
35, 36	1 Feb 1989 (SI 1989/1)
37–41	12 Oct 1988 (SI 1988/1676)
42	Repealed
43	31 Jul 1989 (SI 1989/1085)
44–47	29 Sep 1988 (s 171(6))
48	Repealed
49	12 Oct 1988 (SI 1988/1676)
50	5 Jan 1989 (SI 1988/2073)
51–57	12 Oct 1988 (SI 1988/1676)
58	Repealed
59	12 Oct 1988 (SI 1988/1676)
60–62	5 Jan 1989 (SI 1988/2073)
63	Repealed
64	29 Sep 1988 (s 171(6))
65	Repealed
66, 67	29 Jul 1988 (s 171(5))
68, 69	Repealed
70	12 Oct 1988 (SI 1988/1676)
71, 72	3 Apr 1989 (SI 1989/264)
72AA	Inserted (E, W) by Proceeds of Crime Act 1995, s 2 (qv)
72A	Inserted (E, W) by Criminal Justice Act 1993, s 28 (qv)
73	3 Apr 1989 (SI 1989/264)
73A	Inserted (E, W) by Proceeds of Crime Act 1995, s 4 (qv)
74	3 Apr 1989 (SI 1989/264)
74A	Inserted (E, W) by Proceeds of Crime Act 1995, s 5 (qv)
74B	Inserted (E, W) by Proceeds of Crime Act 1995, s 6 (qv)
74C	Inserted (E, W) by Proceeds of Crime Act 1995, s 7 (qv)
75	3 Apr 1989 (SI 1989/264)
75A	Inserted (E, W) by Proceeds of Crime Act 1995, s 9 (qv), subject to a saving contained in s 16(6) thereof
76–89	3 Apr 1989 (SI 1989/264)
90–93	Repealed
93A	Inserted by Criminal Justice Act 1993, s 29 (qv)
93B	Inserted by Criminal Justice Act 1993, s 30 (qv)

Criminal Justice Act 1988 (c 33)—*contd*

Section

93C		Inserted by Criminal Justice Act 1993, s 31 (qv)
93D		Inserted by Criminal Justice Act 1993, s 32 (qv)
93E		Inserted (S) by Criminal Justice Act 1993, s 33 (qv)
93F		Inserted by Criminal Justice Act 1993, s 35 (qv)
93G		Inserted by Criminal Justice Act 1993, s 77, Sch 4, paras 1, 3 (qv)
93H		Inserted (E, W) by Proceeds of Crime Act 1995, s 11 (qv)
93I		Inserted (E, W) by Proceeds of Crime Act 1995, s 12 (qv)
93J		Inserted (E, W) by Proceeds of Crime Act 1995, s 13 (qv)
94		3 Apr 1989 (SI 1989/264)
95		Repealed
96, 97		12 Oct 1988 (SI 1988/1676)
98		Repealed
99		3 Apr 1989 (SI 1989/264)
100		3 Apr 1989 (SI 1989/264); ceased to have effect on 3 Dec 1990 by virtue of s 100(7) and SI 1990/1359
101, 102		3 Apr 1989 (SI 1989/264)
103	(1)	Repealed
	(2)	See Sch 5, Pt II below
104, 105		Repealed
106		12 Oct 1988 (SI 1988/1676)
107		Repealed
108–117		Repealed (*never in force*)
118		5 Jan 1989 (SI 1988/2073)
119		15 Feb 1990 (SI 1989/1085)
120		5 Jan 1989 (SI 1988/2073)
121, 122		12 Oct 1988 (SI 1988/1676)
123		1 Oct 1988 (SI 1988/1408)
124		1 Nov 1988 (SI 1988/1817)
125		1 Oct 1988 (SI 1988/1408)
126–129		Repealed
130		5 Jan 1989 (SI 1988/2073)
131		12 Oct 1988 (SI 1988/1676)
132		Repealed
133		12 Oct 1988 (SI 1988/1676)
134, 135		29 Sep 1988 (s 171(6))
136, 137		Repealed[1]
138	(1)	29 Sep 1988 (s 171(6))
	(2), (3)	Repealed
139		29 Sep 1988 (s 171(6))

Criminal Justice Act 1988 (c 33)—*contd*

Section

139A, 139B			Inserted by Offensive Weapons Act 1996, s 4(1) (qv)
140			29 Sep 1988 (s 171(6))
141			29 Jul 1988 (s 171(5))
141A			Inserted by Offensive Weapons Act 1996, s 6(1) (qv)
142–144			29 Jul 1988 (s 171(5))
145			12 Oct 1988 (SI 1988/1676)
146			See Sch 13 below
147, 148			12 Oct 1988 (SI 1988/1676)
149			Repealed
150			*Not in force*
151	(1)–(4)		*Not in force*
	(5)		3 Apr 1989 (SI 1989/264)
152			5 Jan 1989 (SI 1988/2073)
153			5 Jan 1989 (SI 1988/2073); prospectively repealed by Criminal Justice and Police Act 2001, s 137, Sch 7, Pt 6[4]
154			5 Jan 1989 (SI 1988/2073)
155–157			12 Oct 1988 (SI 1988/1676)
158			29 Sep 1988 (s 171(6))
159			31 Jul 1989 (SI 1989/1085)
160, 161			29 Sep 1988 (s 171(6))
162			1 Sep 1988 (s 171(7))
163–165			Repealed
166	(1)		29 Jul 1988 (s 171(5))
	(2), (3)		1 Oct 1986 (retrospective; s 166(4))
	(4), (5)		29 Jul 1988 (s 171(5))
167–169			29 Jul 1988 (s 171(5))
170	(1)		See Sch 15 below
	(2)		See Sch 16 below
171–173			29 Jul 1988 (s 171(5))

Schedule

1			Repealed[1]
2			3 Apr 1989 (except in relation to a trial, or proceedings before a magistrates' court acting as examining justices, which began before that date) (SI 1989/264)
3			1 Feb 1989 (SI 1989/1)
4			3 Apr 1989 (SI 1989/264)
5, Pt	I, para	1–17	Repealed
	II, para	18–23	23 Jan 1989 (SI 1989/50)
6, 7			Repealed (*never in force*)
8			1 Oct 1988 (SI 1988/1408)
9			1 Nov 1988 (SI 1988/1817)
10, 11			Repealed
12			12 Oct 1988 (SI 1988/1676)

Criminal Justice Act 1988 (c 33)—*contd*

Schedule

13		31 Jul 1989 (SI 1989/1085)
14		Repealed
15, para	1–4	12 Oct 1988 (SI 1988/1676)
	5, 6	3 Apr 1989 (SI 1989/264)
	7	29 Jul 1988 (s 171(5)); ceased to have effect on 3 Dec 1990 by virtue of para 7(2) and SI 1990/1359
	8	12 Oct 1988 (SI 1988/1676)
	9	29 Jul 1988 (s 171(5))
	10	12 Oct 1988 (SI 1988/1676)
	11, 12	1 Oct 1988 (SI 1988/1408)
	13–15	29 Jul 1988 (s 171(5))
	16	*Not in force*
	17	29 Jul 1988 (so far as relating to para 19) (s 171(5))
		12 Oct 1988 (so far as relating to para 18) (SI 1988/1676)
	18	Repealed (S)
		Ceased to have effect (E, W)
	19	29 Jul 1988 (s 171(5))
	20	12 Oct 1988 (so far as relating to paras 21–24, 26–29, 31) (SI 1988/1676)
		31 Jul 1989 (so far as relating to paras 25, 30, 32) (SI 1989/1085)
	21–24	12 Oct 1988 (SI 1988/1676)
	25	31 Jul 1989 (SI 1989/1085)
	26–29	12 Oct 1988 (SI 1988/1676)
	30	31 Jul 1989 (SI 1989/1085)
	31	12 Oct 1988 (SI 1988/1676)
	32	31 Jul 1989 (SI 1989/1085)
	33, 34	Repealed
	35	1 Oct 1988 (SI 1988/1408)
	36	29 Jul 1988 (s 171(5))
	37–39	Repealed (*para 38 partly never in force*)
	40	Repealed (*never in force*)
	41, 42	Repealed
	43	Spent
	44	31 Jul 1989 (except in relation to any register of electors or any part of any such register required to be used for elections in the twelve months ending on 15 Feb 1990) (SI 1990/1085)
	45	29 Jul 1988 (s 171(5))
	46	5 Jan 1989 (SI 1988/2073)
	47	3 Apr 1989 (SI 1989/264)
	48	29 Jul 1988 (s 171(5))
	49	12 Oct 1988 (SI 1988/1676)
	50, 51	29 Jul 1988 (s 171(5))

Criminal Justice Act 1988 (c 33)—*contd*

Schedule

15, para	52	Repealed
	53	29 Sep 1988 (s 171(6)); prospectively repealed by Youth Justice and Criminal Evidence Act 1999, s 67, Sch 6[2]
	54, 55	Repealed
	56	1 Feb 1989 (SI 1989/1)
	57	Repealed
	58, 59	12 Oct 1988 (SI 1988/1676)
	60–62	29 Sep 1988 (s 171(6))
	63	Repealed
	64	Spent
	65	29 Jul 1988 (so far as relating to paras 67, 70) (s 171(5))
		29 Sep 1988 (so far as relating to para 66) (s 171(6))
		12 Oct 1988 (otherwise) (SI 1988/1676)
	66	29 Sep 1988 (s 171(6))
	67	29 Jul 1988 (s 171(5))
	68	12 Oct 1988 (SI 1988/1676); repealed by Criminal Procedure and Investigations Act 1996, s 80, Sch 5(10), with effect in accordance with provision made by order under Sch 1, Pt III, para 39 to 1996 Act[3]
	69	12 Oct 1988 (SI 1988/1676)
	70	29 Jul 1988 (s 171(5))
	71	1 Feb 1989 (so far as relating to para 76) (SI 1989/1)
		3 Apr 1989 (so far as relating to paras 72, 74, 75, 77) (SI 1989/264)
		31 Jul 1989 (so far as relating to para 73) (SI 1989/1085)
	72	3 Apr 1989 (SI 1989/264)
	73	31 Jul 1989 (SI 1989/1085)
	74, 75	3 Apr 1989 (SI 1989/264)
	76	1 Feb 1989 (SI 1989/1)
	77	3 Apr 1989 (SI 1989/264)
	78	31 Jul 1989 (SI 1989/1085)
	79	Repealed
	80	1 Feb 1989 (SI 1989/1)
	81	Repealed
	82	12 Oct 1988 (SI 1988/1676)
	83–88	Repealed
	89	29 Jul 1988 (s 171(5))
	90	Spent
	91	29 Jul 1988 (s 171(5))

Criminal Justice Act 1988 (c 33)—*contd*

Schedule

15, para	92–96	Repealed
	97–104	29 Jul 1988 (s 171(5))
	105	Repealed
	106–110	3 Apr 1989 (SI 1989/264)
	111–113	29 Jul 1988 (s 171(5))
	114	29 Jul 1988 (s 171(5)); repealed by Criminal Procedure and Investigations Act 1996, s 80, Sch 5(12), with effect in accordance with s 72 of, and Sch 3, para 8 to, 1996 Act[3]
	115–117	29 Jul 1988 (s 171(5))
	118	12 Oct 1988 (SI 1988/1676)
16		29 Jul 1988 (repeals of or in Criminal Justice Act 1967, s 49; Children and Young Persons Act 1969, s 29; Criminal Justice Act 1987) (s 171(5))
		29 Sep 1988 (repeals of or in Prevention of Corruption Act 1916; Criminal Justice Act 1967, Sch 3; Criminal Justice Act 1972, s 28(3); Sexual Offences (Amendment) Act 1976; Protection of Children Act 1978; Cable and Broadcasting Act 1984; Police and Criminal Evidence Act 1984, s 24(2)(e)) (s 171(6))
		1 Oct 1988 (repeals of or in Prison Act 1952; Criminal Justice Act 1961; Firearms Act 1968 (E, W only); Children and Young Persons Act 1969, ss 16(10), 22(5), 34(1)(f); Powers of Criminal Courts Act 1973, s 57(3); Criminal Law Act 1977, Sch 12; Reserve Forces Act 1980; Criminal Justice Act 1982, ss 4–7, 12(1)–(5), (8), (9), 14, 20(1), Sch 8, paras 3(c), 7(d); Repatriation of Prisoners Act 1984 (E, W)) (SI 1988/1408)
		12 Oct 1988 (repeals of or in Criminal Law Act 1826, s 30; Offences Against the Person Act 1861, ss 42–44; Criminal Justice Act 1925, s 39; Children and Young Persons Act 1933, ss 1(5), (6), 38(1), Sch 1; Children and Young Persons (Scotland)

Criminal Justice Act 1988 (c 33)—*contd*
Schedule
16—*contd*

Act 1937, s 12(5), (6); Criminal
Appeal Act 1968, ss 10(3)(d), 42;
Road Traffic Act 1972, s 100;
Criminal Justice Act 1972, Sch 5;
Powers of Criminal Courts
Act 1973, ss 22(5), 34A(1)(c), Sch 3,
paras 2(4)(b), 7, Sch 5, para 29;
Juries Act 1974, s 16(2); Criminal
Law Act 1977, Sch 5, para 2, Sch 6;
Magistrates' Courts Act 1980;
Criminal Justice Act 1982, ss 43,
74, 75, 80(1); Video Recordings
Act 1984, s 15(2), (4), (5); Police
and Criminal Evidence Act 1984,
s 65; Cinemas Act 1985, Sch 2,
para 11; Local Government
Act 1985, s 15(5); Coroners
Act 1988, Sch 3, para 14)
(SI 1988/1676)
1 Nov 1988 (repeals of or in Prisons
(Scotland) Act 1952; Firearms
Act 1968 (S only); Fire Precautions
Act 1971, s 40(2)(b); Repatriation
of Prisoners Act 1984 (S only))
(SI 1988/1817)
5 Jan 1989 (repeals of or in Offences
Against the Person Act 1861, ss 46,
47; Juries Act 1974, s 12(1)(a);
Criminal Law Act 1977, s 43; Drug
Trafficking Offences Act 1986,
s 6(1)(b), (3), (5)) (SI 1988/2073)
23 Jan 1989 (repeals of or in Drug
Trafficking Offences Act 1986,
ss 10(1), 15(5)(b), (c), 17(1),
38(11)) (SI 1989/50)
3 Apr 1989 (repeals of or in Police
and Criminal Evidence Act 1984,
s 68, Sch 3, paras 1–7, 13 (except
in relation to a trial, or proceedings
before a magistrates' court acting as
examining justices, which began
before that date); Administration of
Justice Act 1970, s 41(8); Insolvency
Act 1985, Sch 8, para 24; Drug
Trafficking Offences Act 1986,
ss 19, 25) (SI 1989/264)
31 Jul 1989 (repeal in Criminal
Appeal Act 1968, s 7(1))
(SI 1989/1085)

Criminal Justice Act 1988 (c 33)—*contd*
Schedule

16—*contd*   1 Jan 2000 (repeals of Power of
                                              Criminal Courts Act 1973, ss 39,
                                              40) (SI 1999/3425)
                                              Not in force (otherwise)

[1]   Extradition Act 1989, s 38(4) provided for s 136(1) of, and Sch 1, para 4 to, this Act to come into
      force immediately before 27 Sep 1989 and those provisions were then repealed on that date by
      s 37(1) of, and Sch 2 to, the 1989 Act

[2]   Orders made under Youth Justice and Criminal Evidence Act 1999, s 68(3), bringing the
      prospective repeals into force will be noted to that Act

[3]   Orders appointing such days will be noted to the appropriate provision of that Act

[4]   Orders made under Criminal Justice and Police Act 2001, s 138, bringing the prospective repeal
      into force will be noted to that Act

Dartford-Thurrock Crossing Act 1988 (c 20)

Local application only

Duchy of Lancaster Act 1988 (c 10)

RA: 3 May 1988

3 May 1988 (RA)

Education Reform Act 1988 (c 40)

RA: 29 Jul 1988

Commencement provisions: s 236; Education Reform Act 1988 (Commencement No 1)
   Order 1988, SI 1988/1459; Education Reform Act 1988 (Commencement No 2)
   Order 1988, SI 1988/1794; Education Reform Act 1988 (Commencement No 3)
   Order 1988, SI 1988/2002; Education Reform Act 1988 (Commencement No 4)
   Order 1988, SI 1988/2271 (as amended by SI 1989/501, SI 1990/391);
   Education Reform Act 1988 (Commencement No 5) Order 1989,
   SI 1989/164; Education Reform Act 1988 (Commencement No 6) Order 1989,
   SI 1989/501 (also amends SI 1988/2271); Education Reform Act 1988
   (Commencement No 7) Order 1989, SI 1989/719; Education Reform Act 1988
   (Commencement No 8 and Amendment) Order 1990, SI 1990/391 (also
   amends SI 1988/2271); Education Reform Act 1988 (Commencement No 9)
   Order 1991, SI 1991/409

Section

1–119   Repealed
120   1 Apr 1989 (SI 1988/2271)
121   21 Nov 1988 (except Southampton
                                              Institute of Higher Education)
                                              (SI 1988/1794)
                                              1 Feb 1989 (exception noted above)
                                              (SI 1988/2271)
122   21 Nov 1988 (SI 1988/1794)

Education Reform Act 1988 (c 40)—*contd*

Section

122A	Inserted by Further and Higher Education Act 1992, s 74(1) (qv)
123, 124	21 Nov 1988 (SI 1988/1794)
124A–124D	Inserted by Further and Higher Education Act 1992, s 71(1) (qv)
125	21 Nov 1988 (SI 1988/1794)
125A	Inserted by Teaching and Higher Education Act 1998, s 41(1) (qv)
126–129	21 Nov 1988 (SI 1988/1794)
129A, 129B	Inserted by Further and Higher Education Act 1992, s 73(1) (qv)
130	21 Nov 1988 (SI 1988/1794)
131, 132	Repealed
133	1 Nov 1988 (SI 1988/1794)
134	Repealed
135	21 Nov 1988 (SI 1988/1794)
136	1 Nov 1988 (SI 1988/1794)
137, 138	29 Jul 1988 (s 236(1))
139–155	Repealed
156	29 Jul 1988 (s 236(1)); repealed in relation to designated institutions by Further and Higher Education Act 1992, ss 73(2), 85(1), 93(2), Sch 9 (qv)
157–165	29 Jul 1988 (s 236(1))
166, 167	Repealed
168–199	29 Jul 1988 (s 236(1))
200	Repealed
201–208	29 Jul 1988 (s 236(1))
209	Repealed
210, 211	1 May 1989 (SI 1989/719)
212, 213	Repealed
214–216	30 Nov 1988 (SI 1988/2002)
217	29 Jul 1988 (s 236(1))
218	1 Apr 1989 (SI 1988/2002)
218A	Inserted by Criminal Justice and Court Services Act 2000, s 74, Sch 7, para 83 (qv)
219	Substituted by Education Act 1996, s 582(1), Sch 37, Pt I, para 77 (qv)
220	Repealed
221	29 Jul 1988 (s 236(1))
222, 223	Repealed
224	29 Jul 1988 (s 236(1))
225	Repealed
226	21 Nov 1988 (SI 1988/1794)
227	Repealed
228, 229	21 Nov 1988 (SI 1988/1794)
230–233	29 Jul 1988 (s 236(1))

Education Reform Act 1988 (c 40)—*contd*

Section		
234		Repealed
235, 236		29 Jul 1988 (s 236(1))
237	(1)	See Sch 12 below
	(2)	See Sch 13 below
238		29 Jul 1988 (s 236(1))
Schedule		
1–5		Repealed
6		29 Jul 1988 (s 236(1))
7		21 Nov 1988 (SI 1988/1794)
7A		Inserted by Further and Higher Education Act 1992, s 71(4), Sch 6 (qv)
8		29 Jul 1988 (so far as relating to Education Assets Board) (s 236(1))
		1 Nov 1988 (otherwise) (SI 1988/1754)
		Schedule repealed in relation to Universities Funding Council and Polytechnics and Colleges Funding Council, by Further and Higher Education Act 1992, s 93(1), Sch 8, Pt I, paras 27, 60 (qv)
9–11		29 Jul 1988 (s 236(1))
12, para	1–28	Repealed
	29	29 Jul 1988 (s 236(1))
	30, 31	Repealed
	32	29 Jul 1988 (s 236(1))
	33–40	Repealed
	41–46	1 Apr 1990 (s 236(4))
	47–49	Repealed
	50–53	1 Apr 1990 (s 236(4))
	54–64	Repealed
	65	1 Apr 1989 (SI 1988/2271)
	66	Spent
	67	29 Jul 1988 (s 236(1)) (also purportedly brought into force on 1 Jan 1989 by SI 1988/2271)
	68	Repealed
	69	1 Apr 1989 (SI 1988/2271)
	70	Repealed
	71–75	1 Apr 1989 (SI 1988/2271)
	76, 77	Repealed
	78	1 Apr 1989 (SI 1988/2271)
	79–85	Repealed
	86–98	1 Apr 1989 (SI 1988/2271)
	99	Repealed
	100, 101	1 Apr 1989 (SI 1988/2271)
	102, 103	Repealed
	104, 105	1 Apr 1989 (SI 1988/2271)

Education Reform Act 1988 (c 40)—*contd*

Schedule

12, para	106	Repealed
	107	1 Apr 1989 (SI 1988/2271)
13, Pt	I	1 Apr 1990 (s 236(5))
	II	30 Nov 1988 (repeals of Education Act 1967, s 3; Education Act 1980, Sch 3, para 14) (SI 1988/2002)

1 Jan 1989 (repeals of Education Act 1944, ss 25, 29(2)–(4); Education Act 1946, s 7; Education (No 2) Act 1968 (subject to transitional provisions)) (SI 1988/2271)

1 Apr 1989 (repeal of Education Act 1944, s 61) (SI 1988/1794)

1 Apr 1989 (repeals of Education Act 1980, s 27; Education Act 1981, Sch 3, para 5) (SI 1988/2002)

1 Apr 1989 (repeals of or in Education Act 1944, ss 8(1)(b), 42–46, 50, 52(1), 54, 60, 62(2), 69, 84, 114; Education Act 1946, s 8(3); London Government Act 1963, s 31(1), (4); Industrial Training Act 1964, s 16; Local Government Act 1972, ss 81(4)(a), 104(2); Sex Discrimination Act 1975, ss 24(2)(a), 25(6)(c)(ii); Race Relations Act 1976, ss 19(6)(c)(ii), 78(1); Education (No 2) Act 1986, s 56) (SI 1988/2271)

1 Aug 1989 (repeals of or in Education (No 2) Act 1986, ss 17(1), (4), 18(3), (4), (6), (8), 19(3), 20) (SI 1988/2271)

1 May 1989 (repeals of or in Education Act 1946, s 1(1); Employment Protection (Consolidation) Act 1978, s 29(1)(e); Education Act 1980, s 35(5), Sch 1, para 25; Local Government, Planning and Land Act 1980, Sch 10, Pt I; Local Government Act 1985, s 22; Education (No 2) Act 1986, ss 29, 47(5)(a)(ii), Sch 4, para 4; Local Government Act 1987, s 2) (SI 1989/719)

Education Reform Act 1988 (c 40)—*contd*

Schedule

13, Pt	II—*contd*		31 Mar 1990 (repeals in Local Government Act 1974) (SI 1990/391)
			Not in force (repeal in Education Act 1980, s 35(3))

Electricity (Financial Provisions) (Scotland) Act 1988 (c 37)

Whole Act repealed

Employment Act 1988 (c 19)

RA: 26 May 1988

Commencement provisions: s 34(2); Employment Act 1988 (Commencement No 1) Order 1988, SI 1988/1118; Employment Act 1988 (Commencement No 2) Order 1988, SI 1988/2042

Section				
1–24				Repealed
25, 26				26 May 1988 (RA)
27				Repealed
28, 29				26 May 1988 (RA)
30				Repealed
31				26 May 1988 (RA)
32	(1)			26 May 1988 (RA)
	(2)			Repealed
33	(1)			See Sch 3 below
	(2)			See Sch 4 below
34	(1)			26 May 1988 (RA)
	(2), (3)			Repealed
	(4), (5)			26 May 1988 (RA)
	(6)	(a), (b)		Repealed
		(c)		26 May 1988 (RA)
Schedule				
1				Repealed
2				26 May 1988 (RA)
3, Pt	I, para	1–6		Repealed
	II, para	7–10		Repealed
		11	(1)	Repealed
			(2)	26 May 1988 (RA)
		12	(1)	Repealed
			(2)	26 May 1988 (RA)
			(3)	Repealed
		13		26 May 1988 (RA)
		14	(1)	26 May 1988 (RA)
			(2)	Repealed
		15		26 May 1988 (RA)

Employment Act 1988 (c 19)—*contd*
Schedule

4	26 May 1988 (repeals of or in Parliamentary Commissioner Act 1967, Sch 2; Employment and Training Act 1973, ss 4(2), 5(1), (4), 11(3), 12(4); Social Security Act 1975, s 20(1); House of Commons Disqualification Act 1975, Sch 1, Pt III; Northern Ireland Assembly Disqualification Act 1975, Sch 1, Pt III; Employment Protection Act 1975, Sch 14, para 2(1); Social Security (Miscellaneous Provisions) Act 1977, s 22(6); Social Security (No 2) Act 1980, s 7(7)) (RA)
	26 Jul 1988 (repeals of or in Trade Union Act 1913, s 4(1F); Trade Union (Amalgamations, etc) Act 1964, s 4(6), Sch 1; Employment Protection (Consolidation) Act 1978, ss 23(1), (2A), (2B)[1],58(1), (3)–(12)[1], 58A, 153(1); Employment Act 1980, s 15(2); Employment Act 1982, s 10(1), (2), Sch 3, para 16; Trade Union Act 1984, ss 3, 6(6), 9(1)) (SI 1988/1118)
	26 Jul 1989 (repeals of or in Trade Union Act 1984, ss 1(1)–(3), 8(1)) (SI 1988/1118)

[1] Note: repeal of Employment Protection (Consolidation) Act 1978, ss 23(2A), (2B), 58(3)–(12) effected on 26 Jul 1988 by virtue of the bringing into force on that date of s 11 (now repealed) (SI 1988/1118)

Environment and Safety Information Act 1988 (c 30)

RA: 29 Jul 1988

Commencement provisions: s 5(2)

1 Apr 1989 (s 5(2))

European Communities (Finance) Act 1988 (c 46)

Whole Act repealed

Farm Land and Rural Development Act 1988 (c 16)

RA: 10 May 1988

10 May 1988 (RA)

Finance Act 1988 (c 39)

Budget Day: 15 Mar 1988

RA: 29 Jul 1988

Details of the commencement of Finance Acts are not set out in this work

---

Firearms (Amendment) Act 1988 (c 45)

RA: 15 Nov 1988

Commencement provisions: s 27(3); Firearms (Amendment) Act 1988 (Commencement No 1) Order 1988, SI 1988/2209; Firearms (Amendment) Act 1988 (Commencement No 2) Order 1989, SI 1989/853 (amended by SI 1989/1673); Firearms (Amendment) Act 1988 (Commencement No 3) Order 1990, SI 1990/2620

Section		
1		1 Feb 1989 (subject to transitional provisions) (SI 1988/2209)
2	(1), (2)	1 Jul 1989 (subject to transitional provisions) (SI 1989/853)
	(3)	1 Jul 1989 (SI 1989/853)
3	(1)	1 Jul 1989 (SI 1989/853)
	(2)	1 Jul 1989 (subject to transitional provisions) (SI 1989/853)
4		Repealed
5, 6		1 Jul 1990 (SI 1989/853)
7	(1)	1 Feb 1989 (subject to transitional provisions) (SI 1988/2209)
	(2)	1 Jul 1989 (subject to transitional provisions) (SI 1989/853)
	(3)	1 Jul 1989 (SI 1989/853)
8, 9		1 Feb 1988 (SI 1988/2209)
10		Repealed
11		1 Jul 1989 (SI 1989/853)
12		1 Feb 1989 (SI 1989/2209)
13	(1)	1 Jul 1989 (SI 1989/853)
	(2)–(5)	1 Feb 1989 (SI 1988/2209)
14		1 Feb 1989 (SI 1988/2209)
15		Substituted by Firearms (Amendment) Act 1997, s 45 (qv)
15A		Repealed (*never in force*)
16		1 Feb 1989 (SI 1988/2209)
16A		Inserted by Armed Forces Act 1996, s 28(2) (qv)
17, 18		1 Oct 1989 (SI 1989/853)
18A		Inserted (1 Jan 1993) by Firearms Acts (Amendment) Regulations 1992, SI 1992/2823, reg 9
19		See Schedule below

Firearms (Amendment) Act 1988 (c 45)—*contd*

Section

20	(1), (2)	1 Jul 1989 (for purpose of enabling Secretary of State to make an order under Firearms Act 1968, s 6(1A), which is to come into force on the date on which this section comes into force for all other purposes) (SI 1989/853 as amended by Firearms (Amendment) Act 1988 (Commencement No 2) Order (Amendment) Order 1989, SI 1989/1673, art 3)
		2 Apr 1991 (otherwise) (SI 1990/2620)
	(3)	2 Apr 1991 (SI 1990/2620)
21, 22		1 Feb 1989 (SI 1988/2209)
23	(1)–(3)	1 Feb 1989 (SI 1988/2209)
	(4)–(6)	1 Jul 1989 (SI 1989/853)
	(7)	1 Feb 1989 (SI 1988/2209)
	(8)	1 Oct 1989 (except in relation to a person who is in Great Britain on 1 Oct 1989) (SI 1989/853)
		31 Oct 1989 (exception noted above) (SI 1989/853)
24	(1)	1 Feb 1989 (SI 1988/2209)
	(2)	1 Jul 1989 (SI 1989/853)
25		1 Feb 1989 (SI 1988/2209)
26, 27		15 Nov 1988 (s 27(3))
Schedule		1 Jul 1989 (SI 1989/853)

Foreign Marriage (Amendment) Act 1988 (c 44)

RA: 2 Nov 1988

Commencement provisions: s 7(3); Foreign Marriage (Amendment) Act 1988 (Commencement) Order 1990, SI 1990/522

12 Apr 1990 (SI 1990/522)

Health and Medicines Act 1988 (c 49)

RA: 15 Nov 1988

Commencement provisions: ss 19(2), 26(1)–(5); Health and Medicines Act 1988 (Commencement No 1) Order 1988, SI 1988/2107; Health and Medicines Act 1988 (Commencement No 2) Order 1989, SI 1989/111; Health and Medicines Act 1988 (Commencement No 3) Order 1989, SI 1989/337; Health and Medicines Act 1988 (Commencement No 4) Order 1989, SI 1989/826; Health and Medicines Act 1988 (Commencement No 5) Order 1989, SI 1989/1174 (revoked); Health and Medicines Act 1988 (Commencement No 6) Order 1989, SI 1989/1229 (revoking SI 1989/1174); Health and Medicine Act 1988 (Commencement No 7) Order 1989, SI 1989/1896; Health and Medicines Act 1988 (Commencement No 8) Order 1989, SI 1989/1984

Health and Medicines Act 1988 (c 49)—*contd*

Section

1–6			15 Nov 1988 (s 26(3), (4))
7			15 Jan 1989 (s 26(1)–(5))
8	(1)	(a)	15 Oct 1989 (except words 'or section 19 of the National Health Service (Scotland) Act 1978') (SI 1989/1896)
			31 Oct 1989 (exception noted above) (SI 1989/1984)
		(b)	9 Jun 1989 (SI 1989/826)
	(2)		9 Jun 1989 (except words '(a) or') (SI 1989/826)
			15 Oct 1989 (words '(a) or' except so far as they have effect for the purposes of any list maintained under National Health Service (Scotland) Act 1978, s 19) (SI 1989/1896)
			31 Oct 1989 (exception noted above) (SI 1989/1984)
	(3)–(7)		9 Jun 1989 (SI 1989/826)
9			1 Apr 1990 (SI 1989/826)
10			15 Jan 1989 (s 26(1)–(5))
11	(1)		7 Mar 1989 (SI 1989/337)
	(2)		1 Apr 1989 (SI 1989/337)
	(3)		7 Mar 1989 (for purposes of regulations as to charges authorised by National Health Service Act 1977, s 78(1A)) (SI 1989/337)
			1 Apr 1989 (otherwise) (SI 1989/337)
	(4)		7 Mar 1989 (SI 1989/337)
	(5)		1 Apr 1989 (SI 1989/337)
	(6)		7 Mar 1989 (for purposes of regulations as to charges authorised by National Health Service (Scotland) Act 1978, s 70(1A)) (SI 1989/337)
			1 Apr 1989 (otherwise) (SI 1989/337)
	(7)		1 Jan 1989 (SI 1989/2107)
	(8)		1 Apr 1989 (SI 1989/337)
12	(1)–(3)		1 Apr 1989 (SI 1989/337)
	(4), (5)		Repealed
13	(1)		7 Mar 1989 (for purposes of adding National Health Service Act 1977, s 38(2)–(6) and of adding s 38(7) thereof up to the words 'are to be made' thereto) (SI 1989/337)
			1 Apr 1989 (otherwise) (SI 1989/337)

Health and Medicines Act 1988 (c 49)—*contd*

Section

13	(2)	7 Mar 1989 (for purposes of any regulations made to come into force on or after 1 Apr 1989) (SI 1989/337)
		1 Apr 1989 (otherwise) (SI 1989/337)
	(3)	7 Mar 1989 (SI 1989/337)
	(4)	7 Mar 1989 (for purposes of adding National Health Service (Scotland) Act 1978, s 26(1A)–(1E) and of adding s 26(1F) thereof up to the words 'are to be made' thereto) (SI 1989/337)
		1 Apr 1989 (otherwise) (SI 1989/337)
	(5)	7 Mar 1989 (SI 1989/337)
	(6), (7)	Repealed
14		Repealed
15, 16		15 Jan 1989 (s 26(1)–(5))
17	(1), (2)	15 Jan 1989 (s 26(1)–(5))
	(3)	15 Nov 1988 (s 26(3), (4))
	(3A)	Inserted by National Health Service (Primary Care) Act 1997, s 41(10), Sch 2, para 64(4) (qv)
18		15 Jan 1989 (s 26(1)–(5))
19		26 Nov 1987 (retrospective; s 192))
20		15 Jan 1989 (s 26(1)–(5))
21, 22		15 Nov 1988 (s 26(3), (4))
23, 24		15 Jan 1989 (s 26(1)–(5))
25	(1)	See Sch 2 below
	(2)	See Sch 3 below
26–28		15 Nov 1988 (s 26(3), (4))

Schedule

1		15 Nov 1988 (s 26(3), (4))
2, para	1	15 Jan 1989 (so far as relates to paras 2, 6, 7) (s 26(1)–(5))
		7 Mar 1989 (so far as relates to para 8(1), (2)) (SI 1989/337)
		1 Apr 1989 (so far as relates to paras 5, 8(3)) (SI 1989/337)
		9 Jun 1989 (so far as relates to para 4) (SI 1989/826)
		15 Oct 1989 (so far as relates to para 3) (SI 1989/1896)
	2	15 Jan 1989 (s 26(1)–(5))
	3	Repealed
	4	9 Jun 1989 (SI 1989/826)
	5	1 Apr 1989 (SI 1989/337)
	6, 7	15 Jan 1989 (s 26(1)–(5))

Health and Medicines Act 1988 (c 49)—*contd*

Schedule

2, para	8	(1)	7 Mar 1989 (for purposes of any regulations made to come into force on or after 1 Apr 1989) (SI 1989/337) 1 Apr 1989 (otherwise) (SI 1989/337)
		(2)	7 Mar 1989 (SI 1989/337)
		(3)	1 Apr 1989 (SI 1989/337)
	9		15 Jan 1989 (so far as relates to paras 13, 14) (s 26(1)–(5)) 7 Mar 1989 (so far as relates to para 15(1), (2)) (SI 1989/337) 1 Apr 1989 (so far as relates to paras 12, 15(3)) (SI 1989/337) 9 Jun 1989 (so far as relates to para 11) (SI 1989/826) 31 Oct 1989 (so far as relates to para 10) (SI 1989/1984)
	10		31 Oct 1989 (SI 1989/1984)
	11		Repealed
	12		1 Apr 1989 (SI 1989/337)
	13, 14		15 Jan 1989 (s 26(1)–(5))
	15	(1)	7 Mar 1989 (for purposes of any regulations made to come into force on or after 1 Apr 1989) (SI 1989/337) 1 Apr 1989 (otherwise) (SI 1989/337)
		(2)	7 Mar 1989 (SI 1989/337)
		(3)	1 Apr 1989 (SI 1989/337)
3			15 Nov 1988 (repeal of National Health Service Act 1977, s 28(4)) (s 26(3), (4)) 1 Jan 1989 (repeals of or in National Health Service Act 1977, s 79(1)(d) and word 'or' preceding it; National Health Service (Scotland) Act 1978, s 71(1)(d) and word 'or' preceding it) (SI 1989/2107) 15 Jan 1989 (repeals of or in Health Services and Public Health Act 1968, s 63(3); National Health Service Act 1977, ss 5(1)(a), 58, 61, 62, 63(2), 66A; National Health Service (Scotland) Act 1978, ss 39, 50, 53, 54, 55(2), 58A; Health Services Act 1980, ss 10, 11) (s 26(1)–(5))

Health and Medicines Act 1988 (c 49)—*contd*
Schedule
3—*contd*

27 Feb 1989 (repeals of or in National Health Service Act 1966; Superannuation Act 1972; Health Services Act 1980, ss 17, 19; Health and Social Security Act 1984, s 8; Companies Consolidation (Consequential Provisions) Act 1985) (SI 1989/111)

1 Apr 1989 (otherwise) (SI 1989/337)

Housing Act 1988 (c 50)

RA: 15 Nov 1988

Commencement provisions: ss 132(8), 141(2), (3); Housing Act 1988 (Commencement No 1) Order 1988, SI 1988/2056; Housing Act 1988 (Commencement No 2) Order 1988, SI 1988/2152; Housing Act 1988 (Commencement No 3) Order 1989, SI 1989/203; Housing Act 1988 (Commencement No 4) Order 1989, SI 1989/404; Housing Act 1988 (Commencement No 5 and Transitional Provisions) Order 1991, SI 1991/954; Housing Act 1988 (Commencement No 6) Order 1992, SI 1992/324

Section		
1–8		15 Jan 1989 (s 141(3))
8A		Inserted by Housing Act 1996, s 150 (qv)
9–14		15 Jan 1989 (s 141(3))
14A, 14B		Inserted (1 Apr 1993) by Local Government Finance (Housing) (Consequential Amendments) Order 1993, SI 1993/651, art 2(2), Sch 2, para 8
15–19		15 Jan 1989 (s 141(3))
19A		Inserted by Housing Act 1996, s 96(1) (qv)
20		15 Jan 1989 (s 141(3))
20A		Inserted by Housing Act 1996, s 97 (qv)
21–39		15 Jan 1989 (s 141(3))
40	(1)	15 Jan 1989 (s 141(3))
	(2)	Repealed
	(3)	15 Jan 1989 (s 141(3))
	(4), (5)	15 Jan 1989 (s 141(3)); prospectively repealed by Courts and Legal Services Act 1990, s 125(7), Sch 20[1]
41	(1)	Repealed
	(2)–(4)	15 Jan 1989 (s 141(3))
41A		Inserted by Social Security (Consequential Provisions) Act 1992, s 4, Sch 2, para 103 (qv)

Housing Act 1988 (c 50)—*contd*

Section

41B		Inserted (1 Apr 1993) by Local Government Finance (Housing) (Consequential Amendments) Order 1993, SI 1993/651, art 2(1), Sch 1, para 18 (as substituted by Local Government Finance (Housing) (Consequential Amendments) (Amendment) Order 1993, SI 1993/1120, art 2)
42–45		15 Jan 1989 (s 141(3))
46, 47		Repealed[2]
48, 49		Repealed
50–53		1 Apr 1989 (SI 1989/404)
54, 55		1 Apr 1989 (SI 1989/404); prospectively repealed (S) by Housing (Scotland) Act 2001, s 112, Sch 10, para 15(1), (5)[4]
56		Repealed
57		15 Jan 1989 (SI 1988/2152)
58		Repealed
59	(1)	15 Jan 1989 (SI 1988/2152)
	(1A), (1B)	Inserted (1 Oct 1996) by Housing Act 1996 (Consequential Provisions) Order 1996, SI 1996/2325, art 5, Sch 2, paras 18(1), 19(b), (c)
	(2), (3)	See Sch 6 below
	(4)	1 Apr 1989 (SI 1989/404)
60–69		15 Nov 1988 (RA)
70		Repealed
71–84		15 Nov 1988 (RA)
84A		Inserted by Leasehold Reform, Housing and Urban Development Act 1993, s 125(5) (qv)
85–92		15 Nov 1988 (RA)
93–114		Repealed
115–118		15 Jan 1989 (s 141(3))
119		See Sch 13 below
120		15 Jan 1989 (s 141(3))
121		Repealed
122		10 Mar 1989 (SI 1989/203)
123		15 Jan 1989 (s 141(3))
124		10 Mar 1989 (SI 1989/203)
125, 126		15 Jan 1989 (s 141(3))
127		5 Apr 1989 (SI 1989/404)
128		21 Feb 1992 (SI 1992/324); prospectively repealed by Housing (Scotland) Act 2001, s 112, Sch 10, para 15(1), (7)[4]

Housing Act 1988 (c 50)—*contd*

Section

129		1 Apr 1989 (SI 1989/404)
130		15 Jan 1989 (s 141(3))
131		15 Jan 1989 (s 141(3)); prospectively repealed by Local Government and Housing Act 1989, s 194, Sch 12, Pt II[3]
132		9 Jun 1988 (retrospective; s 132(8))
133		15 Nov 1988 (RA; s 141(2), (3))
134		15 Nov 1988 (RA; s 141(2), (3)); prospectively repealed by Housing (Scotland) Act 2001, s 112, Sch 10, para 15(1), (7)[4]
135	(1)	21 Feb 1992 (SI 1992/324); prospectively repealed by Housing (Scotland) Act 2001, s 112, Sch 10, para 15(1), (7)[4]
	(2)	See Sch 16 below; prospectively repealed by Housing (Scotland) Act 2001, s 112, Sch 10, para 15(1), (7)[4]
	(3)	21 Feb 1992 (SI 1992/324); prospectively repealed by Housing (Scotland) Act 2001, s 112, Sch 10, para 15(1), (7)[4]
136		Repealed
137		15 Jan 1989 (s 141(3))
138, 139		15 Nov 1988 (RA; s 141(2), (3))
140	(1)	See Sch 17 below
	(2)	See Sch 18 below
141		15 Nov 1988 (RA; s 141(2), (3))

Schedule

1, 2			15 Jan 1989 (s 141(3))
2A			Inserted by Housing Act 1996, s 96(2), Sch 7 (qv)
3, 4			15 Jan 1989 (s 141(3))
5			Repealed[2]
6, para	1		Repealed
	2		Repealed[2]
	3–6		Repealed
	7		1 Apr 1989 (SI 1989/404) (E, W) Repealed (S)
	8	(1)	1 Apr 1989 (SI 1989/404) (E, W) Repealed (S)
		(2)	15 Jan 1989 (SI 1988/2152) (E, W) Repealed (S)
	9–23		Repealed
	24		1 Apr 1989 (SI 1989/404)
	25		15 Jan 1989 (SI 1988/2152) (E, W) Repealed (S)

Housing Act 1988 (c 50)—*contd*

Schedule

6, para	26	(a)	15 Jan 1989 (SI 1988/2152) (E, W)
			Repealed (S)
		(b), (c)	Repealed
	27		*Not in force*
	28		1 Apr 1989 (SI 1989/404)
	29		1 Apr 1989 (except for purposes of hostel deficit grant payable under Housing Associations Act 1985, s 55) (SI 1989/404)
	30, 31		1 Apr 1989 (SI 1989/404)
	32		1 Apr 1989 (SI 1989/404) (S)
			Repealed (E, W)
	33–35		1 Apr 1989 (SI 1989/404)
	36		1 Apr 1989 (SI 1989/404) (S)
			Repealed (E, W)
7–11			15 Nov 1988 (RA)
12			Repealed
13			15 Jan 1989 (subject to transitional provisions) (SI 1988/2152)
14, 15			15 Jan 1989 (s 141(3))
16			21 Feb 1992 (SI 1992/324); prospectively repealed by Housing (Scotland) Act 2001, s 112, Sch 10, para 15(1), (9)[4]
17, para	1–16		15 Jan 1989 (SI 1988/2152)
	17	(1)	5 Apr 1989 (SI 1989/404)
		(2)	15 Jan 1989 (SI 1988/2152)
	18		Repealed
	19–26		15 Jan 1989 (subject to transitional provision for para 21) (SI 1988/2152)
	27		Repealed
	28–32		15 Jan 1989 (subject to transitional provision for para 21) (SI 1988/2152)
	33, 34		Repealed
	35–37		15 Jan 1989 (SI 1988/2152)
	38, 39		Repealed
	40		15 Jan 1989 (SI 1988/2152)
	41		10 Mar 1989 (SI 1989/203)
	42–55		15 Jan 1989 (SI 1988/2152)
	56, 57		Repealed
	58–65		15 Jan 1989 (SI 1988/2152)
	66		1 Apr 1989 (SI 1989/404)
	67–70		15 Jan 1989 (SI 1988/2152)
	71, 72		Repealed
	73–76		15 Jan 1989 (SI 1988/2152)
	77, 78		2 Jan 1989 (SI 1988/2152)
	79		*Not in force*

Housing Act 1988 (c 50)—*contd*

Schedule

17, para	80	Repealed
	81–84	15 Jan 1989 (SI 1988/2152)
	85–88	2 Jan 1989 (SI 1988/2152)
	89	1 Apr 1989 (SI 1989/404)
	90	2 Jan 1989 (SI 1988/2152)
	91	Repealed
	92	Repealed[2]
	93	Repealed (retrospectively to 1 Dec 1988)
	94–106	Repealed[2]
	107	Repealed
	108–116	Repealed[2]
18		2 Jan 1989 (repeal in Housing (Scotland) Act 1988, s 38) (SI 1988/2152)

15 Jan 1989 (repeals of or in Reserve and Auxiliary Forces (Protection of Civil Interests) Act 1951; Rent (Agriculture) Act 1976; Rent Act 1977; Protection from Eviction Act 1977; Housing Act 1980; Local Government Act 1985; Housing Act 1985; Housing and Planning Act 1986, ss 7, 12, 13, Sch 4; Landlord and Tenant Act 1987, ss 3, 4, 60; Housing (Scotland) Act 1988, Sch 9, para 6) (subject to transitional provisions) (SI 1988/2152)

1 Apr 1989 (repeals of or in Housing Associations Act 1985, except s 55 and ss 56, 57 in relation to hostel deficit grants; Housing and Planning Act 1986 (so far as not yet in force); Housing (Scotland) Act 1986; Landlord and Tenant Act 1987 (so far as not yet in force); Local Government Act 1988; Housing (Scotland) Act 1988 (so far as not yet in force)) (SI 1989/404)

1 Apr 1991 (repeals of or in Housing Associations Act 1985, ss 55–57, except in relation to hostel deficit grant payable to an association for a period which expires before 1 Apr 1991) (SI 1991/954)

Not in force (otherwise)

Housing Act 1988 (c 50)—*contd*

1   Orders made under Courts and Legal Services Act 1990, s 124, bringing the prospective repeal into force will be noted to that Act

2   The repeal of ss 46, 47 of, and Sch 5, Sch 17, paras 92, 94–106, 108–116 to, this Act by the Government of Wales Act 1998, ss 140, 152, Sch 16, paras 59, 62, 63, 73, Sch 18, Pts IV, VI, does not affect the validity of anything done by, or in relation to (i) the Development Board for Rural Wales before its functions ceased to exist and (ii) Housing for Wales before its functions are transferred to the Secretary of State; see ss 131(1), 141(1) of the 1998 Act

3   Orders made under Local Government and Housing Act 1989, s 195(2), bringing the prospective repeal into force will be noted to that Act

4   Orders made under Housing (Scotland) Act 2001, s 113, bringing the repeals into force will be noted to that Act

---

Housing (Scotland) Act 1988 (c 43)

RA: 2 Nov 1988

Commencement provisions: s 74(2); Housing (Scotland) Act 1988 Commencement Order 1988, SI 1988/2038

Section		
1	(1), (2)	Repealed
	(3)	1 Dec 1988 (SI 1988/2038)
2		1 Dec 1988 (SI 1988/2038)
2A–11		Repealed
12	(1)	2 Jan 1989 (SI 1988/2038)
	(2)	See Sch 4 below
13–25		2 Jan 1989 (SI 1988/2038)
25A, 25B		Inserted (1 Apr 1993) by Local Government Finance (Housing) (Consequential Amendments) (Scotland) Order 1993, SI 1993/658, art 2, Sch 2, para 5
26–35		2 Jan 1989 (SI 1988/2038)
36–40		2 Jan 1989 (s 74(2)(b))
41–45		2 Jan 1989 (SI 1988/2038)
46	(1), (2)	2 Jan 1989 (SI 1988/2038)
	(3), (4)	See Sch 6 below
47, 48		2 Jan 1989 (SI 1988/2038)
48A		Inserted by Social Security (Consequential Provisions) Act 1992, s 4, Sch 2, para 102 (qv)
49–55		2 Jan 1989 (SI 1988/2038)
56–64		1 Apr 1989 (SI 1988/2038)
65		2 Jan 1989 (s 74(2)(b))
66		2 Jan 1989 (SI 1988/2038)
67		2 Jan 1989 (s 74(2)(b))
68		2 Jan 1989 (SI 1988/2038)
69		2 Nov 1988 (s 74(2)(a))
70		Repealed
71		2 Jan 1989 (s 74(2)(b))
72	(1)	See Schs 7, 8 below
	(2)	See Sch 9 below
	(3)	See Sch 10 below

Housing (Scotland) Act 1988 (c 43)—*contd*

Section			
73			1 Dec 1988 (SI 1988/2038)
74			2 Nov 1988 (s 74(2)(a))
Schedule			
1			Repealed
2, para	1		1 Apr 1989 (SI 1988/2038)
	2		1 Apr 1989 (SI 1988/2038); prospectively repealed by Housing (Scotland) Act 2001, s 112, Sch 10, para 14(1), (11)²
	3	(a)	1 Dec 1988 (SI 1988/2038); prospectively repealed by Housing (Scotland) Act 2001, s 112, Sch 10, para 14(1), (11)²
		(b)	1 Apr 1989 (SI 1988/2038)
	4		1 Apr 1989 (SI 1988/2038); prospectively repealed by Housing (Scotland) Act 2001, s 112, Sch 10, para 14(1), (11)²
	5		1 Apr 1989 (SI 1988/2038)
	6		Repealed
	7–13		1 Apr 1989 (SI 1988/2038)
	14		1 Apr 1989 (SI 1988/2038); prospectively repealed by Housing (Scotland) Act 2001, s 112, Sch 10, para 14(1), (11)²
	15–17		1 Apr 1989 (SI 1988/2038)
3			Repealed
4–6			2 Jan 1989 (SI 1988/2038)
7			2 Nov 1988 (s 74(2)(a))
8			2 Jan 1989 (s 74(2)(b))
9, para	1–5		2 Jan 1989 (SI 1988/2038)
	6–9		Repealed
	10		2 Jan 1989 (SI 1988/2038); prospectively repealed by Housing (Scotland) Act 2001, s 112, Sch 10, para 14(1), (15)²
	11–16		2 Jan 1989 (SI 1988/2038)
	17		1 Apr 1989 (SI 1988/2038)
	18–20		2 Apr 1989 (SI 1988/2038)
	21		2 Apr 1989 (SI 1988/2038); prospectively repealed by Housing (Scotland) Act 2001, s 112, Sch 10, para 14(1), (15)²
10			2 Jan 1989 (repeals of or in Housing (Scotland) Act 1987, ss 62(11)–(13), 151) (s 74(2)(b))
			2 Jan 1989 (repeals of or in Rent (Scotland) Act 1984, ss 66(1), 68, 70(2), 71(1)) (SI 1988/2038)

Housing (Scotland) Act 1988 (c 43)—*contd*

Schedule

10—*contd*   1 Apr 1989 (repeal of Housing
                                                      (Scotland) Act 1987, Sch 16,
                                                      para 1(b)) (s 74(2)(c))
                                                  1 Apr 1989 (otherwise)[1] (SI 1988/2038)

[1]   Entry relating to Housing Associations Act 1985 in Sch 10 was repealed on 1 Apr 1989 by Housing
      Act 1988, s 140, Sch 18

[2]   Orders made under Housing (Scotland) Act 2001, s 113, bringing the repeals into force will be
      noted to that Act

Immigration Act 1988 (c 14)

RA: 10 May 1988

Commencement provisions: s 12(3), (4); Immigration Act 1988 (Commencement No 1)
      Order 1988, SI 1988/1133; Immigration Act 1988 (Commencement No 2)
      Order 1991, SI 1991/1001; Immigration Act 1988 (Commencement No 3)
      Order 1994, SI 1994/1923

Section

1–4		1 Aug 1988 (subject to exceptions in relation to ss 1, 2, 4) (SI 1988/1133)
5		Repealed
6		10 Jul 1988 (s 12(3))
7	(1)	20 Jul 1994 (SI 1994/1923)
	(2), (3)	10 Jul 1988 (s 12(3))
8, 9		10 Jul 1988 (s 12(3)); prospectively repealed by Immigration and Asylum Act 1999, s 169(1), (3), Sch 14, paras 85, 86, Sch 16[1]
10–12		10 Jul 1988 (s 12(3))
Schedule		
para	1	16 May 1991 (SI 1991/1001)
	2–10	10 Jul 1988 (s 12(3))

[1]   Orders made under Immigration and Asylum Act 1999, s 170, bringing the prospective repeals into
      force will be noted to that Act

Income and Corporation Taxes Act 1988 (c 1)

RA: 9 Feb 1988

Commencement provisions: as provided for by s 843. In general, the Act came into
      force in relation to tax for the year 1988–89 and subsequent years of assessment,
      and for company accounting periods ending after 5 April 1988; but this is
      subject to a contrary intention, in particular as provided by ss 96, 380–384, 393,
      394 (repealed), 400, 470(3) (repealed)[1], 703, 729(12)[2], 812

[1]   Appointed day for the purposes of s 470(3): 29 Apr 1988 (Income and Corporation Taxes Act 1988
      (Appointed Day) Order 1988, SI 1988/745)

[2]   Appointed day for the purposes of s 729(12): 9 Jun 1988 (SI 1988/1002) (Income and Corporation
      Taxes Act 1988 (Appointed Day No 2) Order 1988, SI 1988/1002)

Land Registration Act 1988 (c 3)

RA: 15 Mar 1988

Commencement provisions: s 3(2); Land Registration Act 1988 (Commencement) Order 1990, SI 1990/1359

3 Dec 1990 (SI 1990/1359)

Landlord and Tenant Act 1988 (c 26)

RA: 29 Jul 1988

Commencement provisions: s 7(2)

29 Sep 1988 (s 7(2))

Legal Aid Act 1988 (c 34)

RA: 29 Jul 1988

Commencement provisions: s 47; Legal Aid Act 1988 (Commencement No 1) Order 1988, SI 1988/1361; Legal Aid Act 1988 (Commencement No 2) (Scotland) Order 1988, SI 1988/1388; Legal Aid Act 1988 (Commencement No 3) Order 1989, SI 1989/288; Legal Aid Act 1988 (Commencement No 4) Order 1991, SI 1991/790

Section		
1–32		Repealed
33		1 Apr 1989 (SI 1989/288)
34–43		Repealed
44		See Sch 4 below
45, 46		Repealed
47		29 Jul 1988 (RA)
Schedule		
1–3		Repealed
4, para	1, 2	29 Jul 1988 (SI 1988/1388)
	3	*Not in force*
	4	29 Jul 1988 (SI 1988/1388)
	5	*Not in force*
	6–9	29 Jul 1988 (SI 1988/1388)
5		1 Apr 1989 (SI 1989/288)
6–8		Repealed

Licensing Act 1988 (c 17)

RA: 19 May 1988

Commencement provisions: s 20(3); Licensing Act 1988 (Commencement No 1) Order 1988, SI 1988/1187; Licensing Act 1988 (Commencement No 2) Order 1988, SI 1988/1333

Section	
1	22 Aug 1988 (SI 1988/1333)
2	1 Aug 1988 (SI 1988/1187)
3	22 Aug 1988 (SI 1988/1333)
4	1 Aug 1988 (SI 1988/1187)

Licensing Act 1988 (c 17)—*contd*

Section			
5			22 Aug 1988 (SI 1988/1333)
6–8			1 Aug 1988 (SI 1988/1187)
9			22 Aug 1988 (SI 1988/1333)
10			1 Aug 1988 (SI 1988/1187)
11			22 Aug 1988 (SI 1988/1333)
12			1 Mar 1989 (SI 1988/1333)
13, 14			22 Aug 1988 (SI 1988/1333)
15			1 Mar 1989 (SI 1988/1333)
16			Repealed
17, 18			1 Aug 1988 (SI 1988/1187)
19	(1)		See Sch 3 below
	(2)		See Sch 4 below
20			1 Aug 1988 (SI 1988/1187)
Schedule			
1, 2			22 Aug 1988 (SI 1988/1333)
3, para	1		22 Aug 1988 (SI 1988/1333)
	2		1 Aug 1988 (SI 1988/1187)
	3–6		1 Mar 1989 (SI 1988/1333)
	7		22 Aug 1988 (SI 1988/1333)
	8	(a)	22 Aug 1988 (SI 1988/1333)
		(b)	1 Aug 1988 (SI 1988/1187)
	9		22 Aug 1988 (SI 1988/1333)
	10		1 Aug 1988 (SI 1988/1187)
	11–14		22 Aug 1988 (SI 1988/1333)
	15	(a)	22 Aug 1988 (SI 1988/1333)
		(b)	1 Mar 1989 (SI 1988/1333)
	16		1 Aug 1988 (SI 1988/1187)
	17		Repealed
	18		1 Aug 1988 (SI 1988/1187)
	19		22 Aug 1988 (SI 1988/1333)
4			1 Aug 1988 (repeals of or in Licensing Act 1964, ss 9(5), 71(3), 72(2), 73(1), 92(4), 169) (SI 1988/1187)
			22 Aug 1988 (repeals of or in Licensing Act 1964, ss 2(3)(b), 6(4), 7, 60, 62(2), 80(2), 95, 151(5), Sch 2, para 9; Finance Act 1967; Criminal Law Act 1977; Magistrates' Courts Act 1980; Licensing (Restaurant Meals) Act 1987) (SI 1988/1333)

Licensing (Retail Sales) Act 1988 (c 25)

RA: 29 Jul 1988

Commencement provisions: s 4(2); Licensing (Retail Sales) Act 1988 (Commencement) Order 1988, SI 1988/1670

1 Nov 1988 (SI 1988/1670)

Local Government Act 1988 (c 9)

RA: 24 Mar 1988

Commencement provisions: passim; Local Government Act 1988 (Commencement No 1) Order 1988, SI 1988/979; Local Government Act 1988 (Commencement No 2) (Scotland) Order 1988, SI 1988/1043

Section		
1–16		Repealed
17–22		7 Apr 1988 (s 23)
23–26		24 Mar 1988 (RA)
27		24 May 1988 (ss 27(3), 28(2), 29(2), 30(3))
28		24 May 1988 (ss 27(3), 28(2), 29(2), 30(3)) (E, W)
		Repealed (S)
29		24 May 1988 (ss 27(3), 28(2), 29(2), 30(3))
30		Repealed
31		See Sch 5 below
32		Repealed
33		11 Feb 1988 (s 33(4))
34		The day any authority or body concerned was established (s 34(2))
35		24 May 1988 (s 35(5))
36		Repealed
37		24 Mar 1988 (RA)
38		24 May 1988 (s 38(4))
39		24 May 1988 (s 39(6))
40		24 Mar 1988 (RA)
41		24 Mar 1988 (RA); but see Sch 7 below
42		24 Mar 1988 (RA)
Schedule		
1		24 Mar 1988 (RA)
2		7 Apr 1988 (s 23)
3		24 May 1988 (s 29(2))
4		Repealed
5, para	1	24 May 1988 (s 31(2))
	2	*Not in force*
	3–6	24 May 1988 (s 31(2))
6		Repealed
7, Pt	I	7 Apr 1988 (s 23)
	II	24 May 1988 (s 29(2))
	III	24 Jun 1988 or 1 Oct 1988 (dependent on relationship to s 32 and Sch 6 noted above) (SI 1988/979; SI 1988/1043)
	IV	29 May 1988 (Sch 7, Pt IV)

Local Government Finance Act 1988 (c 41)

RA: 29 Jul 1988

Commencement provisions: ss 111(5), 131(8), 132(6), 143(1), (2), 150, Schs 12, 13; Local Government Finance Act 1988 (Commencement) (Scotland) Order 1988, SI 1988/1456 (partially revoked by SI 1990/573); Local Government Finance Act 1988 Commencement (Scotland) Amendment Order 1990, SI 1990/573 (partially revokes SI 1988/1456)

Section	
1–40	29 Jul 1988 (RA); repealed, with savings, by Local Government Finance Act 1992, ss 117(2), 118, Sch 14 (qv)
41	29 Jul 1988 (RA)
41A	Inserted by Local Government (Wales) Act 1994, s 37 (qv)
42	29 Jul 1988 (RA)
42A, 42B	Inserted by Local Government and Rating Act 1997, s 1, Sch 1, para 1 (qv)
43, 44	29 Jul 1988 (RA)
44A	Inserted (retrospective to 29 Jul 1988) by Local Government and Housing Act 1989, s 139, Sch 5, para 22
45, 46	29 Jul 1988 (RA)
46A	Inserted (retrospective to 29 Jul 1988) by Local Government and Housing Act 1989, s 139, Sch 5, para 25
47–56	29 Jul 1988 (RA)
57	Substituted (retrospective to 29 Jul 1988) by Local Government and Housing Act 1989, s 139, Sch 5, para 31 (qv)
58	29 Jul 1988 (RA)
59	Substituted (retrospective to 29 Jul 1988) by Local Government and Housing Act 1989, s 139, Sch 5, para 32 (qv)
60–65	29 Jul 1988 (RA)
65A	Inserted by Local Government and Rating Act 1997, s 3, subject to a transitional provision (qv)
66, 67	29 Jul 1988 (RA)
68–73	29 Jul 1988 (RA); repealed, with savings, by Local Government Finance Act 1992, s 117(2), 118(1), Sch 14 (qv)
74	29 Jul 1988 (RA)

Local Government Finance Act 1988 (c 41)—*contd*
Section

74A	Inserted by Local Government and Housing Act 1989, s 139, Sch 5, paras 1, 54, 79(3) (qv); repealed, with savings, by Local Government Finance Act 1992, ss 117(2), 118(1), Sch 14 (qv)
75	29 Jul 1988 (RA)
75A	Inserted by Local Government and Housing Act 1989, s 139, Sch 5, paras 1, 56, 79(1) (qv); repealed, with savings, by Local Government Finance Act 1992, ss 117(2), 118(1), Sch 14 (qv)
76	29 Jul 1988 (RA)
77	29 Jul 1988 (RA); repealed (except as regards a case where a notice has been served before 16 Nov 1989; see Local Government and Housing Act 1989, ss 139, 194(4), Sch 5, paras 1, 57, 79(3), Sch 12, Pt II) (qv)
78	29 Jul 1988 (RA)
78A	Inserted by Local Government Finance Act 1992, s 104, Sch 10, Pt II, para 10 (qv)
79	29 Jul 1988 (RA)
80, 81	29 Jul 1988 (RA); repealed, with savings, by Local Government Finance Act 1992, ss 104, 117(2), 118(1), Sch 10, Pt II, para 12, Sch 14 (qv)
82	29 Jul 1988 (RA); substituted (savings) by Local Government Finance Act 1992, ss 104, 118(1), Sch 10, Pt II, para 13 (qv)
83	29 Jul 1988 (RA)
84	29 Jul 1988 (RA); repealed, with savings, by Local Government Finance Act 1992, ss 104, 117(2), 118(1), Sch 10, Pt II, para 14, Sch 14 (qv)
84A–84C	Inserted by Local Government Finance Act 1992, s 104, Sch 10, Pt II, para 15 (qv)
85–88	29 Jul 1988 (RA)

Local Government Finance Act 1988 (c 41)—*contd*

Local Government Finance Act 1988 (c 41)—*contd*

Section

116	29 Sep 1988 (s 111(5))
117, 118	29 Jul 1988 (RA)
119	Repealed
120–126	29 Jul 1988 (RA)
127	29 Jul 1988 (RA) (subject to prescribed savings made under s 127(2); section forbids levies under London Regional Transport Act 1984, s 13, after 31 Mar 1990)
128–134	Repealed
135–139	29 Jul 1988 (RA)
139A	Inserted by Local Government and Housing Act 1989, s 139, Sch 5, para 68 (qv)
140, 141	29 Jul 1988 (RA)
141A, 141B	Inserted (retrospective to 29 Jul 1988) by Local Government and Housing Act 1989, s 139, Sch 5, paras 1, 71 (repealed), 79(3); repealed, with savings, by Local Government Finance Act 1992, ss 117(2), 118(1), Sch 14 (qv)
142–145	29 Jul 1988 (RA)
145A	Inserted (retrospective to 29 Jul 1988) by Local Government and Housing Act 1989, s 139, Sch 5, paras 1, 73 (repealed), 79(3); repealed, with savings, by Local Government Finance Act 1992, ss 117(2), 118(1), Sch 14 (qv)
146–149	29 Jul 1988 (RA)
150	22 Aug 1988 (SI 1988/1456)
151, 152	29 Jul 1988 (RA)

Schedule

1–4	29 Jul 1988 (RA); repealed, with savings, by Local Government Finance Act 1992, ss 117(2), 118(1), Sch 14 (qv)
4A	Inserted (retrospective to 29 Jul 1988) by Local Government and Housing Act 1989, s 139, Sch 5, para 36
5–7	29 Jul 1988 (RA)
7A	Inserted (retrospective to 29 Jul 1988) by Local Government and Housing Act 1989, s 139, Sch 5, para 40
8–11	29 Jul 1988 (RA)
12, Pt I, para 1	31 Mar 1990 (as regards qualifying dates after that date) (Sch 12, Pt I, para 1(2))

Local Government Finance Act 1988 (c 41)—*contd*

Schedule

12, Pt	I, para	2, 3	Repealed
	II, para	4	22 Aug 1988 (SI 1988/1456)
		5, 6	Repealed
		7	1 Apr 1990 (SI 1988/1456)
		8–10	Repealed
		11, 12	1 Apr 1990 (SI 1988/1456)
		13	Repealed
		14	22 Aug 1988 (SI 1988/1456)
		15–17	Repealed
		18–21	22 Aug 1988 (only for purposes of and in relation to the community charge and the community water charge in respect of the financial year 1989–90 and each subsequent financial year) (SI 1988/1456); 1 Apr 1989 (otherwise) (SI 1988/1456); prospectively repealed by Local Government Finance Act 1992, s 117(2), Sch 14[2]
		22	22 Aug 1988 (SI 1988/1456); prospectively repealed by Local Government Finance Act 1992, s 117(2), Sch 14[2]
		23	Repealed
		24–26	22 Aug 1988 (SI 1988/1456); prospectively repealed by Local Government Finance Act 1992, s 117(2), Sch 14[2]
		27	Repealed
		28	22 Aug 1988 (SI 1988/1456); prospectively repealed by Local Government Finance Act 1992, s 117(2), Sch 14[2]
		29, 30	1 Oct 1988 (SI 1988/1456); prospectively repealed by Local Government Finance Act 1992, s 117(2), Sch 14[2]
		31–34	22 Aug 1988 (SI 1988/1456); prospectively repealed by Local Government Finance Act 1992, s 117(2), Sch 14[2]
		35	22 Aug 1988 (only for purposes of and in relation to the personal community charge and the personal community water charge in respect of the financial year 1989–90 and each subsequent financial year) (SI 1988/1456)

Local Government Finance Act 1988 (c 41)—*contd*

Schedule

12, Pt	II, para	35—*contd*	1 Apr 1989 (otherwise) (SI 1988/1456)
			Para prospectively repealed by Local Government Finance Act 1992, s 117(2), Sch 14[2]
		36	22 Aug 1988 (SI 1988/1456); prospectively repealed by Local Government Finance Act 1992, s 117(2), Sch 14[2]
		37	Repealed
		38	22 Aug 1988 (SI 1988/1456); prospectively repealed by Local Government Finance Act 1992, s 117(2), Sch 14[2]
	III, para	39	1 Apr 1989 (S) (Sch 12, Pt III, para 39(3))
			1 Apr 1990 (E, W) (Sch 12, Pt III, para 39(2))
		40	29 Jul 1988 (RA)
		41	Repealed
		42	1 Apr 1989 (S) (Sch 12, Pt III, para 42(3))
			1 Apr 1990 (E, W) (Sch 12, Pt III, para 42(2))
12A			Inserted (retrospective to 29 Jul 1988) by Local Government and Housing Act 1989, s 139, Sch 5, paras 1, 74 (repealed), 79(3); repealed, with savings, by Local Government Finance Act 1992, ss 117(2), 118(1), Sch 14 (qv)
13, Pt	I		1 Apr 1990 (subject to any saving under s 117(8)) (Sch 13, Pt I)
	II		1 Apr 1990 (Sch 13, Pt II)
	III		See s 127 above
	IV		22 Aug 1988 (repeals of or in Abolition of Domestic Rates Etc (Scotland) Act 1987, ss 4(1), 11(11), 17(5), 30(2), Sch 2) (SI 1988/1456)
			15 Sep 1988 (repeals in s 2 of 1987 Act) (SI 1988/1456)
			1 Oct 1988 (repeals in s 20 of 1987 Act) (SI 1988/1456)
			1 Apr 1989 (repeal in Acquisition of Land (Authorisation Procedure) (Scotland) Act 1947, s 5) (SI 1988/1456)

Local Government Finance Act 1988 (c 41)—*contd*

Schedule

13, Pt	IV—*contd*	1 Apr 1990 (otherwise, except repeal in Abolition of Domestic Rates Act (Scotland) Act 1987, s 24) (SI 1988/1456, as amended by SI 1990/573) *Not in force* (exception noted above)

1   S 101 previously repealed by Local Government Finance and Valuation Act 1991, s 1(1), subject to savings in s 1(3) thereof

2   Orders made under Local Government Finance Act 1992, s 119, bringing the prospective repeal into force will be noted to that Act

---

Malicious Communications Act 1988 (c 27)

RA: 29 Jul 1988

Commencement provisions: s 3(2)

Section

1	29 Sep 1988 (s 3(2))
2, 3	29 Jul 1988 (RA)

Matrimonial Proceedings (Transfers) Act 1988 (c 18)

RA: 19 May 1988

19 May 1988 (RA)

Merchant Shipping Act 1988 (c 12)

RA: 3 May 1988

Commencement provisions: s 58(2)–(4); Merchant Shipping Act 1988 (Commencement No 1) Order 1988, SI 1988/1010; Merchant Shipping Act 1988 (Commencement No 2) Order 1988, SI 1988/1907; Merchant Shipping (Transitional Provisions—Fishing Vessels) Order 1988, SI 1988/1911[1]; Merchant Shipping Act 1988 (Commencement No 3) Order 1989, SI 1989/353; Merchant Shipping Act 1988 (Commencement No 4) Order 1994, SI 1994/1201

Section

1–35	Repealed
36, 37	4 Jul 1988 (SI 1988/1010)
38–49	Repealed
50, 51	4 Jul 1988 (SI 1988/1010); repealed (as from 1 May 1994, with savings for any instrument made under s 50) by Merchant Shipping (Registration, etc) Act 1993, s 8(4), Sch 5, Pt II (repealed)
52	Repealed
53	4 Jul 1988 (SI 1988/1010); repealed (as from 1 Jan 1996, except for purposes of s 37) by Merchant Shipping Act 1995, s 314(1), Sch 12 (qv)

Merchant Shipping Act 1988 (c 12)—*contd*

Section

54		Repealed
55		4 Jul 1988 (SI 1988/1010); repealed (as from 1 Jan 1996, except for purposes of s 37) by Merchant Shipping Act 1995, s 314(1), Sch 12 (qv)
56		4 Jul 1988 (SI 1988/1010)); repealed (as from 1 May 1994, with savings for instruments made under the section) by Merchant Shipping (Registration, etc) Act 1993, s 8(4), Sch 5, Pt II (repealed)
57	(1)	Repealed
	(2)	4 Jul 1988 (SI 1988/1010)
	(3)–(5)	Repealed
58	(1)–(3)	4 Jul 1988 (SI 1988/1010)
	(4)	Spent
	(5)	4 Jul 1988 (SI 1988/1010)

Schedule

1–8	Repealed

[1]   Specifies how certain references in documents under law in force before commencement of the 1988 Act are to be construed after commencement; provided that no fishing vessels to be registered under law in force before commencement during the period 17–30 Nov 1988 inclusive; and provided that no entries relating to fishing vessels to be made in registers of ships kept under Merchant Shipping Act 1894, Pt I except entries closing the registry

---

Motor Vehicles (Wearing of Rear Seat Belts by Children) Act 1988 (c 23)

RA: 28 Jun 1988

Commencement provisions: s 3(2)

Section

1	Repealed
2, 3	28 Jun 1988 (RA)

Multilateral Investment Guarantee Agency Act 1988 (c 8)

RA: 24 Mar 1988

Commencement provisions: s 9(2); Multilateral Investment Guarantee Agency Act 1988 (Commencement) Order 1988, SI 1988/715

12 Apr 1988 (SI 1988/715)

Norfolk and Suffolk Broads Act 1988 (c 4)

Local application only

Protection Against Cruel Tethering Act 1988 (c 31)

RA: 29 Jul 1988

Commencement provisions: s 2(2)

29 Sep 1988 (s 2(2))

Protection of Animals (Amendment) Act 1988 (c 29)

RA: 29 Jul 1988

Commencement provisions: s 3(4)

29 Sep 1988 (s 3(4))

Public Utility Transfers and Water Charges Act 1988 (c 15)

RA: 10 May 1988

Commencement provisions: s 8(2) (repealed); Public Utility Transfers and Water
    Charges Act 1988 (Commencement No 1) Order 1988, SI 1988/879; Public
    Utility Transfers and Water Charges Act 1988 (Commencement No 2)
    Order 1988, SI 1988/1165

Section		
1		10 May 1988 (RA); prospectively repealed by Water Act 1989, s 190(3), Sch 27, Pt II[1]
2, 3		Repealed
4		18 May 1988 (SI 1988/879); repealed by Water Act 1989, s 190(3), Sch 27, Pt I (qv), but continues to apply in accordance with Water Consolidation (Consequential Provisions) Act 1991, s 2, Sch 2, para 11(1)
5		Repealed
6, 7		18 May or 11 Jul 1988 (SI 1988/879); and 1 Oct 1988 (SI 1988/1165); repealed, with savings for orders made under s 6, by Water Act 1989, s 190(2), (3), Sch 26, para 54(3), Sch 27, Pt I (qv)
8	(1)	10 May 1988 (RA); prospectively repealed by Water Act 1989, s 190(3), Sch 27, Pt II[1]
	(2)	Repealed
	(3)	10 May 1988 (RA); prospectively repealed by Water Act 1989, s 190(3), Sch 27, Pt II[1]
Schedule		
1–3		Repealed

---

[1]   Orders made under Water Act 1989, s 194(4), bringing the prospective repeal into force will be
      noted to that Act

Rate Support Grants Act 1988 (c 51)

RA: 15 Nov 1988

15 Nov 1988 (RA)

Regional Development Grants (Termination) Act 1988 (c 11)

RA: 3 May 1988

3 May 1988 (RA)

Road Traffic Act 1988 (c 52)

RA: 15 Nov 1988

Commencement provisions: s 197(2)

15 May 1989 (subject, in the case of ss 15, 195(3), (4), to transitory modifications specified in Road Traffic (Consequential Provisions) Act 1988, Sch 5 (now repealed) which applied until 21 Jul 1989 (Road Traffic Act 1988 (Appointed Day for Section 15) Order 1989, SI 1989/1086) or 1 Sep 1989 (Road Traffic Act 1988 (Appointed Day for Section 15) (No 2) Order 1989, SI 1989/1260)) (s 197(2))

Road Traffic (Consequential Provisions) Act 1988 (c 54)

RA: 15 Nov 1988

Commencement provisions: s 8(2), (3)

Section			
1–3			15 May 1989 (s 8(2), (3))
4			See Schs 2, 3 below
5			15 May 1989 (s 8(2), (3))
6			Repealed
7, 8			15 May 1989 (s 8(2), (3))
Schedule			
1			15 May 1989 (s 8(2), (3))
2, para	1		Repealed
	2–7		15 May 1989 (s 8(2), (3))
	8, 9		Repealed
	10–14		15 May 1989 (s 8(2), (3))
	15–20		*Not in force*
	21–33		Repealed
3, para	1, 2		15 May 1989 (s 8(2), (3))
	3		Repealed
	4, 5		15 May 1989 (s 8(2), (3))
	6	(1)–(5)	Repealed
		(6)–(8)	15 May 1989 (s 8(2), (3))
	7		15 May 1989 (s 8(2), (3))

Road Traffic (Consequential Provisions) Act 1988 (c 54)—*contd*

Schedule

3, para	8		Repealed
	9, 10		15 May 1989 (s 8(2), (3))
	11		Repealed
	12–14		15 May 1989 (s 8(2), (3))
	15		Repealed
	16–18		15 May 1989 (s 8(2), (3))
	19, 20		Repealed
	21–31		15 May 1989 (s 8(2), (3))
	32		Repealed
	33		15 May 1989 (s 8(2), (3))
	34		Repealed
	35, 36		15 May 1989 (s 8(2), (3))
	37	(1), (2)	Repealed
		(3)	15 May 1989 (s 8(2), (3))
	38, 39		15 May 1989 (s 8(2), (3))
4			15 May 1989 (s 8(2), (3))
5			Repealed

Road Traffic Offenders Act 1988 (c 53)

RA: 15 Nov 1988

Commencement provisions: s 99(2)–(5)

Section

1–19		15 May 1989 (s 99(2)–(5))
20		Substituted by Road Traffic Act 1991, s 23 (qv)
21–23		15 May 1989 (s 99(2)–(5))
24		Substituted by Road Traffic Act 1991, s 24 (qv)
25		15 May 1989 (s 99(2)–(5))
26		Substituted by Road Traffic Act 1991, s 25 (qv)
27	(1)	15 May 1989 (s 99(2)–(5))
	(2)	Repealed
	(3)	15 May 1989 (s 99(2)–(5))
	(4)	15 May 1989 (E, W) (s 99(2)–(5)) Not in force (S)
	(5)	Inserted by Access to Justice Act 1999, s 90, Sch 13, para 144(1), (3) (qv)
28		Substituted by Road Traffic Act 1991, s 27 (qv)
29		Substituted by Road Traffic Act 1991, s 28 (qv)
30		15 May 1989 (E, W) (s 99(2)–(5))

Road Traffic Offenders Act 1988 (c 53)—*contd*

Section

30—*contd*		15 May 1989 (S) (so far as relates to ss 75–77) (s 99(2)–(5))
		Not in force (otherwise) (S)
31–33		15 May 1989 (s 99(2)–(5))
33A		Prospectively inserted (S) by Criminal Justice (Scotland) Act 1995, s 117(1), Sch 6, Pt II, para 188 (repealed); substituted by Criminal Procedure (Consequential Provisions) (Scotland) Act 1995, s 5, Sch 4, para 71(1), (6) (qv)
34		15 May 1989 (s 99(2)–(5))
34A–34C		Inserted by Road Traffic Act 1991, s 30 (qv)
35		15 May 1989 (s 99(2)–(5))
36		Substituted by Road Traffic Act 1991, s 32 (qv)
37–41		15 May 1989 (s 99(2)–(5))
41A		Inserted by Road Traffic Act 1991, s 48, Sch 4, para 97 (qv)
42–47		15 May 1989 (s 99(2)–(5))
48		Substituted by Road Traffic Act 1991, s 48, Sch 4, para 101 (qv)
49–51		15 May 1989 (s 99(2)–(5))
52	(1)–(3)	15 May 1989 (s 99(2)–(5))
	(4)	*Not in force*
53		Substituted by Road Traffic Act 1991, s 48, Sch 4, para 102 (qv)
54–58		15 May 1989 (E, W) (s 99(2)–(5))
		Not in force (S)
59	(1)–(5)	*Not in force*
	(6)	Repealed
60		Repealed
61		15 May 1989 (E, W) (s 99(2)–(5))
		Not in force (S)
62–74		15 May 1989 (s 99(2)–(5))
75–77		Substituted by Road Traffic Act 1991, s 34 (qv)
78–91		15 May 1989 (s 99(2)–(5))
91A, 91B		Inserted (1 Jan 1997) by Driving Licences (Community Driving Licence) Regulations 1996, SI 1996/1974, reg 3, Sch 2, paras 4, 5
92–99		15 May 1989 (s 99(2)–(5))
Schedule		
1–5		15 May 1989 (s 99(2)–(5))

School Boards (Scotland) Act 1988 (c 47)

RA: 15 Nov 1988

Commencement provisions: s 24(2); School Boards (Scotland) Act 1988 (Commencement) Order 1989, SI 1989/272

Section

1, 2	1 Apr 1989 (SI 1989/272)
2A, 2B	Inserted by Education (Scotland) Act 1996, s 28(2) (qv)
3	Substituted by Education (Scotland) Act 1996, s 29(1) (qv)
4, 5	1 Apr 1989 (SI 1989/272)
5A	Inserted by Education (Scotland) Act 1996, s 30 (qv)
6–17	1 Apr 1989 (SI 1989/272)
17A	Inserted by Education (Scotland) Act 1996, s 31, Sch 4, para 6 (qv)
18–23	1 Apr 1989 (SI 1989/272)
24	15 Nov 1988 (RA)

Schedule

1–3		1 Apr 1989 (SI 1989/272)
4, para	1–5	1 Nov 1989 (SI 1989/272)
	6	1 Apr 1989 (SI 1989/272)
	7	1 Nov 1989 (SI 1989/272)

Scotch Whisky Act 1988 (c 22)

RA: 28 Jun 1988

Commencement provisions: s 5(2); Scotch Whisky Act 1988 (Commencement and Transitional Provisions) Order 1990, SI 1990/997

Section

1–3	30 Apr 1990 (SI 1990/997)
4, 5	28 Jun 1988 (RA; note that SI 1990/997 also purports to bring s 5 into force on 30 Apr 1990)

Social Security Act 1988 (c 7)

RA: 15 Mar 1988

Commencement provisions: s 18(1)–(4); Social Security Act 1988 (Commencement No 1) Order 1988, SI 1988/520; Social Security Act 1988 (Commencement No 2) Order 1988, SI 1988/1226; Social Security Act 1988 (Commencement No 3) Order 1988, SI 1988/1857

Section

1–11	Repealed
12	15 Mar 1988 (s 18(1), (2))
13, 14	17 Mar 1988 (SI 1988/520)
15	15 Mar 1988 (s 18(1), (2))
15A	Inserted by Social Security Act 1990, s 21(1), Sch 6, para 8(10) (qv)

Social Security Act 1988 (c 7)—*contd*

Section

16	(1)	See Sch 4 below
	(2)	See Sch 5 below
17		Repealed
18–20		15 Mar 1988 (s 18(1), (2))

Schedule

1–3		Repealed
4, para	1	6 Apr 1988 (SI 1988/520)
	2	12 Sep 1988 (SI 1988/1226)
	3–20	Repealed
	21	Spent
	22–30	Repealed
5		15 Mar 1988 (repeals of or in Social Security Act 1975, ss 45, 45A, 46, 47B, 66; Social Security Act 1980, Sch 1; Social Security Act 1985, s 13(4)(a)) (s 18(1), (2))
		6 Apr 1988 (repeals in Social Security Act 1986, s 50(1)) (SI 1988/520)
		11 Apr 1988 (repeals of or in Emergency Laws (Re-enactments and Repeals) Act 1964; Health Services and Public Health Act 1968; Social Security Act 1975, ss 59A, 69; Adoption Act 1976; National Health Service Act 1977; Adoption (Scotland) Act 1978; National Health Service (Scotland) Act 1978; Social Security Act 1985, s 14; Social Security Act 1986, ss 20(6), 23(8), 32, 33(1), 34(1)(a), 51(2), 52(6), 53(10), 63(7), 84(1), Sch 3) (SI 1988/520)
		12 Sep 1988 (repeal of Social Security Act 1986, Sch 10, para 45) (SI 1988/1226)
		2 Oct 1988 (repeals in Social Security Act 1975, Sch 3) (SI 1988/520)

Solicitors (Scotland) Act 1988 (c 42)

RA: 29 Jul 1988

Commencement provisions: s 7(2)

29 Jan 1989 (s 7(2))

Welsh Development Agency Act 1988 (c 5)

Whole Act repealed

1989

Antarctic Minerals Act 1989 (c 21)

RA: 21 Jul 1989

Commencement provisions: s 20(2)

Whole Act repealed, except ss 14, 20, by Antarctic Act 1994, s 33, Schedule (this Act was never brought into force)

Appropriation Act 1989 (c 25)

Whole Act repealed

Atomic Energy Act 1989 (c 7)

RA: 25 May 1989

Commencement provisions: s 7(2); Atomic Energy Act 1989 (Commencement) Order 1989, SI 1989/1317

1 Sep 1989 (SI 1989/1317)

Brunei (Appeals) Act 1989 (c 36)

RA: 16 Nov 1989

Commencement provisions: s 2(2); Brunei (Appeals) Act 1989 (Commencement) Order 1989, SI 1989/2450

1 Feb 1990 (SI 1989/2450)

Children Act 1989 (c 41)

RA: 16 Nov 1989

Commencement provisions: s 108(2), (3); Children Act 1989 (Commencement and Transitional Provisions) Order 1991, SI 1991/828; Children Act 1989 (Commencement No 2—Amendment and Transitional Provisions) Order 1991, SI 1991/1990

Section		
1–4		14 Oct 1991 (SI 1991/828)
5	(1)–(10)	14 Oct 1991 (SI 1991/828)
	(11), (12)	1 Feb 1992 (SI 1991/828, SI 1991/1990)
	(13)	14 Oct 1991 (SI 1991/828)

Children Act 1989 (c 41)—*contd*

Section

6–17	14 Oct 1991 (SI 1991/828)
17A	Inserted by Carers and Disabled Children Act 2000, s 7(1) (qv); substituted, partly prospectively, by Health and Social Care Act 2001, 58[4]
17B	Prospectively inserted by Carers and Disabled Children Act 2000, s 7(1)[1]
18, 19	14 Oct 1991 (SI 1991/828)
19A–19C	Inserted by Children (Leaving Care) Act 2000, s 1 (qv)
20–23	14 Oct 1991 (SI 1991/828)
23A–23C	Inserted by Children (Leaving Care) Act 2000, s 2(4) (qv)
23D, 23E	Inserted by Children (Leaving Care) Act 2000, s 3 (qv)
24	14 Oct 1991 (SI 1991/828); substituted (in part prospectively) by Children (Leaving Care) Act 2000, s 4[3]
24A–24C	Inserted (in part prospectively) by Children (Leaving Care) Act 2000, s 4[3]
24D	Inserted by Children (Leaving Care) Act 2000, s 5 (qv)
25–38	14 Oct 1991 (SI 1991/828)
38A, 38B	Inserted by Family Law Act 1996, s 52, Sch 6, para 1 (qv)
39–44	14 Oct 1991 (SI 1991/828)
44A, 44B	Inserted by Family Law Act 1996, s 52, Sch 6, para 3 (qv)
45–53	14 Oct 1991 (SI 1991/828)
54	Repealed
55–65	14 Oct 1991 (SI 1991/828)
65A	Prospectively inserted by Care Standards Act 2000, s 116, Sch 4, para 14(14)[2]
66–70	14 Oct 1991 (SI 1991/828)
71–78	14 Oct 1991 (SI 1991/828); prospectively repealed by Care Standards Act 2000, s 79(5) (W)[2]; prospectively repealed by Regulation of Care (Scotland) Act 2001, s 80(1), Sch 4 (S)[5] Repealed (E)
79	14 Oct 1991 (SI 1991/828); prospectively repealed by Regulation of Care (Scotland) Act 2001, s 80(1), Sch 4 (S)[5]

Children Act 1989 (c 41)—*contd*

Section

79A-79X		Inserted (in part prospectively) by Care Standards Act 2000, s 79(1) (E, W)[2]
80–87		14 Oct 1991 (SI 1991/828)
87A		Inserted (E, W) by Deregulation and Contracting Out Act 1994, s 38 (qv); substituted (E) by Care Standards Act 2000, s 106(1) (qv); prospectively substituted (W) by Care Standards Act 2000, s 106(1)[2]
87B		Inserted (E, W) by Deregulation and Contracting Out Act 1994, s 38 (qv)
87C, 87D		Inserted by Care Standards Act 2000, ss 107, 108 (qv)
88	(1)	See Sch 10 below
	(2)	14 Oct 1991 (SI 1991/828)
89		Repealed
90–95		14 Oct 1991 (SI 1991/828)
96	(1), (2)	14 Oct 1991 (SI 1991/828)
	(3)–(7)	16 Nov 1989 (s 108(2))
97, 98		14 Oct 1991 (SI 1991/828)
99		Repealed
100–107		14 Oct 1991 (SI 1991/828)
108		16 Nov 1989 (RA)

Schedule

1–8		14 Oct 1991 (SI 1991/828)
9		14 Oct 1991 (SI 1991/828); prospectively repealed by Care Standards Act 2000, s 79(5) (W)[2]
		Repealed (E)
9A		Inserted (in part prospectively) by Care Standards Act 2000, s 79(2), Sch 3[2]
10, para	1–20	14 Oct 1991 (SI 1991/828)
	21	1 May 1991 (SI 1991/828)
	22–28	14 Oct 1991 (SI 1991/828)
	29	Repealed
	30–46	14 Oct 1991 (SI 1991/828)
11		14 Oct 1991 (SI 1991/828)
12, para	1–3	14 Oct 1991 (SI 1991/828)
	4	Repealed
	5–7	14 Oct 1991 (SI 1991/828)
	8	Repealed
	9	14 Oct 1991 (SI 1991/828)
	10	Repealed
	11–17	14 Oct 1991 (SI 1991/828)
	18	Repealed
	19, 20	14 Oct 1991 (SI 1991/828)

Children Act 1989 (c 41)—*contd*

Schedule

12, para	21–25	Repealed
	26–34	14 Oct 1991 (SI 1991/828)
	35	Spent
	36	Repealed
	37–44	14 Oct 1991 (SI 1991/828)
	45	Repealed
13–15		14 Oct 1991 (SI 1991/828)

[1]   Orders made under Carers and Disabled Children Act 2000, s 12(2) bringing the prospective insertions into force will be noted to that Act

[2]   Orders made under Care Standards Act 2000, s 122 bringing the prospective insertions into force will be noted to that Act

[3]   Orders made under Children (Leaving Care) Act 2000, s 8 bringing the prospective amendments into force will be noted to that Act

[4]   Orders made under Health and Social Care Act 2001, s 70(2) bringing the prospective substitution into force will be noted to that Act

[5]   Orders made under Regulation of Care (Scotland) Act 2001, s 81(2) bringing the prospective repeals into force will be noted to that Act

---

Civil Aviation (Air Navigation Charges) Act 1989 (c 9)

Whole Act repealed

Common Land (Rectification of Registers) Act 1989 (c 18)

RA: 21 Jul 1989

21 Jul 1989 (RA)

Companies Act 1989 (c 40)

RA: 16 Nov 1989

Commencement provisions: s 215(1)–(3); Companies Act 1989 (Commencement No 1) Order 1990, SI 1990/98; Companies Act 1989 (Commencement No 2) Order 1990, SI 1990/142; Companies Act 1989 (Commencement No 3, Transitional Provisions and Transfer of Functions under the Financial Services Act 1986) Order 1990, SI 1990/354 (which contains transitional provisions in relation to self-regulating organisations and professional bodies); Companies Act 1989 (Commencement No 4, Transitional and Saving Provisions) Order 1990, SI 1990/355, as amended by SI 1990/1707, SI 1990/2569, SI 1993/3246; Companies Act 1989 (Commencement No 5 and Transitional and Saving Provisions) Order 1990, SI 1990/713; Companies Act 1989 (Commencement No 6 and Transitional and Savings Provisions) Order 1990, SI 1990/1392, as amended by SI 1990/1707; Companies Act 1989 (Commencement No 7, Transitional and Saving Provisions) Order 1990, SI 1990/1707; Companies Act 1989 (Commencement No 8 and Transitional and Saving Provisions) Order 1990, SI 1990/2569; Companies Act 1989 (Commencement No 9 and Saving and Transitional Provisions) Order 1991, SI 1991/488; Companies Act 1989

Companies Act 1989 (c 40)—*contd*
(Commencement No 10 and Saving Provisions) Order 1991, SI 1991/878;
Companies Act 1989 (Commencement No 11) Order 1991, SI 1991/1452;
Companies Act 1989 (Commencement No 12 and Transitional Provision)
Order 1991, SI 1991/1996; Companies Act 1989 (Commencement No 13)
Order 1991, SI 1991/2173; Companies Act 1989 (Commencement No 14 and
Transitional Provision) Order 1991, SI 1991/2945; Companies Act 1989
(Commencement No 15 and Transitional and Savings Provisions) Order 1995,
SI 1995/1352; Companies Act 1989 (Commencement No 16) Order 1995,
SI 1995/1591; Companies Act 1989 (Commencement No 17) Order 1998,
SI 1998/1747

Section	
1	1 Mar 1990 (so far as relates to s 15 below) (SI 1990/142)
	1 Apr 1990 (so far as relates to any section or part thereof brought into force by SI 1990/355) (SI 1990/355)[1]
	7 Jan 1991 (so far as relates to any section or part thereof brought into force by SI 1990/2569) (SI 1990/2569)
	1 Jul 1992 (so far as relates to s 11) (subject to transitional provisions) (SI 1991/2945)
2–6	1 Apr 1990 (SI 1990/355)[1]
7	1 Apr 1990 (except so far as relates to Companies Act 1985, s 233(5)) (SI 1990/355)[1]
	7 Jan 1991 (exception noted above) (SI 1990/2569)[2]
8–10	1 Apr 1990 (SI 1990/355)[1]
11	1 Apr 1990 (except so far as relates to Companies Act 1985, s 242A) (SI 1990/355)[1]
	1 Jul 1992 (exception noted above) (subject to transitional provisions) (SI 1991/2945)
12	7 Jan 1991 (SI 1990/2569)[2]
13, 14	1 Apr 1990 (SI 1990/355)[1]
15	1 Mar 1990 (SI 1990/142)
16–22	1 Apr 1990 (SI 1990/355)[1]
23	See Sch 10 below
24	1 Mar 1990 (for purposes of ss 30–33, 37–40, 41(1), (3)–(6), 42–45, 47(1), 48(1), (2), 49–54, Schs 11, 12, 14) (SI 1990/142)
	1 Oct 1991 (otherwise) (SI 1991/1996)
25–27	1 Oct 1991 (SI 1991/1996)

Companies Act 1989 (c 40)—*contd*
Section

28		1 Oct 1991 (subject to transitional provisions in SI 1991/1996, art 4) (SI 1991/1996)
29		1 Oct 1991 (SI 1991/1996)
30		1 Mar 1990 (SI 1990/142)
31		1 Mar 1990 (so far as relates to recognition of supervisory bodies under Sch 11 and for purpose of enabling Secretary of State to approve a qualification under s 31(4), (5)) (SI 1990/142)
		1 Oct 1991 (otherwise) (SI 1991/1996)
32, 33		1 Mar 1990 (SI 1990/142)
34		1 Oct 1991 (SI 1991/1996)
35, 36		26 Jun 1991 (SI 1991/1452)
37–40		1 Mar 1990 (SI 1990/142)
41	(1)	1 Mar 1990 (for purposes of an application under this section or under provisions specified under s 24 above or of any requirement imposed under such provisions) (SI 1990/142)
		1 Oct 1991 (otherwise) (SI 1991/1996)
	(2)	1 Oct 1991 (SI 1991/1996)
	(3)	1 Mar 1990 (SI 1990/142)
	(4)	1 Mar 1990 (for purposes of an application under this section or under provisions specified under s 24 above or of any requirement imposed under such provisions) (SI 1990/142)
		1 Oct 1991 (otherwise) (SI 1991/1996)
	(5), (6)	1 Mar 1990 (for purposes of s 41(3)) (SI 1990/142)
		1 Oct 1991 (otherwise) (SI 1991/1996)
42–44		1 Mar 1990 (for purposes of ss 30–33, 37–40, 41(1), (3)–(6), 42–45, 47(1), 48(1), (2), 49–54, Schs 11, 12, 14) (SI 1990/142)
		1 Oct 1991 (otherwise) (SI 1991/1996)
45		1 Mar 1990 (SI 1990/142)
46		*Not in force*
47	(1)	1 Mar 1990 (SI 1990/142)
	(2)–(6)	*Not in force*
48	(1), (2)	1 Mar 1990 (SI 1990/142)
	(3)	*Not in force*

Companies Act 1989 (c 40)—*contd*

Section

49		1 Mar 1990 (for purposes of ss 30–33, 37–40, 41(1), (3)–(6), 42–45, 47(1), 48(1), (2), 49–54, Schs 11, 12, 14) (SI 1990/142)
		1 Oct 1991 (otherwise) (SI 1991/1996)
50, 51		1 Mar 1990 (SI 1990/142)
52–54		1 Mar 1990 (for purposes of ss 30–33, 37–40, 41(1), (3)–(6), 42–45, 47(1), 48(1), (2), 49–54, Schs 11, 12, 14) (SI 1990/142)
		1 Oct 1991 (otherwise) (SI 1991/1996)
55–64		21 Feb 1990 (SI 1990/142)
65	(1)	21 Feb 1990 (SI 1990/142)
	(2)	21 Feb 1990 (except so far as refers to Pt VII (ss 154–191) and so far as s 65(2)(g) refers to a body established under s 46) (SI 1990/142)
		25 Apr 1991 (so far as not already in force, except so far as s 65(2)(g) refers to a body established under s 46) (SI 1991/878)
		Not in force (exception noted above)
	(3)–(7)	21 Feb 1990 (SI 1990/142)
66–71		21 Feb 1990 (SI 1990/142)
72–79		Repealed
80		21 Feb 1990 (except so far as refers to Pt VII (ss 154–191)) (SI 1990/142)
		25 Apr 1991 (exception noted above) (SI 1991/878)
81		Repealed
82–86		21 Feb 1990 (SI 1990/142)
87	(1)–(3)	21 Feb 1990 (SI 1990/142)
	(4)	21 Feb 1990 (except so far as refers to Pt VII (ss 154–191)) (SI 1990/142)
		25 Apr 1991 (exception noted above) (SI 1991/878)
	(5), (6)	21 Feb 1990 (SI 1990/142)
88–91		21 Feb 1990 (SI 1990/142)
92–107		*Not in force*
108–110		4 Feb 1991 (SI 1990/2569)[2]
111		Repealed
112		4 Feb 1991 (SI 1990/2569)[2]
113, 114		1 Apr 1990 (SI 1990/355)
115		1 Apr 1990 (SI 1990/355)[3]
116, 117		1 Apr 1990 (SI 1990/355)
118–123		1 Apr 1990 (SI 1990/355)[3]
124		Repealed
125		7 Jan 1991 (SI 1990/2569)
126		1 Jul 1991 (SI 1991/488)[4]

Companies Act 1989 (c 40)—*contd*

Section

127	(1), (2)	7 Jan 1991 (SI 1990/2569)
	(3)	1 Jul 1991 (SI 1991/488)
	(4)	7 Jan 1991 (SI 1990/2569)
	(5), (6)	1 Jul 1991 (SI 1991/488)
	(7)	7 Jan 1991 (so far as inserts in Companies Act 1985, Sch 22, a reference to ss 706, 707, 715A of 1985 Act, as inserted by ss 125, 127(1) of this Act) (SI 1990/2569)
		1 Jul 1991 (otherwise) (SI 1991/488)
128		*Not in force*
129		1 Nov 1990 (SI 1990/1392)
130		31 Jul 1990 (SI 1990/1392)
131		1 Apr 1990 (not to be construed as affecting any right, privilege, obligation or liability acquired, accrued or incurred before 1 Apr 1990; see SI 1990/355, art 11) (SI 1990/355)
132		1 Apr 1990 (SI 1990/355)
133		*Not in force*
134	(1)–(3)	31 May 1990 (SI 1990/713)
	(4)	1 Nov 1991 (SI 1991/1996)
	(5), (6)	31 May 1990 (SI 1990/713)
135		7 Jan 1991 (SI 1990/2569)
136		1 Apr 1990 (SI 1990/355; see, however, saving in art 12 thereof)
137	(1)	1 Apr 1990 (SI 1990/355)
	(2)	1 Apr 1990 (for purposes of a director's report of a company within meaning of Companies Act 1985, s 735 (except in relation to a financial year commencing before 23 Dec 1989; see SI 1990/355, art 13)) (SI 1990/355)
		Not in force (otherwise)
138		31 Jul 1990 (SI 1990/1392)[5]
139		1 Oct 1990 (SI 1990/1707)[6]
140	(1)–(6)	3 Jul 1995 (subject to transitional provisions and savings) (SI 1995/1352)
	(7), (8)	*Not in force*
141		16 Nov 1989 (s 215(1))
142		*Not in force*
143		1 Nov 1991 (SI 1991/1996)
144		1 Nov 1990 (SI 1990/1392)[7]
145		See Sch 19 below
146		1 Apr 1990 (SI 1990/142)
147–150		16 Nov 1989 (s 215(1))

Companies Act 1989 (c 40)—*contd*

Section

151	1 Apr 1990 (SI 1990/142)
152	1 Mar 1990 (SI 1990/142)
153	See Sch 20 below
154, 155	25 Mar 1991 (Pt VII (ss 154–191, Schs 21, 22) brought into force only insofar as is necessary to enable regulations to be made under ss 155(4), (5), 156(1) (so far as it relates to Sch 21), 158(4), (5), 160(5), 173(4), (5), 174(2)–(4), 185, 186, 187(3), Sch 21, para 2(3)) (SI 1991/488)
	25 Apr 1991 (otherwise) (SI 1991/878)
156	Repealed
157	25 Mar 1991 (see note to ss 154–156) (SI 1991/488)
	25 Apr 1991 (otherwise) (SI 1991/878)[8]
158, 159	25 Mar 1991 (see note to ss 154–156) (SI 1991/488)
	25 Apr 1991 (otherwise) (SI 1991/878)
160	25 Mar 1991 (see note to ss 154–156) (SI 1991/488)
	25 Apr 1991 (so far as not already in force, except insofar as imposing a duty (i) on any person where conflict with enactments in force in Northern Ireland relating to insolvency would arise, and (ii) on a relevant office-holder appointed under the general law of insolvency for the time being in force in Northern Ireland) (SI 1991/878)[8]
	1 Oct 1991 (exception noted above) (SI 1991/2173)
161	25 Mar 1991 (see note to ss 154–156) (SI 1991/488)
	25 Apr 1991 (otherwise) (SI 1991/878)
162	25 Mar 1991 (see note to ss 154–156) (SI 1991/488)
	25 Apr 1991 (otherwise, except so far as would require an exchange or clearing house to supply a copy of a report to any relevant office-holder appointed under the general law of insolvency for the time being in force in Northern Ireland) (SI 1991/878)

Companies Act 1989 (c 40)—*contd*
Section

162—*contd*		1 Oct 1991 (exception noted above) (SI 1991/2173)
163–165		25 Mar 1991 (see note to ss 154–156) (SI 1991/488)
		25 Apr 1991 (otherwise) (SI 1991/878)
166		25 Mar 1991 (see note to ss 154–156) (SI 1991/488)
		25 Apr 1991 (so far as not already in force, except where would enable a direction to be given, where an order, appointment or resolution corresponding to those mentioned in s 166(6) has been made or passed in relation to the person in question under the general law of insolvency for the time being in force in Northern Ireland) (SI 1991/878)[8]
		1 Oct 1991 (exception noted above) (SI 1991/2173)
167		25 Mar 1991 (see note to ss 154–156) (SI 1991/488)
		25 Apr 1991 (otherwise, except where enabling an application to be made by a relevant office-holder appointed by, or in consequence of, or in connection with, an order or resolution corresponding to those mentioned in s 167(1) made or passed under the general law of insolvency for the time being in force in Northern Ireland) (SI 1991/878)
		1 Oct 1991 (exception noted above) (SI 1991/2173)
168		Repealed
169	(1)	Repealed
169	(2), (3)	25 Mar 1991 (see note to ss 154–156) (SI 1991/488)
		25 Apr 1991 (otherwise) (SI 1991/878)
	(3A)	Inserted (1 Dec 2001) Financial Services and Markets Act 2000 (Consequential Amendments and Repeals) Order 2001, SI 2001/3649, art 83(1), (4)
	(4)	Repealed
	(5)	25 Mar 1991 (see note to ss 154–156) (SI 1991/488)
		25 Apr 1991 (otherwise) (SI 1991/878)

Companies Act 1989 (c 40)—*contd*
Section

170		25 Mar 1991 (see note to ss 154–156) (SI 1991/488)
		Not in force (otherwise)
171		Repealed
172		25 Mar 1991 (see note to ss 154–156) (SI 1991/488)
		Not in force (otherwise)
173		25 Mar 1991 (see note to ss 154–156) (SI 1991/488)
		25 Apr 1991 (otherwise) (SI 1991/878)
174, 175		25 Mar 1991 (see note to ss 154–156) (SI 1991/488)
		25 Apr 1991 (otherwise) (SI 1991/878)[8]
176		25 Mar 1991 (see note to ss 154–156) (SI 1991/488)
		4 Jul 1995 (otherwise) (SI 1995/1591)
177		25 Mar 1991 (see note to ss 154–156) (SI 1991/488)
		25 Apr 1991 (otherwise) (SI 1991/878)[8]
178		25 Mar 1991 (see note to ss 154–156) (SI 1991/488)
		Not in force (otherwise)
179, 180		25 Mar 1991 (see note to ss 154–156) (SI 1991/488)
		25 Apr 1991 (otherwise) (SI 1991/878)[8]
181		25 Mar 1991 (see note to ss 154–156) (SI 1991/488)
		4 Jul 1995 (otherwise) (SI 1995/1591)
182, 183		25 Mar 1991 (see note to ss 154–156) (SI 1991/488)
		25 Apr 1991 (otherwise) (SI 1991/878)
184	(1)	25 Mar 1991 (see note to ss 154–156) (SI 1991/488)
		25 Apr 1991 (so far as not already in force, except so far as has effect in relation to any relevant office-holder appointed under general law of insolvency for the time being in force in Northern Ireland) (SI 1991/878)
		1 Oct 1991 (exception noted above) (SI 1991/2173)
	(2)–(5)	25 Mar 1991 (see note to ss 154–156) (SI 1991/488)
		25 Apr 1991 (otherwise) (SI 1991/878)
185, 186		25 Mar 1991 (see note to ss 154–156) (SI 1991/488)
		10 Aug 1998 (otherwise) (SI 1998/1747)

Companies Act 1989 (c 40)—*contd*

Companies Act 1989 (c 40)—*contd*

Schedule

10[10], para	35	(2)	(b)	7 Jan 1991 (SI 1990/2569)
		(3)		1 Apr 1990 (SI 1990/355)[1]
	36, 37			Repealed
	38, 39			1 Apr 1990 (SI 1990/355)[1]
11, 12				1 Mar 1990 (SI 1990/142)
13				*Not in force*
14				1 Mar 1990 (SI 1990/142)
15, 16				*Not in force*
17				31 Jul 1990 (SI 1990/1392)
18				1 Nov 1990 (SI 1990/1392)[7]
19, para	1			1 Mar 1990 (SI 1990/142)
	2–6			1 Oct 1990 (SI 1990/1707)[6]
	7			1 Oct 1990 (SI 1990/1707)
	8, 9			1 Mar 1990 (SI 1990/142)
	10			7 Jan 1991 (SI 1990/2569)
	11			4 Feb 1991 (SI 1990/2569)
	12			1 Mar 1990 (SI 1990/142)
	13			*Not in force*
	14			1 Oct 1990 (SI 1990/1707)
	15–18			1 Apr 1990 (SI 1990/355)
	19			1 Mar 1990 (SI 1990/142)
	20			3 Jul 1995 (SI 1995/1352)
	21			1 Mar 1990 (SI 1990/142)
20, para	1			1 Apr 1990 (SI 1990/142)
	2–12			16 Nov 1989 (s 215(1))
	13			1 Apr 1990 (SI 1990/142)
	14–16			16 Nov 1989 (s 215(1))
	17			1 Apr 1990 (SI 1990/142)
	18–20			16 Nov 1989 (s 215(1))
	21–24			Repealed
	25			16 Nov 1989 (s 215(1))
	26			Repealed
21–23				Repealed
24				16 Nov 1989 (repeals of or in Fair Trading Act 1973, ss 71, 74, 88, 89, Sch 9) (s 215(1))
				21 Feb 1990 (repeals of or in Companies Act 1985, ss 435, 440, 443, 446, 447, 449, 452, 735A; Financial Services Act 1986, ss 94, 105, 179, 180, 198(1); Banking Act 1987, s 84(1)) (SI 1990/142)
				1 Mar 1990 (repeals of or in Company Directors Disqualification Act 1986, s 21(2)) (SI 1990/142)
				1 Mar 1990 (repeal in Financial Services Act 1986, s 199(9)) (SI 1990/355)

Companies Act 1989 (c 40)—*contd*
Schedule
24—*contd*

15 Mar 1990 (repeals of or in
Financial Services Act 1986,
ss 48, 55, 119, 159, 160,
Sch 11, paras 4, 10, 14)
(SI 1990/354)

1 Apr 1990 (repeals of or in Fair
Trading Act 1973, ss 46(3), 85)
(SI 1990/142)

1 Apr 1990 (repeals of or in
Harbours Act 1964, s 42(6)
(subject to transitional or saving
provisions); Companies
Act 1985, ss 716, 717, 744
(definition of 'authorised
institution'), 746, Schs 2, 4, 9,
11, 22 (entry relating to
ss 384–393), 24 (except entries
relating to ss 245(1), (2), 365(3),
389(10)) (subject to transitional
or saving provisions); Insolvency
Act 1985, Sch 6, paras 23, 45;
Insolvency Act 1986, Sch 13,
Pt 1 (entries relating to ss 222(4),
225); Financial Services
Act 1986, Sch 16, para 22)
(SI 1990/355)

31 May 1990 (repeals of or in
Companies Act 1985, ss 201,
202(1), 209(1)(j)) (SI 1990/713)

31 Jul 1990 (repeals of or in
Companies Act 1985, s 651(1),
Sch 22 (entry relating to s 36(4));
Building Societies Act 1986,
Schs 15, 18) (SI 1990/1392)

1 Oct 1990 (repeals of or in
Companies Act 1985, ss 466(2),
733(3), Sch 22 (entries relating
to ss 363–365), Sch 24 (entries
relating to s 365(3)); Insolvency
Act 1986, Sch 13, Pt I (entry
relating to s 733(3))
(SI 1990/1707)[6]

7 Jan 1991 (repeals of or in
Companies Act 1985, s 708(1)(b),
Sch 15, 24 (entries relating to
s 245(1), (2))) (SI 1990/2569)[2,6]

1 Jul 1991 (repeal of Companies
Act 1985, ss 712, 715)
(SI 1991/488)

Companies Act 1989 (c 40)—*contd*
Schedule
24—*contd*

> 1 Oct 1991 (repeals of or in Companies Act 1985, ss 389, 460(1); Financial Services Act 1986, s 196(3); Income and Corporation Taxes Act 1988, s 565(6)(b)) (SI 1991/1996)
>
> 1 Nov 1991 (repeals of or in Companies Act 1985, ss 169(5), 175(6)(b), 191(1), (3)(a), (b), 219(1), 288(3), 318(7), 356(1), (2), (4), 383(1)–(3), Sch 13, para 25) (SI 1991/1996)
>
> 3 Jul 1995 (repeals of or in Companies Act 1985, ss 464(5)(c), 744 (definition "annual return")) (SI 1995/1352)
>
> *Not in force* (otherwise)

Note: erroneous repeal of Financial Services Act 1986, s 199(1), by s 212, Sch 24, brought into force on 21 Feb 1990 by SI 1990/142, art 7(d), was revoked by SI 1990/355, art 16, as from 1 Mar 1990

[1] Subject to transitional and saving provisions set out in SI 1990/355, arts 6–9, Sch 2, as amended by SI 1990/2569, art 8, SI 1993/3246, reg 5(2), the principal effect being (with certain exceptions) that the existing rules relating to accounts and reports of companies continue to apply for financial years of a company commencing before 23 Dec 1989

[2] Subject to transitional and saving provisions set out in SI 1990/2569, arts 6, 7

[3] Subject to transitional and saving provisions set out in SI 1990/355, art 10, Sch 4, as amended by SI 1990/1707, art 8, with regard to annual returns and auditors

[4] Subject to transitional and saving provisions set out in SI 1991/488, arts 3, 4

[5] Subject to the saving provision set out in SI 1990/1392, art 5

[6] Subject to transitional and saving provisions set out in SI 1990/1707, arts 4–6

[7] Subject to the transitional provisions set out in SI 1990/1392, art 6

[8] Subject to saving provisions set out in SI 1991/878, art 3

[9] Subject to the saving provision set out in SI 1990/1392, art 7

[10] See, as to transitional and savings provisions, SI 1990/355, art 8, Sch 3

[11] Orders made under Coal Industry Act 1994, s 68, bringing the prospective repeal into force will be noted to that Act

---

Consolidated Fund Act 1989 (c 2)

Whole Act repealed

Consolidated Fund (No 2) Act 1989 (c 46)

Whole Act repealed

Continental Shelf Act 1989 (c 35)

RA: 27 Jul 1989

27 Jul 1989 (RA)

Control of Pollution (Amendment) Act 1989 (c 14)

RA: 6 Jul 1989

Commencement provisions: s 11(2); Control of Pollution (Amendment) Act 1989 (Commencement) Order 1991, SI 1991/1618

Section		
1	(1), (2)	1 Apr 1992 (SI 1991/1618)
	— (3)	16 Jul 1991 (SI 1991/1618)
	(4)–(6)	1 Apr 1992 (SI 1991/1618)
2		16 Jul 1991 (SI 1991/1618)
3		16 Jul 1991 (so far as relates to making of regulations) (SI 1991/1618)
		14 Oct 1991 (otherwise) (SI 1991/1618)
4	(1)–(5)	14 Oct 1991 (SI 1991/1618)
	(6)	16 Jul 1991 (SI 1991/1618)
	(7), (8)	14 Oct 1991 (SI 1991/1618)
	(9)	Inserted by Environment Act 1995, s 120(1), Sch 22, para 37(1), (3) (qv)
5	(1), (2)	1 Apr 1992 (SI 1991/1618)
	(3)	16 Jul 1991 (so far as relates to making of regulations) (SI 1991/1618)
		1 Apr 1992 (otherwise) (SI 1991/1618)
	(4), (5)	1 Apr 1992 (SI 1991/1618)
	(6)	16 Jul 1991 (so far as relates to making of regulations) (SI 1991/1618)
		1 Apr 1992 (otherwise) (SI 1991/1618)
	(7)	1 Apr 1992 (SI 1991/1618)
6		16 Jul 1991 (so far as relates to making of regulations) (SI 1991/1618)
		14 Oct 1991 (otherwise) (SI 1991/1618)
7		14 Oct 1991 (SI 1991/1618)
8–10		16 Jul 1991 (SI 1991/1618)
10A		Inserted by Environment Act 1995, s 118(1) (qv)
11		16 Jul 1991 (SI 1991/1618)

Control of Smoke Pollution Act 1989 (c 17)

Whole Act repealed

Dangerous Dogs Act 1989 (c 30)

RA: 27 Jul 1989

Commencement provisions: s 2(4)

27 Aug 1989 (s 2(4))

Disabled Persons (Northern Ireland) Act 1989 (c 10)

RA: 25 May 1989

Commencement provisions: s 12(2); Disabled Persons (1989 Act) (Commencement No 1) Order (Northern Ireland) 1989, SR 1989/474; Disabled Persons (1989 Act) (Commencement No 2) Order (Northern Ireland) 1990, SR 1990/456

Section		
1–3		*Not in force*
4		1 Apr 1991 (except para (b)) (SR 1990/456)
		Not in force (exception noted above)
5, 6		1 Apr 1991 (SR 1990/456)
7		*Not in force*
8	(1)	1 Apr 1991 (SR 1990/456)
	(2), (3)	*Not in force*
9, 10		7 Dec 1989 (SR 1989/474)
11	(1)	7 Dec 1989 (SR 1989/474)
	(1A)	Inserted by Children (Northern Ireland) Order 1995, SI 1995/755 (NI 2), art 185(1), Sch 9, para 170(2)
	(2), (3)	7 Dec 1989 (SR 1989/474)
	(4)	1 Apr 1991 (SR 1990/456)
12		7 Dec 1989 (SR 1989/474)

Dock Work Act 1989 (c 13)

RA: 3 Jul 1989

Commencement provisions: s 8(3), (4); National Dock Labour Board (Date of Dissolution) Order 1990, SI 1990/1158

Section		
1–6		3 Jul 1989 (s 8(3))
7	(1)	See Sch 1 below
	(2), (3)	3 Jul 1989 (s 8(3))
	(4)	Repealed
	(5)	3 Jul 1989 (s 8(3))
8		3 Jul 1989 (s 8(3))
Schedule		
1, Pt	I	3 Jul 1989 (s 8(3))
	II	30 Jun 1990 (SI 1990/1158)
2		3 Jul 1989 (s 8(3))

Elected Authorities (Northern Ireland) Act 1989 (c 3)

RA: 15 Mar 1989

Commencement provisions: s 13(2); Elected Authorities (Northern Ireland) Act 1989
(Commencement No 1) Order 1989, SI 1989/1093

Section		
1	(1)	Substituted for original sub-ss (1), (2) by Representation of the People Act 2000, s 8, Sch 3, paras 1, 2 (qv)
	(2)	Substituted as noted to sub-s (1) ante
	(3), (4)	15 Mar 1989 (RA)
2–4		15 Mar 1989 (RA)
5		*Not in force*
6, 7		15 Mar 1989 (RA)
8	(1)	15 Mar 1989 (RA)
	(2)	*Not in force*
9–13		15 Mar 1989 (RA)
Schedule		
1		15 Mar 1989 (so far as relates to Representation of the People Act 1983, ss 3, 4) (RA)
		27 Jun 1989 (so far as relates to Representation of the People Act 1983, ss 53, 201, 202(1), Sch 2) (SI 1989/1093)
		1 Aug 1989 (otherwise except so far as relates to Representation of the People Act 1983, ss 49, 50) (SI 1989/1093)
		16 Feb 1990 (so far as relates to Representation of the People Act 1983, ss 49, 50) (SI 1989/1093)
2, 3		15 Mar 1989 (RA)

Electricity Act 1989 (c 29)

RA: 27 Jul 1989

Commencement provisions: s 113(2); Electricity Act 1989 (Commencement No 1) Order 1989, SI 1989/1369; Electricity Act 1989 (Commencement No 2) Order 1990, SI 1990/117; Electricity Act 1989 (Commencement No 3) Order 2001, SI 2001/3419

Section	
1, 2	Repealed
3	Substituted by Utilities Act 2000, s 13 (qv)
3A–3D	Inserted by Utilities Act 2000, ss 13–16 (qv)
4	31 Mar 1990 (SI 1990/117)
5	Substituted by Utilities Act 2000, s 29 (qv)

Electricity Act 1989 (c 29)—*contd*

Section

6, 6A, 6B	Substituted by Utilities Act 2000, s 30 (qv)
7	31 Mar 1990 (SI 1990/117)
7A, 7B	Inserted by Utilities Act 2000, ss 41, 72 (qv)
8	31 Mar 1990 (SI 1990/117)
8A	Inserted by Utilities Act 2000, s 33(3) (qv)
9–11	31 Mar 1990 (SI 1990/117)
11A	Inserted by Utilities Act 2000, s 35 (qv)
12–14	31 Mar 1990 (SI 1990/117)
14A	Inserted by Utilities Act 2000, s 39 (qv)
15	31 Mar 1990 (SI 1990/117)
15A	Inserted by Utilities Act 2000, s 68, (qv)
16	Substituted by Utilities Act 2000, s 44 (qv)
16A	Inserted by Utilities Act 2000, s 44 (qv)
17	Substituted by Utilities Act 2000, s 44 (qv)
18	Repealed
19, 20	31 Mar 1990 (SI 1990/117)
21, 22	Substituted by Utilities Act 2000, ss 48, 49 (qv)
23–27	31 Mar 1990 (SI 1990/117)
27A–27F	Inserted by Utilities Act 2000, s 59(1) (qv)
28–31	31 Mar 1990 (SI 1990/117)
32	Substituted by Utilities Act 2000, s 62 (qv)
32A–32C	Inserted by Utilities Act 2000, ss 63–65 (qv)
33	Repealed
34–39	31 Mar 1990 (SI 1990/117)
39A, 39B	Inserted by Utilities Act 2000, s 54(2) (qv)
40	31 Mar 1990 (SI 1990/117)
40A–40C	Inserted by Utilities Act 2000, ss 55, 56, 61 (qv)
41	31 Mar 1990 (SI 1990/117)
41A	Inserted by Utilities Act 2000, s 70 (qv)
42	31 Mar 1990 (SI 1990/117)
42A	Substituted by Utilities Act 2000, s 58 (qv)
42AA	Inserted by Utilities Act 2000, s 20(6) (qv)
42B	Repealed
42C	Inserted by Utilities Act 2000, s 61 (qv)
43	31 Mar 1990 (SI 1990/117)
43A, 43B	Inserted by Utilities Act 2000, s 69 (qv)

Electricity Act 1989 (c 29)—*contd*
Section

44		Substituted by Utilities Act 2000, s 73(1) (qv)
44A		Prospectively inserted by Competition and Service (Utilities) Act 1992, s 23[1]
45		Repealed
46		Substituted by Utilities Act 2000, s 22(2) (qv)
46A		Inserted by Utilities Act 2000, s 23(2) (qv)
47–49		31 Mar 1990 (SI 1990/117)
49A		Inserted by Utilities Act 2000, s 42 (qv)
50–55		Repealed
56		31 Mar 1990 (SI 1990/117)
56A–56G		Inserted by Utilities Act 2000, ss 18(6), 43 (qv)
57		Repealed
58–63		31 Mar 1990 (SI 1990/117)
64		1 Oct 1989 (definition 'prescribed' for purposes of Schs 14, 15) (SI 1989/1369) 31 Mar 1990 (otherwise) (SI 1990/117)
65–69		1 Oct 1989 (SI 1989/1369)
70		See Sch 10 below
71–84		31 Mar 1990 (SI 1990/117)
85		1 Mar 1990 (SI 1990/117)
86		1 Sep 1989 (SI 1989/1369)
87, 88		31 Mar 1990 (SI 1990/117)
89		1 Oct 1989 (SI 1989/1369)
90		See Sch 11 below
91, 92		1 Oct 1989 (SI 1989/1369)
93		31 Mar 1990 (SI 1990/117)
94, 95		1 Oct 1989 (SI 1989/1369)
96		31 Mar 1990 (SI 1990/117)
97		See Sch 12 below
98, 99		31 Mar 1990 (SI 1990/117)
100	(1)	31 Mar 1990 (SI 1990/117)
	(2)–(6)	31 Mar 1990 (SI 1990/117); repealed (1 Mar 2005) by Competition Act 1989 (Transitional, Consequential and Supplemental Provisions) Order 2000, SI 2000/311, art 23
101–103		31 Mar 1990 (SI 1990/117)
104		See Sch 14 below
105		See Sch 15 below
106, 107		1 Sep 1989 (SI 1989/1369)
108, 109		31 Mar 1990 (SI 1990/117)
110, 111		1 Sep 1989 (SI 1989/1369)

Electricity Act 1989 (c 29)—*contd*

Section

112	(1)–(3)		31 Mar 1990 (SI 1990/117)
	(4)		See Sch 18 below
113			1 Sep 1989 (SI 1989/1369)

Schedule

1, 2			Repealed
3–5			31 Mar 1990 (SI 1990/117)
6			Substituted by Utilities Act 2000, s 51(2), Sch 4 (qv)
7–9			31 Mar 1990 (SI 1990/117)
10			1 Oct 1989 (SI 1989/1369)
11			31 Mar 1990 (SI 1990/117)
12			1 Oct 1989 (SI 1989/1369)
13			31 Mar 1990 (SI 1990/117)
14, 15			1 Oct 1989 (SI 1989/1369)
16			31 Mar 1990 (SI 1990/117)
17, para	1, 2		31 Mar 1990 (SI 1990/117)
	3	(a)	31 Mar 1990 (SI 1990/117)
		(b)	9 Nov 2001 (SI 2001/3419)
	4–40		31 Mar 1990 (SI 1990/117)
18			31 Mar 1990 (except repeals of or in Electricity Act 1947, ss 1(2), (3), 3(1), (7), (8), 64(3), (4), 67(1), 69, Sch 1, column 1; Electricity Act 1957, ss 2(1), 3(1), (6), (7), 40(1), 42, Sch 4, Pt I; House of Commons Disqualification Act 1975, Sch 1, Pt II; Electricity (Scotland) Act 1979, s 1, Sch 1, paras 2–6; National Audit Act 1983, Sch 4; Income and Corporation Taxes Act 1988, s 511(1)–(3), (6)) (SI 1990/117) 9 Nov 2001 (exceptions noted above) (SI 2001/3419)

---

[1] Orders made under Competition and Service (Utilities) Act 1992, s 56, bringing the prospective insertion into force will be noted to that Act

---

Employment Act 1989 (c 38)

RA: 16 Nov 1989

Commencement provisions: s 30(2)–(4); Employment Act 1989 (Commencement and Transitional Provisions) Order 1990, SI 1990/189; Employment Act 1989 (Commencement No 2) Order 1997, SI 1997/134

Section

1–7			16 Jan 1990 (s 30(3))
8			16 Nov 1989 (s 30(2))
9	(1), (2)		16 Jan 1990 (s 30(3))

Employment Act 1989 (c 38)—*contd*

Section

9	(3)	26 Feb 1990 (SI 1990/189)
	(4)–(6)	16 Jan 1990 (s 30(3))
10	(1), (2)	See Sch 3 below
	(3)–(6)	16 Nov 1989 (s 30(2))
11, 12		16 Nov 1989 (s 30(2))
13–20		Repealed
21		16 Jan 1990 (s 30(3))
22–28		16 Nov 1989 (s 30(2))
29	(1), (2)	16 Nov 1989 (s 30(2))
	(3)	See Sch 6 below
	(4)	See Sch 7 below
	(5)	See Sch 8 below
	(6)	See Sch 9 below
30		16 Nov 1989 (s 30(2))

Schedule

1, 2		16 Jan 1990 (s 30(3))
3, Pt	I, II	16 Jan 1990 (except repeals of or in Employment of Women, Young Persons and Children Act 1920, s 1(3), Sch, Pt II; Factories Act 1961, s 119A) (s 30(3))
		26 Feb 1990 (repeals of or in Employment of Women, Young Persons and Children Act 1920, s 1(3), Sch, Pt II) (SI 1990/189)
		3 Mar 1997 (otherwise) (SI 1997/134)
	III	16 Jan 1990 (s 30(3))
4, 5		16 Nov 1989 (s 30(2))
6, para	1, 2	26 Feb 1990 (SI 1990/189)
	3–5	Repealed
	6	3 Mar 1997 (SI 1997/134)
	7, 8	16 Jan 1990 (s 30(3))
	9–12	16 Nov 1989 (s 30(2))
	13	Repealed
	14, 15	16 Nov 1989 (s 30(2))
	16	16 Jan 1990 (s 30(3))
	17–26	Repealed
	27–29	16 Nov 1989 (s 30(2))
	30	16 Jan 1990 (s 30(3))
7, Pt	I	16 Nov 1989 (s 30(2))
	II	16 Jan 1990 (s 30(3))
	III	26 Feb 1990 (except repeals of or in Factories Act 1961, s 119A; Employment Medical Advisory Service Act 1972, s 5(1), s 8(1) (so far as relates to Factories Act 1961, s 119A); Employment and Training Act 1973, Sch 3, para 6) (SI 1990/189)

Employment Act 1989 (c 38)—*contd*

Schedule

7, Pt	III—*contd*	3 Mar 1997 (otherwise) (SI 1997/134)
8		16 Jan 1990 (s 30(3))
9		16 Nov 1989 (s 30(2))

Extradition Act 1989 (c 33)

RA: 27 Jul 1989

Commencement provisions: s 38(2), (3)

Section

1–6			27 Sep 1989 (s 38(2))
7	(1), (2)		27 Sep 1989 (s 38(2))
	(2A)		Inserted by Criminal Justice and Public Order Act 1994, s 158(1), (3) (qv)
	(3)		27 Jul 1989 (s 38(3))
	(4)–(6)		27 Sep 1989 (s 38(2))
	(7)		Inserted by Criminal Justice and Public Order Act 1994, s 168(1), Sch 9, para 37(1) (qv)
8, 9			27 Sep 1989 (s 38(2))
10	(1), (2)		27 Sep 1989 (s 38(2))
	(3)		27 Jul 1989 (s 38(3))
	(4)–(13)		27 Sep 1989 (s 38(2))
	(14)		Inserted (1 Jul 1997) by Hong Kong (Extradition) Order 1997, SI 1997/1178, art 2, Schedule, para 7, subject to transitional provisions
11–13			27 Sep 1989 (s 38(2))
14	(1)		27 Sep 1989 (s 38(2))
	(2), (3)		27 Jul 1989 (s 38(3))
	(4)		27 Sep 1989 (s 38(2))
15–19			27 Sep 1989 (s 38(2))
19A			Inserted (1 Jul 1997) by Hong Kong (Extradition) Order 1997, SI 1997/1178, art 2, Schedule, para 10, subject to transitional provisions
20–37			27 Sep 1989 (s 38(2))
38			27 Jul 1989 (s 38(3))
Schedule			
1, para	1–8		27 Sep 1989 (s 38(3))
	9	(1)	27 Sep 1989 (s 38(2))
		(2)	27 Jul 1989 (s 38(3))
		(3), (4)	27 Sep 1989 (s 38(2))
	10–20		27 Sep 1989 (s 38(2))
2			27 Sep 1989 (s 38(2))

Fair Employment (Northern Ireland) Act 1989 (c 32)

Whole Act repealed

Finance Act 1989 (c 26)

Budget Day: 14 Mar 1989

RA: 27 Jul 1989

Details of the commencement of Finance Acts are not set out in this work

---

Football Spectators Act 1989 (c 37)

RA: 16 Nov 1989

Commencement provisions: s 27(2), (3); Football Spectators Act 1989 (Commencement No 1) Order 1990, SI 1990/690; Football Spectators Act 1989 (Commencement No 2) Order 1990, SI 1990/926; Football Spectators Act 1989 (Commencement No 3) Order 1991, SI 1991/1071; Football Spectators Act 1989 (Commencement No 4) Order 1993, SI 1993/1690

Section			
1	(1), (2)		22 Mar 1990 (SI 1990/690)
	(3)		*Not in force*
	(4)	(a)	22 Mar 1990 (SI 1990/690)
		(b)	*Not in force*
	(5), (6)		*Not in force*
	(7), (8)		22 Mar 1990 (SI 1990/690)
	(8A)		Inserted by Football (Offences and Disorder) Act 1999, s 2(3) (qv)
	(9)–(11)		22 Mar 1990 (SI 1990/690)
2–7			*Not in force*
8			1 Jun 1990 (SI 1990/690)
9			1 Aug 1993 (SI 1993/1690)
10	(1)–(5)		1 Jun 1990 (SI 1990/690)
	(6), (7)		*Not in force*
	(8)	(a), (b)	1 Jun 1990 (SI 1990/690)
		(c)	*Not in force*
	(9)–(11)		1 Jun 1990 (SI 1990/690)
	(12)	(a), (b)	*Not in force*
		(c), (d)	1 Jun 1990 (SI 1990/690)
	(13)–(17)		1 Jun 1990 (SI 1990/690)
11, 12			1 Jun 1990 (SI 1990/690)
13			3 Jun 1991 (SI 1991/1071)
14–17			Ss 14–17 substituted for new ss 14–14J by Football (Disorder) Act 2000, s 1, Sch 1, paras 1, 2 (qv)
18–21			24 Apr 1990 (SI 1990/690)
21A–21D			Inserted by Football (Disorder) Act 2000, s 1, Sch 1, paras 1, 4 (qv)

Football Spectators Act 1989 (c 37)—*contd*

Section

22	(1)	22 Mar 1990 (SI 1990/690)
	(1A)	Inserted by Football (Offences and Disorder) Act 1999, s 5(2) (qv)
	(2)–(4)	24 Apr 1990 (SI 1990/690)
	(5)	Substituted for new sub-ss (5), (5A) by Football (Offences and Disorder) Act 1999, s 5(3) (qv)
	(5A)	Inserted as noted above
	(6), (7)	24 Apr 1990 (SI 1990/690)
	(8)	Substituted by Football (Disorder) Act 2000, s 1(2), Sch 2, paras 9, 17(b) (qv)
	(9)–(11)	Substituted by Football (Offences and Disorder) Act 1999, s 5(5) (qv)
	(12)	22 Mar 1990 (SI 1990/690)
22A		Inserted by Football (Disorder) Act 2000, s 1, Sch 2, paras 9, 18 (qv)
23–26		24 Apr 1990 (SI 1990/690)
27		16 Nov 1989 (RA)

Schedule

1	Substituted by Football (Disorder) Act 2000, s 1, Sch 1, paras 1, 5 (qv)
2	1 Jun 1990 (SI 1990/690)

Hearing Aid Council (Amendment) Act 1989 (c 12)

RA: 3 Jul 1989

Commencement provisions: s 6(2)

Section

1–4	3 Sep 1989 (s 6(2))
5	1 Jan 1990 (s 6(2))
6	3 Sep 1989 (s 6(2))

Human Organ Transplants Act 1989 (c 31)

RA: 27 Jul 1989

Commencement provisions: s 7(3); Human Organ Transplants Act 1989 (Commencement) Order 1989, SI 1989/2106

Section

1		28 Jul 1989 (s 7(3))
2	(1)	1 Apr 1990 (SI 1989/2106)
	(2)–(7)	27 Jul 1989 (RA)
3–7		27 Jul 1989 (RA)

International Parliamentary Organisations (Registration) Act 1989 (c 19)

RA: 21 Jul 1989

21 Jul 1989 (RA)

Law of Property (Miscellaneous Provisions) Act 1989 (c 34)

RA: 27 Jul 1989

Commencement provisions: s 5; Law of Property (Miscellaneous Provisions) Act 1989
  (Commencement) Order 1990, SI 1990/1175

Section

1	(1)–(7)	31 Jul 1990 (SI 1990/1175)
	(8)	See Sch 1 below
	(9)–(11)	31 Jul 1990 (SI 1990/1175)
2, 3		27 Sep 1989 (s 5)
4		See Sch 2 below
5, 6		27 Jul 1989 (RA)

Schedule

1	31 Jul 1990 (SI 1990/1175)
2	27 Sep 1989 (repeal of Law of
	Property Act 1925, s 40) (s 5)
	31 Jul 1990 (otherwise) (SI 1990/1175)

Licensing (Amendment) Act 1989 (c 20)

RA: 21 Jul 1989

Commencement provisions: s 2(2)

21 Sep 1989 (s 2(2))

Local Government and Housing Act 1989 (c 42)

RA: 16 Nov 1989

Commencement provisions: ss 154(3), 195(2), (3) (and individually as noted below: passim);
  Local Government and Housing Act 1989 (Commencement No 1) Order 1989,
  SI 1989/2180; Local Government and Housing Act 1989 (Commencement No 2)
  Order 1989, SI 1989/2186; Local Government and Housing Act 1989
  (Commencement No 3) Order 1989, SI 1989/2445; Local Government and
  Housing Act 1989 (Commencement No 4) Order 1990, SI 1990/191; Local
  Government and Housing Act 1989 (Commencement No 5 and Transitional
  Provisions) Order 1990, SI 1990/431; Local Government and Housing Act 1989
  (Commencement No 6 and Miscellaneous Provisions) Order 1990, SI 1990/762;
  Local Government and Housing Act 1989 (Commencement No 7) Order 1990,
  SI 1990/961; Local Government and Housing Act 1989 (Commencement No 8
  and Transitional Provisions) Order 1990, SI 1990/1274, as amended by
  SI 1990/1335; Local Government and Housing Act 1989 (Commencement No 9
  and Saving) Order 1990, SI 1990/1552; Local Government and Housing Act 1989
  (Commencement No 10) Order 1990, SI 1990/2581; Local Government and
  Housing Act 1989 (Commencement No 11 and Savings) Order 1991, SI 1991/344;
  Local Government and Housing Act 1989 (Commencement No 12) Order 1991,
  SI 1991/953; Local Government and Housing Act 1989 (Commencement No 13)
  Order 1991, SI 1991/2940; Local Government and Housing Act 1989
  (Commencement No 14) Order 1992, SI 1992/760; Local Government and
  Housing Act 1989 (Commencement No 15) Order 1993, SI 1993/105; Local
  Government and Housing Act 1989 (Commencement No 16) Order 1993,
  SI 1993/2410; Local Government and Housing Act 1989 (Commencement No 17)
  Order 1995, SI 1995/841; Local Government and Housing Act 1989
  (Commencement No 18) Order 1996, SI 1996/1857

Local Government and Housing Act 1989 (c 42)—*contd*

Abbreviation: "orders etc" means "so far as confers on Secretary of State powers to make orders, regulations or determinations, to give or make directions, to specify matters, to require information, to impose conditions or to give guidance or approvals, or make provision with respect to the exercise of any such power"

Section

1	(1)–(4)	1 Mar 1990 (SI 1989/2445)
	(5), (6)	29 Nov 1989 (SI 1989/2186)
	(7), (8)	1 Mar 1990 (SI 1989/2445)
2		29 Nov 1989 (SI 1989/2186)
3		16 Nov 1989 (RA)
4, 5		16 Jan 1990 (ss 4(7), 5(9))
5A		Inserted (11 Jul 2001) by Local Authorities (Executive and Alternative Arrangements) (Modification of Enactments and Other Provisions) (England) Order 2001, SI 2001/2237 (E)
6, 7		16 Jan 1990 (ss 6(8), 7(3))
8		16 Nov 1989 (RA)
9		16 Jan 1990 (orders etc) (SI 1989/2445)
		1 Aug 1990 (E, W) (otherwise) (SI 1990/1552)
		Not in force (S) (otherwise)
10		1 Apr 1990 (SI 1990/431)
11		16 Nov 1989 (RA; note s 11(4))
12		16 Jan 1990 (s 12(3))
13		16 Jan 1990 (orders etc) (SI 1989/2445)
		1 Aug 1990 (so far as not already in force, except in relation to a parish or community council until 1 Jan 1991) (SI 1990/1552)
14		16 Jan 1990 (orders etc) (SI 1989/2445)
		Not in force (otherwise)
15		16 Jan 1990 (orders etc) (SI 1989/2445)
		1 Aug 1990 (E, W) (otherwise) (SI 1990/1552)
		Not in force (S) (otherwise)
16		1 Aug 1990 (E, W) (SI 1990/1552)
		Not in force (S)
17		16 Jan 1990 (orders etc) (SI 1989/2445)
		1 Aug 1990 (E, W) (otherwise) (SI 1990/1552)
		Not in force (S) (otherwise)
18		16 Jan 1990 (SI 1989/2445)
19		16 Jan 1990 (orders etc) (SI 1989/2445)

Local Government and Housing Act 1989 (c 42)—*contd*

Section

19—*contd*		8 May 1992 (otherwise) (SI 1992/760); prospectively repealed (S) by Ethical Standards in Public Life etc (Scotland) Act 2000 (asp 7), s 36, Sch 4[2]; prospectively repealed (E, W) by Local Government Act 2000, s 107, Sch 5, para 25, Sch 6[3]
20		16 Jan 1990 (SI 1989/2445)
21		16 Nov 1989 (RA)
22		16 Jan 1990 (SI 1989/2445)
23		1 Apr 1990 (SI 1990/431)
24		16 Nov 1989 (RA) (note s 24(3))
25–29		1 Apr 1990 (SI 1990/431)
30	(1)	3 May 1990 (SI 1990/961)
	(2)	3 May 1990 (so far as amends Local Government Act 1972, s 83(1)) (SI 1990/961)
		1 Jan 1991 (otherwise) (SI 1990/2581)
31		16 Jan 1990 (SI 1989/2445); prospectively repealed (E, W) by Local Government Act 2000, s 107, Sch 5, para 26, Sch 6[3]
32		3 May 1990 (SI 1990/961)
33–35		Repealed (E, W) by Local Government Act 2000, s 107, Sch 5, para 27; Sch 6, as from 28 Jul 2001[4]
36		16 Jan 1990 (orders etc) (SI 1989/2445)
		1 Apr 1990 (otherwise) (SI 1990/431)
37, 38		1 Apr 1990 (SI 1990/431)
39–66		16 Jan 1990 (SI 1989/2445)
67–70		16 Jan 1990 (orders etc) (SI 1989/2445)
		7 Oct 1993 (otherwise) (SI 1993/2410)
71	(1)	16 Jan 1990 (orders etc) (SI 1989/2445)
		1 Apr 1995 (for purposes of sub-ss (4)–(6) only) (SI 1995/841)
		Not in force (otherwise)
	(2), (3)	16 Jan 1990 (orders etc) (SI 1989/2445)
		Not in force (otherwise)
	(4)	16 Jan 1990 (orders etc) (SI 1989/2445)
		1 Apr 1995 (subject to a transitional provision) (otherwise) (SI 1995/841)
	(5)	16 Jan 1990 (orders etc) (SI 1989/2445)
		1 Apr 1995 (for purposes of para (a) only) (subject to a transitional provision) (SI 1995/841)
		Not in force (otherwise)
	(6)	16 Jan 1990 (orders etc) (SI 1989/2445)
		1 Apr 1995 (otherwise) (SI 1995/841)

Local Government and Housing Act 1989 (c 42)—*contd*

Section

71	(7)	16 Jan 1990 (orders etc) (SI 1989/2445)
		Not in force (otherwise)
	(8)	16 Jan 1990 (orders etc) (SI 1989/2445)
		1 Apr 1995 (SI 1995/841) (otherwise)
72		16 Jan 1990 (orders etc) (SI 1989/2445)
		7 Oct 1993 (otherwise) (SI 1993/2410)
73		7 Oct 1993 (SI 1993/2410)
74		16 Nov 1989 (RA)
75		See Sch 4 below
76–78		16 Nov 1989 (RA)
78A, 78B		Inserted by Housing Act 1996, s 222, Sch 18, Pt II, para 4 (qv)
79, 80		16 Nov 1989 (RA)
80A		Inserted by Housing Act 1996, s 222, Sch 18, Pt II, para 5 (qv)
81		Repealed
82–88		16 Nov 1989 (RA)
89–92		16 Jan 1990 (orders etc) (SI 1989/2445)
		1 Apr 1990 (otherwise) (SI 1990/431)
93, 94		1 Apr 1990 (SI 1990/431)
95, 96		16 Jan 1990 (orders etc) (SI 1989/2445)
		1 Apr 1990 (otherwise) (SI 1990/431)
97		1 Apr 1990 (SI 1990/431)
98		16 Jan 1990 (orders etc) (SI 1989/2445)
		1 Apr 1990 (otherwise) (SI 1990/431)
99		16 Jan 1990 (SI 1989/2445)
100		1 Apr 1990 (SI 1990/431)
101–138		Repealed
139		See Sch 5 below
140, 141		Repealed (with savings)
142		1 Dec 1989 (for purposes of, and in relation to, financial year 1990–91 and each subsequent financial year) (SI 1989/2180); prospectively repealed by Local Government Finance Act 1992, s 117(2), Sch 14[1]
143, 144		1 Dec 1989 (SI 1989/2180); prospectively repealed by Local Government Finance Act 1992, s 117(2), Sch 14[1]
145		See Sch 6 below
146		Repealed
147–149		16 Nov 1989 (RA)
150–152		16 Jan 1990 (s 152(7))
153		16 Nov 1989 (RA)
154		1 Jan 1992 (SI 1991/2940)
155		1 Apr 1990 (s 155(7))
156		1 Apr 1990 (SI 1990/431)
157, 158		16 Nov 1989 (RA)

Local Government and Housing Act 1989 (c 42)—*contd*

Section

159			1 Dec 1989 (SI 1989/2180)
160			Repealed
161			16 Nov 1989 (RA)
162			16 Jan 1990 (SI 1989/2445)
163			16 Nov 1989 (RA)
164			Repealed
165	(1)		See Sch 9 below
	(2)		1 Apr 1990 (SI 1990/431)
	(3)–(9)		1 Mar 1990 (SI 1990/191)
166			16 Nov 1989 (RA)
167, 168			16 Jan 1990 (SI 1989/2445)
169	(1)		1 Apr 1990 (SI 1990/431)
	(2)	(a)	1 Apr 1990 (SI 1990/431)
		(b), (c)	1 Jul 1990 (SI 1990/1274)
		(d)	Substituted by Housing Grants, Construction and Regeneration Act 1996, s 103, Sch 1, para 15 (qv)
	(3)–(9)		1 Apr 1990 (SI 1990/431)
170			1 Apr 1990 (SI 1989/2180)
171			16 Jan 1990 (SI 1989/2445)
172	(1)–(5)		1 Mar 1990 (SI 1989/2445)
	(6)–(8)		16 Jan 1990 (SI 1989/2445)
	(9)		1 Mar 1990 (SI 1989/2445)
173			1 Mar 1990 (SI 1989/2445)
174			Repealed
175			16 Jan 1990 (SI 1989/2445)
176			16 Jan 1990 (SI 1989/2180)
177			16 Jan 1990 (SI 1989/2180); prospectively repealed by Housing (Scotland) Act 2001, s 112, Sch 10, para 16[5]
178			16 Jan 1990 (SI 1989/2180)
179			1 Dec 1989 (SI 1989/2180); prospectively repealed by Housing (Scotland) Act 2001, s 112, Sch 10, para 16[5]
180			16 Jan 1990 (SI 1989/2445)
181			16 Nov 1989 (RA); prospectively repealed by Housing (Scotland) Act 2001, s 112, Sch 10, para 16[5]
182			16 Jan 1990 (S) (SI 1989/2445) Repealed (E, W)
183			1 Apr 1990 (SI 1990/431)
184			16 Nov 1989 (RA)
185			16 Jan (SI 1989/2180)
186			1 Apr 1990 (SI 1990/431)
187			16 Nov 1989 (RA)
188			Repealed
189			16 Nov 1989 (RA)

Local Government and Housing Act 1989 (c 42)—*contd*

Section

190–193		16 Nov 1989 (RA)
194	(1)	See Sch 11 below
	(2)–(4)	See Sch 12 below
195		16 Nov 1989 (RA)

Schedule

1		16 Jan 1990 (orders etc) (SI 1989/2445)
		1 Aug 1990 (E, W) (otherwise) (SI 1990/1552)
		Not in force (S) (otherwise)
2		16 Jan 1990 (orders etc) (SI 1989/2445)
		1 Apr 1990 (otherwise) (SI 1990/431)
3		16 Jan 1990 (SI 1989/2445)
4		16 Nov 1989 (RA)
5, para	1★	16 Nov 1989 (RA)
	2–18	Repealed
	19–32★	16 Nov 1989 (RA)
	33★	Repealed
	34–42★	16 Nov 1989 (RA)
	43	Repealed
	44–48★	16 Nov 1989 (RA)
	49–54	Repealed
	55★	16 Nov 1989 (RA)
	56	Repealed
	57★	16 Nov 1989 (RA)
	58, 59	Repealed
	60	16 Jan 1990 (SI 1989/2445)
	61	Repealed
	62★	16 Nov 1989 (RA)
	63–65	Repealed
	66	16 Jan 1990 (para 79(1))
	67–69★	16 Nov 1989 (RA)
	70, 71	Repealed
	72★	16 Nov 1989 (RA)
	73, 74	Repealed
	75, 76★	16 Nov 1989 (RA)
	77, 78	Repealed
	79, 80★	16 Nov 1989 (RA)
6, para	1, 2	1 Apr 1990 (SI 1989/2180)
	3, 4	1 Dec 1989 (for purposes of, and in relation to, financial year 1990–91 and each subsequent financial year) (SI 1989/2180)
	5, 6	1 Dec 1989 (SI 1989/2180)
	7, 8	Repealed
	9	1 Apr 1990 (SI 1989/2180)
	10	1 Apr 1990 (SI 1989/2180); prospectively repealed by Local Government Finance Act 1992, s 117(2), Sch 14[1]

Local Government and Housing Act 1989 (c 42)—*contd*

Schedule

6, para	11, 12		1 Dec 1989 (SI 1989/2180); prospectively repealed by Local Government Finance Act 1992, s 117(2), Sch 14[1]
	13–15		1 Apr 1990 (SI 1989/2180); prospectively repealed by Local Government Finance Act 1992, s 117(2), Sch 14[1]
	16–21		Repealed
	22		1 Apr 1990 (SI 1989/2180); prospectively repealed by Local Government Finance Act 1992, s 117(2), Sch 14[1]
	23		1 Dec 1989 (SI 1989/2180); prospectively repealed (S) by Ethical Standards in Public Life etc (Scotland) Act 2000 (asp 7), s 36, Sch 4[2]
	24–27		1 Dec 1989 (SI 1989/2180); prospectively repealed by Local Government Finance Act 1992, s 117(2), Sch 14[1]
	28, 29		1 Dec 1989 (for purposes of, and in relation to, financial year 1990–91 and each subsequent financial year) (SI 1989/2180); prospectively repealed by Local Government Finance Act 1992, s 117(2), Sch 14[1]
7			16 Nov 1989 (RA)
8			Repealed
9, para	1	(1)–(5)	1 Apr 1990 (SI 1990/431)
		(6)	1 Jul 1990 (SI 1990/1274)
	2		1 Apr 1990 (SI 1990/431)
	3		1 Jul 1990 (SI 1990/1274)
	4–43		1 Apr 1990 (SI 1990/431)
	44		16 Jan 1990 (for purposes of Housing Act 1985, s 369) (SI 1989/2445)
			1 Apr 1990 (otherwise) (SI 1990/431)
	45–47		Repealed
	48–55		1 Apr 1990 (SI 1990/431)
	56	(1), (2)	16 Jan 1990 (SI 1989/2445)
		(3), (4)	1 Apr 1990 (SI 1990/431)
	57, 58		1 Jul 1990 (SI 1990/1274)
	59		1 Apr 1990 (SI 1990/431)
	60		1 Jul 1990 (SI 1990/1274)
	61, 62		1 Apr 1990 (SI 1990/431)
	63		Repealed
	64, 65		1 Jul 1990 (SI 1990/1274)
	66		Repealed

Local Government and Housing Act 1989 (c 42)—*contd*

Schedule

9, para	67–70		1 Apr 1990 (SI 1990/431)
	71	(a), (b)	1 Apr 1990 (SI 1990/431)
		(c), (d)	1 Jul 1990 (SI 1990/1274)
	72–83		1 Apr 1990 (SI 1990/431)
	84		16 Jan 1990 (orders etc) (SI 1989/2445)
			1 Apr 1990 (otherwise) (SI 1990/431)
	85		1 Apr 1990 (except so far as relating to Housing Act 1985, s 605(1)(e)) (SI 1990/431)
			1 Jul 1990 (exception noted above) (SI 1990/1274)
	86–91		1 Apr 1990 (SI 1990/431)
10			1 Apr 1990 (SI 1990/431)
11, para	1, 2		1 Apr 1990 (SI 1990/431)
	3		*Not in force*
	4		Repealed
	5–13		1 Apr 1990 (SI 1990/431)[6]
	14		25 Jan 1993 (SI 1993/105)
	15		Repealed (*never in force*)
	16		1 Apr 1990 (SI 1990/431)
	17, 18		*Not in force*
	19, 20		Repealed
	21		*Not in force*
	22, 23		1 Apr 1990 (SI 1990/431); prospectively repealed (E, W) by Local Government Act 2000, s 107, Sch 6[2]
	24, 25		*Not in force*
	26		27 Feb 1991 (in relation only to power to make regulations relating to prescribed amount in Local Government Act 1972, s 173(1)) (SI 1991/344)
			1 Apr 1991 (otherwise) (SI 1991/344)
	27		1 Apr 1990 (orders etc) (SI 1990/431)
			1 Apr 1991 (otherwise) (SI 1991/344)
	28	(1), (2)	1 Jul 1990 (orders etc) (SI 1990/1274)
			1 Apr 1991 (otherwise) (SI 1991/344)
		(3)	16 Jan 1990 (orders etc) (SI 1989/2445)
			1 Apr 1991 (otherwise) (SI 1991/344)
		(4)	16 Jan 1990 (SI 1989/2445)
	29		1 Apr 1991 (SI 1991/344)
	30		8 May 1992 (SI 1992/760)
	31, 32		1 Apr 1990 (SI 1990/431)
	33		1 Apr 1990 (SI 1990/431); prospectively repealed (S) by Ethical Standards in Public Life etc (Scotland) Act 2000 (asp 7), s 36, Sch 4[2]

Local Government and Housing Act 1989 (c 42)—*contd*

Schedule

11, para	34		1 Apr 1991 (SI 1991/344)
	35	(1), (2)	*Not in force*
		(3)	16 Jan 1990 (orders etc) (SI 1989/2445)
			Not in force (otherwise)
		(4)	16 Jan 1990 (SI 1989/2445)
	36		*Not in force*
	37		16 Jan 1990 (SI 1989/2445)
	38–41		1 Apr 1990 (SI 1990/431)
	42		16 Jan 1990 (SI 1989/2445)
	43		Repealed
	44–48		1 Apr 1990 (SI 1990/431)
	49		16 Jan 1990 (SI 1989/2445)
	50		1 Apr 1990 (SI 1990/431)
	51, 52		Repealed
	53	(1)	16 Jan 1990 (SI 1989/2445)
		(2)	1 Apr 1990 (SI 1990/431)
	54		1 Apr 1990 (SI 1990/431)
	55–57		*Not in force*
	58		16 Jan 1990 (SI 1989/2445)
	59		1 Apr 1990 (SI 1990/431)
	60		*Not in force*
	61		1 Dec 1989 (SI 1989/2180)
	62		1 Apr 1990 (SI 1990/431)
	63		Repealed
	64, 65		1 Apr 1990 (SI 1990/431)
	66–69		Repealed
	70–74		1 Apr 1990 (SI 1990/431)
	75, 76		Repealed
	77–81		16 Jan 1990 (SI 1989/2445)
	82		Repealed
	83, 84		16 Jan 1990 (SI 1989/2445)
	85–87		1 Apr 1990 (SI 1990/431)
	88		16 Jan 1990 (orders etc) (SI 1989/2445)
			1 Apr 1990 (otherwise) (SI 1990/431)
	89		16 Jan 1990 (SI 1989/2445)
	90, 91		1 Jul 1990 (SI 1990/1274)
	92		*Not in force*
	93, 94		16 Jan 1990 (SI 1989/2180)
	95		1 Dec 1989 (SI 1989/2180)
	96		1 Apr 1990 (SI 1990/431)
	97		*Not in force*
	98		Repealed
	99, 100		16 Jan 1990 (SI 1989/2180)
	101, 102		1 Apr 1990 (SI 1990/431)
	103		16 Jan 1990 (SI 1989/2445)
	104–106		16 Nov 1989 (RA)
	107		Repealed

Local Government and Housing Act 1989 (c 42)—*contd*

Schedule

11, para	108	1 Apr 1990 (SI 1990/431)
	109, 110	Repealed
	111, 112	16 Jan 1990 (SI 1989/2445)
	113	Repealed
12, Pt	I	1 Apr 1990 (SI 1990/431)[6]
	II	1 Dec 1989 (repeals of or in Valuation and Rating (Scotland) Act 1956, s 22(4); Local Government (Scotland) Act 1973, s 110A(2); Local Government Finance Act 1988, s 128(2), Sch 12, para 16; Housing (Scotland) Act 1988, s 2(6)) (SI 1988/2180)
		16 Jan 1990 (repeals of or in Housing (Scotland) Act 1987, s 61(10)(a)(v)) (SI 1989/2180)
		16 Jan 1990 (repeals of or in Race Relations Act 1976, s 47; Housing Act 1985, ss 107, 417–420, 423(2), 434, 459, Sch 14; Social Security Act 1986, s 30(10); Housing and Planning Act 1986, s 1; Housing (Scotland) Act 1987, s 80; Housing Act 1988, s 129(5)(b)) (SI 1989/2445)
		1 Mar 1990 (repeals of or in Housing Act 1985, ss 312–314, Sch 12 (in relation to any financial year beginning on or after 1 Apr 1990)) (SI 1990/191)
		1 Apr 1990 (repeals of or in Local Government (Financial Provisions etc) (Scotland) Act 1962, s 4(3), (4), Sch 1; Water (Scotland) Act 1980, s 40(7); Local Government Finance Act 1988, Sch 12, para 37) (SI 1989/2180)
		1 Apr 1990 (repeals of or in Land Compensation Act 1961, s 10, Sch 2; Local Government Act 1972, ss 101, 110; Land Compensation Act 1973, ss 29, 37, 39, 73; Local Government Act 1974, ss 23, 24, 25, 34; Housing Act 1974, Sch 13; Housing Act 1985, so far as not already in force *except* those of or in ss 370–372, 374, 379(1), 381(4) (figure '370'), 460–520, 524–526,

Local Government and Housing Act 1989 (c 42)—*contd*

Schedule

12, Pt   II—*contd*

567, 569); Housing (Consequential
Provisions) Act 1985, Sch 2;
Housing and Planning Act 1986,
s 42(1)(d), Sch 5; Local Government
Act 1988, s 25, Sch 3; Housing
Act 1988, s 130(2)) (SI 1990/431)[6]

1 Jul 1990 (repeals of or in Local
Authorities (Expenditure Powers)
Act 1983; Housing Act 1985,
ss 370–372, 374, 379(1), 381(4)
(figure '370'), 460–520, 567, 569)
(subject to transitional provisions)
(SI 1990/1274)

1 Aug 1990 (repeals of or in Local
Government Act 1972, s 102(3)
(except in relation to a parish or
community council until
1 Jan 1991); Local Government
Act 1985, s 33) (SI 1990/1552)

1 Apr 1991 (repeals of or in Local
Government Act 1972, ss 177,
177A, 178; Local Government
(Scotland) Act 1973, ss 45, 45A,
49A; Education Act 1980; Local
Government, Planning and Land
Act 1980; Local Government
Act 1985, Sch 14; Local
Government Act 1986; Norfolk
and Suffolk Broads Act 1988)
(SI 1991/344)

22 Jul 1996 (repeals in Education
(Grants and Awards) Act 1984;
Education (Amendment)
Act 1986) (SI 1996/1857)

Not in force (otherwise)

★Note: certain amendments made by Sch 5 above (except those made by paras 7, 8, 12,
49(3), 52, 54, 57, 60, 63, 66 or 68) to Local Government Finance Act 1988 are, by
virtue of para 79(3) thereof, retrospective in effect

[1]   Orders made under Local Government Finance Act 1992, s 119, bringing the prospective repeals
into force will be noted to that Act

[2]   Orders made under Ethical Standards in Public Life etc (Scotland) Act 2000, s 37(2), bringing the
prospective repeals into force will be noted to that Act

[3]   Orders made under Local Government Act 2000, s 108, bringing the prospective repeal into force
will be noted to that Act

[4]   The Secretary of State may by order provide for the repeals to be brought into force in relation to
England or Wales before the time appointed by s 108(4) of this Act (ie, 28 Jul 2001)

[5]   Orders made under Housing (Scotland) Act 2001, s 113, bringing the prospective repeals into force
will be noted to that Act

[6]   For savings and transitional provisions see SI 1990/431, Sch 1

National Maritime Museum Act 1989 (c 8)

RA: 5 May 1989

Commencement provisions: s 3(3); National Maritime Museum Act 1989 (Commencement) Order 1989, SI 1989/1028

7 Jul 1989 (SI 1989/1028)

Official Secrets Act 1989 (c 6)

RA: 11 May 1989

Commencement provisions: s 16(6); Official Secrets Act 1989 (Commencement) Order 1990, SI 1990/199

1 Mar 1990 (SI 1990/199)

Opticians Act 1989 (c 44)

RA: 16 Nov 1989

Commencement provisions: s 38

16 Feb 1990 (s 38)

Parking Act 1989 (c 16)

RA: 21 Jul 1989

Commencement provisions: s 5(2); Parking Act 1989 (Commencement) Order 1990, SI 1990/933

16 May 1990 (SI 1990/933)

Pesticides (Fees and Enforcement) Act 1989 (c 27)

RA: 27 Jul 1989

Commencement provisions: s 3(2)
Section

1	27 Jul 1989 (RA)
2	27 Sep 1989 (s 3(2))
3	27 Jul 1989 (RA)

Petroleum Royalties (Relief) and Continental Shelf Act 1989 (c 1)

RA: 7 Feb 1989

7 Feb 1989 (RA)

Police Officers (Central Service) Act 1989 (c 11)

RA: 3 Jul 1989

3 Jul 1989 (RA)

Prevention of Terrorism (Temporary Provisions) Act 1989 (c 4)

Whole Act repealed

Prisons (Scotland) Act 1989 (c 45)

RA: 16 Nov 1989

Commencement provisions: s 46(2)

16 Feb 1990 (s 46(2))

Representation of the People Act 1989 (c 28)

RA: 27 Jul 1989

Commencement provisions: s 8(2); Representation of the People Act 1989 (Commencement No 1) Order 1989, SI 1989/1318; Representation of the People Act 1989 (Commencement No 2) Order 1990, SI 1990/519

Section		
1–4		Repealed
5–8		1 Sep 1989 (SI 1989/1318)

Road Traffic (Driver Licensing and Information Systems) Act 1989 (c 22)

RA: 21 Jul 1989

Commencement provisions: s 17(2); Road Traffic (Driver Licensing and Information Systems) Act 1989 (Commencement No 1) Order 1989, SI 1989/1843; Road Traffic (Driver Licensing and Information Systems) Act 1989 (Commencement No 2) Order 1990, SI 1990/802; Road Traffic (Driver Licensing and Information Systems) Act 1989 (Commencement No 3) Order 1990, SI 1990/2228; Road Traffic (Driver Licensing and Information Systems) Act 1989 (Commencement No 4) Order 1990, SI 1990/2610

Section		
1	(1)–(5)	1 Apr 1991 (SI 1990/2610)
	(6)	See Sch 1 below
	(7)	1 Jun 1990 (so far as relates to definitions 'the 1981 Act', 'the 1988 Act') (SI 1990/802)
		1 Apr 1991 (otherwise) (SI 1990/2610)
2		1 Apr 1991 (SI 1990/2610)
3		1 Jun 1990 (SI 1990/802)
4		1 Apr 1991 (SI 1990/2610)
5	(1)	1 Jun 1990 (except so far as relates to s 5(5)) (SI 1990/802)
		1 Apr 1991 (exception noted above) (SI 1990/2610)
	(2)	1 Jun 1990 (SI 1990/802)
	(3)	Repealed
	(4)	1 Jun 1990 (SI 1990/802)
	(5)	1 Apr 1991 (SI 1990/2610)
	(6)–(10)	1 Jun 1990 (SI 1990/802)

**Road Traffic (Driver Licensing and Information Systems) Act 1989
(c 22)**—*contd*

Section

6			1 Dec 1990 (SI 1990/2228); prospectively repealed by Transport Act 2000, s 274, Sch 31, Pt V(1)[1]
7			See Sch 3 below
8–15			1 Jun 1990 (SI 1990/802)
16			See Sch 6 below
17			8 Nov 1989 (SI 1989/1843)

Schedule

1, para	1–9		1 Apr 1991 (SI 1990/2610)
	10		Repealed
	11		1 Jun 1990 (SI 1990/802); prospectively repealed by s 16 of, and Sch 6 to, this Act
	12		1 Apr 1991 (SI 1990/2610)
2			1 Apr 1991 (SI 1990/2610)
3, para	1–5		1 Apr 1991 (SI 1990/2610)
	6		1 Dec 1990 (SI 1990/2228)
	7		1 Jun 1990 (SI 1990/802)
	8	(a)	1 Apr 1991 (SI 1991/2610)
		(b) (i)	1 Apr 1991 (SI 1990/2610)
		(ii), (iii)	1 Jun 1990 (SI 1990/802)
		(c)–(e)	1 Apr 1991 (SI 1990/2610)
	9	(a), (c)	1 Apr 1991 (SI 1990/2610)
		(b), (d)	1 Jun 1990 (SI 1990/802)
	10		1 Dec 1990 (SI 1990/2228)
	11	(a)	Repealed
		(b)	1 Jun 1990 (SI 1990/802)
		(c)	1 Dec 1990 (SI 1990/2228)
		(d)	1 Jun 1990 (SI 1990/802)
	12	(a)	1 Apr 1991 (SI 1990/2610)
		(b), (c)	1 Jun 1990 (SI 1990/802)
	13		Spent
	14		1 Jun 1990 (SI 1990/802)
	15	(a)	1 Jun 1990 (SI 1990/802)
		(b)–(d)	1 Apr 1991 (SI 1990/2610)
		(e)	1 Jun 1990 (so far as relates to definitions 'NI driving licence', 'NI licence') (SI 1990/802) 1 Apr 1991 (so far as relates to definition 'passenger carrying vehicle') (SI 1990/2610)
		(f)	1 Jun 1990 (SI 1990/802)
		(g)	1 Dec 1990 (SI 1990/2228)
	16, 17		1 Jun 1990 (SI 1990/802)
	18	(a)	1 Apr 1991 (SI 1990/2610)
		(b)–(d)	1 Dec 1990 (SI 1990/2228); prospectively repealed by Transport Act 2000, s 274, Sch 31, Pt V(1)[1]

**Road Traffic (Driver Licensing and Information Systems) Act 1989
(c 22)**—*contd*

Schedule

3, para	19		1 Jun 1990 (SI 1990/802)
	20		1 Apr 1991 (SI 1990/2610)
	21		Repealed
	22, 23		1 Apr 1991 (SI 1990/2610)
	24, 25		1 Jun 1990 (SI 1990/802)
	26		8 Nov 1989 (SI 1989/1843)
	27	(a)–(c)	1 Apr 1991 (SI 1990/2610)
		(d)	Repealed
		(e)	1 Apr 1991 (SI 1990/2610)
	28	(a), (b)	1 Jun 1990 (SI 1990/802)
		(c), (d)	1 Apr 1991 (SI 1990/2610)
	29		8 Nov 1989 (so far as relates to offences under Sch 1, para 10(4), (5)) (SI 1989/1843)
			1 Apr 1991 (otherwise) (SI 1990/2610)
	30	(a)	1 Jun 1990 (SI 1990/802)
		(b), (c)	1 Apr 1991 (SI 1990/2610)
		(d)	8 Nov 1989 (so far as relates to offences under Sch 1, para 10(4), (5)) (SI 1989/1843)
			1 Apr 1991 (otherwise) (SI 1990/2610)
4, 5			1 Jun 1990 (SI 1990/802)
6			1 Jun 1990 (repeals of or in Road Traffic Act 1988, s 97(1); Road Traffic Offenders Act 1988, s 45(3), Sch 2, Pt I (entry relating to s 45 of that Act)) (SI 1990/802)
			1 Dec 1990 (repeals in Road Traffic Act 1988, s 97(3)) (SI 1990/2228)
			1 Apr 1991 (otherwise, except repeal of Road Traffic (Driver Licensing and Information Systems) Act 1989, Sch 1, para 11) (SI 1990/2610)
			Not in force (exception noted above)

[1] Orders made under Transport Act 2000, s 275, bringing the prospective repeals into force will be noted to that Act

---

Security Service Act 1989 (c 5)

RA: 27 Apr 1989

Commencement provisions: s 7(2); Security Service Act 1989 (Commencement) Order 1989, SI 1989/2093

18 Dec 1989 (SI 1989/2093)

Self-Governing Schools etc (Scotland) Act 1989 (c 39)

RA: 16 Nov 1989

Commencement provisions: s 81; Self-Governing Schools etc (Scotland) Act 1989 (Commencement) Order 1990, SI 1990/86; Self-Governing Schools etc (Scotland) Act 1989 (Commencement No 2) Order 1990, SI 1990/1108; Self-Governing Schools etc (Scotland) Act 1989 (Commencement No 3) Order 1997, SI 1997/391

Section		
1–12		16 Nov 1989 (s 81(1)); prospectively repealed by Standards in Scotland's Schools etc Act 2000 (asp 6), s 60(2), Sch 3[1]
13–22		Repealed
23		16 Nov 1989 (s 81(1)); prospectively repealed by Standards in Scotland's Schools etc Act 2000 (asp 6), s 60(2), Sch 3[1]
24		Repealed
25–53		16 Nov 1989 (s 81(1)); prospectively repealed by Standards in Scotland's Schools etc Act 2000 (asp 6), s 60(2), Sch 3[1]
54–66		Repealed
67		1 Feb 1990 (SI 1990/86)
68		16 Nov 1989 (s 81(1))
69	(1), (2)	1 Feb 1990 (SI 1990/86)
	(2)	1 Feb 1990 (SI 1990/86); prospectively repealed by Standards in Scotland's Schools etc Act 2000 (asp 6), s 60(2), Sch 3[1]
	(3)	Repealed
70		19 Feb 1997 (SI 1997/391)
71		16 Nov 1989 (s 81(1))
72		1 Jun 1990 (SI 1990/1108)
73–75		1 Feb 1990 (SI 1990/86)
76		1 Feb 1990 (SI 1990/86); prospectively repealed by Standards in Scotland's Schools etc Act 2000 (asp 6), s 60(2), Sch 3[1]
77–81		16 Nov 1989 (s 81(1))
82	(1)	16 Nov 1989 (s 81(1))
	(2)	1 Feb 1990 (SI 1990/86)
83		16 Nov 1989 (s 81(1))
Schedule		
1, 2		16 Nov 1989 (s 81(1)); prospectively repealed by Standards in Scotland's Schools etc Act 2000 (asp 6), s 60(2), Sch 3[1]
3–5		Repealed

Self-Governing Schools etc (Scotland) Act 1989 (c 39)—*contd*

Schedule

6		16 Nov 1989 (s 81(1)); prospectively repealed by Standards in Scotland's Schools etc Act 2000 (asp 6), s 60(2), Sch 3[1]
7–9		16 Nov 1989 (s 81(1)); prospectively repealed by Standards in Scotland's Schools etc Act 2000 (asp 6), s 60(2), Sch 3[1]
10, para	1, 2	1 Feb 1990 (SI 1990/86)
	3	16 Nov 1989 (s 81(1)); prospectively repealed by Standards in Scotland's Schools etc Act 2000 (asp 6), s 60(2), Sch 3[1]
	4	Repealed
	5, 6	16 Nov 1989 (s 81(1))
	7	Repealed
	8 (1)–(6)	16 Nov 1989 (s 81(1))
	(7)	1 Feb 1990 (SI 1990/86)
	(8)	16 Nov 1989 (s 81(1))
	(9)–(11)	1 Feb 1990 (SI 1990/86)
	(12)	16 Nov 1989 (s 81(1))
	(13)–(18)	1 Feb 1990 (SI 1990/86)
	(19), (20)	1 Feb 1990 (SI 1990/86); prospectively repealed by Standards in Scotland's Schools etc Act 2000 (asp 6), s 60(2), Sch 3[1]
	(21)	1 Feb 1990 (SI 1990/86)
	(22)	16 Nov 1989 (s 81(1))
	9, 10	16 Nov 1989 (s 81(1))
11		1 Feb 1990 (SI 1990/86)

[1] Orders made under Standards in Scotland's Schools etc Act 2000, s 61(2), bringing the prospective amendments into force will be noted to that Act

---

Social Security Act 1989 (c 24)

RA: 21 Jul 1989

Commencement provisions: s 33(2), (3); Social Security Act 1989 (Commencement No 1) Order 1989, SI 1989/1238; Social Security Act 1989 (Commencement No 2) Order 1989, SI 1989/1262; Social Security Act 1989 (Commencement No 3) Order 1990, SI 1990/102; Social Security Act 1989 (Commencement No 4) Order 1990, SI 1990/312 (correcting defect in SI 1990/102); Social Security Act 1989 (Commencement No 5) Order 1994, SI 1994/1661

Section

1–3	Repealed
4	21 Jul 1989 (RA)
5	Repealed
6	21 Jul 1989 (RA)

Social Security Act 1989 (c 24)—*contd*

Section				
7–21				Repealed
22	(1)–(6)			Repealed
	(7)			See Sch 4 below
	(8)			Repealed
23				See Sch 5 below
24				See Sch 6 below
25	(1)–(3)			1 Mar 1990 (for purposes of regulations expressed to come into force on 1 Jan 1991) (SI 1990/102)
				1 Jan 1991 (otherwise) (SI 1990/102)
	(4)–(6)			1 Jan 1991 (SI 1990/102)
26				Spent
27				Repealed
28–30				21 Jul 1989 (RA)
31	(1)			See Sch 8 below
	(2)			See Sch 9 below
	(3)			21 Jul 1989 (RA)
32				Repealed
33				21 Jul 1989 (RA)
Schedule				
1–3				Repealed
4, para	1–21			Repealed
	22, 23			3 Sep 1990 (SI 1990/102)
	24			Repealed
5, para	1			23 Jun 1994 (for purpose of giving effect to paras 5, 6 so far as brought into force by SI 1994/1661) (SI 1994/1661)
				Not in force (otherwise)
	2	(1), (2)		23 Jun 1994 (for purpose of giving effect to paras 5, 6 so far as brought into force by SI 1994/1661) (SI 1994/1661)
				Not in force (otherwise)
		(3)		*Not in force*
		(4)	(a), (b)	*Not in force*
			(c)	23 Jun 1994 (for purpose of giving effect to paras 5, 6 so far as brought into force by SI 1994/1661) (SI 1994/1661)
				Not in force (otherwise)
			(d)–(g)	*Not in force*
		(5)		23 Jun 1994 (for purpose of giving effect to paras 5, 6 so far as brought into force by SI 1994/1661) (SI 1994/1661)
				Not in force (otherwise)
		(6)–(8)		*Not in force*

Social Security Act 1989 (c 24)—*contd*

Schedule

5, para	2	(9)		23 Jun 1994 (for purpose of giving effect to paras 5, 6 so far as brought into force by SI 1994/1661) (SI 1994/1661)
				Not in force (otherwise)
	3	(1)		23 Jun 1994 (for purpose of giving effect to paras 5, 6 so far as brought into force by SI 1994/1661) (SI 1994/1661)
				Not in force (otherwise)
		(2)		*Not in force*
		(3), (4)		23 Jun 1994 (for purpose of giving effect to paras 5, 6 so far as brought into force by SI 1994/1661) (SI 1994/1661)
				Not in force (otherwise)
	4			Repealed (*never in force*)
	5	(1)		23 Jun 1994 (SI 1994/1661)
		(2)	(a)	23 Jun 1994 (SI 1994/1661)
			(b), (c)	*Not in force*
		(3)		23 Jun 1994 (SI 1994/1661)
	6	(1), (2)		23 Jun 1994 (SI 1994/1661)
		(3)	(a)	23 Jun 1994 (SI 1994/1661)
			(b), (c)	*Not in force*
		(4)		23 Jun 1994 (SI 1994/1661)
	7	(a)–(c)		23 Jun 1994 (for purpose of giving effect to paras 5, 6 so far as brought into force by SI 1994/1661) (SI 1994/1661)
				Not in force (otherwise)
		(d)		*Not in force*
		(e)		23 Jun 1994 (for purpose of giving effect to paras 5, 6 so far as brought into force by SI 1994/1661) (SI 1994/1661)
				Not in force (otherwise)
	8			*Not in force*
	9, 10			23 Jun 1994 (for purpose of giving effect to paras 5, 6 so far as brought into force by SI 1994/1661) (SI 1994/1661)
				Not in force (otherwise)
	11			Repealed
	12			*Not in force*
	13–15			Repealed (para 14 *never in force*)
6, para	1–20			Repealed
	21			21 Jul 1989 (RA)
7				Repealed
8, para	1–9			Repealed

Social Security Act 1989 (c 24)—*contd*

Schedule

8, para	10	21 Jul 1989 (RA)
	11	Repealed
	12, 13	21 Jul 1989 (RA)
	14–18	Repealed
	19	25 Jul 1989 (SI 1989/1262 (superseding SI 1989/1238))
9		21 Jul 1989 (repeals consequential on bringing into force of provisions listed in s 33(3)(a)–(f) on 21 Jul 1989) (RA)
		1 Oct 1989 (repeals of or in Social Security Act 1973, s 51(7); Social Security Act 1975, ss 14(6), 15(6)(a), 27(3)–(5), 28(1)(a), 29(5)(a), 30(1), (3), (6)(a), 39(1)(b), 41(1), 48(2), (3), Sch 20 (in definition 'week'); Social Security Pensions Act 1975, ss 8(1), 11, 45(3), Sch 4, para 39; Social Security (Miscellaneous Provisions) Act 1977, s 21(1); Social Security Act 1979, Sch 1, para 17; Social Security and Housing Benefits Act 1982; Social Security Act 1986, ss 50(1), 63(1)(a)(ii), Sch 6, para 3, Sch 10, para 96) (SI 1989/1238)
		5 Oct 1989 (repeals of or in Social Security Act 1975, s 4(6F); Social Security Contributions Act 1982, s 4(4), Sch 1, para 1(4)) (SI 1989/1238)
		9 Oct 1989 (repeals of or in Merchant Shipping Act 1970, s 17(10); Social Security Act 1975, ss 20(1A), 26(7); Social Security Act 1986, s 26(3) and second paragraph of rubric at end of Sch 9) (SI 1989/1238)
		1 Feb 1990 (repeal of Social Security (Contributions) Act 1982, s 4(4)) (SI 1990/312)
		6 Apr 1990 (repeals of or in Social Security Act 1975, ss 100(3), 101(6), (7), 112(4), (5), Sch 10, para 1(7), 2(2), Sch 11, para 4, Sch 13, para 8, 9, Sch 20, definition 'local office') (SI 1990/102)
		Not in force (otherwise)

Statute Law (Repeals) Act 1989 (c 43)

RA: 16 Nov 1989

Commencement provisions: s 3(2); Statute Law (Repeals) Act 1989 (Commencement)
    Order 1992, SI 1992/1275

Section	
1–3	16 Nov 1989 (RA)
Schedule	
1	16 Nov 1989 (except repeal of Federation of Malaya Independence Act 1957, s 3; Malaysia Act 1963, s 5) (RA)
	1 Jun 1992 (exceptions noted above) (SI 1992/1275)
2	16 Nov 1989 (RA)

Transport (Scotland) Act 1989 (c 23)

RA: 21 Jul 1989

Commencement provisions: s 12(2)

Section	
1–17	21 Sep 1989 (s 12(2))
18	21 Jul 1989 (s 12(2))

Water Act 1989 (c 15)

RA: 6 Jul 1989

Commencement provisions: s 194(2)–(5); Water Act 1989 (Commencement No 1)
    Order 1989, SI 1989/1146; Water Authorities (Transfer of Functions)
    (Appointed Day) Order 1989, SI 1989/1530; Water Act 1989 (Commencement
    No 2 and Transitional Provisions) Order 1989, SI 1989/1557; Water Act 1989
    (Commencement No 3) (Scotland) Order 1989, SI 1989/1561; Water Act 1989
    (Commencement No 4) Order 1989, SI 1989/2278

Abbreviation: "rel sub leg" means "so far as relating to the making of subordinate
    legislation"

Section		
1	(1)–(5)	Repealed
	(6)	See Sch 1 below
2, 3		Repealed
4		6 Jul 1989 (rel sub leg) (s 194(2))
		7 Jul 1989 (otherwise) (E, W) (SI 1989/1146)
		1 Sep 1989 (otherwise) (NI) (SI 1989/1557)
		1 Sep 1989 (otherwise) (S) (SI 1989/1561)
5	(1)–(4)	Repealed
	(5)	See Sch 3 below

Water Act 1989 (c 15)—*contd*

Section

6	(1)–(7)	Repealed
	(8)	1 Sep 1989 (SI 1989/1146; SI 1989/1530; SI 1989/1561)
7–10		Repealed
11	(1)–(8)	Repealed
	(9)	7 Jul 1989 (E, W) (SI 1989/1146) 1 Sep 1989 (NI) (SI 1989/1557)
12–68		Repealed (*s 13 never in force in relation to Scotland*)
69		1 Sep 1989 (s 194(3))
70	(1), (2)	1 Sep 1989 (s 194(3))
	(3)–(5)	Repealed
71–82		Repealed
83		6 Jul 1989 (rel sub leg) (s 194(2)) 1 Sep 1989 (otherwise) (s 194(3))
84		1 Sep 1989 (s 194(3))
85, 86		6 Jul 1989 (rel sub leg) (s 194(2)) 1 Sep 1989 (otherwise) (s 194(3))
87, 88		1 Sep 1989 (s 194(3))
89		6 Jul 1989 (rel sub leg) (s 194(2)) 1 Sep 1989 (otherwise) (s 194(3))
90, 91		1 Sep 1989 (s 194(3))
92		6 Jul 1989 (rel sub leg) (s 194(2)) 1 Sep 1989 (otherwise) (s 194(3))
93, 94		1 Sep 1989 (s 194(3))
95		6 Jul 1989 (rel sub leg) (s 194(2)) 1 Sep 1989 (otherwise) (s 194(3))
96		1 Sep 1989 (s 194(3))
97–135		Repealed
136		1 Sep 1989 (S) (s 194(3)) Repealed (E, W)
137	(1)–(8)	Repealed
	(9)	6 Jul 1989 (rel sub leg) (s 194(2)) 1 Sep 1989 (otherwise) (s 194(3))
	(10), (11)	Repealed
138		Repealed
139	(1)–(5)	Repealed
	(6)	1 Sep 1989 (s 194(3))
140		Repealed
141	(1)–(4)	1 Sep 1989 (S) (s 194(3)) Repealed (E, W)
	(5), (6)	1 Sep 1989 (s 194(3))
	(7)	1 Sep 1989 (S) (s 194(3)) Repealed (E, W)
142	(1)	Repealed
	(2)	1 Sep 1989 (s 194(3))
143–167		Repealed
168		See Sch 22 below
169		See Sch 23 below

Water Act 1989 (c 15)—*contd*

Section

170, 171		Repealed
172		1 Sep 1989 (S) (SI 1989/1561)
		Repealed (E, W)
173		6 Jul 1989 (rel sub leg) (s 194(2))
		1 Sep 1989 (otherwise)
		(SI 1989/1146; SI 1989/1530)
174	(1)–(7)	6 Jul 1989 (rel sub leg) (s 194(2))
		7 Jul 1989 (otherwise) (SI 1989/1146)
	(8)	Inserted by Water Consolidation
		(Consequential Provisions)
		Act 1991, s 2(1), Sch 1, para 50(1),
		(2)(e) (qv)
175		1 Sep 1989 (SI 1989/1146;
		SI 1989/1530)
176		Repealed
177		7 Jul 1989 (SI 1989/1146)
178–182		Repealed
183, 184		1 Sep 1989 (SI 1989/1146;
		SI 1989/1530)
185		6 Jul 1989 (s 194(2))
186		Repealed
187		7 Jul 1989 (SI 1989/1146)
188		Repealed
189	(1)	6 Jul 1989 (definitions 'the 1945 Act',
		'the 1973 Act', 'the Authority',
		'contravention', 'the Director',
		'disposal' (and cognate expressions),
		'enactment', 'holding company',
		'information', 'local statutory
		provision', 'the Minister',
		'modifications' (and cognate
		expressions), 'sewer', 'statutory
		water company', 'subordinate
		legislation', 'successor company',
		'transfer date', 'water authority')
		(rel sub leg) (s 194(2))
		7 Jul 1989 (definitions listed above)
		(otherwise) (SI 1989/1146)
		Repealed (otherwise)
	(2)–(5)	Repealed
	(6), (7)	6 Jul 1989 (rel sub leg) (s 194(2))
		7 Jul 1989 (otherwise) (SI 1989/1146)
	(8)	Repealed
	(9), (10)	6 Jul 1989 (rel sub leg) (s 194(2))
		7 Jul 1989 (otherwise) (SI 1989/1146)
190		See Schs 25–27 below (6 Jul 1989 (rel
		sub leg)) (s 194(2))
191	(1)–(5)	6 Jul 1989 (s 194(2))
	(6)	7 Jul 1989 (SI 1989/1146)

Water Act 1989 (c 15)—*contd*

Section

192			7 Jul 1989 (SI 1989/1146)
193			6 Jul 1989 (rel sub leg) (s 194(2))
			7 Jul 1989 (otherwise) (SI 1989/1146)
194			6 Jul 1989 (s 194(2))

Schedule

1			Repealed
2			6 Jul 1989 (rel sub leg) (s 194(2))
			7 Jul 1989 (otherwise) (E, W) (SI 1989/1146)
			1 Sep 1989 (otherwise) (NI) (SI 1989/1557)
			1 Sep 1989 (otherwise) (S) (SI 1989/1561)
3, para	1–5		Repealed
	6, 7		7 Jul 1989 (E, W) (SI 1989/1146)
			1 Sep 1989 (NI) (SI 1989/1557)
			1 Sep 1989 (S) (SI 1989/1561)
4, para	1–5		Repealed
	6		1 Sep 1989 (SI 1989/1146; SI 1989/1530; SI 1989/1557; SI 1989/1561)
5			6 Jul 1989 (rel sub leg) (S) (s 194(2))
			1 Sep 1989 (otherwise) (S) (s 194(3))
			Repealed (E, W)
6, 7			Repealed
8, para	1		Repealed
	2	(1)–(10)	Repealed
		(11)	1 Sep 1989 (s 194(3))
		(12)	Repealed
	3–5		Repealed
	6, 7		1 Sep 1989 (s 194(3))
9–14			Repealed
15, para	1		1 Sep 1989 (S) (s 194(3))
			Repealed (E, W)
	2–13		Repealed
	14		1 Sep 1989 (S) (s 194(3))
			Repealed (E, W)
	15–41		Repealed
16			Repealed
17, para	1		1 Sep 1989 (s 194(3))
	2		6 Jul 1989 (s 194(2))
	3		1 Sep 1989 (s 194(3))
	4		*Not in force*
	5–9		1 Sep 1989 (s 194(3))
18–21			Repealed
22			1 Sep 1989 (s 194(3))
23			1 Sep 1989 (except so far as relates to Control of Pollution Act 1974, s 33) (S) (s 194(3))

Water Act 1989 (c 15)—*contd*
Schedule

23—*contd*		31 May 1991 (exception noted above) (S) (SI 1991/1172)
		Not in force (so far as relates to Control of Pollution Act 1984, ss 33 (E, W), 47, 48)
24		Repealed
25		1 Sep 1989 (for transitional provisions, see SI 1989/1557, art 6) (SI 1989/1146; SI 1989/1530; SI 1989/1557; SI 1989/1561)
26		6 Jul 1989 (rel sub leg) (s 194(2))
		1 Sep 1989 (otherwise) (s 194(3))
27, Pt	I	1 Sep 1989 (s 194(3))
	II	1 Sep 1989 (repeals of or in Water Act 1945, s 41(7), Sch 3, ss 75–77; Rating and Valuation (Miscellaneous Provisions) Act 1955, s 11; Trustee Investments Act 1961, Sch 4, para 3; Water Act 1973, ss 34(1), (3), 35(1), (2), Sch 6, Pt I, Sch 8, para 50) (SI 1989/1557; note savings therein)
		1 Apr 1990 (repeals of or in Water Act 1945, s 59(3), Sch 3, ss 74, 81) (SI 1989/1557)
		Not in force (otherwise)

1990

Access to Health Records Act 1990 (c 23)

RA: 13 Jul 1990

Commencement provisions: s 12(2)

1 Nov 1991 (s 12(2))

Agricultural Holdings (Amendment) Act 1990 (c 15)

RA: 29 Jun 1990

Commencement provisions: s 3(2)

29 Jul 1990 (s 3(2))

Appropriation Act 1990 (c 28)

Whole Act repealed

Australian Constitution (Public Record Copy) Act 1990 (c 17)

RA: 29 Jul 1990

29 Jul 1990 (RA)

Aviation and Maritime Security Act 1990 (c 31)

RA: 26 Jul 1990

Commencement provisions: s 54(2)

Section	
1	26 Sep 1990 (s 54(2))
2–4	26 Jul 1990 (RA)
5	26 Sep 1990 (s 54(2))
6, 7	26 Jul 1990 (RA)
8	See Sch 1 below
9–17	26 Sep 1990 (s 54(2))
18–36	26 Jul 1990 (RA)
37–40	26 Sep 1990 (s 54(2))
41–44	26 Jul 1990 (RA)
45	See Sch 2 below
46–52	26 Jul 1990 (RA)
53 (1)	See Sch 3 below

Aviation and Maritime Security Act 1990 (c 31)—*contd*

Section

53	(2)	See Sch 4 below
54		26 Jul 1990 (RA)

Schedule

1, para	1		26 Sep 1990 (s 54(2))
	2	(1)–(5)	26 Jul 1990 (RA)
		(6)	26 Sep 1990 (s 54(2))
		(7)	26 Jul 1990 (RA)
	3		26 Jul 1990 (RA)
	4–6		26 Sep 1990 (s 54(2))
	7–10		26 Jul 1990 (RA)
	11	(1)–(4)	26 Jul 1990 (RA)
		(5)	26 Sep 1990 (s 54(2))
2			26 Jul 1990 (RA)
3			26 Sep 1990 (s 54(2))
4			26 Jul 1990 (except repeals of or in Criminal Jurisdiction Act 1975, Aviation Security Act 1982, ss 11(5)(a), 14(7)(a), 20(5); Extradition Act 1989) (RA) 26 Sep 1990 (exception noted above) (s 54(2))

British Nationality (Hong Kong) Act 1990 (c 34)

RA: 26 Jul 1990

Commencement provisions: s 6(4); British Nationality (Hong Kong) Act 1990 (Commencement) Order 1990, SI 1990/2210

Section

1	(1)	See Sch 1 below
	(2), (3)	7 Nov 1990 (SI 1990/2210)
	(4)	See Sch 2 below
	(5)	7 Nov 1990 (SI 1990/2210)
2	(1)	7 Nov 1990 (SI 1990/2210)
	(2)	*Not in force*
	(3)	7 Nov 1990 (SI 1990/2210)
3–6		7 Nov 1990 (SI 1990/2210)

Schedule

1, 2	7 Nov 1990 (SI 1990/2210)

Broadcasting Act 1990 (c 42)

RA: 1 Nov 1990

Commencement provisions: s 204(2); Broadcasting Act 1990 (Commencement No 1 and Transitional Provisions) Order 1990, SI 1990/2347

Section

1	(1), (2)	1 Dec 1990 (SI 1990/2347)
	(3)	See Sch 1 below
2	(1)	1 Jan 1991 (SI 1990/2347)
	(2)–(6)	1 Dec 1990 (SI 1990/2347)

Broadcasting Act 1990 (c 42)—*contd*
Section

3–9		1 Dec 1990 (SI 1990/2347)
10		1 Jan 1991 (SI 1990/2347)
11		1 Dec 1990 (SI 1990/2347)
12–17		1 Jan 1991 (SI 1990/2347)
17A		Inserted by Broadcasting Act 1996, s 86(1) (qv)
18–21		1 Jan 1991 (SI 1990/2347)
21A		Inserted by Broadcasting Act 1996, s 78 (qv)
22		1 Jan 1991 (SI 1990/2347)
23	(1)–(5)	1 Jan 1993 (SI 1990/2347)
	(6)	See Sch 3 below
24, 25		1 Jan 1993 (SI 1990/2347)
26		1 Jan 1991 (SI 1990/2347)
27		1 Jan 1993 (SI 1990/2347)
28–31		1 Jan 1991 (SI 1990/2347)
31A		Inserted by Broadcasting Act 1996, s 75 (qv)
32, 33		1 Jan 1991 (SI 1990/2347)
34, 35		1 Jan 1991 (for purposes of enabling conditions of type specified in ss 34(2), 35(1) to be included in a Channel 3 or Channel 5 licence or a licence to provide Channel 4) (SI 1990/2347)
		1 Jan 1993 (otherwise) (SI 1990/2347)
36–42		1 Jan 1991 (SI 1990/2347)
42A, 42B		Inserted by Broadcasting Act 1996, s 85 (qv)
43		Substituted (30 Dec 1998) by Television Broadcasting Regulations 1998, SI 1998/3196, reg 2, Schedule, para 2
44		Repealed
45		1 Dec 1990 (SI 1990/2347)
45A		Inserted by Broadcasting Act 1996, s 89 (qv)
46, 47		1 Dec 1990 (SI 1990/2347)
48–55		1 Jan 1991 (SI 1990/2347)
56	(1), (2)	1 Jan 1991 (SI 1990/2347)
	(3)	See Sch 6 below
57–60		1 Jan 1991 (SI 1990/2347)
61		Substituted by Broadcasting Act 1996, s 80(1), (3) (qv)
61A		Inserted by Broadcasting Act 1996, s 81(1) (qv)
62–66		1 Jan 1991 (SI 1990/2347)
66A		Inserted by Broadcasting Act 1996, s 136, Sch 8, para 3 (qv)

Broadcasting Act 1990 (c 42)—*contd*

Section

67–70		1 Jan 1991 (SI 1990/2347)
71		1 Dec 1990 (SI 1990/2347)
72–76		1 Jan 1991 (SI 1990/2347)
76A		Inserted by Broadcasting Act 1996, s 86(3) (qv)
77, 78		1 Jan 1991 (SI 1990/2347)
78A		Inserted by Broadcasting Act 1996, s 91(1) (qv)
79–82		1 Jan 1991 (SI 1990/2347)
83	(1), (2)	1 Dec 1990 (SI 1990/2347)
	(3)	See Sch 8 below
84–103		1 Jan 1991 (SI 1990/2347)
103A		Inserted by Broadcasting Act 1996, s 92 (qv)
104		1 Jan 1991 (SI 1990/2347)
104A, 104B		Inserted by Broadcasting Act 1996, s 94(1) (qv)
105, 106		1 Jan 1991 (SI 1990/2347)
106A		Inserted by Broadcasting Act 1996, s 93 (qv)
107–111		1 Jan 1991 (SI 1990/2347)
111A, 111B		Inserted by Broadcasting Act 1996, ss 96, 136, Sch 8, para 7 (qv)
112–125		1 Jan 1991 (SI 1990/2347)
126, 127		1 Dec 1990 (SI 1990/2347)
128, 129		1 Jan 1991 (SI 1990/2347)
130–133		1 Dec 1990 (SI 1990/2347)
134–140		1 Jan 1991 (SI 1990/2347)
141		1 Dec 1990 (SI 1990/2347)
142–161		Repealed
162	(1)	1 Jan 1991 (SI 1990/2347)
	(2)	See Sch 15 below
163–170		1 Jan 1991 (SI 1990/2347)
171		See Sch 16 below
172–174		1 Jan 1991 (SI 1990/2347)
175		1 Feb 1991 (SI 1990/2347)
176		See Sch 17 below
177–179		1 Jan 1991 (SI 1990/2347)
180		See Sch 18 below
181		1 Jan 1991 (SI 1990/2347)
182		Repealed
183		See Sch 19 below
184		1 Jan 1991 (SI 1990/2347)
185		1 Jan 1991 (for purposes of enabling conditions of type specified in s 185(3) to be included in a Channel 3 or Channel 5 licence or a licence to provide Channel 4) (SI 1990/2347)

Broadcasting Act 1990 (c 42)—*contd*

Section

185—*contd*		1 Jan 1993 (otherwise) (SI 1990/2347)
186		1 Jan 1991 (SI 1990/2347)
187		1 Jan 1993 (SI 1990/2347)
188–193		1 Jan 1991 (SI 1990/2347)
194		Repealed
194A		Inserted by Broadcasting Act 1996, s 77 (qv)
195–197		1 Jan 1991 (SI 1990/2347)
198–202		1 Dec 1990 (SI 1990/2347)
203	(1)	See Sch 20 below
	(2)	1 Jan 1991 (SI 1990/2347)
	(3)	See Sch 21 below
	(4)	See Sch 22 below
204		1 Dec 1990 (SI 1990/2347)

Schedule

1, 2		1 Dec 1990 (SI 1990/2347)
3		1 Jan 1993 (SI 1990/2347)
4–7		1 Jan 1991 (SI 1990/2347)
8, 9		1 Dec 1990 (SI 1990/2347)
10–12		1 Jan 1991 (SI 1990/2347)
13, 14		Repealed
15, 16		1 Jan 1991 (SI 1990/2347)
17		1 Jan 1991 (for purposes of enabling publication of information about programmes to be included in a programme service on or after that date) (SI 1990/2347)
		1 Mar 1991 (otherwise) (SI 1990/2347)
18		1 Apr 1991 (SI 1990/2347)
19		1 Jan 1991 (SI 1990/2347)
20, para	1	1 Jan 1991 (SI 1990/2347)
	2, 3	Repealed
	4–9	1 Jan 1991 (SI 1990/2347)
	10	1 Jan 1991 (SI 1990/2347); prospectively repealed by Private Hire Vehicles (London) Act 1998, s 39(2), Sch 2[1]
	11–13	1 Jan 1991 (SI 1990/2347)
	14, 15	Repealed
	16–18	1 Jan 1991 (SI 1990/2347)
	19	Repealed
	20, 21	1 Jan 1991 (SI 1990/2347)
	22	Repealed
	23–25	1 Jan 1991 (SI 1990/2347)
	26, 27	1 Jan 1991 (SI 1990/2347); prospectively repealed by Youth Justice and Criminal Evidence Act 1999, s 67, Sch 6[2]
	28–35	1 Jan 1991 (SI 1990/2347)

Broadcasting Act 1990 (c 42)—*contd*
Schedule

20, para	36	1 Jan 1991 (except so far as replaces reference to Independent Broadcasting Authority until that Authority is dissolved by order under s 127(3)) (SI 1990/2347)
		Not in force (exception noted above)
	37	Repealed
	38–46	1 Jan 1991 (SI 1990/2347)
	47	1 Jan 1991 (SI 1990/2347); repealed by Criminal Procedure and Investigations Act 1996, ss 79(4), 80, Sch 4, para 36, Sch 5(4), (12), with effect in accordance with s 72 of, and Sch 3, para 8 to 1996 Act[3]
	48, 49	1 Jan 1991 (SI 1990/2347)
	50	Repealed
	51	1 Jan 1991 (SI 1990/2347)
	52	1 Jan 1991 (SI 1990/2347); repealed by Criminal Procedure and Investigations Act 1996, ss 79(4), 80, Sch 4, para 36, Sch 5(4), (12), with effect in accordance with s 72 of, and Sch 3, para 8 to 1996 Act[3]
	53, 54	1 Jan 1991 (SI 1990/2347)
21		1 Dec 1990 (repeal of or in Cable and Broadcasting Act 1984, s 8(1)(a), (b)) (SI 1990/2347)
		1 Jan 1991 (all remaining repeals except repeals of or in Wireless Telegraphy (Blind Persons) Act 1955; Wireless Telegraphy Act 1967; entries for Cable Authority and Independent Broadcasting Authority in House of Commons Disqualification Act 1975, Sch 1, Pt II; Northern Ireland Assembly Disqualification Act 1975, Sch 1, Pt II) (subject to transitional provisions; see SI 1990/2347, art 3(3)) (SI 1990/2347)
		1 Apr 1991 (repeals of or in Wireless Telegraphy (Blind Persons) Act 1955; Wireless Telegraphy Act 1967) (SI 1990/2347)
		Not in force (entries for Cable Authority and Independent Broadcasting Authority in House

Broadcasting Act 1990 (c 42)—*contd*
Schedule

21—*contd*		of Commons Disqualification Act 1975, Sch 1, Pt II; Northern Ireland Assembly Disqualification Act 1975, Sch 1, Pt II)
22, para	1–3	1 Dec 1990 (SI 1990/2347)
	4–7	1 Jan 1991 (SI 1990/2347)

1   Orders made under Private Hire Vehicles (London) Act 1998, s 40(2), bringing the prospective repeal into force will be noted to that Act

2   Orders made under Youth Justice and Criminal Evidence act 1999, s 68(3), bringing the prospective repeals into force will be noted to that Act

3   This repeal has effect in accordance with provision made by order under the Criminal Procedure and Investigations Act 1996, Sch 3, para 8. Such orders will be noted thereunder

---

Caldey Island Act 1990 (c 44)

Local application only

Capital Allowances Act 1990 (c 1)

Whole Act repealed

Care of Cathedrals Measure 1990 (No 2)

RA: 26 Jul 1990

Commencement provisions: s 21(2)

The provisions of this Measure were brought into force on the following dates by an instrument made by the Archbishops of Canterbury and York and dated 28 Sep 1990 (made under s 21(2))

Section

1, 2		1 Mar 1991
3	(1), (2)	1 Mar 1991
	(3)	See Sch 1 below
4	(1), (2)	1 Mar 1991
	(3)	See Sch 2 below
5–12		1 Mar 1991
13		1 Oct 1990
14, 15		1 Mar 1991
16		Repealed
17–21		1 Oct 1990
Schedule		
1, 2		1 Mar 1991

Civil Aviation Authority (Borrowing Powers) Act 1990 (c 2)

RA: 19 Mar 1990

19 Mar 1990 (RA)

Clergy (Ordination) Measure 1990 (No 1)

RA: 22 Feb 1990

22 Feb 1990 (RA)

Coal Industry Act 1990 (c 3)

RA: 19 Mar 1990

Commencement provisions: s 6(2)

Whole Act repealed, except ss 1, 3, 6(1), (3), which are prospectively repealed by Coal Industry Act 1994, s 67(8), Sch 11, Pt III; orders made under the 1994 Act, s 68, bringing the prospective repeals into force will be noted to that Act

Computer Misuse Act 1990 (c 18)

RA: 26 Jun 1990

Commencement provisions: s 18(2)

29 Aug 1990 (s 18(2))

Consolidated Fund Act 1990 (c 4)

Whole Act repealed

Consolidated Fund (No 2) Act 1990 (c 46)

Whole Act repealed

Contracts (Applicable Law) Act 1990 (c 36)

RA: 26 Jul 1990

Commencement provisions: s 7; Contracts (Applicable Law) Act 1990 (Commencement No 1) Order 1991, SI 1991/707

Section		
1		1 Apr 1991 (SI 1991/707)
2	(1)	1 Apr 1991 (so far as relates to Rome Convention and Luxembourg Convention as defined in s 1) (SI 1991/707)
		Not in force (otherwise)
	(1A)	Inserted (20 May 1993) by Insurance Companies (Amendment) Regulations 1993, SI 1993/174, reg 9; substituted (1 Dec 2001) by Financial Services and Markets Act 2000 (Consequential Amendments and Repeals) Order 2001, SI 2001/3649, art 320

Contracts (Applicable Law) Act 1990 (c 36)—*contd*

Section

2	(2), (3)		1 Apr 1991 (SI 1991/707)
	(4)		See Schs 1–3 below
3	(1), (2)		*Not in force*
	(3)	(a)	1 Apr 1991 (SI 1991/707)
		(b)	*Not in force*
4			1 Apr 1991 (SI 1991/707)
5			See Sch 4 below
6–9			1 Apr 1991 (SI 1991/707)

Schedule

1–3	1 Apr 1991 (SI 1991/707)
3A	Inserted by Contracts (Applicable Law) Act 1990 (Amendment) Order 1994, SI 1994/1900, art 9, Schedule[1]
3B	Inserted by Contracts (Applicable Law) Act 1990 (Amendment) Order 2000, SI 2000/1825, art 7, Schedule[2]
4	1 Apr 1991 (SI 1991/707)

[1] That order came into force on 1 Dec 1997, the date on which the Convention on the accession of Spain and Portugal to the Rome Convention and to the Brussels Protocol entered into force in respect of the United Kingdom, which date was notified in the *London Gazette*, 22 Oct 1997

[2] That order comes into force on the date on which the Convention on the accession of the Republic of Austria, the Republic of Finland and the Kingdom of Sweden to the Rome Convention and to the Brussels Protocol enters into force in respect of the United Kingdom, which date shall be notified in the *London Gazette*

Courts and Legal Services Act 1990 (c 41)

RA: 1 Nov 1990

Commencement provisions: s 124; Courts and Legal Services Act 1990 (Commencement No 1) Order 1990, SI 1990/2170; Courts and Legal Services Act 1990 (Commencement No 2) Order 1990, SI 1990/2484; Courts and Legal Services Act 1990 (Commencement No 3) Order 1991, SI 1991/608; Courts and Legal Services Act 1990 (Commencement No 4) Order 1991, SI 1991/985; Courts and Legal Services Act 1990 (Commencement No 5) Order 1991, SI 1991/1364; Courts and Legal Services Act 1990 (Commencement No 6) Order 1991, SI 1991/1883; Courts and Legal Services Act 1990 (Commencement No 7) Order 1991, SI 1991/2730; Courts and Legal Services Act 1990 (Commencement No 8) Order 1992, SI 1992/1221; Courts and Legal Services Act 1990 (Commencement No 9) Order 1993, SI 1993/2132; Courts and Legal Services Act 1990 (Commencement No 10) Order 1995, SI 1995/641

Section

1	1 Nov 1990 (RA)
2, 3	1 Jul 1991 (SI 1991/1364)
4	1 Oct 1991 (SI 1991/1883)
5	1 Nov 1990 (RA)
6	1 Jan 1991 (s 124(2)(a))

Courts and Legal Services Act 1990 (c 41)—*contd*

Section

7	(1)	23 Jul 1993 (except so far as relates to s 7(2)) (SI 1993/2132)
		1 Oct 1993 (exception noted above) (SI 1993/2132)
	(2)	1 Oct 1993 (SI 1993/2132)
	(3), (4)	Repealed
8		1 Jan 1991 (s 124(2)(a))
9		1 Jan 1991 (SI 1990/2484)
10	(1)	Substituted by Maintenance Enforcement Act 1991, s 11(1), Sch 2, para 11 (qv)
	(2)	1 Jul 1991 (SI 1991/1364)
	(3)–(5)	Repealed
11		1 Jan 1991 (s 124(2)(a))
12–14		*Not in force*
15		1 Jul 1991 (SI 1991/1364)
16		1 Jan 1991 (s 124(2)(a))
17, 18		1 Apr 1991 (SI 1991/608)
18A		Inserted by Access to Justice Act 1999, s 35(2) (qv)
19, 20		Repealed
21	(1)–(5)	1 Jan 1991 (SI 1990/2484)
	(6)	See Sch 3 below
22, 23		1 Jan 1991 (SI 1990/2484)
24	(1), (2)	1 Jan 1991 (SI 1990/2484)
	(3)	Repealed
25–28		1 Jan 1991 (SI 1990/2484)
29		Substituted for original ss 29, 30 by Access to Justice Act 1999, s 41, Sch 5, para 1, subject to transitional provisions (qv)
30		See note to s 29 ante
31		Substituted for original ss 31–33 by Access to Justice Act 1999, s 36 (qv)
31A		Inserted by Access to Justice Act 1999, s 37 (qv)
31B		Inserted by Access to Justice Act 1999, s 38 (qv)
31C		Inserted by Access to Justice Act 1999, s 39 (qv)
32, 33		See note to s 31 ante
34	(1)–(7)	1 Apr 1991 (SI 1991/608)
	(8)	See Sch 5 below
35		1 Apr 1991 (SI 1991/608)
36–39		*Not in force*
40		1 Apr 1991 (SI 1991/608)
41	(1)–(10)	*Not in force*
	(11)	See Sch 6 below
42		*Not in force*

Courts and Legal Services Act 1990 (c 41)—*contd*

Section

43	(1)–(3)		*Not in force*
	(4)		See Sch 7 below
	(5)–(12)		*Not in force*
44–52			*Not in force*
53	(1)–(6)		1 Apr 1991 (except in relation to exemptions under s 55) (SI 1991/608)
			Not in force (exception noted above)
	(7)		See Sch 8 below
	(8), (9)		1 Apr 1991 (except in relation to exemptions under s 55) (SI 1991/608)
			Not in force (exception noted above)
54			*Not in force*
55	(1)–(3)		*Not in force*
	(4)		See Sch 9 below
56, 57			1 Jul 1991 (SI 1991/1364)
58			Substituted for new ss 58, 58A by Access to Justice Act 1999, s 27(1) (qv)
58A			Inserted as noted to s 58 above
58B			Prospectively inserted by Access to Justice Act 1999, s 28[1]
59			Repealed
60–62			1 Jan 1991 (SI 1990/2484)
63	(1)	(a)	1 Apr 1991 (SI 1991/608)
		(b), (c)	*Not in force*
	(2)		1 Apr 1991 (SI 1991/608)
	(3)		*Not in force*
64, 65			1 Jan 1991 (s 124(2)(a))
66			1 Jan 1991 (SI 1990/2484)
67			Repealed
68			1 Jan 1991 (SI 1990/2484)
69			1 Apr 1991 (SI 1991/608)
70			1 Jan 1991 (except so far as relates to authorised practitioners) (SI 1990/2484)
			Not in force (exception noted above)
71	(1)		1 Jan 1991 (SI 1990/2484)
	(2)		See Sch 10 below
	(3)–(5)		1 Jan 1991 (SI 1990/2484)
	(6)		Substituted by Access to Justice Act 1999, s 43, Sch 6, para 9 (qv)
	(7), (8)		Repealed
72, 73			1 Jan 1991 (s 124(2)(a))
74	(1)–(3)		1 Jan 1991 (SI 1990/2484)
	(4)–(7)		1 Jul 1991 (SI 1991/1364)
75			See Sch 11 below
76–78			1 Jan 1991 (SI 1990/2484)

Courts and Legal Services Act 1990 (c 41)—*contd*

Section

79	(1)	1 Jan 1992 (SI 1991/2730)
	(2)	See Sch 12 below
80		1 Jan 1992 (SI 1991/2730)
81		See Sch 13 below
82		6 Mar 1995 (SI 1995/641)
83, 84		1 Jan 1991 (SI 1990/2484)
85		1 Jan 1991 (s 124(2)(a))
86		1 Jul 1991 (SI 1991/1364)
87, 88		1 Jan 1991 (s 124(2)(a))
89	(1)–(7)	14 Oct 1991 (SI 1991/1883)
	(8)	See Sch 14 below
	(9)	14 Oct 1991 (SI 1991/1883)
90–92		1 Jan 1991 (s 124(2)(a))
93	(1), (2)	1 Apr 1991 (SI 1991/608)
	(3)	See Sch 15 below
	(4)	1 Apr 1991 (SI 1991/608)
94–98		1 Jan 1991 (s 124(2)(a))
99		Repealed
100		1 Apr 1991 (SI 1991/608)
101–103		Repealed
104–107		*Not in force*
108		Repealed
109, 110		1 Jan 1991 (s 124(2)(a))
111		1 May 1991 (SI 1991/985)
112		1 Oct 1991 (SI 1991/1883)
113–115		1 Apr 1991 (SI 1991/608)
116	(1)	See Sch 16, Pt I below
	(2)	See Sch 16, Pt II below
	(3)	1 Jan 1992 (SI 1991/2730)
117		Repealed
118		1 Jan 1991 (SI 1990/2484)
119–124		1 Nov 1990 (RA)
125	(1)	1 Nov 1990 (RA)
	(2)	See Sch 17 below
	(3)	See Sch 18 below
	(4), (5)	1 Oct 1991 (SI 1991/1883)
	(6)	See Sch 19 below
	(7)	See Sch 20 below

Schedule

1, 2	Repealed
3	1 Jan 1991 (SI 1990/2484)
4	Substituted by Access to Justice Act 1999, s 41, Sch 5, para 2, subject to transitional provisions (qv)
5	1 Apr 1991 (SI 1991/608)
6, 7	*Not in force*
8	1 Apr 1991 (except in relation to exemptions under s 55) (SI 1991/608)

Courts and Legal Services Act 1990 (c 41)—*contd*

Schedule

8—*contd*			*Not in force* (exception noted above)
9			*Not in force*
10, 11			1 Jan 1991 (SI 1990/2484)
12			1 Jan 1992 (SI 1991/2730)
13			*Not in force*
14			14 Oct 1991 (SI 1991/1883)
15			1 Apr 1991 (SI 1991/608)
16, Pt	I, para	1, 2	14 Oct 1991 (SI 1991/1883)
		3–5	Repealed
		6	14 Oct 1991 (SI 1991/1883)
		7	Repealed
		8	1 Jan 1991 (SI 1990/2484)
		9–16	14 Oct 1991 (SI 1991/1883)
		17	Repealed
		18–33	14 Oct 1991 (SI 1991/1883)
	II, para	34–42	14 Oct 1991 (SI 1991/1883)
17, para	1		1 Jan 1991 (s 124(2)(b))
	2, 3		1 Nov 1990 (RA)
	4		1 Apr 1991 (SI 1991/608)
	5		*Not in force*
	6		1 Jul 1991 (SI 1991/1364)
	7, 8		1 Apr 1991 (SI 1991/608)
	9		1 Jan 1991 (SI 1990/2484)
	10		1 Apr 1991 (SI 1991/608)
	11		Repealed
	12		1 Jan 1991 (s 124(2)(b))
	13		1 Apr 1991 (SI 1991/608)
	14		14 Oct 1991 (SI 1991/1883)
	15		1 Jan 1991 (SI 1990/2484)
	16		1 Jan 1991 (s 124(2)(b))
	17, 18		1 Jul 1991 (SI 1991/1364)
	19		Repealed (*never in force*)
	20		1 Jan 1991 (s 124(2)(b))
18, para	1		1 Jan 1991 (so far as relates to Legal Services Ombudsman) (SI 1990/2484)
			1 Apr 1991 (so far as relates to Lord Chancellor's Advisory Committee on Legal Education and Conduct) (SI 1991/608)
			Not in force (otherwise)
	2		Repealed
	3		1 Jan 1991 (SI 1990/2484)
	4		*Not in force*
	5		1 Apr 1991 (SI 1991/608)
	6		*Not in force*
	7, 8		1 Jan 1991 (s 124(2)(c))
	9, 10		1 Jul 1991 (SI 1991/1364)
	11, 12		*Not in force*

Courts and Legal Services Act 1990 (c 41)—*contd*
Schedule

18, para	13	1 Jun 1992 (SI 1992/1221)
	14–16	1 Jan 1991 (s 124(2)(c))
	17, 18	1 Jul 1991 (SI 1991/1364)
	19	*Not in force*
	20	1 Jan 1991 (SI 1990/2484)
	21	Repealed
	22, 23	*Not in force*
	24	Repealed
	25	1 Jan 1991 (SI 1990/2484)
	26–30	1 Jan 1992 (SI 1991/2730)
	31	*Not in force*
	32	1 Jan 1991 (SI 1990/2484)
	33–35	1 Jan 1992 (SI 1991/2730)
	36–40	1 Jan 1991 (SI 1990/2484)
	41	1 Apr 1991 (SI 1991/608)
	42	1 Jan 1991 (SI 1990/2484)
	43–46	1 Jul 1991 (SI 1991/1364)
	47	1 Jan 1991 (SI 1990/2484)
	48, 49	1 Apr 1991 (SI 1991/608)
	50	1 Jan 1991 (SI 1990/2484)
	51	Repealed
	52	1 Apr 1991 (SI 1991/608)
	53	1 May 1991 (SI 1991/985)
	54	14 Oct 1991 (SI 1991/1883)
	55	1 Jan 1991 (s 124(2)(c))
	56	1 Apr 1991 (SI 1991/608)
	57	1 Jan 1991 (s 124(2)(c))
	58	1 Apr 1991 (SI 1991/608)
	59–63	Repealed
19, para	1	1 Jan 1991 (s 124(2)(d))
	2, 3	Repealed
	4–8	1 Jan 1991 (SI 1990/2484)
	9	1 Jan 1992 (SI 1991/2730)
	10, 11	1 Jan 1991 (SI 1990/2484)
	12, 13	1 Jul 1991 (SI 1991/1364)
	14, 15	1 Apr 1991 (SI 1991/608)
	16	1 Jan 1991 (SI 1990/2484)
	17	1 Apr 1991 (SI 1991/608)
20		1 Nov 1990 (repeal of Administration of Justice Act 1956, s 53) (SI 1990/2170)
		1 Jan 1991 (repeals of or in Public Notaries Act 1801, ss 10, 14; Summary Jurisdiction Act 1857; Naval Agency and Distribution Act 1864; War Pensions (Administrative Provisions) Act 1919; Pensions Appeal Tribunals Act 1943; Lands

Courts and Legal Services Act 1990 (c 41)—*contd*

Schedule

20—*contd*

Tribunal Act 1949; Courts-Martial (Appeals) Act 1951; Barristers (Qualification for Office) Act 1961; Superannuation (Miscellaneous Provisions) Act 1967; Superannuation (Miscellaneous Provisions) Act (Northern Ireland) 1969; Courts Act 1971; Administration of Justice Act 1973; Solicitors Act 1974, ss 3–5, 7, 20(2)(c), 39, 45, 82, Sch 3, para 7; Social Security Act 1975; House of Commons Disqualification Act 1975; Ministerial and other Salaries Act 1975; Justices of the Peace Act 1979; Social Security Act 1980; Judicial Pensions Act 1981, s 33, Sch 1, Pt I; Supreme Court Act 1981, ss 12(4), 94, 100(5), 101(2), 102(6), 103(6); County Courts Act 1984, ss 10, 60(1), (2); Prosecution of Offences Act 1985, s 4(5); Administration of Justice Act 1985, ss 3(1), 63, Sch 1, paras 4, 11, Sch 2, paras 8, 15, Sch 7, para 4; Coroners Act 1988) (SI 1990/2484)

1 Apr 1991 (repeals of or in Commissioners for Oaths Act 1889, s 1; Arbitration Act 1950, s 12(6)(b); Solicitors Act 1974, ss 2(2), 44A, 47A, 81(5); County Courts Act 1984, s 143(2); Prosecution of Offences Act 1985, s 15(1); Administration of Justice Act 1985, ss 1, 3(2), 26(3), 65(5), Sch 2, para 19, Sch 3, para 8, Sch 7, para 5) (SI 1991/608)

1 Jul 1991 (repeals of or in Public Notaries Act 1801, ss 1–5, 7–9; Public Notaries Act 1833; Public Notaries Act 1843; Small Debts Act 1845; Welsh Church Act 1914; Administration of Justice Act 1956, s 37; Administration of Justice Act 1969, s 29; County Courts Act 1984, ss 19, 20, 22, 29, 34, 43, 44, 89(3), 105, 106, Sch 1) (SI 1991/1364)

Courts and Legal Services Act 1990 (c 41)—*contd*
Schedule

20—*contd*	14 Oct 1991 (repeals of or in Maintenance Orders Act 1950; Family Law Reform Act 1969; Children and Young Persons Act 1969; Administration of Justice Act 1970; Maintenance Orders (Reciprocal Enforcement of Orders) Act 1972; Domestic Proceedings and Magistrates' Courts Act 1978; Magistrates' Courts Act 1980; Matrimonial and Family Proceedings Act 1984; Family Law Reform Act 1987; Children Act 1989) (SI 1991/1883)
	1 Jan 1992 (repeals of or in Judicial Pensions Act 1981, ss 18(3), 20(6), 22(5), 24, 25, Sch 1, para 15(3)) (SI 1991/2730)
	1 Jun 1992 (repeals of or in Solicitors Act 1974, ss 7, 33(4); County Courts Act 1984, s 45; Administration of Justice Act 1985, s 9(8), Sch 2, para 4(2)) (SI 1992/1221)
	1 Oct 1993 (repeal of words in Supreme Court Act 1981, s 18) (SI 1993/2132)
	Not in force (otherwise)

---

[1]   Orders made under Access to Justice Act 1999, s 108(1) bringing the prospective insertion into force will be noted to that Act

---

Criminal Justice (International Co-operation) Act 1990 (c 5)

RA: 5 Apr 1990

Commencement provisions: s 32(2); Criminal Justice (International Co-operation) Act 1990 (Commencement No 1) Order 1991, SI 1991/1072; Criminal Justice (International Co-operation) Act 1990 (Commencement No 2) Order 1991, SI 1991/2108

Section

1, 2		10 Jun 1991 (SI 1991/1072)
3	(1), (2)	10 Jun 1991 (SI 1991/1072)
	(3)	23 Apr 1991 (for purpose of making any Order in Council, order, rules, or regulations) (SI 1991/1072)
		10 Jun 1991 (otherwise) (SI 1991/1072)
	(4)–(10)	10 Jun 1991 (SI 1991/1072)
4	(1), (2)	10 Jun 1991 (SI 1991/1072)

Criminal Justice (International Co-operation) Act 1990 (c 5)—*contd*

Section

4	(2A), (2B)	Inserted by Criminal Justice and Public Order Act 1994, s 164(1) (qv)
	(3)–(5)	10 Jun 1991 (SI 1991/1072)
	(6)	See Sch 1 below
5, 6		10 Jun 1991 (SI 1991/1072)
7	(1)–(6)	10 Jun 1991 (SI 1991/1072)
	(7)	23 Apr 1991 (for purpose of making any Order in Council, order, rules, or regulations) (SI 1991/1072)
		10 Jun 1991 (otherwise) (SI 1991/1072)
	(8)	10 Jun 1991 (SI 1991/1072)
	(8A), (8B)	Prospectively inserted by Criminal Justice and Police Act 2001, Sch 2, para 24[2]
	(9)	10 Jun 1991 (SI 1991/1072)
8	(1)–(4)	10 Jun 1991 (SI 1991/1072)
	(5)	23 Apr 1991 (for purpose of making any Order in Council, order, rules, or regulations) (SI 1991/1072)
		10 Jun 1991 (otherwise) (SI 1991/1072)
	(6)	10 Jun 1991 (SI 1991/1072)
	(7), (8)	Prospectively inserted by Criminal Justice and Police Act 2001, Sch 2, para 25[2]
9, 10		23 Apr 1991 (for purpose of making any Order in Council, order, rules, or regulations) (SI 1991/1072)
		10 Jun 1991 (otherwise) (SI 1991/1072)
11		10 Jun 1991 (SI 1991/1072)
12	(1)	1 Jul 1991 (SI 1991/1072)
	(1A)	Inserted by Criminal Justice (International Co-operation) (Amendment) Act 1998, s 1 (qv)
	(2)–(4)	1 Jul 1991 (SI 1991/1072)
	(5)	23 Apr 1991 (for purpose of making any Order in Council, order, rules, or regulations) (SI 1991/1072)
		1 Jul 1991 (otherwise) (SI 1991/1072)
13		23 Apr 1991 (for purpose of making any Order in Council, order, rules, or regulations) (SI 1991/1072)
		1 Jul 1991 (otherwise) (SI 1991/1072)
14		Repealed (E, W, NI)[1]
		1 Jul 1991 (S) (1991/1072)
15		Spent (E, W)
		Repealed (S)
16, 17		Repealed
18–22		1 Jul 1991 (SI 1991/1072)

Criminal Justice (International Co-operation) Act 1990 (c 5)—*contd*

Section				
23				1 Jul 1991 (SI 1991/1072)
23A				Repealed (E, W, NI)
				Inserted by Criminal Justice Act 1993, s 77, Sch 4, para 5 (qv) (S)
24				1 Jul 1991 (SI 1991/1072)
25, 26				Repealed
26A, 26B				Repealed *(never in force)*
27–29				Repealed
30	(1)			10 Jun 1991 (SI 1991/1072)
	(2)			Repealed
	(3)			Repealed *(never in force)*
31	(1)			See Sch 4 below
	(2)			Repealed
	(3)			See Sch 5 below
	(4)			1 Jul 1991 (SI 1991/1072)
32	(1)–(3)			10 Jun 1991 (SI 1991/1072)
	(4)			23 Apr 1991 (for purpose of making any Order in Council, order, rules, or regulations) (SI 1991/1072)
				10 Jun 1991 (otherwise) (SI 1991/1072)

Schedule				
1				10 Jun 1991 (SI 1991/1072)
2				23 Apr 1991 (for purpose of making any Order in Council, order, rules, or regulations) (SI 1991/1072)
				1 Jul 1991 (otherwise) (SI 1991/1072)
3, para	1	(1)	(a), (b)	1 Jul 1991 (SI 1991/1072)
			(c)	23 Apr 1991 (for purpose of making any Order in Council, order, rules, or regulations) (SI 1991/1072)
				1 Jul 1991 (otherwise) (SI 1991/1072)
		(2), (3)		1 Jul 1991 (SI 1991/1072)
	2–9			1 Jul 1991 (SI 1991/1072)
4, para	1			1 Jul 1991 (SI 1991/1072)
	2			10 Jun 1991 (SI 1991/1072)
	3			1 Jul 1991 (SI 1991/1072)
	4, 5			Repealed
	6–8			10 Jun 1991 (SI 1991/1072)
5				10 Jun 1991 (repeals of or in Extradition Act 1873, s 5; Evidence (Proceedings in Other Jurisdictions) Act 1975, s 5; Suppression of Terrorism Act 1978, s 1(3)(d) (and word 'and' immediately preceding it), (4), (5)(b) (and word 'and' immediately preceding it); Criminal Justice Act 1988, s 29) (SI 1991/1072)
				1 Jul 1991 (otherwise) (SI 1991/1072)

Criminal Justice (International Co-operation) Act 1990 (c 5)—*contd*

1   S 14(3), (5) previously repealed (15 Feb 1994) by Criminal Justice Act 1993, s 79(14), Sch 6, Pt I

2   Orders made under Criminal Justice and Police Act 2001, s 138(2)–(4) bringing the prospective insertions into force will be noted to that Act

Education (Student Loans) Act 1990 (c 6)

Whole Act repealed

Employment Act 1990 (c 38)

RA: 1 Nov 1990

Commencement provisions: s 18(2)–(4); Employment Act 1990 (Commencement and Transitional Provisions) Order 1990, SI 1990/2378; Employment Act 1990 (Commencement and Transitional Provisions) Amendment Order 1991, SI 1991/89 (corrects defect in SI 1990/2378)

Section

1–12	Repealed
13	1 Feb 1991 (SI 1990/2378)
14	Repealed
15	1 Nov 1990 (s 18(2))
16	Repealed
17	1 Nov 1990 (s 18(2))
18	1 Nov 1990 (RA)

Schedule

1–3	Repealed

Enterprise and New Towns (Scotland) Act 1990 (c 35)

RA: 26 Jul 1990

Commencement provisions: s 39(1), (3); Enterprise and New Towns (Scotland) Act 1990 Commencement Order 1990, SI 1990/1840

Section

1		1 Oct 1990 (for purpose of establishing Scottish Enterprise and Highlands and Islands Enterprise, and bringing into force Sch 1) (SI 1990/1840)
		1 Apr 1991 (otherwise) (SI 1990/1840)
2–14		1 Apr 1991 (SI 1990/1840)
14A		Inserted by Trade Union Reform and Employment Rights Act 1993, s 47(5) (qv)
15–18		1 Apr 1991 (SI 1990/1840)
19, 20		26 Jul 1990 (for purposes of Sch 3, paras 4, 5) (s 39(1), (3))
		1 Apr 1991 (otherwise) (SI 1990/1840)
21	(1)–(3)	1 Apr 1991 (SI 1990/1840)

Enterprise and New Towns (Scotland) Act 1990 (c 35)—*contd*

Section

21	(4)	1 Oct 1990 (SI 1990/1840)
	(5)	Inserted by Local Government etc (Scotland) Act 1994, s 180(1), Sch 13, para 164(1), (2)(b) (qv)
22		1 Oct 1990 (SI 1990/1840)
23	(1)–(3)	1 Apr 1991 (SI 1990/1840)
	(4)	See Sch 3 below
24		1 Apr 1991 (SI 1990/1840)
25	(1)	See Sch 2 below
	(1A), (1B)	Inserted by Public Finance and Accountability Act 2000, s 8, Sch 1, para 4(2) (qv)
	(2)–(4)	Repealed
26	(1), (2)	1 Oct 1990 (SI 1990/1840)
	(3)	1 Apr 1991 (SI 1990/1840)
	(3A), (3B)	Inserted by Public Finance and Accountability Act, s 8, Sch 1, para 4(3) (qv)
	(4)	1 Apr 1991 (SI 1990/1840)
27		1 Oct 1990 (SI 1990/1840)
28		1 Apr 1991 (SI 1990/1840)
29, 30		1 Oct 1990 (SI 1990/1840)
31, 32		1 Apr 1991 (SI 1990/1840)
33–35		1 Oct 1990 (SI 1990/1840)
36, 37		26 Jul 1990 (s 39(1), (3))
38	(1)	See Sch 4 below
	(2)	See Sch 5 below
	(3), (4)	1 Apr 1991 (SI 1990/1840)
39, 40		26 Jul 1990 (RA)

Schedule

1		1 Oct 1990 (SI 1990/1840)
2, para	1	1 Oct 1990 (SI 1990/1840)
	2–6	1 Apr 1991 (SI 1990/1840)
3, para	1–3	1 Apr 1991 (SI 1990/1840)
	4, 5	26 Jul 1990 (s 39(1), (3))
	6–9	1 Apr 1991 (SI 1990/1840)
4, para	1	1 Oct 1990 (SI 1990/1840)
	2–5	1 Apr 1991 (SI 1990/1840)
	6	1 Oct 1990 (SI 1990/1840)
	7–18	1 Apr 1991 (SI 1990/1840)
5		26 Jul 1990 (s 39(1), (3))

Entertainments (Increased Penalties) Act 1990 (c 20)

RA: 13 Jul 1990

13 Jul 1990 (RA)

Environmental Protection Act 1990 (c 43)

RA: 1 Nov 1990

Commencement provisions: ss 130(4), 131(3), 164(2), (3); Environmental Protection Act 1990 (Commencement No 1) Order 1990, SI 1990/2226; Environmental Protection Act 1990 (Commencement No 2) Order 1990, SI 1990/2243; Environmental Protection Act 1990 (Commencement No 3) Order 1990, SI 1990/2565; Environmental Protection Act 1990 (Commencement No 4) Order 1990, SI 1990/2635 (also amends SI 1990/2565); Environmental Protection Act 1990 (Commencement No 5) Order 1991, SI 1991/96; Environmental Protection Act 1990 (Commencement No 6 and Appointed Day) Order 1991, SI 1991/685; Environmental Protection Act 1990 (Commencement No 7) Order 1991, SI 1991/1042; Environmental Protection Act 1990 (Commencement No 8) Order 1991, SI 1991/1319; Environmental Protection Act 1990 (Commencement No 9) Order 1991, SI 1991/1577; Environmental Protection Act 1990 (Commencement No 10) Order 1991, SI 1991/2829; Environmental Protection Act 1990 (Commencement No 11) Order 1992, SI 1992/266; Environmental Protection Act 1990 (Commencement No 12) Order 1992, SI 1992/3253; Environmental Protection Act 1990 (Commencement No 13) Order 1993, SI 1993/274; Environmental Protection Act 1990 (Commencement No 14) Order 1994, SI 1994/780; Environmental Protection Act 1990 (Commencement No 15) Order 1994, SI 1994/1096, as amended by SI 1994/2487, SI 1994/3234; Environmental Protection Act 1990 (Commencement No 15) (Amendment) Order 1994, SI 1994/2487 (amending SI 1994/1096); Environmental Protection Act 1990 (Commencement No 16) Order 1994, SI 1994/2854; Environmental Protection Act 1990 (Commencement No 15) (Amendment No 2) Order 1994, SI 1994/3234 (amending SI 1994/1096); Environmental Protection Act 1990 (Commencement No 17) Order 1995, SI 1995/2152; Environmental Protection Act 1990 (Commencement No 18) Order 1996, SI 1996/3056

Section	
1, 2	1 Jan 1991 (SI 1990/2635); prospectively repealed by Pollution Prevention and Control Act 1999, s 6(2), Sch 3[1]
3	19 Dec 1991 (SI 1990/2635); prospectively repealed by Pollution Prevention and Control Act 1999, s 6(2), Sch 3[1]
4	1 Jan 1991 (SI 1990/2635); prospectively repealed by Pollution Prevention and Control Act 1999, s 6(2), Sch 3[1]
5	Repealed
6–15	1 Jan 1991 (SI 1990/2635); prospectively repealed by Pollution Prevention and Control Act 1999, s 6(2), Sch 3[1]
16–18	Repealed

Environmental Protection Act 1990 (c 43)—*contd*

Section

19–28			1 Jan 1991 (SI 1990/2635); prospectively repealed by Pollution Prevention and Control Act 1999, s 6(2), Sch 3[1]
29, 30			31 May 1991 (SI 1991/1319)
31			Repealed
32			See Sch 2 below
33	(1)	(a), (b)	See note at end of entry for this Act
		(c)	1 Apr 1992 (SI 1991/2829)
	(2)		1 Apr 1992 (so far as relates to s 33(1)(c)) (SI 1991/2829)
			See note at end of entry for this Act (otherwise)
	(3), (4)		13 Dec 1991 (SI 1991/2829)
	(5)		See note at end of entry for this Act
	(6)–(9)		1 Apr 1992 (so far as relates to s 33(1)(c)) (SI 1991/2829)
			See note at end of entry for this Act (otherwise)
34	(1)–(3)		1 Apr 1992 (SI 1991/2829)
	(3A)		Inserted by Environment Act 1995, s 120(1), Sch 22, para 65 (qv)
	(4)		1 Apr 1992 (SI 1991/2829)
	(4A)		Inserted by Deregulation and Contracting Out Act 1994, s 33 (qv)
	(5)		13 Dec 1991 (SI 1991/2829)
	(6)		1 Apr 1992 (SI 1991/2829)
	(7)–(9)		13 Dec 1991 (SI 1991/2829)
	(10)		1 Apr 1992 (SI 1991/2829)
	(11)		13 Dec 1991 (SI 1991/2829)
35	(1)–(5)		See note at end of entry for this Act
	(6)		18 Feb 1993 (SI 1993/274)
	(7)		See note at end of entry for this Act
	(7A)–(7C)		Inserted by Environment Act 1995, s 120(1), Sch 22, para 66 (qv)
	(8)–(11)		See note at end of entry for this Act
	(11A)		Inserted (1 Aug 2000) by Pollution Prevention and Control (England and Wales) Regulations 2000, SI 2000/1973, reg 39, Sch 10, para 5
	(12)		See note at end of entry for this Act
35A			Inserted by Environment Act 1995, s 120(1), Sch 22, para 67 (qv)
36	(1)		18 Feb 1993 (SI 1993/274)
	(1A)		Inserted (subject to a saving in SI 1996/186, art 4) by Environment Act 1995, s 120(1), Sch 22, para 68(1), (2) (qv)

Environmental Protection Act 1990 (c 43)—*contd*

Section

36	(2)–(4)	See note at end of entry for this Act
	(5), (6)	Repealed
	(7)–(9)	See note at end of entry for this Act
	(9A)	Inserted by Environment Act 1995, s 120(1), Sch 22, para 68(1), (5) (qv)
	(10)–(14)	Substituted for original sub-s (10) (subject to a saving in SI 1996/186, art 4) by Environment Act 1995, s 120(1), Sch 22, para 68(1), (6) (qv); sub-s (12), as so substituted, repealed
36A		Inserted by Environment Act 1995, s 120(1), Sch 22, para 69 (qv)
37	(1), (2)	See note at end of entry for this Act
	(3)	18 Feb 1993 (so far as enables Secretary of State to give directions) (SI 1993/274)
		See note at end of entry for this Act (otherwise)
	(4)–(6)	See note at end of entry for this Act
	(7)	Added by Environment Act 1995, s 120(1), Sch 22, para 70(3) (qv)
37A		Inserted by Environment Act 1995, s 120(1), Sch 22, para 71 (qv)
38	(1)–(6)	See note at end of entry for this Act
	(7)	18 Feb 1993 (so far as enables Secretary of State to give directions) (SI 1993/274)
		See note at end of entry for this Act (otherwise)
	(8), (9)	See note at end of entry for this Act
	(9A)–(9C)	Inserted by Environment Act 1995, s 120(1), Sch 22, para 72(1) (qv)
	(10)–(12)	See note at end of entry for this Act
	(13)	Added by Environment Act 1995, s 120(1), Sch 22, para 72(2) (qv)
39	(1), (2)	See note at end of entry for this Act
	(3)	18 Feb 1993 (SI 1993/274)
	(4)–(7)	See note at end of entry for this Act
	(8)	Repealed
	(9)–(11)	See note at end of entry for this Act
	(12)–(14)	Inserted by Environment Act 1995, s 120(1), Sch 22, para 73(1), (6) (qv); sub-s (13), as so inserted, repealed
40	(1), (2)	See note at end of entry for this Act
	(3)	18 Feb 1993 (SI 1993/274)
	(4)–(6)	See note at end of entry for this Act
41		Repealed

Environmental Protection Act 1990 (c 43)—*contd*

Section

42	(1)	See note at end of entry for this Act
	(2)	Repealed
	(3)–(6)	See note at end of entry for this Act
	(6A)	Inserted by Environment Act 1995, s 120(1), Sch 22, para 76(1), (7) (qv)
	(7)	See note at end of entry for this Act
	(8)	18 Feb 1993 (so far as enables Secretary of State to give directions) (SI 1993/274)
		See note at end of entry for this Act (otherwise)
43	(1), (2)	See note at end of entry for this Act
	(2A)	Inserted by Environment Act 1995, s 120(1), Sch 22, para 77 (qv)
	(3)–(7)	See note at end of entry for this Act
	(8)	18 Feb 1993 (SI 1993/274)
44		Substituted by Environment Act 1995, s 112, Sch 19, para 4(1) (qv)
44A		Inserted by Environment Act 1995, s 92(1) (qv)
44B		Inserted (S) by Environment Act 1995, s 92(1) (qv)
45	(1)	14 Feb 1992 (so far as enables orders or regulations to be made) (SI 1992/266)
		1 Apr 1992 (otherwise) (SI 1992/266)
	(2)	14 Feb 1992 (so far as enables orders or regulations to be made) (SI 1992/266)
		1 Apr 1992 (otherwise) (S) (SI 1992/266)
		Not in force (otherwise) (E, W)
	(3)–(12)	14 Feb 1992 (so far as enable orders or regulations to be made) (SI 1992/266)
		1 Apr 1992 (otherwise) (SI 1992/266)
46, 47		1 Apr 1992 (SI 1992/266)
48	(1)–(6)	1 Apr 1992 (SI 1992/266)
	(7)	*Not in force*
	(8), (9)	1 Apr 1992 (SI 1992/266)
49		1 Aug 1991 (SI 1991/1577)
50		Repealed
51		31 May 1991 (SI 1991/1319)
52	(1)	1 Apr 1992 (SI 1992/266)
	(2)	*Not in force*
	(3)–(7)	1 Apr 1992 (SI 1992/266)
	(8)	13 Dec 1991 (so far as relates to s 52(1), (3)) (SI 1991/2829)

Environmental Protection Act 1990 (c 43)—*contd*

Section

52	(8)—*contd*	*Not in force* (otherwise)
	(9)–(11)	1 Apr 1992 (SI 1992/266)
53		1 Apr 1992 (SI 1992/266)
54	(1)–(13)	1 May 1994 (SI 1994/1096)
	(14)	18 Feb 1993 (SI 1993/274)
	(15)–(17)	1 May 1994 (SI 1994/1096)
		Section prospectively repealed by Environment Act 1995, s 120(3), Sch 24[2]
55, 56		1 Apr 1992 (SI 1992/266)
57		See note at end of entry for this Act
58, 59		1 May 1994 (SI 1994/1096)
60		31 May 1991 (so far as relates to anything deposited at a place for deposit of waste, or in a receptacle for waste, provided by a waste disposal contractor under arrangements made with a waste disposal authority) (SI 1991/1319)
		1 May 1994 (otherwise) (SI 1994/1096)
61		Repealed (*never in force in relation to W, S*)
62		11 Aug 1995 (SI 1995/2152)
63	(1)	18 Feb 1993 (SI 1993/274)
	(2)	*Not in force*; prospectively substituted by Environment Act 1995, s 120(1), Sch 22, para 81[2]
	(3), (4)	*Not in force*
63A		Inserted by Waste Minimisation Act 1998, s 1 (qv)
64	(1)	18 Feb 1993 (SI 1993/274)
	(2)	1 May 1994 (SI 1994/1096)
	(2A)	Inserted by Environment Act 1995, s 120(1), Sch 22, para 82(1), (2) (qv)
	(3)	1 May 1994 (SI 1994/1096)
	(4)	18 Feb 1993 (SI 1993/274)
	(5)	Substituted by Environment Act 1995, s 120(1), Sch 22, para 82(1), (4) (qv)
	(6), (7)	1 May 1994 (SI 1994/1096)
	(8)	18 Feb 1993 (SI 1993/274)
65	(1)	1 May 1994 (SI 1994/1096)
	(2)	18 Feb 1993 (so far as enables Secretary of State to give directions) (SI 1993/274)
		1 May 1994 (otherwise) (SI 1994/1096)
	(3), (4)	1 May 1994 (SI 1994/1096)

Environmental Protection Act 1990 (c 43)—*contd*

Section

66	(1)–(5)		1 May 1994 (SI 1994/1096)
	(6)		Substituted by Environment Act 1995, s 120(1), Sch 22, para 83(2) (qv)
	(7)		18 Feb 1993 (so far as enables Secretary of State to give directions) (SI 1993/274)
			1 May 1994 (otherwise) (SI 1994/1096)
	(8)–(11)		1 May 1994 (SI 1994/1096)
67–70			Repealed
71			31 May 1991 (SI 1991/1319)
72			Repealed
73	(1)–(5)		1 Apr 1992 (SI 1992/266)
	(6)–(9)		1 May 1994 (SI 1994/1096)
74	(1)–(5)		1 May 1994 (SI 1994/1096)
	(6)		18 Feb 1993 (SI 1993/274)
	(7)		1 May 1994 (SI 1994/1096)
75			31 May 1991 (SI 1991/1319)
76			Substituted by Environment Act 1995, s 118(3) (qv)
77			31 May 1991 (SI 1991/1319)
78			13 Dec 1991 (SI 1991/2829)
78A–78YC			Inserted by Environment Act 1995, s 57 (qv)
79, 80			1 Jan 1991 (s 164(2))
80A			Inserted (E, W) by Noise and Statutory Nuisance Act 1993, s 3(6) (qv)
81			1 Jan 1991 (s 164(2))
81A, 81B			Inserted (E, W) by Noise and Statutory Nuisance Act 1993, s 10(2) (qv)
82			1 Jan 1991 (s 164(2))
83			Repealed
84			1 Jan 1991 (s 164(2))
85			Repealed
86	(1)		13 Feb 1991 (E, W) (SI 1991/96)
			1 Apr 1991 (S) (SI 1991/1042)
	(2)	(a)	14 Jan 1991 (SI 1991/96)
		(aa)	Inserted by Local Government (Wales) Act 1994, s 22(3), Sch 9, para 17(6) (qv)
		(b)–(e)	14 Jan 1991 (SI 1991/96)
	(3)		1 Apr 1991 (SI 1991/1042)
	(4), (5)		13 Feb 1991 (E, W) (SI 1991/96)
			1 Apr 1991 (S) (SI 1991/1042)
	(6)–(8)		14 Jan 1991 (SI 1991/96)
	(9)	(a), (b)	13 Feb 1991 (SI 1991/96)

Environmental Protection Act 1990 (c 43)—*contd*

Section

86	(9)	(bb)	Inserted by Local Government (Wales) Act 1994, s 22(3), Sch 9, para 17(7) (qv)
		(c)	13 Feb 1991 (SI 1991/96)
	(10)		1 Apr 1991 (SI 1991/1042)
	(11)		14 Jan 1991 (SI 1991/96)
	(12)		1 Jun 1991 (SI 1991/1042)
	(13)		13 Feb 1991 (E, W) (SI 1991/96)
			1 Apr 1991 (S) (SI 1991/1042)
	(14), (15)		14 Jan 1991 (SI 1991/96)
87	(1), (2)		13 Feb 1991 (E, W) (SI 1991/96)
			1 Apr 1991 (S) (SI 1991/1042)
	(3)	(a)–(e)	13 Feb 1991 (E, W) (SI 1991/96)
			1 Apr 1991 (S) (SI 1991/1042)
		(f)	1 Jun 1991 (SI 1991/1042)
	(4)–(6)		13 Feb 1991 (E, W) (SI 1991/96)
			1 Apr 1991 (S) (SI 1991/1042)
	(7)		1 Apr 1991 (SI 1991/1042)
88	(1)–(4)		13 Feb 1991 (E, W) (SI 1991/96)
			1 Apr 1991 (S) (SI 1991/1042)
	(5)		14 Jan 1991 (SI 1991/96)
	(6)		13 Feb 1991 (E, W) (SI 1991/96)
			1 Apr 1991 (S) (SI 1991/1042)
	(7)		14 Jan 1991 (SI 1991/96)
	(8)		13 Feb 1991 (E, W) (SI 1991/96)
			1 Apr 1991 (S) (SI 1991/1042)
	(9)	(a)	13 Feb 1991 (E, W) (SI 1991/96)
			1 Apr 1991 (S) (SI 1991/1042)
		(b)	14 Jan 1991 (SI 1991/96)
		(c), (d)	Repealed
		(e)	13 Feb 1991 (E, W) (SI 1991/96)
	(10)		13 Feb 1991 (E, W) (SI 1991/96)
			1 Apr 1991 (S) (SI 1991/1042)
89	(1)	(a)–(f)	1 Apr 1991 (SI 1991/1042)
		(g)	1 Jun 1991 (SI 1991/1042)
	(2), (3)		1 Apr 1991 (SI 1991/1042)
	(4)		14 Jan 1991 (SI 1991/96)
	(5), (6)		1 Apr 1991 (SI 1991/1042)
	(7)–(9)		13 Nov 1990 (SI 1990/2243)
	(10)		1 Apr 1991 (SI 1991/1042)
	(11)–(13)		13 Nov 1990 (SI 1990/2243)
	(13A)–(13C)		Inserted (1 Jul 1999) by Scotland Act 1998 (Consequential Modifications) (No 2) Order 1999, SI 1999/1820, art 4, Sch 2, Pt I, para 102
	(14)		1 Apr 1991 (SI 1991/1042)
90	(1), (2)		14 Jan 1991 (SI 1991/96)
	(3)–(6)		1 Jun 1991 (SI 1991/1042)

Environmental Protection Act 1990 (c 43)—*contd*

Section

90	(7)		14 Jan 1991 (SI 1991/96)
91	(1)	(a)–(f)	1 Apr 1991 (SI 1991/1042)
		(g)	1 Jun 1991 (SI 1991/1042)
	(2)–(13)		1 Apr 1991 (SI 1991/1042)
92	(1)	(a)–(c)	1 Apr 1991 (SI 1991/1042)
		(d)	1 Jun 1991 (SI 1991/1042)
	(2)–(10)		1 Apr 1991 (SI 1991/1042)
93			1 Apr 1991 (SI 1991/1042)
94	(1), (2)		14 Jan 1991 (SI 1991/96)
	(3)–(9)		1 Apr 1991 (SI 1991/1042)
95			1 Apr 1991 (SI 1991/1042)
96	(1)		1 Apr 1991 (SI 1991/1042)
	(2), (3)		14 Jan 1991 (SI 1991/96)
97			1 Jan 1991 (s 164(2))
98	(1)		13 Feb 1991 (E, W) (SI 1991/96)
			1 Apr 1991 (S) (SI 1991/1042)
	(2)		13 Feb 1991 (SI 1991/96)
	(3), (4)		1 Apr 1991 (SI 1991/1042)
	(5), (6)		13 Feb 1991 (E, W) (SI 1991/96)
			1 Apr 1991 (S) (SI 1991/1042)
	(7)–(9)		Added (16 Jun 1999) by Railways Act 1993 (Consequential Modifications) Order 1999, SI 1999/1443, art 2(3)
99			See Sch 4 below
100–105			Repealed
106	(1)–(3)		1 Feb 1993 (SI 1992/3253)
	(4), (5)		1 Apr 1991 (SI 1991/1042)
	(6), (7)		1 Feb 1993 (SI 1992/3253)
107	(1)–(7)		1 Feb 1993 (SI 1992/3253)
	(8)		1 Apr 1991 (SI 1991/1042)
	(9)–(11)		1 Feb 1993 (SI 1992/3253)
108	(1)	(a)	1 Feb 1993 (so far as relates to import or acquisition of genetically modified organisms) (SI 1992/3253)
			Not in force (otherwise)
		(b)	1 Apr 1991 (SI 1991/1042)
	(2)		*Not in force*
	(3)	(a)	*Not in force*
		(b)	1 Apr 1991 (SI 1991/1042)
	(4)		*Not in force*
	(5)		1 Apr 1991 (SI 1991/1042)
	(6)		*Not in force*
	(7)		1 Apr 1991 (SI 1991/1042)
	(8)		*Not in force*
	(9)		1 Apr 1991 (SI 1991/1042)
	(10)		1 Jan 1993 (SI 1992/3253)
109			*Not in force*

Environmental Protection Act 1990 (c 43)—*contd*

Section

110			1 Feb 1993 (so far as relates to import, acquisition, release or marketing of genetically modified organisms) (SI 1992/3253)
			Not in force (otherwise)
111	(1), (2)		1 Apr 1991 (SI 1991/1042)
	(3)		*Not in force*
	(4), (5)		1 Apr 1991 (SI 1991/1042)
	(6)		1 Feb 1993 (SI 1992/3253)
	(6A)		Inserted (1 Feb 1993) by Genetically Modified Organisms (Deliberate Release) Regulations 1992, SI 1992/3280, reg 13
	(7)		1 Apr 1991 (SI 1991/1042)
	(8)–(10)		1 Feb 1993 (SI 1992/3253)
	(11)		1 Apr 1991 (SI 1991/1042)
112	(1), (2)		1 Feb 1993 (SI 1992/3253)
	(3), (4)		*Not in force*
	(5)–(7)		1 Feb 1993 (SI 1992/3253)
113			1 Apr 1991 (SI 1991/1042)
114	(1)–(3)		1 Apr 1991 (SI 1991/1042)
	(4), (5)		1 Feb 1993 (SI 1992/3253)
115	(1)–(3)		1 Feb 1993 (SI 1992/3253)
	(4)		1 Apr 1991 (SI 1991/1042)
	(5)–(10)		1 Feb 1993 (SI 1992/3253)
116			1 Feb 1993 (so far as relates to import, acquisition, release or marketing of genetically modified organisms) (SI 1992/3253)
			Not in force (otherwise)
117			1 Feb 1993 (SI 1992/3253)
118	(1)	(a)	1 Feb 1993 (SI 1992/3253)
		(b)	*Not in force*
		(c)	1 Feb 1993 (SI 1992/3253)
		(d)	*Not in force*
		(e)–(l)	1 Feb 1993 (SI 1992/3253)
		(m)	1 Feb 1993 (so far as relates to s 111) (SI 1992/3253)
			Not in force (otherwise)
		(n), (o)	1 Feb 1993 (SI 1992/3253)
	(2)–(10)		1 Feb 1993 (SI 1992/3253)
119–121			1 Feb 1993 (SI 1992/3253)
122	(1)	(a), (b)	1 Apr 1991 (so far as empower Secretary of State to make regulations) (SI 1991/1042)
			Not in force (otherwise)
		(c)–(h)	1 Apr 1991 (so far as empower Secretary of State to make regulations) (SI 1991/1042)

Environmental Protection Act 1990 (c 43)—*contd*

Section

122	(1)	(c)–(h)—*contd*	1 Feb 1993 (otherwise) (SI 1992/3253)
	(2), (3)		1 Feb 1993 (SI 1992/3253)
	(4)		1 Apr 1991 (SI 1991/1042)
123	(1)–(6)		1 Feb 1993 (SI 1992/3253)
	(7)		1 Apr 1991 (SI 1991/1042)
	(8)		1 Feb 1993 (SI 1992/3253)
	(9)		1 Apr 1991 (SI 1991/1042)
124, 125			1 Apr 1991 (SI 1991/1042)
126			Substituted by Food Standards Act 1999, s 18, Sch 3, para 18 (qv)
127			1 Feb 1993 (SI 1992/3253)
128	(1)–(4)		5 Nov 1990 (save for amendments) (SI 1990/2226)
			1 Apr 1991 (otherwise) (SI 1991/685)
	(5)		See Schs 6, 7 below
129			5 Nov 1990 (SI 1990/2226)
130			1 Apr 1991 (SI 1991/685)
131			5 Nov 1990 (SI 1990/2226)[3]
132	(1)	(a)	1 Apr 1991 (SI 1991/685)[3]
		(b)–(e)	5 Nov 1990 (save for amendments) (SI 1990/2226)[3]
			1 Apr 1991 (otherwise) (SI 1991/685)[3]
	(2), (3)		5 Nov 1990 (SI 1990/2226)[3]
133, 134			5 Nov 1990 (SI 1990/2226)[3]
135	(1), (2)		5 Nov 1990 (SI 1990/2226)
	(3)		See Sch 10, Pt I below
136	(1), (2)		5 Nov 1990 (SI 1990/2226)
	(3)		See Sch 10, Pt II below
137	(1)–(3)		5 Nov 1990 (SI 1990/2226)
	(4)		See Sch 10, Pt III below
138			5 Nov 1990 (SI 1990/2226)
139			See Sch 11 below
140	(1)–(4)		1 Jan 1991 (s 164(2))
	(5)		See Sch 12 below
	(6)–(11)		1 Jan 1991 (s 164(2))
141			1 Jan 1991 (s 164(2))
142	(1), (2)		1 Jan 1991 (s 164(2))
	(3)		See Sch 12 below
	(4)–(7)		1 Jan 1991 (s 164(2))
143	(1)		Repealed (E)
			14 Feb 1992 (W) (SI 1992/266)
			Not in force (S)
	(2)–(4)		Repealed (E) (*never in force*)
			Not in force (otherwise)
	(5), (6)		Repealed (E)
			14 Feb 1992 (W) (SI 1992/266)
			Not in force (S)
			Remainder of section repealed
144			See Sch 13 below

Environmental Protection Act 1990 (c 43)—*contd*

Section

145, 146		1 Jan 1991 (s 164(2))
147		31 May 1991 (SI 1991/1319)
148		Repealed
149–151		14 Feb 1992 (so far as enable orders or regulations to be made) (SI 1992/266)
		1 Apr 1992 (otherwise) (SI 1992/266)
152		10 Jul 1991 (SI 1991/1577)
153–155		1 Jan 1991 (s 164(2))
156		1 Apr 1991 (SI 1991/1042)
157		1 Jan 1991 (s 164(2))
158		1 Apr 1991 (SI 1991/1042)
159		1 Jan 1991 (SI 1990/2635)
160, 161		1 Jan 1991 (s 164(2))
162	(1)	See Sch 15 below
	(2)	See Sch 16 below
	(3)	1 Apr 1992 (SI 1992/266)
	(4)	*Not in force*
	(5)	1 Jan 1991 (s 164(2))
163		1 Jan 1991 (s 164(2))
164		1 Nov 1990 (RA)

Schedule

1		1 Jan 1991 (SI 1990/2635); prospectively repealed by Pollution Prevention and Control Act 1999, s 6(2), Sch 3[1]
2		31 May 1991 (SI 1991/1319)
2A		Inserted by Environment Act 1995, s 92(2), Sch 12 (qv)
2B		Prospectively inserted by Environment Act 1995, s 120(1), Sch 22, para 95[2]
3, 4		1 Jan 1991 (s 164(2))
5		Repealed
6–9		5 Nov 1990 (save for amendments) (SI 1990/2226)
		1 Apr 1991 (otherwise) (SI 1991/685)
10, 11		5 Nov 1990 (SI 1990/2226)
12		1 Jan 1991 (s 164(2))
13, Pt	I	1 Jan 1992 (SI 1991/2829)
	II	Repealed
14		1 Jan 1991 (s 164(2)); repealed, subject to an exception, by Merchant Shipping Act 1995, s 314(1), Sch 12 (qv)
15, para	1	Repealed
	2	1 Apr 1991 (SI 1991/1042)

Environmental Protection Act 1990 (c 43)—*contd*

Schedule

15, para	3		1 Apr 1992 (SI 1992/266)
	4, 5		1 Jan 1991 (s 164(2))
	6–8		Repealed
	9		1 Jan 1991 (s 164(2))
	10	(1)	1 Apr 1992 (SI 1991/2829)
		(2)	Repealed
		(3)	14 Jan 1991 (SI 1991/96)
	11		1 Apr 1991 (SI 1991/1042)
	12		Repealed
	13, 14		1 Apr 1991 (SI 1991/1042)
	15	(1)–(5)	14 Jan 1991 (SI 1991/96)
		(6)–(9)	Repealed
	16		Repealed
	17		*Not in force*
	18		Repealed
	19		1 Apr 1992 (SI 1992/266)
	20		1 Apr 1991 (SI 1991/1042)
	21		18 Feb 1993 (SI 1993/274)
	22		1 Jan 1991 (so far as inserts Public Health (Control of Disease) Act 1984, s 7(4)(m)) (s 164(2)) 1 Apr 1991 (otherwise) (SI 1991/1042)
	23		Repealed
	24		1 Jan 1991 (s 164(2))
	25		*Not in force*
	26		See note at end of entry for this Act
	27		1 May 1994 (SI 1994/1096)
	28–30		Repealed
	31	(1)–(3)	31 May 1991 (SI 1991/1319)
		(4) (a)	31 May 1991 (SI 1991/1319)
		(b)	1 Jan 1991 (s 164(2))
		(c)	Repealed
		(5) (a)	1 Apr 1992 (SI 1991/2829)
		(b)	31 May 1991 (SI 1991/1319)
		(c)	Repealed
		(6)	1 Apr 1992 (SI 1991/2829)
16, Pt	I		Repeal of Alkali, &c Works Regulation Act 1906 brought into force, for purposes of application of 1906 Act to activities which fall within a description of a process which has been but has ceased to be a prescribed process (a) on 1 Dec 1994, or, if later, (b) on date on which that description of process ceases to be a prescribed process (SI 1994/2854)

Environmental Protection Act 1990 (c 43)—*contd*

Schedule

16, Pt	I—*contd*	16 Dec 1996 (repeals of or in Alkali, &c Works Regulation Act 1906 (so far as not already repealed); Health and Safety at Work etc Act 1974; Environmental Protection Act 1990) (E, W) (SI 1996/3056)
		Not in force (otherwise)
	II	31 May 1991 (repeals of or in Control of Pollution Act 1974, s 2; Control of Pollution (Amendment) Act 1989, ss 7(2), 9(1)) (SI 1991/1319)
		1 Apr 1992 (repeal of Control of Pollution (Amendment) Act 1989, s 9(2)) (SI 1991/2829)
		1 Apr 1992 (repeals of or in Control of Pollution Act 1974, ss 12, 13, 14(1)–(5), (7)–(11) (except so far as relate to industrial waste in England and Wales), 15; Civic Government (Scotland) Act 1982) (SI 1992/266)
		1 May 1994 (repeal of Control of Pollution Act 1974, s 1) (SI 1994/1096)
		1 May 1994 (S) (repeal of Control of Pollution Act 1974, s 11) (SI 1994/1096)
		In relation to repeal of Control of Pollution Act 1974, ss 3–10, 18, 27, see note at end of entry for this Act
		Not in force (otherwise)
	III	1 Jan 1991 (s 164(2))
	IV	1 Apr 1991 (SI 1991/1042)
	V	1 Jan 1991 (SI 1990/2635)
	VI	1 Apr 1991 (repeals of or in Countryside Act 1968; Wildlife and Countryside Act 1981) (SI 1991/685)
		1 Apr 1992 (repeals in Nature Conservancy Council Act 1973) (SI 1991/2829
		Not in force (otherwise)
	VII	1 Jan 1992 (repeals in Planning (Hazardous Substances) Act 1990) (SI 1991/2829)
		18 Feb 1993 (repeals in Town and Country Planning (Scotland) Act 1972) (SI 1993/274)

Environmental Protection Act 1990 (c 43)—*contd*

Schedule

16, Pt	VII—*contd*	1 May 1993 (repeal in Housing and Planning Act 1986) (SI 1993/274)
		Not in force (otherwise)
	VIII	*Not in force*
	IX	1 Jan 1991 (repeal of Control of Pollution Act 1974, s 100) (s 164(2))
		1 Apr 1992 (repeals of or in Dogs Act 1906; Civic Government (Scotland) Act 1982; Local Government Act 1988) (SI 1992/266)
		18 Feb 1993 (repeals of Criminal Justice Act 1982, s 43; Criminal Justice Act 1988, s 58) (SI 1993/274)

Ss 33 (so far as not already in force), 35–40 (so far as not already in force), 42 (so far as not already in force), 43 (so far as not already in force), 57, 162(1) (so far as relates to Sch 15, para 26), (2) (so far as relates to repeals in Sch 16, Pt II of Control of Pollution Act 1974, ss 3–10, 18, 27) all brought into force on 1 May 1994 by SI 1994/1096, save for purposes of their application to certain activities specified in art 2(2) of that Order. In relation to such activities, those provisions come into force in accordance with art 3 of the Order, as amended by SI 1994/2487, SI 1994/3234

[1]   Orders made under Pollution Prevention and Control Act 1999, s 7(3), bringing the prospective repeals into force will be noted to that Act

[2]   Orders made under Environment Act 1995, s 125(3), bringing the prospective amendments into force will be noted to that Act

[3]   1 Apr 1991 was the day appointed by SI 1991/685 as the day on and after which the Nature Conservancy Councils exercised functions under ss 132–134

Finance Act 1990 (c 29)

Budget Day: 20 Mar 1990

RA: 26 Jul 1990

Details of the commencement of Finance Acts are not set out in this work

---

Food Safety Act 1990 (c 16)

RA: 29 Jun 1990

Commencement provisions: s 60(2)–(4); Food Safety Act 1990 (Commencement No 1) Order 1990, SI 1990/1383; Food Safety Act 1990 (Commencement No 2) Order 1990, SI 1990/2372; Food Safety Act 1990 (Commencement No 3) Order 1992, SI 1992/57

Section

1	(1), (2)	3 Jul 1990 (for purposes of ss 13, 51) (SI 1990/1383)
		1 Dec 1990 (otherwise) (SI 1990/2372)

Food Safety Act 1990 (c 16)—*contd*
Section

1	(3), (4)	3 Jul 1990 (for purposes of s 13) (SI 1990/1383)
		1 Dec 1990 (otherwise) (SI 1990/2372)
2, 3		3 Jul 1990 (for purposes of s 13) (SI 1990/1383)
		1 Dec 1990 (otherwise) (SI 1990/2372)
4		Repealed
5, 6		3 Jul 1990 (for purposes of s 13) (SI 1990/1383)
		1 Dec 1990 (otherwise) (SI 1990/2372)
7	(1), (2)	1 Jan 1991 (SI 1990/2372)
	(3)	3 Jul 1990 (for purposes of s 13) (SI 1990/1383)
		1 Jan 1991 (otherwise) (SI 1990/2372)
8–12		1 Jan 1991 (SI 1990/2372)
13		29 Jun 1990 (s 60(2))
14, 15		1 Jan 1991 (SI 1990/2372)
16	(1), (2)	1 Dec 1990 (SI 1990/2372)
	(3)	See Sch 1 below
	(4), (5)	1 Dec 1990 (SI 1990/2372)
17–19		1 Dec 1990 (SI 1990/2372)
20		3 Jul 1990 (for purposes of s 13) (SI 1990/1383)
		1 Jan 1991 (otherwise) (SI 1990/2372)
21	(1)	3 Jul 1990 (for purposes of s 13) (SI 1990/1383)
		1 Jan 1991 (otherwise) (SI 1990/2372)
	(2)–(4)	1 Jan 1991 (SI 1990/2372)
	(5), (6)	3 Jul 1990 (for purposes of s 13) (SI 1990/1383)
		1 Jan 1991 (otherwise) (SI 1990/2372)
22		3 Jul 1990 (for purposes of s 13) (SI 1990/1383)
		1 Jan 1991 (otherwise) (SI 1990/2372)
23, 24		1 Jan 1991 (SI 1990/2372)
25		Repealed
26		1 Dec 1990 (SI 1990/2372)
27	(1)	1 Jan 1991 (SI 1990/2372)
	(2)	1 Dec 1990 (SI 1990/2372)
	(3), (4)	1 Jan 1991 (SI 1990/2372)
	(5)	1 Dec 1990 (SI 1990/2372)
28	(1)	1 Jan 1991 (SI 1990/2372)
	(2)	1 Dec 1990 (SI 1990/2372)
29		3 Jul 1990 (for purposes of s 13) (SI 1990/1383)
		1 Jan 1991 (otherwise) (SI 1990/2372)
30, 31		1 Dec 1990 (SI 1990/2372)
32–36		3 Jul 1990 (for purposes of s 13) (SI 1990/1383)

Food Safety Act 1990 (c 16)—*contd*

Section

32–36—*contd*		1 Jan 1991 (otherwise) (SI 1990/2372)
36A		Inserted by Food Standards Act 1999, s 40(1), Sch 5, para 16 (qv)
37–39		1 Jan 1991 (SI 1990/2372)
40		1 Dec 1990 (SI 1990/2372)
41, 42		3 Jul 1990 (for purposes of s 13) (SI 1990/1383)
		1 Jan 1991 (otherwise) (SI 1990/2372)
43		1 Jan 1991 (SI 1990/2372)
44		3 Jul 1990 (for purposes of s 13) (SI 1990/1383)
		1 Jan 1991 (otherwise) (SI 1990/2372)
45		1 Dec 1990 (SI 1990/2372)
46		3 Jul 1990 (for purposes of s 13) (SI 1990/1383)
		1 Jan 1991 (otherwise) (SI 1990/2372)
47		1 Jan 1991 (SI 1990/2372)
48	(1)–(3)	3 Jul 1990 (for purposes of s 13) (SI 1990/1383)
		1 Dec 1990 (otherwise) (SI 1990/2372)
	(4)	1 Dec 1990 (SI 1990/2372)
	(4A), (4B)	Inserted by Food Standards Act 1999, s 40(1), Sch 5, para 21 (qv)
	(5)	1 Dec 1990 (SI 1990/2372)
49	(1)	3 Jul 1990 (for purposes of s 13) (SI 1990/1383)
		1 Jan 1991 (otherwise) (SI 1990/2372)
	(2)	1 Dec 1990 (SI 1990/2372)
	(3)–(5)	3 Jul 1990 (for purposes of s 13) (SI 1990/1383)
		1 Jan 1991 (otherwise) (SI 1990/2372)
50		3 Jul 1990 (for purposes of s 13) (SI 1990/1383)
		1 Jan 1991 (otherwise) (SI 1990/2372)
51		29 Jun 1990 (s 60(2))
52		See Sch 2 below
53	(1)	3 Jul 1990 (for purposes of ss 13, 51) (SI 1990/1383)
		1 Dec 1990 (otherwise) (SI 1990/2372)
	(2)–(4)	3 Jul 1990 (for purposes of s 13) (SI 1990/1383)
		1 Dec 1990 (otherwise) (SI 1990/2372)
	(5)	1 Dec 1990 (SI 1990/2372)
54		1 Apr 1992 (SI 1990/2372)
55	(1)	1 Jan 1991 (SI 1990/2372)
	(2)–(6)	Repealed
56		1 Jan 1991 (SI 1990/2372)
57	(1)	Repealed

Food Safety Act 1990 (c 16)—*contd*

Section

57	(2)	3 Jul 1990 (for purposes of s 13) (SI 1990/1383)
		1 Dec 1990 (otherwise) (SI 1990/2372)
58	(1)	3 Jul 1990 (for purposes of s 13) (SI 1990/1383)
		1 Jan 1991 (otherwise) (SI 1990/2372)
	(2)–(4)	1 Jan 1991 (SI 1990/2372)
59	(1)	See Sch 3 below
	(2)	1 Dec 1990 (SI 1990/2372)
	(3)	See Sch 4 below
	(4)	See Sch 5 below
60		1 Jan 1991 (SI 1990/2372)

Schedule

1		1 Dec 1990 (SI 1990/2372)
2, para	1–11	1 Jan 1991 (SI 1990/2372)
	12–15	29 Jun 1990 (s 60(2))
	16	1 Jan 1991 (SI 1990/2372)
3, para	1–13	1 Jan 1991 (SI 1990/2372)
	14	Repealed
	15–28	1 Jan 1991 (SI 1990/2372)
	29, 30	13 Jul 1990 (for purposes of s 51) (SI 1990/1383)
		1 Jan 1991 (otherwise) (SI 1990/2372)
	31–38	1 Jan 1991 (SI 1990/2372)
4		1 Dec 1990 (SI 1990/2372)
5		1 Dec 1990 (so far as relates to Public Analysts (Scotland) Regulations 1956, SI 1956/1162 or Public Analysts Regulations 1957, SI 1957/237, repeals of or in Food and Drugs (Scotland) Act 1956, ss 27, 29, 56 and Food Act 1984, ss 76(2), 79(5)) (SI 1990/2372)
		1 Jan 1991 (all repeals so far as not already in force except those of or in Food Act 1984, s 13 so far as relating to regulations (see following notes), ss 16–20, 62–67, ss 92, 93 (so far as relate to ss 16 and 18), s 132(1) so far as relates to regulations (see following notes)) (SI 1990/2372)
		1 Apr 1991 (repeals of Food Act 1984, ss 13, 132(1), so far as relate to Food Hygiene (Amendment) Regulations 1990, SI 1990/1431 (except reg 3(b), Sch 1 thereof)) (SI 1990/2372)

Food Safety Act 1990 (c 16)—*contd*

Section

5—*contd*	1 Apr 1992 (repeals of Food Act 1984, ss 13, 132(1), so far as relate to Food Hygiene (Amendment) Regulations 1990, reg 3(b), Sch 1) (SI 1990/2372)
	3 Apr 1992 (repeals of or in Food Act 1984, ss 16–20, Pt IV (ss 62–67), ss 92 (so far as relates to s 16(2)), 93 (so far as relates to s 18(4))) (SI 1992/57)

Gaming (Amendment) Act 1990 (c 26)

RA: 13 Jul 1990

Commencement provisions: s 2(2), (3); Gaming (Amendment) Act 1990 (Commencement) Order 1991, SI 1991/59

Section

1		See Schedule below
2		13 Sep 1990 (s 2(2))
Schedule		
para	1, 2	13 Sep 1990 (s 2(2))
	3, 4	1 Apr 1991 (SI 1991/59)
	5–10	13 Sep 1990 (s 2(2))

Government Trading Act 1990 (c 30)

RA: 26 Jul 1990

Commencement provisions: s 4(3); Government Trading Act 1990 (Appointed Day) Order 1991, SI 1991/132

Section

1		26 Jul 1990 (RA)
2		See Sch 1 below
3		26 Jul 1990 (RA)
4		See Sch 2, Pt I below
5		See Sch 2, Pt II below
Schedule		
1		26 Jul 1990 (RA)
2, Pt	I	11 Feb 1991 (SI 1991/132)
	II	26 Jul 1990 (RA)

Greenwich Hospital Act 1990 (c 13)

RA: 29 Jun 1990

29 Jun 1990 (RA)

Horses (Protective Headgear for Young Riders) Act 1990 (c 25)

RA: 13 Jul 1990

Commencement provisions: s 5(2); Horses (Protective Headgear for Young Riders)
  Act 1990 (Commencement) Order 1992, SI 1992/1200

Section
1–3	30 Jun 1992 (SI 1992/1200)
4, 5	13 Jul 1990 (s 5(2))

Human Fertilisation and Embryology Act 1990 (c 37)

RA: 1 Nov 1990

Commencement provisions: s 49(2); Human Fertilisation and Embryology Act 1990
  (Commencement No 1) Order 1990, SI 1990/2165; Human Fertilisation and
  Embryology Act 1990 (Commencement No 2 and Transitional Provision)
  Order 1991, SI 1991/480; Human Fertilisation and Embryology Act 1990
  (Commencement No 3 and Transitional Provisions) Order 1991, SI 1991/1400;
  Human Fertilisation and Embryology Act 1990 (Commencement No 4—
  Amendment of Transitional Provisions) Order 1991, SI 1991/1781; Human
  Fertilisation and Embryology Act 1990 (Commencement No 5) Order 1994,
  SI 1994/1776

Section

1		1 Aug 1991 (SI 1991/1400)[1]
2	(1)	7 Nov 1990 (so far as relates to definition of 'the Authority') (SI 1990/2165)
		1 Aug 1991 (otherwise) (SI 1991/1400)[1]
	(2), (3)	1 Aug 1991 (SI 1991/1400)[1]
3		1 Aug 1991 (SI 1991/1400)[1]
3A		Inserted by Criminal Justice and Public Order Act 1994, s 156(1), (2) (qv)
4		1 Aug 1991 (SI 1991/1400)[1]
5	(1), (2)	7 Nov 1990 (SI 1990/2165)
	(3)	See Sch 1 below
6, 7		7 Nov 1990 (SI 1990/2165)
8		1 Aug 1991 (SI 1991/1400)[1]
9	(1)–(4)	1 Aug 1991 (SI 1991/1400)[1]
	(5)	8 Jul 1991 (for purpose of making regulations) (SI 1991/1400)
		1 Aug 1991 (otherwise) (SI 1991/1400)[1]
	(6)–(11)	1 Aug 1991 (SI 1991/1400)[1]
10		8 Jul 1991 (for purpose of making regulations) (SI 1991/1400)
		1 Aug 1991 (otherwise) (SI 1991/1400)[1]
11–13		1 Aug 1991 (SI 1991/1400)[1]
14	(1)–(4)	1 Aug 1991 (SI 1991/1400)[1]

Human Fertilisation and Embryology Act 1990 (c 37)—*contd*

Section

14	(5)		8 Jul 1991 (for purpose of making regulations) (SI 1991/1400)
			1 Aug 1991 (otherwise) (SI 1991/1400)[1]
15			1 Aug 1991 (SI 1991/1400)[1]
16	(1)		8 Jul 1991 (for purpose of requiring that an application for a licence be made in an approved form and be accompanied by initial fee) (SI 1991/1400)
			1 Aug 1991 (otherwise) (SI 1991/1400)[1]
	(2)–(5)		1 Aug 1991 (SI 1991/1400)[1]
	(6)		8 Jul 1991 (for purpose of fixing amount of initial fee) (SI 1991/1400)
			1 Aug 1991 (otherwise) (SI 1991/1400)[1]
	(7)		1 Aug 1991 (SI 1991/1400)[1]
17–25			1 Aug 1991 (SI 1991/1400)[1]
26			7 Nov 1990 (SI 1990/2165)
27–29			1 Aug 1991 (SI 1991/1400)[1]
30	(1)–(8)		1 Nov 1994 (SI 1994/1776)
	(9), (10)		5 Jul 1994 (SI 1994/1776)
	(11)		1 Nov 1994 (SI 1994/1776)
31, 32			1 Aug 1991 (SI 1991/1400)[1]
33	(1)		7 Nov 1990 (SI 1990/2165)
	(2)	(a)	1 Aug 1991 (SI 1991/1400)[1]
		(b)	7 Nov 1990 (SI 1990/2165)
	(3)		1 Aug 1991 (SI 1991/1400)[1]
	(4)		7 Nov 1990 (SI 1990/2165)
	(5), (6)		1 Aug 1991 (SI 1991/1400)[1]
	(6A)–(6G)		Inserted by Human Fertilisation and Embryology (Disclosure of Information) Act 1992, s 1(1), (3) (qv)
	(7)		1 Aug 1991 (SI 1991/1400)[1]
	(8)		Repealed
	(9)		Added by Human Fertilisation and Embryology (Disclosure of Information) Act 1992, s 1(1), (4) (qv)
34, 35			1 Aug 1991 (SI 1991/1400)[1]
36			7 Nov 1990 (SI 1990/2165)
37			1 Apr 1991 (subject to transitional provisions) (SI 1991/480)
38, 39			1 Aug 1991 (SI 1991/1400)[1]
40			7 Nov 1990 (SI 1990/2165)
41	(1), (2)		1 Aug 1991 (SI 1991/1400)[1]

Human Fertilisation and Embryology Act 1990 (c 37)—*contd*

Section

41	(3)	8 Jul 1991 (SI 1991/1400)
	(4)	8 Jul 1991 (so far as relates to s 41(3)) (SI 1991/1400)
		1 Aug 1991 (otherwise) (SI 1991/1400)[1]
	(5)	7 Nov 1990 (so far as relates to s 33(1), (2)(b), (4)) (SI 1990/2165)
		1 Aug 1991 (otherwise) (SI 1991/1400)[1]
	(6)	7 Nov 1990 (so far as relates to s 40) (SI 1990/2165)
		1 Aug 1991 (otherwise) (SI 1991/1400)[1]
	(7), (8)	1 Aug 1991 (SI 1991/1400)[1]
	(9)	7 Nov 1990 (so far as relates to s 40) (SI 1990/2165)
		1 Aug 1991 (otherwise) (SI 1991/1400)[1]
	(10), (11)	1 Aug 1991 (SI 1991/1400)[1]
42		7 Nov 1990 (SI 1990/2165)
43	(1)	8 Jul 1991 (for purpose of making regulations) (SI 1991/1400)
		1 Aug 1991(otherwise) (SI 1991/1400)[1]
	(2), (3)	1 Aug 1991 (SI 1991/1400)[1]
44		1 Aug 1991 (SI 1991/1400)[1]
45		8 Jul 1991 (SI 1991/1400)
46, 47		1 Aug 1991 (SI 1991/1400)[1]
48	(1)	7 Nov 1990 (so far as relates to provisions brought into force by SI 1990/2165) (SI 1990/2165)
		1 Apr 1991 (so far as relates to provisions brought into force by SI 1991/480) (SI 1991/480)
		8 Jul 1991 (so far as relates to provisions brought into force by SI 1991/1400) (SI 1991/1400)
		1 Aug 1991 (otherwise, except so far as relates to s 30) (SI 1991/1400)[1]
		5 Jul 1994 (so far as relates to s 30(9), (10)) (SI 1994/1776)
		1 Nov 1994 (so far as relates to s 30(1)–(8), (11)) (SI 1994/1776)
	(2)	Repealed
49	(1), (2)	7 Nov 1990 (SI 1990/2165)
	(3), (4)	1 Aug 1991 (SI 1991/1400)[1]
	(5)	See Sch 4 below
	(6), (7)	7 Nov 1990 (SI 1990/2165)

Human Fertilisation and Embryology Act 1990 (c 37)—*contd*
Schedule
1   7 Nov 1990 (SI 1990/2165)
2–4   1 Aug 1991 (SI 1991/1400)[1]

---

1   Subject to transitional provisions set out in SI 1991/1400, arts 3, 4, as amended by SI 1991/1781,
     art 2

Import and Export Control Act 1990 (c 45)

RA: 6 Dec 1990

6 Dec 1990 (RA)

Landlord and Tenant (Licensed Premises) Act 1990 (c 39)

RA: 1 Nov 1990

Commencement provisions: s 2(3)
Section
1   (1)   1 Jan 1991 (s 2(3))
                     (2), (3)   1 Jan 1991 (subject to transitional
                                               provisions) (s 2(3))
                     (4)   1 Jan 1991 (s 2(3))
2   1 Jan 1991 (s 2(3))

Law Reform (Miscellaneous Provisions) (Scotland) Act 1990 (c 40)

RA: 1 Nov 1990

Commencement provisions: s 75(2)–(4); Law Reform (Miscellaneous Provisions) (Scotland) Act 1990 Commencement (No 1) Order 1990, SI 1990/2328; Law Reform (Miscellaneous Provisions) (Scotland) Act 1990 (Commencement No 2) Order 1990, SI 1990/2624; Law Reform (Miscellaneous Provisions) (Scotland) Act 1990 (Commencement No 3) Order 1991, SI 1991/330; Law Reform (Miscellaneous Provisions) (Scotland) Act 1990 (Commencement No 4) Order 1991, SI 1991/822; Law Reform (Miscellaneous Provisions) (Scotland) Act 1990 (Commencement No 5) Order 1991, SI 1991/850; Law Reform (Miscellaneous Provisions) (Scotland) Act 1990 (Commencement No 6) Order 1991, SI 1991/1252; Law Reform (Miscellaneous Provisions) (Scotland) Act 1990 (Commencement No 7) Order 1991, SI 1991/1903; Law Reform (Miscellaneous Provisions) (Scotland) Act 1990 (Commencement No 8) Order 1991, SI 1991/2151; Law Reform (Miscellaneous Provisions) (Scotland) Act 1990 (Commencement No 9) Order 1991, SI 1991/2862; Law Reform (Miscellaneous Provisions) (Scotland) Act 1990 (Commencement No 10) Order 1992, SI 1992/1599; Law Reform (Miscellaneous Provisions) (Scotland) Act 1990 (Commencement No 11) Order 1993, SI 1993/641; Law Reform (Miscellaneous Provisions) (Scotland) Act 1990 (Commencement No 12) Order 1993, SI 1993/2253; Law Reform (Miscellaneous Provisions) (Scotland) Act 1990 (Commencement No 13) Order 1995, SI 1995/364; Law Reform (Miscellaneous Provisions) (Scotland) Act 1990 (Commencement No 13) Order 1996, SI 1996/2894, as amended by SI 1996/2966[1]

Law Reform (Miscellaneous Provisions) (Scotland) Act 1990 (c 40)—*contd*

Section

1, 2			27 Jul 1992 (SI 1992/1599)
3	(1)		4 Jul 1992 (for purpose of power to make order) (SI 1992/1599)
			27 Jul 1992 (otherwise) (SI 1992/1599)
	(2)–(4)		27 Jul 1992 (SI 1992/1599)
4	(1)–(3)		30 Sep 1992 (SI 1992/1599)
	(4)		4 Jul 1992 (SI 1992/1599)
5	(1), (2)		30 Sep 1992 (SI 1992/1599)
	(3)		4 Jul 1992 (SI 1992/1599)
	(4)		30 Sep 1992 (SI 1992/1599)
	(5)		4 Jul 1992 (SI 1992/1599)
	(6)–(14)		30 Sep 1992 (SI 1992/1599)
6			27 Jul 1992 (SI 1992/1599)
7	(1)–(4)		27 Jul 1992 (SI 1992/1599)
	(5)		4 Jul 1992 (for purpose of power to make regulations) (SI 1992/1599)
			27 Jul 1992 (otherwise) (SI 1992/1599)
	(6)–(12)		27 Jul 1992 (SI 1992/1599)
8			27 Jul 1992 (SI 1992/1599)
9	(1)–(4)		27 Jul 1992 (SI 1992/1599)
	(5)		4 Jul 1992 (for purpose of power to make orders) (SI 1992/1599)
			27 Jul 1992 (otherwise) (SI 1992/1599)
	(6), (7)		27 Jul 1992 (SI 1992/1599)
10–12			15 Sep 1993 (SI 1993/2253)
13, 14			27 Jul 1992 (SI 1992/1599)
15	(1)–(4)		27 Jul 1992 (SI 1992/1599)
	(5)	(a)	27 Jul 1992 (SI 1992/1599)
		(b)	4 Jul 1992 (for purpose of power to make orders) (SI 1992/1599)
			27 Jul 1992 (otherwise) (SI 1992/1599)
		(c)	27 Jul 1992 (SI 1992/1599)
		(d)	4 Jul 1992 (for purpose of power to make orders) (SI 1992/1599)
			27 Jul 1992 (otherwise) (SI 1992/1599)
	(6)–(10)		27 Jul 1992 (SI 1992/1599)
	(11)		4 Jul 1992 (SI 1992/1599)
16	(1)–(3)		1 Apr 1991 (SI 1991/822)
	(4)		See Sch 1, Pt I below
17	(1), (2)		1 Mar 1997 (SI 1996/2894)
	(3)		30 Sep 1991 (SI 1991/2151)
	(4)–(10)		1 Mar 1997 (SI 1996/2894)
	(11)–(15)		30 Sep 1991 (SI 1991/2151)
	(16)–(24)		1 Mar 1997 (SI 1996/2894)
18	(1)–(9)		1 Mar 1997 (SI 1996/2894)
	(10), (11)		30 Sep 1991 (SI 1991/2151)
	(12)–(15)		1 Mar 1997 (SI 1996/2894)
19			*Not in force*
20	(1)–(11)		1 Mar 1997 (SI 1996/2894)

Law Reform (Miscellaneous Provisions) (Scotland) Act 1990 (c 40)—*contd*

Section

20	(12)		See Sch 1, Pt II below
	(13)–(17)		1 Mar 1997 (SI 1996/2894)
21			1 Mar 1997 (SI 1996/2894)
22	(1)	(a)	1 Mar 1997 (SI 1996/2894)
		(b)	*Not in force*
	(2)	(a), (b)	1 Mar 1997 (SI 1996/2894)
		(c)	*Not in force*
23			1 Apr 1991 (SI 1991/822)
24			3 Jun 1991 (SI 1991/1252)
25	(1)–(5)		*Not in force*
	(6)		See Sch 2 below
26–29			*Not in force*
30			3 Jun 1991 (SI 1991/1252)
31			17 Mar 1993 (SI 1993/641)
32			17 Mar 1993 (for purpose of provisions relating to making of rules and orders in Solicitors (Scotland) Act 1980, s 60A(2), (3), (5)–(8)) (SI 1993/641)
			Not in force (otherwise)
33			3 Jun 1991 (SI 1991/1252)
34	(1)		1 Apr 1991 (SI 1991/822)
	(1A)–(1F)		Inserted by Scottish Legal Services Ombudsman and Commissioner for Local Administration in Scotland Act 1997, s 1(3) (qv)
	(2)		3 Jun 1991 (SI 1991/1252)
	(2A), (2B)		Inserted by Scottish Legal Services Ombudsman and Commissioner for Local Administration in Scotland Act 1997, s 1(5) (qv)
	(3)		Repealed
	(4)		Substituted by Scottish Legal Services Ombudsman and Commissioner for Local Administration in Scotland Act 1997, s 1(7) (qv)
	(5)–(8)		3 Jun 1991 (SI 1991/1252)
	(9)	(a)–(c)	1 Apr 1991 (SI 1991/822)
		(d), (e)	1 Mar 1997 (SI 1996/2894)
		(f)	*Not in force*
		(g)	1 Mar 1997 (SI 1996/2894)
		(h)	*Not in force*
	(10)		See Sch 3 below
34A, 34B			Inserted by Scottish Legal Services Ombudsman and Commissioner for Local Administration in Scotland Act 1997, ss 2, 3 (qv)
35			1 Apr 1991 (SI 1991/822)
36	(1)		20 Jul 1992 (SI 1992/1599)

Law Reform (Miscellaneous Provisions) (Scotland) Act 1990 (c 40)—*contd*

Section

36	(2)		4 Jul 1992 (for purpose of power to make act of sederunt) (SI 1992/1599)
			20 Jul 1992 (otherwise) (SI 1992/1599)
	(3)		4 Jul 1992 (for purpose of power to make act of sederunt under Solicitors' (Scotland) Act 1980, s 61A) (SI 1992/1599)
			20 Jul 1992 (otherwise) (SI 1992/1599)
	(4)		*Not in force*
37			20 Jul 1992 (SI 1992/1599)
38, 39			30 Sep 1991 (SI 1991/2151)
40–42			30 Sep 1991 (SI 1991/2151)
43			3 Jun 1991 (SI 1991/1252)
44			1 Apr 1991 (SI 1991/822)
45–48			1 Jan 1991 (s 75(3)(a))
49	(1)–(7)		1 Jan 1991 (s 75(3)(a))
	(8)		See Sch 5 below
	(9)–(11)		1 Jan 1991 (s 75(3)(a))
50–55			1 Jan 1991 (s 75(3)(a))
56, 57			Repealed
58, 59			30 Sep 1991 (for purposes of proceedings in any sheriff court in sheriffdom of Glasgow and Strathkelvin or Lothian and Borders) (SI 1991/2151)
			3 Apr 1995 (otherwise) (SI 1995/364)
60			30 Sep 1991 (SI 1991/2151)
61			1 Apr 1991 (SI 1991/850)
62			Repealed
63			1 Dec 1990 (SI 1990/2328)
64, 65			1 Jan 1991 (SI 1990/2624)
66			See Sch 7 below
67			1 Jan 1991 (s 73(3)(b))
68			1 Apr 1991 (SI 1991/330)
69			1 Mar 1991 (SI 1991/330)
70			1 Jan 1991 (s 75(3)(b))
71			Repealed
72			Repealed
73	(1)	(a)	17 Mar 1993 (SI 1993/641)
		(b)–(e)	1 Apr 1991 (SI 1991/822)
	(2)		17 Mar 1993 (SI 1993/641)
74	(1)		See Sch 8 below
	(2)		See Sch 9 below
75			1 Nov 1990 (RA)
Schedule			
1, Pt	I		1 Apr 1991 (SI 1991/822)
	II		1 Mar 1997 (SI 1996/2894)
2			*Not in force*

Law Reform (Miscellaneous Provisions) (Scotland) Act 1990 (c 40)—*contd*
Schedule

3, 4				1 Apr 1991 (SI 1991/822)
5				1 Jan 1991 (s 75(3)(a))
6				Repealed
7				1 Jan 1991 (s 75(3)(a))
8, Pt	I, para	1–18		31 Dec 1991 (SI 1991/2892)
	II, para	19, 20		1 Mar 1997 (SI 1996/2894)
		21		1 Jan 1991 (s 75(3)(b))
		22	(1)	1 Mar 1997 (for all purposes except in relation to a recognised financial institution) (SI 1996/2894)
				Not in force (exception noted above)
			(2)	1 Mar 1997 (SI 1996/2894)
		23		1 Apr 1991 (SI 1991/822)
		24, 25		1 Mar 1997 (SI 1996/2894)
		26		1 Jan 1991 (SI 1990/2624)
		27	(1), (2)	3 Jun 1991 (SI 1991/1252)
			(3)	1 Nov 1990 (s 75(4))
		28		1 Apr 1991 (SI 1991/850)
		29	(1)–(4)	3 Jun 1991 (SI 1991/1252)
			(5) (a), (b)	1 Mar 1997 (except in relation to a recognised financial institution) (SI 1996/2894)
				Not in force (exception noted above)
			(c)	17 Mar 1993 (SI 1993/641)
			(d)	1 Mar 1997 (except in relation to a recognised financial institution) (SI 1996/2894)
				Not in force (exception noted above)
			(6) (a)	1 Jan 1991 (SI 1990/2624)
			(b)	1 Jan 1991 (in so far as it relates to insertion of Solicitors (Scotland) Act 1980, s 32(2B)) (SI 1990/2624)
				1 Mar 1997 (otherwise, except in relation to a recognised financial institution) (SI 1996/2894)
				Not in force (exception noted above)
			(c)	*Not in force*
			(7)	1 Jan 1991 (SI 1990/2624)
			(8)–(14)	3 Jun 1991 (SI 1991/1252)
			(15) (a)	3 Jun 1991 (SI 1991/1252)
			(b)–(d)	17 Mar 1993 (SI 1993/641)
			(e)	3 Jun 1991 (SI 1991/1252)
			(f)	17 Mar 1993 (SI 1993/641)
			(16), (17)	3 Jun 1991 (SI 1991/1252)
		30		20 Jul 1992 (SI 1992/1599)
		31, 32		1 Jan 1991 (SI 1990/2624)
		33		Repealed
		34		1 Jan 1991 (s 75(3)(b))

Law Reform (Miscellaneous Provisions) (Scotland) Act 1990 (c 40)—*contd*

Schedule

8, Pt	II, para	35		1 Dec 1990 (SI 1990/2328)
		36	(1)	*Not in force*
			(2)–(5)	30 Sep 1991 (SI 1991/2151)
			(6)	26 Aug 1991 (SI 1991/1903)
			(7)–(9)	*Not in force*
			(10)–(15)	30 Sep 1991 (SI 1991/2151)
			(16)	*Not in force*
		37		1 Jan 1991 (SI 1990/2624)
		38		3 Jun 1991 (SI 1991/1252)
		39		Repealed
9				1 Dec 1990 (repeals of or in Companies Act 1985, ss 38(1), 39(3), 186, 188(2), 462(2); Insolvency Act 1986, s 53(3); Companies Act 1989, s 130(3), Sch 17, paras 1(2), 2(4), 8, 10) (SI 1990/2328)
				1 Jan 1991 (repeals of or in Matrimonial Homes (Family Protection) (Scotland) Act 1981, ss 6(3)(e), 8; Representation of the People Act 1983, s 42(3)(b)) (SI 1990/2624)
				1 Apr 1991 (repeals of or in Unfair Contract Terms Act 1977, ss 15(1), 25(3)(d), (4)) (SI 1991/330)
				3 Jun 1991 (repeals of or in Solicitors (Scotland) Act 1980, ss 20(1), 31(3), 63(1), Sch 4, paras 1, 17) (SI 1991/1252)
				15 Aug 1991 (repeals of or in House of Commons Disqualification Act 1975, Sch 1; Solicitors (Scotland) Act 1980, ss 49, 65(1), Sch 5) (SI 1991/1252)
				26 Aug 1991 (repeal of Legal Aid Act 1988, Sch 4, para 3(c)) (SI 1991/1903)
				30 Sep 1991 (repeals of or in Solicitors (Scotland) Act 1980, s 29; Legal Aid (Scotland) Act 1986, s 13(2)) (SI 1991/2151)
				17 Mar 1993 (repeals of or in Licensing (Scotland) Act 1976, ss 6, 18(1), 55, 61, 97(2), 131, 132, 133(4), Sch 4, paras 1, 12–17, 19–22; Solicitors (Scotland) Act 1980, s 27; Family Law (Scotland) Act 1985,

Law Reform (Miscellaneous Provisions) (Scotland) Act 1990 (c 40)—*contd*

Schedule

9—*contd*   s 8(1)(a); Law Reform
                                                              (Miscellaneous Provisions)
                                                              (Scotland) Act 1985, Sch 1, Pt I,
                                                              para 5) (SI 1993/641)
                                                              1 Mar 1997 (repeals of or in Probate
                                                              and Legacy Duties Act 1808;
                                                              Confirmation of Executors
                                                              (Scotland) Act 1858; Intestates
                                                              Widows and Children (Scotland)
                                                              Act 1875; Small Testate Estates
                                                              (Scotland) Act 1876; Executors
                                                              (Scotland) Act 1900)
                                                              (SI 1996/2894)
                                                              Not in force (otherwise)

[1]   The effect of this amendment is to change the commencement date from 5 Dec 1996 to 1 Mar 1997.
       (*Note:* it is thought that SI 1996/2894 should have been numbered as Commencement No 14)

Licensing (Low Alcohol Drinks) Act 1990 (c 21)

RA: 13 Jul 1990

Commencement provisions: s 3(2)

1 Jan 1994 (s 3(2)) (no day prior to that date was appointed by the Secretary of
State)

Marriage (Registration of Buildings) Act 1990 (c 33)

RA: 26 Jul 1990

Commencement provisions: s 2(2)

26 Sep 1990 (s 2(2))

National Health Service and Community Care Act 1990 (c 19)

RA: 29 Jun 1990

Commencement provisions: s 67(2); National Health Service and Community Care
    Act 1990 (Commencement No 1) Order 1990, SI 1990/1329 (as amended by
    SI 1990/2511); National Health Service and Community Care Act 1990
    (Commencement No 2) (Scotland) Order 1990, SI 1990/1520; National Health
    Service and Community Care Act 1990 (Commencement No 3 and
    Transitional Provisions) (Scotland) Order 1990, SI 1990/1793 (as amended by
    SI 1990/2510, SI 1992/799); National Health Service and Community Care
    Act 1990 (Commencement No 4 and Transitional Provision) Order 1990,
    SI 1990/2218; National Health Service and Community Care Act 1990
    (Commencement No 5 and Revocation) (Scotland) Order 1990, SI 1990/2510;
    National Health Service and Community Care Act 1990 (Commencement
    No 6–Amendment, and Transitional and Saving Provisions) Order 1990,

National Health Service and Community Care Act 1990 (c 19)—*contd*
SI 1990/2511; National Health Service and Community Care Act 1990
(Commencement No 7) Order 1991, SI 1991/388; National Health Service and
Community Care Act 1990 (Commencement No 8 and Transitional Provisions)
(Scotland) Order 1991, SI 1991/607; National Health Service and Community
Care Act 1990 (Commencement No 9) Order 1992, SI 1992/567; National
Health Service and Community Care Act 1990 (Commencement No 3 and
Transitional Provisions) (Scotland) (Amendment) Order 1992, SI 1992/799
(amending SI 1990/1793); National Health Service and Community Care Act 1990
(Commencement No 10) Order 1992, SI 1992/2975; National Health Service
and Community Care Act 1990 (Commencement No 11) (Scotland) Order 1994,
SI 1994/2658

Section

1	(1), (2)	Repealed
	(3)	See Sch 1, Pt III below
	(4), (5)	Repealed
2		Repealed
3	(1)	Substituted by Health Authorities Act 1995, ss 2(1), Sch 1, Pt II, paras 65, 67(a) (qv)
	(2)	1 Apr 1991 (SI 1990/1329)
	(3), (4)	Repealed
	(5), (6)	1 Apr 1991 (SI 1990/1329)
	(6A)	Inserted (1 Apr 1991) by Health and Personal Social Services (Northern Ireland Consequential Amendments) Order 1991, SI 1991/195, art 7(1), (2)
	(7), (8)	1 Apr 1991 (SI 1990/1329)
4	(1), (2)	6 Mar 1991 (so far as relate to a reference under s 4(4)) (SI 1991/388)
		1 Apr 1991 (otherwise) (SI 1990/1329)
	(3)	1 Apr 1991 (SI 1990/1329)
	(4)	6 Mar 1991 (SI 1991/388)
	(5), (6)	6 Mar 1991 (so far as relate to a reference under s 4(4)) (SI 1991/388)
		1 Apr 1991 (otherwise) (SI 1990/1329)
	(7), (8)	1 Apr 1991 (SI 1990/1329)
	(9)	6 Mar 1991 (so far as relates to a reference under s 4(4)) (SI 1991/388)
		1 Apr 1991 (otherwise) (SI 1990/1329)
	(10)	Added (1 Apr 1991) by Health and Personal Social Services (Northern Ireland Consequential Amendments) Order 1991, SI 1991/195, art 7(1), (5)
4A		Inserted by National Health Service (Primary Care) Act 1997, s 31(1) (qv)

National Health Service and Community Care Act 1990 (c 19)—*contd*
Section

5		See Sch 2 below
6–8		5 Jul 1990 (SI 1990/1329)
9		See Sch 3 below
10, 11		5 Jul 1990 (SI 1990/1329)
12	(1)	17 Sep 1990 (subject to transitional provisions) (SI 1990/1329)
	(2)	Repealed
	(3)	17 Sep 1990 (subject to transitional provisions) (SI 1990/1329)
	(4)	1 Oct 1991 (subject to savings) (SI 1990/2511)
	(5)	Repealed
13		Repealed
14		Repealed (E, W)
15–17		Repealed (E, W)
		1 Apr 1991 (SI 1990/1329); s 15(4) prospectively repealed (S) by Health Act 1999, ss 1, 65, Sch 5[1]
18	(1)	1 Apr 1991 (SI 1990/1329); prospectively repealed by Health Act 1999, s 65, Sch 4, para 80, Sch 5[1]
	(2)	Repealed
	(3)–(7)	1 Apr 1991 (SI 1990/1329); prospectively repealed by Health Act 1999, s 65, Sch 4, para 80, Sch 5[1]
	(8)	Inserted by National Health Service (Primary Care) Act 1997, s 41(10), Sch 2, para 65(10) (qv); prospectively repealed by Health Act 1999, s 65, Sch 4, para 80, Sch 5[1]
19		Repealed
20	(1)	Repealed
	(2)	1 Oct 1990 (SI 1990/1329)
	(3)–(8)	Repealed
21		17 Sep 1990 (SI 1990/1329)
22		1 Jan 1991 (SI 1990/1329); prospectively repealed by Health and Social Care Act 2001, s 67, Sch 6, Pt 1[3]
23	(1)	1 Jan 1991 (subject to transitional provisions) (SI 1990/1329, as amended by SI 1990/2511)
	(2)–(8)	Repealed
24		17 Sep 1990 (SI 1990/1329)
25		1 Apr 1991 (SI 1990/1329)
26	(1)	5 Jul 1990 (SI 1990/1329)

National Health Service and Community Care Act 1990 (c 19)—*contd*
Section

26	(2)	(a)	5 Jul 1990 (SI 1990/1329)
		(b)	Repealed
		(c)	5 Jul 1990 (SI 1990/1329)
		(d)	5 Jul 1990 (so far as relates to definition 'National Health Service trust') (SI 1990/1329) 1 Apr 1991 (otherwise) (SI 1990/1329)
		(e)	5 Jul 1990 (SI 1990/1329)
		(f)	17 Sep 1990 (SI 1990/1329)
		(g)	5 Jul 1990 (SI 1990/1329)
		(h)	1 Apr 1991 (SI 1990/1329)
		(i)	5 Jul 1990 (SI 1990/1329)
27	(1), (2)		31 Mar 1991 (so far as have effect in relation to members of a Health Board or management committee of Common Services Agency for Scottish Health Service) (SI 1990/1793) 30 Jun 1992 (otherwise) (SI 1990/1793, as amended by SI 1992/799)
	(3)		See Sch 5 below
28			17 Sep 1990 (SI 1990/1793)
29	(1), (2)		17 Sep 1990 (SI 1990/1793)
	(3)	(a)	24 Jul 1990 (subject to a transitional provision and saving) (SI 1990/1520)
		(b), (c)	24 Jul 1990 (SI 1990/1520)
	(4)		24 Jul 1990 (SI 1990/1520)
30			1 Apr 1991 (SI 1990/1793)
31			24 Jul 1990 (SI 1990/1520)
32			See Sch 6 below
33			24 Jul 1990 (SI 1990/1520)
34			17 Sep 1990 (so far as relates to provisions of ss 87A, 87B(1) (so far as s 87B(1) provides for meaning of 'recognised fund-holding practice' and 'allotted sum'), to be inserted into National Health Service (Scotland) Act 1978) (SI 1990/1793) 1 Apr 1991 (otherwise) (SI 1990/1793) Section prospectively repealed by Health Act 1999, s 65(2), Sch 5[1]
35			1 Apr 1992 (SI 1990/1793); prospectively repealed by Health Act 1999, s 65(2), Sch 5[1]
36	(1)		See Sch 7 below
	(2)–(8)		17 Sep 1990 (SI 1990/1793)

National Health Service and Community Care Act 1990 (c 19)—*contd*
Section

37		17 Sep 1990 (SI 1900/1793)
38		1 Apr 1991 (SI 1991/607)
39	(1)–(3)	1 Apr 1991 (subject, in case of s 39(2), to transitional provisions) (SI 1991/607)
	(4)	1 Apr 1991 (except repeal in second paragraph of National Health Service (Scotland) Act 1978, s 23(5)) (SI 1991/607)
		Not in force (exception noted above)
	(5)–(8)	1 Apr 1991 (SI 1991/607)
40, 41		17 Sep 1990 (SI 1990/1793)
42	(1)	1 Apr 1993 (SI 1992/2975)
	(2)	Repealed
	(3)–(5)	1 Apr 1993 (SI 1992/2975)
	(6), (7)	1 Apr 1991 (SI 1990/2218)
43		1 Apr 1993 (SI 1992/2975); prospectively repealed by Health and Social Care Act 2001, s 67, Sch 6, Pt 3[3]
44		1 Apr 1993 (SI 1992/2975)
45		12 Apr 1993 (SI 1992/2975)
46		1 Apr 1991 (SI 1990/2218)
47		1 Apr 1993 (SI 1992/2975)
48		1 Apr 1991 (SI 1990/2218)
49		10 Dec 1992 (SI 1992/2975)
50		1 Apr 1991 (SI 1990/2218)
51–54		1 Apr 1991 (SI 1990/2510)
55		1 Apr 1993 (SI 1992/2975)
56		1 Apr 1991 (so far as relates to insertion of Social Work (Scotland) Act 1968, s 13B) (SI 1990/2510) 1 Apr 1993 (otherwise) (SI 1992/2975)
57		1 Apr 1993 (SI 1992/2975); prospectively repealed by Health and Social Care Act 2001, s 67, Sch 6, Pt 3[3]
58		1 Apr 1991 (SI 1990/2510)
59	(1)	Repealed
	(2)	5 Jul 1990 (SI 1990/1329)
	(3)	1 Apr 1991 (SI 1991/607)
60		See Sch 8 below
61		17 Sep 1990 (SI 1990/1329)
62		Repealed
63		1 Apr 1991 (SI 1990/1329)
64, 65		5 Jul 1990 (SI 1990/1329)
66	(1)	See Sch 9 below
	(2)	See Sch 10 below

National Health Service and Community Care Act 1990 (c 19)—*contd*

Section

67				29 Jun 1990 (s 67(2))

Schedule

1, Pt	I, II			Repealed
	III, para	6		Repealed
		7		26 Jul 1990 (so far as has effect in relation to Regional Health Authorities) (SI 1990/1329) 17 Sep 1990 (otherwise) (SI 1990/1329)
		8, 9		26 Jul 1990 (SI 1990/1329)
		10		26 Jul 1990 (so far as has effect in relation to Regional Health Authorities) (SI 1990/1329) 17 Sep 1990 (otherwise) (SI 1990/1329)
2, 3				5 Jul 1990 (SI 1990/1329)
4				Repealed
5				17 Sep 1990 (SI 1990/1793)
6				24 Jul 1990 (SI 1990/1520)
7, para	1			See paras 2–13 below
	2			Repealed
	3	(1)		See sub-paras (2)–(7) below
		(2)	(a)	1 Dec 1994 (SI 1994/2658)
			(b)–(d)	Repealed
		(3)–(7)		Repealed
	4–6			Repealed
	7			1 Apr 1995 (SI 1994/2658)
	8–12			Repealed
	13			1 Dec 1994 (SI 1994/2658)
	14			1 Apr 1995 (SI 1994/2658)
	15			1 Dec 1994 (SI 1994/2658)
8				1 Apr 1991 (SI 1990/1329)
9, para	1			24 Jul 1990 (SI 1990/1520)
	2			5 Jul 1990 (SI 1990/1329)
	3, 4			24 Jul 1990 (SI 1990/1520)
	5	(1)–(3)		1 Apr 1993 (SI 1992/2975)
		(4)		5 Jul 1990 (SI 1990/1329)
		(5)		1 Apr 1993 (SI 1992/2975)
		(6), (7)		1 Apr 1991 (SI 1990/2218)
		(8)		1 Apr 1991 (SI 1990/2218; SI 1990/2510)
		(9)	(a)	1 Apr 1993 (SI 1992/2975)
			(b)	1 Apr 1991 (SI 1990/2510)
	6–9			5 Jul 1990 (SI 1990/1329)
	10	(1)		*Not in force*
		(2)–(6)		1 Apr 1991 (SI 1990/2510)
		(7), (8)		1 Apr 1993 (SI 1992/2975)
		(9)–(11)		1 Apr 1991 (SI 1990/2510)
		(12)		24 Jul 1990 (SI 1990/1520)

National Health Service and Community Care Act 1990 (c 19)—*contd*

Schedule

9, para	10	(13)		1 Apr 1991 (SI 1990/2510)
		(14)	(a)	1 Apr 1991 (SI 1990/2510)
			(b)	24 Jul 1990 (SI 1990/1520)
	11	(a)		1 Apr 1993 (SI 1992/2975)
		(b)		1 Apr 1991 (SI 1990/2218)
		(c)		1 Apr 1991 (so far as relates to s 46) (SI 1990/2218)
				1 Apr 1993 (otherwise) (SI 1992/2975)
	12			1 Apr 1991 (SI 1990/2218)
	13			5 Jul 1990 (SI 1990/1329)
	14			24 Jul 1990 (SI 1990/1520)
	15			Repealed
	16			10 Dec 1992 (SI 1992/2975)
	17			5 Jul 1990 (SI 1990/1329)
	18	(1)	(a)	17 Sep 1990 (SI 1990/1329); prospectively repealed by Health and Social Care Act 2001, s 67, Sch 6, Pt 2[3]
			(b)	Repealed
			(c)	17 Sep 1990 (SI 1990/1329); prospectively repealed by Health and Social Care Act 2001, s 67, Sch 6[3]
		(2)		17 Sep 1990 (SI 1990/1329)
		(3)–(9)		5 Jul 1990 (SI 1990/1329)
		(10), (11)		Repealed
		(12), (13)		5 Jul 1990 (SI 1990/1329)
		(14)		1 Apr 1993 (SI 1992/2975)
	19	(1)–(3)		17 Sep 1990 (SI 1990/1793)
		(4), (5)		24 Jul 1990 (SI 1990/1520)
		(6)		17 Sep 1990 (SI 1990/1793)
		(7)	(a) (i)	17 Sep 1990 (SI 1990/1793)
			(ii)	24 Jul 1990 (SI 1990/1520)
			(iii), (iv)	17 Sep 1990 (SI 1990/1793)
			(b)–(d)	17 Sep 1990 (SI 1990/1793)
		(8)		17 Sep 1990 (SI 1990/1793)
		(9)–(14)		24 Jul 1990 (SI 1990/1520)
		(15)		17 Sep 1990 (SI 1990/1793)
		(16), (17)		24 Jul 1990 (SI 1990/1520)
		(18)		Repealed
		(19)		24 Jul 1990 (SI 1990/1520)
		(20)		17 Sep 1990 (SI 1990/1793)
		(21)		24 Jul 1990 (SI 1990/1520)
		(22)	(a)	17 Sep 1990 (SI 1990/1793)
			(b)	24 Jul 1990 (SI 1990/1520)
			(c)	24 Jul 1990 (so far as relates to definition 'National Health Service trust') (SI 1990/1520)
				1 Apr 1991 (otherwise) (SI 1990/1793)
			(d)	24 Jul 1990 (SI 1990/1520)

National Health Service and Community Care Act 1990 (c 19)—*contd*
Schedule

9, para	19	(22)	(e)	17 Sep 1990 (SI 1990/1793)
		(23)		1 Apr 1991 (SI 1990/1793)
		(24)		24 Jul 1990 (SI 1990/1520)
	20			Repealed
	21	(a), (b)		5 Jul 1990 (SI 1990/1329)
		(c)		24 Jul 1990 (SI 1990/1520)
	22			Repealed
	23			5 Jul 1990 (SI 1990/1329)
	24	(1), (2)		5 Jul 1990 (SI 1990/1329)
		(3)	(a), (b)	5 Jul 1990 (SI 1990/1329)
			(c)	17 Sep 1990 (SI 1990/1329)
		(4)		Repealed
		(5)		5 Jul 1990 (SI 1990/1329)
		(6)		Repealed (*never in force*)
		(7)–(9)		5 Jul 1990 (SI 1990/1329)
	25	(1)		1 Apr 1993 (SI 1992/2975)
		(2)		12 Apr 1993 (SI 1992/2975)
	26			5 Jul 1990 (SI 1990/1329)
	27			Repealed (E)
				5 Jul 1990 (SI 1990/1329); prospectively repealed (W) by Care Standards Act 2000, S 117(2), Sch 6[2]
	28			24 Jul 1990 (SI 1990/1520)
	29			Repealed
	30	(1)	(a)	5 Jul 1990 (SI 1990/1329)
			(b), (c)	*Not in force*
		(2)		5 Jul 1990 (SI 1990/1329)
	31			Repealed
	32, 33			5 Jul 1990 (SI 1990/1329)
	34			17 Sep 1990 (SI 1990/1329)
	35–37			5 Jul 1990 (SI 1990/1329)
10				5 Jul 1990 (repeals of or in National Health Service Act 1977, ss 8(5), 10(7)) (SI 1990/1329)
				17 Sep 1990 (repeals of or in National Health Service Act 1977, ss 8(1)–(3), 11(1), 12(a), 13(1), 14, 16, 18(3), 41(b), 55, 91(3)(b), 97(6), 99(1)(b), Sch 5, para 8; Health Services Act 1980, s 22, Sch 1; Public Health (Control of Disease) Act 1984) (SI 1990/1329)
				17 Sep 1990 (repeals of or in National Health Service (Scotland) Act 1978, ss 5, 6, 10(4), 85(1)(a), 108(1), Sch 3; Health and Medicines Act 1988, Sch 2, para 11) (SI 1990/1793)

National Health Service and Community Care Act 1990 (c 19)—*contd*
Schedule
10—*contd*

                                  1 Oct 1990 (repeals of or in National
Health Service Act 1977,
s 98(1)(b), (3); Local Government
and Housing Act 1989)
(SI 1990/1329)

1 Jan 1991 (repeals of or in National
Health Service Act 1977, s 33(7))
(SI 1990/1329)

1 Jan 1991 (repeals of National Health
Service (Scotland) Act 1978,
s 23(7)) (SI 1990/1793)

1 Apr 1991 (repeals of or in Nursing
Homes Registration (Scotland)
Act 1938; Fire Precautions
Act 1971; Health Services Act 1976;
National Health Service Act 1977,
Sch 5, para 15(2); National Health
Service (Scotland) Act 1978;
Employment Protection
(Consolidation) Act 1978; Health
Services Act 1980, ss 12–15,
Schs 2–4; Registered Homes
Act 1984; National Health Service
(Amendment) Act 1986)
(SI 1990/1329)

1 Apr 1991 (repeals of or in National
Health Service (Scotland)
Act 1978, ss 7(2), 57(3))
(SI 1990/1793)

1 Apr 1991 (repeals of or in National
Assistance Act 1948, ss 35(2), (3),
36, 54 (so far as s 54 relates to
England and Wales, and subject to
a transitional provision (see
SI 1990/2218, art 3)); Health
Services and Public Health Act 1968,
s 45(5); Chronically Sick and
Disabled Persons Act 1970, s 2(1)
(so far as relates to England and
Wales)) (SI 1990/2218)

1 Apr 1991 (so far as they apply to
Scotland, repeals of or in National
Assistance Act 1948, s 54; Social
Work (Scotland) Act 1968, s 1(4);
National Health Service (Scotland)
Act 1978, ss 13A, 13B, Sch 15,
para 15 ; Mental Health (Scotland)
Act 1984, s 13(1)(c)) (S)
(SI 1990/2510)

National Health Service and Community Care Act 1990 (c 19)—*contd*
Schedule
10—*contd*

6 Apr 1992 (repeal of National
Assistance Act 1948, s 22(7))
(E, W) (SI 1992/567)
10 Dec 1992 (repeal in Children
Act 1975, s 99(1)(b))
(SI 1992/2975)
1 Apr 1993 (repeals of or in National
Assistance Act 1948, ss 21(8), 26;
National Health Service Act 1977,
Sch 8, para 2; Mental Health
Act 1983, ss 124(3), 135(6); Social
Security Act 1986, Sch 10,
para 32(2); Local Government
Act 1988, Sch 1, para 2(4)(b);
Local Government Finance
Act 1988, Sch 1, para 9(2)(b))
(SI 1992/2975)
1 Apr 1995 (repeals of National
Health Service (Scotland)
Act 1978, s 86(2); National Health
Service and Community Care
Act 1990, s 36(5)) (SI 1994/2658)
Not in force (otherwise)

[1] Orders made under Health Act 1999, s 67(1), bringing the prospective repeals into force will be noted to that Act

[2] Orders made under Care Standards Act 2000, s 122, bringing the prospective repeals into force will be noted to that Act

[3] Orders made under Health and Social Care Act 2001, s 70(2), bringing the prospective repeals into force will be noted to that Act

---

Pakistan Act 1990 (c 14)

RA: 29 Jun 1990

Commencement provisions: s 2(3)

1 Oct 1989 (retrospective; s 2(3))

Pensions (Miscellaneous Provisions) Act 1990 (c 7)

RA: 24 May 1990

Commencement provisions: ss 1(8), 14(3)
Section

1	(1)		24 Jul 1990 (s 14(3))
	(2)	(a)	24 Jul 1990 (s 14(3))
		(b)	1 Jan 1992 (s 1(8))
	(3)		24 Jul 1990 (s 14(3))
	(4)		1 Jan 1993 (s 1(8))
	(5)–(8)		24 Jul 1990 (S 14(3))

Pensions (Miscellaneous Provisions) Act 1990 (c 7)—*contd*

Section

2–11	24 Jul 1990 (s 14(3))
12	24 May 1990 (RA)
13	24 Jul 1990 (s 14(3))
14	24 May 1990 (RA)

Planning (Consequential Provisions) Act 1990 (c 11)

RA: 24 May 1990

Commencement provisions: s 7(2), Sch 4, para 1(3), (4); Planning (Consequential Provisions) Act 1990 (Appointed Day No 1 and Transitional Provisions) Order 1991, SI 1991/2698[1]

24 Aug 1990 (s 7(2))

[1] This order appointed 2 Jan 1992 as the appointed day under Sch 4, para 1(3)(a) for the purposes of paras 3–16 of that Schedule (transitory modifications), but only for the purposes of awards of costs in relation to proceedings which give rise to a hearing

Planning (Hazardous Substances) Act 1990 (c 10)

RA: 24 May 1990

Commencement provisions: s 41(2), (3); Planning (Hazardous Substances) Act 1990 (Commencement and Transitional Provisions) Order 1992, SI 1992/725

11 Mar 1992 (so far as provisions of this Act confer on the Secretary of State a power, or impose upon him a duty, to make regulations, or make provision with respect to the exercise of any such power or duty, for the purpose only of enabling or requiring the Secretary of State to make regulations) (SI 1992/725)

1 Jun 1992 (otherwise) (SI 1992/725)

See, for transitory provisions, Planning (Consequential Provisions) Act 1990, s 6, Sch 4; those transitory provisions partially ceased to have effect on 2 Jan 1992 (SI 1991/2698), so that on that day para 6(8) of the Schedule to this Act came partially into force

Planning (Listed Buildings and Conservation Areas) Act 1990 (c 9)

RA: 24 May 1990

Commencement provisions: s 94(2)

24 Aug 1990 (s 94(2))

See, for transitory provisions, Planning (Consequential Provisions) Act 1990, s 6, Sch 4; those transitory provisions partially ceased to have effect on 2 Jan 1992 (SI 1991/2698), so that on that day, Sch 3, para 6(8) to this Act came partially into force

Property Services Agency and Crown Suppliers Act 1990 (c 12)

RA: 29 Jun 1990

29 Jun 1990 (RA)

Representation of the People Act 1990 (c 32)

Whole Act repealed

Rights of Way Act 1990 (c 24)

RA: 13 Jul 1990

Commencement provisions: s 6(2)

13 Aug 1990 (s 6(2))

Social Security Act 1990 (c 27)

RA: 13 Jul 1990

Commencement provisions: s 23(2), (3); Social Security Act 1990 (Commencement No 1) Order 1990, SI 1990/1446; Social Security Act 1990 (Commencement No 2) Order 1990, SI 1990/1942; Social Security Act 1990 (Commencement No 3) Order 1991, SI 1991/558; Social Security Act 1990 (Commencement No 4) Order 1992, SI 1992/632; Social Security Act 1990 (Commencement No 5) Order 1992, SI 1992/1532; Social Security Act 1990 (Commencement No 6) Order 1997, SI 1997/1370

Section			
1–5			Repealed
6	(1)–(3)		Repealed
	(4), (5)		13 Jul 1990 (s 23(2), (3))
7			See Sch 1 below
8–14			Repealed
15	(1)		Substituted by Housing Grants, Construction and Regeneration Act 1996, s 142 (qv)
	(2)–(10)		13 Jul 1990 (s 23(2), (3))
	(11)		9 Jun 1997 (SI 1997/1370)
16			Repealed
17	(1)–(9)		Repealed
	(10)		6 Apr 1992 (SI 1992/632)
18–20			13 Jul 1990 (s 23(2), (3))
21	(1)		See Sch 6 below
	(2)		See Sch 7 below
	(3)		13 Jul 1990 (s 23(2), (3))
22			Repealed
23			13 Jul 1990 (s 23(2), (3))
Schedule			
1, para	1–4		Repealed
	5	(1), (2)	Repealed
		(3)	13 Jul 1990 (s 23(2), (3))
		(4)	Repealed
	6		Repealed
	7		13 Jul 1990 (s 23(2), (3))
2–5			Repealed
6, para	1		Repealed

Social Security Act 1990 (c 27)—*contd*

Schedule

6	2		13 Jul 1990 (s 23(2), (3))
	3		Repealed
	4	(1), (2)	Repealed
		(3)	13 Jul 1990 (s 23(2), (3))
	5–7		Repealed
	8	(1)	Repealed
		(2)	Spent
		(3)	Repealed
		(4)	13 Jul 1990 (s 23(2), (3))
		(5)	Repealed
		(6)	Spent
		(7), (8)	Repealed
		(9), (10)	13 Jul 1990 (s 23(2), (3))
		(11)	Repealed
		(12)	13 Jul 1990 (s 23(2), (3))
	9–12		Repealed
	13		13 Jul 1990 (s 23(2), (3))
	14–26		Repealed
	27		13 Jul 1990 (s 23(2), (3))
	28		Repealed
	29		13 Jul 1990 (so far as consequential on any preceding provision brought into force on 13 Jul 1990) (s 23(2), (3))
			Not in force (otherwise)
	30		Repealed
	31	(a), (b)	Repealed
		(c)–(e)	1 Oct 1990 (SI 1990/1942); now superseded
7			13 Jul 1990 (so far as consequential on any preceding provision brought into force on 13 Jul 1990) (s 23(2), (3))
			1 Oct 1990 (repeals of or in Social Security Act 1975, ss 59B(1), (3), (4), (7)(b), (8), 152(6); Social Security Pensions Act 1975, ss 33(2), 56B–56D, 56E(1)(c), 56F–56K, 56L(1)(a), (5)(b), (c), 56M, 56N; Social Security and Housing Benefits Act 1982, s 46(3); Social Security Act 1985, s 31(1), Sch 5, para 35; Social Security Act 1986, s 85(4)(a); Social Security Act 1988, s 2(8), (8A); Social Security Act 1989, Sch 1, para 8(3), (4), (7), Sch 2, Pt II, paras 1(2), 4(b)) (SI 1990/1942)

Social Security Act 1990 (c 27)—*contd*
Schedule

7—*contd*	21 Oct 1990 (repeals of or in Social Security Act 1986, s 79) (SI 1990/1942)
	28 Feb 1991 (repeals in Social Security Pensions Act 1975, Sch 1A, paras 1, 2, 11, 12) (SI 1990/1942)
	9 Jun 1997 (repeals of Housing (Scotland) Act 1987, ss 252, 253) (SI 1997/1370)
	Not in force (otherwise)

Terms and Quarter Days (Scotland) Act 1990 (c 22)

RA: 13 Jul 1990

Commencement provisions: s 3(2)
Section

1	(1)–(4)	13 Jul 1991 (s 3(2))
	(5), (6)	13 Jul 1990 (RA)
	(7)	13 Jul 1991 (s 3(2))
2		13 Jul 1991 (s 3(2))
3		13 Jul 1990 (RA)

Town and Country Planning Act 1990 (c 8)

RA: 24 May 1990

Commencement provisions: s 337(2)

24 Aug 1990 (s 337(2))

See, for transitory provisions, Planning (Consequential Provisions) Act 1990, s 6, Sch 4; those transitory provisions partially ceased to have effect on 2 Jan 1992 (SI 1991/2698), so that on that day, s 322 of, and Sch 6, para 6(5) to, this Act came partially into force

---

1991

Age of Legal Capacity (Scotland) Act 1991 (c 50)

RA: 25 Jul 1991

Commencement provisions: s 11(2)

25 Sep 1991 (s 11(2))

Agricultural Holdings (Scotland) Act 1991 (c 55)

RA: 25 Jul 1991

Commencement provisions: s 89(2)

25 Sep 1991 (s 89(2))

Agriculture and Forestry (Financial Provisions) Act 1991 (c 33)

RA: 25 Jul 1991

Commencement provisions: ss 1(2)–(5), 5(2); Agricultural Mortgage Corporation (Specified Day for Repeals) Order 1991, SI 1991/1937; Scottish Agricultural Securities Corporation (Specified Day for Repeals) Order 1991, SI 1991/1978

Section

1	(1)	See Schedule below
	(2)–(7)	25 Jul 1991 (RA)
2		25 Sep 1991 (s 5(2))
3–5		25 Jul 1991 (RA)
Schedule		
Pt	I	25 Sep 1991 (SI 1991/1937)
	II	25 Sep 1991 (by virtue of s 1(3), SI 1991/1937)
	III	25 Sep 1991 (SI 1991/1978)
	IV	25 Sep 1991 (by virtue of s 1(5), SI 1991/1978)

Appropriation Act 1991 (c 32)

Whole Act repealed

Armed Forces Act 1991 (c 62)

RA: 25 Jul 1991

Commencement provisions: s 27(2)–(4); Armed Forces Act 1991 (Commencement No 1) Order 1991, SI 1991/2719; Armed Forces Act 1991 (Commencement No 2) Order 1996, SI 1996/1173

Section

1	Repealed
2–5	1 Jan 1992 (SI 1991/2719)

Armed Forces Act 1991 (c 62)—*contd*

Armed Forces Act 1991 (c 62)—*contd*
Schedule
3—*contd*

Forces Act 1982; Armed Forces Act 1986, Sch 1, para 12(3), (5); Children Act 1989) (SI 1991/2719)

1 Jun 1996 (repeals of Army Act 1955, s 216(4); Air Force Act 1955, s 214(4); Naval Discipline Act 1957, s 125(3); Armed Forces Act 1981, s 14 (except in relation to any order made under this section on or before 31 May 1996); Armed Forces Act 1986, s 13) (SI 1996/1173)

Arms Control and Disarmament (Inspections) Act 1991 (c 41)

RA: 25 Jul 1991

Commencement provisions: s 6(2); Arms Control and Disarmament (Inspections) Act 1991 (Commencement) Order 1992, SI 1992/1750

Section
1–5	17 Jul 1992 (SI 1992/1750)
6	25 Jul 1991 (RA)
Schedule	17 Jul 1992 (SI 1992/1750)

Atomic Weapons Establishment Act 1991 (c 46)

RA: 25 Jul 1991

Commencement provisions: s 6(2)

25 Sep 1991 (s 6(2))

Badgers Act 1991 (c 36)

Whole Act repealed

Badgers (Further Protection) Act 1991 (c 35)

Whole Act repealed

Breeding of Dogs Act 1991 (c 64)

RA: 25 Jul 1991

Commencement provisions: s 3(2)

25 Sep 1991 (s 3(2))

British Railways Board (Finance) Act 1991 (c 63)

RA: 25 Jul 1991

25 Jul 1991 (RA)

Whole Act prospectively repealed by Transport Act 2000, s 274, Sch 31, Pt IV

British Technology Group Act 1991 (c 66)

RA: 22 Oct 1991

Commencement provisions: ss 1(1), 11(2), 18(2)–(4); British Technology Group
   Act 1991 (Appointed Day) Order 1991, SI 1991/2721

Section		
1	(1)–(5)	22 Oct 1991 (s 18(3))
	(6)	See Sch 1 below
2		22 Oct 1991 (s 18(3))
3–6		6 Jan 1992 (ss 1(1), 18(2); SI 1991/2721)
7		22 Oct 1991 (s 18(3))
8–13		6 Jan 1992 (ss 1(1), 18(2); SI 1991/2721)
14		22 Oct 1991 (s 18(3))
15		6 Jan 1992 (ss 1(1), 18(2); SI 1991/2721)
16	(1)	22 Oct 1991 (s 18(3))
	(2)	6 Jan 1992 (ss 1(1), 18(2); SI 1991/2721)
17	(1)	6 Jan 1992 (ss 1(1), 18(2); SI 1991/2721)
	(2)	See Sch 2 below
	(3)	See Sch 3 below
18		22 Oct 1991 (s 18(3))
Schedule		
1, para	1	22 Oct 1991 (s 18(3))
	2–5	6 Jan 1992 (ss 1(1), 18(2); SI 1991/2721)
2, Pt	I	6 Jan 1992 (ss 1(1), 18(2); SI 1991/2721)
	II	*Not in force*
	III	1 Jul 1996 (SI 1996/1448)
3		6 Jan 1992 (ss 1(1), 18(2); SI 1991/2721)

Caravans (Standard Community Charge and Rating) Act 1991 (c 2)

RA: 12 Feb 1991

12 Feb 1991 (RA)

Care of Churches and Ecclesiastical Jurisdiction Measure 1991 (No 1)

RA: 25 Jul 1991

Commencement provisions: s 33(2)

1 Mar 1993 (the day appointed by the Archbishops of Canterbury and York under s 33(2))

Census (Confidentiality) Act 1991 (c 6)

RA: 7 Mar 1991

7 Mar 1991 (RA)

Child Support Act 1991 (c 48)

RA: 25 Jul 1991

Commencement provisions: s 58(2)–(7); Child Support Act 1991 (Commencement No 1) Order 1992, SI 1992/1431; Child Support Act 1991 (Commencement No 2) Order 1992, SI 1992/1938; Child Support Act 1991 (Commencement No 3 and Transitional Provisions) Order 1992, SI 1992/2644, as amended by SI 1993/966; Child Support Act 1991 (Commencement No 3 and Transitional Provisions) (Amendment) Order 1993, SI 1993/966 (amending SI 1992/2644, Schedule, which contains transitional provisions)

Section			
1, 2			5 Apr 1993 (SI 1992/2644)
3	(1), (2)		5 Apr 1993 (SI 1992/2644)
	(3)	(a), (b)	5 Apr 1993 (SI 1992/2644)
		(c)	17 Jun 1992 (SI 1992/1431)
	(4)–(7)		5 Apr 1993 (SI 1992/2644)
4	(1)–(3)		5 Apr 1993 (subject to transitional provisions) (SI 1992/2644, as amended by SI 1993/966)
	(4)		17 Jun 1992 (SI 1992/1431)
	(5), (6)		5 Apr 1993 (subject to transitional provisions) (SI 1992/2644, as amended by SI 1993/966)
	(7), (8)		17 Jun 1992 (SI 1992/1431)
	(9)		5 Apr 1993 (subject to transitional provisions) (SI 1992/2644, as amended by SI 1993/966)
	(10)		Added by Child Support Act 1995, s 18(1) (qv)
	(11)		Added by Child Support Act 1995, s 18(1) (qv)
5	(1), (2)		5 Apr 1993 (SI 1992/2644)
	(3)		17 Jun 1992 (SI 1992/1431)
6	(1)		17 Jun 1992 (so far as confers power to prescribe kinds of benefit for purposes of s 6(1)) (SI 1992/1431)

Child Support Act 1991 (c 48)—*contd*

Section

6	(1)—*contd*	5 Apr 1993 (otherwise) (SI 1992/2644) Subsection prospectively substituted by Child Support, Pensions and Social Security Act 2000, s 3 (substitution in force for the purpose of making regulations and Acts of Sederunt)[2]
	(2)–(8)	5 Apr 1993 (SI 1992/2644); prospectively substituted as noted to sub-s (1) above[2]
	(9), (10)	17 Jun 1992 (SI 1992/1431); prospectively substituted as noted to sub-s (1) above[2]
	(11), (12)	5 Apr 1993 (SI 1992/2644); prospectively substituted as noted to sub-s (1) above[2]
	(13)	17 Jun 1992 (SI 1992/1431); prospectively substituted as noted to sub-s (1) above[2]
	(14)	5 Apr 1993 (SI 1992/2644); prospectively substituted as noted to sub-s (1) above[2]
7	(1)–(4)	5 Apr 1993 (subject to transitional provisions) (SI 1992/2644, as amended by SI 1993/966)
	(5)	17 Jun 1992 (SI 1992/1431)
	(6), (7)	5 Apr 1993 (subject to transitional provisions) (SI 1992/2644, as amended by SI 1993/966)
	(8), (9)	17 Jun 1992 (SI 1992/1431)
	(10)	Added by Child Support Act 1995, s 18(2) (qv)
8	(1)–(3)	5 Apr 1993 (subject to transitional provisions) (SI 1992/2644, as amended by SI 1993/966)
	(3A)	Inserted by Child Support Act 1995, s 18(3) (qv); prospectively substituted by Child Support, Pensions and Social Security Act 2000, s 26, Sch 3, para 11(5)(c)[2]
	(4)	5 Apr 1993 (subject to transitional provisions) (SI 1992/2644, as amended by SI 1993/966)
	(5)	17 Jun 1992 (SI 1992/1431)
	(6)–(8)	5 Apr 1993 (SI 1992/2644)
	(9)	17 Jun 1992 (SI 1992/1431)
	(10)	5 Apr 1993 (SI 1992/2644)
	(11) (a)–(e)	5 Apr 1993 (SI 1992/2644)

Child Support Act 1991 (c 48)—*contd*

Section

8	(11)	(f)	17 Jun 1992 (SI 1992/1431)
9			5 Apr 1993 (subject to transitional provisions) (SI 1992/2644, as amended by SI 1993/966)
10			17 Jun 1992 (SI 1992/1431)
11	(1)		5 Apr 1993 (SI 1992/2644); prospectively substituted by Child Support, Pensions and Social Security Act 2000, s 1(1)[2]
	(1A)–(1C)		Inserted by Child Support Act 1995, s 19 (qv); prospectively substituted as noted to sub-s(1) above[2]
	(2), (3)		Prospectively substituted as noted to sub-s(1) above[2]
	(4)–(8)		Prospectively added by Child Support, Pensions and Social Security Act 2000, s 1(1)[2]
12	(1), (1A)		Substituted for new subs (1) by Social Security Act 1998, s 86(1), Sch 7, para 25 (qv); prospectively substituted by Child Support, Pensions and Social Security Act 2000, s 4 (substitution in force for the purpose of making regulations and Acts of Sederunt)[2]
	(2), (3)		17 Jun 1992 (SI 1992/1431); prospectively substituted as noted to sub-ss (1), (1A) above[2]
	(4)		5 Apr 1993 (SI 1992/2644); prospectively substituted as noted to sub-ss (1), (1A) above[2]
	(5)		17 Jun 1992 (SI 1992/1431); prospectively substituted as noted to sub-ss (1), (1A) above[2]
13			Repealed
14	(1)		17 Jun 1992 (SI 1992/1431)
	(1A)		Inserted by Child Support Act 1995, s 30(5), Sch 3, paras 2, 3(1) (qv)
	(2), (2A)		Repealed
	(3)		17 Jun 1992 (SI 1992/1431)
	(4)		See Sch 2 below
14A			Inserted by Child Support, Pensions and Social Security Act 2000, s 13 (qv)
15			5 Apr 1993 (SI 1992/2644)
16			Repealed
17			Substituted, together with ss 18, 19, for new s 17 by Social Security Act 1998, s 41 (qv)

Child Support Act 1991 (c 48)—*contd*

Section

18, 19			Substituted, as noted to s 17
20			Repealed (*partly never in force*)
20A, 21			Repealed
22	(1), (2)		1 Sep 1992 (SI 1992/1938)
	(3), (4)		17 Jun 1992 (SI 1992/1431)
	(5)		See Sch 4 below
23			1 Sep 1992 (SI 1992/1938)
23A			Inserted by Child Support, Pensions and Social Security Act 2000, s 10 (qv)
24	(1)		5 Apr 1993 (SI 1992/2644)
	(1A)		Repealed
	(2), (3)		5 Apr 1993 (SI 1992/2644)
	(4)		Substituted by Social Security Act 1998, s 86, Sch 7, para 30, Sch 8 (qv)
	(5)		5 Apr 1993 (SI 1992/2644)
	(6), (7)		17 Jun 1992 (SI 1992/1431)
	(8)		5 Apr 1993 (SI 1992/2644)
	(9)		1 Sep 1992 (SI 1992/1938)
25	(1)		5 Apr 1993 (SI 1992/2644)
	(2)	(a)	17 Jun 1992 (SI 1992/1431)
		(b)	5 Apr 1993 (SI 1992/2644)
	(3)	(a), (b)	5 Apr 1993 (SI 1992/2644)
		(c)	17 Jun 1992 (SI 1992/1431)
	(3A), (3B)		Inserted by Child Support Act 1995, s 30(5), Sch 3, paras 2, 8(1) (qv)
	(4)		5 Apr 1993 (SI 1992/2644)
	(5), (6)		17 Jun 1992 (SI 1992/1431)
26			5 Apr 1993 (SI 1992/2644)
27			5 Apr 1993 (SI 1992/2644); substituted by Child Support, Pensions and Social Security Act 2000, s 83(5), Sch 8, para 13 (qv)
27A			Inserted by Child Support Act 1995, s 21 (qv)
28			5 Apr 1993 (SI 1992/2644)
28ZA–28ZD			Inserted by Social Security Act 1998, ss 43, 44 (qv)
28A			Inserted by Child Support Act 1995, s 1(1) (qv); prospectively substituted by Child Support, Pensions and Social Security Act 2000, s 5 (substitution in force for the purpose of making regulations and Acts of Sederunt)[2]
28B	(1)–(3)		Inserted by Child Support Act 1995, s 2 (qv); prospectively substituted as noted to s 28A above[2]
	(4), (5)		Repealed

Child Support Act 1991 (c 48)—*contd*

Section

28B	(6)	Prospectively inserted by Child Support Act 1995, s 2[1]; substituted by Social Security Act 1998, s 86, Sch 7, para 35, Sch 8 (qv); prospectively substituted as noted to s 28A above[2]
28C		Inserted by Child Support Act 1995, ss 3–8 (qv); prospectively substituted as noted to s 28A above[2]
28D, 28E		Inserted by Child Support Act 1995, ss 3–8 (qv)
28F		Inserted by Child Support Act 1995, ss 3–8 (qv); prospectively substituted as noted to s 28A above[2]
28G		Substituted by Child Support, Pensions and Social Security Act 2000, s 7 (qv)
28H		Inserted by Child Support Act 1995, s 8(qv); substituted by Social Security Act 1998, s 86(1), Sch 7, para 39 (qv); prospectively repealed by Child Support, Pensions and Social Security Act 2000, ss 26, 85, Sch 3, para 11(14), Sch 9, Pt I[2]
28I	(1)–(3)	Prospectively inserted by Child Support Act 1995, s 9[1]; prospectively repealed by Child Support, Pensions and Social Security Act 2000, ss 26, 85, Sch 3, para 11(14), Sch 9, Pt I[2]
	(4), (5)	Inserted by Child Support Act 1995, s 9 (qv); prospectively repealed as noted to S 28H above[2]
28J		Prospectively inserted by Child Support, Pensions and Social Security Act 2000, s 20(1) (substitution in force for the purpose of making regulations and Acts of Sederunt)[2]
29	(1)	5 Apr 1993 (SI 1992/2644)
	(2), (3)	17 Jun 1992 (SI 1992/1431)
30	(1)	17 Jun 1992 (SI 1992/1431)
	(2)	*Not in force*; prospectively substituted by Child Support, Pensions and Social Security Act 2000, s 26, Sch 3, para 11(15)[2]
	(3)	5 Apr 1993 (SI 1992/2644)

Child Support Act 1991 (c 48)—*contd*
Section

30	(4), (5)			17 Jun 1992 (SI 1992/1431)
	(5A)			Prospectively added by Child Support Act 1995, s 30(5), Sch 3, paras 2, 9[1]
31	(1)–(7)			5 Apr 1993 (SI 1992/2644)
	(8)			17 Jun 1992 (SI 1992/1431)
32	(1)–(5)			17 Jun 1992 (SI 1992/1431)
	(6)			5 Apr 1993 (SI 1992/2644)
	(7)–(9)			17 Jun 1992 (SI 1992/1431)
	(10)–(11)			5 Apr 1993 (SI 1992/2644)
33				5 Apr 1993 (SI 1992/2644)
34	(1)			17 Jun 1992 (SI 1992/1431)
	(2)			*Not in force*
35	(1)			5 Apr 1993 (SI 1992/2644)
	(2)	(a)		5 Apr 1993 (SI 1992/2644)
		(b)		17 Jun 1992 (SI 1992/1431)
	(3)–(6)			5 Apr 1993 (SI 1992/2644)
	(7), (8)			17 Jun 1992 (SI 1992/1431)
36				5 Apr 1993 (SI 1992/2644)
37	(1)			5 Apr 1993 (SI 1992/2644)
	(2), (3)			*Not in force*
38				5 Apr 1993 (SI 1992/2644)
39				17 Jun 1992 (SI 1992/1431)
39A				Inserted by Child Support, Pensions and Social Security Act 2000, s 16(1) (qv)
40	(1), (2)			Repealed
	(3)			5 Apr 1993 (SI 1992/2644)
	(4)	(a)	(i)	5 Apr 1993 (SI 1992/2644)
			(ii)	17 Jun 1992 (SI 1992/1431)
		(b)		5 Apr 1993 (SI 1992/2644)
	(5)–(7)			5 Apr 1993 (SI 1992/2644)
	(8)			17 Jun 1992 (SI 1992/1431)
	(9), (10)			5 Apr 1993 (SI 1992/2644)
	(11)			17 Jun 1992 (SI 1992/1431)
	(12)–(14)			Substituted by Child Support, Pensions and Social Security Act 2000, s 17(1) (qv)
40A				Inserted by Child Support, Pensions and Social Security Act 2000, s 17(2) (qv)
40B				Inserted by Child Support, Pensions and Social Security Act 2000, s 16(3) (qv)
41	(1)			5 Apr 1993 (SI 1992/2644)
	(2), (2A)			Substituted (for sub-s (2)) by Child Support Act 1995, s 30(5), Sch 3, paras 2, 11 (qv)

Child Support Act 1991 (c 48)—*contd*

Section

41	(3), (4)		17 Jun 1992 (SI 1992/1431); prospectively repealed by Child Support, Pensions and Social Security Act 2000, ss 18(1), 85, Sch 9, Pt I[2]
	(5)		5 Apr 1993 (SI 1992/2644); prospectively repealed as noted to sub-ss (3), (4) above[2]
	(6)		5 Apr 1993 (SI 1992/2644)
41A			Prospectively inserted by Child Support Act 1995, s 22[1]; prospectively substituted by Child Support, Pensions and Social Security Act 2000, s 18(2) (substitution in force for the purpose of making regulations and Acts of Sederunt)[2]
41B			Inserted by Child Support Act 1995, s 23 (qv)
42			17 Jun 1992 (SI 1992/1431)
43	(1)	(a)	5 Apr 1993 (SI 1992/2644); prospectively substituted by Child Support, Pensions and Social Security Act 2000, s 21 (amendments in force for the purpose of making regulations and Acts of Sederunt)[2]
		(b)	17 Jun 1992 (SI 1992/1431); prospectively substituted as noted to sub-s (1)(a) above[2]
	(2)	(a)	17 Jun 1992 (SI 1992/1431) ; prospectively substituted as noted to sub-s (1)(a) above[2]
		(b)	5 Apr 1993 (SI 1992/2644) ; prospectively substituted as noted to sub-s (1)(a) above[2]
	(3)		Added by Social Security Act 1998, s 86(1), Sch 7, para 40 (qv) ; prospectively substituted as noted to sub-s (1)(a) above[2]
44	(1), (2)		5 Apr 1993 (SI 1992/2644)
	(2A)		Inserted by Child Support, Pensions and Social Security Act 2000, s 22(3) (qv)
	(3)		17 Jun 1992 (SI 1992/1431); prospectively repealed by Child Support, Pensions and Social Security Act 2000, ss 22(4), 85, Sch 9, Pt I[2]

Child Support Act 1991 (c 48)—*contd*
Section

45			17 Jun 1992 (SI 1992/1431)
46	(1)–(6)		5 Apr 1993 (SI 1992/2644); prospectively substituted by Child Support, Pensions and Social Security Act 2000, s 19 (substitution in force for the purpose of making regulations and Acts of Sederunt)[2]
	(7), (8)		Substituted for new sub-s (7) by Social Security Act 1998, s 86, Sch 7, para 43, Sch 8 (qv); prospectively substituted as noted to sub-ss (1)–(6) above[2]
	(9), (10)		5 Apr 1993 (SI 1992/2644); prospectively substituted as noted to sub-ss (1)–(6) above[2]
	(11)		17 Jun 1992 (SI 1992/1431); prospectively substituted as noted to sub-ss (1)–(6) above[2]
46A, 46B			Inserted by Social Security Act 1998, s 86(1), Sch 7, para 44 (qv)
47			17 Jun 1992 (SI 1992/1431)
48			5 Apr 1993 (SI 1992/2644)
49			17 Jun 1992 (SI 1992/1431)
50	(1)–(4)		5 Apr 1993 (SI 1992/2644)
	(5)		17 Jun 1992 (SI 1992/1431)
	(6)		5 Apr 1993 (SI 1992/2644)
	(7)	(a)–(c)	5 Apr 1993 (SI 1992/2644)
		(d)	17 Jun 1992 (SI 1992/1431)
	(8)		5 Apr 1993 (SI 1992/2644)
51, 52			17 Jun 1992 (SI 1992/1431)
53			5 Apr 1993 (SI 1992/2644)
54, 55			17 Jun 1992 (SI 1992/1431)
56	(1)		25 Jul 1991 (s 58(2))
	(2)–(4)		Repealed
57			17 Jun 1992 (SI 1992/1431)
58	(1)–(11)		25 Jul 1991 (s 58(2))
	(12)		*Not in force*
	(13)		See Sch 5 below
	(14)		25 Jul 1991 (s 58(2))
Schedule			
1, para	1	(1), (2)	5 Apr 1993 (SI 1992/2644); Sch 1, Pt I prospectively substituted by Child Support, Pensions and Social Security Act 2000, s 1(3), Sch 1 (substitution in force for purpose of making regulations and Acts of Sederunt)[2]

Child Support Act 1991 (c 48)—*contd*
Schedule

1, para	1	(3)	17 Jun 1992 (SI 1992/1431); prospectively substituted as noted to para 1(1), (2) above[2]
		(4)	5 Apr 1993 (SI 1992/2644) ; prospectively substituted as noted to para 1(1), (2) above[2]
		(5)	17 Jun 1992 (SI 1992/1431) ; prospectively substituted as noted to para 1(1), (2) above[2]
	2	(1)	17 Jun 1992 (SI 1992/1431); prospectively substituted as noted to para 1(1), (2) above[2]
		(2), (3)	5 Apr 1993 (SI 1992/2644); prospectively substituted as noted to para 1(1), (2) above[2]
	3		5 Apr 1993 (SI 1992/2644); prospectively substituted as noted to para 1(1), (2) above[2]
	4	(1)	17 Jun 1992 (SI 1992/1431); prospectively substituted as noted to para 1(1), (2) above[2]
		(2)	5 Apr 1993 (SI 1992/2644); prospectively substituted as noted to para 1(1), (2) above[2]
		(3)	17 Jun 1992 (SI 1992/1431); prospectively substituted as noted to para 1(1), (2) above[2]
	5	(1), (2)	17 Jun 1992 (SI 1992/1431); prospectively substituted as noted to para 1(1), (2) above[2]
		(3)	5 Apr 1993 (SI 1992/2644); prospectively substituted as noted to para 1(1), (2) above[2]
		(4)	17 Jun 1992 (SI 1992/1431); prospectively substituted as noted to para 1(1), (2) above[2]
	6	(1)	5 Apr 1993 (SI 1992/2644); prospectively substituted as noted to para 1(1), (2) above[2]
		(2)–(6)	17 Jun 1992 (SI 1992/1431); prospectively substituted as noted to para 1(1), (2) above[2]
		(7)–(11)	5 Apr 1993 (SI 1992/2644); prospectively substituted as noted to para 1(1), (2) above[2]
	7–9		17 Jun 1992 (SI 1992/1431); prospectively substituted as noted to para 1(1), (2) above[2]

Child Support Act 1991 (c 48)—*contd*

Schedule

1, para	10		5 Apr 1993 (SI 1992/2644); prospectively substituted as noted to para 1(1), (2) above[2]
	10A–10C		Prospectively inserted by Child Support, Pensions and Social Security Act 2000, s 1(3), Sch 1 (in force for purpose of making regulations and Acts of Sederunt)[2]
	11		17 Jun 1992 (SI 1992/1431)
	12		5 Apr 1993 (SI 1992/2644)
	13		5 Apr 1993 (SI 1992/2644); prospectively repealed by Child Support, Pensions and Social Security Act 2000, ss 26, 85, Sch 3, para 11(22)(a), Sch 9, Pt I[2]
	14		17 Jun 1992 (SI 1992/1431)
	15		5 Apr 1993 (SI 1992/2644)
	16	(1)	5 Apr 1993 (SI 1992/2644)
		(2)–(4)	5 Apr 1993 (SI 1992/2644); prospectively repealed by Child Support, Pensions and Social Security Act 2000, ss 26, 85, Sch 3, para 11(22)(c)(ii), Sch 9, Pt I[2]
		(4A)	Inserted by Child Support Act 1995, s 14(2) (qv); prospectively repealed by Child Support, Pensions and Social Security Act 2000, ss 26, 85, Sch 3, para 11(22)(c)(ii), Sch 9, Pt I[2]
		(5)	17 Jun 1992 (SI 1992/1431); prospectively repealed by Child Support, Pensions and Social Security Act 2000, ss 26, 85, Sch 3, para 11(22)(c)(ii), Sch 9, Pt I[2]
		(6)–(9)	5 Apr 1993 (SI 1992/2644); prospectively repealed by Child Support, Pensions and Social Security Act 2000, ss 26, 85, Sch 3, para 11(22)(c)(ii), Sch 9, Pt I[2]
		(10), (11)	17 Jun 1992 (SI 1992/1431)
2, para	1		5 Apr 1993 (SI 1992/2644)
	1A		Inserted by Welfare Reform and Pensions Act 1999, s 80 (qv)
	2		Repealed
3			Repealed
4			1 Sep 1992 (SI 1992/1938)
4A			Inserted by Child Support Act 1995, s 1(2), Sch 1 (qv); prospectively substituted by Child Support,

Child Support Act 1991 (c 48)—*contd*
Schedule

4A—*contd*		Pensions and Social Security Act 2000, s 6(1), Sch 2, Pt I (substitution in force for purpose of making regulations and Acts of Sederunt)[2]
4B		Inserted by Child Support Act 1995, s 6(2), Sch 2 (qv); prospectively substituted by Child Support, Pensions and Social Security Act 2000, s 6(2), Sch 2, Pt II (substitution in force for purpose of making regulations and Acts of Sederunt)[2]
4C		Inserted by Social Security Act 1998, s 86(1), Sch 7, para 54 (qv); prospectively repealed by Child Support, Pensions and Social Security Act 2000, s 85, Sch 9, Pt I[1]
5, para	1, 2	Repealed
	3, 4	1 Sep 1992 (SI 1992/1938)
	5–8	5 Apr 1993 (SI 1992/2644)

[1]   Orders made under Child Support Act 1995, s 30(4), bringing the prospective amendments into force will be noted to that Act

[2]   Orders made under Child Support, Pensions and Social Security Act 2000, s 84, bringing the prospective amendments into force will be noted to that Act

---

Children and Young Persons (Protection from Tobacco) Act 1991 (c 23)

RA: 27 Jun 1991

Commencement provisions: s 8(2); Children and Young Persons (Protection from Tobacco) Act 1991 (Commencement No 1) Order 1991, SI 1991/2500; Children and Young Persons (Protection from Tobacco) Act 1991 (Commencement No 2) Order 1992, SI 1992/332; Children and Young Persons (Protection from Tobacco) Act 1991 (Commencement No 3) Order 1992, SI 1992/3227

Section

1–3		1 Mar 1992 (SI 1992/332)
4	(1), (2)	20 Feb 1993 (SI 1992/3227)
	(3)	17 Dec 1992 (SI 1992/3227)
	(4)–(8)	20 Feb 1993 (SI 1992/3227)
	(9)	17 Dec 1992 (SI 1992/3227)
5–7		1 Mar 1992 (SI 1992/332)
8	(1)	1 Mar 1992 (SI 1992/332)
	(2)	27 Jun 1991 (RA)
	(3)–(5)	1 Mar 1992 (SI 1992/332)
	(6), (7)	11 Nov 1991 (NI) (SI 1992/2500)
		1 Mar 1992 (otherwise) (SI 1992/332)

Civil Jurisdiction and Judgments Act 1991 (c 12)

RA: 9 May 1991

Commencement provisions: s 5(3); Civil Jurisdiction and Judgments Act 1991
(Commencement) Order 1992, SI 1992/745

1 May 1992 (SI 1992/745)

Coal Mining Subsidence Act 1991 (c 45)

RA: 25 Jul 1991

Commencement provisions: s 54(2), (3); Coal Mining Subsidence Act 1991
(Commencement) Order 1991, SI 1991/2508

30 Nov 1991 (subject to transitional provision with respect to s 34(1)(a)) (SI 1991/2508)

Community Charges (General Reduction) Act 1991 (c 9)

RA: 28 Mar 1991

28 Mar 1991 (RA)

Community Charges (Substitute Setting) Act 1991 (c 8)

Whole Act repealed

Consolidated Fund Act 1991 (c 7)

Whole Act repealed

Consolidated Fund (No 2) Act 1991 (c 10)

Whole Act repealed

Consolidated Fund (No 3) Act 1991 (c 68)

Whole Act repealed

Criminal Justice Act 1991 (c 53)

RA: 25 Jul 1991

Commencement provisions: s 102(2), (3); Criminal Justice Act 1991 (Commencement
No 1) Order 1991, SI 1991/2208; Criminal Justice Act 1991 (Commencement
No 2 and Transitional Provisions) Order 1991, SI 1991/2706; Criminal Justice
Act 1991 (Commencement No 3) Order 1992, SI 1992/333 (as amended by
SI 1992/2118, SI 1999/1280); Criminal Justice Act 1991 (Commencement No 3
(Amendment) and Transitional Provisions and Savings) (Scotland) Order 1992,
SI 1992/2118 (amending SI 1992/333); Criminal Justice Act 1991
(Commencement No 4) Order 1994, SI 1994/3191; Criminal Justice Act 1991
(Commencement No 3) (Amendment) Order 1999, SI 1999/1280 (amending
SI 1992/333)

Criminal Justice Act 1991 (c 53)—*contd*

Section

1–15		Repealed
16		1 Oct 1992 (SI 1992/333)
17		1 Oct 1992 (but does not apply in relation to any offence committed before 1 Oct 1992) (SI 1992/333, as amended by SI 1992/2118)
18–20		Repealed
20A		Inserted by Criminal Justice and Public Order Act 1994, s 168(1), Sch 9, para 43 (qv)
21, 22		Repealed
23, 24		1 Oct 1992 (SI 1992/333)
25		Repealed
26	(1), (2)	1 Oct 1992 (SI 1992/333)
	(3)	Repealed
	(4), (5)	31 Oct 1991 (SI 1991/2208)
27		1 Oct 1992 (SI 1992/333)
28, 29		Repealed
30		1 Oct 1992 (SI 1992/333)
31		Repealed
32	(1)	Substituted by Criminal Justice and Public Order Act 1994, s 149 (qv)
	(2), (3)	1 Oct 1992 (SI 1992/333)
	(3A)	Inserted by Crime and Disorder Act 1998, s 119, Sch 8, para 79 (qv)
	(4)	Repealed
	(5), (6)	1 Oct 1992 (SI 1992/333)
	(7)	See Sch 5 below
33		1 Oct 1992 (SI 1992/333); prospectively repealed by Crime (Sentences) Act 1997, s 56(2), Sch 6 (repealed)[1]
33A		Inserted by Crime and Disorder Act 1998, ss 119, 120(1), Sch 8, para 81, Sch 9, para 12(1), (4), subject to transitional provisions (qv)
34		Repealed
34A		Inserted by Crime and Disorder Act 1998, ss 99, 120(1), Sch 9, paras 10, 12(1), (5), subject to transitional provisions (qv)
35–37		1 Oct 1992 (SI 1992/333); repealed, partly prospectively, by Crime (Sentences) Act 1997, s 56(2), Sch 6 (repealed)[1]
37A		Inserted by Crime and Disorder Act 1998, s 100(1) (qv)

Criminal Justice Act 1991 (c 53)—*contd*

Section

38		Repealed
38A		Inserted by Crime and Disorder Act 1998, s 100(2) (qv)
39		1 Oct 1992 (SI 1992/333); repealed, partly prospectively, by Crime (Sentences) Act 1997, s 56(2), Sch 6 (repealed)[1]
40		1 Oct 1992 (SI 1992/333); repealed, partly prospectively, by Crime (Sentences) Act 1997, s 56(2), Sch 6 (repealed)[1]; repealed (25 Aug 2000) by Powers of Criminal Courts (Sentencing) Act 2000, s 165(4), Sch 12, Pt I (qv)
40A		Inserted by Crime and Disorder Act 1998, ss 105, 120(1), Sch 9, paras 12(1), (6), 14 (qv)
41–43		1 Oct 1992 (SI 1992/333); repealed, partly prospectively by Crime (Sentences) Act 1997, s 56(2), Sch 6 (repealed)[1]
44		Substituted by Crime and Disorder Act 1998, ss 59, 120(1), Sch 9, para 12(1), (7) (qv); repealed (25 Aug 2000), as it applies to persons sentenced for sexual offences committed before 30 Sep 1998, by Powers of Criminal Courts (Sentencing) Act 2000, s 165(4), Sch 12, Pt I (qv)
44A		Inserted by Crime and Disorder Act 1998, s 60 (qv)
45–47		1 Oct 1992 (SI 1992/333); prospectively repealed by Crime (Sentences) Act 1997, s 56(2), Sch 6 (repealed)[1]
48		Repealed
49–51		1 Oct 1992 (SI 1992/333); repealed, partly prospectively by Crime (Sentences) Act 1997, s 56(2), Sch 6 (repealed)[1]
52		1 Oct 1992 (SI 1992/333); prospectively repealed by Youth Justice and Criminal Evidence Act 1999, s 67, Sch 6[5]
53	(1)–(4)	1 Oct 1992 (SI 1992/333)
	(5)	See Sch 6 below
	(6), (7)	1 Oct 1992 (SI 1992/333)

Criminal Justice Act 1991 (c 53)—*contd*

Section

53	(8)		Inserted, partly prospectively, by Crime and Disorder Act 1998, s 119, Sch 8, para 93[2]
54			1 Oct 1992 (SI 1992/333); prospectively repealed by Youth Justice and Criminal Evidence Act 1999, s 67, Sch 6[5]
55, 56			1 Oct 1992 (SI 1992/333)
57, 58			Repealed
59			1 Oct 1992 (SI 1992/333)
60	(1)		1 Oct 1992 (SI 1992/333)
	(2)	(a)	1 Oct 1992 (SI 1992/333)
		(b), (c)	1 Jun 1999 (SI 1999/1280)
	(3)		14 Oct 1991 (SI 1991/2208)
61			1 Oct 1992 (SI 1992/333)
61A			Prospectively inserted by Criminal Justice and Public Order Act 1994, s 21[3]
62–64			Repealed
65			1 Oct 1992 (SI 1992/333); prospectively repealed by Crime (Sentences) Act 1997, s 56(2), Sch 6 (repealed)[1]
66, 67			Repealed
68			See Sch 8 below
69, 70			1 Oct 1992 (SI 1992/333)
71			See Sch 9 below
72			1 Oct 1992 (SI 1992/333)
73–75			Repealed
76–78			1 Apr 1992 (SI 1992/333)
79			1 Apr 1992 (SI 1992/333); repealed, partly prospectively, by Police and Magistrates' Courts Act 1994, s 93, Sch 9, Pt II (qv)
80–82			31 Oct 1991 (SI 1991/2208)
83, 84			Substituted by Criminal Justice and Public Order Act 1994, ss 95, 96 (qv)
85–88			31 Oct 1991 (SI 1991/2208)
88A			Inserted by Criminal Justice and Public Order Act 1994, s 99 (qv)
89	(1)		31 Oct 1991 (SI 1991/2208)
	(2)		See Sch 10 below
	(3)		31 Oct 1991 (SI 1991/2208)
90, 91			31 Oct 1991 (SI 1991/2208)
92	(1)		31 Oct 1991 (SI 1991/2208)
	(1A)		Inserted by Criminal Justice and Public Order Act 1994, s 98 (qv)
	(2)		1 Apr 1992 (SI 1992/333)

Criminal Justice Act 1991 (c 53)—*contd*

Section

92	(3)		*Not in force* (due to come into force on day appointed by order made by Secretary of State under s 62(1)) (SI 1992/333)
	(4)		Inserted by Criminal Justice and Public Order Act 1994, s 93(7) (qv)
93	(1)		Repealed
	(2)		31 Oct 1991 (SI 1991/2208); prospectively repealed by Police and Magistrates' Courts Act 1994, s 93, Sch 9, Pt II[4]
	(3), (4)		Repealed
94			Repealed
95			31 Oct 1991 (SI 1991/2208)
96, 97			Repealed
98			31 Oct 1991 (SI 1991/2208)
99	(1)		14 Oct 1991 (except definitions 'child' and 'young person') (SI 1991/2208) 1 Oct 1992 (exceptions noted above) (SI 1992/333)
	(2)		1 Oct 1992 (SI 1992/333)
100			See Sch 11 below
101	(1)		See Sch 12 below
	(2)		See Sch 13 below
102			14 Oct 1991 (SI 1991/2208)

Schedule

1, 2			Repealed
3, 4			1 Oct 1992 (SI 1992/333)
5			Substituted by Criminal Justice and Public Order Act 1994, s 168(2), Sch 10, para 70 (qv)
6			1 Oct 1992 (SI 1992/333)
7			Repealed
8, para	1	(1)	*Not in force*
		(2)	1 Oct 1992 (SI 1992/333)
		(3)	1 Oct 1992 (except to the extent that would otherwise apply to Children and Young Persons Act 1933, s 34) (SI 1992/333) *Not in force* (exception noted above)
	2		1 Oct 1992 (SI 1992/333); prospectively repealed by Criminal Justice and Court Services Act 2000, ss 74, 75, Sch 7, paras 103, 112, Sch 8[6]
	3–6		1 Oct 1992 (SI 1992/333)
9			1 Oct 1992 (SI 1992/333)

Criminal Justice Act 1991 (c 53)—*contd*

Schedule

10				31 Oct 1991 (SI 1991/2208)
11, para	1			1 Oct 1992 (SI 1992/333); prospectively repealed by Youth Justice and Criminal Evidence Act 1999, s 67, Sch 6[5]
	2	(1)		1 Oct 1992 (SI 1992/333)
		(2)	(a)	1 Oct 1992 (SI 1992/333)
			(b)	1 Jun 1999 (SI 1999/1280)
		(3)		1 Oct 1992 (SI 1992/333)
		(4)	(a), (b)	1 Oct 1992 (SI 1992/333)
			(c)	1 Jun 1999 (SI 1999/1280)
	3			1 Oct 1992 (SI 1992/333)
	4–17			Repealed
	18			1 Apr 1992 (SI 1992/333)
	19			Repealed
	20			1 Oct 1992 (SI 1992/333)
	21			Repealed
	22, 23			1 Oct 1992 (SI 1992/333)
	24			Repealed
	25			1 Oct 1992 (SI 1992/333)
	26			Repealed
	27, 28			1 Oct 1992 (SI 1992/333)
	29			1 Apr 1992 (SI 1992/333)
	30–34			Repealed
	35			1 Oct 1992 (SI 1992/333)
	36			14 Oct 1991 (SI 1991/2208)
	37			1 Oct 1992 (SI 1992/333)
	38, 39			Repealed
	40, 41			1 Oct 1992 (SI 1992/333)
12, para	1–6			Repealed
	6A			Inserted by Powers of Criminal Courts (Sentencing) Act 2000, s 165(1), Sch 9, para 149 (qv)
	7			25 Oct 1991 (SI 1991/2208)
	8–13			1 Oct 1992 (SI 1992/333)
	14			Repealed
	15	(1), (2)		1 Oct 1992 (SI 1992/333)
		(3)–(5)		*Not in force* (due to come into force on day appointed by order made by Secretary of State under s 62(1)) (SI 1992/333)
	16	(1)		1 Oct 1992 (SI 1992/333)
		(2)–(4)		1 Jun 1999 (SI 1999/1280)
	17			Repealed
	18, 19			1 Oct 1992 (SI 1992/333)
	20, 21			Repealed
	22			1 Oct 1992 (SI 1992/333)
	23			14 Oct 1991 (SI 1991/2208)

Criminal Justice Act 1991 (c 53)—*contd*
Schedule

12, para	24	1 Oct 1992 (SI 1992/333)
13		31 Oct 1991 (repeal of Metropolitan Police Act 1839, s 11) (SI 1991/2208)
		1 Oct 1992 (otherwise, except repeal in Criminal Justice Act 1967, s 67(6)) (SI 1992/333)
		1 Jun 1999 (exception noted above) (SI 1999/1280)

[1]   The prospective repeals by Crime (Sentences) Act 1997, Sch 6 have been repealed by Crime and Disorder Act 1998, ss 119, 120(2), Sch 8, paras 138, 139, Sch 10, and accordingly have no effect

[2]   Orders made under Crime and Disorder 1998, s 121, bringing the prospective amendments into force will be noted to that Act

[3]   Orders made under Criminal Justice and Public Order Act 1994, s 172, bringing the prospective insertion into force will be noted to that Act

[4]   Orders made under Police and Magistrates' Courts Act 1994, s 121, bringing the prospective repeal into force will be noted to that Act

[5]   Orders made under Youth Justice and Criminal Evidence Act 1999, s 68(3), bringing the prospective repeals into force will be noted to that Act

[6]   Orders made under Criminal Justice and Court Services Act 2000, s 80, bringing the prospective repeal into force will be noted to that Act

Criminal Procedure (Insanity and Unfitness to Plead) Act 1991 (c 25)

RA: 27 Jun 1991

Commencement provisions: s 9(2); Criminal Procedure (Insanity and Unfitness to Plead) Act 1991 (Commencement) Order 1991, SI 1991/2488

1 Jan 1992 (SI 1991/2488)

Crofter Forestry (Scotland) Act 1991 (c 18)

Whole Act repealed

Dangerous Dogs Act 1991 (c 65)

RA: 25 Jul 1991

Commencement provisions: s 10(4); Dangerous Dogs Act 1991 (Commencement and Appointed Day) Order 1991, SI 1991/1742
Section

1–4	12 Aug 1991 (SI 1991/1742)
4A	Inserted by Dangerous Dogs (Amendment) Act 1997, s 2, subject to transitional provisions (qv)
4B	Inserted by Dangerous Dogs (Amendment) Act 1997, s 3(1), subject to transitional provisions (qv)

Dangerous Dogs Act 1991 (c 65)—*contd*
Section

5–7	12 Aug 1991 (SI 1991/1742)
8	25 Jul 1991 (s 10(4))
9, 10	12 Aug 1991 (SI 1991/1742)

Deer Act 1991 (c 54)

RA: 25 Jul 1991

Commencement provisions: s 18(3)

25 Oct 1991 (s 18(3))

Development Board for Rural Wales Act 1991 (c 1)

RA: 12 Feb 1991

12 Feb 1991 (RA)

Whole Act repealed; note however s 131 of Government of Wales Act 1998 which
contains transitional provisions in relation to the continuance by the Welsh
Development Agency (which takes over from the Development Board for
Rural Wales) of anything which relates to the functions of the Board or to any
property, rights or liabilities transferred by it which was in the process of being
done by the Board when its functions ceased to exist

Diocesan Boards of Education Measure 1991 (No 2)

RA: 12 Jul 1991

Commencement provisions: s 13(3)

1 Aug 1991 (the day appointed by the Archbishops of Canterbury and York under
s 13(3))

**Disability Living Allowance and Disability Working Allowance Act 1991
(c 21)**

RA: 27 Jun 1991

Commencement provisions: s 15(2), (3); Disability Living Allowance and Disability
Working Allowance Act 1991 (Commencement No 1) Order 1991, SI 1991/1519;
Disability Living Allowance and Disability Working Allowance Act 1991
(Commencement No 2) Order 1991, SI 1991/2617
Section

1		Repealed
2	(1)	Repealed
	(2), (3)	6 Apr 1992 (SI 1991/2617)
3		Repealed
4	(1)	Repealed
	(2)	See Sch 2 below
5, 6		Repealed
7	(1)	Repealed
	(2)	See Sch 3 below

**Disability Living Allowance and Disability Working Allowance Act 1991
(c 21)**—*contd*

Section

8, 9			Repealed
10			See Sch 4 below
11–14			Repealed
15			27 Jun 1991 (s 15(2), (3))

Schedule

1			Repealed
2, para	1–5		Repealed
	6, 7		3 Feb 1992 (for purposes of making claims for, and determination of claims and questions relating to, disability living allowance, or for purposes of making by persons who will have attained the age of 65 on 6 Apr 1992 of claims for, and determination of claims and questions relating to, attendance allowance) (SI 1991/2617)
			6 Apr 1992 (otherwise) (SI 1991/2617)
	8–11		Repealed
	12		3 Feb 1992 (for purposes noted to Sch 2, paras 6, 7 above) (SI 1991/2617)
	13		Repealed
	14		3 Feb 1992 (for purposes noted to Sch 2, paras 6, 7 above) (SI 1991/2617)
			6 Apr 1992 (otherwise) (SI 1991/2617)
	15–17		Repealed
	18		3 Feb 1992 (for purposes noted to Sch 2, paras 6, 7 above) (SI 1991/2617)
			6 Apr 1992 (otherwise) (SI 1991/2617)
	19–21		Repealed
	22		3 Feb 1992 (for purposes noted to Sch 2, paras 6, 7 above) (SI 1991/2617)
			6 Apr 1992 (otherwise) (SI 1992/2617)
3, Pt	I, para	1–8	Repealed
	II, para	9	19 Nov 1991 (for purposes of making regulations expressed to come into force on or after 3 Feb 1992) (SI 1991/2617)
			10 Mar 1992 (for purposes of making claims for, and determination of claims and questions relation to, disability working allowance) (SI 1991/2617)
			6 Apr 1992 (otherwise) (SI 1991/2617)

Disability Living Allowance and Disability Working Allowance Act 1991 (c 21)—*contd*
Schedule

3, Pt	II, para	10, 11	Spent
		12	Repealed
		13–15	Spent
4			6 Apr 1992 (SI 1991/2617)

Export and Investment Guarantees Act 1991 (c 67)

RA: 22 Oct 1991

Commencement provisions: s 15(6); Export and Investment Guarantees Act 1991 (Commencement) Order 1991, SI 1991/2430

23 Oct 1991 (SI 1991/2430)

Finance Act 1991 (c 31)

Budget Day: 19 Mar 1991

RA: 25 Jul 1991

Details of the commencement of Finance Acts are not set out in this work

Football (Offences) Act 1991 (c 19)

RA: 27 Jun 1991

Commencement provisions: s 6(2); Football (Offences) Act 1991 (Commencement) Order 1991, SI 1991/1564

10 Aug 1991 (SI 1991/1564)

Foreign Corporations Act 1991 (c 44)

RA: 25 Jul 1991

Commencement provisions: s 2(3)

25 Sep 1991 (s 2(3))

Forestry Act 1991 (c 43)

RA: 25 Jul 1991

Commencement provisions: s 2(2)

25 Sep 1991 (s 2(2))

Land Drainage Act 1991 (c 59)

RA: 25 Jul 1991

Commencement provisions: s 76(2)

1 Dec 1991 (s 76(2))

Local Government Finance and Valuation Act 1991 (c 51)

Whole Act repealed

Local Government Finance (Publicity for Auditors' Reports) Act 1991 (c 15)

Whole Act repealed

Maintenance Enforcement Act 1991 (c 17)

RA: 27 Jun 1991

Commencement provisions: s 12(2); Maintenance Enforcement Act 1991 (Commencement No 1) Order 1991, SI 1991/2042; Maintenance Enforcement Act 1991 (Commencement No 2) Order 1992, SI 1992/455

Section		
1–8		1 Apr 1992 (SI 1992/455)
9		Repealed
10		See Sch 1 below
11	(1)	See Sch 2 below
	(2)	See Sch 3 below
12		27 Jun 1991 (RA)
Schedule		
1, para	1–14	1 Apr 1992 (SI 1992/455)
	15–17	Repealed
	18, 19	1 Apr 1992 (SI 1992/455)
	20	Repealed
	21	1 Apr 1992 (SI 1992/455)
2, para	1	1 Apr 1992 (SI 1992/455)
	2	Repealed
	3	1 Apr 1992 (SI 1992/455)
	4	Repealed
	5–10	1 Apr 1992 (SI 1992/455)
	11	14 Oct 1991 (SI 1991/2042)
3		1 Apr 1992 (SI 1992/455)

Medical Qualifications (Amendment) Act 1991 (c 38)

RA: 25 Jul 1991

Commencement provisions: s 2(2); Medical Qualifications (Amendment) Act 1991 (Commencement) Order 1992, SI 1992/804

Section	
1	30 Mar 1992 (SI 1992/804)
2	25 Jul 1991 (RA)

Mental Health (Detention) (Scotland) Act 1991 (c 47)

RA: 25 Jul 1991

Commencement provisions: s 4(2); Mental Health (Detention) (Scotland) Act 1991 (Commencement) Order 1992, SI 1992/357

9 Mar 1992 (SI 1992/357)

Ministerial and other Pensions and Salaries Act 1991 (c 5)

RA: 28 Feb 1991

28 Feb 1991 (RA)

Motor Vehicles (Safety Equipment for Children) Act 1991 (c 14)

RA: 27 Jun 1991

27 Jun 1991 (RA)

Namibia Act 1991 (c 4)

RA: 28 Feb 1991

Commencement provisions: s 2(2)

21 Mar 1990 (s 2(2))

Natural Heritage (Scotland) Act 1991 (c 28)

RA: 27 Jun 1991

Commencement provisions: s 28(2); Natural Heritage (Scotland) Act 1991 (Commencement No 1) Order 1991, SI 1991/2187; Natural Heritage (Scotland) Act 1991 (Commencement No 2) Order 1991, SI 1991/2633

Section		
1		27 Nov 1991 (SI 1991/2633)
2	(1)	27 Nov 1991 (SI 1991/2633)
	(2)	1 Apr 1992 (SI 1991/2633)
3		27 Nov 1991 (SI 1991/2633)
4–7		1 Apr 1992 (SI 1991/2633)
8		27 Nov 1991 (SI 1991/2633)
9		1 Apr 1992 (SI 1991/2633)
10, 11		27 Nov 1991 (SI 1991/2633)
12, 13		1 Apr 1992 (SI 1991/2633)
14	(1), (2)	27 Nov 1991 (SI 1991/2633)
	(3), (4)	1 Apr 1992 (SI 1991/2633)
	(5)	27 Nov 1991 (SI 1991/2633)
15–26		1 Oct 1991 (SI 1991/2187)
26A		Inserted by Environment Act 1995, s 120(1), Sch 22, para 96(1), (6) (qv)
27	(1)	See Sch 10 below
	(2)	See Sch 11 below
28		27 Nov 1991 (SI 1991/2633)
Schedule		
1		27 Nov 1991 (SI 1991/2633)
2, 3		1 Apr 1992 (SI 1991/2633)
4		27 Nov 1991 (SI 1991/2633)
5–9		1 Oct 1991 (SI 1991/2187)
10, para	1	Repealed

Natural Heritage (Scotland) Act 1991 (c 28)—*contd*

Schedule

10, para	2	27 Nov 1991 (so far as inserts reference to Scottish Natural Heritage in Superannuation Act 1965, s 39(1), para 7) (SI 1991/2633)
		1 Apr 1992 (otherwise) (SI 1991/2633)
	3	27 Nov 1991 (SI 1991/2633)
	4	1 Apr 1992 (SI 1991/2633)
	5	1 Oct 1991 (SI 1991/2187)
	6	Repealed
	7	1 Oct 1991 (SI 1991/2187)
	8	1 Apr 1992 (SI 1991/2633)
	9	1 Oct 1991 (SI 1991/2187)
	10	27 Nov 1991 (SI 1991/2633)
	11–13	1 Apr 1992 (SI 1991/2633)
11		1 Oct 1991 (repeals of or in Spray Irrigation (Scotland) Act 1964; Water (Scotland) Act 1980, ss 77–79, Schs 5, 6) (SI 1991/2187)
		1 Apr 1992 (otherwise) (SI 1991/2633)

New Roads and Street Works Act 1991 (c 22)

RA: 27 Jun 1991

Commencement provisions: s 170(1); New Roads and Street Works Act 1991 (Commencement No 1) (Scotland) Order 1991, SI 1991/2286; New Roads and Street Works Act 1991 (Commencement No 1) Order 1991, SI 1991/2288; New Roads and Street Works Act 1991 (Commencement No 4) (Scotland) Order 1992, SI 1992/1671; New Roads and Street Works Act 1991 (Commencement No 3) Order 1992, SI 1992/1686; New Roads and Street Works Act 1991 (Commencement No 5 and Transitional Provisions and Savings) Order 1992, SI 1992/2984; New Roads and Street Works Act 1991 (Commencement No 6 and Transitional Provisions and Savings) (Scotland) Order 1992, SI 1992/2990

Section

1–5		1 Nov 1991 (SI 1991/2288)
6	(1), (2)	1 Nov 1991 (SI 1991/2288)
	(3)	See Sch 2 below
	(4)–(6)	1 Nov 1991 (SI 1991/2288)
7–26		1 Nov 1991 (SI 1991/2288)
27–42		21 Oct 1991 (SI 1991/2286)
43, 44		1 Nov 1991 (SI 1991/2286)
45–47		21 Oct 1991 (SI 1991/2286)
48, 49		14 Jul 1992 (SI 1992/1686)
50	(1)–(3)	1 Jan 1993 (SI 1992/2984)
	(4)	See Sch 3 below
	(5)–(7)	1 Jan 1993 (SI 1992/2984)
51		1 Jan 1993 (SI 1992/2984)

New Roads and Street Works Act 1991 (c 22)—*contd*

Section

52		14 Jul 1992 (SI 1992/1686)
53	(1)–(3)	28 Nov 1992 (SI 1992/2984)
	(4)–(6)	14 Jul 1992 (SI 1992/1686)
54		14 Jul 1992 (SI 1992/1686)
55		28 Nov 1992 (for purpose of making regulations) (SI 1992/2984)
		1 Jan 1993 (otherwise) (SI 1992/2984)
56		14 Jul 1992 (SI 1992/1686)
57, 58		28 Nov 1992 (SI 1992/2984)
59	(1), (2)	1 Jan 1993 (SI 1992/2984)
	(3)	14 Jul 1992 (SI 1992/1686)
	(4)–(6)	1 Jan 1993 (SI 1992/2984)
60	(1)	1 Jan 1993 (SI 1992/2984)
	(2)	14 Jul 1992 (SI 1992/1686)
	(3)	1 Jan 1993 (SI 1992/2984)
61		1 Jan 1993 (SI 1992/2984)
62		14 Jul 1992 (SI 1992/1686)
63	(1)	See Sch 4 below
	(2)–(4)	14 Jul 1992 (SI 1992/1686)
64		14 Jul 1992 (SI 1992/1686)
65	(1), (2)	1 Apr 1993 (SI 1992/2984)
	(3)	14 Jul 1992 (SI 1992/1686)
	(4)–(6)	1 Apr 1993 (SI 1992/2984)
66		1 Jan 1993 (SI 1992/2984)
67		14 Jul 1992 (SI 1992/1686)
68, 69		1 Jan 1993 (SI 1992/2984)
70	(1)–(3)	1 Jan 1993 (SI 1992/2984)
	(4)	14 Jul 1992 (SI 1992/1686)
	(5)–(7)	1 Jan 1993 (SI 1992/2984)
71		14 Jul 1992 (SI 1992/1686)
72–74		1 Jan 1993 (SI 1992/2984)
74A, 74B		Inserted by Transport Act 2000, s 255(1) (qv)
75		14 Jul 1992 (SI 1992/1686)
76–78		1 Jan 1993 (SI 1992/2984)
79, 80		*Not in force*
81	(1), (2)	1 Jan 1993 (SI 1992/2984)
	(3), (4)	14 Jul 1992 (SI 1992/1686)
	(5)–(7)	1 Jan 1993 (SI 1992/2984)
82, 83		1 Jan 1993 (SI 1992/2984)
84	(1)	1 Jan 1993 (SI 1992/2984)
	(2)	14 Jul 1992 (SI 1992/1686)
	(3), (4)	1 Jan 1993 (SI 1992/2984)
85–87		14 Jul 1992 (SI 1992/1686)
88–96		1 Jan 1993 (SI 1992/2984)
97–99		14 Jul 1992 (SI 1992/1686)
100–103		1 Jan 1993 (SI 1992/2984)
104–106		14 Jul 1992 (SI 1992/1686)
107, 108		14 Jul 1992 (SI 1992/1671)

New Roads and Street Works Act 1991 (c 22)—*contd*

Section

109, 110		1 Jan 1993 (SI 1992/2990)
111		14 Jul 1992 (SI 1992/1671)
112	(1)–(3)	30 Nov 1992 (SI 1992/2990)
	(4)	14 Jul 1992 (SI 1992/1671)
	(4A)	Inserted by Local Government etc (Scotland) Act 1994, s 149(b) (qv)
	(5), (6)	14 Jul 1992 (SI 1992/1671)
113		14 Jul 1992 (SI 1992/1671)
114		30 Nov 1992 (for purpose of making regulations) (SI 1992/2990)
		1 Jan 1993 (otherwise) (SI 1992/2990)
115		14 Jul 1992 (SI 1992/1671)
116, 117		30 Nov 1992 (SI 1992/2990)
118	(1), (2)	1 Jan 1993 (SI 1992/2990)
	(3)	14 Jul 1992 (SI 1992/1671)
	(4)–(6)	1 Jan 1993 (SI 1992/2990)
119	(1)	1 Jan 1993 (SI 1992/2990)
	(2)	14 Jul 1992 (SI 1992/1671)
	(3)	1 Jan 1993 (SI 1992/2990)
120		1 Jan 1993 (SI 1992/2990)
121		14 Jul 1992 (SI 1992/1671)
122	(1)	See Sch 6 below
	(2)–(5)	14 Jul 1992 (SI 1992/1671)
123		14 Jul 1992 (SI 1992/1671)
124	(1), (2)	1 Apr 1993 (SI 1992/2990)
	(3)	14 Jul 1992 (SI 1992/1671)
	(4)–(6)	1 Apr 1993 (SI 1992/2990)
125		1 Jan 1993 (SI 1992/2990)
126		14 Jul 1992 (SI 1992/1671)
127, 128		1 Jan 1993 (SI 1992/2990)
129	(1)–(3)	1 Jan 1993 (SI 1992/2990)
	(4)	14 Jul 1992 (SI 1992/1671)
	(5)–(7)	1 Jan 1993 (SI 1992/2990)
130		14 Jul 1992 (SI 1992/1671)
131–133		1 Jan 1993 (SI 1992/2990)
134		14 Jul 1992 (SI 1992/1671)
135–137		1 Jan 1993 (SI 1992/2990)
138, 139		*Not in force*
140	(1), (2)	1 Jan 1993 (SI 1992/2990)
	(3), (4)	14 Jul 1992 (SI 1992/1671)
	(5)–(7)	1 Jan 1993 (SI 1992/2990)
141, 142		1 Jan 1993 (SI 1992/2990)
143	(1)	1 Jan 1993 (SI 1992/2990)
	(2)	14 Jul 1992 (SI 1992/1671)
	(3), (4)	1 Jan 1993 (SI 1992/2990)
144–146		14 Jul 1992 (SI 1992/1671)
147–155		1 Jan 1993 (SI 1992/2990)
156–158		14 Jul 1992 (SI 1992/1671)
159–162		1 Jan 1993 (SI 1992/2990)

New Roads and Street Works Act 1991 (c 22)—*contd*

Section

163–165				14 Jul 1992 (SI 1992/1671)
166	(1)			21 Oct 1991 (S) (so far as relates to offence committed under Pt II (ss 27–47)) (SI 1991/2286)
				1 Nov 1991 (EW) (SI 1991/2288)
				1 Jan 1993 (S) (otherwise) (SI 1992/2990)
	(2)			21 Oct 1991 (so far as relates to offence committed under Pt II (ss 27–47)) (SI 1991/2286)
				1 Jan 1993 (otherwise) (SI 1992/2990)
167	(1)–(3)			21 Oct 1991 (S) (so far as relate to Pt II (ss 27–47)) (SI 1991/2286)
				1 Nov 1991 (EW) (SI 1991/2288)
				Not in force (S) (otherwise)
	(4), (5)			14 Jul 1992 (S) (SI 1992/1671)
				14 Jul 1992 (EW) (SI 1992/1686)
	(6)			21 Oct 1991 (S) (so far as relates to Pt II (ss 27–47)) (SI 1991/2286)
				1 Nov 1991 (EW) (SI 1991/2288)
				Not in force (S) (otherwise)
168	(1)			See Sch 8 below
	(2)			See Sch 9 below
169	(1)			1 Nov 1991 (SI 1991/2288)
	(2)			14 Jul 1992 (SI 1992/1671)
	(3)			*Not in force*
170, 171				1 Nov 1991 (SI 1991/2288)

Schedule

1, 2				1 Nov 1991 (SI 1991/2288)
3				1 Jan 1993 (SI 1992/2984)
4				14 Jul 1992 (SI 1992/1686)
5				1 Jan 1993 (SI 1992/2984)
6				14 Jul 1992 (SI 1992/1671)
7				1 Jan 1993 (SI 1992/2990)
8, Pt	I, para	1–16		1 Jan 1993 (SI 1992/2984)
	II, para	17–25		1 Nov 1991 (SI 1991/2286; SI 1991/2288)
		26		Repealed
		27–78		1 Nov 1991 (SI 1991/2286; SI 1991/2288)
		79		Repealed
		80		1 Nov 1991 (SI 1991/2286; SI 1991/2288)
	III, para	81–92		1 Jan 1993 (SI 1992/2990)
		93	(a)	21 Oct 1991 (SI 1991/2286)
			(b)	1 Jan 1993 (SI 1992/2990)
			(c)	21 Oct 1991 (SI 1991/2286)
		94	(a)	1 Jan 1993 (SI 1992/2990)

New Roads and Street Works Act 1991 (c 22)—*contd*
Schedule

8, Pt	III, para	94	(b)		21 Oct 1991 (SI 1991/2286)
		95			1 Jan 1993 (SI 1992/2990)
		96, 97			21 Oct 1991 (SI 1991/2286)
	IV, para	98			Repealed
		99	(1), (2)		1 Nov 1991 (SI 1991/2286; SI 1991/2288)
			(3)	(a)	1 Nov 1991 (SI 1991/2288)
				(b)	1 Jan 1993 (SI 1992/2990)
		100, 101			1 Jan 1993 (SI 1992/2984; SI 1992/2990)
		102			1 Nov 1991 (SI 1991/2286)
		103			1 Jan 1993 (SI 1992/2990)
		104			Repealed
		105			1 Jan 1993 (SI 1992/2990)
		106			1 Jan 1993 (SI 1992/2984)
		107			Repealed
		108			1 Jan 1993 (SI 1992/2990)
		109			1 Jan 1993 (SI 1992/2984; SI 1992/2990)
		110			Repealed
		111			1 Jan 1993 (SI 1992/2984; SI 1992/2990)
		112			1 Nov 1991 (SI 1991/2288)
		113–115			1 Jan 1993 (SI 1992/2984; SI 1992/2990)
		116			1 Nov 1991 (SI 1991/2288)
		117			1 Nov 1991 (SI 1991/2286; SI 1991/2288)
		118	(1), (2)		1 Nov 1991 (SI 1991/2286; SI 1991/2288)
			(3)		1 Jan 1993 (SI 1992/2984; SI 1992/2990)
		119	(1)–(6)		1 Jan 1993 (SI 1992/2984; SI 1992/2990)
			(7)		1 Jan 1993 (SI 1992/2990)
		120			Repealed
		121	(1)		1 Nov 1991 (SI 1991/2286; SI 1991/2288)
			(2)		1 Jan 1993 (SI 1992/2984; SI 1992/2990)
			(3)		1 Nov 1991 (SI 1991/2286; SI 1991/2288)
			(4)		1 Nov 1991 (SI 1991/2288)
		122			Repealed
		123			1 Jan 1993 (SI 1992/2984; SI 1992/2990)
		124			1 Jan 1993 (SI 1992/2990)
		125			1 Jan 1993 (SI 1992/2984; SI 1992/2990)

New Roads and Street Works Act 1991 (c 22)—*contd*
Schedule

8, Pt	IV, para	126	(1), (2)	1 Nov 1991 (SI 1991/2288)
			(3)	1 Jan 1993 (SI 1992/2984)
		127		1 Jan 1993 (SI 1992/2990)
9				21 Oct 1991 (repeal in Roads (Scotland) Act 1984, s 143(2)(b)(ii)) (SI 1991/2286)
				1 Nov 1991 (repeals of or in Road Traffic Regulation Act 1984, ss 1(2), (4), (5), 3(1), 5(2), 16(3), (4), 17(6), 19(3), 23(5), 34(1), 55(5), 68(1)(a), 86(4), 91, 106(8), 124(2), 132(6), 132A, Sch 9, paras 20(1), 21, 27(1); Roads (Scotland) Act 1984, s 127, Sch 7, paras 2, 3(a), (b), 4, Sch 9, paras 93(2)–(22), (23)(a), (24)–(38), (40), (42), (44)(a), (b), (d), (e), (45)(b); Transport Act 1985, s 137(1); Road Traffic Offenders Act 1988, Sch 3 (the entry relating to Road Traffic Regulation Act 1984, s 29(3)); Environmental Protection Act 1990, Sch 8, para 7) (S) (SI 1991/2286)
				1 Nov 1991 (repeals of or in Road Traffic Regulation Act 1984; Transport Act 1985; Road Traffic Offenders Act 1988; Environmental Protection Act 1990) (EW) (SI 1991/2288)
				1 Nov 1991 (repeals in Local Government Act 1985, Sch 5) (SI 1991/2288)
				1 Jan 1993 (otherwise) (SI 1992/2984; 1992/2990)

Northern Ireland (Emergency Provisions) Act 1991 (c 24)

Whole Act repealed

Oversea Superannuation Act 1991 (c 16)

RA: 27 Jun 1991

Commencement provisions: s 3(2)

27 Aug 1991 (s 3(2))

Planning and Compensation Act 1991 (c 34)

RA: 25 Jul 1991

Commencement provisions: s 84(2)–(4); Planning and Compensation Act 1991 (Commencement No 1 and Transitional Provisions) Order 1991, SI 1991/2067; Planning and Compensation Act 1991 (Commencement No 2 and Transitional Provisions) (Scotland) Order 1991, SI 1991/2092; Planning and Compensation Act 1991 (Commencement No 3) Order 1991, SI 1991/2272; Planning and Compensation Act 1991 (Commencement No 4 and Transitional Provisions) Order 1991, SI 1991/2728; Planning and Compensation Act 1991 (Commencement No 5 and Transitional Provisions) Order 1991, SI 1991/2905; Planning and Compensation Act 1991 (Commencement No 6) (Scotland) Order 1992, SI 1992/71; Planning and Compensation Act 1991 (Commencement No 7 and Transitional Provisions) Order 1992, SI 1992/334; Planning and Compensation Act 1991 (Commencement No 8) Order 1992, SI 1992/665; Planning and Compensation Act 1991 (Commencement No 9 and Transitional Provision) Order 1992, SI 1992/1279; Planning and Compensation Act 1991 (Commencement No 10 and Transitional Provision) Order 1992, SI 1992/1491; Planning and Compensation Act 1991 (Commencement No 11 and Transitional Provisions) Order 1992, SI 1992/1630; Planning and Compensation Act 1991 (Commencement No 12 and Transitional Provisions) (Scotland) Order 1992, SI 1992/1937; Planning and Compensation Act 1991 (Commencement No 13 and Transitional Provision) Order 1992, SI 1992/2413; Planning and Compensation Act 1991 (Commencement No 14 and Transitional Provision) Order 1992, SI 1992/2831; Planning and Compensation Act 1991 (Commencement No 15) (Scotland) Order 1993, SI 1993/275; Planning and Compensation Act 1991 (Commencement No 16) (Scotland) Order 1994, SI 1994/398; Planning and Compensation Act 1991 (Commencement No 17 and Transitional Provision) (Scotland) Order 1994, SI 1994/3292; Planning and Compensation Act 1991 (Commencement No 18 and Transitional Provision) (Scotland) Order 1995, SI 1995/2045

Abbreviation: "rules, etc" means "so much of the provision as enables provision to be made by rules of court, confers on the Secretary of State a power or imposes on him a duty to make or to make provision by development order or other order or regulations or to give or revoke directions, or makes provision with respect to the exercise of any such power or performance of any such duty, is brought into force on the specified date"

Section	
1	2 Jan 1992 (SI 1991/2905)
2	27 Jul 1992 (SI 1992/1630)
3	25 Nov 1991 (rules, etc) (SI 1991/2728)
	2 Jan 1992 (otherwise) (SI 1991/2905)
4	2 Jan 1992 (except so far as relates to breach of condition notices) (SI 1991/2905)
	27 Jul 1992 (exception noted above) (SI 1992/1630)
5	25 Nov 1991 (rules, etc) (SI 1991/2728)

Planning and Compensation Act 1991 (c 34)—*contd*

Section

5—*contd*		2 Jan 1992 (otherwise) (SI 1991/2905)
6	(1)–(4)	2 Jan 1992 (SI 1991/2905)
	(5)	25 Nov 1991 (rules, etc) (SI 1991/2728)
		2 Jan 1992 (otherwise) (SI 1991/2905)
	(6)	13 Oct 1991 (SI 1991/2272)
7–9		2 Jan 1992 (SI 1991/2905)
10		25 Nov 1991 (rules, etc) (SI 1991/2728)
		27 Jul 1992 (otherwise) (SI 1992/1630)
11		2 Jan 1992 (SI 1991/2905)
12	(1)	25 Oct 1991 (so far as substitutes Town and Country Planning Act 1990, s 106) (SI 1991/2272)
		25 Nov 1991 (so far as substitutes Town and Country Planning Act 1990, ss 106A, 106B) (rules, etc) (SI 1991/2728)
		9 Nov 1992 (otherwise) (SI 1992/2831)
	(2), (3)	25 Oct 1991 (SI 1991/2272)
13	(1)	27 Jul 1992 (SI 1992/1279)
	(2)	25 Nov 1991 (rules, etc) (SI 1991/2728)
		27 Jul 1992 (otherwise) (SI 1992/1279)
	(3)	27 Jul 1992 (SI 1992/1279)
14		2 Jan 1992 (SI 1991/2905)
15		25 Sep 1991 (SI 1991/2067)
16		25 Nov 1991 (rules, etc) (SI 1991/2728)
		17 Jul 1992 (otherwise) (SI 1992/1491)
17, 18		25 Sep 1991 (SI 1991/2067)
19		25 Nov 1991 (rules, etc) (SI 1991/2728)
		2 Jan 1992 (otherwise, except so far as relates to Town and Country Planning Act 1990, Sch 1, para 4(1), as it concerns applications for consent to the display of advertisements) (SI 1991/2905)
		6 Apr 1992 (exception noted above) (SI 1992/665)
20		25 Nov 1991 (rules, etc) (SI 1991/2728)
		17 Jul 1992 (otherwise) (SI 1992/1491)
21		See Sch 1 below
22		25 Sep 1991 (SI 1991/2067)
23	(1)–(6)	2 Jan 1992 (SI 1991/2905)
	(7)	25 Nov 1991 (so far as relates to Town and Country Planning Act 1990, s 214A(2)) (rules, etc) (SI 1991/2728)

Planning and Compensation Act 1991 (c 34)—*contd*

Section

23	(7)—*contd*	2 Jan 1992 (otherwise) (SI 1991/2905)
	(8)	2 Jan 1992 (SI 1991/2905)
24		6 Apr 1992 (SI 1992/665)
25		See Sch 3 below
26		25 Sep 1991 (SI 1991/2067)
27		See Sch 4 below
28		See Sch 5 below
29		25 Sep 1991 (SI 1991/2067)
30		2 Jan 1992 (subject to certain exceptions and savings; see SI 1991/2728, arts 3, 4) (SI 1991/2728)
		Not in force (exceptions referred to above)
31	(1)	25 Sep 1991 (SI 1991/2067)
	(2), (3)	25 Jul 1991 (s 84(4))
	(4)	See Sch 6 below
	(5), (6)	25 Sep 1991 (SI 1991/2067)
	(7), (8)	25 Jul 1991 (s 84(4))
32		See Sch 7 below
33–59		Repealed
60	(1)–(5)	Repealed
	(6)	See Sch 12 below
	(7), (8)	Repealed
61		See Sch 13 below
62–69		25 Sep 1991 (SI 1991/2067)
70		See Sch 15 below
71–78		25 Sep 1991 (SI 1991/2092)
79		See Sch 17 below
80		25 Sep 1991 (EW) (except in relation to entries noted to Sch 18 below) (SI 1991/2067)
		25 Sep 1991 (S) (except in relation to entries noted to Sch 18 below) (SI 1991/2092)
		2 Jan 1992 (EW) (otherwise) (SI 1991/2728)
		30 Aug 1995 (S) (otherwise) (SI 1995/2045)
81		25 Sep 1991 (SI 1991/2067)
82		26 Mar 1992 (SI 1992/334)
83		25 Oct 1991 (SI 1991/2272)
84	(1)–(5)	25 Jul 1991 (RA)
	(6)	See Sch 19 below
	(7)–(9)	25 Jul 1991 (RA)
Schedule		
1, 2		25 Sep 1991 (SI 1991/2067)
3, para	1	25 Sep 1991 (SI 1991/2067)
	2–6	2 Jan 1992 (SI 1991/2905)

Planning and Compensation Act 1991 (c 34)—*contd*

Schedule

3, para	7	25 Nov 1991 (rules, etc) (SI 1991/2728)
		2 Jan 1992 (otherwise) (SI 1991/2905)
	8–14	2 Jan 1992 (SI 1991/2905)
	15	25 Nov 1991 (rules, etc) (SI 1991/2728)
		2 Jan 1992 (otherwise) (SI 1991/2905)
	16–32	2 Jan 1992 (SI 1991/2905)
4, para	1, 2	25 Nov 1991 (rules, etc) (SI 1991/2728)
		10 Feb 1992 (otherwise) (SI 1991/2905)
	3	10 Feb 1992 (SI 1991/2905)
	4–25	25 Nov 1991 (rules, etc) (SI 1991/2728)
		10 Feb 1992 (otherwise) (SI 1991/2905)
	26	10 Feb 1992 (SI 1991/2905)
	27–38	25 Nov 1991 (rules, etc) (SI 1991/2728)
		10 Feb 1992 (otherwise) (SI 1991/2905)
	39	Repealed
	40–51	25 Nov 1991 (rules, etc) (SI 1991/2728)
		10 Feb 1992 (otherwise) (SI 1991/2905)
5		25 Nov 1991 (rules, etc) (SI 1991/2728)
		9 Nov 1992 (otherwise; but note that amendments do not apply with respect to proposals which are or have been made available for inspection in accordance with Town and Country Planning Act 1990, Sch 7, para 5 or 6 before 12 Oct 1992 but simplified planning zone scheme had not yet come into operation on that date) (SI 1992/2413)
6, para	1	25 Jul 1991 (s 84(4))
	2–4	25 Sep 1991 (SI 1991/2067)
	5	25 Jul 1991 (s 84(4))
	6–12	25 Sep 1991 (SI 1991/2067)
	13	25 Jul 1991 (s 84(4))
	14–49	25 Sep 1991 (SI 1991/2067)
7, para	1	27 Jul 1992 (SI 1992/1630)
	2	2 Jan 1992 (SI 1991/2905)
	3	27 Jul 1992 (SI 1992/1630)

Planning and Compensation Act 1991 (c 34)—*contd*

Schedule

7, para	4		2 Jan 1992 (SI 1991/2905)
	5		2 Jan 1992 (except so far as relates to reference to s 187A) (SI 1991/2905)
			27 Jul 1992 (exception noted above) (SI 1992/1630)
	6		25 Oct 1991 (SI 1991/2272)
	7		2 Jan 1992 (SI 1991/2905)
	8		25 Sep 1991 (SI 1991/2067)
	9	(1)	2 Jan 1992 (SI 1991/2905)
		(2) (a)	10 Feb 1992 (SI 1991/2905)
		(b)	27 Jul 1992 (SI 1992/1630)
		(c)	25 Sep 1991 (SI 1991/2067)
		(d)	2 Jan 1992 (so far as relates to reference to s 171C) (SI 1991/2905)
			9 Nov 1992 (otherwise) (SI 1992/2831)
		(e)	2 Jan 1992 (SI 1991/2905)
		(f)	2 Jan 1992 (so far as relates to reference to s 187B) (SI 1991/2905)
			27 Jul 1992 (otherwise) (SI 1992/1630)
		(g)	2 Jan 1992 (SI 1991/2905)
		(h)	25 Oct 1991 (SI 1991/2272)
		(i)	2 Jan 1992 (except so far as relates to substitution of reference to 'section 316(1) to (3)' by reference to 'section 316') (SI 1991/2905)
			17 Jul 1992 (exception noted above) (SI 1992/1491)
	10	(1)	25 Sep 1991 (SI 1991/2067)
		(2)	27 Jul 1992 (SI 1992/1279)
	11		2 Jan 1992 (SI 1991/2905)
	12		27 Jul 1992 (SI 1992/1630)
	13		2 Jan 1992 (SI 1991/2905)
	14, 15		17 Jul 1992 (SI 1992/1491)
	16		2 Jan 1992 (SI 1991/2905)
	17		17 Jul 1992 (SI 1992/1491)
	18, 19		2 Jan 1992 (so far as relate to inclusion in Town and Country Planning Act 1990, ss 77(4), 79(4), of reference to s 73A) (SI 1991/2905)
			17 Jul 1992 (otherwise) (SI 1992/1491)
	20–23		2 Jan 1992 (SI 1991/2905)
	24	(1) (a)	2 Jan 1992 (SI 1991/2905)
		(b)	27 Jul 1992 (SI 1992/1630)
		(2), (3)	2 Jan 1992 (SI 1991/2905)
	25		2 Jan 1992 (SI 1991/2905)

Planning and Compensation Act 1991 (c 34)—*contd*

Schedule

7, para				
26				2 Jan 1992 (except so far as relates to breach of condition notices) (SI 1991/2905)
				27 Jul 1992 (exception noted above) (SI 1992/1630)
27–29				2 Jan 1992 (SI 1991/2905)
30				27 Jul 1992 (SI 1992/1630)
31				2 Jan 1992 (SI 1991/2905)
32, 33				27 Jul 1992 (SI 1992/1630)
34				17 Jul 1992 (SI 1992/1491)
35				2 Jan 1992 (SI 1991/2905)
36				25 Sep 1991 (SI 1991/2067)
37				17 Jul 1992 (SI 1992/1491)
38				6 Apr 1992 (SI 1992/665)
39–41				27 Jul 1992 (SI 1992/1630)
42				2 Jan 1992 (SI 1991/2905)
43, 44				27 Jul 1992 (SI 1992/1630)
45	(1)			2 Jan 1992 (SI 1991/2905)
	(2)			2 Jan 1992 (except so far as relates to reference to s 187A) (SI 1991/2905)
				27 Jul 1992 (exception noted above) (SI 1992/1630)
46				27 Jul 1992 (SI 1992/1630)
47				2 Jan 1992 (SI 1991/2905)
48				25 Nov 1991 (rules, etc) (SI 1991/2728)
				17 Jul 1992 (otherwise) (SI 1992/1491)
49				25 Nov 1991 (rules, etc) (SI 1991/2728)
				27 Jul 1992 (otherwise) (SI 1992/1630)
50				2 Jan 1992 (SI 1991/2905)
51				25 Sep 1991 (SI 1991/2067)
52	(1)			2 Jan 1992 (SI 1991/2905)
	(2)	(a)		2 Jan 1992 (except so far as relates to definition 'breach of condition notice') (SI 1991/2905)
				27 Jul 1992 (exception noted above) (SI 1992/1630)
		(b)		2 Jan 1992 (SI 1991/2905)
		(c)		27 Jul 1992 (but not relating to demolition of building on land where, before 27 Jul 1992, planning permission has been granted under Town and Country Planning Act 1990, Pt III, or has been deemed to have been granted under that Pt of that Act, for the redevelopment of the land) (SI 1992/1279)

Planning and Compensation Act 1991 (c 34)—*contd*

Schedule

7, para	52	(2)	(d)	27 Jul 1992 (SI 1992/1630)
			(e)	17 Jul 1992 (SI 1992/1491)
			(f), (g)	2 Jan 1992 (SI 1991/2905)
		(3)		17 Jul 1992 (SI 1992/1491)
		(4)		2 Jan 1992 (SI 1991/2905)
	53	(1)		See sub-paras (2)–(9) below
		(2)		27 Jul 1992 (SI 1992/1630)
		(3)		2 Jan 1992 (except so far as relates to applications for consent to the display of advertisements) (SI 1991/2905)
				6 Apr 1992 (exception noted above) (SI 1992/665)
		(4)		17 Jul 1992 (SI 1992/1491)
		(5)		2 Jan 1992 (so far as confers on the Secretary of State a power to make provision by development order) (SI 1991/2905)
				9 Nov 1992 (otherwise; but note that does not apply to application for planning permission or application for approval of matter reserved under outline planning permission (within meaning of Town and Country Planning Act 1990, s 92, made before 6 Nov 1992 nor to any alteration to that application accepted by the authority) (SI 1992/2831)
		(6)		2 Jan 1992 (so far as relates to insertion of the words 'planning contravention notices under s 171C or') (SI 1991/2905)
				27 Jul 1992 (otherwise) (SI 1992/1630)
		(7), (8)		2 Jan 1992 (SI 1991/2905)
		(9)		25 Oct 1991 (SI 1991/2272)
	54	(1)		25 Sep 1991 (SI 1991/2067)
		(2)		9 Nov 1992 (SI 1992/2831)
		(3)	(a)	25 Sep 1991 (SI 1991/2067)
			(b)	9 Nov 1992 (SI 1992/2831)
			(c)	2 Jan 1992 (SI 1991/2905)
			(d)	27 Jul 1992 (SI 1992/1630)
			(e)	2 Jan 1992 (SI 1991/2905)
			(f)	9 Nov 1992 (SI 1992/2831)
			(g)	27 Jul 1992 (SI 1992/1630)
		(4)		17 Jul 1992 (SI 1992/1491)
	55			17 Jul 1992 (SI 1992/1491)
	56			25 Sep 1991 (SI 1991/2067)
	57	(1)		25 Sep 1991 (SI 1991/2067)

Planning and Compensation Act 1991 (c 34)—*contd*

Schedule

7, para	57	(2)	(a)	2 Jan 1992 (so far as relates to omission of reference to s 63) (SI 1991/2905)
				27 Jul 1992 (otherwise) (SI 1992/1630)
			(b)	25 Sep 1991 (SI 1991/2067)
			(c)	2 Jan 1992 (SI 1991/2905)
			(d), (e)	17 Jul 1992 (SI 1992/1491)
			(f)	9 Nov 1992 (SI 1992/2831)
			(g)	2 Jan 1992 (so far as relates to references to ss 196A–196C) (SI 1991/2905)
				27 Jul 1992 (otherwise) (SI 1992/1630)
			(h), (i)	2 Jan 1992 (SI 1991/2905)
			(j), (k)	17 Jul 1992 (SI 1992/1491)
		(3)	(a)	17 Jul 1992 (SI 1992/1491)
			(b)	25 Sep 1991 (SI 1991/2067)
			(c)	2 Jan 1992 (SI 1991/2905)
			(d)	2 Jan 1992 (except so far as relates to s 187A) (SI 1991/2905)
				27 Jul 1992 (exception noted above) (SI 1992/1630)
		(4)		25 Sep 1991 (SI 1991/2067)
		(5)		17 Jul 1992 (except so far as relates to omission of reference to Pt IV) (SI 1992/1491)
				27 Jul 1992 (exception noted above) (SI 1992/1630)
		(6)	(a), (b)	17 Jul 1992 (SI 1992/1491)
			(c)	27 Jul 1992 (SI 1992/1630)
			(d)	17 Jul 1992 (SI 1992/1491)
	58–61			2 Jan 1992 (SI 1991/2905)
8–11				Repealed
12				25 Sep 1991 (SI 1991/2092)
13, para	1			25 Sep 1992 (SI 1992/1937)
	2–43			Repealed
	44			Repealed (*never in force*)
	45–47			Repealed
14				25 Sep 1991 (SI 1991/2067)
15, para	1–31			25 Sep 1991 (SI 1991/2067)
	32			2 Jan 1992 (SI 1991/2728)
16, 17				25 Sep 1991 (SI 1991/2092)
18, Pt	I			25 Sep 1991 (EW) (except entries relating to Planning (Hazardous Substances) Act 1990) (SI 1991/2067)
				25 Sep 1991 (S) (except entries relating to Town and Country Planning (Scotland) Act 1972, ss 56J(8), 56K(12)) (SI 1991/2092)

Planning and Compensation Act 1991 (c 34)—*contd*

Schedule

18, Pt	I—*contd*	2 Jan 1992 (EW) (exception noted above) (SI 1991/2728
		30 Aug 1995 (S) (exception noted above) (SI 1995/2045)
	II	25 Sep 1991 (SI 1991/2067; SI 1991/2092))
19, Pt	I	25 Sep 1991 (repeals of or in Town and Country Planning Act 1990, ss 55(6), 97(5), 219(6), 336(1) (definitions of 'development consisting of the winning and working of minerals', 'mineral compensation modifications', 'relevant order', 'restriction on the winning and working of minerals' and 'special consultations'), Sch 1, para 1(2), Sch 5, para 1(6), Sch 11, Sch 16, Pt III (entries relating to ss 312(2), 324(4)); Planning (Listed Buildings and Conservation Areas) Act 1990, s 9(5)) (SI 1991/2067)
		2 Jan 1992 (repeals of or in Town and Country Planning Act 1990, ss 63, 69(1), (3), 178(2), 186(1)(c), 190(4), 210(3), (5), 285, 324, 336(1) (definition of 'planning permission'), Sch 1, para 4(1) (except so far as concerns applications for consent to the display of advertisements), Sch 16 (entry relating to s 285); Planning (Listed Buildings and Conservation Areas) Act 1990, ss 38(2), 39(7), 42(7), 55(6), 88(6), 90(6)(b), 92(2)(b); Planning (Hazardous Substances) Act 1990, ss 25(1)(c), 36(5); Planning (Consequential Provisions) Act 1990, Sch 2, para 38) (SI 1991/2905)
		10 Feb 1992 (repeals of or in Town and Country Planning Act 1990, ss 12(4)(a), 14(3), 21(2), 22, 23(2)–(4), (9), (10), 49, 50, 51(1), 52(2), (3), 53(1), (2)(b), (g), (5), 284(1)(a), 287(1)–(3), (5), 306(2), Sch 2, Pt I, paras 3, 5, 6, Pt II, paras 3–16, 18, Sch 13; Planning (Consequential Provisions) Act 1990, Sch 4) (SI 1991/2905)

Planning and Compensation Act 1991 (c 34)—*contd*
Schedule
19, Pt   I—*contd*   6 Apr 1992 (repeal of Town and
                                                                            Country Planning Act 1990, Sch 1,
                                                                            para 4(1) (so far as not already in
                                                                            force)) (SI 1992/665)
                                                                            17 Jul 1992 (repeals of or in Town
                                                                            and Country Planning Act 1990,
                                                                            ss 74(2), 198(4)(a), 220(3)(a),
                                                                            336(1) (definition of "owner"), (9),
                                                                            Sch 16, Pt I, entries relating to
                                                                            ss 77, 78, 79, Pt V) (SI 1992/1491)
                                                                            27 Jul 1992 (repeals of or in Local
                                                                            Government (Miscellaneous
                                                                            Provisions) Act 1976, s 7(5)(a)(iii);
                                                                            Town and Country Planning
                                                                            Act 1990, ss 64, 188(1), 196,
                                                                            250(2), 266(3), 284(3)(g),
                                                                            286(1)(b), 290, 336(1) (so far as
                                                                            not already in force), Sch 6,
                                                                            para 2(1)(c), (8), Sch 16, Pt IV;
                                                                            Planning (Consequential
                                                                            Provisions) Act 1990, Sch 2,
                                                                            paras 3(2), 35(1)(b))
                                                                            (SI 1992/1630)
                                                                            9 Nov 1992 (repeals of or in Town
                                                                            and Country Planning Act 1990,
                                                                            Sch 1, para 9(2), (3), Sch 7,
                                                                            para 13(2)(e)) (SI 1992/2831)
                                                                            Not in force (otherwise)
                II   25 Jul 1991 (repeals of Land
                                                                            Compensation Act 1961,
                                                                            s 15(4)(a), (b); Land Compensation
                                                                            Act 1973, s 5(3)(a), (b); Town and
                                                                            Country Planning Act 1990, s 114;
                                                                            Planning (Listed Buildings and
                                                                            Conservation Areas) Act 1990,
                                                                            s 27) (s 84(4))
                                                                            25 Sep 1991 (otherwise)
                                                                            (SI 1991/2067)
                III   25 Sep 1991 (SI 1991/2067)
                IV   25 Jul 1991 (repeals of Town and
                                                                            Country Planning (Scotland)
                                                                            Act 1972, ss 158, 160) (s 84(4))
                                                                            25 Sep 1991 (repeal in Land
                                                                            Compensation (Scotland) Act 1973,
                                                                            Sch 2, Pt II) (SI 1991/2067)
                                                                            25 Sep 1991 (repeals of or in Land
                                                                            Compensation (Scotland) Act 1963;
                                                                            Gas Act 1965; Public Expenditure
                                                                            and Receipts Act 1968; Town and

Planning and Compensation Act 1991 (c 34)—*contd*
Schedule

19, Pt	IV—*contd*	Country Planning (Scotland) Act 1972, ss 19(5), 35, 36, 58(2)(a), 106, Pt VII (except s 145), 155(5), (6), 156, 157(1), (3), (4), 158, 160, 169(3), 231(3)(c), 244(2), 245, 246, 248, 249, 263, 264, 265(5) (the words 'Part VII of'), 275(1) (definitions of 'new development' and 'previous apportionment'), Sch 6, paras 3–9, 12, Sch 19, Pt I; Land Compensation (Scotland) Act 1973, ss 5(3)(a), (b), 27(1), (5), 31(6), 48(9)(b); Local Government, Planning and Land Act 1980; Civil Aviation Act 1982; Airports Act 1986) (SI 1991/2092)
		26 Mar 1992 (repeals of or in Town and Country Planning (Scotland) Act 1972, ss 85(5), (11), 88(1), (2), 93(1)(k), (5), 98(1), (3), 166(2)(c), 265 (so far as not already in force), 275(1) (in definition 'planning permission', words from 'and in construing' to the end)) (SI 1992/334)
		25 Sep 1992 (repeals of or in Town and Country Planning (Scotland) Act 1972, ss 51, 91(3), (5), 201(5) (definition of 'lawful access'), 214(3), 234, 275(1) (definition of 'established use certificate')) (subject to transitional provisions) (SI 1992/1937)
		3 Feb 1995 (repeal in Town and Country Planning (Scotland) Act 1972, s 28(1)) (SI 1994/3292)
		30 Aug 1995 (repeals of or in Town and Country Planning (Scotland) Act 1972, s 61(6), Sch 6A, para 12(2)(e), Sch 7, para 2(1)(c), Schs 12–15) (SI 1995/2045)
		Not in force (otherwise)
	V	25 Sep 1991 (SI 1991/2067)

Note: the orders bringing this Act into force, as noted above, contain numerous transitional and saving provisions which are too complex to set out in this work

Ports Act 1991 (c 52)

RA: 25 Jul 1991

Commencement provisions: ss 32(8), 42(2); Ports Act 1991 (Transfer of Local Lighthouses: Appointed Day) Order 1992, SI 1992/2381

Section	
1–15	25 Jul 1991 (RA)
15A	Inserted by Finance Act 1995, s 159(1) (qv)
16–30	25 Jul 1991 (RA)
31–34	Repealed
35–42	25 Jul 1991 (RA)
Schedule	
1, 2	25 Jul 1991 (RA)

Property Misdescriptions Act 1991 (c 29)

RA: 27 Jun 1991

27 Jun 1991 (RA)

Radioactive Material (Road Transport) Act 1991 (c 27)

RA: 27 Jun 1991

Commencement provisions: s 9(3)

Section		
1–7		27 Aug 1991 (s 9(3))
8		27 Jun 1991 (RA)
9	(1)	27 Aug 1991 (s 9(3))
	(2)	See Schedule below
	(3), (4)	27 Aug 1991 (s 9(3))
Schedule		27 Aug 1991 (s 9(3))

Registered Homes (Amendment) Act 1991 (c 20)

RA: 27 Jun 1991

Commencement provisions: s 2(2); Registered Homes (Amendment) Act 1991 (Commencement) Order 1992, SI 1992/2240

1 Apr 1993 (SI 1992/2240)

Whole Act repealed in relation to England, and prospectively repealed by Care Standards Act 2000, s 117(2), Sch 6, in relation to Wales; orders made under the 2000 Act, s 122, bringing the prospective repeal into force will be noted to that Act in the service to this work

Representation of the People Act 1991 (c 11)

RA: 9 May 1991

Commencement provisions: s 3(2); Representation of the People Act 1991 (Commencement) Order 1991, SI 1991/1634

22 Jul 1991 (SI 1991/1634)

Road Traffic Act 1991 (c 40)

RA: 25 Jul 1991

Commencement provisions: s 84(1); Road Traffic Act 1991 (Commencement No 1) Order 1991, SI 1991/2054; Road Traffic Act 1991 (Commencement No 2) Order 1992, SI 1992/199; Road Traffic Act 1991 (Commencement No 3) Order 1992, SI 1992/421; Road Traffic Act 1991 (Commencement No 4 and Transitional Provisions) Order 1992, SI 1992/1286 (as amended by SI 1992/1410); Road Traffic Act 1991 (Commencement No 4 and Transitional Provisions) (Amendment) Order 1992, SI 1992/1410 (amending SI 1992/1286); Road Traffic Act 1991 (Commencement No 5 and Transitional Provisions) Order 1992, SI 1992/2010; Road Traffic Act 1991 (Commencement No 6) Order 1993, SI 1993/975; Road Traffic Act 1991 (Commencement No 6 and Transitional Provisions) Order 1993, SI 1993/1461, as amended by SI 1993/1686, SI 1993/2229; Road Traffic Act 1991 (Commencement No 6 and Transitional Provisions) (Amendment) Order 1993, SI 1993/1686; Road Traffic Act 1991 (Commencement No 7 and Transitional Provisions) Order 1993, SI 1993/2229; Road Traffic Act 1991 (Commencement No 8 and Transitional Provisions) Order 1993, SI 1993/2803; Road Traffic Act 1991 (Commencement No 9 and Transitional Provisions) Order 1993, SI 1993/3238 (as amended by SI 1994/81); Road Traffic Act 1991 (Commencement No 10 and Transitional Provisions) Order 1994, SI 1994/81 (amending SI 1993/3238); Road Traffic Act 1991 (Commencement No 11 and Transitional Provisions) Order 1994, SI 1994/1482; Road Traffic Act 1991 (Commencement No 12 and Transitional Provisions) Order 1994, SI 1994/1484; Road Traffic Act 1991 (Commencement No 13) (Scotland) Order 1997, SI 1997/1580; Road Traffic Act 1991 (Commencement No 14) (Scotland) Order 1997, SI 1997/2260; Road Traffic Act 1991 (Commencement No 15 and Transitional Provisions) Order 1998, SI 1998/967 (amending SI 1993/1461, SI 1993/2229, SI 1993/2803, SI 1993/3238, SI 1994/81, SI 1994/1482, SI 1994/1484)

Section		
1–21		1 Jul 1992 (SI 1992/1286)
22		See Sch 1 below
23–25		1 Jul 1992 (SI 1992/1286)
26		See Sch 2 below
27–34		1 Jul 1992 (SI 1992/1286)
35	(1)	1 Oct 1991 (so far as relates to s 35(2), (5)) (SI 1991/2054)
		2 Mar 1992 (otherwise) (SI 1992/199)
	(2)	1 Oct 1991 (SI 1991/2054)
	(3), (4)	2 Mar 1992 (SI 1992/199)
	(5)	1 Oct 1991 (SI 1991/2054)
	(6)	2 Mar 1992 (SI 1992/199)
36–38		Repealed
39, 40		1 Jul 1992 (SI 1992/1286)
41, 42		5 Jul 1993 (EW) (SI 1993/1461, as amended by SI 1993/1686)
		10 Oct 1997 (S) (SI 1997/2260)
43		1 Oct 1991 (EW) (SI 1991/2054)
		16 Jun 1997 (S) (SI 1997/1580)
44		1 Oct 1991 (SI 1991/2054)

Road Traffic Act 1991 (c 40)—*contd*

Section

45, 46		1 Jul 1992 (SI 1992/1286)
47		Repealed
48		See Sch 4 below
49		1 Jul 1992 (SI 1992/1286)
50, 63		Repealed
64	(1)	Ss 64(1), 65, 66(1)–(6), 67(4), (6),

68(2)(b), 69, 81 (so far as relates
to Sch 7 as noted below),
Sch 7, para 5(2), (3), brought
into force, subject to transitional
provisions relating to ss 66(2),
67(4), (6), 68(2)(b), on various
dates and in respect of various
London boroughs as follows—

5 Jul 1993 (only in London borough
of Wandsworth) (subject to
transitional provisions)
(SI 1993/1461)

4 Oct 1993 (only in London
boroughs of Bromley,
Hammersmith and Fulham and
Lewisham) (SI 1993/2229)

6 Dec 1993 (only in London
boroughs of Camden, Hackney
and Hounslow) (SI 1993/2803)

31 Jan 1994 (only in London borough
of Richmond upon Thames)
(SI 1993/3238, as amended by
SI 1994/81)

5 Apr 1994 (only in London borough
of Southwark) (SI 1994/81)

4 Jul 1994 (only in City of London
and London boroughs of Barking
and Dagenham, Barnet, Brent,
Croydon, Ealing, Enfield,
Greenwich, Haringey, Harrow,
Havering, Hillingdon, Islington,
Royal borough of Kensington
and Chelsea, Royal borough of
Kingston upon Thames,
Lambeth, Merton, Newham,
Redbridge, Sutton, Tower
Hamlets, Waltham Forest, City
of Westminster)
(SI 1994/1482)

4 Jul 1994 (only in London borough
of Bexley, and not in relation to
ss 67(4), (6), 68(2)(b), 69)
(SI 1994/1484)

Road Traffic Act 1991 (c 40)—*contd*

Section

64	(1)—*contd*		10 Apr 1998 (in relation to ss 67(4), 68(2)(b), 69 (so far as those provisions are not already in force)) (SI 1998/967)
			Not in force (otherwise)
	(2)		1 Oct 1991 (SI 1991/2054)
65			See s 64 above
66	(1)–(4)		See s 64 above
	(4A)		Inserted in relation to Common Council of the City of London and council of any London borough other than Tower Hamlets, by London Local Authorities Act 1995, s 8 (qv)
	(5), (6)		See s 64 above
	(7)		See Sch 6 below
67	(1)–(3)		5 Jul 1993 (subject to transitional provisions) (SI 1993/1461)
	(4)		See s 64 above
	(5)		5 Jul 1993 (subject to transitional provisions) (SI 1993/1461)
	(6)		See s 64 above
	(7)		5 Jul 1993 (subject to transitional provisions) (SI 1993/1461)
68	(1)		5 Jul 1993 (subject to transitional provisions) (SI 1993/1461)
	(2)	(a)	5 Jul 1993 (subject to transitional provisions) (SI 1993/1461)
		(b)	See s 64 above
	(3), (4)		5 Jul 1993 (subject to transitional provisions) (SI 1993/1461)
69			See s 64 above
70–72			5 Jul 1993 (SI 1993/1461)
73			1 Oct 1991 (SI 1991/2054)
74			Substituted for new ss 74, 74A by Greater London Authority Act 1999, s 284 (qv)
74A			Inserted as noted to s 74 ante
75, 76			1 Oct 1991 (SI 1991/2054)
76A			Inserted by Greater London Authority Act 1999, s 286 (qv)
77, 78			1 Oct 1991 (SI 1991/2054)
79			5 Jul 1993 (SI 1993/1461)
80			Repealed
81			See Sch 7 below
82			1 Oct 1991 (SI 1991/2054)
83			See Sch 8 below
84–87			25 Jul 1991 (RA)

Road Traffic Act 1991 (c 40)—*contd*

Schedule

1, 2			1 Jul 1992 (SI 1992/1286)
3			1 Oct 1991 (EW) (SI 1991/2054)
			16 Jun 1997 (S) (SI 1997/1580)
4, para	1		Repealed
	2, 3		1 Jul 1992 (SI 1992/1286)
	4, 5		Repealed
	6–26		1 Jul 1992 (SI 1992/1286)
	27, 28		1 Oct 1991 (SI 1991/2054)
	29, 30		1 Jul 1992 (SI 1992/1286)
	31–35		1 Oct 1991 (SI 1991/2054)
	36		1 Apr 1992 (SI 1992/421)
	37–49		1 Jul 1992 (SI 1992/1286)
	50		1 Apr 1992 (SI 1992/421)
	51, 52		1 Jul 1992 (SI 1992/1286)
	53		1 Jul 1992 (SI 1992/1286); prospectively repealed by Road Traffic (Vehicle Testing) Act 1999, s 7(2)(b)[2]
	54–72		1 Jul 1992 (SI 1992/1286)
	73	(1)	1 Apr 1992 (so far as relates to para 73(2), (3)) (SI 1992/421)
			1 Jul 1992 (otherwise) (SI 1992/1286)
		(2), (3)	1 Apr 1992 (SI 1992/421)
		(4)–(6)	1 Jul 1992 (SI 1992/1286)
	74		1 Jul 1992 (SI 1992/1286)
	75		1 Apr 1992 (SI 1992/421); prospectively repealed by Road Traffic (Vehicle Testing) Act 1999, s 7(2)(b)[2]
	76–78		1 Jul 1992 (SI 1992/1286)
	79		Repealed
	80–84		1 Jul 1992 (SI 1992/1286)
	85		1 Apr 1993 (for purposes of summary criminal proceedings in Scotland commenced on or after that date) (SI 1993/975)
			Not in force (otherwise)
	86–101		1 Jul 1992 (SI 1992/1286)
	102		1 Apr 1992 (but does not apply to offence alleged to have been committed before 1 Apr 1992) (SI 1992/199)
	103–105		1 Jul 1992 (SI 1992/1286)
	106		1 Oct 1991 (SI 1991/2054)
	107–114		1 Jul 1992 (SI 1992/1286)
5			Repealed
6			5 Jul 1993 (SI 1993/1461)
7, para	1		Repealed
	2		1 Jul 1992 (SI 1992/1286)

Road Traffic Act 1991 (c 40)—*contd*
Schedule

7, para	3, 4		1 Oct 1991 (SI 1991/2054)
	5	(1)	1 Oct 1991 (SI 1991/2054)
		(2), (3)	See s 64 above
		(4)	1 Oct 1991 (SI 1991/2054)
	6		10 Apr 1998 (SI 1998/967)
	7		1 Oct 1991 (SI 1991/2054)
	8		1 Sep 1992 (subject to transitional provisions with respect to a notice of a proposal to exercise a power to which Local Government Act 1985, Sch 5, para 5(2), applies, given before 1 Sep 1992) (SI 1992/2010)
	9–11		1 Oct 1991 (SI 1991/2054)
	12		10 Apr 1998 (SI 1998/967)
8			1 Oct 1991 (repeals of or in Chronically Sick and Disabled Persons Act 1970, s 21(5); Road Traffic Regulation Act 1984, ss 35(9), 51(5), 55(4)(c), 99(2), 104(10), 105(3)(b), 106(2)–(6), (9), (10), 117(3)) (SI 1991/2054)
			1 Apr 1992 (repeal of Road Traffic Act 1988, s 41(3)(b), (c)) (SI 1992/421)
			1 Jul 1992 (otherwise, except repeals in Public Passenger Vehicles Act 1981, s 66A; Road Traffic Regulation Act 1984, s 102) (SI 1992/1286)
			5 Jul 1993 (repeals in Road Traffic Regulation Act 1984, s 102) (SI 1993/1461)
			Not in force (repeal in Public Passenger Vehicles Act 1981, s 66A)

[1]   Orders made under Police Act 1997, s 135(1), bringing the prospective repeal into force will be noted to that Act

[2]   Orders made under Road Traffic (Vehicle Testing) Act 1999, s 9(2), bringing the prospective repeals into force will be noted to that Act

Road Traffic (Temporary Restrictions) Act 1991 (c 26)

RA: 27 Jun 1991

Commencement provisions: s 2(7); Road Traffic (Temporary Restrictions) Act 1991 (Commencement) Order 1992, SI 1992/1218

1 Jul 1992 (SI 1992/1218)

School Teachers' Pay and Conditions Act 1991 (c 49)

RA: 25 Jul 1991

Commencement provisions: s 6(5); School Teachers' Pay and Conditions Act 1991 (Commencement No 1) Order 1991, SI 1991/1874; School Teachers' Pay and Conditions Act 1991 (Commencement No 2 and Transitional Provision) Order 1992, SI 1992/532; School Teachers' Pay and Conditions Act 1991 (Commencement No 3) Order 1992, SI 1992/988; School Teachers' Pay and Conditions Act 1991 (Commencement No 4) Order 1992, SI 1992/3070

Section		
1		22 Aug 1991 (SI 1991/1874)
2	(1)	6 Mar 1992 SI 1992/532)
	(2)	Repealed
	(3)–(6)	6 Mar 1992 (SI 1992/532)
	(7)	4 Dec 1992 (SI 1992/3070)
	(8)	6 Mar 1992 (SI 1992/532)
	(9)	30 Mar 1992 (SI 1992/988)
3		6 Mar 1992 (SI 1992/532); substituted by School Standards and Framework Act 1998, s 13, subject to a saving in s 144(7), Sch 32, Pt II, para 7 (qv)
3A		Inserted by Education Act 1993, s 289; substituted by Education Act 1996, s 582(1), Sch 37, Pt I, para 101(1)(b), (3) (qv)
4, 5		22 Aug 1991 (SI 1991/1874)
6	(1)	22 Aug 1991 (SI 1991/1874)
	(2)	Repealed
	(3)	See Sch 2 below
	(4), (5)	22 Aug 1991 (SI 1991/1874)
Schedule		
1		22 Aug 1991 (SI 1991/1874)
2		6 Mar 1992 (SI 1992/532)

Smoke Detectors Act 1991 (c 37)

RA: 25 Jul 1991

Commencement provisions: s 7(3)

Not in force

Social Security (Contributions) Act 1991 (c 42)

Whole Act repealed

Statute Law Revision (Isle of Man) Act 1991 (c 61)

RA: 25 Jul 1991

25 Jul 1991 (RA)

Statutory Sick Pay Act 1991 (c 3)

RA: 12 Feb 1991

Commencement provisions: s 4(2); Statutory Sick Pay Act 1991 (Commencement) Order 1991, SI 1991/260

Section		
1, 2		Repealed
3	(1)	12 Feb 1991 (s 4(2))
	(2)	See Schedule below
	(3)–(5)	Repealed
	(6)	12 Feb 1991 (s 4(2))
4		12 Feb 1991 (s 4(2))
Schedule		6 Apr 1991 (SI 1991/260)

Statutory Water Companies Act 1991 (c 58)

RA: 25 Jul 1991

Commencement provisions: s 17(2)

1 Dec 1991 (s 17(2))

War Crimes Act 1991 (c 13)

RA: 9 May 1991

Commencement provisions: s 3(4)

Section		
1	(1)–(3)	9 May 1991 (s 3(4))
	(4)	Repealed or spent
2, 3		9 May 1991 (s 3(4))
Schedule		Repealed

Water Consolidation (Consequential Provisions) Act 1991 (c 60)

RA: 25 Jul 1991

Commencement provisions: s 4(2)

1 Dec 1991 (s 4(2))

Water Industry Act 1991 (c 56)

RA: 25 Jul 1991

Commencement provisions: s 223(2)

1 Dec 1991 (s 223(2))

Water Resources Act 1991 (c 57)

RA: 25 Jul 1991

Commencement provisions: s 225(2)

1 Dec 1991 (s 225(2))

Welfare of Animals at Slaughter Act 1991 (c 30)

RA: 27 Jun 1991

Commencement provisions: s 7(2)

27 Aug 1991 (s 7(2))

Welsh Development Agency Act 1991 (c 69)

Whole Act repealed

Wildlife and Countryside (Amendment) Act 1991 (c 39)

RA: 25 Jul 1991

Commencement provisions: s 3(3)

25 Sep 1991 (s 3(3))

1992

Access to Neighbouring Land Act 1992 (c 23)

RA: 16 Mar 1992

Commencement provisions: s 9(2); Access to Neighbouring Land Act 1992 (Commencement) Order 1992, SI 1992/3349

31 Jan 1993 (SI 1992/3349)

Aggravated Vehicle-Taking Act 1992 (c 11)

RA: 6 Mar 1992

Commencement provisions: s 4(2); Aggravated Vehicle-Taking Act 1992 (Commencement) Order 1992, SI 1992/764

1 Apr 1992 (SI 1992/764)

Appropriation Act 1992 (c 22)

Whole Act repealed

Appropriation (No 2) Act 1992 (c 47)

Whole Act repealed

Army Act 1992 (c 39)

RA: 16 Mar 1992

Commencement provisions: s 5

1 Jul 1992 (s 5)

Bingo Act 1992 (c 10)

RA: 6 Mar 1992

Commencement provisions: s 2(2)

6 May 1992 (s 2(2))

Boundary Commissions Act 1992 (c 55)

RA: 12 Nov 1992

12 Nov 1992 (RA)

Car Tax (Abolition) Act 1992 (c 58)

RA: 3 Dec 1992

Commencement provisions: s 5

13 Nov 1992 (s 5)

Carriage of Goods by Sea Act 1992 (c 50)

RA: 16 Jul 1992

Commencement provisions: s 6(3)

16 Sep 1992 (s 6(3))

Charities Act 1992 (c 41)

RA: 16 Mar 1992

Commencement provisions: s 79(2); Charities Act 1992 (Commencement No 1 and Transitional Provisions) Order 1992, SI 1992/1900; Charities Act 1992 (Commencement No 2) Order 1994, SI 1994/3023

Section	
1	1 Sep 1992 (except definitions 'financial year', 'independent examiner' and 'special trust' in sub-s (1), and except sub-s (3) (now repealed)) (SI 1992/1900)
	Not in force (exception noted above)
2–28	Repealed
29, 30	1 Sep 1992 (SI 1992/1900)
31–35	Repealed
36	1 Jan 1993 (SI 1992/1900)
37–48	Repealed
49, 50	1 Sep 1992 (SI 1992/1900)
51–57	Repealed
58	1 Mar 1995 (SI 1994/3023)
59	28 Nov 1994 (regulations, etc) (SI 1994/3023)
	1 Mar 1995 (otherwise) (SI 1994/3023)
60–63	1 Mar 1995 (SI 1994/3023)
64	28 Nov 1994 (regulations, etc) (SI 1994/3023)
	1 Mar 1995 (otherwise) (SI 1994/3023)
65–74	*Not in force*
75–79	1 Sep 1992 (SI 1992/1900)
Schedule	
1–4	Repealed
5	1 Sep 1992 (SI 1992/1900)
6, para 1	1 Jan 1993 (SI 1992/1900)

Charities Act 1992 (c 41)—*contd*
Schedule

6, para	2		1 Sep 1992 (SI 1992/1900); repealed by Finance Act 1999, s 139, Sch 20, Pt V(5), in relation to instruments executed on or after 6 Feb 2000
	3–8		1 Jan 1993 (SI 1992/1900)
	9		*Not in force*
	10	(a)	1 Sep 1992 (SI 1992/1900)
		(b)	*Not in force*
	11, 12		1 Sep 1992 (SI 1992/1900)
	13	(1)	1 Jan 1993 (SI 1992/1900)
		(2)	Repealed (*never in force*)
		(3)	1 Jan 1993 (SI 1992/1900)
	14–17		1 Sep 1992 (SI 1992/1900)
7			1 Sep 1992 (repeals of or in War Charities Act 1940; National Assistance Act 1948, s 41; Trading Representations (Disabled Persons) Act 1958, s 1(2)(b); Mental Health Act 1959, s 8(3); Charities Act 1960, ss 4(6), 6(6), (9) (subject to transitional provisions), 7(4), 16(2), 19(6), 22(6), (9), 30C(1)(c), 31, 45(3), 46, Sch 1, para 1(3), Sch 6; Local Government Act 1966, Sch 3, Pt II, column 1, para 20; Local Authority Social Services Act 1970, Sch 1; Local Government Act 1972, s 210(8); Health and Social Services and Social Security Adjudications Act 1983, s 30(3); National Heritage Act 1983, Sch 4, paras 13, 14; Companies Consolidation (Consequential Provisions) Act 1985, Sch 2; Charities Act 1985 (except s 1) (subject to transitional provisions); Finance Act 1986, s 33) (SI 1992/1900)
			1 Jan 1993 (repeals of or in Charitable Trustees Incorporation Act 1872, ss 2, 4, 5, 7, Schedule; Charities Act 1960, ss 27 (subject to transitional provisions), 29, 44) (SI 1992/1900)
			Not in force (otherwise)

Cheques Act 1992 (c 32)

RA: 16 Mar 1992

Commencement provisions: s 4(2)

16 Jun 1992 (s 4(2))

Church of England (Miscellaneous Provisions) Measure 1992 (No 1)

RA: 6 Mar 1992

Commencement provisions: s 19(2)

The provisions of this Measure were brought into force on the following dates
by instruments made by the Archbishops of Canterbury and York, and dated
27 May 1992 and 11 Jul 1992 (made under s 19(2))

Section		
1		1 Jun 1992
2, 3		11 Jul 1992
4		*Not in force*
5–14		1 Jun 1992
15		11 Jul 1992
16–19		1 Jun 1992
Schedule		
1		*Not in force*
2		1 Jun 1992
3, para	1	11 Jul 1992
	2–4	1 Jun 1992
	5	11 Jul 1992
	6–11	1 Jun 1992
	12	11 Jul 1992
	13–27	1 Jun 1992
4, Pt	I	1 Jun 1992
	II	1 Jun 1992 (except entry relating to Cremation Act 1902, s 11)
		11 Jul 1992 (exception noted above)

Civil Service (Management Functions) Act 1992 (c 61)

RA: 17 Dec 1992

17 Dec 1992 (RA)

Coal Industry Act 1992 (c 17)

RA: 6 Mar 1992

Commencement provisions: s 3(4); Coal Industry Act 1992 (Commencement) Order
1993, SI 1993/2514

Section	
1	6 Mar 1992 (RA)
2	20 Nov 1993 (SI 1993/2514)

Coal Industry Act 1992 (c 17)—*contd*

Section

3	(1), (2)	6 Mar 1992 (RA)
	(3)	See Schedule below
	(4), (5)	6 Mar 1992 (RA)
Schedule		
Pt	I	6 Mar 1992 (RA)
	II	20 Nov 1993 (SI 1993/2514)

Whole Act repealed by Coal Industry Act 1994, s 67(8), Sch 11, Pt III, as from a day to be appointed by order under s 68(4), (5) of that Act; any such order bringing the prospective repeal into force will be noted to that Act

---

Community Care (Residential Accommodation) Act 1992 (c 49)

RA: 16 Jul 1992

Commencement provisions: s 2(2); Community Care (Residential Accommodation) Act 1992 (Commencement) Order 1992, SI 1992/2976

Section

1	1 Apr 1993 (SI 1992/2976)
2	16 Jul 1992 (RA)

Competition and Service (Utilities) Act 1992 (c 43)

RA: 16 Mar 1992

Commencement provisions: s 56(2); Competition and Service (Utilities) Act 1992 (Commencement No 1) Order 1992, dated 29 May 1992 (note that, due to a drafting error, commencement orders under this Act are not made by statutory instrument)

Abbreviation: "No 1" means the Competition and Service (Utilities) Act 1992 (Commencement No 1) Order 1992

Section

1–4		1 Jul 1992 (No 1)
5		1 Sep 1992 (No 1)
6	(1)	1 Jul 1992 (except so far as inserts Telecommunications Act 1984, s 27G(8)) (No 1)
		Not in force (exception noted above)
	(2)	1 Jul 1992 (No 1)
7		1 Jul 1992 (except so far as inserts Telecommunications Act 1984, s 27H(4)) (No 1)
		Not in force (exception noted above)
8–13		1 Jul 1992 (No 1)
14–16		Repealed
17		*Not in force*
18		1 Jul 1992 (No 1)
19, 20		Repealed
21		1 Jul 1992 (No 1)

Competition and Service (Utilities) Act 1992 (c 43)—*contd*

Section

22		Repealed
23		*Not in force*
24–33		1 Jul 1992 (No 1)
34, 35		1 Sep 1992 (No 1)
36		*Not in force*
37		30 May 1992 (No 1)
38		Repealed
39–50		1 Jul 1992 (No 1)
51		1 Sep 1992 (No 1)
52, 53		1 Jul 1992 (No 1)
54		16 Mar 1992 (s 56(2))
55		30 May 1992 (No 1)
56	(1)–(5)	16 Mar 1992 (s 56(2))
	(6)	See Sch 1 below
	(7)	See Sch 2 below
Schedule		
1, para	1–4	1 Jul 1992 (No 1)
	5, 6	Repealed
	7–30	1 Jul 1992 (No 1)
	31	1 Sep 1992 (No 1)
2		1 Jul 1992 (No 1)

Consolidated Fund Act 1992 (c 1)

Whole Act repealed

Consolidated Fund (No 2) Act 1992 (c 21)

Whole Act repealed

Consolidated Fund (No 3) Act 1992 (c 59)

Whole Act repealed

Education (Schools) Act 1992 (c 38)

RA: 16 Mar 1992

Commencement provisions: s 21(3); Education (Schools) Act 1992 (Commencement No 1) Order 1992, SI 1992/1157; Education (Schools) Act 1992 (Commencement No 2 and Transitional Provision) Order 1993, SI 1993/1190; Education (Schools) Act 1992 (Commencement No 3) Order 1993, SI 1993/1491; Education (Schools) Act 1992 (Commencement No 4) Order 1996, SI 1996/1325

Whole Act repealed in relation to England and Wales; ss 17, 21(5) (extent provision) remain in force in relation to Scotland (as from 1 May 1993 (SI 1993/1190)

Finance Act 1992 (c 20)

Budget Day: 10 Mar 1992

RA: 16 Mar 1992

Details of the commencement of Finance Acts are not set out in this work

Finance (No 2) Act 1992 (c 48)

Budget Day: 10 Mar 1992

RA: 16 Jul 1992

Details of the commencement of Finance Acts are not set out in this work

Firearms (Amendment) Act 1992 (c 31)

RA: 16 Mar 1992

16 Mar 1992 (RA)

Friendly Societies Act 1992 (c 40)

RA: 16 Mar 1992

Commencement provisions: s 126(2); Friendly Societies Act 1992 (Commencement No 1) Order 1992, SI 1992/1325; Friendly Societies Act 1992 (Commencement No 2) Order 1992, SI 1992/3117; Friendly Societies Act 1992 (Commencement No 3 and Transitional Provisions) Order 1993, SI 1993/16; Friendly Societies Act 1992 (Commencement No 4) Order 1993, SI 1993/197; Friendly Societies Act 1992 (Commencement No 5 and Savings) Order 1993, SI 1993/1186; Friendly Societies Act 1992 (Commencement No 6 and Transitional Provisions) Order 1993, SI 1993/2213; Friendly Societies Act 1992 (Commencement No 7 and Transitional Provisions and Savings) Order 1993, SI 1993/3226; Friendly Societies Act 1992 (Commencement No 8) Order 1994, SI 1994/2543

Section		
1–4		Substituted (1 Dec 2001) by Financial Services and Markets Act 2000 (Mutual Societies) Order 2001, SI 2001/2617, art 13(1), Sch 3, Pt I, paras 53, 54
5	(1)–(5)	1 Feb 1993 (SI 1993/16)
	(6)	See Sch 3 below
	(7)	1 Feb 1993 (SI 1993/16)
6–26		1 Feb 1993 (SI 1993/16)
27	(1)–(4)	13 Jan 1993 (for purpose of management and administration of incorporated friendly societies) (SI 1993/16)
		1 Jan 1994 (otherwise) (SI 1993/2213)
	(5)	See Sch 11 below

Friendly Societies Act 1992 (c 40)—*contd*
Section

28, 29	13 Jan 1993 (for purpose of management and administration of incorporated friendly societies) (SI 1993/16)
	1 Jan 1994 (otherwise) (subject to transitional provisions) (SI 1993/2213)
30	See Sch 12 below
31–36A	Repealed
37	13 Jan 1993 (for purpose of control of conduct of business by incorporated friendly societies) (SI 1993/16)
	13 Sep 1993 (otherwise) (SI 1993/2213)
38–51	Repealed
52	13 Jan 1993 (for purpose of regulation of business of incorporated friendly societies) (SI 1993/16)
	28 Apr 1993 (otherwise) (SI 1993/1186)
52A, 53	Repealed
54	13 Jan 1993 (for purpose of regulation of business of incorporated friendly societies) (SI 1993/16)
	28 Apr 1993 (otherwise) (SI 1993/1186)
55	13 Jan 1993 (for purpose of regulation of business of incorporated friendly societies) (SI 1993/16)
	1 Jan 1994 (otherwise) (SI 1993/2213)
55A	Inserted (1 Sep 1994) by Friendly Societies Act 1992 (Amendment) Regulations 1994, SI 1994/1984, reg 14(1)
56, 57, 57A	Repealed
58, 58A	Substituted (1 Dec 2001) by Financial Services and Markets Act 2000 (Mutual Societies) Order 2001, SI 2001/2617, art 13(1), Sch 3, Pt I, paras 53, 75
59–61	Substituted (1 Dec 2001) by Financial Services and Markets Act 2000 (Mutual Societies) Order 2001, SI 2001/2617, art 13(1), Sch 3, Pt I, paras 53, 75
62	13 Jan 1993 (for purpose of regulation of business of incorporated friendly societies) (SI 1993/16)

Friendly Societies Act 1992 (c 40)—*contd*
Section

62—*contd*		28 Apr 1993 (otherwise) (SI 1993/1186)
62A		Inserted (1 Dec 2001) by Financial Services and Markets Act 2000 (Mutual Societies) Order 2001, SI 2001/2617, art 13(1), Sch 3, Pt I, paras 53, 77
63, 63A		Substituted (1 Dec 2001) by Financial Services and Markets Act 2000 (Mutual Societies) Order 2001, SI 2001/2617, art 13(1), Sch 3, Pt I, paras 53, 78
64		Substituted (1 Dec 2001) by Financial Services and Markets Act 2000 (Mutual Societies) Order 2001, SI 2001/2617, art 13(1), Sch 3, Pt I, paras 53, 78
65–67		13 Jan 1993 (for purpose of regulation of business of incorporated friendly societies) (SI 1993/16) 28 Apr 1993 (otherwise) (SI 1993/1186)
67A–67D		Repealed
68, 69		13 Jan 1993 (for purpose of accounts and audit of incorporated friendly societies) (SI 1993/16) 1 Jan 1994 (otherwise) (SI 1993/2213)
70	(1)–(4)	13 Jan 1993 (for purpose of accounts and audit of incorporated friendly societies) (SI 1993/16) 1 Jan 1994 (otherwise) (SI 1993/2213)
	(5)–(7)	13 Jan 1993 (for purpose of accounts and audit of incorporated friendly societies) (SI 1993/16) 13 Sep 1993 (otherwise) (SI 1993/2213)
	(8)–(11)	13 Jan 1993 (for purpose of accounts and audit of incorporated friendly societies) (SI 1993/16) 1 Jan 1994 (otherwise) (SI 1993/2213)
71	(1), (2)	13 Jan 1993 (for purpose of accounts and audit of incorporated friendly societies) (SI 1993/16) 13 Sep 1993 (so far as confers powers to make regulations for purposes of section) (SI 1993/2213) 1 Jan 1994 (otherwise) (SI 1993/2213)
	(3)	13 Jan 1993 (for purpose of accounts and audit of incorporated friendly societies) (SI 1993/16)

Friendly Societies Act 1992 (c 40)—*contd*

Section

71	(3)—*contd*	1 Jan 1994 (otherwise) (SI 1993/2213)
72	(1)	13 Jan 1993 (for purpose of accounts and audit of incorporated friendly societies) (SI 1993/16)
		1 Jan 1994 (otherwise) (SI 1993/2213)
	(2)	See Sch 14 below
73–78		13 Jan 1993 (for purpose of accounts and audit of incorporated friendly societies) (SI 1993/16)
		1 Jan 1994 (otherwise) (SI 1993/2213)
79		Repealed
80		13 Jan 1993 (subject to transitional provisions) (SI 1993/16)
81		13 Jan 1993 (SI 1993/16)
82	(1)–(4)	13 Jan 1993 (SI 1993/16)
	(5)	1 Jan 1994 (SI 1993/3226)
83		13 Jan 1993 (SI 1993/16)
84		1 Jan 1993 (subject to transitional provisions) (SI 1992/3117)
85–90		13 Sep 1993 (subject to transitional provisions) (SI 1993/2213)
90A		Repealed
91, 92		13 Sep 1993 (subject to transitional provisions) (SI 1993/2213)
93	(1)–(4)	1 Feb 1993 (SI 1993/16)
	(5)–(15)	1 Jan 1994 (SI 1993/2213)
94		1 Feb 1993 (SI 1993/16)
95		See Sch 16 below
96		1 Jan 1994 (SI 1993/3226)
97		Repealed (*never in force*)
98		Repealed
99		1 Feb 1993 (SI 1993/16)
100, 101		Repealed
102–113		1 Feb 1993 (SI 1993/16)
114		Substituted (1 Dec 2001) by Financial Services and Markets Act 2000 (Consequential Amendments and Repeals) Order 2001, SI 2001/3649, art 204(1)
115		1 Feb 1993 (SI 1993/16)
116–119		8 Jun 1992 (SI 1992/1325)
119A		Inserted (1 Sep 1994) by Friendly Societies Act 1992 (Amendment) Regulations 1994, SI 1994/1984, reg 31
119B		Repealed
120	(1)	See Sch 21 below
	(2)	See Sch 22 below
121		8 Jun 1992 (SI 1992/1325)

Friendly Societies Act 1992 (c 40)—*contd*

Section			
122			Repealed
123			8 Jun 1992 (SI 1992/1325)
124			1 Jan 1994 (SI 1993/3226)
125			1 Feb 1993 (SI 1993/16)
126			8 Jun 1992 (SI 1992/1325)
Schedule			
1			Repealed
2			1 Feb 1993 (SI 1993/16)
3, para	1–8		1 Feb 1993 (SI 1993/16)
	9	(1)	1 Feb 1993 (SI 1993/16)
		(2)	Repealed
		(3)–(7)	1 Feb 1993 (SI 1993/16)
	10–15		1 Feb 1993 (SI 1993/16)
4–6			1 Feb 1993 (SI 1993/16)
7			Repealed
8–10			1 Feb 1993 (SI 1993/16)
11, para	1–15		13 Jan 1993 (for purpose of committee of management of incorporated friendly societies) (SI 1993/16)
			1 Jan 1994 (otherwise) (SI 1993/2213)
	16		13 Jan 1993 (for purpose of committee of management of incorporated friendly societies) (SI 1993/16)
			13 Sep 1993 (otherwise) (SI 1993/2213)
12, para	1–6		13 Jan 1993 (for purpose of meetings and resolutions of incorporated friendly societies) (SI 1993/16)
			1 Jan 1994 (otherwise) (SI 1993/2213)
	7		13 Jan 1993 (for purpose of meetings and resolutions of incorporated friendly societies) (SI 1993/16)
			13 Sep 1993 (otherwise) (SI 1993/2213)
	8, 9		13 Jan 1993 (for purpose of meetings and resolutions of incorporated friendly societies) (SI 1993/16)
			1 Jan 1994 (otherwise) (SI 1993/2213)
13, 13A–13C			Repealed
14, para	1–6		13 Jan 1993 (for purpose of auditors of incorporated friendly societies) (SI 1993/16)
			1 Jan 1994 (otherwise) (SI 1993/2213)
	7	(1)	1 Jan 1994 (SI 1993/2213)
		(2)	Repealed
		(3)	1 Jan 1994 (SI 1993/2213)
		(4)	Repealed

Friendly Societies Act 1992 (c 40)—*contd*

Schedule

14, para	7	(5)–(7)		1 Jan 1994 (SI 1993/2213)
	8–16			13 Jan 1993 (for purpose of auditors of incorporated friendly societies) (SI 1993/16)
				1 Jan 1994 (otherwise) (SI 1993/2213)
	17			13 Jan 1993 (for purpose of auditors of incorporated friendly societies) (SI 1993/16)
				13 Sep 1993 (otherwise) (SI 1993/2213)
15				13 Sep 1993 (SI 1993/2213)
16, para	1			See paras 2–52 below
	2	(1)	(a)	13 Jan 1993 (SI 1993/16)
			(b)	1 Jan 1994 (SI 1993/3226)
		(2)		1 Jan 1994 (SI 1993/3226)
		(3)		13 Jan 1993 (SI 1993/16)
	3			Repealed
	4	(a)		1 Feb 1993 (SI 1993/16)
		(b)		1 Jan 1994 (subject to transitional provisions) (SI 1993/2213)
		(c)		1 Feb 1993 (SI 1993/16)
	5–7			1 Feb 1993 (SI 1993/16)
	8, 9			1 Jan 1994 (SI 1993/2213)
	10			1 Feb 1993 (SI 1993/16)
	11, 12			1 Jan 1994 (subject to transitional provisions) (SI 1993/2213)
	13, 14			1 Jan 1994 (SI 1993/3226)
	15			1 Jan 1994 (SI 1993/2213)
	16			1 Feb 1993 (SI 1993/16)
	17			1 Jan 1994 (SI 1993/2213)
	18	(a)		1 Jan 1994 (SI 1993/2213)
		(b)		1 Jan 1994 (SI 1993/3226)
	19			1 Feb 1993 (SI 1993/16)
	20, 21			1 Jan 1994 (SI 1993/3226)
	22, 23			1 Jan 1994 (subject to transitional provisions) (SI 1993/2213)
	24			1 Feb 1993 (so far as repeals Friendly Societies Act 1974, ss 70–73, 75) (subject to transitional provisions) (SI 1993/16)
				Not in force (repeal of Friendly Societies Act 1974, s 74)
	25, 26			13 Jan 1993 (subject to transitional provisions) (SI 1993/16)
	27			1 Jan 1994 (SI 1993/3226)
	28			13 Jan 1993 (SI 1993/16)
	29			13 Sep 1993 (subject to transitional provisions) (SI 1993/2213)

Friendly Societies Act 1992 (c 40)—*contd*
Schedule

16, para	30		Repealed
	31		13 Sep 1993 (SI 1993/2213)
	32		1 Feb 1993 (insertion of Friendly Societies Act 1974, s 84A(1)–(7)) (SI 1993/16)[2]
			1 Jan 1994 (insertion of Friendly Societies Act 1974, s 84A(8)) (SI 1993/3226)
	33		13 Sep 1993 (subject to transitional provisions) (SI 1993/2213)
	34–36		28 Apr 1993 (SI 1993/1186)
	37		1 Feb 1993 (SI 1993/16)
	38	(a)	1 Feb 1993 (subject to transitional provisions) (SI 1993/16)
		(b)	28 Apr 1993 (SI 1993/1186)
		(c)	28 Apr 1993 (so far as relates to Friendly Societies Act 1974, s 93(3)(a), (b)) (SI 1993/1186)
			1 Jan 1994 (so far as relates to Friendly Societies Act 1974, s 93(3)(c)) (SI 1993/3226)
	39–41		28 Apr 1993 (SI 1993/1186)
	42	(a)	1 Feb 1993 (SI 1993/16)
		(b), (c)	1 Jan 1994 (SI 1993/3226)
	43		1 Jan 1994 (SI 1993/2213)
	44		1 Jan 1994 (SI 1993/3226)
	45		1 Feb 1993 (SI 1993/16)
	46		1 Jan 1994 (SI 1993/3226)
	47		Repealed
	48	(a)	1 Jan 1994 (SI 1993/3226)
		(b)	1 Feb 1993 (SI 1993/16)
		(c), (d)	1 Jan 1994 (SI 1993/3226)
		(e)	1 Feb 1993 (SI 1993/16)
	49, 50		1 Jan 1994 (SI 1993/3226)
	51		1 Jan 1994 (SI 1993/2213)
	52		1 Feb 1993 (SI 1993/16)
17			Repealed (*never in force*)
18			Repealed
19			Repealed (*paras 8, 10, 26, 28 never in force*)
20			Repealed
21, Pt	I, para	1	1 Feb 1993 (SI 1993/16)
		2–4	1 Jan 1993 (SI 1992/3117)
		5–9	1 Feb 1993 (SI 1993/16)
		10	Repealed
		11	1 Feb 1993 (SI 1993/16)
		12–17	Repealed
		18, 19	1 Jan 1994 (SI 1993/3226)
	II		1 Jan 1994 (SI 1993/3226)

Friendly Societies Act 1992 (c 40)—*contd*
Schedule

22, Pt	I	13 Jan 1993 (repeals of or in Friendly Societies Act 1974, ss 76(1)(c), (d), (e), (5), 77, 78(1), (2), (3), 79(1), 80(1)) (subject to transitional provisions) (SI 1993/16)
		1 Feb 1993 (repeals of or in Industrial Assurance Act 1923, ss 2(1) (words "and anything which under" to the end), 4, 7, 8(3), Sch 1; Industrial Assurance and Friendly Societies Act 1948, ss 6, 7, 10(1)(b), (c) (and words from "and shall, on demand" to the end of sub-s (1)), (2), (3), 11, Sch 1; Friendly Societies Act 1974, ss 8, 11(1), 13(2), 15 (words "society or", in each place they appear⁴),17, 70–73, 75) (subject to transitional provisions) (SI 1993/16)
		1 Feb 1993 (in relation to incorporated friendly societies which are collecting societies, repeals of or in: Industrial Assurance Act 1923, ss 8(2), (4), 15, 16, 18, 19(1)–(3), 35; Industrial Assurance and Friendly Societies Act 1948, s 13(3)) (SI 1993/16)
		5 Feb 1993 (repeals of Industrial Assurance Act 1923, s 8(1)(b), in relation to collecting societies (as defined by s 1(1A) thereof) to which the criteria of prudent management described in Friendly Societies Act 1992, s 50(3) apply; Friendly Societies Act 1974, Sch 5) (SI 1993/197)
		28 Apr 1993 (in relation to incorporated friendly societies, repeals of or in Financial Services Act 1986, ss 139(3)–(5), 207(1), Sch 11, paras 1, 26(1), (3), 27, 38(1)(a), 43, Sch 15, para 14(1), (3)) (SI 1993/1186)
		28 Apr 1993 (repeals of or in Friendly Societies Act 1974, ss 6(2), 16, 88, 89, 106; Industrial Assurance Act 1948, s 17A(2)) (SI 1993/1186)

Friendly Societies Act 1992 (c 40)—*contd*
Schedule
22, Pt   I—*contd*

13 Sep 1993 (repeals of or in Industrial
Assurance Act 1923, ss 36, 38;
Friendly Societies Act 1974, s 82,
Sch 9, para 5) (subject to transitional
provisions) (SI 1993/2213)

1 Jan 1994 (so far as not brought into
force on 1 Feb and 28 Apr 1993 by
SI 1993/16, SI 1993/1186) (repeals
of or in Industrial Assurance
Act 1923, ss 8(2), (4), 15, 16, 18,
19(1)–(3), 35; Industrial Assurance
and Friendly Societies Act 1948,
s 13(3); Financial Services Act 1986,
ss 139(3)–(5), 207(1), Sch 11, paras 1,
26(1), (3), 27, 38(1)(a), 43, Sch 15,
para 14(1), (3) (SI 1993/2213)

1 Jan 1994 (repeals of or in Loan
Societies Act 1840; Friendly
Societies Act 1896; Industrial
Assurance Act 1923, ss 20(1)(b),
31, 44, 45(2); Industrial Assurance
and Friendly Societies Act 1929;
Industrial Assurance and Friendly
Societies Act 1948, ss 1, 4, 23(1),
Schs 2, 3; Friendly Societies
Act 1955, s 3(2); Industrial
Assurance Act 1948 (Amendment)
Act 1958; Friendly Societies A
ct 1974, ss 9(2), (3), 27, 28, 30(5),
46, 53(3), 107(1), Schs 1, 2, 3,
Sch 9, paras 2, 6, 8, 10(1); Banking
Act 1987, s 84(1); Income and
Corporation Taxes Act 1988;
Companies Act 1989) (subject to
transitional provisions)
(SI 1993/2213)

1 Jan 1994 (repeals of or in Industrial
Assurance and Friendly Societies
Act 1948, ss 2, 10(1)(a) (words
"signed by two of the committee of
management and by the secretary"
only); Consumer Credit Act 1974,
s 189(1); Friendly Societies Act 1974,
ss 98, 111(6), 115, 117(3), Sch 3;
Finance Act 1984; Friendly Societies
Act 1984, s 3; Companies Act 1985,
s 449; Building Societies Act 1986,
s 7; Banking Act 1987, s 96, Sch 2)
(SI 1993/3226)

Friendly Societies Act 1992 (c 40)—*contd*
Schedule

22, Pt	I—*contd*	1 Nov 1994 (repeal of Industrial Assurance Act 1923, s 2(1) (so far as not already in force), (2)) (SI 1994/2543)
		Repealed (repeal of Trade Union and Labour Relations (Consolidation) 1992, s 19(2))
		Not in force (otherwise)
	II	1 Jan 1994 (except so far as repeals Industrial Assurance (Northern Ireland) Order 1979, SI 1979/1574, arts 4(1) (other than words "and in the exercise and performance of his powers and duties as Registrar under the Friendly Societies Act in relation to collecting societies" which are repealed), (3), 5, 9(1)(a) (other than words "signed by two of the committee of management and by the secretary" which are repealed)) (subject to transitional provisions) (SI 1993/3226)
		1 Nov 1994 (revocation of Industrial Assurance (Northern Ireland) Order 1979, SI 1979/1574, art 4(1) (so far as not already in force), (3)) (SI 1994/2543)
		Not in force (repeal of Industrial Assurance (Northern Ireland) Order 1979, SI 1979/1574, arts 5, 9(1)(a) (part))

[1]   Note that SI 1993/16 purports to bring into force Sch 16, para 32 (except sub-para (8)). As para 32 contains no sub-paragraphs, it is thought that it was intended to bring into force s 84A(1)–(7) of the 1974 Act, but not sub-s (8) thereof. Note also that SI 1993/2213 purports to bring Sch 16, para 32 (except s 84A(8)) into force for all remaining purposes on 13 Sep 1993

[2]   Note that the repeal of those words by the Friendly Societies Act 1992, s 120(2), Sch 22, Pt I, is made to the Friendly Societies Act 1974, s 16, and not to s 15 thereof

---

Further and Higher Education Act 1992 (c 13)

RA: 6 Mar 1992

Commencement provisions: s 94(3); Further and Higher Education Act 1992 (Commencement No 1 and Transitional Provisions) Order 1992, SI 1992/831 (as amended by SI 1992/2041); Further and Higher Education Act 1992 (Commencement No 1 and Transitional Provisions) (Amendment) Order 1992, SI 1992/2041 (amending SI 1992/831); Further and Higher Education Act 1992 (Commencement No 2) Order 1992, SI 1992/2377; Further and Higher Education Act 1992 (Commencement No 2) Order 1992, SI 1992/3057; Further and Higher Education Act 1992 (Commencement No 3) Order 1996, SI 1996/1897

Further and Higher Education Act 1992 (c 13)—*contd*

Section

1–14		Repealed
15	(1)–(3)	6 May 1992 (SI 1992/831)
	(4)	30 Sep 1992 (SI 1992/831)
	(5)–(7)	6 May 1992 (SI 1992/831)
16		30 Sep 1992 (SI 1992/831)
17		6 May 1992 (SI 1992/831)
18–22		30 Sep 1992 (SI 1992/831)
22A		Inserted by Teaching and Higher Education Act 1998, s 41(2) (qv)
23, 24		30 Sep 1992 (SI 1992/831)
25		Substituted by School Standards and Framework Act 1998, s 140(1), Sch 30, para 36 (qv)
26		30 Sep 1992 (except in respect of persons employed by a local authority to work solely at the institution the corporation is established to conduct and who are so employed in connection with an arrangement for the supply by that local authority of goods or services for the purposes of that institution in pursuance of a bid prepared under Local Government Act 1988, s 7) (SI 1992/831, as amended by SI 1992/2041)
		Not in force (exception noted above)
27		30 Sep 1992 (SI 1992/831)
28, 29		6 May 1992 (SI 1992/831)
30		Substituted by Learning and Skills Act 2000, s 143(2) (qv)
31–33		6 May 1992 (SI 1992/831)
34, 35		1 Apr 1993 (SI 1992/831)
36		30 Sep 1992 (SI 1992/831)
37, 38		1 Apr 1993 (SI 1992/831)
39–43		6 May 1992 (SI 1992/831)
44, 45		1 Apr 1993 (in respect of institutions which, before they became institutions within the further education sector, were schools maintained by a local education authority or grant-maintained schools) (SI 1992/831)
		Not in force (otherwise)
46–50		1 Apr 1993 (SI 1992/831)
51		30 Sep 1992 (SI 1992/831)
52		1 Apr 1993 (SI 1992/831)
52A		Inserted by School Standards and Framework Act 1998, s 113 (qv)

Further and Higher Education Act 1992 (c 13)—*contd*

Section

53			30 Sep 1992 (SI 1992/831)
54	(1)		6 May 1992 (SI 1992/831)
	(2)		1 Apr 1993 (SI 1992/831)
55	(1)–(3)		Repealed
	(4)–(6)		1 Apr 1993 (SI 1992/831)
	(7)	(a)	Repealed
		(c)	1 Apr 1993 (SI 1992/831)
56			Repealed
57			Substituted by Learning and Skills Act 2000, s 149, Sch 9, para 34 (qv)
58			30 Sep 1992 (SI 1992/831)
59			Repealed
60			1 Apr 1993 (SI 1992/831)
60A			Repealed
61			6 May 1992 (SI 1992/831)
61A			Inserted by Learning and Skills Act 2000, s 149, Sch 9, para 37 (qv)
62			6 May 1992 (SI 1992/831)
63			1 Apr 1993 (SI 1992/831)
64			6 May 1992 (SI 1992/831)
65			1 Apr 1993 (SI 1992/831); prospectively repealed by Special Educational Needs and Disability Act 2001, ss 34(1), 42(6), Sch 9[1]
66			1 Apr 1993 (SI 1992/831)
67	(1)		1 Apr 1993 (SI 1992/831)
	(2)–(5)		6 May 1992 (SI 1992/831)
68–73			6 May 1992 (SI 1992/831)
74			1 Apr 1993 (SI 1992/831)
75–84			6 May 1992 (SI 1992/831)
85			1 Apr 1993 (SI 1992/831)
86			Repealed
87			30 Sep 1992 (SI 1992/831)
88–92			6 May 1992 (SI 1992/831)
93	(1)		See Sch 8 below
	(2)		See Sch 9 below
94			6 May 1992 (SI 1992/831)

Schedule

1			6 May 1992 (SI 1992/831)
2			Repealed
3			6 May 1992 (SI 1992/831)
4, 5			30 Sep 1992 (SI 1992/831)
5A			Repealed
6			6 May 1992 (SI 1992/831)
7			30 Sep 1992 (SI 1992/831)
8, Pt	I, para	1–18	Repealed
		19, 20	1 Apr 1993 (SI 1992/831)
		21	30 Sep 1992 (SI 1992/831)
		22, 23	1 Apr 1993 (SI 1992/831)

Further and Higher Education Act 1992 (c 13)—*contd*

Schedule

8, Pt	I, para	24–26		Repealed
		27		6 May 1992 (SI 1992/831)
		28, 29		Repealed
		30		1 Apr 1993 (SI 1992/831)
		31		6 May 1992 (SI 1992/831)
		32	(a)	1 Apr 1993 (SI 1992/831)
			(b)	6 May 1992 (SI 1992/831)
		33		1 Apr 1993 (SI 1992/831)
		34		6 May 1992 (SI 1992/831)
		35		1 Apr 1993 (SI 1992/831)
		36	(a)	6 May 1992 (SI 1992/831)
			(b)	1 Apr 1993 (SI 1992/831)
		37	(a)	1 Apr 1993 (SI 1992/831)
			(b)	6 May 1992 (SI 1992/831)
		38		6 May 1992 (SI 1992/831)
		39–42		1 Apr 1993 (SI 1992/831)
		43		6 May 1992 (SI 1992/831)
		44–47		1 Apr 1993 (SI 1992/831)
		48		6 May 1992 (SI 1992/831)
		49		1 Apr 1993 (SI 1992/831)
		50, 51		Repealed
		52		1 Apr 1993 (SI 1992/831)
		53, 54		Repealed
		55		1 Apr 1993 (SI 1992/831)
		56, 57		Repealed
		58		1 Apr 1993 (SI 1992/831)
		59		6 May 1992 (SI 1992/831)
		60		1 Apr 1993 (SI 1992/831)
		61–64		Repealed
		65		6 May 1992 (subject to saving in relation to any matter notified to the Secretary of State by the Education Assets Board pursuant to Education Reform Act 1988, Sch 10, para 3, before 6 May 1992) (SI 1992/831)
		66, 67		1 Apr 1993 (SI 1992/831)
	II, para	68		6 May 1992 (SI 1992/831)
		69		Repealed
		70–74		1 Apr 1993 (SI 1992/831)
		75, 76		6 May 1992 (SI 1992/831)
		77		1 Aug 1993 (SI 1992/831)
		78, 79		6 May 1992 (SI 1992/831)
		80		1 Aug 1993 (SI 1992/831)
		81		1 Apr 1993 (SI 1992/831)
		82		Repealed
		83		1 Apr 1993 (SI 1992/831)
		84, 85		6 May 1992 (SI 1992/831)
		86		1 Aug 1993 (SI 1992/831)

Further and Higher Education Act 1992 (c 13)—*contd*

Schedule

8, Pt	II, para	87		6 May 1992 (SI 1992/831)
		88, 89		Repealed
		90–92		1 Apr 1993 (SI 1992/831)
		93	(a)	1 Apr 1993 (SI 1992/831)
			(b)	6 May 1992 (SI 1992/831)
		94, 95		1 Apr 1993 (SI 1992/831)
9				6 May 1992 (repeals of or in Education Reform Act 1988, ss 122(2)–(5), 129(3), (4), 136(3)–(7), 137(2) (expression 'or 129(3)'), 156 (so far as relates to institutions designated under Education Reform Act 1988, s 129), 219(2)(e), 227(2)–(4), 232(3) (expression 'or 227'), 232(4)(b) (expression '227'), Sch 7, para 19) (SI 1992/831)
				1 Apr 1993 (repeals of or in Education Act 1944, ss 8(3), 67(4A), 85(2), (3), 114(1), (1A), (1B), (1C); Education (Miscellaneous Provisions) Act 1948, s 3(3); Superannuation Act 1972, Sch 1; House of Commons Disqualification Act 1975, Sch 1, Pt III; Education (No 2) Act 1986, ss 43(5)(c), (7), 49(3)(d), (da), 51(2)(b), (5), (6), 58(3), (4), (5)(a), (ab); Education Reform Act 1988, ss 120, 124(4), 131, 132, 134, Pt II, Chapter III (ss 139–155), s 156 (so far as still in force), ss 157, 158(2), 159(2)(b), 161(1)(c), 205(6), 211(c), 218(10)(b), 219, 221(1)(c), (3), 222(2)(b), (3)(c), 230(1), (3)(c)(ii), 232(2), 234(2)(b), 235(2)(a), (h), Sch 12, paras 68, 69(2), 70, 100(2), 101(4); Environmental Protection Act 1990, s 98(2)(a)) (SI 1992/831)
				1 Aug 1993 (repeal in Education Reform Act 1988, s 105(2)(b)) (SI 1992/831)

---

[1]   Orders made under the Special Educational Needs and Disability Act 2001, s 43(3), bringing the prospective repeal into force will be noted to that Act in the service to this work

Further and Higher Education (Scotland) Act 1992 (c 37)

RA: 16 Mar 1992

Commencement provisions: s 63(2); Further and Higher Education (Scotland) Act 1992 (Commencement No 1 and Saving Provisions) Order 1992, SI 1992/817; Further and Higher Education (Scotland) Act 1992 (Commencement No 2) Order 1998, SI 1998/2886

Section

1	(1), (2)	1 Apr 1993 (SI 1992/817)
	(3)–(5)	16 May 1992 (SI 1992/817)
	(6)	1 Apr 1993 (SI 1992/817)
2		1 Apr 1993 (SI 1992/817)
3	(1)–(4)	1 Apr 1993 (SI 1992/817)
	(5)	16 May 1992 (SI 1992/817)
	(6)	1 Apr 1993 (SI 1992/817)
4, 5		1 Apr 1993 (SI 1992/817)
6		16 May 1992 (SI 1992/817)
7–10		21 Nov 1998 (SI 1998/2886)
11, 12		16 May 1992 (SI 1992/817)
13, 14		1 Apr 1993 (SI 1992/817)
15		16 May 1992 (SI 1992/817)
16		1 Sep 1992 (SI 1992/817)
17		1 Apr 1993 (SI 1992/817)
18		16 May 1992 (SI 1992/817)
19–25		1 Apr 1993 (SI 1992/817)
26–36		16 May 1992 (SI 1992/817)
37		1 Jun 1992 (SI 1992/817)
38		16 May 1992 (SI 1992/817)
39		1 Jun 1992 (so far as relates to institutions for whose activities the Council are considering providing financial support) (SI 1992/817)
		1 Apr 1993 (otherwise) (SI 1992/817)
40, 41		1 Apr 1993 (SI 1992/817)
42	(1)	1 Jun 1992 (SI 1992/817)
	(2), (3)	1 Apr 1993 (SI 1992/817)
	(3A)–(3G)	Inserted by Teaching and Higher Education 1998, s 31(2) (qv)
	(4)	1 Jun 1992 (SI 1992/817)
43	(1)	1 Jun 1992 (SI 1992/817)
	(2)	1 Apr 1993 (SI 1992/817)
	(3)–(8)	1 Jun 1992 (SI 1992/817)
44		25 Apr 1992 (for purpose of authorising the making under s 44 of an Order which is expressed to come into force on or after 16 May 1992) (SI 1992/817)
		16 May 1992 (otherwise) (SI 1992/817)
45–49		16 May 1992 (SI 1992/817)
50, 51		1 Jun 1992 (SI 1992/817)
52		16 May 1992 (SI 1992/817)

Further and Higher Education (Scotland) Act 1992 (c 37)—*contd*

Section			
53			1 Apr 1993 (SI 1992/817)
54	(1), (2)		1 Jun 1992 (SI 1992/817)
	(3)		1 Apr 1993 (SI 1992/817)
55–58			16 May 1992 (SI 1992/817)
59			Repealed
59A			Inserted by Teaching and Higher Education Act 1998, s 37 (qv)
60, 61			16 May 1992 (SI 1992/817)
62	(1)		See Sch 8 below
	(2)		See Sch 9 below
	(3)		See Sch 10 below
63			25 Apr 1992 (SI 1992/817)
Schedule			
1			21 Nov 1998 (SI 1998/2886)
2			16 May 1992 (SI 1992/817)
3, 4			1 Sep 1992 (SI 1992/817)
5, 6			16 May 1992 (SI 1992/817)
7			1 Jun 1992 (SI 1992/817)
8			16 May 1992 (SI 1992/817)
9, para	1		16 May 1992 (SI 1992/817)
	2	(a)	1 Apr 1993 (SI 1992/817)
		(b), (c)	16 May 1992 (SI 1992/817)
	3		16 May 1992 (SI 1992/817)
	4	(1), (2)	16 May 1992 (SI 1992/817)
		(3)	1 Jun 1992 (so far as relates to the Scottish Higher Education Funding Council) (SI 1992/817) 21 Nov 1998 (otherwise) (SI 1998/2886)
		(4)–(6)	16 May 1992 (SI 1992/817)
	5	(1), (2)	16 May 1992 (SI 1992/817)
		(3)	1 Jun 1992 (so far as relates to the Scottish Higher Education Funding Council) (SI 1992/817) 21 Nov 1998 (otherwise) (SI 1998/2886)
		(4)	Repealed
		(5)	16 May 1992 (SI 1992/817)
	6		Repealed
	7	(1)	16 May 1992 (SI 1992/817)
		(2)–(6)	1 Apr 1993 (SI 1992/817)
		(7)	16 May 1992 (SI 1992/817)
	8	(1), (2)	16 May 1992 (SI 1992/817)
		(3)	1 Apr 1993 (SI 1992/817)
	9		1 Apr 1993 (SI 1992/817)
	10		1 Jun 1992 (SI 1992/817)
	11		1 Apr 1993 (SI 1992/817)
	12	(1), (2)	16 May 1992 (SI 1992/817)
		(3)	1 Apr 1993 (SI 1992/817)

Further and Higher Education (Scotland) Act 1992 (c 37)—*contd*
Schedule

9, para	13	(a)	1 Apr 1993 (SI 1992/817)
		(b), (c)	16 May 1992 (SI 1992/817)
10			16 May 1992 (repeals of or in Employment Protection (Consolidation) Act 1978, s 29; Education (Scotland) Act 1980, ss 3, 7, 77, 135(1)) (SI 1992/817)
			1 Apr 1993 (repeals of or in School Boards (Scotland) Act 1988, ss 8, 22; Self-Governing Schools etc (Scotland) Act 1989, ss 54–66, 80) (SI 1992/817)

[1] Orders made under the Race Relations (Amendment) Act 2000, s 10, bringing the prospective repeal into force will be noted to that Act in the service to this work

---

Human Fertilisation and Embryology (Disclosure of Information) Act 1992 (c 54)

RA: 16 Jul 1992

16 Jul 1992 (RA)

Licensing (Amendment) (Scotland) Act 1992 (c 18)

RA: 6 Mar 1992

Commencement provisions: s 2(2); Licensing (Amendment) (Scotland) Act 1992 (Commencement and Savings) Order 1992, SI 1992/819
Section

1	15 Apr 1992 (subject to savings with respect to any licence temporarily transferred under Licensing (Scotland) Act 1976, s 25(1), before 15 Apr 1992) (SI 1992/819)
2	6 Mar 1992 (RA)

Local Government Act 1992 (c 19)

RA: 6 Mar 1992

Commencement provisions: s 30(2), (3); Local Government Act 1992 (Commencement No 1) Order 1992, SI 1992/2371; Local Government Act 1992 (Commencement No 2) Order 1992, SI 1992/3241; Local Government Act 1992 (Commencement No 3) Order 1993, SI 1993/3169; Local Government Act 1992 (Commencement No 4) Order 1994, SI 1994/1445; Local Government Act 1992 (Commencement No 5) Order 1996, SI 1996/1888
Section

1–11	Repealed (*s 8 never in force*)
12	6 Mar 1992 (RA)

Local Government Act 1992 (c 19)—*contd*

Section

13	Substituted (1 Apr 2002) by Local Government Commission for England (Transfer of Functions) Order 2001, SI 2001/3962, art 8, Sch 1, para 1
14, 15	6 Mar 1992 (RA)
15A	Inserted (1 Apr 2002) by Local Government Commission for England (Transfer of Functions) Order 2001, SI 2001/3962, art 8, Sch 1, para 4
16–23	6 Mar 1992 (RA)
24	31 Oct 1992 (SI 1992/2371)
25–30	6 Mar 1992 (RA)

Schedule

1		Repealed
2		6 Mar 1992 (RA)
3		31 Oct 1992 (SI 1992/2371)
4, Pt	I	6 May 1992 (repeal in Local Government Finance Act 1982, s 15(1)) (s 30(2))
		8 Aug 1996 (repeals in Local Government, Planning and Land Act 1980) (SI 1996/1888)
		Not in force (otherwise)
	II	31 Oct 1992 (SI 1992/2371)

Local Government Finance Act 1992 (c 14)

RA: 6 Mar 1992

Commencement provisions: s 119(2); Local Government Finance Act 1992 (Commencement No 1) Order 1992, SI 1992/473; Local Government Finance Act 1992 (Commencement No 2) Order 1992, SI 1992/818; Local Government Finance Act 1992 (Commencement No 3) Order 1992, SI 1992/1460; Local Government Finance Act 1992 (Commencement No 4) Order 1992, SI 1992/1755; Local Government Finance Act 1992 (Commencement No 5 and Transitional Provisions) Order 1992, SI 1992/2183; Local Government Finance Act 1992 (Commencement No 6 and Transitional Provisions) Order 1992, SI 1992/2454, as amended by SI 1993/194; Local Government Finance Act 1992 (Commencement No 7 and Amendment) Order 1993, SI 1993/194 (amending SI 1992/2454); Local Government Finance Act 1992 (Commencement No 8 and Transitional Provisions) Order 1993, SI 1993/575; Local Government Finance Act 1992 (Commencement No 9 and Transitional Provision) Order 1994, SI 1994/3152; Local Government Finance Act 1992 (Commencement No 10) Order 1996, SI 1996/918

Section

1–22	6 Mar 1992 (RA)
22A	Inserted by Local Government (Wales) Act 1994, s 36 (qv)

Local Government Finance Act 1992 (c 14)—*contd*

Section

23–52			6 Mar 1992 (RA)
52A–52Z			Inserted by Local Government Act 1999, s 30, Sch 1, para 1 (qv)
53–64			Repealed
65–94			6 Mar 1992 (RA)
94A			Inserted (S) by Local Government etc (Scotland) Act 1994, s 24 (qv)
95			Repealed
96–98			6 Mar 1992 (RA)
99	(1)		6 Mar 1992 (RA)
	(2)		1 Apr 1993 (SI 1993/575)
	(3)		6 Mar 1992 (RA)
100–103			6 Mar 1992 (RA)
104			See Sch 10 below
105, 106			6 Mar 1992 (RA)
107			See Sch 11 below
108			6 Mar 1992 (RA)
108A			Inserted (S) by Local Government etc (Scotland) Act 1994, s 167 (qv)
109			6 Mar 1992
110	(1)		1 Oct 1992 (subject to transitional provisions in relation to any financial year beginning before 1 Apr 1993) (SI 1992/2183)
	(2), (3)		31 Mar 1995 (subject to a saving) (SI 1994/3152)
	(4)		1 Oct 1992 (subject to transitional provisions in relation to any financial year beginning before 1 Apr 1993) (SI 1992/2183)
111			1 Apr 1993 (SI 1993/575)
112–116			6 Mar 1992 (RA)
117	(1)		See Sch 13 below
	(2)		See Sch 14 below
118, 119			6 Mar 1992 (RA)

Schedule

1–9			6 Mar 1992 (RA)
10, para	1		18 Jun 1992 (SI 1992/1460)
	2		7 Mar 1992 (SI 1992/473)
	3		1 Apr 1992 (SI 1992/473)
	4		7 Mar 1992 (so far as enables provision to be made by regulations) (SI 1992/473) 1 Apr 1992 (otherwise) (SI 1992/473)
	5–24		6 Mar 1992 (RA)
11, para	1–27		Repealed
	28		6 Mar 1992 (RA)
	29	(a)	1 Apr 1993 (SI 1993/575)
		(b)	6 Mar 1992 (RA)

Local Government Finance Act 1992 (c 14)—*contd*

Schedule

11, para	30		1 Apr 1993 (SI 1993/575)
	31	(a)	Repealed
		(b)	1 Oct 1992 (subject to transitional provisions in relation to any financial year beginning before 1 Apr 1993) (SI 1992/2183)
	32–34		Repealed
	35		1 Apr 1993 (SI 1993/575)
	36, 37		Repealed
	38	(a)–(c)	Repealed
		(d)	6 Mar 1992 (RA)
		(e)	Repealed
		(f)	6 Mar 1992 (RA)
12			6 Mar 1992 (RA)
13, para	1		1 Apr 1993 (SI 1993/194)
	2		1 Apr 1993 (SI 1993/575)
	3–5		1 Apr 1993 (SI 1992/2454)
	6–8		2 Nov 1992 (SI 1992/2454)
	9		1 Apr 1993 (SI 1993/575)
	10, 11		1 Apr 1992 (SI 1992/818)
	12–14		2 Nov 1992 (SI 1992/2454)
	15–25		6 Mar 1992 (RA)
	26		2 Nov 1992 (SI 1992/2454)
	27, 28		1 Apr 1993 (SI 1993/194)
	29		Repealed
	30		2 Nov 1992 (SI 1992/2454)
	31		Repealed
	32		1 Feb 1993 (SI 1993/194, amending SI 1992/2454); prospectively repealed by Local Government Act 2000, s 107, Sch 6[5]
	33		*Not in force*
	34		1 Apr 1993 (SI 1992/2454)
	35		1 Apr 1993 (SI 1993/575); prospectively repealed (S) by Ethical Standards in Public Life etc (Scotland) Act 2000 (asp 7), s 36, Sch 4[4]
	36		1 Oct 1992 (subject to transitional provisions in relation to any financial year beginning before 1 Apr 1993) (SI 1992/2183)
	37		Repealed
	38		1 Oct 1992 (so far as relates to Local Government (Scotland) Act 1973, s 110A) (subject to transitional provisions in relation to any financial year beginning before 1 Apr 1993) (SI 1992/2183)

Local Government Finance Act 1992 (c 14)—*contd*

Schedule

13, para	38—*contd*		1 Apr 1993 (otherwise) (SI 1993/575)
	39		1 Apr 1996 (SI 1996/918)
	40		1 Apr 1993 (SI 1993/575)
	41		1 Apr 1992 (SI 1992/818)
	42		6 Mar 1992 (RA)
	43		1 Oct 1992 (subject to transitional provisions in relation to any financial year beginning before 1 Apr 1993) (SI 1992/2183)
	44	(a), (b)	Repealed
		(c)	6 Mar 1992 (RA)
		(d)	Repealed
	45–47		6 Mar 1992 (RA)
	48		Repealed
	49		1 Oct 1992 (subject to transitional provisions in relation to any financial year beginning before 1 Apr 1993) (SI 1992/2183)
	50–52		2 Nov 1992 (SI 1992/2454)
	53–56		1 Apr 1993 (SI 1993/575)
	57		1 Apr 1993 (SI 1992/2454)
	58		Repealed
	59–74		6 Mar 1992 (RA)
	75		Repealed
	76–88		6 Mar 1992 (RA)
	89		1 Apr 1992 (SI 1992/818)
	90, 91		2 Nov 1992 (SI 1992/2454)
	92		6 Mar 1992 (RA)
	93		Repealed
	94		1 Apr 1993 (SI 1993/194); repealed, except for certain purposes by Social Security Act 1998, s 86(2), Sch 8[3]
	95		1 Aug 1992 (subject to transitional provisions in relation to any financial year beginning before 1 Apr 1993) (SI 1992/1755); prospectively repealed by Environment Act 1995, s 120(3), Sch 24[1]
	96–98		1 Aug 1992 (subject to transitional provisions in relation to any financial year beginning before 1 Apr 1993) (SI 1992/1755)
	99, 100		6 Mar 1992 (RA)
14[2]			6 Mar 1992 (repeals of or in Local Government Finance Act 1988 (except Sch 12); Social Security Contributions and Benefits Act 1992; Social Security Administration Act 1992) (RA)

Local Government Finance Act 1992 (c 14)—*contd*
Schedule
14²—*contd*

1 Apr 1992 (repeals of or in Local
Government (Financial Provisions)
(Scotland) Act 1963, s 10; Local
Government (Scotland) Act 1975,
s 37(1); Local Government,
Planning and Land Act 1980, s 46;
Abolition of Domestic Rates etc
(Scotland) Act 1987, Sch 1, para 19;
Local Government Finance
Act 1988, Sch 12, para 5; Local
Government and Housing Act 1989,
Sch 6, para 8) (SI 1992/818)

1 Aug 1992 (repeals of or in Local
Government and Housing
Act 1989, Sch 5, para 30(4); Water
Resources Act 1991, ss 11, 135,
136 (subject to transitional
provisions)) (SI 1992/1755)

1 Oct 1992 (repeals of or in Local
Government (Scotland) Act 1973,
s 110A; Abolition of Domestic
Rates Etc (Scotland) Act 1987,
ss 3A, 9, 10(7A), 11B, 28, Sch 2,
paras 1(2), 2(1), Sch 5, paras 2–5,
9, 10, 14, 15, 17–19, 21, 25; Local
Government Finance Act 1988,
Sch 12, paras 10, 13) (subject to
transitional provisions in relation to
any financial year beginning before
1 Apr 1993)) (SI 1992/2183)

1 Apr 1993 (repeals of or in
Education Reform Act 1988,
s 81(8A); Local Government and
Housing Act 1989, s 146 (subject
to transitional provisions), Sch 5,
paras 2–18, 43, 49–54, 55(3), 56,
58, 59, 61, 63–65, 70, 71, 73, 74,
76(3), 77, 78, Sch 11, para 98;
Community Charges (Substitute
Setting) Act 1991) (SI 1992/2454)

1 Apr 1993 (repeal of Local
Government Finance and
Valuation Act 1991) (SI 1993/194)

1 Apr 1993 (repeals of or in
Registration of Births, Deaths and
Marriages (Scotland) Act 1965,
s 28B; Local Government (Scotland)
Act 1966, Sch 1, Pt I, para 2A;
Local Government (Scotland)

Local Government Finance Act 1992 (c 14)—*contd*
Schedule
14[2]—*contd*

Act 1973, ss 110, 118(1)(b); Local Government (Scotland) Act 1975, Sch 3, para 31; Water (Scotland) Act 1980, ss 41(2), (2A), 54(3)(b), 109(1); Debtors (Scotland) Act 1987, s 106; Abolition of Domestic Rates Etc (Scotland) Act 1987, ss 1–7, 14, 18(2A), 20(10), 25(1), (3), 26(1), (2), 27, 33, Sch 1, Sch 3, paras 1–4, 5(1), 7, Sch 5, paras 1, 6, 12, 13, 16, 19A, 20, 22–24, 26–49; Local Government Finance Act 1988, Sch 12, paras 8, 15, 17, 23, 27; Local Government and Housing Act 1989, ss 140, 141, Sch 6, paras 20, 21; Environmental Protection Act 1990, Sch 15, para 1; Caravans (Standard Community Charge and Rating) Act 1991, s 2) (subject to transitional provisions) (SI 1993/575)

1 Apr 1996 (repeals of Local Government (Scotland) Act 1973, s 111(1)(a), (b), (d); Water (Scotland) Act 1980, s 9(6)) (SI 1996/918)

Not in force (otherwise)

[1]   Orders made under Environment Act 1995, s 125(3), bringing the prospective repeal into force will be noted to that Act

[2]   For savings in relation to the repeals of the Abolition of Domestic Rates (Scotland) Act 1987, Sch 2, para 7A, and the Local Government Finance Act 1988, Sch 4, para 6, see the Local Government Finance Act 1992 (Recovery of Community Charge) Saving Order 1993, SI 1993/1780

[3]   For those purposes, see SI 1999/3178

[4]   Orders made under Ethical Standards in Public Life etc (Scotland) Act 2000, s 37(2), bringing the prospective repeals into force will be noted to that Act

[5]   Orders made under Local Government Act 2000, s 108, bringing the prospective repeal into force will be noted to that Act

---

Maintenance Orders (Reciprocal Enforcement) Act 1992 (c 56)

RA: 12 Nov 1992

Commencement provisions: s 3; Maintenance Orders (Reciprocal Enforcement) Act 1992 (Commencement) Order 1993, SI 1993/618

5 Apr 1993 (SI 1993/618)

Mauritius Republic Act 1992 (c 45)

RA: 18 Jun 1992

18 Jun 1992 (RA; but note that s 1 deemed to have come into force on 12 Mar 1992
(s 1(4))

Medicinal Products: Prescription by Nurses etc Act 1992 (c 28)

RA: 16 Mar 1992

Commencement provisions: s 6(2); Medicinal Products: Prescription by Nurses etc
Act 1992 (Commencement No 1) Order 1994, SI 1994/2408; Medicinal
Products: Prescription by Nurses etc Act 1992 (Commencement No 2)
Order 1996, SI 1996/1505

Section	
1	3 Oct 1994 (SI 1994/2408)
2	3 Oct 1994 (SI 1994/2408); prospectively repealed by Health and Social Care Act 2001, s 67, Sch 6, Pt 2[1]
3	1 Jul 1996 (SI 1996/1505)
4–6	16 Mar 1992 (RA)

[1]   Orders made under Health and Social Care Act 2001, s 70(2), bringing the prospective repeal into
     force will be noted to that Act

Museums and Galleries Act 1992 (c 44)

RA: 16 Mar 1992

Commencement provisions: s 11(4); Museums and Galleries Act 1992 (Commencement)
Order 1992, SI 1992/1874

Section			
1–8			1 Sep 1992 (SI 1992/1874)
9			1 Apr 1993 (SI 1992/1874)
10, 11			1 Sep 1992 (SI 1992/1874)
Schedule			
1–7			1 Sep 1992 (SI 1992/1874)
8, para	1	(1)–(6)	1 Sep 1992 (SI 1992/1874)
		(7)	Repealed
		(8), (9)	1 Sep 1992 (SI 1992/1874)
	2		Repealed
	3		1 Sep 1992 (SI 1992/1874)
	4		Repealed
	5–9		1 Sep 1992 (SI 1992/1874)
	10		Repealed
	11–14		1 Sep 1992 (SI 1992/1874)
9			1 Sep 1992 (except repeal of Charities Act 1960, Sch 2, paras (da)–(dd)[1]) (SI 1992/1874)

[1]   Entry relating to Charities Act 1960, Sch 2, paras (da)–(dd) (never in force) now repealed by
     Charities Act 1993, s 98(2), Sch 7

Non-Domestic Rating Act 1992 (c 46)

RA: 18 Jun 1992

Commencement provisions: s 10(2); Non-Domestic Rating Act 1992 (Commencement No 1) Order 1992, SI 1992/1486; Non-Domestic Rating Act 1992 (Commencement No 2) Order 1992, SI 1992/1642

Section

1–4		16 Jul 1992 (SI 1992/1642)
5	(1)	16 Jul 1992 (SI 1992/1642)
	(2)	23 Jun 1992 (SI 1992/1486)
6		16 Jul 1992 (SI 1992/1642)
7		23 Jun 1992 (SI 1992/1486)
8		16 Jul 1992 (SI 1992/1642)
9		23 Jun 1992 (SI 1992/1486)
10		18 Jun 1992 (RA)

Nurses, Midwives and Health Visitors Act 1992 (c 16)

Whole Act repealed

Offshore Safety Act 1992 (c 15)

RA: 6 Mar 1992

Commencement provisions: s 7(3); Offshore Safety Act 1992 (Commencement No 1) Order 1993, SI 1993/2406; Offshore Safety Act 1992 (Commencement No 2) Order 1996, SI 1996/487

Section

1			6 Mar 1992 (RA)
2	(1), (2)		6 Mar 1992 (RA)
	(3)	(a)	6 Mar 1992 (RA)
		(b)	Repealed
		(c)	1 Mar 1996 (SI 1996/487)
	(4)		6 Mar 1992 (RA)
3	(1)	(a)	30 Nov 1993 (SI 1993/2406)
		(b)	6 Mar 1992 (RA)
		(c), (d)	Repealed
		(e)	30 Nov 1993 (SI 1993/2406)
	(2)		30 Nov 1993 (SI 1993/2406)
	(3)	(a)	6 Mar 1992 (RA)
		(b)	1 Mar 1996 (SI 1996/487)
		(c), (d)	6 Mar 1992 (RA)
	(4)		6 Mar 1992 (RA)
4–6			6 Mar 1992 (RA)
7	(1)		6 Mar 1992 (RA)
	(2)		See Sch 2 below
	(3), (4)		6 Mar 1992 (RA)

Schedule

1	30 Nov 1993 (SI 1993/2406)
2	6 Mar 1992 (except repeals in Continental Shelf Act 1964; Gas Act 1986, s 47(5)) (RA)

Offshore Safety Act 1992 (c 15)—*contd*
Schedule
2—*contd*   30 Nov 1993 (repeal in Continental
                                          Shelf Act 1964) (SI 1993/2406)
                                        1 Mar 1996 (repeal, for certain
                                          purposes, of Gas Act 1986, s 47(5))
                                          (SI 1996/487)

Offshore Safety (Protection Against Victimisation) Act 1992 (c 24)

Whole Act repealed

Parliamentary Corporate Bodies Act 1992 (c 27)

RA: 16 Mar 1992

16 Mar 1992 (RA)

Prison Security Act 1992 (c 25)

RA: 16 Mar 1992

Commencement provisions: s 3(2)

16 May 1992 (s 3(2))

Protection of Badgers Act 1992 (c 51)

RA: 16 Jul 1992

Commencement provisions: s 15(3)

16 Oct 1992 (s 15(3))

Sea Fish (Conservation) Act 1992 (c 60)

RA: 17 Dec 1992

Commencement provisions: s 11(1), (2)
Section
1   (1)   17 Dec 1992 (RA)
               (2)   17 Jan 1993 (except in relation to
                                          vessels of an overall length of 10
                                          metres or less until such day as may
                                          be appointed) (s 11(1), (2))
                                        Not in force (exception noted above)
               (3)   17 Dec 1992 (RA)
               (4), (5)   17 Jan 1993 (s 11(1))
2   17 Dec 1992 (RA)
3   17 Jan 1993 (s 11(1))
4   17 Dec 1992 (RA)
5   17 Jan 1993 (s 11(1))
6–13   17 Dec 1992 (RA)

Sea Fisheries (Wildlife Conservation) Act 1992 (c 36)

RA: 16 Mar 1992

Commencement provisions: s 2(2)

16 May 1992 (s 2(2))

Severn Bridges Act 1992 (c 3)

Local application only

Sexual Offences (Amendment) Act 1992 (c 34)

RA: 16 Mar 1992

Commencement provisions: s 8(3)–(5); Sexual Offences (Amendment) Act 1992 (Commencement) Order 1992, SI 1992/1336

Section	
1–7	1 Aug 1992 (SI 1992/1336)
8	16 Mar 1992 (s 8(3))

Social Security Administration Act 1992 (c 5)

RA: 13 Feb 1992

Commencement provisions: s 192(4)

1 Jul 1992 (s 192(4); but note transitory modifications in Social Security (Consequential Provisions) Act 1992, Sch 4)

Social Security Administration (Northern Ireland) Act 1992 (c 8)

RA: 13 Feb 1992

Commencement provisions: s 168(4)

1 Jul 1992 (s 168(4); but note transitory modifications in Social Security (Consequential Provisions) (Northern Ireland) Act 1992, Sch 4)

Social Security (Consequential Provisions) Act 1992 (c 6)

RA: 13 Feb 1992

Commencement provisions: s 7(2), Sch 4, para 1(3); Social Security (Consequential Provisions) Act 1992 Appointed Day Order 1993, SI 1993/1025[1]

1 Jul 1992 (s 7(2))

[1] This order appointed 19 Apr 1993 as the appointed day in respect of Sch 4, paras 8, 9

Social Security (Consequential Provisions) (Northern Ireland) Act 1992 (c 9)

RA: 13 Feb 1992

Commencement provisions: s 7(2)

1 Jul 1992 (s 7(2))

Social Security Contributions and Benefits Act 1992 (c 4)

RA: 13 Feb 1992

Commencement provisions: s 177(4)

1 Jul 1992 (s 177(4); but note transitory modifications in Social Security (Consequential Provisions) Act 1992, Sch 4; those transitory modifications partially ceased to have effect on 19 Apr 1993 (SI 1993/1025) so that, on that day, Sch 2, para 6(2) to this Act came into force)

Social Security Contributions and Benefits (Northern Ireland) Act 1992 (c 7)

RA: 13 Feb 1992

Commencement provisions: s 173(4)

1 Jul 1992 (s 173(4); but note transitory modifications in Social Security (Consequential Provisions) (Northern Ireland) Act 1992, Sch 4)

Social Security (Mortgage Interest Payments) Act 1992 (c 33)

RA: 16 Mar 1992

16 Mar 1992 (RA; but note that s 1(1) ceased to have effect on 1 Jul 1992, by virtue of s 1(2))

Sporting Events (Control of Alcohol etc) (Amendment) Act 1992 (c 57)

RA: 3 Dec 1992

3 Dec 1992 (RA)

Stamp Duty (Temporary Provisions) Act 1992 (c 2)

RA: 13 Feb 1992

Whole Act repealed by Finance Act 1999, s 139, Sch 20, Pt V(2), in relation to instruments executed, or bearer instruments issued, on or after 1 Oct 1999, subject to savings

Commencement provisions: s 1(4)
Section
1	16 Jan 1992 (s 1(4))
2, 3	13 Feb 1992 (RA)

Still-Birth (Definition) Act 1992 (c 29)

RA: 16 Mar 1992

Commencement provisions: s 4(2)
Section
1, 2	1 Oct 1992 (s 4(2))
3	16 Mar 1992 (RA)
4	1 Oct 1992 (s 4(2))

Taxation of Chargeable Gains Act 1992 (c 12)

RA: 6 Mar 1992

Commencement provisions: s 289

Except where the context otherwise requires, this Act has effect in relation to tax for the year 1992–93 and subsequent years of assessment, and tax for the accounting periods of companies beginning on or after 6 Apr 1992 (s 289)

Timeshare Act 1992 (c 35)

RA: 16 Mar 1992

Commencement provisions: s 13(2); Timeshare Act 1992 (Commencement) Order 1992, SI 1992/1941

12 Oct 1992 (SI 1992/1941)

Tourism (Overseas Promotion) (Wales) Act 1992 (c 26)

RA: 16 Mar 1992

Commencement provisions: s 3

16 May 1992 (s 3)

Trade Union and Labour Relations (Consolidation) Act 1992 (c 52)

RA: 16 Jul 1992

Commencement provisions: s 302

16 Oct 1992 (s 302)

Traffic Calming Act 1992 (c 30)

RA: 16 Mar 1992

Commencement provisions: s 3

16 May 1992 (s 3)

Transport and Works Act 1992 (c 42)

RA: 16 Mar 1992

Commencement provisions: s 70; Transport and Works Act 1992 (Commencement No 1) Order 1992, SI 1992/1347; Transport and Works Act 1992 (Commencement No 2) Order 1992, SI 1992/2043; Transport and Works Act 1992 (Commencement No 3 and Transitional Provisions) Order 1992, SI 1992/2784; Transport and Works Act 1992 (Commencement No 4) Order 1992, SI 1992/3144; Transport and Works Act 1992 (Commencement No 5 and Transitional Provisions) Order 1994, SI 1994/718; Transport and Works Act 1992 (Commencement No 6) Order 1996, SI 1996/1609; Transport and Works Act 1992 (Commencement No 7) Order 1998, SI 1998/274

Transport and Works Act 1992 (c 42)—*contd*

Section

1–6			1 Jan 1993 (SI 1992/2784)
6A			Inserted by Transport and Works (Assessment of Environmental Effects) Regulations 1998, SI 1998/2226, regs 1(2), 3
7–25			1 Jan 1993 (SI 1992/2784)
26–40			7 Dec 1992 (SI 1992/2043)
41			31 Jan 1993 (SI 1992/3144)
42–44			Repealed
45, 46			15 Jul 1992 (SI 1992/1347)
47	(1)		See Sch 2 below
	(2)		31 Jan 1993 (SI 1992/3144)
48			31 Jan 1993 (SI 1992/3144)
49			15 Jul 1992 (SI 1992/1347)
50			8 Jul 1996 (SI 1996/1609)
51			31 Jan 1993 (SI 1992/3144)
52–56			8 Jul 1996 (SI 1996/1609)
57–60			15 Jul 1992 (SI 1992/1347)
61			31 Jan 1993 (SI 1992/3144)
62			8 Jul 1996 (SI 1996/1609)
63			15 Jul 1992 (subject to transitional provisions with respect to certain Harbour Revision Orders and Harbour Empowerment Orders) (SI 1992/1347)
64			31 Jan 1993 (SI 1992/3144)
65	(1)	(a)	15 Jul 1992 (SI 1992/1347)
		(b)	1 Jan 1993 (except words "in section 25, the words 'and shall not be opened' onwards,"; and "section 48,") (SI 1992/2784)
			5 Apr 1994 (words "in section 25, the words 'and shall not be opened' onwards,") (subject to transitional provisions) (SI 1994/718)
			8 Jul 1996 (words "section 48,") (SI 1996/1609)
		(c), (d)	1 Jan 1993 (SI 1992/2784)
		(e)	15 Jul 1992 (SI 1992/1347)
		(f)	1 Jan 1993 (SI 1992/2784)
	(2)		15 Jul 1992 (SI 1992/1347)
66, 67			15 Jul 1992 (SI 1992/1347)
68	(1)		See Sch 4 below
	(2)		*Not in force*
69			15 Jul 1992 (SI 1992/1347)
70–72			16 Mar 1992 (s 70)
Schedule			
1			1 Jan 1993 (SI 1992/2784)

Transport and Works Act 1992 (c 42)—*contd*
Schedule

2	22 Dec 1992 (for purpose of conferring on Secretary of State power to make regulation in relation to rail crossing extinguishment orders or rail crossing diversion orders) (SI 1992/3144)
	31 Jan 1993 (otherwise) (SI 1992/3144)
3	15 Jul 1992 (subject to transitional provisions with respect to certain Harbour Revision Orders and Harbour Empowerment Orders) (SI 1992/1347)
4, Pt I	15 Jul 1992 (repeals of or in British Railways Act 1965; London Transport Act 1965; Criminal Justice Act 1967; London Transport Act 1977; British Railways Act 1977) (subject to transitional provisions with respect to certain Harbour Revision Orders and Harbour Empowerment Orders) (SI 1992/1347)
	7 Dec 1992 (repeal in Railway Regulation Act 1842) (SI 1992/2043)
	1 Jan 1993 (repeals of or in Tramways Act 1870 (except words 'and shall not be opened' onwards in s 25, and s 48); Municipal Corporations Act 1882; Military Tramways Act 1887; Light Railways Act 1896; Railways (Electrical Power) Act 1903; Light Railways Act 1912; Railways Act 1921; Transport Act 1962; Administration of Justice Act 1965; Transport Act 1968 (expect ss 124, 125(4)); Local Government Act 1972; Supply Powers Act 1975; Administration of Justice Act 1982; Telecommunications Act 1984; Roads (Scotland) Act 1984; Insolvency Act 1986) (subject to transitional provisions) (SI 1992/2784)
	31 Jan 1993 (repeals of or in Regulation of Railways Act 1871, s 3; Highways Act 1980) (SI 1992/3144)

Transport and Works Act 1992 (c 42)—*contd*

Schedule

4, Pt	I—*contd*	5 Apr 1994 (repeals of Tramways Act 1870, s 25 (words "and shall not be opened" onwards); Road and Rail Traffic Act 1933, s 41; Transport Act 1968, s 125(4)) (subject to transitional provisions) (SI 1994/718)
		8 Jul 1996 (repeals of Tramways Act 1870, s 48; Transport Act 1968, s 124, subject to a saving) (SI 1996/1609)
		26 Feb 1998 (repeals of or in Town Police Clauses Act 1889; Notice of Accidents Act 1894; Notice of Accidents Act 1906; Road and Rail Traffic Act 1933, s 43; Transport Charges &c (Miscellaneous Provisions) Act 1954; Public Service Vehicles (Arrest of Offenders) Act 1975; Channel Tunnel Act 1987) (SI 1998/274)
		Not in force (otherwise)
	II	15 Jul 1992 (subject to transitional provisions with respect to certain Harbour Revision Orders and Harbour Empowerment Orders) (SI 1992/1347)

Tribunals and Inquiries Act 1992 (c 53)

RA: 16 Jul 1992

Commencement provisions: s 19(2)

1 Oct 1992 (s 19(2))

1993

Agriculture Act 1993 (c 37)

RA: 27 Jul 1993

Commencement provisions: ss 1(2)–(4), 21(2), (3), 26(2)–(4), 54(2), 55(3), 65(2), (3); Agriculture Act 1993 (Commencement No 1) Order 1993, SI 1993/2038; Potato Marketing Scheme (Commencement of Revocation Period) Order 1996, SI 1996/336

Section

1	(1)	1 Nov 1994 (SI 1994/2921)
	(2)–(5)	27 Jul 1993 (RA)
2–11		27 Jul 1993 (RA)
12		See Sch 2 below
13–20		27 Jul 1993 (RA)
21	(1)	Day on which s 1(1) comes into force completely (ie 1 Nov 1994) (s 21(2), (3), SI 1994/2922)
	(2), (3)	27 Jul 1993 (RA)
22–25		27 Jul 1993 (RA)
26	(1)	1 Jul 1996 (SI 1996/336)
	(2)–(5)	27 Jul 1993 (RA)
27–35		27 Jul 1993 (RA)
36		See Sch 4 below
37–49		27 Jul 1993 (RA)
50–53		27 Sep 1993 (s 65(2))
54		27 Jul 1993 (RA)
55		4 Aug 1993 (SI 1993/2038)
56–58		27 Jul 1993 (RA)
59		4 Aug 1993 (SI 1993/2038)
60–65		27 Jul 1993 (RA)

Schedule

1–4	27 Jul 1993 (RA)
5	27 Jul 1993 (except so far as repeals relate to potatoes and revocation of Potato Marketing Scheme, para 67) (RA)
	4 Aug 1993 (exceptions noted above) (SI 1993/2038)

Appropriation Act 1993 (c 33)

Whole Act repealed

Asylum and Immigration Appeals Act 1993 (c 23)

RA: 1 Jul 1993

Commencement provisions: s 14; Asylum and Immigration Appeals Act 1993
(Commencement and Transitional Provisions) Order 1993, SI 1993/1655

Section

1	1 Jul 1993 (except so far as relates to ss 4–11) (RA)
	26 Jul 1993 (exception noted above) (SI 1993/1655)
2	1 Jul 1993 (RA)
3–9	Repealed
9A	Inserted by Asylum and Immigration Act 1996, s 12(2), Sch 3, para 3 (qv)
10, 11	Repealed
12	Repealed
13–16	1 Jul 1993 (RA)
Schedule	
1, 2	Repealed

Bail (Amendment) Act 1993 (c 26)

RA: 20 Jul 1993

Commencement provisions: s 2(2); Bail (Amendment) Act 1993 (Commencement)
Order 1994, SI 1994/1437

Section

1	27 Jun 1994 (SI 1994/1437)
2	20 Jul 1993 (s 2(2))

Bankruptcy (Scotland) Act 1993 (c 6)

RA: 18 Feb 1993

Commencement provisions: s 12(3)–(6); Bankruptcy (Scotland) Act 1993 Commencement
and Savings Order 1993, SI 1993/438

Section

1–7			1 Apr 1993 (SI 1993/438)
8, 9			18 Feb 1993 (s 12(3))
10			1 Apr 1993 (SI 1993/438)
11	(1), (2)		1 Apr 1993 (SI 1993/438)
	(3)		See Sch 1 below
	(4)		See Sch 2 below
12			18 Feb 1993 (s 12(3))
Schedule			
1, para	1–21		1 Apr 1993 (SI 1993/438)
	22	(1)–(4)	1 Apr 1993 (SI 1993/438)
		(5)	18 Feb 1993 (s 12(3))
	23		18 Feb 1993 (s 12(3))
	24–30		1 Apr 1993 (SI 1993/438)

Bankruptcy (Scotland) Act 1993 (c 6)—*contd*
Schedule

1, para	31	(1)–(3)	1 Apr 1993 (SI 1993/438)
		(4), (5)	18 Feb 1993 (s 12(3))
	32		1 Apr 1993 (SI 1993/438)
2			1 Apr 1993 (SI 1993/438)

British Coal and British Rail (Transfer Proposals) Act 1993 (c 2)

RA: 19 Jan 1993

19 Jan 1993 (RA); *whole Act prospectively repealed* in relation to British Railways Board by Railways Act 1993, s 152(1), Sch 12, para 32; *whole Act also prospectively repealed* by Coal Industry Act 1994, s 67(8), Sch 11, Pt III. Orders made under those Acts bringing the prospective repeal into force will be noted to those Acts

Cardiff Bay Barrage Act 1993 (c 42)

Local application only

Carrying of Knives etc (Scotland) Act 1993 (c 13)

Whole Act repealed

Charities Act 1993 (c 10)

RA: 27 May 1993

Commencement provisions: s 99; Charities Act 1993 (Commencement and Transitional Provisions) Order 1995, SI 1995/2695
Section

1–4		1 Aug 1993 (s 99(1))
5	(1)	1 Aug 1993 (subject to transitional provisions) (s 99(1), (4))
	(2)	1 Aug 1993 (s 99(1))
	(2A)	Inserted by Welsh Language Act 1993, s 32(3) (qv)
	(3)–(6)	1 Aug 1993 (s 99(1))
6–11		1 Aug 1993 (s 99(1))
12		Repealed
13–40		1 Aug 1993 (s 99(1))
41–49		15 Oct 1995 (for purposes of making orders or regulations) (SI 1995/2695) 1 Mar 1996 (otherwise, subject to a transitional provision) (SI 1995/2695)
50–68		1 Aug 1993 (s 99(1))
69		1 Mar 1996 (SI 1995/2695)
70, 71		Repelaed
72, 73		1 Aug 1993 (s 99(1))

Charities Act 1993 (c 10)—*contd*

Section

74	(1)	(a)	1 Aug 1993 (subject to transitional provisions) (s 99(1), (4))
		(b)	1 Aug 1993 (s 99(1))
	(2)–(12)		1 Aug 1993 (s 99(1))
75	(1)	(a)	1 Aug 1993 (s 99(1))
		(b)	1 Aug 1993 (subject to transitional provisions) (s 99(1), (4))
	(2)–(10)		1 Aug 1993 (s 99(1))
76–97			1 Aug 1993 (s 99(1))
98	(1)		See Sch 6 below
	(2)		See Sch 7 below
99, 100			1 Aug 1993 (s 99(1))

Schedule

1–5			1 Aug 1993 (s 99(1))
6, para	1–4		1 Aug 1993 (s 99(1))
	5		1 Aug 1993 (s 99(1)); repealed by Finance Act 1999, s 139, Sch 20, Pt V(5), in relation to instruments executed on or after 6 Feb 2000
	6–15		1 Aug 1993 (s 99(1))
	16		Repealed
	17–20		1 Aug 1993 (s 99(1))
	21	(1), (2)	1 Aug 1993 (s 99(1))
		(3)	Repealed
		(4), (5)	1 Aug 1993 (s 99(1))
	22–30		1 Aug 1993 (s 99(1))
7			1 Aug 1993 (subject to transitional provisions) (s 99(1)–(3))
8			1 Aug 1993 (s 99(1))

Clean Air Act 1993 (c 11)

RA: 27 May 1993

Commencement provisions: s 68(2)

27 Aug 1993 (s 68(2))

Consolidated Fund Act 1993 (c 4)

Whole Act repealed

Consolidated Fund (No 2) Act 1993 (c 7)

Whole Act repealed

Consolidated Fund (No 3) Act 1993 (c 52)

Whole Act repealed

Criminal Justice Act 1993 (c 36)

RA: 27 Jul 1993

Commencement provisions: s 78; Criminal Justice Act 1993 (Commencement No 1) Order 1993, SI 1993/1968; Criminal Justice Act 1993 (Commencement No 2 Transitional Provisions and Savings) (Scotland) Order 1993, SI 1993/2035; Criminal Justice Act 1993 (Commencement No 3) Order 1993, SI 1993/2734; Criminal Justice Act 1993 (Commencement No 4) Order 1994, SI 1994/71; Criminal Justice Act 1993 (Commencement No 5) Order 1994, SI 1994/242; Criminal Justice Act 1993 (Commencement No 6) Order 1994, SI 1994/700; Criminal Justice Act 1993 (Commencement No 7) Order 1994, SI 1994/1951; Criminal Justice Act 1993 (Commencement No 8) Order 1995, SI 1995/43; Criminal Justice Act 1993 (Commencement No 9) Order 1995, SI 1995/1958; Criminal Justice Act 1993 (Commencement No 10) Order 1999, SI 1999/1189; Criminal Justice Act 1993 (Commencement No 11) Order 1999, SI 1999/1499

Section		
1–4		1 Jun 1999 (SI 1999/1189)
5	(1)	Repealed (*never in force*)
	(2)	1 Jun 1999 (SI 1999/1189)
	(3)–(5)	1 Jun 1999 (SI 1999/1499)
6		1 Jun 1999 (SI 1999/1189)
7–16		Repealed
17		15 Feb 1994 (SI 1994/71)
18		Repealed
19		1 Apr 1994 (SI 1994/700)
20–23		1 Dec 1993 (SI 1993/2734)
24	(1)–(11)	Repealed
	(12)–(15)	3 Feb 1995 (SI 1995/43)
25		Repealed
26		1 Apr 1994 (SI 1994/700)
27, 28		3 Feb 1995 (SI 1995/43)
29–31		15 Feb 1994 (SI 1994/71)
32		1 Apr 1994 (SI 1994/700)
33		15 Feb 1994 (SI 1994/71)
34, 35		1 Dec 1993 (SI 1993/2734)
36–51		Repealed
52–64		1 Mar 1994 (SI 1994/242)
65		20 Sep 1993 (SI 1993/1968)
66		Repealed
67	(1)	16 Aug 1993 (E, W) (SI 1993/1968)
		16 Aug 1993 (S) (subject to savings) (SI 1993/2035)
	(2)	Repealed
68, 69		Repealed
70, 71		27 Sep 1993 (s 78(1))
72		22 Aug 1994 (SI 1994/1951)
73		1 Dec 1993 (SI 1993/2734)
74		15 Feb 1994 (SI 1994/71)
75, 76		27 Jul 1993 (s 78(2))
77		1 Apr 1994 (SI 1994/700)
78		27 Jul 1993 (partly) (RA)

Criminal Justice Act 1993 (c 36)—*contd*

Section

78—*contd*		15 Feb 1994 (otherwise) (SI 1994/71)
79	(1)–(5)	27 Jul 1993 (s 78(2))
	(6)	Repealed
	(7)–(10)	27 Jul 1993 (s 78(2))
	(11)	Repealed
	(12)	27 Jul 1993 (s 78(2))
	(13)	See Sch 5 below
	(14)	See Sch 6 below

Schedule

1, 2		1 Mar 1994 (SI 1994/242)
3		20 Sep 1993 (SI 1993/1968)
4		1 Apr 1994 (SI 1994/700)
5, para	1	14 Aug 1995 (SI 1995/1958)
	2, 3	Repealed
	4	1 Mar 1994 (SI 1994/242)
	5–13	Repealed
	14	15 Feb 1994 (SI 1994/71)
	15	Repealed
	16	1 Mar 1994 (SI 1994/242)
	17	Repealed
6, Pt	I	27 Jul 1993 (repeals in Criminal Procedure (Scotland) Act 1975; Prisoners and Criminal Proceedings (Scotland) Act 1993) (s 78(2))
		20 Sep 1993 (repeals in Magistrates' Courts Act 1980; Criminal Justice Act 1991) (SI 1993/1968)
		15 Feb 1994 (repeals of or in Drug Trafficking Offences Act 1986, ss 1(5)(b)(iii), 27(5); Criminal Justice Act 1988, ss 48 (E, W only), 98; Prevention of Terrorism (Temporary Provisions) Act 1989; Criminal Justice (International Co-operation) Act 1990; Northern Ireland (Emergency Provisions) Act 1991, ss 50(2), 67(6)) (SI 1994/71)
		1 Mar 1994 (repeals of or in Company Securities (Insider Dealing) Act 1985; Financial Services Act 1986; Banking Act 1987; Criminal Justice Act 1987; Companies Act 1989) (SI 1994/242)

Criminal Justice Act 1993 (c 36)—*contd*
Schedule
6, Pt   I—*contd*   3 Feb 1995 (repeals of or in Northern
                                                 Ireland (Emergency Provisions)
                                                 Act 1991, ss 48(3), 51(3))
                                                 (SI 1995/43)
                                                 Not in force (otherwise)
                II   1 Mar 1994 (SI 1994/242)

Crofters (Scotland) Act 1993 (c 44)

RA: 5 Nov 1993

Commencement provisions: ss 28(17), 64(2)
Section
1–27   5 Jan 1994 (s 64(2))
28   *Not in force*
29–64   5 Jan 1994 (s 64(2))
Schedule
1–7   5 Jan 1994 (s 64(2))

Damages (Scotland) Act 1993 (c 5)

RA: 18 Feb 1993

Commencement provisions: s 8(3)

18 Apr 1993 (s 8(3))

Disability (Grants) Act 1993 (c 14)

RA: 27 May 1993

27 May 1993 (RA)

Education Act 1993 (c 35)

Whole Act repealed

European Communities (Amendment) Act 1993 (c 32)

RA: 20 Jul 1993

Commencement provisions: s 7

23 Jul 1993 (s 7)

European Economic Area Act 1993 (c 51)

RA: 5 Nov 1993

5 Nov 1993 (RA)

European Parliamentary Elections Act 1993 (c 41)

RA: 5 Nov 1993

Commencement provisions: s 3(3); European Parliamentary Elections Act 1993 (Commencement) Order 1994, SI 1994/1089

Section
1, 2	Repealed, subject to a saving
3	5 Nov 1993 (RA)

Schedule	Repealed

Finance Act 1993 (c 34)

Budget Day: 16 Mar 1993

RA: 27 Jul 1993

Details of the commencement of Finance Acts are not set out in this work

Foreign Compensation (Amendment) Act 1993 (c 16)

RA: 27 May 1993

Commencement provisions: s 3(1)

27 Jul 1993 (s 3(1))

Gas (Exempt Supplies) Act 1993 (c 1)

RA: 19 Jan 1993

Commencement provisions: s 4(2); Gas (Exempt Supplies) Act 1993 (Commencement) Order 1994, SI 1994/2568

31 Oct 1994 (SI 1994/2568)

Health Service Commissioners Act 1993 (c 46)

RA: 5 Nov 1993

Commencement provisions: s 22(4)

5 Feb 1994 (s 22(4))

Incumbents (Vacation of Benefices) (Amendment) Measure 1993 (No 1)

RA: 27 Jul 1993

Commencement provisions: s 16(2)

The provisions of this Measure are brought into force on 1 Sep 1994 by an appointed day notice signed by the Archbishops of Canterbury and York and dated 25 Jul 1994 (made under s 16(2))

Judicial Pensions and Retirement Act 1993 (c 8)

RA: 29 Mar 1993

Commencement provisions: s 31(2); Judicial Pensions and Retirement Act 1993 (Commencement) Order 1995, SI 1995/631

31 Mar 1995 (SI 1995/631)

Leasehold Reform, Housing and Urban Development Act 1993 (c 28)

RA: 20 Jul 1993

Commencement provisions: ss 138(2), 188(2), (3); Leasehold Reform, Housing and Urban Development Act 1993 (Commencement and Transitional Provisions No 1) Order 1993, SI 1993/2134; Leasehold Reform, Housing and Urban Development Act 1993 (Commencement No 2) (Scotland) Order 1993, SI 1993/2163; Leasehold Reform, Housing and Urban Development Act 1993 (Commencement and Transitional Provisions No 3) Order 1993, SI 1993/2762; Leasehold Reform, Housing and Urban Development Act 1993 (Commencement No 4) Order 1994, SI 1994/935

Section		
1–8		1 Nov 1993 (SI 1993/2134)
8A		Inserted by Housing Act 1996, s 106, Sch 9, para 3(1), (3) (qv)
9–25		1 Nov 1993 (SI 1993/2134)
26	(1)–(3)	1 Nov 1993 (SI 1993/2134)
	(3A)	Inserted by Housing Act 1996, s 107(4), Sch 10, paras 1, 9 (qv)
	(4)–(8)	1 Nov 1993 (SI 1993/2134)
	(9)	2 Sep 1993 (SI 1993/2134)
27–37		1 Nov 1993 (SI 1993/2134)
37A, 37B		Inserted by Housing Act 1996, s 116, Sch 11, para 2(1) (qv)
38–58		1 Nov 1993 (SI 1993/2134)
58A		Inserted by Housing Act 1996, s 117 (qv)
59–61		1 Nov 1993 (SI 1993/2134)
61A, 61B		Inserted by Housing Act 1996, s 116, Sch 11, para 3(1) (qv)
62–66		1 Nov 1993 (SI 1993/2134)
67, 68		1 Nov 1993 (subject to savings) (SI 1993/2134)
69–74		1 Nov 1993 (SI 1993/2134)
75		2 Sep 1993 (so far as confers on Secretary of State a power to make orders, regulations or declarations) (SI 1993/2134)
		1 Nov 1993 (otherwise) (SI 1993/2134)
76–84		1 Nov 1993 (SI 1993/2134)
85, 86		1 Nov 1993 (subject to savings) (SI 1993/2134)

Leasehold Reform, Housing and Urban Development Act 1993 (c 28)—*contd*

Section

87	1 Nov 1993 (SI 1993/2134)
88	2 Sep 1993 (so far as confers on Secretary of State a power to make orders, regulations or declarations) (SI 1993/2134)
	1 Nov 1993 (otherwise) (SI 1993/2134)
89, 90	1 Nov 1993 (SI 1993/2134)
91	2 Sep 1993 (so far as confers on Secretary of State a power to make orders, regulations or declarations) (SI 1993/2134)
	1 Nov 1993 (otherwise) (SI 1993/2134)
92, 93	1 Nov 1993 (SI 1993/2134)
93A	Inserted by Housing Act 1996, s 113 (qv)
94–97	1 Nov 1993 (SI 1993/2134)
98	2 Sep 1993 (SI 1993/2134)
99	2 Sep 1993 (so far as confers on Secretary of State a power to make orders, regulations or declarations) (SI 1993/2134)
	1 Nov 1993 (otherwise) (SI 1993/2134)
100	2 Sep 1993 (SI 1993/2134)
101–103	1 Nov 1993 (SI 1993/2134)
104–107	11 Oct 1993 (subject to savings) (SI 1993/2134)
108	2 Sep 1993 (so far as confers on Secretary of State a power to make orders, regulations or declarations) (SI 1993/2134)
	11 Oct 1993 (otherwise) (subject to savings) (SI 1993/2134)
109–120	11 Oct 1993 (subject to savings) (SI 1993/2134)
121	1 Dec 1993 (subject to transitional provisions) (SI 1993/2762)
122	1 Feb 1994 (subject to transitional provisions) (SI 1993/2762)
123	11 Oct 1993 (SI 1993/2134)
124, 125	11 Oct 1993 (subject to savings) (SI 1993/2134)
126, 127	20 Jul 1993 (RA)
128, 129	11 Oct 1993 (SI 1993/2134)
130, 131	Repealed
132	10 Nov 1993 (so far as confers on the Secretary of State a power to make regulations) (SI 1993/2762)
	1 Apr 1994 (otherwise) (SI 1994/935)

Leasehold Reform, Housing and Urban Development Act 1993 (c 28)—*contd*

Section

133		11 Oct 1993 (subject to savings) (SI 1993/2134)
134		Repealed
135–137		20 Jul 1993 (RA)
138		1 Jan 1993 (s 138(2))
139, 140		20 Jul 1993 (RA)
141–143		27 Sep 1993 (SI 1993/2163); prospectively repealed by Housing (Scotland) Act 2001, s 112, Sch 10, para 20[1]
144, 145		27 Sep 1993 (SI 1993/2163)
146, 147		1 Apr 1994 (SI 1993/2163); prospectively repealed by Housing (Scotland) Act 2001, s 112, Sch 10, para 20[1]
148		27 Sep 1993 (SI 1993/2163); prospectively repealed by Housing (Scotland) Act 2001, s 112, Sch 10, para 20[1]
149–151		20 Jul 1993 (RA)
152		1 Apr 1994 (SI 1993/2163); prospectively repealed by Housing (Scotland) Act 2001, s 112, Sch 10, para 20[1]
153		1 Apr 1994 (SI 1993/2163)
154–157		27 Sep 1993 (SI 1993/2163)
158–173		10 Nov 1993 (SI 1993/2762)
174		Repealed
175		10 Nov 1993 (SI 1993/2762)
176		11 Oct 1993 (SI 1993/2134)
177		10 Nov 1993 (SI 1993/2762)
178		11 Oct 1993 (subject to savings) (SI 1993/2134)
179		11 Oct 1993 (SI 1993/2134)
180		11 Oct 1993 (except so far as relates to insertion of s 165A(2) of the 1980 Act) (SI 1993/2134) 10 Nov 1993 (otherwise) (SI 1993/2762)
181	(1)	20 Jul 1993 (RA)
	(2)	Repealed (subject to transitional provisions)
	(3)	10 Nov 1993 (SI 1993/2762)
	(4)	Repealed (subject to transitional provisions))
182		11 Oct 1993 (SI 1993/2134)
183		10 Nov 1993 (SI 1993/2762)
184		1 Apr 1994 (subject to transitional provisions) (SI 1994/935)

Leasehold Reform, Housing and Urban Development Act 1993 (c 28)—*contd*

Section

185		10 Nov 1993 (SI 1993/2762)
186		20 Jul 1993 (RA)
187	(1)	See Sch 21 below
	(2)	See Sch 22 below
188		20 Jul 1993 (RA)

Schedule

1–15		1 Nov 1993 (SI 1993/2134)
16		11 Oct 1993 (subject to savings) (SI 1993/2134)
17–20		10 Nov 1993 (SI 1993/2762)
21, para	1	1 Nov 1993 (SI 1993/2134)
	2	*Not in force*
	3	10 Nov 1993 (SI 1993/2762)
	4	2 Sep 1993 (SI 1993/2134)
	5	1 Nov 1993 (subject to savings) (SI 1993/2134)
	6	10 Nov 1993 (SI 1993/2762)
	7	2 Sep 1993 (SI 1993/2134)
	8	10 Nov 1993 (SI 1993/2762)
	9	1 Nov 1993 (SI 1993/2134)
	10	11 Oct 1993 (SI 1993/2134)
	11–25	11 Oct 1993 (subject to savings) (SI 1993/2134)
	26	1 Nov 1993 (SI 1993/2134)
	27	2 Sep 1993 (SI 1993/2134)
	28, 29	10 Nov 1993 (SI 1993/2762)
	30	1 Nov 1993 (SI 1993/2134)
	31, 32	10 Nov 1993 (SI 1993/2762)
22		20 Jul 1993 (repeal in Local Government and Housing Act 1989, s 80(1)) (RA)
		2 Sep 1993 (repeals of Housing Act 1988, s 41(1); Local Government and Housing Act 1989, Sch 11, para 51) (SI 1993/2134)
		27 Sep 1993 (repeals in Housing Scotland Act 1987) (SI 1993/2163)
		11 Oct 1993 (repeals in Local Government, Planning and Land Act 1980; Housing Act 1988, s 69(2)) (SI 1993/2134)
		11 Oct 1993 (repeals of or in Housing Act 1985, ss 124(3), 128(6), 132–135, 137, 138(1), 139(3), 140(5), 142, 153A(1), 153B(1), 164(6), 166(6), 169(3), 171C(2), 171H, 177, 180, 181(1), 182(1), 187, 188, Schs 6, 7–9; Housing

Leasehold Reform, Housing and Urban Development Act 1993 (c 28)—*contd*
Schedule
22—*contd*   and Planning Act 1986, Sch 5,
                                     para 5; Housing Act 1988, s 79;
                                     Local Government and Housing
                                     Act 1989, s 164) (subject to
                                     savings) (SI 1993/2134)
                                   1 Nov 1993 (repeals in Housing
                                     Act 1980; Housing (Consequential
                                     Provisions) Act 1985)
                                     (SI 1993/2134)
                                   1 Nov 1993 (repeals in Landlord and
                                     Tenant Act 1987) (subject to
                                     savings) (SI 1993/2134)
                                   10 Nov 1993 (repeal in Land
                                     Compensation Act 1961)
                                     (SI 1993/2762)
                                   1 Apr 1994 (repeal of English
                                     Industrial Estates Corporation
                                     Act 1981) (subject to transitional
                                     provisions) (SI 1994/935)
                                   Not in force (otherwise)

[1]   Orders made under Housing (Scotland) Act 2001, s 113, bring the repeals into force will be noted
      to that Act

Licensing (Amendment) (Scotland) Act 1993 (c 20)

RA: 1 Jul 1993

1 Jul 1993 (RA)

Local Government (Amendment) Act 1993 (c 27)

RA: 20 Jul 1993

Commencement provisions: s 3(2)

20 Sep 1993 (s 3(2))

Local Government (Overseas Assistance) Act 1993 (c 25)

RA: 20 Jul 1993

Commencement provisions: s 2(2)

20 Sep 1993 (s 2(2))

Merchant Shipping (Registration, etc) Act 1993 (c 22)

Whole Act repealed

National Lottery etc Act 1993 (c 39)

RA: 21 Oct 1993

Commencement provisions: s 65; National Lottery etc Act 1993 (Commencement No 1 and Transitional Provisions) Order 1993, SI 1993/2632; National Lottery etc Act 1993 (Commencement No 2 and Transitional Provisions) Order 1994, SI 1994/1055; National Lottery etc Act 1993 (Commencement No 3) Order 1994, SI 1994/2659

Section		
1, 2		25 Oct 1993 (SI 1993/2632)
3		Repealed
3A		Inserted by National Lottery Act 1998, s 1(3) (qv)
4–10		25 Oct 1993 (SI 1993/2632)
10A		Inserted by National Lottery Act 1998, s 2(1), (5) (in relation to any contravention after 2 Sep 1998 of a condition in a licence under the 1993 Act, ss 5, 6 whenever grants) (qv)
10B		Inserted by National Lottery Act 1998, s 3 (qv)
11–15		25 Oct 1993 (SI 1993/2632)
16		21 Dec 1993 (SI 1993/2632)
17		25 Oct 1993 (SI 1993/2632)
18		21 Dec 1993 (subject to transitional provisions) (SI 1993/2632)
19		25 Oct 1993 (SI 1993/2632); prospectively repealed by Police Act 1997, ss 133(d), 134(2), Sch 10[1]
20		25 Oct 1993 (SI 1993/2632)
21–25		21 Dec 1993 (SI 1993/2632)
25A–25C		Inserted by National Lottery Act 1998, ss 11(1), 12(1), 13 (qv)
25D		Inserted (1 Jul 1999) by Scotland Act 1998 (Modification of Functions) Order 1999, SI 1999/1756, arts 2, 8(1), Schedule, para 15(2), subject to a saving
26	(1)	25 Oct 1993 (SI 1993/2632)
	(2)	21 Dec 1993 (SI 1993/2632)
	(3)	25 Oct 1993 (SI 1993/2632)
	(3A)	Inserted by National Lottery Act 1998, s 11(2) (qv)
	(4)	25 Oct 1993 (SI 1993/2632)
	(4A)	Inserted by National Lottery Act 1998, s 11(4) (qv)
	(5)	25 Oct 1993 (SI 1993/2632)

National Lottery etc Act 1993 (c 39)—*contd*

Section

26A	Inserted (1 Jul 1999) by Scotland Act 1998 (Modification of Functions) Order 1999, SI 1999/1756, arts 2, 8(1), Schedule, para 15(3), subject to a saving
27–39	21 Dec 1993 (SI 1993/2632)
40–43	25 Oct 1993 (SI 1993/2632)
43A–43C	Inserted by National Lottery Act 1998, s 7(2) (qv)
43CC	Inserted (1 Jul 1999) by Scotland Act 1998 (Modification of Functions) Order 1999, SI 1999/1756, arts 2, 8(1), Schedule, para 15(10), subject to a saving
43D	Inserted by National Lottery Act 1998, s 7(2)(qv)
44	25 Oct 1993 (SI 1993/2632)
45–47	21 Dec 1993 (SI 1993/2632)
48, 49	3 May 1994 (subject to transitional provisions relating to s 48(3)) (SI 1994/1055)
50	3 Oct 1994 (SI 1994/1055)
51–55	3 May 1994 (subject to transitional provisions relating to s 52(4), (7), (8)) (SI 1994/1055)
56–59	14 Nov 1994 (SI 1994/2659)
60–63	25 Oct 1993 (SI 1993/2632)
64	See Sch 10 below
65, 66	25 Oct 1993 (SI 1993/2632)

Schedule

1	25 Oct 1993 (SI 1993/2632)
2	Repealed
2A	Inserted by National Lottery Act 1998, s 1(5), Sch 1, Pt II, para 7 (qv)
3	25 Oct 1993 (SI 1993/2632)
3A	Inserted by National Lottery Act 1998, s 12(3), Sch 3 (qv)
4, 5	21 Dec 1993 (SI 1993/2632)
6	25 Oct 1993 (SI 1993/2632)
6A	Inserted by National Lottery Act 1998, s 7(3), Sch 2 (qv)
7, 8	3 May 1994 (subject to transitional provisions relating to Sch 7, Pt I, para 7) (SI 1994/1055)
9	3 Oct 1994 (SI 1994/1055)

National Lottery etc Act 1993 (c 39)—*contd*

Schedule

10   21 Dec 1993 (repeals in Revenue
                                     Act 1898; National Heritage
                                     Act 1980) (SI 1993/2632)
                                   3 May 1994 (otherwise) (SI 1994/1055)

1   Orders made under Police Act 1997, s 135, bringing the prospective repeal into force will be noted
     to that Act

Noise and Statutory Nuisance Act 1993 (c 40)

RA: 5 Nov 1993

Commencement provisions: s 12
Section
1–5   5 Jan 1994 (s 12(1))
6   Repealed
7, 8   5 Jan 1994 (s 12(1))
9   *Not in force*
10–14   5 Jan 1994 (s 12(1))
Schedule
1   Repealed
2   5 Jan 1994 (s 12(1))
3   *Not in force*

Non-Domestic Rating Act 1993 (c 17)

RA: 27 May 1993

Commencement provisions: s 6(2); Non-Domestic Rating Act 1993 (Commencement
    No 1) Order 1993, SI 1993/1418; Non-Domestic Rating Act 1993
    (Commencement No 2) Order 1993, SI 1993/1512
Section
1   (1)   6 Jul 1993 (SI 1993/1512)
           (2)   4 Jun 1993 (SI 1993/1418)
           (3)–(5)   6 Jul 1993 (SI 1993/1512);
                                     sub-ss (3), (4) superseded by
                                     Non-Domestic Rating Act 1994,
                                     s 1(2), (3)
2, 3   6 Jul 1993 (SI 1993/1512)
4   4 Jun 1993 (SI 1993/1418)
5, 6   6 Jul 1993 (SI 1993/1512)

Ordination of Women (Financial Provisions) Measure 1993 (No 3)

RA: 5 Nov 1993

5 Nov 1993 (RA)

Osteopaths Act 1993 (c 21)

RA: 1 Jul 1993

Commencement provisions: s 42(2)–(5); Osteopaths Act 1993 (Commencement No 1 and Transitional Provision) Order 1997, SI 1997/34; Osteopaths Act 1993 (Commencement No 2) Order 1998, SI 1998/872; Osteopaths Act 1993 (Commencement No 3) Order 1998, SI 1998/1138; Osteopaths Act 1993 (Commencement No 4) Order 1999, SI 1999/1767; Osteopaths Act 1993 (Commencement No 5) Order 2000, SI 2000/217; Osteopaths Act 1993 (Commencement No 6 and Transitional Provision) Order 2000, SI 2000/1065; Osteopaths Act 1993 (Commencement No 7) Order 2002, SI 2002/500

Section			
1	(1)		14 Jan 1997 (SI 1997/34)
	(2)		14 Jan 1997 (for limited purposes referred to in SI 1997/34, art 2, Schedule) (SI 1997/34)
			9 May 1998 (otherwise) (SI 1998/1138)
	(3)		14 Jan 1997 (so far as it relates to the other provisions of the Act brought into force by SI 1997/34) (SI 1997/34)
			1 Apr 1998 (so far as it relates to the other provisions of the Act brought into force by SI 1998/872) (SI 1998/872)
			9 May 1998 (so far as it relates to the other provisions of the Act brought into force by SI 1998/1138) (SI 1998/1138)
			8 Mar 2000 (otherwise) (SI 2000/217)
	(4)		See Schedule below
	(5)	(a)	1 Apr 1998 (SI 1998/872)
		(b)	1 Apr 1998 (SI 1998/872)[1]
			5 Jul 1999 (otherwise) (SI 1999/1767)
		(c), (d)	1 Apr 1998 (SI 1998/872)[1]
			8 Mar 2000 (otherwise) (SI 2000/217)
	(6)		1 Apr 1998 (SI 1998/872)
	(7)		1 Apr 1998 (SI 1998/872)[1]
			5 Jul 1999 (so far as relates to the other provisions of this Act brought into force by SI 1999/1767) (SI 1999/1767)
			8 Mar 2000 (otherwise) (SI 2000/217)
	(8)		14 Jan 1997 (SI 1997/34)
	(9)		1 Apr 1998 (SI 1998/872)[1]
			5 Jul 1999 (so far as relates to the other provisions of this Act brought into force by SI 1999/1767) (SI 1999/1767)
			8 Mar 2000 (otherwise) (SI 2000/217)
	(10)–(12)		14 Jan 1997 (SI 1997/34)

Osteopaths Act 1993 (c 21)—*contd*

Section

2	(1)		14 Jan 1997 (SI 1997/34)
	(2)		14 Jan 1997 (SI 1997/34)
	(3)		9 May 1998 (SI 1998/1138)
	(4)–(6)		14 Jan 1997 (SI 1997/34)
3, 4			1 Apr 1998 (for limited purposes referred to in SI 1998/872, art 2(1)(b)) (SI 1998/872)
			9 May 1998 (otherwise) (SI 1998/1138)
5			8 Mar 2000 (SI 2000/217)
6	(1)		9 May 1998 (SI 1998/1138)
	(2)		1 Apr 1998 (SI 1998/872)
	(3)	(a)	9 May 1998 (SI 1998/1138)
		(b)–(l)	1 Apr 1998 (SI 1998/872)
		(m)	9 May 1998 (SI 1998/1138)
	(4)	(a)	1 Apr 1998 (SI 1998/872)
		(b)–(e)	9 May 1998 (SI 1998/1138)
	(5)		9 May 1998 (SI 1998/1138)
7	(1), (2)		5 Jul 1999 (so far as they relate to the other provisions of this Act brought into force by SI 1999/1767) (SI 1999/1767)
			8 Mar 2000 (otherwise) (SI 2000/217)
	(3)		9 May 2000 (SI 2000/1065)
8			8 Mar 2000 (SI 2000/217)
9	(1)–(1B)		9 May 1998 (SI 1998/1138)
	(1C)		8 Mar 2000 (SI 2000/217)
	(2)–(5)		9 May 1998 (SI 1998/1138)
10	(1)		9 May 1998 (SI 1998/1138)
	(2)		5 Jul 1999 (except the words "or section 8, or under rules made by virtue of section 8(8),") (SI 1999/1767)
			8 Mar 2000 (otherwise) (SI 2000/217)
	(3)–(12)		5 Jul 1999 (SI 1999/1767)
11			1 Apr 1998 (SI 1998/872)
12			9 May 1998 (SI 1998/1138)
13			1 Apr 1998 (SI 1998/872)
14–16			9 May 1998 (SI 1998/1138)
17			8 Mar 2000 (SI 2000/217)
18			9 May 1998 (SI 1998/1138)
19			1 Apr 1998 (SI 1998/872)
20, 21			5 Jul 1999 (SI 1999/1767)
22–26			8 Mar 2000 (SI 2000/217)
27, 28			5 Jul 1999 (SI 1999/1767)
29			9 May 1998 (SI 1998/1138)
30, 31			8 Mar 2000 (SI 2000/217)
32	(1)		9 May 2000 (subject to a transitional provision) (SI 2000/1065)

Osteopaths Act 1993 (c 21)—*contd*

Section

32	(2)	8 Mar 2000 (SI 2000/217)
	(3)	8 Mar 2000 (except so far as relates to s 32(1)) (SI 2000/217)
		9 May 2000 (exception noted above) (SI 2000/1065)
33		9 May 1998 (SI 1998/1138)
34		14 Jan 1997 (SI 1997/34)
35	(1), (2)	14 Jan 1997 (SI 1997/34)
	(3)	8 Mar 2000 (SI 2000/217)
	(4)	14 Jan 1997 (SI 1997/34)
36	(1), (2)	14 Jan 1997 (SI 1997/34)
	(3)	8 Mar 2000 (SI 2000/217)
	(4)–(6)	14 Jan 1997 (SI 1997/34)
37		1 Apr 1998 (SI 1998/872)
38		Repealed
39		1 Apr 1998 (SI 1998/872); prospectively repealed by Police Act 1997, ss 133(c), 134(2), Sch 10[2]
40		14 Jan 1997 (SI 1997/34)
41		14 Jan 1997 (so far as relates to definitions "the General Council", "prescribed" and "the Registrar") (SI 1997/34)
		1 Apr 1998 (otherwise, except definitions "interim suspension order", "provisionally registered osteopath", "registered address", "unacceptable professional conduct" and "visitor") (SI 1998/872)
		5 Jul 1999 (exceptions noted above) (SI 1999/1767)
42	(1)–(6)	14 Jan 1997 (SI 1997/34)
	(7)	14 Jan 1997 (words "This Act extends to the United Kingdom") (SI 1997/34)
		9 May 1998 (otherwise) (SI 1998/1138)

Schedule

para	1, 2	14 Jan 1997 (SI 1997/34)
	3	3 Mar 2002 (SI 2002/500)
	4	14 Jan 1997 (SI 1997/34)
	5	14 Jan 1997 (subject to a transitional provision) (SI 1997/34)
	6	14 Jan 1997 (SI 1997/34)
	7	8 Mar 2000 (SI 2000/217)
	8	14 Jan 1997 (SI 1997/34)
	9, 10	3 Mar 2002 (SI 2002/500)

Osteopaths Act 1993 (c 21)—*contd*
Schedule

para				
11				14 Jan 1997 (SI 1997/34)
12				3 Mar 2002 (SI 2002/500)
13				14 Jan 1997 (SI 1997/34)
14	(1)			3 Mar 2002 (SI 2002/500)
	(2)			14 Jan 1997 (subject to a transitional provision) (SI 1997/34)
	(3)	(a)–(c)		14 Jan 1997 (SI 1997/34)
		(d)		3 Mar 2002 (SI 2002/500)
	(4)			3 Mar 2002 (SI 2002/500)
	(5)	(a)		3 Mar 2002 (SI 2002/500)
		(b)		1 Apr 1998 (SI 1998/872)
15				14 Jan 1997 (SI 1997/34)
16–21				1 Apr 1998 (SI 1998/872)[1]
				5 Jul 1999 (so far as not already in force, in relation to the Investigating Committee only) (SI 1999/1767)
				8 Mar 2000 (otherwise) (SI 2000/217)
22				5 Jul 1999 (in relation to the Investigating Committee only) (SI 1999/1767)
				8 Mar 2000 (otherwise) (SI 2000/217)
23				1 Apr 1998 (SI 1998/872)[1]
				5 Jul 1999 (so far as not already in force, in relation to the Investigating Committee only) (SI 1999/1767)
				8 Mar 2000 (otherwise) (SI 2000/217)
24	(1)			1 Apr 1998 (SI 1998/872)[1]
				5 Jul 1999 (so far as not already in force, in relation to the Investigating Committee only) (SI 1999/1767)
				8 Mar 2000 (otherwise) (SI 2000/217)
	(2)			8 Mar 2000 (SI 2000/217)
25–29				1 Apr 1998 (SI 1998/872)
30–33				1 Apr 1998 (SI 1998/872)[1]
				5 Jul 1999 (otherwise) (SI 1999/1767)
34–41				1 Apr 1998 (SI 1998/872)[1]
				8 Mar 2000 (otherwise) (SI 2000/217)
42–48				14 Jan 1997 (SI 1997/34)

[1]   For the purpose only of enabling the Investigating Committee, the Professional Conduct Committee and the Health Committee and any sub-committees of those committees to be established and to carry out work preparatory to the exercise of any function which may be, or if the relevant provision were in force could become, exercisable under any provision of the Act

[2]   Orders made under Police Act 1997, s 135, bringing the prospective repeal into force will be noted to that Act

Pension Schemes Act 1993 (c 48)

RA: 5 Nov 1993

Commencement provisions: s 193(2), (3); Pension Schemes Act 1993 (Commencement
  No 1) Order 1994, SI 1994/86

Section

1	7 Feb 1994 (SI 1994/86)
2–5	Repealed
6–12	7 Feb 1994 (SI 1994/86)
12A–12D	Inserted by Pensions Act 1995, s 136(5) (qv)
13–15	7 Feb 1994 (SI 1994/86)
15A	Inserted by Welfare Reform and Pensions Act 1999, s 32(3) (qv)
16–21	7 Feb 1994 (SI 1994/86)
22	Repealed
23	7 Feb 1994 (SI 1994/86)
24	Repealed
25–28	7 Feb 1994 (SI 1994/86)
28A, 28B	Inserted by Pensions Act 1995, s 143 (qv)
29–32	7 Feb 1994 (SI 1994/86)
32A	Inserted by Pensions Act 1995, s 146(1) (qv)
33	7 Feb 1994 (SI 1994/86)
33A	Inserted by Pensions Act 1995, s 147 (qv)
34	7 Feb 1994 (SI 1994/86)
35, 36	7 Feb 1994 (SI 1994/86); prospectively repealed by Pensions Act 1995, ss 151, 177, Sch 5, paras 18, 38, Sch 7, Pt III[1]
37	Substituted by Pensions Act 1995, s 151, Sch 5, paras 18, 39 (qv)
38–42	7 Feb 1994 (SI 1994/86)
42A, 42B	Inserted by Pensions Act 1995, s 137(5) (qv)
43–45	7 Feb 1994 (SI 1994/86)
45A, 45B	Inserted by Pensions Act 1995, s 138(5) (qv)
46, 47	7 Feb 1994 (SI 1994/86)
48	Repealed
48A	Inserted by Pensions Act 1995, s 140(1) (qv)
49	Substituted by Pensions Act 1995, s 126(c), Sch 4, Pt III, para 16 (qv)
50–58	7 Feb 1994 (SI 1994/86)
59	Repealed
60–63	7 Feb 1994 (SI 1994/86)
64–66	Repealed
67, 68	7 Feb 1994 (SI 1994/86)

Pension Schemes Act 1993 (c 48)—*contd*

Pension Schemes Act 1993 (c 48)—*contd*

Section

172, 173		Repealed
174		7 Feb 1994 (SI 1994/86)
175		Substituted by Pensions Act 1995, s 165 (qv)
176–180		7 Feb 1994 (SI 1994/86)
180A		Inserted (1 Dec 2001) by Financial Services and Markets Act 2000 (Consequential Amendments and Repeals) Order 2001, SI 2001/3649, art 126
181–186		7 Feb 1994 (SI 1994/86)
187		Repealed
188	(1), (2)	See Sch 5 below
	(3)	7 Feb 1994 (SI 1994/86)
189		7 Feb 1994 (SI 1994/86)
190		See Schs 7, 8 below
191–193		7 Feb 1994 (SI 1994/86)

Schedule

1		Repealed
2–4		7 Feb 1994 (SI 1994/86)
5, Pt	I	7 Feb 1994 (SI 1994/86)
	II	*Not in force*
	III, IV	7 Feb 1994 (SI 1994/86)
6		7 Feb 1994 (SI 1994/86)
7		*Not in force*
8, 9		7 Feb 1994 (SI 1994/86)

[1] Orders made under Pensions Act 1995, s 180, bringing the prospective repeals into force will be noted to that Act

[2] Orders made under Social Security Act 1998, s 87, bringing the prospective repeal into force will be noted to that Act

---

Pension Schemes (Northern Ireland) Act 1993 (c 49)

RA: 5 Nov 1993

Commencement provisions: s 186(2), (3); Pension Schemes (1993 Act) (Commencement No 1) Order (Northern Ireland) 1994, SR 1994/17

Section

1–11	7 Feb 1994 (SR 1994/17)
11A	Inserted, partly prospectively, by Welfare Reform and Pensions (Northern Ireland) Order 1999, SI 1999/3147 (NI 11), art 29(3)[1]
12–64	7 Feb 1994 (SR 1994/17)
64A–64D	Inserted, partly prospectively, by Welfare Reform and Pensions (Northern Ireland) Order 1999, SI 1999/3147 (NI 11), art 33[1]

Pension Schemes (Northern Ireland) Act 1993 (c 49)—*contd*

Section		
65–97		7 Feb 1994 (SR 1994/17)
97A–97Q		Inserted, partly prospectively, by Welfare Reform and Pensions (Northern Ireland) Order 1999, SI 1999/3147 (NI 11), art 34[1]
98–107		7 Feb 1994 (SR 1994/17)
107A, 107B		Inserted, partly prospectively, by Welfare Reform and Pensions (Northern Ireland) Order 1999, SI 1999/3147 (NI 11), art 11[1]
108–155		7 Feb 1994 (SR 1994/17)
155A		Inserted, partly prospectively, by Welfare Reform and Pensions (Northern Ireland) Order 1999, SI 1999/3147, (NI 11), art 14[1]
156–175		7 Feb 1994 (SR 1994/17)
175A		Inserted (1 Dec 2001) by Financial Services and Markets Act 2000 (Consequential Amendments and Repeals) Order 2001, SI 2001/3649, art 137(1)
176–181		7 Feb 1994 (SR 1994/17)
182	(1), (2)	See Sch 4 below
	(3)	7 Feb 1994 (SR 1994/17)
183		7 Feb 1994 (SR 1994/17)
184		See Schs 6, 7 below
185, 186		7 Feb 1994 (SR 1994/17)
Schedule		
1–3		7 Feb 1994 (SR 1994/17)
4, Pt	I	7 Feb 1994 (SR 1994/17)
	II	*Not in force*
	III	7 Feb 1994 (SR 1994/17)
5		7 Feb 1994 (SR 1994/17)
6		*Not in force*
7, 8		7 Feb 1994 (SR 1994/17)

1   For the commencement of these insertions, see orders made under Welfare Reform and Pensions (Northern Ireland) Order 1999, SI 1999/3147 (NI 11), art 1(2)

Priests (Ordination of Women) Measure 1993 (No 2)

RA: 5 Nov 1993

Commencement provisions: s 12(2)

The provisions of this Measure are brought into force on 1 Feb 1994 by an appointed day notice signed by the Archbishops of Canterbury and York and dated 31 Jan 1994 (made under s 12)

Prisoners and Criminal Proceedings (Scotland) Act 1993 (c 9)

RA: 29 Mar 1993

Commencement provisions: s 48(2)–(4); Prisoners and Criminal Proceedings (Scotland) Act 1993 Commencement, Transitional Provisions and Savings Order 1993, SI 1993/2050

Section		
1		1 Oct 1993 (SI 1993/2050)
1A		Inserted by Crime and Disorder Act 1998, s 111(1) (qv)
2, 3		1 Oct 1993 (SI 1993/2050)
3A		Inserted by Crime and Disorder Act 1998, s 88 (qv)
4, 5		1 Oct 1993 (SI 1993/2050)
6	(1)	1 Oct 1993 (SI 1993/2050)
	(2), (3)	Repealed
7	(1)	1 Oct 1993 (SI 1993/2050)
	(1A), (1B)	Inserted by Criminal Justice and Public Order Act 1994, s 130(1) (qv)
	(2)	1 Oct 1993 (SI 1993/2050)
	(2A)–(2C)	Inserted by Crime and Disorder Act 1998, s 119, Sch 8, para 101, subject to transitional provisions (qv)
	(3), (4)	1 Oct 1993 (SI 1993/2050)
	(4A)	Inserted by Crime and Disorder Act 1998, s 119, Sch 8, para 101, subject to transitional provisions (qv)
	(5)	1 Oct 1993 (SI 1993/2050)
	(6)	18 Aug 1993 (for purpose of enabling orders to be made so as to come into force on or after 1 Oct 1993) (SI 1993/2050)
		1 Oct 1993 (otherwise) (SI 1993/2050)
	(7)	1 Oct 1993 (SI 1993/2050)
8		Repealed
9, 10		1 Oct 1993 (SI 1993/2050)
10A		Inserted by Convention Rights (Compliance) (Scotland) Act 2001, s 3(2) (qv)
11–19		1 Oct 1993 (SI 1993/2050)
20	(1), (2)	1 Oct 1993 (SI 1993/2050)
	(3)	18 Aug 1993 (for purpose of enabling orders to be made so as to come into force on or after 1 Oct 1993) (SI 1993/2050)
		1 Oct 1993 (otherwise) (SI 1993/2050)
	(4)	18 Aug 1993 (for purpose of enabling rules to be made, and directions to be given, so as to come into force on or after 1 Oct 1993) (SI 1993/2050)

Prisoners and Criminal Proceedings (Scotland) Act 1993 (c 9)—*contd*

Section

20	(4)—*contd*	1 Oct 1993 (otherwise) (SI 1993/2050)
	(4A)	Inserted by Convention Rights (Compliance) (Scotland) Act 2001, s 5(1)(c) (qv)
	(5)	18 Aug 1993 (for purpose of enabling rules to be made, and directions to be given, so as to come into force on or after 1 Oct 1993) (SI 1993/2050)
		1 Oct 1993 (otherwise) (SI 1993/2050)
	(6)	1 Oct 1993 (SI 1993/2050)
21–23		1 Oct 1993 (SI 1993/2050)
24, 25		18 Aug 1993 (SI 1993/2050)
26		1 Oct 1993 (SI 1993/2050)
26A		Inserted by Crime and Disorder Act 1998, s 87 (qv)
27	(1)	18 Aug 1993 (for purpose of enabling an order to be made so as to come into force on or after 1 Oct 1993) (SI 1993/2050)
		1 Oct 1993 (otherwise) (SI 1993/2050)
	(2), (3)	18 Aug 1993 (for purpose of enabling an order to be made so as to come into force on or after 1 Oct 1993) (SI 1993/2050)
		1 Oct 1993 (otherwise) (SI 1993/2050)
	(4)	1 Oct 1993 (SI 1993/2050)
	(5)	Substituted by Crime and Disorder Act 1998, s 111(3) (qv)
	(6), (7)	1 Oct 1993 (SI 1993/2050)
	(8)	Inserted by Crime and Disorder Act 1998, s 119, Sch 8, para 107 (qv)
28–35		Repealed
36		18 Sep 1993 (subject to a saving) (SI 1993/2050)
37–43		Repealed
44		1 Oct 1993 (SI 1993/2050)
45, 46		18 Aug 1993 (SI 1993/2050)
47	(1)	See Sch 5 below
	(2)	See Sch 6 below
	(3)	See Sch 7 below
48		29 Mar 1993 (s 48(4))
Schedule		
1, 2		1 Oct 1993 (subject to a saving) (SI 1993/2050)
3, 4		Repealed
5, para	1	Repealed
	2–4	1 Oct 1993 (SI 1993/2050)

Prisoners and Criminal Proceedings (Scotland) Act 1993 (c 9)—*contd*
Schedule

5, para	5		29 Mar 1993 (s 48(4))
	6	(1)–(4)	18 Aug 1993 (SI 1993/2050)
		(5)	1 Oct 1993 (SI 1993/2050)
		(6)	18 Aug 1993 (SI 1993/2050)
		(7)	1 Oct 1993 (SI 1993/2050)
		(8)	18 Aug 1993 (SI 1993/2050)
		(9)	1 Oct 1993 (SI 1993/2050)
6			1 Oct 1993 (SI 1993/2050)
7			18 Sep 1993 (repeals of or in Criminal Procedure (Scotland) Act 1975, ss 108, 289D, 328; Criminal Justice (Scotland) Act 1980, Sch 3; Criminal Justice (Scotland) Act 1987, s 62) (subject to savings) (SI 1993/2050)
			1 Oct 1993 (otherwise) (subject to savings) (SI 1993/2050)

Probation Service Act 1993 (c 47)

Whole Act repealed

Protection of Animals (Scotland) Act 1993 (c 15)

RA: 27 May 1993

Commencement provisions: s 2(2)

27 Jul 1993 (s 2(2))

Radioactive Substances Act 1993 (c 12)

RA: 27 May 1993

Commencement provisions: s 51(2)

27 Aug 1993 (s 51(2))

Railways Act 1993 (c 43)

RA: 5 Nov 1993

Commencement provisions: s 154(2); Railways Act 1993 (Commencement No 1) Order 1993, SI 1993/3237; Railways Act 1993 (Commencement No 2) Order 1994, SI 1994/202; Railways Act 1993 (Commencement No 3) Order 1994, SI 1994/447; Railways Act 1993 (Commencement No 4 and Transitional Provision) Order 1994, SI 1994/571; Railways Act 1993 (Commencement No 5 and Transitional Provisions) Order 1994, SI 1994/1648; Railways Act 1993 (Commencement No 6) Order 1994, SI 1994/2142

Section

1	5 Nov 1993 (s 154(2))
2, 3	1 Apr 1994 (SI 1994/571)

Railways Act 1993 (c 43)—*contd*

Section

4	(1)	24 Dec 1993 (for purposes of functions of Secretary of State under s 33) (SI 1993/3237)
		22 Feb 1994 (for purpose of functions of Regulator under s 70) (SI 1994/447)
		21 Mar 1994 (otherwise) (SI 1994/571)
	(2)	22 Feb 1994 (for purpose of functions of Regulator under s 70) (SI 1994/447)
		21 Mar 1994 (otherwise) (SI 1994/571)
	(3)	24 Dec 1993 (for purposes of functions of Secretary of State under s 33) (SI 1993/3237)
		22 Feb 1994 (for purpose of functions of Regulator under s 70) (SI 1994/447)
		21 Mar 1994 (otherwise) (SI 1994/571)
	(4)	21 Mar 1994 (SI 1994/571)
	(5), (6)	22 Feb 1994 (for purpose of functions of Regulator under s 70) (SI 1994/447)
		21 Mar 1994 (otherwise) (SI 1994/571)
	(7)	24 Dec 1993 (for purposes of functions of Secretary of State under s 33) (SI 1993/3237)
	(7A), (7B)	Inserted by Competition Act 1998, s 54(2), Sch 10, Pt II, para 6(3) (qv)
		21 Mar 1994 (otherwise) (SI 1994/571)
	(8)	21 Mar 1994 (SI 1994/571)
	(9)	24 Dec 1993 (for purposes of definitions "environment" and "through ticket") (SI 1993/3237)
		21 Mar 1994 (otherwise) (SI 1994/571)
5		Repealed
6	(1)	1 Apr 1994 (SI 1994/571)
	(1A)	Inserted (27 Jun 1998) by Railways Regulations 1998, SI 1998/1340, reg 21(1), (2)
	(2)	6 Jan 1994 (SI 1993/3237)
	(2A)	Inserted (27 Jun 1998) by Railways Regulations 1998, SI 1998/1340, reg 21(1), (4)
	(3), (4)	1 Apr 1994 (SI 1994/571)
7		1 Apr 1994 (SI 1994/571)
7A		Inserted by Transport Act 2000, s 216, Sch 17, Pt I, paras 1, 3 (qv)
8–15		1 Apr 1994 (SI 1994/571)
15A–15C		Inserted by Transport Act 2000, s 242(2) (qv)

Railways Act 1993 (c 43)—*contd*

Section

16		1 Apr 1994 (SI 1994/571)
16A–16I		Inserted by Transport Act 2000, s 223 (qv)
17–19		2 Apr 1994 (SI 1994/571)
19A		Inserted by Transport Act 2000, s 231(1) (qv)
20–22		2 Apr 1994 (SI 1994/571)
22A–22C		Inserted by Transport Act 2000, s 232(2) (qv)
23	(1), (2)	1 Apr 1994 (SI 1994/571)
	(3), (4)	6 Jan 1994 (SI 1993/3237)
24		1 Apr 1994 (SI 1994/571)
25	(1), (2)	6 Jan 1994 (for purpose of providing definition "public sector operator") (SI 1993/3237)
		1 Apr 1994 (otherwise) (SI 1994/571)
	(3)–(9)	Repealed
26		1 Apr 1994 (SI 1994/571)
26A–26C		Inserted by Transport Act 2000, s 212(4) (qv)
27, 28		1 Apr 1994 (SI 1994/571)
29	(1)–(7)	1 Apr 1994 (SI 1994/571)
	(8)	6 Jan 1994 (SI 1993/3237)
30		Substituted by Transport Act 2000, s 212(5) (qv)
31		1 Apr 1994 (SI 1994/571)
32, 33		Repealed
34–43		1 Apr 1994 (SI 1994/571)
44		Repealed
45, 46		1 Apr 1994 (SI 1994/571)
46A		Inserted by Transport Act 2000, s 238 (qv)
46B		Inserted by Transport Act 2000, s 216, Sch 17, Pt II, paras 17, 25(3) (qv)
47		Substituted for ss 47, 47A, 47B by Transport Act 2000, s 215, Sch 16, paras 8, 31 (qv)
48–50		1 Apr 1994 (SI 1994/571)
51–53		Repealed
54	(1)	1 Apr 1994 (SI 1994/571)
	(2)	21 Mar 1994 (SI 1994/571)
	(3)	21 Mar 1994 (for purpose of definitions "franchising functions", in relation to the Franchising Director, and "railway investment") (SI 1994/571)
		1 Apr 1994 (otherwise) (SI 1994/571)
55–57		1 Apr 1994 (SI 1994/571)

Railways Act 1993 (c 43)—*contd*

Section

86			1 Apr 1994 (SI 1994/571); prospectively repealed by Transport Act 2000, s 274, Sch 31, Pt IV[1]
87	(1)		6 Jan 1994 (for purpose of enabling Secretary of State to transfer functions to himself) (SI 1993/3237)
			1 Apr 1994 (otherwise) (SI 1994/571)
			Subsection prospectively repealed by Transport Act 2000, s 274, Sch 31, Pt IV[1]
	(2)		6 Jan 1994 (SI 1993/3237); prospectively repealed by Transport Act 2000, s 274, Sch 31, Pt IV[1]
	(3), (4)		1 Apr 1994 (SI 1994/571); prospectively repealed by Transport Act 2000, s 274, Sch 31, Pt IV[1]
	(5)		6 Jan 1994 (SI 1993/3237); prospectively repealed by Transport Act 2000, s 274, Sch 31, Pt IV[1]
88–92			6 Jan 1994 (SI 1993/3237); prospectively repealed by Transport Act 2000, s 274, Sch 31, Pt IV[1]
93	(1), (2)		6 Jan 1994 (SI 1993/3237); prospectively repealed by Transport Act 2000, s 274, Sch 31, Pt IV[1]
	(3)	(a)	6 Jan 1994 (SI 1993/3237); prospectively repealed by Transport Act 2000, s 274, Sch 31, Pt IV[1]
		(b)	1 Apr 1994 (SI 1994/571); prospectively repealed by Transport Act 2000, s 274, Sch 31, Pt IV[1]
	(4)–(13)		6 Jan 1994 (SI 1993/3237); prospectively repealed by Transport Act 2000, s 274, Sch 31, Pt IV[1]
94–112			6 Jan 1994 (SI 1993/3237); prospectively repealed by Transport Act 2000, s 274, Sch 31, Pt IV[1]
113			Repealed

Railways Act 1993 (c 43)—*contd*
Section

114–116		6 Jan 1994 (SI 1993/3237); prospectively repealed by Transport Act 2000, s 274, Sch 31, Pt IV[1]
117		2 Feb 1994 (SI 1994/202)
118–121		8 Mar 1994 (SI 1994/571)
122–124		1 Apr 1994 (SI 1994/571)
125–129		Repealed
130		6 Jan 1994 (SI 1993/3237)
131		Repealed (subject to transitional provisions and savings in Competition Act 1998, s 74(2), Sch 13)
132	(1)–(4)	8 Mar 1994 (SI 1994/571)
	(5)	Repealed
	(6), (7)	8 Mar 1994 (SI 1994/571)
	(8)	See Sch 10 below
	(9), (10)	8 Mar 1994 (SI 1994/571)
133		8 Mar 1994 (SI 1994/571)
134	(1)	See Sch 11 below
	(2), (3)	6 Jan 1994 (SI 1993/3237)
135,136		1 Apr 1994 (SI 1994/571)
137		Repealed
138		21 Mar 1994 (SI 1994/571)
139		Repealed
140		15 Jul 1994 (subject to transitional provisions) (SI 1994/1648); prospectively repealed in relation to England and Wales by Transport Act 2000, s 274, Sch 31, Pt V(2) and repealed in relation to Scotland[1]
141		Repealed
142–144		24 Dec 1993 (SI 1993/3237)
145	(1)–(5)	24 Dec 1993 (except for purposes of sub-s (5)(a), (b)(i)) (SI 1993/3237) 1 Apr 1994 (exceptions noted above) (SI 1994/571)
	(5A)	Inserted by Transport Act 2000, s 252, Sch 27, paras 17, 41(1), (3) (qv)
	(6)	24 Dec 1993 (except for purposes of sub-s (5)(a), (b)(i)) (SI 1993/3237) 1 Apr 1994 (exceptions noted above) (SI 1994/571)
	(6A)	Inserted by Competition Act 1998, ss 54(3), 74(3), Sch 10, Pt IV, para 15(10) (qv)
	(7)	1 Apr 1994 (SI 1994/571)
146–149		24 Dec 1993 (SI 1993/3237)

Railways Act 1993 (c 43)—*contd*
Section

150	(1)–(3)		24 Dec 1993 (SI 1993/3237)
	(4)		1 Apr 1994 (SI 1994/571)
151	(1)		24 Dec 1993 (for purposes of definitions "the Board", "body corporate", "company", "contravention", "the Franchising Director", "functions", "local authority", "the Monopolies Commission", "notice", "the Regulator", "subsidiary" and "wholly owned subsidiary") (SI 1993/3237)
			6 Jan 1994 (otherwise) (SI 1993/3237)
	(2)–(4)		6 Jan 1994 (SI 1993/3237)
	(5)		24 Dec 1993 (SI 1993/3237)
	(6)–(9)		6 Jan 1994 (SI 1993/3237)
152	(1)		See Sch 12 below
	(2)		Repealed
	(3)		See Sch 14 below
153			6 Jan 1994 (SI 1993/3237)
154			24 Dec 1993 (SI 1993/3237)

Schedule

1			5 Nov 1993 (s 154(2))
2, 3			1 Apr 1994 (SI 1994/571)
4			2 Apr 1994 (SI 1994/571)
4A			Inserted by Transport Act 2000, s 231(2), Sch 24 (qv)
5–7			1 Apr 1994 (SI 1994/571)
8, 9			6 Jan 1994 (SI 1993/3237); prospectively repealed by Transport Act 2000, s 274, Sch 31, Pt IV[1]
10, para	1, 2		8 Mar 1994 (subject to transitional provisions) (SI 1994/571)
	3	(1)	8 Mar 1994 (so far as repeals Transport Act 1962, ss 69, 71) (SI 1994/571)
			Not in force (otherwise)
		(2), (3)	8 Mar 1994 (SI 1994/571)
11, para	1–8		6 Jan 1994 (SI 1993/3237)
	9	(1), (2)	6 Jan 1994 (SI 1993/3237)
		(3)	6 Jan 1994 (for purpose of inserting Transport Act 1980, s 52D(6)–(8)) (SI 1993/3237)
			16 Aug 1994 (otherwise) (SI 1994/2142)
		(4)	6 Jan 1994 (SI 1993/3237)
	10		6 Jan 1994 (SI 1993/3237)
	11		16 Aug 1994 (SI 1994/2142)
	12–14		6 Jan 1994 (SI 1993/3237)

Railways Act 1993 (c 43)—*contd*
Schedule

12, para	1–3		1 Apr 1994 (SI 1994/571)
	4		6 Jan 1994 (SI 1993/3237)
	5		6 Jan 1994 (SI 1993/3237); prospectively repealed by Transport Act 2000, s 274, Sch 31, Pt IV[1]
	6	(1)–(5)	6 Jan 1994 (SI 1993/3237)
		(6)	1 Apr 1994 (SI 1994/571)
		(7)	Repealed
	7, 8		6 Jan 1994 (SI 1993/3237)
	9		1 Apr 1994 (SI 1994/571)
	10–13		6 Jan 1994 (SI 1993/3237)
	14	(1)–(3)	6 Jan 1994 (SI 1993/3237)
		(4)–(6)	1 Apr 1994 (SI 1994/571)
	15–22		1 Apr 1994 (SI 1994/571)
	23, 24		6 Jan 1994 (SI 1993/3237)
	25		1 Apr 1994 (SI 1994/571)
	26		6 Jan 1994 (SI 1993/3237)
	27		1 Apr 1994 (SI 1994/571)
	28		6 Jan 1994 (SI 1993/3237)
	29		1 Apr 1994 (SI 1994/571)
	30, 31		6 Jan 1994 (SI 1993/3237)
	32		*Not in force*; prospectively repealed by Transport Act 2000, s 274, Sch 31, Pt IV[1]
13			Repealed
14			6 Jan 1994 (repeals of or in British Transport Commission Act 1950, s 43; Transport Act 1962, ss 4, 5, 13, 53; Transport Act 1968, ss 42, 45, 50, 137) (SI 1993/3237)
			8 Mar 1994 (repeals of Transport Act 1962, ss 54(1)(b), (2), 69, 71) (SI 1994/571)
			31 Mar 1994 (repeal of Transport Act 1981, Pt I, Sch 1) (SI 1994/571)
			1 Apr 1994 (all repeals so far as not already in force except repeals of Transport Act 1962, s 70, Railways Act 1974, s 8, Transport Act 1981, s 36) (SI 1994/571)
			15 Jul 1994 (repeals of Railways Act 1974, s 8, Transport Act 1981, s 36) (subject to transitional provisions) (SI 1994/1648)
			Not in force (repeal of Transport Act 1962, s 70)

[1]   Orders made under Transport Act 2000, s 275, bringing the prospective repeal into force will be noted to that Act

Reinsurance (Acts of Terrorism) Act 1993 (c 18)

RA: 27 May 1993

27 May 1993 (RA)

Representation of the People Act 1993 (c 29)

RA: 20 Jul 1993

20 Jul 1993 (RA)

Road Traffic (Driving Instruction by Disabled Persons) Act 1993 (c 31)

RA: 20 Jul 1993

Commencement provisions: s 7(2); Road Traffic (Driving Instruction by Disabled Persons) Act 1993 (Commencement) Order 1996, SI 1996/1980

9 Sep 1996 (SI 1996/1980)

Scottish Land Court Act 1993 (c 45)

RA: 5 Nov 1993

Commencement provisions: s 2(3)

5 Jan 1994 (s 2(3))

Sexual Offences Act 1993 (c 30)

RA: 20 Jul 1993

Commencement provisions: s 2(2)

20 Sep 1993 (s 2(2))

Social Security Act 1993 (c 3)

RA: 29 Jan 1993

29 Jan 1993 (RA; but note s 5(2))

Statute Law (Repeals) Act 1993 (c 50)

RA: 5 Nov 1993

Commencement provisions: s 4(2), (3); Statute Law (Repeals) Act 1993 (Commencement) Order 1996, SI 1996/509

Section

1	(1)	See Sch 1 below
	(2)	See Sch 2 below
2–4		5 Nov 1993 (RA)

Statute Law (Repeals) Act 1993 (c 50)—*contd*

Schedule

1	5 Nov 1993[1] (except repeals of Shipbuilding (Redundancy Payments) Act 1978, Shipbuilding Act 1985, s 1) (RA)
	1 Apr 1996 (exceptions noted above) (SI 1996/509)
2	5 Nov 1993 (RA)

---

[1]   By s 4(2), repeals of National Loans Act 1939, Sch 2, para 5, Bank of England Act 1946, Sch 1, para 10, Coal Industry Nationalisation Act 1946, s 33(8) have effect, so far as relating to stock registered in the National Savings Stock Register, on the coming into force of the first regulations made by virtue of the National Debt Act 1972, s 3(1)(bb)

Trade Union Reform and Employment Rights Act 1993 (c 19)

RA: 1 Jul 1993

Commencement provisions: ss 7(4), 52; Trade Union Reform and Employment Rights Act 1993 (Commencement No 1 and Transitional Provisions) Order 1993, SI 1993/1908; Trade Union Reform and Employment Rights Act 1993 (Commencement No 2 and Transitional Provisions) Order 1993, SI 1993/2503; Trade Union Reform and Employment Rights Act 1993 (Commencement No 3 and Transitional Provisions) Order 1994, SI 1994/1365

Section

1, 2		30 Aug 1993 (subject to transitional provisions) (SI 1993/1908)
3		See Sch 1 below
4–6		30 Aug 1993 (subject to transitional provisions) (SI 1993/1908)
7	(1)	1 Apr 1996 (s 7(4))
	(2)–(4)	1 Apr 1996 (SI 1993/1908)
8, 9		1 Jan 1994 (SI 1993/1908)
10–12		30 Aug 1993 (SI 1993/1908)
13		30 Aug 1993 (subject to transitional provisions) (SI 1993/1908)
14		30 Nov 1993 (SI 1993/1908)
15, 16		30 Aug 1993 (SI 1993/1908)
17		30 Aug 1993 (subject to transitional provisions) (SI 1993/1908)
18	(1)	30 Aug 1993 (SI 1993/1908)
	(2)	30 Aug 1993 (subject to transitional provisions) (SI 1993/1908)
19–21		30 Aug 1993 (subject to transitional provisions) (SI 1993/1908)
22		30 Aug 1993 (SI 1993/1908)
23–31		Repealed (s 31 *never in force*)
32		30 Nov 1993 (SI 1993/2503)
33		30 Aug 1993 (SI 1993/1908)
34		30 Aug 1993 (subject to transitional provisions) (SI 1993/1908)

Trade Union Reform and Employment Rights Act 1993 (c 19)—*contd*

Section

35		30 Aug 1993 (SI 1993/1908)
36–38		Repealed
39	(1)	Repealed
	(2)	See Sch 6 below
40–42		Repealed
43, 44		30 Aug 1993 (SI 1993/1908)
45		30 Nov 1993 (so far as substitutes 1973 Act, s 10(7)) (SI 1993/2503)
		1 Apr 1994 (otherwise) (E, S) (SI 1993/2503)
		1 Apr 1995 (otherwise) (SI 1993/2503)
46		1 Apr 1994 (E, S) (SI 1993/2503)
		1 Apr 1995 (otherwise) (SI 1993/2503)
47, 48		30 Aug 1993 (SI 1993/1908)
49	(1)	See Sch 7 below
	(2)	See Sch 8 below
50		See Sch 9 below
51		See Sch 10 below
52–55		1 Jul 1993 (RA)

Schedule

1		30 Aug 1993 (subject to transitional provisions) (SI 1993/1908)
2–5		Repealed
6		30 Aug 1993 (SI 1993/1908)
7, para	1	30 Aug 1993 (SI 1993/1908)
	2–7	Repealed
	8–10	30 Nov 1993 (SI 1993/2503)
	11	Repealed
	12	30 Nov 1993 (SI 1993/2503)
	13, 14	Repealed
	15	30 Aug 1993 (SI 1993/1908)
	16	Repealed
	17–19	30 Aug 1993 (SI 1993/1908)
	20	Repealed
	21–27	30 Aug 1993 (SI 1993/1908)
8, para	1	1 Apr 1994 (E, S) (SI 1993/2503)
		1 Apr 1995 (otherwise) (SI 1993/2503)
	2	Repealed
	3–5	1 Apr 1994 (E, S) (SI 1993/2503)
		1 Apr 1995 (otherwise) (SI 1993/2503)
	6, 7	Repealed
	8, 9	1 Apr 1994 (E, S) (SI 1993/2503)
		1 Apr 1995 (otherwise) (SI 1993/2503)
	10–32	Repealed
	33, 34	1 Apr 1994 (E, S) (SI 1993/2503)
		1 Apr 1995 (otherwise) (SI 1993/2503)
	35–37	Repealed
	38	30 Aug 1993 (SI 1993/1908)
	39	Repealed

Trade Union Reform and Employment Rights Act 1993 (c 19)—*contd*

Schedule

8, para	40, 41		30 Aug 1993 (SI 1993/1908)
	42		1 Jan 1994 (SI 1993/1908)
	43	(a)	1 Jan 1994 (SI 1993/1908)
		(b)	30 Aug 1993 (SI 1993/1908)
	44, 45		1 Jan 1994 (SI 1993/1908)
	46, 47		30 Aug 1993 (SI 1993/1908)
	48		30 Nov 1993 (SI 1993/1908)
	49		30 Aug 1993 (SI 1993/1908)
	50, 51		30 Nov 1993 (SI 1993/1908)
	52–57		30 Aug 1993 (SI 1993/1908)
	58–60		Repealed
	61		30 Aug 1993 (SI 1993/1908)
	62	(a)	1 Jan 1994 (SI 1993/1908)
		(b)	30 Aug 1993 (SI 1993/1908)
	63		30 Aug 1993 (SI 1993/1908)
	64	(a)	1 Jan 1994 (SI 1993/1908)
		(b), (c)	30 Aug 1993 (SI 1993/1908)
	65		30 Aug 1993 (SI 1993/1908)
	66	(a)	1 Jan 1994 (SI 1993/1908)
		(b)	30 Aug 1993 (SI 1993/1908)
	67		Repealed
	68–75		30 Aug 1993 (SI 1993/1908)
	76, 77		30 Aug 1993 (so far as relate to s 57A of the 1978 Act) (SI 1993/1908)
			10 Jun 1994 (otherwise) (SI 1994/1365)[1]
	78		30 Aug 1993 (SI 1993/1908)
	79–84		Repealed
	85		30 Nov 1993 (SI 1993/2503)
	86, 87		Repealed
	88, 89		30 Aug 1993 (SI 1993/1908)
9, para	1		30 Aug 1993 (SI 1993/1908)
	2		30 Aug 1993 (subject to transitional provisions) (SI 1993/1908)
	3		Repealed
	4, 5		30 Aug 1993 (SI 1993/1908)
10			30 Aug 1993 (repeals of or in Factories Act 1961; Contracts of Employment and Redundancy Payments Act (Northern Ireland) 1965; Transport Act 1968; House of Commons Disqualification Act 1975; Northern Ireland Assembly Disqualification Act 1975; Industrial Relations (Northern Ireland) Order 1976; Employment Protection (Consolidation) Act 1978, ss 18, 53, 55, 64A, 93–95, 100, 123, 149, Schs 12, 13;

Trade Union Reform and Employment Rights Act 1993 (c 19)—*contd*
Schedule
10—*contd*

Employment Act 1980, s 8,
Sch 1; Transfer of Undertakings
(Protection of Employment)
Regulations 1981; Wages Act 1986;
Income and Corporation Taxes
Act 1988; Enterprise and New
Towns (Scotland) Act 1990;
Offshore Safety (Protection Against
Victimisation) Act 1992; Trade
Union and Labour Relations
(Consolidation) Act 1992, ss 24,
34, 43, 52, 65, 74, 78, 118, 135,
154, 188, 190, 209, 246, 249, 256,
273, 283, 299, Sch 2, paras 15, 34)
(SI 1993/1908)

15 Oct 1993 (repeal in Employment
Protection (Consolidation)
Act 1978, Sch 9, para 1A)
(SI 1993/2503)

30 Nov 1993 (repeals in Trade Union
and Labour Relations
(Consolidation) Act 1992, ss 67,
288, 290, 291) (SI 1993/1908)

30 Nov 1993 (repeals of or in
Employment Protection
(Consolidation) Act 1978, ss 11(3),
(7), 128(4), 133(1), 138(1), (2)
(so far as words repealed relate to
sub-ss (4), (5)), 139(1), 146(4),
Sch 9, para 8; Employment
Act 1982; Dock Work Act 1989;
Employment Act 1989; Trade
Union and Labour Relations
(Consolidation) Act 1992,
s 277(2), Sch 2, para 24(3))
(SI 1993/2503)

1 Jan 1994 (repeal in Trade Union
and Labour Relations
(Consolidation) Act 1992, s 32)
(SI 1993/1908)

1 Apr 1994 (E, S) and 1 Apr 1995
(otherwise) (repeals in Finance
Act 1969; Chronically Sick and
Disabled Persons Act 1970;
Employment and Training Act 1973;
Education (Scotland) Act 1980;
Agricultural Training Board
Act 1982; Industrial Training
Act 1982) (SI 1993/2503)

Trade Union Reform and Employment Rights Act 1993 (c 19)—*contd*
Schedule

10—*contd*	10 Jun 1994 (so far as not already in force, except repeal of words "subject to subsections (3)–(5)" in Employment Protection (Consolidation) Act 1978, s 138, so far as they relate to sub-s (3)) (SI 1994/1365)[1]
	1 Apr 1996 (repeals of Trade Union and Labour Relations (Consolidation) Act 1992, ss 115, 116) (SI 1993/1908)
	Not in force (otherwise)

[1] By SI 1994/1365, art 3(1), the amendments and repeals made by provisions of this Act brought into force by that Order have effect only in relation to women whose expected week of childbirth begins on or after 16 Oct 1994

Video Recordings Act 1993 (c 24)

RA: 20 Jul 1993

Commencement provisions: s 6(2)

20 Sep 1993 (s 6(2))

Welsh Language Act 1993 (c 38)

RA: 21 Oct 1993

Commencement provisions: s 36; Welsh Language Act 1993 (Commencement) Order 1994, SI 1994/115

Section		
1–29		21 Dec 1993 (s 36(1))
30	(1)	25 Jan 1994 (so far as enables prescription of description of documents for purpose of Companies Act 1985, s 710B(3)(a) and so far as enables prescription of manner in which a translation is to be certified for purpose of s 710B(8) of the 1985 Act) (SI 1994/115)
		1 Feb 1994 (otherwise) (SI 1994/115)
	(2)–(5)	1 Feb 1994 (SI 1994/115)
	(6)	25 Jan 1994 (so far as enables prescription of description of documents for purpose of Companies Act 1985, s 710B(3)(a) and so far as enables prescription of manner in which a translation is to be certified for purpose of s 710B(8) of the 1985 Act) (SI 1994/115)

Welsh Language Act 1993 (c 38)—*contd*

1994

Antarctic Act 1994 (c 15)

RA: 5 Jul 1994

Commencement provisions: s 35; Antarctic Act 1994 (Commencement) Order 1995, SI 1995/2748; Antarctic Act 1994 (Commencement) Order 1996, SI 1996/2666; Antarctic Act 1994 (Commencement) Order 1997, SI 1997/1411; Antarctic Act 1994 (Commencement) (No 2) Order 1997, SI 1997/2298; Antarctic Act 1994 (Commencement) (No 3) Order 1997, SI 1997/3068

Section	
1, 2	1 Nov 1995 (SI 1995/2748)
3, 4	14 Jan 1998 (SI 1997/3068)
5	1 Jun 1997 (SI 1997/1411)
6	1 Oct 1997 (SI 1997/2298)
7	1 Nov 1996 (SI 1996/2666)
8–32	1 Nov 1995 (SI 1995/2748)
33	See Schedule below
34–36	1 Nov 1995 (SI 1995/2748)
Schedule	1 Nov 1995 (except repeals of Antarctic Treaty Act 1967, ss 6, 7(2)(b), (7), 8, 9, 10, 11) (SI 1995/2748)
	Not in force (exception noted above)

Appropriation Act 1994 (c 24)

Whole Act repealed

Care of Cathedrals (Supplementary Provisions) Measure 1994 (No 2)

RA: 21 Jul 1994

Commencement provisions: s 11(2)

The provisions of this Measure are brought into force on 1 Oct 1994 by an appointed day notice signed by the Archbishops of Canterbury and York and dated 25 Jul 1994 (made under s 11(2))

Chiropractors Act 1994 (c 17)

RA: 5 Jul 1994

Commencement provisions: s 44(2)–(6); Chiropractors Act 1994 (Commencement No 1 and Transitional Provision) Order 1998, SI 1998/2031; Chiropractors Act 1994 (Commencement No 2) Order 1999, SI 1999/1309; Chiropractors Act 1994 (Commencement No 3) Order 1999, SI 1999/1496; Chiropractors Act 1994 (Commencement No 4) Order 2000, SI 2000/2388; Chiropractors Act 1994

Chiropractors Act 1994 (c 17)—*contd*
(Commencement Order No 5 and Transitional Provision) Order 2001,
SI 2001/2028; Chiropractors Act 1994 (Commencement No 6) Order 2002,
SI 2002/312

Section

1	(1)	14 Aug 1998 (SI 1998/2031)
	(2)	14 Aug 1998 (for the purpose of enabling Chiropractic Council to prepare for the exercise of any functions which may be, or if the relevant provisions were in force could become, exercisable under any provision of the Act including this subsection) (SI 1998/2031)
		13 May 1999 (so far as relates to the other provisions of this Act brought into force by SI 1999/1309) (SI 1999/1309)
		15 Jun 1999 (so far as relates to the other provisions of this Act brought into force by SI 1999/1496) (SI 1999/1496)
		7 Sep 2000 (so far as relates to other provisions of this Act brought into force by SI 2000/2388) (SI 2000/2388)
		Not in force (otherwise)
	(3)	14 Aug 1998 (so far as relates to the other provisions of this Act brought into force by SI 1998/2031) (SI 1998/2031)
		13 May 1999 (so far as relates to the other provisions of this Act brought into force by SI 1999/1309) (SI 1999/1309)
		15 Jun 1999 (so far as relates to the other provisions of this Act brought into force by SI 1999/1496) (SI 1999/1496)
		7 Sep 2000 (so far as relates to other provisions of this Act brought into force by SI 2000/2388) (SI 2000/2388)
		Not in force (otherwise)
		14 Aug 1998 (so far as relates to Sch 1, Pt I, paras 1, 2, 4–6, 8, 11, 13, 14(2), (3)(a)–(c), 15) (SI 1998/2031)
		13 May 1999 (so far as relates to Sch 1, Pt 1, paras 7, 14(5)(b)) (SI 1999/1309)

Chiropractors Act 1994 (c 17)—*contd*
Section

1	(4)	1 Feb 2002 (so far as relates to Sch 1, Pt 1, paras 9, 10, 14(5)(a)) (SI 2002/312)
		16 Jun 2002 (so far as it relates to Sch 1, Pt 1, paras 3 (insofar as it relates to elected members), 14(1), (3)(d), (4)) (SI 2002/312)
		15 Feb 2003 (so far as it relates to Sch 1, Pt 1, para 12 (for the purpose of enabling consultation on appointments by the Education Committee)) (SI 2002/312)
		16 Jun 2003 (so far as relates to Sch 1, Pt 1, para 12 (otherwise)) (SI 2001/312)
		16 Jun 2003 (so far as relates to Sch 1, Pt 1, para 3 (insofar as it relates to education members and members appointed by the Secretary of State)) (SI 2001/312)
		16 Jun 2004 (so far as relates to Sch 1, Pt 1, para 3 (otherwise)) (SI 2002/312)
	(5)–(7)	13 May 1999 (so far as they relate to the Education Committee) (SI 1999/1309)
		7 Sep 2000 (otherwise) (SI 2000/2388)
	(8)	14 Aug 1998 (SI 1998/2031)
	(9)	13 May 1999 (so far as relates to the provisions of Sch 1, Pt II brought into force by SI 1999/1309) (SI 1999/1309)
		7 Sep 2000 (so far as not already in force) (SI 2000/2388)
		Not in force (otherwise)
	(10)–(12)	14 Aug 1998 (SI 1998/2031)
2	(1), (2)	14 Aug 1998 (SI 1998/2031)
	(3)	15 Jun 1999 (SI 1999/1496)
	(4)–(6)	14 Aug 1998 (SI 1998/2031)
3, 4		15 Jun 1999 (SI 1999/1496)
5		*Not in force*
6		15 Jun 1999 (SI 1999/1496)
7	(1)–(2)	7 Sep 2000 (SI 2000/2388)
	(3)	15 Jun 2001 (SI 2001/2028)
8	(1)–(7)	7 Sep 2000 (SI 2000/2388)
	(8)	7 Sep 2000 (so far as relates to restoration to register of conditionally registered chiropractors) (SI 2000/2388)

Chiropractors Act 1994 (c 17)—*contd*

Section

8	(8)—*contd*	*Not in force* (otherwise)
9		15 Jun 1999 (SI 1999/1496)
10	(1)	15 Jun 1999 (SI 1999/1496)
	(2)–(12)	7 Sep 2000 (SI 2000/2388)
11–16		13 May 1999 (SI 1999/1309)
17		*Not in force*
18		13 May 1999 (SI 1999/1309)
19		15 Jun 1999 (SI 1999/1496)
20–28		7 Sep 2000 (SI 2000/2388)
29		15 Jun 1999 (SI 1999/1496)
30, 31		7 Sep 2000 (SI 2000/2388)
32	(1)	15 Jun 2001 (subject to a transitional provision) (SI 2001/2028)
	(2)	7 Sep 2000 (SI 2000/2388)
	(3)	7 Sep 2000 (so far as relates to sub-s (2)) (SI 2000/2388)
		15 Jun 2001 (otherwise) (SI 2001/2028)
33		13 May 1999 (SI 1999/1309)
34		14 Aug 1998 (SI 1998/2031)
35	(1), (2)	14 Aug 1998 (SI 1998/2031)
	(3)	7 Sep 2000 (SI 2000/2388)
	(4)	14 Aug 1998 (SI 1998/2031)
36	(1), (2)	14 Aug 1998 (SI 1998/2031)
	(3)	15 Jun 1999 (SI 1999/1496)
	(4)–(6)	14 Aug 1998 (SI 1998/2031)
37		15 Jun 1999 (SI 1999/1496)
38		Repealed
39		13 May 1999 (SI 1999/1309)
40		15 Jun 1999 (SI 1999/1496); prospectively repealed by Police Act 1997, ss 133(e), 134(2), Sch 10[1]
41		14 Aug 1998 (SI 1998/2031)
42		See Sch 2 below
43		14 Aug 1998 (so far as it provides the definitions "the General Council", "prescribed" and "the Registrar") (SI 1998/2031)
		13 May 1999 (so far as it provides the definitions "recognised qualification", "the required standard of proficiency", "the statutory committees" and "visitor") (SI 1999/1309)
		15 Jun 1999 (so far as it provides the definitions "conditionally registered chiropractor", "fully registered chiropractor", "opening of the register", "the register", "registered", "registered address",

Chiropractors Act 1994 (c 17)—*contd*

Section

43—*contd*			"registered chiropractor" and "unacceptable professional conduct") (SI 1999/1496)
			7 Sep 2000 (so far as provides the definition "interim suspension order") (SI 2000/2388)
			Not in force (otherwise)
44	(1)		14 Aug 1998 (SI 1998/2031)
	(2)		5 Jul 1994 (s 44(2))
	(3)–(6)		14 Aug 1998 (SI 1998/2031)
	(7)		See Sch 1, Pt III below
	(8)		14 Aug 1998 (so far as it relates to provisions of this Act already in force or brought into force by SI 1998/2031) (SI 1998/2031)
			13 May 1999 (so far as it relates to the provisions of this Act brought into force by SI 1999/1309) (SI 1999/1309)
			15 Jun 1999 (otherwise) (SI 1999/1496)

Schedule

1, Pt	I, para	1, 2		14 Aug 1998 (SI 1998/2031)
		3		16 Jun 2002 (in so far as it relates to elected members) (SI 2002/312)
				16 Jun 2003 (in so far as relates to education members and the member appointed by Secretary of State) (SI 2002/312)
				16 Jun 2004 (otherwise) (SI 2002/312)
		4		14 Aug 1998 (SI 1998/2031)
		5		14 Aug 1998 (subject to a transitional provision) (SI 1998/2031)
		6		14 Aug 1998 (SI 1998/2031)
		7		13 May 1999 (SI 1999/1309)
		8		14 Aug 1998 (SI 1998/2031)
		9, 10		1 Feb 2002 (SI 2002/312)
		11		14 Aug 1998 (SI 1998/2031)
		12		15 Feb 2003 (for purposes of enabling consultation on appointments by the Education Committee) (SI 2002/312)
				16 Jun 2003 (otherwise) (SI 2002/312)
		13		14 Aug 1998 (SI 1998/2031)
		14	(1)	16 Jun 2002 (SI 2002/312)
			(2)	14 Aug 1998 (subject to a transitional provision) (SI 1998/2031)
			(3) (a)–(c)	14 Aug 1998 (SI 1998/2031)
			(d)	16 Jun 2002 (SI 2002/312)
			(4)	16 Jun 2002 (SI 2002/312)

Chiropractors Act 1994 (c 17)—*contd*

Section

1, Pt	I, para	14	(5)	(a)	1 Feb 2002 (SI 2002/312)
				(b)	13 May 1999 (SI 1999/1309)
		15			14 Aug 1998 (SI 1998/2031)
	II, para	16, 17			13 May 1999 (SI 1999/1309)
		18–20			13 May 1999 (so far as they relate to the Education Committee) (SI 1999/1309)
					7 Sep 2000 (otherwise) (SI 2000/2388)
		21	(1)		7 Sep 2000 (SI 2000/2388)
			(2)		13 May 1999 (so far as relates to the Education Committee) (SI 1999/1309)
					7 Sep 2000 (otherwise) (SI 2000/2388)
		22, 23			13 May 1999 (so far as they relate to the Education Committee) (SI 1999/1309)
					7 Sep 2000 (otherwise) (SI 2000/2388)
		24			7 Sep 2000 (SI 2000/2388)
		25–29			13 May 1999 (SI 1999/1309)
		30–41			7 Sep 2000 (SI 2000/2388)
	III				14 Aug 1998 (SI 1998/2031)
2					5 Jul 1994 (s 44(2))

[1]   Orders made under Police Act 1997, s 135, bringing the prospective repeal into force will be noted to that Act

---

Church of England (Legal Aid) Measure 1994 (No 3)

RA: 21 Jul 1994

Commencement provisions: s 8(2)

The provisions of this Measure are brought into force on 1 Sep 1994 by an appointed day notice signed by the Archbishops of Canterbury and York and dated 25 Jul 1994 (made under s 8(2))

Coal Industry Act 1994 (c 21)

RA: 5 Jul 1994

Commencement provisions: s 68(2)–(6); Coal Industry Act 1994 (Commencement No 1) Order 1994, SI 1994/2189; Coal Industry Act 1994 (Commencement No 2 and Transitional Provision) Order 1994, SI 1994/2552; Coal Industry (Restructuring Date) Order 1994, SI 1994/2553; Coal Industry Act 1994 (Commencement No 3) Order 1994, SI 1994/3063; Coal Industry Act 1994 (Commencement No 4) Order 1995, SI 1995/159; Coal Industry Act 1994 (Commencement No 5) Order 1995, SI 1995/273; Coal Industry Act 1994 (Commencement No 6) and Membership of the British Coal Corporation (Appointed Day) Order 1995, SI 1995/1507

Section

1	19 Sep 1994 (SI 1994/2189)
2, 3	31 Oct 1994 (SI 1994/2552)

Coal Industry Act 1994 (c 21)—*contd*

Section		
4–6		19 Sep 1994 (SI 1994/2189)
7–9		5 Jul 1994 (s 68(4), (6))
10, 11		31 Oct 1994 (SI 1994/2553)
12–14		5 Jul 1994 (s 68(4), (6))
15, 16		31 Oct 1994 (SI 1994/2552)
17		5 Jul 1994 (s 68(4), (6))
18		31 Oct 1994 (SI 1994/2553)
19, 20		31 Oct 1994 (SI 1994/2552)
21		19 Sep 1994 (SI 1994/2189)
22	(1)	31 Oct 1994 (SI 1994/2552)
	(2)	*Not in force*
	(3)	31 Oct 1994 (SI 1994/2552)
23		31 Oct 1994 (SI 1994/2553)
24		31 Jan 1995 (SI 1995/159)
25–30		31 Oct 1994 (SI 1994/2552)
31–34		31 Oct 1994 (SI 1994/2553)
35		31 Oct 1994 (SI 1994/2552)
36		31 Oct 1994 (SI 1994/2553)
37		31 Oct 1994 (SI 1994/2552)
38–44		31 Oct 1994 (SI 1994/2553)
45–47		31 Oct 1994 (SI 1994/2552)
48–53		31 Oct 1994 (SI 1994/2553)
54		5 Jul 1994 (s 68(4), (6))
55		31 Oct 1994 (SI 1994/2553)
56–61		31 Oct 1994 (SI 1994/2552)
62–66		5 Jul 1994 (s 68(4), (6))
67	(1)	See Sch 9 below
	(2)–(6)	5 Jul 1994 (s 68(4), (6))
	(7)	See Sch 10 below
	(8)	See Sch 11 below
68		5 Jul 1994 (s 68(4), (6))
Schedule		
1		19 Sep 1994 (SI 1994/2189)
2		5 Jul 1994 (s 68(4), (6))
3		31 Oct 1994 (SI 1994/2552)
4		19 Sep 1994 (SI 1994/2189)
5		31 Oct 1994 (SI 1994/2552)
6–8		31 Oct 1994 (SI 1994/2553)
9, para	1–6	31 Oct 1994 (SI 1994/2553)
	7	*Not in force*
	8	31 Oct 1994 (SI 1994/2552)
	9, 10	31 Oct 1994 (SI 1994/2553)
	11	Repealed
	12	31 Oct 1994 (SI 1994/2552)
	13	Repealed
	14–18	31 Oct 1994 (SI 1994/2553)
	19	Repealed (subject to transitional provisions)
	20–23	31 Oct 1994 (SI 1994/2553)

Coal Industry Act 1994 (c 21)—*contd*
Schedule

9, para	24		*Not in force*
	25–28		31 Oct 1994 (SI 1994/2553)
	29, 30		*Not in force*
	31–38		31 Oct 1994 (SI 1994/2553)
	39	(1)	31 Oct 1994 (SI 1994/2553)
		(2), (3)	1 Nov 1994 (SI 1994/2552)
		(4)	31 Oct 1994 (SI 1994/2553)
	40–44		31 Oct 1994 (SI 1994/2553)
	45		*Not in force*
10			31 Oct 1994 (SI 1994/2552)
11, Pt	I		5 Jul 1994 (s 68(4), (6))
	II		31 Oct 1994 (SI 1994/2553)
	III		31 Oct 1994 (repeals of or in Coal Act 1938; Coal Act 1943; Coal Industry Nationalisation Act 1946, ss 52, 57, 58, 63(2); Opencast Coal Act 1958; Land Commission Act 1967; Electricity Act 1989) (SI 1994/2552)

1 Nov 1994 (repeals in Town and Country Planning (Scotland) Act 1972; Town and Country Planning Act 1990) (SI 1994/2552)

24 Dec 1994 (repeals of or in Coal Industry Nationalisation Act 1946, s 45 (for purposes specified in sub-s (1) thereof); Housing and Planning Act 1986, Sch 8, para 8; Coal Industry Act 1987, Sch 1, paras 9, 17, 20) (SI 1994/3063)

1 Mar 1995 (repeals of or in Coal Industry Nationalisation Act 1946, s 4 (subject to a saving in relation to sub-s (6)); Coal Consumers' Councils (Northern Irish Interests) Act 1962 (subject to a saving in relation to s 2); Chronically Sick and Disabled Persons Act 1970, s 14(1)) (SI 1995/273)

30 Jun 1995 (repeals of or in Coal Industry Nationalisation Act 1946, s 2(2), (3), (5); Coal Industry Act 1949, s 1(2), (4)) (SI 1995/1507)
Not in force (otherwise)

	IV	*Not in force*

Consolidated Fund Act 1994 (c 4)

Whole Act repealed

Consolidated Fund (No 2) Act 1994 (c 41)

Whole Act repealed

Criminal Justice and Public Order Act 1994 (c 33)

RA: 3 Nov 1994

Commencement provisions: ss 82(3), 172(2)–(4), (6); Criminal Justice and Public Order Act 1994 (Commencement No 1) Order 1994, SI 1994/2935; Criminal Justice and Public Order Act 1994 (Commencement No 2) Order 1994, SI 1994/3192; Criminal Justice and Public Order Act 1994 (Commencement No 3) Order 1994, SI 1994/3258; Criminal Justice and Public Order Act 1994 (Commencement No 4) Order 1995, SI 1995/24; Criminal Justice and Public Order Act 1994 (Commencement No 5 and Transitional Provisions) Order 1995, SI 1995/127; Criminal Justice and Public Order Act 1994 (Commencement No 6) Order 1995, SI 1995/721; Criminal Justice and Public Order Act 1994 (Commencement No 7) Order 1995, SI 1995/1378; Criminal Justice and Public Order Act 1994 (Commencement No 8 and Transitional Provision) Order 1995, SI 1995/1957; Criminal Justice and Public Order Act 1994 (Commencement No 9) Order 1996, SI 1996/625; Criminal Justice and Public Order Act 1994 (Commencement No 10) Order 1996, SI 1996/1608; Criminal Justice and Public Order Act 1994 (Commencement No 11 and Transitional Provision) Order 1997, SI 1997/882; Criminal Justice and Public Order Act 1994 (Commencement No 12 and Transitional Provision) Order 1998, SI 1998/277; Criminal Justice and Public Order Act 1994 (Commencement No 13) Order 2002, SI 2002/447

Section	
1–4	Repealed, subject to transitional provisions
5–15	3 Nov 1994 (s 172(4))
16	Repealed
17, 18	3 Feb 1995 (subject to a saving relating to s 17) (SI 1995/127)
19	30 May 1995 (SI 1995/1378)
20	Repealed
21	*Not in force*
22	8 Mar 1996 (SI 1996/625)
23, 24	3 Feb 1995 (subject to a saving relating to s 23) (SI 1995/127)
25–30	10 Apr 1995 (SI 1995/721)
31–33	3 Feb 1995 (subject to a saving relating to s 31) (SI 1995/127)
34–39	10 Apr 1995 (SI 1995/721)
40–43	3 Feb 1995 (SI 1995/127)
44	Repealed (deemed to have been enacted with this repeal)
45	See Sch 5 below
46, 47	3 Feb 1995 (subject to a saving relating to s 50) (SI 1995/127)
48	Repealed
49	3 Feb 1995 (subject to a saving relating to s 50) (SI 1995/127)

Criminal Justice and Public Order Act 1994 (c 33)—*contd*
Section

50		3 Feb 1995 (subject to a saving relating to s 50) (SI 1995/127); prospectively repealed by Youth Justice and Criminal Evidence Act 1999, s 67, Sch 6[1]
51		3 Feb 1995 (subject to a saving relating to s 50) (SI 1995/127)
52		11 Jan 1995 (SI 1994/3258)
53		2 Feb 1995 (SI 1995/24)
54–60		10 Apr 1995 (SI 1995/721)
60AA		Inserted by Anti-terrorism, Crime and Security Act 2001, s 94(1) (qv)
60A, 60B		Inserted by Crime and Disorder Act 1998, ss 26, 27(2) (qv)
61		3 Nov 1994 (s 172(4))
62		10 Apr 1995 (SI 1995/721)
63		3 Nov 1994 (s 172(4))
64	(1)–(3)	3 Feb 1995 (so far as relating to powers conferred on a constable by s 63) (SI 1995/127)
		Not in force (otherwise)
	(4)–(6)	10 Apr 1995 (SI 1995/721)
65		3 Nov 1994 (s 172(4))
66	(1)–(5)	10 Apr 1995 (SI 1995/721)
	(6)	3 Feb 1995 (SI 1995/127)
	(7)–(9)	10 Apr 1995 (SI 1995/721)
	(10)–(13)	3 Feb 1995 (SI 1995/127)
67	(1), (2)	10 Apr 1995 (SI 1995/721)
	(3)–(5)	3 Feb 1995 (SI 1995/127)
	(6), (7)	10 Apr 1995 (SI 1995/721)
	(8), (9)	3 Feb 1995 (SI 1995/127)
68–71		3 Nov 1994 (s 172(4))
72–74		3 Feb 1995 (SI 1995/127)
75, 76		24 Aug 1995 (SI 1995/1957)
77–80		3 Nov 1994 (s 172(4))
81–83		Repealed
84–88		3 Feb 1995 (subject to a saving relating to s 88) (SI 1995/127)
89		1 Nov 1995 (subject to a transitional provision) (SI 1995/1957)
90		3 Nov 1994 (s 172(4))
91, 92		3 Feb 1995 (SI 1995/127)
93–101		3 Nov 1994 (s 172(4))
102–117		3 Feb 1995 (SI 1995/127)
118–125		10 Apr 1995 (SI 1995/721)
126–128		3 Nov 1994 (s 172(4))
129		Repealed
130, 131		3 Feb 1995 (SI 1995/127)
132		Repealed

Criminal Justice and Public Order Act 1994 (c 33)—*contd*
Section

133–140		3 Feb 1995 (note that s 134(3) only comes into force on that date for purpose of making rules under Prisons (Scotland) Act 1989, s 18(3A)—s 134(3) and otherwise comes into force on 1 Jun 1995) (subject to savings relating to s 134(3)) (SI 1995/127)
141		Repealed
142–144		3 Nov 1994 (s 172(4))
145		Repealed
146–148		3 Nov 1994 (s 172(4))
149		1 Jul 1996 (SI 1996/1608)
150		3 Nov 1994 (s 172(4))
151		9 Jan 1995 (SI 1994/3192)
152–155		3 Feb 1995 (SI 1995/127)
156		10 Apr 1995 (SI 1995/721)
157		3 Feb 1995 (subject to a saving) (SI 1995/127)
158	(1)	3 Nov 1994 (s 172(4))
	(2)	1 Apr 1997 (SI 1997/882)
	(3), (4)	3 Nov 1994 (s 172(4))
	(5)–(8)	1 Apr 1997 (subject to transitional provisions relating to sub-ss (5), (8)) (SI 1997/882)
159	(1), (2)	19 Dec 1994 (SI 1994/2935)
	(3)	20 Mar 2002 (SI 2002/447)
	(4)	19 Dec 1994 (SI 1994/2935)
	(5)	1 Apr 1997 (SI 1997/882)
160		3 Feb 1995 (SI 1995/127)
161		Repealed
162–164		3 Feb 1995 (SI 1995/127)
165		*Not in force*
166, 167		3 Nov 1994 (s 172(4))
168	(1)	See Sch 9 below
	(2)	See Sch 10 below
	(3)	See Sch 11 below
169, 170		3 Feb 1995 (SI 1995/127)
171, 172		3 Nov 1994 (s 172(4))
Schedule		
1, 2		3 Nov 1994 (s 172(4))
3		10 Apr 1995 (SI 1995/721)
4		Repealed (deemed to have been enacted with this repeal)
5		4 Sep 1995 (SI 1995/1957)
6		3 Feb 1995 (SI 1995/127)
7		10 Apr 1995 (SI 1995/721)
8		3 Feb 1995 (subject to a saving) (SI 1995/127)

Criminal Justice and Public Order Act 1994 (c 33)—*contd*

Schedule

9, para	1–6	3 Feb 1995 (SI 1995/127)
	7	Repealed
	8, 9	3 Feb 1995 (subject to a saving relating to para 15) (SI 1995/127)
	10	Repealed
	11, 12	3 Feb 1995 (subject to a saving relating to para 15) (SI 1995/127)
	13	3 Feb 1995 (subject to a saving relating to para 15) (SI 1995/127); prospectively repealed by Youth Justice and Criminal Evidence Act 1999, s 67, Sch 6[1]
	14	3 Feb 1995 (SI 1995/127)
	15, 16	Repealed
	17–20	3 Feb 1995 (SI 1995/127)
	21	Repealed
	22–27	3 Feb 1995 (SI 1995/127)
	28	Repealed
	29–32	3 Feb 1995 (subject to a saving relating to para 33) (SI 1995/127)
	33	3 Feb 1995 (subject to a saving relating to para 33) (SI 1995/127); prospectively repealed by Youth Justice and Criminal Evidence Act 1999, s 67, Sch 6[1]
	34	9 Jan 1995 (SI 1994/3192)
	35–37	3 Feb 1995 (save for para 37(3)) (SI 1995/127) 10 Apr 1995 (para 37(3)) (SI 1995/721)
	38	*Not in force*
	39	3 Feb 1995 (subject to a saving relating to para 40) (SI 1995/127); prospectively repealed by Police (Amendment) (Northern Ireland) Order 1995, SI 1995/2993 (NI 17), art 32(2), Sch 2[2]
	40–42	Repealed
	43	3 Feb 1995 (SI 1995/127)
	44, 45	Repealed
	46	3 Nov 1994 (s 172(4))
	47–51	Repealed
	52, 53	3 Feb 1995 (SI 1995/127)
10, para	1–3	10 Apr 1995 (SI 1995/721)
	4, 5	Repealed
	6	10 Apr 1995 (SI 1995/721)
	7, 8	3 Feb 1995 (SI 1995/127)
	9	1 Mar 1998 (SI 1998/277)
	10	10 Apr 1995 (SI 1995/721)
	11	3 Feb 1995 (SI 1995/127)

Criminal Justice and Public Order Act 1994 (c 33)—*contd*

Schedule

10, para	12	1 Mar 1998 (SI 1998/277)
	13, 14	Repealed
	15	10 Apr 1995 (SI 1995/721)
	16	1 Mar 1998 (SI 1998/277)
	17	Repealed
	18	3 Feb 1995 (SI 1995/127)
	19–23	10 Apr 1995 (SI 1995/721)
	24	1 Mar 1998 (SI 1998/277)
	25	3 Feb 1995 (SI 1995/127)
	26	3 Nov 1994 (s 172(4), (6))
	27	Repealed
	28, 29	3 Feb 1995 (SI 1995/127)
	30	1 Mar 1998 (SI 1998/277)
	31	3 Feb 1995 (SI 1995/127)
	32	10 Apr 1995 (SI 1995/721); prospectively repealed by Youth Justice and Criminal Evidence Act 1999, s 67, Sch 6[1]
	33, 34	10 Apr 1995 (SI 1995/721)
	35	3 Nov 1994 (s 172(4), (6))
	36	3 Nov 1994 (s 172(4), (6)); prospectively repealed by Youth Justice and Criminal Evidence Act 1999, s 67, Sch 6[1]
	37, 38	3 Feb 1995 (SI 1995/127)
	39	1 Mar 1998 (SI 1998/277)
	40	9 Jan 1995 (SI 1994/3192)
	41	10 Apr 1995 (SI 1995/721)
	42	Repealed
	43, 44	10 Apr 1995 (SI 1995/721)
	45	3 Feb 1995 (SI 1995/127)
	46	1 Mar 1998 (SI 1998/277)
	47	Repealed
	48	10 Apr 1995 (SI 1995/721)
	49	Repealed
	50	1 Mar 1998 (SI 1998/277)
	51	10 Apr 1995 (SI 1995/721)
	52	3 Feb 1995 (SI 1995/127)
	53	24 Aug 1995 (SI 1995/1957)
	54–58	10 Apr 1995 (SI 1995/721)
	59, 60	3 Nov 1994 (s 172(4), (6))
	61, 62	10 Apr 1995 (SI 1995/721)
	63	Repealed
	64	9 Jan 1995 (so far as substitutes for reference to s 41 references to ss 41 and 41B in Prisons (Scotland) Act 1989, s 19(4)) (SI 1994/3192)
		3 Feb 1995 (so far as not already in force) (SI 1995/127)

Criminal Justice and Public Order Act 1994 (c 33)—*contd*

Schedule

10, para	65–67	Repealed
	68	3 Feb 1995 (SI 1995/127)
	69	9 Jan 1995 (SI 1994/3192)
	70	1 Jul 1996 (SI 1996/1608)
	71	10 Apr 1995 (SI 1995/721)
	72, 73	Repealed
11[3]		3 Nov 1994 (repeals in Sexual Offences Act 1967; Caravan Sites Act 1968; Sexual Offences (Amendment) Act 1976; Public Order Act 1986; Criminal Justice (Scotland) Act 1980; Homosexual Offences (Northern Ireland) Order 1982, SI 1982/1536) (s 172(4))[4]
		9 Jan 1995 (repeals of or in Magistrates' Courts Act 1980, s 24; Criminal Justice Act 1988, s 126; Criminal Justice Act 1991, s 64; Criminal Justice Act 1993, s 67(2)) (SI 1994/3192)
		3 Feb 1995 (repeals of or in Indictable Offences Act 1848; Sexual Offences Act 1956; Children and Young Persons Act 1963; Police (Scotland) Act 1967; Children and Young Persons Act 1969; Police Act 1969[5]; Police Act (Northern Ireland) 1970; Juries Act 1974; Rehabilitation of Offenders Act 1974; Criminal Law Act 1977, s 38; Protection of Children Act 1978; Magistrates' Courts Act 1980, ss 22(1), 38(2)(b); Criminal Justice Act 1982, s 12(6), (7), (11); Video Recordings Act 1984; Prisons (Scotland) Act 1989; Broadcasting Act 1990; Northern Ireland (Emergency Provisions) Act 1991; Criminal Justice Act 1991 (so far as not already in force); Parole Board (Transfer of Functions) Order 1992, SI 1992/1829; Video Recordings Act 1993; Criminal Justice Act 1993 (so far as not already in force)) (SI 1995/127)

Criminal Justice and Public Order Act 1994 (c 33)—*contd*
Schedule
11³—*contd*

10 Apr 1995 (repeals in Criminal
Evidence Act 1898; Criminal
Evidence Act (Northern Ireland)
1923; Bail Act 1976; Police and
Criminal Evidence Act 1984;
Criminal Evidence (Northern
Ireland) Order 1988,
SI 1988/1987) (SI 1995/721)
4 Sep 1995 (repeals in Prosecution of
Offences Act 1985, Criminal
Justice Act 1988, ss 25, 34, 160)
(SI 1995/1957)
1 Mar 1998 (repeals of or in Prison
Act 1952, s 43(1), the word "and"
at end of para (b); Criminal Justice
Act 1967, s 67(5), word "and" at
end of para (a); Criminal Justice
Act 1982, Sch 14, para 8)
(SI 1998/277)
20 Mar 2002 (repeals in Backing of
Warrants (Republic of Ireland)
Act 1965) (SI 2002/447)
Not in force (otherwise)

1   Orders made under Youth Justice and Criminal Evidence Act 1999, s 68(3), bringing the prospective repeals into force will be noted to that Act Orders made under Crime and Disorder Act 1998, s 121(2), bringing the prospective repeals into force will be noted to that Act

2   For the commencement of this repeal, see orders made under Police (Amendment) (Northern Ireland) Order 1995, SI 1995/2993 (NI 17), art 1(2), bringing the prospective repeal into force will be noted to that Act

3   Certain repeals made by Sch 11 have been repealed by Criminal Procedure and Investigations Act 1996, s 44, and Sch 11 is deemed to have been enacted as such

4   In relation to repeal of Criminal Justice Act 1991, s 50(4), note that s 150 of this Act (which also effects that repeal) is brought into force on 3 Nov 1994 as noted above

5   The entry relating to Children and Young Persons Act 1969, s 57(4) is to be treated as always having been an entry relating to Children and Young Persons Act 1969, s 57(4), by virtue of Youth Justice and Criminal Evidence Act 1999, s 67, Sch 4, para 24, as from a day to be appointed under s 68(3) of the 1999 Act

Deregulation and Contracting Out Act 1994 (c 40)

RA: 3 Nov 1994

Commencement provisions: s 82(2)–(7); Deregulation and Contracting Out Act 1994 (Commencement No 1) Order 1994, SI 1994/3037; Deregulation and Contracting Out Act 1994 (Commencement No 2) Order 1994, SI 1994/3188; Industrial Relations (Deregulation and Contracting Out Act 1994) (Commencement) Order (Northern Ireland) 1994, SR 1994/488; Deregulation and Contracting Out Act 1994 (Commencement No 3) Order 1995, SI 1995/1433; Deregulation and Contracting Out Act 1994 (Commencement No 4 and Transitional Provisions) Order 1995, SI 1995/2835

Deregulation and Contracting Out Act 1994 (c 40)—*contd*

Section

1–5		Repealed
6		3 Nov 1994 (s 82(3))
7		3 Jan 1995 (s 82(2))
8		3 Jan 1995 (SI 1994/3188)
9		3 Jan 1995 (s 82(2))
10, 11		Repealed
12	(1)–(6)	Repealed
	(7)	See Sch 4 below
13	(1)	See Sch 5 below
	(2)	See Sch 6 below
14		3 Nov 1994 (s 82(3))
15		3 Jan 1995 (s 82(2))
16, 17		Repealed
18		3 Nov 1994 (s 82(3))
19		3 Jan 1995 (SI 1994/3188)
20, 21		3 Jan 1995 (s 82(2))
22–24		1 Dec 1994 (SI 1994/3037)
25–30		3 Nov 1994 (s 82(3))
31		3 Jan 1995 (s 82(2))
32–34		3 Nov 1994 (s 82(3))
35		See Sch 10 below
36	(1)	3 Jan 1995 (subject to transitional provisions) (SI 1994/3188)
	(2)	Repealed
37		3 Nov 1994 (s 82(3))
38		1 Jan 1996 (SI 1995/2835)
39		See Sch 11 below
40		3 Nov 1994 (s 82(3))
41–57		Repealed
58		3 Jan 1995 (SI 1994/3188)
59		1 Jan 1996 (subject to transitional provisions) (SI 1995/2835)
60		1 Apr 1995 (subject to transitional provisions) (SI 1994/3188)
61		1 Jan 1996 (subject to transitional provisions) (SI 1995/2835)
62		3 Jan 1995 (SI 1994/3188)
63		1 Jan 1996 (subject to transitional provisions) (SI 1995/2835)
64		3 Jan 1995 (SI 1994/3188)
65, 66		1 Jan 1996 (subject to transitional provisions) (SI 1995/2835)
67		3 Jan 1995 (SI 1994/3188)
68		See Sch 14 below
69–79		3 Jan 1995 (s 82(2))
80		1 Jan 1996 (subject to transitional provisions) (SI 1995/2835)
81		See Sch 17 below
82		3 Nov 1994 (s 82(3))

Deregulation and Contracting Out Act 1994 (c 40)—*contd*

Schedule

1				Repealed
2–4				3 Jan 1995 (s 82(2))
5				1 Jul 1995 (SI 1995/1433)
6, para	1, 2			1 Jul 1995 (so far as enables regulations to be made under Companies (Northern Ireland) Order 1986, SI 1986/1032, arts 603B(6)(f), 603C(2)(f)) (SI 1995/1433)
				1 Nov 1995 (otherwise) (SI 1995/1433)
	3, 4			1 Nov 1995 (SI 1995/1433)
7				3 Jan 1995 (SI 1994/3188)
8				Repealed
9				3 Jan 1995 (s 82(2))
10				3 Jan 1995 (SI 1994/3188)
11				3 Nov 1994 (amendments relating to Road Traffic Regulation Act 1984; Charities Act 1993) (s 82(3))
				3 Jan 1995 (amendments relating to Fair Trading Act 1973, ss 93A, 133; Energy Act 1976; Competition Act 1980; Building Societies Act 1986; Financial Services Act 1986; Companies Act 1989; Companies (Northern Ireland) Order 1990) (s 82(2))
				3 Jan 1995 (amendments relating to Licensing Act 1964; Fair Trading Act 1973, s 77) (SI 1994/3188)
				1 Jul 1995 (amendment relating to Company Directors Disqualification Act 1986) (SI 1995/1433)
				1 Nov 1995 (amendment relating to Companies (Northern Ireland) Order 1989, SI 1989/2404) (SI 1995/1433)
12, 13				Repealed
14, para	1			See paras 2–8 below
	2			1 Jan 1996 (subject to transitional provisions) (SI 1995/2835)
	3			3 Jan 1995 (SI 1994/3188)
	4			1 Jan 1996 (subject to transitional provisions) (SI 1995/2835)
	5	(1)		1 Jan 1996 (subject to transitional provisions) (SI 1995/2835)
		(2)	(a)	1 Jan 1996 (subject to transitional provisions) (SI 1995/2835)
			(b)	3 Jan 1995 (SI 1994/3188)
	6–8			1 Jan 1996 (subject to transitional provisions) (SI 1995/2835)

Deregulation and Contracting Out Act 1994 (c 40)—*contd*

Schedule

15, 16	3 Jan 1995 (s 82(2))
17	3 Nov 1994 (repeals in Road Traffic Regulation Act 1984; Weights and Measures Act 1985; Charities Act 1992; Charities Act 1993) (s 82(3))
	1 Dec 1994 (repeals of or in Shops Act 1950; Shops (Airports) Act 1962; Shops (Early Closing Days) Act 1965; Local Government Act 1972; Local Government (Scotland) Act 1973; Cinemas Act 1985; Employment Act 1989; Sunday Trading Act 1994) (SI 1994/3037)
	3 Jan 1995 (repeals in Fair Trading Act 1973; Competition Act 1980; Telecommunications Act 1984; Gas Act 1986; Building Societies Act 1986; Financial Services Act 1986; Electricity Act 1989; Companies Act 1989; Companies (Northern Ireland) Order 1990; Electricity (Northern Ireland) Order 1992; Railways Act 1993) (s 82(2))
	3 Jan 1995 (repeals of or in Merchant Shipping Act 1894; Licensing Act 1964; Employment Agencies Act 1973; House of Commons Disqualification Act 1975; Employment Protection Act 1975; Employment Protection (Consolidation) Act 1978; Merchant Shipping Act 1979; Public Passenger Vehicles Act 1981, ss 14A(3), 17(2)(b), 27; Employment (Miscellaneous Provisions) (Northern Ireland) Order 1981, SI 1981/839; Income and Corporation Taxes Act 1988) (SI 1994/3188)
	1 Jan 1996 (so far as not already in force) (SI 1995/2835)

Drug Trafficking Act 1994 (c 37)

RA: 3 Nov 1994

Commencement provisions: s 69(2)

3 Feb 1995 (s 69(2))

Education Act 1994 (c 30)

RA: 21 Jul 1994

Commencement provisions: s 26; Education Act 1994 (Commencement) Order 1994, SI 1994/2204

Section		
1–11		21 Sep 1994 (SI 1994/2204)
11A		Inserted by Education Act 1996, s 582(1), Sch 37, Pt I, para 126 (qv)
12–18		21 Sep 1994 (SI 1994/2204)
18A		Inserted by Teaching and Higher Education Act 1998, s 20 (qv)
19–21		21 Sep 1994 (SI 1994/2204)
22	(1), (2)	21 Sep 1994 (SI 1994/2204)
	(3)–(5)	1 Apr 1995 (SI 1994/2204)
	(6)–(9)	21 Sep 1994 (SI 1994/2204)
23–27		21 Sep 1994 (SI 1994/2204)
Schedule		
1, 2		21 Sep 1994 (SI 1994/2204)

European Union (Accessions) Act 1994 (c 38)

RA: 3 Nov 1994

3 Nov 1994 (RA)

Finance Act 1994 (c 9)

Budget Day: 30 Nov 1993

RA: 3 May 1994

Details of the commencement of Finance Acts are not set out in this work

Firearms (Amendment) Act 1994 (c 31)

RA: 21 Jul 1994

Commencement provisions: s 4(2)

21 Sep 1994 (s 4(2))

Inshore Fishing (Scotland) Act 1994 (c 27)

RA: 21 Jul 1994

Commencement provisions: s 5(1); Inshore Fishing (Scotland) Act 1994 (Commencement) Order 1994, SI 1994/2124

8 Aug 1994 (SI 1994/2124)

Insolvency Act 1994 (c 7)

RA: 24 Mar 1994

24 Mar 1994 (RA; but note ss 1(7), 2(4), 3(5), Sch 1, para 3)

Insolvency (No 2) Act 1994 (c 12)

RA: 26 May 1994

Commencement provisions: s 6(2)

26 Jul 1994 (s 6(2))

Intelligence Services Act 1994 (c 13)

RA: 26 May 1994

Commencement provisions: s 12(2); Intelligence Services Act 1994 (Commencement) Order 1994, SI 1994/2734

15 Dec 1994 (SI 1994/2734; though note that for purposes of making any Order in Council under s 12(4) it is brought into force on 2 Nov 1994)

Land Drainage Act 1994 (c 25)

RA: 21 Jul 1994

Commencement provisions: s 3(2)

21 Sep 1994 (s 3(2))

Law of Property (Miscellaneous Provisions) Act 1994 (c 36)

RA: 3 Nov 1994

Commencement provisions: s 23; Law of Property (Miscellaneous Provisions) Act 1994 (Commencement No 1) Order 1995, SI 1995/145; Law of Property (Miscellaneous Provisions) Act 1994 (Commencement No 2) Order 1995, SI 1995/1317

Section		
1–20		1 Jul 1995 (SI 1995/1317)
21	(1)	See Sch 1 below
	(2)–(4)	1 Jul 1995 (SI 1995/1317)
22–24		1 Jul 1995 (SI 1995/1317)
Schedule		
1, para	1	1 Jul 1995 (SI 1995/1317)
	2	15 Feb 1995 (SI 1995/145)
	3	1 Jul 1995 (SI 1995/1317)
	4	Repealed
	5–12	1 Jul 1995 (SI 1995/1317)
2		1 Jul 1995 (SI 1995/1317)

Local Government etc (Scotland) Act 1994 (c 39)

RA: 3 Nov 1994

Commencement provisions: s 184(2), (3); Local Government etc (Scotland) Act 1994 (Commencement No 1) Order 1994, SI 1994/2850, as amended by SI 1994/3150; Local Government etc (Scotland) Act 1994 (Commencement No 2) Order 1994, SI 1994/3150; Local Government etc (Scotland) Act 1994 (Commencement No 3) Order 1995, SI 1995/702; Local Government etc (Scotland) Act 1994 (Commencement No 4) Order 1995, SI 1995/1898; Local Government etc (Scotland) Act 1994 (Commencement No 5) Order 1995, SI 1995/2866; Local Government etc (Scotland) Act 1994 (Commencement No 6 and Saving) Order 1995, SI 1995/3326; Local Government etc (Scotland) Act 1994 (Commencement No 7 and Savings) Order 1996, SI 1996/323; Local Government etc (Scotland) Act 1994 (Commencement No 8) Order 1998, SI 1998/2532

Section		
1		8 Nov 1994 (SI 1994/2850)
2–4		6 Apr 1995 (SI 1995/702)
5		8 Nov 1994 (SI 1994/2850)
6		1 Apr 1996 (SI 1996/323)
7		8 Nov 1994 (SI 1994/2850)
8–11		4 Jan 1995 (SI 1994/2850)
12		8 Nov 1994 (SI 1994/2850)
13–17		4 Jan 1995 (SI 1994/2850)
18, 19		6 Apr 1995 (SI 1995/702)
20		1 Apr 1996 (SI 1995/702)
21, 22		1 Apr 1996 (SI 1996/323)
23		6 Apr 1995 (SI 1995/702)
24		4 Jan 1995 (SI 1994/2850)
25–29		6 Apr 1995 (SI 1995/702) (but note s 29(1) effective from 1 Apr 1996)
30–32		1 Apr 1996 (SI 1996/323)
33		Repealed
34		4 Jan 1995 (SI 1994/2850)
35		1 Apr 1996 (SI 1996/323)
36		6 Apr 1995 (subject to a transitional provision) (SI 1995/702)
37		Repealed (*never in force*)
38		4 Jan 1995 (SI 1994/2850)
39		6 Apr 1995 (SI 1995/702)
40		4 Jan 1995 (SI 1994/2850)
41		1 Apr 1996 (SI 1996/323)
42, 43		6 Apr 1995 (SI 1995/702)
44		4 Jan 1995 (SI 1994/2850)
45		1 Apr 1996 (SI 1996/323)
46		19 Feb 1996 (SI 1996/323)
47		4 Jan 1995 (SI 1994/2850)
48		1 Apr 1996 (SI 1996/323)
49, 50		4 Jan 1995 (SI 1994/2850)
51	(1), (2)	1 Apr 1996 (SI 1996/323)
	(3)	4 Jan 1995 (SI 1994/2850)

Local Government etc (Scotland) Act 1994 (c 39)—*contd*

Section

51	(4), (5)	1 Apr 1996 (SI 1996/323)
52		1 Apr 1996 (SI 1995/702)
53		1 Apr 1996 (SI 1996/323)
54	(1)–(4)	1 Apr 1996 (SI 1996/323)
	(5)	Repealed
55, 56		6 Apr 1995 (SI 1995/702)
57		8 Nov 1994 (SI 1994/2850)
58		1 Aug 1995 (so far as enables a new local authority to enter into an agreement with any other new local authority for carrying out an activity or service on and after 1 Apr 1996) (SI 1995/702)
		1 Apr 1996 (otherwise) (SI 1996/323)
59		6 Apr 1995 (SI 1995/702)
60		4 Jan 1995 (SI 1994/2850)
61		8 Nov 1994 (SI 1994/2850)
62–64		17 Jul 1995 (SI 1995/1898)
65	(1)	1 Apr 1996 (SI 1996/323)
	(2)	17 Jul 1995 (SI 1995/1898)
66		17 Jul 1995 (SI 1995/1898)
67		Repealed
67A		Inserted by Water Industry Act 1999, s 12(1) (qv)
68	(1)	Repealed
	(2)	Substituted for new sub-ss (2), (2A) by Water Industry Act 1999, s 15(1), Sch 3, para 10(1), (3) (qv)
	(3)	1 Apr 1996 (SI 1996/323)
	(4), (5)	30 Oct 1995 (SI 1995/2866)
69–71		30 Oct 1995 (SI 1995/2866)
72		1 Apr 1996 (SI 1996/323)
73, 74		17 Jul 1995 (SI 1995/1898)
75		1 Apr 1996 (SI 1996/323)
75A		Inserted by Water Industry Act 1999, s 13 (qv)
76, 77		17 Jul 1995 (SI 1995/1898)
78		1 Apr 1996 (SI 1996/323)
79	(1)–(3)	17 Jul 1995 (SI 1995/1898)
	(4)	1 Apr 1996 (SI 1996/323)
	(5)	17 Jul 1995 (SI 1995/1898)
80		1 Apr 1996 (SI 1996/323)
81		17 Jul 1995 (SI 1995/1898)
82		1 Apr 1996 (SI 1996/323)
83–87		17 Jul 1995 (SI 1995/1898)
88		Substituted by Public Finance and Accountability (Scotland) Act 2000, s 26, Sch 3, para 12(2) (qv)
89, 90		17 Jul 1995 (SI 1995/1898)

Local Government etc (Scotland) Act 1994 (c 39)—*contd*

Section

91–96		10 Mar 1995 (SI 1995/702)
97	(1)–(5)	4 Jan 1995 (SI 1994/2850)
	(6)	8 Nov 1994 (SI 1994/2850)
	(7), (8)	4 Jan 1995 (SI 1994/2850)
98		17 Jul 1995 (SI 1995/1898)
99, 100		1 Apr 1996 (SI 1996/323)
101		4 Jan 1995 (subject to a transitional provision) (SI 1994/2850)
102		1 Apr 1996 (SI 1996/323)
103		30 Jun 1999 (SI 1998/2532)
104		4 Jan 1995 (SI 1994/2850)
105–112		1 Apr 1996 (SI 1996/323)
113–115		4 Jan 1995 (SI 1994/2850)
116		17 Jul 1995 (SI 1995/1898)
117		1 Apr 1996 (SI 1996/323)
118	(1)	17 Jul 1995 (SI 1995/1898)
	(2), (3)	1 Apr 1996 (SI 1996/323)
119		1 Apr 1996 (SI 1996/323)
120	(1)	17 Jul 1995 (SI 1995/1898)
	(2)	1 Apr 1996 (SI 1996/323)
121		1 Apr 1996 (SI 1996/323)
122, 123		17 Jul 1995 (SI 1995/1898)
124		4 Jan 1995 (SI 1994/2850)
125		8 Nov 1994 (SI 1994/2850)
125A		Prospectively inserted by Environment Act 1995, s 116, Sch 21, para 6[1]
126		4 Jan 1995 (SI 1994/2850)
127–131		6 Apr 1995 (except so far as s 127(1) provides for the transfer of functions referred to therein or repeals Social Work (Scotland) Act 1968, s 36(1)) (SI 1995/702)
		1 Apr 1996 (exceptions relating to s 127(1) noted above) (SI 1996/323)
132		1 Apr 1996 (SI 1996/323)
133–136		6 Apr 1995 (SI 1995/702)
137	(1)	8 Nov 1994 (so far as applies to s 12) (SI 1994/2850)
		4 Jan 1995 (otherwise) (SI 1994/2850)
	(2)–(5)	4 Jan 1995 (SI 1994/2850)
138		6 Apr 1995 (SI 1995/702)
139		Repealed
140		1 Apr 1996 (SI 1996/323)
141		4 Jan 1995 (SI 1994/2850)
142		1 Apr 1996 (SI 1996/323)
143		4 Jan 1995 (SI 1994/2850)
144, 145		1 Apr 1996 (SI 1996/323)

Local Government etc (Scotland) Act 1994 (c 39)—*contd*

Section

146–151		4 Jan 1995 (SI 1994/2850)
152		1 Apr 1995 (SI 1994/3150)
153		4 Jan 1995 (SI 1994/3150)
154–156		1 Apr 1995 (SI 1994/3150)
157		Repealed
158, 159		1 Apr 1995 (SI 1994/3150)
160, 161		4 Jan 1995 (SI 1994/3150)
162	(1)	1 Apr 1995 (SI 1994/3150)
	(2)	1 Apr 1996 (SI 1996/323)
163		3 Nov 1994 (RA)
164	(1), (2)	1 Apr 1995 (SI 1995/702)
	(3)–(5)	1 Apr 1996 (SI 1996/323)
165–167		4 Jan 1995 (SI 1994/2850)
168		1 Apr 1995 (subject to a transitional provision) (SI 1995/702)
169		6 Apr 1995 (SI 1995/702)
170		4 Jan 1995 (SI 1994/2850)
171		30 Oct 1995 (so far as enables a local authority to comply with their duties under Local Government (Scotland) Act 1973, s 171A(5) before the beginning of the financial year commencing 1 Apr 1996, and so far as enables the Secretary of State to approve under s 171A(6) of the 1973 Act the proposals submitted by the local authority under sub-s (5) of that section) (SI 1995/2866) 1 Apr 1996 (otherwise) (SI 1995/2866)
172, 173		4 Jan 1995 (SI 1994/2850)
174		1 Apr 1996 (SI 1996/323)
175		4 Jan 1995 (SI 1994/2850)
176		1 Apr 1996 (SI 1995/2866)
177	(1)	See sub-ss (2), (3) below
	(2)	6 Apr 1995 (so far as relates to entry in House of Commons Disqualification Act 1975, Sch 1, Pt II, concerning Scottish Children's Reporter Administration) (SI 1995/702) 17 Jul 1995 (so far as relates to entry in House of Commons Disqualification Act 1975, Sch 1, Pt II, concerning East of Scotland Water Authority, North of Scotland Water Authority and West of Scotland Water Authority) (SI 1995/1898)

Local Government etc (Scotland) Act 1994 (c 39)—*contd*

Section

177	(2)—*contd*				30 Oct 1995 (otherwise) (SI 1995/2866)
	(3)				8 Nov 1994 (so far as relates to entry in House of Commons Disqualification Act 1975, Pt III, concerning any member of the staff commission) (SI 1994/2850)
					6 Apr 1995 (so far as not already in force) (SI 1995/702)
178					8 Nov 1994 (SI 1994/2850)
179					4 Jan 1995 (SI 1994/2850)
180	(1)				See Sch 13 below
	(2)				See Sch 14 below
181	(1), (2)				8 Nov 1994 (SI 1994/2850)
	(3)–(7)				6 Apr 1995 (SI 1995/702)
	(8), (9)				8 Nov 1994 (SI 1994/2850)
182					4 Jan 1995 (SI 1994/2850)
183	(1)				8 Nov 1994 (SI 1994/2850)
	(2)				1 Apr 1996 (SI 1996/323)
	(3)				6 Apr 1995 (SI 1995/702)
	(4), (5)				1 Apr 1996 (SI 1996/323)
	(6)				6 Apr 1995 (SI 1995/702)
184					8 Nov 1994 (SI 1994/2850)

Schedule

1, 2					8 Nov 1994 (SI 1994/2850)
3					6 Apr 1995 (SI 1995/702)
4					Repealed
5					4 Jan 1995 (SI 1994/2850)
6					1 Apr 1996 (SI 1995/702)
7, 8					17 Jul 1995 (SI 1995/1898)
9					Repealed
9A					Inserted by Water Industry Act 1999, s 12(4), Sch 2 (qv)
10					1 Apr 1996 (SI 1996/323)
11					10 Mar 1995 (SI 1995/702)
12					6 Apr 1995 (SI 1995/702)
13, para	1, 2				1 Apr 1996 (SI 1996/323)
	3				4 Jan 1995 (SI 1994/2850)
	4	(1)			4 Jan 1995 (SI 1994/2850)
		(2)			1 Apr 1996 (SI 1996/323)
		(3)			4 Jan 1995 (SI 1994/2850)
	5, 6				1 Apr 1996 (SI 1996/323)
	7				*Not in force;* prospectively repealed by Merchant Shipping Act 1995, s 314(1), Sch 12[2]
	8–26				1 Apr 1996 (SI 1996/323)
	27	(1), (2)			4 Jan 1995 (SI 1994/2850)
		(3)	(a)	(i)	4 Jan 1995 (SI 1994/2850)
				(ii)	1 Apr 1996 (SI 1996/323)

Local Government etc (Scotland) Act 1994 (c 39)—*contd*
Schedule

13, para	27	(3)	(b)–(o)	1 Apr 1996 (SI 1996/323)
			(p)	6 Apr 1995 (SI 1995/702)
			(q)	1 Apr 1996 (SI 1996/323)
		(4)		1 Apr 1996 (SI 1996/323)
	28–33			1 Apr 1996 (SI 1996/323)
	34			*Not in force*
	35, 36			1 Apr 1996 (SI 1996/323)
	37			Repealed
	38	(1)		See sub-paras (2)–(8) below
		(2)–(7)		Repealed
		(8)		1 Apr 1996 (SI 1996/323)
	39			1 Apr 1996 (SI 1996/323)
	40			Repealed
	41–56			1 Apr 1996 (SI 1996/323)
	57			1 Apr 1995 (SI 1994/3150)
	58, 59			1 Apr 1996 (SI 1996/323)
	60	(1)		4 Jan 1995 (SI 1994/2850)
		(2)		1 Apr 1996 (SI 1996/323)
		(3)	(a)–(c)	4 Jan 1995 (SI 1994/2850)
			(d)	1 Apr 1996 (SI 1996/323)
		(4)		1 Apr 1995 (SI 1994/3150)
		(5)		1 Apr 1996 (SI 1996/323)
	61			1 Apr 1996 (SI 1996/323)
	62			*Not in force*
	63–66			1 Apr 1996 (SI 1996/323)
	67	(1), (2)		1 Apr 1995 (SI 1994/3150)
		(3), (4)		1 Apr 1996 (SI 1996/323)
		(5)		1 Apr 1995 (SI 1994/3150)
	68–70			1 Apr 1996 (SI 1996/323)
	71	(1)		4 Jan 1995 (SI 1994/2850)
		(2)–(5)		1 Apr 1996 (SI 1996/323)
		(6)		4 Jan 1995 (SI 1994/2850)
		(7)–(17)		1 Apr 1996 (SI 1996/323)
	72	(1), (2)		1 Apr 1995 (SI 1995/702)
		(3)–(9)		1 Apr 1996 (SI 1996/323)
	73, 74			1 Apr 1996 (SI 1996/323)
	75	(1)		4 Jan 1995 (SI 1994/2850)
		(2)	(a)	1 Apr 1996 (SI 1996/323)
			(b)	4 Jan 1995 (subject to a transitional provision) (SI 1994/2850)
			(c)	1 Apr 1996 (SI 1996/323)
			(d)	4 Jan 1995 (subject to a transitional provision) (SI 1994/2850)
			(e)	4 Jan 1995 (SI 1994/2850)
		(3)–(12)		1 Apr 1996 (SI 1996/323)
		(13)	(a) (i)	1 Apr 1996 (SI 1996/323)
			(ii)	4 Jan 1995 (SI 1994/2850)
			(b), (c)	1 Apr 1996 (SI 1996/323)

Local Government etc (Scotland) Act 1994 (c 39)—*contd*

Schedule

13, para	75	(14)		4 Jan 1995 (subject to a transitional provision) (SI 1994/2850)
		(15), (16)		1 Apr 1996 (SI 1996/323)
		(17)	(a)–(c)	1 Apr 1996 (SI 1996/323)
			(d)	4 Jan 1995 (subject to a transitional provision) (SI 1994/2850)
		(18)	(a), (b)	1 Apr 1996 (SI 1996/323)
			(c)	4 Jan 1995 (SI 1994/2850)
		(19)	(a)	1 Apr 1996 (SI 1996/323)
			(b)	4 Jan 1995 (subject to a transitional provision) (SI 1994/2850)
		(20)		4 Jan 1995 (subject to a transitional provision) (SI 1994/2850)
		(21)–(23)		1 Apr 1996 (SI 1996/323)
		(24)		4 Jan 1995 (subject to a transitional provision) (SI 1994/2850)
		(25)	(a)	1 Apr 1996 (SI 1996/323)
			(b)	17 Jul 1995 (SI 1995/1898)
		(26)–(28)		1 Apr 1996 (SI 1996/323)
	76–81			1 Apr 1996 (SI 1996/323)
	82			Repealed
	83, 84			1 Apr 1996 (SI 1996/323)
	85	(1), (2)		1 Apr 1996 (SI 1996/323)
		(3)	(a)	Repealed
			(b) (i)	Repealed
			(ii)	1 Apr 1996 (SI 1996/323)
			(c)	1 Apr 1996 (SI 1996/323)
		(4)		Repealed
	86, 87			1 Apr 1996 (SI 1996/323)
	88			Repealed
	89–91			1 Apr 1996 (SI 1996/323)
	92	(1)		4 Jan 1995 (SI 1994/2850)
		(2)–(8)		1 Apr 1996 (SI 1996/323)
		(9)		1 Apr 1996 (SI 1996/323); prospectively repealed (S) by Ethical Standards in Public Life etc (Scotland) Act 2000 (asp 7), s 36, Sch 4[3]
		(10)–(19)		1 Apr 1996 (SI 1996/323)
		(20)		4 Jan 1995 (SI 1994/2850)
		(21)		1 Apr 1996 (SI 1996/323)
		(22)		4 Jan 1995 (SI 1994/2850)
		(23), (24)		1 Apr 1996 (SI 1996/323)
		(25)		1 Apr 1995 (SI 1995/702)
		(26), (27)		4 Jan 1995 (SI 1994/2850)
		(28)–(33)		1 Apr 1996 (SI 1996/323)
		(34), (35)		Repealed (*never in force*)
		(36)–(47)		1 Apr 1996 (SI 1996/323)
		(48)		*Not in force*

Local Government etc (Scotland) Act 1994 (c 39)—*contd*

Schedule

13, para	92	(49)–(56)		1 Apr 1996 (SI 1996/323)
		(57)		Repealed
		(58), (59)		1 Apr 1996 (SI 1996/323)
		(60)		Repealed
		(61)–(69)		1 Apr 1996 (SI 1996/323)
		(70)		4 Jan 1995 (SI 1994/2850)
		(71)–(74)		1 Apr 1996 (SI 1996/323)
	93	(1)		See sub-paras (2), (3) below
		(2)		Repealed
		(3)		1 Apr 1996 (SI 1996/323)
	94			1 Apr 1996 (SI 1996/323)
	95	(1)		4 Jan 1995 (SI 1994/2850)
		(2)		Repealed
		(3)		1 Apr 1996 (SI 1996/323)
		(4)		Repealed
		(5)–(7)		1 Apr 1996 (SI 1996/323)
		(8), (9)		Repealed (*never in force*)
		(10)		1 Apr 1996 (SI 1996/323)
	96–99			1 Apr 1996 (SI 1996/323)
	100	(1)		4 Jan 1995 (SI 1994/2850)
		(2)		1 Apr 1995 (SI 1994/3150)
		(3)		*Not in force*
		(4), (5)		1 Apr 1995 (SI 1994/3150)
		(6)	(a) (i)	6 Apr 1995 (SI 1995/702)
			(ii)	1 Apr 1996 (SI 1996/323)
			(b)	1 Apr 1996 (SI 1996/323)
		(7), (8)		1 Apr 1996 (SI 1996/323)
		(9)	(a)–(e)	1 Apr 1996 (SI 1996/323)
			(f), (g)	4 Jan 1995 (SI 1994/2850)
			(h)	31 Mar 1996 (SI 1996/323)
			(i)	1 Apr 1996 (SI 1996/323)
			(j)	*Not in force*
	101, 102			1 Apr 1996 (SI 1996/323)
	103			Repealed
	104–107			1 Apr 1996 (SI 1996/323)
	108			Repealed
	109–115			1 Apr 1996 (SI 1996/323)
	116			Repealed (sub-para (6) *never in force*)
	117, 118			1 Apr 1996 (SI 1996/323)
	119	(1)		4 Jan 1995 (SI 1994/2850)
		(2)–(4)		1 Apr 1996 (SI 1996/323)
		(5)	(a)–(c)	1 Apr 1996 (SI 1996/323)
			(d)	4 Jan 1995 (SI 1994/2850)
			(e)	1 Apr 1996 (SI 1996/323)
		(6)		1 Apr 1996 (SI 1996/323)
		(7)	(a), (b)	1 Apr 1996 (SI 1996/323)
			(c) (i)	1 Apr 1996 (SI 1996/323)
			(ii)	4 Jan 1995 (SI 1994/2850)
			(d)	1 Apr 1996 (SI 1996/323)

Local Government etc (Scotland) Act 1994 (c 39)—*contd*

Schedule

13, para	119	(8)–(33)		1 Apr 1996 (SI 1996/323)
		(34)		4 Jan 1995 (SI 1994/2850)
		(35)		1 Apr 1996 (SI 1996/323)
		(36)		4 Jan 1995 (SI 1994/2850)
		(37)–(41)		1 Apr 1996 (SI 1996/323)
		(42)–(45)		4 Jan 1995 (SI 1994/2850)
		(46)		4 Jan 1995 (so far as relates to definition "wholesome" in Water (Scotland) Act 1980, s 76L(1)) (SI 1994/2850)
				1 Apr 1996 (otherwise) (SI 1996/323)
		(47)–(50)		1 Apr 1996 (SI 1996/323)
		(51)		4 Jan 1995 (SI 1994/2850)
		(52)		1 Apr 1996 (SI 1996/323)
		(53)	(a) (i)–(iii)	1 Apr 1996 (SI 1996/323)
			(iv)	4 Jan 1995 (SI 1994/2850)
			(v)	1 Apr 1996 (SI 1996/323)
			(vi)	4 Jan 1995 (SI 1994/2850)
			(b)	1 Apr 1996 (SI 1996/323)
		(54)		1 Apr 1996 (except paras (a)(ii), (h)(ii) which are now repealed) (SI 1996/323)
		(55)–(58)		1 Apr 1996 (SI 1996/323)
	120–128			1 Apr 1996 (SI 1996/323)
	129	(1)		4 Jan 1995 (SI 1994/2850)
		(2)–(19)		1 Apr 1996 (SI 1996/323)
		(20)	(a)	1 Apr 1996 (SI 1996/323)
			(b)	4 Jan 1995 (SI 1994/2850)
		(21), (22)		1 Apr 1996 (SI 1996/323)
	130–148			1 Apr 1996 (SI 1996/323)
	149			Repealed (*never in force*)
	150–153			1 Apr 1996 (SI 1996/323)
	154			Repealed
	155			1 Apr 1996 (SI 1996/323)
	156	(1)		4 Jan 1995 (SI 1994/2850)
		(2)		1 Apr 1996 (SI 1996/323)
		(3), (4)		4 Jan 1995 (SI 1994/2850)
		(5), (6)		1 Apr 1996 (SI 1996/323)
	157–161			1 Apr 1996 (SI 1996/323)
	162	(1), (2)		22 Dec 1995 (subject to a saving) (SI 1995/3326)
		(3), (4)		1 Apr 1996 (SI 1995/3326)
	163–172			1 Apr 1996 (except para 167(2), (4), (5), (7), (9) which are now repealed) (SI 1996/323)
	173			1 Apr 1996 (SI 1996/323); repealed (25 Aug 2000) by Powers of Criminal Courts (Sentencing) Act 2000, s 165(4), Sch 12, Pt I (qv)

Local Government etc (Scotland) Act 1994 (c 39)—*contd*
Schedule

13, para	174, 175		1 Apr 1996 (SI 1996/323)
	176	(1)	31 Dec 1994 (SI 1994/3150)
		(2)	19 Feb 1996 (subject to a saving) (SI 1996/323)
		(3)–(9)	1 Apr 1996 (SI 1996/323)
		(10)	19 Feb 1996 (subject to a saving) (SI 1996/323)
		(11)	1 Apr 1996 (SI 1996/323)
		(12)	(a) 1 Apr 1996 (SI 1996/323)
			(b) 19 Feb 1996 (subject to a saving) (SI 1996/323)
			(c), (d) 1 Apr 1996 (SI 1996/323)
		(13)–(15)	1 Apr 1996 (SI 1996/323)
		(16)	(a)–(c) 19 Feb 1996 (subject to a saving) (SI 1996/323)
			(d) 1 Apr 1996 (SI 1996/323)
		(17), (18)	1 Apr 1996 (SI 1996/323)
		(19)	(a) 1 Apr 1996 (SI 1996/323)
			(b) 31 Dec 1994 (subject to a transitional provision) (SI 1994/3150)
			(c), (d) 4 Jan 1995 (SI 1994/2850)
	177		4 Jan 1995 (SI 1994/2850)
	178–184		1 Apr 1996 (SI 1996/323)
14			4 Jan 1995 (repeals of or in Burial Grounds (Scotland) Act 1855; Fire Services Act 1947, ss 15(2), 36(2); Local Government (Scotland) Act 1973, s 84(2), (4); Water (Scotland) Act 1980, ss 64–67, 76H(8), 76L(1) (definition "wholesome" only), 109(1) (definition "owner" only); Civic Government (Scotland) Act 1982, s 121) (SI 1994/2850)
			4 Jan 1995 (repeals of Local Government (Scotland) Act 1973, s 116(6); Local Government (Miscellaneous Provisions) (Scotland) Act 1981, Sch 2, paras 41, 42; Water Act 1989, Sch 25, para 60(2)) (SI 1994/3150)
			1 Apr 1995 (repeals of or in Sporting Lands Rating (Scotland) Act 1886; Local Government (Scotland) Act 1947, ss 243, 243A, 243B, 244; Valuation and Rating (Scotland) Act 1956, s 22A; Local Government and Miscellaneous Financial Provisions (Scotland) Act 1958, s 7; Local Government

Local Government etc (Scotland) Act 1994 (c 39)—*contd*

Schedule

14—*contd*

(Scotland) Act 1966; Town and Country Planning (Scotland) Act 1972, Sch 21; Local Government (Scotland) Act 1973, Sch 9, para 11; Local Government (Scotland) Act 1975, Sch 6, Pt II, paras 6, 13, 34; Local Government Planning and Land Act 1980, Sch 32 para 33 (except repeal of definition "rates" in sub-para (4)); Local Government (Miscellaneous Provisions) (Scotland) Act 1981, s 6, Sch 3, para 26; Local Government and Planning (Scotland) Act 1982, s 4; Rating and Valuation (Amendment) (Scotland) Act 1984, ss 6, 7, Sch 2, para 7; Local Government Finance Act 1988, s 128, Sch 12, Pt II, para 6; Water Act 1989, Sch 25, para 22; Local Government and Housing Act 1989, Sch 6, para 7; Local Government Finance Act 1992, Sch 13, para 75) (SI 1994/3150)

1 Apr 1995 (repeals of or in Local Government (Scotland) Act 1973, ss 83(4B)(d), 96(5), 100(3); Criminal Procedure (Scotland) Act 1975, Sch 7D, para 59; Local Government (Scotland) Act 1975, Sch 3, para 22(1), head (c) and para 24A; Local Government Act 1988, Sch 6, para 11; Local Government Finance Act 1992, Sch 7, para 1(6)) (SI 1995/702)

1 Apr 1996 (repeals in Prisons (Scotland) Act 1989, ss 14(2), 16(2)) (SI 1995/3326)

19 Feb 1996 (repeals of or in Local Government Finance Act 1992, ss 93(1)(a), 97(2), 112(2)(d), Sch 2, Sch 11, Pts I, II, and paras 26, 27) (subject to a saving) (SI 1996/323)

1 Apr 1996 (repeals of or in Rural Water Supplies and Sewerage Act 1944; Fire Services Act 1947 (remainder); Local Government (Scotland) Act 1947 (remainder);

Local Government etc (Scotland) Act 1994 (c 39)—*contd*
Schedule
14—*contd*

National Assistance Act 1948;
Coast Protection Act 1949;
National Parks and Access to the
Countryside Act 1949; Rural
Water Supplies and Sewerage
Act 1955; Valuation and Rating
(Scotland) Act 1956(remainder);
Deer (Scotland) Act 1959; Caravan
Sites and Control of Development
Act 1960; Flood Prevention
(Scotland) Act 1961; Registration
of Births, Deaths and Marriages
(Scotland) Act 1965; Police
(Scotland) Act 1967; Water
(Scotland) Act 1967; Countryside
(Scotland) Act 1967; New Towns
(Scotland) Act 1968; Health
Services and Public Health Act 1968;
Sewerage (Scotland) Act 1968;
Social Work (Scotland) Act 1968;
Transport Act 1968; Rural Water
Supplies and Sewerage (Scotland)
Act 1970; Rural Water Supplies
and Sewerage Act 1971; Town and
Country Planning (Scotland)
Act 1972 (remainder); Local
Government (Scotland) Act 1973,
ss 1, 2, 3, 3A, 4, 5, 11, 24(5),
31(4), 47(4), (5), 51(1), (3), 56(6),
(9), 63(2), (5), 64(5), 69(4), 74(3),
83(2), (2A), (2B), (3A), 87(1), (2),
(3), 90A, 106(1), 109, 111(1),
116(1)–(5), (7), (8), 118(1), (5),
127, 131, 132, 133(1), 134(1),
137(1), 138(1), 140, 142, 143,
146(7), 148(1), 153(1), (2), (3),
154(1), (2), (3), (3A), (3B), 154A,
154B, 155(1), 156(1), 159, 161,
163(1), (2), (3), 166(1), (2), 168,
170A(5), 170B(2), 171(1), (2), 173,
174, 176, 177, 179, 181, 182, 183,
202(1), (1A), (13), 215(3)–(7),
222–224, 226, 230, 235(1), 236(2),
Schs 1, 2, Sch 6, para 2, Sch 9,
para 53, Schs 10, 13, 14, Sch 17,
paras 1, 2, Schs 20, 22, Sch 27, Pt II,
paras 159, 180, 182; Control of
Pollution Act 1974, s 106(3);
District Courts (Scotland) Act1975;

Local Government etc (Scotland) Act 1994 (c 39)—*contd*

Schedule

14—*contd*

House of Commons Disqualification Act 1975; Local Government (Scotland) Act 1975, ss 1(3), (7), 4, 6(1A), 7(1A), 13, 16, 23(1), (2), 29A(3), Sch 3, paras 1(4), 22(2), 28(1), Sch 6, Pt II, paras 23, 53; Children Act 1975; Licensing (Scotland) Act 1976; Supplementary Benefits Act 1976; National Health Service (Scotland) Act 1978; Inner Urban Areas Act 1978; Reserve Forces Act 1980; Education (Scotland) Act 1980; Water (Scotland) Act 1980 (remainder); Local Government, Planning and Land Act 1980 (remainder); Local Government (Miscellaneous Provisions) (Scotland) Act 1981, s 11, Sch 3, paras 24, 28, 38; Civil Aviation Act 1982; Local Government and Planning (Scotland) Act 1982 (remainder); Civic Government (Scotland) Act 1982 (remainder); Representation of the People Act 1983; Road Traffic Regulation Act 1984; Roads (Scotland) Act 1984; Water (Fluoridation) Act 1985; Housing Associations Act 1985; Disabled Persons (Services, Consultation and Representation) Act 1986; Housing (Scotland) Act 1987; Local Government Act 1988 (remainder); Housing (Scotland) Act 1988; School Boards (Scotland) Act 1988; Electricity Act 1989; Local Government and Housing Act 1989 (remainder); Environmental Protection Act 1990, ss 53(4), 88(9), 90(3), 92(1), 93(1), 95(1); New Roads and Street Works Act 1991; Natural Heritage (Scotland) Act 1991; Planning and Compensation Act 1991; Social Security Contributions and Benefits Act 1992; Social Security Administration Act 1992; Local Government Finance Act 1992,

Local Government etc (Scotland) Act 1994 (c 39)—*contd*

Schedule

14—*contd*

ss 74(1), 84(1), (2), 85(2), (3), (4),
(5), 86(4), (10), (11), 87(9), 90(3),
94(9), 95, 99(1), (2), 107(1), Sch 9,
paras 9, 25, Sch 11, paras 24, 25,
31–34, 36, 37, 38, Sch 13, paras 37,
93; Railways Act 1993) (subject to
a saving relating to Local
Government (Scotland) Act 1973,
s 223) (SI 1996/323)
Not in force (otherwise)

1   Orders made under Environment Act 1995, s 125(3), bringing the prospective insertion into force will be noted to that Act

2   Orders made under Merchant Shipping Act 1995, s 314(3), Sch 14, para 5(2), bringing the prospective repeal into force will be noted to that Act

3   Orders made under Ethical Standards in Public Life etc (Scotland) Act 2000, s 37(2), bringing the prospective repeals into force will be noted to that Act

Local Government (Wales) Act 1994 (c 19)

RA: 5 Jul 1994

Commencement provisions: s 66(2)–(4); Local Government (Wales) Act 1994 (Commencement No 1) Order 1994, SI 1994/2109; Local Government (Wales) Act 1994 (Commencement No 2) Order 1994, SI 1994/2790; Local Government (Wales) Act 1994 (Commencement No 3) Order 1995, SI 1995/546, as amended by SI 1995/851; Local Government (Wales) Act 1994 (Commencement No 4) Order 1995, SI 1995/852; Local Government (Wales) Act 1994 (Commencement No 5) Order 1995, SI 1995/2490; Local Government (Wales) Act 1994 (Commencement No 6) Order 1995, SI 1995/3198; Local Government (Wales) Act 1994 (Commencement No 7) Order 1996, SI 1996/396

Section

1   (1), (2)   5 Jul 1994 (s 66(2)(a))
     (3)   See Sch 2 below
     (4)   See sub-ss (5)–(8) below
     (5), (6)   24 Oct 1994 (in relation to sub-ss (5),
                     (6), for interpretation of Pt IV of
                     Local Government Act 1972)
                     (subject to a saving) (SI 1994/2790)
                     20 Mar 1995 (in relation to sub-s (5),
                     for interpretation of Local
                     Government Act 1972, ss 21, 25,
                     26, 79, 80, 270(1), (3) and s 17 of
                     this Act) (subject to a saving)
                     (SI 1995/546)
                     3 Apr 1995 (in relation to sub-ss (5),
                     (6), for interpretation of provisions
                     of Local Government Act 1972
                     falling to be applied in
                     consequence of SI 1995/852)
                     (subject to a saving) (SI 1995/852)

Local Government (Wales) Act 1994 (c 19)—*contd*

Section

1	(5), (6)—*contd*	1 Oct 1995 (in relation to sub-s (5), for interpretation of Local Government Finance Act 1982, Pt III) (subject to a transitional provision) (SI 1995/2490)
		1 Apr 1996 (otherwise) (SI 1995/3198)
	(7)	5 Jul 1994 (s 66(2)(a))
	(8)	24 Oct 1994 (for interpretation of Pt IV of Local Government Act 1972) (subject to a saving) (SI 1994/2790)
		20 Mar 1995 (for interpretation of Local Government Act 1972, ss 21, 25, 26, 79, 80, 270(1), (3) and s 17 of this Act) (subject to a saving) (SI 1995/546)
		3 Apr 1995 (for interpretation of provisions of Local Government Act 1972 falling to be applied in consequence of SI 1995/852) (subject to a saving) (SI 1995/852)
		1 Oct 1995 (for interpretation of Environment Act 1995, s 65(4), Sch 7, para 2) (SI 1995/2490)
		1 Apr 1996 (otherwise) (SI 1995/3198)
2		20 Mar 1995 (subject to a saving) (SI 1995/546)
3		5 Jul 1994 (s 66(2)(a))
4		20 Mar 1995 (subject to a saving) (SI 1995/546)
5		3 Apr 1995 (subject to a saving) (SI 1995/852)
6, 7		5 Jul 1994 (s 66(2)(a))
8–13		1 Apr 1996 (SI 1995/3198)
14, 15		3 Apr 1995 (SI 1995/852)
16		1 Apr 1996 (SI 1995/3198)
17		20 Mar 1995 (only for purposes of legislative provisions specified in SI 1995/546, art 5, and subject to a transitional provision) (SI 1995/546, as amended by SI 1995/851)
		1 Apr 1996 (otherwise) (SI 1996/396)
18	(1)–(6)	3 Apr 1995 (for purposes specified in SI 1995/852, art 4(2), and subject to savings) (SI 1995/852)
		1 Apr 1996 (otherwise) (SI 1995/852)
	(7)	1 Apr 1996 (SI 1995/3198)
19		3 Apr 1995 (SI 1995/852)
20	(1)–(3)	1 Apr 1996 (SI 1995/3198)

Local Government (Wales) Act 1994 (c 19)—*contd*

Section

20	(4)	See Sch 6 below
21		Repealed
22	(1)–(5)	See Schs 7–11 below
	(6)	1 Apr 1996 (SI 1996/396)
23	(1)	1 Apr 1996 (SI 1995/3198)
	(2)–(6)	3 Apr 1995 (SI 1995/852)
24		Repealed
25–38		3 Apr 1995 (subject to a saving relating to s 35) (SI 1995/852)
39, 40		5 Jul 1994 (s 66(2)(a))
41		15 Aug 1994 (SI 1994/2109)
42		3 Apr 1995 (SI 1995/852)
43		5 Jul 1994 (s 66(2)(a))
44, 45		3 Apr 1995 (SI 1995/852)
46–48		5 Jul 1994 (s 66(2)(a))
49, 50		1 Apr 1996 (SI 1995/3198)
51		3 Apr 1995 (SI 1995/852)
52		15 Aug 1994 (SI 1994/2109)
53		3 Apr 1995 (SI 1995/852)
54, 55		5 Jul 1994 (s 66(2)(a))
56–60		3 Apr 1995 (SI 1995/852)
61		1 Apr 1996 (SI 1996/396)
62		1 Apr 1996 (SI 1995/3198)
63, 64		5 Jul 1994 (s 66(2)(a))
65		15 Aug 1994 (SI 1994/2109)
66	(1)–(4)	5 Jul 1994 (s 66(2)(c))
	(5)	See Sch 15 below
	(6)	See Sch 16 below
	(7)	See Sch 17 below
	(8)	See Sch 18 below
	(9)	5 Jul 1994 (s 66(2)(c))

Schedule

1		5 Jul 1994 (s 66(2)(b))
2, para	1–3	1 Apr 1996 (SI 1995/3198)
	4, 5	24 Oct 1994 (subject to a saving) (SI 1994/2790)
	6, 7	1 Apr 1996 (SI 1995/3198)
	8, 9	3 Apr 1995 (SI 1995/852)
	10	Repealed
	11, 12	1 Apr 1996 (SI 1995/3198)
	13	1 Oct 1995 (SI 1995/2490)
3		5 Jul 1994 (s 66(2)(b))
4, 5		1 Apr 1996 (SI 1995/3198)
6, para	1	1 Apr 1996 (SI 1996/396)
	2	3 Apr 1995 (SI 1995/852)
	3–12	Repealed (paras 5–10 *never in force*)
	13	Repealed
	14–17	1 Apr 1996 (SI 1996/396)
	18	Repealed (*never in force*)

Local Government (Wales) Act 1994 (c 19)—*contd*
Schedule

6, para	19, 20		1 Apr 1996 (SI 1996/396)
	21		3 Apr 1995 (SI 1995/852)
	22		1 Apr 1996 (SI 1996/396)
	23		Repealed
	24	(1)	Repealed (sub-para (1)(a) *never in force*)
		(2)–(9)	1 Apr 1996 (SI 1996/396)
		(10)	(a)	1 Apr 1996 (SI 1996/396)
			(b)	1 Oct 1995 (SI 1995/2490)
		(11)–(16)	1 Apr 1996 (SI 1996/396)
		(17)	(a)	1 Oct 1995 (SI 1995/2490)
			(b)	1 Apr 1996 (SI 1996/396)
		(18), (19)	1 Apr 1996 (SI 1996/396)
	25–27		1 Apr 1996 (SI 1996/396)
	28, 29		Repealed (*never in force*)
7, para	1		3 Apr 1995 (for purposes specified in SI 1995/852, art 4(5), and subject to a transitional provision) (SI 1995/852)
			1 Apr 1996 (otherwise) (SI 1996/396)
	2–26		1 Apr 1996 (SI 1996/396)
	27	(1)–(3)	1 Apr 1996 (SI 1996/396)
		(4)	1 Oct 1995 (SI 1995/2490)
	28–43		1 Apr 1996 (SI 1996/396)
8, para	1, 2		1 Apr 1996 (SI 1996/396)
	3	(1)	1 Apr 1996 (SI 1996/396)
		(2)	1 Oct 1995 (for purposes specified in SI 1995/2490, art 4(2), and subject to a transitional provision) (SI 1995/2490)
			1 Apr 1996 (otherwise) (SI 1995/2490)
		(3)–(5)	1 Apr 1996 (SI 1996/396)
	4–11		1 Apr 1996 (SI 1996/396)
9, para	1–3		1 Apr 1996 (SI 1996/396)
	4, 5		Repealed
	6–16		1 Apr 1996 (SI 1996/396)
	17	(1)	1 Apr 1996 (SI 1996/396); prospectively repealed by Pollution Prevention and Control Act 1999, s 6(2), Sch 3[1]
		(2), (3)	1 Apr 1996 (SI 1996/396)
		(4)	Repealed (*never in force*)
		(5)–(11)	1 Apr 1996 (SI 1996/396)
		(12)	Repealed
		(13)	1 Apr 1996 (SI 1996/396)
	18		1 Apr 1996 (SI 1996/396)
10, para	1–10		1 Apr 1996 (SI 1996/396)
	11	(1)	Repealed (*never in force*)
		(2)–(4)	1 Apr 1996 (SI 1996/396)
	12, 13		1 Apr 1996 (SI 1996/396)

Local Government (Wales) Act 1994 (c 19)—*contd*

Schedule

10, para	14		3 Apr 1995 (SI 1995/852)
11, para	1, 2		1 Apr 1996 (SI 1996/396)
	3	(1), (2)	Repealed (*never in force*)
		(3)–(11)	1 Apr 1996 (SI 1996/396)
	4, 5		1 Apr 1996 (SI 1996/396)
12			3 Apr 1995 (subject to savings) (SI 1995/852)
13, 14			5 Jul 1994 (s 66(2)(b))
15, para	1		24 Oct 1994 (SI 1994/2790)
	2		1 Apr 1996 (SI 1996/396)
	3		3 Apr 1995 (SI 1995/852)
	4, 5		1 Apr 1996 (SI 1996/396)
	6		20 Mar 1995 (SI 1995/546)
	7		24 Oct 1994 (subject to a saving) (SI 1994/2790)
	8	(1)–(4)	1 Apr 1996 (SI 1996/396)
		(5)	24 Oct 1994 (subject to a saving) (SI 1994/2790)
	9	(1)–(3)	1 Apr 1996 (SI 1996/396)
		(4) (a)	1 Apr 1996 (SI 1996/396)
		(b)	24 Oct 1994 (subject to a saving) (SI 1994/2790)
	10	(1)	1 Oct 1995 (SI 1995/2490)
		(2), (3)	1 Apr 1996 (SI 1996/396)
	11	(1)	1 Apr 1996 (SI 1996/396)
		(2)	24 Oct 1994 (subject to a saving) (SI 1994/2790)
	12	(a)	1 Apr 1996 (SI 1996/396)
		(b)	24 Oct 1994 (subject to a saving) (SI 1994/2790)
	13–17		1 Apr 1996 (SI 1996/396)
	18, 19		24 Oct 1994 (subject to a saving) (SI 1994/2790)
	20		3 Apr 1995 (subject to a saving) (SI 1995/852)
	21, 22		1 Apr 1996 (SI 1996/396)
	23		3 Apr 1995 (SI 1995/852)
	24		1 Apr 1996 (SI 1996/396)
	25		1 Apr 1996 (SI 1996/396); prospectively repealed by Local Government Act 2000, s 107, Sch 16[2]
	26		3 Apr 1995 (subject to a saving) (SI 1995/852)
	27–51		1 Apr 1996 (SI 1996/396)
	52		1 Oct 1995 (SI 1995/2490)
	53, 54		1 Apr 1996 (SI 1996/396)
	55		3 Apr 1995 (subject to a saving) (SI 1995/852)

Local Government (Wales) Act 1994 (c 19)—*contd*

Schedule

15, para	56			1 Apr 1996 (SI 1996/396)
	57			24 Oct 1994 (subject to a saving) (SI 1994/2790)
	58–61			1 Oct 1995 (SI 1995/2490)
	62–66			1 Apr 1996 (SI 1996/396)
16, para	1–7			1 Apr 1996 (SI 1996/396)
	8			Repealed
	9–10			1 Apr 1996 (SI 1996/396)
	11			Repealed (*never in force*)
	12			1 Oct 1995 (for purposes specified in SI 1995/2490, art 5(2), and subject to a transitional provision) (SI 1995/2490)
				1 Apr 1996 (otherwise) (SI 1995/2490)
	13–25			1 Apr 1996 (SI 1996/396)
	26			1 Oct 1995 (for purposes specified in SI 1995/2490, art 5(4), and subject to a transitional provision) (SI 1995/2490)
				1 Apr 1996 (otherwise) (SI 1995/2490)
	27–34			1 Apr 1996 (SI 1996/396)
	35			Repealed
	36–39			1 Apr 1996 (SI 1996/396)
	40	(1)		1 Apr 1996 (SI 1996/396)
		(2)	(a)	1 Apr 1996 (SI 1996/396)
			(b)	Repealed (*never in force*)
		(3)		1 Apr 1996 (SI 1996/396)
	41–52			1 Apr 1996 (SI 1996/396)
	53			Repealed (subject to transitional provisions)
	54			Repealed, subject to a saving
	55, 56			1 Apr 1996 (SI 1996/396)
	57	(1)–(5)		3 Apr 1995 (subject to a saving) (SI 1995/852)
		(6)		Repealed (*never in force*)
	58			Repealed (subject to transitional provisions)
	59–66			1 Apr 1996 (SI 1996/396)
	67			Repealed (*never in force*)
	68	(1)–(5)		1 Apr 1996 (SI 1996/396)
		(6)		20 Mar 1995 (subject to savings and transitional provisions) (SI 1995/546)
		(7)		20 Mar 1995 (but not in respect of Representation of the People Act 1983, s 35(1A)(b)) (subject to a saving) (SI 1995/546)
				1 Apr 1996 (otherwise) (SI 1996/396)

Local Government (Wales) Act 1994 (c 19)—*contd*

Schedule

16, para	68	(8), (9)	20 Mar 1995 (subject to savings and transitional provisions in respect of sub-para (8)) (SI 1995/546)
		(10)–(12)	1 Apr 1996 (SI 1996/396)
		(13)–(16)	20 Mar 1995 (subject to transitional provisions in respect of sub-para (16)) (SI 1995/546)
		(17), (18)	1 Apr 1996 (SI 1996/396)
		(19)	20 Mar 1995 (SI 1995/546)
		(20)	1 Apr 1996 (SI 1996/396)
	69		1 Apr 1996 (SI 1996/396)
	70		Repealed (*never in force*)
	71–77		1 Apr 1996 (SI 1996/396)
	78		Repealed
	79–81		1 Apr 1996 (SI 1996/396)
	82	(1), (2)	Repealed
		(3)	3 Apr 1995 (for purposes of orders made under Coroners Act 1988, s 4A, and subject to transitional provisions) (SI 1995/852)
			1 Apr 1996 (otherwise) (SI 1995/852)
		(4)	3 Apr 1995 (subject to transitional provisions) (SI 1995/852)
		(5)	3 Apr 1995 (only in respect of Coroners Act 1988, s 4A(1), (2), (7), (9), (10)) (SI 1995/852)
			1 Apr 1996 (otherwise) (SI 1996/396)
		(6)–(8)	1 Apr 1996 (SI 1996/396)
		(9)	Repealed
		(10)	1 Apr 1996 (SI 1996/396)
	83		1 Apr 1996 (SI 1996/396)
	84–86		3 Apr 1995 (SI 1995/852)
	87		1 Apr 1996 (SI 1996/396)
	88		3 Apr 1995 (SI 1995/852)
	89–92		1 Apr 1996 (SI 1996/396)
	93		Repealed (*never in force*)
	94, 95		1 Apr 1996 (SI 1996/396)
	96, 97		3 Apr 1995 (SI 1995/852)
	98		Repealed, in relation to the limitation of council tax and precepts as regards the financial year beginning with 1 Apr 2000 and subsequent financial years
	99–104		1 Apr 1996 (SI 1996/396)
	105		Repealed
	106		3 Apr 1995 (SI 1995/852)
	107, 108		1 Apr 1996 (SI 1996/396)
	109		Repealed
17, para	1		5 Jul 1994 (s 66(2)(b))

Local Government (Wales) Act 1994 (c 19)—*contd*

Schedule

17, para	2, 3	3 Apr 1995 (SI 1995/852)
	4	5 Jul 1994 (s 66(2)(b))
	5	3 Apr 1995 (SI 1995/852)
	6	5 Jul 1994 (s 66(2)(b))
	7, 8	20 Mar 1995 (SI 1995/546)
	9	5 Jul 1994 (s 66(2)(b))
	10–12	3 Apr 1995 (SI 1995/852)
	13	Repealed
	14	3 Apr 1995 (SI 1995/852)
	15	1 Apr 1996 (SI 1995/3198)
	16	1 Apr 1996 (SI 1996/396)
	17	1 Apr 1996 (SI 1995/3198)
	18–23	3 Apr 1995 (SI 1995/852)
18		24 Oct 1994 (repeals in Local Government Act 1972, ss 55(5)(a), 59(2), 72(2)) (subject to a saving) (SI 1994/2790)
		20 Mar 1995 (repeals in Representation of the People Act 1983, ss 35(1), 36(3)(b)) (SI 1995/546)
		3 Apr 1995 (repeals in Local Government Act 1972, 74(3), (4); Local Government, Planning and Land Act 1980, ss 4(7), 20(1); Town and Country Planning Act 1990, ss 1(3), 2(1)) (SI 1995/852)
		1 Oct 1995 (repeals of or in Local Government Act 1972, Sch 4, Pt IV, Sch 8, para 8, Sch 10, Sch 11, para 3(2)(b), (c)) (SI 1995/2490)
		1 Jan 1996 (subject to a saving) (repeal in European Parliamentary Elections Act 1978, Sch 2, para 5A(4)(a)) (SI 1995/3198)
		1 Apr 1996 (repeals of or in Game Licences Act 1860; Finance Act 1908; Public Health Act 1936; Education Act 1944; Coast Protection Act 1949; Disabled Persons (Employment) Act 1958; Opencast Coal Act 1958; Caravan Sites and Control of Development Act 1960; Pipe-lines Act 1962; Licensing Act 1964; Harbours Act 1964; Public Libraries and Museums Act 1964; Gas Act 1965;

Local Government (Wales) Act 1994 (c 19)—*contd*
Schedule
18—*contd*

Agriculture Act 1967; Slaughter of
Poultry Act 1967; Theatres
Act 1968; Mines and Quarries
(Tips) Act 1969; Post Office
Act 1969; Agriculture Act 1970;
Chronically Sick and Disabled
Persons Act 1970; Fire Precautions
Act 1971; Poisons Act 1972; Local
Government Act 1972, ss 30, 60(5),
67(5)(f), 69(4), 76(2), (3), 97(1),
(2), (3), 195(3), 200, 207, 213(1),
226(5), 227(1), (2), 245(6)–(9),
Sch 11, para 1(2)(c), (d), Sch 26,
paras 4(a), 11(1); Employment
Agencies Act 1973; Breeding of
Dogs Act 1973; Slaughterhouses
Act 1974; Health and Safety at
Work etc Act 1974; Consumer
Credit Act 1974; Control of
Pollution Act 1974; Reservoirs
Act 1975; Guard Dogs Act 1975;
Safety of Sports Grounds Act 1975;
Dangerous Wild Animals Act 1976;
Development of Rural Wales
Act 1976; European Parliamentary
Elections Act 1978, Sch 1,
para 4(5)(a); Ancient Monuments
and Archaeological Areas Act
1979; Local Government, Planning
and Land Act 1980, ss 116(4)(a),
165(9)(a), Sch 32, para 2(2)(a)(ii);
Zoo Licensing Act 1981; Wildlife
and Countryside Act 1981; Civil
Aviation Act 1982; Representation
of the People Act 1983, ss 8(2),
18(2), 36(5), 39(6)(b), 52(4)(a);
Level Crossings Act 1983;
Telecommunications Act 1984;
Road Traffic Regulation Act 1984;
Cinemas Act 1985; Representation
of the People Act 1985; Transport
Act 1985; Airports Act 1986;
GasAct 1986; Building Societies
Act 1986; Fire Safety and Safety of
Places of Sport Act 1987; Road
Traffic Act 1988; Road Traffic
Offenders Act 1988; Electricity
Act 1989; Children Act 1989;
Town and Country Planning

Local Government (Wales) Act 1994 (c 19)—*contd*

Schedule

18—*contd*

Act 1990, Sch 1, para 8(1), (2)(a);
Planning (Listed Buildings and
Conservation Areas) Act 1990;
Food Safety Act 1990;
Broadcasting Act 1990;
Environmental Protection Act 1990,
ss 30(3)(a), 143(6)(b), 149(11);
Caldey Island Act 1990; Road
Traffic Act 1991; Coal Mining
Subsidence Act 1991; Severn
Bridges Act 1992; Social Security
Administration Act 1992; Clean
Air Act 1993; Radioactive
Substances Act 1993; Health
Service Commissioners Act 1993)
(SI 1996/396)

[1] Orders made under Pollution Prevention and Control Act 1999, s 7(3), bringing the prospective repeal into force will be noted to that Act in the service to this work

[2] Orders made under Local Government Act 2000, s 108, bringing the prospective repeal into force will be noted to that Act in the service to this work

Marriage Act 1994 (c 34)

RA: 3 Nov 1994

Commencement provisions: s 3(2); Marriage Act 1994 (Commencement No 1) Order 1994, SI 1994/3116; Marriage Act 1994 (Commencement No 2) Order 1995, SI 1995/424

Section

1	(1)	1 Apr 1995 (SI 1995/424)
	(2)	24 Feb 1995 (so far as inserts Marriage Act 1949, ss 46A, 46B(2)) (SI 1995/424)
		1 Apr 1995 (otherwise) (SI 1995/424)
	(3)	See Schedule below
2	(1)	1 Jan 1995 (so far as inserts Marriage Act 1949, s 35(2A)) (SI 1994/3116)
		1 Apr 1995 (so far as not already in force) (SI 1995/424)
	(2)	1 Jan 1995 (SI 1994/3116)
3		1 Jan 1995 (SI 1994/3116)

Schedule

para	1	See paras 2–8 below
	2–4	1 Apr 1995 (SI 1995/424)
	5	24 Feb 1995 (SI 1995/424)
	6–9	1 Apr 1995 (SI 1995/424)

Mental Health (Amendment) Act 1994 (c 6)

RA: 24 Mar 1994

Commencement provisions: s 2(3)

14 Apr 1994 (s 2(3))

Merchant Shipping (Salvage and Pollution) Act 1994 (c 28)

Whole Act repealed

New Towns (Amendment) Act 1994 (c 5)

RA: 24 Mar 1994

24 Mar 1994 (RA)

Non-Domestic Rating Act 1994 (c 3)

RA: 24 Feb 1994

24 Feb 1994 (RA)

Parliamentary Commissioner Act 1994 (c 14)

RA: 5 Jul 1994

Commencement provisions: s 3(2)

5 Sep 1994 (s 3(2))

Pastoral (Amendment) Measure 1994 (No 1)

RA: 24 Mar 1994

Commencement provisions: s 15(2)

The provisions of this Measure are brought into force on 1 Apr 1994 by an appointed day notice signed by the Archbishops of Canterbury and York and dated 25 Mar 1994 (made under s 15(2))

Police and Magistrates' Courts Act 1994 (c 29)

RA: 21 Jul 1994

Commencement provisions: s 94; Police and Magistrates' Courts Act 1994 (Commencement No 1 and Transitional Provisions) Order 1994, SI 1994/2025; Police and Magistrates' Courts Act 1994 (Commencement No 2) Order 1994, SI 1994/2151; Police and Magistrates' Courts Act 1994 (Commencement No 3 and Transitional Provisions) Order 1994, SI 1994/2594; Police and Magistrates' Courts Act 1994 (Commencement No 4 and Transitional Provisions) (Scotland) Order 1994, SI 1994/3075; Police and Magistrates' Courts Act 1994 (Commencement No 5 and Transitional Provisions) Order 1994, SI 1994/3262,

Police and Magistrates' Courts Act 1994 (c 29)—*contd*

as amended by SI 1995/246 and SI 1995/899; Police and Magistrates' Courts Act 1994 (Commencement No 5 and Transitional Provisions) (Amendment) Order 1995, SI 1995/246, and Police and Magistrates' Courts Act 1994 (Commencement No 5 and Transitional Provisions) (Amendment No 2) Order 1995, SI 1995/899 (both amending transitional provisions set out in SI 1994/3262); Police and Magistrates' Courts Act 1994 (Commencement No 6 and Transitional Provisions) Order 1995, SI 1995/42; Police and Magistrates' Courts Act 1994 (Commencement No 7 and Transitional Provisions) (Scotland) Order 1995, SI 1995/492, as amended by SI 1995/3003; Police and Magistrates' Courts Act 1994 (Commencement No 8 and Transitional Provisions) Order 1995, SI 1995/685; Police and Magistrates' Courts Act 1994 (Commencement No 9 and Amendment) Order 1995, SI 1995/3003; Police and Magistrates' Courts Act 1994 (Commencement No 10 and Savings) (Scotland) Order 1996, SI 1996/1646

Section		
1–26		Repealed
27		1 Nov 1994 (for purposes of any financial year beginning on or after 1 Apr 1995, and subject to SI 1994/2025, art 7(3), (4)) (SI 1994/2025)
28, 29		Repealed
30		15 Mar 1995 (for purposes of issuing a basic credit approval under Local Government and Housing Act 1989, s 53, to a new police authority in respect of the financial year beginning on 1 Apr 1995) (SI 1994/3262)
		1 Apr 1995 (otherwise) (SI 1994/3262)
31		1 Oct 1994 (for purposes specified in SI 1994/2025, art 6(1) and subject to modifications specified in art 6(3)–(6) thereof) (SI 1994/2025)
		1 Apr 1995 (otherwise) (SI 1994/3262)
32		Repealed
33		1 Oct 1994 (SI 1994/2025)
34–38		Repealed (*never in force*)
39	(1)	Repealed
	(2), (3)	1 Apr 1995 (SI 1994/3262)
	(4)–(7)	1 Oct 1994 (SI 1994/2025)
40		1 Apr 1995 (SI 1994/3262)
41		8 Aug 1994 (SI 1994/2025)
42		1 Oct 1994 (SI 1994/2025)
43		See Sch 4 below
44		See Sch 5 below
45		Repealed
46		8 Aug 1994 (SI 1994/2025)
47	(1)	13 Dec 1995 (SI 1995/3003)[1]

Police and Magistrates' Courts Act 1994 (c 29)—*contd*

Police and Magistrates' Courts Act 1994 (c 29)—*contd*

Section

59—*contd*			1 Apr 1995 (otherwise) (SI 1994/3075, but see further SI 1995/492 below)
			1 Apr 1995 (so far as not already in force (though already brought fully into force by SI 1994/3075)) (SI 1995/492)
60			21 Jul 1994 (so far as relates to service in accordance with arrangements made under Police (Scotland) Act 1967, s 12A(2)) (s 94(3)(c))
			1 Apr 1995 (otherwise) (SI 1995/492)
61			1 Aug 1996 (SI 1996/1646)
62			1 Jan 1995 (SI 1994/3075)
63	(1)		1 Jan 1995 (SI 1994/3075)
	(2)		1 Apr 1995 (SI 1995/492)
	(3)		1 Aug 1996 (subject to a saving) (SI 1996/1646)
	(4)		21 Jul 1994 (so far as relates to service in accordance with arrangements made under Police (Scotland) Act 1967, s 12A(2)) (s 94(3)(c))
			1 Apr 1995 (otherwise) (SI 1995/492)
	(5)		1 Apr 1995 (SI 1995/492)
	(6)		1 Jan 1995 (SI 1994/3075)
	(7)	(a)	21 Jul 1994 (so far as relates to service in accordance with arrangements made under Police (Scotland) Act 1967, s 12A(2)) (s 94(3)(c))
			1 Apr 1995 (otherwise) (SI 1995/492)
		(b)	1 Jan 1995 (SI 1994/3075)
	(8)		1 Aug 1996 (subject to a saving) (SI 1996/1646)
	(9)	(a)	13 Dec 1995 (SI 1995/3003)[1]
		(b)	1 Jan 1995 (SI 1994/3075)
	(10)		1 Aug 1996 (subject to a saving) (SI 1996/1646)
64			1 Apr 1996 (SI 1995/492)
65			8 Aug 1994 (SI 1994/2025)
66–90			Repealed
91	(1)		See Sch 8 below
	(2)		Repealed
	(3)		Repealed (subject to a saving)
92			1 Nov 1994 (SI 1994/2594)
93			See Sch 9 below
94			21 Jul 1994 (RA)
95			Repealed
96, 97			21 Jul 1994 (RA)
Schedule			
1–3			Repealed

Police and Magistrates' Courts Act 1994 (c 29)—*contd*

Schedule

4, para	1–4		1 Apr 1995 (SI 1994/3262)
	5		1 Oct 1994 (for purposes specified in SI 1994/2025, art 6(1) and subject to modifications specified in art 6(3)–(6) thereof) (SI 1994/2025)
			1 Apr 1995 (otherwise) (SI 1994/3262)
	6		Repealed
	7		1 Oct 1994 (for purposes specified in SI 1994/2025, art 6(1) and subject to modifications specified in art 6(3)–(6) thereof) (SI 1994/2025)
			1 Apr 1995 (otherwise) (SI 1994/3262)
			Para prospectively repealed by Local Government Act 2000, s 107(2), Sch 6[2]
	8–14		1 Oct 1994 (for purposes specified in SI 1994/2025, art 6(1) and subject to modifications specified in art 6(3)–(6) thereof) (SI 1994/2025)
			1 Apr 1995 (otherwise) (SI 1994/3262)
	15	(1)	1 Oct 1994 (for purposes specified in SI 1994/2025, art 6(1) and subject to modifications specified in art 6(3)–(6) thereof) (SI 1994/2025)
			1 Apr 1995 (otherwise) (SI 1994/3262)
		(2)	1 Apr 1995 (SI 1994/3262)
		(3), (4)	1 Oct 1994 (for purposes specified in SI 1994/2025, art 6(1) and subject to modifications specified in art 6(3)–(6) thereof) (SI 1994/2025)
			1 Apr 1995 (otherwise) (SI 1994/3262)
	16–24		1 Oct 1994 (for purposes specified in SI 1994/2025, art 6(1) and subject to modifications specified in art 6(3)–(6) thereof) (SI 1994/2025)
			1 Apr 1995 (otherwise) (SI 1994/3262)
	25–28		Repealed
	29–39		1 Oct 1994 (for purposes specified in SI 1994/2025, art 6(1) and subject to modifications specified in art 6(3)–(6) thereof) (SI 1994/2025)
			1 Apr 1995 (otherwise) (SI 1994/3262)
	40		Repealed
	41		1 Oct 1994 (for purposes specified in SI 1994/2025, art 6(1) and subject to modifications specified in art 6(3)–(6) thereof) (SI 1994/2025)
			1 Apr 1995 (otherwise) (SI 1994/3262)
	42		1 Apr 1995 (SI 1994/3262)

Police and Magistrates' Courts Act 1994 (c 29)—*contd*

Section

4, para	43–48		1 Oct 1994 (for purposes specified in SI 1994/2025, art 6(1) and subject to modifications specified in art 6(3)–(6) thereof) (SI 1994/2025)
	49		Repealed
	50		1 Oct 1994 (for purposes specified in SI 1994/2025, art 6(1) and subject to modifications specified in art 6(3)–(6) thereof) (SI 1994/2025)
	51		Repealed
	52, 53		1 Oct 1994 (for purposes specified in SI 1994/2025, art 6(1) and subject to modifications specified in art 6(3)–(6) thereof) (SI 1994/2025)
			1 Apr 1995 (otherwise) (SI 1994/3262)
	54		Repealed
	55–63		1 Oct 1994 (for purposes specified in SI 1994/2025, art 6(1) and subject to modifications specified in art 6(3)–(6) thereof) (SI 1994/2025)
			1 Apr 1995 (otherwise) (SI 1994/3262)
5, para	1–16		Repealed (paras 11 (partly), 12 *never in force*)
	17–20		21 Jul 1994 (so far as relate to service in accordance with arrangements made under Police Act 1964, s 15A(2), Police (Scotland) Act 1967, s 12A(2)) (s 94(3)(c))
			1 Apr 1995 (otherwise) (SI 1994/3262)
	21, 22		Repealed
	23		1 Apr 1995 (SI 1994/3262)
	24–34		Repealed
	35		1 Apr 1995 (SI 1994/3262)
	36		Repealed
	37, 38		1 Apr 1995 (SI 1994/3262)
	39	(a)	Repealed
		(b)	1 Aug 1996 (SI 1996/1646)
	40	(1)	1 Aug 1996 (SI 1996/1646)
		(2)	Repealed (*never in force*)
		(3)	1 Aug 1996 (SI 1996/1646)
6			1 Aug 1996 (subject to a saving) (SI 1996/1646)
7			Repealed (*never in force*)
8, Pt	I		Repealed (paras 1, 19 (partly), 23 *never in force*)
	II, para	24	Repealed (*never in force*)
		25	Repealed
		26–32	1 Apr 1995 (SI 1995/685)
		33 (1)–(4)	1 Apr 1995 (SI 1995/685)

Police and Magistrates' Courts Act 1994 (c 29)—*contd*
Section

8, Pt	II, para	33	(5)	Repealed (*never in force*)
			(6)	1 Apr 1995 (SI 1995/685)
		34		1 Apr 1995 (SI 1995/685)
		35		Repealed
9, Pt	I			8 Aug 1994 (repeals of or in Metropolitan Police Act 1856; Police Act 1964, ss 25(5) (for certain purposes), 33(5); Drug Trafficking Offences Act 1986) (SI 1994/2025)

9, Pt   I

8 Aug 1994 (repeals of or in
Metropolitan Police Act 1856;
Police Act 1964, ss 25(5) (for
certain purposes), 33(5); Drug
Trafficking Offences Act 1986)
(SI 1994/2025)
23 Aug 1994 (repeals in Police
Act (Northern Ireland) 1970)
(SI 1994/2151)
1 Oct 1994 (repeals in Licensing
Act 1902; Police Negotiating
Board Act 1980; Local
Government Act 1985, s 30(2))
(SI 1994/2025)
31 Dec 1994 (repeals in Police
Act 1964, s 12) (SI 1994/3262)
1 Jan 1995 (repeals of or in Police
(Scotland) Act 1967, ss 24(3),
38(1)–(3), (5), Sch 4) (SI 1994/3075)
1 Apr 1995 (all entries so far as relate
to enactments as they apply in
England and Wales, *except* those in
respect of Metropolitan Police
Act 1856; Licensing Act 1902;
Police Act 1964, ss 12, 33(5),
53(1), 60; Police Negotiating
Board Act 1980; Police and
Criminal Evidence Act 1984,
ss 67(8), 85(8), 90(3), (4), (6), (8),
91, 92, 94, 97(4), 99(2), 101, 103,
104(1), (2), 105, Sch 4; Local
Government Act 1985, s 30(2);
Drug Trafficking Offences Act 1986;
Courts and Legal Services
Act 1990; Police Act (Northern
Ireland) 1970) (SI 1994/3262)
1 Apr 1995 (repeal of Police
Act 1964, s 25(5) (for remaining
purposes)) (SI 1994/3262)
1 Apr 1995 (S) (repeals in Police
(Overseas Service) Act 1945;
Police Act 1969; Police Pensions
Act 1976; Overseas Development
and Cooperation Act 1980)
(SI 1995/492)

Police and Magistrates' Courts Act 1994 (c 29)—*contd*
Section

9, Pt   I—*contd*   1 Apr 1995 (repeals in Police
(Scotland) Act 1967, ss 6(2), 7(1),
31(2), (4)) (subject to transitional
provisions) (SI 1995/492)
13 Dec 1995 (repeals of or in Police
(Scotland) Act 1967, ss 7(2), 14(1),
26(2)(d), 51(1); Police and
Criminal Evidence Act 1984,
Sch 4, para 11) (SI 1995/3003)[1]
1 Apr 1996 (repeal in Police
(Scotland) Act 1967, s 8(1))
(SI 1995/492)
1 Aug 1996 (repeals in Police
(Scotland) Act 1967 so far as not
already in force, subject to savings)
(SI 1996/1646)
Not in force (otherwise, but entries
relating to Police Act 1964,
ss 53(1), 60(1), 60(2); Police and
Criminal Evidence Act 1984
(except s 108, Schs 4, 6); Courts
and Legal Services Act 1990 have
been repealed by Police Act 1996,
s 103, Sch 9, Pt I)

        II   1 Nov 1994 (repeals of or in Justices
of the Peace Act 1979, ss 12(7),
18(2), 19(3), (4), 21(1), 23(1),
24(1)(a), (2), (5), 24A(1), 70
(definition "joint committee area"
only) and (for purpose specified in
entry to s 79 of this Act above),
repeal of s 35 of the 1979 Act)
(SI 1994/2594)
1 Apr 1995 (repeals of or in Reserve
and Auxiliary Forces (Protection of
Civil Interests) Act 1951, s 48;
Administration of Justice Act 1964,
Sch 3, Pt II, para 29; Gaming
Act 1968, Sch 2, para 2(2); Juries
Act 1974, Sch 1, Pt I, Group B;
Justices of the Peace Act 1979,
ss 22(2), 26(1), (2), (4), (5),
27(1)–(5), (7), (9), 28(1A), 30(1),
35 (so far as not already in force),
36–38, 53(6), 57, 63(2), (4);
Magistrates' Courts Act 1980,
ss 68(7), 141(3), 145(1)(d); Local
Government Act 1985, s 12;
Criminal Justice Act 1988,

Police and Magistrates' Courts Act 1994 (c 29)—*contd*

Section

9, Pt	II—*contd*	ss 164(3), 165; Courts and Legal Services Act 1990, s 10(3)–(5), Sch 18, para 25; Criminal Justice Act 1991, s 76(3), 79 (so far as applies to Justices of the Peace Act 1979, s 55(2)), 93(1), Sch 11, paras 40(2)(k), 41(2)(c)) (subject to transitional provisions) (SI 1995/685) *Not in force* (otherwise)

1   Note that these provisions were to come into force on 1 Apr 1996 by virtue of SI 1995/492, which was subsequently amended by SI 1995/3003

2   Orders made under the Local Government Act 2000, s 108, bringing the prospective repeal into force will be noted to that Act in the service to this work

---

Race Relations (Remedies) Act 1994 (c 10)

RA: 3 May 1994

Commencement provisions: s 3(3)

3 Jul 1994 (s 3(3))

Road Traffic Regulation (Special Events) Act 1994 (c 11)

RA: 3 May 1994

3 May 1994 (RA)

Sale and Supply of Goods Act 1994 (c 35)

RA: 3 Nov 1994

Commencement provisions: s 8(2)

3 Jan 1995 (s 8(2))

Sale of Goods (Amendment) Act 1994 (c 32)

RA: 3 Nov 1994

Commencement provisions: s 3(3)

3 Jan 1995 (s 3(3))

Social Security (Contributions) Act 1994 (c 1)

RA: 10 Feb 1994

10 Feb 1994 (RA; but note ss 1(2), 2(3), 3(2))

Social Security (Incapacity for Work) Act 1994 (c 18)

RA: 5 Jul 1994

Commencement provisions: s 16(2), (3); Social Security (Incapacity for Work) Act 1994
(Commencement) Order 1994, SI 1994/2926

Section

1		13 Apr 1995 (SI 1994/2926)
2	(1)	18 Nov 1994 (for purpose of authorising the making of regulations expressed to come into force on 13 Apr 1995) (SI 1994/2926) 13 Apr 1995 (otherwise) (SI 1994/2926)
	(2)	13 Apr 1995 (SI 1994/2926)
	(3)	18 Nov 1994 (SI 1994/2926)
	(4)	13 Apr 1995 (SI 1994/2926)
	(5)	18 Nov 1994 (for purpose of authorising the making of regulations expressed to come into force on 13 Apr 1995) (SI 1994/2926) 13 Apr 1995 (otherwise) (SI 1994/2926)
	(6)	13 Apr 1995 (SI 1994/2926)
	(7)	18 Nov 1994 (SI 1994/2926)
3	(1)	18 Nov 1994 (for purpose of authorising the making of regulations expressed to come into force on 13 Apr 1995) (SI 1994/2926) 13 Apr 1995 (otherwise) (SI 1994/2926)
	(2)	13 Apr 1995 (SI 1994/2926)
4		18 Nov 1994 (SI 1994/2926)
5, 6		18 Nov 1994 (for purpose of authorising the making of regulations expressed to come into force on 13 Apr 1995) (SI 1994/2926) 13 Apr 1995 (otherwise) (SI 1994/2926)
7		18 Nov 1994 (SI 1994/2926)
8	(1)	6 Apr 1995 (SI 1994/2926)
	(2)	18 Nov 1994 (SI 1994/2926)
	(3), (4)	6 Apr 1995 (SI 1994/2926)
9	(1)–(3)	Repealed
	(4)	18 Nov 1994 (SI 1994/2926)
10	(1)	18 Nov 1994 (for purpose of authorising the making of regulations expressed to come into force on 13 Apr 1995) (SI 1994/2926)

Social Security (Incapacity for Work) Act 1994 (c 18)—*contd*

Section

10	(1)—*contd*	13 Apr 1995 (otherwise) (SI 1994/2926)
	(2)	13 Apr 1995 (SI 1994/2926)
	(3)	18 Nov 1994 (for purpose of authorising the making of regulations expressed to come into force on 13 Apr 1995) (SI 1994/2926)
		13 Apr 1995 (otherwise) (SI 1994/2926)
11		13 Apr 1995 (SI 1994/2926)
12		18 Nov 1994 (SI 1994/2926)
13		13 Apr 1995 (SI 1994/2926)
14–16		5 Jul 1994 (s 16(2))

Schedule

1, 2	13 Apr 1995 (SI 1994/2926)

State Hospitals (Scotland) Act 1994 (c 16)

RA: 5 Jul 1994

Commencement provisions: s 3(2), (3); State Hospitals (Scotland) Act 1994 Commencement Order 1995, SI 1995/576

1 Apr 1995 (SI 1995/576)

Statutory Sick Pay Act 1994 (c 2)

RA: 10 Feb 1994

Commencement provisions: s 5(2)

Section

1	6 Apr 1994 (s 5(2))
2–5	10 Feb 1994 (s 5(2))

Sunday Trading Act 1994 (c 20)

RA: 5 Jul 1994

Commencement provisions: ss 1, 9(3); Sunday Trading Act 1994 Appointed Day Order 1994, SI 1994/1841

Section

1		5 Jul 1994 (RA)
2–4		26 Aug 1994 (SI 1994/1841)
5		Repealed
6–8		5 Jul 1994 (RA)
9	(1)	5 Jul 1994 (RA)
	(2)	26 Aug 1994 (SI 1994/1841)
	(3), (4)	5 Jul 1994 (RA)

Sunday Trading Act 1994 (c 20)—*contd*
Schedule

1–3		26 Aug 1994 (SI 1994/1841)
4, para	1–23	Repealed
	24	26 Aug 1994 (SI 1994/1841)
5		26 Aug 1994 (SI 1994/1841)

Trade Marks Act 1994 (c 26)

RA: 21 Jul 1994

Commencement provisions: s 109; Trade Marks Act 1994 (Commencement) Order 1994, SI 1994/2550

31 Oct 1994 (SI 1994/2550; though note that, for certain purposes relating to the making of subordinate legislation, ss 4(4), 13(2), 25(1), (5), (6), 34(1), 35(5), 38(1), (2), 39(3), 40(4), 41(1), (3), 43(2), (3), (5), (6), 44(3), 45(2), 63(2), (3), 64(4), 65(1), (3)–(5), 66(2), 67(1), (2), 68(1), (3), 69, 76(1), 78, 79, 80(3), 81, 82, 88, 90, Sch 1, para 6(2), Sch 2, para 7(2), Sch 3, paras 10(2), 11(2), 12, 14(5) are brought into force on 29 Sep 1994, and note that ss 66(1), 80(1), (3) are brought into force on that date for certain purposes relating to the exercise of the registrar's powers)

Transport Police (Jurisdiction) Act 1994 (c 8)

RA: 24 Mar 1994

Commencement provisions: s 2(2)

1 Apr 1994 (s 2(2))

Value Added Tax Act 1994 (c 23)

RA: 5 Jul 1994

Commencement provisions: s 101(1)

1 Sep 1994 (s 101(1))

Vehicle Excise and Registration Act 1994 (c 22)

RA: 5 Jul 1994

Commencement provisions: s 66, Sch 4, para 9

1 Sep 1994 (s 66; though note that by Sch 4, para 9 to the Act, s 20 and the references thereto in ss 45(1)(b), 57(5) do not come into force until a day to be appointed by the Secretary of State)

1995

Activity Centres (Young Persons' Safety) Act 1995 (c 15)

RA: 28 Jun 1995

Commencement provisions: s 5

28 Aug 1995 (s 5)

Agricultural Tenancies Act 1995 (c 8)

RA: 9 May 1995

Commencement provisions: s 41(2)

1 Sep 1995 (s 41(2))

Appropriation Act 1995 (c 19)

Whole Act repealed

Atomic Energy Authority Act 1995 (c 37)

RA: 8 Nov 1995

8 Nov 1995 (RA)

Building Societies (Joint Account Holders) Act 1995 (c 5)

RA: 1 May 1995

1 May 1995 (RA) (and see s 2(2))

Carers (Recognition and Services) Act 1995 (c 12)

RA: 28 Jun 1995

Commencement provisions: s 5(2)

1 Apr 1996 (s 5(2))

Charities (Amendment) Act 1995 (c 48)

RA: 8 Nov 1995

8 Nov 1995 (RA)

Child Support Act 1995 (c 34)

RA: 19 Jul 1995

Commencement provisions: s 30(3), (4); Child Support Act 1995 (Commencement No 1) Order 1995, SI 1995/2302; Child Support Act 1995 (Commencement No 2) Order 1995, SI 1995/3262; Child Support Act 1995 (Commencement No 3) Order 1996, SI 1996/2630

Section		
1	(1)	14 Oct 1996 (for the purpose of regulations under Child Support Act 1991, s 28A) (SI 1996/2630)
		2 Dec 1996 (otherwise) (SI 1996/2630)
		Prospectively repealed by Child Support, Pensions and Social Security Act 2000, s 85, Sch 9, Pt I[1]
	(2)	See Sch 1 below; prospectively repealed by Child Support, Pensions and Social Security Act 2000, s 85, Sch 9, Pt I[1]
2		14 Oct 1996 (in respect of insertion of Child Support Act 1991, s 28B(2), (3), for the purpose of regulations under s 28B(2) thereof) (SI 1996/2630)
		2 Dec 1996 (in respect of insertion of Child Support Act 1991, s 28B(1), (2) (so far as not already in force), (3) (so far as not already in force), (4), (5)) (SI 1996/2630)
		Not in force (otherwise)
		Prospectively repealed by Child Support, Pensions and Social Security Act 2000, s 85, Sch 9, Pt I[1]
3		14 Oct 1996 (for the purpose of regulations under Child Support Act 1991, s 28C) (SI 1996/2630)
		2 Dec 1996 (otherwise) (SI 1996/2630)
		Prospectively repealed by Child Support, Pensions and Social Security Act 2000, s 85, Sch 9, Pt I[1]
4		2 Dec 1996 (SI 1996/2630)
5		14 Oct 1996 (for the purpose of regulations under Child Support Act 1991, s 28E) (SI 1996/2630)
		2 Dec 1996 (otherwise) (SI 1996/2630)
6	(1)	14 Oct 1996 (for the purpose of regulations under Child Support Act 1991, s 28F) (SI 1996/2630)

Child Support Act 1995 (c 34)—*contd*
Section

6	(1)—*contd*	2 Dec 1996 (otherwise) (SI 1996/2630)
		Prospectively repealed by Child Support, Pensions and Social Security Act 2000, s 85, Sch 9, Pt I[1]
	(2)	See Sch 2 below
7		14 Oct 1996 (for the purpose of regulations under Child Support Act 1991, s 28G) (SI 1996/2630)
		2 Dec 1996 (otherwise) (SI 1996/2630)
		Prospectively repealed as noted to s 1(1) above[1]
8		2 Dec 1996 (SI 1996/2630); Prospectively repealed by Child Support, Pensions and Social Security Act 2000, s 85, Sch 9, Pt I[1]
9		22 Jan 1996 (in respect of insertion of Child Support Act 1991, s 28I(4)) (SI 1995/3262)
		14 Oct 1996 (in respect of the insertion of Child Support Act 1991, s 28I(5)) (SI 1996/2630)
		Not in force (otherwise)
		Prospectively repealed by Child Support, Pensions and Social Security Act 2000, s 85, Sch 9, Pt I[1]
10		Prospectively repealed by Child Support, Pensions and Social Security Act 2000, ss 23, 85, Sch 9, Pt I[1]
11		22 Jan 1996 (SI 1995/3262); prospectively repealed by Child Support, Pensions and Social Security Act 2000, s 85, Sch 9, Pt I[1]
12, 13		Repealed
14		22 Jan 1996 (SI 1995/3262)
15, 16		Repealed
17		18 Dec 1995 (SI 1995/3262)
18		4 Sep 1995 (SI 1995/2302)
19		4 Sep 1995 (SI 1995/2302); prospectively repealed by Child Support, Pensions and Social Security Act 2000, s 85, Sch 9, Pt I[1]
20, 21		4 Sep 1995 (SI 1995/2302)

Child Support Act 1995 (c 34)—*contd*

Section			
22			*Not in force*; prospectively repealed by Child Support, Pensions and Social Security Act 2000, s 85, Sch 9, Pt I[1]
23			4 Sep 1995 (so far as inserts Child Support Act 1991, s 41B(1), (2), (7)) (SI 1995/2302)
			1 Oct 1995 (otherwise) (SI 1995/2302)
24			Repealed
25			1 Oct 1995 (SI 1995/2302)
26	(1)–(3)		4 Sep 1995 (SI 1995/2302)
	(4)	(a)	14 Oct 1996 (SI 1996/2630)
		(b)	4 Sep 1995 (SI 1995/2302)
		(c)	1 Oct 1995 (SI 1995/2302); prospectively repealed by Child Support, Pensions and Social Security Act 2000, s 85, Sch 9, Pt I[1]
	(5), (6)		4 Sep 1995 (SI 1995/2302)
27, 28			4 Sep 1995 (SI 1995/2302)
29			19 Jul 1995 (s 30(3))
30	(1)–(4)		19 Jul 1995 (s 30(3))
	(5)		See Sch 3 below
	(6)		19 Jul 1995 (s 30(3))
Schedule			
1			14 Oct 1996 (for the purpose of regulations under Child Support Act 1991, Sch 4A) (SI 1996/2630)
			2 Dec 1996 (otherwise) (SI 1996/2630); prospectively repealed by Child Support, Pensions and Social Security Act 2000, s 85, Sch 9, Pt I[1]
2			14 Oct 1996 (for the purpose of regulations under Child Support Act 1991, Sch 4B) (SI 1996/2630)
			2 Dec 1996 (otherwise) (SI 1996/2630)
			Prospectively repealed by Child Support, Pensions and Social Security Act 2000, s 85, Sch 9, Pt I[1]
3, para	1		1 Oct 1995 (so far as inserts Income and Corporation Taxes Act 1988, s 617(2)(ae)) (SI 1995/2302)
			14 Oct 1996 (otherwise) (SI 1996/2630)
	2		4 Sep 1995 (SI 1995/2302)
	3	(1)	1 Oct 1995 (SI 1995/2302)
		(2)	Repealed

Child Support Act 1995 (c 34)—*contd*

Schedule

3, para	4–6	Repealed (para 5 *never in force*)
	7	2 Dec 1996 (SI 1996/2630)
	8	4 Sep 1995 (SI 1995/2302)
	9	*Not in force*
	10	4 Sep 1995 (SI 1995/2302)
	11	1 Oct 1995 (SI 1995/2302)
	12	1 Oct 1995 (SI 1995/2302); prospectively repealed by Child Support, Pensions and Social Security Act 2000, s 85, Sch 9, Pt I[1]
	13	*Not in force*
	14	4 Sep 1995 (SI 1995/2302)
	15	4 Sep 1995 (SI 1995/2302); prospectively repealed by Child Support, Pensions and Social Security Act 2000, s 85, Sch 9, Pt I[1]
	16	4 Sep 1995 (SI 1995/2302)
	17	Repealed
	18	18 Dec 1995 (SI 1995/3262)
	19	4 Sep 1995 (SI 1995/2302)
	20	14 Oct 1996 (SI 1996/2630)

[1]   Orders made under Child Support, Pensions and Social Security Act 2000, s 86, bringing the prospective amendments into force will be noted to that Act

---

Children (Scotland) Act 1995 (c 36)

RA: 19 Jul 1995

Commencement provisions: s 105(1), (2); Children (Scotland) Act 1995 (Commencement No 1) Order 1995, SI 1995/2787; Children (Scotland) Act 1995 (Commencement No 2 and Transitional Provisions) Order 1996, SI 1996/2203, as amended by SI 1996/2708, SI 1997/137; Children (Scotland) Act 1995 (Commencement No 3) Order 1996, SI 1996/3201[1], as amended by SI 1997/744; Children (Scotland) Act 1995 (Commencement No 4) Order 2001, SSI 2001/475; Children (Scotland) Act 1995 (Commencement No 5) Order 2002, SSI 2002/12

Section

1	(1)–(3)	1 Nov 1995 (for purpose of bringing into force ss 15, 103, Sch 4, para 12) (SI 1995/2787)
		1 Nov 1996 (otherwise) (SI 1996/2203)
	(4)	1 Nov 1996 (SI 1996/2203)
2		1 Nov 1996 (SI 1996/2203)
3		1 Nov 1996 (subject to transitional provisions) (SI 1996/2203)

Children (Scotland) Act 1995 (c 36)—*contd*
Section

4	1 Sep 1996 (for purpose of making regulations so as to come into force on or after 1 Nov 1996) (SI 1996/2203)
	1 Nov 1996 (otherwise) (SI 1996/2203)
5, 6	1 Nov 1996 (SI 1996/2203)
7	1 Nov 1996 (subject to transitional provisions) (SI 1996/2203)
8–10	1 Nov 1996 (SI 1996/2203)
11	1 Nov 1996 (subject to transitional provisions) (SI 1996/2203)
12–14	1 Nov 1996 (SI 1996/2203)
15	1 Nov 1995 (SI 1995/2787)
16	1 Apr 1997 (SI 1996/3201)
17	12 Dec 1996 (for the purpose of enabling directions, rules or regulations to be made so as to come into force on or after 1 Apr 1997) (SI 1996/3201)
	1 Apr 1997 (otherwise) (SI 1996/3201)
18	1 Apr 1997 (SI 1996/3201)
19, 20	12 Dec 1996 (for the purpose of enabling directions, rules or regulations to be made so as to come into force on or after 1 Apr 1997) (SI 1996/3201)
	1 Apr 1997 (otherwise) (SI 1996/3201)
21–30	1 Apr 1997 (SI 1996/3201)
31	12 Dec 1996 (for the purpose of enabling directions, rules or regulations to be made so as to come into force on or after 1 Apr 1997) (SI 1996/3201)
	1 Apr 1997 (otherwise) (SI 1996/3201)
32	1 Apr 1997 (SI 1996/3201)
33	12 Dec 1996 (for the purpose of enabling directions, rules or regulations to be made so as to come into force on or after 1 Apr 1997) (SI 1996/3201)
	1 Apr 1997 (otherwise) (SI 1996/3201)
34	1 Apr 1997 (SI 1996/3201)
35	1 Nov 1995 (SI 1995/2787)
36	1 Apr 1997 (SI 1996/3201)
37	1 Nov 1995 (SI 1995/2787)

Children (Scotland) Act 1995 (c 36)—*contd*
Section

38	12 Dec 1996 (for the purpose of enabling directions, rules or regulations to be made so as to come into force on or after 1 Apr 1997) (SI 1996/3201)
	1 Apr 1997 (otherwise) (SI 1996/3201)
39	1 Apr 1997 (SI 1996/3201)
40	12 Dec 1996 (for the purpose of enabling directions, rules or regulations to be made so as to come into force on or after 1 Apr 1997) (SI 1996/3201)
	1 Apr 1997 (otherwise) (SI 1996/3201)
41	1 Apr 1997 (SI 1996/3201)
42	12 Dec 1996 (for the purpose of enabling directions, rules or regulations to be made so as to come into force on or after 1 Apr 1997) (SI 1996/3201)
	1 Apr 1997 (otherwise) (SI 1996/3201)
43–48	1 Apr 1997 (SI 1996/3201)
49	Repealed
50–53	1 Apr 1997 (SI 1996/3201)
54	1 Nov 1996 (subject to transitional provisions) (SI 1996/2203)
55–61	1 Apr 1997 (SI 1996/3201)
62	12 Dec 1996 (for the purpose of enabling directions, rules or regulations to be made so as to come into force on or after 1 Apr 1997) (SI 1996/3201)
	1 Apr 1997 (otherwise) (SI 1996/3201)
63–69	1 Apr 1997 (SI 1996/3201)
70	12 Dec 1996 (for the purpose of enabling directions, rules or regulations to be made so as to come into force on or after 1 Apr 1997) (SI 1996/3201)
	1 Apr 1997 (otherwise) (SI 1996/3201)
71–73	1 Apr 1997 (SI 1996/3201)
74, 75	12 Dec 1996 (for the purpose of enabling directions, rules or regulations to be made so as to come into force on or after 1 Apr 1997) (SI 1996/3201)
	1 Apr 1997 (otherwise) (SI 1996/3201)
76–86	1 Apr 1997 (SI 1996/3201)

Children (Scotland) Act 1995 (c 36)—*contd*

Section

87		12 Dec 1996 (for the purpose of enabling directions, rules or regulations to be made so as to come into force on or after 1 Apr 1997) (SI 1996/3201)
		1 Apr 1997 (otherwise) (SI 1996/3201)
88–90		1 Apr 1997 (SI 1996/3201)
91		1 Oct 1996 (SI 1996/2203)
92		1 Apr 1997 (SI 1996/3201)
93		1 Nov 1996 (SI 1996/2203)
94		12 Dec 1996 (for the purpose of enabling directions, rules or regulations to be made so as to come into force on or after 1 Apr 1997) (SI 1996/3201)
		1 Apr 1997 (otherwise) (SI 1996/3201)
95–97		1 Apr 1997 (SI 1996/3201)
98	(1)	See Sch 2 below
	(2)	1 Nov 1996 (SI 1996/2203)
99		1 Nov 1995 (SI 1995/2787)
100		1 Apr 1997 (SI 1996/3201)
101		12 Dec 1996 (for the purpose of enabling directions, rules or regulations to be made so as to come into force on or after 1 Apr 1997) (SI 1996/3201)
		22 Jan 2002 (otherwise) (SSI 2001/475)
102		1 Apr 1997 (SI 1996/3201)
103, 104		1 Nov 1995 (SI 1995/2787)
105	(1), (2)	19 Jul 1995 (RA)
	(3)	See Sch 3 below
	(4)	See Sch 4 below
	(5)	See Sch 5 below
	(6)–(10)	19 Jul 1995 (RA)
Schedule		
1		1 Apr 1997 (SI 1996/3201)
2, para	1	1 Nov 1996 (SI 1996/2203)
	2	1 Apr 1997 (SI 1996/3201)
	3	12 Dec 1996 (for the purposes of inserting Adoption (Scotland) Act 1978, s 3(3)(aa), for the purpose of enabling regulations to be made, so as to come into force on or after 1 Apr 1997) (SI 1996/3201)
		1 Apr 1997 (otherwise) (SI 1996/3201)
	4	1 Apr 1997 (SI 1996/3201)

Children (Scotland) Act 1995 (c 36)—*contd*

Schedule

2, para	5			12 Dec 1996 (for the purpose of amending Adoption Act 1978, s 9, and inserting s 9(3A) for the purpose of enabling regulations to be made so as to come into force on or after 1 Apr 1997) (SI 1996/3201)
				1 Apr 1997 (otherwise) (SI 1996/3201)
	6			1 Apr 1997 (SI 1996/3201)
	7	(a)	(i)	1 Nov 1996 (SI 1996/2203)
			(ii)	1 Apr 1997 (SI 1996/3201)
		(b), (c)		1 Nov 1996 (SI 1996/2203)
		(d)		1 Apr 1997 (SI 1996/3201)
	8	(a)		1 Nov 1996 (SI 1996/2203)
		(b)		1 Apr 1997 (SI 1996/3201)
	9	(a)		1 Nov 1996 (SI 1996/2203)
		(b)		1 Apr 1997 (SI 1996/3201)
	10			1 Apr 1997 (SI 1996/3201)
	11	(a)		1 Apr 1997 (SI 1996/3201)
		(b), (c)		1 Nov 1996 (SI 1996/2203)
		(d)		1 Apr 1997 (SI 1996/3201)
	12	(a)		1 Apr 1997 (SI 1996/3201)
		(b)	(i)	1 Nov 1996 (SI 1996/2203)
			(ii)	1 Apr 1997 (SI 1996/3201)
		(c), (d)		1 Apr 1997 (SI 1996/3201)
	13	(a)	(i)	1 Apr 1997 (SI 1996/3201)
			(ii)	1 Nov 1996 (SI 1996/2203)
		(b)		1 Apr 1997 (SI 1996/3201)
		(c)	(i)	1 Apr 1997 (SI 1996/3201)
			(ii)	1 Nov 1996 (SI 1996/2203)
		(d)		1 Nov 1996 (SI 1996/2203)
		(e), (f)		1 Apr 1997 (SI 1996/3201)
	14			1 Nov 1996 (SI 1996/2203)
	15, 16			1 Apr 1997 (SI 1996/3201)
	17	(a)		1 Apr 1997 (SI 1996/3201)
		(b)		1 Nov 1996 (SI 1996/2203)
	18			1 Apr 1997 (SI 1996/3201)
	19			12 Dec 1996 (for the purpose of substituting new Adoption (Scotland) Act 1978, s 27(1), (2), for the purpose of enabling regulations to be made, so as to come into force on or after 1 Apr 1997) (SI 1996/3201)
				1 Apr 1997 (otherwise) (SI 1996/3201)
	20–22			1 Apr 1997 (SI 1996/3201)
	23			1 Nov 1996 (SI 1996/2203)
	24			1 Apr 1997 (SI 1996/3201)

Children (Scotland) Act 1995 (c 36)—*contd*
Schedule

2, para	25			12 Dec 1996 (for the purpose of inserting Adoption (Scotland) Act 1978, s 51A, for the purpose of enabling regulations to be made, so as to come into force on or after 1 Apr 1998, or enabling the Secretary of State to make a direction) (SI 1996/3201) 1 Apr 1997 (so far as it relates to insertion of Adoption (Scotland) Act 1978, s 51B) (SI 1996/3201) 1 Apr 1998 (otherwise) (SI 1996/3201)
	26			1 Nov 1996 (SI 1996/2203)
	27, 28			1 Apr 1997 (SI 1996/3201)
	29	(a)	(i), (ii)	1 Apr 1997 (SI 1996/3201)
			(iii)	1 Nov 1996 (SI 1996/2203)
			(iv)	1 Apr 1997 (SI 1996/3201)
			(v), (vi)	1 Nov 1996 (SI 1996/2203)
			(vii)	1 Apr 1997 (SI 1996/3201)
		(b), (c)		1 Apr 1997 (SI 1996/3201)
3, para	1–6			1 Apr 1997 (SI 1996/3201)
	7			1 Nov 1996 (SI 1996/2203)
	8–11			1 Apr 1997 (SI 1996/3201)
4, para	1–6			1 Nov 1996 (SI 1996/2203)
	7	(1)–(5)		1 Nov 1996 (SI 1996/2203)
		(6)	(a)	1 Nov 1996 (SI 1996/2203)
			(b), (c)	1 Apr 1997 (SI 1996/3201)
	8, 9			1 Nov 1996 (SI 1996/2203)
	10	(a)		Repealed
		(b)		1 Nov 1996 (SI 1996/2203)
	11			1 Nov 1996 (SI 1996/2203)
	12, 13			1 Nov 1995 (SI 1995/2787)
	14			1 Nov 1996 (SI 1996/2203)
	15	(1)		1 Nov 1996 (SI 1996/2203)
		(2)–(4)		12 Dec 1996 (for the purpose of amending Social Work (Scotland) Act 1968 for the purpose of enabling regulations to be made, so as to come into force on or after 1 Apr 1997) (SI 1996/3201) 1 Apr 1997 (otherwise) (SI 1996/3201)
		(5)		1 Nov 1996 (SI 1996/2203)
		(6)–(16)		12 Dec 1996 (for the purpose of amending Social Work (Scotland) Act 1968 for the purpose of enabling regulations to be made, so as to come into force on or after 1 Apr 1997) (SI 1996/3201) 1 Apr 1997 (otherwise) (SI 1996/3201)

Children (Scotland) Act 1995 (c 36)—*contd*

Schedule

4, para	15	(17)	(a)	(i)	12 Dec 1996 (for the purpose of amending Social Work (Scotland) Act 1968 for the purpose of enabling regulations to be made, so as to come into force on or after 1 Apr 1997) (SI 1996/3201) 1 Apr 1997 (otherwise) (SI 1996/3201)
				(ii)	1 Nov 1996 (SI 1996/2203)
			(b)		12 Dec 1996 (for the purpose of amending Social Work (Scotland) Act 1968 for the purpose of enabling regulations to be made, so as to come into force on or after 1 Apr 1997) (SI 1996/3201) 1 Apr 1997 (otherwise) (SI 1996/3201)
		(18), (19)			12 Dec 1996 (for the purpose of amending Social Work (Scotland) Act 1968 for the purpose of enabling regulations to be made, so as to come into force on or after 1 Apr 1997) (SI 1996/3201) 1 Apr 1997 (otherwise) (SI 1996/3201)
		(20)	(a), (b)		12 Dec 1996 (for the purpose of amending Social Work (Scotland) Act 1968 for the purpose of enabling regulations to be made, so as to come into force on or after 1 Apr 1997) (SI 1996/3201) 1 Apr 1997 (otherwise) (SI 1996/3201)
			(c)		1 Nov 1996 (SI 1996/2203)
			(d)		12 Dec 1996 (for the purpose of amending Social Work (Scotland) Act 1968 for the purpose of enabling regulations to be made, so as to come into force on or after 1 Apr 1997) (SI 1996/3201) 1 Apr 1997 (otherwise) (SI 1996/3201)
		(21)–(27)			12 Dec 1996 (for the purpose of amending Social Work (Scotland) Act 1968 for the purpose of enabling regulations to be made, so as to come into force on or after 1 Apr 1997) (SI 1996/3201) 1 Apr 1997 (otherwise) (SI 1996/3201)

Children (Scotland) Act 1995 (c 36)—*contd*
Schedule

4, para	15	(28)	(a)–(c)	12 Dec 1996 (for the purpose of amending Social Work (Scotland) Act 1968 for the purpose of enabling regulations to be made, so as to come into force on or after 1 Apr 1997) (SI 1996/3201)
				1 Apr 1997 (otherwise) (SI 1996/3201)
			(d), (e)	1 Nov 1996 (SI 1996/2203)
			(f)–(k)	12 Dec 1996 (for the purpose of amending Social Work (Scotland) Act 1968 for the purpose of enabling regulations to be made, so as to come into force on or after 1 Apr 1997) (SI 1996/3201)
				1 Apr 1997 (otherwise) (SI 1996/3201)
		(29), (30)		12 Dec 1996 (for the purpose of amending Social Work (Scotland) Act 1968 for the purpose of enabling regulations to be made, so as to come into force on or after 1 Apr 1997) (SI 1996/3201)
				1 Apr 1997 (otherwise) (SI 1996/3201)
	16, 17			1 Apr 1997 (SI 1996/3201)
	18	(1)		See sub-paras (2), (3) below
		(2)		1 Nov 1995 (SI 1995/2787)
		(3)		1 Nov 1996 (SI 1996/2203)
	19, 20			1 Nov 1996 (SI 1996/2203)
	21, 22			1 Apr 1997 (SI 1996/3201)
	23	(1)		1 Nov 1996 (SI 1996/2203)
		(2), (3)		1 Apr 1997 (SI 1996/3201)
		(4)	(a)	1 Nov 1996 (for purpose of the substitution of Rehabilitation of Offenders Act 1974, s 7(2)(c)) (SI 1996/2203)
				1 Apr 1997 (otherwise) (SI 1996/3201)
			(b)	1 Apr 1997 (SI 1996/3201)
			(c)	1 Nov 1996 (SI 1996/2203)
	24			Repealed
	25			1 Apr 1997 (SI 1996/3201)
	26	(1)–(3)		1 Nov 1996 (SI 1996/2203)
		(4)	(a)	1 Nov 1996 (SI 1996/2203)
			(b)	1 Apr 1997 (SI 1996/3201)
			(c)	1 Nov 1996 (SI 1996/2203)
		(5)–(7)		1 Nov 1996 (SI 1996/2203)
		(8)		1 Apr 1997 (except in so far as relates to Children Act 1975, s 103) (SI 1996/3201)
				22 Jan 2002 (exception noted above) (SSI 2002/12)

Children (Scotland) Act 1995 (c 36)—*contd*

Schedule

4, para	26	(9), (10)		1 Apr 1997 (SI 1996/3201)
	27			Repealed
	28	(1)		1 Nov 1996 (SI 1996/2203)
		(2)–(4)		1 Apr 1997 (SI 1996/3201)
		(5)	(a)	1 Nov 1996 (SI 1996/2203)
			(b)–(d)	1 Apr 1997 (SI 1996/3201)
	29			Repealed
	30, 31			1 Nov 1996 (SI 1996/2203)
	32			1 Apr 1997 (SI 1996/3201)
	33	(1)		1 Nov 1996 (SI 1996/2203)
		(2), (3)		1 Apr 1997 (SI 1996/3201)
		(4)		1 Nov 1996 (SI 1996/2203)
	34			1 Nov 1996 (SI 1996/2203)
	35			1 Apr 1997 (SI 1996/3201)
	36			1 Nov 1996 (SI 1996/2203)
	37	(1)		1 Nov 1996 (SI 1996/2203)
		(2)–(4)		1 Apr 1997 (SI 1996/3201)
		(5)		1 Nov 1996 (SI 1996/2203)
		(6)	(a) (i), (ii)	1 Nov 1996 (SI 1996/2203)
			(iii), (iv)	1 Apr 1997 (SI 1996/3201)
			(b), (c)	1 Apr 1997 (SI 1996/3201)
	38			1 Nov 1996 (SI 1996/2203)
	39	(1)		1 Nov 1996 (SI 1996/2203)
		(2)	(a)	1 Nov 1996 (SI 1996/2203)
			(b)	1 Apr 1997 (SI 1996/3201)
		(3)	(a)	1 Nov 1996 (SI 1996/2203)
			(b)	1 Apr 1997 (SI 1996/3201)
		(4)		1 Nov 1996 (SI 1996/2203)
		(5)	(a)	1 Apr 1997 (SI 1996/3201)
			(b)	1 Nov 1996 (SI 1996/2203)
			(c), (d)	1 Apr 1997 (SI 1996/3201)
	40	(a)		1 Apr 1997 (SI 1996/3201)
		(b)		1 Nov 1995 (SI 1995/2787)
	41			1 Nov 1996 (SI 1996/2203)
	42			1 Apr 1997 (SI 1996/3201); prospectively repealed by Housing (Scotland) Act 2001, s 112, Sch 10, para 23[2]
	43			1 Nov 1996 (SI 1996/2203)
	44			1 Apr 1997 (SI 1996/3201)
	45			1 Nov 1995 (SI 1995/2787)
	46, 47			1 Nov 1996 (SI 1996/2203)
	48	(1)		1 Nov 1996 (SI 1996/2203)
		(2), (3)		1 Apr 1997 (SI 1996/3201)
		(4)		1 Nov 1996 (SI 1996/2203)
		(5)		1 Apr 1997 (SI 1996/3201)
	49			1 Apr 1997 (SI 1996/3201)
	50–52			1 Nov 1996 (SI 1996/2203)
	53	(1)		See sub-paras (2)–(5) below

Children (Scotland) Act 1995 (c 36)—*contd*

Schedule

4, para	53	(2)	1 Nov 1996 (SI 1996/2203)
		(3)	1 Nov 1995 (SI 1995/2787)
		(4), (5)	1 Nov 1996 (SI 1996/2203)
	54	(1)	1 Nov 1996 (SI 1996/2203)
		(2)–(4)	1 Apr 1997 (SI 1996/3201)
		(5)	1 Nov 1996 (SI 1996/2203)
	55–60		1 Apr 1997 (SI 1996/3201)
5			1 Nov 1995 (repeals in Registration of Births, Deaths and Marriages (Scotland) Act 1965, s 43) (SI 1995/2787)
			1 Nov 1996 (repeals of or in Lands Clauses Consolidation (Scotland) Act 1845; Judicial Factors Act 1849; Improvement of Land Act 1864; Judicial Factors (Scotland) Act 1880; Sheriff Courts (Scotland) Act 1907; Children and Young Persons (Scotland) Act 1937; Nursing Homes Registration (Scotland) Act 1938; Reserve and Auxiliary Forces (Protection of Civil Interests) Act 1951; Matrimonial Proceedings (Children) Act 1958; Social Work (Scotland) Act 1968, ss 5B(5), 94(1) relating to the definition "guardian"; Maintenance Orders (Reciprocal Enforcement) Act 1972; Guardianship Act 1973; Rehabilitation of Offenders Act 1974, s 7(2) (the words from "In the application" to the end); Children Act 1975, ss 47–49, 53; Adoption (Scotland) Act 1978, ss 12(3)(b), (4), 14(1), 15(1), (3), 65(1) relating to the definition "guardian"; Law Reform (Husband and Wife) (Scotland) Act 1984; Mental Health (Scotland) Act 1984, s 55(4); Family Law (Scotland) Act 1985; Law Reform (Parent and Child) (Scotland) Act 1986; Disabled Persons (Services, Consultation and Representation) Act 1986; Family Law Act 1986; Court of Session Act 1988; Children Act 1989; Child Support Act 1991; Age of Legal Capacity (Scotland) Act 1991; Education Act 1993) (SI 1996/2203)

Children (Scotland) Act 1995 (c 36)—*contd*
Schedule
5—*contd*

1 Apr 1997 (repeals of or in Social Work (Scotland) Act 1968 (so far as not already in force); Children and Young Persons Act 1969; Social Work (Scotland) Act 1972; Local Government (Scotland) Act 1973; Rehabilitation of Offenders Act 1974 (so far as not already in force); Criminal Procedure (Scotland) Act 1975; Children Act 1975, ss 73–84, 99, 100, 102, 105, 107, Sch 3, paras 52–57; Adoption (Scotland) Act 1978 (so far as not already in force); Education (Scotland) Act 1980; Criminal Justice (Scotland) Act 1980; Solvent Abuse (Scotland) Act 1983; Health and Social Services and Social Security Adjudications Act 1983; Mental Health (Scotland) Act 1984 (so far as not already in force); Foster Children (Scotland) Act 1984; Child Abduction and Custody Act 1985; Civil Evidence (Scotland) Act 1988; Local Government and Housing Act 1989; Prisoners and Criminal Proceedings (Scotland) Act 1993; Local Government etc (Scotland) Act 1994) (SI 1996/3201)
22 Jan 2002 (repeal of Children Act 1975, s 103) (SSI 2002/12)
Not in force (repeal relating to Trusts (Scotland) Act 1921)

[1] For transitional provisions see SI 1996/3201, arts 4–6

[2] Orders under Housing (Scotland) Act 2001, s 113, bringing the repeal into force will be noted to that Act

Church of England (Miscellaneous Provisions) Measure 1995 (No 2)

RA: 19 Jul 1995

Commencement provisions: s 15(2)

The provisions of this Measure (except s 6) were brought into force on 1 Sep 1995 by an instrument made by the Archbishops of Canterbury and York and dated 26 Jul 1995 (made under s 15(2))

Civil Evidence Act 1995 (c 38)

RA: 8 Nov 1995

Commencement provisions: s 16(2); Civil Evidence Act 1995 (Commencement No 1) Order 1996, SI 1996/3217

Section

1–9		31 Jan 1997 (SI 1996/3217)
10		*Not in force*; prospectively repealed (NI) by Civil Evidence (Northern Ireland) Order 1997, SI 1997/2983 (NI 21), art 13(2), Sch 2, subject to savings[1]
11–15		31 Jan 1997 (SI 1996/3217)
16	(1), (2)	31 Jan 1997 (SI 1996/3217)
	(3)	31 Jan 1997 (SI 1996/3217); substituted (26 Apr 1999) by Civil Procedure (Modification of Enactments) Order 1999, SI 1999/1217, art 4(a)
	(3A)	Inserted (26 Apr 1999) by Civil Procedure (Modification of Enactments) Order 1999, SI 1999/1217, art 4(b)
	(4)	31 Jan 1997 (SI 1996/3217)
	(5)	*Not in force*; prospectively repealed (NI) by Civil Evidence (Northern Ireland) Order 1997, SI 1997/2983 (NI 21), art 13(2), Sch 2, subject to savings[1]
	(6)	31 Jan 1997 (SI 1996/3217)

Schedule

1, 2	31 Jan 1997 (SI 1996/3217)

[1]   For the commencement of these repeals, see orders made under Civil Evidence (Northern Ireland) Order 1997, SI 1997/2983 (NI 21), art 1(2), (3)

Civil Evidence (Family Mediation) (Scotland) Act 1995 (c 6)

RA: 1 May 1995

Commencement provisions: s 3(3)

19 Feb 1996 (but Act not to apply to any civil proceedings in which any evidence has been given or heard (in whole or in part) at any time prior to that date) (SI 1996/125)

Commonwealth Development Corporation Act 1995 (c 9)

Whole Act repealed

Consolidated Fund Act 1995 (c 2)

Whole Act repealed

Consolidated Fund (No 2) Act 1995 (c 54)

Whole Act repealed

Criminal Appeal Act 1995 (c 35)

RA: 19 Jul 1995

Commencement provisions. s 32; Criminal Appeal Act 1995 (Commencement No 1 and Transitional Provisions) Order 1995, SI 1995/3061; Criminal Appeal Act 1995 (Commencement No 2) Order 1996, SI 1996/3041; Criminal Appeal Act 1995 (Commencement No 3) Order 1996, SI 1996/3149; Criminal Appeal Act 1995 (Commencement No 4 and Transitional Provisions) Order 1997, SI 1997/402

Section

Section			
1, 2			1 Jan 1996 (subject to transitional provisions) (SI 1995/3061)
3			31 Mar 1997 (subject to transitional provisions) (SI 1997/402)
4			1 Jan 1996 (subject to transitional provisions) (SI 1995/3061)
5			31 Mar 1997 (subject to transitional provisions) (SI 1997/402)
6			1 Jan 1996 (subject to transitional provisions) (SI 1995/3061)
7			1 Jan 1996 (subject to transitional provisions, and except in so far as relating to references by the Criminal Cases Review Commission) (SI 1995/3061)
			31 Mar 1997 (exception noted above) (SI 1997/402)
8	(1)–(6)		12 Dec 1996 (for the purposes of making recommendations and appointments) (SI 1996/3041)
			1 Jan 1997 (otherwise) (SI 1996/3149)
	(7)		See Sch 1 below
9–25			31 Mar 1997 (subject to transitional provisions) (SI 1997/402)
26–28			1 Jan 1996 (subject to transitional provisions) (SI 1995/3061)
29			See Schs 2, 3 below
30			1 Jan 1996 (subject to transitional provisions) (SI 1995/3061)
31	(1)	(a)	1 Jan 1997 (SI 1996/3149)
		(b)	1 Jan 1996 (subject to transitional provisions) (SI 1995/3061)
	(2)		1 Jan 1996 (subject to transitional provisions) (SI 1995/3061)
32–34			1 Jan 1996 (subject to transitional provisions) (SI 1995/3061)

Criminal Appeal Act 1995 (c 35)—*contd*
Schedule

1, para	1, 2		12 Dec 1996 (for the purposes of making recommendations and appointments) (SI 1996/3041) 1 Jan 1997 (otherwise) (SI 1996/3149)
	3–11		1 Jan 1997 (SI 1996/3149)
2, para	1, 2		Repealed
	3		31 Mar 1997 (subject to transitional provisions) (SI 1997/402)
	4	(1)–(3)	1 Jan 1996 (subject to transitional provisions) (SI 1995/3061)
		(4)	31 Mar 1997 (subject to transitional provisions) (SI 1997/402)
		(5)	1 Jan 1996 (subject to transitional provisions) (SI 1995/3061)
	5, 6		1 Jan 1996 (subject to transitional provisions) (SI 1995/3061)
	7–11		1 Jan 1997 (SI 1996/3149)
	12	(1)–(4)	1 Jan 1996 (subject to transitional provisions) (SI 1995/3061)
		(5)	31 Mar 1997 (subject to transitional provisions) (SI 1997/402)
		(6)	1 Jan 1996 (subject to transitional provisions) (SI 1995/3061)
	13, 14		31 Mar 1997 (subject to transitional provisions) (SI 1997/402)
	15		1 Jan 1996 (subject to transitional provisions) (SI 1995/3061)
	16		31 Mar 1997 (subject to transitional provisions) (SI 1997/402)
	17		Repealed
	18		31 Mar 1997 (subject to transitional provisions) (SI 1997/402); prospectively repealed by Criminal Evidence (Northern Ireland) Order 1999, SI 1999/2789 (NI 8), art 40(3), Sch 3[1]
	19		31 Mar 1997 (subject to transitional provisions) (SI 1997/402)
3			1 Jan 1996 (so far as relates to repeals of or in Criminal Appeal Act 1968, s 23(3), Courts-Martial (Appeals) Act 1968, the Criminal Law Act 1977, Magistrates' Courts Act 1980, Criminal Appeal (Northern Ireland) Act 1980, ss 16(1), 25(3), Supreme Court Act 1981, Criminal Justice Act 1988,

Criminal Appeal Act 1995 (c 35)—*contd*
Schedule

3—*contd* . Criminal Procedure (Insanity and
Unfitness to Plead) Act 1991,
Sch 3, para 3(1), and subject to
transitional provisions)
(SI 1995/3061)
31 Mar 1997 (otherwise) (subject to
transitional provisions)
(SI 1997/402)

[1] For the commencement of this repeal, see orders made under Criminal Evidence (Northern Ireland) Order 1999, SI 1999/2789 (NI 8), art 1(2)

Criminal Injuries Compensation Act 1995 (c 53)

RA: 8 Nov 1995

8 Nov 1995 (RA)

Criminal Justice (Scotland) Act 1995 (c 20)

Whole Act repealed by Criminal Procedure (Consequential Provisions) Act 1995, s 6(1), Sch 5, subject to savings for prospective amendments; see s 4, Sch 3, paras 3, 16 thereto

Commencement provisions: s 118(2), (3) (repealed as noted above); Criminal Justice (Scotland) Act 1995 (Commencement No 1, Transitional Provisions and Savings) Order 1995, SI 1995/2295; Criminal Justice (Scotland) Act 1995 (Commencement No 2, Transitional Provisions and Savings) Order 1996, SI 1996/517 (bringing into force, subject to transitional provisions and savings, and with the exception of s 66 (repealed), all of the provisions of this Act (in so far as not already in force) on 5 Mar 1996 and 31 Mar 1996)

Criminal Law (Consolidation) (Scotland) Act 1995 (c 39)

RA: 8 Nov 1995

Commencement provisions: s 53(2)

1 Apr 1996 (s 53(2)), subject to transitional provisions and savings in Criminal Procedure (Consequential Provisions) (Scotland) Act 1995, in particular for consolidated provisions which are not in force at that date; see s 4, Sch 3 thereto

Criminal Procedure (Consequential Provisions) (Scotland) Act 1995 (c 40)

RA: 8 Nov 1995

Commencement provisions: s 7(2)

1 Apr 1996 (s 7(2)), subject to transitional provisions and savings, in particular for amendments by consolidated enactments which are not in force at that date; see s 4, Sch 3 thereto

Criminal Procedure (Scotland) Act 1995 (c 46)

RA: 8 Nov 1995

Commencement provisions: s 309(2)

1 Apr 1996 (s 309(2)), subject to transitional provisions and savings in Criminal Procedure (Consequential Provisions) (Scotland) Act 1995, in particular for consolidated provisions which are not in force at that date; see s 4, Sch 3 thereto

Crown Agents Act 1995 (c 24)

RA: 19 Jul 1995

19 Jul 1995 (RA) (note that certain provisions of this Act have effect as from "the appointed day" or as from the dissolution of the Crown Agents— 21 Mar 1997 is the appointed day under s 1(1) (Crown Agents Act 1995 (Appointed Day) Order 1997, SI 1997/1139) and as at 17 August 2001 no such dissolution order had been made under s 8(4))

Disability Discrimination Act 1995 (c 50)

RA: 8 Nov 1995

Commencement provisions: s 70(2), (3); Disability Discrimination Act 1995 (Commencement No 1) Order 1995, SI 1995/3330; Disability Discrimination Act 1995 (Commencement No 1) Order (Northern Ireland) 1996, SR 1996/1; Disability Discrimination Act 1995 (Commencement No 2) Order 1996, SI 1996/1336; Disability Discrimination Act 1995 (Commencement No 2) Order (Northern Ireland) 1996, SR 1996/219; Disability Discrimination Act 1995 (Commencement No 3 and Saving and Transitional Provisions) Order 1996, SI 1996/1474; Disability Discrimination Act 1995 (Commencement No 3 and Saving and Transitional Provisions) Order (Northern Ireland) 1996, SR 1996/280; Disability Discrimination Act 1995 (Commencement No 4) Order 1996, SI 1996/3003; Disability Discrimination Act 1995 (Commencement No 4) Order (Northern Ireland) 1996, SR 1996/560; Disability Discrimination Act 1995 (Commencement No 5) Order 1998, SI 1998/1282; Disability Discrimination Act (Commencement No 5) Order (Northern Ireland) 1998, SR 1998/183; Disability Discrimination Act 1995 (Commencement No 6) Order 1999, SI 1999/1190; Disability Discrimination Act (Commencement No 6) Order (Northern Ireland) 1999, SR 1999/196; Disability Discrimination Act 1995 (Commencement No 7) Order 2000, SI 2000/1969; Disability Discrimination Act 1995 (Commencement No 7) Order (Northern Ireland) 2001, SR 2001/163; Disability Discrimination Act 1995 (Commencement No 8) Order 2000, SI 2000/2989; Disability Discrimination Act 1995 (Commencement No 9) Order 2001, SI 2001/2030; Disability Discrimination Act 1995 (Commencement No 8) Order (Northern Ireland) 2001, SR 2001/439

In its application to Northern Ireland, this Act is modified; see Sch 8 to this Act

Section

1–3   17 May 1996 (E, W, S) (SI 1996/1336)
                                                                       30 May 1996 (NI) (SR 1996/219)

Disability Discrimination Act 1995 (c 50)—*contd*

Section

4			2 Dec 1996 (SI 1996/1474; SR 1996/280)
5	(1)–(5)		2 Dec 1996 (SI 1996/1474; SR 1996/280)
	(6), (7)		6 Jun 1996 (E, W, S) (SI 1996/1474) 11 Jul 1996 (NI) (SR 1996/280)
6	(1)–(7)		2 Dec 1996 (SI 1996/1474; SR 1996/280)
	(8)–(10)		6 Jun 1996 (E, W, S) (SI 1996/1474) 11 Jul 1996 (NI) (SR 1996/280)
	(11), (12)		2 Dec 1996 (SI 1996/1474; SR 1996/280)
7			2 Dec 1996 (SI 1996/1474; SR 1996/280)
8	(1)–(5)		2 Dec 1996 (SI 1996/1474; SR 1996/280)
	(6), (7)		6 Jun 1996 (E, W, S) (SI 1996/1474) 11 Jul 1996 (NI) (SR 1996/280)
	(8)		2 Dec 1996 (SI 1996/1474; SR 1996/280)
9–11			2 Dec 1996 (SI 1996/1474; SR 1996/280)
12	(1), (2)		2 Dec 1996 (SI 1996/1474; SR 1996/280)
	(3)		6 Jun 1996 (E, W, S) (SI 1996/1474) 11 Jul 1996 (NI) (SR 1996/280)
	(4), (5)		2 Dec 1996 (SI 1996/1474; SR 1996/280)
	(6)		6 Jun 1996 (E, W, S) (SI 1996/1474) 11 Jul 1996 (NI) (SR 1996/280)
13			2 Dec 1996 (SI 1996/1474; SR 1996/280)
14	(1)		2 Dec 1996 (SI 1996/1474; SR 1996/280)
	(2)		1 Oct 1999 (SI 1999/1190; SR 1999/196)
	(3)		2 Dec 1996 (SI 1996/1474; SR 1996/280)
	(4), (5)		1 Oct 1999 (SI 1999/1190; SR 1999/196)
	(6)		6 Jun 1996 (E, W, S) (SI 1996/1474) 11 Jul 1996 (NI) (SR 1996/280)
15	(1)	(a)	1 Oct 1999 (SI 1999/1190; SR 1999/196)
		(b)	*Not in force*
	(2)–(10)		1 Oct 1999 (SI 1999/1190; SR 1999/196)
16	(1), (2)		2 Dec 1996 (SI 1996/1474; SR 1996/280)

Disability Discrimination Act 1995 (c 50)—*contd*

Section

16	(3)		17 May 1996 (E, W, S) (so far as it relates to definitions "sub-lease" and "sub-tenancy") (SI 1996/1336)
			30 May 1996 (NI) (so far as it relates to definitions "sub-lease" and "sub-tenancy") (SR 1996/219)
			2 Dec 1996 (otherwise) (SI 1996/3003; SR 1996/560)
	(4)		2 Dec 1996 (SI 1996/1474; SR 1996/280)
	(5)		See Sch 4, paras 1–4 below
17	(1), (2)		2 Dec 1996 (SI 1996/1474; SR 1996/280)
	(3)		6 Jun 1996 (E, W, S) (SI 1996/1474) 11 Jul 1996 (NI) (SR 1996/280)
	(4)		2 Dec 1996 (SI 1996/1474; SR 1996/280)
18	(1), (2)		2 Dec 1996 (SI 1996/1474; SR 1996/280)
	(3), (4)		6 Jun 1996 (E, W, S) (SI 1996/1474) 11 Jul 1996 (NI) (SR 1996/280)
19	(1)	(a)	2 Dec 1996 (SI 1996/1474; SR 1996/280)
		(b)	1 Oct 1999 (SI 1999/1190; SR 1999/196)
		(c), (d)	2 Dec 1996 (SI 1996/1474; SR 1996/280)
	(2)–(4)		2 Dec 1996 (SI 1996/1474; SR 1996/280)
	(5)	(a), (b)	2 Dec 1996 (SI 1996/1474; SR 1996/280); prospectively repealed by Special Educational Needs and Disability Act 2001, ss 38(5)(a), 42(6), Sch 9[2]
		(aa), (ab)	Inserted by Learning and Skills Act 2000, s 149, Sch 9, para 49 (qv); prospectively repealed by Special Educational Needs and Disability Act 2001, ss 38(5)(a), 42(6), Sch 9[2]
		(c)	6 Jun 1996 (E, W, S) (SI 1996/1474) 11 Jul 1996 (NI) (SI 1996/280)
	(5A)		Prospectively inserted by Special Educational Needs and Disability Act 2001, s 38(6)[2]
	(6)		2 Dec 1996 (SI 1996/1474; SR 1996/280); prospectively repealed by Special Educational Needs and Disability Act 2001, ss 38(5)(b), 42(6), Sch 9[2]

Disability Discrimination Act 1995 (c 50)—*contd*

Section

20	(1)		2 Dec 1996 (SI 1996/1474; SR 1996/280)
	(2)		1 Oct 1999 (SI 1999/1190; SR 1999/196)
	(3), (4)		2 Dec 1996 (SI 1996/1474; SR 1996/280)
	(5)		1 Oct 1999 (SI 1999/1190; SR 1999/196)
	(6)–(8)		6 Jun 1996 (E, W, S) (SI 1996/1474) 11 Jul 1996 (NI) (SR 1996/280)
	(9)		1 Oct 1999 (SI 1999/1190; SR 1999/196)
21	(1)		1 Oct 1999 (SI 1999/1190; SR 1999/196)
	(2)	(a)–(c)	1 Oct 2004 (SI 2001/2030; SR 2001/439)
		(d)	1 Oct 1999 (SI 1999/1190; SR 1999/196)
	(3)		26 Apr 1999 (SI 1999/1190; SR 1999/196)
	(4)		1 Oct 1999 (SI 1999/1190; SR 1999/196)
	(5)		26 Apr 1999 (SI 1999/1190; SR 1999/196)
	(6)		1 Oct 1999 (SI 1999/1190; SR 1999/196)
	(7)–(9)		*Not in force*
	(10)		1 Oct 1999 (E, W, S) (SI 1999/1190; SR 1999/196)
22, 23			2 Dec 1996 (SI 1996/1474; SR 1996/280)
24	(1)–(4)		2 Dec 1996 (SI 1996/1474; SR 1996/280)
	(5)		6 Jun 1996 (E, W, S) (SI 1996/1474) 11 Jul 1996 (NI) (SR 1996/280)
25, 26			2 Dec 1996 (SI 1996/1474; SR 1996/280)
27	(1), (2)		1 Oct 2004 (SI 2001/2030; SR 2001/439)
	(3)		9 May 2001 (SI 2001/2030) 31 Dec 2001 (NI) (SR 2001/439)
	(4)		1 Oct 2004 (SI 2001/2030; SR 2001/439)
	(5)		See Sch 4, paras 5–9 below
28			Substituted (25 Apr 2000) by Disability Rights Commission Act 1999, s 10, Equality (Disability, etc) (Northern Ireland) Order 2000, SI 2000/1110 (NI 2), art 12

Disability Discrimination Act 1995 (c 50)—*contd*

Disability Discrimination Act 1995 (c 50)—*contd*
Section

Disability Discrimination Act 1995 (c 50)—*contd*

Disability Discrimination Act 1995 (c 50)—*contd*

Section

52	(11)—*contd*	2 Jan 1996 (NI) (SR 1996/1); prospectively repealed by Equality (Disability, etc) (Northern Ireland) Order 2000, SI 2000/1110 (NI 2), art 16, Sch 2
	(12)	Repealed
53	(1)–(3)	Repealed
	(4)–(7)	6 Jun 1996 (E, W, S) (SI 1996/1474); prospectively repealed by Disability Rights Commission Act 1999, s 14(2), Sch 5[1]
		11 Jul 1996 (NI) (SR 1996/280); prospectively repealed by Equality (Disability, etc) (Northern Ireland) Order 2000, SI 2000/1110 (NI 2), art 16, Sch 2
	(8), (9)	Repealed
53A		Inserted (E, W, S) by Disability Rights Commission Act 1999, s 9(1)[1]
54	(1)–(7)	Repealed
	(8)	6 Jun 1996 (E, W, S) (SI 1996/1474); prospectively repealed by Disability Rights Commission Act 1999, s 14(2), Sch 5[1]
		11 Jul 1996 (NI) (SR 1996/280); prospectively repealed by Equality (Disability, etc) (Northern Ireland) Order 2000, SI 2000/1110 (NI 2), art 16, Sch 2
	(9)	Repealed (E, W, S)
		11 Jul 1996 (NI) (SR 1996/280); prospectively repealed by Equality (Disability, etc) (Northern Ireland) Order 2000, SI 2000/1110 (NI 2), art 16, Sch 2
54A		Inserted (NI) (25 Apr 2000) by Equality (Disability, etc) (Northern Ireland) Order 2000, SI 2000/1110 (NI 2), art 11
55		2 Dec 1996 (SI 1996/1474; SR 1996/280)
56		6 Jun 1996 (E, W, S) (SI 1996/1474) 11 Jul 1996 (NI) (SR 1996/280)
57, 58		2 Dec 1996 (SI 1996/1474; SR 1996/280)
59		17 May 1996 (E, W, S) (SI 1996/1336) 30 May 1996 (NI) (SR 1996/219)

Disability Discrimination Act 1995 (c 50)—*contd*

Disability Discrimination Act 1995 (c 50)—*contd*

Schedule

4, para	4—*contd*	30 May 1996 (NI) (SR 1996/219)
	5–7	1 Oct 2004 (SI 2001/2030; SR 2001/439)
	8, 9	9 May 2001 (SI 2001/2030)
		31 Dec 2001 (SR 2001/439)
	10–14	Prospectively inserted by Special Educational Needs and Disability Act 2001, s 31(2), Sch 6[2]
4A		Prospectively inserted by Special Educational Needs and Disability Act 2001, s 11(2), Sch 2[2]
4B		Prospectively inserted by Special Educational Needs and Disability Act 2001, s 26(2), Sch 4[2]
4C		Prospectively inserted by Special Educational Needs and Disability Act 2001, s 29, Sch 5[2]
5		Repealed (E, W, S)
		2 Jan 1996 (NI) (SR 1996/1); prospectively repealed by Equality (Disability, etc) (Northern Ireland) Order 2000, SI 2000/1110 (NI 2), art 16, Sch 2
6		2 Dec 1996 (SI 1996/1474; SR 1996/280)
7		2 Dec 1996 (repeals of or in Disabled Persons (Employment) Act 1944, ss 1, 6–14, 19, 21, subject to a saving and transitional provisions; Disabled Persons (Employment) Act 1958) (E, W, S) (SI 1996/1474)
		2 Dec 1996 (repeals of Disabled Persons (Employment) Act (Northern Ireland) 1945, ss 1, 6–14, 19, 21 subject to saving and transitional provisions; Disabled Persons (Employment) Act (Northern Ireland) 1960) (NI) (SR 1996/280)
		Not in force (otherwise)
8		8 Nov 1995 (s 70(2))

[1] Orders made under Disability Rights Commission Act 1999, s 16(2) bringing the prospective amendments into force will be noted to that Act

[2] Orders made under Special Educational Needs and Disability Act 2001, s 43, bringing the prospective insertions into force will be noted to that Act

Environment Act 1995 (c 25)

RA: 19 Jul 1995

Commencement provisions: s 125(2)–(5); Environment Act 1995 (Commencement No 1) Order 1995, SI 1995/1983; Environment Act 1995 (Commencement No 2) Order 1995, SI 1995/2649; Environment Act 1995 (Commencement No 3) Order 1995, SI 1995/2765; Environment Act 1995 (Commencement No 4 and Saving Provisions) Order 1995, SI 1995/2950; Environment Act 1995 (Commencement No 5) Order 1996, SI 1996/186; Environment Act (Commencement No 6 and Repeal Provisions) Order 1996, SI 1996/2560; Environment Act 1995 (Commencement No 7) (Scotland) Order 1996, SI 1996/2857; Environment Act 1995 (Commencement No 8 and Saving Provisions) Order 1996, SI 1996/2909; Environment Act 1995 (Commencement No 9 and Transitional Provisions) Order 1997, SI 1997/1626; Environment Act 1995 (Commencement No 10) Order 1997, SI 1997/3044; Environment Act 1995 (Commencement No 11) Order 1998, SI 1998/604; Environment Act 1995 (Commencement No 12 and Transitional Provisions) (Scotland) Order 1998, SI 1998/781; Environment Act 1995 (Commencement No 13) (Scotland) Order 1998, SI 1998/3272; Environment Act 1995 (Commencement No 14) Order 1999, SI 1999/803; Environment Act 1995 (Commencement No 15) Order 1999, SI 1999/1301; Environment Act 1995 (Commencement No 16 and Saving Provision) (England) Order 2000, SI 2000/340; Environment Act 1995 (Commencement No 17 and Savings Provision) (Scotland) Order 2000, SI 2000/180; Environment Act 1995 (Commencement No 18) (Scotland) Order 2000, SI 2000/1986; Environment Act 1995 (Commencement No 18) (England and Wales) Order 2000, SI 2000/3033; Environment Act 1995 (Commencement No 19) (Scotland) Order 2000, SI 2000/433; Environment Act 1995 (Commencement and Saving Provision) (Wales) Order 2001, SI 2001/2351[5]; Environment Act 1995 (Commencement No 20 and Saving Provision) (Wales) Order 2001, SI 2001/3211[6]

Section		
1		28 Jul 1995 (SI 1995/1983)
2		1 Apr 1996 (SI 1996/186)
3	(1)	1 Apr 1996 (SI 1996/186)
	(2)–(8)	28 Jul 1995 (SI 1995/1983)
4		28 Jul 1995 (SI 1995/1983)
5	(1)	1 Apr 1996 (SI 1996/186)
	(2)	1 Feb 1996 (SI 1996/186)
	(3), (4)	1 Apr 1996 (SI 1996/186)
	(5)	1 Feb 1996 (SI 1996/186)
6		1 Apr 1996 (SI 1996/186)
7		28 Jul 1995 (SI 1995/1983)
8		1 Apr 1996 (SI 1996/186)
9		28 Jul 1995 (SI 1995/1983)
10, 11		1 Apr 1996 (SI 1996/186)
12		28 Jul 1995 (SI 1995/1983)
13		1 Apr 1996 (SI 1996/186)
14		See Sch 4 below
15–18		1 Apr 1996 (SI 1996/186)
19		See Sch 5 below

Environment Act 1995 (c 25)—*contd*
Section

20–23		12 Oct 1995 (SI 1995/2649)
24		*Not in force*
25–29		1 Apr 1996 (SI 1996/186)
30–32		12 Oct 1995 (SI 1995/2649)
33–35		1 Apr 1996 (SI 1996/186)
36		12 Oct 1995 (SI 1995/2649)
37	(1), (2)	28 Jul 1995 (SI 1995/1983)
	(3)–(8)	1 Apr 1996 (SI 1996/186)
	(9)	28 Jul 1995 (SI 1995/1983)
38–40		28 Jul 1995 (SI 1995/1983)
41		21 Sep 1995 (so far as confers power to make schemes imposing charges) (SI 1995/1983)
		1 Feb 1996 (so far as confers power on Secretary of State to make regulations and makes provision in relation to the exercise of that power) (SI 1996/186)
		1 Apr 1996 (otherwise) (SI 1996/186)
42		21 Sep 1995 (SI 1995/1983)
43–46		28 Jul 1995 (SI 1995/1983)
46A		Inserted by Public Finance and Accountability Act 2000, s 26, Sch 3, para 13(3) (qv)
47–52		28 Jul 1995 (SI 1995/1983)
53, 54		1 Apr 1996 (SI 1996/186)
55	(1)–(6)	1 Apr 1996 (SI 1996/186)
	(7)–(10)	1 Feb 1996 (SI 1996/186)
56		28 Jul 1995 (SI 1995/1983)
57		21 Sep 1995 (so far as it confers power on Secretary of State to make regulations or orders, give directions or issue guidance, or so far as makes provision with respect to the exercise of any such power) (SI 1995/1983)
		1 Apr 2000 (E) (otherwise) (SI 2000/340)
		14 Jul 2000 (S) (except so far as inserts Environmental Protection Act 1990, s 78S) (SI 2000/180)
		14 Jul 2000 (S) (otherwise) (SI 2000/1986)
		15 Sep 2001 (W) (otherwise) (SI 2001/3211)
58		21 Sep 1995 (so far as it confers power on Secretary of State to make regulations or orders, give directions or issue guidance, or so

Environment Act 1995 (c 25)—*contd*
Section

58—*contd*			far as makes provision with respect to the exercise of any such power) (SI 1995/1983)
			1 Jul 1998 (otherwise) (SI 1998/604)
59			12 Oct 1995 (so far as confers power on Secretary of State to make regulations) (SI 1995/2649)
			1 Jan 1999 (otherwise) (SI 1998/3272)
60	(1), (2)		1 Jul 1998 (SI 1998/604)
	(3), (4)		1 Jul 1997 (subject to transitional provisions) (SI 1997/1626)
	(5)	(a)	1 Jul 1997 (subject to transitional provisions) (SI 1997/1626)
		(b)	1 Jul 1998 (SI 1998/604)
	(6)		1 Jul 1998 (SI 1998/604)
	(7)		1 Jul 1997 (subject to transitional provisions) (SI 1997/1626)
61–73			19 Sep 1995 (s 125(2))
74			19 Jul 1995 (s 125(3))
75–77			19 Sep 1995 (s 125(2))
78			See Sch 10 below
79			19 Sep 1995 (s 125(2))
80			1 Feb 1996 (SI 1996/186)
81			1 Apr 1996 (SI 1996/186)
82–86			23 Dec 1997 (SI 1997/3044)
86A			Inserted by Greater London Authority Act 1999, s 368 (qv)
87–89			1 Feb 1996 (SI 1996/186)
90			See Sch 11 below
91			1 Feb 1996 (SI 1996/186)
92			1 Apr 1996 (SI 1996/186)
93, 94			21 Sep 1995 (SI 1995/1983)
94A			Inserted by Competition Act 1998, s 3(1)(b), Sch 2, Pt IV, para 6(1), (4) (qv)
95			21 Sep 1995 (SI 1995/1983)
96	(1)		See Schs 13, 14 below (E, W)
	(2)		1 Nov 1995 (E, W) (SI 1995/2765)
	(3)		Repealed (E, W)
	(4)		1 Nov 1995 (E, W) (so far as repeals Town and Country Planning Act 1990, s 105) (SI 1995/2765)
			1 Jan 1997 (E, W) (so far as it relates to repeal of Town and Country Planning (Scotland) Act 1972, s 251A) (SI 1996/2857)
	(5), (6)		1 Nov 1995 (E, W) (SI 1995/2765)
			Repealed (S)
97–103			21 Sep 1995 (SI 1995/1983)

Environment Act 1995 (c 25)—*contd*

Section			
104			1 Apr 1996 (SI 1996/186)
105			See Sch 15 below
106			See Sch 16 below
107			See Sch 17 below
108	(1)–(13)		1 Apr 1996 (SI 1996/186)
	(14)		See Sch 18 below
	(15), (16)		1 Apr 1996 (SI 1996/186)
109–111			1 Apr 1996 (SI 1996/186)
112			See Sch 19 below
113			1 Apr 1996 (SI 1996/186)
114	(1)–(3)		1 Apr 1996 (SI 1996/186)
	(4)		See Sch 20 below
115			1 Apr 1996 (SI 1995/2950; SI 1996/186)
116			See Sch 21 below
117			1 Feb 1996 (SI 1996/186)
118	(1)–(3)		1 Feb 1996 (SI 1996/186)
	(4), (5)		1 Feb 1996 (so far as confers power to make orders or make provision in relation to the exercise of that power) (SI 1996/186)
			Not in force (otherwise)
	(6)		1 Feb 1996 (SI 1996/186)
119			1 Feb 1996 (SI 1996/186)
120	(1)		28 Jul 1995 (so far as confers powers to make regulations) (SI 1995/1983)
			See Sch 22 below (otherwise)
	(2)		See Sch 23 below
	(3)		See Sch 24 below
	(4)–(6)		28 Jul 1995 (SI 1995/1983)
121–124			28 Jul 1995 (SI 1995/1983)
125			19 Jul 1995 (s 125(3))
Schedule			
1			28 Jul 1995 (SI 1995/1983)
2			28 Jul 1995 (so far as relates to s 3) (SI 1995/1983)
			12 Oct 1995 (so far as relates to s 22) (SI 1995/2649)
3			28 Jul 1995 (SI 1995/1983)
4, 5			1 Apr 1996 (SI 1996/186)
6			12 Oct 1995 (SI 1995/2649)
7, para	1–6		19 Sep 1995 (s 125(2))
	7	(1)	19 Sep 1995 (s 125(2))
		(2)	1 Apr 1997 (SI 1996/2560)
		(3)–(5)	19 Sep 1995 (s 125(2))
	8		19 Sep 1995 (s 125(2))

Environment Act 1995 (c 25)—*contd*

Schedule

7, para	9, 10		19 Sep 1995 (s 125(2)); prospectively repealed by Local Government Act 2000, s 107, Sch 6[4]
	11–18		19 Sep 1995 (s 125(2))
	19		Repealed
	20		19 Sep 1995 (s 125(2))
8, 9			19 Sep 1995 (s 125(2))
10, para	1		Repealed
	2	(1)	23 Nov 1995 (SI 1995/2950)
		(2)	1 Apr 1996 (SI 1995/2950)
		(3)–(6)	23 Nov 1995 (SI 1995/2950)
		(7)	Repealed
		(8)	23 Nov 1995 (SI 1995/2950)
		(9)	(a)	23 Nov 1995 (SI 1995/2950)
			(b)	1 Apr 1996 (SI 1995/2950)
			(c), (d)	23 Nov 1995 (SI 1995/2950)
	3–7		23 Nov 1995 (SI 1995/2950)
	8	(1)	1 Apr 1996 (SI 1995/2950)
		(2)	23 Nov 1995 (SI 1995/2950)
		(3)	1 Apr 1996 (SI 1995/2950)
	9		23 Nov 1995 (SI 1995/2950)
	10	(1)	23 Nov 1995 (SI 1995/2950)
		(2)	(a)	Spent (*never in force*)
			(b)	1 Apr 1997 (SI 1996/2560)
		(3)	23 Nov 1995 (SI 1995/2950)
	11, 12		23 Nov 1995 (SI 1995/2950)
	13		1 Apr 1996 (SI 1995/2950)
	14, 15		23 Nov 1995 (SI 1995/2950)
	16		Repealed
	17, 18		23 Nov 1995 (SI 1995/2950)
	19, 20		Repealed
	21		23 Nov 1995 (SI 1995/2950)
	22	(1)	Repealed
		(2)	1 Apr 1997 (SI 1996/2560)
		(3)	1 Apr 1996 (SI 1995/2950)
		(4)	(a), (b)	1 Apr 1996 (SI 1995/2950)
			(c)	1 Apr 1997 (SI 1996/2560)
		(5)	1 Apr 1996 (SI 1995/2950)
		(6)	1 Apr 1997 (SI 1996/2560)
		(7)	Repealed
	23–26		23 Nov 1995 (SI 1995/2950)
	27		1 Apr 1997 (SI 1996/2560)
	28–31		23 Nov 1995 (SI 1995/2950)
	32	(1)–(13)	23 Nov 1995 (subject to a saving in relation to sub-para (2)) (SI 1995/2950)
		(14)	1 Apr 1997 (SI 1996/2560)
		(15)–(17)	23 Nov 1995 (SI 1995/2950)
		(18)	Spent

Environment Act 1995 (c 25)—*contd*

Schedule

10, para	33	(1)–(5)	23 Nov 1995 (SI 1995/2950)
		(6)–(8)	1 Apr 1997 (SI 1996/2560)
	34		23 Nov 1995 (SI 1995/2950)
	35		23 Nov 1995 (so far as adds Local Government Finance Act 1992, s 35(5)(c) and the word "or" immediately preceding it) (SI 1995/2950)
			1 Apr 1997 (otherwise) (SI 1996/2560)
	36, 37		23 Nov 1995 (SI 1995/2950)
	38	(1)	23 Nov 1995 (SI 1995/2950)
		(2)	1 Apr 1997 (SI 1996/2560)
11, para	1		23 Dec 1997 (SI 1997/3044)
	2, 3		1 Feb 1996 (SI 1996/186)
	4		23 Dec 1997 (SI 1997/3044)
	5		1 Feb 1996 (SI 1996/186)
12			1 Apr 1996 (SI 1996/186)
13, 14			1 Nov 1995 (E, W) (SI 1995/2765)
			Repealed (S)
15, para	1, 2		1 Apr 1996 (SI 1996/186)
	3		1 Feb 1996 (SI 1996/186)
	4		1 Apr 1996 (SI 1996/186)
	5	(1)	1 Feb 1996 (SI 1996/186)
		(2), (3)	1 Apr 1996 (SI 1996/186)
	6–12		1 Apr 1996 (SI 1996/186)
	13		1 Jan 1999 (SI 1995/1983)
	14	(1)	1 Jan 1999 (SI 1995/1983)
		(2), (3)	1 Apr 1996 (SI 1996/186)
		(4)	1 Jan 1999 (SI 1995/1983)
	15, 16		1 Apr 1996 (SI 1996/186)
	17		1 Jan 1999 (SI 1995/1983)
	18, 19		1 Apr 1996 (SI 1996/186)
	20		1 Jan 1999 (SI 1995/1983)
	21–24		1 Apr 1996 (SI 1996/186)
	25		21 Sep 1995 (SI 1995/1983)
	26	(1)	21 Sep 1995 (SI 1995/1983)
		(2)	1 Jan 1999 (SI 1995/1983)
16–20			1 Apr 1996 (SI 1996/186)
21, para	1	(1)	1 Dec 2000 (SI 2000/3033)
		(2)–(8)	*Not in force*
	2	(1)–(3)	21 Sep 1995 (SI 1995/1983)
		(4)	1 Jul 1997 (except for purposes of the application of substituted Water Resources Act 1991, s 222 to Pt II of the Act) (subject to transitional provisions) (SI 1997/1626)
			Not in force (exception noted above)
	3		*Not in force*

Environment Act 1995 (c 25)—*contd*

Schedule

21, para	4			8 Apr 1998 (subject to transitional provisions) (SI 1998/781)
	5, 6			*Not in force*
22, para	1			1 Apr 1996 (SI 1996/186)
	2			1 Feb 1996 (SI 1996/186)
	3			1 Apr 1996 (SI 1996/186)
	4			28 Jul 1995 (SI 1995/1983)
	5–12			1 Apr 1996 (SI 1996/186)
	13			1 Feb 1996 (SI 1996/186)
	14			1 Apr 1996 (SI 1996/186)
	15			12 Oct 1995 (SI 1995/2649)
	16			Repealed (*never in force*)
	17, 18			1 Apr 1996 (SI 1996/186)
	19–26			1 Apr 1996 (SI 1996/186); prospectively repealed by s 120(3) of, and Sch 24 to, this Act[2]
	27	(a)		1 Apr 1996 (SI 1996/186)
		(b), (c)		*Not in force*
				Paragraph prospectively repealed by s 120(3) of, and Sch 24 to, this Act[2]
	28			1 Apr 1996 (SI 1996/186)
	29	(1)		See sub-paras (2)–(35) below
		(2)–(20)		1 Apr 1996 (SI 1996/186)
		(21)	(a) (i)	*Not in force*
			(ii)	1 Apr 1996 (SI 1996/186)
			(b)–(e)	*Not in force*
		(22)		12 Oct 1995 (so far as confers power on Secretary of State to make regulations) (SI 1995/2649)
				Not in force (otherwise)
		(23)–(25)		1 Apr 1996 (SI 1996/186)
		(26)		*Not in force*
		(27)–(35)		1 Apr 1996 (SI 1996/186)
	30			1 Apr 1996 (SI 1996/186)
	31			28 Jul 1995 (SI 1995/1983)
	32–34			1 Apr 1996 (SI 1996/186)
	35			Repealed
	36			1 Feb 1996 (SI 1996/186)
	37	(1)		21 Sep 1995 (SI 1995/1983)
		(2)	(a)	1 Apr 1998 (SI 1998/604)
			(b)	1 Feb 1996 (SI 1996/186)
		(3)		1 Apr 1996 (SI 1996/186)
		(4)		21 Sep 1995 (SI 1995/1983)
		(5)–(8)		1 Apr 1996 (SI 1996/186)
	38, 39			Repealed
	40, 41			1 Apr 1996 (SI 1996/186)
	42			28 Jul 1995 (SI 1995/1983)
	43, 44			1 Feb 1996 (SI 1996/186)

Environment Act 1995 (c 25)—*contd*
Schedule

22, para	45		1 Apr 1996 (SI 1996/186); prospectively repealed by Pollution Prevention and Control Act 1999, s 6(2), Sch 3[3]
	46	(1)–(4)	1 Apr 1996 (SI 1996/186); prospectively repealed by Pollution Prevention and Control Act 1999, s 6(2), Sch 3[3]
		(5)	23 Dec 1997 (SI 1997/3044); prospectively repealed by Pollution Prevention and Control Act 1999, s 6(2), Sch 3[3]
		(6)–(11)	1 Apr 1996 (SI 1996/186); prospectively repealed by Pollution Prevention and Control Act 1999, s 6(2), Sch 3[3]
	47–50		1 Apr 1996 (SI 1996/186); prospectively repealed by Pollution Prevention and Control Act 1999, s 6(2), Sch 3[3]
	51	(1)–(3)	12 Oct 1995 (SI 1995/2649); prospectively repealed by Pollution Prevention and Control Act 1999, s 6(2), Sch 3[3]
		(4)	1 Apr 1996 (SI 1996/186); prospectively repealed by Pollution Prevention and Control Act 1999, s 6(2), Sch 3[3]
		(5)	12 Oct 1995 (SI 1995/2649); prospectively repealed by Pollution Prevention and Control Act 1999, s 6(2), Sch 3[3]
	52		1 Apr 1996 (SI 1996/186); prospectively repealed by Pollution Prevention and Control Act 1999, s 6(2), Sch 3[3]
	53		12 Oct 1995 (SI 1995/2649); prospectively repealed by Pollution Prevention and Control Act 1999, s 6(2), Sch 3[3]
	54–61		1 Apr 1996 (SI 1996/186); prospectively repealed by Pollution Prevention and Control Act 1999, s 6(2), Sch 3[3]
	62–66		1 Apr 1996 (SI 1996/186)
	67		1 Feb 1996 (so far as confers power to make regulations or makes provision in relation to the exercise of that power) (SI 1996/186)

Environment Act 1995 (c 25)—*contd*

Schedule

22, para	67—*contd*		1 Apr 1998 (so far as it imposes a duty, or confers power, to make regulations) (SI 1998/604)
			1 Apr 1999 (otherwise) (SI 1999/803)
	68	(1)	1 Apr 1996 (SI 1996/186)
		(2)	1 Apr 1996 (so far as requires an application to be accompanied by the prescribed charge) (subject to a saving) (SI 1996/186)
			1 Apr 1998 (otherwise) (SI 1998/604)
		(3), (4)	1 Apr 1996 (subject to a saving relating to sub-para (3)) (SI 1996/186)
		(5)	1 Apr 1998 (SI 1998/604)
		(6)	1 Apr 1996 (subject to a saving) (SI 1996/186)
	69		1 Apr 1998 (so far as confers power to make regulations) (SI 1998/604)
			1 Apr 1999 (otherwise) (SI 1999/803)
	70	(1), (2)	1 Apr 1996 (SI 1996/186)
		(3)	1 Apr 1999 (SI 1999/803)
	71		1 Apr 1998 (so far as confers power to make regulations) (SI 1998/604)
			1 Apr 1999 (otherwise) (SI 1999/803)
	72	(1)	1 Apr 1998 (so far as confers power to make regulations) (SI 1998/604)
			1 Apr 1999 (otherwise) (SI 1999/803)
		(2)	1 Apr 1996 (SI 1996/186)
	73	(1)	1 Apr 1996 (SI 1996/186)
		(2)	1 Apr 1996 (so far as requires an application to be accompanied by the prescribed charge) (SI 1996/186)
			1 Apr 1998 (otherwise) (SI 1998/604)
		(3)–(6)	1 Apr 1996 (SI 1996/186)
	74		1 Apr 1996 (so far as requires an application to be accompanied by the prescribed charge) (SI 1996/186)
			1 Apr 1998 (otherwise) (SI 1998/604)
	75		1 Apr 1996 (SI 1996/186)
	76	(1)	21 Sep 1995 (SI 1995/1983)
		(2)	1 Apr 1996 (SI 1996/186)
		(3)	21 Sep 1995 (SI 1995/1983)
		(4)–(7)	1 Apr 1996 (SI 1996/186)
		(8) (a)	19 Jul 1995 (s 125(3))
		(b)	1 Apr 1996 (SI 1996/186)
	77, 78		1 Apr 1996 (SI 1996/186)
	79		1 Apr 2000 (E) (SI 2000/340)

Environment Act 1995 (c 25)—*contd*
Schedule

22, para	79—*contd*		14 Jul 2000 (S) (SI 2000/180)
			15 Sep 2001 (W) (SI 2001/3211)
	80	(1), (2)	21 Sep 1995 (SI 1995/1983)
		(3)	1 Apr 1996 (SI 1996/186)
	81		*Not in force*
	82	(1)	See sub-paras (2)–(5) below
		(2)–(4)	1 Apr 1996 (SI 1996/186)
		(5)	21 Sep 1995 (so far as confers power on Secretary of State to make regulations or makes provision with respect to the exercise of any such power) (SI 1995/1983)
			1 Apr 1996 (otherwise) (SI 1996/186)
	83–87		1 Apr 1996 (SI 1996/186)
	88		*Not in force*
	89		1 Apr 2000 (E) (subject to a saving) (SI 2000/340)
			14 Jul 2000 (S) (subject to a saving) (SI 2000/180)
			15 Sep 2001 (W) (subject to a saving) (SI 2001/3211)
	90		1 Apr 1996 (SI 1996/186)
	91, 92		1 Apr 2000 (E) (SI 2000/340)
			14 Jul 2000 (S) (SI 2000/180)
			15 Sep 2001 (W) (SI 2001/3211)
	93, 94		1 Apr 1996 (SI 1996/186)
	95		*Not in force*
	96–101		1 Apr 1996 (SI 1996/186)
	102		1 Feb 1996 (SI 1996/186)
	103		1 Feb 1996 (so far as confers power to issue guidance or makes provision in relation to the exercise of that power) (SI 1996/186)
			1 Apr 1996 (otherwise) (SI 1996/186)
	104–132		1 Apr 1996 (SI 1996/186)
	133	(1)	21 Sep 1995 (SI 1995/1983)
		(2)	1 Apr 1996 (SI 1996/186)
	134		1 Apr 1996 (SI 1996/186)
	135		19 Jul 1995 (s 125(3))
	136		1 Apr 1996 (SI 1996/186)
	137–139		21 Sep 1995 (SI 1995/1983)
	140, 141		1 Apr 1996 (SI 1996/186)
	142		21 Nov 1996 (so far as confers power to make regulations) (SI 1996/2909)
			31 Dec 1996 (otherwise) (SI 1996/2909)
	143		21 Nov 1996 (so far as confers power to make regulations) (SI 1996/2909)

Environment Act 1995 (c 25)—*contd*

Schedule

22, para	143—*contd*			31 Dec 1996 (otherwise) (SI 1996/2909)
	144–146			1 Apr 1996 (SI 1996/186)
	147			21 Sep 1995 (SI 1995/1983)
	148–152			1 Apr 1996 (SI 1996/186)
	153			21 Sep 1995 (SI 1995/1983)
	154–160			1 Apr 1996 (SI 1996/186)
	161			29 Apr 1999 (SI 1999/1301)
	162			21 Sep 1995 (so far as confers power on Secretary of State to make regulations or makes provision with respect to the exercise of any such power) (SI 1995/1983)
				16 Mar 1999 (so far as confers power to make regulations in relation to Water Resources Act 1991, ss 161A–161D) (SI 1999/803)
				29 Apr 1999 (otherwise) (SI 1999/1301)
	163			29 Apr 1999 (SI 1999/1301)
	164–168			1 Apr 1996 (SI 1996/186)
	169, 170			21 Nov 1996 (so far as confers power to make regulations) (SI 1996/2909)
				31 Dec 1996 (otherwise) (SI 1996/2909)
	171–181			1 Apr 1996 (SI 1996/186)
	182			21 Sep 1995 (SI 1995/1983); prospectively repealed by s 120(3) of, Sch 24 to, this Act[2]
	183			21 Nov 1996 (so far as confers power to make regulations) (SI 1996/2909)
				31 Dec 1996 (otherwise, but subject to savings) (SI 1996/2909)
	184, 185			1 Apr 1996 (SI 1996/186)
	186			*Not in force*
	187	(1)		21 Sep 1995 (SI 1995/1983)
		(2)		1 Apr 1996 (SI 1996/186)
	188–191			1 Apr 1996 (SI 1996/186)
	192			21 Sep 1995 (SI 1995/1983)
	193–212			1 Apr 1996 (SI 1996/186)
	213	(1)		28 Jul 1995 (SI 1995/1983)
		(2)	(a)	1 Apr 1996 (SI 1996/186)
			(b)	28 Jul 1995 (SI 1995/1983)
		(3)		28 Jul 1995 (SI 1995/1983)
		(4)		1 Apr 1996 (SI 1996/186)
		(5)		Repealed
	214–222			1 Apr 1996 (SI 1996/186)

Environment Act 1995 (c 25)—*contd*

Schedule

22, para	223	(1)	(a), (b)	1 Apr 1996 (SI 1996/186)
			(c)	28 Jul 1995 (SI 1995/1983)
		(2)		1 Apr 1996 (SI 1996/186)
	224–230			1 Apr 1996 (SI 1996/186)
	231			1 Apr 1996 (SI 1996/186); prospectively repealed by s 120(3) of, Sch 24 to, this Act²
	232	(1)		1 Feb 1996 (SI 1996/186)
		(2)		*Not in force*
	233			1 Apr 1996 (SI 1996/186)
23, para	1–6			1 Apr 1996 (SI 1996/186)
	7			*Not in force*
	8–10			1 Apr 1996 (SI 1996/186)
	11			*Not in force*
	12, 13			1 Apr 1996 (SI 1996/186)
	14	(1)–(4)		1 Apr 1996 (SI 1996/186)
		(5), (6)		1 Jan 1999 (SI 1995/1983)
		(7)		1 Apr 1996 (SI 1996/186)
		(8)		1 Jan 1999 (definitions "grating" and "the substitution date")
				1 Apr 1996 (otherwise) (SI 1996/186)
	15			*Not in force*
	16–24			1 Apr 1996 (SI 1996/186)
24				21 Sep 1995 (repeal of Water Resources Act 1991, ss 68, 69(5), 126(6), 129(4)) (SI 1995/1983)
				1 Nov 1995 (repeal of Town and Country Planning Act 1990, s 105) (SI 1995/2765)
				1 Feb 1996 (repeals in Local Government etc (Scotland) Act 1994, except the repeal in relation to s 165(6)) (SI 1996/186)
				1 Apr 1996 (repeals of or in Public Health (Scotland) Act 1897; Alkali, &c, Works Regulation Act 1906; Rivers (Prevention of Pollution) (Scotland) Act 1951; Mines and Quarries Act 1954; Rivers (Prevention of Pollution) (Scotland) Act 1965; Nuclear Installations Act 1965; Parliamentary Commissioner Act 1967; Sewerage (Scotland) Act 1968; Hovercraft Act 1968; Agriculture Act 1970; Local Government Act 1972, s 223(2); Clyde River Purification Act 1972; Local Government (Scotland)

Environment Act 1995 (c 25)—*contd*
Schedule
24—*contd*

Act 1973; Health and Safety at
Work etc Act 1974; Control of
Pollution Act 1974 (except repeal
relating to s 30(1)); Clean Air
Enactments (Repeals and
Modifications) Regulations 1974;
House of Commons
Disqualification Act 1975;
Northern Ireland Assembly
Disqualification Act 1975; Local
Government (Scotland) Act 1975;
Salmon and Freshwater Fisheries
Act 1975, ss 5(2), 10, 15; Water
(Scotland) Act 1980; Roads
(Scotland) Act 1984; Control of
Industrial Air Pollution (Transfer
of Powers of Enforcement)
Regulations 1987; Control of
Pollution (Amendment) Act 1989,
ss 7(2), (8), 11(3); Water Act 1989;
Environmental Protection Act 1990
(except repeals relating to
ss 33(1), 36(11), (12), 39(12),
(13), 54, 61, 75(3), 88, 143, Sch 8);
Natural Heritage (Scotland)
Act 1991; Water Industry
Act 1991 (except repeals in s 4(6));
Water Resources Act 1991,
ss 1–14, 16–19, 58, 105(1), 113(1),
114, 117, 121–124, 131, 132, 144,
146, 150–153, 187, 196, 202(5),
206(2), 209(1), (2), (4), 213–215,
218, 219, 221(1), Schs 1, 3, 4;
Land Drainage Act 1991, s 72(1);
Water Consolidation
(Consequential Provisions)
Act 1991; Clean Air Act 1993;
Radioactive Substances Act 1993;
Noise and Statutory Nuisance
Act 1993; Local Government
(Wales) Act 1994, Sch 9, para
17(4), Sch 11, para 3(1), (2);
Local Government etc (Scotland)
Act 1994, s 165(6))
(SI 1996/186)

31 Dec 1996 (repeals in Water
Resources Act 1991, ss 91,
190(1)) (subject to savings
relating to s 91)[1] (SI 1996/2909)

Environment Act 1995 (c 25)—*contd*
Schedule
24—*contd*

1 Jan 1997 (repeal of Town and
Country Planning (Scotland)
Act 1972, s 251A) (SI 1996/2857)

1 Apr 1997 (repeals of or in National
Parks and Access to the
Countryside Act 1949; Caravan
Sites and Control of Development
Act 1960; Agriculture Act 1967;
Countryside Act 1968; Local
Government Act 1972; Local
Government Act 1974; Welsh
Development Agency Act 1975;
Race Relations Act 1976; Local
Government, Planning and Land
Act 1980 (except repeals relating to
s 103(2)(c) and Sch 2, para 9(2),
(3)); Highways Act 1980;
Acquisition of Land Act 1981;
Wildlife and Countryside Act 1981;
Local Government (Miscellaneous
Provisions) Act 1982; Derelict
Land Act 1982; Litter Act 1983;
Local Government Act 1985;
Housing Act 1985; Norfolk and
Suffolk Broads Act 1988; Local
Government Act 1988; Local
Government Finance Act 1988;
Electricity Act 1989; Local
Government and Housing Act 1989
(except repeal relating to the word
"and" in s 21(1)); Town and
Country Planning Act 1990
(remainder); Planning (Listed
Buildings and Conservation Areas)
Act 1990; Planning (Hazardous
Substances) Act 1990; Planning
(Consequential Provisions) Act 1990;
Environmental Protection Act 1990
(remainder, except repeals relating
to ss 33(1), 54, 61, 75(3), 143);
Planning and Compensation
Act 1991; Water Industry Act 1991
(remainder); Water Resources
Act 1991 (remainder, except repeal
relating to s 190(1)); Land
Drainage Act 1991; Local
Government Finance Act 1992
(except repeal relating to Sch 13,
para 95); Local Government

Environment Act 1995 (c 25)—*contd*
Schedule
24—*contd*

(Overseas Assistance) Act 1993;
Local Government (Wales)
Act 1994 (remainder, except
repeals relating to Sch 9,
para 17(12), Sch 16, para 65(5));
Environment Act 1995 (except
repeals relating to Sch 22)
(SI 1996/2560)
1 Jan 1999 (repeals in Salmon and
Freshwater Fisheries Act 1975,
ss 30, 41(1)) (SI 1995/1983)
1 Apr 2000 (E) (repeals of or in
Environmental Protection
Act 1990, ss 61, 143)
(SI 2000/340)
14 Jul 2000 (S) (repeals of or in
Environmental Protection
Act 1990, ss 61, 143)
(SI 2000/180)
15 Sep 2001 (W) (repeals of or in
Environmental Protection
Act 1990, ss 61, 143)
(SI 2001/3211)
Not in force (otherwise)

[1]   Repeal relating to s 91 has already been brought into force by SI 1996/2560

[2]   Orders made under s 125 of this Act, bringing the prospective repeals into force will be noted to this Act

[3]   Orders made under Pollution Prevention and Control Act 1999, s 7(3), bringing the prospective amendment into force will be noted to that Act

[4]   Orders made under Local Government Act 2000, s 108, bringing the prospective repeal into force will be noted to that Act

[5]   SI 2001/2351 was made by the National Assembly for Wales and purported to bring into force certain provisions of this Act; the National Assembly for Wales subsequently found it did not have the power to make that commencement order and those provisions are now now brought into force on a later date by SI 2001/3211

[6]   For saving see SI 2001/3211, art 3

European Communities (Finance) Act 1995 (c 1)

Whole Act repealed

Finance Act 1995 (c 4)

Budget Day: 29 Nov 1994

RA: 1 May 1995

Details of the commencement of Finance Acts are not set out in this work

---

Gas Act 1995 (c 45)

RA: 8 Nov 1995

Commencement provisions: s 18(2)–(4); Gas Act 1995 (Appointed Day and Commencement) Order 1996, SI 1996/218

Section

1, 2		Repealed
3–7		1 Mar 1996 (SI 1996/218)
8	(1)	1 Mar 1996 (SI 1996/218)
	(2)	Repealed
9, 10		1 Mar 1996 (SI 1996/218)
11	(1)–(5)	8 Nov 1995 (RA)
	(6), (7)	1 Mar 1996 (SI 1996/218)
12		1 Mar 1996 (SI 1996/218)
13		8 Nov 1995 (RA)
14–16		1 Mar 1996 (SI 1996/218)
17	(1), (2)	8 Nov 1995 (RA)
	(3), (4)	1 Mar 1996 (SI 1996/218)
	(5)	See Sch 6 below
18		8 Nov 1995 (RA)

Schedule

1	1 Mar 1996 (SI 1996/218); prospectively repealed by Utilities Act 2000, s 108, Sch 8[1]
2–4	1 Mar 1996 (SI 1996/218)
5	8 Nov 1995 (RA)
6	8 Nov 1995 (RA) (so far as relating to Gas Act 1986, s 62(7)) 1 Mar 1996 (otherwise) (SI 1996/218)

[1] Orders made under Utilities Act 2000, s 110(2), bringing the prospective amendments into force will be noted to that Act

Geneva Conventions (Amendment) Act 1995 (c 27)

RA: 19 Jul 1995

Commencement provisions: s 7(2); Geneva Conventions (Amendment) Act 1995 (Commencement) Order 1998, SI 1998/1505

20 Jul 1998 (SI 1998/1505)

Goods Vehicles (Licensing of Operators) Act 1995 (c 23)

RA: 19 Jul 1995

Commencement provisions: ss 50(2), 61; Goods Vehicles (Licensing of Operators) Act 1995 (Commencement and Transitional Provisions) Order 1995, SI 1995/2181

Section

1–49	1 Jan 1996 (subject to transitional provisions) (SI 1995/2181)
50	*Not in force*
51–62	1 Jan 1996 (SI 1995/2181)

Goods Vehicles (Licensing of Operators) Act 1995 (c 23)—*contd*

Schedule

1	1 Jan 1996 (SI 1995/2181)
1A	Inserted by Transport Act 2000, s 262(2), Sch 30 (qv)
2–4	1 Jan 1996 (SI 1995/2181)
5	*Not in force*
6–8	1 Jan 1996 (SI 1995/2181)

Health Authorities Act 1995 (c 17)

RA: 28 Jun 1995

Commencement provisions: ss 1(2), 2(3), 4(2), 5(2), 8(1)

Section

1	(1)	28 Jun 1995 (regulations etc)[1] (s 8(1))
		1 Apr 1996 (otherwise) (s 1(2))
	(2)	28 Jun 1995 (RA)
2	(1)	See Sch 1 below
	(2), (3)	28 Jun 1995 (RA)
3		28 Jun 1995 (RA)[2]
4	(1)	See Sch 2 below
	(2)	28 Jun 1995 (RA)
5	(1)	See Sch 3 below
	(2)	28 Jun 1995 (RA)
6–10		28 Jun 1995 (RA)

Schedule

1	28 Jun 1995 (regulations etc)[1] (s 8(1))
	1 Apr 1996 (otherwise) (s 2(3))
2	28 Jun 1995 (regulations etc)[1] (s 8(1))
	1 Apr 1996 (otherwise) (s 4(2))
3	28 Jun 1995 (repeal in National Health Service Act 1977, s 18(3)) (RA)
	1 Apr 1996 (otherwise) (s 5(2))

[1]   "regulations etc" means "so far as is necessary for enabling the making of any regulations, orders, directions, schemes or appointments" (s 8(1))

[2]   Whole section (apart from sub-s (8)) repealed as from 1 Apr 1996 (s 3(10))

Home Energy Conservation Act 1995 (c 10)

RA: 28 Jun 1995

Commencement provisions: s 9(2), (3); Home Energy Conservation Act 1995 (Commencement) Order (Northern Ireland) 1995, SR 1995/455; Home Energy Conservation Act 1995 (Commencement No 2) (England) Order 1995, SI 1995/3340; Home Energy Conservation Act 1995 (Commencement No 3) (Scotland) Order 1996, SI 1996/2797; Home Energy Conservation Act 1995 (Commencement No 4) (Wales) Order 1996, SI 1996/3181

Section

1, 2	1 Apr 1996 (NI, E) (SR 1995/455; SI 1995/3340)
	1 Dec 1996 (S) (SI 1996/2797)

Home Energy Conservation Act 1995 (c 10)—*contd*

Section

1, 2—*contd*		1 Apr 1997 (W) (SI 1996/3181)
3	(1)	1 Jan 1996 (NI) (SR 1995/455)
		15 Jan 1996 (E) (SI 1995/3340)
		1 Dec 1996 (S) (SI 1996/2797)
		10 Jan 1997 (W) (SI 1996/3181)
	(2)–(4)	1 Apr 1996 (NI, E) (SR 1995/455; SI 1995/3340)
		1 Dec 1996 (S) (SI 1996/2797)
		1 Apr 1997 (W) (SI 1996/3181)
4	(1), (2)	1 Jan 1996 (NI) (SR 1995/455)
		15 Jan 1996 (E) (SI 1995/3340)
		1 Dec 1996 (S) (SI 1996/2797)
		10 Jan 1997 (W) (SI 1996/3181)
	(3)	1 Apr 1996 (NI, E) (SR 1995/455; SI 1995/3340)
		1 Dec 1996 (S) (SI 1996/2797)
		1 Apr 1997 (W) (SI 1996/3181)
5–9		1 Apr 1996 (NI, E) (SR 1995/455; SI 1995/3340)
		1 Dec 1996 (S) (SI 1996/2797)
		1 Apr 1997 (W) (SI 1996/3181)

Insurance Companies (Reserves) Act 1995 (c 29)

Whole Act repealed

Jobseekers Act 1995 (c 18)

RA: 28 Jun 1995

Commencement provisions: s 41(2), (3); Jobseekers Act 1995 (Commencement No 1) Order 1995, SI 1995/3228; Jobseekers Act 1995 (Commencement No 2) Order 1996, SI 1996/1126; Jobseekers Act 1995 (Commencement No 3) Order 1996, SI 1996/1509; Jobseekers Act 1995 (Commencement No 4) Order 1996, SI 1996/2208

Section

1			7 Oct 1996 (SI 1996/2208)
2	(1)	(a), (b)	7 Oct 1996 (SI 1996/2208)
		(c)	12 Dec 1995 (for purpose of authorising regulations to be made) (SI 1995/3228)
			7 Oct 1996 (otherwise) (SI 1996/2208)
		(d)	7 Oct 1996 (SI 1996/2208)
	(2), (3)		7 Oct 1996 (SI 1996/2208)
	(3A)		Inserted by Social Security Act 1998, s 86(1), Sch 7, para 133 (qv)
	(4)	(a)	7 Oct 1996 (SI 1996/2208)

Jobseekers Act 1995 (c 18)—*contd*

Section

2	(4)	(b)		12 Dec 1995 (for purpose of authorising regulations to be made) (SI 1995/3228)
				7 Oct 1996 (otherwise) (SI 1996/2208)
		(c)		7 Oct 1996 (SI 1996/2208)
3	(1)	(a)–(e)		7 Oct 1996 (SI 1996/2208)
		(f)	(i), (ii)	7 Oct 1996 (SI 1996/2208)
			(iii)	12 Dec 1995 (for purpose of authorising regulations to be made) (SI 1995/3228)
				7 Oct 1996 (otherwise) (SI 1996/2208)
	(2)–(4)			12 Dec 1995 (for purpose of authorising regulations to be made) (SI 1995/3228)
				7 Oct 1996 (otherwise) (SI 1996/2208)
3A, 3B				Inserted by Welfare Reform and Pensions Act 1999, s 59, Sch 7, para 4(2) (qv)
4	(1)	(a)		7 Oct 1996 (SI 1996/2208)
		(b)		12 Dec 1995 (for purpose of authorising regulations to be made) (SI 1995/3228)
				7 Oct 1996 (otherwise) (SI 1996/2208)
	(2)			12 Dec 1995 (for purpose of authorising regulations to be made) (SI 1995/3228)
				7 Oct 1996 (otherwise) (SI 1996/2208)
	(3)			7 Oct 1996 (SI 1996/2208)
	(3A)			Inserted by Welfare Reform and Pensions Act 1999, s 59, Sch 7, para 5(3) (qv)
	(4), (5)			12 Dec 1995 (for purpose of authorising regulations to be made) (SI 1995/3228)
				7 Oct 1996 (otherwise) (SI 1996/2208)
	(6)–(11)			7 Oct 1996 (SI 1996/2208)
	(11A)			Inserted by Welfare Reform and Pensions Act 1999, s 59, Sch 7, para 5(4) (qv)
	(12)			12 Dec 1995 (for purpose of authorising regulations to be made) (SI 1995/3228)
				7 Oct 1996 (otherwise) (SI 1996/2208)
4A				Inserted by Welfare Reform and Pensions Act 1999, s 59, Sch 7, para 6 (qv)
5	(1), (2)			7 Oct 1996 (SI 1996/2208)
	(3)			12 Dec 1995 (for purpose of authorising regulations to be made) (SI 1995/3228)

Jobseekers Act 1995 (c 18)—*contd*

Section

5	(3)—*contd*	7 Oct 1996 (otherwise) (SI 1996/2208)
6	(1)	7 Oct 1996 (SI 1996/2208)
	(2)–(5)	12 Dec 1995 (for purpose of authorising regulations to be made) (SI 1995/3228)
		7 Oct 1996 (otherwise) (SI 1996/2208)
	(6)	7 Oct 1996 (SI 1996/2208)
	(7), (8)	12 Dec 1995 (for purpose of authorising regulations to be made) (SI 1995/3228)
		7 Oct 1996 (otherwise) (SI 1996/2208)
	(9)	7 Oct 1996 (SI 1996/2208)
7	(1)	7 Oct 1996 (SI 1996/2208)
	(2)–(6)	12 Dec 1995 (for purpose of authorising regulations to be made) (SI 1995/3228)
		7 Oct 1996 (otherwise) (SI 1996/2208)
	(7)	7 Oct 1996 (SI 1996/2208)
	(8)	12 Dec 1995 (for purpose of authorising regulations to be made) (SI 1995/3228)
		7 Oct 1996 (otherwise) (SI 1996/2208)
8		12 Dec 1995 (for purpose of authorising regulations to be made) (SI 1995/3228)
		7 Oct 1996 (otherwise) (SI 1996/2208)
9	(1)	12 Dec 1995 (for purpose of authorising regulations to be made) (SI 1995/3228)
		7 Oct 1996 (otherwise) (SI 1996/2208)
	(2)–(7)	7 Oct 1996 (SI 1996/2208)
	(8)	12 Dec 1995 (for purpose of authorising regulations to be made) (SI 1995/3228)
		7 Oct 1996 (otherwise) (SI 1996/2208)
	(9)	7 Oct 1996 (SI 1996/2208); repealed, partly prospectively, by Social Security Act 1998, s 86, Sch 7, para 136, Sch 8[1]
	(10)–(12)	12 Dec 1995 (for purpose of authorising regulations to be made) (SI 1995/3228)
		7 Oct 1996 (otherwise) (SI 1996/2208)
	(13)	12 Dec 1995 (SI 1995/3228)
10	(1)	12 Dec 1995 (for purpose of authorising regulations to be made) (SI 1995/3228)
		7 Oct 1996 (otherwise) (SI 1996/2208)
	(2)–(5)	7 Oct 1996 (SI 1996/2208)

Jobseekers Act 1995 (c 18)—*contd*
Section

10	(6)	(a), (b)	7 Oct 1996 (SI 1996/2208)
		(c)	12 Dec 1995 (for purpose of authorising regulations to be made) (SI 1995/3228)
			7 Oct 1996 (otherwise) (SI 1996/2208)
		(d)	7 Oct 1996 (SI 1996/2208)
	(7)		12 Dec 1995 (for purpose of authorising regulations to be made) (SI 1995/3228)
			7 Oct 1996 (otherwise) (SI 1996/2208)
	(8)		7 Oct 1996 (SI 1996/2208); repealed, partly prospectively, by Social Security Act 1998, s 86, Sch 7, para 137, Sch 8[1]
11	(1)		7 Oct 1996 (SI 1996/2208)
	(2)		12 Dec 1995 (for purpose of authorising regulations to be made) (SI 1995/3228)
			7 Oct 1996 (otherwise) (SI 1996/2208)
	(3), (4)		7 Oct 1996 (SI 1996/2208)
	(5)		12 Dec 1995 (for purpose of authorising regulations to be made) (SI 1995/3228)
			7 Oct 1996 (otherwise) (SI 1996/2208)
	(6)		7 Oct 1996 (SI 1996/2208)
	(7), (8)		12 Dec 1995 (for purpose of authorising regulations to be made) (SI 1995/3228)
			7 Oct 1996 (otherwise) (SI 1996/2208)
	(9)		7 Oct 1996 (SI 1996/2208)
			Section repealed, partly prospectively, by Social Security Act 1998, s 86, Sch 7, para 138, Sch 8[1]
12, 13			12 Dec 1995 (for purpose of authorising regulations to be made) (SI 1995/3228)
			7 Oct 1996 (otherwise) (SI 1996/2208)
14			7 Oct 1996 (SI 1996/2208)
15	(1)		12 Dec 1995 (for purpose of authorising regulations to be made) (SI 1995/3228)
			7 Oct 1996 (otherwise) (SI 1996/2208)
	(2)	(a)–(c)	7 Oct 1996 (SI 1996/2208)
		(d)	12 Dec 1995 (for purpose of authorising regulations to be made) (SI 1995/3228)
			7 Oct 1996 (otherwise) (SI 1996/2208)
	(3), (4)		7 Oct 1996 (SI 1996/2208)

Jobseekers Act 1995 (c 18)—*contd*

Section

15	(5), (6)		12 Dec 1995 (for purpose of authorising regulations to be made) (SI 1995/3228)
			7 Oct 1996 (otherwise) (SI 1996/2208)
	(7)–(10)		7 Oct 1996 (SI 1996/2208)
15A			Inserted by Welfare Reform and Pensions Act 1999, s 59, Sch 7, para 10 (qv)
16			7 Oct 1996 (SI 1996/2208)
17	(1)		12 Dec 1995 (for purpose of authorising regulations to be made) (SI 1995/3228)
			7 Oct 1996 (otherwise) (SI 1996/2208)
	(1A)		Inserted by Welfare Reform and Pensions Act 1999, s 59, Sch 7, para 11 (qv)
	(2), (3)		7 Oct 1996 (SI 1996/2208)
	(4), (5)		7 Oct 1996 (SI 1996/2208); substituted, partly prospectively, by Social Security Act 1998, s 86(1), Sch 7, para 140(3)[1]
18			7 Oct 1996 (SI 1996/2208)
19	(1)		7 Oct 1996 (SI 1996/2208)
	(1A)		Inserted by Welfare Reform and Pensions Act 1999, s 59, Sch 7, para 12 (qv)
	(2)		12 Dec 1995 (for purpose of authorising regulations to be made) (SI 1995/3228)
			7 Oct 1996 (otherwise) (SI 1996/2208)
	(3)		7 Oct 1996 (SI 1996/2208)
	(4)		12 Dec 1995 (for purpose of authorising regulations to be made) (SI 1995/3228)
			7 Oct 1996 (otherwise) (SI 1996/2208)
	(5), (6)		7 Oct 1996 (SI 1996/2208)
	(7), (8)		12 Dec 1995 (for purpose of authorising regulations to be made) (SI 1995/3228)
			7 Oct 1996 (otherwise) (SI 1996/2208)
	(9)		7 Oct 1996 (SI 1996/2208)
	(10)	(a)	12 Dec 1995 (SI 1995/3228)
		(b)	7 Oct 1996 (SI 1996/2208)
		(c)	12 Dec 1995 (for purpose of authorising regulations to be made) (SI 1995/3228)
			7 Oct 1996 (otherwise) (SI 1996/2208)
20	(1), (2)		7 Oct 1996 (SI 1996/2208)

Jobseekers Act 1995 (c 18)—*contd*
Section

20	(3)–(8)		12 Dec 1995 (for purpose of authorising regulations to be made) (SI 1995/3228)
			7 Oct 1996 (otherwise) (SI 1996/2208)
20A, 20B			Inserted by Welfare Reform and Pensions Act 1999, s 59, Sch 7, para 13 (qv)
21, 22			12 Dec 1995 (for purpose of authorising regulations to be made) (SI 1995/3228)
			7 Oct 1996 (otherwise) (SI 1996/2208)
23	(1)		12 Dec 1995 (for purpose of authorising regulations to be made) (SI 1995/3228)
			7 Oct 1996 (otherwise) (SI 1996/2208)
	(2)		7 Oct 1996 (SI 1996/2208)
	(3), (4)		12 Dec 1995 (for purpose of authorising regulations to be made) (SI 1995/3228)
			7 Oct 1996 (otherwise) (SI 1996/2208)
	(5)		7 Oct 1996 (SI 1996/2208)
24, 25			7 Oct 1996 (SI 1996/2208)
26			12 Dec 1995 (for purpose of authorising regulations to be made) (SI 1995/3228)
			7 Oct 1996 (otherwise) (SI 1996/2208)
27			12 Dec 1995 (for purpose of authorising regulations to be made) (SI 1995/3228)
			6 Apr 1996 (otherwise) (SI 1995/3228)
28			12 Dec 1995 (for purpose of authorising regulations to be made) (SI 1995/3228)
			1 Apr 1996 (otherwise) (SI 1995/3228)
29			1 Jan 1996 (SI 1995/3228)
30			1 Apr 1996 (SI 1995/3228)
31			12 Dec 1995 (for purpose of authorising regulations to be made) (SI 1995/3228)
			7 Oct 1996 (otherwise) (SI 1996/2208)
32			7 Oct 1996 (SI 1996/2208)
33, 34			Repealed
35–37			12 Dec 1995 (SI 1995/3228)
38	(1)	(a)	7 Oct 1996 (SI 1996/2208)
		(b)	6 Apr 1996 (SI 1995/3228)
	(2)–(4)		7 Oct 1996 (SI 1996/2208)
	(5)		6 Apr 1996 (SI 1995/3228)
	(6)–(8)		7 Oct 1996 (SI 1996/2208)

Jobseekers Act 1995 (c 18)—*contd*

Section

38	(9)	Inserted by the Social Security Contributions (Transfer of Functions, etc) Act 1999, s 1(1), Sch 1, para 66(1), (6) (qv)
39		28 Jun 1995 (s 41(2))
40		12 Dec 1995 (for purpose of authorising regulations to be made) (SI 1995/3228) 7 Oct 1996 (otherwise) (SI 1996/2208)
41	(1)–(3)	28 Jun 1995 (s 41(2))
	(4)	See Sch 2 below
	(5)	See Sch 3 below
	(6)	28 Jun 1995 (s 41(2))

Schedule

1			12 Dec 1995 (for purpose of authorising regulations to be made) (SI 1995/3228) 7 Oct 1996 (otherwise) (SI 1996/2208)
2, para	1		7 Oct 1996 (SI 1996/2208)
	2, 3		Repealed
	4–9		7 Oct 1996 (SI 1996/2208)
	10		11 Jun 1996 (SI 1996/1509)
	11		7 Oct 1996 (SI 1996/2208)
	12		2 Sep 1996 (SI 1996/2208)
	13		7 Oct 1996 (SI 1996/2208)
	14		2 Sep 1996 (SI 1996/2208)
	15–16		7 Oct 1996 (SI 1996/2208)
	17		Repealed
	18		11 Jun 1996 (SI 1996/1509)
	19, 20		7 Oct 1996 (SI 1996/2208)
	21		11 Jun 1996 (SI 1996/1509)
	22–29		7 Oct 1996 (SI 1996/2208)
	30	(1)–(4)	7 Oct 1996 (SI 1996/2208)
		(5)	12 Dec 1995 (for purpose of authorising regulations to be made) (SI 1995/3228) 7 Oct 1996 (otherwise) (SI 1996/2208)
	31–37		7 Oct 1996 (SI 1996/2208)
	38–40		22 Apr 1996 (SI 1996/1126)
	41–47		Repealed
	48		7 Oct 1996 (SI 1996/2208)
	49–51		11 Jun 1996 (SI 1996/1509)
	52		Repealed
	53		11 Jun 1996 (SI 1996/1509)
	54		Repealed
	55, 56		11 Jun 1996 (SI 1996/1509)

Jobseekers Act 1995 (c 18)—*contd*

Schedule

2, para	57, 58	Repealed
	59–61	11 Jun 1996 (SI 1996/1509)
	62, 63	Repealed
	64	11 Jun 1996 (SI 1996/1509)
	65	7 Oct 1996 (SI 1996/2208)
	66	11 Jun 1996 (SI 1996/1509)
	67–70	22 Apr 1996 (SI 1996/1126)
	71, 72	11 Jun 1996 (SI 1996/1509)
	73	22 Apr 1996 (SI 1996/1126)
	74	11 Jun 1996 (SI 1996/1509)
	75, 76	22 Apr 1996 (SI 1996/1126)
3		1 Apr 1996 (repeals of Supplementary Benefits Act 1976, s 30, Sch 5)
		7 Oct 1996 (otherwise) (SI 1996/2208)

[1]   Orders made under Social Security Act 1998, s 87(2), bringing the prospective substitutions and repeals into force will be noted to that Act

---

Land Registers (Scotland) Act 1995 (c 14)

RA: 28 Jun 1995

Commencement provisions: s 2(2); Land Registers (Scotland) Act 1995 (Commencement) Order 1996, SI 1996/94

1 Apr 1996 (SI 1996/94)

Landlord and Tenant (Covenants) Act 1995 (c 30)

RA: 19 Jul 1995

Commencement provisions: s 31; Landlord and Tenant (Covenants) Act 1995 (Commencement) Order 1995, SI 1995/2963

1 Jan 1996 (SI 1995/2963)

Law Reform (Succession) Act 1995 (c 41)

RA: 8 Nov 1995

8 Nov 1995 (RA)

Licensing (Sunday Hours) Act 1995 (c 33)

RA: 19 Jul 1995

Commencement provisions: s 5; Licensing (Sunday Hours) Act 1995 (Commencement) Order 1995, SI 1995/1930

6 Aug 1995 (SI 1995/1930)

Medical (Professional Performance) Act 1995 (c 51)

RA: 8 Nov 1995

Commencement provisions: s 6; Medical (Professional Performance) Act 1995 (Commencement No 1) Order 1996, SI 1996/271; Medical (Professional Performance) Act 1995 (Commencement No 2) Order 1996, SI 1996/1631; Medical (Professional Performance) Act 1995 (Commencement No 3) Order 1997, SI 1997/1315; Medical (Professional Performance) Act 1995 (Commencement No 4) Order 2000, SI 2000/1344

Section			
1			1 Jul 1997 (SI 1997/1315)
2			18 May 2000 (SI 2000/1344)
3			1 May 1996 (SI 1996/271)
4			See Schedule below
5, 6			1 May 1996 (SI 1996/271)
7	(1)		1 May 1996 (SI 1996/271)
	(2)		1 May 1996 (so far as relates to provisions brought into force by SI 1996/271) (SI 1996/271)
			1 Sep 1996 (so far as relates to provisions brought into force by SI 1996/1631) (SI 1996/1631)
			1 Jan 1997 (so far as relates to provisions brought into force by SI 1996/1631) (SI 1996/1631)
			1 Jul 1997 (so far as relates to provisions brought into force by SI 1997/1315) (SI 1997/1315)
			18 May 2000 (otherwise) (SI 2000/1344)
Schedule			
para	1		See paras 2–27 below
	2		1 Jan 1997 (SI 1996/1631)
	3		18 May 2000 (SI 2000/1344)
	4–6		1 May 1996 (SI 1996/271)
	7–9		1 Jul 1997 (SI 1997/1315)
	10	(a), (b)	1 Jul 1997 (SI 1997/1315)
		(c)	1 May 1996 (SI 1996/271)
	11		1 Jul 1997 (SI 1997/1315)
	12		1 Sep 1996 (for the purpose of enabling the General Medical Council in accordance with rules to determine the membership of its statutory committees as from 1 Jan 1997) (SI 1996/1631)
			1 Jan 1997 (otherwise) (SI 1996/1631)
	13		1 Jan 1997 (SI 1996/1631)
	14		1 Sep 1996 (SI 1996/1631)
	15–21		1 Jul 1997 (SI 1997/1315)
	22	(a)	1 Jul 1997 (SI 1997/1315)
		(b)	1 May 1996 (SI 1996/271)

Medical (Professional Performance) Act 1995 (c 51)—*contd*
Schedule

para			
23–27			1 Jul 1997 (SI 1997/1315)
28	(a)		1 May 1996 (SI 1996/271)
	(b)		1 Jul 1997 (SI 1997/1315)
29	(a)		1 May 1996 (SI 1996/271)
	(b)		1 Jul 1997 (SI 1997/1315)
30	(a)		1 May 1996 (SI 1996/271)
	(b)		1 Jul 1997 (SI 1997/1315)

Mental Health (Patients in the Community) Act 1995 (c 52)

RA: 8 Nov 1995

Commencement provisions: s 7(2)

1 Apr 1996 (s 7(2))

Merchant Shipping Act 1995 (c 21)

RA: 19 Jul 1995

Commencement provisions: s 316(2), Sch 14, para 5; Merchant Shipping Act 1995 (Appointed Day No 2) Order 1997, SI 1997/3107

Section		
1–56		1 Jan 1996 (s 316(2))
57		1 Jan 1996 (s 316(2)); prospectively repealed by Merchant Shipping Act 1995, s 214(3), Sch 14, para 6
58, 59		1 Jan 1996 (s 316(2))
60		*Not in force*
61–79		1 Jan 1996 (s 316(2))
80	(1)	1 Jan 1996 (s 316(2))
	(2)	*Not in force*
	(3)	1 Jan 1996 (s 316(2))
	(4)	*Not in force*
81–88		1 Jan 1996 (s 316(2))
89, 90		Repealed
91–100		1 Jan 1996 (s 316(2))
100A–100G		Inserted by Merchant Shipping and Maritime Security Act 1997, ss 1, 10, 11 (qv)
101–110		1 Jan 1996 (s 316(2))
111		*Not in force*
112–114		1 Jan 1996 (s 316(2))
115		*Not in force*
116		1 Feb 1998 (SI 1997/3107)
117		1 Jan 1996 (s 316(2))
118		*Not in force*
119	(1)	1 Jan 1996 (s 316(2))
	(2), (3)	*Not in force*

Merchant Shipping Act 1995 (c 21)—*contd*
Section

120–126		1 Jan 1996 (s 316(2))
127		*Not in force*
128–130		1 Jan 1996 (s 316(2))
130A–130E		Inserted by Merchant Shipping and Maritime Security Act 1997, s 5 (qv)
131–136		1 Jan 1996 (s 316(2))
136A		Inserted by Pollution Prevention and Control Act 1999, s 6(1), Sch 2, para 13 (qv)
137, 138		1 Jan 1996 (s 316(2))
138A		Inserted, subject to a saving, by Merchant Shipping and Maritime Security Act 1997, s 3 (qv)
139–182		1 Jan 1996 (s 316(2))
182A–182C		Inserted by Merchant Shipping and Maritime Security Act 1997, s 14(1) (qv)
183–192		1 Jan 1996 (s 316(2))
192A		Inserted by Merchant Shipping and Maritime Security Act 1997, s 16 (qv)
193–201		1 Jan 1996 (s 316(2))
202		Repealed
203–222		1 Jan 1996 (s 316(2))
222A		Inserted by Merchant Shipping and Maritime Security Act 1997, s 20 (qv)
223–256		1 Jan 1996 (s 316(2))
256A		Inserted (1 Jul 1999) by Scotland Act 1998 (Consequential Modifications) (No 2) Order 1999, SI 1999/1820, art 4, Sch 2, Pt I, para 119
257–277		1 Jan 1996 (s 316(2))
277A		Inserted (1 Dec 1997) by Merchant Shipping (Oil Pollution) (Jersey) Order 1997, SI 1997/2598, art 3
278–302		1 Jan 1996 (s 316(2))
302A		Inserted by Merchant Shipping and Maritime Security Act 1997, s 13, Sch 2, para 1 (qv)
303–313		1 Jan 1996 (s 316(2))
313A		Inserted by Maritime Shipping and Maritime Security Act 1997, s 29(1), Sch 6, para 20 (qv)
314	(1)	See Sch 12 below
	(2)–(4)	1 Jan 1996 (s 316(2))
315, 316		1 Jan 1996 (s 316(2))

Merchant Shipping Act 1995 (c 21)—*contd*

Schedule

1, 2	1 Jan 1996 (s 316(2))
3	Repealed
4, 5	1 Jan 1996 (s 316(2))
5A	Inserted by Maritime Shipping and Maritime Security Act 1997, s 14(2), Sch 3 (qv)
6–8	1 Jan 1996 (s 316(2))
9	Repealed
10, 11	1 Jan 1996 (s 316(2))
11A	Inserted by Maritime Shipping and Maritime Security Act 1997, s 13, Sch 2, para 2 (qv)
12	1 Jan 1996 (except repeals in Aliens Restriction (Amendment) Act 1919, Local Government etc (Scotland) Act 1994) (s 316(2))
	Not in force (exceptions noted above)
13, 14	1 Jan 1996 (s 316(2))

National Health Service (Amendment) Act 1995 (c 31)

RA: 19 Jul 1995

Commencement provisions: s 14(3), (4); National Health Service (Amendment) Act 1995 (Commencement No 1 and Saving) Order 1995, SI 1995/3090; National Health Service (Amendment) Act 1995 (Commencement No 2 and Saving) (Scotland) Order 1995, SI 1995/3214; National Health Service (Amendment) Act 1995 (Commencement No 3) Order 1996, SI 1996/552

Section

1	21 Dec 1995 (subject to transitional provisions) (for the purposes of amending National Health Service Act 1977 in relation to general medical services and general dental services only) (SI 1995/3090)
	1 Apr 1996 (otherwise) (SI 1996/552)
	Section prospectively repealed by Health Act 1999, s 65(2), Sch 5[1]
2	21 Dec 1995 (subject to transitional provisions) (for the purposes of amending National Health Service Act 1977 in relation to general medical services and general dental services only) (SI 1995/3090)
	1 Apr 1996 (otherwise) (SI 1996/552)
3	21 Dec 1995 (subject to transitional provisions) (SI 1995/3090); prospectively repealed by the Health Act 1999, s 65(2), Sch 5[1]

National Health Service (Amendment) Act 1995 (c 31)—*contd*

Section

4–6		Repealed
7		1 Jan 1996 (subject to transitional provisions) (for the purposes of amending National Health Service (Scotland) Act 1978 in relation to general medical services and general dental services only) (SI 1995/3214)
		1 Apr 1996 (otherwise) (SI 1996/552)
		Section prospectively repealed by Health Act 1999, s 65(2), Sch 5[1]
8		1 Jan 1996 (subject to transitional provisions) (for the purposes of amending National Health Service (Scotland) Act 1978 in relation to general medical services and general dental services only) (SI 1995/3214)
		1 Apr 1996 (otherwise) (SI 1996/552)
9		1 Jan 1996 (subject to transitional provisions) (SI 1995/3214); prospectively repealed by Health Act 1999, s 65(2), Sch 5[1]
10–12		1 Jan 1996 (subject to transitional provisions) (SI 1995/3214)
13		19 Jul 1995 (RA)
14	(1)	19 Jul 1995 (RA)
	(2)	See Schedule below
	(3), (4)	19 Jul 1995 (RA)
	(5)	Repealed (E)
		19 Jul 1995 (RA); prospectively repealed by Health and Social Care Act 2001, s 67(2), Sch 6, Pt I (W)[2]
	(6)	19 Jul 1995 (RA)
Schedule		21 Dec 1995 (subject to transitional provisions) (repeals in National Health Service Act 1977, Health Authorities Act 1995) (SI 1995/3090)
		1 Jan 1996 (subject to transitional provisions) (repeals in National Health Service (Scotland) Act 1978) (SI 1995/3214)

[1] Orders made under Health Act 1999, s 67(1), bringing the prospective repeals into force will be noted to that Act

[2] Orders made under Health and Social Care Act 2001, s 70(2), bringing the prospective repeal into force will be noted to that Act

Northern Ireland (Remission of Sentences) Act 1995 (c 47)

RA: 8 Nov 1995

Commencement provisions: s 2; Northern Ireland (Remission of Sentences) Act 1995 (Commencement) Order 1995, SI 1995/2945

17 Nov 1995 (SI 1995/2945)

Olympic Symbol etc (Protection) Act 1995 (c 32)

RA: 19 Jul 1995

Commencement provisions: s 19(2); Olympic Symbol etc (Protection) Act 1995 (Commencement) Order 1995, SI 1995/2472

20 Sep 1995 (SI 1995/2472)

Pensions Act 1995 (c 26)

RA: 19 Jul 1995

Commencement provisions: ss 135, 150(2), 180, Sch 4; Pensions Act 1995 (Commencement No 1) Order 1995, SI 1995/2548; Pensions Act 1995 (Commencement No 2) Order 1995, SI 1995/3104; Pensions Act 1995 (Commencement No 3) Order 1996, SI 1996/778; Pensions Act 1995 (Commencement No 4) Order 1996, SI 1996/1412; Pensions Act 1995 (Commencement) (No 5) Order 1996, SI 1996/1675; Pensions Act 1995 (Commencement No 6) Order 1996, SI 1996/1843; Pensions Act 1995 (Commencement No 7) Order 1996, SI 1996/1853[1]; Pensions Act 1995 (Commencement No 8) Order 1996, SI 1996/2637; Pensions Act 1995 (Commencement No 9) Order 1997, SI 1997/216; Pensions Act 1995 (Commencement No 10) Order 1997, SI 1997/664

Section		
1	(1)–(4)	1 Apr 1996 (SI 1996/778)
	(5)	See Sch 1 below
	(6)	1 Apr 1996 (SI 1996/778)
2		1 Apr 1996 (SI 1996/778)
3	(1)	6 Apr 1997 (SI 1997/664)
	(2)	16 Oct 1996 (for purpose of making regulations) (SI 1996/2637)
		6 Apr 1997 (otherwise) (SI 1997/664)
	(3), (4)	6 Apr 1997 (SI 1997/664)
4–9		6 Apr 1997 (SI 1997/664)
10	(1)	1 Jun 1996 (for purpose of authorising the making of regulations) (SI 1996/1412)
		6 Apr 1997 (otherwise) (SI 1997/664)
	(2), (3)	6 Apr 1996 (for purpose of authorising the making of regulations) (SI 1996/778)
		6 Apr 1997 (otherwise) (SI 1997/664)
	(4)–(8)	6 Apr 1997 (SI 1997/664)

Pensions Act 1995 (c 26)—*contd*

Section

10	(8A)	Inserted by Welfare Reform and Pensions Act 1999, s 18, Sch 2, para 11 (qv)
	(9)	6 Apr 1997 (SI 1997/664)
11–15		6 Apr 1997 (SI 1997/664)
16		6 Apr 1996 (for purpose of authorising the making of regulations) (SI 1996/778)
17		6 Apr 1996 (for purpose of authorising the making of regulations) (SI 1996/778); prospectively repealed by Child Support, Pensions and Social Security Act 2000, ss 43(9), 85, Sch 9, Pt III(1)[6]
18		6 Apr 1996 (for purpose of authorising the making of regulations) (SI 1996/778)
18A		Prospectively inserted by Child Support, Pensions and Social Security Act 2000, s 45(1)[6]
19, 20		6 Apr 1996 (for purpose of authorising the making of regulations) (SI 1996/778); prospectively repealed by Child Support, Pensions and Social Security Act 2000, ss 44(10), 85, Sch 9, Pt III(1)[6]
		6 Apr 1997 (otherwise) (SI 1997/664)
21	(1), (2)	6 Apr 1996 (for purpose of authorising the making of regulations) (SI 1996/778)
		6 Apr 1997 (otherwise) (SI 1997/664)
	(2A)	Prospectively inserted by Child Support, Pensions and Social Security Act 2000, s 46(4)[6]
	(3)	6 Apr 1996 (for purpose of authorising the making of regulations) (SI 1996/778)
		6 Oct 1996 (for purpose of any transitional provision in regulations made under ss 16–21) (SI 1996/778)
		6 Apr 1997 (otherwise) (SI 1997/664)
	(4)	6 Apr 1996 (for purpose of authorising the making of regulations) (SI 1996/778)

Pensions Act 1995 (c 26)—*contd*

Pensions Act 1995 (c 26)—*contd*

Section

40, 41—*contd*		6 Apr 1997 (otherwise) (SI 1997/664)
42–46		Repealed (*never in force*)
47		6 Apr 1996 (for purpose of authorising the making of regulations) (SI 1996/778)
		6 Apr 1997 (otherwise) (SI 1997/664)
48	(1)	6 Apr 1997 (SI 1997/664)
	(2)	*Not in force*
	(3)–(6)	6 Apr 1997 (SI 1997/664)
	(7)–(13)	*Not in force*
49		6 Apr 1996 (for purpose of authorising the making of regulations) (SI 1996/778)
49A		Inserted by Child Support, Pensions and Social Security Act 2000, s 49(3) (qv)
50, 51		6 Apr 1996 (for purpose of authorising the making of regulations) (SI 1996/778)
		6 Apr 1997 (otherwise) (SI 1997/664)
51A		Inserted by Child Support, Pensions and Social Security Act 2000, s 51(2) (qv)
52–54		6 Apr 1997 (SI 1997/664)
55		4 Feb 1997 (SI 1997/216)
56–61		6 Apr 1996 (for purpose of authorising the making of regulations) (SI 1996/778)
		6 Apr 1997 (otherwise) (SI 1997/664)
62–66		4 Dec 1995 (for purpose of authorising the making of regulations under ss 63(5), 64(2), (3), 66(4)) (SI 1995/3104)
		1 Jan 1996 (otherwise) (SI 1995/3104)
66A		Inserted by Child Support, Pensions and Social Security Act 2000, s 55 (qv)
67		6 Apr 1996 (for purpose of authorising the making of regulations) (SI 1996/778)
		6 Apr 1997 (otherwise) (SI 1997/664)
68		6 Apr 1996 (for purpose of authorising the making of regulations) (SI 1996/778)
		6 Oct 1996 (for purpose of any transitional provision in regulations made under ss 16–21) (SI 1996/778)
		6 Apr 1997 (otherwise) (SI 1997/664)

Pensions Act 1995 (c 26)—*contd*
Section

69			6 Apr 1996 (for purpose of authorising the making of regulations) (SI 1996/778)
			6 Apr 1997 (otherwise) (SI 1997/664)
70, 71			6 Apr 1997 (SI 1997/664)
71A			Prospectively inserted by Child Support, Pensions and Social Security Act 2000, s 48[6]
72			6 Apr 1997 (SI 1997/664)
72A			Inserted by Child Support, Pensions and Social Security Act 2000, s 49(1) (qv)
72B, 72C			Inserted by Child Support, Pensions and Social Security Act 2000, s 50 (qv)
73			6 Apr 1996 (for purpose of authorising the making of regulations) (SI 1996/778)
			6 Apr 1997 (otherwise) (SI 1997/664)
74	(1)		16 Oct 1996 (for purpose of making regulations) (SI 1996/2637)
			6 Apr 1997 (otherwise) (SI 1997/664)
	(2), (3)		6 Apr 1996 (for purpose of authorising the making of regulations) (SI 1996/778)
			6 Apr 1997 (otherwise) (SI 1997/664)
	(4)		6 Apr 1997 (SI 1997/664)
	(5)	(a)	16 Oct 1996 (for purpose of making regulations) (SI 1996/2637)
			6 Apr 1997 (otherwise) (SI 1997/664)
		(b)	6 Apr 1996 (for purpose of authorising the making of regulations) (SI 1996/778)
			6 Apr 1997 (otherwise) (SI 1997/664)
75–77			6 Apr 1996 (for purpose of authorising the making of regulations) (SI 1996/778)
			6 Apr 1997 (otherwise) (SI 1997/664)
78	(1)–(3)		1 Aug 1996 (SI 1996/1412)
	(4)		6 Apr 1997 (SI 1997/664)
	(5)		1 Aug 1996 (SI 1996/1412)
	(5A), (5B)		Inserted (1 Dec 2001) by Financial Services and Markets Act 2000 (Consequential Amendments and Repeals) Order 2001, SI 2001/3649, art 145(1), (3)
	(6)		1 Jun 1996 (for purpose of authorising the making of regulations) (SI 1996/1412)
			1 Aug 1996 (otherwise) (SI 1996/1412)

Pensions Act 1995 (c 26)—*contd*

Section

78	(7)			1 Aug 1996 (SI 1996/1412)
	(8)			See Sch 2 below
79				6 Apr 1997 (SI 1997/664)
80	(1)–(3)			6 Apr 1997 (SI 1997/664)
	(4)			4 Feb 1997 (for purpose of authorising the making of regulations) (SI 1997/216) 6 Apr 1997 (otherwise) (SI 1997/216)
	(5)			6 Apr 1997 (SI 1997/664)
81	(1)	(a), (b)		6 Apr 1997 (SI 1997/664)
		(c)		1 Jun 1996 (for purpose of authorising the making of regulations) (SI 1996/1412) 6 Apr 1997 (otherwise) (SI 1997/664)
		(d), (e)		6 Apr 1997 (SI 1997/664)
	(2)			1 Jun 1996 (for purpose of authorising the making of regulations) (SI 1996/1412) 6 Apr 1997 (otherwise) (SI 1997/664)
	(2A)			Inserted by Welfare Reform and Pensions Act 1999, s 17(2) (qv)
	(3)	(a)–(e)		6 Apr 1997 (SI 1997/664)
		(f)	(i)	1 Jun 1996 (for purpose of authorising the making of regulations) (SI 1996/1412) 6 Apr 1997 (otherwise) (SI 1997/664)
			(ii)	6 Apr 1997 (SI 1997/664)
	(4)–(6)			6 Apr 1997 (SI 1997/664)
	(7)			6 Mar 1997 (for purpose of making regulations relating to the compensation regulations) (SI 1997/664) 6 Apr 1997 (otherwise) (SI 1997/664)
	(8)			6 Apr 1997 (SI 1997/664)
82	(1)			1 Jun 1996 (for purpose of authorising the making of regulations) (SI 1996/1412) 6 Apr 1997 (otherwise) (SI 1997/664)
	(2)–(5)			6 Apr 1997 (SI 1997/664)
83	(1)			6 Apr 1997 (SI 1997/664)
	(2)			1 Jun 1996 (for purpose of authorising the making of regulations) (SI 1996/1412) 6 Apr 1997 (otherwise) (SI 1997/664)
	(3)	(a)		1 Jun 1996 (for purpose of authorising the making of regulations) (SI 1996/1412) 6 Apr 1997 (otherwise) (SI 1997/664)
		(b)		6 Apr 1997 (SI 1997/664)

Pensions Act 1995 (c 26)—*contd*
Section

83	(4)		Inserted by Welfare Reform and Pensions Act 1999, s 17(6) (qv)
84	(1)	(a)	6 Apr 1997 (SI 1997/664)
		(b)	1 Jun 1996 (for purpose of authorising the making of regulations) (SI 1996/1412)
			6 Apr 1997 (otherwise) (SI 1997/664)
	(2), (3)		1 Jun 1996 (for purpose of authorising the making of regulations) (SI 1996/1412)
			6 Apr 1997 (otherwise) (SI 1997/664)
85	(1), (2)		6 Apr 1997 (SI 1997/664)
	(3)	(a)	1 Aug 1996 (SI 1996/1412)
		(b)	6 Apr 1997 (SI 1997/664)
86			1 Jun 1996 (for purpose of authorising the making of regulations) (SI 1996/1412)
			6 Apr 1997 (otherwise) (SI 1997/664)
87–89			6 Apr 1996 (for purpose of authorising the making of regulations) (SI 1996/778)
			6 Apr 1997 (otherwise) (SI 1997/664)
90			2 Oct 1995 (SI 1995/2548)
91	(1), (2)		6 Apr 1996 (for purpose of authorising the making of regulations) (SI 1996/778)
			6 Apr 1997 (otherwise) (SI 1997/664)
	(3)		Repealed (*partly never in force*)
	(4)–(7)		6 Apr 1996 (for purpose of authorising the making of regulations) (SI 1996/778)
			6 Apr 1997 (otherwise) (SI 1997/664)
92–94			6 Apr 1996 (for purpose of authorising the making of regulations) (SI 1996/778)
			6 Apr 1997 (otherwise) (SI 1997/664)
95			Repealed (*partly never in force*)
96	(1)		6 Apr 1997 (SI 1997/664)
	(2)		1 Jun 1996 (for purpose of authorising the making of regulations) (SI 1996/1412)
			6 Apr 1997 (otherwise) (SI 1997/664)
	(3), (4)		6 Apr 1997 (SI 1997/664)
	(5)		1 Jun 1996 (for purpose of authorising the making of regulations) (SI 1996/1412)
			6 Apr 1997 (otherwise) (SI 1997/664)
	(6)		6 Apr 1997 (SI 1997/664)
97–115			6 Apr 1997 (SI 1997/664)

Pensions Act 1995 (c 26)—*contd*

Section

116	(1)	16 Jul 1996 (SI 1996/1853)
	(2), (3)	6 Apr 1997 (SI 1997/664)
117		1 Jan 1996 (so far as relates to s 39) (SI 1995/3104)
		4 Dec 1995 and 1 Jan 1996 (so far as relates to ss 62–66) (SI 1995/3104)
		6 Oct 1996 (for purpose of any transitional provision in regulations made under ss 16–21) (SI 1996/778)
		6 Apr 1997 (otherwise) (SI 1997/664)
118		6 Apr 1996 (so far as relates to authorising the making of regulations relating to certain provisions of Pt I of this Act) (SI 1996/778)
		16 Oct 1996 (otherwise) (SI 1996/2637)
119		6 Apr 1996 (SI 1996/778)
120		4 Dec 1995 and 1 Jan 1996 (so far as relates to ss 62–66) (SI 1995/3104)
		6 Apr 1996 (otherwise) (SI 1996/778)
121		1 Jan 1996 (so far as relates to s 39) (SI 1995/3104)
		4 Dec 1995 and 1 Jan 1996 (so far as relates to ss 62–66) (SI 1995/3104)
		6 Apr 1996 (otherwise) (SI 1996/778)
122		See Sch 3 below
123	(1), (2)	6 Apr 1997 (SI 1997/664)
	(3)	6 Apr 1996 (SI 1996/778)
124		1 Jan 1996 (so far as relates to s 39) (SI 1995/3104)
		4 Dec 1995 and 1 Jan 1996 (so far as relates to ss 62–66) (SI 1995/3104)
		6 Apr 1996 (otherwise) (SI 1996/778)
125	(1)	6 Apr 1996 (so far as relates to authorising the making of regulations relating to certain provisions of Pt I of this Act) (SI 1996/778)
		6 Apr 1997 (otherwise) (SI 1997/664)
	(2)–(4)	6 Apr 1996 (so far as relates to authorising the making of regulations relating to certain provisions of Pt I of this Act) (SI 1996/778)
		16 Oct 1996 (otherwise) (SI 1996/2637)

Pensions Act 1995 (c 26)—*contd*

Section

126		See Sch 4 below
127–134		19 Jul 1995 (s 180(2))
135		*Not in force*
136		6 Apr 1996 (for purpose of authorising the making of regulations) (SI 1996/778)
		6 Apr 1997 (otherwise) (SI 1996/778)
137	(1)	13 Mar 1996 (for purpose of authorising the making of orders) (SI 1996/778)
		6 Apr 1996 (for purpose of authorising the making of regulations) (SI 1996/778)
		6 Apr 1997 (otherwise) (SI 1997/664)
	(2)	Repealed
	(3)–(5)	13 Mar 1996 (for purpose of authorising the making of orders) (SI 1996/778)
		6 Apr 1996 (for purpose of authorising the making of regulations) (SI 1996/778)
		6 Apr 1997 (otherwise) (SI 1997/664)
	(6), (7)	6 Apr 1996 (for purpose of authorising the making of regulations) (SI 1996/778)
		6 Apr 1997 (otherwise) (SI 1997/664)
138	(1)–(4)	6 Apr 1997 (SI 1997/664)
	(5)	13 Mar 1996 (for purpose of authorising the making of orders) (SI 1996/778)
		6 Apr 1997 (otherwise) (SI 1997/664)
139		6 Apr 1996 (for purpose of authorising the making of regulations) (SI 1996/778)
		6 Apr 1997 (otherwise) (SI 1997/664)
140	(1)	6 Apr 1996 (for purpose of authorising the making of regulations) (SI 1996/778)
		6 Apr 1997 (otherwise) (SI 1997/664)
	(2)	13 Mar 1996 (for purpose of authorising the making of regulations) (SI 1996/778)
		6 Apr 1996 (otherwise) (SI 1996/778)
	(3)	6 Apr 1997 (subject to savings) (SI 1997/664)
141		6 Apr 1996 (for purpose of authorising the making of regulations) (SI 1996/778)
		6 Apr 1997 (otherwise) (SI 1997/664)

Pensions Act 1995 (c 26)—*contd*

Section

142–144		13 Mar 1996 (for purpose of authorising the making of regulations) (SI 1996/778) 6 Apr 1996 (otherwise) (SI 1996/778)
145		*Not in force*
146		13 Mar 1996 (for purpose of authorising the making of regulations) (SI 1996/778) 6 Apr 1996 (otherwise) (SI 1996/778)
147		6 Apr 1997 (SI 1997/664)
148		6 Apr 1996 (SI 1996/778)
149		1 Jun 1996 (for purpose of authorising the making of regulations) (SI 1996/778) 6 Apr 1997 (otherwise) (SI 1997/664)
150		6 Apr 1997 (SI 1997/664)
151		See Sch 5 below
152–154		6 Apr 1996 (for purpose of authorising the making of regulations) (SI 1996/778) 6 Apr 1997 (otherwise) (SI 1997/664)
155		6 Apr 1996 (for purpose of authorising the making of regulations relating to Pension Schemes Act 1993, s 113) (SI 1996/778) 1 Jun 1996 (for purpose of authorising the making of other regulations) (SI 1996/1412) 6 Apr 1997 (otherwise) (SI 1997/664)
156		2 Oct 1995 (SI 1995/2548)
157	(1)	6 Apr 1997 (SI 1997/664)
	(2)	1 Jun 1996 (for purpose of authorising the making of regulations) (SI 1996/1412) 6 Apr 1997 (otherwise) (SI 1997/664)
	(3)–(6)	6 Apr 1997 (SI 1997/664)
	(7)	6 Apr 1997 (SI 1997/664); prospectively repealed by Child Support, Pensions and Social Security Act 2000, s 85, Sch 9, Pt III(3)[6]
	(8)–(12)	6 Apr 1997 (SI 1997/664)
158		1 Jun 1996 (for purpose of authorising the making of regulations) (SI 1996/1412) 16 Oct 1996 (for purpose of making rules) (SI 1996/2637) 6 Apr 1997 (otherwise) (SI 1997/664)
159		6 Apr 1997 (SI 1997/664)

Pensions Act 1995 (c 26)—*contd*

Section

160	1 Jun 1996 (for purpose of authorising the making of regulations) (SI 1996/1412)
	6 Apr 1997 (otherwise) (SI 1997/664)
161	6 Apr 1997 (subject to savings) (SI 1997/664)
162–164	6 Apr 1997 (SI 1997/664)
165	16 Oct 1996 (for purpose of making regulations) (SI 1996/2637)
	6 Apr 1997 (otherwise) (SI 1997/664)
166	27 Jun 1996 (in relation to the insertion of Matrimonial Causes Act 1973, s 25D(2)–(4)) (SI 1996/1675)
	1 Aug 1996 (otherwise, but subject to savings) (SI 1996/1675)[2]
167	15 Jul 1996 (for the purpose of bringing into force the provisions relating to the making of regulations in Family Law (Scotland) Act 1985, ss 10(8), (9), (10), 12A(8)–(10)) (SI 1996/1843)
	19 Aug 1996 (otherwise, but subject to savings) (SI 1996/1843)
168	19 Jul 1995 (s 180(2))
169	2 Oct 1995 (SI 1995/2548)
170, 171	19 Jul 1995 (s 180(2))
172	2 Oct 1995 (SI 1995/2548)
173	See Sch 6 below
174, 175	2 Oct 1995 (so far as they relate to s 172) (SI 1995/2548)
	4 Dec 1995 and 1 Jan 1996 (so far as relates to ss 62–66) (SI 1995/3104)
	6 Apr 1996 (otherwise) (SI 1996/778)
176	6 Apr 1996 (SI 1996/778)
177	See Sch 7 below
178	6 Apr 1997 (SI 1997/664)
179	19 Jul 1995 (s 180(2))
180, 181	See ss 1–179 above

Schedule

1, para	1–12	1 Apr 1996 (SI 1996/778)
	13	1 Jun 1996 (SI 1996/1412)
	14–17	1 Apr 1996 (SI 1996/778)
	18	6 Apr 1997 (SI 1997/664)
	19, 20	1 Apr 1996 (SI 1996/778)
2, para	1–11	1 Aug 1996 (SI 1996/1412)
	12	4 Feb 1997 (for purpose of authorising the making of regulations) (SI 1997/216)

Pensions Act 1995 (c 26)—*contd*

Schedule

2, para	12—*contd*			6 Apr 1997 (otherwise) (SI 1997/216)
	13			1 Aug 1996 (SI 1996/1412)
	14	(1)–(4)		1 Aug 1996 (SI 1996/1412)
		(5)		6 Apr 1997 (SI 1997/664)
	15			6 Apr 1997 (SI 1997/664)
	16, 17			1 Aug 1996 (SI 1996/1412)
	18	(1)		1 Aug 1996 (SI 1996/1412)
		(2)		6 Apr 1997 (SI 1997/664)
	19, 20			1 Aug 1996 (SI 1996/1412)
3, para	1–10			Repealed (*never in force*)
	11			Repealed
	12–16			6 Apr 1997 (SI 1997/664)
	17–19			Repealed
	20–22			6 Apr 1997 (SI 1997/664)
	23			16 Oct 1996 (for purpose of making regulations) (SI 1996/2637)
				1 Apr 1997 (otherwise) (SI 1997/664)
	24			6 Apr 1997 (SI 1997/664)
	25			6 Apr 1997 (subject to savings) (SI 1997/664)
	26			6 Apr 1997 (SI 1997/664)
	27			6 Apr 1997 (subject to savings) (SI 1997/664)
	28			6 Apr 1997 (SI 1997/664)
	29			1 Jan 1996 (SI 1995/3104)
	30, 31			6 Apr 1997 (SI 1997/664)
	32–37			1 Jan 1996 (SI 1995/3104)
	38			6 Apr 1997 (SI 1997/664)
	39	(a)		6 Apr 1997 (SI 1997/664)
		(b)		1 Jan 1996 (SI 1995/3104)
		(c), (d)		6 Apr 1997 (SI 1997/664)
	40, 41			6 Apr 1997 (SI 1997/664)
	42			1 Jan 1996 (SI 1995/3104)
	43			6 Apr 1997 (SI 1997/664); prospectively repealed by Child Support, Pensions and Social Security Act 2000, s 85, Sch 9, Pt III(2)[6]
	44	(a)	(i)	1 Jan 1996 (SI 1995/3104)
			(ii)	16 Oct 1996 (for purpose of making regulations) (SI 1996/2637)
				6 Apr 1997 (otherwise) (SI 1997/664)
		(b)		6 Apr 1997 (SI 1997/664)
	45, 46			6 Apr 1997 (SI 1997/664)
	47			1 Jan 1996 (SI 1995/3104)
4				19 Jul 1995 (s 180(2))[3]
5, para	1–7			6 Apr 1997 (SI 1997/664)
	8			Repealed
	9, 10			6 Apr 1997 (SI 1997/664)

Pensions Act 1995 (c 26)—*contd*

Schedule

5, para	11		Repealed
	12–19		6 Apr 1997 (SI 1997/664)
	20		1 Apr 1997 (SI 1997/664)
	21		6 Apr 1996 (for purpose of authorising the making of regulations so far as relates to Pension Schemes Act 1993, ss 11(5)(d), 34(2)(a), 50(4), 163(6)) (SI 1996/778)
			6 Apr 1997 (otherwise) (SI 1997/664)
	22		Repealed
	23–27		6 Apr 1997 (SI 1997/664)
	28	(a)	6 Apr 1996 (for purpose of authorising the making of regulations) (SI 1996/778)
			6 Apr 1997 (otherwise) (SI 1997/664)
		(b)	6 Apr 1997 (SI 1997/664)
	29–32		6 Apr 1997 (SI 1997/664)
	33	(a)	6 Apr 1997 (SI 1997/664)
		(b)	6 Apr 1996 (for purpose of authorising the making of regulations) (SI 1996/778)
			6 Apr 1997 (otherwise) (SI 1997/664)
	34	(a)	Repealed
		(b)	6 Apr 1997 (SI 1997/664)
	35		6 Apr 1996 (for purpose of authorising the making of regulations) (SI 1996/778)
			6 Apr 1997 (otherwise) (SI 1997/664)
	36		1 Jun 1996 (for purpose of authorising the making of regulations) (SI 1996/1412)
			6 Apr 1997 (otherwise) (SI 1997/664)
	37		6 Apr 1996 (for purpose of authorising the making of regulations) (SI 1996/778)
			6 Apr 1997 (otherwise) (SI 1997/664)
	38		*Not in force*
	39		6 Apr 1996 (for purpose of authorising the making of regulations) (SI 1996/778)
			6 Apr 1997 (otherwise) (SI 1997/664)
	40–44		6 Apr 1997 (SI 1997/664)
	45	(a)	6 Apr 1997 (SI 1997/664)
		(b)	6 Apr 1996 (for purpose of authorising the making of regulations) (SI 1996/778)
			6 Apr 1997 (otherwise) (SI 1997/664)
		(c)	6 Apr 1997 (SI 1997/664)

Pensions Act 1995 (c 26)—*contd*
Schedule

5, para	46		6 Apr 1996 (for purpose of authorising the making of regulations) (SI 1996/778)
			6 Apr 1997 (otherwise) (SI 1997/664)
	47		6 Apr 1997 (SI 1997/664)
	48	(a), (b)	6 Apr 1997 (SI 1997/664)
		(c)	6 Apr 1996 (for purpose of authorising the making of regulations) (SI 1996/778)
			6 Apr 1997 (otherwise) (SI 1997/664)
		(d)	6 Apr 1997 (SI 1997/664)
	49	(a)	6 Apr 1996 (for purpose of authorising the making of regulations) (SI 1996/778)
			6 Apr 1997 (otherwise) (SI 1997/664)
		(b)	6 Apr 1997 (SI 1997/664)
	50–64		6 Apr 1997 (subject to savings) (SI 1997/664)
	65		6 Apr 1996 (for purpose of authorising the making of regulations) (SI 1996/778)
			6 Apr 1997 (otherwise) (SI 1997/664)
	66–69		6 Apr 1997 (SI 1997/664)
	70	(a), (b)	6 Apr 1997 (subject to savings) (SI 1997/664)
		(c)	6 Apr 1996 (for purpose of authorising the making of regulations) (SI 1996/778)
			6 Apr 1997 (otherwise) (SI 1997/664)
			Paragraph repealed, partly prospectively, by Social Security Act 1998, s 86(2), Sch 8[4]
	71		6 Apr 1997 (subject to savings) (SI 1997/664)
	72		6 Apr 1997 (SI 1997/664)
	73		1 Apr 1997 (SI 1997/664)
	74–79		6 Apr 1997 (SI 1997/664)
	80	(a)–(e)	6 Apr 1997 (SI 1997/664)
		(f)	16 Oct 1996 (for purpose of making regulations) (SI 1996/2637)
			6 Apr 1997 (otherwise) (SI 1997/664)
			Sub-para 80(f) prospectively repealed by Welfare Reform and Pensions Act 1999, s 88, Sch 13, Pt I[5]
	81–83		6 Apr 1997 (SI 1997/664)
	84		6 Apr 1996 (for purpose of authorising the making of regulations) (SI 1996/778)
			6 Apr 1997 (otherwise) (SI 1997/664)

Pensions Act 1995 (c 26)—*contd*
Schedule

6, para	1		2 Oct 1995 (SI 1995/2548)
	2, 3		6 Apr 1997 (SI 1997/664)
	4, 5		6 Apr 1996 (for purpose of authorising the making of regulations) (SI 1996/778)
			6 Apr 1997 (otherwise) (SI 1997/664)
	6	(a), (b)	6 Apr 1997 (SI 1997/664)
		(c)	6 Apr 1996 (for purpose of authorising the making of regulations) (SI 1996/778)
			6 Apr 1997 (otherwise) (SI 1997/664)
		(d)	6 Apr 1997 (SI 1997/664)
		(e)	6 Apr 1996 (for purpose of authorising the making of regulations) (SI 1996/778)
			6 Apr 1997 (otherwise) (SI 1997/664)
	7, 8		6 Apr 1997 (SI 1997/664)
	9		6 Apr 1996 (SI 1996/778)
	10–16		6 Apr 1997 (SI 1997/664)
7, Pt	I		6 Apr 1997 (subject to savings relating to Pension Schemes Act 1993, ss 108, 114) (SI 1997/664)
	II		Has effect in accordance with Sch 4 (s 180(2))
	III		6 Apr 1996 (so far as relates to Pension Schemes Act 1993, s 48(2)(b), (c)) (SI 1996/778)
			6 Apr 1997 (otherwise, except repeals relating to Pension Schemes Act 1993, ss 35, 36, and subject to savings relating to 1993 Act, ss 55–68, 170(1), 171(1)) (SI 1997/664)
			Not in force (exceptions noted above)
	IV		19 Jul 1995 (repeal in Pensions (Increase) Act 1971) (s 180(2))
			6 Apr 1997 (otherwise, subject to savings relating to Pension Schemes Act 1993, ss 136–140) (SI 1997/664)

[1]   SI 1996/1853 (originally issued as Commencement No 6) was renumbered as Commencement No 7 by the Pensions Act 1995 (Commencement No 6: SI 1996/1853: C 38) (Amendment) Order 1996, SI 1996/2150

[2]   Orders under Matrimonial Causes Act 1973, s 23 requiring periodical payments made by a pension fund to a spouse without pension rights may not be ordered so as to commence before 6 Apr 1997

[3]   Certain provisions of Sch 4 have effect as follows—para 2 has effect on or after 6 Apr 2010 (para 2(2)); para 4 has effect in relation to any person attaining pensionable age on or after 6 Apr 2010 (para 4(2)); para 6(1) comes into force on 6 Apr 2010; and para 6(2)–(4) have effect in relation to incremental periods beginning on or after that date (para 6(5)); paras 18, 19 have effect on or after 6 Apr 2010 (para 20)

Pensions Act 1995 (c 26)—*contd*

4 Orders made under Social Security Act 1998, s 87(2), bringing the prospective repeals into force will be noted to that Act

5 Orders made under Welfare Reform and Pensions Act 1999, s 89, bringing the prospective amendments into force will be noted to that Act

6 Orders made under Child Support, Pensions and Social Security Act 2000, s 86, bringing the prospective amendments into force will be noted to that Act

Prisoners (Return to Custody) Act 1995 (c 16)

RA: 28 Jun 1995

Commencement provisions: s 3(2); Prisoners (Return to Custody) Act 1995 (Commencement) Order 1995, SI 1995/2021

5 Sep 1995 (SI 1995/2021)

Private International Law (Miscellaneous Provisions) Act 1995 (c 42)

RA: 8 Nov 1995

Commencement provisions: s 16; Private International Law (Miscellaneous Provisions) Act 1995 (Commencement) Order 1996, SI 1996/995; Private International Law (Miscellaneous Provisions) Act 1995 (Commencement No 2) Order 1996, SI 1996/2515

Section

1, 2	1 Nov 1996 (SI 1996/2515)
3	Repealed *(never in force)*
4	1 Nov 1996 (SI 1996/2515)
5–8	8 Jan 1996 (s 16(2))
9–15	1 May 1996 (SI 1996/995)
16–19	8 Nov 1995 (RA)
Schedule	8 Jan 1996 (s 16(2))

Proceeds of Crime Act 1995 (c 11)

RA: 28 Jun 1995

Commencement provisions: s 16(3)–(6); Proceeds of Crime Act 1995 (Commencement) Order 1995, SI 1995/2650

Section

1–13	1 Nov 1995 (SI 1995/2650)
14	28 Jun 1995 (s 16(4))
15	1 Nov 1995 (SI 1995/2650)
16	28 Jun 1995 (s 16(4))
Schedule	
1, 2	1 Nov 1995 (SI 1995/2650)

Proceeds of Crime (Scotland) Act 1995 (c 43)

RA: 8 Nov 1995

Commencement provisions: s 50(2)

1 Apr 1996 (s 50(2)), subject to transitional provisions and savings in Criminal Procedure (Consequential Provisions) (Scotland) Act 1995, in particular for consolidated provisions which are not in force at that date; see s 4, Sch 3 thereto

Requirements of Writing (Scotland) Act 1995 (c 7)

RA: 1 May 1995

Commencement provisions: s 15(2)

1 Aug 1995 (s 15(2))

Road Traffic (New Drivers) Act 1995 (c 13)

RA: 28 Jun 1995

Commencement provisions: s 10(2), (3); Road Traffic (New Drivers) Act 1995
(Commencement) Order 1997, SI 1997/267

Section		
1–4		1 Jun 1997 (SI 1997/267)
5	(1), (2)	1 Mar 1997 (SI 1997/267)
	(3)–(7)	1 Jun 1997 (SI 1997/267)
	(8)–(10)	1 Mar 1997 (SI 1997/267)
6		See Sch 1 below
7–9		1 Jun 1997 (SI 1997/267)
10	(1)	1 Mar 1997 (SI 1997/267)
	(2)–(4)	1 Jun 1997 (SI 1997/267)
	(5)	1 Mar 1997 (SI 1997/267)
Schedule		
1, para	1–10	1 Jun 1997 (SI 1997/267)
	11	1 Mar 1997(SI 1997/267)
2		1 Jun 1997 (SI 1997/267)

Sale of Goods (Amendment) Act 1995 (c 28)

RA: 19 Jul 1995

Commencement provisions: s 3(2)

19 Sep 1995 (s 3(2))

Shipping and Trading Interests (Protection) Act 1995 (c 22)

RA: 19 Jul 1995

Commencement provisions: s 9(4)

1 Jan 1996 (s 9(4))

South Africa Act 1995 (c 3)

RA: 23 Mar 1995

23 Mar 1995 (RA)

Statute Law (Repeals) Act 1995 (c 44)

RA: 8 Nov 1995

8 Nov 1995 (RA)

Team and Group Ministries Measure 1995 (No 1)

RA: 28 Jun 1995

Commencement provisions: s 20(2); Order dated 12 Feb 1996
Section

1	1 May 1996 (order dated 12 Feb 1996)
2	28 Jun 1995 (s 20(2))
3–12	1 May 1996 (order dated 12 Feb 1996)
13	12 Feb 1996 (order dated 12 Feb 1996)
14–19	1 May 1996 (order dated 12 Feb 1996)
20	See ss 1–19 above
Schedule	
1, 2	1 May 1996 (order dated 12 Feb 1996)

Town and Country Planning (Costs of Inquiries etc) Act 1995 (c 49)

RA: 8 Nov 1995

8 Nov 1995 (RA)

1996

Appropriation Act 1996 (c 45)

Whole Act repealed

Arbitration Act 1996 (c 23)

RA: 17 Jun 1996

Commencement provisions: s 109; Arbitration Act 1996 (Commencement No 1) Order 1996, SI 1996/3146

Section		
1–84		31 Jan 1997 (subject to transitional provisions) (SI 1996/3146)
85–87		*Not in force*
88–90		31 Jan 1997 (subject to transitional provisions) (SI 1996/3146)
91		17 Dec 1996 (so far as it relates to the power to make orders) (SI 1996/3146)
		31 Jan 1997 (otherwise, and subject to transitional provisions) (SI 1996/3146)
92–104		31 Jan 1997 (subject to transitional provisions) (SI 1996/3146)
105		17 Dec 1996 (SI 1996/3146)
106		31 Jan 1997 (subject to transitional provisions) (SI 1996/3146)
107	(1)	See Sch 3 below
	(2)	See Sch 4 below
108–110		17 Dec 1996 (SI 1996/3146)
Schedule		
1, 2		31 Jan 1997 (subject to transitional provisions) (SI 1996/3146)
3, para	1	Spent
	2, 3	31 Jan 1997 (subject to transitional provisions) (SI 1996/3146)
	4	Repealed
	5–17	31 Jan 1997 (subject to transitional provisions) (SI 1996/3146)
	18	Repealed
	19–30	31 Jan 1997 (subject to transitional provisions) (SI 1996/3146)

Arbitration Act 1996 (c 23)—*contd*
Schedule

3, para	31	Repealed
	32–35	31 Jan 1997 (subject to transitional provisions) (SI 1996/3146)
	36	17 Dec 1996 (so far as it relates to the provision that may be made by county court rules) (SI 1996/3146)
		31 Jan 1997 (otherwise, and subject to transitional provisions) (SI 1996/3146)
	37–40	31 Jan 1997 (subject to transitional provisions) (SI 1996/3146)
	41	Repealed
	42	31 Jan 1997 (subject to transitional provisions) (SI 1996/3146)
	43	Repealed
	44–50	31 Jan 1997 (subject to transitional provisions) (SI 1996/3146)
	51	Repealed
	52, 53	31 Jan 1997 (subject to transitional provisions) (SI 1996/3146)
	54	31 Jan 1997 (subject to transitional provisions) (SI 1996/3146); prospectively repealed by Social Security Act 1998, s 86(2), Sch 8[1]
	55	31 Jan 1997 (subject to transitional provisions) (SI 1996/3146)
		Repealed, partly prospectively, by Social Security (Northern Ireland) Order 1998, SI 1998/1506 (NI 10), art 78(2), Sch 7[2]
	56–58	31 Jan 1997 (subject to transitional provisions) (SI 1996/3146)
	59	Repealed
	60–62	31 Jan 1997 (subject to transitional provisions) (SI 1996/3146)
4		17 Dec 1996 (repeal relating to the County Courts (Northern Ireland) Order 1980 (NI 3), so far as it relates to the provision that may be made by county court rules) (SI 1996/3146)
		31 Jan 1997 (otherwise, and subject to transitional provisions) (SI 1996/3146)

[1] Orders made under Social Security Act 1998, s 87, bringing the prospective repeal into force will be noted to that Act

[2] For the commencement of this repeal, see orders made under Social Security (Northern Ireland) Order 1998, SI 1998/1506 (NI 10), art 1(2)

Armed Forces Act 1996 (c 46)

RA: 24 Jul 1996

Commencement provisions: s 36; Armed Forces Act 1996 (Commencement No 1) Order 1996, SI 1996/2474; Armed Forces Act 1996 (Commencement No 2) Order 1997, SI 1997/304; Armed Forces Act 1996 (Commencement No 3 and Transitional Provisions) Order 1997, SI 1997/2164; Armed Forces Act 1996 (Commencement No 4) Order 2001, SI 2001/1519

Section		
1		Repealed
2		1 Oct 1996 (SI 1996/2474)
3, 4		1 May 2001 (SI 2001/1519)
5		See Sch 1 below
6		1 Oct 1996 (with a saving for any service disciplinary proceedings which began on or before 30 Sep 1996) (SI 1996/2474)
7		1 Oct 1996 (SI 1996/2474)
8		*Not in force*
9		1 Apr 1997 (with savings) (SI 1997/304)
10		See Sch 3 below
11, 12		1 Oct 1996 (with a saving for convictions on or before 30 Sep 1996) (SI 1996/2474)
13, 14		1 Oct 1996 (SI 1996/2474)
15		1 Apr 1997 (with savings) (SI 1997/304)
16		See Sch 5 below
17		1 Apr 1997 (with savings) (SI 1997/304)
18, 19		1 Oct 1996 (SI 1996/2474)
20		1 Oct 1997 (SI 1997/2164)
21	(1)–(3)	1 Oct 1997 (SI 1997/2164)
	(4)	1 Oct 1997 (subject to transitional provisions) (SI 1997/2164)
	(5), (6)	1 Oct 1997 (SI 1997/2164)
22	(1)–(3)	1 Oct 1997 (SI 1997/2164)
	(4)	1 Oct 1997 (subject to transitional provisions) (SI 1997/2164)
	(5)–(7)	1 Oct 1997 (SI 1997/2164)
23		1 Oct 1997 (subject to transitional provisions) (SI 1997/2164)
24	(1)	1 Oct 1997 (SI 1997/2164)
	(2)	1 Oct 1997 (subject to transitional provisions) (SI 1997/2164)
25	(1)	1 Oct 1997 (SI 1997/2164)
	(2)	1 Oct 1997 (subject to transitional provisions) (SI 1997/2164)
26, 27		1 Oct 1997 (SI 1997/2164)

Armed Forces Act 1996 (c 46)—*contd*

Armed Forces Act 1996 (c 46)—*contd*

Schedule

7, Pt	III—*contd*	1 May 2001 (otherwise, except repeals of or in Mental Health Act 1983, s 46; Mental Health (Scotland) Act 1984, s 69; Mental Health (Northern Ireland) Order 1986, SI 1986/595 (NI 4), art 52) (SI2001/1519)
		Not in force (exceptions noted above)

Asylum and Immigration Act 1996 (c 49)

RA: 24 Jul 1996

Commencement provisions: s 13(3); Asylum and Immigration Act 1996 (Commencement No 1) Order 1996, SI 1996/2053; Asylum and Immigration Act 1996 (Commencement No 2) Order 1996, SI 1996/2127; Asylum and Immigration Act 1996 (Commencement No 3 and Transitional Provisions) Order 1996, SI 1996/2970

Section		
1–3		Repealed
4		1 Oct 1996 (SI 1996/2053); prospectively repealed by Immigration and Asylum Act 1999, s 169(3), Sch 16[1]
5, 6		1 Oct 1996 (SI 1996/2053)
7		Repealed
8	(1), (2)	1 Dec 1996 (for the purpose only of making orders) (SI 1996/2970)
		27 Jan 1997 (otherwise, but subject to a saving for employment beginning before 27 Jan 1997) (SI 1996/2970)
	(3)–(8)	27 Jan 1997 (subject to a saving for employment beginning before 27 Jan 1997) (SI 1996/2970)
8A		Inserted by Immigration and Asylum Act 1999, s 22 (qv)
9–11		Repealed
12	(1)	See Sch 2 below
	(2)	See Sch 3 below
	(3)	See Sch 4 below
13		26 Jul 1996 (SI 1996/2053)
Schedule		
1		Repealed
2, para	1	Repealed
	2	1 Oct 1996 (SI 1996/2053)
	3	Repealed
	4–7	1 Oct 1996 (SI 1996/2053)
	8–12	1 Sep 1996 (SI 1996/2053)

Asylum and Immigration Act 1996 (c 49)—*contd*

Schedule

2, para	13	1 Oct 1996 (SI 1996/2053)
3, para	1, 2	Repealed
	3	1 Sep 1996 (SI 1996/2053)
	4	*Not in force*
	5	Repealed
4		1 Sep 1996 (repeal relating to Asylum and Immigration Appeals Act 1993) (SI 1996/2053)
		1 Oct 1996 (repeal relating to Immigration Act 1971) (SI 1996/2053)

[1]   Orders made under Immigration and Asylum Act 1999, s 170, bringing the prospective repeal into force will be noted to that Act

Audit (Miscellaneous Provisions) Act 1996 (c 10)

RA: 29 Apr 1996

Commencement provisions: s 1(2)

Section

1–6	Repealed
7	29 Apr 1996 (RA)

Broadcasting Act 1996 (c 55)

RA: 24 Jul 1996

Commencement provisions: s 149(1), (2); Broadcasting Act 1996 (Commencement No 1 and Transitional Provisions) Order 1996, SI 1996/2120; Broadcasting Act 1996 (Commencement No 2) Order 1997, SI 1997/1005; Broadcasting Act 1996 (Commencement No 3) Order 1998, SI 1998/188

Section

1	1 Oct 1996 (SI 1996/2120)
2	15 Sep 1996 (for the purposes of the notification by the independent analogue broadcasters of their intention to provide their respective services for broadcasting in digital form) (SI 1996/2120)
	1 Oct 1996 (otherwise) (SI 1996/2120)
3–40	1 Oct 1996 (SI 1996/2120)
41	1 Oct 1996 (except for the purposes of the notification by the independent national broadcasters of their intention to provide a service for broadcasting in digital form pursuant to s 41(2) of this Act) (SI 1996/2120)

Broadcasting Act 1996 (c 55)—*contd*

Section

41—*contd*			29 Jan 1998 (exception noted above) (SI 1998/188)
42–72			1 Oct 1996 (SI 1996/2120)
73			See Sch 2 below
74–78			24 Jul 1996 (s 149(1))
79			1 Oct 1996 (SI 1996/2120)
80			24 Jul 1996 (s 149(1))
81			1 Oct 1996 (SI 1996/2120)
82			*Not in force*
83			24 Jul 1996 (s 149(1))
84			1 Oct 1996 (SI 1996/2120)
85			1 Apr 1997 (SI 1997/1005)
86			1 Oct 1996 (SI 1996/2120)
87			1 Nov 1996 (SI 1996/2120)
88			24 Jul 1996 (s 149(1))
89			1 Nov 1996 (SI 1996/2120)
90			24 Jul 1996 (s 149(1))
91			1 Oct 1996 (SI 1996/2120)
92			24 Jul 1996 (s 149(1))
93, 94			1 Nov 1996 (SI 1996/2120)
95			1 Apr 1997 (SI 1997/1005)
96			1 Nov 1996 (SI 1996/2120)
97			1 Oct 1996 (SI 1996/2120)
98			Substituted (19 Jan 2000) by Television Broadcasting Regulations 2000, SI 2000/54, reg 3, Schedule, para 1
99–101			1 Oct 1996 (SI 1996/2120)
101A, 101B			Inserted (19 Jan 2000) by Television Broadcasting Regulations 2000, SI 2000/54, reg 3, Schedule, para 4
102, 103			1 Oct 1996 (SI 1996/2120)
104			10 Aug 1996 (subject to a transitional provision) (SI 1996/2120)
104A			Inserted (19 Jan 2000) by Television Broadcasting Regulations 2000, SI 2000/54, reg 3, Schedule, reg 8
105			1 Oct 1996 (SI 1996/2120)
106–130			1 Apr 1997 (SI 1997/1005)
131–136			24 Jul 1996 (s 149(1))
137, 138			1 Oct 1996 (SI 1996/2120)
139			1 Nov 1996 (SI 1996/2120)
140, 141			Repealed
142			1 Oct 1996 (SI 1996/2120)
143–146			1 Nov 1996 (SI 1996/2120)
147	(1)		24 Jul 1996 (s 149(1))
	(2)	(a), (b)	1 Oct 1996 (SI 1996/2120)

Broadcasting Act 1996 (c 55)—*contd*

Section

147	(2)	(c)	1 Apr 1997 (SI 1997/1005)
		(d)	1 Oct 1996 (SI 1996/2120)
148	(1)		See Sch 10 below
	(2)		See Sch 11 below
149, 150			24 Jul 1996 (s 149(1))

Schedule

1		1 Oct 1996 (SI 1996/2120)
2, para	1–5	10 Aug 1996 (in relation to the interpretation of Broadcasting Act 1990, Sch 2, Pt IV, paras 12, 13) (SI 1996/2120)
		1 Nov 1996 (otherwise) (SI 1996/2120)
	6	1 Nov 1996 (SI 1996/2120)
	7, 8	24 Jul 1996 (so far as relating to BBC companies) (s 149(1))
		1 Nov 1996 (otherwise) (SI 1996/2120)
	9	24 Jul 1996 (so far as relating to BBC companies) (s 149(1))
		1 Oct 1996 (otherwise) (SI 1996/2120)
	10	1 Nov 1996 (except so far as relating to Broadcasting Act 1990, Sch 2, Pt III, paras 1(2)(b), 2(7)) (SI 1996/2120)
		1 Apr 1997 (exception noted above) (SI 1997/1005)
	11	10 Aug 1996 (so far as relates to Broadcasting Act 1990, Sch 2, Pt IV, paras 12[1], 13 and in relation to paras 1, 2, 3, 9, 10, 14 of that substituted Part in so far as those paras apply to the interpretation of the said paras 12, 13 to the 1990 Act) (subject to a transitional provision) (SI 1996/2120)
		1 Nov 1996 (otherwise, except so far as relating to Broadcasting Act 1990, Sch 2, Pt IV, para 15)[2] (SI 1996/2120)
		1 Apr 1997 (otherwise) (SI 1997/1005)
	12, 13	1 Nov 1996 (SI 1996/2120)
3, 4		1 Apr 1997 (SI 1997/1005)
5–8		24 Jul 1996 (s 149(1))
9		1 Oct 1996 (SI 1996/2120)
10, para	1–11	1 Oct 1996 (SI 1996/2120)

Broadcasting Act 1996 (c 55)—*contd*
Schedule

10, para	12		1 Apr 1997 (SI 1997/1005)
	13		1 Nov 1996 (SI 1996/2120)
	14		1 Oct 1996 (SI 1996/2120)
	15		Repealed
	16		1 Oct 1996 (so far as relating to a multiplex service) (SI 1996/2120)
			1 Apr 1997 (otherwise) (SI 1997/1005)
	17, 18		1 Apr 1997 (SI 1997/1005)
	19		24 Jul 1996 (so far as relating to BBC companies) (s 149(1))
			1 Oct 1996 (otherwise) (SI 1996/2120)
	20		1 Apr 1997 (SI 1997/1005)
	21	(a)	1 Oct 1996 (SI 1996/2120)
		(b)	1 Nov 1996 (SI 1996/2120)
		(c)	1 Oct 1996 (SI 1996/2120)
	22–26		1 Apr 1997 (SI 1997/1005)
	27, 28		1 Oct 1996 (SI 1996/2120)
	29		Repealed
	30		1 Oct 1996 (SI 1996/2120)
	31		1 Oct 1996 (so far as relating to anything done under ss 1–72 of this Act) (SI 1996/2120)
			1 Apr 1997 (otherwise) (SI 1997/1005)
	32		1 Oct 1996 (except so far as relating to anything done in pursuance of ss 115(4), (6), 116(5), 117 of this Act) (SI 1996/2120)
			1 Apr 1997 (otherwise) (SI 1997/1005)
11, Pt	I		24 Jul 1996 (repeals of or in Broadcasting Act 1990, ss 32(9), 45(8), (9), 47(11), (12)) (s 149(1))
			1 Oct 1996 (repeals of or in Broadcasting Act 1990, ss 2(1)(a), (4), 32(10), (13)(a), 72(2)(d), 84(1)(b), 182, Sch 20, para 50) (SI 1996/2120)
			1 Nov 1996 (repeals of or in Broadcasting Act 1990, s 104(5), (6)(a), Sch 2) (SI 1996/2120)
			1 Apr 1997 (otherwise) (SI 1997/1005)
	II		1 Oct 1996 (revocation of Cable (Excepted Programmes) Order 1991, SI 1991/1246) (SI 1996/2120)

Broadcasting Act 1996 (c 55)—*contd*

Schedule

11, Pt	II—*contd*	1 Nov 1996 (revocations of or in Broadcasting (Restrictions on the Holding of Licences) Order 1991, SI 1991/1176; Broadcasting (Restrictions on the Holding of Licences) (Amendment) Order 1993, SI 1993/3199; Broadcasting (Restrictions on the Holding of Licences) (Amendment) Order 1995, SI 1995/1924) (SI 1996/2120)

[1] For the purposes of the Broadcasting Act 1990, Sch 2, Pt IV, para 12(5)(b), as substituted, any determination made before 1 Nov 1996, is to be taken to have been made on that date

[2] 1 Nov 1996 is the "relevant day" for the purposes of the Broadcasting Act 1990, Sch 2, Pt IV, para 9(5), where the holder of any licence specified in the substituted Sch 2, Pt IV, paras 9(4), 10(2), 11(1), (3) of the 1990 Act, becomes connected with a national or local newspaper by virtue of the commencement of Sch 2, Pt I of this Act

Channel Tunnel Rail Link Act 1996 (c 61)

Local application only

Chemical Weapons Act 1996 (c 6)

RA: 3 Apr 1996

Commencement provisions: s 39(1); Chemical Weapons Act 1996 (Commencement) Order 1996, SI 1996/2054

Section

1–30	16 Sep 1996 (SI 1996/2054)
30A	Inserted by Anti-terrorism, Crime and Security Act 2001, s 46 (qv)
31–38	16 Sep 1996 (SI 1996/2054)
39	3 Apr 1996 (RA)
Schedule	16 Sep 1996 (SI 1996/2054)

Civil Aviation (Amendment) Act 1996 (c 39)

RA: 18 Jul 1996

18 Jul 1996 (RA)

Commonwealth Development Corporation Act 1996 (c 28)

Whole Act repealed

Community Care (Direct Payments) Act 1996 (c 30)

RA: 4 Jul 1996

Commencement provisions: s 7(2); Community Care (Direct Payments) Act 1996 (Commencement) Order 1997, SI 1997/756
Section

1	1 Apr 1997 (SI 1997/756); prospectively repealed by Health and Social Care Act 2001, s 67, Sch 6, Pt 3[1]
2, 3	1 Apr 1997 (SI 1997/756); prospectively repealed by Health and Social Care Act 2001, s 67(2), Sch 6, Pt 3[1]
4, 5	1 Apr 1997 (SI 1997/756)
6	4 Jul 1996 (s 7(2))
7	1 Apr 1997 (SI 1997/756)

[1]   Orders made under Health and Social Care Act 2001, s 70(2), bringing the prospective repeal into force are noted to that Act

Consolidated Fund Act 1996 (c 4)

Whole Act repealed

Consolidated Fund (No 2) Act 1996 (c 60)

Whole Act repealed

Criminal Procedure and Investigations Act 1996 (c 25)

RA: 4 Jul 1996

The text of this Act states clearly the dates from which the provisions are to have effect. For information on orders appointing such dates see the note "Orders under this section" to the relevant provision of this Act in the service to Halsbury's Statutes

Damages Act 1996 (c 48)

RA: 24 Jul 1996

Commencement provisions: s 8(3)

24 Sep 1996 (s 8(3))

Deer (Amendment) (Scotland) Act 1996 (c 44)

Whole Act repealed

Deer (Scotland) Act 1996 (c 58)

RA: 24 Jul 1996

Commencement provisions: s 48(6)

18 Nov 1996 (s 48(6))

Defamation Act 1996 (c 31)

RA: 4 Jul 1996

Commencement provisions: s 19; Defamation Act 1996 (Commencement No 1) Order 1999, SI 1999/817; Defamation Act 1996 (Commencement No 2) Order 2000, SI 2000/222; Defamation Act 1996 (Commencement No 3 and Transitional Provision) (Scotland) Order 2001, SSI 2001/98[1]

Section		
1		4 Sep 1996 (s 19)
2		28 Feb 2000 (E, W) (SI 2000/222)
		31 Mar 2001 (S) (SSI 2001/98)
3	(1)–(7)	28 Feb 2000 (E, W) (SI 2000/222)
		31 Mar 2001 (S) (SSI 2001/98)
	(8)	28 Feb 2000 (E, W) (SI 2000/222)
		Not in force (otherwise)
	(9)	31 Mar 2001 (S) (SSI 2001/98)
	(10)	28 Feb 2000 (E, W) (SI 2000/222)
		31 Mar 2001 (S) (SSI 2001/98)
4		28 Feb 2000 (E, W) (SI 2000/222)
		31 Mar 2001 (S) (SSI 2001/98)
5, 6		4 Sep 1996 (s 19)
7–10		28 Feb 2000 (E, W) (SI 2000/222)
		Not in force (otherwise)
11		*Not in force*
12, 13		4 Sep 1996 (s 19)
14, 15		1 Apr 1999 (SI 1999/817)
16		See Sch 2 below
17	(1)	4 Sep 1996 (so far as relates to ss 1, 5, 6, 12, 13, 16, Sch 2 (so far as consequential to ss 1, 5, 6, 12, 13, 16)) (s 19)
		1 Apr 1999 (so far as applies to ss 14, 15, Sch 1) (SI 1999/817)
		28 Feb 2000 (E, W) (otherwise) (SI 2000/222)
		31 Mar 2001 (S) (otherwise) (SSI 2001/98)
	(2)	4 Sep 1996 (so far as relates to ss 1, 5, 6, 12, 13, 16, Sch 2 (so far as consequential to ss 1, 5, 6, 12, 13, 16)) (s 19)
		1 Apr 1999 (so far as applies to ss 14, 15, Sch 1) (SI 1999/817)

Defamation Act 1996 (c 31)—*contd*

Section

17	(2)—*contd*	31 Mar 2001 (S) (otherwise) (SSI 2001/98)
		Not in force (otherwise)
18–20		4 Jul 1996 (RA)

Schedule

1	1 Apr 1999 (SI 1999/817)
2	4 Sep 1996 (so far as consequential on ss 1, 5, 6, 12, 13, 16) (s 19)
	1 Apr 1999 (so far as consequential on ss 14, 15, 17, Sch 1, except repeals of Defamation Act 1952, ss 4, 16(3); Defamation Act (Northern Ireland) 1955, ss 4, 14(2); Broadcasting Act 1990, Sch 20, para 3) (SI 1999/817)
	28 Feb 2000 (E, W) (otherwise, except repeals of or in Defamation Act (Northern Ireland) 1955; Local Government Act (Northern Ireland) 1972; British Nationality Act 1981, Sch 7 (entry relating to Defamation Act (Northern Ireland) 1955); Local Government (Access to Information) Act 1985, Sch 2, para 3; Education and Libraries (Northern Ireland) Order 1986, SI 1986/594 (NI 3); Broadcasting Act 1990, Sch 20, para 3) (subject to a saving in relation to Defamation Act 1952, s 4) (SI 2000/222)
	31 Mar 2001 (S) (so far as extends to and is not already in force in relation to Scotland) (SSI 2001/98)[1]
	Not in force (otherwise)

[1] For transitional provision, see SSI 2001/98, art 4

Dogs (Fouling of Land) Act 1996 (c 20)

RA: 17 Jun 1996

Commencement provisions: s 8(2)

17 Aug 1996 (s 8(2))

Education Act 1996 (c 56)

RA: 24 Jul 1996

Commencement provisions: s 583(2), (3); the Education Act 1996 (Commencement No 1) Order 1996, SI 1996/2904; Education Act 1996 (Commencement No 2 and Appointed Day) Order 1997, SI 1997/1623; Education Act 1996 (Commencement No 3) Order 1997, SI 1997/2352

Section		
1–7		1 Nov 1996 (s 583(2))
8		1 Sep 1997 (SI 1997/1623)
9–13		1 Nov 1996 (s 583(2))
13A		Inserted by School Standards and Framework Act 1998, s 5 (qv)
14		1 Nov 1996 (s 583(2))
15		Repealed
15A		Inserted by School Standards and Framework Act 1998, s 140(1), Sch 30, para 63 (qv)
15B		Inserted by Learning and Skills Act 2000, s 149, Sch 9, para 55 (qv)
16, 17		1 Nov 1996 (s 583(2))
18		1 Nov 1996 (s 583(2)); prospectively substituted by School Standards and Framework Act 1998, s 128(1)[1]
19		1 Nov 1996 (s 583(2))
20–28		Repealed
29		1 Nov 1996 (s 583(2))
30–89		Repealed
90, 91		Repealed, subject to savings
92, 93		Repealed
94, 95		Repealed, subject to savings
96–100		Repealed
101–126		Repealed, subject to savings
127–211		Repealed
212		Repealed, subject to a saving
213–243		Repealed
244–254		Repealed, subject to savings
255–311		Repealed
312–315		1 Nov 1996 (s 583(2))
316, 316A		1 Nov 1996 (s 583(2))
		Substituted, partly prospectively, for original s 316, by Special Educational Needs and Disability Act 2001, s 1[2]
317	(1)–(5)	1 Nov 1996 (s 583(2))
	(6)	1 Jan 1997 (SI 1996/2904)
		Sub-ss (6), (7), (7A) prospectively substituted for original sub-ss (6), (7) by Special Educational Needs and Disability Act 2001, s 14(2)[2]

Education Act 1996 (c 56)—*contd*
Section

317	(7)	1 Nov 1996 (s 583(2))
		Prospectively substituted as noted to sub-s (6) above
	(7A)	Prospectively substituted as noted to sub-s (6) above
317A		Inserted by Special Educational Needs and Disability Act 2001, s 7(1) (qv)
318–326		1 Nov 1996 (s 583(2))
326A		Inserted by Special Educational Needs and Disability Act 2001, s 5 (qv)
327–329		1 Nov 1996 (s 583(2))
329A		Inserted by Special Educational Needs and Disability Act 2001, s 8 (qv)
330		Repealed
331–332		1 Nov 1996 (s 583(2))
332A		Inserted by Special Educational Needs and Disability Act 2001, s 2 (qv)
332B		Inserted by Special Educational Needs and Disability Act 2001, s 3 (qv)
333–336		1 Nov 1996 (s 583(2))
336A		Inserted by Special Educational Needs and Disability Act 2001, s 4 (qv)
337		Substituted by School Standards and Framework Act 1998, s 140(1), Sch 30, para 81, Sch 31 (qv)
338–341		Repealed
342		Substituted by School Standards and Framework Act 1998, s 140(1), Sch 30, para 82 (qv)
343–346		Repealed
347		1 Nov 1996 (s 583(2))
348		1 Sep 1997 (SI 1997/1623)
349–357		1 Nov 1996 (s 583(2))
358–361		Repealed
362–369		1 Nov 1996 (s 583(2))
370–374		Repealed
375		1 Nov 1996 (s 583(2))
376–389		Repealed
390–392		1 Nov 1996 (s 583(2))
393		Repealed
394–399		1 Nov 1996 (s 583(2))
400, 401		Repealed
402–410		1 Nov 1996 (s 583(2))
411–413		Repealed
413A, 413B		Repealed (*never in force*)
414–432		Repealed
433–435		1 Nov 1996 (s 583(2))
436		Repealed
437–447		1 Nov 1996 (s 583(2))

Education Act 1996 (c 56)—*contd*

Section

448	Repealed
449	Substituted by School Standards and Framework Act 1998, s 140(1), Sch 30, para 119 (qv)
450–472	1 Nov 1996 (s 583(2))
473A, 473B	Inserted by Criminal Justice and Court Services Act 2000, s 74, Sch 7, paras 127, 129 (qv)
474–478	1 Nov 1996 (s 583(2))
479–481	Repealed, subject to savings
482, 483	1 Nov 1996 (s 583(2))
483A	Inserted by Learning and Skills Act 2000, s 133 (qv)
483–493	1 Nov 1996 (s 583(2))
494	Substituted by School Standards and Framework Act 1998, s 140(1), Sch 30, para 128 (qv)
495–497	1 Nov 1996 (s 583(2))
497A, 497B	Inserted by School Standards and Framework Act 1998, s 8 (qv)
498, 499	1 Nov 1996 (s 583(2))
500–505	Repealed
506–509	1 Nov 1996 (s 583(2))
509A	Inserted by School Standards and Framework Act 1998, s 124 (qv)
510–512	1 Nov 1996 (s 583(2))
512A	Inserted by School Standards and Framework Act 1998, s 116 (qv)
513–515	1 Nov 1996 (s 583(2))
516	Repealed
517	1 Nov 1996 (s 583(2)); prospectively repealed by School Standards and Framework Act 1998, s 140(1), (3), Sch 30, para 138, Sch 31[1]
518	Substituted by School Standards and Framework Act 1998, s 129, subject to transitional provisions (qv)
519–527	1 Nov 1996 (s 583(2))
527A	Inserted by Education Act 1997, s 9 (qv)
528	1 Aug 1997 (E) (SI 1997/1623) 30 Oct 1997 (W) (SI 1997/2352); prospectively repealed by Special Educational Needs and Disability Act 2001, ss 34(3), 42(6), Sch 9 [2]
529–533	1 Nov 1996 (s 583(2))
534	Repealed
535	1 Nov 1996 (s 583(2))

Education Act 1996 (c 56)—*contd*

Section

536			Repealed
537			1 Nov 1996 (s 583(2))
537A			Inserted by Education Act 1997, s 20 (qv); substituted by School Standards and Framework Act 1998, s 140(1), Sch 30, para 153, subject to saving and transitional provisions (qv)
538			1 Nov 1996 (s 583(2))
539			Repealed
540–547			1 Nov 1996 (s 583(2))
548			Substituted by School Standards and Framework Act 1998, s 131(1) (qv)
549, 550			Repealed
550A, 550B			Inserted by Education Act 1997, ss 4, 5 (qv)
551			1 Nov 1996 (s 583(2))
552			Repealed
553–566			1 Nov 1996 (s 583(2))
567			Repealed
568, 569			1 Nov 1996 (s 583(2))
570	(1)	(a)	1 Nov 1996 (s 583(2))
		(b)	Repealed
		(c)	1 Nov 1996 (s 583(2))
	(2), (3)		1 Nov 1996 (s 583(2))
571–574			1 Nov 1996 (s 583(2))
575			Repealed
576			1 Nov 1996 (s 583(2))
577			Repealed
578–581			1 Nov 1996 (s 583(2))
582	(1)		See Sch 37 below
	(2)		See Sch 38 below
	(3), (4)		1 Nov 1996 (s 583(2))
583			1 Nov 1996 (s 583(2))

Schedule

1			1 Nov 1996 (s 583(2))
2–10			Repealed
11–13			1 Nov 1996 (s 583(2)); prospectively repealed by School Standards and Framework Act 1998, s 140(1), (3), Sch 30, paras 57, 185, Sch 31[1]
14–16			Repealed
17–19			1 Nov 1996 (s 583(2)); prospectively repealed by School Standards and Framework Act 1998, s 140(1), (3), Sch 30, paras 57, 185, Sch 31[1]
20, 21			Repealed

Education Act 1996 (c 56)—*contd*
Schedule

22		1 Nov 1996 (s 583(2))
		Repealed, partly prospectively, by School Standards and Framework Act 1998, s 140(1), (3), Sch 30, para 185, Sch 31[1]
23–25		1 Nov 1996 (s 583(2)); prospectively repealed by School Standards and Framework Act 1998, s 140(1), (3), Sch 30, para 185, Sch 31[1]
25A		Inserted by Education Act 1997, s 8(2), Sch 1 (qv) ; prospectively repealed by School Standards and Framework Act 1998, s 140(1), (3), Sch 30, para 185, Sch 31[1]
26, 27		1 Nov 1996 (s 583(2))
28–30		Repealed
31		1 Nov 1996 (s 583(2))
32–33B		Repealed
34		1 Nov 1996 (s 583(2))
35		Repealed, subject to savings
36		1 Nov 1996 (s 583(2))
37, Pt	I	1 Nov 1996 (s 583(2))
	II	1 Sep 1997 (SI 1997/1623)
38, Pt	I	1 Nov 1996 (s 583(2))
	II	1 Sep 1997 (SI 1997/1623)
	III	1 Nov 1996 (s 583(2))
39		1 Nov 1996 (s 583(2))
40		Repealed

[1]   Orders made under School Standards and Framework Act 1998, s 145, bringing the prospective amendments into force will be noted to that Act

[2]   Orders made under Special Educational Needs and Disability Act 2001, s 43, bringing the prospective amendments into force will be noted to that Act

---

Education (Scotland) Act 1996 (c 43)

RA: 18 Jul 1996

Commencement provisions: s 37(2); Education (Scotland) Act 1996 (Commencement) Order 1996, SI 1996/2250; Education (Scotland) Act 1996 (Commencement No 2) Order 1997, SI 1997/365

Section

1		18 Sep 1996 (SI 1996/2250)
2–8		1 Apr 1997 (SI 1997/365)
9–22		18 Sep 1996 (SI 1996/2250)
23–27		Repealed
28–35		18 Sep 1996 (SI 1996/2250)
36	(1)	See Sch 5 below
	(2)	See Sch 6 below
	(3)	18 Sep 1996 (SI 1996/2250)
37		18 Sep 1996 (SI 1996/2250)

Education (Scotland) Act 1996 (c 43)—*contd*

Schedule

1–4		18 Sep 1996 (SI 1996/2250)
5, para	1–5	18 Sep 1996 (SI 1996/2250)
	6–9	1 Apr 1997 (SI 1997/365)
6		18 Sep 1996 (repeals of or in Education (Scotland) Act 1980, ss 2, 19(1), 20, 65F; School Boards (Scotland) Act 1988; Self-Governing Schools etc (Scotland) Act 1989) (SI 1996/2250)
		1 Apr 1997 (otherwise) (SI 1997/365)

Education (Student Loans) Act 1996 (c 9)

Whole Act repealed; subject to savings and transitional provisions

Employment Rights Act 1996 (c 18)

RA: 22 May 1996

Commencement provisions: s 243

22 Aug 1996 (s 243)

Employment Tribunals Act 1996 (c 17)

RA: 22 May 1996

Commencement provisions: s 46

22 Aug 1996 (s 46)

Energy Conservation Act 1996 (c 38)

RA: 18 Jul 1996

Commencement provisions: s 2(2); Energy Conservation Act 1996 (Commencement No 1) (Scotland) Order 1996, SI 1996/2796; Energy Conservation Act (Commencement) Order (Northern Ireland) 1996, SR 1996/559; Energy Conservation Act 1996 (Commencement No 3 and Adaptations) Order 1997, SI 1997/47

1 Dec 1996 (S)

5 Dec 1996 (NI)

14 Jan 1997 (E, W) (for the purposes of Home Energy Conservation Act 1995, ss 3(1), 4(1), (2)); 1 Apr 1997 (E, W) (otherwise)

Family Law Act 1996 (c 27)

RA: 4 Jul 1996

Commencement provisions: s 67(2), (3); Family Law Act 1996 (Commencement No 1)
   Order 1997, SI 1997/1077; Family Law Act 1996 (Commencement No 2)
   Order 1997, SI 1997/1892; Family Law Act 1996 (Commencement) (No 3)
   Order 1998, SI 1998/2572

Section			
1			21 Mar 1997 (SI 1997/1077)
2–15			*Not in force*
16			Repealed
17			Repealed
18–21			*Not in force*
22			21 Mar 1997 (SI 1997/1077)
23–25			*Not in force*
26–29			Repealed
30–56			1 Oct 1997 (SI 1997/1892)
57			28 Jul 1997 (SI 1997/1892)
58, 59			1 Oct 1997 (SI 1997/1892)
60			*Not in force*
61–63			1 Oct 1997 (SI 1997/1892)
64			*Not in force*
65			4 Jul 1996 (s 67(2))
66	(1)		See Sch 8 below
	(2)		See Sch 9 below
	(3)		See Sch 10 below
67			4 Jul 1996 (s 67(2))
Schedule			
1–3			*Not in force*
4–6			1 Oct 1997 (SI 1997/1892)
7, para	1		1 Oct 1997 (SI 1997/1892)
	2	(1)	1 Oct 1997 (SI 1997/1892)
		(2)	1 Oct 1997 (subject to a transitional provision) (SI 1997/1892)
	3–6		1 Oct 1997 (SI 1997/1892)
	7	(1), (2)	1 Oct 1997 (SI 1997/1892)
		(3)	1 Oct 1997 (subject to a transitional provision) (SI 1997/1892)
		(3A)	Inserted (12 Feb 1997) by Housing Act 1996 (Consequential Amendments) Order 1997, SI 1997/74, art 2, Schedule, para 10
		(4)	1 Oct 1997 (subject to a transitional provision) (SI 1997/1892)
		(5)	1 Oct 1997 (SI 1997/1892)
		(6)	1 Oct 1997 (subject to a transitional provision) (SI 1997/1892)
	8–11		1 Oct 1997 (SI 1997/1892)
	12		1 Oct 1997 (subject to a transitional provision) (SI 1997/1892)

Family Law Act 1996 (c 27)—*contd*

Schedule

7, para	13	(1)		1 Oct 1997 (subject to a transitional provision) (SI 1997/1892)
		(2)		1 Oct 1997 (SI 1997/1892)
	14, 15			1 Oct 1997 (SI 1997/1892)
8, Pt	I, para	1–10		*Not in force*
		11, 11A		Substituted by Welfare Reform and Pensions Act 1999, s 84, Sch 12, para 66(4) (qv) (original para 11 *never in force*)
		12–15		*Not in force*
		16	(1)–(3)	*Not in force*
			(3A)	Inserted by Welfare Reform and Pensions Act 1999, s 84, Sch 12, para 66(6) (qv)
			(4)	*Not in force*
			(4A)	Inserted by Welfare Reform and Pensions Act 1999, s 84, Sch 12, para 66(8) (qv)
			(5) (a)	1 Nov 1998 (SI 1998/2572)
			(b)	*Not in force*
			(6) (a)	*Not in force*
			(b)	1 Nov 1998 (SI 1998/2572)
			(7)	1 Nov 1998 (subject to transitional provisions) (SI 1998/2572)
			(8)–(9)	Inserted by Welfare Reform and Pensions Act 1999, s 84, Sch 12, para 66(9) (qv)
		16A		Inserted by Welfare Reform and Pensions Act 1999, s 84, Sch 12, paras 64, 66(1), (10) (qv)
		17–25		*Not in force*
		25A		Inserted by Welfare Reform and Pensions Act 1999, s 84, Sch 12, paras 64, 66(1), (13) (qv)
		26–38		*Not in force*
		39		Repealed (*never in force*)
		40–43		*Not in force*
		43A		Inserted by Welfare Reform and Pensions Act 1999, s 84, Sch 12, paras 64, 66(1), (17) (qv)
	II			Repealed
	III, para	45–51		1 Oct 1997 (SI 1997/1892)
		52		1 Oct 1997 (subject to a transitional provision) (SI 1997/1892)
		53–60		1 Oct 1997 (SI 1997/1892)
		61		Repealed
9, para	1, 2			*Not in force*
	3, 4			28 Jul 1997 (SI 1997/1892)
	5, 6			*Not in force*

Family Law Act 1996 (c 27)—*contd*
Schedule

9, para	7–15	1 Oct 1997 (SI 1997/1892)
10		21 Mar 1997 (repeal relating to Legal Aid Act 1988) (SI 1997/1077)
		1 Oct 1997 (repeals of or in Domestic Violence and Matrimonial Proceedings Act 1976; Domestic Proceedings and Magistrates' Courts Act 1978, ss 16–18, 28(2), Sch 2, para 53; Matrimonial Homes Act 1983; Administration of Justice Act 1985, s 34(2), Sch 2, para 37; Housing (Consequential Provisions) Act 1985, Sch 2, para 56; Housing Act 1988, Sch 17, paras 33, 34; Children Act 1989, s 8(4); Courts and Legal Services Act 1990, s 58(10), Sch 18, para 21; Private International Law (Miscellaneous Provisions) Act 1995, Schedule, para 3) (SI 1997/1892)
		Not in force (otherwise)

Finance Act 1996 (c 8)

Budget Day: 28 Nov 1995

RA: 29 Apr 1996

Details of the commencement of Finance Acts are not set out in this work

---

Health Service Commissioners (Amendment) Act 1996 (c 5)

RA: 21 Mar 1996

Commencement provisions: s 14; Health Service Commissioners (Amendment) Act 1996 (Commencement) Order 1996, SI 1996/970

1 Apr 1996 (SI 1996/970)

Hong Kong Economic and Trade Office Act 1996 (c 63)

RA: 18 Dec 1996

18 Dec 1996 (RA)

Hong Kong (Overseas Public Servants) Act 1996 (c 2)

RA: 29 Feb 1996

29 Feb 1996 (RA)

Hong Kong (War Wives and Widows) Act 1996 (c 41)

RA: 18 Jul 1996

18 Jul 1996 (RA)

Housing Act 1996 (c 52)

RA: 24 Jul 1996

Commencement provisions: s 232; Housing Act 1996 (Commencement No 1) Order 1996, SI 1996/2048; Housing Act 1996 (Commencement No 2 and Savings) Order 1996, SI 1996/2212; Housing Act 1996 (Commencement No 3 and Transitional Provisions) Order 1996, SI 1996/2402; Housing Act 1996 (Commencement No 4) Order 1996, SI 1996/2658; Housing Act 1996 (Commencement No 5 and Transitional Provisions) Order 1996, SI 1996/2959; Housing Act 1996 (Commencement No 6 and Savings) Order 1997, SI 1997/66; Housing Act 1996 (Commencement No 7 and Savings) Order 1997, SI 1997/225; Housing Act 1996 (Commencement No 8) Order 1997, SI 1997/350; Housing Act 1996 (Commencement No 9) Order 1997, SI 1997/596; Housing Act 1996 (Commencement No 10 and Transitional Provisions) Order 1997, SI 1997/618; Housing Act 1996 (Commencement No 11 and Savings) Order 1997, SI 1997/1851; Housing Act 1996 (Commencement No 12 and Transitional Provision) Order 1998, SI 1998/1768; Housing Act 1996 (Commencement No 13) Order 2001, SI 2001/3164

Abbreviation: "orders etc" means "so much of the provision as to confer on the Corporation or the Secretary of State a power to consult, to make determinations, directions, orders or regulations or prepare schemes"

Section

1		1 Oct 1996 (subject to transitional provisions) (SI 1996/2402)
2	(1)–(6)	1 Oct 1996 (subject to transitional provisions) (SI 1996/2402)
	(7), (8)	1 Aug 1996 (SI 1996/2048)
3	(1)	1 Oct 1996 (subject to transitional provisions) (SI 1996/2402)
	(2)	1 Aug 1996 (for the purpose of conferring upon the Secretary of State, the Housing Corporation or Housing for Wales a power to consult, to make determinations, to give consents and to delegate functions) (SI 1996/2048)
		1 Oct 1996 (otherwise) (subject to transitional provisions) (SI 1996/2402)
	(3), (4)	1 Oct 1996 (subject to transitional provisions) (SI 1996/2402)
4		1 Oct 1996 (subject to transitional provisions) (SI 1996/2402)
5		1 Aug 1996 (SI 1996/2048)

Housing Act 1996 (c 52)—*contd*

Section

6		1 Oct 1996 (subject to savings and transitional provisions) (SI 1996/2402)
7		See Sch 1 below
8		1 Oct 1996 (subject to transitional provisions) (SI 1996/2402)
9	(1)	1 Oct 1996 (subject to transitional provisions) (SI 1996/2402)
	(1A)	Inserted by Government of Wales Act 1998, s 140, Sch 16, para 84(3), subject to transitional provisions (qv)
	(2)	1 Oct 1996 (subject to transitional provisions) (SI 1996/2402)
	(3)	1 Aug 1996 (SI 1996/2048)
	(4)–(8)	1 Oct 1996 (subject to savings and transitional provisions) (SI 1996/2402)
10–15		1 Oct 1996 (subject to transitional provisions) (SI 1996/2402)
16		1 Apr 1997 (subject to a saving relating to sub-s (2)(c)) (SI 1997/618)
17		1 Aug 1996 (SI 1996/2048)
18	(1)	1 Apr 1997 (SI 1997/618)
	(2)	1 Oct 1996 (orders etc) (SI 1996/2402) 1 Apr 1997 (otherwise) (SI 1997/618)
	(3), (4)	1 Apr 1997 (SI 1997/618)
	(5)	Substituted by Government of Wales Act 1998, s 140, Sch 16, para 85(2), subject to transitional provisions (qv)
	(6)	1 Apr 1997 (SI 1997/618)
	(7)	1 Oct 1996 (orders etc) (SI 1996/2402) 1 Apr 1997 (otherwise) (SI 1997/618)
	(8)	1 Apr 1997 (SI 1997/618)
19		1 Apr 1997 (SI 1997/618)
20	(1), (2)	1 Apr 1997 (SI 1997/618)
	(3)	1 Oct 1996 (orders etc) (SI 1996/2402) 1 Apr 1997 (otherwise) (SI 1997/618)
	(4)	1 Apr 1997 (SI 1997/618)
21	(1), (2)	1 Apr 1997 (SI 1997/618)
	(3)	1 Oct 1996 (orders etc) (SI 1996/2402) 1 Apr 1997 (otherwise) (SI 1997/618)
	(4)	1 Apr 1997 (SI 1997/618)
22, 23		1 Oct 1996 (subject to transitional provisions) (SI 1996/2402)

Housing Act 1996 (c 52)—*contd*

Section

24		1 Aug 1996 (for the purposes of conferring upon the Secretary of State, the Housing Corporation or Housing for Wales a power to consult, to make determinations, to give consents and to delegate functions) (SI 1996/2048)
		1 Apr 1997 (otherwise) (SI 1997/618)
25		1 Oct 1996 (orders etc) (SI 1996/2402)
		1 Apr 1997 (otherwise) (SI 1997/618)
26		1 Apr 1997 (SI 1997/618)
27		1 Oct 1996 (orders etc) (SI 1996/2402)
		1 Apr 1997 (otherwise) (SI 1997/618)
28	(1), (2)	1 Apr 1997 (SI 1997/618)
	(3)	1 Oct 1996 (for the purpose of enabling a determination to be made under Housing Act 1988, s 52(2), as amended by this Act) (SI 1996/2402)
		1 Apr 1997 (otherwise) (SI 1997/618)
	(4)	1 Aug 1996 (SI 1996/2048)
	(5), (6)	1 Apr 1997 (SI 1997/618)
29		1 Aug 1996 (for the purposes of conferring upon the Secretary of State, the Housing Corporation or Housing for Wales a power to consult, to make determinations, to give consents and to delegate functions) (SI 1996/2048)
		1 Apr 1997 (otherwise) (SI 1997/618)
30–34		1 Oct 1996 (subject to transitional provisions) (SI 1996/2402)
35	(1)–(3)	1 Apr 1997 (SI 1997/618)
	(4)	1 Apr 1998 (SI 1997/618)
	(5)	1 Apr 1997 (SI 1997/618)
36	(1), (2)	1 Aug 1996 (SI 1996/2048)
	(3), (4)	Substituted by Government of Wales Act 1998, s 140, Sch 16, para 87, subject to transitional provisions (qv)
	(5), (6)	1 Aug 1996 (SI 1996/2048)
	(7)	1 Oct 1996 (subject to transitional provisions) (SI 1996/2402)
37, 38		1 Oct 1996 (subject to transitional provisions) (SI 1996/2402)
39–50		1 Oct 1996 (SI 1996/2402)
51	(1)	See Sch 2 below

Housing Act 1996 (c 52)—*contd*

Section

51	(2)–(6)	1 Apr 1997 (SI 1997/618)
52–54		1 Aug 1996 (SI 1996/2048)
55	(1)	See Sch 3 below
	(2), (3)	1 Aug 1996 (SI 1996/2048)
56–64		1 Aug 1996 (SI 1996/2048)
65, 66		1 Oct 1996 (orders etc) (SI 1996/2402)
		3 Mar 1997 (otherwise) (SI 1997/350)
67–71		3 Mar 1997 (SI 1997/350)
72		1 Oct 1996 (orders etc) (SI 1996/2402)
		3 Mar 1997 (otherwise) (SI 1997/350)
73		*Not in force*
74		3 Mar 1997 (SI 1997/350)
75		1 Oct 1996 (orders etc) (SI 1996/2402)
		3 Mar 1997 (otherwise) (SI 1997/350)
76, 77		1 Oct 1996 (SI 1996/2402)
78, 79		3 Mar 1997 (SI 1997/350)
80	(1), (2)	3 Mar 1997 (SI 1997/350)
	(3)	1 Oct 1996 (SI 1996/2402)
81, 82		24 Sep 1996 (s 232(2))
83	(1), (2)	1 Sep 1997 (subject to savings) (SI 1997/1851)
		11 Aug 1998 (otherwise, subject to a transitional provision) (SI 1998/1768)
	(3)	23 Aug 1996 (for the purpose of conferring power to make orders, regulations or rules) (SI 1996/2212)
		1 Sep 1997 (otherwise, but subject to savings) (SI 1997/1851)
		11 Aug 1998 (otherwise, subject to a transitional provision) (SI 1998/1768)
	(4)–(6)	1 Sep 1997 (subject to savings) (SI 1997/1851)
		11 Aug 1998 (otherwise, subject to a transitional provision) (SI 1998/1768)
84		1 Oct 1996 (SI 1996/2212)
85		24 Sep 1996 (s 232(2))
86	(1)–(3)	1 Sep 1997 (subject to savings) (SI 1997/1851)
	(4), (5)	23 Aug 1996 (for the purpose of conferring power to make orders, regulations or rules) (SI 1996/2212)
		1 Sep 1997 (otherwise, but subject to savings) (SI 1997/1851)
	(6)	1 Sep 1997 (subject to savings) (SI 1997/1851)

Housing Act 1996 (c 52)—*contd*

Section

87		*Not in force*
88–91		1 Oct 1996 (subject to savings) (SI 1996/2212)
92	(1)	See Sch 6 below
	(2)	1 Oct 1996 (subject to savings) (SI 1996/2212)
	(3)	1 Oct 1996 (subject to savings) (SI 1996/2212)
93		1 Oct 1996 (subject to savings) (SI 1996/2212)
94, 95		24 Sep 1996 (s 232(2))
96	(1)	28 Feb 1997 (SI 1997/225)
	(2)	See Sch 7 below
97		28 Feb 1997 (SI 1997/225)
98		28 Feb 1997 (subject to savings) (SI 1997/225)
99, 100		28 Feb 1997 (SI 1997/225)
101, 102		28 Feb 1997 (subject to savings) (SI 1997/225)
103		28 Feb 1997 (SI 1997/225)
104		See Sch 8 below
105		1 Oct 1996 (subject to savings) (SI 1996/2212)
106		See Sch 9 below
107–109		1 Oct 1996 (subject to savings) (SI 1996/2212)
110		24 Jul 1996 (s 232(1))
111–115		1 Oct 1996 (subject to savings) (SI 1996/2212)
116, 117		1 Oct 1996 (SI 1996/2212)
118		1 Apr 1997 (subject to transitional provisions) (SI 1997/618)
119		23 Aug 1996 (for the purpose of conferring power to make orders, regulations or rules) (SI 1996/2212)
		Not in force (otherwise)
120		24 Jul 1996 (s 232(1))
121		See Sch 12 below
122		1 Apr 1997 (SI 1997/618)
123		See Sch 13 below
124–128		12 Feb 1997 (SI 1997/66)
129	(1), (2)	12 Feb 1997 (SI 1997/66)
	(3), (4)	1 Oct 1996 (SI 1996/2402)
	(5), (6)	12 Feb 1997 (SI 1997/66)
130–134		12 Feb 1997 (SI 1997/66)
135		1 Oct 1996 (SI 1996/2402)
136, 137		12 Feb 1997 (SI 1997/66)
138	(1)–(3)	12 Feb 1997 (SI 1997/66)
	(4)–(6)	1 Oct 1996 (SI 1996/2402)

Housing Act 1996 (c 52)—*contd*

Section

139, 140			1 Oct 1996 (SI 1996/2402)
141	(1)		See Sch 14 below
	(2), (3)		1 Oct 1996 (SI 1996/2402)
142, 143			1 Oct 1996 (SI 1996/2402)
144–146			12 Feb 1997 (subject to savings) (SI 1997/66)
147			1 Oct 1996 (orders etc) (SI 1996/2402)
			12 Feb 1997 (otherwise, but subject to savings) (SI 1997/66)
148–151			28 Feb 1997 (subject to savings) (SI 1997/225)
152–154			1 Sep 1997 (SI 1997/1851)
155	(1)		1 Sep 1997 (SI 1997/1851)
	(2)	(a)	1 Sep 1997 (SI 1997/1851)
		(b)	15 Oct 2001 (SI 2001/3164)
	(3)–(7)		15 Oct 2001 (SI 2001/3164)
156			15 Oct 2001 (SI 2001/3164)
157, 158			1 Sep 1997 (SI 1997/1851)
159			1 Apr 1997 (SI 1996/2959)
160	(1)–(3)		1 Apr 1997 (SI 1996/2959)
	(4), (5)		1 Oct 1996 (SI 1996/2402)
161	(1)		1 Apr 1997 (SI 1996/2959)
	(2)		1 Oct 1996 (orders etc) (SI 1996/2402)
			1 Apr 1997 (otherwise) (SI 1996/2959)
	(2A)		Inserted by Immigration and Asylum Act 1999, s 117(3) (qv)
	(3)		1 Oct 1996 (orders etc) (SI 1996/2402)
			1 Apr 1997 (otherwise) (SI 1996/2959)
	(4)–(6)		1 Apr 1997 (SI 1996/2959)
162	(1)–(3)		1 Apr 1997 (SI 1996/2959)
	(4)		1 Oct 1996 (orders etc) (SI 1996/2402)
			1 Apr 1997 (otherwise) (SI 1996/2959)
	(5)		1 Apr 1997 (SI 1996/2959)
163	(1)–(6)		1 Apr 1997 (SI 1996/2959)
	(7)		1 Oct 1996 (orders etc) (SI 1996/2402)
			1 Apr 1997 (otherwise) (SI 1996/2959)
164			1 Apr 1997 (SI 1996/2959)
165	(1), (2)		1 Oct 1996 (SI 1996/2402)
	(3), (4)		1 Apr 1997 (SI 1996/2959)
	(5)		1 Oct 1996 (SI 1996/2402)
	(6)		1 Apr 1997 (SI 1996/2959)
166			1 Apr 1997 (SI 1996/2959)
167	(1), (2)		23 Oct 1996 (for the purposes of requiring a local housing authority to consult on an allocation scheme prior to its adoption and enabling them to adopt a scheme) (SI 1996/2658)
			1 Apr 1997 (otherwise) (SI 1996/2959)

Housing Act 1996 (c 52)—*contd*
Section

167	(3)–(5)	1 Oct 1996 (SI 1996/2402)
	(6)–(8)	23 Oct 1996 (for the purposes of requiring a local housing authority to consult on an allocation scheme prior to its adoption and enabling them to adopt a scheme) (SI 1996/2658)
		1 Apr 1997 (otherwise) (SI 1996/2959)
168		1 Apr 1997 (SI 1996/2959)
169		1 Oct 1996 (SI 1996/2402)
170, 171		1 Apr 1997 (SI 1996/2959)
172		1 Oct 1996 (SI 1996/2402)
173		See Sch 16 below
174		1 Oct 1996 (SI 1996/2402)
175, 176		20 Jan 1997 (SI 1996/2959)
177	(1), (2)	20 Jan 1997 (SI 1996/2959)
	(3)	1 Oct 1996 (SI 1996/2402)
178–181		20 Jan 1997 (SI 1996/2959)
182		1 Oct 1996 (SI 1996/2402)
183	(1)	20 Jan 1997 (SI 1996/2959)
	(2)	1 Oct 1996 (SI 1996/2402)
	(3)	20 Jan 1997 (SI 1996/2959)
184		20 Jan 1997 (SI 1996/2959)
185	(1)	20 Jan 1997 (SI 1996/2959)
	(2)	1 Oct 1996 (orders etc) (SI 1996/2402)
		20 Jan 1997 (otherwise) (SI 1996/2959)
	(2A)	Inserted by Immigration and Asylum Act 1999, s 117(4) (qv)
	(3)	1 Oct 1996 (orders etc) (SI 1996/2402)
		20 Jan 1997 (otherwise) (SI 1996/2959)
	(4)	20 Jan 1997 (SI 1996/2959)
186		20 Jan 1997 (SI 1996/2959); prospectively repealed by Immigration and Asylum Act 1999, ss 117(5), 169(3), Sch 16[1]
187–188		20 Jan 1997 (SI 1996/2959)
189	(1)	20 Jan 1997 (SI 1996/2959)
	(2)–(4)	1 Oct 1996 (SI 1996/2402)
190–193		20 Jan 1997 (SI 1996/2959)
194	(1)–(5)	20 Jan 1997 (SI 1996/2959)
	(6)	1 Oct 1996 (orders etc) (SI 1996/2402)
		20 Jan 1997 (otherwise) (SI 1996/2959)
195–197		20 Jan 1997 (SI 1996/2959)
198	(1)–(3)	20 Jan 1997 (SI 1996/2959)
	(4)–(7)	1 Oct 1996 (orders etc) (SI 1996/2402)
		20 Jan 1997 (otherwise) (SI 1996/2959)
199	(1)–(4)	20 Jan 1997 (SI 1996/2959)
	(5)	1 Oct 1996 (SI 1996/2402)
200–202		20 Jan 1997 (SI 1996/2959)

Housing Act 1996 (c 52)—*contd*
Section

203	(1), (2)		1 Oct 1996 (SI 1996/2402)
	(3)–(6)		20 Jan 1997 (SI 1996/2959)
	(7)		1 Oct 1996 (SI 1996/2402)
	(8)		20 Jan 1997 (SI 1996/2959)
204–206			20 Jan 1997 (SI 1996/2959)
207	(1)–(3)		20 Jan 1997 (SI 1996/2959)
	(4)–(6)		1 Oct 1996 (orders etc) (SI 1996/2402)
			20 Jan 1997 (otherwise) (SI 1996/2959)
208, 209			20 Jan 1997 (SI 1996/2959)
210	(1)		20 Jan 1997 (SI 1996/2959)
	(2)		1 Oct 1996 (SI 1996/2402)
211–214			20 Jan 1997 (SI 1996/2959)
215			1 Oct 1996 (SI 1996/2402)
216	(1), (2)		20 Jan 1997 (SI 1996/2959)
	(3)		See Sch 17 below
217, 218			1 Oct 1996 (SI 1996/2402)
219, 220			24 Sep 1996 (SI 1996/2402)
221			24 Sep 1996 (s 232(2))
222			See Sch 18 below
223–226			24 Jul 1996 (s 232(1))
227			See Sch 19 below
228–233			24 Jul 1996 (s 232(1))

Schedule

1, para	1			1 Oct 1996 (subject to transitional provisions) (SI 1996/2402)
	2	(1)		1 Oct 1996 (subject to transitional provisions) (SI 1996/2402)
		(2)	(a)–(e)	1 Oct 1996 (subject to transitional provisions) (SI 1996/2402)
			(f)	1 Aug 1996 (for the purpose of conferring upon the Secretary of State, the Housing Corporation or Housing for Wales a power to consult, to make determinations, to give consents and to delegate functions) (SI 1996/2048)
				1 Oct 1996 (otherwise) (subject to transitional provisions) (SI 1996/2402)
		(3), (4)		1 Oct 1996 (subject to transitional provisions) (SI 1996/2402)
	3	(1), (2)		1 Aug 1996 (SI 1996/2048)
		(3)		1 Oct 1996 (subject to transitional provisions) (SI 1996/2402)
	4–15			1 Oct 1996 (subject to transitional provisions) (SI 1996/2402)
	16	(1), (2)		1 Aug 1996 (SI 1996/2048)
		(3)–(5)		1 Oct 1996 (subject to transitional provisions) (SI 1996/2402)

Housing Act 1996 (c 52)—*contd*

Schedule

1, para	17, 18		1 Oct 1996 (subject to transitional provisions) (SI 1996/2402)
	19		1 Oct 1996 (subject to transitional provisions) (SI 1996/2402)
	20–26		1 Oct 1996 (subject to transitional provisions) (SI 1996/2402)
	27	(1)–(3)	1 Oct 1996 (subject to transitional provisions) (SI 1996/2402)
		(4)	1 Aug 1996 (for the purpose of conferring upon the Secretary of State, the Housing Corporation or Housing for Wales a power to consult, to make determinations, to give consents and to delegate functions) (SI 1996/2048) 1 Oct 1996 (otherwise) (subject to transitional provisions) (SI 1996/2402)
		(5), (6)	1 Oct 1996 (subject to transitional provisions) (SI 1996/2402)
	28, 29		1 Oct 1996 (subject to transitional provisions) (SI 1996/2402)
2, para	1		1 Apr 1997 (subject to a saving for complaints against any social landlord which is or at any time was registered with Housing for Wales) (SI 1997/618)
	2–6		1 Aug 1996 (subject to a saving for complaints against any social landlord which is or at any time was registered with Housing for Wales) (SI 1996/2048)
	7–9		1 Apr 1997 (subject to a saving for complaints against any social landlord which is or at any time was registered with Housing for Wales) (SI 1997/618)
	10		1 Aug 1996 (subject to a saving for complaints against any social landlord which is or at any time was registered with Housing for Wales) (SI 1996/2048)
	11	(1)	1 Aug 1996 (subject to a saving for complaints against any social landlord which is or at any time was registered with Housing for Wales) (1996/2048)

Housing Act 1996 (c 52)—*contd*
Schedule

2, para	11	(2)	1 Apr 1997 (subject to a saving for complaints against any social landlord which is or at any time was registered with Housing for Wales) (SI 1997/618)
		(3), (4)	1 Aug 1996 (subject to a saving for complaints against any social landlord which is or at any time was registered with Housing for Wales) (SI 1996/2048)
3, para	1	(1)–(4)	1 Oct 1996 (subject to transitional provisions and savings) (SI 1996/2402)
		(5)	1 Apr 1997 (SI 1997/618)
	2		Repealed
	3–5		1 Oct 1996 (subject to transitional provisions and savings) (SI 1996/2402)
	6		1 Aug 1996 (SI 1996/2048)
	7		1 Aug 1996 (for the purposes of enabling a determination to be made under Housing Associations Act 1985, s 87(3) with respect to financial assistance under that section) (SI 1996/2048)
			1 Oct 1996 (otherwise) (subject to transitional provisions and savings) (SI 1996/2402)
	8		1 Oct 1996 (subject to transitional provisions and savings) (SI 1996/2402)
	9		Repealed
	10, 11		1 Oct 1996 (subject to transitional provisions and savings) (SI 1996/2402)
4			1 Oct 1996 (SI 1996/2212)
5			*Not in force*
6, Pt	I–III		1 Oct 1996 (SI 1996/2212)
	IV, para	1	1 Oct 1996 (subject to savings) (SI 1996/2212)
		2	1 Oct 1996 (subject to savings) (SI 1996/2212)
		3–5	1 Oct 1996 (subject to savings) (SI 1996/2212)
		6	1 Oct 1996 (subject to savings) (SI 1996/2212)
		7	23 Aug 1996 (for the power of conferring power to make orders, regulations or rules) (SI 1996/2212)

Housing Act 1996 (c 52)—*contd*
Schedule

6, Pt	IV, para	7—*contd*	1 Oct 1996 (otherwise, but subject to savings) (SI 1996/2212)
		8–11	1 Oct 1996 (subject to savings) (SI 1996/2212)
7			23 Aug 1996 (so far as relates to the insertion of Housing Act 1988, Sch 2A, paras 7(2)(a), 9(2)(a) for the purpose of conferring power to make orders, regulations or rules) (SI 1996/2212)
			28 Feb 1997 (otherwise) (SI 1997/225)
8			28 Feb 1997 (SI 1997/225)
9, para	1		23 Aug 1996 (for the purpose of conferring power to make orders, regulations or rules) (SI 1996/2212)
			1 Apr 1997 (otherwise and subject to savings) (SI 1997/618)
	2–5		1 Apr 1997 (subject to savings) (SI 1997/618)
10, 11			1 Oct 1996 (SI 1996/2212)
12, 13			1 Apr 1997 (SI 1997/618)
14			12 Feb 1997 (SI 1997/66)
15			*Not in force*
16, para	1		1 Apr 1997 (SI 1996/2959)
	2		1 Apr 1997 (subject to transitional provisions) (SI 1996/2959)
	3		Repealed
17			20 Jan 1997 (SI 1996/2959)
18, para	1–23		1 Oct 1996 (SI 1996/2402)
	24		24 Sep 1996 (s 232(2))
	25		1 Oct 1996 (SI 1996/2402)
	26–29		24 Sep 1996 (s 232(2))
	30		24 Sep 1996 (SI 1996/2402)
19, Pt	I		1 Oct 1996 (subject to savings) (SI 1996/2402)
	II		3 Mar 1997 (SI 1997/596)
	III		1 Oct 1996 (repeals in Landlord and Tenant Act 1987 subject to savings) (SI 1996/2212)
			1 Sep 1997 (repeals in Landlord and Tenant Act 1985; Arbitration Act 1996) (SI 1997/1851)
			Not in force (otherwise)
	IV		28 Feb 1997 (SI 1997/225)
	V		1 Oct 1996 (except repeal in Leasehold Reform, Housing and Urban Development Act 1993, s 39(3) and subject to savings) (SI 1996/2212)

Housing Act 1996 (c 52)—*contd*
Schedule

19, Pt	V—*contd*	1 Apr 1997 (exception noted above) (SI 1997/618)
	VI	1 Apr 1997 (subject to transitional provisions and savings) (SI 1997/618)
	VII	1 Apr 1997 (SI 1996/2959)
	VIII	20 Jan 1997 (subject to transitional provisions) (SI 1996/2959)
	IX	1 Oct 1996 (except repeal in Housing Act 1988, s 79(2)(a) and subject to savings) (SI 1996/2402)
		Not in force (exception noted above)
	X–XIII	1 Oct 1996 (subject to savings) (SI 1996/2402)
	XIV	24 Sep 1996 (repeals in Housing Act 1985) (s 232(2))
		24 Sep 1996 (repeal in Local Government (Wales) Act 1994) (SI 1996/2402)
		Not in force (otherwise)

[1] Orders made under Immigration and Asylum Act 1999, s 170, bringing the prospective amendments into force will be noted to that Act

Housing Grants, Construction and Regeneration Act 1996 (c 53)

RA: 24 Jul 1996

Commencement provisions: s 150(1)–(3); Housing Grants, Construction and Regeneration Act 1996 (Commencement No 1) Order 1996, SI 1996/2352; Housing Grants, Construction and Regeneration Act 1996 (Commencement No 2 and Revocation, Savings, Supplementary and Transitional Provisions) Order 1996, SI 1996/2842; Housing Grants, Construction and Regeneration Act 1996 (Commencement No 3) Order 1997, SI 1997/2846; Housing Grants, Construction and Regeneration Act (England and Wales) (Commencement No 4) Order 1998, SI 1998/650; Housing Grants, Construction and Regeneration (Scotland) (Commencement No 5) Order 1998, SI 1998/894

Abbreviation: "orders etc" means "so far as confers on the Secretary of State or the Lord Advocate a power to consult, to make orders, regulations or determinations, to give directions, guidance, approvals or consents, to specify matters, or to impose conditions"

Section

1	17 Dec 1996 (SI 1996/2842)
2, 3	11 Sep 1996 (orders etc) (SI 1996/2352)
	17 Dec 1996 (otherwise) (SI 1996/2842)
4–6	17 Dec 1996 (SI 1996/2842)
7	11 Sep 1996 (orders etc) (SI 1996/2352)

Housing Grants, Construction and Regeneration Act 1996 (c 53)—*contd*

Section

7—*contd*	17 Dec 1996 (otherwise) (SI 1996/2842)
8–11	17 Dec 1996 (SI 1996/2842)
12	11 Sep 1996 (orders etc) (SI 1996/2352)
	17 Dec 1996 (otherwise) (SI 1996/2842)
13–16	17 Dec 1996 (SI 1996/2842)
17	11 Sep 1996 (orders etc) (SI 1996/2352)
	17 Dec 1996 (otherwise) (SI 1996/2842)
18	17 Dec 1996 (SI 1996/2842)
19	11 Sep 1996 (orders etc) (SI 1996/2352)
	17 Dec 1996 (otherwise) (SI 1996/2842)
20–24	17 Dec 1996 (SI 1996/2842)
25	11 Sep 1996 (orders etc) (SI 1996/2352)
	17 Dec 1996 (otherwise) (SI 1996/2842)
26	17 Dec 1996 (SI 1996/2842)
27	11 Sep 1996 (orders etc) (SI 1996/2352)
	17 Dec 1996 (otherwise) (SI 1996/2842)
28, 29	17 Dec 1996 (SI 1996/2842)
30	11 Sep 1996 (orders etc) (SI 1996/2352)
	17 Dec 1996 (otherwise) (SI 1996/2842)
31	13 Nov 1996 (so far as confers on the Secretary of State a power to make regulations) (SI 1996/2842)
	17 Dec 1996 (otherwise) (SI 1996/2842)
32	17 Dec 1996 (SI 1996/2842)
33	11 Sep 1996 (orders etc) (SI 1996/2352)
	17 Dec 1996 (otherwise) (SI 1996/2842)
34–43	17 Dec 1996 (SI 1996/2842)
44–47	11 Sep 1996 (orders etc) (SI 1996/2352)
	17 Dec 1996 (otherwise) (SI 1996/2842)
48–50	17 Dec 1996 (SI 1996/2842)

Housing Grants, Construction and Regeneration Act 1996 (c 53)—*contd*
Section

51, 52	11 Sep 1996 (orders etc) (SI 1996/2352) 17 Dec 1996 (otherwise) (SI 1996/2842)
53–60	17 Dec 1996 (SI 1996/2842)
61	11 Sep 1996 (orders etc) (SI 1996/2352) 17 Dec 1996 (otherwise) (SI 1996/2842)
62	17 Dec 1996 (SI 1996/2842)
63, 64	11 Sep 1996 (orders etc) (SI 1996/2352) 17 Dec 1996 (otherwise) (SI 1996/2842)
65, 66	17 Dec 1996 (SI 1996/2842)
67, 68	11 Sep 1996 (orders etc) (SI 1996/2352) 17 Dec 1996 (otherwise) (SI 1996/2842)
69–73	17 Dec 1996 (SI 1996/2842)
74	11 Sep 1996 (SI 1996/2352)
75	17 Dec 1996 (SI 1996/2842)
76	11 Sep 1996 (orders etc) (SI 1996/2352) 17 Dec 1996 (otherwise) (SI 1996/2842)
77, 78	17 Dec 1996 (SI 1996/2842)
79	11 Sep 1996 (SI 1996/2352)
80–84	17 Dec 1996 (SI 1996/2842)
85	11 Sep 1996 (orders etc) (SI 1996/2352) 17 Dec 1996 (otherwise) (SI 1996/2842)
86	11 Sep 1996 (SI 1996/2352)
87	11 Sep 1996 (orders etc) (SI 1996/2352) 17 Dec 1996 (otherwise) (SI 1996/2842)
88	17 Dec 1996 (SI 1996/2842)
89	11 Sep 1996 (SI 1996/2352)
90, 91	17 Dec 1996 (SI 1996/2842)
92	11 Sep 1996 (orders etc) (SI 1996/2352) 17 Dec 1996 (otherwise) (SI 1996/2842)
93	17 Dec 1996 (SI 1996/2842)
94	11 Sep 1996 (SI 1996/2352)
95–100	17 Dec 1996 (SI 1996/2842)
101	11 Sep 1996 (orders etc) (SI 1996/2352)

Housing Grants, Construction and Regeneration Act 1996 (c 53)—*contd*
Section

101—*contd*	17 Dec 1996 (otherwise) (SI 1996/2352)
102	11 Sep 1996 (orders etc) (SI 1996/2352)
	17 Dec 1996 (otherwise, and subject to transitional provisions) (SI 1996/2842)
103	17 Dec 1996 (SI 1996/2842)
104–106	11 Sep 1996 (orders etc) (SI 1996/2352)
	1 May 1998 (E, W) (otherwise) (SI 1998/650)
	1 May 1998 (S) (otherwise) (SI 1998/894)
107	1 May 1998 (E, W) (SI 1998/650)
	1 May 1998 (S) (SI 1998/894)
108	11 Sep 1996 (orders etc) (SI 1996/2352)
	1 May 1998 (E, W) (otherwise) (SI 1998/650)
	1 May 1998 (S) (otherwise) (SI 1998/894)
109–113	1 May 1998 (E, W) (SI 1998/650)
	1 May 1998 (S) (SI 1998/894)
114	11 Sep 1996 (orders etc) (SI 1996/2352)
	1 May 1998 (E, W) (otherwise) (SI 1998/650)
	1 May 1998 (S) (otherwise) (SI 1998/894)
115–117	1 May 1998 (E, W) (SI 1998/650)
	1 May 1998 (S) (SI 1998/894)
118–125	Repealed
126–130	24 Sep 1996 (s 150(2))
131–135	11 Sep 1996 (orders etc) (SI 1996/2352)
	16 Dec 1997 (otherwise) (SI 1997/2846)
136–138	16 Dec 1997 (SI 1997/2846)
139, 140	11 Sep 1996 (orders etc) (SI 1996/2352)
	16 Dec 1997 (otherwise) (SI 1997/2846)
141–145	24 Sep 1996 (s 150(2))
146	24 Jul 1996 (s 150(1))
147	See Sch 3 below
148–151	24 Jul 1996 (s 150(1))
Schedule	
1	17 Dec 1996 (SI 1996/2842)

Housing Grants, Construction and Regeneration Act 1996 (c 53)—*contd*
Schedule

2		Repealed
3, Pt	I	17 Dec 1996 (subject to savings and transitional provisions relating to Local Government and Housing Act 1989) (SI 1996/2842)
	II	1 Apr 1997 (SI 1996/2842)
	III	24 Sep 1996 (s 150(2))

Humber Bridge (Debts) Act 1996 (c 1)

RA: 29 Feb 1996

29 Feb 1996 (RA)

Law Reform (Year and a Day Rule) Act 1996 (c 19)

RA: 17 Jun 1996

Commencement provisions: s 3(3)
Section

1	17 Jun 1996 (subject to a saving) (RA)
2	17 Aug 1996 (but applies to the institution of proceedings after 17 Aug 1996 in any case where the death occurred between 17 Jun 1996 and 17 Aug 1996) (s 3(3))
3	17 Jun 1996 (RA)

Licensing (Amendment) (Scotland) Act 1996 (c 36)

RA: 18 Jul 1996

Commencement provisions: s 3(2); Licensing (Amendment) (Scotland) Act 1996 Commencement Order 1996, SI 1996/2670

21 Oct 1996 (SI 1996/2670)

London Regional Transport Act 1996 (c 21)

RA: 17 Jun 1996

Commencement provisions: s 6(2)

17 Aug 1996 (s 6(2))

Marriage Ceremony (Prescribed Words) Act 1996 (c 34)

RA: 18 Jul 1996

Commencement provisions: s 2(2); Marriage Ceremony (Prescribed Words) Act 1996 (Commencement) Order 1996, SI 1996/2506

1 Feb 1997 (SI 1996/2506)

National Health Service (Residual Liabilities) Act 1996 (c 15)

RA: 22 May 1996

22 May 1996 (RA)

Noise Act 1996 (c 37)

RA: 18 Jul 1996

Commencement provisions: s 14(2); Noise Act 1996 (Commencement No 1) Order 1996, SI 1996/2219; Noise Act 1996 (Commencement No 2) Order 1997, SI 1997/1695

Section

1–9		23 Jul 1997 (SI 1997/1695)
10	(1)–(6)	23 Jul 1997 (SI 1997/1695)
	(7)	19 Sep 1996 (SI 1996/2219)
	(8)	19 Sep 1996 (so far as relates to the power of a local authority under Environmental Protection Act 1990, s 81(3), to abate a statutory nuisance by virtue of s 79(1)(g) of that Act) (SI 1996/2219)
		23 Jul 1997 (otherwise) (SI 1997/1695)
	(9)	See Schedule below
11, 12		19 Sep 1996 (so far as relates to the power of a local authority under Environmental Protection Act 1990, s 81(3), to abate a statutory nuisance by virtue of s 79(1)(g) of that Act) (SI 1996/2219)
		23 Jul 1997 (otherwise) (SI 1997/1695)
13		19 Sep 1996 (SI 1996/2219)
14	(1)–(3)	19 Sep 1996 (SI 1996/2219)
	(4)	23 Jul 1997 (SI 1997/1695)
Schedule		19 Sep 1996 (so far as relates to the power of a local authority under Environmental Protection Act 1990, s 81(3), to abate a statutory nuisance by virtue of s 79(1)(g) of that Act) (SI 1996/2219)
		23 Jul 1997 (otherwise) (SI 1997/1695)

Non-Domestic Rating (Information) Act 1996 (c 13)

RA: 22 May 1996

22 May 1996 (RA)

Northern Ireland (Emergency Provisions) Act 1996 (c 22)

Whole Act repealed by Terrorism Act 2000, ss 2(1)(b), 125, Sch 16, Pt I, subject to s 2(2), Sch 1 of the 2000 Act which preserves certain provisions of the 1996 Act, in some cases with amendment, for a transitional period

Northern Ireland (Entry to Negotiations, etc) Act 1996 (c 11)

Whole Act repealed

Nursery Education and Grant-Maintained Schools Act 1996 (c 50)

RA: 24 Jul 1996

Commencement provisions: s 11(3); Nursery Education and Grant-Maintained Schools Act 1996 (Commencement No 1) Order 1996, SI 1996/2022; Nursery Education and Grant-Maintained Schools Act 1996 (Commencement No 2) Order 1996, SI 1996/3192

Section		
1–4		1 Sep 1996 (SI 1996/2022)
5		Repealed
6		1 Sep 1996 (SI 1996/2022)
7		Repealed
8–11		1 Sep 1996 (SI 1996/2022)
Schedule		
1		Repealed
2–4		1 Sep 1996 (SI 1996/2022)

Offensive Weapons Act 1996 (c 26)

RA: 4 Jul 1996

Commencement provisions: ss 4(4), 6(3); Offensive Weapons Act 1996 (Commencement No 1) Order 1996, SI 1996/2071; Offensive Weapons Act 1996 (Commencement No 2) Order 1996, SI 1996/3063

Section		
1–3		4 Jul 1996 (RA)
4	(1)–(3)	1 Sep 1996 (SI 1996/2071)
	(4)	4 Jul 1996 (RA)
5		4 Jul 1996 (RA)
6	(1), (2)	1 Jan 1997 (SI 1996/3063)
	(3)	4 Jul 1996 (RA)
7		4 Jul 1996 (RA)

Party Wall etc Act 1996 (c 40)

RA: 18 Jul 1996

Commencement provisions: s 22(2); Party Wall etc Act 1996 (Commencement) Order 1997, SI 1997/670

1 Jul 1997 (SI 1997/670) (subject to transitional provisions relating to ss 1, 2 and 6)

Police Act 1996 (c 16)

RA: 22 May 1996

Commencement provisions: s 104; Police Act 1996 (Commencement and Transitional Provisions) Order 1999, SI 1999/533

Section

1–5		22 Aug 1996 (s 104(1))
5A–5C		Inserted by Greater London Authority Act 1999, s 310(1) (qv)
6–9		22 Aug 1996 (s 104(1))
9A		Inserted by Greater London Authority Act 1999, s 314 (qv)
9B		Inserted by Greater London Authority Act 1999, s 315 (qv)
9C		Inserted by Greater London Authority Act 1999, s 316 (qv)
9D		Inserted by Greater London Authority Act 1999, s 317 (qv)
9E		Inserted by Greater London Authority Act 1999, s 318 (qv)
9F		Inserted by Greater London Authority Act 1999, s 319 (qv)
9FA		Inserted by Criminal Justice and Police Act 2001, s 122(1) (qv)
9G		Inserted by Greater London Authority Act 1999, s 320 (qv)
9H		Inserted by Greater London Authority Act 1999, s 322 (qv)
10–11		22 Aug 1996 (s 104(1))
11A		Inserted by Criminal Justice and Police Act 2001, s 123 (qv)
12		22 Aug 1996 (s 104(1))
12A		Inserted by Criminal Justice and Police Act 2001, s 124(2) (qv)
13–20		22 Aug 1996 (s 104(1))
20A		Inserted by Greater London Authority Act 1999, s 325, Sch 27, para 78 (qv)
21–49		22 Aug 1996 (s 104(1))
50	(1), (2)	22 Aug 1996 (s 104(1))
	(3)	1 Apr 1999 (SI 1999/533)
	(4)–(8)	22 Aug 1996 (s 104(1))
51–64		22 Aug 1996 (s 104(1))
65–74		1 Apr 1999 (SI 1999/533)
75		1 Apr 1999 (subject to transitional provisions) (SI 1999/533)
76–84		1 Apr 1999 (SI 1999/533)
85		1 Apr 1999 (subject to transitional provisions) (SI 1999/533)
86, 87		1 Apr 1999 (SI 1999/533)
88		22 Aug 1996 (s 104(1))

Police Act 1996 (c 16)—*contd*

Section		
89–96		22 Aug 1996 (s 104(1))
96A, 96B		Inserted by Greater London Authority Act 1999, s 325, Sch 27, para 104 (qv)
97–102		22 Aug 1996 (s 104(1))
103	(1)	See Sch 7 below
	(2)	See Sch 8 below
	(3)	See Sch 9 below
104–106		22 Aug 1996 (s 104(1))
Schedule		
1, 2		22 Aug 1996 (s 104(1))
2A		Inserted by Greater London Authority Act 1999, s 310(2), Sch 26 (qv)
3, 4		22 Aug 1996 (s 104(1))
5		1 Apr 1999 (E, W) (SI 1999/533)
6		1 Apr 1999 (SI 1999/533)
7, para	1–16	22 Aug 1996 (s 104(1))
	17	Repealed
	18–20	22 Aug 1996 (s 104(1))
	21	22 Aug 1996 (s 104(1)); prospectively repealed by Local Government Act 2000, s 107, Sch 6[1]
	22–30	22 Aug 1996 (s 104(1))
	31	Repealed
	32–41	22 Aug 1996 (s 104(1))
	42	Repealed
	43	1 Apr 1999 (SI 1999/533)
	44	22 Aug 1996 (s 104(1))
	45, 46	1 Apr 1999 (SI 1999/533)
	47	22 Aug 1996 (s 104(1))
8, para	1–11	22 Aug 1996 (s 104(1))
	12	1 Apr 1999 (SI 1999/533)
	13	22 Aug 1996 (s 104(1))
9, Pt	I	22 Aug 1996 (s 104(1))
	II	1 Apr 1999 (SI 1999/533)
	III	22 Aug 1996 (s 104(1))

[1] Orders made under the Local Government Act 2000, s 108, bringing the prospective repeal into force will be noted to that Act in the service to this work

---

Prevention of Terrorism (Additional Powers) Act 1996 (c 7)

Whole Act repealed

Prisoners' Earnings Act 1996 (c 33)

RA: 18 Jul 1996

Commencement provisions: s 5(2)

Not in force

Public Order (Amendment) Act 1996 (c 59)

RA: 17 Oct 1996

17 Oct 1996 (RA)

Railway Heritage Act 1996 (c 42)

RA: 18 Jul 1996

Commencement provisions: s 8(3)

18 Sep 1996 (s 8(3))

Rating (Caravans and Boats) Act 1996 (c 12)

RA: 29 Apr 1996

29 Apr 1996 (RA)

Reserve Forces Act 1996 (c 14)

RA: 22 May 1996

Commencement provisions: ss 121(2), 132(4); Reserve Forces Act 1996 (Commencement No 1) Order 1997, SI 1997/305

Section		
1–120		1 Apr 1997 (SI 1997/305)
121		Repealed
122–130		1 Apr 1997 (SI 1997/305)
131	(1)	1 Apr 1997 (SI 1997/305)
	(2)	See Sch 11 below
Schedule		
1–5		1 Apr 1997 (SI 1997/305)
6		Repealed
7–10		1 Apr 1997 (SI 1997/305)
11		1 Apr 1997 (except repeals relating to Reserve Forces Act 1980 ss 10, 11, 13(2)–(4), 16, 17, 18(1), (2), 19, 20(1), 21, 22, 24–26, 28, 29, 30(1), (2), 31, 32, 34(1)–(3), 35, 36, 38, 39(1)(a), (b), 40–42, 44, 47, 50, 57, 58, 63, 67, 69, 70, 83(1), (2), 87, 93, 100, 101, 120, 139(1), 141–144, 145(1)(b), (2), 146(1)(b), (2), 154(1), 155, Sch 2, Sch 8, paras 1, 4, 5(1), (3), 6–8, 10–15, 16(2), (3), (5)–(10), 17, 19, 20) (SI 1997/305) *Not in force* (exception noted above)

School Inspections Act 1996 (c 57)

RA: 24 Jul 1996

Commencement provisions: s 48(2)

1 Nov 1996 (s 48(2))

Security Service Act 1996 (c 35)

RA: 18 Jul 1996

Commencement provisions: s 4(2); the Security Service Act 1996 (Commencement) Order 1996, SI 1996/2454

14 Oct 1996 (SI 1996/2454)

Sexual Offences (Conspiracy and Incitement) Act 1996 (c 29)

RA: 4 Jul 1996

Commencement provisions: s 7(2); Sexual Offences (Conspiracy and Incitement) Act 1996 (Commencement) Order 1996, SI 1996/2262

1 Oct 1996 (SI 1996/2262)

Social Security (Overpayments) Act 1996 (c 51)

RA: 24 Jul 1996

24 Jul 1996 (RA)

Statutory Instruments (Production and Sale) Act 1996 (c 54)

RA: 24 Jul 1996

24 Jul 1996 (RA)

Theft (Amendment) Act 1996 (c 62)

RA: 18 Dec 1996

18 Dec 1996 (RA)

Trading Schemes Act 1996 (c 32)

RA: 4 Jul 1996

Commencement provisions: s 5(2); Trading Schemes Act 1996 (Commencement) Order 1997, SI 1997/29

6 Feb 1997 (SI 1997/29)

Treasure Act 1996 (c 24)

RA: 4 Jul 1996

Commencement provisions: s 15(2); Treasure Act 1996 (Commencement No 1) Order 1997, SI 1997/760; Treasure Act 1996 (Commencement No 2) Order 1997, SI 1997/1977

Section	
1–10	24 Sep 1997 (SI 1997/1977)
11	13 Mar 1997 (SI 1997/760)
12–15	24 Sep 1997 (SI 1997/1977)

Trusts of Land and Appointment of Trustees Act 1996 (c 47)

RA: 24 Jul 1996

Commencement provisions: s 27(2); Trusts of Land and Appointment of Trustees Act 1996 (Commencement) Order 1996, SI 1996/2974

1 Jan 1997 (SI 1996/2974)

Wild Mammals (Protection) Act 1996 (c 3)

RA: 29 Feb 1996

Commencement provisions: s 7(2)

29 Apr 1996 (s 7(2))

1997

Appropriation Act 1997 (c 31)

Whole Act repealed

Appropriation (No 2) Act 1997 (c 57)

RA: 31 Jul 1997

31 Jul 1997 (RA)

Architects Act 1997 (c 22)

RA: 19 Mar 1997

Commencement provisions: s 28(2); Architects Act 1997 (Commencement) Order 1997, SI 1997/1672

Section		
1–27		21 Jul 1997 (SI 1997/1672)
28		19 Mar 1997 (RA)
Schedule		
1–3		21 Jul 1997 (SI 1997/1672)

Birds (Registration Charges) Act 1997 (c 55)

RA: 21 Mar 1997

21 Mar 1997 (RA)

British Nationality (Hong Kong) Act 1997 (c 20)

RA: 19 Mar 1997

19 Mar 1997 (RA)

Building Societies Act 1997 (c 32)

RA: 21 Mar 1997

Commencement provisions: s 47(3); Building Societies Act 1997 (Commencement No 1) Order 1997, SI 1997/1307; Building Societies Act 1997 (Commencement No 2) Order 1997, SI 1997/1427; Building Societies Act 1997 (Commencement No 3) Order 1997, SI 1997/2668

Section		
1, 2		1 Dec 1997 (SI 1997/2668)[1]
3	(1)	1 Dec 1997 (SI 1997/2668)[1]
	(2)	See Sch 1 below

Building Societies Act 1997 (c 32)—*contd*

Section

4–6			1 Dec 1997 (SI 1997/2668)[1]
7	(1)		1 Dec 1997 (SI 1997/2668)
	(2)		See Sch 2 below
8–10			1 Dec 1997 (SI 1997/2668)[1]
11			9 Jun 1997 (SI 1997/1427)
12	(1)	(a)	1 Dec 1997 (so far as relates to Building Societies Act 1986, s 13(7), Sch 4) (SI 1997/2668)
			1 Dec 1997 (otherwise) (SI 1997/2668)[1]
		(b)–(d)	1 Dec 1997 (SI 1997/2668)[1]
	(2)		1 Dec 1997 (SI 1997/2668)
	(3)		1 Dec 1997 (SI 1997/2668)[1]
	(4)		1 Dec 1997 (SI 1997/2668)
13	(1)		1 Dec 1997 (SI 1997/2668)[1]
	(2)		See Sch 3 below
14, 15			1 Dec 1997 (SI 1997/2668)[1]
16			Repealed
17	(1)		9 Jun 1997 (SI 1997/1427)
	(2)		See Sch 4 below
18			9 Jun 1997 (SI 1997/1427)
19–24			Repealed
25–29			1 Dec 1997 (SI 1997/2668)[1]
30	(1), (2)		1 Dec 1997 (SI 1997/2668)
	(3)		See Sch 5 below
31			9 Jun 1997 (SI 1997/1427)
32–35			Repealed
36			1 Dec 1997 (SI 1997/2668)
37			9 Jun 1997 (SI 1997/1427)
38			1 Dec 1997 (SI 1997/2668)[1]
39	(1)		1 Dec 1997 (SI 1997/2668)
	(2)		See Sch 6 below
40, 41			21 Mar 1997 (RA)
42			9 Jun 1997 (SI 1997/1427)
43			See Sch 7 below
44			Repealed
45	(1)		9 Jun 1997 (SI 1997/1427)
	(2)		1 Dec 1997 (SI 1997/2668)[1]
46	(1)		See Sch 8 below
	(2)		See Sch 9 below
47			21 Mar 1997 (RA)

Schedule

1			1 Dec 1997 (SI 1997/2668)[1]
2			1 Dec 1997 (SI 1997/2668)
3			Repealed
4			9 Jun 1997 (SI 1997/1427)
5, 6			1 Dec 1997 (SI 1997/2668)
7, para	1		Repealed
	2		2 Dec 1997 (SI 1997/2668)

Building Societies Act 1997 (c 32)—*contd*

Schedule

7, para	3–15			Repealed
	16			1 Dec 1997 (SI 1997/2668)[1]
	17	(1)		9 Jun 1997 (SI 1997/1427)
		(2)–(4)		1 Dec 1997 (SI 1997/2668)[1]
		(5)	(a), (b)	1 Dec 1997 (SI 1997/2668)[1]
			(c)	9 Jun 1997 (SI 1997/1427)
		(6)–(8)		9 Jun 1997 (SI 1997/1427)
	18–20			Repealed
	21–25			1 Dec 1997 (SI 1997/2668)[1]
	26			9 Jun 1997 (SI 1997/1427)
	27	(1)		1 Dec 1997 (SI 1997/2668)[1]
		(2), (3)		9 Jun 1997 (SI 1997/1427)
	28			9 Jun 1997 (SI 1997/1427)
	29	(1)		1 Dec 1997 (SI 1997/2668)[1]
		(2)		Repealed
		(3), (4)		1 Dec 1997 (SI 1997/2668)[1]
	30–32			1 Dec 1997 (SI 1997/2668)[1]
	33	(1)		1 Dec 1997 (SI 1997/2668)[1]
		(2)		9 Jun 1997 (SI 1997/1427)
	34			1 Dec 1997 (SI 1997/2668)[1]
	35, 36			Repealed
	37, 38			9 Jun 1997 (SI 1997/1427)
	39, 40			1 Dec 1997 (SI 1997/2668)[1]
	41	(a)		1 Dec 1997 (SI 1997/2668)
		(b)		1 Dec 1997 (SI 1997/2668)[1]
	42			1 Dec 1997 (SI 1997/2668)[1]
	43, 44			1 Dec 1997 (SI 1997/2668)
	45	(1)		9 Jun 1997 (SI 1997/1427)
		(2), (3)		1 Dec 1997 (SI 1997/2668)[1]
		(4)		9 Jun 1997 (SI 1997/1427)
	46			1 Dec 1997 (SI 1997/2668)
	47			1 Dec 1997 (SI 1997/2668)[1]
	48			1 Dec 1997 (SI 1997/2668)
	49			1 Dec 1997 (SI 1997/2668)[1]
	50			1 Dec 1997 (SI 1997/2668)
	51			Repealed
	52			1 Dec 1997 (SI 1997/2668)[1]
	53	(1)	(a)	1 Dec 1997 (for purpose of defining expressions used in provisions falling within SI 1997/2668, Schedule, Pt I) (SI 1997/2668) 1 Dec 1997 (otherwise) (SI 1997/2668)[1]
			(b)	9 Jun 1997 (SI 1997/1427)
			(c)	1 Dec 1997 (for purpose of defining expressions used in provisions falling within SI 1997/2668, Schedule, Pt I) (SI 1997/2668)

Building Societies Act 1997 (c 32)—*contd*
Schedule

7, para	53	(1)	(c)—*contd*	1 Dec 1997 (otherwise) (SI 1997/2668)[1]
			(d)	9 Jun 1997 (for purpose of construing the words "connected undertaking" in Building Societies Act 1986, ss 43A(3)(c), 52(5A), (6), (9)) (SI 1997/1427)
				1 Dec 1997 (for purpose of defining expressions used in provisions falling within SI 1997/2668, Schedule, Pt I) (SI 1997/2668)
				1 Dec 1997 (otherwise) (SI 1997/2668)[1]
			(e)–(o)	1 Dec 1997 (for purpose of defining expressions used in provisions falling within SI 1997/2668, Schedule, Pt I) (SI 1997/2668)
				1 Dec 1997 (otherwise) (SI 1997/2668)[1]
		(2)		1 Dec 1997 (SI 1997/2668)[1]
		(3)	(a)	9 Jun 1997 (SI 1997/1427)
			(b)	1 Dec 1997 (SI 1997/2668)[1]
		(4), (5)		9 Jun 1997 (SI 1997/1427)
	54			1 Dec 1997 (SI 1997/2668)[1]
	55			Repealed
	56	(1)–(8)		1 Dec 1997 (SI 1997/2668)[1]
		(9)		9 Jun 1997 (SI 1997/1427)
		(10)		1 Dec 1997 (SI 1997/2668)[1]
	57			1 Dec 1997 (SI 1997/2668)[1]
	58			Repealed
	59			1 Dec 1997 (SI 1997/2668)[1]
	60	(1)		9 Jun 1997 (SI 1997/1427)
		(2), (3)		1 Dec 1997 (SI 1997/2668)[1]
	61			1 Dec 1997 (SI 1997/2668)
	62, 63			Repealed
	64	(1)–(4)		1 Dec 1997 (SI 1997/2668)[1]
		(5)		Repealed
	65			1 Dec 1997 (SI 1997/2668)
	66	(1)	(a)	1 Dec 1997 (SI 1997/2668)[1]
			(b)	1 Dec 1997 (SI 1997/2668)
		(2)–(4)		1 Dec 1997 (SI 1997/2668)
	67	(a)		1 Dec 1997 (SI 1997/2668)[1]
		(b)		1 Dec 1997 (so far as relates to Building Societies Act 1986, Sch 20, paras 2–4, 18) (SI 1997/2668)
				1 Dec 1997 (so far as relates to Building Societies Act 1986, Sch 20, paras 7–13, 15, 17) (SI 1997/2668)[1]

Building Societies Act 1997 (c 32)—*contd*
Schedule

7, para	67	(b)—*contd*	2 Dec 1997 (otherwise) (SI 1997/2668)
8, para	1–3		Repealed
	4–8		1 Dec 1997 (SI 1997/2668)[1]
	9, 10		21 Mar 1997 (s 47(3)(b))
9			21 Mar 1997 (repeals and revocations in Building Societies Act 1986, s 100; Building Societies (Transfer of Business) Regulations 1988, SI 1988/1153) (s 47(3)(c))

1 Dec 1997 (repeals and revocations of or in Solicitors Act 1974, s 86; Building Societies Act 1986, ss 13(7), 28(2), 41, 84(1), 95, 108, 119(3)(a), Sch 4, Sch 12, Pt II, Sch 16, para 1(5), Sch 20, paras 2–4, 18; Credit Institutions (Protection of Depositors) Regulations 1995, SI 1995/1442) (SI 1997/2668)

1 Dec 1997 (repeals and revocations of or in Home Purchase Assistance and Housing Corporation Guarantee Act 1978; Housing (Northern Ireland) Order 1981, SI 1981/156 (NI 3); Housing Act 1985; Building Societies Act 1986, s 9(3), Pt III (so far as not already repealed), s 33, Pt V, ss 38–40, 51, 52(3), 60(17), 65(10), 71(10A), 79(5), 82, 97(3), 105, 118, 119(1), 122(1), Schs 2, 10, 18, Sch 20, paras 1, 7–13, 15, 17; Banking Act 1987; Deregulation and Contracting Out Act 1994) (SI 1997/2668)[1]

2 Dec 1997 (otherwise) (SI 1997/2668)

[1]   Applies to any existing building society which sends the central office a record of alterations to its purpose or principal purpose, its powers and its rules, in accordance with Sch 8, para 1(1) to the Act, where the alterations are specified as taking effect on or before 1 Dec 1997, and the record of the alterations is registered by the central office under Sch 8, para 1(3) to the Act on or before 1 Dec 1997, and also to any building society registered after 30 Nov 1997. In the case of any other existing building society, these provisions come into force on the date on which the record of alterations to its purpose or principal purpose, its powers and its rules takes effect under Sch 8, paras 1(5), 2(6) to the Act, or as the case may be, is registered under para 3(3)(a) to that Schedule

Building Societies (Distributions) Act 1997 (c 41)

RA: 21 Mar 1997

Commencement provisions: s 2(2)

22 Jan 1997 (s 2(2))

This Act applies to any transfer of business of a building society where the decision of the board of directors of the building society to enter the transfer is made public after 22 Jan 1997

Civil Procedure Act 1997 (c 12)

RA: 27 Feb 1997

Commencement provisions: s 11(2); Civil Procedure Act 1997 (Commencement No 1) Order 1997, SI 1997/841; Civil Procedure Act 1997 (Commencement No 2) Order 1999, SI 1999/1009

Section				
1	(1)			27 Apr 1997 (SI 1997/841)
	(2)			See Sch 1 below
	(3)			27 Apr 1997 (SI 1997/841)
2–9				27 Apr 1997 (SI 1997/841)
10				See Sch 2 below
11				27 Feb 1997 (RA)
Schedule				
1				27 Apr 1997 (SI 1997/841)
2, para	1	(1)		27 Apr 1997 (SI 1997/841)
		(2)		Repealed
		(3)		26 Apr 1999 (SI 1999/1009)
		(4)	(a), (b)	26 Apr 1999 (SI 1999/1009)
			(c)	27 Apr 1997 (SI 1997/841)
			(d)	26 Apr 1999 (SI 1999/1009)
		(5)–(7)		26 Apr 1999 (SI 1999/1009)
	2	(1), (2)		27 Apr 1997 (SI 1997/841)
		(3)		26 Apr 1999 (SI 1999/1009)
		(4), (5)		27 Apr 1997 (SI 1997/841)
		(6)–(9)		26 Apr 1999 (SI 1999/1009)
	3	(a)		14 Mar 1997 (SI 1997/841)
		(b)		26 Apr 1999 (SI 1999/1009)
	4			27 Apr 1997 (SI 1997/841)

Confiscation of Alcohol (Young Persons) Act 1997 (c 33)

RA: 21 Mar 1997

Commencement provisions: s 2(2); Confiscation of Alcohol (Young Persons) Act 1997 (Commencement) Order 1997, SI 1997/1725

Section	
1	1 Aug 1997 (SI 1997/1725)
2	21 Mar 1997 (RA)

Consolidated Fund Act 1997 (c 15)

Whole Act repealed

Consolidated Fund (No 2) Act 1997 (c 67)

Whole Act repealed

Contract (Scotland) Act 1997 (c 34)

RA: 21 Mar 1997

Commencement provisions: s 4(2)

21 Jun 1997 (s 4(2))

Crime and Punishment (Scotland) Act 1997 (c 48)

RA: 21 Mar 1997

Commencement provisions: s 65(2)–(4); Crime and Punishment (Scotland) Act 1997 (Commencement and Transitional Provisions) Order 1997, SI 1997/1712; Crime and Punishment (Scotland) Act 1997 (Commencement No 2 and Transitional and Consequential Provisions) Order 1997, SI 1997/2323; Crime and Punishment (Scotland) Act 1997 (Commencement No 3) Order 1997, SI 1997/2694; Crime and Punishment (Scotland) Act 1997 (Commencement No 4) Order 1997, SI 1997/3004; Crime and Punishment (Scotland) Act 1997 (Commencement No 5 and Transitional Provisions and Savings) Order 1999, SI 1999/652

Section	
1	*Not in force*
2	20 Oct 1997 (SI 1997/2323)
3	20 Oct 1997 (for purpose of inserting Criminal Procedure (Scotland) Act 1995, s 205C(1) for the purpose of the interpretation of s 205B of that Act) (SI 1997/2323)
	Not in force (otherwise)
4	Repealed (*never in force*)
5	20 Oct 1997 (for purpose of enabling the Secretary of State to make regulations, notify courts and make arrangements, including contractual arrangements, under Criminal Procedure (Scotland) Act 1995, ss 245A–245C) (SI 1997/2323)
	1 Jul 1998 (otherwise) (SI 1997/2323)
6–11	1 Jan 1998 (SI 1997/2323)
12	1 Aug 1997 (SI 1997/1712)
13	*Not in force*

Crime and Punishment (Scotland) Act 1997 (c 48)—*contd*

Crime and Punishment (Scotland) Act 1997 (c 48)—*contd*

Section

25				1 Jan 1998 (for purpose of inserting Criminal Procedure (Scotland) Act 1995, ss 194A, 194E, 194G, Sch 9A) (SI 1997/3004)
				1 Apr 1999 (otherwise, subject to transitional provisions and savings) (SI 1999/652)
26–32				1 Aug 1997 (SI 1997/1712)
33–41				Repealed (*never in force*)
42–44				1 Jan 1998 (SI 1997/2323)
45, 46				21 Mar 1997 (RA)
47	(1)	(a), (b)		1 Aug 1997 (SI 1997/1712)
		(c)		17 Nov 1997 (SI 1997/2694)
		(d)		1 Aug 1997 (SI 1997/1712)
	(2)–(5)			1 Aug 1997 (SI 1997/1712)
48				17 Nov 1997 (SI 1997/2694)
49				1 Oct 1997 (for purpose of bringing into force Legal Aid (Scotland) Act 1986, ss 25A(5), (6) (for purposes of enabling the Scottish Legal Aid Board to determine the form of the application for entry on the Register and to specify the documents which are to accompany the application), 25B) (SI 1997/2323)
				1 Apr 1998 (for purpose of bringing into force Legal Aid (Scotland) Act 1986, ss 25A(1), (5)–(15), 25F(1)) (SI 1997/2323)
				1 Oct 1998 (for purpose of bringing into force Legal Aid (Scotland) Act 1986, ss 25A(2)–(4), 25C–25E, 25F(2), (3)) (SI 1997/2323)
50–54				1 Oct 1997 (SI 1997/2323)
55, 56				1 Aug 1997 (SI 1997/1712)
57	(1)			1 Aug 1997 (subject to a transitional provision) (SI 1997/1712)
	(2)			1 Aug 1997 (SI 1997/1712)
58–61				1 Aug 1997 (SI 1997/1712)
62	(1)			See Sch 1 below
	(2)			See Sch 3 below
63	(1)	(a)	(i)	20 Oct 1997 (SI 1997/2323)
			(ii)	1 Jan 1998 (SI 1997/3004)
			(iii)	1 Aug 1997 (SI 1997/1712)
		(b)		1 Oct 1997 (SI 1997/2323)
		(c)		1 Aug 1997 (SI 1997/1712)
	(2)			1 Aug 1997 (SI 1997/1712)

Crime and Punishment (Scotland) Act 1997 (c 48)—*contd*

Section				
64				1 Aug 1997 (SI 1997/1712)
65	(1)			1 Aug 1997 (SI 1997/1712)
	(2)–(4)			*Not in force*
	(5)			1 Aug 1997 (SI 1997/1712)
	(6)			*Not in force*
	(7)			1 Aug 1997 (SI 1997/1712)
Schedule				
1, para	1			Repealed (*never in force*)
	2			1 Aug 1997 (SI 1997/1712)
	3			*Not in force*
	4, 5			1 Jan 1998 (SI 1997/3004)
	6			1 Aug 1997 (SI 1997/1712)
	7			1 Jan 1998 (SI 1997/3004)
	8			1 Aug 1997 (SI 1997/1712)
	9	(1)		1 Aug 1997 (SI 1997/1712)
		(2)		1 Jan 1998 (SI 1997/2323)
		(3)	(a)	1 Jan 1998 (SI 1997/2323)
			(b)	1 Aug 1997 (SI 1997/1712)
		(4)–(6)		1 Aug 1997 (SI 1997/1712)
		(7)		Repealed (*never in force*)
		(8), (9)		1 Jan 1998 (SI 1997/2323)
		(10)–(14)		1 Aug 1997 (SI 1997/1712)
		(15), (16)		1 Jan 1998 (SI 1997/2323)
	10	(1)		1 Aug 1997 (SI 1997/1712)
		(2)	(a)	Repealed (*never in force*)
			(b)	1 Aug 1997 (SI 1997/1712)
		(3)		20 Oct 1997 (SI 1997/2323)
	11			1 Aug 1997 (SI 1997/1712)
	12	(1)		1 Aug 1997 (SI 1997/1712)
		(2)–(4)		1 Oct 1997 (SI 1997/2323)
		(5), (6)		20 Oct 1997 (SI 1997/2323)
		(7)		1 Aug 1997 (SI 1997/1712)
		(8)–(10)		1 Oct 1997 (SI 1997/2323)
	13	(1), (2)		1 Jan 1998 (SI 1997/2323)
		(3)		Repealed (*never in force*)
		(4)		1 Jan 1998 (SI 1997/2323)
	14	(1)		20 Oct 1997 (SI 1997/2323)
		(2)	(a)	Repealed (*never in force*)
			(b)	20 Oct 1997 (SI 1997/2323)
		(3)	(a)–(d)	20 Oct 1997 (SI 1997/2323)
			(e)	Repealed (*never in force*)
		(4)–(7)		Repealed (*never in force*)
		(8)		20 Oct 1997 (SI 1997/2323)
		(9)		Repealed (*never in force*)
		(10)	(a)	Repealed (*never in force*)
			(b)	20 Oct 1997 (SI 1997/2323)
		(11)	(a)	Superseded
			(b)	Repealed (*never in force*)
		(12)–(15)		Repealed (*never in force*)

Crime and Punishment (Scotland) Act 1997 (c 48)—*contd*

Schedule

1, para	14	(16)		Substituted by Crime and Disorder Act 1998, s 119, Sch 8, para 141(2) (qv)
		(17)		Repealed (*never in force*)
		(18)		20 Oct 1997 (SI 1997/2323)
	15			1 Jan 1998 (SI 1997/2323)
	16, 17			1 Aug 1997 (SI 1997/1712)
	18	(1)		1 Aug 1997 (SI 1997/1712)
		(2)	(a)	*Not in force*
			(b)	1 Aug 1997 (SI 1997/1712)
		(3)–(8)		1 Aug 1997 (SI 1997/1712)
	19, 20			1 Aug 1997 (SI 1997/1712)
	21	(1), (2)		1 Aug 1997 (SI 1997/1712)
		(3)		Repealed (*never in force*)
		(4)		1 Aug 1997 (SI 1997/1712)
		(5)–(8)		1 Jan 1998 (SI 1997/2323)
		(9)–(15)		1 Aug 1997 (SI 1997/1712)
		(16)		1 Apr 1999 (subject to transitional provisions and savings) (SI 1999/652)
		(17)		1 Aug 1997 (SI 1997/1712)
		(18)		1 Apr 1999 (subject to transitional provisions and savings) (SI 1999/652)
		(19)–(22)		1 Aug 1997 (SI 1997/1712)
		(23)		20 Oct 1997 (except for purpose of inserting references to s 205A into Criminal Procedure (Scotland) Act 1995) (SI 1997/2323)
				Not in force (exception noted above)
		(24)		*Not in force*
		(25)		20 Oct 1997 (except for purpose of inserting references to s 205A into Criminal Procedure (Scotland) Act 1995) (SI 1997/2323)
				Not in force (exception noted above)
		(26)		1 Apr 1999 (subject to transitional provisions and savings) (SI 1999/652)
		(27), (28)		1 Jul 1998 (SI 1997/2323)
		(29)		*Not in force*
		(30)		1 Aug 1997 (SI 1997/1712)
		(31)		20 Oct 1997 (except for purpose of inserting references to s 205A into Criminal Procedure (Scotland) Act 1995) (SI 1997/2323)
				Not in force (exception noted above)
		(32)		1 Aug 1997 (SI 1997/1712)
		(33)	(a)	20 Oct 1997 (SI 1997/2323)

Crime and Punishment (Scotland) Act 1997 (c 48)—*contd*

Schedule

1, para	21	(33)	(b)	1 Apr 1999 (subject to transitional provisions and savings) (SI 1999/652)
		(34)	(a)	1 Apr 1999 (subject to transitional provisions and savings) (SI 1999/652)
			(b)	1 Aug 1997 (SI 1997/1712)
		(35)		1 Jan 1998 (SI 1997/2323)
2				Repealed (*never in force*)
3				1 Aug 1997 (repeals of or in Police (Scotland) Act 1967; Social Work (Scotland) Act 1968; Sexual Offences (Scotland) Act 1976; Video Recordings Act 1993; Criminal Justice (Scotland) Act 1995; Environment Act 1995; Children (Scotland) Act 1995; Criminal Procedure (Consequential Provisions) (Scotland) Act 1995; Criminal Procedure (Scotland) Act 1995 (except ss 18, 44, 53, 63, 124, 252)) (SI 1997/1712)
				20 Oct 1997 (repeals of or in Repatriation of Prisoners Act 1984; Prisoners and Criminal Proceedings (Scotland) Act 1993, s 2(2)) (SI 1997/2323)
				17 Nov 1997 (repeal of Criminal Procedure (Scotland) Act 1995, s 18(7)) (SI 1997/2694)
				1 Jan 1998 (repeals of or in Mental Health (Scotland) Act 1984; Prisons (Scotland) Act 1989, s 3(1); Criminal Procedure (Scotland) Act 1995, ss 53, 63, 252(2)) (SI 1997/2323)
				1 Apr 1999 (repeal of Criminal Procedure (Scotland) Act 1995, s 124(3)–(5), subject to transitional provisions and savings) (SI 1999/652)
				Repealed (repeals in or of Prisons (Scotland) Act 1989, s 39(7); Prisoners and Criminal Proceedings (Scotland) Act 1993, ss 1, 3, 5–7, 9, 12, 14(4), 16, 17, 20, 24, 27(2), (3), (5), (6), Sch 1, in s 27(1), definitions "short term

Crime and Punishment (Scotland) Act 1997 (c 48)—*contd*

Schedule

3—*contd*　　　　　　　　　　　　　prisoner", "long term prisoner",
and in definition "supervised release
order", words from "but" to the
end; Criminal Procedure (Scotland)
Act 1995, s 44) (*never in force*)

Not in force (otherwise)

Crime (Sentences) Act 1997 (c 43)

RA: 21 Mar 1997

Commencement provisions: s 57(2); Crime (Sentences) Act 1997 (Commencement)
(No 1) Order 1997, SI 1997/1581; Crime (Sentences) Act 1997 (Commencement
No 2 and Transitional Provisions) Order 1997, SI 1997/2200; Crime
(Sentences) Act 1997 (Commencement No 3) Order 1999, SI 1999/3096

Section		
1–7		Repealed
8, 9		Repealed (*never in force*)
9A		Inserted by Crime and Disorder Act 1998, ss 107(1), (5), subject to a transitional provision (qv)
10–27		Repealed (*never in force*)
28–30		1 Oct 1997 (SI 1997/2200)
31	(1), (2)	1 Oct 1997 (SI 1997/2200)
	(2A)	Inserted by Crime and Disorder Act 1998, s 119, Sch 8, para 131
	(3)–(5)	1 Oct 1997 (SI 1997/2200)
	(6)	1 Oct 1997 (subject to transitional provisions) (SI 1997/2200)
32		1 Oct 1997 (SI 1997/2200)
33	(1)	1 Oct 1997 (subject to a transitional provision) (SI 1997/2200)
	(2)–(5)	1 Oct 1997 (SI 1997/2200)
34		1 Oct 1997 (SI 1997/2200)
35		1 Jan 1998 (SI 1997/2200)
36–39		Repealed
40		1 Jan 1998 (SI 1997/2200)
41		See Sch 1 below
42		See Sch 2 below
43, 44		Repealed
45		1 Oct 1997 (SI 1997/2200)
46		1 Oct 1997 (subject to a saving) (SI 1997/2200)
47		1 Oct 1997 (SI 1997/2200)
48		See Sch 3 below
49		1 Oct 1997 (SI 1997/2200)
50, 51		Repealed
52		1 Oct 1997 (subject to a saving) (SI 1997/2200)

Crime (Sentences) Act 1997 (c 43)—*contd*

Section

53, 54			1 Oct 1997 (SI 1997/2200)
55	(1)		See Sch 4 below
	(2)	(a)	Repealed
		(b)	1 Oct 1997 (SI 1997/2200); Prospectively repealed by Armed Forces Act 2001, s 38, Sch 7, Pt 2[1]
56	(1)		See Sch 5 below
	(2)		See Sch 6 below
57			1 Oct 1997 (SI 1997/2200)

Schedule

1, para	1–13		1 Oct 1997 (subject to savings) (SI 1997/2200)
	14		25 Jun 1997 (subject to savings) (SI 1997/1581)
	15–18		1 Oct 1997 (subject to savings) (SI 1997/2200)
	19		25 Jun 1997 (subject to savings) (SI 1997/1581)
	20		1 Oct 1997 (subject to savings) (SI 1997/2200)
2, para	1–3		1 Oct 1997 (SI 1997/2200)
	4		Repealed (*never in force*)
	5–7		1 Oct 1997 (SI 1997/2200)
	8		Repealed (*never in force*)
	9–11		1 Oct 1997 (SI 1997/2200)
3			1 Oct 1997 (SI 1997/2200)
4, para	1	(1)	1 Oct 1997 (so far as relates to offences whose corresponding civil offences are offences to which s 2 would apply) (SI 1997/2200) *Not in force* (otherwise) Prospectively repealed by Armed Forces Act 2001, s 38, Sch 7, Pt 2[1]
		(2)	1 Oct 1997 (SI 1997/2200)
		(3)	*Not in force*
		(4)	1 Oct 1997 (SI 1997/2200) Prospectively repealed by Armed Forces Act 2001, s 38, Sch 7, Pt 2[1]
		(5)	*Not in force*
	2	(1)	1 Oct 1997 (so far as relates to offences whose corresponding civil offences are offences to which s 2 would apply) (SI 1997/2200) *Not in force* (otherwise) Prospectively repealed by Armed Forces Act 2001, s 38, Sch 7, Pt 2[1]
		(2)	1 Oct 1997 (SI 1997/2200)
		(3)	*Not in force*

Crime (Sentences) Act 1997 (c 43)—*contd*

Schedule

4, para	2	(4)		1 Oct 1997 (SI 1997/2200)
				Prospectively repealed by Armed Forces Act 2001, s 38, Sch 7, Pt 2[1]
		(5)		*Not in force*
	3	(1)		1 Oct 1997 (so far as relates to offences whose corresponding civil offences are offences to which s 2 would apply) (SI 1997/2200)
				1 Dec 2000 (otherwise) (SI 1999/3096)
				Prospectively repealed by Armed Forces Act 2001, s 38, Sch 7, Pt 2[1]
		(2)		1 Oct 1997 (SI 1997/2200)
		(3)		1 Dec 1999 (SI 1999/3096)
		(4)		1 Oct 1997 (SI 1997/2200); prospectively repealed by Armed Forces Act 2001, s 38, Sch 7, Pt 2[1]
		(5)		*Not in force*
	4			1 Oct 1997 (SI 1997/2200); prospectively repealed by Armed Forces Act 2001, s 38, Sch 7, Pt 2[1]
	5	(1)		Repealed
		(2)		1 Oct 1997 (SI 1997/2200)
	6	(1)	(a)	1 Oct 1997 (SI 1997/2200)
			(b)	Repealed (*never in force*)
		(2)		*Not in force*
	7			*Not in force*
	8			Repealed
	9			Repealed (*never in force*)
	10	(1)		1 Oct 1997 (SI 1997/2200)
		(2)		1 Jan 1998 (SI 1997/2200)
	11			Repealed (*never in force*)
	12	(1)		1 Oct 1997 (SI 1997/2200)
		(2)		1 Oct 1997 (so far as relates to offences the sentences for which would otherwise fall to be imposed under s 3(2)) (SI 1997/2200)
				1 Dec 1999 (otherwise) (SI 1999/3096)
		(3)		1 Oct 1997 (SI 1997/2200)
		(4)		Repealed (*never in force*)
		(5)–(19)		1 Oct 1997 (SI 1997/2200)
	13			1 Oct 1997 (so far as relates to sentences required by ss 2(2), 3(2)) (SI 1997/2200)
				1 Dec 1999 (otherwise) (SI 1999/3096)
	14			*Not in force*

Crime (Sentences) Act 1997 (c 43)—*contd*
Schedule

4, para	15	(1)–(9)	Repealed
		(10)	1 Oct 1997 (subject to transitional provisions) (SI 1997/2200)
		(11)–(13)	Repealed
	16		1 Oct 1997 (SI 1997/2200)
	17		Repealed
5, para	1–4		Repealed (*never in force*)
	5		1 Oct 1997 (SI 1997/2200)
	6		Repealed (*never in force*)
	7		1 Oct 1997 (SI 1997/2200)
	8		Repealed
	9–13		1 Oct 1997 (SI 1997/2200)
6			1 Oct 1997 (so far as relates to repeals of or in Criminal Justice Act 1961; Powers of Criminal Courts Act 1973; Mental Health Act 1983; Criminal Justice Act 1991, ss 4(1), 12, 34, 35(2), (3), 36(1) (so far as relating to life prisoners), 36(2) (the words "or life"), 37(3) (so far as relating to life prisoners), 37(4), (5), 39(1) (the words "or life"), 39(5)(a) (the word "other"), 39(5)(b) (the words "direction or"), 43(2), (3) (the words "(whether short–term, long–term or life prisoners)", "or (2)"), 48, 51(1) (the definitions "discretionary life prisoner", "life prisoner"), 51(3)) (subject to savings) (SI 1997/2200) *Not in force* (otherwise)

[1] Orders under the Armed Forces Act 2001, s 39, bringing the prospective repeals into force will be noted to that Act

---

Criminal Evidence (Amendment) Act 1997 (c 17)

RA: 19 Mar 1997

19 Mar 1997 (RA)

Dangerous Dogs (Amendment) Act 1997 (c 53)

RA: 21 Mar 1997

Commencement provisions: s 6(3); Dangerous Dogs (Amendment) Act 1997 (Commencement) Order 1997, SI 1997/1151

8 Jun 1997 (SI 1997/1151)

Education Act 1997 (c 44)

RA: 21 Mar 1997

Commencement provisions: s 58(3), (4); Education Act 1997 (Commencement No 1) Order 1997, SI 1997/1153; Education Act 1997 (Commencement No 2 and Transitional Provisions) Order 1997, SI 1997/1468; Education Act 1997 (Commencement No 3 and Transitional Provisions) Order 1998, SI 1998/386; Education Act 1997 (Commencement No 4) Order 2001, SI 2001/1215

Section		
1–3		Repealed
4		1 Sep 1998 (SI 1998/386)
5		1 Sep 1998 (subject to transitional provisions) (SI 1998/386)
6–8		Repealed
9		1 Apr 1998 (SI 1998/386)
10–14		Repealed (s 13 *never in force*)
15		1 Nov 1997 (SI 1997/1468)
16	(1)	1 Apr 1998 (E) (SI 1998/386)
		1 Apr 1999 (W) (SI 1998/386)
	(2), (3)	1 Nov 1997 (SI 1997/1468)
	(4)	1 Nov 1997 (E) (SI 1997/1468)
		1 Nov 1998 (W) (SI 1998/386)
	(5)	1 Apr 1998 (E) (SI 1998/386)
		1 Apr 1999 (W) (SI 1998/386)
	(6)	1 Nov 1997 (SI 1997/1468)
17	(1)–(3)	1 Aug 1998 (E) (SI 1998/386)
		1 Sep 1999 (W) (SI 1998/386)
	(4)	1 Nov 1997 (SI 1997/1468)
	(5)–(7)	1 Aug 1998 (E) (SI 1998/386)
		1 Sep 1999 (W) (SI 1998/386)
	(8)	1 Nov 1997 (SI 1997/1468)
18		1 Nov 1997 (SI 1997/1468)
19		1 Apr 1998 (SI 1998/386)
20		14 Jun 1997 (SI 1997/1468)
21	(1)–(4)	1 Oct 1997 (SI 1997/1468)
	(5)	See Sch 4 below
22–26		1 Oct 1997 (SI 1997/1468)
27	(1)–(4)	1 Oct 1997 (SI 1997/1468)
	(5)	See Sch 5 below
28–32		1 Oct 1997 (SI 1997/1468)
33		1 Mar 1998 (SI 1998/386)
34, 35		1 Sep 1997 (SI 1997/1468)
36		1 Dec 1997 (SI 1997/1468)
37	(1)–(4)	Repealed
	(5)	1 Sep 2001 (SI 2001/1215)
38–41		1 Sep 1997 (SI 1997/1468)
42		See Sch 6 below
43		1 Sep 1998 (SI 1998/386)
44–46		1 Sep 1997 (SI 1997/1468)
47		1 Sep 1998 (SI 1998/386)
48		1 Dec 1997 (SI 1997/1468)

Education Act 1997 (c 44)—*contd*

Section

49	(1)		1 Oct 1997 (so far as relates to s 49(2), (3)) (SI 1997/1468)
			1 Mar 1998 (otherwise) (SI 1998/386)
	(2), (3)		1 Oct 1997 (SI 1997/1468)
	(4)		1 Mar 1998 (SI 1998/386)
50			Repealed
51			1 Sep 1997 (SI 1997/1468)
52	(1)–(3)		1 Aug 1998 (SI 1998/386)
	(4)		Repealed
	(5)		Repealed (*never in force*)
53			1 Oct 1997 (SI 1997/1468)
54			21 Mar 1997 (s 58(4))
55, 56			14 Jun 1997 (SI 1997/1468)
57	(1)		See Sch 7 below
	(2), (3)		Repealed
	(4)		See Sch 8 below
58			21 Mar 1997 (s 58(4))

Schedule

1–3			Repealed
4, 5			1 Oct 1997 (SI 1997/1468)
6			1 Sep 1997 (subject to transitional provisions) (SI 1997/1468)
7, para	1		1 Oct 1997 (SI 1997/1468)
	2	(1)	1 Oct 1997 (except so far as it provides that the definition of "public body" ceases to include SCAA) (SI 1997/1468)
			1 Mar 1998 (exception noted above) (SI 1998/386)
		(2)	1 Oct 1997 (SI 1997/1468)
	3	(1)	1 Oct 1997 (except so far as it omits entry relating to SCAA) (SI 1997/1468)
			1 Mar 1998 (exception noted above) (SI 1998/386)
		(2)	1 Mar 1998 (SI 1998/386)
	4	(1)	1 Oct 1997 (SI 1997/1468)
		(2)	1 Oct 1997 (except so far as it omits entry relating to SCAA) (SI 1997/1468)
			1 Mar 1998 (exception noted above) (SI 1998/386)
		(3), (4)	1 Oct 1997 (SI 1997/1468)
	5		Repealed
	6		1 Oct 1997 (subject to transitional provisions) (SI 1997/1468); repealed in relation to payments made on or after such date after 7 Apr 2000 as the treasury may appoint

Education Act 1997 (c 44)—*contd*

Schedule

7, para	7		1 Oct 1997 (subject to transitional provisions) (SI 1997/1468)
	8		1 Aug 1998 (SI 1998/386)
	9		1 Sep 1997 (SI 1997/1468)
	10		1 Sep 1998 (SI 1998/386)
	11–14		1 Aug 1998 (SI 1998/386)
	15–22		Repealed
	23, 24		1 Aug 1998 (SI 1998/386)
	25		Repealed
	26		1 Oct 1997 (so far as it repeals Education Act 1996, ss 360, 361) (SI 1997/1468)
			1 Mar 1998 (otherwise) (SI 1998/386)
	27–29		1 Oct 1997 (subject to transitional provisions) (SI 1997/1468)
	30	(a)	1 Oct 1997 (SI 1997/1468)
		(b)	1 Sep 2001 (SI 2001/1215)
	31–35		Repealed
	36		1 Aug 1998 (SI 1998/386)
	37		14 Jun 1997 (SI 1997/1468)
	38		1 Sep 1998 (SI 1998/386)
	39		14 Jun 1997 (SI 1997/1468)
	40		Repealed (*never in force*)
	41–43		14 Jun 1997 (SI 1997/1468)
	44		14 Jun 1997 (so far as it inserts reference to "school year" into Education Act 1996, s 580) (SI 1997/1468)
			1 Sep 1997 (otherwise) (SI 1997/1468)
	45–51		Repealed (para 49 partly *never in force*)
8			4 Apr 1997 (repeal in Education Act 1996, s 479(2)) (SI 1997/1153)
			14 Jun 1997 (repeals of or in Education Act 1996, ss 355(5), 571(2)) (SI 1997/1468)
			1 Sep 1997 (repeal of Education Act 1996, s 423(6)) (SI 1997/1468)
			1 Oct 1997 (repeals of or in Superannuation Act 1972 (to the extent that the provisions relate to the Curriculum and Assessment Authority for Wales); House of Commons Disqualification Act 1975 (to the extent that the provisions relate to the Curriculum and Assessment Authority for Wales); Education Act 1996, ss 360, 361, Schs 30, 37 (except in so far as Sch 37 relates to SCAA) (SI 1997/1468)

Education Act 1997 (c 44)—*contd*
Schedule

8—*contd*	1 Mar 1998 (repeals of or in Superannuation Act 1972 (to the extent that the provisions relate to SCAA); House of Commons Disqualification Act 1975 (to the extent that the provisions relate to NCVQ and SCAA); Education Act 1996, ss 358, 359, Schs 29, 37 (in so far as Sch 37 relates to SCAA)) (SI 1998/386)
	1 Aug 1998 (repeal in Education Act 1996, s 312(2)(c)) (SI 1998/386)
	1 Sep 1998 (repeals in Education Act 1996, ss 4(2), 19(1), (4), Sch 16, para 15(1)) (SI 1998/386)
	1 Sep 2001 (repeals of or in Education Act 1996, ss 400, 401, 408(4)(f)[1] (SI 2001/1215)

[1]   SI 2001/1215 purports to bring into force the repeal of words in s 408(4)(l). It is thought that this is a printing error as the words repealed are contained in s 408(4)(f) and there is no mention of s 408(4)(l) in Sch 8 to the 1997 Act.

Education (Schools) Act 1997 (c 59)

RA: 31 Jul 1997

Commencement provisions: s 7(3); Education (Schools) Act 1997 (Commencement) Order 1997, SI 1997/2774

Section		
1, 2		1 Sep 1997 (s 7(3)(a))
3, 4		31 Jul 1997 (RA)
5	(1)	31 Jul 1997 (RA)
	(2)	1 Dec 1997 (SI 1997/2774)
6	(1)	Repealed
	(2)	31 Jul 1997 (RA)
	(3)	See Schedule below
7		31 Jul 1997 (RA)
Schedule		
Pt	I	1 Sep 1997 (s 7(3)(a))
	II	1 Dec 1997 (SI 1997/2774)

Finance Act 1997 (c 16)

Budget Day: 26 Nov 1996

RA: 19 Mar 1997

Details of the commencement of Finance Acts are not set out in this work

Finance (No 2) Act 1997 (c 58)

Budget Day: 2 Jul 1997

RA: 31 Jul 1997

Details of the commencement of Finance Acts are not set out in this work

---

Firearms (Amendment) Act 1997 (c 5)

RA: 27 Feb 1997

Commencement provisions: s 53(3); Firearms (Amendment) Act 1997 (Commencement) (No 1) Order 1997, SI 1997/1076; Firearms (Amendment) Act 1997 (Commencement) (No 2) Order 1997, SI 1997/1535; Firearms (Amendment) Act 1997 (Commencement) (No 2) (Amendment) Order 1997, SI 1997/1536

Section		
1	(1)	1 Jul 1997 (SI 1997/1535)
	(2)	1 Jul 1997 (subject to a saving) (SI 1997/1536)
	(3)	1 Jul 1997 (subject to a saving) (SI 1997/1535)
	(4)–(8)	1 Jul 1997 (SI 1997/1535)
	(9)	Repealed
2–8		1 Jul 1997 (SI 1997/1535)
9		1 Jul 1997 (subject to a saving) (SI 1997/1536)
10		1 Jul 1997 (SI 1997/1535)
11–14		Repealed (*never in force*)
15		10 Jun 1997 (SI 1997/1535)
16–18		17 Mar 1997 (for purposes of making a compensation scheme) (SI 1997/1076)
		1 Jul 1997 (otherwise) (SI 1997/1535)
19–31		Repealed (*never in force*)
32–36		1 Oct 1997 (SI 1997/1535)
37, 38		1 Jul 1997 (SI 1997/1535)
39		1 Oct 1997 (SI 1997/1535)
40		1 Jul 1997 (SI 1997/1535)
41		1 Jul 1997 (subject to a saving) (SI 1997/1535)
42, 43		1 Jul 1997 (SI 1997/1535)
44, 45		1 Oct 1997 (SI 1997/1535)
46		Repealed (*never in force*)
47–50		1 Jul 1997 (SI 1997/1535)
51		10 Jun 1997 (SI 1997/1535)
52		See Sch 2, 3 below
53		27 Feb 1997 (RA)
Schedule		
1		Repealed (*never in force*)
2, para	1, 2	1 Jul 1997 (SI 1997/1535)
	3	1 Oct 1997 (SI 1997/1535)

Firearms (Amendment) Act 1997 (c 5)—*contd*
Schedule

2, para	4	1 Jul 1997 (SI 1997/1535)
	5, 6	1 Oct 1997 (SI 1997/1535)
	7, 8	1 Jul 1997 (SI 1997/1535)
	9	*Not in force*
	10–12	1 Jul 1997 (SI 1997/1535)
	13	Repealed (*never in force*)
	14–20	1 Jul 1997 (SI 1997/1535)
3		1 Jul 1997 (repeals of or in Firearms Act 1968, ss 5, 5A, 23, 28; Firearms (Amendment) Act 1988, ss 9, 10, 12; Firearms (Amendment) Act 1992) (SI 1997/1535)
		1 Oct 1997 (repeals of or in Firearms Act 1968, ss 42, 54, Sch 6; Firearms (Amendment) Act 1988, s 4) (SI 1997/1535)
		Not in force (otherwise)

Firearms (Amendment) (No 2) Act 1997 (c 64)

RA: 27 Nov 1997

Commencement provisions: s 3(3), (4); Firearms (Amendment) (No 2) Act 1997 (Commencement) Order 1997, SI 1997/3114
Section

1		1 Feb 1998 (subject to savings) (SI 1997/3114)
2	(1), (2)	17 Dec 1997 (SI 1997/3114)
	(3), (4)	17 Dec 1997 (for purposes of making a compensation scheme) (SI 1997/3114)
		1 Feb 1998 (otherwise, but subject to savings) (SI 1997/3114)
	(5), (6)	17 Dec 1997 (SI 1997/3114)
	(7)	See Schedule below
3		27 Nov 1997 (RA)
Schedule		17 Dec 1997 (repeals of or in Firearms Act 1968, s 32(2B); Firearms (Amendment) Act 1988; Firearms (Amendment) Act 1997, ss 11–14, 19–31, 45(2), 46, 49(2), 50(1), Sch 1, Sch 2, para 13) (SI 1997/3114)
		1 Feb 1998 (so far as not already in force) (subject to savings) (SI 1997/3114)

Flood Prevention and Land Drainage (Scotland) Act 1997 (c 36)

RA: 21 Mar 1997

Commencement provisions: s 9(2)–(4); Flood Prevention and Land Drainage (Scotland) Act 1997 (Commencement) Order 1997, SI 1997/1322

Section		
1		26 May 1997 (SI 1997/1322)
2		28 Jul 1997 (SI 1997/1322)
3–5		26 May 1997 (SI 1997/1322)
6	(1)	21 Mar 1997 (s 9(2))
	(2)	1 Apr 1999 (s 9(3))
7		21 Mar 1997 (s 9(2))
8		See Schedule below
9		21 Mar 1997 (s 9(2))
Schedule		1 Apr 1999 (repeals of or in Land Drainage (Scotland) Act 1930; Land Drainage (Scotland) Act 1941) (SI 1997/1322)
		26 May 1997 (otherwise) (SI 1997/1322)

Horserace Totalisator Board Act 1997 (c 1)

RA: 27 Feb 1997

27 Feb 1997 (RA)

Justices of the Peace Act 1997 (c 25)

RA: 19 Mar 1997

Commencement provisions: s 74(1)–(4)

19 Jun 1997 (s 74(1); but note sub-ss (2)–(4))

Knives Act 1997 (c 21)

RA: 19 Mar 1997

Commencement provisions: s 11(2), (3); Knives Act 1997 (Commencement) (No 1) Order 1997, SI 1997/1906; Knives Act 1997 (Commencement) (No 2) Order 1999, SI 1999/5

Section	
1–7	1 Sep 1997 (SI 1997/1906)
8	1 Mar 1999 (SI 1999/5)
9, 10	1 Sep 1997 (SI 1997/1906)
11	19 Mar 1997 (s 11(2))

Land Registration Act 1997 (c 2)

RA: 27 Feb 1997

Commencement provisions: s 5; Land Registration Act 1997 (Commencement) Order 1997, SI 1997/3036

Section	
1	1 Apr 1998 (SI 1997/3036)
2, 3	27 Apr 1997 (s 5(3))

Land Registration Act 1997 (c 2)—*contd*
Section

4	(1)	See Sch 1 below
	(2)	See Sch 2 below
5		27 Apr 1997 (s 5(3))

Schedule

1, Pt	I	1 Apr 1998 (in relation to dispositions made on or after 1 Apr 1998) (SI 1997/3036)
	II	27 Apr 1997 (s 5(3))
2, Pt	I	1 Apr 1998 (SI 1997/3036)
	II	27 Apr 1997 (s 5(3))

Law Officers Act 1997 (c 60)

RA: 31 Jul 1997

Commencement provisions: s 3(3)

30 Sep 1997 (s 3(3))

Lieutenancies Act 1997 (c 23)

RA: 19 Mar 1997

Commencement provisions: s 9(2)

1 Jul 1997 (s 9(2))

Local Government and Rating Act 1997 (c 29)

RA: 19 Mar 1997

Commencement provisions: s 34(1)–(3); Local Government and Rating Act 1997 (Commencement No 1) Order 1997, SI 1997/1097; Local Government and Rating Act 1997 (Commencement No 2) Order 1997, SI 1997/2752; Local Government and Rating Act 1997 (Commencement No 3) Order 1997, SI 1997/2826; Local Government and Rating Act 1997 (Commencement No 4) Order 1998, SI 1998/694; Local Government and Rating Act 1997 (Commencement No 5 and Transitional Provision) Order 1998, SI 1998/2329

Section

1	19 Nov 1997 (subject to a saving) (SI 1997/2752)
2	1 Apr 1997 (SI 1997/1097)
3	1 Apr 2000 (subject to a transitional provision) (SI 1998/2329)
4	1 Oct 1998 (SI 1998/2329)
5	See Sch 2 below
6	1 Apr 2000 (subject to a transitional provision) (SI 1998/2329)
7	1 Oct 1998 (SI 1998/2329)
8	1 Dec 1997 (subject to a transitional provision) (SI 1997/2826)

Local Government and Rating Act 1997 (c 29)—*contd*

Section

9–25			19 May 1997 (s 34(2))
26–31			19 May 1997 (SI 1997/1097)
32			19 Mar 1997 (s 34(3))
33	(1)		See Sch 3 below
	(2)		See Sch 4 below
34, 35			19 Mar 1997 (s 34(3))

Schedule

1			19 Nov 1997 (subject to a saving) (SI 1997/2752)
2			1 Dec 1997 (subject to a transitional provision) (SI 1997/2826)
3, para	1		19 May 1997 (SI 1997/1097)
	2		1 Apr 1997 (SI 1997/1097)
	3		1 Apr 2000 (subject to a transitional provision) (SI 1998/2329)
	4–10		19 May 1997 (s 34(2))
	11–16		19 May 1997 (SI 1997/1097)
	17		18 Mar 1998 (SI 1998/694)
	18–20		1 Apr 2000 (subject to a transitional provision) (SI 1998/2329)
	21		Repealed
	22		1 Apr 1997 (so far as relates to Local Government Finance Act 1988, s 47(7) only) (SI 1997/1097)
			1 Apr 2000 (otherwise) (subject to a transitional provision) (SI 1998/2329)
	23		1 Apr 1997 (SI 1997/1097)
	24–28		1 Apr 2000 (subject to a transitional provision) (SI 1998/2329)
	29	(a)	1 Apr 2000 (subject to a transitional provision) (SI 1998/2329)
		(b)	1 Dec 1997 (subject to a transitional provision) (SI 1997/2826)
4			19 May 1997 (except repeals of or in Valuation and Rating (Scotland) Act 1956, s 20; Local Government Act 1972, ss 9(2), (3), (5), 11(5), 12(1); National Heritage Act 1983, Sch 1, paras 2(5), 12(5), 22(3), 32(5), Sch 3, para 2(5); National Heritage (Scotland) Act 1985, s 20; Dockyard Services Act 1986, s 3(1); Local Government Finance Act 1988, ss 64(4)(d), (5)–(7D), 65(9), Sch 5, paras 10, 14(3); National Maritime Museum Act 1989, s 1(6); Local Government and Housing Act 1989, Sch 5, paras 33, 35(2)) (SI 1997/1097)

Local Government and Rating Act 1997 (c 29)—*contd*

Schedule

4—*contd*	18 Mar 1998 (repeals in Local Government Act 1972) (SI 1998/694)
	1 Apr 2000 (otherwise) (subject to a transitional provision) (SI 1998/2329)

Local Government (Contracts) Act 1997 (c 65)

RA: 27 Nov 1997

Commencement provisions: s 12(2); Local Government (Contracts) Act 1997 (Commencement No 1) Order 1997, SI 1997/2843; Local Government (Contracts) Act 1997 (Commencement No 2) Order 1997, SI 1997/2878

Section

1			27 Nov 1997 (RA)
2			30 Dec 1997 (E, W) (SI 1997/2843)
			1 Jan 1998 (S) (SI 1997/2878)
3	(1)		30 Dec 1997 (E, W) (SI 1997/2843)
			1 Jan 1998 (S) (SI 1997/2878)
	(2)	(a)–(d)	30 Dec 1997 (E, W) (SI 1997/2843)
			1 Jan 1998 (S) (SI 1997/2878)
		(e), (f)	1 Dec 1997 (so far as they confer power on the Secretary of State to make regulations) (E, W) (SI 1997/2843)
			2 Dec 1997 (so far as they confer power on the Secretary of State to make regulations) (S) (SI 1997/2878)
			30 Dec 1997 (otherwise) (E, W) (SI 1997/2843)
			1 Jan 1998 (otherwise) (S) (SI 1997/2878)
		(g)	30 Dec 1997 (E, W) (SI 1997/2843)
			1 Jan 1998 (S) (SI 1997/2878)
	(3)		1 Dec 1997 (so far as it confers power on the Secretary of State to make regulations) (E, W) (SI 1997/2843)
			2 Dec 1997 (so far as it confers power on the Secretary of State to make regulations) (S) (SI 1997/2878)
			30 Dec 1997 (otherwise) (E, W) (SI 1997/2843)
			1 Jan 1998 (otherwise) (S) (SI 1997/2878)
	(4)		30 Dec 1997 (E, W) (SI 1997/2843)
			1 Jan 1998 (S) (SI 1997/2878)
4–9			30 Dec 1997 (E, W) (SI 1997/2843)
			1 Jan 1998 (S) (SI 1997/2878)
10–12			27 Nov 1997 (RA)

Local Government Finance (Supplementary Credit Approvals) Act 1997 (c 63)

RA: 6 Nov 1997

6 Nov 1997 (RA)

Local Government (Gaelic Names) (Scotland) Act 1997 (c 6)

RA: 27 Feb 1997

Commencement provisions: s 2(2)

27 Apr 1997 (s 2(2))

Merchant Shipping and Maritime Security Act 1997 (c 28)

RA: 19 Mar 1997

Commencement provisions: s 31(3), (4); Merchant Shipping and Maritime Security
  Act 1997 (Commencement No 1) Order 1997, SI 1997/1082; Merchant
  Shipping and Maritime Security Act 1997 (Commencement No 2) Order 1997,
  SI 1997/1539

Section		
1		23 Mar 1997 (SI 1997/1082)
2–4		17 Jul 1997 (SI 1997/1539)
5		19 Mar 1997 (s 31(4))
6, 7		17 Jul 1997 (SI 1997/1539)
8		19 Mar 1997 (s 31(4))
9		See Sch 1 below
10		23 Mar 1997 (SI 1997/1082)
11, 12		19 Mar 1997 (s 31(4))
13		See Sch 2 below
14	(1)	17 Jul 1997 (SI 1997/1539)
	(2)	See Sch 3 below
15		17 Jul 1997 (SI 1997/1539)
16		19 Mar 1997 (s 31(4))
17–23		17 Jul 1997 (SI 1997/1539)
24		19 Mar 1997 (s 31(4))
25		See Sch 4 below
26	(1)	See Sch 5 below
	(2)–(6)	17 Jul 1997 (SI 1997/1539)
27		17 Jul 1997 (SI 1997/1539)
28		19 Mar 1997 (s 31(4))
29	(1)	See Sch 6 below
	(2)	See Sch 7 below
30, 31		19 Mar 1997 (s 31(4))
Schedule		
1, para	1–5	23 Mar 1997 (SI 1997/1082)
	6	*Not in force*
2		19 Mar 1997 (s 31(4))
3–5		17 Jul 1997 (SI 1997/1539)
6, para	1–15	17 Jul 1997 (SI 1997/1539)

Merchant Shipping and Maritime Security Act 1997 (c 28)—*contd*
Schedule

16			19 Mar 1997 (s 31(4))
17			17 Jul 1997 (SI 1997/1539)
18	(1)		23 Mar 1997 (SI 1997/1082)
	(2)		17 Jul 1997 (SI 1997/1539)
	(3)		23 Mar 1997 (SI 1997/1082)
	(4)		17 Jul 1997 (SI 1997/1539)
	(5)		23 Mar 1997 (SI 1997/1082)
19	(1)		23 Mar 1997 (SI 1997/1082)
	(2)	(a)	17 Jul 1997 (SI 1997/1539)
		(b), (c)	23 Mar 1997 (SI 1997/1082)
		(d)	17 Jul 1997 (SI 1997/1539)
	(3)		23 Mar 1997 (SI 1997/1082)
20			23 Mar 1997 (SI 1997/1082)
7, Pt	I		23 Mar 1997 (repeals of or in Merchant Shipping Act 1995, ss 85(3), 86(5), (6)) (SI 1997/1082) 17 Jul 1997 (otherwise) (SI 1997/1539)
	II		17 Jul 1997 (SI 1997/1539)

Ministerial and other Salaries Act 1997 (c 62)

RA: 6 Nov 1997

6 Nov 1997 (RA)

National Health Service (Primary Care) Act 1997 (c 46)

RA: 21 Mar 1997

Commencement provisions: s 41(2), (3); National Health Service (Primary Care) Act 1997 (Commencement No 1) Order 1997, SI 1997/1780; National Health Service (Primary Care) Act 1997 (Commencement No 2) Order 1997, SI 1997/2457; National Health Service (Primary Care) Act 1997 (Commencement No 3) Order 1997, SI 1997/2620; National Health Service (Primary Care) Act 1997 (Commencement No 4) Order 1998, SI 1998/631; National Health Service (Primary Care) Act 1997 (Commencement No 5) Order 1998, SI 1998/1998; National Health Service (Primary Care) Act 1997 (Commencement No 6) Order 1998, SI 1998/2840; National Health Service (Primary Care) Act 1997 (Commencement No 7) (Scotland) Order 2001, SSI 2001/58

Section

1, 2	28 Nov 1997 (SI 1997/2620)
3	14 Aug 1998 (SI 1998/1998)
4	22 Aug 1997 (so far as relates to pilot schemes under which personal medical services are provided) (SI 1997/1780) 30 Oct 1997 (otherwise) (SI 1997/2620)

National Health Service (Primary Care) Act 1997 (c 46)—*contd*
Section

5, 6			28 Nov 1997 (so far as they relate to pilot schemes under which personal medical services are provided) (SI 1997/2620)
			1 Apr 1998 (otherwise) (SI 1998/631)
7, 8			1 Apr 1998 (so far as they relate to pilot schemes under which personal medical services are provided) (SI 1998/631)
			1 Oct 1998 (otherwise) (SI 1998/1998)
8A			Inserted, partly prospectively, by Health Act 1999, s 6(1)[1]
8ZA			Inserted, partly prospectively, by Health and Social Care Act 2001, s 26(2)[2]
9	(1), (2)		15 Aug 1997 (SI 1997/1780)
	(3)		1 Apr 1998 (so far as it relates to pilot schemes under which personal medical services are provided) (SI 1998/631)
			1 Oct 1998 (otherwise) (SI 1998/1998)
10			15 Aug 1997 (SI 1997/1780)
11, 12			1 Apr 1998 (SI 1998/631)
13	(1)		15 Aug 1997 (SI 1997/1780)
	(2)		1 Apr 1998 (SI 1998/631)
	(3)–(8)		15 Aug 1997 (SI 1997/1780)
	(9)		1 Apr 1998 (SI 1998/631)
14			Repealed
15			1 Apr 1998 (SI 1998/631)
16			30 Oct 1997 (so far as relates to pilot schemes under which personal medical services are provided) (SI 1997/2620)
			11 May 1998 (otherwise) (SI 1998/631)
17			1 Oct 1998 (SI 1998/1998)
18	(1)		15 Aug 1997 (SI 1997/1780)
	(2)	(a)	15 Aug 1997 (SI 1997/1780)
		(b)	28 Nov 1997 (so far as relates to pilot schemes under which personal medical services are provided) (SI 1997/2620)
			1 Apr 1998 (otherwise) (SI 1998/631)
	(3)		15 Aug 1997 (SI 1997/1780)
19			Repealed
20			1 Oct 1998 (SI 1998/1998)
21	(1)		*Not in force*

National Health Service (Primary Care) Act 1997 (c 46)—*contd*
Section

21	(2), (3)		5 Mar 2001(S) (so far as relates to personal medical services) (SSI 2001/58)
			Not in force (otherwise)
22	(1)		*Not in force*
	(2)		5 Mar 2001(S) (so far as relates to personal medical services) (SSI 2001/58)
			Not in force (otherwise)
23			1 Apr 1998 (SI 1998/631)
24			1 Oct 1998 (SI 1998/1998)
25	(1)		*Not in force*
	(2)		5 Mar 2001(S) (so far as relates to personal medical services) (SSI 2001/58)
			Not in force (otherwise)
26			*Not in force*
27, 28			15 Aug 1997 (SI 1997/1780)
29			1 Apr 1998 (SI 1998/631)
30			15 Aug 1997 (SI 1997/1780)
31			1 Sep 1997 (SI 1997/1780)
32			10 Dec 1998 (SI 1998/2840)
33			*Not in force*
34, 35			1 Apr 1998 (SI 1998/631)
36			14 Oct 1997 (subject to a saving) (SI 1997/2457)
37			1 Apr 1998 (SI 1998/631)
38–40			21 Mar 1997 (s 41(2))
41	(1)–(9)		21 Mar 1997 (s 41(2))
	(10)		See Sch 2 below
	(11)		*Not in force*
	(12)		See Sch 3 below
	(13), (14)		21 Mar 1997 (s 41(2))
Schedule			
1			1 Apr 1998 (subject to transitional provisions relating to paras 1(2)(c), 2(2), (4)) (SI 1998/631)
2, Pt	I, para	1, 2	1 Apr 1998 (SI 1998/631)
		3	1 Apr 1998 (so far as it relates to any of paras 4–31 already in force or brought into force by SI 1998/631) (SI 1998/631)
			1 Oct 1998 (so far as it relates to any of paras 4–31 brought into force by SI 1998/1998) (SI 1998/1998)
			10 Dec 1998 (so far as it relates to paras 9–11, 28 brought into force by SI 1998/2840) (SI 1998/2840)
			Not in force (otherwise)

National Health Service (Primary Care) Act 1997 (c 46)—*contd*
Schedule

2, Pt	I, para	4	1 Apr 1998 (SI 1998/631)
		5	1 Apr 1998 (SI 1998/631)
		6–8	1 Apr 1998 (SI 1998/631)
		9, 10	10 Dec 1998 (subject to a saving) (SI 1998/2840)
		11	10 Dec 1998 (subject to a saving) (SI 1998/2840); prospectively repealed by Health and Social Care Act 2001, s 67, Sch 6, Pt 1[2]
		12	1 Oct 1998 (SI 1998/1998)
		13	15 Aug 1997 (SI 1997/1780); prospectively repealed by Health and Social Care Act 2001, s 67, Sch 6, Pt 2[2]
		14	15 Aug 1997 (SI 1997/1780)
		15–18	1 Oct 1998 (SI 1998/1998)
		19	*Not in force*
		20	15 Aug 1997 (SI 1997/1780)
		21	1 Apr 1998 (so far as it relates to pilot schemes under which personal medical services are provided) (SI 1998/631)
			1 Oct 1998 (otherwise) (SI 1998/1998)
		22, 23	1 Apr 1998 (subject to a saving) (SI 1998/631)
		24–26	1 Apr 1998 (SI 1998/631)
		27	15 Aug 1997 (SI 1997/1780)
		28	1 Apr 1998 (for the purpose of inserting the definition "section 28C arrangements") (SI 1998/631)
			10 Dec 1998 (for the purpose of inserting the definition "medical list") (SI 1998/2840)
			Not in force (otherwise)
		29	1 Apr 1998 (SI 1998/631); prospectively repealed by Health and Social Care Act 2001, s 67, Sch 6, Pt 1[2]
		30, 31	1 Apr 1998 (SI 1998/631)
		32	1 Apr 1998 (so far as it relates to any of paras 33–60 already in force or brought into force by SI 1998/631) (SI 1998/631)
			1 Oct 1998 (so far as it relates to any of paras 33–60 brought into force by SI 1998/1998) (SI 1998/1998)
			Not in force (otherwise)
		33	*Not in force*

National Health Service (Primary Care) Act 1997 (c 46)—*contd*
Schedule

2, Pt	I, para	34	5 Mar 2001 (S) (SSI 2001/58)
		35–39	1 Apr 1998 (SI 1998/631)
		40–42	*Not in force*
		43	1 Oct 1998 (SI 1998/1998)
		44, 45	15 Aug 1997 (SI 1997/1780)
		46	*Not in force*
		47–50	1 Oct 1998 (SI 1998/1998)
		51	15 Aug 1997 (SI 1997/1780)
		52	1 Oct 1998 (SI 1998/1998)
		53, 54	1 Apr 1998 (SI 1998/631); prospectively repealed by Health Act 1999, s 65(2), Sch 5[1]
		55	*Not in force*; prospectively repealed by Health Act 1999, s 65(2), Sch 5[1]
		56	5 Mar 2001(S) (SSI 2001/58)
		57	1 Apr 1998 (for the purpose of inserting the definition "section 17C arrangements") (SI 1998/631) 5 Mar 2001 (S) (for purpose of inserting the definition "personal medical services") (SSI 2001/58) *Not in force* (otherwise)
		58–61	1 Apr 1998 (SI 1998/631)
		62	18 Nov 1998 (subject to a saving) (SI 1998/2840)
		63	1 Apr 1998 (SI 1998/631)
		64	(1)	1 Apr 1998 (so far as it relates to paras 64(2), (4)) (SI 1998/631) *Not in force* (otherwise)
			(2)	1 Apr 1998 (SI 1998/631)
			(3)	*Not in force*
			(4)	1 Apr 1998 (SI 1998/631)
		65	(1)	1 Apr 1998 (SI 1998/631)
			(2)	*Not in force*
			(3)–(7)	Repealed (*never in force*)
			(8)–(10)	1 Apr 1998 (SI 1998/631); prospectively repealed by Health Act 1999, s 65(2), Sch 5[1]
			(11)	1 Apr 1998 (SI 1998/631)
		66–68	1 Apr 1998 (SI 1998/631)
	II, para	69	*Not in force*; prospectively repealed by Health Act 1999, s 65(2), Sch 5[1]
		70–75	*Not in force*
		76	*Not in force*; prospectively repealed by Health and Social Care Act 2001, s 67, Sch 6, Pt 2[2]
		77, 78	*Not in force*; prospectively repealed by Health Act 1999, s 65(2), Sch 5[1]
		79–81	*Not in force*

National Health Service (Primary Care) Act 1997 (c 46)—*contd*
Schedule

3, Pt	I	1 Apr 1998 (repeals of or in National Health Service Act 1977, ss 29(2), 97A(9)(c)(i) (subject to a saving), Sch 10, National Health Service (Scotland) Act 1978, s 19(2), Sch 9, National Health Service and Community Care Act 1990, s 12(1)(c), Health Authorities Act 1995, Sch 1, paras 6(c), 36) (SI 1998/631)
		1 Oct 1998 (repeals of or in National Health Service Act 1977, s 36(1)(c), National Health Service (Scotland) Act 1978, s 25(2)(c)) (SI 1998/1998)
		10 Dec 1998 (repeals in National Health Service Act 1977 (so far as not already in force), Health Services Act 1980, Health and Social Security Act 1984, Health and Medicines Act 1988, National Health Service and Community Care Act 1990 (so far as not already in force), Health Authorities Act 1995 (so far as not already in force)) (subject to a saving) (SI 1998/2840)
		Not in force (otherwise)
	II	*Not in force*
	III	10 Dec 1998 (SI 1998/2840)

1   Orders made under Health Act 1999, s 67(1), bringing the prospective insertion and repeals into force are noted to that Act

2   Orders made under Health and Social Care Act 2001, s 70(2), bringing the prospective insertion and repeals into force are noted to that Act

---

National Health Service (Private Finance) Act 1997 (c 56)

RA: 15 Jul 1997

15 Jul 1997 (RA)

National Heritage Act 1997 (c 14)

RA: 27 Feb 1997

Commencement provisions: s 4(2); National Heritage Act 1997 (Commencement) Order 1998, SI 1998/292

Section	
1–3	4 Mar 1998 (SI 1998/292)
4	27 Feb 1997 (RA)
Schedule	4 Mar 1998 (SI 1998/292)

Northern Ireland Arms Decommissioning Act 1997 (c 7)

RA: 27 Feb 1997

Commencement provisions: s 7(6); Northern Ireland Arms Decommissioning Act 1997
(Commencement of Section 7) Order 1997, SI 1997/2111

Section
1–6	27 Feb 1997 (RA)
7	1 Sep 1997 (SI 1997/2111)
8–11	27 Feb 1997 (RA)
Schedule	27 Feb 1997 (RA)

Nurses, Midwives and Health Visitors Act 1997 (c 24)

RA: 19 Mar 1997

Commencement provisions: s 24(2)

19 Jun 1997 (s 24(2)). *Whole Act prospectively repealed* by the Health Act 1999,
ss 60(3), 65, Sch 5; orders made under the 1999 Act, s 67(1) bringing the
prospective repeal into force will be noted to that Act

Pensions Measure 1997 (No 1)

RA: 21 Mar 1997

Commencement provisions: s 11(2)

The provisions of this Measure were brought into force on 1 Jan 1998 by an
instrument made by the Archbishops of Canterbury and York dated 28 Nov 1997
(made under s 11(2))

Pharmacists (Fitness to Practise) Act 1997 (c 19)

RA: 19 Mar 1997

Commencement provisions: s 2(1), (2)
Section
1	*Not in force*
2, 3	19 Mar 1997 (RA)
Schedule	*Not in force*

Planning (Consequential Provisions) (Scotland) Act 1997 (c 11)

RA: 27 Feb 1997

Commencement provisions: s 6
Section
1, 2		27 May 1997 (s 6(2))
3	(1)	See Sch 1 below
	(2), (3)	27 May 1997 (s 6(2))
4		See Sch 2 below
5	(1)	See Sch 3 below
	(2)	27 May 1997 (s 6(2))
6		27 May 1997 (s 6(2))

Planning (Consequential Provisions) (Scotland) Act 1997 (c 11)—*contd*

Schedule

1, Pt	I	27 May 1997 (except repeal relating to Town and Country Planning (Scotland) Act 1997, s 186) (s 6(2)) *Not in force* (exception noted above)
	II, III	27 May 1997 (s 6(2))
2, 3		27 May 1997 (s 6(2))

Planning (Hazardous Substances) (Scotland) Act 1997 (c 10)

RA: 27 Feb 1997

Commencement provisions: s 40(2)

27 May 1997 (s 40(2))

Planning (Listed Buildings and Conservation Areas) (Scotland) Act 1997 (c 9)

RA: 27 Feb 1997

Commencement provisions: s 83(2)

27 May 1997 (s 83(2))

Plant Varieties Act 1997 (c 66)

RA: 27 Nov 1997

Commencement provisions: s 54(2)–(4); Plant Varieties Act 1997 (Commencement) Order 1998, SI 1998/1028

Section	
1–32	8 May 1998 (SI 1998/1028)
33	Repealed
34–48	8 May 1998 (SI 1998/1028)
49	27 Nov 1997 (s 54(2))
50–52	8 May 1998 (SI 1998/1028)
53, 54	27 Nov 1997 (s 54(2))
Schedule	
1–4	8 May 1998 (SI 1998/1028)

Police Act 1997 (c 50)

RA: 21 Mar 1997

Commencement provisions: s 135; Police Act 1997 (Commencement No 1 and Transitional Provisions) Order 1997, SI 1997/1377; Police Act 1997 (Commencement No 2) Order 1997, SI 1997/1696; Police Act 1997 (Commencement No 3 and Transitional Provisions) Order 1997, SI 1997/1930; Police Act 1997 (Commencement No 4 and Transitional Provisions) Order 1997, SI 1997/2390, as amended by SI 1998/354; Police Act 1997 (Commencement No 5 and Transitional Provisions) Order 1998, SI 1998/354; Police Act 1997 (Commencement No 6) Order 1999, SI 1999/151; Police Act 1997 (Commencement No 7) Order 2001, SI 2001/1097; Police Act 1997 (Commencement No 8) (Scotland) Order 2001, SSI 2001/482; Police Act 1997 (Commencement No 9) Order 2002, SI 2002/413

Police Act 1997 (c 50)—*contd*

Section

1	(1)–(6)		25 Jun 1997 (for purposes of the appointment of members of the Service Authority for the National Criminal Intelligence Service) (SI 1997/1377)
			23 Jul 1997 (otherwise) (SI 1997/1377)
	(7)		See Schs 1, 2 below
2	(1)–(3)		1 Apr 1998 (SI 1998/354)
	(3A), (3B)		Inserted by Football (Disorder) Act 2000, s 2
	(4), (5)		1 Apr 1998 (SI 1998/354)
	(6)		1 Sep 1997 (so far as relates to any directions given under s 27) (SI 1997/1930)
			8 Oct 1997 (so far as relates to any directions given under Sch 3 below) (SI 1997/1930)
			1 Apr 1998 (otherwise) (SI 1998/354)
3	(1)		1 Apr 1998 (SI 1998/354)
	(2), (3)		1 Sep 1997 (SI 1997/1930)
	(4)	(a)	1 Sep 1997 (subject to a transitional provision) (SI 1997/1930)
		(b)–(d)	1 Sep 1997 (SI 1997/1930)
		(e)	Inserted by Criminal Justice and Police Act 2001, s 128, Sch 6, para 4(b)
4			31 Oct 1997 (subject to a transitional provision) (SI 1997/2390)
5			1 Apr 1998 (SI 1998/354)
6			23 Jul 1997 (SI 1997/1377)
7			Repealed
8, 9			31 Oct 1997 (subject to transitional provisions) (SI 1997/2390)
9A			Inserted by Criminal Justice and Police Act 2001, s 117
10–12			1 Apr 1998 (SI 1998/354)
13–16			23 Jul 1997 (SI 1997/1377)
16A			Inserted by Criminal Justice and Police Act 2001, s 110
17, 17A			Substituted for original s 17 by Criminal Justice and Police Act 2001, s 111
18			Repealed
18A			Inserted (1 Jul 1999) by Scotland Act 1998 (Cross-Border Public Authorities) (Adaptation of Functions etc) Order 1999, SI 1999/1747, arts 3, 4, Sch 18, paras 1, 2(1), (10)
19			31 Oct 1997 (SI 1997/2390)

Police Act 1997 (c 50)—*contd*

Section

20			1 Apr 1998 (SI 1998/354)
21			31 Oct 1997 (SI 1997/2390)
21A			Inserted by Criminal Justice and Police Act 2001, s 112
22	(1)–(3)		1 Apr 1998 (SI 1998/354)
	(4)–(8)		31 Oct 1997 (subject to a transitional provision) (SI 1997/2390)
	(9)		Added (1 Jul 1999) by Scotland Act 1998 (Consequential Modifications) (No 2) Order 1999, SI 1999/1820, art 4, Sch 2, Pt I, para 131(1), (2)
23, 24			1 Apr 1998 (SI 1998/354)
25			Substituted (1 Jul 1999) by Scotland Act 1998 (Cross–Border Public Authorities) (Adaptation of Functions etc) Order 1999, SI 1999/1747, arts 3, 4, Sch 18, paras 1, 2(1), (11)
26	(1)		1 Sep 1997 (SI 1997/1930)
	(2)	(a)	1 Sep 1997 (SI 1997/1930)
		(b)	1 Sep 1997 (subject to a transitional provision) (SI 1997/1930)
		(c)–(e)	1 Sep 1997 (SI 1997/1930)
		(f)	1 Sep 1997 (subject to a transitional provision) (SI 1997/1930)
		(g)	1 Sep 1997 (SI 1997/1930)
		(h)	Added (1 Jul 1999) by Scotland Act 1998 (Cross–Border Public Authorities) (Adaptation of Functions etc) Order 1999, SI 1999/1747, arts 3, 4, Sch 18, paras 1, 2(1), (12)
27			1 Sep 1997 (SI 1997/1930)
28			31 Oct 1997 (SI 1997/2390)
29–36			1 Apr 1998 (SI 1998/354)
37			31 Oct 1997 (SI 1997/2390)
38			31 Oct 1997 (for purpose of making orders) (SI 1997/2390)
			1 Apr 1998 (otherwise) (SI 1998/354)
39			31 Oct 1997 (SI 1997/2390)
40–43			1 Apr 1998 (SI 1998/354)
44			Repealed
45, 46			25 Jun 1997 (SI 1997/1377)
47	(1)–(6)		25 Jun 1997 (for purposes of the appointment of members of the Service Authority for the National Crime Squad) (SI 1997/1377)
			23 Jul 1997 (otherwise) (SI 1997/1377)

Police Act 1997 (c 50)—*contd*

Section

47	(7)		See Schs 1, 2 below
48	(1)–(6)		1 Apr 1998 (SI 1998/354)
	(7)		1 Sep 1997 (so far as relates to any directions given under s 72) (SI 1997/1930)
			8 Oct 1997 (so far as relates to any directions given under Sch 5) (SI 1997/1930)
			1 Apr 1998 (otherwise) (SI 1998/354)
49	(1)		1 Apr 1998 (SI 1998/354)
	(2), (3)		1 Sep 1997 (SI 1997/1930)
	(4)	(a)	1 Sep 1997 (subject to a transitional provision) (SI 1997/1930)
		(ba)	Inserted by Criminal Justice and Police Act 2001, s 128, Sch 6, para 13(b)
		(b), (c)	1 Sep 1997 (SI 1997/1930)
50			31 Oct 1997 (subject to a transitional provision) (SI 1997/2390)
51			1 Apr 1998 (SI 1998/354)
52			23 Jul 1997 (SI 1997/1377)
53			Repealed
54, 55			31 Oct 1997 (subject to transitional provisions) (SI 1997/2390)
55A			Inserted by Criminal Justice and Police Act 2001, s 120
56, 57			1 Apr 1998 (SI 1998/354)
58–61			23 Jul 1997 (SI 1997/1377)
61A			Inserted by Criminal Justice and Police Act 2001, s 113
62, 62A			Substituted for original s 62 by Criminal Justice and Police Act 2001, s 114
63			Repealed
64			31 Oct 1997 (SI 1997/2390)
65			1 Apr 1998 (SI 1998/354)
66			31 Oct 1997 (SI 1997/2390)
66A			Inserted by Criminal Justice and Police Act 2001, s 115
67, 68			Repealed
69			1 Apr 1998 (SI 1998/354)
70			1 Sep 1997 (SI 1997/1930)
71	(1)		1 Sep 1997 (SI 1997/1930)
	(2)	(a)	1 Sep 1997 (SI 1997/1930)
		(b)	1 Sep 1997 (subject to a transitional provision) (SI 1997/1930)
		(c)–(e)	1 Sep 1997 (SI 1997/1930)
		(f)	1 Sep 1997 (subject to a transitional provision) (SI 1997/1930)

Police Act 1997 (c 50)—*contd*

Section

71	(2)	(g)	Inserted by Criminal Justice and Police Act 2001, s 128, Sch 6, para 18(b)
	(3)		1 Sep 1997 (SI 1997/1930)
72			1 Sep 1997 (SI 1997/1930)
73			31 Oct 1997 (SI 1997/2390)
74–80			1 Apr 1998 (SI 1998/354)
81			31 Oct 1997 (SI 1997/2390)
82			31 Oct 1997 (for purpose of making orders) (SI 1997/2390)
			1 Apr 1998 (otherwise) (SI 1998/354)
83			31 Oct 1997 (SI 1997/2390)
84–87			1 Apr 1998 (SI 1998/354)
88			See Sch 6 below
89, 90			25 Jun 1997 (SI 1997/1377)
91	(1)–(5)		1 Sep 1997 (SI 1997/1930)
	(6)		Substituted (1 Jul 1999) by Scotland Act 1998 (Cross-Border Public Authorities) (Adaptation of Functions etc) Order 1999, SI 1999/1747, arts 3, 5, Sch 6, paras 1, 2(1), (2)(b)
	(7), (8)		1 Sep 1997 (SI 1997/1930)
	(8A)		Inserted (1 Jul 1999) by Scotland Act 1998 (Cross-Border Public Authorities) (Adaptation of Functions etc) Order 1999, SI 1999/1747, arts 3, 5, Sch 6, paras 1, 2(1), (2)(d)
	(9)		1 Sep 1997 (SI 1997/1930)
	(9A)		Inserted (1 Jul 1999) by Scotland Act 1998 (Cross-Border Public Authorities) (Adaptation of Functions etc) Order 1999, SI 1999/1747, arts 3, 5, Sch 6, paras 1, 2(1), (2)(g)
	(10)		22 Feb 1999 (SI 1999/151)
92–95			22 Feb 1999 (SI 1999/151)
96			1 Sep 1997 (for purpose of making orders) (SI 1997/1930)
			22 Feb 1999 (otherwise) (SI 1999/151)
97–100			22 Feb 1999 (SI 1999/151)
101, 102			Repealed
103–105			22 Feb 1999 (SI 1999/151)
106			Repealed
107–108			22 Feb 1999 (SI 1999/151)
109	(1)		1 Sep 1997 (SI 1997/1930)
	(2)		See Sch 8 below

Police Act 1997 (c 50)—*contd*

Section

109	(3)		1 Sep 1997 (for purpose of making orders) (SI 1997/1930)
			1 Apr 1998 (otherwise) (SI 1998/354)
	(3A)		Inserted (1 Jul 1999) by Scotland Act 1998 (Cross-Border Public Authorities) (Adaptation of Functions, etc) Order 1999, SI 1999/1747, arts 3, 4, Sch 20, paras 1, 2(1), (2)
	(4)		1 Apr 1998 (SI 1998/354)
	(5)		1 Sep 1997 (for purpose of making orders) (SI 1997/1930)
			1 Apr 1998 (otherwise) (SI 1998/354)
	(6)		1 Apr 1998 (SI 1998/354)
110			1 Apr 1998 (SI 1998/354)
111	(1)	(a), (b)	1 Sep 1997 (SI 1997/1930)
		(c), (d)	1 Apr 1998 (SI 1998/354)
	(2)	(a)–(c)	1 Sep 1997 (SI 1997/1930)
		(d), (e)	1 Apr 1998 (SI 1998/354)
	(3)	(a), (b)	1 Sep 1997 (SI 1997/1930)
		(c), (d)	1 Apr 1998 (SI 1998/354)
112			*Not in force*
113–119			1 Mar 2002 (SI 2002/413)
120	(1), (2)		1 May 2001 (E, W) (SI 2001/1097)
			1 Feb 2002 (S) (SSI 2001/482)
	(3)		19 Mar 2001 (E, W) (SI 2001/1097)
			1 Jan 2002 (S) (SSI 2001/482)
	(4)–(7)		1 May 2001 (E, W) (SI 2001/1097)
			1 Feb 2002 (S) (SSI 2001/482)
120A			Inserted by Criminal Justice and Police Act 2001, s 134(1)
121			1 Mar 2002 (SI 2002/413)
122	(1), (2)		19 Mar 2001 (E, W) (SI 2001/1097)
			1 Jan 2002 (S) (SSI 2001/482)
	(3)		1 Mar 2002 (SI 2002/413)
123, 124			1 Mar 2002 (SI 2002/413)
125			19 Mar 2001 (E, W) (SI 2001/1097)
			1 Jan 2002 (S) (SSI 2001/482)
126, 127			1 Mar 2002 (SI 2002/413)
128			25 Jun 1997 (SI 1997/1377)
129	(a)		*Not in force*
	(b)–(d)		25 Jun 1997 (SI 1997/1377)
			Not in force (exception noted above)
130–132			Repealed
133			*Not in force*
133A			Inserted by Regulation of Investigatory Powers Act 2000, s 82(1), Sch 4, para 8(13)
134	(1)		See Sch 9 below

Police Act 1997 (c 50)—*contd*

Section

134	(2)			See Sch 10 below
135–138				21 Mar 1997 (RA)

Schedule

1				25 Jun 1997 (for purposes of the appointment of members of the Service Authority for the National Criminal Intelligence Service and members of the Service Authority for the National Crime Squad) (SI 1997/1377)
				23 Jul 1997 (otherwise) (SI 1997/1377)
2				25 Jun 1997 (for purposes of the appointment of members of the Service Authority for the National Criminal Intelligence Service and members of the Service Authority for the National Crime Squad) (SI 1997/1377)
				23 Jul 1997 (otherwise) (SI 1997/1377)
2A				Inserted (in part prospectively) by Criminal Justice and Police Act 2001, s 128, Sch 6, Pt 1, para 21
3–5				Repealed
6, paras	1–4			Repealed
	5			1 Sep 1997 (SI 1997/1930)
	6			31 Oct 1997 (subject to a transitional provision) (SI 1997/2390)
	7			1 Apr 1998 (SI 1998/354)
	8–13			Repealed
	14			Repealed (*never in force*)
	15–24			Repealed
	25, 26			Repealed (*never in force*)
	27, 28			Repealed
	29			31 Oct 1997 (subject to a transitional provision) (SI 1997/2390)
	30–32			Repealed
7				Repealed
8, para	1	(1)		1 Sep 1997 (SI 1997/1930)
		(2)		1 Sep 1997 (subject to a modification) (SI 1997/1930)
		(2A)		Inserted (1 Jul 1999) by Scotland Act 1998 (Cross-Border Public Authorities) (Adaptation of Functions etc) Order 1999, SI 1999/1747, arts 3, 4, Sch 20, paras 1, 2(1), (4)(b)
		(3)	(a)–(d)	1 Sep 1997 (SI 1997/1930)
			(e), (f)	*Not in force*

Police Act 1997 (c 50)—*contd*
Schedule

8, para	1	(3)	(g)	Substituted (1 Jul 1999) by Scotland Act 1998 (Cross–Border Public Authorities) (Adaptation of Functions etc) Order 1999, SI 1999/1747, arts 3, 4, Sch 20, paras 1, 2(1), (4)(c)
	2	(1)–(4)		1 Sep 1997 (SI 1997/1930)
		(4A), (4B)		Inserted (1 Jul 1999) by Scotland Act 1998 (Cross–Border Public Authorities) (Adaptation of Functions etc) Order 1999, SI 1999/1747, arts 3, 4, Sch 20, paras 1, 2(1), (5)(b)
		(5)		1 Sep 1997 (SI 1997/1930)
		(5A)[1]		Inserted (1 Jul 1999) by Scotland Act 1998 (Cross–Border Public Authorities) (Adaptation of Functions etc) Order 1999, SI 1999/1747, arts 3, 4, Sch 20, paras 1, 2(1), (5)(d)
		(6)		*Not in force*
	3			1 Apr 1998 (SI 1998/354)
	4			1 Sep 1997 (SI 1997/1930)
	5–7			1 Apr 1998 (SI 1998/354)
	8	(1)		1 Sep 1997 (SI 1997/1930)
		(2)		1 Apr 1998 (SI 1998/354)
	9			1 Sep 1997 (SI 1997/1930)
	10			1 Sep 1997 (except the reference to para 1(3)(e) in sub-para (1)(a) and the reference to para 1(3)(f) in sub-para (1)(b)) (SI 1997/1930)
				Not in force (exceptions noted above)
	11			1 Sep 1997 (SI 1997/1930)
	12, 13			1 Apr 1998 (SI 1998/354)
	13A			Inserted (1 Jul 1999) by Scotland Act 1998 (Cross–Border Public Authorities) (Adaptation of Functions etc) Order 1999, SI 1999/1747, arts 3, 4, Sch 20, paras 1, 2(1), (8)
	14–17			1 Apr 1998 (SI 1998/354)
	18			1 Sep 1997 (SI 1997/1930)
9, para	1, 2			1 Apr 1998 (SI 1998/354)
	3			1 Sep 1997 (SI 1997/1930)
	4–7			1 Apr 1998 (SI 1998/354)
	8, 9			1 Sep 1997 (SI 1997/1930)
	10–12			1 Apr 1998 (SI 1998/354)
	13, 14			31 Oct 1997 (SI 1997/2390)

Police Act 1997 (c 50)—*contd*
Schedule

9, para	15–18		1 Apr 1998 (SI 1998/354)
	19		Repealed
	20		1 Apr 1998 (SI 1998/354)
	21–23		Repealed
	24		1 Apr 1998 (SI 1998/354)
	25		Repealed
	26		1 Apr 1998 (SI 1998/354)
	27		23 Jul 1997 (so far as relates to members of the service authorities for the National Crime Intelligence Service and the National Crime Squad) (SI 1997/1377) 1 Apr 1998 (otherwise) (SI 1998/354)
	28		23 Jul 1997 (SI 1997/1377)
	29	(1), (2)	1 Apr 1998 (SI 1998/354)
		(3)	1 Sep 1997 (SI 1997/1930)
	30, 31		1 Apr 1998 (SI 1998/354)
	32		1 Apr 1998 (SI 1998/354); prospectively repealed by Police (Northern Ireland) Act 2000, s 78(4), Sch 8
	33, 34		1 Apr 1998 (SI 1998/354)
	35, 36		Repealed
	37		1 Apr 1998 (SI 1998/354); prospectively repealed by Police (Northern Ireland) Act 2000, s 78(4), Sch 8
	38, 39		Repealed
	40		23 Jul 1997 (SI 1997/1377)
	41		23 Jul 1997 (so far as relates to members of the service authorities for the National Crime Intelligence Service and the National Crime Squad) (SI 1997/1377) 1 Apr 1998 (otherwise) (SI 1998/354)
	42, 43		Repealed
	44		1 Apr 1998 (SI 1998/354)
	45		Repealed
	46–48		1 Apr 1998 (SI 1998/354)
	49		Repealed
	50		31 Oct 1997 (SI 1997/2390)
	51–53		Repealed
	54		1 Apr 1998 (SI 1998/354)
	55		Repealed
	56		1 Apr 1998 (SI 1998/354)

Police Act 1997 (c 50)—*contd*
Schedule

9, para	57	31 Oct 1997 (SI 1997/2390)
	58–62	1 Apr 1998 (SI 1998/354)
	63	Repealed
	64	1 Apr 1998 (SI 1998/354)
	65	1 Mar 2002 (SI 2002/413)
	66	31 Oct 1997 (SI 1997/2390)
	67, 68	Repealed
	69–71	1 Apr 1998 (SI 1998/354)
	72, 73	31 Oct 1997 (SI 1997/2390)
	74–80	1 Apr 1998 (SI 1998/354)
	81	31 Oct 1997 (SI 1997/2390)
	82, 83	1 Sep 1997 (SI 1997/1930)
	84, 85	1 Apr 1998 (SI 1998/354)
	86	31 Oct 1997 (SI 1997/2390)
	87	1 Apr 1998 (SI 1998/354)
	88	23 Jul 1997 (SI 1997/1377)
	89, 90	1 Apr 1998 (SI 1998/354)
	91	31 Oct 1997 (SI 1997/2390)
	92	1 Apr 1998 (SI 1998/354)
10		1 Apr 1998 (repeals in Police (Scotland) Act 1967; Leasehold Reform Act 1967; Local Government Act 1972; Police Pensions Act 1976; Local Government (Miscellaneous Provisions) Act 1976; Security Service Act 1989; Aviation and Maritime Security Act 1990; Environment Act 1995; Police Act 1996; Security Service Act 1996) (SI 1998/354)
		1 Mar 2002 (repeal in Road Traffic Act 1991) (SI 2002/413)
		Not in force (otherwise)

[1]   SI 1999/1747 refers to this insertion as sub-para (5) but it is assumed that it should refer to it as sub-para (5A) as noted

[2]   Orders made under Local Government Act 2000, s 108, bringing the prospective repeal into force will be noted to that Act

Police and Firemen's Pensions Act 1997 (c 52)

RA: 21 Mar 1997

Commencement provisions: s 4
Section

1	21 Mar 1997 (RA)
2, 3	21 May 1997 (s 4(2))
4	21 Mar 1997 (RA)

Police (Health and Safety) Act 1997 (c 42)

RA: 21 Mar 1997

Commencement provisions: s 9(2); Police (Health and Safety) Act 1997 (Commencement) Order 1998, SI 1998/1542

Section
1–6	1 Jul 1998 (SI 1998/1542)
7–9	21 Mar 1997 (s 9(2))

Police (Insurance of Voluntary Assistants) Act 1997 (c 45)

RA: 21 Mar 1997

21 Mar 1997 (RA)

Police (Property) Act 1997 (c 30)

RA: 19 Mar 1997

Commencement provisions: s 7(2)

19 May 1997 (s 7(2)). *Whole Act repealed*, in relation to Northern Ireland

Policyholders Protection Act 1997 (c 18)

Whole Act repealed

Prisons (Alcohol Testing) Act 1997 (c 38)

RA: 21 Mar 1997

Commencement provisions: s 3(2)

21 May 1997 (s 3(2))

Protection from Harassment Act 1997 (c 40)

RA: 21 Mar 1997

Commencement provisions: s 15(1)–(3); Protection from Harassment Act 1997 (Commencement) (No 1) Order 1997, SI 1997/1418; Protection from Harassment Act 1997 (Commencement) (No 2) Order 1997, SI 1997/1498; Protection from Harassment Act 1997 (Commencement No 3) Order 1998, SI 1998/1902

Section
1, 2		16 Jun 1997 (SI 1997/1418)
3	(1), (2)	16 Jun 1997 (SI 1997/1498)
	(3)–(9)	1 Sep 1998 (SI 1998/1902)
4, 5		16 Jun 1997 (SI 1997/1418)
6		16 Jun 1997 (SI 1997/1498)
7–12		16 Jun 1997 (SI 1997/1418)
13–16		21 Mar 1997 (RA)

Public Entertainments Licences (Drug Misuse) Act 1997 (c 49)

RA: 21 Mar 1997

Commencement provisions: s 4(2); Public Entertainments Licences (Drug Misuse) Act 1997
(Commencement and Transitional Provisions) Order 1998, SI 1998/1009

Section

1–3	1 May 1998 (subject to a transitional provision relating to ss 1(5), 2(5)) (SI 1998/1009)
4	21 Mar 1997 (RA)

Referendums (Scotland and Wales) Act 1997 (c 61)

RA: 31 Jul 1997

31 Jul 1997 (RA)

Road Traffic Reduction Act 1997 (c 54)

RA: 21 Mar 1997

Commencement provisions: s 4(3); Road Traffic Reduction Act 1997 (Commencement)
(Scotland) Order 2000, SI 2000/101; Road Traffic Reduction Act 1997
(Commencement) (England and Wales) Order 2000, SI 2000/735

10 Mar 2000 (E, W) (SI 2000/735)

21 Apr 2000 (S) (SI 2000/101)

Scottish Legal Services Ombudsman and Commissioner for Local Administration in Scotland Act 1997 (c 35)

RA: 21 Mar 1997

Commencement provisions: s 11; Scottish Legal Services Ombudsman and
Commissioner for Local Administration in Scotland Act 1997 (Commencement)
Order 1998, SI 1998/252

Section

1–7		21 May 1997 (s 11(2))
8	(1)	21 May 1997 (s 11(2))
	(2)	21 May 1997 (repeal of Local Government (Scotland) Act 1975, s 23(1)(ee)) (s 11(2)) 1 Apr 1998 (otherwise) (SI 1998/252)
	(3)	1 Apr 1998 (SI 1998/252)
	(4)–(6)	21 May 1997 (s 11(2))
9		21 May 1997 (s 11(2))
10		See Schedule below
11		21 Mar 1997 (RA)

Scottish Legal Services Ombudsman and Commissioner for Local Administration in Scotland Act 1997 (c 35)—*contd*

Schedule   21 May 1997 (repeals of or in Local
                                        Government (Scotland) Act 1975,
                                        ss 23(1)(ee), 29A(3), 32(2A); Local
                                        Government and Housing Act 1989,
                                        s 27(2); Law Reform (Miscellaneous
                                        Provisions) (Scotland) Act 1990,
                                        ss 33(3), (4), 34(2), (3), Sch 1,
                                        paras 1, 7, 8; Local Government etc
                                        (Scotland) Act 1994, Sch 13,
                                        para 100(6)(a)) (s 11(2))
                                        1 Apr 1998 (otherwise) (SI 1998/252)

Sea Fisheries (Shellfish) (Amendment) Act 1997 (c 3)

RA: 27 Feb 1997

27 Feb 1997 (RA)

Sex Offenders Act 1997 (c 51)

RA: 21 Mar 1997

Commencement provisions: s 10(2); Sex Offenders Act 1997 (Commencement) Order 1997, SI 1997/1920

1 Sep 1997 (SI 1997/1920)

Sexual Offences (Protected Material) Act 1997 (c 39)

RA: 21 Mar 1997

Commencement provisions: s 11(2)

Not in force

Social Security Administration (Fraud) Act 1997 (c 47)

RA: 21 Mar 1997

Commencement provisions: s 25(1), (2); Social Security Administration (Fraud) Act 1997 (Commencement No 1) Order 1997, SI 1997/1577; Social Security Administration (Fraud) Act 1997 (Commencement No 2) Order 1997, SI 1997/2056; Social Security Administration (Fraud) Act 1997 (Commencement No 3) Order 1997, SI 1997/2417; Social Security Administration (Fraud) Act 1997 (Commencement No 4) Order 1997, SI 1997/2669; the Social Security Administration (Fraud) Act 1997 (Commencement No 5) Order 1997, SI 1997/2766; Social Security Administration (Fraud) Act 1997 (Commencement No 6) Order 1998, 1998/2779; Social Security Administration (Fraud) Act 1997 (Commencement No 7) Order 1999, SI 1999/1046

Section
1–2   1 Jul 1997 (SI 1997/1577)
3   1 Jul 1997 (except so far as it inserts
                                        s 122E(3), (4) into Social Security
                                        Administration Act 1992)
                                        (SI 1997/1577)

Social Security Administration (Fraud) Act 1997 (c 47)—*contd*

Social Security Administration (Fraud) Act 1997 (c 47)—*contd*

Schedule

1, para	8	18 Dec 1997 (SI 1997/2766)
	9–14	1 Jul 1997 (SI 1997/1577)
2		1 Jul 1997 (except repeal of Social Security Administration Act 1992, s 128A and the heading preceding that section) (SI 1997/1577)
		Not in force (exception noted above)

[1] Orders made under Social Security Act 1998, s 87(2), bringing the prospective repeals into force will be noted to that Act

[2] Orders made under Social Security Fraud Act 2001, s 20(1), bringing the prospective repeals into force will be noted to that Act

Social Security (Recovery of Benefits) Act 1997 (c 27)

RA: 19 Mar 1997

Commencement provisions: s 34(2); Social Security (Recovery of Benefits) Act 1997 (Commencement) Order 1997, SI 1997/2085

Section

1	(1)	6 Oct 1997 (SI 1997/2085)
	(2)	3 Sep 1997 (for purpose of conferring on the Secretary of State the powers to make regulations, so far as it relates to Sch 1, Pt I, paras 4, 8) (SI 1997/2085)
		6 Oct 1997 (otherwise) (SI 1997/2085)
	(3), (4)	6 Oct 1997 (SI 1997/2085)
2, 3		6 Oct 1997 (SI 1997/2085)
4	(1)–(8)	6 Oct 1997 (SI 1997/2085)
	(9)	3 Sep 1997 (for purpose of conferring on the Secretary of State the powers to make regulations) (SI 1997/2085)
		6 Oct 1997 (otherwise) (SI 1997/2085)
5–10		6 Oct 1997 (SI 1997/2085)
11	(1)–(4)	6 Oct 1997 (SI 1997/2085)
	(5)	3 Sep 1997 (for purpose of conferring on the Secretary of State the powers to make regulations) (SI 1997/2085)
		6 Oct 1997 (otherwise) (SI 1997/2085)
	(6)	3 Sep 1997 (for purpose of conferring on the Secretary of State the powers to make regulations) (SI 1997/2085)
		6 Oct 1997 (otherwise) (SI 1997/2085)

Social Security (Recovery of Benefits) Act 1997 (c 27)—*contd*

Section

11	(6)—*contd*	Sub-section repealed, except for certain purposes, by Social Security Act 1998, s 86, Sch 7, para 150, Sch 8[1]
12	(1), (2)	6 Oct 1997 (SI 1997/2085); sub-ss (1), (2) substituted for new sub-s (1), except for certain purposes, by Social Security Act 1998, s 86, Sch 7, para 151, Sch 8[1]
	(3)–(5)	6 Oct 1997 (SI 1997/2085)
	(6)	3 Sep 1997 (for purpose of conferring on the Secretary of State the powers to make regulations) (SI 1997/2085)
		6 Oct 1997 (otherwise) (SI 1997/2085); sub-s (6) repealed, except for certain purposes by Social Security Act 1998, s 6, Sch 7, para 151, Sch 8
	(7)	3 Sep 1997 (for purpose of conferring on the Secretary of State the powers to make regulations) (SI 1997/2085)
		6 Oct 1997 (otherwise) (SI 1997/2085)
	(8)	6 Oct 1997 (SI 1997/2085); repealed, except for certain purposes, by Social Security Act 1998, s 86, Sch 7, para 151, Sch 8[1]
13	(1), (2)	6 Oct 1997 (SI 1997/2085)
	(3)	3 Sep 1997 (for purpose of conferring on the Secretary of State the powers to make regulations) (SI 1997/2085)
		6 Oct 1997 (otherwise) (SI 1997/2085)
	(4)	6 Oct 1997 (SI 1997/2085); repealed, except for certain purposes, by Social Security Act 1998, s 86, Sch 7, para 152, Sch 8[1]
14	(1)	6 Oct 1997 (SI 1997/2085)
	(2)–(4)	3 Sep 1997 (for purpose of conferring on the Secretary of State the powers to make regulations) (SI 1997/2085)
		6 Oct 1997 (otherwise) (SI 1997/2085)
15		6 Oct 1997 (SI 1997/2085)
16	(1), (2)	3 Sep 1997 (for purpose of conferring on the Secretary of State the powers to make regulations) (SI 1997/2085)

Social Security (Recovery of Benefits) Act 1997 (c 27)—*contd*

Section

16	(1), (2)—*contd*	6 Oct 1997 (otherwise) (SI 1997/2085)
	(3), (4)	6 Oct 1997 (SI 1997/2085)
17		6 Oct 1997 (SI 1997/2085)
18, 19		3 Sep 1997 (for purpose of conferring on the Secretary of State the powers to make regulations) (SI 1997/2085) 6 Oct 1997 (otherwise) (SI 1997/2085)
20		6 Oct 1997 (SI 1997/2085)
21	(1), (2)	6 Oct 1997 (SI 1997/2085)
	(3)	3 Sep 1997 (for purpose of conferring on the Secretary of State the powers to make regulations) (SI 1997/2085) 6 Oct 1997 (otherwise) (SI 1997/2085)
	(4)–(6)	6 Oct 1997 (SI 1997/2085)
22		6 Oct 1997 (SI 1997/2085)
23	(1), (2)	3 Sep 1997 (for purpose of conferring on the Secretary of State the powers to make regulations) (SI 1997/2085) 6 Oct 1997 (otherwise) (SI 1997/2085)
	(3), (4)	6 Oct 1997 (SI 1997/2085)
	(5)	3 Sep 1997 (for purpose of conferring on the Secretary of State the powers to make regulations) (SI 1997/2085) 6 Oct 1997 (otherwise) (SI 1997/2085)
	(6)	6 Oct 1997 (SI 1997/2085)
	(7)	3 Sep 1997 (for purpose of conferring on the Secretary of State the powers to make regulations) (SI 1997/2085) 6 Oct 1997 (otherwise) (SI 1997/2085)
	(8)	6 Oct 1997 (SI 1997/2085)
24		6 Oct 1997 (SI 1997/2085)
25		19 Mar 1997 (RA)
26–28		6 Oct 1997 (SI 1997/2085)
29–32		19 Mar 1997 (RA)
33		6 Oct 1997 (SI 1997/2085)
34		19 Mar 1997 (RA)
Schedule		
1–4		6 Oct 1997 (SI 1997/2085)

[1] As to those purposes, see SI 1999/3178

Special Immigration Appeals Commission Act 1997 (c 68)

RA: 17 Dec 1997

Commencement provisions: s 9(2); Special Immigration Appeals Commission Act 1997 (Commencement No 1) Order 1998, SI 1998/1336; Special Immigration Appeals Commission Act 1997 (Commencement No 2) Order 1998, SI 1998/1892

Section

1, 2	3 Aug 1998 (SI 1998/1892)
2A	Inserted, partly prospectively, by Immigration and Asylum Act 1999, s 169(1), Sch 14, para 121[1]
3, 4	3 Aug 1998 (SI 1998/1892)
5	11 Jun 1998 (SI 1998/1336)
6, 7	3 Aug 1998 (SI 1998/1892)
7A	Inserted by Immigration and Asylum Act 1999, s 169(1), Sch 14, para 124
8	11 Jun 1998 (SI 1998/1336)
9	17 Dec 1997 (RA)

Schedule

1–3	3 Aug 1998 (SI 1998/1892)

[1]   Orders made under Immigration and Asylum Act 1999, s 170, bringing the prospective insertion into force will be noted to that Act

Supreme Court (Offices) Act 1997 (c 69)

RA: 17 Dec 1997

17 Dec 1997 (RA)

Telecommunications (Fraud) Act 1997 (c 4)

RA: 27 Feb 1997

Commencement provisions: s 3(3)

27 Apr 1997 (s 3(3))

Town and Country Planning (Scotland) Act 1997 (c 8)

RA: 27 Feb 1997

Commencement provisions: s 278(2)

27 May 1997 (s 278(2)) (except as provided in the Planning (Consequential Provisions) (Scotland) Act 1997, Sch 3)

Transfer of Crofting Estates (Scotland) Act 1997 (c 26)

RA: 19 Mar 1997

Commencement provisions: s 8(2); Transfer of Crofting Estates (Scotland) Act 1997 Commencement Order 1997, SI 1997/1430

6 Jun 1997 (SI 1997/1430)

United Nations Personnel Act 1997 (c 13)

RA: 27 Feb 1997

Commencement provisions: s 10(2)

27 Apr 1997 (s 10(2))

Welsh Development Agency Act 1997 (c 37)

RA: 21 Mar 1997

Commencement provisions: s 2(3)

21 May 1997 (s 2(3))

1998

Animal Health (Amendment) Act 1998 (c 13)

RA: 21 May 1998

Commencement provisions: s 2(2)

21 Jul 1998 (s 2(2))

Appropriation Act 1998 (c 28)

Whole Act repealed

Audit Commission Act 1998 (c 18)

RA: 11 Jun 1998

Commencement provisions: s 55(2)

11 Sep 1998 (s 55(2))

Bank of England Act 1998 (c 11)

RA: 23 Apr 1998

Commencement provisions: s 46; Bank of England Act 1998 (Commencement) Order 1998, SI 1998/1120

1 Jun 1998 (SI 1998/1120)

Community Care (Residential Accommodation) Act 1998 (c 19)

RA: 11 Jun 1998

Commencement provisions: s 3(2)

11 Aug 1998 (s 3(2))

Competition Act 1998 (c 41)

RA: 9 Nov 1998

Commencement provisions: s 76(2), (3); Competition Act 1998 (Commencement No 1) Order 1998, SI 1998/2750; Competition Act 1998 (Commencement No 2) Order 1998, SI 1998/3166; Competition Act 1998 (Commencement No 3) Order 1999, SI 1999/505; Competition Act 1998 (Commencement No 4) Order 1999, SI 1999/2859; Competition Act 1998 (Commencement No 5) Order 2000, SI 2000/344

Section

1	(a)	*Not in force*
	(b)–(d)	1 Mar 2000 (SI 2000/344)

Competition Act 1998 (c 41)—*contd*

Section

2			1 Mar 2000 (SI 2000/344)
3	(1)	(a)	11 Jan 1999 (SI 1998/3166)
		(b)	See Sch 2 below
		(c), (d)	11 Jan 1999 (SI 1998/3166)
	(2)–(6)		11 Jan 1999 (SI 1998/3166)
4–11			1 Mar 2000 (SI 2000/344)
12	(1), (2)		1 Mar 2000 (SI 2000/344)
	(3)		11 Jan 1999 (SI 1998/3166)
13–18			1 Mar 2000 (SI 2000/344)
19			11 Jan 1999 (SI 1998/3166)
20–37			1 Mar 2000 (SI 2000/344)
38	(1)–(7)		11 Jan 1999 (SI 1998/3166)
	(8)–(10)		1 Mar 2000 (SI 2000/344)
39–44			1 Mar 2000 (SI 2000/344)
45			1 Apr 1999 (SI 1999/505)
46, 47			1 Mar 2000 (SI 2000/344)
48			1 Apr 1999 (SI 1999/505)
49	(1), (2)		1 Mar 2000 (SI 2000/344)
	(3)		1 Apr 1999 (SI 1999/505)
	(4)		1 Mar 2000 (SI 2000/344)
50			11 Jan 1999 (SI 1998/3166)
51, 52			26 Nov 1998 (SI 1998/2750)
53			11 Jan 1999 (SI 1998/3166)
54	(1)		1 Mar 2000 (SI 2000/344)
	(2), (3)		See Sch 10 below
	(4)–(7)		11 Jan 1999 (SI 1998/3166)
55	(1)–(5)		1 Mar 2000 (SI 2000/344)
	(6)		11 Jan 1999 (SI 1998/3166)
	(7), (8)		1 Mar 2000 (SI 2000/344)
56			1 Mar 2000 (SI 2000/344)
57			11 Jan 1999 (SI 1998/3166)
58			1 Mar 2000 (SI 2000/344)
59			26 Nov 1998 (for the purposes of ss 51, 52, Sch 9) (SI 1998/2750)
			11 Jan 1999 (so far as not already in force) (SI 1998/3166)
60			11 Jan 1999 (SI 1998/3166)
61–65			1 Mar 2000 (SI 2000/344)
66–68			1 Apr 1999 (SI 1999/505)
69			11 Jan 1999 (SI 1998/3166)
70			1 Mar 2000 (SI 2000/344)
71			9 Nov 1998 (s 76(2))
72, 73			1 Mar 2000 (SI 2000/344)
74	(1)		See Sch 12 below
	(2)		See Sch 13 below
	(3)		See Sch 14 below
75, 76			9 Nov 1998 (s 76(2))

Schedule

1			11 Jan 1999 (SI 1998/3166)

Competition Act 1998 (c 41)—*contd*

Schedule

2, para	1–5			1 Mar 2000 (SI 2000/344)
	6			11 Jan 1999 (SI 1998/3166)
3, 4				11 Jan 1999 (SI 1998/3166)
5, para	1–6			1 Mar 2000 (SI 2000/344)
	7			*Not in force*
6, para	1–6			1 Mar 2000 (SI 2000/344)
	7			*Not in force*
7				1 Apr 1999 (SI 1999/505)
8, Pt	I, para	1		1 Apr 1999 (SI 1999/505)
		2–4		1 Mar 2000 (SI 2000/344)
	II			1 Apr 1999 (SI 1999/505)
9				26 Nov 1998 (SI 1998/2750)
10, para	1			1 Apr 1999 (SI 1999/505)
	2–8			26 Nov 1998 (for the purposes of ss 51, 52, Sch 9) (subject to a saving) (SI 1998/2750) 1 Mar 2000 (otherwise) (SI 2000/344)
	9	(1), (2)		1 Apr 1999 (SI 1999/505)
		(3), (4)		1 Mar 2000 (SI 2000/344)
		(5)		1 Apr 1999 (SI 1999/505)
		(6)		1 Mar 2000 (SI 2000/344)
		(7)	(a)	1 Mar 2000 (SI 2000/344)
			(b)	11 Jan 1999 (SI 1998/3166)
		(8)		1 Mar 2000 (SI 2000/344)
	10	(1), (2)		1 Apr 1999 (SI 1999/505)
		(3)–(5)		1 Mar 2000 (SI 2000/344)
		(6)	(a)	1 Mar 2000 (SI 2000/344)
			(b)	11 Jan 1999 (SI 1998/3166)
		(7)		1 Mar 2000 (SI 2000/344)
	11	(a)		1 Mar 2000 (SI 2000/344)
		(b)		11 Jan 1999 (SI 1998/3166)
	12	(1), (2)		1 Apr 1999 (SI 1999/505)
		(3)–(5)		1 Mar 2000 (SI 2000/344)
		(6)		1 Apr 1999 (SI 1999/505)
		(7)	(a)	1 Mar 2000 (SI 2000/344)
			(b)	11 Jan 1999 (SI 1998/3166)
		(8)		1 Mar 2000 (SI 2000/344)
	13	(1)		1 Apr 1999 (SI 1999/505)
		(2)		1 Mar 2000 (SI 2000/344)
		(3)		1 Apr 1999 (SI 1999/505)
		(4)–(7)		1 Mar 2000 (SI 2000/344)
		(8)		1 Apr 1999 (SI 1999/505)
		(9)		1 Mar 2000 (SI 2000/344)
		(10)	(a)	1 Mar 2000 (SI 2000/344)
			(b)	11 Jan 1999 (SI 1998/3166)
	14	(a)		1 Mar 2000 (SI 2000/344)
		(b)		11 Jan 1999 (SI 1998/3166)
	15	(1), (2)		1 Apr 1999 (SI 1999/505)

Competition Act 1998 (c 41)—*contd*

Schedule				
10, para	15	(3)–(8)		1 Mar 2000 (SI 2000/344)
		(9)	(a)	1 Mar 2000 (SI 2000/344)
			(b)	11 Jan 1999 (SI 1998/3166)
		(10)		1 Mar 2000 (SI 2000/344)
	16			1 Mar 2000 (SI 2000/344)
	17	(1), (2)		1 Apr 1999 (SI 1999/505)
		(3)–(5)		1 Mar 2000 (SI 2000/344)
		(6)		1 Apr 1999 (SI 1999/505)
		(7)	(a)	1 Mar 2000 (SI 2000/344)
			(b)	11 Jan 1999 (SI 1998/3166)
		(8), (9)		1 Mar 2000 (SI 2000/344)
	18	(1), (2)		1 Apr 1999 (SI 1999/505)
		(3)–(5)		1 Mar 2000 (SI 2000/344)
		(6)	(a)	1 Mar 2000 (SI 2000/344)
			(b)	11 Jan 1999 (SI 1998/3166)
		(7)		1 Mar 2000 (SI 2000/344)
11				1 Mar 2000 (SI 2000/344)
12, para	1	(1), (2)		1 Apr 1999 (SI 1999/505)
		(3)	(a), (b)	10 Nov 1999 (SI 1999/2859)
			(c)	1 Mar 2000 (SI 2000/344)
			(d)	10 Nov 1999 (SI 1999/2859)
		(4)–(8)		1 Mar 2000 (SI 2000/344)
		(9)–(13)		1 Apr 1999 (SI 1999/505)
		(14)		11 Jan 1999 (SI 1998/3166)
		(15)		1 Apr 1999 (SI 1999/505)
	2			1 Mar 2000 (SI 2000/344)
	3	(a)		1 Mar 2000 (SI 2000/344)
		(b)		11 Jan 1999 (SI 1998/3166)
	4	(1)		1 Apr 1999 (SI 1999/505)
		(2)		1 Mar 2000 (SI 2000/344)
		(3)		1 Apr 1999 (SI 1999/505)
		(4)–(8)		1 Mar 2000 (SI 2000/344)
		(9)		11 Jan 1999 (SI 1998/3166)
		(10)		1 Mar 2000 (SI 2000/344)
		(11)		11 Jan 1999 (SI 1998/3166)
		(12)		1 Apr 1999 (SI 1999/505)
		(13)–(15)		1 Mar 2000 (SI 2000/344)
	5			1 Mar 2000 (SI 2000/344)
	6	(a)		1 Apr 1999 (SI 1999/505)
		(b)		1 Mar 2000 (SI 2000/344)
	7	(1), (2)		1 Apr 1999 (SI 1999/505)
		(3)–(5)		1 Mar 2000 (SI 2000/344)
	8, 9			1 Mar 2000 (SI 2000/344)
	10	(a)		1 Mar 2000 (SI 2000/344)
		(b)		11 Jan 1999 (SI 1998/3166)
	11–13			1 Mar 2000 (SI 2000/344)
	14	(1)		1 Apr 1999 (SI 1999/505)
		(2)		1 Mar 2000 (SI 2000/344)
		(3)		1 Apr 1999 (SI 1999/505)

Competition Act 1998 (c 41)—*contd*

Schedule

12, para	15		1 Apr 1999 (SI 1999/505)
	16, 17		1 Mar 2000 (SI 2000/344)
	18	(a)	1 Mar 2000 (SI 2000/344)
		(b)	11 Jan 1999 (SI 1998/3166)
	19		1 Mar 2000 (SI 2000/344)
	20	(1), (2)	1 Apr 1999 (SI 1999/505)
		(3)–(6)	1 Mar 2000 (SI 2000/344)
	21		1 Mar 2000 (SI 2000/344)
13, para	1–7		9 Nov 1998 (s 76(2))
	8, 9		1 Mar 2000 (SI 2000/344)
	10	(1)–(4)	1 Mar 2000 (SI 2000/344)
		(5)	11 Jan 1999 (SI 1998/3166)
		(6)	1 Mar 2000 (SI 2000/344)
	11		11 Jan 1999 (for the purpose of prescribing modifications to Restrictive Trade Practices Act 1976) (SI 1998/3166)
			Not in force (otherwise)
	12	(1)	11 Jan 1999 (for the purpose of prescribing modifications to Restrictive Trade Practices Act 1976) (SI 1998/3166)
			1 Mar 2000 (otherwise) (SI 2000/344)
		(2)	1 Mar 2000 (SI 2000/344)
	13–18		1 Mar 2000 (SI 2000/344)
	19	(1), (2)	1 Mar 2000 (SI 2000/344)
		(3)	11 Jan 1999 (SI 1998/3166)
	20–34		1 Mar 2000 (SI 2000/344)
	35		9 Nov 1998 (s 76(2))
	36–39		1 Mar 2000 (SI 2000/344)
	40, 41		10 Nov 1999 (SI 1999/2859)
	42–46		1 Mar 2000 (SI 2000/344)
14, Pt	I		11 Jan 1999 (repeals of or in Fair Trading Act 1973, s 83, Competition Act 1980, s 22) (SI 1998/3166)
			1 Apr 1999 (repeals of or in Fair Trading Act 1973, ss 4, 45, 81, 135, Sch 3) (SI 1999/505)
			10 Nov 1999 (repeals of or in Fair Trading Act 1973, ss 10(2), 54(5), Sch 8, para 3(1), (2)) (SI 1999/2859)
			1 Mar 2000 (otherwise) (except repeal of Restrictive Practices Court Act 1976) (SI 2000/344)
			Not in force (exception noted above)

Competition Act 1998 (c 41)—*contd*
Schedule

14, Pt	II	1 Apr 1999 (repeal of entry relating to Fair Trading Act 1973 in Agricultural Marketing Northern Ireland) Order 1982, SI 1982/1080) (SI 1999/505)
		1 Mar 2000 (otherwise) (SI 2000/344)

Consolidated Fund Act 1998 (c 4)

Whole Act repealed

Consolidated Fund (No 2) Act 1998 (c 49)

Whole Act repealed

Crime and Disorder Act 1998 (c 37)

RA: 31 Jul 1998

Commencement provisions: s 121(2); Crime and Disorder Act 1998 (Commencement No 1) Order 1998, SI 1998/1883; Crime and Disorder Act 1998 (Commencement No 2 and Transitional Provisions) Order 1998, SI 1998/2327, as amended by SI 1998/2412, SI 1998/2906; Crime and Disorder Act 1998 (Commencement No 3 and Appointed Day) Order 1998, SI 1998/3263; Crime and Disorder Act 1998 (Commencement No 4) Order 1999, SI 1999/1279; Crime and Disorder Act 1998 (Commencement No 5) Order 1999, SI 1999/2976; Crime and Disorder Act 1998 (Commencement No 6) Order 1999, SI 1999/3426; Crime and Disorder Act 1998 (Commencement No 7) Order 2000, SI 2000/924

Section		
1		1 Apr 1999 (SI 1998/3263)
2, 3		1 Dec 1998 (SI 1998/2327)
4		1 Dec 1998 (so far as relating to a sex offender order) (SI 1998/2327)
		1 Apr 1999 (otherwise) (SI 1998/3263)
5–9		30 Sep 1998 (SI 1998/2327)
10	(1)–(5)	30 Sep 1998 (SI 1998/2327)
	(6), (7)	1 Jun 2000 (SI 2000/924)
11, 12		30 Sep 1998 (SI 1998/2327)
13	(1), (2)	30 Sep 1998 (SI 1998/2327)
	(3)	1 Jun 2000 (SI 2000/924)
14, 15		30 Sep 1998 (SI 1998/2327)
16		1 Dec 1998 (SI 1998/2327)
17, 18		30 Sep 1998 (SI 1998/2327)
19		1 Apr 1999 (SI 1998/3263)
20		1 Dec 1998 (SI 1998/2327)
21		1 Dec 1998 (for the purposes of sex offender orders made under s 20, and orders made under s 20(4)(a)) (SI 1998/2327)

Crime and Disorder Act 1998 (c 37)—*contd*

Section

21—*contd*		1 Apr 1999 (otherwise) (SI 1998/3263)
22	(1)–(5)	1 Dec 1998 (for the purposes of their application to an order under s 20(4)(a), and to a sex offender order made under s 20) (SI 1998/2327)
		1 Apr 1999 (otherwise) (SI 1998/3263)
	(6), (7)	1 Dec 1998 (SI 1998/2327)
23, 24		1 Dec 1998 (SI 1998/2327)
25		1 Mar 1999 (SI 1998/3263)
26		1 Dec 1998 (for the purpose of making regulations under Criminal Justice and Public Order Act 1994, s 60A) (SI 1998/2327)
		1 Mar 1999 (otherwise) (SI 1998/3263)
27		1 Mar 1999 (SI 1998/3263)
28–37		30 Sep 1998 (SI 1998/2327)
38	(1)–(3)	30 Sep 1998 (in the areas of the counties of Bedfordshire, Devon and Hampshire, the Isle of Wight, the cities of Portsmouth, Sheffield, Southampton and Westminster, the Royal borough of Kensington and Chelsea, the London boroughs of Hammersmith and Fulham, and Lewisham, the Metropolitan boroughs of St Helens and Wolverhampton, and the boroughs of Blackburn with Darwen, and Luton) (subject to transitional provisions) (SI 1998/2327)
		1 Apr 2000 (otherwise) (SI 2000/924)
	(4)	30 Sep 1998 (subject to transitional provisions) (SI 1998/2327)[1]
	(5)	30 Sep 1998 (in the areas of the counties of Bedfordshire, Devon and Hampshire, the Isle of Wight, the cities of Portsmouth, Sheffield, Southampton and Westminster, the Royal borough of Kensington and Chelsea, the London boroughs of Hammersmith and Fulham, and Lewisham, the Metropolitan boroughs of St Helens and Wolverhampton, and the boroughs of Blackburn with Darwen, and Luton) (subject to transitional provisions) (SI 1998/2327)
		1 Apr 2000 (otherwise) (SI 2000/924)

Crime and Disorder Act 1998 (c 37)—*contd*

Section

39		30 Sep 1998 (in the areas of the counties of Bedfordshire, Devon and Hampshire, the Isle of Wight, the cities of Portsmouth, Sheffield, Southampton and Westminster, the Royal borough of Kensington and Chelsea, the London boroughs of Hammersmith and Fulham, and Lewisham, the Metropolitan boroughs of St Helens and Wolverhampton, and the boroughs of Blackburn with Darwen, and Luton) (subject to transitional provisions) (SI 1998/2327)
		1 Apr 2000 (otherwise) (SI 2000/924)
40		30 Sep 1998 (in the areas of the counties of Bedfordshire, Devon and Hampshire, the Isle of Wight, the cities of Portsmouth, Sheffield, Southampton and Westminster, the Royal borough of Kensington and Chelsea, the London boroughs of Hammersmith and Fulham, and Lewisham, the Metropolitan boroughs of St Helens and Wolverhampton, and the boroughs of Blackburn with Darwen, and Luton) (subject to transitional provisions) (SI 1998/2327)
		1 Jan 2000 (otherwise) (SI 1999/3426)
41	(1)–(10)	1 Aug 1998 (for the purpose of making appointments) (SI 1998/1883)
		30 Sep 1998 (otherwise) (SI 1998/2327)
	(11)	See Sch 2 below
42		30 Sep 1998 (SI 1998/2327)
43	(1)	30 Sep 1998 (SI 1998/2327)
	(2)–(8)	1 Jun 1999 (SI 1999/1279)
44, 45		1 Jun 1999 (SI 1999/1279)
46		30 Sep 1998 (in the petty sessions areas of Bromley, Croydon, and Sutton, the petty sessional divisions of Aberconwy, Arfon, Blackburn, Darwen and Ribble Valley, Burnley and Pendle, Colwyn, Corby, Daventry, Dyffryn Clwyd, Eifionydd and Pwllheli, Gateshead, Kettering, Meirionnydd, Newcastle-under-Lyme and Pirehill

Crime and Disorder Act 1998 (c 37)—*contd*
Section

46—*contd*		North, Newcastle-upon-Tyne, Northampton, Rhuddlan, Staffordshire Moorlands, Stoke-on-Trent, Towcester, Wellingborough, and Ynys Mon/Anglesey) (SI 1999/2327) 1 Nov 1999 (otherwise) (SI 1999/2976)
47		30 Sep 1998 (SI 1998/2327)
48		30 Sep 1998 (SI 1998/2327); prospectively repealed by Access to Justice Act 1999, s 106, Sch 15, Pt V(2)[2]
49	(1)	30 Sep 1998 (in the petty sessions areas of Bromley, Croydon, and Sutton, the petty sessional divisions of Aberconwy, Arfon, Blackburn, Darwen and Ribble Valley, Burnley and Pendle, Colwyn, Corby, Daventry, Dyffryn Clwyd, Eifionydd and Pwllheli, Gateshead, Kettering, Meirionnydd, Newcastle-under-Lyme and Pirehill North, Newcastle-upon-Tyne, Northampton, Rhuddlan, Staffordshire Moorlands, Stoke-on-Trent, Towcester, Wellingborough, and Ynys Mon/Anglesey) (SI 1999/2327) 1 Nov 1999 (otherwise) (SI 1999/2976)
	(2)	1 Aug 1998 (SI 1998/1883)
	(3)–(5)	30 Sep 1998 (in the petty sessions areas of Bromley, Croydon, and Sutton, the petty sessional divisions of Aberconwy, Arfon, Blackburn, Darwen and Ribble Valley, Burnley and Pendle, Colwyn, Corby, Daventry, Dyffryn Clwyd, Eifionydd and Pwllheli, Gateshead, Kettering, Meirionnydd, Newcastle-under-Lyme and Pirehill North, Newcastle-upon-Tyne, Northampton, Rhuddlan, Staffordshire Moorlands, Stoke-on-Trent, Towcester, Wellingborough, and Ynys Mon/Anglesey) (SI 1999/2327) 1 Nov 1999 (otherwise) (SI 1999/2976)
50		30 Sep 1998 (SI 1998/2327)

Crime and Disorder Act 1998 (c 37)—*contd*
Section

51		4 Jan 1999 (for the purpose of sending any person for trial under s 51 from the petty sessions areas of Bromley, Croydon, and Sutton, the petty sessional divisions of Aberconwy, Arfon, Blackburn, Darwen and Ribble Valley, Burnley and Pendle, Colwyn, Corby, Daventry, Dyffryn Clwyd, Eifionydd and Pwllheli, Gateshead, Kettering, Meirionnydd, Newcastle-under-Lyme and Pirehill North, Newcastle-upon-Tyne, Northampton, Rhuddlan, Staffordshire Moorlands, Stoke-on-Trent, Towcester, Wellingborough, and Ynys Mon/Anglesey) (SI 1998/2327)
		Not in force (otherwise)
52	(1)–(5)	4 Jan 1999 (for the purpose of sending any person for trial under s 51 from the petty sessions areas of Bromley, Croydon, and Sutton, the petty sessional divisions of Aberconwy, Arfon, Blackburn, Darwen and Ribble Valley, Burnley and Pendle, Colwyn, Corby, Daventry, Dyffryn Clwyd, Eifionydd and Pwllheli, Gateshead, Kettering, Meirionnydd, Newcastle-under-Lyme and Pirehill North, Newcastle-upon-Tyne, Northampton, Rhuddlan, Staffordshire Moorlands, Stoke-on-Trent, Towcester, Wellingborough, and Ynys Mon/Anglesey) (SI 1998/2327)
		Not in force (otherwise)
	(6)	See Sch 3 below
53–57		30 Sep 1998 (SI 1998/2327)
58		Repealed
59		30 Sep 1998 (subject to transitional provisions) (SI 1998/2327)
60		30 Sep 1998 (SI 1998/2327)
61–64		Repealed
65, 66		30 Sep 1998 (in the areas, for the purpose of reprimanding or warning a person under s 65, of the county of Hampshire, the Isle of Wight, the cities of Portsmouth, Sheffield, Southampton and

Crime and Disorder Act 1998 (c 37)—*contd*
Section

65, 66—*contd*		Westminster, the Royal borough of Kensington and Chelsea, the London borough of Hammersmith and Fulham, the Metropolitan borough of Wolverhampton, and the borough of Blackburn with Darwen) (SI 1998/2327)
		1 Apr 2000 (in the areas, for the purpose of reprimanding or warning a person under s 65, of the counties of Oxfordshire, Norfolk, the cities of Cardiff, Sunderland, the London boroughs of Lewisham, Greenwich, Southwark, the Metropolitan borough of Gateshead) (SI 2000/924)
		1 Jun 2000 (otherwise) (SI 2000/924)
67–79		Repealed
80, 81		1 Jul 1999 (SI 1998/3263)
82		Repealed
83		30 Sep 1998 (SI 1998/2327)
84, 85		Repealed
86		30 Sep 1998 (subject to transitional provisions) (SI 1998/2327)
87–96		30 Sep 1998 (SI 1998/2327)
97		30 Sep 1998 (for the purpose of making an order under Children and Young Persons Act 1969, s 23) (SI 1998/2327)
		1 Jun 1999 (otherwise) (SI 1999/1279)
98		1 Jun 1999 (SI 1999/1279)
99		28 Jan 1999 (SI 1998/3263)
100	(1)	30 Sep 1998 (for the purpose of making orders under Criminal Justice Act 1991, s 37A) (subject to a transitional provision) (SI 1998/2327)
		28 Jan 1999 (otherwise) (SI 1998/3263)
	(2)	28 Jan 1999 (SI 1998/3263)
101		30 Sep 1998 (SI 1998/2327)
102		Repealed
103		1 Jan 1999 (SI 1998/3263)
104–108		30 Sep 1998 (SI 1998/2327)
109		31 Jul 1998 (s 121(2))
110		30 Sep 1998 (SI 1998/2327)
111	(1)–(7)	30 Sep 1998 (SI 1998/2327)
	(8)	31 Jul 1998 (s 121(2))
112, 113		30 Sep 1998 (SI 1998/2327)
114		1 Aug 1998 (SI 1998/1883)

Crime and Disorder Act 1998 (c 37)—*contd*

Section			
115			30 Sep 1998 (SI 1998/2327)
116, 117			1 Aug 1998 (SI 1998/1883)
118			30 Sep 1998 (SI 1998/2327)
119			See Sch 8 below
120	(1)		30 Sep 1998 (SI 1998/2327)
	(2)		See Sch 10 below
121			31 Jul 1998 (s 121(2))

Schedule			
1			1 Dec 1998 (SI 1998/2327)
2, para	1, 2		1 Aug 1998 (for the purpose of making appointments under s 41 and para 1) (SI 1998/1883)
			30 Sep 1998 (otherwise) (SI 1998/2327)
	3–11		30 Sep 1998 (SI 1998/2327)
3, para	1		30 Sep 1998 (for the purpose of making regulations) (SI 1998/2327)
			4 Jan 1999 (for the purpose of sending any person for trial under s 51 from the petty sessions areas of Bromley, Croydon, and Sutton, the petty sessional divisions of Aberconwy, Arfon, Blackburn, Darwen and Ribble Valley, Burnley and Pendle, Colwyn, Corby, Daventry, Dyffryn Clwyd, Eifionydd and Pwllheli, Gateshead, Kettering, Meirionnydd, Newcastle-under-Lyme and Pirehill North, Newcastle-upon-Tyne, Northampton, Rhuddlan, Staffordshire Moorlands, Stoke-on-Trent, Towcester, Wellingborough, and Ynys Mon/Anglesey) (SI 1998/2327)
			Not in force (otherwise)
	2	(1)–(6)	4 Jan 1999 (for the purpose of sending any person for trial under s 51 from the petty sessions areas of Bromley, Croydon, and Sutton, the petty sessional divisions of Aberconwy, Arfon, Blackburn, Darwen and Ribble Valley, Burnley and Pendle, Colwyn, Corby, Daventry, Dyffryn Clwyd, Eifionydd and Pwllheli, Gateshead, Kettering, Meirionnydd, Newcastle-under-Lyme and Pirehill North, Newcastle-upon-Tyne, Northampton, Rhuddlan,

Crime and Disorder Act 1998 (c 37)—*contd*

Schedule

3, para	2	(1)–(6)—*contd*	Staffordshire Moorlands, Stoke-on-Trent, Towcester, Wellingborough, and Ynys Mon/Anglesey) (SI 1998/2327)
			Not in force (otherwise)
		(7)	30 Sep 1998 (for the purpose of making rules) (SI 1998/2327)
			4 Jan 1999 (for the purpose of sending any person for trial under s 51 from the petty sessions areas of Bromley, Croydon, and Sutton, the petty sessional divisions of Aberconwy, Arfon, Blackburn, Darwen and Ribble Valley, Burnley and Pendle, Colwyn, Corby, Daventry, Dyffryn Clwyd, Eifionydd and Pwllheli, Gateshead, Kettering, Meirionnydd, Newcastle-under-Lyme and Pirehill North, Newcastle-upon-Tyne, Northampton, Rhuddlan, Staffordshire Moorlands, Stoke-on-Trent, Towcester, Wellingborough, and Ynys Mon/Anglesey) (SI 1998/2327)
			Not in force (otherwise)
	3–15		4 Jan 1999 (for the purpose of sending any person for trial under s 51 from the petty sessions areas of Bromley, Croydon, and Sutton, the petty sessional divisions of Aberconwy, Arfon, Blackburn, Darwen and Ribble Valley, Burnley and Pendle, Colwyn, Corby, Daventry, Dyffryn Clwyd, Eifionydd and Pwllheli, Gateshead, Kettering, Meirionnydd, Newcastle-under-Lyme and Pirehill North, Newcastle-upon-Tyne, Northampton, Rhuddlan, Staffordshire Moorlands, Stoke-on-Trent, Towcester, Wellingborough, and Ynys Mon/Anglesey) (SI 1998/2327)
			Not in force (otherwise)
4, 5			Repealed
6			30 Sep 1998 (SI 1998/2327)
7			30 Sep 1998 (subject to transitional provisions) (SI 1998/2327)

Crime and Disorder Act 1998 (c 37)—*contd*

Schedule

8, para	1			1 Apr 2000 (subject to transitional provisions and savings) (SI 1999/3426)
	2			Repealed
	3			Repealed (*partly never in force*)
	4			Repealed
	5	(1)	(a)	4 Jan 1999 (for the purpose of sending any person for trial under s 51 from the petty sessions areas of Bromley, Croydon, and Sutton, the petty sessional divisions of Aberconwy, Arfon, Blackburn, Darwen and Ribble Valley, Burnley and Pendle, Colwyn, Corby, Daventry, Dyffryn Clwyd, Eifionydd and Pwllheli, Gateshead, Kettering, Meirionnydd, Newcastle-under-Lyme and Pirehill North, Newcastle-upon-Tyne, Northampton, Rhuddlan, Staffordshire Moorlands, Stoke-on-Trent, Towcester, Wellingborough, and Ynys Mon/Anglesey) (SI 1998/2327)
				Not in force (otherwise)
			(b)	1 Jun 1999 (SI 1999/1279)
		(2)		4 Jan 1999 (for the purpose of sending any person for trial under s 51 from the petty sessions areas of Bromley, Croydon, and Sutton, the petty sessional divisions of Aberconwy, Arfon, Blackburn, Darwen and Ribble Valley, Burnley and Pendle, Colwyn, Corby, Daventry, Dyffryn Clwyd, Eifionydd and Pwllheli, Gateshead, Kettering, Meirionnydd, Newcastle-under-Lyme and Pirehill North, Newcastle-upon-Tyne, Northampton, Rhuddlan, Staffordshire Moorlands, Stoke-on-Trent, Towcester, Wellingborough, and Ynys Mon/Anglesey) (SI 1998/2327)
				Not in force (otherwise)
	6			1 Apr 2000 (SI 1999/3426)
	7			1 Apr 2000 (subject to transitional provisions and savings) (SI 1999/3426)

Crime and Disorder Act 1998 (c 37)—*contd*

Schedule

8, para	8	4 Jan 1999 (for the purpose of sending any person for trial under s 51 from the petty sessions areas of Bromley, Croydon, and Sutton, the petty sessional divisions of Aberconwy, Arfon, Blackburn, Darwen and Ribble Valley, Burnley and Pendle, Colwyn, Corby, Daventry, Dyffryn Clwyd, Eifionydd and Pwllheli, Gateshead, Kettering, Meirionnydd, Newcastle-under-Lyme and Pirehill North, Newcastle-upon-Tyne, Northampton, Rhuddlan, Staffordshire Moorlands, Stoke-on-Trent, Towcester, Wellingborough, and Ynys Mon/Anglesey) (SI 1998/2327) *Not in force* (otherwise)
	9, 10	Repealed
	11	30 Sep 1998 (SI 1998/2327)
	12	4 Jan 1999 (for the purpose of sending any person for trial under s 51 from the petty sessions areas of Bromley, Croydon, and Sutton, the petty sessional divisions of Aberconwy, Arfon, Blackburn, Darwen and Ribble Valley, Burnley and Pendle, Colwyn, Corby, Daventry, Dyffryn Clwyd, Eifionydd and Pwllheli, Gateshead, Kettering, Meirionnydd, Newcastle-under-Lyme and Pirehill North, Newcastle-upon-Tyne, Northampton, Rhuddlan, Staffordshire Moorlands, Stoke-on-Trent, Towcester, Wellingborough, and Ynys Mon/Anglesey) (SI 1998/2327) *Not in force* (otherwise)
	13	30 Sep 1998 (SI 1998/2327)
	14	1 Apr 2000 (SI 1999/3426)
	15	1 Apr 2000 (subject to transitional provisions and savings) (SI 1999/3426)
	16–21	Repealed
	22	1 Apr 2000 (SI 1999/3426)
	23	30 Sep 1998 (in the areas of the counties of Bedfordshire, Devon and Hampshire, the Isle of Wight, the cities of Portsmouth, Sheffield,

Crime and Disorder Act 1998 (c 37)—*contd*

Schedule

8, para	23—*contd*		Southampton and Westminster, the Royal borough of Kensington and Chelsea, the London boroughs of Hammersmith and Fulham, and Lewisham, the Metropolitan boroughs of St Helens and Wolverhampton, and the boroughs of Blackburn with Darwen, and Luton) (SI 1998/2327)
			1 Apr 2000 (otherwise) (SI 2000/924)
	24		30 Sep 1998 (SI 1998/2327)
	25–34		Repealed
	35		1 Apr 2000 (SI 1999/3426)
	36		1 Dec 1998 (SI 1998/2327)
	37		4 Jan 1999 (for the purpose of sending any person for trial under s 51 from the petty sessions areas of Bromley, Croydon, and Sutton, the petty sessional divisions of Aberconwy, Arfon, Blackburn, Darwen and Ribble Valley, Burnley and Pendle, Colwyn, Corby, Daventry, Dyffryn Clwyd, Eifionydd and Pwllheli, Gateshead, Kettering, Meirionnydd, Newcastle-under-Lyme and Pirehill North, Newcastle-upon-Tyne, Northampton, Rhuddlan, Staffordshire Moorlands, Stoke-on-Trent, Towcester, Wellingborough, and Ynys Mon/Anglesey) (SI 1998/2327)
			Not in force (otherwise)
	38		30 Sep 1998 (SI 1998/2327)
	39		1 Apr 2000 (SI 1999/3426)
	40	(1)	30 Sep 1998 (SI 1998/2327)
		(2)	4 Jan 1999 (for the purpose of sending any person for trial under s 51 from the petty sessions areas of Bromley, Croydon, and Sutton, the petty sessional divisions of Aberconwy, Arfon, Blackburn, Darwen and Ribble Valley, Burnley and Pendle, Colwyn, Corby, Daventry, Dyffryn Clwyd, Eifionydd and Pwllheli, Gateshead, Kettering, Meirionnydd, Newcastle-under-Lyme and Pirehill North, Newcastle-upon-Tyne, Northampton, Rhuddlan, Staffordshire Moorlands,

Crime and Disorder Act 1998 (c 37)—*contd*

Schedule

8, para	40	(2)—*contd*	Stoke-on-Trent, Towcester, Wellingborough, and Ynys Mon/Anglesey) (SI 1998/2327)
			Not in force (otherwise)
	41		1 Apr 2000 (SI 1999/3426)
	42, 43		30 Sep 1998 (SI 1998/2327)
	44		Repealed (*partly never in force*)
	45		4 Jan 1999 (for the purpose of sending any person for trial under s 51 from the petty sessions areas of Bromley, Croydon, and Sutton, the petty sessional divisions of Aberconwy, Arfon, Blackburn, Darwen and Ribble Valley, Burnley and Pendle, Colwyn, Corby, Daventry, Dyffryn Clwyd, Eifionydd and Pwllheli, Gateshead, Kettering, Meirionnydd, Newcastle-under-Lyme and Pirehill North, Newcastle-upon-Tyne, Northampton, Rhuddlan, Staffordshire Moorlands, Stoke-on-Trent, Towcester, Wellingborough, and Ynys Mon/Anglesey) (SI 1998/2327)
			Not in force (otherwise)
	46, 47		Repealed
	48		4 Jan 1999 (for the purpose of sending any person for trial under s 51 from the petty sessions areas of Bromley, Croydon, and Sutton, the petty sessional divisions of Aberconwy, Arfon, Blackburn, Darwen and Ribble Valley, Burnley and Pendle, Colwyn, Corby, Daventry, Dyffryn Clwyd, Eifionydd and Pwllheli, Gateshead, Kettering, Meirionnydd, Newcastle-under-Lyme and Pirehill North, Newcastle-upon-Tyne, Northampton, Rhuddlan, Staffordshire Moorlands, Stoke-on-Trent, Towcester, Wellingborough, and Ynys Mon/Anglesey) (SI 1998/2327)
			Not in force (otherwise)
	49		Repealed (*partly never in force*)
	50, 51		Repealed
	52	(1)	Repealed
		(2)	Repealed (*partly never in force*)
	53		Repealed

Crime and Disorder Act 1998 (c 37)—*contd*

Schedule

8, para	54	30 Sep 1998 (SI 1998/2327)
	55	31 Jul 1998 (s 121(2))
	56–60	30 Sep 1998 (SI 1998/2327)
	61	30 Sep 1998 (in the areas, for the purpose of reprimanding or warning a person under s 65, of the county of Hampshire, the Isle of Wight, the cities of Portsmouth, Sheffield, Southampton and Westminster, the Royal borough of Kensington and Chelsea, the London borough of Hammersmith and Fulham, the Metropolitan borough of Wolverhampton, and the borough of Blackburn with Darwen) (SI 1998/2327)
		1 Apr 2000 (in the areas, for the purpose of reprimanding or warning a person under s 65, of the counties of Oxfordshire, Norfolk, the cities of Cardiff, Sunderland, the London boroughs of Lewisham, Greenwich, Southwark, the Metropolitan borough of Gateshead) (SI 2000/924)
		1 Jun 2000 (otherwise) (SI 2000/924)
		Para prospectively repealed by Criminal Justice and Police Act 2001, s 137, Sch 7, Pt 2(1)[3]
	62	30 Sep 1998 (SI 1998/2327)
	63–66	4 Jan 1999 (for the purpose of sending any person for trial under s 51 from the petty sessions areas of Bromley, Croydon, and Sutton, the petty sessional divisions of Aberconwy, Arfon, Blackburn, Darwen and Ribble Valley, Burnley and Pendle, Colwyn, Corby, Daventry, Dyffryn Clwyd, Eifionydd and Pwllheli, Gateshead, Kettering, Meirionnydd, Newcastle-under-Lyme and Pirehill North, Newcastle-upon-Tyne, Northampton, Rhuddlan, Staffordshire Moorlands, Stoke-on-Trent, Towcester, Wellingborough, and Ynys Mon/Anglesey) (SI 1998/2327)
		Not in force (otherwise)
	67	Repealed (*partly never in force*)
	68–71	30 Sep 1998 (SI 1998/2327)

Crime and Disorder Act 1998 (c 37)—*contd*

Schedule

8, para	72–78		Repealed
	79–82		30 Sep 1998 (SI 1998/2327)
	83	(1)	(a)	30 Sep 1998 (SI 1998/2327)
			(b)	1 Jan 1999 (SI 1998/3263)
		(2), (3)		1 Jan 1999 (SI 1998/3263)
		(4)–(6)		30 Sep 1998 (SI 1998/2327)
	84		30 Sep 1998 (SI 1998/2327)
	85		Repealed
	86		*Not in force*
	87		30 Sep 1998 (SI 1998/2327)
	88	(1), (2)		30 Sep 1998 (SI 1998/2327)
		(3)	(a)	1 Jan 1999 (SI 1998/3263)
			(b)	30 Sep 1998 (SI 1998/2327)
	89		30 Sep 1998 (SI 1998/2327)
	90		*Not in force*
	91		30 Sep 1998 (SI 1998/2327)
	92		Repealed
	93		4 Jan 1999 (for the purpose of sending any person for trial under s 51 from the petty sessions areas of Bromley, Croydon, and Sutton, the petty sessional divisions of Aberconwy, Arfon, Blackburn, Darwen and Ribble Valley, Burnley and Pendle, Colwyn, Corby, Daventry, Dyffryn Clwyd, Eifionydd and Pwllheli, Gateshead, Kettering, Meirionnydd, Newcastle-under-Lyme and Pirehill North, Newcastle-upon-Tyne, Northampton, Rhuddlan, Staffordshire Moorlands, Stoke-on-Trent, Towcester, Wellingborough, and Ynys Mon/Anglesey) (SI 1998/2327) *Not in force* (otherwise)
	94, 95		30 Sep 1998 (in the areas of the counties of Bedfordshire, Devon and Hampshire, the Isle of Wight, the cities of Portsmouth, Sheffield, Southampton and Westminster, the Royal borough of Kensington and Chelsea, the London boroughs of Hammersmith and Fulham, and Lewisham, the Metropolitan boroughs of St Helens and Wolverhampton, and the boroughs of Blackburn with Darwen, and Luton) (SI 1998/2327)

Crime and Disorder Act 1998 (c 37)—*contd*

Schedule

8, para	94, 95—*contd*	1 Apr 2000 (otherwise) (SI 2000/924)
	96	Repealed
	97	30 Sep 1998 (SI 1998/2327)
	98	30 Sep 1998 (subject to transitional provisions)(SI 1998/2327)
	99	31 Jul 1998 (s 121(2))
	100–103	30 Sep 1998 (subject to transitional provisions) (SI 1998/2327)
	104	30 Sep 1998 (subject to transitional provisions) (SI 1998/2327)
	105–108	30 Sep 1998 (SI 1998/2327)
	109, 110	Repealed
	111	1 Apr 2000 (SI 1999/3426)
	112	Repealed
	113	30 Sep 1998 (SI 1998/2327)
	114	1 Apr 2000 (SI 1999/3426)
	115, 116	30 Sep 1998 (SI 1998/2327)
	117	31 Jul 1998 (s 121(2))
	118–124	30 Sep 1998 (SI 1998/2327)
	125 (a)	4 Jan 1999 (for the purpose of sending any person for trial under s 51 from the petty sessions areas of Bromley, Croydon, and Sutton, the petty sessional divisions of Aberconwy, Arfon, Blackburn, Darwen and Ribble Valley, Burnley and Pendle, Colwyn, Corby, Daventry, Dyffryn Clwyd, Eifionydd and Pwllheli, Gateshead, Kettering, Meirionnydd, Newcastle-under-Lyme and Pirehill North, Newcastle-upon-Tyne, Northampton, Rhuddlan, Staffordshire Moorlands, Stoke-on-Trent, Towcester, Wellingborough, and Ynys Mon/Anglesey) (SI 1998/2327)
		Not in force (otherwise)
	(b)	1 Jun 1999 (SI 1999/1279)
	126	4 Jan 1999 (for the purpose of sending any person for trial under s 51 from the petty sessions areas of Bromley, Croydon, and Sutton, the petty sessional divisions of Aberconwy, Arfon, Blackburn, Darwen and Ribble Valley, Burnley and Pendle, Colwyn, Corby, Daventry, Dyffryn Clwyd, Eifionydd and Pwllheli, Gateshead, Kettering, Meirionnydd, Newcastle-under-Lyme and Pirehill

Crime and Disorder Act 1998 (c 37)—*contd*

Schedule

8, para	126—*contd*			North, Newcastle-upon-Tyne, Northampton, Rhuddlan, Staffordshire Moorlands, Stoke-on-Trent, Towcester, Wellingborough, and Ynys Mon/Anglesey) (SI 1998/2327)
				Not in force (otherwise)
	127	(a)		Repealed (*never in force in part*)
		(b)		1 Jun 1999 (SI 1999/1279)
	128, 129			4 Jan 1999 (for the purpose of sending any person for trial under s 51 from the petty sessions areas of Bromley, Croydon, and Sutton, the petty sessional divisions of Aberconwy, Arfon, Blackburn, Darwen and Ribble Valley, Burnley and Pendle, Colwyn, Corby, Daventry, Dyffryn Clwyd, Eifionydd and Pwllheli, Gateshead, Kettering, Meirionnydd, Newcastle-under-Lyme and Pirehill North, Newcastle-upon-Tyne, Northampton, Rhuddlan, Staffordshire Moorlands, Stoke-on-Trent, Towcester, Wellingborough, and Ynys Mon/Anglesey) (SI 1998/2327)
				Not in force (otherwise)
	130			30 Sep 1998 (SI 1998/2327)
	131	(1), (2)		30 Sep 1998 (in the areas of the counties of Bedfordshire, Devon and Hampshire, the Isle of Wight, the cities of Portsmouth, Sheffield, Southampton and Westminster, the Royal borough of Kensington and Chelsea, the London boroughs of Hammersmith and Fulham, and Lewisham, the Metropolitan boroughs of St Helens and Wolverhampton, and the boroughs of Blackburn with Darwen, and Luton) (SI 1998/2327)
				1 Apr 2000 (otherwise) (SI 2000/924)
		(3)		30 Sep 1998 (SI 1998/2327)
	132–134			30 Sep 1998 (SI 1998/2327)
	135	(1)		30 Sep 1998 (SI 1998/2327)
		(2)	(a)	1 Apr 2000 (SI 1999/3426)
			(b)	30 Sep 1998 (SI 1998/2327)
		(3)–(8)		30 Sep 1998 (SI 1998/2327)
		(9), (10)		1 Apr 2000 (SI 1999/3426)

Crime and Disorder Act 1998 (c 37)—*contd*
Schedule

8, para	136–143		30 Sep 1998 (SI 1998/2327)
	144		1 Apr 2000 (SI 1999/3426)
9, para	1, 2		30 Sep 1998 (SI 1998/2327)
	3, 4		Repealed
	5		30 Sep 1998 (in the areas, for the purpose of reprimanding or warning a person under s 65, of the county of Hampshire, the Isle of Wight, the cities of Portsmouth, Sheffield, Southampton and Westminster, the Royal borough of Kensington and Chelsea, the London borough of Hammersmith and Fulham, the Metropolitan borough of Wolverhampton, and the borough of Blackburn with Darwen) (SI 1998/2327)
			1 Apr 2000 (in the areas, for the purpose of reprimanding or warning a person under s 65, of the counties of Oxfordshire, Norfolk, the cities of Cardiff, Sunderland, the London boroughs of Lewisham, Greenwich, Southwark, the Metropolitan borough of Gateshead) (SI 2000/924)
			1 Jun 2000 (otherwise) (SI 2000/924)
	6		30 Sep 1998 (SI 1998/2327)
	7		1 Jul 1999 (SI 1998/3263)
	8		30 Sep 1998 (SI 1998/2327)
	9		7 Aug 1998 (SI 1998/1883)
	10		28 Jan 1999 (SI 1998/3263)
	11		30 Sep 1998 (SI 1998/2327)
	12	(1)	30 Sep 1998 (SI 1998/2327)
		(2)	1 Jan 1999 (SI 1998/3263)
		(3)–(9)	30 Sep 1998 (SI 1998/2327)
	13–15		30 Sep 1998 (SI 1998/2327)
10			30 Sep 1998 (repeals of or in Treason Act 1790, Treason Act 1795; Treason by Women Act (Ireland) 1796; Treason Act 1817; Treason Felony Act 1848; Sentence of Death (Expectant Mothers) Act 1931; Children and Young Persons Act 1933; Criminal Justice Act (Northern Ireland) 1945; Criminal Justice Act 1967, s 56(3), (13), Criminal Appeal Act 1968; Children and Young Persons

Crime and Disorder Act 1998 (c 37)—*contd*
Schedule
10—*contd*

Act 1969; Criminal Justice Act 1972;
Powers of Criminal Courts
Act 1973, ss 1B, 1C, in s 2(1), the
words "For the purposes" to
"available evidence", ss 11 (subject
to transitional provisions), 14, 31,
32, Schs 1A, 5; Bail Act 1976;
Magistrates' Courts Act 1980,
ss 38, 38A, 108, Sch 7; Criminal
Justice Act 1982, ss 3, 18, 19, 66,
Sch 14; Family Law Reform
Act 1987; Criminal Justice Act 1988;
Prisons (Scotland) Act 1989;
Criminal Justice Act 1991, ss 6, 33,
37(4), Schs 2, 11; Prisoners and
Criminal Proceedings (Scotland)
Act 1993 (subject to transitional
provisions); Criminal Justice and
Public Order Act 1994, ss 35,
130(4); Criminal Procedure
(Scotland) Act 1995; Crime
(Sentences) Act 1997, ss 1, 8,
10–27, 35, 43, 54, Schs 1, 2, 4–6;
Crime and Punishment (Scotland)
Act 1997; Police Act 1997)
(SI 1998/2327)

30 Sep 1998 (repeals of Powers of
Criminal Courts Act 1973, in
s 2(1) (the words "by a probation
officer"); Crime (Sentences)
Act 1997, s 31(2)) (in the areas of
the counties of Bedfordshire,
Devon and Hampshire, the Isle of
Wight, the cities of Portsmouth,
Sheffield, Southampton and
Westminster, the Royal borough
of Kensington and Chelsea, the
London boroughs of Hammersmith
and Fulham, and Lewisham, the
Metropolitan boroughs of St
Helens and Wolverhampton, and
the boroughs of Blackburn with
Darwen, and Luton) (SI 1998/2327)

1 Jan 1999 (repeals of or in Criminal
Justice Act 1991, ss 37(1), 38, 45)
(SI 1998/3263)

4 Jan 1999 (repeals in Magistrates'
Courts Act 1980, ss 125, 126) (for
the purpose of sending any person

Crime and Disorder Act 1998 (c 37)—*contd*
Schedule
10—*contd*

for trial under s 51 from the petty
sessions areas of Bromley, Croydon,
and Sutton, the petty sessional
divisions of Aberconwy, Arfon,
Blackburn, Darwen and Ribble
Valley, Burnley and Pendle,
Colwyn, Corby, Daventry, Dyffryn
Clwyd, Eifionydd and Pwllheli,
Gateshead, Kettering, Meirionnydd,
Newcastle-under-Lyme and Pirehill
North, Newcastle-upon-Tyne,
Northampton, Rhuddlan,
Staffordshire Moorlands,
Stoke-on-Trent, Towcester,
Wellingborough, and Ynys
Mon/Anglesey) (SI 1998/2327)

1 Jun 1999 (repeals of Criminal
Justice Act 1991, s 62; Criminal
Justice and Public Order Act 1994,
s 20) (SI 1999/1279)

1 Apr 2000 (repeals of or in Criminal
Justice Act 1967, ss 56(6), 67;
Powers of Criminal Courts
Act 1973, ss 1, 42; Magistrates'
Courts Act 1980, 37; Criminal
Justice Act 1982, ss 1A–1C;
Criminal Justice Act 1991, ss 31,
61, Sch 12; Probation Service
Act 1993, s 17; Criminal Justice
and Public Order Act 1994, ss 1–4,
Sch 10; Drug Trafficking Act 1994,
s 2) (subject to transitional
provisions and savings)
(SI 1999/3426)

1 Apr 2000 (repeals of Powers
of Criminal Courts Act 1973,
s 2(1) (the words "by a
probation officer"); Crime
(Sentences) Act 1997, s 31(2))
(so far as not already in force)
(SI 2000/924)

Not in force (otherwise)

---

1   The transitional provision relating to s 38(4)(c) of this Act (contained in SI 1998/2327, art 9) is
      revoked by SI 2000/924, art 6, as from 1 April 2000

2   Orders made under Access to Justice Act 1999, s 108(1) bringing the prospective repeal into force
      will be noted to that Act

3   Orders made under Criminal Justice and Police Act 2001, s 138 bringing the prospective repeal
      into force will be noted to that Act

Criminal Justice (International Co-operation) (Amendment) Act 1998 (c 27)

RA: 9 Jul 1998

Commencement provisions: s 2(2)

9 Sep 1998 (s 2(2))

Criminal Justice (Terrorism and Conspiracy) Act 1998 (c 40)

RA: 4 Sep 1998

4 Sep 1998 (RA)

Criminal Procedure (Intermediate Diets) (Scotland) Act 1998 (c 10)

RA: 8 Apr 1998

8 Apr 1998 (RA)

Data Protection Act 1998 (c 29)

RA: 16 Jul 1998

Commencement provisions: s 75(2), (3); Data Protection Act 1998 (Commencement) Order 2000, SI 2000/183

Section

1–3		16 Jul 1998 (s 75(2))
4–6		1 Mar 2000 (SI 2000/183)
7	(1), (2)	1 Mar 2000 (SI 2000/183)
	(3)	Substituted by Freedom of Information Act 2000, s 73, Sch 6, para 1 (qv)
	(4)–(6)	1 Mar 2000 (SI 2000/183)
	(7)	16 Jul 1998 (so far as conferring power to make subordinate legislation) (s 75(2))
		1 Mar 2000 (otherwise) (SI 2000/183)
	(8)–(11)	1 Mar 2000 (SI 2000/183)
8	(1)	16 Jul 1998 (so far as conferring power to make subordinate legislation) (s 75(2))
		1 Mar 2000 (otherwise) (SI 2000/183)
	(2)–(7)	1 Mar 2000 (SI 2000/183)
9	(1), (2)	1 Mar 2000 (SI 2000/183)
	(3)	16 Jul 1998 (so far as conferring power to make subordinate legislation) (s 75(2))
		1 Mar 2000 (otherwise) (SI 2000/183)
9A		Inserted, partly prospectively by Freedom of Information Act 2000, s 69(2)[1]
10	(1)	1 Mar 2000 (SI 2000/183)

Data Protection Act 1998 (c 29)—*contd*

Section

10	(2)	16 Jul 1998 (so far as conferring power to make subordinate legislation) (s 75(2))
		1 Mar 2000 (otherwise) (SI 2000/183)
	(3)–(5)	1 Mar 2000 (SI 2000/183)
11		1 Mar 2000 (SI 2000/183)
12	(1)–(4)	1 Mar 2000 (SI 2000/183)
	(5)	16 Jul 1998 (so far as conferring power to make subordinate legislation) (s 75(2))
		1 Mar 2000 (otherwise) (SI 2000/183)
	(6)–(9)	1 Mar 2000 (SI 2000/183)
12A		Inserted by s 72 of, and Sch 13, para 1 to, this Act to have effect during the period beginning with the commencement of s 72 (1 Mar 2000) and ending on 23 Oct 2007
13–16		1 Mar 2000 (SI 2000/183)
17	(1), (2)	1 Mar 2000 (SI 2000/183)
	(3)	16 Jul 1998 (so far as conferring power to make subordinate legislation) (s 75(2))
		1 Mar 2000 (otherwise) (SI 2000/183)
	(4)	1 Mar 2000 (SI 2000/183)
18	(1)	1 Mar 2000 (SI 2000/183)
	(2)	16 Jul 1998 (so far as conferring power to make subordinate legislation) (s 75(2))
		1 Mar 2000 (otherwise) (SI 2000/183)
	(3)	1 Mar 2000 (SI 2000/183)
	(4)–(6)	16 Jul 1998 (so far as conferring power to make subordinate legislation) (s 75(2))
		1 Mar 2000 (otherwise) (SI 2000/183)
19	(1), (2)	1 Mar 2000 (SI 2000/183)
	(3), (4)	16 Jul 1998 (so far as conferring power to make subordinate legislation) (s 75(2))
		1 Mar 2000 (otherwise) (SI 2000/183)
	(5), (6)	1 Mar 2000 (SI 2000/183)
	(7)	16 Jul 1998 (so far as conferring power to make subordinate legislation) (s 75(2))
		1 Mar 2000 (otherwise) (SI 2000/183)
20	(1)	16 Jul 1998 (so far as conferring power to make subordinate legislation) (s 75(2))
		1 Mar 2000 (otherwise) (SI 2000/183)
	(2)–(4)	1 Mar 2000 (SI 2000/183)

Data Protection Act 1998 (c 29)—*contd*

Section

21		1 Mar 2000 (SI 2000/183)
22	(1)	16 Jul 1998 (so far as conferring power to make subordinate legislation) (s 75(2))
		1 Mar 2000 (otherwise) (SI 2000/183)
	(2)–(6)	1 Mar 2000 (SI 2000/183)
	(7)	16 Jul 1998 (so far as conferring power to make subordinate legislation) (s 75(2))
		1 Mar 2000 (otherwise) (SI 2000/183)
23	(1)	16 Jul 1998 (so far as conferring power to make subordinate legislation) (s 75(2))
		1 Mar 2000 (otherwise) (SI 2000/183)
	(2)	1 Mar 2000 (SI 2000/183)
24	(1), (2)	1 Mar 2000 (SI 2000/183)
	(3)	16 Jul 1998 (so far as conferring power to make subordinate legislation) (s 75(2))
		1 Mar 2000 (otherwise) (SI 2000/183)
	(4), (5)	1 Mar 2000 (SI 2000/183)
25	(1)	16 Jul 1998 (s 75(2))
	(2), (3)	1 Mar 2000 (SI 2000/183)
	(4)	16 Jul 1998 (s 75(2))
26		16 Jul 1998 (s 75(2))
27–29		1 Mar 2000 (SI 2000/183)
30	(1)–(3)	16 Jul 1998 (so far as conferring power to make subordinate legislation) (s 75(2))
		1 Mar 2000 (otherwise) (SI 2000/183)
	(4), (5)	1 Mar 2000 (SI 2000/183)
31		1 Mar 2000 (SI 2000/183)
32	(1), (2)	1 Mar 2000 (SI 2000/183)
	(3)	16 Jul 1998 (so far as conferring power to make subordinate legislation) (s 75(2))
		1 Mar 2000 (otherwise) (SI 2000/183)
	(4)–(6)	1 Mar 2000 (SI 2000/183)
33		1 Mar 2000 (SI 2000/183)
33A		Prospectively inserted by Freedom of Information Act 2000, s 70(1)[1]
34, 35		1 Mar 2000 (SI 2000/183)
35A		Prospectively inserted by Freedom of Information Act 2000, s 73, Sch 6, para 2[1]
36, 37		1 Mar 2000 (SI 2000/183)
38		16 Jul 1998 (so far as conferring power to make subordinate legislation) (s 75(2))

Data Protection Act 1998 (c 29)—*contd*

Section

38—*contd*		1 Mar 2000 (otherwise) (SI 2000/183)
39		1 Mar 2000 (SI 2000/183)
40	(1)–(8)	1 Mar 2000 (SI 2000/183)
	(9)	16 Jul 1998 (so far as conferring power to make subordinate legislation) (s 75(2))
		1 Mar 2000 (otherwise) (SI 2000/183)
	(10)	1 Mar 2000 (SI 2000/183)
41–50		1 Mar 2000 (SI 2000/183)
51	(1), (2)	1 Mar 2000 (SI 2000/183)
	(3)	16 Jul 1998 (so far as conferring power to make subordinate legislation) (s 75(2))
		1 Mar 2000 (otherwise) (SI 2000/183)
	(4)–(9)	1 Mar 2000 (SI 2000/183)
52, 53		1 Mar 2000 (SI 2000/183)
54	(1)	1 Mar 2000 (SI 2000/183)
	(2)–(4)	16 Jul 1998 (so far as conferring power to make subordinate legislation) (s 75(2))
		1 Mar 2000 (otherwise) (SI 2000/183)
	(5)–(8)	1 Mar 2000 (SI 2000/183)
55		1 Mar 2000 (SI 2000/183)
56	(1)–(6)	*Not in force*
	(6A)	Prospectively inserted by Freedom of Information Act 2000, s 68(4)[1]
	(7)	*Not in force*
	(8)	16 Jul 1998 (so far as conferring power to make subordinate legislation) (s 75(2))
		Not in force (otherwise)
	(9), (10)	*Not in force*
57–61		1 Mar 2000 (SI 2000/183)
62		1 Mar 2000 (subject to transitional provisions) (SI 2000/183)
63		1 Mar 2000 (SI 2000/183)
63A		Prospectively inserted by Freedom of Information Act 2000, s 73, Sch 6, para 3[1]
64	(1), (2)	1 Mar 2000 (SI 2000/183)
	(3)	16 Jul 1998 (so far as conferring power to make subordinate legislation) (s 75(2))
		1 Mar 2000 (otherwise) (SI 2000/183)
67–71		16 Jul 1998 (s 75(2))
72–74		1 Mar 2000 (SI 2000/183)
75		16 Jul 1998 (s 75(2))
Schedule		
1		1 Mar 2000 (SI 2000/183)

Data Protection Act 1998 (c 29)—*contd*

Schedule

2, para	1–5		1 Mar 2000 (SI 2000/183)
	6	(1)	1 Mar 2000 (SI 2000/183)
		(2)	16 Jul 1998 (so far as conferring power to make subordinate legislation) (s 75(2))
			1 Mar 2000 (otherwise) (SI 2000/183)
3, para	1		1 Mar 2000 (SI 2000/183)
	2	(1)	1 Mar 2000 (SI 2000/183)
		(2)	16 Jul 1998 (so far as conferring power to make subordinate legislation) (s 75(2))
			1 Mar 2000 (otherwise) (SI 2000/183)
	3–6		1 Mar 2000 (SI 2000/183)
	7	(1)	1 Mar 2000 (SI 2000/183)
		(2)	16 Jul 1998 (so far as conferring power to make subordinate legislation) (s 75(2))
			1 Mar 2000 (otherwise) (SI 2000/183)
	8		1 Mar 2000 (SI 2000/183)
	9	(1)	1 Mar 2000 (SI 2000/183)
		(2)	16 Jul 1998 (so far as conferring power to make subordinate legislation) (s 75(2))
			1 Mar 2000 (otherwise) (SI 2000/183)
	10		16 Jul 1998 (so far as conferring power to make subordinate legislation) (s 75(2))
			1 Mar 2000 (otherwise) (SI 2000/183)
4, para	1–3		1 Mar 2000 (SI 2000/183)
	4	(1)	1 Mar 2000 (SI 2000/183)
		(2)	16 Jul 1998 (so far as conferring power to make subordinate legislation) (s 75(2))
			1 Mar 2000 (otherwise) (SI 2000/183)
	5–9		1 Mar 2000 (SI 2000/183)
5, para	1–15		1 Mar 2000 (SI 2000/183)
	16, 17		Repealed
6, para	1–6		1 Mar 2000 (SI 2000/183)
	7		16 Jul 1998 (so far as conferring power to make subordinate legislation) (s 75(2))
			1 Mar 2000 (otherwise) (SI 2000/183)
	8		1 Mar 2000 (SI 2000/183)
7, para	1–3		1 Mar 2000 (SI 2000/183)
	4		16 Jul 1998 (so far as conferring power to make subordinate legislation) (s 75(2))
			1 Mar 2000 (otherwise) (SI 2000/183)
	5		1 Mar 2000 (SI 2000/183)

Data Protection Act 1998 (c 29)—*contd*
Schedule

7, para	6	(1)	1 Mar 2000 (SI 2000/183)
		(2)	16 Jul 1998 (so far as conferring power to make subordinate legislation) (s 75(2))
			1 Mar 2000 (otherwise) (SI 2000/183)
		(3)	1 Mar 2000 (SI 2000/183)
	7–11		1 Mar 2000 (SI 2000/183)
8–10			1 Mar 2000 (SI 2000/183)
11, 12			16 Jul 1998 (s 75(2))
13–16			1 Mar 2000 (SI 2000/183)

1   Orders made under Freedom of Information Act 2000, s 87, bringing the prospective amendments into force will be noted to that Act

Education (Student Loans) Act 1998 (c 1)

Whole Act repealed, subject to savings and transitional provisions in SI 1998/2004

Employment Rights (Dispute Resolution) Act 1998 (c 8)

RA: 8 Apr 1998

Commencement provisions: s 17(1), (2); Employment Rights (Dispute Resolution) Act 1998 (Commencement No 1 and Transitional and Saving Provisions) Order 1998, SI 1998/1658

Section

1, 2		1 Aug 1998 (SI 1998/1658)
3	(1)–(3)	1 Aug 1998 (subject to a transitional provision) (SI 1998/1658)
	(4)–(6)	1 Aug 1998 (SI 1998/1658)
4		*Not in force*
5		1 Aug 1998 (SI 1998/1658)
6		1 Aug 1998 (subject to a transitional provision) (SI 1998/1658)
7		1 Aug 1998 (SI 1998/1658)
8	(1), (2)	1 Aug 1998 (subject to a transitional provision) (SI 1998/1658)
	(3)	1 Aug 1998 (SI 1998/1658)
	(4)	1 Aug 1998 (subject to a transitional provision) (SI 1998/1658)
	(5)	1 Aug 1998 (SI 1998/1658)
9, 10		1 Aug 1998 (SI 1998/1658)
11		1 Oct 1998 (subject to a saving) (SI 1998/1658)
12		1 Aug 1998 (SI 1998/1658)
13		1 Jan 1999 (subject to a transitional provision) (SI 1998/1658)
14		1 Aug 1998 (subject to a saving) (SI 1998/1658)

Employment Rights (Dispute Resolution) Act 1998 (c 8)—*contd*

Section

15		See Schs 1, 2 below
16–18		8 Apr 1998 (s 17(1))

Schedule

1, para	1–11		1 Aug 1998 (SI 1998/1658)
	12	(1), (2)	1 Aug 1998 (SI 1998/1658)
		(3)	1 Aug 1998 (subject to a transitional provision) (SI 1998/1658)
		(4)	1 Aug 1998 (SI 1998/1658)
	13–16		1 Aug 1998 (SI 1998/1658)
	17	(1)	1 Aug 1998 (SI 1998/1658)
		(2)	8 Apr 1998 (amendment made by this sub-paragraph is deemed always to have had effect) (s 17(1), (3))
		(3)	1 Aug 1998 (SI 1998/1658)
	18		1 Aug 1998 (subject to a saving) (SI 1998/1658)
	19–21		1 Jan 1999 (subject to a transitional provision) (SI 1998/1658)
	22		1 Aug 1998 (SI 1998/1658)
	23		1 Jan 1999 (subject to a transitional provision) (SI 1998/1658)
	24, 25		1 Aug 1998 (SI 1998/1658)
	26		1 Jan 1999 (subject to a transitional provision) (SI 1998/1658)
2			1 Aug 1998 (except repeals in Employment Rights Act 1996, ss 166(2)(a), 168(1)(a)) (subject to a transitional provision and savings) (SI 1998/1658)
			1 Oct 1998 (exceptions noted above) (subject to a saving) (SI 1998/1658)

European Communities (Amendment) Act 1998 (c 21)

RA: 11 Jun 1998

11 Jun 1998 (RA)

Finance Act 1998 (c 36)

RA: 31 Jul 1998

Details of the commencement of Finance Acts are not set out in this work

Fossil Fuel Levy Act 1998 (c 5)

Whole Act repealed

Government of Wales Act 1998 (c 38)

RA: 31 Jul 1998

Commencement provisions: s 158; Government of Wales Act 1998 (Commencement
No 1) Order 1998, SI 1998/2244; Government of Wales Act 1998
(Commencement No 2) Order 1998, SI 1998/2789; Government of Wales
Act 1998 (Commencement No 3) Order 1999, SI 1999/118; Government of
Wales Act 1998 (Commencement No 4) Order 1999, SI 1999/782;
Government of Wales Act 1998 (Commencement No 5) Order 1999,
SI 1999/1290; Government of Wales Act 1998 (Commencement No 6)
Order 2001, SI 2001/1756

Section		
1–34		1 Dec 1998 (SI 1998/2789)
34A		Inserted by Political Parties, Elections and Referendums Act 2000, s 158(1), Sch 21, para 12(1), (4) (qv)
35–49		1 Dec 1998 (SI 1998/2789)
50, 51		31 Jul 1998 (s 158(1))
52–101		1 Dec 1998 (SI 1998/2789)
101A		Inserted, partly prospectively, by Government Resources and Accounts Act 2000, s 29(1), Sch 1, paras 21, 24[1]
102, 103		1 Dec 1998 (SI 1998/2789)
104	(1)–(4)	1 Jul 1999 (SI 1999/1290)
	(4A), (4B)	Inserted by Learning and Skills Act 2000, s 149, Sch 9, para 92(1), (3) (qv)
	(5)	1 Jul 1999 (SI 1999/1290)
	(6)	See Sch 6 below
105	(1)–(3)	14 May 2001 (SI 2001/1756)[2]
	(4)	14 May 2001 (SI 2001/1756)[3]
	(5)	See Sch 7 below
106		1 Dec 1998 (SI 1998/2789)
107		1 Apr 1999 (SI 1999/782)
108–110		1 Dec 1998 (SI 1998/2789)
111	(1)	1 Feb 1999 (SI 1999/118)
	(2)	See Sch 9 below
112		See Sch 10 below
113–115		1 Dec 1998 (SI 1998/2789)
116–118		1 Apr 1999 (SI 1999/782)
119–124		1 Dec 1998 (SI 1998/2789)
125		See Sch 12 below
126		1 Oct 1998 (SI 1998/2244)
127		See Sch 13 below
128		See Sch 14 below
129	(1)	1 Oct 1998 (SI 1998/2244)
	(2)	See Sch 15 below
130	(1)–(3)	1 Oct 1998 (SI 1998/2244)
	(4), (5)	2 Sep 1998 (SI 1998/2244)
131		1 Oct 1998 (SI 1998/2244)

Government of Wales Act 1998 (c 38)—*contd*

Section

132	(1)		2 Sep 1998 (SI 1998/2244)
	(2)–(5)		1 Oct 1998 (SI 1998/2244)
	(6)		2 Sep 1998 (SI 1998/2244)
	(7)		1 Oct 1998 (SI 1998/2244)
133	(1), (2)		1 Oct 1998 (SI 1998/2244)
	(3), (4)		2 Sep 1998 (SI 1998/2244)
134, 135			1 Oct 1998 (SI 1998/2244)
136	(1)–(3)		1 Oct 1998 (SI 1998/2244)
	(4), (5)		2 Sep 1998 (SI 1998/2244)
137			1 Oct 1998 (SI 1998/2244)
138	(1)		2 Sep 1998 (SI 1998/2244)
	(2)–(5)		1 Oct 1998 (SI 1998/2244)
	(6)		2 Sep 1998 (SI 1998/2244)
	(7)		1 Oct 1998 (SI 1998/2244)
139	(1), (2)		1 Oct 1998 (SI 1998/2244)
	(3), (4)		2 Sep 1998 (SI 1998/2244)
140	(1)–(4)		1 Nov 1998 (SI 1998/2244)
	(5), (6)		2 Sep 1998 (SI 1998/2244)
141			1 Nov 1998 (SI 1998/2244)
142	(1)		2 Sep 1998 (SI 1998/2244)
	(2)–(6)		1 Nov 1998 (SI 1998/2244)
	(7), (8)		2 Sep 1998 (SI 1998/2244)
143	(1), (2)		1 Nov 1998 (SI 1998/2244)
	(3), (4)		2 Sep 1998 (SI 1998/2244)
144–149			1 Dec 1998 (SI 1998/2789)
150			2 Sep 1998 (SI 1998/2244)
151			31 Jul 1998 (s 158(1))
152			See Sch 18 below
153–159			31 Jul 1998 (s 158(1))

Schedule

1–5			1 Dec 1998 (SI 1998/2789)
6, para	1, 2		1 May 1999 (SI 1999/1290
	3–9		1 Jul 1999 (SI 1999/1290)
7, para	1	(1), (2)	1 Apr 1999 (SI 1999/782)
		(3)	14 May 2001 (SI 2001/1756) [2]
	2–7		14 May 2001 (SI 2001/1756) [2]
	8		1 Apr 1999 (SI 1999/782)
	9	(1)	14 May 2001 (SI 2001/1756) [2]
		(2)	1 Apr 1999 (so far as relates to an examination under National Audit Act 1983, s 6) (SI 1999/782)
			14 May 2001 (otherwise) (SI 2001/1756) [2]
	10, 11		14 May 2001 (SI 2001/1756) [2]
8			1 Dec 1998 (SI 1998/2789)
9, Pt	I		1 Feb 1999 (SI 1999/118)
	II, para	14–16	1 Jul 1999 (SI 1999/1290)
	17	(1)–(8)	1 Jul 1999 (SI 1999/1290)
		(9)	1 May 1999 (SI 1999/1290)

Government of Wales Act 1998 (c 38)—*contd*

Schedule

9, Pt	II, para	17	(10)	1 Jul 1999 (SI 1999/1290)
		18–27		1 Jul 1999 (SI 1999/1290)
		28		Inserted by Freedom of Information Act 2000, s 76(2), Sch 7, para 8 (qv)
10, para	1			1 Apr 1999 (SI 1999/782)
	2			1 Jul 1999 (SI 1999/1290)
	3	(1), (2)		1 Apr 1999 (SI 1999/782)
		(3), (4)		1 Jul 1999 (SI 1999/1290)
	4			1 Apr 1999 (SI 1999/782)
	5			1 Jul 1999 (SI 1999/1290)
	6, 7			1 Apr 1999 (SI 1999/782)
	8–12			1 Jul 1999 (SI 1999/1290)
	13, 14			1 Apr 1999 (SI 1999/782)
	15	(1), (2)		1 Apr 1999 (SI 1999/782)
		(3)		1 Jul 1999 (SI 1999/1290)
		(4)		1 Apr 1999 (SI 1999/782)
	16, 17			1 Jul 1999 (SI 1999/1290)
11				1 Dec 1998 (SI 1998/2789)
12, para	1			1 Feb 1999 (SI 1999/118)
	2–4			1 Apr 1999 (SI 1999/782)
	5, 6			1 Jul 1999 (SI 1999/1290)
	7			1 Apr 1999 (SI 1999/782)
	8, 9			1 Jul 1999 (SI 1999/1290)
	10–14			1 Apr 1999 (SI 1999/782)
	15	(1), (2)		1 Apr 1999 (SI 1999/782)
		(3)		1 Jul 1999 (SI 1999/1290)
	16			1 Apr 1999 (SI 1999/782)
	17			1 Jul 1999 (SI 1999/1290)
	18, 19			1 Feb 1999 (SI 1999/118)
	20–30			1 Apr 1999 (SI 1999/782)
	31, 32			1 Feb 1999 (SI 1999/118)
	33–36			1 Apr 1999 (SI 1999/782)
13–15				1 Oct 1998 (SI 1998/2244)
16				1 Nov 1998 (SI 1998/2244)
17				1 Dec 1998 (SI 1998/2789)
18, Pt	I			1 Feb 1999 (repeal in Finance Act 1989, s 182) (SI 1999/118)
				1 Apr 1999 (repeals of or in Health Service Commissioners Act 1993, ss 2(2)(b), 18(3); Health Authorities Act 1995) (SI 1999/782)
				1 Jul 1999 (otherwise) (SI 1999/1290)
	II			1 Apr 1999 (except the reference to the General Teaching Council for Wales) (SI 1999/782)
				Not in force (exception noted above)
	III–V			1 Oct 1998 (SI 1998/2244)
	VI			1 Nov 1998 (SI 1998/2244)
	VII			2 Sep 1998 (SI 1998/2244)

Government of Wales Act 1998 (c 38)—*contd*

1   Orders made under Government Resources and Accounts Act 2000, s 30(1), (2), bringing the prospective insertion into force will be noted to that Act

2   This provision does not apply in relation to the financial year beginning on 1 April 2000, or any earlier financial year; see SI 2001/1756, art 2(2)

3   This provision does not apply in relation to the financial year beginning on 1 April 2001, or any earlier financial year; see SI 2001/1756, art 2(3)

Greater London Authority (Referendum) Act 1998 (c 3)

RA: 23 Feb 1998

23 Feb 1998 (RA)

Human Rights Act 1998 (c 42)

RA: 9 Nov 1998

Commencement provisions: s 22(2), (3); Human Rights Act 1998 (Commencement) Order 1998, SI 1998/2882; Human Rights Act 1998 (Commencement No 2) Order 2000, SI 2000/1851

Section

1–17		2 Oct 2000 (SI 2000/1851)
18		9 Nov 1998 (s 22(2))
19		24 Nov 1998 (SI 1998/2882)
20		9 Nov 1998 (s 22(2))
21	(1)–(4)	2 Oct 2000 (SI 2000/1851)
	(5)	9 Nov 1998 (s 22(2))
22		9 Nov 1998 (s 22(2))

Schedule

1–3	2 Oct 2000 (SI 2000/1851)
4	9 Nov 1998 (s 22(2))

Landmines Act 1998 (c 33)

RA: 28 Jul 1998

Commencement provisions: s 29(2); Landmines Act 1998 (Commencement) Order 1999, SI 1999/448

Section

1–28	1 Mar 1999 (SI 1999/448)
29	28 Jul 1998 (s 29(2))

Late Payment of Commercial Debts (Interest) Act 1998 (c 20)

RA: 11 Jun 1998

Commencement provisions: s 17(2); Late Payment of Commercial Debts (Interest) Act 1998 (Commencement No 1) Order 1998, SI 1998/2479; Late Payment of Commercial Debts (Interest) Act 1998 (Commencement No 2) Order 1999, SI 1999/1816; Late Payment of Commercial Debts (Interest) Act 1998 (Commencement No 3) Order 2000, SI 2000/2225; Late Payment of Commercial Debts (Interest) Act 1998 (Commencement No 4) Order 2000, SI 2000/2740

Section

1–16	1 Nov 1998 (in relation to contracts for the supply of goods or services made on or after 1 Nov 1998 made

Late Payment of Commercial Debts (Interest) Act 1998 (c 20)—*contd*

Section

1–16—*contd*	between a small business supplier and a purchaser who is a United Kingdom public authority, or made between a small business supplier and a large business supplier) (SI 1998/2479)
	1 Jul 1999 (in relation to contracts for the supply of goods or services made on or after 1 Jul 1999 between a small business supplier and any purchaser who is a United Kingdom public authority) (SI 1999/1816)
	1 Sept 2000 (in relation to contracts for the supply of goods or services made on or after 1 Sept 2000 between a small business supplier and the Comptroller and Auditor General for Northern Ireland, the Metropolitan Police Authority or the London Fire and Emergency Planning Authority) (SI 2000/2225)
	1 Nov 2000 (in relation to contracts for the supply of goods or services made on or after 1 Nov 2000 between a small business supplier and a small business purchaser) (SI 2000/2740)
	Not in force (otherwise)
17	11 Jun 1998 (s 17(2))

Magistrates' Court (Procedure) Act 1998 (c 15)

RA: 21 May 1998

Commencement provisions: s 5(2), (3); Magistrates' Court (Procedure) Act 1998 (Commencement No 1) Order 1998, SI 1998/1837; Magistrates' Courts (Procedure) Act 1998 (Commencement No 2) Order 1999, SI 1999/1197

Section

1	4 May 1999 (in cases where a summons is issued on or after that date) (SI 1999/1197)
2	1 Sep 1998 (subject to a transitional provision) (SI 1998/1837)
3	1 Sep 1998 (in relation to where the information is substantiated on oath, or the accused is convicted, on or after 1 Sep 1998) (SI 1998/1837)
4	1 Sep 1998 (SI 1998/1837)
5	21 May 1998 (s 5(2))

National Institutions Measure 1998 (No 1)

RA: 2 Jul 1998

Commencement provisions: s 15; Instrument of the Archbishops of 14 October 1998

1 Jan 1999 (Instrument of the Archbishops of 14 October 1998)

National Lottery Act 1998 (c 22)

RA: 2 Jul 1998

Commencement provisions: s 27(3)–(5); National Lottery Act 1998 (Commencement) Order 1999, SI 1999/650

Section		
1		1 Apr 1999 (SI 1999/650)
2–5		2 Sep 1998 (s 27(5))
6–12		2 Jul 1998 (s 27(4))
13, 14		2 Sep 1998 (s 27(5))
15–25		2 Jul 1998 (s 27(4))
26		See Sch 5 below
27		2 Jul 1998 (s 27(4))
Schedule		
1		1 Apr 1999 (SI 1999/650)
2–4		2 Jul 1998 (s 27(4))
5, Pt	I	1 Apr 1999 (SI 1999/650)
	II	2 Jul 1998 (repeals in National Lottery etc Act 1993, s 22, Sch 5, paras 2, 3, 6) (s 27(4))
		2 Sep 1998 (otherwise) (s 27(5))

National Minimum Wage Act 1998 (c 39)

RA: 31 Jul 1998

Commencement provisions: s 56(2); National Minimum Wage Act 1998 (Commencement No 1 and Transitional Provisions) Order 1998, SI 1998/2574; National Minimum Wage Act 1998 (Commencement No 2 and Transitional Provisions) Order 1999, SI 1999/685

Section		
1	(1), (2)	1 Apr 1999 (SI 1998/2574)
	(3), (4)	31 Jul 1998 (so far as confers power to make subordinate legislation) (s 56(2))
		1 Apr 1999 (otherwise) (SI 1998/2574)
	(5)	1 Apr 1999 (SI 1998/2574)
2	(1)	31 Jul 1998 (so far as confers power to make subordinate legislation) (s 56(2))
		Not in force (otherwise)
	(2)–(8)	*Not in force*
3	(1)	*Not in force*

National Minimum Wage Act 1998 (c 39)—*contd*

Section

3	(1A)	Inserted (6 Mar 1999) by National Minimum Wage Act 1998 (Amendment) Regulations 1999, SI 1999/583, reg 2
	(2)	31 Jul 1998 (so far as confers power to make subordinate legislation) (s 56(2))
		Not in force (otherwise)
	(3), (4)	*Not in force*
4	(1)	31 Jul 1998 (so far as confers power to make subordinate legislation) (s 56(2))
		Not in force (otherwise)
	(2)	*Not in force*
5–8		1 Nov 1998 (SI 1998/2574)
9		31 Jul 1998 (so far as confers power to make subordinate legislation) (s 56(2))
		Not in force (otherwise)
10, 11		1 Apr 1999 (SI 1998/2574)
12	(1), (2)	31 Jul 1998 (so far as confers power to make subordinate legislation) (s 56(2))
		1 Apr 1999 (otherwise) (SI 1998/2574)
	(3), (4)	1 Apr 1999 (SI 1998/2574)
13		1 Nov 1998 (SI 1998/2574)
14–20		1 Apr 1999 (SI 1998/2574)
21	(1)–(3)	1 Apr 1999 (SI 1998/2574)
	(4)	31 Jul 1998 (so far as confers power to make subordinate legislation) (s 56(2))
		1 Apr 1999 (otherwise) (SI 1998/2574)
	(5)–(8)	1 Apr 1999 (SI 1998/2574)
22		1 Apr 1999 (SI 1998/2574)
23, 24		1 Nov 1998 (SI 1998/2574)
25		1 Nov 1998 (subject to transitional provisions) (SI 1998/2574)
26	(1)–(4)	1 Nov 1998 (subject to transitional provisions) (SI 1998/2574)
	(5), (6)	Repealed (sub-s (5) *never in force*)
27, 28		1 Apr 1999 (SI 1998/2574)
29		1 Nov 1998 (SI 1998/2574)
30		1 Nov 1998 (so far as it relates to s 24) (SI 1998/2574)
		1 Apr 1999 (otherwise) (SI 1998/2574)
31–33		1 Apr 1999 (SI 1998/2574)
34–40		1 Nov 1998 (SI 1998/2574)

National Minimum Wage Act 1998 (c 39)—*contd*

Section

41		31 Jul 1998 (so far as confers power to make subordinate legislation) (s 56(2))
		Not in force (otherwise)
42	(1)	*Not in force*
	(2)	31 Jul 1998 (so far as confers power to make subordinate legislation) (s 56(2))
		Not in force (otherwise)
	(3)–(5)	*Not in force*
43, 44		1 Nov 1998 (SI 1998/2574)
44A		Inserted by Employment Relations Act 1999, s 22 (qv)
45		1 Nov 1998 (SI 1998/2574)
46		1 Apr 1999 (SI 1999/685)
47	(1)	1 Apr 1999 (SI 1999/685)
	(2)	31 Jul 1998 (so far as confers power to make subordinate legislation) (s 56(2))
		1 Apr 1999 (otherwise) (SI 1999/685)
	(3)	1 Apr 1999 (SI 1999/685)
	(4)	31 Jul 1998 (so far as confers power to make subordinate legislation) (s 56(2))
		1 Apr 1999 (otherwise) (SI 1999/685)
	(5), (6)	1 Apr 1999 (SI 1999/685)
48		1 Nov 1998 (SI 1998/2574)
49	(1)–(8)	1 Nov 1998 (SI 1998/2574)
	(9), (10)	*Not in force*
	(11)	31 Jul 1998 (so far as confers power to make subordinate legislation) (s 56(2))
		1 Nov 1998 (otherwise) (SI 1998/2574)
50		1 Nov 1998 (SI 1998/2574)
51		*Not in force*
52		1 Nov 1998 (SI 1998/2574)
53		See Sch 3 below
54, 55		1 Nov 1998 (SI 1998/2574)
56		31 Jul 1998 (s 56(2))
Schedule		
1		1 Nov 1998 (SI 1998/2574)
2, para	1, 2	1 Apr 1999 (subject to transitional provisions) (SI 1999/685)
	3	1 Apr 1999 (except the words "(f) any reference to a pay reference period shall be disregarded") (subject to transitional provisions) (SI 1999/685)
		Not in force (exception noted above)

National Minimum Wage Act 1998 (c 39)—*contd*

Schedule

2, para	4–12	1 Apr 1999 (subject to transitional provisions) (SI 1999/685)
	13	1 Apr 1999 (except the words "(f) any reference to a pay reference period shall be disregarded") (subject to transitional provisions) (SI 1999/685)
		Not in force (exception noted above)
	14–25	1 Apr 1999 (subject to transitional provisions) (SI 1999/685)
	26	1 Apr 1999 (except the words "(f) any reference to a pay reference period shall be disregarded") (subject to transitional provisions) (SI 1999/685)
		Not in force (exception noted above)
	27	1 Apr 1999 (subject to transitional provisions) (SI 1999/685)
3		1 Nov 1998 (repeals in Employment Tribunals Act 1996; Employment Rights Act 1996) (SI 1998/2574)
		1 Apr 1999 (repeals in Agricultural Wages Act 1948; Agricultural Wages (Scotland) Act 1949) (subject to transitional provisions) (SI 1999/685)
		Not in force (repeal in Employment Rights (Northern Ireland) Order 1996, SI 1996/1919)

Northern Ireland Act 1998 (c 47)

RA: 19 Nov 1998

Commencement provisions: s 101(2), (3); Northern Ireland Act 1998 (Commencement No 1) Order 1999, SI 1999/340; Northern Ireland Act 1998 (Commencement No 2) Order 1999, SI 1999/1753; Northern Ireland Act 1998 (Commencement No 3) Order 1999, SI 1999/2204; Northern Ireland Act 1998 (Commencement No 4) Order 1999, SI 1999/2936; Northern Ireland Act 1998 (Appointed Day) Order 1999, SI 1999/3208; Northern Ireland Act 1998 (Commencement No 5) Order 1999, SI 1999/3209

Section

1, 2	2 Dec 1999 (SI 1999/3209)
3	19 Nov 1998 (s 101(2))
4	2 Dec 1999 (SI 1999/3209)
5–19	2 Dec 1999 (SI 1999/3208)
19A	Inserted by Disqualifications Act 2000, s 2 (qv)
20–30	2 Dec 1999 (SI 1999/3208)

Northern Ireland Act 1998 (c 47)—*contd*

Section

31–39		2 Dec 1999 (SI 1999/3209)
40	(1)–(3)	2 Dec 1999 (SI 1999/3209)
	(3A)	Inserted by Disqualifications Act 2000, s 3(2) (qv)
	(4)–(9)	2 Dec 1999 (SI 1999/3209)
	(10)	See Sch 5 below
41–48		2 Dec 1999 (SI 1999/3209)
49	(1)	1 Mar 1999 (SI 1999/340)
	(2)–(4)	2 Dec 1999 (SI 1999/3209)
50–54		2 Dec 1999 (SI 1999/3209)
55		19 Nov 1998 (s 101(2))
56–67[1]		2 Dec 1999 (SI 1999/3209)
68	(1)–(3)	15 Feb 1999 (for the purpose of making appointments to the Northern Ireland Human Rights Commission) (SI 1999/340)
		1 Mar 1999 (otherwise) (SI 1999/340)
	(4)	See Sch 7 below
69	(1), (2)	1 Mar 1999 (SI 1999/340)
	(3)	1 Mar 1999 (so far as provides for the Commission to advise the Secretary of State) (SI 1999/340)
		2 Dec 1999 (otherwise) (SI 1999/3209)
	(4)	2 Dec 1999 (SI 1999/3209)
	(5)	1 Jun 1999 (SI 1999/340)
	(6)–(11)	1 Mar 1999 (SI 1999/340)
70		1 Jun 1999 (SI 1999/340)
71	(1)	1 Jun 1999 (to the extent that it makes provision about s 69(5) of this Act) (SI 1999/340)
		2 Dec 1999 (otherwise) (SI 1999/3209)
	(2)	1 Jun 1999 (SI 1999/340)
	(3), (4)	2 Dec 1999 (SI 1999/3209)
	(5)	1 Jun 1999 (SI 1999/340)
72		1 Mar 1999 (SI 1999/340)
73	(1)	15 Feb 1999 (for the purpose of making appointments to the Equality Commission for Northern Ireland and appointing the Chief Commissioner and the Deputy Chief Commissioner) (SI 1999/340)
		2 Aug 1999 (otherwise, except for the purposes of Employment and Treatment (Northern Ireland) Order 1998, SI 1998/3162, Sch 4, para 6) (SI 1999/2204)
		1 Oct 1999 (exception noted above) (SI 1999/2204)

Northern Ireland Act 1998 (c 47)—*contd*

Section

73	(2)–(4)		2 Aug 1999 (SI 1999/2204)
	(5)		See Sch 8 below
74	(1)–(4)		1 Oct 1999 (SI 1999/2204)
	(5), (6)		21 Jun 1999 (for the purpose of making orders) (SI 1999/1753)
			1 Oct 1999 (otherwise) (SI 1999/2204)
75	(1), (2)		1 Jan 2000 (SI 1999/2204)
	(3)	(a)	1 Mar 1999 (for the purpose of making designations under s 75(3)(a), (d)) (SI 1999/340)
			1 Jan 2000 (otherwise) (SI 1999/2204)
		(b), (c)	1 Jan 2000 (SI 1999/2204)
		(cc)	Inserted by Police (Northern Ireland) Act 2000, s 78(1), Sch 6, para 24(1), (2) (qv)
		(d)	1 Mar 1999 (for the purpose of making designations under s 75(3)(a), (d)) (SI 1999/340)
			1 Jan 2000 (otherwise) (SI 1999/2204)
	(4)		See Sch 9 below
	(5)		1 Jan 2000 (SI 1999/2204)
76–78			2 Dec 1999 (SI 1999/3209)
79			See Sch 10 below
80, 81			2 Dec 1999 (SI 1999/3209)
82	(1), (2)		2 Dec 1999 (SI 1999/3209)
	(3)–(5)		1 Mar 1999 (SI 1999/340)
83–85			2 Dec 1999 (SI 1999/3209)
86			19 Nov 1998 (s 101(2))
87–89			2 Dec 1999 (SI 1999/3209)
90			2 Aug 1999 (SI 1999/2204)
91	(1)		See Sch 11 below
	(2)–(6)		1 Mar 1999 (SI 1999/340)
	(7)–(9)		2 Aug 1999 (SI 1999/2204)
92	(1), (2)		2 Aug 1999 (SI 1999/2204)
	(3), (4)		1 Mar 1999 (SI 1999/340)
93			19 Nov 1998 (s 101(2))
94			2 Dec 1999 (SI 1999/3209)
95	(1)–(4)		2 Dec 1999 (SI 1999/3209)
	(5)		See Sch 12 below
96			19 Nov 1998 (s 101(2))
97			1 Mar 1999 (SI 1999/340)
98			19 Nov 1998 (s 101(2))
99			See Sch 13 below
100	(1)		See Sch 14 below
	(2)		See Sch 15 below
101			19 Nov 1998 (s 101(2))

Schedule

1–4		2 Dec 1999 (SI 1999/3209)
5, para	1–5	2 Dec 1999 (SI 1999/3209)

Northern Ireland Act 1998 (c 47)—*contd*
Schedule

5, para	6		28 Oct 1999 (SI 1999/2936)
6			2 Dec 1999 (SI 1999/3209)
7, para	1, 2		15 Feb 1999 (for the purpose of making appointments to the Northern Ireland Human Rights Commission) (SI 1999/340)
			1 Mar 1999 (otherwise) (SI 1999/340)
	3–11		1 Mar 1999 (SI 1999/340)
8, para	1, 2		15 Feb 1999 (for the purpose of making appointments to the Equality Commission for Northern Ireland and appointing the Chief Commissioner and Deputy Chief Commissioner) (SI 1999/340)
			2 Aug 1999 (otherwise) (SI 1999/2204)
	3		2 Aug 1999 (SI 1999/2204)
	3A		Inserted by Equality (Disability, etc) (Northern Ireland) Order 2000, SI 2000/1110 (NI 2), art 18
	4–12		2 Aug 1999 (SI 1999/2204)
9, para	1	(a)	1 Jan 2000 (SI 1999/2204)
		(b)	1 Oct 1999 (except for the purposes of para 2 of this Schedule) (SI 1999/2204)
			1 Jan 2000 (exception noted above) (SI 1999/2204)
		(c)	1 Jan 2000 (SI 1999/2204)
	2–12		1 Jan 2000 (SI 1999/2204)
10, para	1–37		2 Dec 1999 (SI 1999/3209)
	38		1 Mar 1999 (SI 1999/340)
	39–41		2 Dec 1999 (SI 1999/3209)
11, para	1–3		15 Feb 1999 (for the purpose of making appointments and nominations in connection with the Tribunal established under s 91 of this Act) (SI 1999/340)
			2 Aug 1999 (otherwise) (SI 1999/2204)
	4–7		2 Aug 1999 (SI 1999/2204)
	8		15 Feb 1999 (for the purpose of making appointments and nominations in connection with the Tribunal established under s 91 of this Act) (SI 1999/340)
			2 Aug 1999 (otherwise) (SI 1999/2204)
	9–11		2 Aug 1999 (SI 1999/2204)
12, para	1		1 Oct 1999 (SI 1999/2204)
	2–12		2 Dec 1999 (SI 1999/3209)
	13		1 Oct 1999 (SI 1999/2204)
13, para	1		Repealed (*never in force*)

Northern Ireland Act 1998 (c 47)—*contd*

Schedule

13, para	2	1 Oct 1999 (SI 1999/2204)
	3–9	2 Dec 1999 (SI 1999/3209)
	10	Repealed (*never in force*)
	11–15	2 Dec 1999 (SI 1999/3209)
	16	Repealed
	17	2 Dec 1999 (SI 1999/3209)
	18	Repealed
	19	1 Oct 1999 (SI 1999/2204)
	20	19 Nov 1998 (s 101(2))
	21	2 Dec 1999 (SI 1999/3209)
14, para	1	1 Jun 1999 (so far as refers to s 71 of this Act) (SI 1999/340)
		2 Dec 1999 (otherwise) (SI 1999/3209)
	2–17	2 Dec 1999 (SI 1999/3209)
	18	2 Aug 1999 (SI 1999/2204)
	19–23	2 Dec 1999 (SI 1999/3209)
15		19 Nov 1998 (repeal of Northern Ireland Constitution Act 1973, s 31(4)–(6)) (s 101(2))
		1 Mar 1999 (repeal of Northern Ireland Constitution Act 1973, s 20) (SI 1999/340)
		1 Oct 1999 (repeals of or in House of Commons Disqualification Act 1975; Northern Ireland Assembly Disqualification Act 1975, Sch 1; Sex Discrimination (Northern Ireland) Order 1976; Commissioner for Complaints (Northern Ireland) Order 1996, Sch 2; Race Relations (Northern Ireland) Order 1997) (SI 1999/2204)
		2 Dec 1999 (so far as not already in force, except repeals of or in Fair Employment (Northern Ireland) Act 1976; Fair Employment (Northern Ireland) Act 1989; Northern Ireland (Emergency Provisions) Act 1996; Northern Ireland Act 1998) (SI 1999/3209)
		Not in force (exceptions noted above)

[1] S 56 of this Act ceases to have effect for any period during which the Northern Ireland Act 2000, s 1 is in force

Northern Ireland (Elections) Act 1998 (c 12)

Whole Act repealed, subject to transitional provisions

Northern Ireland (Emergency Provisions) Act 1998 (c 9)

Whole Act repealed

Northern Ireland (Sentences) Act 1998 (c 35)

RA: 28 Jul 1998

Commencement provisions: s 22; Northern Ireland (Sentences) Act 1998
  (Commencement) Order 1998, SI 1998/1858

28 Jul 1998 (SI 1998/1858)

Nuclear Explosions (Prohibition and Inspections) Act 1998 (c 7)

RA: 18 Mar 1998

Commencement provisions: s 15(1)

Not in force

Pesticides Act 1998 (c 26)

RA: 9 Jul 1998

Commencement provisions: s 3(b)

9 Sep 1998 (s 3(b))

Petroleum Act 1998 (c 17)

RA: 11 Jun 1998

Commencement provisions: s 52; Petroleum Act 1998 (Commencement No 1)
  Order 1999, SI 1999/161

Section		
1–4		15 Feb 1999 (SI 1999/161)
5	(1)–(4)	11 Jun 1998 (s 52(1))
	(5)–(10)	15 Feb 1999 (SI 1999/161)
	(11)	11 Jun 1998 (s 52(1))
6–17		15 Feb 1999 (SI 1999/161)
17A–17H		Inserted (10 Aug 2000) by Gas (Third Party Access and Accounts) Regulations 2000, SI 2000/1937, reg 2(4), Sch 4, para 4
18–49		15 Feb 1999 (SI 1999/161)
50		See Sch 4 below
51		See Sch 5 below
52		11 Jun 1998 (s 52(1))
53		15 Feb 1999 (SI 1999/161)
Schedule		
1		11 Jun 1998 (so far as relates to s 5(1)–(4), (11)) (s 52(1)) 15 Feb 1999 (otherwise) (SI 1999/161)

Petroleum Act 1998 (c 17)—*contd*

Schedule

2, 3		15 Feb 1999 (SI 1999/161)
4, para	1–7	15 Feb 1999 (SI 1999/161)
	8	*Not in force*
	9	15 Feb 1999 (SI 1999/161)
	10	Repealed (*never in force*)
	11	*Not in force*
	12	15 Feb 1999 (SI 1999/161)
	13	*Not in force*
	14–21	15 Feb 1999 (SI 1999/161)
	22	15 Feb 1999 (SI 1999/161); repealed (1 Mar 2005) by Competition Act 1998 (Transitional, Consequential and Supplemental Provisions) Order 2000, SI 2000/311, art 34
	23–26	15 Feb 1999 (SI 1999/161)
	27	Repealed
	28–33	15 Feb 1999 (SI 1999/161)
	34	*Not in force*
	35–39	15 Feb 1999 (SI 1999/161)
	40	*Not in force*
	41	15 Feb 1999 (SI 1999/161)
5		15 Feb 1999 (except repeals of Employment (Continental Shelf) Act 1978, Trade Union and Labour Relations (Consolidation) Act 1992, s 287(5), Employment Rights Act 1996, s 201(5)) (SI 1999/161)
		Not in force (exceptions noted above)

Police (Northern Ireland) Act 1998 (c 32)

RA: 24 Jul 1998

Commencement provisions: s 75; Police (1998 Act) (Commencement No 1) Order (Northern Ireland) 1998, SR 1998/346; Police (1998 Act) (Commencement No 2) Order (Northern Ireland) 1999, SR 1999/48; Police (1998 Act) (Commencement No 3) Order (Northern Ireland) 1999, SR 1999/176; Police (Northern Ireland) Act 1998 (Commencement) Order (Northern Ireland) 2000, SI 2000/399[2]

Section

1		Repealed
2		Repealed (*partly never in force*)
3–24		Repealed
25	(1)–(3)	9 Feb 1999 (subject to transitional provisions and savings) (SR 1999/48)
	(4)	*Not in force*

Police (Northern Ireland) Act 1998 (c 32)—*contd*

Section

25	(5)–(8)	9 Feb 1999 (subject to transitional provisions and savings) (SR 1999/48)
26	(1)–(3)	9 Feb 1999 (subject to transitional provisions and savings) (SR 1999/48)
	(4)	1 Apr 1999 (subject to transitional provisions and savings) (SR 1999/176)
	(5), (6)	9 Feb 1999 (subject to transitional provisions and savings) (SR 1999/48)
27, 28		9 Feb 1999 (subject to transitional provisions and savings) (SR 1999/48)
29		1 Apr 1999 (subject to transitional provisions and savings) (SR 1999/176)
30		9 Feb 1999 (subject to transitional provisions and savings) (SR 1999/48)
31		1 Apr 1999 (subject to transitional provisions and savings) (SR 1999/176)
32–35		9 Feb 1999 (subject to transitional provisions and savings) (SR 1999/48)
36–39		Repealed
40	(1), (2)	1 Apr 1999 (subject to transitional provisions and savings) (SR 1999/176)
	(3), (4)	*Not in force*
41–46		1 Apr 1999 (subject to transitional provisions and savings) (SR 1999/176)
47–49		Repealed
50		6 Nov 2000 (SI 2000/399)[2]
51	(1), (2)	6 Nov 2000 (SI 2000/399)[2]
	(3)	See Sch 3 below
	(4), (5)	6 Nov 2000 (SI 2000/399)[2]
52–58		6 Nov 2000 (SI 2000/399)[2]
58A		Inserted by Police (Northern Ireland) Act 2000, s 62(1) (qv)
59–61		6 Nov 2000 (SI 2000/399)[2]
61A		Inserted by Police (Northern Ireland) Act 2000, s 63(1) (qv)
61AA		Inserted by Police (Northern Ireland) Act 2000, s 64 (qv)
62–65		6 Nov 2000 (SI 2000/399)[2]

Police (Northern Ireland) Act 1998 (c 32)—*contd*

Section

66–69		9 Feb 1999 (subject to transitional provisions and savings) (SR 1999/48)
70		Repealed
71, 72		1 Apr 1999 (subject to transitional provisions and savings) (SR 1999/176)
73		Substituted by Police (Northern Ireland) Act 2000, s 78(1), Sch 6, para 23(1), (6)(b) (qv)
74	(1)	See Sch 4 below
	(2)	See Sch 5 below
	(3)	See Sch 6 below
	(4)	1 Apr 1999 (subject to transitional provisions and savings) (SR 1999/176)
75		8 Oct 1998 (SR 1998/346)
76	(1)	8 Oct 1998 (SR 1998/346)
	(2)	*Not in force*
	(3)	1 Apr 1999 (subject to transitional provisions and savings) (SR 1999/176)
77		8 Oct 1998 (SR 1998/346)

Schedule

1, 2		Repealed
3		6 Nov 2000 (SI 2000/399)[2]
4, para	1	1 Apr 1999 (subject to transitional provisions and savings) (SR 1999/176)
	2	9 Feb 1999 (subject to transitional provisions and savings) (SR 1999/48)
	3	Repealed
	4	*Not in force*
	5–7	9 Feb 1999 (subject to transitional provisions and savings) (SR 1999/48)
	8, 9	*Not in force*
	10	Repealed
	11	1 Apr 1999 (subject to transitional provisions and savings) (SR 1999/176)
	12	Repealed
	13, 14	1 Apr 1999 (subject to transitional provisions and savings) (SR 1999/176)
	15, 16	9 Feb 1999 (subject to transitional provisions and savings) (SR 1999/48)

Police (Northern Ireland) Act 1998 (c 32)—*contd*

Schedule

4, para	17		Repealed
	18	(1)	1 Apr 1999 (subject to transitional provisions and savings) (SR 1999/176)
		(2)	Repealed
		(3)	8 Oct 1998 (SR 1998/346)
		(4), (5)	Repealed
		(6)	1 Apr 1999 (subject to transitional provisions and savings) (SR 1999/176)
	19		1 Apr 1999 (subject to transitional provisions and savings) (SR 1999/176)
	20	(1), (2)	1 Apr 1999 (subject to transitional provisions and savings) (SR 1999/176)
		(3)–(5)	*Not in force*
		(6)	Repealed
	21		*Not in force*
	22	(1)	1 Apr 1999 (subject to transitional provisions and savings) (SR 1999/176)[1]
		(2)–(5)	9 Feb 1999 (subject to transitional provisions and savings) (SR 1999/48)[1]
		(6)	Repealed
		(7)	1 Apr 1999 (subject to transitional provisions and savings) (SR 1999/176)
		(8)	*Not in force*
		(9)	9 Feb 1999 (subject to transitional provisions and savings) (SR 1999/48)[1]
	23		1 Apr 1999 (subject to transitional provisions and savings) (SR 1999/176)
	24, 25		Repealed
5, para	1		9 Feb 1999 (subject to transitional provisions and savings) (SR 1999/48)
	2		1 Apr 1999 (subject to transitional provisions and savings) (SR 1999/176)
	3		9 Feb 1999 (subject to transitional provisions and savings) (SR 1999/48)
	4–11		*Not in force*
6			8 Oct 1998 (repeals of Constabulary (Ireland) Act 1836, ss 5, 17;

Police (Northern Ireland) Act 1998 (c 32)—*contd*
Schedule
6—*contd*
Constabulary Act (Northern Ireland) 1922, s 7(1)(c), Sch 2; Police Act (Northern Ireland) 1970, s 15 (subject to transitional provisions); Police and Criminal Evidence (Northern Ireland) Order 1989, art 82) (SR 1998/346)

9 Feb 1999 (repeals of Constabulary (Ireland) Act 1836; Constabulary and Police (Ireland) Act 1919; Game Preservation Act (Northern Ireland) 1928, in s 1, the words "notwithstanding anything in Section 15 of the Constabulary (Ireland) Act 1836, as it applies to the said Constabulary"; Police (Overseas Service) Act 1945, s 3(4); Criminal Justice Act (Northern Ireland) 1953, s 20(2); Fisheries Act (Northern Ireland) 1966, in s 167(1), the words "notwithstanding" to the end, and in s 167(2), the words "as provided" to "any case"; Criminal Justice (Miscellaneous Provisions) Act (Northern Ireland) 1968, s 7(1)(a); Police Act (Northern Ireland) 1970, ss 17, 21, 25, 26, 28, 34; Police (Amendment) (Northern Ireland) Order 1995, in Pt III, Sch 1, the amendments to Police Act (Northern Ireland) 1970) (subject to transitional provisions and savings) (SR 1999/48)

1 Apr 1999 (except repeals in Superannuation Act (Northern Ireland) 1972; Superannuation (Northern Ireland) Order 1972; House of Commons Disqualification Act 1975; Northern Ireland Assembly Disqualification Act 1975; Police (Northern Ireland) Order 1987; Police (Amendment) (Northern Ireland) Order 1995, in Art 2(2), the definition "the 1987 Order" and Pt IV) (subject to transitional provisions and savings) (SR 1999/176)

Not in force (exceptions noted above)

Police (Northern Ireland) Act 1998 (c 32)—*contd*

1   It is assumed that the reference in SR 1999/48, art 3, with regards to Sch 4 para 20 to the Police (Northern Ireland) Act 1998 is a reference to Sch 4, para 22

2   For transitional provisions, see SI 2000/399, arts 4, 5

Private Hire Vehicles (London) Act 1998 (c 34)

RA: 28 Jul 1998

Commencement provisions: s 40(2); Private Hire Vehicles (London) Act 1998 (Commencement No 1) Order 2000, SI 2000/3144

Section

1		22 Jan 2001 (SI 2000/3144)
2		22 Oct 2001 (SI 2000/3144)
3		22 Jan 2001 (SI 2000/3144)
4	(1)	22 Jan 2001 (SI 2000/3144)
	(2)	*Not in force*
	(3), (4)	22 Jan 2001 (SI 2000/3144)
	(5), (6)	22 Oct 2001 (SI 2000/3144)
5	(1)–(4)	22 Oct 2001 (SI 2000/3144)
	(5)	22 Jan 2001 (SI 2000/3144)
6–14		*Not in force*
15	(1)–(3)	22 Jan 2001 (SI 2000/3144)
	(4)	*Not in force*
	(5)	22 Jan 2001 (SI 2000/3144)
16	(1), (2)	22 Jan 2001 (SI 2000/3144)
	(3), (4)	*Not in force*
17–20		22 Jan 2001 (SI 2000/3144)
21	(1)	22 Jan 2001 (SI 2000/3144)
	(2)	*Not in force*
	(3)	22 Jan 2001 (SI 2000/3144)
	(4)	22 Oct 2001 (SI 2000/3144)
22	(1)	22 Jan 2001 (SI 2000/3144)
	(2), (3)	*Not in force*
	(4)	22 Jan 2001 (SI 2000/3144)
	(5), (6)	22 Oct 2001 (SI 2000/3144)
	(7)	*Not in force*
23–29		22 Jan 2001 (SI 2000/3144)
30, 31		*Not in force*
32, 33		22 Jan 2001 (SI 2000/3144)
34	(1), (2)	22 Jan 2001 (SI 2000/3144)
	(3)	*Not in force*
35		*Not in force*
36, 37		22 Jan 2001 (SI 2000/3144)
38		22 Jan 2001 (SI 2000/3144)
		Repealed, partly prospectively, by Greater London Authority Act 1999, ss 254, 423, Sch 21, para 19, Sch 34, Pt V[1]
39		*Not in force*
40		28 Jul 1998 (s 40(2))

Private Hire Vehicles (London) Act 1998 (c 34)—*contd*
Schedule
1, 2   *Not in force*

¹   Orders made under Greater London Authority Act 1999, s 425, bringing the prospective repeal
     into force will be noted to that Act

Public Interest Disclosure Act 1998 (c 23)

RA: 2 Jul 1998

Commencement provisions: s 18(3), (4); Public Interest Disclosure Act 1998
    (Commencement) Order 1999, SI 1999/1547
Section
1   2 Jul 1998 (so far as relates to the
                                              power to make an order under
                                              Employment Rights Act 1996,
                                              s 43F) (s 18(4))
                                              2 Jul 1999 (otherwise) (SI 1999/1547)
2–7   2 Jul 1999 (SI 1999/1547)
8   Repealed
9, 10   2 Jul 1999 (SI 1999/1547)
11   Repealed
12–16   2 Jul 1999 (SI 1999/1547)
17, 18   2 Jul 1998 (s 18(4))

Public Processions (Northern Ireland) Act 1998 (c 2)

RA: 16 Feb 1998

Commencement provisions: s 19(2)–(4); Public Processions (Northern Ireland) Act 1998
    (Commencement) Order 1998, SI 1998/717
Section
1   (1)   16 Feb 1998 (RA)
             (2)   See Sch 1 below
2   2 Mar 1998 (SI 1998/717)
3   (1), (2)   16 Feb 1998 (RA)
             (3)   See Sch 2 below
4   (1)–(4)   16 Feb 1998 (RA)
             (5)   See Sch 2 below
5   16 Feb 1998 (RA)
6, 7   2 Mar 1998 (SI 1998/717)
8   (1)–(5)   2 Mar 1998 (SI 1998/717)
             (6)   16 Feb 1998 (RA)
             (7)–(9)   2 Mar 1998 (SI 1998/717)
9–15   2 Mar 1998 (SI 1998/717)
16, 17   16 Feb 1998 (RA)
18   (1)   See Sch 3 below
             (2)   See Sch 4 below
19   16 Feb 1998 (RA)
Schedule
1, 2   16 Feb 1998 (RA)

Public Processions (Northern Ireland) Act 1998 (c 2)—*contd*
Schedule

3, para	1, 2	16 Feb 1998 (RA)
	3	2 Mar 1998 (SI 1998/717)
4		2 Mar 1998 (SI 1998/717)

Regional Development Agencies Act 1998 (c 45)

RA: 19 Nov 1998

Commencement provisions: s 43; Regional Development Agencies Act 1998 (Commencement No 1) Order 1998, SI 1998/2952; Regional Development Agencies Act 1998 (Commencement No 2) Order 2000, SI 2000/1173
Section

1		25 Nov 1998 (except in so far as it relates to the establishment of a regional development agency for London) (SI 1998/2952)
		3 Jul 2000 (exception noted above) (SI 2000/1173)
2		25 Nov 1998 (for the purposes of regional development agencies established on 25 Nov 1998) (SI 1998/2952)
		8 May 2000 (for the purpose only of enabling the Mayor to consult on the appointment of persons to be members of the London Development Agency) (SI 2000/1173)
		3 Jul 2000 (otherwise) (SI 2000/1173)
3–5		25 Nov 1998 (for the purposes of regional development agencies established on 25 Nov 1998) (SI 1998/2952)
		3 Jul 2000 (otherwise) (SI 2000/1173)
6	(1), (2)	25 Nov 1998 (for the purposes of regional development agencies established on 25 Nov 1998) (SI 1998/2952)
		8 May 2000 (otherwise) (SI 2000/1173)
	(3)–(5)	25 Nov 1998 (for the purposes of regional development agencies established on 25 Nov 1998) (SI 1998/2952)
		3 Jul 2000 (otherwise) (SI 2000/1173)
	(6)	See Sch 3 below
6A		Inserted by Greater London Authority Act 1999, s 305(2) (qv)

Regional Development Agencies Act 1998 (c 45)—*contd*
Section

7			25 Nov 1998 (for the purposes of regional development agencies established on 25 Nov 1998)) (SI 1998/2952)
			3 Jul 2000 (otherwise) (SI 2000/1173)
7A			Inserted by Greater London Authority Act 1999, s 306(2) (qv)
7B			Inserted by Greater London Authority Act 1999, s 307 (qv)
8–26			25 Nov 1998 (for the purposes of regional development agencies established on 25 Nov 1998)) (SI 1998/2952)
			3 Jul 2000 (otherwise) (SI 2000/1173)
26A			Inserted by Greater London Authority Act 1999, s 309, Sch 25, para 16 (qv)
27–30			25 Nov 1998 (for the purposes of regional development agencies established on 25 Nov 1998)) (SI 1998/2952)
			3 Jul 2000 (otherwise) (SI 2000/1173)
30A			Inserted by Greater London Authority Act 1999, s 309, Sch 25, para 18 (qv)
31–42			25 Nov 1998 (for the purposes of regional development agencies established on 25 Nov 1998)) (SI 1998/2952)
			3 Jul 2000 (otherwise) (SI 2000/1173)
43–45			19 Nov 1998 (s 43)

Schedule

1, 2			25 Nov 1998 (for the purposes of regional development agencies established on 25 Nov 1998)) (SI 1998/2952)
			3 Jul 2000 (otherwise) (SI 2000/1173)
2A			Inserted (3 Jul 2000) by London Development Agency (Transitional Provisions) Order 2000, SI 2000/1174, art 2(b)
3	1	(1)	25 Nov 1998 (for the purposes of regional development agencies established on 25 Nov 1998)) (SI 1998/2952)
			8 May 2000 (otherwise) (SI 2000/1173)
		(2)	25 Nov 1998 (for the purposes of regional development agencies established on 25 Nov 1998)) (SI 1998/2952)
			3 Jul 2000 (otherwise) (SI 2000/1173)

Regional Development Agencies Act 1998 (c 45)—*contd*

Schedule

3	2–10	25 Nov 1998 (for the purposes of regional development agencies established on 25 Nov 1998)) (SI 1998/2952)
		8 May 2000 (otherwise) (SI 2000/1173)
	11, 12	25 Nov 1998 (for the purposes of regional development agencies established on 25 Nov 1998)) (SI 1998/2952)
		3 Jul 2000 (otherwise) (SI 2000/1173)
	13	25 Nov 1998 (for the purposes of regional development agencies established on 25 Nov 1998)) (SI 1998/2952)
		8 May 2000 (otherwise) (SI 2000/1173)
4–6		25 Nov 1998 (for the purposes of regional development agencies established on 25 Nov 1998)) (SI 1998/2952)
		3 Jul 2000 (otherwise) (SI 2000/1173)
6A		Inserted by Greater London Authority Act 1999, s 309, Sch 25, para 21 (qv)
7–9		25 Nov 1998 (for the purposes of regional development agencies established on 25 Nov 1998)) (SI 1998/2952)
		3 Jul 2000 (otherwise) (SI 2000/1173)

Registered Establishments (Scotland) Act 1998 (c 25)

RA: 9 Jul 1998

9 Jul 1998 (RA)

Registration of Political Parties Act 1998 (c 48)

RA: 19 Nov 1998

Commencement provisions: s 25; Registration of Political Parties Act 1998 (Commencement) Order 1999, SI 1999/393

Section

1–12	Repealed
13	See Sch 2 below
14	Repealed
15	24 Mar 1999 (SI 1999/393)
16–23	Repealed
20–22	19 Nov 1998 (s 25)
23	See Sch 3 below

Registration of Political Parties Act 1998 (c 48)—*contd*

Section

24	19 Nov 1998 (s 25)
25	Repealed
26	19 Nov 1998 (s 25)

Schedule

1	Repealed
2	24 Mar 1999 (SI 1999/393)
3	Repealed

Road Traffic Reduction (National Targets) Act 1998 (c 24)

RA: 2 Jul 1998

2 Jul 1998 (RA)

School Standards and Framework Act 1998 (c 31)

RA: 24 Jul 1998

Commencement provisions: s 145(3)–(5); School Standards and Framework Act 1998 (Commencement No 1) Order 1998, SI 1998/2048; School Standards and Framework Act 1998 (Commencement No 2 and Supplemental, Saving and Transitional Provisions) Order 1998, SI 1998/2212; School Standards and Framework Act 1998 (Commencement No 3 and Saving and Transitional Provisions) Order 1998, SI 1998/2791; School Standards and Framework Act 1998 (Commencement No 4 and Transitional Provisions) Order 1998, SI 1998/3198; School Standards and Framework Act 1998 (Commencement No 5 and Saving and Transitional Provisions) Order 1999, SI 1999/120; School Standards and Framework Act 1998 (Commencement No 6 and Saving and Transitional Provisions) Order 1999, SI 1999/1016[1]; School Standards and Framework Act 1998 (Commencement No 7 and Saving and Transitional Provisions) Order 1999, SI 1999/2323[2] ; School Standards and Framework Act 1998 (Commencement No 8 and Supplemental Provisions) Order 2001, SI 2001/1195; School Standards and Framework Act 1998 (Commencement No 9 and Supplemental Provisions) Order 2001, SI 2001/2663

Section

1–4		24 Jul 1998 (s 145(4))
5–9		1 Oct 1998 (SI 1998/2212)
10–12		8 Aug 1998 (SI 1998/2048)
13		1 Sep 1998 (SI 1998/2048)
14, 15		1 Oct 1998 (SI 1998/2212)
16	(1)–(5)	1 Oct 1998 (SI 1998/2212)
	(6)–(12)	1 Sep 1999 (SI 1999/2323)
	(13)	1 Oct 1998 (SI 1998/2212)
17–19		1 Oct 1998 (SI 1998/2212)
20, 21		24 Jul 1998 (s 145(4))
22, 23		1 Sep 1999 (SI 1999/2323)
24	(1)	1 Apr 1999 (SI 1999/1016)
	(2)–(5)	1 Oct 1998 (SI 1998/2212)
25		1 Oct 1998 (SI 1998/2212)

School Standards and Framework Act 1998 (c 31)—*contd*

Section

26	(1)	1 Apr 1999 (SI 1999/1016)
	(2)–(8)	1 Oct 1998 (SI 1998/2212)
26A, 26B		Inserted by Learning and Skills Act 2000, s 139(7), Sch 9, para 81 (qv)
27		1 Sep 1999 (SI 1999/2323)
28	(1)–(4)	1 Sep 1999 (SI 1999/2323)
	(5)	1 Apr 1999 (SI 1999/1016)
	(6)–(8)	1 Sep 1999 (SI 1999/2323)
	(9)	1 Feb 1999 (SI 1998/3198)
	(10)	1 Apr 1999 (SI 1999/1016)
	(11), (12)	1 Sep 1999 (SI 1999/2323)
29	(1)–(3)	1 Sep 1999 (SI 1999/2323)
	(4)	1 Apr 1999 (SI 1999/1016)
	(5)–(7)	1 Sep 1999 (SI 1999/2323)
	(8)	1 Feb 1999 (SI 1998/3198)
	(9)	1 Apr 1999 (SI 1999/1016)
	(10)	1 Sep 1999 (SI 1999/2323)
30		1 Sep 1999 (SI 1999/2323)
31	(1)–(3)	1 Sep 1999 (SI 1999/2323)
	(4)	1 Apr 1999 (SI 1999/1016)
	(5)–(8)	1 Sep 1999 (SI 1999/2323)
	(9)	1 Apr 1999 (SI 1999/1016)
32		1 Sep 1999 (SI 1999/2323)
33	(1)–(3)	1 Sep 1999 (SI 1999/2323)
	(4)	1 Feb 1999 (SI 1998/3198)
34		1 Sep 1999 (SI 1999/2323)
35		1 Apr 1999 (SI 1999/1016)
36	(1), (2)	24 Jul 1998 (for purposes of the preparation of instruments of government and the constitution of governing bodies and the exercise (in relation to those or any other matters) of any power to make regulations) (s 145(5)) 1 Sep 1999 (otherwise) (SI 1999/2323)
	(3)	24 Jul 1998 (s 145(4))
37	(1), (2)	24 Jul 1998 (for purposes of the preparation of instruments of government and the constitution of governing bodies and the exercise (in relation to those or any other matters) of any power to make regulations) (s 145(5)) 1 Sep 1999 (otherwise) (SI 1999/2323)
	(3)	1 Sep 1999 (SI 1999/2323)
38	(1), (2)	1 Sep 1999 (SI 1999/2323)
	(3)	1 Oct 1998 (SI 1998/2212)
	(4)	1 Sep 1999 (SI 1999/2323)

School Standards and Framework Act 1998 (c 31)—*contd*

Section

39	(1)	1 Oct 1998 (as far as relates to the power to make regulations) (SI 1998/2212)
		Not in force (otherwise)
	(2), (3)	1 Sep 1999 (SI 1999/2323)
40, 41		1 Sep 1999 (SI 1999/2323)
42	(1), (2)	1 Apr 1999 (so far as relates to the power to make regulations) (SI 1999/1016) 1 Sep 1999 (otherwise) (SI 1999/2323)
	(3)–(5)	1 Sep 1999 (SI 1999/2323)
43	(1)–(3)	1 Sep 1999 (SI 1999/2323)
	(4)	1 Apr 1999 (SI 1999/1016)
44	(1)–(4)	1 Sep 1999 (SI 1999/2323)
	(5), (6)	1 Oct 1998 (SI 1998/2212)
	(7)–(9)	1 Sep 1999 (SI 1999/2323)
45–48		1 Oct 1998 (subject to supplemental, saving and transitional provisions) (SI 1998/2212)
49		1 Apr 1999 (SI 1998/2212)
50	(1), (2)	1 Apr 1999 (SI 1998/2212)
	(3), (4)	1 Oct 1998 (subject to supplemental, saving and transitional provisions) (SI 1998/2212)
	(5)–(7)	1 Apr 1999 (SI 1998/2212)
51		1 Apr 1999 (SI 1998/2212)
52		1 Oct 1998 (subject to supplemental, saving and transitional provisions) (SI 1998/2212)
53		1 Apr 1999 (SI 1998/2212)
54		See Sch 16 below
55		See Sch 17 below
56		1 Sep 1999 (SI 1999/2323)
57		1 Apr 1999 (SI 1999/1016)
58–61		1 Sep 1999 (SI 1999/2323)
62, 63		1 Oct 1998 (SI 1998/2212)
64, 65		1 Sep 1999 (SI 1999/2323)
66	(1)–(7)	1 Sep 1999 (SI 1999/2323)
	(8)	1 Dec 1998 (SI 1998/2212)
67	(1)	1 Sep 1999 (SI 1999/2323)
	(2)	See Sch 18 below
	(3), (4)	1 Sep 1999 (SI 1999/2323)
68		1 Sep 1999 (SI 1999/2323)
69	(1)	1 Sep 1999 (SI 1999/2323)
	(2)–(5)	1 Oct 1998 (SI 1998/2212)
70		1 Sep 1999 (SI 1999/2323)
71	(1)–(6)	1 Sep 1999 (SI 1999/2323)
	(7)	1 Oct 1998 (SI 1998/2212)
72		1 Oct 1998 (SI 1998/2212)

School Standards and Framework Act 1998 (c 31)—*contd*

Section

73, 74			1 Apr 1999 (SI 1999/1016)
75, 76			1 Sep 1999 (SI 1999/2323)
77	(1)		1 Oct 1998 (SI 1998/2212)
	(2)	(a)	1 Oct 1998 (SI 1998/2212)
		(b)	1 Feb 1999 (SI 1998/3198)
	(3)–(9)		1 Oct 1998 (SI 1998/2212)
78–80			1 Sep 1999 (SI 1999/2323)
81			1 Oct 1998 (SI 1998/2212)
82			24 Jul 1998 (s 145(4))
83			1 Sep 1999 (SI 1999/2323)
84, 85			24 Jul 1998 (s 145(4))
86, 87			1 Apr 1999 (SI 1999/1016)
88			1 Oct 1998 (SI 1998/2212)
89	(1)		6 Jan 1999 (subject to transitional provisions) (SI 1998/3198)
	(2)–(8)		1 Oct 1998 (as far as relate to the power to make regulations) (SI 1998/2212)
			6 Jan 1999 (subject to transitional provisions) (otherwise) (SI 1998/3198)
	(9)		6 Jan 1999 (subject to transitional provisions) (SI 1998/3198)
90	(1)–(3)		1 Oct 1998 (as far as relate to the power to make regulations) (SI 1998/2212)
			1 Apr 1999 (otherwise) (SI 1999/1016)
	(4)		1 Apr 1999 (SI 1999/1016)
	(5)		1 Oct 1998 (as far as relates to the power to make regulations) (SI 1998/2212)
			1 Apr 1999 (otherwise) (SI 1999/1016)
	(6)–(8)		1 Apr 1999 (SI 1999/1016)
	(9), (10)		1 Oct 1998 (as far as relate to the power to make regulations) (SI 1998/2212)
			1 Apr 1999 (otherwise) (SI 1999/1016)
91	(1)		1 Apr 1999 (subject to saving and transitional provisions) (SI 1999/1016)
	(2)–(4)		1 Oct 1998 (as far as relate to the power to make regulations) (SI 1998/2212)
			1 Apr 1999 (subject to saving and transitional provisions) (otherwise) (SI 1999/1016)
	(5)		1 Apr 1999 (subject to saving and transitional provisions) (SI 1999/1016)

School Standards and Framework Act 1998 (c 31)—*contd*
Section

91	(6)	1 Oct 1998 (as far as relates to the power to make regulations) (SI 1998/2212)
		1 Apr 1999 (subject to saving and transitional provisions) (otherwise) (SI 1999/1016)
	(7), (8)	1 Apr 1999 (subject to saving and transitional provisions) (SI 1999/1016)
	(9)	1 Oct 1998 (as far as relates to the power to make regulations) (SI 1998/2212)
		1 Apr 1999 (subject to saving and transitional provisions) (otherwise) (SI 1999/1016)
	(10)	1 Apr 1999 (subject to saving and transitional provisions) (SI 1999/1016)
92		1 Oct 1998 (as far as relates to the power to make regulations) (SI 1998/2212)
		1 Apr 1999 (subject to saving and transitional provisions) (otherwise) (SI 1999/1016)
93	(1), (2)	1 Apr 1999 (subject to saving and transitional provisions) (SI 1999/1016)
	(3)	1 Oct 1998 (SI 1998/2212)
	(4)–(7)	1 Sep 1999 (subject to saving and transitional provisions) (SI 1999/1016)
	(8), (9)	1 Oct 1998 (SI 1998/2212)
	(10)	1 Apr 1999 (subject to saving and transitional provisions) (SI 1999/1016)
94–97		1 Apr 1999 (subject to savings and transitional provisions) (SI 1999/1016)
98	(1)–(4)	1 Apr 1999 (SI 1999/1016)
	(5)	1 Oct 1998 (as far as relates to the power to make regulations) (SI 1998/2212)
		1 Apr 1999 (otherwise) (SI 1999/1016)
	(6), (7)	1 Apr 1999 (SI 1999/1016)
	(8)–(10)	1 Oct 1998 (as far as relates to the power to make regulations) (SI 1998/2212)
		1 Apr 1999 (otherwise) (SI 1999/1016)

School Standards and Framework Act 1998 (c 31)—*contd*

Section

99	(1)		1 Oct 1998 (subject to supplemental, saving and transitional provisions) (SI 1998/2212)
	(2)		1 Oct 1998 (SI 1998/2212)
	(3), (4)		1 Apr 1999 (SI 1999/1016)
	(5)		1 Oct 1998 (SI 1998/2212)
100			1 Oct 1998 (so far as relates to s 99(2)(a)) (SI 1998/2212)
			1 Apr 1999 (otherwise) (SI 1999/1016)
101	(1)–(3)		1 Oct 1998 (SI 1998/2212)
	(4)		1 Oct 1998 (subject to supplemental, saving and transitional provisions) (SI 1998/2212)
	(5)		1 Apr 1999 (SI 1999/1016)
102	(1)		1 Oct 1998 (as far as relates to the power to make regulations) (SI 1998/2212)
			1 Apr 1999 (otherwise) (SI 1999/1016)
	(2), (3)		1 Apr 1999 (SI 1999/1016)
	(4)		1 Oct 1998 (as far as relates to the power to make regulations) (SI 1998/2212)
			1 Apr 1999 (otherwise) (SI 1999/1016)
	(5)		1 Apr 1999 (SI 1999/1016)
103	(1), (2)		1 Apr 1999 (SI 1999/1016)
	(3)		1 Oct 1998 (SI 1998/2212)
104	(1)–(3)		1 Sep 1998 (SI 1998/2048)
	(4)	(a)	1 Oct 1998 (SI 1998/2212)
		(b)	1 Sep 1999 (SI 1999/2323)
	(5)–(7)		1 Sep 1998 (SI 1998/2048)
105, 106			1 Oct 1998 (SI 1998/2212)
107			1 Dec 1998 (SI 1998/2212)
108			1 Oct 1998 (SI 1998/2212)
109	(1), (2)		1 Sep 1999 (SI 1999/2323)
	(3), (4)		1 Feb 1999 (SI 1998/3198)
	(5)		1 Sep 1999 (SI 1999/2323)
110, 111			1 Feb 1999 (SI 1998/2212)
112	(1), (2)		1 Oct 1998 (SI 1998/2212)
	(3)		*Not in force*
113			1 Oct 1998 (SI 1998/2212)
114			1 Apr 1999 (SI 1999/1016)
115	(1)		1 Apr 1999 (SI 1999/1016)
	(2), (3)		1 Apr 2001 (E) (SI 2001/1195)
			20 Jul 2001 (W) (SI 2001/2663)
	(4), (5)		1 Apr 1999 (SI 1999/1016)
116			1 Feb 1999 (SI 1998/3198)
117			1 Oct 1998 (SI 1998/2212)
118			1 Apr 1999 (SI 1998/2212)
119			1 Oct 1998 (SI 1998/2212)

School Standards and Framework Act 1998 (c 31)—*contd*

Section

120, 121				1 Apr 1999 (SI 1999/1016)
122, 123				1 Oct 1998 (SI 1998/2212)
124				1 Apr 1999 (SI 1998/2212)
125, 126				Repealed
127				1 Oct 1998 (SI 1998/2212)
128				*Not in force*
129				1 Feb 1999 (subject to transitional provisions) (SI 1999/120)
130				24 Jul 1998 (s 145(4))
131				1 Sep 1999 (SI 1999/2323)
132, 133				1 Apr 1999 (SI 1999/1016)
134	(1)			1 Oct 1998 (SI 1998/2212)
	(2)			Spent (*never in force*)
	(3)			1 Oct 1998 (SI 1998/2212)
135				See Sch 28 below
136				1 Oct 1998 (SI 1998/2212)
137				1 Feb 1999 (subject to transitional provisions) (SI 1999/120)
138, 139				24 Jul 1998 (s 145(4))
140	(1)			See Sch 30 below
	(2)			1 Sep 1999 (SI 1999/2323)
	(3)			See Sch 31 below
	(4)			1 Sep 1999 (SI 1999/2323)
141–145				24 Jul 1998 (s 145(4))

Schedule

1				8 Aug 1998 (SI 1998/2048)
2				24 Jul 1998 (s 145(4))
3				1 Sep 1999 (SI 1999/2323)
4, para	1, 2			1 Oct 1998 (SI 1998/2212)
	3, 4			1 Sep 1999 (SI 1999/2323)
	5			1 Oct 1998 (SI 1998/2212)
	6–10			1 Sep 1999 (SI 1999/2323)
5				1 Oct 1998 (SI 1998/2212)
6, Pt	I, para	1–4		1 Sep 1999 (SI 1999/2323)
		5	(1)–(3)	1 Sep 1999 (SI 1999/2323)
			(4)	1 Feb 1999 (so far as confers power to provide for ss 28, 29, 31 and Sch 6, Pt I to have effect with modifications) (SI 1998/3198)
				1 Sep 1999 (otherwise) (SI 1999/2323)
			(5)–(9)	1 Sep 1999 (SI 1999/2323)
	II, para	6–9		1 Sep 1999 (SI 1999/2323)
		10	(1)–(3)	1 Sep 1999 (SI 1999/2323)
			(4)	1 Feb 1999 (so far as confers power to provide for ss 28, 29, 31 and Sch 6, Pt I to have effect with modifications) (SI 1998/3198)
				1 Sep 1999 (otherwise) (SI 1999/2323)
			(5), (6)	1 Sep 1999 (SI 1999/2323)

School Standards and Framework Act 1998 (c 31)—*contd*

Schedule

6, Pt	III–V		1 Sep 1999 (SI 1999/2323)
7			1 Sep 1999 (SI 1999/2323)
8			1 Apr 1999 (SI 1999/1016)
9, 10			24 Jul 1998 (for purposes of the preparation of instruments of government and the constitution of governing bodies and the exercise (in relation to those or any other matters) of any power to make regulations) (s 145(5))
			1 Sep 1999 (otherwise) (SI 1999/2323)
11, Pt	I		24 Jul 1998 (s 145(4))
	II, para	6	1 Oct 1998 (SI 1998/2212)
		7	1 Sep 1999 (SI 1999/2323)
	III		24 Jul 1998 (s 145(4))
12			24 Jul 1998 (for purposes of the preparation of instruments of government and the constitution of governing bodies and the exercise (in relation to those or any other matters) of any power to make regulations) (s 145(5))
			1 Sep 1999 (otherwise) (SI 1999/2323)
13			1 Sep 1999 (SI 1999/2323)
14			1 Oct 1998 (subject to supplemental, saving and transitional provisions) (SI 1998/2212)
15			1 Apr 1999 (subject to supplemental, saving and transitional provisions) (SI 1998/2212)
16, para	1–29		1 Sep 1999 (SI 1999/2323)
	30		1 Feb 1999 (SI 1999/120)
	31		1 Sep 1999 (SI 1999/2323)
17, para	1	(1)	1 Feb 1999 (SI 1999/120)
		(2), (3)	1 Sep 1999 (SI 1999/2323)
	2–26		1 Sep 1999 (SI 1999/2323)
	27	(1), (2)	1 Sep 1999 (SI 1999/2323)
		(3)	1 Feb 1999 (SI 1999/120)
	28–30		1 Sep 1999 (SI 1999/2323)
18, para	1–3		1 Sep 1999 (SI 1999/2323)
	4		1 Apr 1999 (SI 1999/1016)
	5–18		1 Sep 1999 (SI 1999/2323)
19, para	1		1 Oct 1998 (SI 1998/2212)
	2	(1)–(3)	1 Sep 1999 (SI 1999/2323)
		(4)	1 Oct 1998 (for the purpose of making orders) (SI 1998/2212)
			1 Sep 1999 (otherwise) (SI 1999/2323)
		(5)	1 Sep 1999 (SI 1999/2323)
	3	(1)–(3)	1 Sep 1999 (SI 1999/2323)

School Standards and Framework Act 1998 (c 31)—*contd*

Schedule

19, para	3	(4)		1 Oct 1998 (for the purpose of making orders) (SI 1998/2212)
				1 Sep 1999 (otherwise) (SI 1999/2323)
	4			1 Sep 1999 (SI 1999/2323)
20–22				1 Sep 1999 (SI 1999/2323)
23, para	1–4			1 Sep 1999 (SI 1999/1016)
	5	(1)		1 Oct 1998 (as far as relates to the power to make regulations) (SI 1998/2212)
				1 Sep 1999 (otherwise) (SI 1999/1016)
		(2)–(4)		1 Sep 1999 (SI 1999/1016)
		(5), (6)		1 Oct 1998 (as far as relate to the power to make regulations) (SI 1998/2212)
				1 Sep 1999 (otherwise) (SI 1999/1016)
	6	(1)–(6)		1 Sep 1999 (SI 1999/1016)
		(7)		1 Oct 1998 (as far as relates to the power to make regulations) (SI 1998/2212)
				1 Sep 1999 (otherwise) (SI 1999/1016)
		(8), (9)		1 Sep 1999 (SI 1999/1016)
		(10)		1 Oct 1998 (as far as relates to the power to make regulations) (SI 1998/2212)
				1 Sep 1999 (otherwise) (SI 1999/1016)
		(11)		1 Sep 1999 (SI 1999/1016)
	7, 8			1 Sep 1999 (SI 1999/1016)
	9	(1)		1 Oct 1998 (as far as relates to the power to make regulations) (SI 1998/2212)
				1 Sep 1999 (otherwise) (SI 1999/1016)
		(2)–(5)		1 Sep 1999 (SI 1999/1016)
		(6), (7)		1 Oct 1998 (as far as relate to the power to make regulations) (SI 1998/2212)
				1 Sep 1999 (otherwise) (SI 1999/1016)
	10	(1)–(6)		1 Sep 1999 (SI 1999/1016)
		(7)		1 Oct 1998 (as far as relates to the power to make regulations) (SI 1998/2212)
				1 Sep 1999 (otherwise) (SI 1999/1016)
	11			1 Sep 1999 (SI 1999/1016)
24, 25				1 Apr 1999 (SI 1999/1016)
26				1 Oct 1998 (SI 1998/2212)
27				Repealed
28, Pt	I, para	1–3		1 Oct 1998 (SI 1998/2212)
		4	(1)	1 Jan 2000 (so far as it applies in relation to the inspection of schools in England) (SI 1999/2323)

School Standards and Framework Act 1998 (c 31)—*contd*
Schedule

28, Pt	I, para	4	(1)—*contd*		1 Aug 2000 (so far as it applies in relation to the inspection of schools in Wales) (SI 1999/2323)
			(2)		1 Oct 1998 (subject to a transitional provision) (SI 1998/2212)
		5			*Not in force*
	II				1 Sep 1999 (SI 1999/2323)
29					1 Feb 1999 (SI 1999/120)
30, para	1				1 Sep 1999 (SI 1999/2323)
	2				1 Oct 1998 (SI 1998/2212)
	3				1 Apr 1999 (SI 1999/1016)
	4				1 Apr 1999 (except so far as substitutes Local Government Act 1974, s 25(5)(b)) (SI 1999/1016) 1 Sep 1999 (exception noted above) (SI 1999/2323)
	5–13				1 Sep 1999 (SI 1999/2323)
	14				1 Apr 1999 (subject to transitional provisions and savings) (SI 1999/1016)
	15				1 Sep 1999 (SI 1999/2323)
	16				1 Oct 1998 (SI 1998/2212)
	17–19				1 Sep 1999 (SI 1999/2323)
	20				1 Oct 1998 (SI 1998/2212)
	21–23				1 Sep 1999 (SI 1999/2323)
	24				1 Oct 1998 (SI 1998/2212)
	25				1 Sep 1999 (SI 1999/2323)
	26	(a), (b)			1 Sep 1999 (SI 1999/2323)
		(c), (d)			1 Oct 1998 (SI 1998/2212)
		(e), (f)			1 Sep 1999 (SI 1999/2323)
	27				1 Sep 1999 (SI 1999/2323)
	28	(1)			1 Jun 1999 (for the purpose of making orders under School Teachers' Pay and Conditions Act 1991, to come into force on or after 1 Sep 1999) (SI 1999/1016) 1 Sep 1999 (otherwise) (SI 1999/2323)
		(2)	(a)		1 Jun 1999 (for the purpose of making orders under School Teachers' Pay and Conditions Act 1991, to come into force on or after 1 Sep 1999) (SI 1999/1016) 1 Sep 1999 (otherwise) (SI 1999/2323)
			(b)		Repealed (*never in force*)
			(c)		1 Jun 1999 (for the purpose of making orders under School Teachers' Pay and Conditions Act 1991, to come into force on or after 1 Sep 1999) (SI 1999/1016)

School Standards and Framework Act 1998 (c 31)—*contd*
Schedule

30, para	28	(2)	(c)—*contd* 1 Sep 1999 (otherwise) (SI 1999/2323)
		(3)	1 Sep 1999 (SI 1999/2323)
	29–32		1 Sep 1999 (SI 1999/2323)
	33		1 Apr 1999 (SI 1998/2212)
	34		Spent
	35–39		1 Sep 1999 (SI 1999/2323)
	40		1 Apr 1999 (SI 1998/2212)
	41, 42		Repealed
	43–46		1 Sep 1999 (SI 1999/2323)
	47		1 Apr 1999 (except so far as substitutes Tribunal and Inquiries Act 1992, Sch 1, para 15(b)) (subject to savings and transitional provisions) (SI 1999/1016)
			1 Sep 1999 (exception noted above) (SI 1999/2323)
	48		1 Feb 1999 (SI 1999/120)
	49–51		1 Sep 1999 (SI 1999/2323)
	52		1 Apr 1999 (SI 1998/2212)
	53		1 Sep 1999 (SI 1999/2323)
	54	(a), (b)	1 Sep 1999 (SI 1999/2323)
		(c)	1 Apr 1999 (SI 1998/2212)
	55		1 Sep 1999 (SI 1999/2323)
	56		1 Apr 1999 (SI 1999/1016)
	57		1 Oct 1998 (SI 1998/2212)
	58–60		1 Sep 1999 (SI 1999/2323)
	61		1 Apr 1999 (SI 1999/1016)
	62, 63		1 Sep 1999 (SI 1999/2323)
	64, 65		*Not in force*
	66		1 Apr 1999 (so far as relates to the repeal of Education Act 1996, ss 21, 22(1)(b), (c), (2), 27) (SI 1999/1016)
			1 Nov 1999 (otherwise) (SI 1999/2323)
	67, 68		1 Nov 1999 (SI 1999/2323)
	69		1 Oct 1998 (so far as it relates to the repeal of Education Act 1996, s 155(1), (4)) (SI 1998/2212)
			10 Mar 1999 (so far as it relates to the repeal of Education Act 1996, ss 54(6)(c), 89(1), (2), 90, 91, 92(1), (2), (4), 94, 95) (subject to savings) (SI 1999/120)
			1 Apr 1999 (so far as it relates to the repeal of Education Act 1996, Pt II, Chapter V) (SI 1998/2212)
			1 Apr 1999 (so far as relates to the repeals of or in Education Act 1996, ss 35(8), 36(3), 37(4), (7)–(9), 42(4),

School Standards and Framework Act 1998 (c 31)—*contd*
Schedule

30, para	69—*contd*	43(2) (the words "(subject to subsections (3) to (6))"), (3)–(6), 139, 155 (so far as not already repealed), 167(1) (the words "(subject to subsection (6)"), (6), 168(3), 169(4), (5) (the words "(subject to subsection (6)"), (6) (SI 1999/1016)
		1 Sep 1999 (otherwise) (SI 1999/2323)
	70	1 Oct 1998 (so far as it relates to the repeal of Education Act 1996, ss 184–199, 200(4), 202, 203, 209, 212 (subject to a saving), 213(2), (3), 232–240, 290) (SI 1998/2212)
		1 Apr 1999 (so far as relates to the repeal of Education Act 1996, ss 183(4), 211, 213 (so far as not already repealed), 214, 215, 216(2) (subject to a transitional provision), (3)–(9), 217, 244 (except in relation to the payment of maintenance grants in respect of any financial year beginning before 1 Apr 1999), 245 (except in so far as they applies to the payment of special purpose grant in England by the Secretary of State on or after 1 Apr 1999), 246–248 (except in so far as they apply to the payment of special purpose and capital grants by the Secretary of State on or after 1 Apr 1999), 249 (except in so far as it applies to the application of ss 250–254 in their application to the payment of capital grant by the Secretary of State on or after 1 Apr 1999), 250, 251, 253 and 254 (except in so far as they apply to the payment of capital grant by the Secretary of State on or after 1 Apr 1999), 255–258, 260, 261(2), (3) (the words "under subsection (1) or (2) any" and "(and, in the case of proposals published under section 268, the funding authority)"), (4), (5), 263(4)(b), 264, 265, 268, 269(2), (3) (the words "under subsection (1) or (2) any" and

School Standards and Framework Act 1998 (c 31)—*contd*
Schedule
30, para   70—*contd*

		"(and, in the case of proposals published under section 268, the funding authority)"), (5), (6), 270(2)(b)(ii), 271–273, 310, (subject to a saving)) (SI 1999/1016)
		1 Sep 1999 (so far as relates to the repeal of Education Act 1996, Pt III, Chapters I–V, s 252, Chapters VII–X) (SI 1999/2323)
		Not in force (otherwise)
71–74		1 Sep 1999 (SI 1999/2323)
75	(1)–(3)	1 Sep 1999 (SI 1999/2323)
	(4)	1 Oct 1998 (SI 1998/2212)
76		1 Sep 1999 (SI 1999/2323)
77	(a)	1 Sep 1999 (SI 1999/2323)
	(b)	1 Oct 1998 (SI 1998/2212)
78–80		1 Sep 1999 (SI 1999/2323)
81		1 Apr 1999 (so far as relates to the repeal of Education Act 1996, ss 338, 339(2), and in 339(4)(a), the words "or the funding authority") (SI 1999/1016)
		1 Sep 1999 (otherwise) (SI 1999/2323)
82		1 Sep 1999 (SI 1999/2323)
83		1 Oct 1998 (so far as it relates to the repeal of Education Act 1996, s 346) (SI 1998/2212)
		1 Apr 1999 (so far as it relates to the repeal of Education Act 1996, s 345) (SI 1999/1016)
		1 Sep 1999 (otherwise) (SI 1999/2323)
84–86		1 Sep 1999 (SI 1999/2323)
87	(a)	1 Oct 1998 (SI 1998/2212)
	(b)	1 Apr 1999 (SI 1999/1016)
88		1 Oct 1998 (SI 1998/2212)
89, 90		1 Sep 1999 (SI 1999/2323)
91		1 Oct 1998 (so far as it relates to the repeal of Education Act 1996, ss 370–373) (SI 1998/2212)
		1 Sep 1999 (otherwise) (SI 1999/2323)
92–95		1 Sep 1999 (SI 1999/2323)
96		1 Apr 1999 (SI 1999/1016)
97–102		1 Sep 1999 (SI 1999/2323)
103	(a)	1 Sep 1999 (SI 1999/2323)
	(b)	1 Oct 1998 (SI 1998/2212)
104, 105		1 Sep 1999 (SI 1999/2323)
106	(a)	1 Sep 1999 (SI 1999/2323)
	(b)	1 Oct 1998 (SI 1998/2212)

School Standards and Framework Act 1998 (c 31)—*contd*

Schedule

30, para	106	(c), (d)	1 Sep 1999 (SI 1999/2323)
	107		1 Sep 1999 (SI 1999/2323)
	108		1 Sep 1999 (SI 1999/1016)
	109		1 Apr 1999 (so far as it relates to the repeal of Education Act 1996, ss 426(6), 428, 431, 432) (SI 1999/1016)
			1 Sep 1999 (so far as it relates to the repeal of Education Act 1996, ss 411, 411A, 412–421, 421A, 422, 423, 423A, 424, 425, 425A, 425B, 426(1)–(5), 426A, 427, 429, 430, 436) (SI 1999/1016)
			Not in force (otherwise)
	110		1 Oct 1998 (SI 1998/2212)
	111–113		1 Sep 1999 (SI 1999/2323)
	114		1 Sep 1999 (except in so far as substitutes Education Act 1996, s 438(5)(b)) (SI 1999/2323)
			Not in force (exception noted above)
	115		1 Sep 1999 (SI 1999/2323)
	116		1 Sep 1999 (except in so far as substitutes Education Act 1996, s 440(3)(b)) (SI 1999/2323)
			Not in force (exception noted above)
	117–124		1 Sep 1999 (SI 1999/2323)
	125, 126		1 Feb 1999 (SI 1999/120)
	127		1 Sep 1999 (SI 1999/2323)
	128		1 Apr 1999 (SI 1998/2212)
	129–131		1 Sep 1999 (SI 1999/2323)
	132		1 Apr 1999 (so far as it relates to the repeal of Education Act 1996, ss 500(2), and in (3), (4) (the words "or (2)" in each place they appear), 501(1)(a), 502(6)) (SI 1999/1016)
			1 Sep 1999 (otherwise) (SI 1999/2323)
	133	(a)	1 Sep 1999 (SI 1999/2323)
		(b)	1 Apr 1999 (SI 1998/2212)
	134–136		1 Sep 1999 (SI 1999/2323)
	137		1 Apr 1999 (SI 1998/2212)
	138		*Not in force*
	139		20 Nov 1998 (for the purpose of making schemes and regulations under Education Act 1996, s 519) (subject to saving and transitional provisions) (SI 1998/2791)
			1 Apr 1999 (otherwise) (SI 1998/2791)
	140–147		1 Sep 1999 (SI 1999/2323)
	148		1 Apr 1999 (SI 1999/1016)

School Standards and Framework Act 1998 (c 31)—*contd*

Schedule

30, para	149–152	1 Sep 1999 (SI 1999/2323)
	153	20 Nov 1998 (subject to saving and transitional provisions) (SI 1998/2791)
	154	1 Sep 1999 (SI 1999/2323)
	155	1 Nov 1999 (SI 1999/2323)
	156–158	1 Sep 1999 (SI 1999/2323)
	159	1 Feb 1999 (SI 1998/2212)
	160 (a)	1 Apr 1999 (SI 1999/1016)
	(b)	1 Sep 1999 (SI 1999/2323)
	161–166	1 Sep 1999 (SI 1999/2323)
	167	1 Apr 1999 (so far as it relates to the repeal of Education Act 1996, s 552(1)–(3)) (SI 1999/1016) 1 Sep 1999 (otherwise) (SI 1999/2323)
	168–176	1 Sep 1999 (SI 1999/2323)
	177	1 Apr 1999 (SI 1999/1016)
	178–181	1 Sep 1999 (SI 1999/2323)
	182	1 Feb 1999 (SI 1999/120)
	183	1 Sep 1999 (SI 1999/2323)
	184 (a)	1 Oct 1998 (SI 1998/2212)
	(b), (c)	1 Sep 1999 (SI 1999/2323)
	185	1 Oct 1998 (so far as it relates to the repeal of Education Act 1996, Sch 4, paras 7, 8, Sch 20, Pt 1, Sch 21) (SI 1998/2212) 1 Apr 1999 (so far as it relates to the repeal of Education Act 1996, Sch 22, para 15) (SI 1998/2212) 1 Apr 1999 (so far as it relates to the repeal of Education Act 1996, Schs 3, 4, 20 (so far as not already repealed)) (SI 1999/1016) 1 Sep 1999 (so far as relates to the repeal of Education Act 1996, Schs 5–10, 14–16) (SI 1999/2323) 1 Nov 1999 (so far as relates to the repeal of Education Act 1996, Sch 2) (SI 1999/2323) *Not in force* (otherwise)
	186–188	1 Sep 1999 (SI 1999/2323)
	189 (a)–(d)	1 Sep 1999 (subject to savings and transitional provisions) (SI 1999/1016)
	(e), (f)	1 Sep 1999 (SI 1999/2323)
	(g)	1 Oct 1998 (SI 1998/2212)
	190	1 Oct 1998 (subject to a saving) (SI 1998/2212)
	191	1 Sep 1999 (SI 1999/2323)

School Standards and Framework Act 1998 (c 31)—*contd*

Schedule

30, para	192	(1)–(3)		1 Sep 1999 (SI 1999/2323)
		(4)	(a)	1 Sep 1999 (SI 1999/2323)
			(b)	1 Apr 1999 (SI 1999/1016)
	193–196			1 Sep 1999 (SI 1999/2323)
	197	(a)		1 Sep 1999 (SI 1999/2323)
		(b)		1 Apr 1999 (SI 1999/1016)
	198	(a)		1 Sep 1999 (SI 1999/2323)
		(b)		1 Apr 1999 (SI 1999/1016)
	199			1 Sep 1999 (SI 1999/2323)
	200, 201			1 Oct 1998 (SI 1998/2212)
	202	(1), (2)		1 Sep 1999 (SI 1999/2323)
		(3), (4)		1 Apr 1999 (SI 1999/1016)
	203–206			1 Sep 1999 (SI 1999/2323)
	207			1 Oct 1998 (SI 1998/2212)
	208	(a), (b)		1 Sep 1999 (SI 1999/2323)
		(c)		1 Feb 1999 (so far as it relates to the repeal of Education Act 1997, s 13) (SI 1998/2212)
				1 Sep 1999 (otherwise) (SI 1999/1016)
	209–215			1 Sep 1999 (SI 1999/2323)
	216			1 Oct 1998 (SI 1998/2212)
	217			1 Sep 1999 (SI 1999/2323)
	218			1 Apr 1999 (SI 1999/1016)
	219			1 Oct 1998 (SI 1998/2212)
	220			1 Sep 1999 (SI 1999/1016)
	221			1 Sep 1999 (SI 1999/2323)
	222	(a)		1 Feb 1999 (so far as relates to the repeal of Education Act 1996, Sch 33B, paras, 1, 2 set out in Education Act 1997, Sch 3) (SI 1998/2212)
				1 Sep 1999 (so far as it relates to the repeal of Education Act 1997, Sch 3, so far as that repeal is not already in force) (SI 1999/1016)
				1 Sep 1999 (otherwise) (SI 1999/2323)
		(b)		1 Oct 1998 (SI 1998/2212)
	223			1 Sep 1999 (so far as it relates to the repeal of Education Act 1997, Sch 7, paras 31–34, 49(3), so far as those repeals are not already in force) (SI 1999/1016)
				1 Sep 1999 (otherwise) (SI 1999/2323)
	224			24 Jul 1998 (s 145(4))
	225			1 Apr 1999 (SI 1999/1016)
31				1 Oct 1998 (repeals of or in Local Government Act 1974; Education Reform Act 1988, Sch 8; School Teachers Pay and Conditions

School Standards and Framework Act 1998 (c 31)—*contd*
Schedule
31—*contd*

Act 1991, s 2(4); Nursery
Education and Grant-Maintained
Schools Act 1996; Education
Act 1996, ss 155(1), (4), 184–199,
200(4), 202, 203, 209, 212 (subject
to a saving), 213(2), (3), 232–240,
290, 346, 357(2), 370–373, 404(3),
433(4), Sch 4, paras 7, 8, Sch 20,
Pt I, Schs 21, 40; School
Inspections Act 1996, Pt II (subject
to a saving), ss 44, 45; Education
Act 1997, ss 42, 52(4), (5), Sch 6,
para 5) (SI 1998/2212)

1 Feb 1999 (so far as relates to the
repeal of Education Act 1996,
Sch 33B, paras, 1, 2 set out in
Education Act 1997, Sch 3;
Education Act 1997, s 13)
(SI 1998/2212)

10 Mar 1999 (so far as relates to the
repeal of Education Act 1996,
ss 54(6)(c), 89(1), (2), 90, 91,
92(1), (2), (4), 94, 95) (subject to
savings) (SI 1999/120)

1 Apr 1999 (repeals of Education
Act 1996, Pt II, Chapter V (subject
to a saving), s 516, Sch 22, para 15)
(SI 1998/2212)

1 Apr 1999 (repeals of or in Public
Records Act 1958; Building
Act 1984, s 4(1)(a)(iv); Education
(No 2) Act 1986, s 49(3)(ba);
Education Act 1996, ss 356(5)(a)(ii),
393, 544(1), and the provisions
repealed by Sch 30, paras 66, 69,
70, 81, 83, 109, 132, 167, 177, 185
to this Act, to the extent that they
are brought into force by
SI 1999/1016 as noted above;
Schools Inspections Act 1996,
ss 11(5)(b), 20(3), 21(4), 46(1);
Education Act 1997, s 50; Audit
Commission Act 1998)
(SI 1999/1016)

1 Sep 1999 (so far it relates to the
repeals of or in Education Acts of
1996 and 1997 by Sch 30,
paras 109, 189, 208, 220, 222, 223
to this Act, to the extent that they

School Standards and Framework Act 1998 (c 31)—*contd*
Schedule
31—*contd*

are brought into force by
SI 1999/1016 as noted above)
(SI 1999/1016)
1 Sep 1999 (so far as relates to the
repeals of or in London
Government Act 1963, s 31;
Superannuation Act 1972, Sch 1
(entry relating to the Schools
Funding Council for Wales); Local
Government Act 1972; House of
Commons Disqualification
Act 1975, Sch 1, Pt III (the entries
"Any member of an education
association in receipt of
renumeration" and "Any member
of the Funding Council for Wales
in receipt of renumeration"; Sex
Discrimination Act 1975, ss 22,
23C, 25; Race Relations Act 1976;
National Health Service Act 1977;
Education (Scotland) Act 1980;
Acquisition of Land Act 1981,
s 17(4)(ab); Representation of the
People Act 1983; Building
Act 1984, s 4(1)(a)(ii), (iii);
Education Reform Act 1988,
ss 166, 167, 197(7), 236(1),
Sch 12; Children Act 1989; School
Teachers' Pay and Conditions
Act 1991, ss 1(5), (6), 2(2), (5), (6);
Diocesan Boards of Education
Measure 1991; Further and Higher
Education Act 1992; Charities
Act 1993; Value Added Tax
Act 1994; Education Act 1994;
Disability Discrimination Act 1995;
Employment Rights Act 1996;
Education Act 1996, ss 391(8), (9),
392(4), 560(6), and the provisions
repealed by Sch 30, paras 58, 62,
69–71, 74, 79, 81, 83, 90–92, 94,
95, 106, 107, 111–118, 120–124,
127, 132, 133(a), 134, 140–143,
149, 151, 152, 158, 160(b),
161–167, 172, 174, 175, 178–181,
183–185, 187–189, to this Act, to
the extent that they are brought
into force by SI 1999/2323 as
noted above; School Inspections

School Standards and Framework Act 1998 (c 31)—*contd*

Schedule

31—*contd*

Act 1996 (the provisions repealed by Sch 30, paras 191, 192, 194, 195, 199, 202, 205, 206 to this Act, to the extent that they are brought into force by SI 1999/2323 as noted above); Education Act 1997 (the provisions repealed by Sch 30, paras 208, 212, 217, 221–223 to this Act, to the extent that they are brought into force by SI 1999/2323 as noted above); Education (Schools) Act 1997) (SI 1999/2323)

1 Nov 1999 (so far as relates to repeals of or in Superannuation Act 1972, Sch 1 (the entry relating to the Funding Agency for Schools); House of Commons Disqualification Act 1975, Sch 1, Pt III (the entry "Any member of the Funding Agency for Schools in receipt of renumeration"); Education Act 1996 (the provisions repealed by Sch 30, paras 66–68, 155, 185 to this Act, to the extent that they are brought into force by SI 1999/2323 as noted above) (SI 1999/2323)

Not in force (otherwise)

32　　　　　　　　　　　　　　　　　24 Jul 1998 (s 145(4))

[1]　For transitional and saving provisions relating to the admission of children to maintained schools see SI 1999/1016, art 6, Sch 4, as amended by SI 1999/2484

[2]　For transitional and saving provisions, see SI 1999/2323, arts 3–23, Schs 5–7, as amended by SI 1999/2484

Scotland Act 1998 (c 46)

RA: 19 Nov 1998

Commencement provisions: s 130; Scotland Act (Commencement) Order 1998, SI 1998/3178

Section

1–18		19 Nov 1998 (RA)
19, 20		6 May 1999 (SI 1998/3178)
21	(1)–(7)	6 May 1999 (SI 1998/3178)
	(8)	See Sch 2 below
22		6 May 1999 (SI 1998/3178)

Scotland Act 1998 (c 46)—*contd*
Section

23			6 May 1999 (for the purpose of enabling the Parliament to require any member of the Scottish Executive or his staff to attend its proceedings for the purpose of giving evidence or to produce documents in his custody or under his control) (SI 1998/3178)
			1 Jul 1999 (otherwise) (SI 1998/3178)
24–26			6 May 1999 (SI 1998/3178)
27			20 May 1999 (SI 1998/3178)
28, 29			1 Jul 1999 (SI 1998/3178)
30			6 May 1999 (SI 1998/3178)
31–36			1 Jul 1999 (SI 1998/3178)
37			25 Jan 1999 (SI 1998/3178)
38	(1), (2)		6 May 1999 (SI 1998/3178)
	(3)		25 Jan 1999 (SI 1998/3178)
	(4)–(6)		6 May 1999 (SI 1998/3178)
39			1 Jul 1999 (SI 1998/3178)
40–43			6 May 1999 (SI 1998/3178)
44	(1)	(a), (b)	6 May 1999 (SI 1998/3178)
		(c)	20 May 1999 (SI 1998/3178)
	(2)–(4)		6 May 1999 (SI 1998/3178)
45–47			6 May 1999 (SI 1998/3178)
48	(1)		6 May 1999 (for the purpose of enabling the First Minister to recommend the appointment of the Lord Advocate and Solicitor General for Scotland to take effect from a date not earlier than 20 May 1999) (SI 1998/3178)
			20 May 1999 (otherwise) (SI 1998/3178)
	(2)–(6)		20 May 1999 (SI 1998/3178)
49, 50			6 May 1999 (SI 1998/3178)
51	(1)–(3)		6 May 1999 (SI 1998/3178)
	(4)		25 Jan 1999 (for the purpose of enabling any delegation of civil service management functions or any determination of payments to be made to come into force not earlier than 6 May 1999) (SI 1998/3178)
			6 May 1999 (otherwise) (SI 1998/3178)
	(5), (6)		6 May 1999 (SI 1998/3178)
	(7)		25 Jan 1999 (for the purpose of enabling any delegation of civil service management functions or

Scotland Act 1998 (c 46)—*contd*

Section

51	(7)—*contd*	any determination of payments to be made to come into force not earlier than 6 May 1999) (SI 1998/3178)
		6 May 1999 (otherwise) (SI 1998/3178)
	(8), (9)	6 May 1999 (SI 1998/3178)
52		6 May 1999 (except so far as relating to the Lord Advocate) (SI 1998/3178)
		20 May 1999 (exception noted above) (SI 1998/3178)
53–55		1 Jul 1999 (SI 1998/3178)
56	(1)	1 Jul 1999 (SI 1998/3178)
	(2)	25 Jan 1999 (for the purpose of enabling subordinate legislation to be made to come into force not earlier than 1 Jul 1999) (SI 1998/3178)
	(3)–(5)	1 Jul 1999 (SI 1998/3178)
57	(1)	1 Jul 1999 (SI 1998/3178)
	(2)	6 May 1999 (SI 1998/3178)
	(3)	20 May 1999 (SI 1998/3178)
58, 59		6 May 1999 (SI 1998/3178)
60		25 Jan 1999 (for the purpose of enabling subordinate legislation to be made to come into force not earlier than 1 Jul 1999) (SI 1998/3178)
		6 May 1999 (otherwise) (SI 1998/3178)
61	(1)–(3)	20 May 1999 (SI 1998/3178)
	(4)	6 May 1999 (SI 1998/3178)
62		25 Jan 1999 (for the purpose of enabling subordinate legislation to be made to come into force not earlier than 20 May 1999) (SI 1998/3178)
		20 May 1999 (otherwise) (SI 1998/3178)
63		6 May 1999 (for the purpose of enabling subordinate legislation to be made to come into force not earlier than 1 Jul 1999) (SI 1998/3178)
		1 Jul 1999 (otherwise) (SI 1998/3178)
64	(1), (2)	1 Apr 1999 (SI 1998/3178)
	(3)–(7)	1 Jul 1999 (SI 1998/3178)
	(8)	1 Apr 1999 (SI 1998/3178)
65–68		1 Jul 1999 (SI 1998/3178)
69		6 May 1999 (SI 1998/3178)

Scotland Act 1998 (c 46)—*contd*

Section

70		1 Jul 1999 (SI 1998/3178)
71	(1)–(5)	1 Jul 1999 (SI 1998/3178)
	(6)	25 Jan 1999 (for the purpose of enabling subordinate legislation to be made to come into force not earlier than 1 Jul 1999) (SI 1998/3178)
		1 Jul 1999 (otherwise) (SI 1998/3178)
	(7), (8)	1 Jul 1999 (SI 1998/3178)
72		1 Jul 1999 (SI 1998/3178)
73–85		6 May 1999 (SI 1998/3178)
86		1 Jul 1999 (SI 1998/3178)
87		20 May 1999 (SI 1998/3178)
88		25 Jan 1999 (for the purpose of enabling subordinate legislation to be made to come into force not earlier than 1 Jul 1999) (SI 1998/3178)
		1 Jul 1999 (otherwise) (SI 1998/3178)
89		6 May 1999 (for the purpose of enabling subordinate legislation to be made to come into force not earlier than 1 Jul 1999) (SI 1998/3178)
		1 Jul 1999 (otherwise) (SI 1998/3178)
90, 91		1 Jul 1999 (SI 1998/3178)
92		6 May 1999 (SI 1998/3178)
93		6 May 1999 (for the purpose of enabling subordinate legislation to be made to come into force not earlier than 1 Jul 1999) (SI 1998/3178)
		1 Jul 1999 (otherwise) (SI 1998/3178)
94, 95		1 Jul 1999 (SI 1998/3178)
96		6 May 1999 (SI 1998/3178)
97		25 Jan 1999 (for the purpose of enabling subordinate legislation to be made to come into force not earlier than 6 May 1999) (SI 1998/3178)
		6 May 1999 (otherwise) (SI 1998/3178)
98–100		6 May 1999 (SI 1998/3178)
101, 102		1 Jul 1999 (SI 1998/3178)
103	(1), (2)	6 May 1999 (SI 1998/3178)
	(3)	25 Jan 1999 (for the purpose of enabling subordinate legislation to be made to come into force not earlier than 6 May 1999) (SI 1998/3178)

Scotland Act 1998 (c 46)—*contd*

Section

103	(3)—*contd*		6 May 1999 (otherwise) (SI 1998/3178)
	(4)		6 May 1999 (SI 1998/3178)
104			1 Jul 1999 (SI 1998/3178)
105, 106			25 Jan 1999 (SI 1998/3178)
107			1 Jul 1999 (SI 1998/3178)
108–111			6 May 1999 (SI 1998/3178)
112–116			19 Nov 1998 (RA)
117–119			1 Jul 1999 (SI 1998/3178)
120			1 Apr 2000 (SI 1998/3178)
121, 122			1 Jul 1999 (SI 1998/3178)
123			6 May 1999 (except so far as relating to the Lord Advocate) (SI 1998/3178)
			20 May 1999 (exception noted above) (SI 1998/3178)
124			1 Jul 1999 (SI 1998/3178)
125	(1)		See Sch 8 below
	(2)		See Sch 9 below
126–132			19 Nov 1998 (RA)

Schedule

1			19 Nov 1998 (RA)
2, para	1		6 May 1999 (SI 1998/3178)
	2	(1)	6 May 1999 (SI 1998/3178)
		(2)–(4)	25 Jan 1999 (for the purpose of enabling subordinate legislation to be made to come into force not earlier than 6 May 1999) (SI 1998/3178)
			6 May 1999 (otherwise) (SI 1998/3178)
	3–6		6 May 1999 (SI 1998/3178)
	7		25 Jan 1999 (for the purpose of enabling subordinate legislation to be made to come into force not earlier than 6 May 1999) (SI 1998/3178)
			6 May 1999 (otherwise) (SI 1998/3178)
3			6 May 1999 (SI 1998/3178)
4			1 Jul 1999 (SI 1998/3178)
5, 6			6 May 1999 (SI 1998/3178)
7			19 Nov 1998 (RA)
8, para	1		1 Jul 1999 (SI 1998/3178)
	2		20 May 1999 (SI 1998/3178)
	3–6		1 Jul 1999 (SI 1998/3178)
	7		20 May 1999 (SI 1998/3178)
	8, 9		1 Jul 1999 (SI 1998/3178)
	10, 11		19 Nov 1998 (RA)
	12		1 Jul 1999 (SI 1998/3178)
	13, 14		6 May 1999 (SI 1998/3178)
	15–17		1 Jul 1999 (SI 1998/3178)

Scotland Act 1998 (c 46)—*contd*

Schedule

8, para	18		6 May 1999 (SI 1998/3178)
	19		19 Nov 1998 (RA)
	20		1 Apr 2000 (SI 1998/3178)
	21, 22		1 Jul 1999 (SI 1998/3178)
	23	(1)	19 Nov 1998 (RA)
		(2), (2A)	Substituted (1 Dec 2001) by Financial Services and Markets Act 2000 (Consequential Amendments and Repeals) Order 2001, SI 2001/3649, art 360
		(3)	19 Nov 1998 (RA)
		(4), (4A)	Substituted (1 Dec 2001) by Financial Services and Markets Act 2000 (Consequential Amendments and Repeals) Order 2001, SI 2001/3649, art 360
		(5)	1 Jul 1999 (SI 1998/3178)
		(6)	19 Nov 1998 (RA)
	24–26		6 May 1999 (SI 1998/3178)
	27		1 Jul 1999 (SI 1998/3178)
	28		6 May 1999 (SI 1998/3178)
	29		1 Jul 1999 (SI 1998/3178)
	30, 31		6 May 1999 (SI 1998/3178)
	32		20 May 1999 (SI 1998/3178)
	33		6 May 1999 (SI 1998/3178)
	34		1 Jul 1999 (SI 1998/3178)
9			20 May 1999 (repeals in House of Commons Disqualification Act 1975, Ministerial and other Salaries Act 1975) (SI 1998/3178) 1 Jul 1999 (otherwise) (SI 1998/3178)

Social Security Act 1998 (c 14)

RA: 21 May 1998

Commencement provisions: s 87(2), (3); Social Security Act 1998 (Commencement No 1) Order 1998, SI 1998/2209; Social Security Act 1998 (Commencement No 2) Order 1998, SI 1998/2780; Social Security Act 1998 (Commencement No 3) Order 1999, SI 1999/418; Social Security Act 1998 (Commencement No 4) Order 1999, SI 1999/526; Social Security Act 1998 (Commencement No 5) Order 1999, SI 1999/528; Social Security Act 1998 (Commencement No 6) Order 1999, SI 1999/1055; Social Security Act 1998 (Commencement No 7 and Consequential and Transitional Provisions) Order 1999, SI 1999/1510[1]; Social Security Act 1998 (Commencement No 8, and Savings and Consequential and Transitional Provisions) Order 1999, SI 1999/1958; Social Security Act 1998 (Commencement No 9, and Savings and Consequential and Transitional Provisions) Order 1999, SI 1999/2422; Social Security Act 1998 (Commencement No 10 and Transitional Provisions) Order 1999, SI 1999/2739[5];

Social Security Act 1998 (c 14)—*contd*
Social Security Act 1998 (Commencement No 11, and Savings and Consequential and Transitional Provisions) Order 1999, SI 1999/2860[6]; Social Security Act 1998 (Commencement No 12 and Consequential and Transitional Provisions) Order 1999, SI 1999/3178[7]; Social Security Act 1998 (Commencement No 13) Order 2001, SI 2001/2316

Section

1	(a)		5 Jul 1999 (for certain purposes)[3] (SI 1999/1958)
			6 Sep 1999 (so far as not already in force for certain purposes)[4] (SI 1999/2422)
			5 Oct 1999 (so far as not already in force for certain purposes)[5] (SI 1999/2739)
			18 Oct 1999 (so far as not already in force for certain purposes)[6] (SI 1999/2860)
			29 Nov 1999 (so far as not already in force for certain purposes)[7] (SI 1999/3178)
			29 Nov 1999 (so far as not already in force except for certain purposes)[7] (SI 1999/3178)
			Not in force (exceptions referred to above)
	(b)		29 Nov 1999 (for certain purposes)[7] (SI 1999/3178)
			29 Nov 1999 (so far as not already in force except for certain purposes)[7] (SI 1999/3178)
			Not in force (exceptions referred to above)
	(c)		1 Jun 1999 (SI 1999/1510)
2	(1)		8 Sep 1998 (SI 1998/2209)
	(2)	(a)	5 Jul 1999 (for certain purposes)[3] (SI 1999/1958)
			6 Sep 1999 (so far as not already in force for certain purposes)[4] (SI 1999/2422)
			5 Oct 1999 (so far as not already in force for certain purposes)[5] (SI 1999/2739)
			18 Oct 1999 (so far as not already in force for certain purposes)[6] (SI 1999/2860)
			29 Nov 1999 (so far as not already in force except for certain purposes)[7] (SI 1999/3178)
			Not in force (exceptions referred to above)

Social Security Act 1998 (c 14)—*contd*
Section

2	(2)	(b)–(h)	8 Sep 1998 (SI 1998/2209)
	(3)		8 Sep 1998 (SI 1998/2209)
3			8 Sep 1998 (SI 1998/2209)
4	(1)	(a)	5 Jul 1999 (for certain purposes[3] and so far as it relates to social security appeal tribunals and medical appeal tribunals) (SI 1999/1958)

5 Jul 1999 (for certain purposes[3] and
  so far as it relates to social security
  appeal tribunals and medical appeal
  tribunals) (SI 1999/1958)
6 Sep 1999 (so far as not already in
  force for certain purposes[4] and so
  far as it relates to social security
  appeal tribunals and medical appeal
  tribunals) (SI 1999/2422)
5 Oct 1999 (so far as not already in
  force for certain purposes[5] and so
  far as it relates to social security
  appeal tribunals and disability
  appeal tribunals) (SI 1999/2739)
18 Oct 1999 (so far as not already in
  force for certain purposes)[6]
  (SI 1999/2860)
29 Nov 1999 (so far as not already in
  force for certain purposes)[7]
  (SI 1999/3178)
29 Nov 1999 (so far as not already in
  force except for certain purposes)[7]
  (SI 1999/3178)
Not in force (exceptions referred to
  above)

(b)   1 Jun 1999 (SI 1999/1510)
(c)   18 Oct 1999 (for certain purposes)[6]
  (SI 1999/2860)
29 Nov 1999 (so far as not already in
  force for certain purposes)[7]
  (SI 1999/3178)
29 Nov 1999 (so far as not already in
  force except for certain purposes)[7]
  (SI 1999/3178)
Not in force (exceptions referred to above)

(2)   (a)   5 Jul 1999 (for certain purposes)[3]
  (SI 1999/1958)
6 Sep 1999 (so far as not already in
  force for certain purposes)[4]
  (SI 1999/2422)
5 Oct 1999 (so far as not already in
  force for certain purposes)[5]
  (SI 1999/2739)
18 Oct 1999 (so far as not already in
  force for certain purposes)[6]
  (SI 1999/2860)

Social Security Act 1998 (c 14)—*contd*

4	(2)	(a)—*contd*	29 Nov 1999 (so far as not already in force for certain purposes)[7] (SI 1999/3178)
			29 Nov 1999 (so far as not already in force except for certain purposes)[7] (SI 1999/3178)
			Not in force (exceptions referred to above)
		(b)	1 Jun 1999 (SI 1999/1510)
		(c)	18 Oct 1999 (for certain purposes)[6] (SI 1999/2860)
			29 Nov 1999 (so far as not already in force for certain purposes)[7] (SI 1999/3178)
			29 Nov 1999 (so far as not already in force except for certain purposes)[7] (SI 1999/3178)
			Not in force (exceptions referred to above)
		(d)	29 Nov 1999 (so far as not already in force for certain purposes)[7] (SI 1999/3178)
			29 Nov 1999 (so far as not already in force except for certain purposes)[7] (SI 1999/3178)
			Not in force (exceptions referred to above)
5			1 Jun 1999 (SI 1999/1510)
6	(1), (2)		1 Jun 1999 (SI 1999/1510)
	(3)		4 Mar 1999 (so far as authorising the making of regulations) (SI 1999/528)
			1 Jun 1999 (otherwise) (SI 1999/1510)
	(4)–(6)		1 Jun 1999 (SI 1999/1510)
7	(1)–(5)		1 Jun 1999 (SI 1999/1510)
	(6)		4 Mar 1999 (so far as authorising the making of regulations) (SI 1999/528)
			1 Jun 1999 (otherwise) (SI 1999/1510)
	(7)		See Sch 1 below
8	(1)	(a)	5 Jul 1999 (for certain purposes)[3] (SI 1999/1958)
			6 Sep 1999 (so far as not already in force for certain purposes)[4] (SI 1999/2422)
			5 Oct 1999 (so far as not already in force for certain purposes)[5] (SI 1999/2739)

Social Security Act 1998 (c 14)—*contd*
Section

8	(1)	(a)—*contd*	18 Oct 1999 (so far as not already in force for certain purposes)[6] (SI 1999/2860)
			29 Nov 1999 (so far as not already in force except for certain purposes)[7] (SI 1999/3178)
			Not in force (exceptions referred to above)
		(b)	29 Nov 1999 (except for certain purposes)[7] (SI 1999/3178)
			Not in force (exceptions referred to above)
		(c)	5 Jul 1999 (for certain purposes)[3] (SI 1999/1958)
			6 Sep 1999 (so far as not already in force for certain purposes)[4] (SI 1999/2422)
			5 Oct 1999 (so far as not already in force for certain purposes)[5] (SI 1999/2739)
			18 Oct 1999 (so far as not already in force for certain purposes)[6] (SI 1999/2860)
			29 Nov 1999 (so far as not already in force except for certain purposes)[7] (SI 1999/3178)
			Not in force (exceptions referred to above)
		(d)	Repealed (*partly never in force*)
	(2)		5 Jul 1999 (for certain purposes)[3] (SI 1999/1958)
			6 Sep 1999 (so far as not already in force for certain purposes)[4] (SI 1999/2422)
			5 Oct 1999 (so far as not already in force for certain purposes)[5] (SI 1999/2739)
			18 Oct 1999 (so far as not already in force for certain purposes)[6] (SI 1999/2860)
			29 Nov 1999 (so far as not already in force except for certain purposes)[7] (SI 1999/3178)
			Not in force (exceptions referred to above)
	(3)	(a)	5 Jul 1999 (for certain purposes)[3] (SI 1999/1958)
			6 Sep 1999 (so far as not already in force for certain purposes)[4] (SI 1999/2422)

Social Security Act 1998 (c 14)—*contd*

Section

8	(3)	(a)—*contd*	18 Oct 1999 (so far as not already in force for certain purposes)[6] (SI 1999/2860)
			29 Nov 1999 (so far as not already in force except for certain purposes)[7] (SI 1999/3178)
			Not in force (exceptions referred to above)
		(b)	18 Oct 1999 (for certain purposes)[6] (SI 1999/2860)
			29 Nov 1999 (so far as not already in force except for certain purposes)[7] (SI 1999/3178)
			Not in force (exceptions referred to above)
		(c)	29 Nov 1999 (except for certain purposes)[7] (SI 1999/3178)
			Not in force (exceptions referred to above)
		(d), (e)	5 Oct 1999 (for certain purposes)[5] (SI 1999/2739)
			29 Nov 1999 (so far as not already in force except for certain purposes)[7] (SI 1999/3178)
			Not in force (exceptions referred to above)
		(f)	29 Nov 1999 (except for certain purposes)[7] (SI 1999/3178)
			Not in force (exceptions referred to above)
		(g)	5 Jul 1999 (for certain purposes)[3] (SI 1999/1958)
			29 Nov 1999 (so far as not already in force except for certain purposes)[7] (SI 1999/3178)
			Not in force (exceptions referred to above)
		(h)	29 Nov 1999 (except for certain purposes)[7] (SI 1999/3178)
			Not in force (exceptions referred to above)
	(4), (5)		5 Jul 1999 (for certain purposes)[3] (SI 1999/1958)
			6 Sep 1999 (so far as not already in force for certain purposes)[4] (SI 1999/2422)
			5 Oct 1999 (so far as not already in force for certain purposes)[5] (SI 1999/2739)

Social Security Act 1998 (c 14)—*contd*

Section

8	(4), (5)—*contd*	18 Oct 1999 (so far as not already in force for certain purposes)[6] (SI 1999/2860)
		29 Nov 1999 (so far as not already in force except for certain purposes)[7] (SI 1999/3178)
		Not in force (exceptions referred to above)
9	(1)	4 Mar 1999 (so far as authorising the making of regulations) (SI 1999/528)
		5 Jul 1999 (for certain purposes)[3] (SI 1999/1958)
		6 Sep 1999 (so far as not already in force for certain purposes)[4] (SI 1999/2422)
		5 Oct 1999 (so far as not already in force for certain purposes)[5] (SI 1999/2739)
		18 Oct 1999 (so far as not already in force for certain purposes)[6] (SI 1999/2860)
		29 Nov 1999 (so far as not already in force except for certain purposes)[7] (SI 1999/3178)
		Not in force (exceptions referred to above)
	(2), (3)	5 Jul 1999 (for certain purposes)[3] (SI 1999/1958)
		6 Sep 1999 (so far as not already in force for certain purposes)[4] (SI 1999/2422)
		5 Oct 1999 (so far as not already in force for certain purposes)[5] (SI 1999/2739)
		18 Oct 1999 (so far as not already in force for certain purposes)[6] (SI 1999/2860)
		29 Nov 1999 (so far as not already in force except for certain purposes)[7] (SI 1999/3178)
		Not in force (exceptions referred to above)
	(4)	4 Mar 1999 (so far as authorising the making of regulations) (SI 1999/528)
		5 Jul 1999 (for certain purposes)[3] (SI 1999/1958)

Social Security Act 1998 (c 14)—*contd*
Section

9	(4)—*contd*	6 Sep 1999 (so far as not already in force for certain purposes)[4] (SI 1999/2422)
		5 Oct 1999 (so far as not already in force for certain purposes)[5] (SI 1999/2739)
		18 Oct 1999 (so far as not already in force for certain purposes)[6] (SI 1999/2860)
		29 Nov 1999 (so far as not already in force except for certain purposes)[7] (SI 1999/3178)
		Not in force (exceptions referred to above)
	(5)	5 Jul 1999 (for certain purposes)[3] (SI 1999/1958)
		6 Sep 1999 (so far as not already in force for certain purposes)[4] (SI 1999/2422)
		5 Oct 1999 (so far as not already in force for certain purposes)[5] (SI 1999/2739)
		18 Oct 1999 (so far as not already in force for certain purposes)[6] (SI 1999/2860)
		29 Nov 1999 (so far as not already in force except for certain purposes)[7] (SI 1999/3178)
		Not in force (exceptions referred to above)
	(6)	4 Mar 1999 (so far as authorising the making of regulations) (SI 1999/528)
		5 Jul 1999 (for certain purposes)[3] (SI 1999/1958)
		6 Sep 1999 (so far as not already in force for certain purposes)[4] (SI 1999/2422)
		5 Oct 1999 (so far as not already in force for certain purposes)[5] (SI 1999/2739)
		18 Oct 1999 (so far as not already in force for certain purposes)[6] (SI 1999/2860)
		29 Nov 1999 (so far as not already in force except for certain purposes)[7] (SI 1999/3178)
		Not in force (exceptions referred to above)

Social Security Act 1998 (c 14)—*contd*
Section

10	(1), (2)	5 Jul 1999 (for certain purposes)[3] (SI 1999/1958)
		6 Sep 1999 (so far as not already in force for certain purposes)[4] (SI 1999/2422)
		5 Oct 1999 (so far as not already in force for certain purposes)[5] (SI 1999/2739)
		18 Oct 1999 (so far as not already in force for certain purposes)[6] (SI 1999/2860)
		29 Nov 1999 (so far as not already in force except for certain purposes)[7] (SI 1999/3178)
		Not in force (exceptions referred to above)
	(3)	4 Mar 1999 (so far as authorising the making of regulations) (SI 1999/528)
		5 Jul 1999 (for certain purposes)[3] (SI 1999/1958)
		6 Sep 1999 (so far as not already in force for certain purposes)[4] (SI 1999/2422)
		5 Oct 1999 (so far as not already in force for certain purposes)[5] (SI 1999/2739)
		18 Oct 1999 (so far as not already in force for certain purposes)[6] (SI 1999/2860)
		29 Nov 1999 (so far as not already in force except for certain purposes)[7] (SI 1999/3178)
		Not in force (exceptions referred to above)
	(4)	Repealed (*partly never in force*)
	(5)	5 Jul 1999 (for certain purposes)[3] (SI 1999/1958)
		6 Sep 1999 (so far as not already in force for certain purposes)[4] (SI 1999/2422)
		5 Oct 1999 (so far as not already in force for certain purposes)[5] (SI 1999/2739)
		18 Oct 1999 (so far as not already in force for certain purposes)[6] (SI 1999/2860)
		29 Nov 1999 (so far as not already in force except for certain purposes)[7] (SI 1999/3178)

Social Security Act 1998 (c 14)—*contd*

Section

10	(5)—*contd*	*Not in force* (exceptions referred to above)
	(6)	4 Mar 1999 (so far as authorising the making of regulations) (SI 1999/528)
		5 Jul 1999 (for certain purposes)[3] (SI 1999/1958)
		6 Sep 1999 (so far as not already in force for certain purposes)[4] (SI 1999/2422)
		5 Oct 1999 (so far as not already in force for certain purposes)[5] (SI 1999/2739)
		18 Oct 1999 (so far as not already in force for certain purposes)[6] (SI 1999/2860)
		29 Nov 1999 (so far as not already in force except for certain purposes)[7] (SI 1999/3178)
		Not in force (exceptions referred to above)
10A		Inserted by Social Security Contributions (Transfer of Functions, etc) Act 1999, s 18, Sch 7, para 24 (qv)
11	(1)	4 Mar 1999 (so far as authorising the making of regulations) (SI 1999/528)
		5 Jul 1999 (for certain purposes)[3] (SI 1999/1958)
		6 Sep 1999 (so far as not already in force for certain purposes[4]) (SI 1999/2422)
		5 Oct 1999 (so far as not already in force for certain purposes)[5] (SI 1999/2739)
		18 Oct 1999 (so far as not already in force for certain purposes)[6] (SI 1999/2860)
		29 Nov 1999 (so far as not already in force except for certain purposes)[7] (SI 1999/3178)
		Not in force (exceptions referred to above)
	(2)	5 Jul 1999 (for certain purposes)[3] (SI 1999/1958)
		6 Sep 1999 (so far as not already in force for certain purposes[4]) (SI 1999/2422)

Social Security Act 1998 (c 14)—*contd*
Section

11	(2)—*contd*	5 Oct 1999 (so far as not already in force for certain purposes)[5] (SI 1999/2739)
		18 Oct 1999 (so far as not already in force for certain purposes)[6] (SI 1999/2860)
		29 Nov 1999 (so far as not already in force except for certain purposes)[7] (SI 1999/3178)
		Not in force (exceptions referred to above)
	(3)	5 Jul 1999 (for certain purposes[3], except the definitions "the current legislation" (so far as it relates to Jobseekers Act 1995 and Social Security (Recovery of Benefits) Act 1997) and "the former legislation" (so far as it relates to Social Security Act 1986, Pt II)) (SI 1999/1958)
		6 Sep 1999 (so far as not already in force for certain purposes[4], except the definitions "the current legislation" (so far as it relates to Jobseekers Act 1995 and Social Security (Recovery of Benefits) Act 1997) and "the former legislation" (so far as it relates to Social Security Act 1986, Pt II)) (SI 1999/2422)
		5 Oct 1999 (so far as not already in force for certain purposes[5], except the definitions "the current legislation" (so far as it relates to Jobseekers Act 1995 and Social Security (Recovery of Benefits) Act 1997) and "the former legislation" (so far as it relates to National Insurance Acts 1965—1974, National Insurance (Industrial Injuries) Acts 1965—1974, Social Security Act 1975)) (SI 1999/2739)
		18 Oct 1999 (so far as not already in force for certain purposes[6], except the definitions "the current legislation" (so far as it relates to Social Security (Recovery of Benefits) Act 1997) and "the

Social Security Act 1998 (c 14)—*contd*

Section

11	(3)—*contd*	former legislation" (so far as it relates to National Insurance Acts 1965—1974, National Insurance (Industrial Injuries) Acts 1965—1974, Social Security Act 1986, Pt II)) (SI 1999/2860)
		29 Nov 1999 (so far as not already in force except for certain purposes)[7] (SI 1999/3178)
		Not in force (exceptions referred to above)
12	(1)	See Schs 2, 3 below
	(2)	Substituted by Social Security Contributions (Transfer of Functions, etc) Act 1999, s 18, Sch 7, para 25(1), (3) (qv)
	(3)	4 Mar 1999 (so far as authorising the making of regulations) (SI 1999/528)
		5 Jul 1999 (for certain purposes)[3] (SI 1999/1958)
		6 Sep 1999 (so far as not already in force for certain purposes)[4] (SI 1999/2422)
		5 Oct 1999 (so far as not already in force for certain purposes)[5] (SI 1999/2739)
		18 Oct 1999 (so far as not already in force for certain purposes)[6] (SI 1999/2860)
		29 Nov 1999 (so far as not already in force except for certain purposes)[7] (SI 1999/3178)
		Not in force (exceptions referred to above)
	(4)	5 Jul 1999 (for certain purposes[3] except so far as relates to Social Security Administration Act 1992, s 74) (SI 1999/1958)
		6 Sep 1999 (so far as not already in force for certain purposes[4], except so far as relates to Social Security Administration Act 1992, s 74) (SI 1999/2422)
		5 Oct 1999 (so far as not already in force for certain purposes[5], except so far as relates to Social Security Administration Act 1992, s 74) (SI 1999/2739)

Social Security Act 1998 (c 14)—*contd*

12	(4)—*contd*	18 Oct 1999 (so far as not already in force for certain purposes)[6] (SI 1999/2860)
		29 Nov 1999 (so far as not already in force except for certain purposes)[7] (SI 1999/3178)
		Not in force (exceptions referred to above)
	(5)	5 Jul 1999 (for certain purposes)[3] (SI 1999/1958)
		29 Nov 1999 (so far as not already in force except for certain purposes)[7] (SI 1999/3178)
		Not in force (exceptions referred to above)
	(6), (7)	4 Mar 1999 (so far as authorising the making of regulations) (SI 1999/528)
		5 Jul 1999 (for certain purposes)[3] (SI 1999/1958)
		6 Sep 1999 (so far as not already in force for certain purposes)[4] (SI 1999/2422)
		5 Oct 1999 (so far as not already in force for certain purposes)[5] (SI 1999/2739)
		18 Oct 1999 (so far as not already in force for certain purposes)[6] (SI 1999/2860)
		29 Nov 1999 (so far as not already in force except for certain purposes)[7] (SI 1999/3178)
		Not in force (exceptions referred to above)
	(8), (9)	5 Jul 1999 (for certain purposes)[3] (SI 1999/1958)
		6 Sep 1999 (so far as not already in force for certain purposes)[4] (SI 1999/2422)
		5 Oct 1999 (so far as not already in force for certain purposes)[5] (SI 1999/2739)
		18 Oct 1999 (so far as not already in force for certain purposes)[6] (SI 1999/2860)
		29 Nov 1999 (so far as not already in force except for certain purposes)[7] (SI 1999/3178)
		Not in force (exceptions referred to above)

Social Security Act 1998 (c 14)—*contd*
Section

13		5 Jul 1999 (for certain purposes)[3] (SI 1999/1958)
		6 Sep 1999 (so far as not already in force for certain purposes)[4] (SI 1999/2422)
		5 Oct 1999 (so far as not already in force for certain purposes)[5] (SI 1999/2739)
		18 Oct 1999 (so far as not already in force for certain purposes)[6] (SI 1999/2860)
		29 Nov 1999 (so far as not already in force except for certain purposes)[7] (SI 1999/3178)
		Not in force (exceptions referred to above)
14	(1)	5 Jul 1999 (for certain purposes)[3] (SI 1999/1958)
		6 Sep 1999 (so far as not already in force for certain purposes)[4] (SI 1999/2422)
		5 Oct 1999 (so far as not already in force for certain purposes)[5] (SI 1999/2739)
		18 Oct 1999 (so far as not already in force for certain purposes)[6] (SI 1999/2860)
		29 Nov 1999 (so far as not already in force except for certain purposes)[7] (SI 1999/3178)
		Not in force (exceptions referred to above)
	(2)	Repealed
	(3)	4 Mar 1999 (so far as authorising the making of regulations) (SI 1999/528)
		5 Jul 1999 (for certain purposes)[3] (SI 1999/1958)
		6 Sep 1999 (so far as not already in force for certain purposes)[4] (SI 1999/2422)
		5 Oct 1999 (so far as not already in force for certain purposes)[5] (SI 1999/2739)
		18 Oct 1999 (so far as not already in force for certain purposes)[6] (SI 1999/2860)
		29 Nov 1999 (so far as not already in force except for certain purposes)[7] (SI 1999/3178)

Social Security Act 1998 (c 14)—*contd*
Section

14	(3)—*contd*	*Not in force* (exceptions referred to above)
	(4)–(9)	5 Jul 1999 (for certain purposes)[3] (SI 1999/1958)
		6 Sep 1999 (so far as not already in force for certain purposes)[4] (SI 1999/2422)
		5 Oct 1999 (so far as not already in force for certain purposes)[5] (SI 1999/2739)
		18 Oct 1999 (so far as not already in force for certain purposes)[6] (SI 1999/2860)
		29 Nov 1999 (so far as not already in force except for certain purposes)[7] (SI 1999/3178)
		Not in force (exceptions referred to above)
	(10), (11)	4 Mar 1999 (so far as authorising the making of regulations) (SI 1999/528)
		5 Jul 1999 (for certain purposes)[3] (SI 1999/1958)
		6 Sep 1999 (so far as not already in force for certain purposes)[4] (SI 1999/2422)
		5 Oct 1999 (so far as not already in force for certain purposes)[5] (SI 1999/2739)
		18 Oct 1999 (so far as not already in force for certain purposes)[6] (SI 1999/2860)
		29 Nov 1999 (so far as not already in force except for certain purposes)[7] (SI 1999/3178)
		Not in force (exceptions referred to above)
	(12)	See Sch 4 below
15	(1)	5 Jul 1999 (for certain purposes)[3] (SI 1999/1958)
		6 Sep 1999 (so far as not already in force for certain purposes)[4] (SI 1999/2422)
		5 Oct 1999 (so far as not already in force for certain purposes)[5] (SI 1999/2739)
		18 Oct 1999 (so far as not already in force for certain purposes)[6] (SI 1999/2860)

Social Security Act 1998 (c 14)—*contd*

Section

15	(1)—*contd*	29 Nov 1999 (so far as not already in force except for certain purposes)[7] (SI 1999/3178)
		Not in force (exceptions referred to above)
	(2), (3)	4 Mar 1999 (so far as authorising the making of regulations) (SI 1999/528)
		5 Jul 1999 (for certain purposes)[3] (SI 1999/1958)
		6 Sep 1999 (so far as not already in force for certain purposes)[4] (SI 1999/2422)
		5 Oct 1999 (so far as not already in force for certain purposes)[5] (SI 1999/2739)
		18 Oct 1999 (so far as not already in force for certain purposes)[6] (SI 1999/2860)
		29 Nov 1999 (so far as not already in force except for certain purposes)[7] (SI 1999/3178)
		Not in force (exceptions referred to above)
	(4), (5)	5 Jul 1999 (for certain purposes)[3] (SI 1999/1958)
		6 Sep 1999 (so far as not already in force for certain purposes)[4] (SI 1999/2422)
		5 Oct 1999 (so far as not already in force for certain purposes)[5] (SI 1999/2739)
		18 Oct 1999 (so far as not already in force for certain purposes)[6] (SI 1999/2860)
		29 Nov 1999 (so far as not already in force except for certain purposes)[7] (SI 1999/3178)
		Not in force (exceptions referred to above)
16	(1)–(3)	4 Mar 1999 (so far as authorising the making of regulations) (SI 1999/528)
		5 Jul 1999 (for certain purposes)[3] (SI 1999/1958)
		6 Sep 1999 (so far as not already in force for certain purposes)[4] (SI 1999/2422)

Social Security Act 1998 (c 14)—*contd*
Section

16	(1)–(3)—*contd*		5 Oct 1999 (so far as not already in force for certain purposes)[5] (SI 1999/2739)
			18 Oct 1999 (so far as not already in force for certain purposes)[6] (SI 1999/2860)
			29 Nov 1999 (so far as not already in force except for certain purposes)[7] (SI 1999/3178)
			Not in force (exceptions referred to above)
	(4)	(a)	8 Sep 1998 (SI 1998/2209); prospectively repealed by Social Security Contributions (Transfer of Functions, etc) Act 1999, s 18, Sch 7, para 28[2]
		(b)	6 Apr 1999 (SI 1998/2209); prospectively repealed by Social Security Contributions (Transfer of Functions, etc) Act 1999, s 18, Sch 7, para 28[2]
	(5)		8 Sep 1998 (SI 1998/2209); prospectively repealed by Social Security Contributions (Transfer of Functions, etc) Act 1999, s 18, Sch 7, para 28[2]
	(6)–(9)		5 Jul 1999 (for certain purposes)[3] (SI 1999/1958)
			6 Sep 1999 (so far as not already in force for certain purposes)[4] (SI 1999/2422)
			5 Oct 1999 (so far as not already in force for certain purposes)[5] (SI 1999/2739)
			18 Oct 1999 (so far as not already in force for certain purposes)[6] (SI 1999/2860)
			29 Nov 1999 (so far as not already in force except for certain purposes)[7] (SI 1999/3178)
			Not in force (exceptions referred to above)
17			4 Mar 1999 (so far as authorising the making of regulations) (SI 1999/528)
			5 Jul 1999 (for certain purposes)[3] (SI 1999/1958)
			6 Sep 1999 (so far as not already in force for certain purposes)[4] (SI 1999/2422)

Social Security Act 1998 (c 14)—*contd*
Section

17—*contd*		5 Oct 1999 (so far as not already in force for certain purposes)[5] (SI 1999/2739)
		18 Oct 1999 (so far as not already in force for certain purposes)[6] (SI 1999/2860)
		29 Nov 1999 (so far as not already in force except for certain purposes)[7] (SI 1999/3178)
		Not in force (exceptions referred to above)
18	(1)	4 Mar 1999 (so far as authorising the making of regulations) (SI 1999/528)
		5 Jul 1999 (for certain purposes)[3] (SI 1999/1958)
		6 Sep 1999 (so far as not already in force for certain purposes)[4] (SI 1999/2422)
		5 Oct 1999 (so far as not already in force for certain purposes)[5] (SI 1999/2739)
		18 Oct 1999 (so far as not already in force for certain purposes)[6] (SI 1999/2860)
		29 Nov 1999 (so far as not already in force except for certain purposes)[7] (SI 1999/3178)
		Not in force (exceptions referred to above)
	(2)	18 Oct 1999 (SI 1999/2860)
19		5 Jul 1999 (for certain purposes)[3] (SI 1999/1958)
		6 Sep 1999 (so far as not already in force for certain purposes)[4] (SI 1999/2422)
		5 Oct 1999 (so far as not already in force for certain purposes)[5] (SI 1999/2739)
		18 Oct 1999 (so far as not already in force for certain purposes)[6] (SI 1999/2860)
		29 Nov 1999 (so far as not already in force except for certain purposes)[7] (SI 1999/3178)
		Not in force (exceptions referred to above)
20	(1), (2)	4 Mar 1999 (so far as authorising the making of regulations) (SI 1999/528)

Social Security Act 1998 (c 14)—*contd*
Section

20	(1), (2)—*contd*	5 Jul 1999 (for certain purposes)[3] (SI 1999/1958)
		6 Sep 1999 (so far as not already in force for certain purposes)[4] (SI 1999/2422)
		5 Oct 1999 (so far as not already in force for certain purposes)[5] (SI 1999/2739)
		18 Oct 1999 (so far as not already in force for certain purposes)[6] (SI 1999/2860)
		29 Nov 1999 (so far as not already in force except for certain purposes)[7] (SI 1999/3178)
		Not in force (exceptions referred to above)
	(3) (a)	4 Mar 1999 (so far as authorising the making of regulations) (SI 1999/528)
		5 Jul 1999 (for certain purposes)[3] (SI 1999/1958)
		6 Sep 1999 (so far as not already in force for certain purposes)[4] (SI 1999/2422)
		5 Oct 1999 (so far as not already in force for certain purposes)[5] (SI 1999/2739)
		18 Oct 1999 (so far as not already in force for certain purposes)[6] (SI 1999/2860)
		29 Nov 1999 (so far as not already in force except for certain purposes)[7] (SI 1999/3178)
		Not in force (exceptions referred to above)
	(b)	4 Mar 1999 (so far as authorising the making of regulations) (SI 1999/528)
		18 Oct 1999 (so far as not already in force for certain purposes)[6] (SI 1999/2860)
		29 Nov 1999 (so far as not already in force except for certain purposes)[7] (SI 1999/3178)
		Not in force (exceptions referred to above)
21–24		4 Mar 1999 (so far as authorising the making of regulations) (SI 1999/528)

Social Security Act 1998 (c 14)—*contd*
Section

21–24—*contd*		5 Jul 1999 (for certain purposes)[3] (SI 1999/1958)
		6 Sep 1999 (so far as not already in force for certain purposes)[4] (SI 1999/2422)
		5 Oct 1999 (so far as not already in force for certain purposes)[5] (SI 1999/2739)
		18 Oct 1999 (so far as not already in force for certain purposes)[6] (SI 1999/2860)
		29 Nov 1999 (so far as not already in force except for certain purposes)[7] (SI 1999/3178)
		Not in force (exceptions referred to above)
24A		Inserted by Social Security Contributions (Transfer of Functions, etc) Act 1999, s 18, Sch 7, para 33 (qv)
25	(1), (2)	5 Jul 1999 (for certain purposes)[3] (SI 1999/1958)
		6 Sep 1999 (so far as not already in force for certain purposes)[4] (SI 1999/2422)
		5 Oct 1999 (so far as not already in force for certain purposes)[5] (SI 1999/2739)
		18 Oct 1999 (so far as not already in force for certain purposes)[6] (SI 1999/2860)
		29 Nov 1999 (so far as not already in force except for certain purposes)[7] (SI 1999/3178)
		Not in force (exceptions referred to above)
	(3) (a)	5 Jul 1999 (for certain purposes)[3] (SI 1999/1958)
		6 Sep 1999 (so far as not already in force for certain purposes)[4] (SI 1999/2422)
		5 Oct 1999 (so far as not already in force for certain purposes)[5] (SI 1999/2739)
		18 Oct 1999 (so far as not already in force for certain purposes)[6] (SI 1999/2860)
		29 Nov 1999 (so far as not already in force except for certain purposes)[7] (SI 1999/3178)

Social Security Act 1998 (c 14)—*contd*
Section

25	(3)	(a)—*contd*	*Not in force* (exceptions referred to above)
		(b)	4 Mar 1999 (so far as authorising the making of regulations) (SI 1999/528)
			5 Jul 1999 (for certain purposes)[3] (SI 1999/1958)
			6 Sep 1999 (so far as not already in force for certain purposes)[4] (SI 1999/2422)
			5 Oct 1999 (so far as not already in force for certain purposes)[5] (SI 1999/2739)
			18 Oct 1999 (so far as not already in force for certain purposes)[6] (SI 1999/2860)
			29 Nov 1999 (so far as not already in force except for certain purposes)[7] (SI 1999/3178)
			Not in force (exceptions referred to above)
	(4)		5 Jul 1999 (for certain purposes)[3] (SI 1999/1958)
			6 Sep 1999 (so far as not already in force for certain purposes)[4] (SI 1999/2422)
			5 Oct 1999 (so far as not already in force for certain purposes)[5] (SI 1999/2739)
			18 Oct 1999 (so far as not already in force for certain purposes)[6] (SI 1999/2860)
			29 Nov 1999 (so far as not already in force except for certain purposes)[7] (SI 1999/3178)
			Not in force (exceptions referred to above)
	(5)	(a), (b)	5 Jul 1999 (for certain purposes)[3] (SI 1999/1958)
			6 Sep 1999 (so far as not already in force for certain purposes)[4] (SI 1999/2422)
			5 Oct 1999 (so far as not already in force for certain purposes)[5] (SI 1999/2739)
			18 Oct 1999 (so far as not already in force for certain purposes)[6] (SI 1999/2860)

Social Security Act 1998 (c 14)—*contd*
Section

25	(5)	(a), (b)—*contd*	29 Nov 1999 (so far as not already in force except for certain purposes)[7] (SI 1999/3178)
			Not in force (exceptions referred to above)
		(c)	4 Mar 1999 (so far as authorising the making of regulations) (SI 1999/528)
			5 Jul 1999 (for certain purposes)[3] (SI 1999/1958)
			6 Sep 1999 (so far as not already in force for certain purposes)[4] (SI 1999/2422)
			5 Oct 1999 (so far as not already in force for certain purposes)[5] (SI 1999/2739)
			18 Oct 1999 (so far as not already in force for certain purposes)[6] (SI 1999/2860)
			29 Nov 1999 (so far as not already in force except for certain purposes)[7] (SI 1999/3178)
			Not in force (exceptions referred to above)
	(6)		5 Jul 1999 (for certain purposes)[3] (SI 1999/1958)
			6 Sep 1999 (so far as not already in force for certain purposes)[4] (SI 1999/2422)
			5 Oct 1999 (so far as not already in force for certain purposes)[5] (SI 1999/2739)
			18 Oct 1999 (so far as not already in force for certain purposes)[6] (SI 1999/2860)
			29 Nov 1999 (so far as not already in force except for certain purposes)[7] (SI 1999/3178)
			Not in force (exceptions referred to above)
26	(1)–(5)		5 Jul 1999 (for certain purposes)[3] (SI 1999/1958)
			6 Sep 1999 (so far as not already in force for certain purposes)[4] (SI 1999/2422)
			5 Oct 1999 (so far as not already in force for certain purposes)[5] (SI 1999/2739)

Social Security Act 1998 (c 14)—*contd*
Section

26	(1)–(5)—*contd*	18 Oct 1999 (so far as not already in force for certain purposes)[6] (SI 1999/2860)
		29 Nov 1999 (so far as not already in force except for certain purposes)[7] (SI 1999/3178)
		Not in force (exceptions referred to above)
	(6) (a), (b)	5 Jul 1999 (for certain purposes)[3] (SI 1999/1958)
		6 Sep 1999 (so far as not already in force for certain purposes)[4] (SI 1999/2422)
		5 Oct 1999 (so far as not already in force for certain purposes)[5] (SI 1999/2739)
		18 Oct 1999 (so far as not already in force for certain purposes)[6] (SI 1999/2860)
		29 Nov 1999 (so far as not already in force except for certain purposes)[7] (SI 1999/3178)
		Not in force (exceptions referred to above)
	(c)	4 Mar 1999 (so far as authorising the making of regulations) (SI 1999/528)
		5 Jul 1999 (for certain purposes)[3] (SI 1999/1958)
		6 Sep 1999 (so far as not already in force for certain purposes)[4] (SI 1999/2422)
		5 Oct 1999 (so far as not already in force for certain purposes)[5] (SI 1999/2739)
		18 Oct 1999 (so far as not already in force for certain purposes)[6] (SI 1999/2860)
		29 Nov 1999 (so far as not already in force except for certain purposes)[7] (SI 1999/3178)
		Not in force (exceptions referred to above)
	(7)	5 Jul 1999 (for certain purposes)[3] (SI 1999/1958)
		6 Sep 1999 (so far as not already in force for certain purposes)[4] (SI 1999/2422)

Social Security Act 1998 (c 14)—*contd*

Social Security Act 1998 (c 14)—*contd*
Section

28	(2)		4 Mar 1999 (so far as authorising the making of regulations) (SI 1999/528)
			5 Jul 1999 (for certain purposes)[3] (SI 1999/1958)
			6 Sep 1999 (so far as not already in force for certain purposes)[4] (SI 1999/2422)
			5 Oct 1999 (so far as not already in force for certain purposes)[5] (SI 1999/2739)
			18 Oct 1999 (so far as not already in force for certain purposes)[6] (SI 1999/2860)
			29 Nov 1999 (so far as not already in force except for certain purposes)[7] (SI 1999/3178)
			Not in force (exceptions referred to above)
	(3)	(a), (b)	4 Mar 1999 (so far as authorising the making of regulations) (SI 1999/528)
			5 Jul 1999 (for certain purposes)[3] (SI 1999/1958)
			6 Sep 1999 (so far as not already in force for certain purposes)[4] (SI 1999/2422)
			5 Oct 1999 (so far as not already in force for certain purposes)[5] (SI 1999/2739)
			18 Oct 1999 (so far as not already in force for certain purposes)[6] (SI 1999/2860)
			29 Nov 1999 (so far as not already in force except for certain purposes)[7] (SI 1999/3178)
			Not in force (exceptions referred to above)
		(c)	4 Mar 1999 (so far as authorising the making of regulations) (SI 1999/528)
			5 Jul 1999 (for certain purposes)[3] (SI 1999/1958)
			29 Nov 1999 (so far as not already in force except for certain purposes)[7] (SI 1999/3178)
			Not in force (exceptions referred to above)
		(d)	4 Mar 1999 (so far as authorising the making of regulations) (SI 1999/528)

Social Security Act 1998 (c 14)—*contd*
Section

28	(3)	(d)—*contd*	18 Oct 1999 (so far as not already in force for certain purposes)[6] (SI 1999/2860)
			29 Nov 1999 (so far as not already in force except for certain purposes)[7] (SI 1999/3178)
			Not in force (exceptions referred to above)
		(e)	4 Mar 1999 (so far as authorising the making of regulations) (SI 1999/528)
			29 Nov 1999 (so far as not already in force except for certain purposes)[7] (SI 1999/3178)
			Not in force (exceptions referred to above)
29, 30			5 Jul 1999 (for certain purposes)[3] (SI 1999/1958)
			Not in force (otherwise)
31	(1)		6 Sep 1999 (SI 1999/2422)
	(2), (3)		4 Mar 1999 (so far as authorising the making of regulations) (SI 1999/528)
			6 Sep 1999 (otherwise) (SI 1999/2422)
32			18 Oct 1999 (SI 1999/2860)
33			29 Nov 1999 (except for certain purposes)[7] (SI 1999/3178)
			Not in force (exceptions referred to above)
34			18 Oct 1999 (SI 1999/2860)
35			*Not in force*
			Repealed, partly prospectively, by Child Support, Pensions and Social Security Act 2000, s 85, Sch 9, Pt VII[8]
36, 37			29 Nov 1999 (except for certain purposes)[7] (SI 1999/3178)
			Not in force (exceptions referred to above)
38	(1)	(a)	4 Mar 1999 (so far as authorising the making of regulations) (SI 1999/528)
			29 Nov 1999 (so far as not already in force except for certain purposes)[7] (SI 1999/3178)
			Not in force (exceptions referred to above)
		(b), (c)	29 Nov 1999 (except for certain purposes)[7] (SI 1999/3178)
			Not in force (exceptions referred to above)

Social Security Act 1998 (c 14)—*contd*
Section

38	(2)	29 Nov 1999 (except for certain purposes)[7] (SI 1999/3178)
		Not in force (exceptions referred to above)
	(3)	4 Mar 1999 (so far as authorising the making of regulations) (SI 1999/528)
		29 Nov 1999 (so far as not already in force except for certain purposes)[7] (SI 1999/3178)
		Not in force (exceptions referred to above)
	(4)–(13)	29 Nov 1999 (except for certain purposes)[7] (SI 1999/3178)
		Not in force (exceptions referred to above)
39	(1), (2)	5 Jul 1999 (for certain purposes)[3] (SI 1999/1958)
		6 Sep 1999 (so far as not already in force for certain purposes)[4] (SI 1999/2422)
		5 Oct 1999 (so far as not already in force for certain purposes)[5] (SI 1999/2739)
		18 Oct 1999 (so far as not already in force for certain purposes)[6] (SI 1999/2860)
		29 Nov 1999 (so far as not already in force except for certain purposes)[7] (SI 1999/3178)
		Not in force (exceptions referred to above)
	(3)	5 Jul 1999 (for certain purposes)[3] (SI 1999/1958)
		6 Sep 1999 (so far as not already in force for certain purposes[4] and so far as relates to the repeal of Social Security Administration Act 1992, s 61A) (subject to a saving) (SI 1999/2422)
		5 Oct 1999 (so far as not already in force for certain purposes)[5] (SI 1999/2739)
		18 Oct 1999 (so far as not already in force for certain purposes[6] and so far as relates to the repeal of Social Security Administration Act 1992, s 63) (subject to a saving) (SI 1999/2860)

Social Security Act 1998 (c 14)—*contd*
Section

39	(3)—*contd*	29 Nov 1999 (so far as not already in force for certain purposes)[7] (SI 1999/3178)
		Not in force (exceptions referred to above)
40		16 Nov 1998 (so far as it introduces the making of regulations) (subject to transitional provisions and savings) (SI 1998/2780)
		7 Dec 1998 (otherwise) (subject to transitional provisions and savings) (SI 1998/2780)
41		4 Mar 1999 (so far as authorising the making of regulations, and in so far as substitutes Child Support Act 1991, s 17(3), (5)) (SI 1999/528)
		1 Jun 1999 (otherwise) (SI 1999/1510)
42		4 Mar 1999 (so far as authorising the making of regulations, and in so far as substitutes Child Support Act 1991, s 20(4)–(6)) (SI 1999/528)
		1 Jun 1999 (otherwise) (SI 1999/1510)
		Prospectively repealed by Child Support, Pensions and Social Security Act 2000, s 85, Sch 9, Pt I[8]
43		4 Mar 1999 (so far as authorising the making of regulations and in so far as inserts Child Support Act 1991, ss 28ZA(2)(b), (4)(c), 28ZB(6)(c)) (SI 1999/528)
		1 Jun 1999 (otherwise) (SI 1999/1510)
44		4 Mar 1999 (so far as authorising the making of regulations and in so far as inserts Child Support Act 1991, s 28ZD) (SI 1999/528)
		1 Jun 1999 (otherwise) (SI 1999/1510)
45		4 Mar 1999 (so far as authorising the making of regulations and in so far as inserts Vaccine Damage Payments Act 1979, s 3A(1), (3), (4)) (SI 1999/528)

Social Security Act 1998 (c 14)—*contd*

Section

45—*contd*		18 Oct 1999 (so far as not already in force for certain purposes)[6] (SI 1999/2860)
		Not in force (otherwise)
46		4 Mar 1999 (so far as authorising the making of regulations, and in so far as substitutes Vaccine Damage Payments Act 1979, s 4(2), (3), and) (SI 1999/528)
		18 Oct 1999 (so far as not already in force for certain purposes)[6] (SI 1999/2860)
		Not in force (otherwise)
47		4 Mar 1999 (so far as authorising the making of regulations) (SI 1999/528)
		18 Oct 1999 (so far as not already in force for certain purposes)[6] (SI 1999/2860)
		Not in force (otherwise)
48, 49		8 Sep 1998 (SI 1998/2209)
50	(1)	21 May 1998 (so far as relating to a sum which is chargeable to tax by virtue of Income and Corporation Taxes Act 1998, s 313) (s 87(2))
		8 Sep 1998 (otherwise) (SI 1998/2209)
	(2)	Repealed, subject to savings
	(3), (4)	21 May 1998 (s 87(2))
51		Repealed, subject to savings
52		Repealed
53		8 Sep 1998 (for the purpose of authorising the making of regulations or orders) (SI 1998/2209)
		6 Apr 1999 (otherwise) (SI 1998/2209)
54		4 Mar 1999 (for the purpose of authorising the making of regulations or schemes) (SI 1999/526)
		6 Apr 1999 (otherwise) (SI 1999/526)
55		8 Sep 1998 (SI 1998/2209)
56	(1)	6 Apr 1999 (SI 1999/526)
	(2)	4 Mar 1999 (for the purpose of authorising the making of regulations or schemes) (SI 1999/526)
		6 Apr 1999 (otherwise) (SI 1999/526)

Social Security Act 1998 (c 14)—*contd*

Section

57	4 Mar 1999 (for the purpose of authorising the making of regulations or schemes) (SI 1999/526)
	6 Apr 1999 (otherwise) (SI 1999/526)
58	Repealed (*never in force*)
59	8 Sep 1998 (subject to a saving) (SI 1998/2209)
60	4 Mar 1999 (for the purpose of authorising the making of regulations or schemes) (SI 1999/526)
	6 Apr 1999 (otherwise) (SI 1999/526)
61	4 Mar 1999 (for the purpose of authorising the making of regulations or schemes, except so far as relates to Social Security Administration Act 1992, s 114A) (SI 1999/526)
	6 Apr 1999 (otherwise, except so far as relates to Social Security Administration Act 1992, s 114A) (SI 1999/526)
	Not in force (exception noted above)
	Section repealed (so far as relates to Social Security Administration Act 1992, s 114A)
62	6 Apr 1999 (SI 1999/526)
63	4 Mar 1999 (for the purpose of authorising the making of regulations or schemes) (SI 1999/526)
	6 Apr 1999 (otherwise) (SI 1999/526)
64	6 Apr 1999 (SI 1999/526)
65	8 Sep 1998 (for purpose of authorising the making of regulations or orders) (SI 1998/2209)
	6 Apr 1999 (otherwise) (SI 1998/2209)
66	21 May 1998 (s 87(2))
67	*Not in force*
68	8 Sep 1998 (SI 1998/2209)
69	21 May 1998 (s 87(2))
70, 71	5 Apr 1999 (subject to a transitional provision) (SI 1999/1055)
72	21 May 1998 (s 87(2))
73	6 Apr 1999 (SI 1998/2209)
74	4 Mar 1999 (so far as authorising the making of regulations) (SI 1999/528)

Social Security Act 1998 (c 14)—*contd*

Section

74—*contd*		29 Nov 1999 (so far as not already in force except for certain purposes)[7] (SI 1999/3178)
		Not in force (exceptions referred to above)
75		5 Oct 1998 (SI 1998/2209)
76		16 Nov 1998 (subject to transitional provisions and savings) (SI 1998/2780)
77–82		21 May 1998 (s 87(2))
83		Repealed (partly prospectively) by Social Security Act 1998, s 86(2), Sch 8
84, 85		21 May 1998 (s 87(2))
86	(1)	See Sch 7 below
	(2)	See Sch 8 below
87		21 May 1998 (s 87(2))

Schedule

1, para	1–6	1 Jun 1999 (SI 1999/1510)
	7	4 Mar 1999 (so far as authorising the making of regulations) (SI 1999/528)
		1 Jun 1999 (otherwise) (SI 1999/1510)
	8, 9	1 Jun 1999 (SI 1999/1510)
	10	31 Mar 2000 (SI 1999/3178)
	11, 12	4 Mar 1999 (so far as authorising the making of regulations) (SI 1999/528)
		1 Jun 1999 (otherwise) (SI 1999/1510)
	13	1 Jun 1999 (SI 1999/1510)
2, para	1	18 Oct 1999 (for certain purposes)[6] (SI 1999/2860)
		29 Nov 1999 (so far as not already in force except for certain purposes)[7] (SI 1999/3178)
		Not in force (exceptions referred to above)
	2	29 Nov 1999 (except for certain purposes)[7] (SI 1999/3178)
		Not in force (exceptions referred to above)
	3	18 Oct 1999 (for certain purposes)[6] (SI 1999/2860)
		29 Nov 1999 (so far as not already in force except for certain purposes)[7] (SI 1999/3178)
		Not in force (exceptions referred to above)

Social Security Act 1998 (c 14)—*contd*

Schedule

2, para	4		5 Jul 1999 (for certain purposes)[3] (SI 1999/1958)
			29 Nov 1999 (so far as not already in force except for certain purposes)[7] (SI 1999/3178)
			Not in force (exceptions referred to above)
	5		5 Jul 1999 (for certain purposes)[3] (SI 1999/1958)
			6 Sep 1999 (so far as not already in force for certain purposes)[4] (SI 1999/2422)
			18 Oct 1999 (so far as not already in force for certain purposes)[6] (SI 1999/2860)
			29 Nov 1999 (so far as not already in force except for certain purposes)[7] (SI 1999/3178)
			Not in force (exceptions referred to above)
	5A		Inserted by Welfare Reform and Pensions Act 1999, s 84, Sch 12, para 87 (qv)
	6	(a)	5 Jul 1999 (for certain purposes)[3] (SI 1999/1958)
			6 Sep 1999 (so far as not already in force for certain purposes)[4] (SI 1999/2422)
			5 Oct 1999 (so far as not already in force for certain purposes)[5] (SI 1999/2739)
			18 Oct 1999 (so far as not already in force for certain purposes)[6] (SI 1999/2860)
			29 Nov 1999 (so far as not already in force except for certain purposes)[7] (SI 1999/3178)
			Not in force (exceptions referred to above)
		(b) (i)	29 Nov 1999 (except for certain purposes)[7] (SI 1999/3178)
			Not in force (exceptions referred to above)
		(ii)	18 Oct 1999 (for certain purposes)[6] (SI 1999/2860)
			29 Nov 1999 (so far as not already in force except for certain purposes)[7] (SI 1999/3178)
			Not in force (exceptions referred to above)

Social Security Act 1998 (c 14)—*contd*
Schedule

2, para	7	5 Jul 1999 (for certain purposes)[3] (SI 1999/1958)
		18 Oct 1999 (so far as not already in force for certain purposes)[6] (SI 1999/2860)
		29 Nov 1999 (so far as not already in force except for certain purposes)[7] (SI 1999/3178)
		Not in force (exceptions referred to above)
	8	5 Jul 1999 (for certain purposes)[3] (SI 1999/1958)
		5 Oct 1999 (so far as not already in force for certain purposes)[5] (SI 1999/2739)
		18 Oct 1999 (so far as not already in force for certain purposes)[6] (SI 1999/2860)
		29 Nov 1999 (so far as not already in force except for certain purposes)[7] (SI 1999/3178)
		Not in force (exceptions referred to above)
		Prospectively substituted by Child Support, Pensions and Social Security Act 2000, s 26, Sch 3, para 15[8]
	9	4 Mar 1999 (so far as authorising the making of regulations) (SI 1999/528)
		5 Jul 1999 (for certain purposes)[3] (SI 1999/1958)
		6 Sep 1999 (so far as not already in force for certain purposes)[4] (SI 1999/2422)
		5 Oct 1999 (so far as not already in force for certain purposes)[5] (SI 1999/2739)
		18 Oct 1999 (so far as not already in force for certain purposes)[6] (SI 1999/2860)
		29 Nov 1999 (so far as not already in force except for certain purposes)[7] (SI 1999/3178)
		Not in force (exceptions referred to above)
3, para	1	4 Mar 1999 (so far as authorising the making of regulations) (SI 1999/528)

Social Security Act 1998 (c 14)—*contd*
Schedule
3, para   1—*contd*

	1—*contd*	5 Jul 1999 (for certain purposes)[3] (SI 1999/1958)
		6 Sep 1999 (so far as not already in force for certain purposes)[4] (SI 1999/2422)
		5 Oct 1999 (so far as not already in force for certain purposes)[5] (SI 1999/2739)
		18 Oct 1999 (so far as not already in force for certain purposes)[6] (SI 1999/2860)
		29 Nov 1999 (so far as not already in force except for certain purposes)[7] (SI 1999/3178)
		Not in force (exceptions referred to above)
	2	5 Jul 1999 (for certain purposes)[3] (SI 1999/1958)
		6 Sep 1999 (so far as not already in force for certain purposes)[4] (SI 1999/2422)
		5 Oct 1999 (so far as not already in force for certain purposes)[5] (SI 1999/2739)
		18 Oct 1999 (so far as not already in force for certain purposes)[6] (SI 1999/2860)
		29 Nov 1999 (so far as not already in force except for certain purposes)[7] (SI 1999/3178)
		Not in force (exceptions referred to above)
	3 (a)	5 Jul 1999 (for certain purposes)[3] (SI 1999/1958)
		6 Sep 1999 (so far as not already in force for certain purposes)[4] (SI 1999/2422)
		5 Oct 1999 (so far as not already in force for certain purposes)[5] (SI 1999/2739)
		18 Oct 1999 (so far as not already in force for certain purposes)[6] (SI 1999/2860)
		29 Nov 1999 (so far as not already in force except for certain purposes)[7] (SI 1999/3178)
		Not in force (exceptions referred to above)

Social Security Act 1998 (c 14)—*contd*
Schedule

3, para	3	(b)	18 Oct 1999 (for certain purposes)[6] (SI 1999/2860)
			29 Nov 1999 (so far as not already in force except for certain purposes)[7] (SI 1999/3178)
			Not in force (exceptions referred to above)
		(c)	5 Jul 1999 (for certain purposes)[3] (SI 1999/1958)
			6 Sep 1999 (so far as not already in force for certain purposes)[4] (SI 1999/2422)
			5 Oct 1999 (so far as not already in force for certain purposes)[5] (SI 1999/2739)
			18 Oct 1999 (so far as not already in force for certain purposes)[6] (SI 1999/2860)
			29 Nov 1999 (so far as not already in force except for certain purposes)[7] (SI 1999/3178)
			Not in force (exceptions referred to above)
		(d)	18 Oct 1999 (for certain purposes)[6] (SI 1999/2860)
			29 Nov 1999 (so far as not already in force except for certain purposes)[7] (SI 1999/3178)
			Not in force (exceptions referred to above)
		(e)	Inserted, partly prospectively, by Child Support, Pensions and Social Security Act 2000, s 66[8]
		(f)	Inserted by Social Security Fraud Act 2001, s 12(2) (qv)
	4		4 Mar 1999 (so far as authorising the making of regulations) (SI 1999/528)
			5 Jul 1999 (for certain purposes)[3] (SI 1999/1958)
			6 Sep 1999 (so far as not already in force for certain purposes)[4] (SI 1999/2422)
			5 Oct 1999 (so far as not already in force for certain purposes)[5] (SI 1999/2739)
			18 Oct 1999 (so far as not already in force for certain purposes)[6] (SI 1999/2860)

Social Security Act 1998 (c 14)—*contd*
Schedule

3, para	4—*contd*	29 Nov 1999 (so far as not already in force except for certain purposes)[7] (SI 1999/3178)
		Not in force (exceptions referred to above)
	5	5 Jul 1999 (for certain purposes[3], except so far as relates to Social Security Administration Act 1992, s 71A) (SI 1999/1958)
		6 Sep 1999 (so far as not already in force for certain purposes[4], except so far as relates to Social Security Administration Act 1992, s 71A) (SI 1999/2422)
		5 Oct 1999 (so far as not already in force for certain purposes[5], except so far as relates to Social Security Administration Act 1992, s 71A) (SI 1999/2739)
		18 Oct 1999 (so far as not already in force for certain purposes)[6] (SI 1999/2860)
		29 Nov 1999 (so far as not already in force except for certain purposes)[7] (SI 1999/3178)
		Not in force (exceptions referred to above)
	6	5 Jul 1999 (for certain purposes)[3] (SI 1999/1958)
		6 Sep 1999 (so far as not already in force for certain purposes)[4] (SI 1999/2422)
		5 Oct 1999 (so far as not already in force for certain purposes)[5] (SI 1999/2739)
		18 Oct 1999 (so far as not already in force for certain purposes)[6] (SI 1999/2860)
		29 Nov 1999 (so far as not already in force except for certain purposes)[7] (SI 1999/3178)
		Not in force (exceptions referred to above)
	7	5 Jul 1999 (for certain purposes)[3] (SI 1999/1958)
		29 Nov 1999 (so far as not already in force except for certain purposes)[7] (SI 1999/3178)
		Not in force (exceptions referred to above)

Social Security Act 1998 (c 14)—*contd*
Schedule

3, para	8	18 Oct 1999 (for certain purposes)[6] (SI 1999/2860)
		29 Nov 1999 (so far as not already in force except for certain purposes)[7] (SI 1999/3178)
		Not in force (exceptions referred to above)
	9	4 Mar 1999 (so far as authorising the making of regulations) (SI 1999/528)
		5 Jul 1999 (for certain purposes)[3] (SI 1999/1958)
		6 Sep 1999 (so far as not already in force for certain purposes)[4] (SI 1999/2422)
		5 Oct 1999 (so far as not already in force for certain purposes)[5] (SI 1999/2739)
		18 Oct 1999 (so far as not already in force for certain purposes)[6] (SI 1999/2860)
		29 Nov 1999 (so far as not already in force except for certain purposes)[7] (SI 1999/3178)
		Not in force (exceptions referred to above)
	10–15	Repealed (*partly never in force*)
	16, 17	18 Oct 1999 (for certain purposes)[6] (SI 1999/2860)
		29 Nov 1999 (so far as not already in force except for certain purposes)[7] (SI 1999/3178)
		Not in force (exceptions referred to above)
	18–29	Repealed (*partly never in force*)
4, para	1–5	5 Jul 1999 (for certain purposes)[3] (SI 1999/1958)
		6 Sep 1999 (so far as not already in force for certain purposes)[4] (SI 1999/2422)
		5 Oct 1999 (so far as not already in force for certain purposes)[5] (SI 1999/2739)
		18 Oct 1999 (so far as not already in force for certain purposes)[6] (SI 1999/2860)
		29 Nov 1999 (so far as not already in force except for certain purposes)[7] (SI 1999/3178)

Social Security Act 1998 (c 14)—*contd*

Schedule

4, para	1–5—*contd*	*Not in force* (exceptions referred to above)
	6	4 Mar 1999 (so far as authorising the making of regulations) (SI 1999/528)
		5 Jul 1999 (for certain purposes)[3] (SI 1999/1958)
		6 Sep 1999 (so far as not already in force for certain purposes)[4] (SI 1999/2422)
		5 Oct 1999 (so far as not already in force for certain purposes)[5] (SI 1999/2739)
		18 Oct 1999 (so far as not already in force for certain purposes)[6] (SI 1999/2860)
		29 Nov 1999 (so far as not already in force except for certain purposes)[7] (SI 1999/3178)
		Not in force (exceptions referred to above)
	7	5 Jul 1999 (for certain purposes)[3] (SI 1999/1958)
		6 Sep 1999 (so far as not already in force for certain purposes)[4] (SI 1999/2422)
		5 Oct 1999 (so far as not already in force for certain purposes)[5] (SI 1999/2739)
		18 Oct 1999 (so far as not already in force for certain purposes)[6] (SI 1999/2860)
		29 Nov 1999 (so far as not already in force except for certain purposes)[7] (SI 1999/3178)
		Not in force (exceptions referred to above)
	8	4 Mar 1999 (so far as authorising the making of regulations) (SI 1999/528)
		5 Jul 1999 (for certain purposes)[3] (SI 1999/1958)
		6 Sep 1999 (so far as not already in force for certain purposes)[4] (SI 1999/2422)
		5 Oct 1999 (so far as not already in force for certain purposes)[5] (SI 1999/2739)

Social Security Act 1998 (c 14)—*contd*
Schedule

4, para	8—*contd*		18 Oct 1999 (so far as not already in force for certain purposes)[6] (SI 1999/2860)
			29 Nov 1999 (so far as not already in force except for certain purposes)[7] (SI 1999/3178)
			Not in force (exceptions referred to above)
	5		4 Mar 1999 (so far as authorising the making of regulations) (SI 1999/528)
			5 Jul 1999 (for certain purposes)[3] (SI 1999/1958)
			6 Sep 1999 (so far as not already in force for certain purposes)[4] (SI 1999/2422)
			5 Oct 1999 (so far as not already in force for certain purposes)[5] (SI 1999/2739)
			18 Oct 1999 (so far as not already in force for certain purposes)[6] (SI 1999/2860)
			29 Nov 1999 (so far as not already in force except for certain purposes)[7] (SI 1999/3178)
			Not in force (exceptions referred to above)
	6		Repealed (in part prospectively) by Social Security Act 1998, s 86(2), Sch 8
7, para	1, 2		1 Jun 1999 (SI 1999/1510)
	3		*Not in force*
	4	(1)	29 Nov 1999 (except for certain purposes)[7] (SI 1999/3178)
			Not in force (exceptions referred to above)
		(2)	1 Jun 1999 (so far as applies to the entries relating to regional or other full-time chairmen of child support appeal tribunals, the Chief Child Support Officer and members of a panel appointed under Tribunals and Inquiries Act 1992, s 6, of persons to act as chairmen of child support appeal tribunals) (SI 1999/1510)
			18 Oct 1999 (so far as not already in force for certain purposes[6] as applies to the entries relating to

Social Security Act 1998 (c 14)—*contd*
Schedule

7, para	4	(2)—*contd*	regional or other full-time chairmen of disability appeal tribunals, members of a panel appointed under Tribunals and Inquiries Act 1992, s 6, of persons to act as chairmen of disability appeal tribunals and members of a panel of persons appointed to serve on a vaccine damage tribunal) (SI 1999/2860)
			29 Nov 1999 (so far as not already in force except for certain purposes)[7] (SI 1999/3178)
			Not in force (exceptions referred to above)
		(3)	1 Jun 1999 (SI 1999/1510)
	5–7		18 Oct 1999 (for certain purposes)[6] (SI 1999/2860)
			Not in force (otherwise)
	8, 9		4 Mar 1999 (so far as authorising the making of regulations) (SI 1999/528)
			18 Oct 1999 (so far as not already in force for certain purposes)[6] (SI 1999/2860)
			Not in force (otherwise)
	10		18 Oct 1999 (for certain purposes)[6] (SI 1999/2860)
			Not in force (otherwise)
	11		5 Jul 1999 (for certain purposes)[3] (SI 1999/1958)
			6 Sep 1999 (so far as not already in force for certain purposes)[4] (SI 1999/2422)
			29 Nov 1999 (so far as not already in force except for certain purposes)[7] (SI 1999/3178)
			Not in force (exceptions referred to above)
	12–14		6 Apr 1999 (SI 1999/526)
	15		18 Oct 1999 (for certain purposes)[6] (SI 1999/2860)
			29 Nov 1999 (so far as not already in force except for certain purposes)[7] (SI 1999/3178)
			Not in force (exceptions referred to above)
	16		6 Apr 1999 (SI 1999/418)

Social Security Act 1998 (c 14)—*contd*

Schedule

7, para	17		18 Oct 1999 (for certain purposes)[6] (SI 1999/2860)
			29 Nov 1999 (so far as not already in force except for certain purposes)[7] (SI 1999/3178)
			Not in force (exceptions referred to above)
	18, 19		1 Jun 1999 (SI 1999/1510)
	20		1 Jun 1999 (SI 1999/1510); prospectively repealed as noted to s 42 above[8]
	21–23		1 Jun 1999 (SI 1999/1510)
	24, 25		1 Jun 1999 (SI 1999/1510); prospectively repealed as noted to s 42 above[8]
	26		1 Jun 1999 (SI 1999/1510)
	27	(a)	8 Sep 1998 (SI 1998/2209)
		(b)	1 Jun 1999 (SI 1999/1510)
	28		Repealed
	29–31		1 Jun 1999 (SI 1999/1510)
	32		Repealed
	33		1 Jun 1999 (SI 1999/1510)
	34		1 Jun 1999 (SI 1999/1510); prospectively repealed as noted to s 42 above[8]
	35	(1)	1 Jun 1999 (SI 1999/1510); prospectively repealed as noted to s 42 above[8]
		(2)	4 Mar 1999 (so far as authorising the making of regulations) (SI 1999/528) 1 Jun 1999 (otherwise) (SI 1999/1510) Prospectively repealed as noted to s 42 above[8]
	36		1 Jun 1999 (SI 1999/1510)
	37, 38		1 Jun 1999 (SI 1999/1510); prospectively repealed by Child Support, Pensions and Social Security Act 2000, s 85, Sch 9, Pt I[8]
	39, 40		4 Mar 1999 (so far as authorising the making of regulations) (SI 1999/528) 1 Jun 1999 (otherwise) (SI 1999/1510) Prospectively repealed by Child Support, Pensions and Social Security Act 2000, s 85, Sch 9, Pt I[8]
	41, 42		1 Jun 1999 (SI 1999/1510)
	43	(1), (2)	1 Jun 1999 (SI 1999/1510); prospectively repealed by Child Support, Pensions and Social Security Act 2000, s 85, Sch 9, Pt I[8]

Social Security Act 1998 (c 14)—*contd*

Schedule

7, para	43	(3)	4 Mar 1999 (so far as authorising the making of regulations) (SI 1999/528) 1 Jun 1999 (otherwise) (SI 1999/1510) Prospectively repealed by Child Support, Pensions and Social Security Act 2000, s 85, Sch 9, Pt I[8]
		(4)	1 Jun 1999 (SI 1999/1510); prospectively repealed by Child Support, Pensions and Social Security Act 2000, s 85, Sch 9, Pt I[8]
	44		4 Mar 1999 (so far as authorising the making of regulations and in so far as relates to the insertions of Child Support Act 1991, ss 46A(2), 46B) (SI 1999/528) 1 Jun 1999 (otherwise) (SI 1999/1510)
	45		1 Jun 1999 (SI 1999/1510)
	46	(a)	16 Nov 1998 (subject to transitional provisions and savings) (SI 1998/2780); prospectively repealed by Child Support, Pensions and Social Security Act 2000, s 85, Sch 9, Pt I[8]
		(b)	4 Mar 1999 (so far as authorising the making of regulations) (SI 1999/528) 1 Jun 1999 (otherwise) (SI 1999/1510) Prospectively repealed by Child Support, Pensions and Social Security Act 2000, s 85, Sch 9, Pt I[8]
	47	(a)	1 Jun 1999 (SI 1999/1510)
		(b)	1 Jun 1999 (so far as relates to the definitions "Chief Child Support Officer", "child support appeal tribunal" and "child support officer") (SI 1999/1510) 29 Nov 1999 (so far as not already in force except for certain purposes)[7] (SI 1999/3178) *Not in force* (exceptions referred to above)
	48		1 Jun 1999 (SI 1999/1510)
	49		8 Sep 1998 (SI 1998/2209)
	50, 51		1 Jun 1999 (SI 1999/1510)
	52	(1)–(3)	1 Jun 1999 (SI 1999/1510)
		(4)	4 Mar 1999 (so far as authorising the making of regulations) (SI 1999/528) 1 Jun 1999 (otherwise) (SI 1999/1510)

Social Security Act 1998 (c 14)—*contd*

Schedule

7, para	53	(1)–(4)	1 Jun 1999 (SI 1999/1510); prospectively repealed by Child Support, Pensions and Social Security Act 2000, s 85, Sch 9, Pt I[8]
		(5)	4 Mar 1999 (so far as authorising the making of regulations) (SI 1999/528)
			1 Jun 1999 (otherwise) (SI 1999/1510)
			Prospectively repealed by Child Support, Pensions and Social Security Act 2000, s 85, Sch 9, Pt I[8]
		(6)	1 Jun 1999 (SI 1999/1510); prospectively repealed by Child Support, Pensions and Social Security Act 2000, s 85, Sch 9, Pt I[8]
	54		4 Mar 1999 (so far as authorising the making of regulations) (SI 1999/528)
			1 Jun 1999 (otherwise) (SI 1999/1510)
			Para prospectively repealed by Child Support, Pensions and Social Security Act 2000, s 85, Sch 9, Pt I[8]
	55		18 Oct 1999 (for certain purposes)[6] (SI 1999/2860)
			29 Nov 1999 (so far as not already in force except for certain purposes)[7] (SI 1999/3178)
			Not in force (exceptions referred to above)
	56		8 Sep 1998 (for purpose of authorising the making of regulations or orders) (SI 1998/2209)
			6 Apr 1999 (otherwise) (SI 1998/2209)
	57		Repealed
	58		Repealed, subject to savings
	59–61		6 Apr 1999 (SI 1999/418)
	62		6 Sep 1999 (for certain purposes)[4] (SI 1999/2422)
			Not in force (otherwise)
	63		5 Jul 1999 (for certain purposes, coming into force immediately before Social Security Contributions (Transfer of Functions) Act 1999, Sch 7, para 4 comes into force)[3] (SI 1999/1958)
	64, 65		5 Jul 1999 (for certain purposes)[3] (SI 1999/1958)
			Not in force (otherwise)
	66–70		5 Jul 1999 (for certain purposes)[3] (SI 1999/1958)

Social Security Act 1998 (c 14)—*contd*

Schedule

7, para	66–70—*contd*		6 Sep 1999 (so far as not already in force for certain purposes)[4] (SI 1999/2422)
			18 Oct 1999 (so far as not already in force for certain purposes)[6] (SI 1999/2860)
			29 Nov 1999 (so far as not already in force except for certain purposes)[7] (SI 1999/3178)
			Not in force (exceptions referred to above)
	71	(a)	5 Jul 1999 (for certain purposes)[3] (SI 1999/1958)
			6 Sep 1999 (so far as not already in force for certain purposes)[4] (SI 1999/2422)
			18 Oct 1999 (so far as not already in force for certain purposes)[6] (SI 1999/2860)
			29 Nov 1999 (so far as not already in force except for certain purposes)[7] (SI 1999/3178)
			Not in force (exceptions referred to above)
		(b), (c)	6 Apr 1999 (SI 1999/418)
		(d)	8 Sep 1998 (for purpose of authorising the making of regulations or orders) (SI 1998/2209)
			6 Apr 1999 (otherwise) (SI 1998/2209)
		(e)	6 Apr 1999 (SI 1999/418)
	72	(1), (2)	29 Nov 1999 (except for certain purposes)[7] (SI 1999/3178)
			Not in force (exceptions referred to above)
		(3), (4)	5 Apr 1999 (subject to a transitional provision) (SI 1999/1055)
		(5)	29 Nov 1999 (except for certain purposes)[7] (SI 1999/3178)
			Not in force (exceptions referred to above)
	73		29 Nov 1999 (except for certain purposes)[7] (SI 1999/3178)
			Not in force (exceptions referred to above)
	74, 75		6 Apr 1999 (SI 1999/418)
	76		6 Sep 1999 (for certain purposes)[4] (SI 1999/2422)
			Not in force (otherwise)
	77	(1)	6 Apr 1999 (SI 1998/2209)

Social Security Act 1998 (c 14)—*contd*

Schedule

7, para	77	(2)–(5)		6 Apr 1999 (SI 1999/418)
		(6)		8 Sep 1998 (SI 1998/2209)
		(7)–(9)		8 Sep 1998 (for purpose of authorising the making of regulations or orders) (SI 1998/2209)
				6 Apr 1999 (otherwise) (SI 1998/2209)
		(10)		Repealed (*never in force*)
		(11)		8 Sep 1998 (for purpose of authorising the making of regulations or orders) (SI 1998/2209)
				6 Apr 1999 (otherwise) (SI 1998/2209)
		(12)		6 Apr 1999 (SI 1998/2209)
		(13)		Repealed (*never in force*)
		(14)–(16)		8 Sep 1998 (for purpose of authorising the making of regulations or orders) (SI 1998/2209)
				6 Apr 1999 (otherwise) (SI 1998/2209)
	78			Repealed (*partly never in force*)
	79	(1)	(a)	5 Jul 1999 (for certain purposes)[3] (SI 1999/1958)
				6 Sep 1999 (so far as not already in force for certain purposes)[4] (SI 1999/2422)
				5 Oct 1999 (so far as not already in force for certain purposes)[5] (SI 1999/2739)
				18 Oct 1999 (so far as not already in force for certain purposes)[6] (SI 1999/2860)
				29 Nov 1999 (so far as not already in force except for certain purposes)[7] (SI 1999/3178)
				Not in force (exceptions referred to above)
			(b)	5 Jul 1999 (for certain purposes)[3] (SI 1999/1958)
				6 Sep 1999 (so far as not already in force for certain purposes)[4] (SI 1999/2422)
				5 Oct 1999 (so far as not already in force for certain purposes)[5] (SI 1999/2739)
				18 Oct 1999 (so far as not already in force for certain purposes)[6] (SI 1999/2860)
				29 Nov 1999 (so far as not already in force except for certain purposes)[7] (SI 1999/3178)

Social Security Act 1998 (c 14)—*contd*

Schedule

7, para	79	(1)	(b)—*contd*	2 Jul 2001 (in so far as relates to housing benefit) (SI 2001/2316)
				Not in force (exceptions referred to above)
		(2)		2 Jul 2001 (SI 2001/2316)
	80			2 Jul 2001 (SI 2001/2316)
	81			5 Jul 1999 (for certain purposes)[3] (SI 1999/1958)
				6 Sep 1999 (so far as not already in force for certain purposes)[4] (SI 1999/2422)
				5 Oct 1999 (so far as not already in force for certain purposes)[5] (SI 1999/2739)
				18 Oct 1999 (so far as not already in force for certain purposes)[6] (SI 1999/2860)
				29 Nov 1999 (so far as not already in force except for certain purposes)[7] (SI 1999/3178)
				Not in force (exceptions referred to above)
	82			18 Oct 1999 (for certain purposes)[6] (SI 1999/2860)
				Not in force (otherwise)
	83			29 Nov 1999 (except for certain purposes)[7] (SI 1999/3178)
				Not in force (exceptions referred to above)
	84			5 Jul 1999 (for certain purposes)[3] (SI 1999/1958)
				29 Nov 1999 (so far as not already in force except for certain purposes)[7] (SI 1999/3178)
				Not in force (exceptions referred to above)
	85			6 Apr 1999 (SI 1999/526)
	86	(1)		6 Apr 1999 (SI 1999/526)
		(2)	(a)	6 Apr 1999 (SI 1998/2209)
			(b)	6 Apr 1999 (SI 1999/526)
		(3)	(a)	6 Apr 1999 (SI 1998/2209)
			(b)	6 Apr 1999 (SI 1999/526)
		(4)		6 Apr 1999 (SI 1998/2209)
		(5)		6 Apr 1999 (SI 1999/526)
		(6)		6 Apr 1999 (SI 1998/2209)
	87			6 Apr 1999 (SI 1999/526)
	88, 89			5 Jul 1999 (for certain purposes)[3] (SI 1999/1958)

Social Security Act 1998 (c 14)—*contd*
Schedule

7, para	88, 89—*contd*	6 Sep 1999 (so far as not already in force for certain purposes)[4] (SI 1999/2422)
		5 Oct 1999 (so far as not already in force for certain purposes)[5] (SI 1999/2739)
		18 Oct 1999 (so far as not already in force for certain purposes)[6] (SI 1999/2860)
		29 Nov 1999 (so far as not already in force except for certain purposes)[7] (SI 1999/3178)
		Not in force (exceptions referred to above)
	90	6 Apr 1999 (SI 1999/418)
	91	Repealed
	92–94	6 Apr 1999 (SI 1999/418)
	95	29 Nov 1999 (except for certain purposes)[7] (SI 1999/3178)
		Not in force (exceptions referred to above)
	96	18 Oct 1999 (for certain purposes)[6] (SI 1999/2860)
		Not in force (otherwise)
	97	29 Nov 1999 (except for certain purposes)[7] (SI 1999/3178)
		Not in force (exceptions referred to above)
	98	18 Oct 1999 (for certain purposes)[6] (SI 1999/2860)
		Not in force (otherwise)
	99 (1)	8 Sep 1998 (SI 1998/2209)
	(2)	6 Apr 1999 (SI 1999/526)
	(3)	6 Apr 1999 (SI 1999/418)
	(4)	8 Sep 1998 (for purpose of authorising the making of regulations or orders) (SI 1998/2209)
		6 Apr 1999 (otherwise) (SI 1998/2209)
	100 (1)	6 Apr 1999 (SI 1998/2209)
	(2)	6 Apr 1999 (SI 1999/526)
	101	5 Jul 1999 (for certain purposes)[3] (SI 1999/1958)
		29 Nov 1999 (so far as not already in force except for certain purposes)[7] (SI 1999/3178)
		Not in force (exceptions referred to above)

Social Security Act 1998 (c 14)—*contd*
Schedule

7, para	102	5 Jul 1999 (for certain purposes, coming into force immediately before Social Security Contributions (Transfer of Functions) Act 1999, Sch 7, para 14 comes into force)[3] (SI 1999/1958)
		6 Sep 1999 (so far as not already in force for certain purposes)[4] (SI 1999/2422)
		18 Oct 1999 (so far as not already in force for certain purposes)[6] (SI 1999/2860)
		29 Nov 1999 (so far as not already in force except for certain purposes)[7] (SI 1999/3178)
		Not in force (exceptions referred to above)
	103	29 Nov 1999 (except for certain purposes)[7] (SI 1999/3178)
		Not in force (exceptions referred to above)
	104	4 Mar 1999 (SI 1999/528)
	105	5 Jul 1999 (subject to transitional provisions and savings) (SI 1999/1958)
	106	5 Jul 1999 (for certain purposes)[3] (SI 1999/1958)
		5 Oct 1999 (so far as not already in force for certain purposes)[5] (SI 1999/2739)
		18 Oct 1999 (so far as not already in force for certain purposes)[6] (SI 1999/2860)
		29 Nov 1999 (so far as not already in force except for certain purposes)[7] (SI 1999/3178)
		Not in force (exceptions referred to above)
	107, 108	5 Jul 1999 (for certain purposes)[3] (SI 1999/1958)
		6 Sep 1999 (so far as not already in force for certain purposes)[4] (SI 1999/2422)
		5 Oct 1999 (so far as not already in force for certain purposes)[5] (SI 1999/2739)
		18 Oct 1999 (so far as not already in force for certain purposes)[6] (SI 1999/2860)

Social Security Act 1998 (c 14)—*contd*
Schedule

7, para	107, 108—*contd*		29 Nov 1999 (so far as not already in force except for certain purposes)[7] (SI 1999/3178)
			Not in force (exceptions referred to above)
	109		6 Sep 1999 (for certain purposes)[4] (SI 1999/2422)
			5 Oct 1999 (so far as not already in force for certain purposes)[5] (SI 1999/2739)
			18 Oct 1999 (so far as not already in force for certain purposes)[6] (SI 1999/2860)
			29 Nov 1999 (so far as not already in force except for certain purposes)[7] (SI 1999/3178)
			Not in force (exceptions referred to above)
	110	(1)	(a) Repealed
			(b) 6 Apr 1999 (SI 1999/418)
		(2)	29 Nov 1999 (except for certain purposes)[7] (SI 1999/3178)
			Not in force (exceptions referred to above)
	111	(a)	29 Nov 1999 (except for certain purposes)[7] (SI 1999/3178)
			Not in force (exceptions referred to above)
		(b)	5 Jul 1999 (for certain purposes)[3] (SI 1999/1958)
			29 Nov 1999 (so far as not already in force except for certain purposes)[7] (SI 1999/3178)
			Not in force (exceptions referred to above)
	112		6 Sep 1999 (so far as not already in force for certain purposes)[4] (SI 1999/2422)
			5 Oct 1999 (so far as not already in force for certain purposes)[5] (SI 1999/2739)
			29 Nov 1999 (so far as not already in force except for certain purposes)[7] (SI 1999/3178)
			Not in force (exceptions referred to above)
	113		29 Nov 1999 (except for certain purposes)[7] (SI 1999/3178)
			Not in force (exceptions referred to above)

Social Security Act 1998 (c 14)—*contd*

Schedule

7, para	114		8 Sep 1998 (for purpose of authorising the making of regulations or orders) (SI 1998/2209)
			6 Apr 1999 (otherwise) (SI 1998/2209)
	115		5 Jul 1999 (for certain purposes)[3] (SI 1999/1958)
			Not in force (otherwise)
	116		29 Nov 1999 (except for certain purposes)[7] (SI 1999/3178)
			Not in force (exceptions referred to above)
	117		18 Oct 1999 (for certain purposes)[6] (SI 1999/2860)
			29 Nov 1999 (so far as not already in force except for certain purposes)[7] (SI 1999/3178)
			Not in force (exceptions referred to above)
	118	(1)	1 Jun 1999 (so far as substitutes the words "paragraph 7(b)" for the words "paragraph 7") (SI 1999/1510)
			18 Oct 1999 (for certain purposes[6] so far as substitutes for the words "paragraph 38(a), 41(b), 41(e) or 43" the words "paragraph 38(a)") (SI 1999/2860)
			29 Nov 1999 (so far as not already in force except for certain purposes)[7] (SI 1999/3178)
			Not in force (exceptions referred to above)
		(2)	18 Oct 1999 (for certain purposes[6] so far as relates to the tribunals specified in Tribunals and Inquiries Act 1992, Sch 1, para 41(b)) (SI 1999/2860)
			29 Nov 1999 (so far as not already in force except for certain purposes)[7] (SI 1999/3178)
			Not in force (exceptions referred to above)
	119		18 Oct 1999 (for certain purposes)[6] (SI 1999/2860)
			Not in force (otherwise)
	120	(a)	*Not in force*
		(b)	29 Nov 1999 (except for certain purposes)[7] (SI 1999/3178)
			Not in force (exceptions referred to above)

Social Security Act 1998 (c 14)—*contd*
Schedule

7, para	121	(1)		4 Mar 1999 (so far as authorising the making of regulations) (SI 1999/528) 1 Jun 1999 (otherwise) (SI 1999/1510)
		(2)	(a)	4 Mar 1999 (so far as authorising the making of regulations) (SI 1999/528) 6 Sep 1999 (so far as not already in force for certain purposes)[4] (SI 1999/2422) 5 Oct 1999 (so far as not already in force for certain purposes)[5] (SI 1999/2739) 18 Oct 1999 (so far as not already in force for certain purposes[6] and so far as relates to Tribunals and Inquiries Act 1992, Sch 1, para 41(b), (e)) (SI 1999/2860) 29 Nov 1999 (so far as not already in force except for certain purposes)[7] (SI 1999/3178) *Not in force* (exceptions referred to above)
			(b)	4 Mar 1999 (so far as authorising the making of regulations) (SI 1999/528) 18 Oct 1999 (so far as not already in force for certain purposes[6] and so far as relates to Tribunals and Inquiries Act 1992, Sch 1, para 41(b), (e)) (SI 1999/2860) 29 Nov 1999 (so far as not already in force except for certain purposes)[7] (SI 1999/3178) *Not in force* (exceptions referred to above)
			(c)	4 Mar 1999 (so far as authorising the making of regulations) (SI 1999/528) 6 Sep 1999 (so far as not already in force for certain purposes)[4] (SI 1999/2422) 5 Oct 1999 (so far as not already in force for certain purposes)[5] (SI 1999/2739) 29 Nov 1999 (so far as not already in force except for certain purposes)[7] (SI 1999/3178) *Not in force* (exceptions referred to above)
	122			1 Jun 1999 (SI 1999/1510)

Social Security Act 1998 (c 14)—*contd*

Schedule

7, para	123	(1)	(a)	6 Sep 1999 (for certain purposes)[4] (SI 1999/2422)
				5 Oct 1999 (so far as not already in force for certain purposes)[5] (SI 1999/2739)
				29 Nov 1999 (so far as not already in force except for certain purposes)[7] (SI 1999/3178)
				Not in force (exceptions referred to above)
			(b)	1 Jun 1999 (SI 1999/1510)
		(2)		1 Jun 1999 (so far as it applies to the entry "Chairman of child support appeal tribunals") (SI 1999/1510)
				18 Oct 1999 (for certain purposes[6] and so far as it applies to the entries relating to chairmen of disability appeal tribunals in Judicial Pensions and Retirement Act 1993, Sch 1, Pt II) (SI 1999/2860)
				29 Nov 1999 (so far as not already in force except for certain purposes)[7] (SI 1999/3178)
				Not in force (exceptions referred to above)
	124	(1)	(a)	6 Sep 1999 (for certain purposes)[4] (SI 1999/2422)
				5 Oct 1999 (so far as not already in force for certain purposes)[5] (SI 1999/2739)
				29 Nov 1999 (so far as not already in force except for certain purposes)[7] (SI 1999/3178)
				Not in force (exceptions referred to above)
			(b)	1 Jun 1999 (SI 1999/1510)
		(2)		1 Jun 1999 (so far as it applies to the entry "Chairman of child support appeal tribunals") (SI 1999/1510)
				18 Oct 1999 (for certain purposes[6] and so far as it applies to the entries relating to chairmen of disability appeal tribunals and vaccine damage tribunals in Judicial Pensions and Retirement Act 1993, Sch 5) (SI 1999/2860)
				29 Nov 1999 (so far as not already in force except for certain purposes)[7] (SI 1999/3178)

Social Security Act 1998 (c 14)—*contd*
Schedule

7, para	124	(2)—*contd*	*Not in force* (exceptions referred to above)
	125		29 Nov 1999 (except for certain purposes)[7] (SI 1999/3178)
			Not in force (exceptions referred to above)
	126–128		6 Apr 1999 (SI 1999/418)
	129		5 Jul 1999 (for certain purposes)[3] (SI 1999/1958)
			29 Nov 1999 (so far as not already in force except for certain purposes)[7] (SI 1999/3178)
			Not in force (exceptions referred to above)
	130	(1)	Repealed (*never in force*)
		(2)	5 Jul 1999 (for certain purposes)[3] (SI 1999/1958)
			Not in force (otherwise)
			Sub-s 130(2) prospectively repealed by Social Security Contributions (Transfer of Functions, etc) Act 1999, s 26(3), Sch 10, Pt I[5]
	131		4 Mar 1999 (so far as authorising the making of regulations) (SI 1999/528)
			5 Jul 1999 (for certain purposes)[3] (SI 1999/1958)
			Not in force (otherwise)
	132		Repealed (*never in force*)
	133		6 Apr 1999 (SI 1999/418)
	134–146		18 Oct 1999 (for certain purposes)[6] (SI 1999/2860)
			Not in force (otherwise)
	147		18 Oct 1999 (for certain purposes)[6] (SI 1999/2860)
			29 Nov 1999 (so far as not already in force except for certain purposes)[7] (SI 1999/3178)
			Not in force (exceptions referred to above)
	148		Repealed (*never in force*)
	149	(1)	4 Mar 1999 (so far as authorising the making of regulations) (SI 1999/528)
			29 Nov 1999 (so far as not already in force except for certain purposes)[7] (SI 1999/3178)
			Not in force (exceptions referred to above)

Social Security Act 1998 (c 14)—*contd*

Schedule

7, para	149	(2)	29 Nov 1999 (except for certain purposes)[7] (SI 1999/3178) *Not in force* (exceptions referred to above)
	150–153		29 Nov 1999 (except for certain purposes)[7] (SI 1999/3178) *Not in force* (exceptions referred to above)
8			8 Sep 1998 (repeals of or in Child Support Act 1991, s 14(2), (2A), Sch 2, para 2; Social Security Contributions and Benefits Act 1992, Sch 2, paras 3(1)(b), 6(2); Social Security Contributions and Benefits (Northern Ireland) Act 1992, paras 3(1)(b), 6(2); Jobseekers Act 1995, Sch 2, para 20(3); Child Support Act 1995, Sch 3, para 3(2)) (SI 1998/2209)

5 Apr 1999 (repeal of Social Security Contributions and Benefits Act 1992, ss 139(3), 140(4)(e)) (subject to a transitional provision) (SI 1999/1055)

6 Apr 1999 (repeals in Social Security Contributions and Benefits Act 1992, Sch 1, para 6(2)(b), Sch 11, para 2(d)) (SI 1998/2209)

6 Apr 1999 (repeals of or in Social Security Administration Act 1992, ss 146, 147(1)–(3), 190(1)(a); Social Security Contributions and Benefits Act 1992, s 122(1); Pensions Act 1995, s 137(2)) (SI 1999/418)

6 Apr 1999 (repeals of or in Social Security Administration Act 1992, ss 118(4), 119(2), 120(1), (5), 121(1), (2)) (SI 1999/526)

1 Jun 1999 (repeals of or in House of Commons Disqualification Act 1975, Sch 1, Pt III (so far as applies to the entries relating to regional or other full-time chairmen of child support appeal tribunals, the Chief Child Support Officer and members of a panel appointed under Tribunals and

Social Security Act 1998 (c 14)—*contd*
Schedule
8—*contd*

Inquiries Act 1992, s 6, of persons to act as chairmen of child support appeal tribunals); Debtors (Scotland) Act 1987; Child Support Act 1991; Social Security Administration Act 1992, Sch 2, para 3; Tribunals and Inquiries Act 1992, Sch 2, para 3; Judicial Pensions and Retirement Act 1993, Sch 1, Pt II (entry relating to chairmen of child support appeal tribunals), Sch 5 (entry relating to chairmen of child support appeal tribunals), Sch 6, para 23(1), Sch 8, para 21(1); Child Support Act 1995) (SI 1999/1510)

5 Jul 1999 (for certain purposes[3] and so far as relates to repeals of Social Security Administration Act 1992, s 164(5)(a); Pension Schemes Act 1993, s 167(4)) (SI 1999/1958)

6 Sep 1999 (repeal of Social Security Administration Act 1992, s 61A) (SI 1999/2422)

18 Oct 1999 (repeal of Social Security Administration Act 1992, s 63) (SI 1999/2860)

18 Oct 1999 (for certain purposes[6] and so far as relates to repeals of or in House of Commons Disqualification Act 1975, Pt III (so far as applies to the entries relating to regional or other full-time chairmen of disability appeal tribunals, members of a panel appointed under Tribunals and Inquiries Act 1992, s 6, of persons to act as chairmen of disability appeal tribunals, members of a panel of persons who may be appointed to serve on a vaccine damage tribunal, and the President of disability appeals tribunals); Vaccine Damage Payments Act 1979, ss 5(1)–(3), (5), 7(3) (the words from "and in relation to" to the end), 12(1); Judicial Pensions and Retirement Act 1993, Sch 1, Pt II, Sch 5 (entries relating to

Social Security Act 1998 (c 14)—*contd*
Schedule
8—*contd*

chairmen of disability appeal tribunals and to chairmen of vaccine damage tribunals); Jobseekers Act 1995, ss 6(6) (the words "("the first determination")"), 7(7) (the words "("the first determination")"), 9(9), 10(8), 11, 28(1)(b), (3), 35(1) (the definition "adjudication officer"), Sch 2, paras 20(3), 41--47, 57) (SI 1999/2860)

29 Nov 1999 (except for certain purposes[7] and so far as relates to repeals of or in House of Commons Disqualification Act 1975; Health and Social Services and Social Security Adjudications Act 1983; Social Security Administration Act 1992, ss 17–70, 116(6), 189(1) (the words "subsection (2) below and to"), (2), (4) (the words "24 or"), (5) (the words "(other than the power conferred by section 24 above)"), (6) (the word "24,"), (10), 190(4), 191 (the definitions "commissioner", "the disablement questions", "5 year general qualification", "President", "10 year general qualification"), 192(5) (the words "section 24;"), Sch 4, Pt I (the entry "Adjudication officers", paras (b)–(d) in the entry "Adjudicating bodies" and the words "A social fund officer" in the entry "The Social Fund"); Social Security (Consequential Provisions) Act 1992; Local Government Finance Act 1992; Tribunals and Inquiries Act 1992; Judicial Pensions and Retirement Act 1993; Pension Schemes Act 1993; Social Security (Incapacity for Work) Act 1994; Deregulation and Contracting Out Act 1994; Pensions Act 1995; Industrial Tribunals Act 1996; Arbitration Act 1996; Social Security (Recovery of Benefits) Act 1997; Social Security

Social Security Act 1998 (c 14)—*contd*
Schedule
8—*contd*

Administration (Fraud) Act 1997;
Social Security Act 1998)
(SI 1999/3178)
2 Jul 2001 (repeals of Social Security
Administration Act 1992, ss
5(1)(n), (o), (4), 6(1)(n), (o)
(SI 2001/2316)
Not in force (exceptions referred to
above)

¹ For transitional provisions see SI 1999/1510, arts 48–50

² Orders made under Social Security Contributions (Transfer of Functions, etc) Act 1999, s 28(3), bringing the prospective insertions and repeals into force will be noted to that Act

³ Subject to transitional provisions and savings, "for certain purposes" means for the purposes of guardian's allowance under the Social Security Contributions and Benefits Act 1992 ("the Act"), Pt III, benefits under Pt V of the Act, child benefit, and any matter to which, by virtue of Pension Schemes Act 1993, s 170, provisions of Chapter II of Pt I of the Act are to apply

⁴ Subject to transitional provisions in SI 1999/2422, art 4, Sch 14, "for certain purposes" means for the purposes of benefits under the Social Security Contributions and Benefits Act 1992 ("the Act"), Pt II (except child's special allowance), severe disablement allowance under ss 68, 69 of the Act, benefits for the aged under ss 78, 79 of the Act, increases for dependants under Pt IV of the Act, and graduated retirement benefit under the National Insurance Act 1965, ss 36, 37

⁵ Subject to transitional provisions in SI 1999/2739, art 3, Sch 2, "for certain purposes" means for the purposes of family credit and disability working allowance under Pt VII of the Social Security Contributions and Benefits Act 1992

⁶ Subject to transitional provisions in SI 1999/2860, art 4, Schs 16--18, "for certain purposes" means for the purposes of (i) attendance allowance, disability living allowance and invalid care allowance under Social Security Contributions and Benefits Act 1992, Pt III, (ii) jobseeker's allowance under Jobseekers Act 1995, Pt I and any sums payable under s 26 of that Act, (iii) vaccine damage payments under Vaccine Damage Payments Act 1979, (iv) decisions whether a person is entitled to be credited with earnings or contributions in accordance with regulations made under Social Security Contributions and Benefits Act 1992, s 22(5), and (v) decisions whether a person was, within the meaning of regulations, precluded from regular employment by responsibilities at home

⁷ Subject to transitional provisions in SI 1999/3178, art 4, Schs 21–23, "for certain purposes" means for the purposes of statutory sick pay and statutory maternity pay under Social Security Contributions and Benefits Act 1992, Pts XI, XII, and (ii) "except for certain purposes" means for the purposes of housing benefit, council Tax benefit and decisions to which the Social Security Contributions (Transfer of Functions, etc) Act 1999 (Commencement No 1 and Transitional Provisions) Order 1999, SI 1999/527, art 4(6), applies

⁸ Orders made under Child Support, Pensions and Social Security Act 2000, s 86, bringing the prospective amendments into force will be noted to that Act

---

Statute Law (Repeals) Act 1998 (c 43)

RA: 19 Nov 1998

Commencement provisions: s 2
Section

1	(1)	See Sch 1 below
	(2)	See Sch 2 below
2, 3		19 Nov 1998 (RA)

Statute Law (Repeals) Act 1998 (c 43)—*contd*

Schedule

1	19 Nov 1998 (except repeal of Public Notaries Act 1843 as it applies to the Isle of Man, repeal in Statute Law (Repeals) Act 1993, s 3(3)) (RA)
	Not in force (exceptions noted above)
2	19 Nov 1998 (RA)

Tax Credits (Initial Expenditure) Act 1998 (c 16)

RA: 21 May 1998

21 May 1998 (RA)

Teaching and Higher Education Act 1998 (c 30)

RA: 16 Jul 1998

Commencement provisions: s 46(2), (3); Teaching and Higher Education Act 1998 (Commencement No 1) Order 1998, SI 1998/1729; Teaching and Higher Education Act 1998 (Commencement No 2 and Transitional Provisions) Order 1998, SI 1998/2004; Teaching and Higher Education Act 1998 (Commencement No 3) Order 1998, SI 1998/2215; Teaching and Higher Education Act 1998 (Commencement No 4 and Transitional Provisions) Order 1998, SI 1998/3237; Teaching and Higher Education Act 1998 (Commencement No 5) Order 1999, SI 1999/987; Teaching and Higher Education Act 1998 (Commencement No 6) Order 2000, SI 2000/970; Teaching and Higher Education Act 1998 (Commencement No 7) Order 2000, SI 2000/2199; Teaching and Higher Education Act 1998 (Commencement No 8) Order 2001, SI 2001/1211

Section

1	(1)		1 Oct 1998 (so far as defines "the Council") (SI 1998/2215)
			1 Sep 2000 (otherwise) (SI 2000/970)
	(2)–(10)		1 Oct 1998 (SI 1998/2215)
2	(1)–(3)		1 Sep 2000 (SI 2000/970)
	(4)		30 Apr 2001 (W) (SI 2001/1211)
			1 Jun 2001 (E) (SI 2001/1211)
	(5)–(7)		1 Sep 2000 (SI 2000/970)
3	(1), (2)		1 Sep 2000 (SI 2000/970)
	(3)	(a)–(c)	1 Sep 2000 (SI 2000/970)
		(d)	5 Apr 2000 (for the purposes of making regulations) (SI 2000/970)
			1 Sep 2000 (otherwise) (SI 2000/970)
	(4)		5 Apr 2000 (for the purposes of making regulations) (SI 2000/970)
			1 Sep 2000 (otherwise) (SI 2000/970)
4, 5			5 Apr 2000 (SI 2000/970)
6			See Sch 2 below

Teaching and Higher Education Act 1998 (c 30)—*contd*

Section

7	(1)–(4)		5 Apr 2000 (SI 2000/970)
	(5)		1 Sep 2000 (SI 2000/970)
8			1 Oct 1998 (SI 1998/2215)
9, 10			1 Sep 2000 (SI 2000/970)
11, 12			5 Apr 2000 (SI 2000/970)
13			1 Sep 2000 (SI 2000/970)
14	(1), (2)		1 Sep 2000 (SI 2000/970)
	(3)		5 Apr 2000 (SI 2000/970)
	(4), (5)		1 Sep 2000 (SI 2000/970)
15			15 Aug 2000 (SI 2000/2199)
16, 17			1 Oct 1998 (SI 1998/2215)
18			*Not in force*
19	(1)–(6)		1 Oct 1998 (SI 1998/2215)
	(6A)		Inserted by Learning and Skills Act 2000, s 139(5) (qv)
	(7)–(9)		1 Apr 1999 (SI 1998/2215)
	(10)	(a)	1 Apr 1999 (SI 1998/2215)
		(b), (c)	1 Oct 1998 (SI 1998/2215)
		(d)	Inserted by Learning and Skills Act 2000, s 139(1), (6) (qv)
	(11), (12)		Inserted by Learning and Skills Act 2000, s 139(7) (qv)
20, 21			1 Oct 1998 (SI 1998/2215)
22–31			16 Jul 1998 (s 46(2))
32, 33			1 Sep 1999 (SI 1999/987)
34			Repealed
35			1 Oct 1998 (SI 1998/2215)
35A			Inserted by Learning and Skills Act 2000, s 81 (qv)
36			Spent
37			1 Jan 1999 (SI 1998/3237)
38			1 Jan 1999 (SI 1998/3237); prospectively repealed by Special Educational Needs and Disability Act 2001, ss 38(15), 42(6), Sch 9[1]
39			1 Feb 1999 (SI 1998/3237)
40, 41			1 Oct 1998 (SI 1998/2215)
42, 43			16 Jul 1998 (s 46(2))
44	(1)		See Sch 3 below
	(2)		See Sch 4 below
45, 46			16 Jul 1998 (s 46(2))
Schedule			
1			1 Oct 1998 (SI 1998/2215)
2	1, 2		28 Feb 2001 (SI 2001/1211)
	3	(1)–(3)	30 Apr 2001 (W) (SI 2001/1211) 1 Jun 2001 (E) (SI 2001/1211)
		(4)	28 Feb 2001 (for the purpose of making regulations) (SI 2001/1211)

Teaching and Higher Education Act 1998 (c 30)—*contd*
Schedule

2	3	(4)—*contd*	30 Apr 2001 (W) (otherwise) (SI 2001/1211)
			1 Jun 2001 (E) (otherwise) (SI 2001/1211)
		(5)	28 Feb 2001 (SI 2001/1211)
	4		30 Apr 2001 (W) (SI 2001/1211)
			1 Jun 2001 (E) (SI 2001/1211)
	5	(1)	28 Feb 2001 (for the purpose of making regulations) (SI 2001/1211)
			30 Apr 2001 (W) (otherwise) (SI 2001/1211)
			1 Jun 2001 (E) (otherwise) (SI 2001/1211)
		(2)	30 Apr 2001 (W) (SI 2001/1211)
			1 Jun 2001 (E) (SI 2001/1211)
	6	(1)	28 Feb 2001 (SI 2001/1211)
		(2), (3)	30 Apr 2001 (W) (SI 2001/1211)
			1 Jun 2001 (E) (SI 2001/1211)
	7, 8		28 Feb 2001 (SI 2001/1211)
3, para	1–3		1 Sep 2000 (SI 2000/970)
	4		18 Jul 1998 (SI 1998/1729)
	5–9		1 Oct 1998 (SI 1998/2215)
	10–14		1 Sep 1999 (SI 1999/987)
	15		1 Oct 1998 (SI 1998/2215)
4			13 Aug 1998 (repeals of Education (Student Loans) Act 1990; Education (Student Loans) Act 1996; Education (Student Loans) Act 1998) (subject to transitional and saving provisions) (SI 1998/2004)
			1 Oct 1998 (repeals in Education Reform Act 1988, ss 218(1)(c), 232(6)) (SI 1998/2215)
			1 Jan 1999 (repeals of or in Education Act 1962; Education Act 1973, s 3; Education Act 1980, s 19, Sch 5; Education (Fees and Awards) Act 1983, s 2(3); Education Reform Act 1988, s 209; Education Act 1996, s 578) (subject to transitional and saving provisions) (SI 1998/3237)
			1 Jan 1999 (repeal of Charities Act 1993, Sch 2, paras (h), (j)) (SI 1998/3237)
			Not in force (otherwise)

[1]   Orders made under Special Educational Needs and Disability Act 2001, s 43, bringing the prospective repeals into force will be noted to that Act

Waste Minimisation Act 1998 (c 44)

RA: 19 Nov 1998

19 Nov 1998 (RA)

***

Wireless Telegraphy Act 1998 (c 6)

RA: 18 Mar 1998

Commencement provisions: s 10(2)

18 Jun 1998 (s 10(2))

***

1999

Access to Justice Act 1999 (c 22)

RA: 27 Jul 1999

Commencement provisions: s 108; Access to Justice Act 1999 (Commencement No 1) Order 1999, SI 1999/2657; Access to Justice Act 1999 (Commencement No 2 and Transitional Provisions) Order 1999, SI 1999/3344; Access to Justice Act 1999 (Commencement No 3, Transitional Provisions and Savings) Order 2000, SI 2000/774[1]; Access to Justice Act 1999 (Commencement No 4 and Transitional Provisions) Order 2000, SI 2000/1920[2] ; Access to Justice Act 1999 (Commencement No 5 and Transitional Provisions) Order 2000, SI 2000/3280[3]; Access to Justice Act 1999 (Commencement No 6 and Transitional Provisions) Order 2001, SI 2001/168[4]; Access to Justice Act 1999 (Commencement No 7, Transitional Provisions and Savings) Order 2001, SI 2001/916[5]; Access to Justice Act 1999 (Commencement No 8) Order 2001, SI 2001/1655

Section	
1–11	1 Apr 2000 (SI 2000/774)
12–18	2 Apr 2001 (SI 2001/916)
19–23	1 Apr 2000 (SI 2000/774)
24	See Sch 4 below
25–27	1 Apr 2000 (SI 2000/774)
28	*Not in force*
29, 30	1 Apr 2000 (SI 2000/774)
31	*Not in force*
32–34	27 Sep 1999 (s 108(3))
35	1 Jan 2000 (SI 1999/3344)
36	27 Sep 1999 (SI 1999/2657)
37–39	31 Jul 2000 (SI 2000/1920)
40	27 Sep 1999 (SI 1999/2657)
41	See Sch 5 below
42	27 Sep 1999 (SI 1999/2657)
43	See Sch 6 below
44	31 Jul 2000 (SI 2000/1920)
45	27 Jul 1999 (s 108(2))
46	27 Sep 1999 (SI 1999/2657)
47	25 May 2001 (SI 2001/1655)
48	See Sch 7 below
49	27 Sep 1999 (SI 1999/2657)
50–52	*Not in force*
53	1 Nov 1999 (SI 1999/2657)
54–65	27 Sep 1999 (s 108(3))
66	Repealed

Access to Justice Act 1999 (c 22)—*contd*

Section

67	(1)	27 Sep 1999 (s 108(3))
	(2)	27 Sep 1999 (in the petty sessions areas of Aberconwy, Arfon, Blackburn, Darwen and Ribble Vally, Bromley, Burnley and Pendle, Colwyn, Corby, Croydon, Daventry, Denbighshire, Dwyfor, Flintshire, Gateshead, Kettering, Meirionnydd, Newcastle-under-Lyme and Pirehill North, Newcastle-upon-Tyne, Northampton, Rhuddlan, Staffordshire Moorlands, Stoke-on-Trent, Sutton, Towcester, Wellingborough, Wrexham Maelor, Ynys Môn/Anglesey) (SI 1999/2657)
		8 Jan 2001 (otherwise) (SI 2000/3280)
	(3)	27 Sep 1999 (s 108(3))
68–70		27 Sep 1999 (s 108(3))
71		1 Jan 2000 (SI 1999/3344)
72–76		27 Sep 1999 (s 108(3))
77		*Not in force*
78	(1)	31 Aug 2000 (SI 2000/1920)
	(2)	See Sch 11 below
79		12 Nov 1999 (SI 1999/2657)
80		*Not in force*
81, 82		27 Sep 1999 (s 108(3))
83	(1)	27 Sep 1999 (so far as it inserts Justices of the Peace Act 1997, s 30B) (SI 1999/2657)
		1 Mar 2000 (so far as it inserts Justices of the Peace Act 1997, ss 30A(1), 30C) (SI 1999/3344)
		1 Apr 2001 (so far as not already in force) (SI 2001/916)
	(2)	31 Aug 2000 (so far as it inserts Justices of the Peace Act 1997, ss 59B, 59C, 59D(4), (5)) (SI 2000/1920)
		1 Apr 2001 (so far as not already in force) (SI 2001/916)
	(3)	See Sch 12 below
84		27 Sep 1999 (s 108(3))
85		1 Jan 2000 (SI 1999/3344)
86, 87		27 Sep 1999 (s 108(3))
88, 89		27 Sep 1999 (SI 1999/2657)
90, 91		1 Apr 2001 (SI 2001/916)
92–95		8 Jan 2001 (SI 2000/3280)
96, 97		19 Feb 2001 (SI 2001/168)

Access to Justice Act 1999 (c 22)—*contd*

Section

98–100			1 Apr 2001 (SI 2001/916)
101–103			1 Apr 2001 (E, W, NI) (SI 2001/916)
			Not in force (S)
104			27 Sep 1999 (s 108(3))
105			See Sch 14 below
106			See Sch 15 below
107			27 Sep 1999 (s 108(3))
108–110			27 Jul 1999 (RA)

Schedule

1–2				*Not in force*
3				2 Apr 2001 (SI 2001/916)
4, para	1, 2			1 Apr 2000 (SI 2000/774)
	3, 4			2 Apr 2001 (SI 2001/916)
	5			Repealed (*never in force*)
	6–8			2 Apr 2001 (SI 2001/916)
	9			Repealed (*never in force*)
	10	(1)		1 Apr 2000 (SI 2000/774)
		(2)		2 Apr 2001 (SI 2001/916)
		(3)	(a)	2 Apr 2001 (SI 2001/916)
			(b)	1 Apr 2000 (SI 2000/774)
		(4), (5)		2 Apr 2001 (SI 2001/916)
	11–15			1 Apr 2000 (SI 2000/774)
	16–18			2 Apr 2001 (SI 2001/916)
	19, 20			1 Apr 2000 (SI 2000/774)
	21–23			2 Apr 2001 (SI 2001/916)
	24, 25			Repealed (*never in force*)
	26			1 Apr 2000 (SI 2000/774)
	27–30			2 Apr 2001 (SI 2001/916)
	31–34			1 Apr 2000 (SI 2000/774)
	35			2 Apr 2001 (SI 2001/916)
	36, 37			1 Apr 2000 (SI 2000/774)
	38–40			2 Apr 2001 (SI 2001/916)
	41–46			1 Apr 2000 (SI 2000/774)
	47			2 Apr 2001 (SI 2001/916)
	48			1 Apr 2000 (SI 2000/774)
	49			2 Apr 2001 (SI 2001/916)
	50–52			1 Apr 2000 (SI 2000/774)
	53–55			2 Apr 2001 (SI 2001/916)
	56			1 Apr 2000 (SI 2000/774)
5				1 Jan 2000 (subject to transitional provisions) (SI 1999/3344)
6, para	1–5			1 Jan 2000 (SI 1999/3344)
	6, 7			27 Sep 1999 (SI 1999/2657)
	8			1 Jan 2000 (SI 1999/3344)
	9, 10			27 Sep 1999 (SI 1999/2657)
	11			1 Jan 2000 (SI 1999/3344)
7				27 Sep 1999 (SI 1999/2657)
8				*Not in force*
9				Repealed

Access to Justice Act 1999 (c 22)—*contd*

Schedule

10		27 Sep 1999 (s 108(3))
11		31 Aug 2000 (SI 2000/1920)
12, para	1–8	1 Apr 2001 (SI 2001/916)
	9	1 Mar 2000 (SI 1999/3344)
	10	1 Apr 2001 (SI 2001/916)
	11	27 Sep 1999 (SI 1999/2657)
	12	1 Mar 2000 (SI 1999/3344)
	13–19	1 Apr 2001 (SI 2001/916)
13		1 Apr 2001 (SI 2001/916)
14		27 Sep 1999 (s 108(3))
15, Pt	I	1 Apr 2000 (repeals of or in Parliamentary Commissioner Act 1967; House of Commons Disqualification Act 1975; Northern Ireland Assembly Disqualification Act 1975; Legal Aid Act 1988, ss 3(5)–(10), 4(5), (8), 5–18, 31, 32, 34–40, 42, 45, 46, Schs 1, 2, Sch 5, paras 2, 4, 5, 6a, 7a, 8, 16–18, 20, 21, Schs 6–8; Children Act 1989 (except s 99(3)); Civil Legal Aid (Matrimonial Proceedings) Regulations 1989, SI 1989/549; Courts and Legal Services Act 1990 (except s 59); Legal Aid Act 1988 (Children Act 1989) Order 1991, SI 1991/1924; Companies Act 1989 (Eligibility for Appointment as Company Auditor) (Consequential Amendments) Regulations 1991, SI 1991/1997; Civil Legal Aid (General) (Amendment) (No 2) Regulations 1991, SI 1991/2036; Social Security (Consequential Provisions) Act 1992; Tribunals and Inquiries Act 1992; Trade Union Reform and Employment Rights Act 1993; Civil Legal Aid (Scope) Regulations 1993, SI 1993/1354; Legal Aid (Scope) Regulations 1994, SI 1994/2768; Employment Rights Act 1996; Family Law Act 1996) (SI 2000/774) 2 Apr 2001 (so far as not already in force) (SI 2001/916)

Access to Justice Act 1999 (c 22)—*contd*
Schedule

15, Pt	II		27 Sep 1999 (repeals of or in Solicitors Act 1974, ss 32(4), 87(1); Courts and Legal Services Act 1990, ss 27(2), (3), (6), 28(2), (3), (5), 71(7), (8), Schs 3, 19) (SI 1999/2657)
			1 Nov 1999 (repeals of or in Public Notaries Act 1801, s 13; Public Notaries Act 1843, s 6; Courts and Legal Services Act 1990, ss 57(11), 113(1), (10)) (SI 1999/2657)
			1 Jan 2000 (repeals of or in House of Commons Disqualification Act 1975; Northern Ireland Assembly Disqualification Act 1975; Administration of Justice Act 1985, ss 9(2)(g), 65, Sch 2; Courts and Legal Services Act 1990, ss 19 (and the heading preceding it), 20, 24(3), 123(1), (f), (2)(e), Schs 1, 2) (SI 1999/3344)
			31 Jul 2000 (otherwise) (SI 2000/1920)
	III		27 Sep 1999 (s 108(3))
	IV		27 Sep 1999 (SI 1999/2657)
	V	(1)	27 Sep 1999 (except repeals of or in Magistrates' Courts Act 1980, s 67(8); Children Act 1989, Sch 11) (s 108(3))
			Not in force (exceptions noted above)
		(2)	*Not in force*
		(3)	31 Aug 2000 (SI 2000/1920)
		(4)	12 Nov 1999 (SI 1999/2657)
		(5)	27 Sep 1999 (s 108(3))
		(6)	1 Mar 2000 (repeals of or in Justices of the Peace Act 1997, s 56(4)) (SI 1999/3344)
			1 Apr 2001 (so far as not already in force) (SI 2001/916)
		(7)	27 Sep 1999 (repeals of or in Justices of the Peace Act 1997, ss 31(2), 40(5), Sch 4, para 15) (SI 1999/2657)
			1 Apr 2001 (so far as not already in force) (SI 2001/916)
		(8)	8 Jan 2001 (so far as relates to repeals of or in Magistrates' Courts Act 1980, s 125(2); Criminal Justice Act 1988, s 65; Courts and Legal Services Act 1990, Sch 17, para 11) (SI 2000/3280)

Access to Justice Act 1999 (c 22)—*contd*

Schedule

15, Pt	V	(8)—*contd*	19 Feb 2001 (otherwise) (SI 2001/168)
	VI		1 Apr 2001 (SI 2001/916)

¹   For transitional and saving provisions, see SI 2000/774, arts 3–11

²   For transitional provisions, see SI 2000/1920, art 4

³   For transitional provisions, see SI 2000/3280, art 3

⁴   For transitional provisions, see SI 2001/168, art 3

⁵   For transitional provisions and savings, see SI 2001/916, art 4, Schs 1, 2

Adoption (Intercountry Aspects) Act 1999 (c 18)

RA: 27 Jul 1999

Commencement provisions: s 18(3); Adoption (Intercountry Aspects) Act 1999 (Commencement No 1) Order 2000, SI 2000/52; Adoption (Intercountry Aspects) Act 1999 (Commencement No 2) (Scotland) Order 2000, SSI 2000/223; Adoption (Intercountry Aspects) Act 1999 (Commencement No 3) Order 2000, SI 2000/2821; Adoption (Intercountry Aspects) Act 1999 (Commencement No 4) (Scotland) Order 2000, SSI 2000/390 ²; Adoption (Intercountry Aspects) Act 1999 (Commencement No 5) Order 2001, SI 2001/1279; Adoption (Intercountry Aspects) Act 1999 (Commencement No 6) Order 2001, SSI 2001/235

Section

1–8		*Not in force*
9		30 Apr 2001 (so far as amends Adoption Act 1976) (SI 2001/1279)
		2 Jul 2001 (so far as amends Adoption (Scotland) Act 1978) (SSI 2001/235)
10		*Not in force*
		Prospectively repealed by Care Standards Act 2000, s 117(2), Sch 6¹
11, 12		*Not in force*
13		31 Jan 2000 (so far as it inserts Adoption Act 1976, s 72(3A)) (SI 2000/52)
		10 Nov 2000 (so far as it inserts Adoption (Scotland) Act 1978, s 65(3A)) (S) (SSI 2000/390)
		Not in force (otherwise)
14		30 Apr 2001 (so far as amends Adoption Act 1976) (SI 2001/1279)
		2 Jul 2001 (so far as amends Adoption (Scotland) Act 1978) (SSI 2001/235)
15		*Not in force*
16	(1)	*Not in force*
	(2)	16 Oct 2000 (SI 2000/2821)

Adoption (Intercountry Aspects) Act 1999 (c 18)—*contd*
Section
17   *Not in force*
18   27 Jul 1999 (RA)
Schedule
1–3   *Not in force*

[1]   Orders made under Care Standards Act 2000, s 122 bringing the prospective repeal into force will
      be noted to that Act

[2]   SSI 2000/390 replaces SSI 2000/223 which incorrectly purported to bring s 13 into force on
      2 June 2000

Appropriation Act 1999 (c 13)

RA: 15 Jul 1999

15 Jul 1999 (RA)

Breeding and Sale of Dogs (Welfare) Act 1999 (c 11)

RA: 30 Jun 1999

Commencement provisions: s 11(2)

31 December 1999 (s 11(2))

Care of Places of Worship Measure 1999 (No 2)

RA: 30 Jun 1999

Commencement provisions: s 7(2)

The provisions of this Measure were brought into force on 1 Jul 2001 by an
    instrument made by the Archbishops of Canterbury and York and dated
    21 Jun 2001 (made under s 7(2))

Cathedrals Measure 1999 (No 1)

RA: 30 Jun 1999

30 Jun 1999 (RA)

Commonwealth Development Corporation Act 1999 (c 20)

RA: 27 Jul 1999

27 Jul 1999 (RA)

Company and Business Names (Chamber of Commerce, Etc) Act 1999 (c 19)

RA: 27 Jul 1999

Commencement provisions: s 5(2) Company and Business Names (Chamber of
    Commerce Etc) Act 1999 (Commencement) Order 2001, SI 2001/258

10 May 2001 (SI 2001/258)

Consolidated Fund Act 1999 (c 4)

RA: 25 Mar 1999

25 Mar 1999 (RA)

Consolidated Fund (No 2) Act 1999 (c 35)

RA: 20 Dec 1999

20 Dec 1999 (RA)

Contracts (Rights of Third Parties) Act 1999 (c 31)

RA: 11 Nov 1999

11 Nov 1999 (RA), but the Act does not apply in relation to contracts entered into before the end of the period of six months beginning on 11 Nov 1999, except in certain limited circumstances

Criminal Cases Review (Insanity) Act 1999 (c 25)

RA: 27 Jul 1999

27 Jul 1999 (RA)

Disability Rights Commission Act 1999 (c 17)

RA: 27 Jul 1999

Commencement provisions: s 16(2); Disability Rights Commission Act 1999 (Commencement No 1 and Transitional Provision) Order 1999, SI 1999/2210; Disability Rights Commission Act 1999 (Commencement No 2 and Transitional Provision) Order 2000, SI 2000/880

Section		
1	(1)–(3)	6 Aug 1999 (SI 1999/2210)
	(4)	25 Apr 2000 (SI 2000/880)
2		25 Apr 2000 (SI 2000/880)
3	(1)–(4)	25 Apr 2000 (SI 2000/880)
	(5)	23 Mar 2000 (in so far as relates to the Secretary of State's regulations powers contained in Sch 3, para 26(a)) (SI 2000/880)
		25 Apr 2000 (otherwise) (SI 2000/880)
4	(1)–(5)	25 Apr 2000 (SI 2000/880)
	(6)	23 Mar 2000 (in so far as bringing into effect the Secretary of State's powers to prescribe any matter in regulations made by him contained in Sch 3, paras 15(3), 16(3), 16(4), 17(4), 18(2), 18(3)(a), (b) of this Act and the Secretary of State's regulation making powers contained in Sch 3 para 26(a) of this Act) (SI 2000/880)
		25 Apr 2000 (otherwise) (SI 2000/880)

Disability Rights Commission Act 1999 (c 17)—*contd*

Section

5–11				25 Apr 2000 (SI 2000/880)
12, 13				6 Aug 1999 (SI 1999/2210)
14	(1)			See Sch 4 below
	(2)			See Sch 5 below
15				6 Aug 1999 (SI 1999/2210)
16				27 Jul 1999 (RA)

Schedule

1				6 Aug 1999 (SI 1999/2210)
2				25 Apr 2000 (SI 2000/880)
3, Pt	I, II			25 Apr 2000 (SI 2000/880)
	III, para	1–14		25 Apr 2000 (SI 2000/880)
		15	(1), (2)	25 Apr 2000 (SI 2000/880)
			(3)	23 Mar 2000 (in so far as relates to the Secretary of State's powers to prescribe any matter in regulations made by him) (SI 2000/880) 25 Apr 2000 (otherwise) (SI 2000/880)
		16	(1), (2)	25 Apr 2000 (SI 2000/880)
			(3), (4)	23 Mar 2000 (in so far as relates to the Secretary of State's powers to prescribe any matter in regulations made by him) (SI 2000/880) 25 Apr 2000 (otherwise) (SI 2000/880)
		17	(1)–(3)	25 Apr 2000 (SI 2000/880)
			(4)	23 Mar 2000 (in so far as relates to the Secretary of State's powers to prescribe any matter in regulations made by him) (SI 2000/880) 25 Apr 2000 (otherwise) (SI 2000/880)
		18	(1)	25 Apr 2000 (SI 2000/880)
			(2), (3)	23 Mar 2000 (in so far as relates to the Secretary of State's powers to prescribe any matter in regulations made by him) (SI 2000/880) 25 Apr 2000 (otherwise) (SI 2000/880)
		19–21		25 Apr 2000 (SI 2000/880)
	IV	22–25		25 Apr 2000 (SI 2000/880)
		26	(a)	23 Mar 2000 (SI 2000/880)
			(b)	25 Apr 2000 (SI 2000/880)
4, para	1, 2			6 Aug 1999 (SI 1999/2210)
	3	(1), (2)		25 Apr 2000 (SI 2000/880)
		(3)		25 Apr 2000 (subject to a transitional provision) (SI 2000/880)
	4			6 Aug 1999 (subject to a transitional provision) (SI 1999/2210)

Disability Rights Commission Act 1999 (c 17)—*contd*
Schedule

5	25 Apr 2000 (repeals of or in House of Commons Disqualification Act 1975; Northern Ireland Assembly Disqualification Act 1975; Disability Discrimination Act 1995, ss 50, 51(1), (2), 52(1)–(10), (12), 53(1)–(3), (8), (9), 54(1)–(7), (9), 70(7), Sch 5) (SI 2000/880) *Not in force* (otherwise)

Employment Relations Act 1999 (c 26)

RA: 27 Jul 1999

Commencement provisions: s 45(1); Employment Relations Act 1999 (Commencement No 1 and Transitional Provisions) Order 1999, SI 1999/2509; Employment Relations Act 1999 (Commencement No 2 and Transitional and Saving Provisions) Order 1999, SI 1999/2830[1]; Employment Relations Act 1999 (Commencement No 3 and Transitional Provision) Order 1999, SI 1999/3374; Employment Relations Act 1999 (Commencement No 4 and Transitional Provision) Order 2000, SI 2000/420; Employment Relations Act 1999 (Commencement No 5 and Transitional Provision) Order 2000, SI 2000/875; Employment Relations Act 1999 (Commencement No 6 and Transitional Provisions) Order 2000, SI 2000/1338; Employment Relations Act 1999 (Commencement No 7 and Transitional Provisions) Order 2000, SI 2000/2242; Employment Relations Act 1999 (Commencement No 8) Order 2001, SI 2001/1187, as amended by SI 2001/1461.

Section

1	(1), (2)	6 Jun 2000 (SI 2000/1338)
	(3)	See Sch 1 below
2		See Sch 2 below
3		25 Oct 1999 (SI 1999/2830)
4		18 Sep 2000 (SI 2000/2242)
5		6 Jun 2000 (SI 2000/1338)
6		6 Jun 2000 (subject to a transitional provision) (SI 2000/1338)
7–9		See Sch 4 below
10–12		4 Sep 2000 (subject to a transitional provision in relation to s 10) (SI 2000/2242)
13	(1)–(3)	25 Oct 1999 (SI 1999/2830)
	(4)–(6)	4 Sep 2000 (SI 2000/2242)
14, 15		4 Sep 2000 (SI 2000/2242)
16		See Sch 5 below
17		*Not in force*
18	(1)–(5)	25 Oct 1999 (SI 1999/2830)
	(6)	Repealed
19–23		25 Oct 1999 (SI 1999/2830)

Employment Relations Act 1999 (c 26)—*contd*

Section

24			22 Feb 2000 (subject to a transitional provision) (SI 2000/420)
25			6 Jun 2000 (SI 2000/1338)
26–28			25 Oct 1999 (SI 1999/2830)
29			See Sch 6 below
30			25 Oct 1999 (SI 1999/2830)
31			See Sch 7 below
32, 33			25 Oct 1999 (SI 1999/2830)
34	(1)–(3)		17 Dec 1999 (subject to a transitional provision) (SI 1999/3374)
	(4)		25 Oct 1999 (SI 1999/2830)
	(5), (6)		17 Dec 1999 (SI 1999/3374)
35			25 Oct 1999 (SI 1999/2830)
36	(1)	(a)	17 Dec 1999 (SI 1999/3374)
		(b)	25 Oct 1999 (so far as repeals Trade Union and Labour Relations (Consolidation) Act 1992, s 159(1)(b)) (SI 1999/2830)
			17 Dec 1999 (otherwise) (SI 1999/3374)
	(2), (3)		17 Dec 1999 (SI 1999/3374)
37			25 Oct 1999 (SI 1999/2830)
38			9 Sep 1999 (SI 1999/2509)
39, 40			25 Oct 1999 (SI 1999/2830)
41			See Sch 8 below
42			9 Sep 1999 (SI 1999/2509)
43			25 Oct 1999 (SI 1999/2830)
44			See Sch 9 below
45–47			27 Jul 1999 (RA)

Schedule

1			6 Jun 2000 (subject to a transitional provision) (SI 2000/1338)
2			25 Oct 1999 (SI 1999/2830)
3			18 Sep 2000 (SI 2000/2242)
4			15 Dec 1999 (SI 1999/2830)
5			24 Apr 2000 (subject to a transitional provision) (SI 2000/875)
6			25 Oct 1999 (SI 1999/2830)
7, para	1, 2		25 Oct 1999 (SI 1999/2830)
	3, 4		*Not in force*
	5		25 Oct 1999 (so far as inserts Employment Agencies Act 1973, s 11A) (SI 1999/2830)
			Not in force (otherwise)
	6		25 Oct 1999 (SI 1999/2830)
	7		*Not in force*
	8		25 Oct 1999 (SI 1999/2830)
8			16 Jul 2001[2] (SI 2001/1187)
9, Pt	1		*Not in force*

Enquiry Bureau 020 7400 2518

Employment Relations Act 1999 (c 26)—*contd*

Schedule

9, Pt	2	15 Dec 1999 (SI 1999/2830)
	3	25 Oct 1999 (except repeal of Trade Union and Labour Relations (Consolidation) Act 1992, Sch A1, para 163) (SI 1999/2830)
		Not in force (exception noted above)
	4—7	25 Oct 1999 (SI 1999/2830)
	8	*Not in force*
	9	25 Oct 1999 (SI 1999/2830)
	10	25 Oct 1999 (repeals of or in Trade Union and Labour Relations (Consolidation) Act 1992, ss 157, 158, 159(1)(b); Employment Rights Act 1996, s 117(4)(b) (and the word "or" before it), (5), (6), 118(2), (3), 125; Employment Rights (Dispute Resolution) Act 1998, s 14(1)) (SI 1999/2830)
		17 Dec 1999 (repeals of or in Trade Union and Labour Relations (Consolidation) Act 1992, ss 159(1)(a), (2), (3), 176(7), (8); Employment Rights Act 1996, ss 120(2), 124(2), 186(2), 208, 227(2)–(4)) (SI 1999/3374)
		Not in force (repeals of or in Employment Rights Act 1996, s 236, Sch 1)
	11	25 Oct 1999 (SI 1999/2830)
	12	16 Jul 2001[2] (SI 2001/1187)

[1] For transitional and saving provisions relating to the provisions brought into force by SI 1999/2830, see Sch 3 of that Order

[2] SI 2001/1187 purported to bring s 41 and Sch 8 into force on 18 April 2001, but was amended by SI 2001/1461, which alters the date for the coming into force of these provisions to 16 July 2001

European Parliamentary Elections Act 1999 (c 1)

RA: 14 Jan 1999

Commencement provisions: s 5(1); European Parliamentary Elections Act 1999 (Commencement) Order 1999, SI 1999/717

Section

1	16 Mar 1999 (so far as confers power to make subordinate legislation) (subject to a saving) (SI 1999/717)
	1 May 1999 (otherwise) (subject to a saving) (SI 1999/717)
2–4	1 May 1999 (subject to a saving) (SI 1999/717)
5, 6	14 Jan 1999 (RA)

European Parliamentary Elections Act 1999 (c 1)—*contd*

Schedule

1	1 May 1999 (subject to a saving) (SI 1999/717)
2	16 Mar 1999 (so far as confers power to make subordinate legislation) (subject to a saving) (SI 1999/717) 1 May 1999 (otherwise) (subject to a saving) (SI 1999/717)
3, 4	1 May 1999 (subject to a saving) (SI 1999/717)

Finance Act 1999 (c 16)

RA: 27 Jul 1999

Details of the commencement of Finance Acts are not set out in this work

---

Food Standards Act 1999 (c 28)

RA: 11 Nov 1999

Commencement provisions: s 43(2); Food Standards Act 1999 (Commencement No 1) Order 2000, SI 2000/92; Food Standards Act 1999 (Commencement No 2) Order 2000, SI 2000/1066

Section

1	(1)	11 Jan 2000 (SI 2000/92)
	(2), (3)	1 Apr 2000 (SI 2000/1066)
2		11 Jan 2000 (SI 2000/92)
3	(1)–(3)	11 Jan 2000 (SI 2000/92)
	(4), (5)	11 Jan 2000 (W, S) (SI 2000/92) 1 Apr 2000 (otherwise) (SI 2000/1066)
	(6)	11 Jan 2000 (so far as (i) it is concerned with the chief executive, and (ii) it is concerned with directors and relates to Wales and Scotland) (SI 2000/92) 1 Apr 2000 (otherwise) (SI 2000/1066)
4		1 Apr 2000 (SI 2000/1066)
5	(1)	11 Jan 2000 (W, S) (SI 2000/92) 1 Apr 2000 (otherwise) (SI 2000/1066)
	(2), (3)	1 Apr 2000 (SI 2000/1066)
	(4)	See Sch 2 below
6–35		1 Apr 2000 (SI 2000/1066)
36	(1)	11 Jan 2000 (so far as it relates to the definitions "Agency", "appropriate authority") (SI 2000/92) 1 Apr 2000 (otherwise) (SI 2000/1066)
	(2)	11 Jan 2000 (SI 2000/92)
	(3)–(5)	1 Apr 2000 (SI 2000/1066)
37–40		1 Apr 2000 (SI 2000/1066)

Food Standards Act 1999 (c 28)—*contd*

Section

41, 42			11 Jan 2000 (SI 2000/92)
43			11 Nov 1999 (RA)

Schedule

1			11 Jan 2000 (SI 2000/92)
2, para	1		11 Jan 2000 (SI 2000/92)
	2–4		1 Apr 2000 (SI 2000/1066)
	5, 6		11 Jan 2000 (SI 2000/92)
	7, 8		1 Apr 2000 (SI 2000/1066)
3, 4			1 Apr 2000 (SI 2000/1066)
5, para	1–5		1 Apr 2000 (SI 2000/1066)
	6	(1)	1 Apr 2000 (SI 2000/1066)
		(2)	11 Nov 1999 (RA)
		(3), (4)	1 Apr 2000 (SI 2000/1066)
		(5)	11 Nov 1999 (RA)
		(6)	1 Apr 2000 (SI 2000/1066)
	7–45		1 Apr 2000 (SI 2000/1066)
6			1 Apr 2000 (SI 2000/1066)

Football (Offences and Disorder) Act 1999 (c 21)

RA: 27 Jul 1999

Commencement provisions: s 12(2)

27 Sep 1999 (s 12(2))

Greater London Authority Act 1999 (c 29)

RA: 11 Nov 1999

Commencement provisions: s 425(2); Greater London Authority Act 1999 (Commencement No 1) Order 1999, SI 1999/3271; Greater London Authority Act 1999 (Commencement No 2) Order 1999, SI 1999/3376; Greater London Authority Act 1999 (Commencement No 3 and Transitional Finance Provisions) Order 1999, SI 1999/3434; Greater London Authority Act 1999 (Commencement No 4 and Adaptation) Order 2000, SI 2000/801; Greater London Authority Act 1999 (Commencement No 5 and Appointment of Reconstitution Day) Order 2000, SI 2000/1094; Greater London Authority Act 1999 (Commencement No 6 and Preliminary Arrangements for the Metropolitan Police Authority) Order 2000, SI 2000/1095; Greater London Authority Act 1999 (Commencement No 7, Transitional Provisions and Amendment) Order 2000, SI 2000/1648; Greater London Authority Act 1999 (Commencement No 8 and Consequential Provisions) Order 2000, SI 2000/3145; Greater London Authority Act 1999 (Commencement No 9) Order 2000, SI 2000/3379; Greater London Authority Act 1999 (Commencement No 10) Order 2001, SI 2001/3603

Section

1–17	14 Dec 1999 (SI 1999/3376)
17A	Inserted by Representation of the People Act 2000, s 14(2) (qv)

Greater London Authority Act 1999 (c 29)—*contd*

Section

18–29		14 Dec 1999 (SI 1999/3376)
30	(1)–(6)	3 Jul 2000 (SI 2000/801)
	(7)	8 May 2000 (SI 2000/801)
	(8)	3 Jul 2000 (SI 2000/801)
	(9)	8 May 2000 (SI 2000/801)
	(10)	3 Jul 2000 (SI 2000/801)
31		11 Nov 1999 (for the purpose of making orders) (s 425(2))
		3 Jul 2000 (otherwise) (SI 2000/801)
32, 33		3 Jul 2000 (SI 2000/801)
34–36		8 May 2000 (SI 2000/801)
37		See Sch 4 below
38–40		8 May 2000 (SI 2000/801)
41–44		3 Jul 2000 (SI 2000/801)
45		8 May 2000 (SI 2000/801)
46–48		3 Jul 2000 (SI 2000/801)
49–59		8 May 2000 (SI 2000/801)
60–62		3 Jul 2000 (SI 2000/801)
63		*Not in force*[1]
64, 65		3 Jul 2000 (SI 2000/801)
66		8 May 2000 (SI 2000/801); prospectively repealed by Local Government Act 2000, s 107, Sch 5, para 34, Sch 6[7]
67–75		8 May 2000 (SI 2000/801)
76		3 Jul 2000 (SI 2000/801)
77	(1)–(3)	3 Jul 2000 (SI 2000/801)
	(4)	See Sch 5 below
	(5)–(7)	3 Jul 2000 (SI 2000/801)
78, 79		3 Jul 2000 (SI 2000/801)
80		8 May 2000 (SI 2000/801)
81		12 Jan 2000 (subject to transitional provisions) (SI 1999/3434)[2]
82	(1), (2)	12 Jan 2000 (subject to transitional provisions) (SI 1999/3434)[2]
	(3)	12 Jan 2000 (so far as relates to the exercise of functions by the London Fire and Civil Defence Authority in respect of the financial year beginning on 1 Apr 2000 and subsequent years) (SI 1999/3434)
		1 Jan 2001 (otherwise)[8] (SI 2000/3379)
83		12 Jan 2000 (subject to transitional provisions) (SI 1999/3434)[2]
84		3 Jul 2000 (SI 1999/3434)
85		12 Jan 2000 (subject to transitional provisions) (SI 1999/3434)[2]

Greater London Authority Act 1999 (c 29)—*contd*

Greater London Authority Act 1999 (c 29)—*contd*

Section

115⁴	(2)	3 Jul 2000 (so far as relates to financial years beginning in or after 2001) (SI 2000/801)
		Not in force (otherwise)¹
	(3)	3 Jul 2000 (SI 2000/801)
116		11 Nov 1999 (for the purpose of making regulations) (s 425(2))
		3 Jul 2000 (otherwise) (SI 2000/801)
117		8 May 2000 (SI 2000/801)
118		3 Jul 2000 (SI 2000/801)
119		11 Nov 1999 (for the purpose of making regulations) (s 425(2))
		3 Jul 2000 (otherwise) (SI 2000/801)
120, 121		3 Jul 2000 (SI 2000/801)
122–124		3 Jul 2000 (so far as relates to capital spending plans for financial years beginning in or after 2001) (SI 2000/801)
		Not in force (otherwise)¹
125		3 Jul 2000 (SI 2000/801)
126		8 May 2000 (SI 2000/801)
127		8 May 2000 (so far as applies to the Greater London Authority) (SI 1999/3434)
		Operative date⁵ (so far as applies to the Metropolitan Police Authority, and for the purposes only of SI 2000/1095, arts 5, 6, which provide for the first meeting of the Authority) (SI 2000/1095)
		3 Jul 2000 (otherwise) (SI 1999/3434)
128–133		8 May 2000 (so far as applies to the Greater London Authority) (SI 1999/3434)
		3 Jul 2000 (otherwise) (SI 1999/3434)
134		8 May 2000 (SI 1999/3434)
135		3 Jul 2000 (SI 1999/3434)
136	(1)	12 Jan 2000 (SI 1999/3434)
	(2)	See Sch 9 below
137		8 May 2000 (SI 1999/3434)
138–140		3 Jul 2000 (SI 1999/3434)
141–153		3 Jul 2000 (SI 2000/801)
154	(1)	8 May 2000 (SI 2000/801)
	(2), (3)	3 Jul 2000 (SI 2000/801)
	(4)	See Sch 10 below
155		3 Jul 2000 (SI 2000/801)
156	(1)–(7)	3 Jul 2000 (SI 2000/801)
	(8)	See Sch 11 below

Greater London Authority Act 1999 (c 29)—*contd*

Greater London Authority Act 1999 (c 29)—*contd*

Section

266—*contd*		3 Jul 2000 (otherwise) (SI 2000/801)
267–269		3 Jul 2000 (SI 2000/801)
270		See Sch 22 below
271		3 Jul 2000 (SI 2000/801)
272		12 Jan 2000 (SI 1999/3434)
273–286		3 Jul 2000 (SI 2000/801)
287	(1)	3 Jul 2000 (SI 2000/801)
	(2)	*Not in force*[6]
	(3)–(5)	3 Jul 2000 (SI 2000/801)
288		1 Apr 2000 (SI 2000/801)
289, 290		3 Jul 2000 (SI 2000/801)
291		8 May 2000 (for the purposes of enabling directions to be given under Road Traffic Regulation Act 1984, s 121B(9)) (SI 2000/801)
		3 Jul 2000 (otherwise) (SI 2000/801)
292–294		3 Jul 2000 (SI 2000/801)
295	(1)	8 May 2000 (except in relation to Transport for London) (SI 2000/801)
		3 Jul 2000 (exception noted above) (SI 2000/801)
	(2)	See Sch 23 below
	(3)	8 May 2000 (except in relation to Transport for London) (SI 2000/801)
		3 Jul 2000 (exception noted above) (SI 2000/801)
296	(1)	8 May 2000 (except in relation to Transport for London) (SI 2000/801)
		3 Jul 2000 (exception noted above) (SI 2000/801)
	(2)	See Sch 24 below
297		1 Apr 2000 (SI 2000/801)
298	(1), (2)	12 Jan 2000 (SI 1999/3434)
	(3)–(9)	3 Jul 2000 (SI 2000/801)
299, 300		3 Jul 2000 (SI 2000/801)
301, 302		*Not in force*[1]
303		1 Apr 2000 (for the purposes of s 297) (SI 2000/801)
		Not in force (otherwise)[1]
304		8 May 2000 (for the purpose only of enabling the Mayor to consult on the appointment of persons to be members of the London Development Agency) (SI 2000/801)

Greater London Authority Act 1999 (c 29)—*contd*

Greater London Authority Act 1999 (c 29)—*contd*

Section

387		8 May 2000 (for the purposes of its application to the Greater London Authority) (SI 1999/3434)
		3 Jul 2000 (other than for the purposes of sub-s (3)(b), so far as not already in force) (SI 1999/3434)
		3 Jul 2000 (otherwise) (SI 2000/801)
388		8 May 2000 (for the purposes of para (a)) (SI 1999/3434)
		3 Jul 2000 (otherwise) (SI 1999/3434)
389, 390		12 Jan 2000 (SI 1999/3434)
391		Repealed
392		8 May 2000 (for the purposes of sub-s (3)(a)) (SI 1999/3434)
		3 Jul 2000 (for the purposes of sub-s (3)(b)) (SI 1999/3434)
		3 Jul 2000 (otherwise) (SI 2000/801)
393		8 May 2000 (for the purposes of its application to the Greater London Authority) (SI 1999/3434)
		3 Jul 2000 (otherwise) (SI 1999/3434)
394		8 May 2000 (SI 2000/801)
395		3 Jul 2000 (SI 2000/801)
396	(1)–(9)	11 Nov 1999 (for the purpose of making regulations) (s 425(2))
		8 May 2000 (otherwise) (SI 2000/801)
	(10)–(12)	1 Apr 2000 (SI 2000/801)
397–400		8 May 2000 (SI 2000/801)
401		12 Jan 2000 (SI 1999/3434)
402, 403		3 Jul 2000 (SI 2000/801)
404		8 May 2000 (SI 2000/801)
405, 406		*Not in force*[1]
407		12 Jan 2000 (SI 1999/3434)
408		*Not in force*[1]
409, 410		12 Jan 2000 (SI 1999/3434)
411		*Not in force*[1]
412		12 Jan 2000 (SI 1999/3434)
413		*Not in force*[1]
414–419		12 Jan 2000 (SI 1999/3434)
420		11 Nov 1999 (s 425(2))
421, 422		12 Jan 2000 (SI 1999/3434)
423		See Sch 34 below
424		14 Dec 1999 (so far as relates to Pt I, Schs 1–3 of this Act) (SI 1999/3376)
		12 Jan 2000 (so far as not already in force and subject to transitional provisions) (SI 1999/3434)[2]
425		11 Nov 1999 (s 425(2))

Greater London Authority Act 1999 (c 29)—*contd*

Schedule

1–3		14 Dec 1999 (SI 1999/3376)
3A		Inserted by Representation of the People Act 2000, s 14(4), Sch 5 (qv)
4		8 May 2000 (SI 2000/801)
5		3 Jul 2000 (SI 2000/801)
6, 7		3 Jul 2000 (SI 1999/3434)
8		*Not in force*[1]
9		3 Jul 2000 (SI 1999/3434)
10		8 May 2000 (SI 2000/801)
11–13		3 Jul 2000 (SI 2000/801)
14, 15		*Not in force*[1]
16		3 Jul 2000 (SI 2000/801)
17, para	1–9	3 Jul 2000 (SI 2000/801)
	10	11 Nov 1999 (for the purpose of making orders) (s 425(2))
		3 Jul 2000 (otherwise) (SI 2000/801)
	11	*Not in force*
18–20		3 Jul 2000 (SI 2000/801)
21, paras	1–18	22 Jan 2001 (SI 2000/3145)
	19	7 Nov 2001 (SI 2001/3603)
22		3 Jul 2000 (SI 2000/801)
23, 24		8 May 2000 (except in relation to Transport for London) (SI 2000/801)
		Not in force (exception noted above)[1]
25		3 Jul 2000 (SI 2000/801)
26		1 Jan 2000 (for the purposes of giving effect to those parts of Police Act 1996, Schs 2A, 3 relating to the appointment of members of the Metropolitan Police Authority) (SI 1999/3271)
		Operative date[5] (for the purposes only of SI 2000/1095, arts 5, 6, which provide for the first meeting of the Metropolitan Police Authority) (SI 2000/1095)
		3 Jul 2000 (otherwise) (SI 2000/1095)
27, para	1	3 Jul 2000 (subject to a transitional provision) (save in so far as Metropolitan Police Act 1829, ss 10–12, relate to the Receiver's functions in relation to purposes other than police purposes) (SI 2000/1648)
		Not in force[1] (saving noted above)
	2	3 Jul 2000 (SI 2000/1648)

Greater London Authority Act 1999 (c 29)—*contd*

Schedule

27, para	3		3 Jul 2000 (so far as Metropolitan Police (Receiver) Act 1861, ss 1, 5, relate to the Receiver's functions in relation to police purposes) (SI 2000/1648)
			Not in force[1] (otherwise)
	4		30 Mar 2000 (subject to adaptation)[3] (SI 2000/801)
	5		3 Jul 2000 (so far as Metropolitan Police Act 1886, ss 2, 4, 6, relate to the Receiver's functions in relation to police purposes) (SI 2000/1648)
			Not in force[1] (otherwise)
	6		3 Jul 2000 (SI 2000/1648)
	7		3 Jul 2000 (so far as Metropolitan Police Act 1887 relates to the Receiver's functions in relation to police purposes) (SI 2000/1648)
			Not in force[1] (otherwise)
	8, 9		*Not in force*[1]
	10		3 Jul 2000 (SI 2000/1648)
	11		3 Jul 2000 (save in so far as Metropolitan Police Act 1899, s 1, relates to the Receiver) (SI 2000/1648)
			Not in force[1] (saving noted above)
	12		3 Jul 2000 (SI 2000/1648)
	13		3 Jul 2000 (save in so far as Crown Lands Act 1936, s 3(2), relates to the Receiver's functions in relation to purposes other than police purposes) (SI 2000/1648)
			Not in force[1] (saving noted above)
	14		*Not in force*[1]
	15–17		3 Jul 2000 (SI 2000/1648)
	18		*Not in force*[1]
	19		3 Jul 2000 (SI 2000/1648)
	20		3 Jul 2000 (subject to a transitional provision) (SI 2000/1648)
	21–28		3 Jul 2000 (SI 2000/1648)
	29		3 Jul 2000 (SI 2000/1648); prospectively repealed by Criminal Justice and Police Act 2001, s 137, Sch 7, Pt 5(1)[9]
	30–38		3 Jul 2000 (SI 2000/1648)
	39	(1)	3 Jul 2000 (SI 2000/1648)
		(2)	(a), (b) 3 Jul 2000 (SI 2000/1648)
			(c) *Not in force*[1]

Greater London Authority Act 1999 (c 29)—*contd*

Schedule

27, para	40	(1)		3 Jul 2000 (SI 2000/1648)
		(2)	(a), (b)	3 Jul 2000 (SI 2000/1648)
			(c)	*Not in force*[1]
	41–61			3 Jul 2000 (SI 2000/1648)
	62			Operative date[5] (for the purposes only of SI 2000/1095, arts 5, 6, which provide for the first meeting of the Metropolitan Police Authority) (SI 2000/1095)
				3 Jul 2000 (otherwise) (SI 2000/1095)
	63			3 Jul 2000 (SI 2000/1648); prospectively repealed by Criminal Justice and Police Act 2001, s 137, Sch 7, Pt 5(1)[9]
	64			3 Jul 2000 (except that the substitution of Local Government and Housing Act 1989, s 157(6)(f), shall not have effect in so far as it relates to the Receiver's functions in relation to purposes other than police purposes) (SI 2000/1648)
				Not in force[1] (exception noted above)
	65			3 Jul 2000 (SI 2000/1648)
	66	(a)		*Not in force*[1]
		(b)		3 Jul 2000 (subject to a transitional provision) (SI 2000/1648)
	67			3 Jul 2000 (SI 2000/1648)
	68			*Not in force*[1]
	69			1 Apr 2000 (SI 1999/3271)
	70–74			3 Jul 2000 (SI 2000/1648)
	75, 76			Operative date[5] (for the purposes only of SI 2000/1095, arts 5, 6, which provide for the first meeting of the Metropolitan Police Authority) (SI 2000/1095)
				3 Jul 2000 (otherwise) (SI 2000/1095)
	77–83			3 Jul 2000 (SI 2000/1648)
	84	(1)		1 Apr 2000 (SI 1999/3271)
		(2)		3 Jul 2000 (SI 2000/1648)
		(3)		1 Apr 2000 (SI 1999/3271)
	85–96			3 Jul 2000 (SI 2000/1648)
	97			3 Jul 2000 (subject to a transitional provision) (SI 2000/1648)
	98–104			3 Jul 2000 (SI 2000/1648)
	105			1 Apr 2000 (SI 1999/3271)

Greater London Authority Act 1999 (c 29)—*contd*

Schedule

27, para	106	1 Jan 2000 (for the purposes of giving effect to those parts of Police Act 1996, Schs 2A, 3 relating to the appointment of members of the Metropolitan Police Authority) (SI 1999/3271)
		3 Jul 2000 (otherwise) (SI 2000/1648)
	107–115	3 Jul 2000 (SI 2000/1648)
	107–109	3 Jul 2000 (SI 2000/1648)
	110, 111	Repealed
	112, 113	3 Jul 2000 (SI 2000/1648)
	114, 115	Repealed
	116	*Not in force*[1]
28		1 May 2000 (for the purpose only of nominating or appointing the first members of the Fire etc Authority) (SI 2000/1094)
		3 Jul 2000 (otherwise) (SI 2000/1094)
29		3 Jul 2000 (SI 2000/1094)
30		8 May 2000 (SI 2000/801)
31		12 Jan 2000 (SI 1999/3434)
32		*Not in force*[1]
33		12 Jan 2000 (SI 1999/3434)
34, Pt	I	12 Jan 2000 (repeals of or in Local Government Finance Act 1992, ss 39(1)(e) (in respect of the exercise of functions in relation to the financial year beginning on 1 Apr 2000 and subsequent years), 43(5A)(b) and the word "and" immediately preceding it, 46(2)(d), (3)(d), (4)) (SI 1999/3434)
		3 Jul 2000 (repeals of or in Public Works Loans Act 1965; National Loans Act 1968) (SI 1999/3434)
		1 Jan 2001 (repeals of or in Local Government Finance Act 1992, ss 39(1)(f), 65(3)) (SI 2000/3379)[8]
		Not in force (otherwise)[1]
	II	3 Jul 2000 (repeals of or in Railways Act 1993, s 2(1)) (SI 2000/801)
		Not in force (otherwise)[1]
	III, IV	3 Jul 2000 (SI 2000/801)
	V	3 Jul 2000 (except repeal of or in Private Hire Vehicles (London) Act 1998, s 38) (SI 2000/801)
		Not in force (exception noted above)[1]
	VI	3 Jul 2000 (SI 2000/801)

Greater London Authority Act 1999 (c 29)—*contd*
Schedule

34, Pt	VII	1 Apr 2000 (repeals of or in Police Act 1996, ss 1(3), 32(5), Sch 2) (SI 1999/3271)
		3 Jul 2000 (repeals of or in Metropolitan Police Act 1856; Riot (Damages) Act 1886; Police (Property) Act 1897; Police Act 1909; Crown Lands Act 1936, ss 1, 3(1); Local Government Act 1948; Metropolitan Magistrates' Courts Act 1959; Leasehold Reform Act 1967; Firearms Act 1968; Local Government Act 1972; Local Government Act 1974; House of Commons Disqualification Act 1975 (except entry relating to the Receiver); Northern Ireland Assembly Disqualification Act 1975 (except entry relating to the Receiver); Local Government, Planning and Land Act 1980; Aviation Security Act 1982; Insurance Companies Act 1982; Road Traffic Regulation Act 1984; Rates Act 1984; Local Government Finance Act 1988; Road Traffic Act 1988; Police Act 1996, ss 22, 25, 26, 28, 29, 32(3), 33, 44, 55, 65, 93, 95, 96, 101, Sch 6; Police (Insurance of Voluntary Assistants) Act 1997; Police Act 1997) (SI 2000/1648)
		Not in force (otherwise)[1]
	VIII	3 Jul 2000 (SI 2000/1094)
	IX	3 Jul 2000 (repeals of or in Local Government Act 1974, s 25(1)) (SI 2000/801)
		Not in force (otherwise)[1]

[1]   But, note that any power of a Minister of the Crown to make regulations or an order under this Act comes into force on 11 Nov 1999 (s 425(2))

[2]   The transitional provisions are set out in the Greater London Authority Act 1999 (Commencement No 3 and Transitional Finance Provisions) Order 1999, SI 1999/3434, Sch 1, Tables 1, 2. The transitional provisions in Tables 1, 2 modify certain provisions of this Act with effect for the financial year beginning on 1 Apr 2000 and the exercise before 3 Jul 2000 or 3 Apr 2001 respectively of functions under those provisions, or under any provisions modified by any of those provisions

[3]   For the adaptation to this provision, see SI 2000/801, art 3

[4]   Ss 113, 115 are modified by SI 2000/862, in relation to the financial year beginning in 2000

Greater London Authority Act 1999 (c 29)—*contd*

5   The "operative date" means the date on which appointments to the Metropolitan Police Authority are first made under Police Act 1996, Sch 2A, para 3(3) (appointment of independent members), as inserted by the Greater London Authority Act 1999, s 310(2), Sch 26

6   SI 2000/801 purported to bring s 287(2) into force on 3 Jul 2000. However SI 2000/1648, art 3, amends SI 2000/801 so as to provide that s 287(2) has not yet come into force

7   Orders made under Greater London Authority Act 2000, s 425(2), bringing the prospective repeal into force will be noted to that Act

8   For saving provisions, see SI 2000/3379, art 3

9   Orders made under the Criminal Justice and Police Act 2001, s 138, bringing the prospective repeals into force will be noted to that Act

---

Health Act 1999 (c 8)

RA: 30 Jun 1999

Commencement provisions: s 67; Health Act 1999 (Commencement No 1) Order 1999, SI 1999/2177; Health Act 1999 (Commencement No 2) Order 1999, SI 1999/2342; Health Act 1999 (Commencement No 3) Order 1999, SI 1999/2540; Health Act 1999 (Commencement No 4) Order 1999, SSI 1999/90; Health Act 1999 (Commencement No 5) Order 1999, SI 1999/2793; Health Act 1999 (Commencement No 6) (Scotland) Order 1999, SSI 1999/115; Health Act 1999 (Commencement No 1) (Wales) Order 1999, SI 1999/3184; Health Act 1999 (Commencement No 7) (Scotland) Order 2000, SSI 2000/38; Health Act 1999 (Commencement No 8) Order 2000, SI 2000/779; Health Act 1999 (Commencement No 9) Order 2000, SI 2000/1041; Health Act 1999 (Commencement No 2) (Wales) Order 2000, SI 2000/1026; Health Act 1999 (Commencement No 3) (Wales) Order 2000, SI 2000/2991; Health Act 1999 (Commencement No 10) Order 2001, SI 2001/270; Health Act 1999 (Commencement No 11) Order 2001, SI 2001/1985

Section		
1		1 Oct 1999 (E) (SI 1999/2540)
		1 Apr 2000 (W) (SI 2000/1026)
2	(1)	8 Sep 1999 (E) (so far as relates to National Health Service Act 1977, s 16A(4), (5), (6), Sch 5A, paras 20(2), (3), 23(3)) (SI 1999/2342)
		4 Jan 2000 (E) (otherwise) (SI 1999/2342)
		Not in force (W)
	(2)	See Sch 1 below
3		1 Apr 2000 (E) (for the purposes of the financial year 2000–2001 and subsequent financial years) (SI 1999/2342)
		Not in force (W)
4	(1)	1 Sep 1999 (E) (so far as it inserts National Health Service Act 1977, Sch 12A, paras 1–3, 7, except in so far as para 7(3) relates to a Primary Care Trust) (SI 1999/2342)

Health Act 1999 (c 8)—*contd*

Section

4	(1)—*contd*		1 Apr 2000 (E) (otherwise, except that the provisions of National Health Service Act 1977, Sch 12A, relating to Primary Care Trusts are brought into force only for the purposes of the financial year 2000–2001 and subsequent financial years) (SI 1999/2342)
			Not in force (E) (exception noted above)
			Not in force (W)
	(2)	(a), (b)	1 Sep 1999 (E) (SI 1999/2342)
			Not in force (W)
		(c)	1 Sep 1999 (E) (so far as it relates to the provisions in s 4(1) brought into force on 1 Sep 1999 by SI 1999/2342) (SI 1999/2342)
			1 Apr 2000 (E) (otherwise, except that the provisions of National Health Service Act 1977, Sch 12A, relating to Primary Care Trusts are brought into force only for the purposes of the financial year 2000–2001 and subsequent financial years) (SI 1999/2342)
			Not in force (E) (exception noted above)
			Not in force (W)
	(3)		1 Sep 1999 (E) (SI 1999/2342)
			Not in force (W)
	(4)		1 Sep 1999 (E) (so far as it relates to the provisions of s 4 brought into force on 1 Sep 1999 by SI 1999/2342) (SI 1999/2342)
			1 Apr 2000 (E) (otherwise, except that the provisions of National Health Service Act 1977, Sch 12A, relating to Primary Care Trusts are brought into force only for the purposes of the financial year 2000–2001 and subsequent financial years) (SI 1999/2342)
			Not in force (E) (exception noted above)
			Not in force (W)
5			4 Jan 2000 (E) (except that the references in National Health Service Act 1977, s 18A to arrangements made under s 28C of

Health Act 1999 (c 8)—*contd*
Section

5—*contd*		the 1977 Act are brought into force for the purposes only of pilot schemes under National Health Service (Primary Care) Act 1997, Pt I) (SI 1999/2342)
		Not in force (E) (exception noted above)
		Not in force (W)
6	(1)	4 Jan 2000 (E) (SI 1999/2342)
		Not in force (W)
	(2)	*Not in force*
7		4 Jan 2000 (E) (SI 1999/2342)
		Not in force (W)
8		1 Sep 1999 (E) (SI 1999/2342)
		Not in force (W)
9		1 Apr 2000 (E) (SI 1999/2793)
		1 Apr 2000 (W) (SI 2000/1041)
10		*Not in force*
11		1 Sep 1999 (E) (except that the references in National Health Service Act 1977, s 44(3) to arrangements made under s 28C of the 1977 Act are brought into force for the purposes only of pilot schemes under National Health Service (Primary Care) Act 1997, Pt I) (SI 1999/2342)
		Not in force (E) (exception noted above)
		1 Apr 2000 (W) (except that the references in National Health Service Act 1977, s 44(3) to arrangements made under s 28C of the 1977 Act are brought into force for the purposes only of pilot schemes under National Health Service (Primary Care) Act 1997, Pt I) (SI 2000/1026)
		Not in force (W) (exception noted above)
12	(1)	1 Sep 1999 (E) (so far as it substitutes National Health Service Act 1977, ss 16D, 17, except in so far as they relate to Primary Care Trusts and s 28 of the 1977 Act) (SI 1999/2342)
		1 Dec 1999 (W) (so far as it substitutes National Health Service Act 1977, ss 16D, 17, except in so far as they relate to Primary Care Trusts, and s 28 of the 1977 Act) (SI 1999/3184)

Health Act 1999 (c 8)—*contd*
Section

12	(1)—*contd*	4 Jan 2000 (E) (otherwise) (SI 1999/2342)
		Not in force (W) (otherwise)
	(2)	1 Sep 1999 (E) (SI 1999/2342)
		1 Dec 1999 (W) (SI 1999/3184)
		Prospectively repealed by Health and Social Care Act 2001, s 67, Sch 6, Pt 1[2]
	(3), (4)	1 Sep 1999 (E) (so far as relates to s 12(1)) (SI 1999/2342)
		1 Dec 1999 (W) (so far as relates to s 12(1)) (SI 1999/3184)
		4 Jan 2000 (E) (otherwise) (SI 1999/2342)
		Not in force (W) (otherwise)
	(5)	1 Sep 1999 (E) (SI 1999/2342)
		1 Dec 1999 (W) (SI 1999/3184)
13, 14		1 Oct 1999 (E) (SI 1999/2540)
		1 Nov 1999 (W) (SI 1999/3184)
15–17		1 Sep 1999 (E) (SI 1999/2342)
		1 Nov 1999 (W) (SI 1999/3184)
18		1 Nov 1999 (E) (except so far as relates to Primary Care Trusts) (SI 1999/2793)
		1 Nov 1999 (W) (except so far as relates to Primary Care Trusts) (SI 1999/3184)
		4 Jan 2000 (E) (exception noted above) (SI 1999/2793)
		Not in force (W) (exception noted above)
19		1 Nov 1999 (SI 1999/2793)
20		1 Nov 1999 (E, W) (except so far as relates to Primary Care Trusts) (SI 1999/2793)
		4 Jan 2000 (E) (otherwise) (SI 1999/2793)
		Not in force (W) (exception noted above)
21		4 Jan 2000 (E) (SI 1999/2793)
		1 Apr 2000 (W) (SI 2000/1041)
22		*Not in force*
23–25		1 Nov 1999 (SI 1999/2793)
26		1 Apr 2000 (E) (SI 1999/2793)
		1 Dec 2000 (W) (except so far as relates to Primary Care Trusts) (SI 2000/2991)
		Not in force (W) (otherwise)

Health Act 1999 (c 8)—*contd*

Section

27			1 Apr 2000 (E) (SI 1999/2793)
			1 Dec 2000 (W) (except so far as National Health Service Act 1977, s 22(1A) relates to Primary Care Trusts) (SI 2000/2991)
			Not in force (W) (otherwise)
28			1 Nov 1999 (W) (except so far as relates to Primary Care Trusts (SI 1999/3184)
			1 Apr 2000 (E) (SI 1999/2793)
			Not in force (W) (exception noted above)
29	(1)		1 Nov 1999 (E) (so far as relates to s 29(2)(a), (3) below) (SI 1999/2793)
			1 Apr 2000 (E) (otherwise) (SI 1999/2793)
			1 Dec 2000 (W) (so far as relates to s 29(2)(a), (3)) (SI 2000/ 2991)
			Not in force (W) (otherwise)
	(2)	(a)	1 Nov 1999 (E) (SI 1999/2793)
			1 Dec 2000 (W) (except so far as National Health Service Act 1977, s 28A(2B) relates to Primary Care Trusts) (SI 2000/ 2991)
			Not in force (W) (otherwise)
		(b)	1 Apr 2000 (E) (SI 1999/2793)
			Not in force (W)
	(3)		1 Nov 1999 (E) (SI 1999/2793)
			1 Dec 2000 (W) (so far as relates to s 29(2)(a)) (SI 2000/ 2991)
			Not in force (W) (otherwise)
30			1 Apr 2000 (E) (SI 1999/2793)
			1 Dec 2000 (W) (except so far as National Health Service Act 1977, s 28BB(2) relates to Primary Care Trusts) (SI 2000/2991)
			Not in force (W) (otherwise)
31			1 Apr 2000 (E) (SI 1999/2793)
			1 Dec 2000 (W) (except so far as relates to Primary Care Trusts) (SI 2000/2991)
			Not in force (W) (otherwise)
32			1 Apr 2000 (E) (SI 1999/2793)
			1 Jan 2001 (W) (SI 2000/2991)
33	(1)–(6)		1 Sep 1999 (except in so far as relates to s 35) (SI 1999/2177)
			Not in force (exception noted above)
	(7), (8)		*Not in force*

Health Act 1999 (c 8)—*contd*

Section

34		3 Aug 1999 (for the purpose only of consulting the industry body) (SI 1999/2177)
		1 Nov 1999 (otherwise) (SI 1999/2177)
35		*Not in force*
36		3 Aug 1999 (for the purpose only of consulting the industry body and so far as relates to the introduction of a limit under s 34) (SI 1999/2177)
		Not in force (otherwise)
37	(1)–(9)	3 Aug 1999 (for the purpose only of consulting the industry body) (SI 1999/2177)
		1 Nov 1999 (otherwise) (SI 1999/2177)
	(10)	3 Aug 1999 (for the purpose only of consulting the industry body) (SI 1999/2177)
		Not in force (otherwise)
38	(1)–(4)	1 Sep 1999 (so far as relates to the exercise of any power conferred by s 33(6)) (SI 1999/2177)
		1 Nov 1999 (so far as relates to the exercise of any power conferred by ss 34, 37) (SI 1999/2177)
		Not in force (otherwise)
	(5)	1 Sep 1999 (so far as relates to the exercise of any power conferred by s 33(6)) (SI 1999/2177)
		1 Nov 1999 (otherwise) (SI 1999/2177)
	(6)	3 Aug 1999 (for the purpose only of consulting the industry body, except in so far as relates to ss 33, 35) (SI 1999/2177)
		1 Sep 1999 (so far as relates to the exercise of any power conferred by s 33(6)) (SI 1999/2177)
		1 Nov 1999 (so far as relates to the exercise of any power conferred by ss 34, 37) (SI 1999/2177)
		Not in force (otherwise)
	(7), (8)	1 Sep 1999 (so far as relates to the exercise of any power conferred by s 33(6)) (SI 1999/2177)
		1 Nov 1999 (so far as relates to the exercise of any power conferred by ss 34, 37) (SI 1999/2177)
		Not in force (otherwise)
39		1 Nov 1999 (E) (SI 1999/2793)
		9 Feb 2001 (W) (SI 2001/270)

Health Act 1999 (c 8)—*contd*

Section

40		*Not in force*; prospectively repealed by Health and Social Care Act 2001, s 67, Sch 6, Pt 1[2]
41		1 Apr 2000 (SI 1999/2793)
42		1 Oct 1999 (SI 1999/2540)
43		1 Oct 1999 (E, W) (SI 1999/2540)
		1 Mar 2000 (S) (SSI 2000/38)
44		1 Oct 1999 (SI 1999/2540)
45–55		1 Oct 1999 (SSI 1999/90)
56		1 Mar 2000 (S) (SSI 2000/38)
57		1 Oct 1999 (SSI 1999/90)
58		*Not in force*
59		14 Oct 1999 (SSI 1999/115)
60	(1), (2)	15 Mar 2000 (SI 2000/779)
	(3)	1 Jul 1999 (repeal of Professions Supplementary to Medicine Act 1960, s 10) (s 67(3))
		11 May 2001 (so far as relates to Nurses, Midwives and Health Visitors Act 1997, s 10(5), Sch 1, para 7(4), Professions Supplementary to Medicine Act 1960, Sch 1, para 16(2) (so far as it provides that not more than one third of members of a committee appointed by the Council or a board under para 16(1) may be persons who are not members of the body appointing the committee) and Sch 2, para 1(1) (so far as it provides that, subject to sub-para (2)(b), a person shall not be eligible for membership of the investigating committee or disciplinary committee set up by a board unless he is a member of that board)) (SI 2001/1985)
		Not in force (otherwise)
	(4)	See Sch 3 below
61		*Not in force*
62–64		3 Aug 1999 (SI 1999/2177)
		1 Oct 1999 (S) (SSI 1999/90)
65	(1)	See Sch 4 below
	(2)	See Sch 5 below
66	(1)	30 Jun 1999 (s 67(4))
	(2)	1 Jul 1999 (s 67(4))
	(3)–(6)	30 Jun 1999 (s 67(4))
67–69		30 Jun 1999 (RA)

Health Act 1999 (c 8)—*contd*
Schedule

1		8 Sep 1999 (E) (so far as inserts National Health Service Act 1977, Sch 5A, paras 20(2), (3), 23(3)) SI 1999/2342)
		4 Jan 2000 (E) (otherwise, except so far as it inserts National Health Service Act 1977, Sch 5A, paras 16, 17) (SI 1999/2342)
		1 Apr 2000 (E) (otherwise, except that the provisions of National Health Service Act 1977, Sch 5A, paras 16, 17 are brought into force only for the purposes of the financial year 2000–2001 and subsequent financial years) (SI 1999/2342)
		Not in force (E) (exception noted above)
		Not in force (W)
2, paras	1–14	1 Nov 1999 (E, W) (SI 1999/2793)
	15–19	1 Nov 1999 (E, W) (SI 1999/2793)
		11 May 2001 (otherwise) (SI 2001/1985)
2A		Inserted, partly prospectively, by Health and Social Care Act 2001, s 48(4), Sch 4[2]
3		15 Mar 2000 (SI 2000/779)
4, para	1	1 Oct 1999 (S) (SSI 1999/90)
		4 Jan 2000 (E) (SI 1999/2342)
		Not in force (otherwise)
	2	1 Oct 1999 (S) (SSI 1999/90)
		Not in force (otherwise)
	3	4 Jan 2000 (E) (SI 1999/2342)
		Not in force (otherwise)
	4	See paras 5–41 below
	5	1 Dec 1999 (W) (SI 1999/3184)
		4 Jan 2000 (E) (SI 1999/2342)
	6	1 Sep 1999 (E) (SI 1999/2342)
		1 Dec 1999 (W) (SI 1999/3184)
	7	4 Jan 2000 (E) (SI 1999/2342)
		Not in force (otherwise)
	8	1 Oct 1999 (E) (so far as relates to fund-holding practices) (SI 1999/2540)
		1 Apr 2000 (W) (so far as relates to fund-holding practices) (SI 2000/1026)
		Not in force (otherwise)

Health Act 1999 (c 8)—*contd*

Schedule

4, para	9			1 Sep 1999 (E) (so far as substitutes National Health Service Act 1977, s 16, except in so far as relates to Primary Care Trusts) (SI 1999/2342)
				1 Dec 1999 (W) (so far as substitutes National Health Service Act 1977, s 16, except in so far as relates to Primary Care Trusts) (SI 1999/3184)
				4 Jan 2000 (E) (otherwise) (SI 1999/2342)
				Not in force (otherwise)
	10, 11			4 Jan 2000 (E) (SI 1999/2342)
				Not in force (otherwise)
	12	(1)		See sub-paras (2), (3) below
		(2)		4 Jan 2000 (E) (SI 1999/2342)
				Not in force (otherwise)
		(3)	(a)	4 Jan 2000 (E) (SI 1999/2342)
				Not in force (otherwise)
			(b)	1 Sep 1999 (E) (SI 1999/2342)
				1 Dec 1999 (W) (SI 1999/3184)
	13			4 Jan 2000 (E) (SI 1999/2342)
				Not in force (otherwise)
	14	(1)		See sub-paras (2)–(4) below
		(2)		1 Nov 1999 (E) (SI 1999/2793)
				1 Dec 2000 (W) (SI 2000/2991)
		(3)		1 Nov 1999 (E) (SI 1999/2793)
				1 Dec 2000 (W) (so far as relates to payments made under National Health Service Act 1977 s 28A(2A)) (SI 2000/2991)
				1 Jan 2001 (W) (otherwise) (SI 2000/2991)
		(4)	(a)	1 Nov 1999 (E) (SI 1999/2793)
				1 Dec 2000 (W) (so far as relates to payments made under National Health Service Act 1977 s 28A(2A)) (SI 2000/2991)
				1 Jan 2001 (W) (otherwise) (SI 2000/2991)
			(b)	1 Nov 1999 (E) (SI 1999/2793)
				1 Dec 2000 (W) (SI 2000/2991)
			(c), (d)	1 Apr 2000 (E) (SI 1999/2793)
				1 Jan 2001 (W) (SI 2000/2991)
			(e)	1 Nov 1999 (E) (so far as relates to payments made under section National Health Service Act 1977, s 28A(2A)) (SI 1999/2793)
				1 Apr 2000 (E) (otherwise) (SI 1999/2793)

Health Act 1999 (c 8)—*contd*
Schedule

4, para			
14		(e)—*contd*	1 Dec 2000 (W) (so far as relates to payments made under National Health Service Act 1977 s 28A(2A)) (SI 2000/2991)
			1 Jan 2001 (W) (otherwise) (SI 2000/2991)
15			1 Oct 1999 (E) (SI 1999/2540)
			1 Dec 1999 (W) (SI 1999/3184)
16			4 Jan 2000 (E) (SI 1999/2540)
			Not in force (otherwise)
17–22			*Not in force*; prospectively repealed by Health and Social Care Act 2001, s 67, Sch 6, Pt 1[2]
23			4 Jan 2000 (E) (SI 1999/2342)
			Not in force (otherwise)
24			1 Sep 1999 (E) (SI 1999/2342)
			1 Apr 2000 (W) (SI 2000/1026)
25			4 Jan 2000 (E) (SI 1999/2342)
			Not in force (otherwise)
26			1 Sep 1999 (E) (SI 1999/2342)
			1 Dec 1999 (W) (SI 1999/3184)
27	(a)		1 Oct 1999 (E) (except so far as substitutes National Health Service Act 1977, s 91(3)(b)–(d), in so far as those paras relate to NHS trusts) (SI 1999/2540)
			4 Jan 2000 (E) (exception noted above) (SI 1999/2342)
			1 Apr 2000 (W) (except so far as substitutes National Health Service Act 1977, s 91(3)(b)–(d), in so far as those paras relate to Primary Care Trusts) (SI 2000/1026)
			Not in force (otherwise)
	(b)		1 Apr 2000 (E) (SI 1999/2793)
			Not in force (otherwise)
28, 29			4 Jan 2000 (E) (SI 1999/2342)
			Not in force (otherwise)
30	(1)		See sub-paras (2)–(4) below
	(2)		1 Sep 1999 (E) (SI 1999/2342)
			1 Dec 1999 (W) (SI 1999/3184)
	(3), (4)		4 Jan 2000 (E) (SI 1999/2342)
			Not in force (otherwise)
31	(1)		See sub-paras (2)–(4) below
	(2)		1 Apr 2000 (E) (SI 1999/2342)
			Not in force (otherwise)
	(3)		1 Sep 1999 (E) (SI 1999/2342)
			1 Dec 1999 (W) (SI 1999/3184)

Health Act 1999 (c 8)—*contd*

Schedule

4, para	31	(4)		1 Apr 2000 (E) (SI 1999/2342)
				Not in force (otherwise)
	32			1 Sep 1999 (E) (SI 1999/2342)
				1 Dec 1999 (W) (SI 1999/3184)
	33			1 Apr 2000 (E) (for the purposes of the financial year 2000–2001 and subsequent financial years) (SI 1999/2342)
				Not in force (otherwise)
	34	(a)		4 Jan 2000 (E) (SI 1999/2342)
				Not in force (otherwise)
		(b)		1 Sep 1999 (E) (SI 1999/2342)
				1 Dec 1999 (W) (SI 1999/3184)
	35			1 Apr 2000 (E) (SI 1999/2342)
				Not in force (otherwise)
	36			1 Nov 1999 (E) (SI 1999/2793)
				Not in force (otherwise)
	37	(1)		See sub-paras (2)–(6) below
		(2), (3)		4 Jan 2000 (E) (SI 1999/2342)
				Not in force (otherwise)
		(4)		1 Sep 1999 (E) (so far as relates to the substitution of National Health Service Act1977, ss 16D, 17) (SI 1999/2342)
				1 Dec 1999 (W) (so far as relates to the substitution of National Health Service Act 1977, ss 16D, 17) (SI 1999/3184)
				4 Jan 2000 (E) (otherwise) (SI 1999/2342)
				Not in force (otherwise)
		(5), (6)		1 Sep 1999 (E) (SI 1999/2342)
				1 Nov 1999 (W) (SI 1999/3184)
	38	(1)		See sub-paras (2), (3) below
		(2)	(a)	4 Jan 2000 (E) (SI 1999/2342)
				Not in force (otherwise)
			(b)	1 Apr 2000 (E, W) (SI 1999/2793)
			(c)	4 Jan 2000 (E) (SI 1999/2342)
				Not in force (otherwise)
			(d)	1 Apr 2000 (E, W) (SI 1999/2793)
		(3)		1 Sep 1999 (E) (so far as inserts National Health Service Act 1977, s 128(1A), except in so far as that subsection relates to s 17A of the 1977 Act and Primary Care Trusts) (SI 1999/2342)

Health Act 1999 (c 8)—*contd*

Schedule

4, para	38	(3)—*contd*	1 Dec 1999 (W) (so far as inserts National Health Service Act 1977, s 128(1A), except in so far as that subsection relates to s 17A of the 1977 Act and Primary Care Trusts) (SI 1999/3184)
			4 Jan 2000 (E) (otherwise) (SI 1999/2342)
			Not in force (otherwise)
	39		1 Sep 1999 (E) (SI 1999/2342)
			1 Dec 1999 (W) (SI 1999/3184)
	40		4 Jan 2000 (E) (SI 1999/2342)
			Not in force (otherwise)
	41		*Not in force*; prospectively repealed by Health and Social Care Act 2001, s 67, Sch 6, Pt 1[2]
	42–47		1 Oct 1999 (SSI 1999/90)
			Not in force (otherwise)
	48–53		*Not in force*
	54–63		1 Oct 1999 (SSI 1999/90)
			Not in force (otherwise)
	64		*Not in force*
	65–69		1 Apr 2000 (E, W) (SI 1999/2793)
	70		1 Oct 1999 (SSI 1999/90)
			Not in force (otherwise)
	71	(a), (b)	1 Oct 1999 (E) (except so far as inserts Hospital Complaints Procedure Act 1985, s 1(1B), and s 1(1C) in so far as it relates to s 1(1B)) (SI 1999/2540)
			1 Oct 1999 (S) (SSI 1999/90)
			4 Jan 2000 (E) (exception noted above) (SI 1999/2342)
			1 Apr 2000 (W) (SI 2000/1026)
		(c)	1 Oct 1999 (E) (except so far as inserts Hospital Complaints Procedure Act 1985, s 1(1B), and s 1(1C) in so far as it relates to s 1(1B)) (SI 1999/2540)
			1 Oct 1999 (S) (SSI 1999/90)
			4 Jan 2000 (E) (exception noted above) (SI 1999/2342)
			Not in force (otherwise)
	72		1 Apr 2000 (E) (SI 1999/2793)
			1 Jan 2001 (W) (SI 2000/2991)
	73		1 Apr 2000 (E, W) (SI 1999/2342)
			11 May 2001 (otherwise) (SI 2001/1985)

Health Act 1999 (c 8)—*contd*
Schedule

4, para	74			See paras 75–84 below
	75			1 Sep 1999 (E) (SI 1999/2342)
				1 Dec 1999 (W) (SI 1999/3184)
	76	(a)	(i)	4 Jan 2000 (E, W) (SI 1999/2342)
			(ii)	1 Nov 1999 (E, W) (SI 1999/2793)
		(b)		1 Sep 1999 (E) (SI 1999/2342)
				1 Dec 1999 (W) (SI 1999/3184)
	77, 78			4 Jan 2000 (E) (SI 1999/2342)
				Not in force (otherwise)
	79	(1)		See sub-paras (2)–(4) below
		(2)	(a)	1 Nov 1999 (W) (SI 1999/3184)
				1 Apr 2000 (E) (SI 1999/2342)
			(b)	1 Apr 2000 (E) (SI 1999/2342)
				Not in force (otherwise)
			(c)	1 Nov 1999 (W) (SI 1999/3184)
				1 Apr 2000 (E) (SI 1999/2342)
		(3), (4)		1 Apr 2000 (E) (SI 1999/2342)
				Not in force (otherwise)
	80			*Not in force*
	81	(1)		See sub-paras (2), (3) below
		(2)	(a)	4 Jan 2000 (E) (SI 1999/2342)
				Not in force (otherwise)
			(b)	1 Nov 1999 (E, W) (SI 1999/2793)
		(3)		4 Jan 2000 (E) (SI 1999/2342)
				Not in force (otherwise)
	82			1 Apr 2000 (E, W) (SI 1999/2342)
	83	(1)		See sub-paras (2)–(7) below
		(2)		4 Jan 2000 (E) (SI 1999/2342)
				Not in force (otherwise)
		(3)		1 Oct 1999 (S) (SSI 1999/90)
				4 Jan 2000 (E) (SI 1999/2342)
				Not in force (otherwise)
		(4)		1 Sep 1999 (E) (SI 1999/2342)
				1 Oct 1999 (S) (SSI 1999/90)
				1 Dec 1999 (W) (subject to a saving)[1] (SI 1999/3184)
		(5)		4 Jan 2000 (E) (SI 1999/2342)
				Not in force (otherwise)
		(6)		1 Oct 1999 (E) (SI 1999/2540)
				1 Apr 2000 (W) (SI 2000/1026)
		(7)		4 Jan 2000 (E) (SI 1999/2342)
				Not in force (otherwise)
	84			1 Sep 1999 (E) (SI 1999/2342)
				1 Apr 2000 (W) (SI 2000/1026)
	85	(1)		See sub-paras (2)–(4) below
		(2)	(a)	4 Jan 2000 (E, W) (SI 1999/2342)
				Not in force (otherwise)
			(b)	*Not in force*
		(3)		1 Oct 1999 (E) (SI 1999/2540)

Health Act 1999 (c 8)—*contd*

Schedule

4, para	85	(3)—*contd*	1 Oct 1999 (S) (SSI 1999/90)
			Not in force (otherwise)
		(4)	1 Oct 1999 (E) (SI 1999/2540)
			1 Oct 1999 (S) (SSI 1999/90)
			1 Apr 2000 (W) (SI 2000/1026)
	86		1 Apr 2000 (E, W) (SI 1999/2342)
			11 May 2001 (otherwise)
			(SI 2001/1985)
	87		4 Jan 2000 (E) (SI 1999/2342)
			Not in force (otherwise)
	88	(1)	See sub-paras (2)–(6) below
		(2)–(4)	1 Oct 1999 (S) (SSI 1999/90)
			4 Jan 2000 (E) (SI 1999/2342)
			Not in force (otherwise)
		(5)	1 Sep 1999 (E) (SI 1999/2342)
			1 Oct 1999 (S) (SSI 1999/90)
			1 Dec 1999 (W) (SI 1999/3184)
		(6)	1 Oct 1999 (E) (SI 1999/2540)
			1 Oct 1999 (S) (SSI 1999/90)
			Not in force (otherwise)
	89		4 Jan 2000 (E) (SI 1999/2342)
			Not in force (otherwise)
	90		1 Oct 1999 (E) (SI 1999/2540)
			1 Apr 2000 (W) (SI 2000/1026)
			Not in force (otherwise)
5			1 Jul 1999 (repeal of Professions Supplementary to Medicine Act 1960, s 10) (s 67(3))

1 Oct 1999 (E) (repeals of or in National Health Service Act 1977, ss 15(1B)–(1D) (so far as relates to fund-holding practices), 28E(4), 98(2B), 128(1) (so far as relates to the definition "fund-holding practice"); National Health Service and Community Care Act 1990, ss 4(2)(f), 14–17, 18(2), 20(2)(b); Health Service Commissioners Act 1993, ss 3(1B), 19; Health Authorities Act 1995, Sch 1, paras 6(c), (d), 50(c), 58(b), 73–76, Sch 2, para 13(5); Health Service Commissioners (Amendment) Act 1996, Sch 1, para 6(2), (7); National Health Service (Primary Care) Act 1997, ss 14, 19, Sch 2, paras 4(3), (4) (so far as relates to fund-holding practices), 65(3)–(7); Audit Commission Act 1998) (SI 1999/2540)

Health Act 1999 (c 8)—*contd*
Schedule
5—*contd*

1 Oct 1999 (S) (repeals of or in
National Health Service Act 1966,
s 10; Local Government (Scotland)
Act 1973, s 97(2)(a)(iii), (2A), (2B)
(the definitions "recognised fund-
holding practice" , "allotted sum");
National Health Service (Scotland)
Act 1978, ss 12E(5), (6), 17A(2)(d),
(j), (3)(a) and the word "and"
following it, 17E(4), 86(1A), (1C),
(5), 87A--87D, Sch 7A, paras 6(2),
16(c) (the words from "which
purposes shall include" to the end),
para 22(1) (the words "or Health
Authority" and in sub-para (c), the
words following "Health Board"),
23, Sch 7B, paras 1(3)--(5), 3(2),
5(2), Sch 16, para 22; Hospital
Complaints Procedure Act 1985,
s 1(1) (the words from "under" to
"functions)" and the words "for
the management of"), (1A) (the
words "for the management of");
Health Service Commissioners
Act 1993, ss 3(1B), 19 (the
definitions "allotted sum",
"recognised fund-holding
practice"); National Health Service
(Primary Care) Act 1997, ss 14, 19)
(SSI 1999/90)
1 Nov 1999 (repeal of National
Health Service and Community
Care Act 1990, ss 62, 65(2) (so far
as it relates to the repeal of s 62)
(SI 1999/2793)
1 Nov 1999 (E, W) (repeal of Health
Service Commissioners Act 1993,
s 15) (SI 1999/2793)
1 Apr 2000 (E, W) (repeal of or in
National Health Service Act 1977,
ss 91(4), 128(1) (so far as it relates
to the definition "special
hospital"); Mental Health
Act 1983) (SI 1999/2793)
1 Apr 2000 (E, W) (repeals of or in
National Health Service Act 1977,
ss 8(4), 13, 27(3), 44(1)(a), (b),
45(2), 65(3), 86(b), 96A(5)(b),
97(7), 97A(5), 99(3), s 15(1B)–(1D)

Health Act 1999 (c 8)—*contd*
Schedule
5—*contd*

(in relation to "fund-holding
practices" only, so far as not
already in force), ss 28E(4), 98(2B),
128(1) (so far as not already in
force), Sch 5, para 10(3); Hospital
Complaints Procedure Act 1985,
s 1(1), (1A); National Health
Service and Community Care
Act 1990, ss 4, 14–17, 18(2),
20(2)(b) (so far as not already in
force), ss 5(1), 8(1), 9(5), (6),
Sch 2, paras 6, 19, 20, Sch 3,
paras 1(3)–(5), 3(3), 5(2); Health
Service Commissioners Act 1993,
ss 3(1B), 19 (so far as not already in
force), 15; Health Authorities
Act 1995, Sch 1, paras 4, 6(c), (d),
50(c), 58(b), 73–76, 85(d), Sch 2,
para 13(5) (so far as not already in
force); Health Service
Commissioners (Amendment)
Act 1996, Sch 1, para 6(2), (7) (so
far as not already in force);
National Health Service (Primary
Care) Act 1997, ss 14, 19 (so far as
not already in force), Sch 2, paras 4
(in relation to "fund-holding
practices" only, so far as not
already in force), para 65(3)–(7);
Audit Commission Act 1998,
ss 6(3), 53(1), (3), Sch 2, para 3 (so
far as not already in force)
(SI 2000/1041)

5 Feb 2001 (E, W) (repeals of or in
National Health Service Act 1977,
ss 22(2)–(6), 28A(4), (8)(a), 122(2);
Health Service Joint Consultative
Committee (Access to Information)
Act 1986) (SI 2001/270)

11 May 2001 (so far as relates to
Nurses, Midwives and Health
Visitors Act 1997, s 10(5), Sch 1,
para 7(4); Professions
Supplementary to Medicine
Act 1960, Sch 1, para 16(2) (so far
as it provides that not more than
one third of members of a
committee appointed by the
Council or a board under para 16(1)

Health Act 1999 (c 8)—*contd*
Schedule
5—*contd*

may be persons who are not
members of the body appointing
the committee) and Sch 2,
para 1(1) (so far as it provides that,
subject to sub-para (2)(b), a person
shall not be eligible for
membership of the investigating
committee or disciplinary
committee set up by a board unless
he is a member of that board))
(SI 2001/1985)
Not in force (otherwise)

1   For saving see SI 1999/3184 art 3

2   Orders under Health and Social Care Act 2001, s 70(2) bringing the prospective insertion and
     repeals into force will be noted to that Act

House of Lords Act 1999 (c 34)

RA: 11 Nov 1999

Commencement provision: s 5
Section
1–4	11 Nov 1999 (s 5(1))
5, 6	11 Nov 1999 (RA)
Schedule	
1, 2	11 Nov 1999 (s 5(1))

Immigration and Asylum Act 1999 (c 33)

RA: 11 Nov 1999

Commencement provisions: s 170(2)–(5); Immigration and Asylum Act 1999
(Commencement No 1) Order 1999, SI 1999/3190; Immigration and Asylum
Act 1999 (Commencement No 2 and Transitional Provisions) Order 2000,
SI 2000/168; Immigration and Asylum Act 1999 (Commencement No 3)
Order 2000, SI 2000/464; Immigration and Asylum Act 1999 (Commencement
No 4) Order 2000, SI 2000/1282; Immigration and Asylum Act 1999
(Commencement No 5 and Transitional Provisions) Order 2000, SI 2000/1985[4];
Immigration and Asylum Act 1999 (Commencement No 6, Transitional and
Consequential Provisions) Order 2000, SI 2000/2444[5]; Immigration and
Asylum Act 1999 (Commencement No 7) Order 2000, SI 2000/2698[6];
Immigration and Asylum Act 1999 (Commencement No 8 and Transitional
Provisions) Order 2000, SI 2000/3099[7]; Immigration and Asylum Act 1999
(Commencement No 9) Order 2001, SI 2001/239; Immigration and Asylum
Act 1999 (Commencement No 10) Order 2001, SI 2001/1394

Section
1, 2	14 Feb 2000 (SI 2000/168)
3	2 Oct 2000 (SI 2000/2444)[5]
4	11 Nov 1999 (s 170(3))
5	*Not in force*

Immigration and Asylum Act 1999 (c 33)—*contd*

Section

6–8		1 Mar 2000 (SI 2000/168)
9		11 Nov 1999 (s 170(3))
10	(1)–(5)	2 Oct 2000 (SI 2000/2444)[1, 5]
	(6)	22 May 2000 (SI 2000/1282)
	(7)–(9)	2 Oct 2000 (SI 2000/2444)[1, 5]
11		2 Oct 2000 (SI 2000/2444)[5]
12	(1)	22 May 2000 (for the purposes of enabling subordinate legislation to be made under it) (SI 2000/1282)
		2 Oct 2000 (otherwise) (SI 2000/2444)[5]
	(2)–(8)	2 Oct 2000 (SI 2000/2444)[5]
13		11 Dec 2000 (SI 2000/3099)
14		1 Mar 2000 (SI 2000/168)
15		11 Nov 1999 (s 170(3))
16, 17		*Not in force*
18		1 Mar 2000 (so far as conferring power to make subordinate legislation) (SI 2000/464)
		3 Apr 2000 (otherwise) (SI 2000/464)
19		3 Apr 2000 (SI 2000/464)
20, 21		1 Jan 2000 (SI 1999/3190)
22		19 Feb 2001 (for purposes of laying a draft code before Parliament and enabling subordinate legislation to be made under Asylum and Immigration Act 1996, s 8A) (SI 2001/239)
		2 May 2001 (otherwise) (SI 2001/1394)
23		2 Oct 2000 (SI 2000/2444)[5]
24		1 Jan 2001 (SI 2000/2698)
25, 26		*Not in force*
27		11 Nov 1999 (s 170(3))
28		14 Feb 2000 (SI 2000/168)
29	(1)	See sub-ss (2)–(4) below
	(2)	14 Feb 2000 (SI 2000/168)
	(3)	2 Oct 2000 (SI 2000/2444)[5]
	(4)	14 Feb 2000 (SI 2000/168)
30		14 Feb 2000 (SI 2000/168)
31		11 Nov 1999 (s 170(3))
32	(1)	3 Apr 2000 (for the purposes of clandestine entrants, within the meaning of s 32(1) of this Act, other than those who (a) within the meaning of Pt II of this Act, arrive in the United Kingdom concealed otherwise than in a vehicle, and (b) are clandestine entrants by virtue of s 32(1)(a) of this Act) (SI 2000/464)

Immigration and Asylum Act 1999 (c 33)—*contd*

Section

32	(1)—*contd*		18 Sep 2000 (for the purposes of s 39 of this Act and any regulations made under it (in addition to the purposes specified in relation to these provisions in SI 2000/464)) (SI 2000/2444)[5] *Not in force* (otherwise)
	(2)	(a)	6 Dec 1999 (so far as conferring power to make subordinate legislation) (SI 1999/3190) 3 Apr 2000 (for the purposes of clandestine entrants, within the meaning of s 32(1) of this Act, other than those who (a) within the meaning of Pt II of this Act, arrive in the United Kingdom concealed otherwise than in a vehicle, and (b) are clandestine entrants by virtue of s 32(1)(a) of this Act) (SI 2000/464) 18 Sep 2000 (for the purposes of s 39 of this Act and any regulations made under it (in addition to the purposes specified in relation to these provisions in SI 2000/464)) (SI 2000/2444)[5] *Not in force* (otherwise)
		(b)	3 Apr 2000 (for the purposes of clandestine entrants, within the meaning of s 32(1) of this Act, other than those who (a) within the meaning of Pt II of this Act, arrive in the United Kingdom concealed otherwise than in a vehicle, and (b) are clandestine entrants by virtue of s 32(1)(a) of this Act) (SI 2000/464) 18 Sep 2000 (for the purposes of s 39 of this Act and any regulations made under it (in addition to the purposes specified in relation to these provisions in SI 2000/464)) (SI 2000/2444)[5] *Not in force* (otherwise)
	(3)		6 Dec 1999 (so far as conferring power to make subordinate legislation) (SI 1999/3190)

Immigration and Asylum Act 1999 (c 33)—*contd*
Section

32	(3)—*contd*	3 Apr 2000 (for the purposes of clandestine entrants, within the meaning of s 32(1) of this Act, other than those who (a) within the meaning of Pt II of this Act, arrive in the United Kingdom concealed otherwise than in a vehicle, and (b) are clandestine entrants by virtue of s 32(1)(a) of this Act) (SI 2000/464)
		18 Sep 2000 (for the purposes of s 39 of this Act and any regulations made under it (in addition to the purposes specified in relation to these provisions in SI 2000/464)) (SI 2000/2444)[5]
		Not in force (otherwise)
	(4)–(9)	3 Apr 2000 (for the purposes of clandestine entrants, within the meaning of s 32(1) of this Act, other than those who (a) within the meaning of Pt II of this Act, arrive in the United Kingdom concealed otherwise than in a vehicle, and (b) are clandestine entrants by virtue of s 32(1)(a) of this Act) (SI 2000/464)
		18 Sep 2000 (for the purposes of s 39 of this Act and any regulations made under it (in addition to the purposes specified in relation to these provisions in SI 2000/464)) (SI 2000/2444)[5]
		Not in force (otherwise)
	(10)	6 Dec 1999 (so far as conferring power to make subordinate legislation) (SI 1999/3190)
		3 Apr 2000 (for the purposes of clandestine entrants, within the meaning of s 32(1) of this Act, other than those who (a) within the meaning of Pt II of this Act, arrive in the United Kingdom concealed otherwise than in a vehicle, and (b) are clandestine entrants by virtue of s 32(1)(a) of this Act) (SI 2000/464)

Immigration and Asylum Act 1999 (c 33)—*contd*

Section

32	(10)—*contd*	18 Sep 2000 (for the purposes of s 39 of this Act and any regulations made under it (in addition to the purposes specified in relation to these provisions in SI 2000/464)) (SI 2000/2444)[5]
		Not in force (otherwise)
33		6 Dec 1999 (SI 1999/3190)
34		3 Apr 2000 (for the purposes of clandestine entrants, within the meaning of s 32(1) of this Act, other than those who (a) within the meaning of Pt II of this Act, arrive in the United Kingdom concealed otherwise than in a vehicle, and (b) are clandestine entrants by virtue of s 32(1)(a) of this Act) (SI 2000/464)
		18 Sep 2000 (for the purposes of s 39 of this Act and any regulations made under it (in addition to the purposes specified in relation to these provisions in SI 2000/464)) (SI 2000/2444)[5]
		Not in force (otherwise)
35	(1)–(6)	3 Apr 2000 (for the purposes of clandestine entrants, within the meaning of s 32(1) of this Act, other than those who (a) within the meaning of Pt II of this Act, arrive in the United Kingdom concealed otherwise than in a vehicle, and (b) are clandestine entrants by virtue of s 32(1)(a) of this Act) (SI 2000/464)
		18 Sep 2000 (for the purposes of s 39 of this Act and any regulations made under it (in addition to the purposes specified in relation to these provisions in SI 2000/464)) (SI 2000/2444)[5]
		Not in force (otherwise)
	(7)–(9)	6 Dec 1999 (so far as conferring power to make subordinate legislation) (SI 1999/3190)
		3 Apr 2000 (for the purposes of clandestine entrants, within the meaning of s 32(1) of this Act, other than those who (a) within

Immigration and Asylum Act 1999 (c 33)—*contd*

Section

35	(7)–(9)—*contd*	the meaning of Pt II of this Act, arrive in the United Kingdom concealed otherwise than in a vehicle, and (b) are clandestine entrants by virtue of s 32(1)(a) of this Act) (SI 2000/464)
		18 Sep 2000 (for the purposes of s 39 of this Act and any regulations made under it (in addition to the purposes specified in relation to these provisions in SI 2000/464)) (SI 2000/2444)[5]
		Not in force (otherwise)
	(10)	3 Apr 2000 (for the purposes of clandestine entrants, within the meaning of s 32(1) of this Act, other than those who (a) within the meaning of Pt II of this Act, arrive in the United Kingdom concealed otherwise than in a vehicle, and (b) are clandestine entrants by virtue of s 32(1)(a) of this Act) (SI 2000/464)
		18 Sep 2000 (for the purposes of s 39 of this Act and any regulations made under it (in addition to the purposes specified in relation to these provisions in SI 2000/464)) (SI 2000/2444)[5]
		Not in force (otherwise)
36	(1)	3 Apr 2000 (for the purposes of clandestine entrants, within the meaning of s 32(1) of this Act, other than those who (a) within the meaning of Pt II of this Act, arrive in the United Kingdom concealed otherwise than in a vehicle, and (b) are clandestine entrants by virtue of s 32(1)(a) of this Act) (SI 2000/464)
		18 Sep 2000 (for the purposes of s 39 of this Act and any regulations made under it (in addition to the purposes specified in relation to these provisions in SI 2000/464)) (SI 2000/2444)[5]
		Not in force (otherwise)

Immigration and Asylum Act 1999 (c 33)—*contd*

Section

36	(2)	(a)	6 Dec 1999 (so far as conferring power to make subordinate legislation) (SI 1999/3190)

3 Apr 2000 (for the purposes of clandestine entrants, within the meaning of s 32(1) of this Act, other than those who (a) within the meaning of Pt II of this Act, arrive in the United Kingdom concealed otherwise than in a vehicle, and (b) are clandestine entrants by virtue of s 32(1)(a) of this Act) (SI 2000/464)

18 Sep 2000 (for the purposes of s 39 of this Act and any regulations made under it (in addition to the purposes specified in relation to these provisions in SI 2000/464)) (SI 2000/2444)[5]

Not in force (otherwise)

(b)   3 Apr 2000 (for the purposes of clandestine entrants, within the meaning of s 32(1) of this Act, other than those who (a) within the meaning of Pt II of this Act, arrive in the United Kingdom concealed otherwise than in a vehicle, and (b) are clandestine entrants by virtue of s 32(1)(a) of this Act) (SI 2000/464)

18 Sep 2000 (for the purposes of s 39 of this Act and any regulations made under it (in addition to the purposes specified in relation to these provisions in SI 2000/464)) (SI 2000/2444)[5]

Not in force (otherwise)

(3)–(5)   3 Apr 2000 (for the purposes of clandestine entrants, within the meaning of s 32(1) of this Act, other than those who (a) within the meaning of Pt II of this Act, arrive in the United Kingdom concealed otherwise than in a vehicle, and (b) are clandestine entrants by virtue of s 32(1)(a) of this Act) (SI 2000/464)

Immigration and Asylum Act 1999 (c 33)—*contd*

Section

36	(3)–(5)—*contd*	18 Sep 2000 (for the purposes of s 39 of this Act and any regulations made under it (in addition to the purposes specified in relation to these provisions in SI 2000/464)) (SI 2000/2444)[5]
		Not in force (otherwise)
37	(1)–(5)	3 Apr 2000 (for the purposes of clandestine entrants, within the meaning of s 32(1) of this Act, other than those who (a) within the meaning of Pt II of this Act, arrive in the United Kingdom concealed otherwise than in a vehicle, and (b) are clandestine entrants by virtue of s 32(1)(a) of this Act) (SI 2000/464)
		18 Sep 2000 (for the purposes of s 39 of this Act and any regulations made under it (in addition to the purposes specified in relation to these provisions in SI 2000/464)) (SI 2000/2444)[5]
		Not in force (otherwise)
	(6)	See Sch 1 below
38		3 Apr 2000 (SI 2000/464)
39		6 Dec 1999 (SI 1999/3190)
40	(1)–(8)	*Not in force*
	(9), (10)	6 Dec 1999 (SI 1999/3190)
	(11)–(13)	*Not in force*
41		*Not in force*
42	(1)–(7)	*Not in force*
	(8)	See Sch 1 below
43		6 Dec 1999 (SI 1999/3190)
44–55		*Not in force*
56, 57		14 Feb 2000 (subject to transitional provisions) (SI 2000/168)
58	(1)	2 Oct 2000 (SI 2000/2444)[5]
	(2)	See Sch 4 below
	(3)–(10)	2 Oct 2000 (SI 2000/2444)[5]
59		2 Oct 2000 (SI 2000/2444)[5]
60	(1)–(5)	2 Oct 2000 (SI 2000/2444)[5]
	(6)	22 May 2000 (SI 2000/1282)
	(7)–(9)	2 Oct 2000 (SI 2000/2444)[5]
	(10)	22 May 2000 (SI 2000/1282)
61–71		2 Oct 2000 (SI 2000/2444)[5]
72	(1), (2)	2 Oct 2000 (SI 2000/2444)[5]

Immigration and Asylum Act 1999 (c 33)—*contd*

Section

72	(3)		22 May 2000 (for the purposes of enabling subordinate legislation to be made under it) (SI 2000/1282)
			2 Oct 2000 (otherwise) (SI 2000/2444)[5]
73			2 Oct 2000 (SI 2000/2444)[5]
74, 75			22 May 2000 (for the purposes of enabling subordinate legislation to be made under them) (SI 2000/1282)
			2 Oct 2000 (otherwise) (SI 2000/2444)[5]
76	(1)–(5)		2 Oct 2000 (SI 2000/2444)[5]
	(6)		22 May 2000 (SI 2000/1282)
77, 78			2 Oct 2000 (SI 2000/2444)[5]
79			*Not in force*
80			22 May 2000 (SI 2000/1282)
81			2 Oct 2000 (SI 2000/2444)[5]
82			22 May 2000 (SI 2000/1282)
83	(1)–(3)		22 May 2000 (SI 2000/1282)
	(4)		See Sch 5 below
	(5)		22 May 2000 (so far as relates to the regulatory functions set out in Sch 5, paras 1(1), (2), (4), 2(1)–(4), (6)–(8), 3(1)–(3), (5)–(7), 4, 5(1)–(3), 6(1), 11–25) (SI 2000/1282)
			30 Oct 2000 (otherwise) (SI 2000/1985)
	(6), (7)		22 May 2000 (SI 2000/1282)
84	(1)		30 Apr 2001 (SI 2001/1394)
	(2)	(a), (b)	30 Oct 2000 (so far as relates to the provisions of s 85 below as commenced by this order) (SI 2000/1985)
			30 Apr 2001 (otherwise) (SI 2001/1394)
		(c)–(f)	30 Apr 2001 (SI 2001/1394)
	(3)		30 Apr 2001 (SI 2001/1394)
	(4)	(a)	30 Oct 2000 (so far as to enable the Commissioner to certify a person as exempt under it) (SI 2000/1985)
			30 Apr 2001 (otherwise) (SI 2001/1394)
		(b), (c)	30 Apr 2001 (SI 2001/1394)
		(d)	30 Oct 2000 (so far as conferring power to make subordinate legislation) (SI 2000/1985)
			30 Apr 2001 (otherwise) (SI 2001/1394)

Immigration and Asylum Act 1999 (c 33)—*contd*
Section

84	(5)	30 Oct 2000 (SI 2000/1985)
	(6)	30 Apr 2001 (SI 2001/1394)
	(7)	30 Oct 2000 (SI 2000/1985)
85	(1), (2)	30 Oct 2000 (SI 2000/1985)
	(3)	See Sch 6 below
86	(1)–(9)	22 May 2000 (SI 2000/1282)
	(10)–(12)	30 Oct 2000 (so far as conferring power to make subordinate legislation) (SI 2000/1985)
		30 Apr 2001 (otherwise) (SI 2001/1394)
87	(1)–(4)	30 Oct 2000 (SI 2000/1985)
	(5)	See Sch 7 below
88, 89		30 Oct 2000 (SI 2000/1985)
90		1 Aug 2000 (so far as conferring power to make subordinate legislation) (SI 2000/1985)
		30 Apr 2001 (otherwise) (SI 2001/1394)
91, 92		30 Apr 2001 (SI 2001/1394)
93		22 May 2000 (SI 2000/1282)
94		11 Nov 1999 (s 170(3))
95	(1), (2)	1 Jan 2000 (so far as conferring power to make subordinate legislation) (SI 1999/3190)
		3 Apr 2000 (otherwise) (SI 2000/464)
	(3)–(8)	6 Dec 1999 (for the purposes of ss 116, 117(1), (2) of (and the amendments to other legislation effected by those sections), and Sch 9, para 3 to, this Act) (SI 1999/3190)
		1 Jan 2000 (so far as conferring power to make subordinate legislation) (SI 1999/3190)
		3 Apr 2000 (otherwise) (SI 2000/464)
	(9)–(11)	1 Jan 2000 (so far as conferring power to make subordinate legislation) (SI 1999/3190)
		3 Apr 2000 (otherwise) (SI 2000/464)
	(12)	1 Jan 2000 (SI 1999/3190)
	(13)	11 Nov 1999 (s 170(3))
96		3 Apr 2000 (SI 2000/464)
97		1 Jan 2000 (so far as conferring power to make subordinate legislation) (SI 1999/3190)
		3 Apr 2000 (otherwise) (SI 2000/464)
98	(1), (2)	3 Apr 2000 (SI 2000/464)

Immigration and Asylum Act 1999 (c 33)—*contd*

Section

98	(3)	1 Mar 2000 (for the purposes of enabling subordinate legislation to be made under s 95 of this Act as applied by s 98(3)) (SI 2000/464)
		3 Apr 2000 (otherwise) (SI 2000/464)
99	(1)–(3)	3 Apr 2000 (SI 2000/464)
	(4), (5)	11 Nov 1999 (s 170(3))
100–103		3 Apr 2000 (SI 2000/464)
104		1 Jan 2000 (SI 1999/3190)
105–109		11 Nov 1999 (s 170(3))
110	(1), (2)	11 Nov 1999 (s 170(3))
	(3)–(7)	3 Apr 2000 (SI 2000/464)
	(8)	11 Nov 1999 (so far as relates to sub-ss (1), (2) above) (s 170(3))
		3 Apr 2000 (otherwise) (SI 2000/464)
	(9)	6 Dec 1999 (SI 1999/3190)
111		11 Nov 1999 (s 170(3))
112, 113		3 Apr 2000 (SI 2000/464)
114		1 Jan 2000 (so far as conferring power to make subordinate legislation) (SI 1999/3190)
		3 Apr 2000 (otherwise) (SI 2000/464)
115		1 Jan 2000 (so far as conferring power to make subordinate legislation) (SI 1999/3190)[2]
		3 Apr 2000 (otherwise) (SI 2000/464)
116		6 Dec 1999 (SI 1999/3190)
117	(1), (2)	6 Dec 1999 (SI 1999/3190)
	(3), (4)	3 Apr 2000 (SI 2000/464)
	(5)	*Not in force*
	(6)	3 Apr 2000 (SI 2000/464)
118, 119		1 Jan 2000 (so far as conferring power to make subordinate legislation) (SI 1999/3190)
		1 Mar 2000 (otherwise) (SI 2000/464)
120, 121		1 Mar 2000 (for the purpose of enabling subordinate legislation to be made under s 95 of this Act as applied by any provision inserted by ss 120, 121) (SI 2000/464)
		3 Apr 2000 (otherwise) (SI 2000/464)
122		1 Mar 2000 (so far as conferring power to make subordinate legislation) (SI 2000/464)
		3 Apr 2000 (otherwise) (SI 2000/464)
123		1 Jan 2000 (so far as conferring power to make subordinate legislation) (SI 1999/3190)
		3 Apr 2000 (otherwise) (SI 2000/464)

Immigration and Asylum Act 1999 (c 33)—*contd*

Section

124			11 Nov 1999 (s 170(3))
125–127			3 Apr 2000 (SI 2000/464)
128–139			14 Feb 2000 (SI 2000/168)
140			11 Nov 1999 (s 170(3))
141–144			11 Dec 2000 (SI 2000/3099)
145			11 Nov 1999 (s 170(3))
146	(1)		11 Nov 1999 (s 170(3))
	(2)		*Not in force*
147			1 Aug 2000 (SI 2000/1985)
148	(1), (2)		2 Apr 2001 (SI 2001/239)
	(3)		1 Aug 2000 (so far as conferring power to make subordinate legislation) (SI 2000/1985)
			2 Apr 2001 (otherwise) (SI 2001/239)
	(4), (5)		*Not in force*
149	(1)		1 Aug 2000 (SI 2000/1985)
	(2)		2 Apr 2001 (SI 2001/239)
	(3)		1 Aug 2000 (SI 2000/1985)
	(4), (5)		2 Apr 2001 (SI 2001/239)
	(6)	(a)	1 Aug 2000 (SI 2000/1985)
		(b)	2 Apr 2001 (SI 2001/239)
	(7), (8)		2 Apr 2001 (SI 2001/239)
	(9)		1 Aug 2000 (SI 2000/1985)
150, 151			2 Apr 2001 (SI 2001/239)
152	(1)		2 Apr 2001 (SI 2001/239)
	(2), (3)		1 Aug 2000 (so far as conferring power to make subordinate legislation) (SI 2000/1985)
			2 Apr 2001 (SI 2001/239)
	(4), (5)		2 Apr 2001 (SI 2001/239)
153			1 Aug 2000 (so far as conferring power to make subordinate legislation) (SI 2000/1985)
			2 Apr 2001 (otherwise) (SI 2001/239)
154	(1)–(6)		*Not in force*
	(7)		See Sch 11 below
155	(1)		2 Apr 2001 (SI 2001/239)
	(2)		See Sch 12 below
156	(1)–(4)		2 Apr 2001 (SI 2001/239)
	(5)		See Sch 13 below
	(6), (7)		2 Apr 2001 (SI 2001/239)
157			1 Aug 2000 (so far as conferring power to make subordinate legislation) (SI 2000/1985)
			2 Apr 2001 (otherwise) (SI 2001/239)
158, 159			2 Apr 2001 (SI 2001/239)
160–163			1 Jan 2001 (SI 2000/2698)
164			*Not in force*

Immigration and Asylum Act 1999 (c 33)—*contd*

Section

165		22 May 2000 (for the purposes of enabling subordinate legislation to be made under Immigration Act 1971, s 31A, as inserted by this section) (SI 2000/1282)
		Not in force (otherwise)
166–168		11 Nov 1999 (s 170(3))
169	(1)	See Sch 14 below
	(2)	See Sch 15 below
	(3)	See Sch 16 below
170		11 Nov 1999 (s 170(3))

Schedule

1, para	1		3 Apr 2000 (for the purposes of s 37 of this Act) (SI 2000/464)
			Not in force (otherwise)
	2		6 Dec 1999 (SI 1999/3190)
	3, 4		3 Apr 2000 (for the purposes of s 37 of this Act) (SI 2000/464)
			Not in force (otherwise)
	5		6 Dec 1999 (SI 1999/3190)
2, 3			14 Feb 2000 (subject to transitional provisions) (SI 2000/168)
4, para	1		22 May 2000 (SI 2000/1282)
	2		2 Oct 2000 (SI 2000/2444)[5]
	3–5		14 Feb 2000 (subject to a transitional provision relating to para 5) (SI 2000/168)
	6		2 Oct 2000 (SI 2000/2444)[5]
	7		Substituted (2 Oct 2000) by Immigration (European Economic Area) Regulations 2000, SI 2000/2326, reg 29(4), Sch 2, para 3(2)
	8, 9		2 Oct 2000 (SI 2000/2444)[5]
	9A		Inserted by Race Relations (Amendment) Act 2000, s 9(1), Sch 2, para 40 (qv)
	10–24		2 Oct 2000 (SI 2000/2444)[5]
5, para	1	(1), (2)	22 May 2000 (SI 2000/1282)
		(3)	30 Oct 2000 (SI 2000/1985)
		(4)	22 May 2000 (SI 2000/1282)
	2	(1)–(4)	22 May 2000 (SI 2000/1282)
		(5)	30 Oct 2000 (SI 2000/1985)
		(6)–(8)	22 May 2000 (SI 2000/1282)
	3	(1)–(3)	22 May 2000 (SI 2000/1282)
		(4)	30 Oct 2000 (SI 2000/1985)
		(5)–(7)	22 May 2000 (SI 2000/1282)
	4		22 May 2000 (SI 2000/1282)
	5	(1)–(3)	22 May 2000 (SI 2000/1282)

Immigration and Asylum Act 1999 (c 33)—*contd*

Schedule

5, para	5	(4), (5)		30 Oct 2000 (SI 2000/1985)
	6	(1)		22 May 2000 (SI 2000/1282)
		(2), (3)		30 Oct 2000 (SI 2000/1985)
	7–10			30 Oct 2000 (SI 2000/1985)
	11–25			22 May 2000 (SI 2000/1282)
6, para	1–4			30 Oct 2000 (SI 2000/1985)
	5	(1)		1 Aug 2000 (so far as conferring power to make subordinate legislation) (SI 2000/1985)
				30 Oct 2000 (otherwise) (SI 2000/1985)
		(2)		30 Oct 2000 (SI 2000/1985)
	6			30 Oct 2000 (SI 2000/1985)
7	1–6			30 Oct 2000 (SI 2000/1985)
	7			1 Aug 2000 (SI 2000/1985)
	8	(1), (2)		30 Oct 2000 (SI 2000/1985)
		(3)		1 Aug 2000 (SI 2000/1985)
	9–13			30 Oct 2000 (SI 2000/1985)
8				1 Jan 2000 (SI 1999/3190)
9				11 Nov 1999 (s 170(3))
10				*Not in force*
11, para	1			3 Apr 2000 (SI 2000/464)
	2	(1)	(a)	1 Aug 2000 (so far as conferring power to make subordinate legislation) (SI 2000/1985)
				2 Apr 2001 (otherwise) (SI 2001/239)
			(b)	2 Apr 2001 (SI 2001/239)
		(2)–(4)		2 Apr 2001 (SI 2001/239)
	3–6			2 Apr 2001 (SI 2001/239)
	7	(1)		3 Apr 2000 (SI 2000/464)
		(2), (3)		1 Aug 2000 (so far as conferring power to make subordinate legislation) (SI 2000/1985)
				2 Apr 2001 (otherwise) (SI 2001/239)
12	1, 2			1 Aug 2000 (so far as conferring power to make subordinate legislation) (SI 2000/1985)
				2 Apr 2001 (otherwise) (SI 2001/239)
	3	(1)–(6)		2 Apr 2001 (SI 2001/239)
		(7)		1 Aug 2000 (so far as conferring power to make subordinate legislation) (SI 2000/1985)
				2 Apr 2001 (otherwise) (SI 2001/239)
	4–7			2 Apr 2001 (SI 2001/239)
13	1			2 Apr 2001 (SI 2001/239)
	2	(1)	(a)	1 Aug 2000 (so far as conferring power to make subordinate legislation) (SI 2000/1985)
				2 Apr 2001 (otherwise) (SI 2001/239)

Immigration and Asylum Act 1999 (c 33)—*contd*

Schedule

13	2	(1)	(b)	2 Apr 2001 (SI 2001/239)
		(2), (3)		2 Apr 2001 (SI 2001/239)
		(4)		1 Aug 2000 (so far as conferring power to make subordinate legislation) (SI 2000/1985)
				2 Apr 2001 (otherwise) (SI 2001/239)
		(5)		2 Apr 2001 (SI 2001/239)
	3			2 Apr 2001 (SI 2001/239)
14, para	1–32			1 Jan 2001 (SI 2000/2698)
	33–36			*Not in force*
	37–42			1 Jan 2001 (SI 2000/2698)
	43			See paras 44–70 below
	44	(1)		14 Feb 2000 (SI 2000/168)
		(2)		2 Oct 2000 (SI 2000/2444)[5]
	45			14 Feb 2000 (SI 2000/168)
	46			2 Oct 2000 (SI 2000/2444)[5]
	47, 48			*Not in force*
	49			14 Feb 2000 (so far as relates to repeal of Immigration Act 1971, s 12) (SI 2000/168)
				2 Oct 2000 (except in relation to Immigration Act 1971, s 22, so far as that section has effect for the purposes of Sch 2, para 25 to that Act) (SI 2000/2444)[5]
				Not in force (exception noted above)
	50, 51			14 Feb 2000 (SI 2000/168)
	52	(1)		See sub-paras (2), (3) below
		(2)		2 Oct 2000 (SI 2000/2444)[5]
		(3)	(a)	1 Mar 2000 (SI 2000/464)
			(b)	3 Apr 2000 (SI 2000/464)
	53			14 Feb 2000 (SI 2000/168)
	54			6 Dec 1999 (SI 1999/3190)
	55			2 Oct 2000 (SI 2000/2444)[5]
	56–60			14 Feb 2000 (SI 2000/168)
	61			11 Dec 2000 (SI 2000/3099)
	62	(1)		14 Feb 2000 (SI 2000/168)
		(2)		11 Nov 1999 (s 170(3))
		(3), (4)		14 Feb 2000 (SI 2000/168)
	63, 64			14 Feb 2000 (SI 2000/168)
	65, 66			2 Oct 2000 (SI 2000/2444)[5]
	67, 68			14 Feb 2000 (SI 2000/168)
	69, 70			2 Oct 2000 (SI 2000/2444)[5]
	71, 72			14 Feb 2000 (subject to transitional provisions) (SI 2000/168)
	73			11 Nov 1999 (s 170(3))
	74			3 Apr 2000 (SI 2000/464)
	75			*Not in force*
	76			3 Apr 2000 (SI 2000/464)

Immigration and Asylum Act 1999 (c 33)—*contd*

Schedule

14, para	77		1 Jan 2001 (SI 2000/2698)
	78, 79		11 Nov 1999 (s 170(3))
	80	(1)	See sub-paras (2)–(4) below
		(2), (3)	14 Feb 2000 (SI 2000/168)
		(4)	*Not in force*
	81, 82		11 Nov 1999 (s 170(3))
	83		See paras 84–86 below
	84		2 Oct 2000 (SI 2000/2444)[5]
	85, 86		*Not in force*
	87, 88		11 Nov 1999 (s 170(3))
	89		Repealed (*never in force*)
	90	(1)	See sub-paras (2)–(4) below
		(2), (3)	14 Feb 2000 (SI 2000/168)
		(4)	*Not in force*
	91		14 Feb 2000 (subject to transitional provisions) (SI 2000/168)
	92, 93		3 Apr 2000 (SI 2000/464)
	94		See paras 95–97 below
	95, 96		14 Feb 2000 (SI 2000/168)
	97		*Not in force*
	98		14 Feb 2000 (subject to transitional provisions) (SI 2000/168)
	99		See paras 100–107 below
	100		*Not in force*
	101		3 Apr 2000 (SI 2000/464)
	102		11 Nov 1999 (s 170(3))
	103–106		2 Oct 2000 (SI 2000/2444)[5]
	107		*Not in force*
	108		See paras 109–115 below
	109		14 Feb 2000 (SI 2000/168)
	110		1 Mar 2000 (SI 2000/464)
	111–113		3 Apr 2000 (SI 2000/464)
	114, 115		2 Oct 2000 (SI 2000/2444)[5]
	116		*Not in force*
	117		6 Dec 1999 (SI 1999/3190)
	118		See paras 119–129 below
	119		Repealed (*never in force*)
	120		2 Oct 2000 (SI 2000/2444)[5]
	121		2 Oct 2000 (so far as relates to Special Immigration Appeals Commission Act 1997, s 2A(1)–(6)) (SI 2000/2444)[5]
			Not in force (otherwise)
	122–124		2 Oct 2000 (SI 2000/2444)[5]
	125		14 Feb 2000 (SI 2000/168)
	126–128		2 Oct 2000 (SI 2000/2444)[5]
	129		1 Aug 2000 (so far as conferring power to make subordinate legislation) (SI 2000/1985)

Immigration and Asylum Act 1999 (c 33)—*contd*

Schedule

14, para	129—*contd*		2 Oct 2000 (otherwise) (SI 2000/2444)[5]
15, para	1		14 Feb 2000 (SI 2000/168)
	2		11 Nov 1999 (s 170(3))
	3		14 Feb 2000 (SI 2000/168)
	4	(a)	*Not in force*
		(b)	14 Feb 2000 (SI 2000/168)
	5, 6		6 Dec 1999 (SI 1999/3190)
	7, 8		*Not in force*
	9		6 Dec 1999 (SI 1999/3190)
	10		*Not in force*
	11, 12		2 Oct 2000 (SI 2000/2444)[1, 5]
	13		11 Nov 1999 (s 170(3))
	14		14 Feb 2000 (SI 2000/168)
16			14 Feb 2000 (repeals of or in Immigration Act 1971, ss 12, 24, 25, Sch 2, paras 21, 26, Sch 5; House of Commons Disqualification Act 1975; Northern Ireland Assembly Disqualification Act 1975; Courts and Legal Services Act 1990; Judicial Pensions and Retirement Act 1993; Asylum and Immigration Act 1996, s 7) (SI 2000/168)
			1 Mar 2000 (repeals of or in Asylum and Immigration Act 1996, s 9; Housing Act 1996, Sch 16, para 3) (SI 2000/464)
			3 Apr 2000 (repeals of or in Social Security Contributions and Benefits Act 1992; Social Security Contributions and Benefits (Northern Ireland) Act 1992; Asylum and Immigration Appeals Act 1993, ss 4, 5, Sch 1; Asylum and Immigration Act 1996, ss 10, 11) (SI 2000/464)[3]
			2 Oct 2000 (repeals of or in Immigration Act 1971, Pt II (ss 13–23), Schs 2, 3 (except s 22 of the 1971 Act, so far as that section has effect for the purposes of Sch 2, para 25 to the 1971 Act) so far as not already in force; Immigration Act 1988, s 5; Asylum and Immigration Appeals Act 1993, ss 7–11, Sch 2; Asylum and Immigration Act 1996, ss 1–3, Schs 2, 3; Special Immigration Appeals Commission Act 1997, s 7(4), Sch 2, para 5) (SI 2000/2444)[5]

Immigration and Asylum Act 1999 (c 33)—*contd*
Schedule
16—*contd*   11 Dec 2000 (repeal of Asylum and
                                          Immigration Act 1993, s 3)
                                          (SI 2000/3099)
                                          1 Jan 2001 (repeals of or in Marriage
                                          Act 1949; Family Law Reform
                                          Act 1969; Marriage (Registrar
                                          General's Licence) Act 1970)
                                          (SI 2000/2698)
                                          Not in force (otherwise)

[1]   But, note that s 10 of, and Sch 15, para 12 to, this Act come into force on the day after that on
        which the "regularisation period" ends. As to the meaning of "regularisation period", see s 9 of the
        1999 Act

[2]   Sub-ss (1), (2) of s 115 are to come into force on the day on which the first regulations made under
        Sch 8 of this Act come into force

[3]   The Queen's Printer's copy of SI 2000/464 erroneously purports to bring into force the repeal by
        Sch 16 to this Act of Asylum and Immigration Act 1996, Sch 1. Sch 16 to this Act does not repeal
        Sch 1 to the 1996 Act; Sch 1 is repealed by Sch 14, para 113 to this Act

[4]   For transitional provisions relating to the provisions brought into force by SI 2000/1985, see art 3
        of that Order

[5]   For transitional provisions relating to the provisions brought into force by SI 2000/2444, see arts 3, 4,
        Sch 2 of that Order

[6]   For transitional provisions relating to the provisions brought into force by SI 2000/2698, see
        SI 2000/3099, art 4, which inserts SI 2000/2698, art 3

[7]   For transitional provisions made by SI 2000/3099, relating to Pt IV of this Act, see art 5 of that
        Order

Local Government Act 1999 (c 27)

RA: 27 Jul 1999

Commencement provisions: s 27; Local Government Act 1999 (Commencement No 1)
    Order 1999, SI 1999/2169; Local Government Act 1999 (Commencement)
    (Wales) Order 1999, SI 1999/2815; Local Government Act 1999 (Commencement
    No 3) (England) Order 2000, SI 2000/1724
Section
1   (1)   (a), (b)   10 Aug 1999 (SI 1999/2169)[2]
                                     1 Oct 1999 (otherwise) (SI 1999/2815)[1]
                      (c)   10 Aug 1999 (SI 1999/2169)[2]
                                     27 Jul 2000 (otherwise) (s 27(1))[1]
                      (d), (e)   10 Aug 1999 (SI 1999/2169)
                      (f)   3 Jul 2000 (SI 2000/1724)[1]
                      (g)   10 Aug 1999 (SI 1999/2169)[2]
                                     1 Oct 1999 (otherwise) (SI 1999/2815)[1]
                      (h)   10 Aug 1999 (SI 1999/2169)[2]
                                     27 Jul 2000 (otherwise) (s 27(1))[1]
                      (i), (j)   3 Jul 2000 (SI 2000/1724)[1]
           (2)   (a)–(c)   10 Aug 1999 (SI 1999/2169)[2]
                                     27 Jul 2000 (otherwise) (s 27(1))[1]
                      (d)   3 Jul 2000 (SI 2000/1724)[1]

Local Government Act 1999 (c 27)—*contd*
Section

1	(3)		1 Oct 1999 (W) (SI 1999/2815)[1]
			27 Jul 2000 (otherwise) (s 27(1))[1]
	(4)	(a), (b)	10 Aug 1999 (SI 1999/2169)
		(c)	3 Jul 2000 (SI 2000/1724)[1]
	(5)	(a)	10 Aug 1999 (SI 1999/2169)[2]
			1 Oct 1999 (otherwise) (SI 1999/2815)[1]
		(b)	10 Aug 1999 (SI 1999/2169)[2]
			27 Jul 2000 (otherwise) (s 27(1))[1]
2	(1)–(3)		27 Sep 1999 (SI 1999/2169)[2]
			1 Oct 1999 (otherwise) (SI 1999/2815)[1]
	(4)		3 Jul 2000 (SI 2000/1724)[1]
	(5)		27 Sep 1999 (SI 1999/2169)[2]
			1 Oct 1999 (otherwise) (SI 1999/2815)[1]
	(6)		27 Sep 1999 (SI 1999/2169)[2]
			27 Jul 2000 (otherwise) (s 27(1))[1]
3	(1)		1 Apr 2000 (SI 1999/2169)[2]
			1 Apr 2000 (otherwise) (SI 1999/2815)[1]
	(2)–(4)		10 Aug 1999 (SI 1999/2169)[2]
			1 Oct 1999 (otherwise) (SI 1999/2815)[1]
4	(1), (2)		27 Sep 1999 (SI 1999/2169)[2]
			1 Oct 1999 (otherwise) (SI 1999/2815)[1]
	(3), (4)		10 Aug 1999 (SI 1999/2169)[2]
			1 Oct 1999 (otherwise) (SI 1999/2815)[1]
	(5)		1 Apr 2000 (SI 1999/2169)[2]
			1 Apr 2000 (otherwise) (SI 1999/2815)[1]
5	(1)		1 Apr 2000 (SI 1999/2169)[2]
			1 Apr 2000 (otherwise) (SI 1999/2815)[1]
	(2)		27 Sep 1999 (SI 1999/2169)[2]
			1 Oct 1999 (otherwise) (SI 1999/2815)[1]
	(3)		1 Apr 2000 (SI 1999/2169)[2]
			1 Apr 2000 (otherwise) (SI 1999/2815)[1]
	(4)–(7)		27 Sep 1999 (SI 1999/2169)[2]
			1 Oct 1999 (otherwise) (SI 1999/2815)[1]
6			27 Sep 1999 (SI 1999/2169)[2]
			1 Oct 1999 (otherwise) (SI 1999/2815)[1]
7			1 Apr 2000 (SI 1999/2169)[2]
			1 Apr 2000 (otherwise) (SI 1999/2815)[1]
8	(1)		1 Apr 2000 (SI 1999/2169)[2]
			1 Apr 2000 (otherwise) (SI 1999/2815)[1]
	(2)–(7)		27 Sep 1999 (SI 1999/2169)[2]
			1 Oct 1999 (otherwise) (SI 1999/2815)[1]
9			1 Apr 2000 (SI 1999/2169)[2]
			1 Apr 2000 (otherwise) (SI 1999/2815)[1]
10	(1)–(3)		1 Apr 2000 (SI 1999/2169)[2]
			1 Apr 2000 (otherwise) (SI 1999/2815)[1]
	(4)		27 Sep 1999 (for the purposes of the issue of guidance by the Secretary of State) (SI 1999/2169)[2]

Local Government Act 1999 (c 27)—*contd*

Section

10	(4)—*contd*		1 Oct 1999 (W) (otherwise) (SI 1999/2815)[1]
			1 Apr 2000 (E) (otherwise) (SI 1999/2815)[1]
11			1 Apr 2000 (SI 1999/2169)[2]
			1 Apr 2000 (otherwise) (SI 1999/2815)[1]
12	(1)		27 Sep 1999 (SI 1999/2169)[2]
			1 Oct 1999 (otherwise) (SI 1999/2815)[1]
	(2), (3)		1 Apr 2000 (SI 1999/2169)[2]
			1 Apr 2000 (otherwise) (SI 1999/2815)[1]
	(4)		10 Aug 1999 (SI 1999/2169)[2]
			1 Oct 1999 (otherwise) (SI 1999/2815)[1]
13			1 Apr 2000 (SI 1999/2169)[2]
			1 Apr 2000 (otherwise) (SI 1999/2815)[1]
14			1 Apr 2000 (SI 1999/2169)
15	(1)–(6)		1 Apr 2000 (SI 1999/2169)[2]
			1 Apr 2000 (otherwise) (SI 1999/2815)[1]
	(7), (8)		27 Sep 1999 (SI 1999/2169)[2]
			1 Apr 2000 (otherwise) (SI 1999/2815)[1]
	(9)–(13)		1 Apr 2000 (SI 1999/2169)[2]
			1 Apr 2000 (otherwise) (SI 1999/2815)[1]
16			27 Sep 1999 (SI 1999/2169)
17			10 Aug 1999 (SI 1999/2169)
18			27 Sep 1999 (SI 1999/2169)
19	(1), (2)		27 Sep 1999 (SI 1999/2169)[2]
			1 Oct 1999 (otherwise) (SI 1999/2815)[1]
	(3)		27 Sep 1999 (SI 1999/2169)[2]
			27 Jul 2000 (otherwise) (s 27(1))[1]
	(4)		27 Sep 1999 (SI 1999/2169)[2]
			1 Oct 1999 (otherwise) (SI 1999/2815)[1]
20			27 Sep 1999 (SI 1999/2169)[2]
			1 Oct 1999 (otherwise) (SI 1999/2815)[1]
21			27 Jul 1999 (RA)
22			27 Sep 1999 (SI 1999/2169)[2]
			1 Oct 1999 (otherwise) (SI 1999/2815)[1]
23	(1)–(3)		27 Sep 1999 (SI 1999/2169)[2]
			1 Oct 1999 (otherwise) (SI 1999/2815)[1]
	(4)		10 Aug 1999 (SI 1999/2169)[2]
			1 Oct 1999 (otherwise) (SI 1999/2815)[1]
	(5), (6)		27 Sep 1999 (SI 1999/2169)[2]
			1 Oct 1999 (otherwise) (SI 1999/2815)[1]
24	(1)		27 Sep 1999 (SI 1999/2169)
	(2), (3)		1 Apr 2000 (SI 1999/2169)
25	(1)		27 Sep 1999 (SI 1999/2169)[2]
			1 Oct 1999 (otherwise) (SI 1999/2815)[1]
	(2)	(a)	27 Sep 1999 (SI 1999/2169)[2]
			1 Oct 1999 (otherwise) (SI 1999/2815)[1]
		(b), (c)	27 Sep 1999 (SI 1999/2169)[2]
			27 Jul 2000 (otherwise) (s 27(1))[1]

Local Government Act 1999 (c 27)—*contd*

Section

25	(2)	(d)–(h)	27 Sep 1999 (SI 1999/2169)[2]
			1 Oct 1999 (otherwise) (SI 1999/2815)[1]
		(i)	27 Sep 1999 (SI 1999/2169)[2]
			27 Jul 2000 (otherwise) (s 27(1))[1]
	(3)		27 Sep 1999 (SI 1999/2169) [2]
			1 Oct 1999 (otherwise) (SI 1999/2815)[1]
26	(1)		27 Sep 1999 (SI 1999/2169)[2]
			1 Oct 1999 (otherwise) (SI 1999/2815)[1]
	(2)	(a), (b)	27 Sep 1999 (SI 1999/2169)[2]
			1 Oct 1999 (otherwise) (SI 1999/2815)[1]
		(c)	10 Aug 1999 (SI 1999/2169)[2]
			1 Oct 1999 (otherwise) (SI 1999/2815)[1]
		(d)	27 Sep 1999 (SI 1999/2169)[2]
			1 Oct 1999 (otherwise) (SI 1999/2815)[1]
	(3), (4)		10 Aug 1999 (SI 1999/2169)[2]
			1 Oct 1999 (otherwise) (SI 1999/2815)[1]
27–29			27 Jul 1999 (RA)
30			See Sch 1 below
31			27 Jul 1999 (RA) (this section applies as regards the financial year beginning with 1 Apr 1999, subject to modifications and subsequent financial years)
32, 33			27 Jul 1999 (RA)
34			See Sch 2 below
35, 36			27 Jul 1999 (RA)

Schedule

1			27 Jul 1999 (RA) (applies in relation to the limitation of council tax and precepts as regards the financial year beginning with 1 Apr 2000 and subsequent financial years)
2			27 Jul 1999 (RA)

[1]   The Secretary of State may by order provide for (i) any of ss 1–13, 15, 19, 20, 22, 23, 25, 26 to be brought into force in relation to England before the time appointed by s 27(1) of this Act (ie 27 July 2000), (ii) any of those sections, in so far as it relates to an authority falling with s 1(1)(d), (e) to be brought into force in relation to Wales before that time, and (iii) any of ss 14, 16–18, 24 to be brought into force before that time, and the National Assembly for Wales may by order provide for any of ss 1–13, 15, 19, 20, 22, 23, 25, 26, except in so far as it relates to an authority falling within s 1(1)(d), (e), to be brought into force in relation to Wales before that time.

[2]   In relation to England, and in relation to Wales so far as they relate to an authority falling within s 1(1)(d), (e) of the Act

Mental Health (Amendment) (Scotland) Act 1999 (c 32)

RA: 11 Nov 1999

Commencement provisions: s 2(2)

11 Jan 2000 (s 2(2))

Mental Health (Public Safety and Appeals) (Scotland) Act 1999 (asp 1)

RA: 13 Sep 1999

13 Sep 1999 (RA)

Northern Ireland (Location of Victims' Remains) Act 1999 (c 7)

RA: 26 May 1999

Commencement provisions: s 2(5); Northern Ireland (Location of Victims' Remains) Act 1999 (Commencement of Section 2) Order 1999, SI 1999/1511

Section

1	26 May 1999 (RA)
2	26 May 1999 (SI 1999/1511)
3–7	26 May 1999 (RA)

Pollution Prevention and Control Act 1999 (c 24)

RA: 27 Jul 1999

Commencement provisions: s 7(3); Pollution Prevention and Control Act 1999 (Commencement No 1) (England and Wales) Order 2000, SI 2000/800

Section

1–5		27 Jul 1999 (RA)
6	(1)	See Sch 2 below
	(2)	*Not in force*
7		27 Jul 1999 (RA)
Schedule		
1		27 Jul 1999 (RA)
2		21 Mar 2000 (E, W) (SI 2000/800)
		Not in force (otherwise)
3		*Not in force*

Protection of Children Act 1999 (c 14)

RA: 15 Jul 1999

Commencement provisions: s 14(2); Protection of Children Act 1999 (Commencement No 1) Order 2000, SI 2000/1459; Protection of Children Act 1999 (Commencement No 2) Order 2000, SI 2000/2337

Section

1			2 Oct 2000 (SI 2000/2337)
2	(1)		2 Oct 2000 (SI 2000/2337)
	(2)	(a)–(c)	1 Sep 2000 (so far as relate to s 3 below) (SI 2000/2337)
			2 Oct 2000 (otherwise) (SI 2000/2337)
		(d)	2 Oct 2000 (SI 2000/2337)
	(3)–(9)		2 Oct 2000 (SI 2000/2337)
	(9A)		Inserted by Care Standards Act 2000, s 94(2) (qv)
	(10)		2 Oct 2000 (SI 2000/2337)

Protection of Children Act 1999 (c 14)—*contd*

Section

2A		Prospectively inserted by Care Standards Act 2000, s 95(1)[1]
2B		Inserted by Care Standards Act 2000, s 96(1) (qv)
2C		Prospectively inserted by Care Standards Act 2000, s 97(1)[1]
2D		Inserted by Care Standards Act 2000, s 98(1) (qv)
3	(1), (2)	5 Jun 2000 (SI 2000/1459)
	(3)	1 Sep 2000 (except so far as provides for inclusion of any individual in list kept by Secretary of State under s 1 above) (SI 2000/2337)
		2 Oct 2000 (otherwise) (SI 2000/2337)
	(4)–(7)	Inserted by Care Standards Act 2000, s 99 (qv)
4		2 Oct 2000 (SI 2000/2337)
4A–4C		Inserted by Criminal Justice and Court Services Act 2000, s 74, Sch 7, paras 154, 155 (qv)
5		1 Sep 2000 (SI 2000/2337)
6		Repealed
7		2 Oct 2000 (SI 2000/2337)
8		*Not in force*
9	(1)–(3)	1 Sep 2000 (for purpose of making regulations) (SI 2000/2337)
	(3A)–(3C)	Inserted by Care Standards Act 2000, s 116, Sch 4, para 26(3) (qv)
	(4)–(6)	1 Sep 2000 (for purpose of making regulations) (SI 2000/2337)
		2 Oct 2000 (otherwise) (SI 2000/2337)
	(7)	*See Schedule below*
10		Repealed (*never in force*)
12		1 Sep 2000 (SI 2000/2337)
13–14		2 Oct 2000 (SI 2000/2337)
Schedule		2 Oct 2000 (SI 2000/2337)

[1] Orders made under Care Standards Act 2000, s 122 bringing the prospective insertions etc into force will be noted to that Act

---

Rating (Valuation) Act 1999 (c 6)

RA: 26 May 1999

Commencement provisions: s 2(1)–(3)
Section

1	1 Apr 1990 (in relation to rating lists compiled before 26 May 1999, subject to a saving) (s 2(2), (3))

Rating (Valuation) Act 1999 (c 6)—*contd*
Section

1—*contd*	26 May 1999 (in relation to rating lists to be compiled on or after 26 May 1999) (s 2(1))
2, 3	26 May 1999 (RA)

Road Traffic (NHS Charges) Act 1999 (c 3)

RA: 10 March 1999

Commencement provisions: s 21(2), (3); Road Traffic (NHS Charges) Act 1999 (Commencement No 1) Order 1999, SI 1999/1075
Section

1–20	5 Apr 1999 (except in relation to military hospitals) (SI 1999/1075)
	Not in force (exception noted above)
21	10 Mar 1999 (RA)

Road Traffic (Vehicle Testing) Act 1999 (c 12)

RA: 30 June 1999

Commencement provisions: s 9(2); Road Traffic (Vehicle Testing) Act 1999 (Commencement No 1) Order 2001, SI 2001/1896
Section

1	(1), (2)	*Not in force*
	(3)	1 Jun 2001 (so far as relates to the insertion of Road Traffic Act 1988, s 45(6B)) (SI 2001/1896)
		Not in force (otherwise)
2		*Not in force*
3		1 Jun 2001 (SI 2001/1896)
4, 5		*Not in force*
6		30 Jun 1999 (RA)
7		*Not in force*
8, 9		30 Jun 1999 (RA)
Schedule		*Not in force*

Scottish Enterprise Act 1999 (c 5)

Whole Act repealed

Social Security Contributions (Transfer of Functions, etc) Act 1999 (c 2)

RA: 25 February 1999

Commencement provisions: s 28(2), (3); Social Security Contributions (Transfer of Functions, etc) Act 1999 (Commencement No 1 and Transitional Provisions) Order 1999, SI 1999/527[1]; Social Security Contributions (Transfer of Functions, etc) Act 1999 (Commencement No 2 and Consequential and Transitional Provisions) Order 1999, SI 1999/1662
Section

1	(1)	See Sch 1 below
	(2)	See Sch 2 below

**Social Security Contributions (Transfer of Functions, etc) Act 1999
(c 2)**—*contd*

Section

2			See Sch 3 below
3	(1), (2)		1 Apr 1999 (SI 1999/527)
	(3)	(a), (b)	1 Apr 1999 (SI 1999/527)
		(c)	Repealed (*never in force*)
		(d)–(f)	1 Apr 1999 (SI 1999/527)
	(4)–(7)		1 Apr 1999 (SI 1999/527)
4	(a)		1 Apr 1999 (except so far as relates to Class 1B contributions) (SI 1999/527)
			6 Apr 1999 (exception noted above) (SI 1999/527)
	(b)		1 Apr 1999 (SI 1999/527)
	(c)		6 Apr 1999 (SI 1999/527)
5			See Sch 5 below
6			See Sch 6 below
7			1 Apr 1999 (SI 1999/527)
8	(1)	(a)–(g)	25 Feb 1999 (so far as conferring power to make subordinate legislation) (s 28(2))
			1 Apr 1999 (otherwise) (SI 1999/527)
		(h)	25 Feb 1999 (so far as conferring power to make subordinate legislation) (s 28(2))
			6 Apr 1999 (otherwise) (SI 1999/527)
		(i)	25 Feb 1999 (so far as conferring power to make subordinate legislation) (s 28(2))
			1 Apr 1999 (otherwise) (SI 1999/527)
		(ia)	Inserted by Child Support, Pensions and Social Security Act 2000, s 77(5) (qv)
		(j)	Repealed
		(k), (l)	25 Feb 1999 (so far as conferring power to make subordinate legislation) (s 28(2))
			6 Apr 1999 (otherwise) (SI 1999/527)
		(m)	25 Feb 1999 (so far as conferring power to make subordinate legislation) (s 28(2))
			1 Apr 1999 (otherwise) (SI 1999/527)
	(2), (3)		25 Feb 1999 (so far as conferring power to make subordinate legislation) (s 28(2))
			1 Apr 1999 (otherwise) (SI 1999/527)
	(4)		Repealed
9, 10			25 Feb 1999 (so far as conferring power to make subordinate legislation) (s 28(2))

Social Security Contributions (Transfer of Functions, etc) Act 1999
(c 2)—*contd*

Section

9, 10—*contd*		1 Apr 1999 (otherwise) (SI 1999/527)
11	(1)–(3)	25 Feb 1999 (so far as conferring power to make subordinate legislation) (s 28(2))
		1 Apr 1999 (otherwise) (SI 1999/527)
	(4)	25 Feb 1999 (so far as conferring power to make subordinate legislation) (s 28(2))
		6 Apr 1999 (otherwise) (SI 1999/527)
12		25 Feb 1999 (so far as conferring power to make subordinate legislation) (s 28(2))
		1 Apr 1999 (otherwise, except for the words from "section 121D" to "and to" in sub-s (4)) (SI 1999/527)
		6 Apr 1999 (exception noted above) (SI 1999/527)
13–15		25 Feb 1999 (so far as conferring power to make subordinate legislation) (s 28(2))
		1 Apr 1999 (otherwise) (SI 1999/527)
16	(1)	5 Jul 1999 (SI 1999/1662)
	(2)	14 Jun 1999 (for the purpose of authorising the making of regulations) (SI 1999/1662)
		5 Jul 1999 (otherwise, subject to a transitional provision) (SI 1999/1662)
	(3)–(7)	5 Jul 1999 (SI 1999/1662)
17		25 Feb 1999 (s 28(2))
18		See Sch 7 below
19		4 Mar 1999 (for purposes connected with the making of regulations) (SI 1999/527)
		1 Apr 1999 (otherwise) (SI 1999/527)
20		25 Feb 1999 (s 28(2))
21		1 Apr 1999 (SI 1999/527)
22	(1)–(3)	1 Apr 1999 (SI 1999/527)
	(4)	25 Feb 1999 (so far as conferring power to make an order) (s 28(2))
		1 Apr 1999 (otherwise) (SI 1999/527)
	(5)	1 Apr 1999 (SI 1999/527)
23		1 Apr 1999 (SI 1999/527)
24, 25		25 Feb 1999 (s 28(2))
26	(1)	See Sch 8 below
	(2)	See Sch 9 below
	(3)	See Sch 10 below
27, 28		25 Feb 1999 (s 28(2))

**Social Security Contributions (Transfer of Functions, etc) Act 1999
(c 2)**—*contd*
Schedule

1, para	1–16		25 Feb 1999 (so far as enabling the Secretary of State to make subordinate legislation conferring functions on the Board) (s 28(2)) 1 Apr 1999 (otherwise) (SI 1999/527)
	17	(a), (b)	25 Feb 1999 (so far as enabling the Secretary of State to make subordinate legislation conferring functions on the Board) (s 28(2)) 1 Apr 1999 (otherwise) (SI 1999/527)
		(c)	25 Feb 1999 (so far as enabling the Secretary of State to make subordinate legislation conferring functions on the Board) (s 28(2)) 1 Apr 1999 (otherwise, except in so far as amends Social Security Contributions and Benefits Act 1992, Sch 1, para 6(8)) (SI 1999/527) *Not in force* (exception noted above)
	18		25 Feb 1999 (so far as enabling the Secretary of State to make subordinate legislation conferring functions on the Board) (s 28(2)) 1 Apr 1999 (otherwise) (SI 1999/527)
	19		Repealed or spent
	20–59		25 Feb 1999 (so far as enabling the Secretary of State to make subordinate legislation conferring functions on the Board) (s 28(2)) 1 Apr 1999 (otherwise) (SI 1999/527)
	60		Repealed
	61–65		25 Feb 1999 (so far as enabling the Secretary of State to make subordinate legislation conferring functions on the Board) (s 28(2)) 1 Apr 1999 (otherwise) (SI 1999/527)
	66	(1), (2)	25 Feb 1999 (so far as enabling the Secretary of State to make subordinate legislation conferring functions on the Board) (s 28(2)) 1 Apr 1999 (otherwise) (SI 1999/527)
		(3)	Repealed
		(4)–(6)	25 Feb 1999 (so far as enabling the Secretary of State to make subordinate legislation conferring functions on the Board) (s 28(2)) 1 Apr 1999 (otherwise) (SI 1999/527)

**Social Security Contributions (Transfer of Functions, etc) Act 1999
(c 2)**—*contd*

Schedule

1, para	67, 68	25 Feb 1999 (so far as enabling the Secretary of State to make subordinate legislation conferring functions on the Board) (s 28(2))
		1 Apr 1999 (otherwise) (SI 1999/527)
2		1 Apr 1999 (except in relation to functions which are, by virtue of SI 1997/664, art 4, exercisable under SI 1984/380, reg 20(2)(b)) (SI 1999/527)
		Not in force (exception noted above)
3		1 Apr 1999 (SI 1999/527)
4		1 Apr 1999 (except so far as relates to Class 1B contributions) (SI 1999/527)
		6 Apr 1999 (exception noted above) (SI 1999/527)
5, para	1	1 Apr 1999 (SI 1999/527)
	2	Repealed
	3, 4	1 Apr 1999 (SI 1999/527)
	5	6 Apr 1999 (SI 1999/527)
	6	1 Apr 1999 (SI 1999/527)
	7	6 Apr 1999 (SI 1999/527)
	8–12	1 Apr 1999 (SI 1999/527)
6		1 Apr 1999 (SI 1999/527)
7, para	1–3	4 Mar 1999 (for purposes connected with the making of regulations) (SI 1999/527)
		1 Apr 1999 (otherwise) (SI 1999/527)
	4	5 Jul 1999 (SI 1999/1662)
	5–8	4 Mar 1999 (for purposes connected with the making of regulations) (SI 1999/527)
		1 Apr 1999 (otherwise) (SI 1999/527)
	9, 10	4 Mar 1999 (for purposes connected with the making of regulations) (SI 1999/527)
		6 Apr 1999 (otherwise) (SI 1999/527)
	11	4 Mar 1999 (for purposes connected with the making of regulations) (SI 1999/527)
		1 Apr 1999 (otherwise) (SI 1999/527)
	12	5 Jul 1999 (SI 1999/1662)
	13	1 Apr 1999 (SI 1999/527)
	14	5 Jul 1999 (SI 1999/1662)
	15, 16	1 Apr 1999 (SI 1999/527)

Social Security Contributions (Transfer of Functions, etc) Act 1999 (c 2)—*contd*

Schedule

7, para	17		4 Mar 1999 (for purposes connected with the making of regulations) (SI 1999/527)
			1 Apr 1999 (otherwise) (SI 1999/527)
	18	(1), (2)	1 Apr 1999 (SI 1999/527)
		(3)	5 Jul 1999 (SI 1999/1662)
	19, 20		5 Jul 1999 (SI 1999/1662)
	21–23		1 Apr 1999 (SI 1999/527)
	24		14 Jun 1999 (for the purpose of authorising the making of regulations) (SI 1999/1662)
			5 Jul 1999 (otherwise) (SI 1999/1662)
	25–27		1 Apr 1999 (SI 1999/527)
	28		*Not in force*
	29–32		1 Apr 1999 (SI 1999/527)
	33		14 Jun 1999 (for the purpose of authorising the making of regulations) (SI 1999/1662)
			5 Jul 1999 (otherwise) (SI 1999/1662)
	34		5 Jul 1999 (SI 1999/1662)
	35		1 Apr 1999 (SI 1999/527)
	36		1 Apr 1999 (so far as relates to Social Security Act 1998, Sch 3, para 23) (SI 1999/527)
			5 Jul 1999 (so far as relates to Social Security Act 1998, Sch 3, para 23) (SI 1999/1662)
			Not in force (otherwise)
8			25 Feb 1999 (s 28(2))
9, para	1, 2		6 Apr 1999 (SI 1999/527)
	3		1 Apr 1999 (SI 1999/527)
	4–7		4 Mar 1999 (for purposes connected with the making of regulations) (SI 1999/527)
			1 Apr 1999 (otherwise) (SI 1999/527)
	8		1 Apr 1999 (SI 1999/527)
10			1 Apr 1999 (except repeals of or in Social Security Administration Act 1992, s 118; Pension Schemes Act 1993, s 167(3); Social Security Act 1998, ss 16, 62, Sch 3, para 23, Sch 7, paras 130, 132) (SI 1999/527)
			6 Apr 1999 (repeals of or in Social Security Administration Act 1992, s 118; Social Security Act 1998, s 62) (SI 1999/527)

Social Security Contributions (Transfer of Functions, etc) Act 1999

(c 2)—*contd*

Schedule

10—*contd*	5 Jul 1999 (repeals of Pension Schemes Act 1993, s 167(3); Social Security Act 1998, Sch 3, para 23, Sch 7, paras 130(1), 132) (SI 1999/1662)
	Not in force (exceptions noted above)

---

[1]   For transitional provisions relating to the provisions brought into force by SI 1999/527, see arts 3–6 of that Order

---

Tax Credits Act 1999 (c 10)

RA: 30 Jun 1999

Commencement provisions: ss 6(4), 14(9), 20(2)

Section

1–5		5 Oct 1999 (s 20(2))
6		6 Apr 2000 (s 6(4))
7–13		5 Oct 1999 (s 20(2))
14	(1)	5 Oct 1999 (so far as relates to s 14(3) of this Act) (s 20(2))
		1 Oct 2000 (otherwise) (s 14(9))
	(2)	1 Oct 2000 (s 14(9))
	(3)	5 Oct 1999 (s 20(2))
	(4)–(9)	1 Oct 2000 (s 14(9))
15–18		5 Oct 1999 (s 20(2))
19	(1)	30 Jun 1999 (RA)
	(2)–(4)	5 Oct 1999 (s 20(2))
20		30 Jun 1999 (RA)
Schedule		
1–6		5 Oct 1999 (s 20(2))

Trustee Delegation Act 1999 (c 15)

RA: 15 Jul 1999

Commencement provisions: s 13(1); Trustee Delegation Act 1999 (Commencement) Order 2000, SI 2000/216

Section

1–12	1 Mar 2000 (SI 2000/216)
13	15 Jul 1999 (RA)
Schedule	1 Mar 2000 (SI 2000/216)

Water Industry Act 1999 (c 9)

RA: 30 Jun 1999

Commencement provisions: s 17(2), (3); Water Industry Act 1999 (Commencement No 1) (Scotland) Order 1999, SSI 1999/133; Water Industry Act 1999 (Commencement No 2) Order 1999, SI 1999/3440

Section

1, 2	30 Jun 1999 (s 17(2))
3	1 Apr 2000 (SI 1999/3440)

Water Industry Act 1999 (c 9)—*contd*

Section

4, 5			30 Jun 1999 (so far as confers power to make subordinate legislation) (s 17(2))
			23 Dec 1999 (otherwise) (SI 1999/3440)
6, 7			30 Jun 1999 (so far as confers power to make subordinate legislation) (s 17(2))
			1 Apr 2000 (otherwise) (SI 1999/3440)
8			30 Jun 1999 (s 17(2))
9–11			1 Apr 2000 (SI 1999/3440)
12			30 Jun 1999 (so far as confers power to make subordinate legislation) (s 17(2))
			1 Nov 1999 (otherwise) (SSI 1999/133)
13			1 Nov 1999 (SSI 1999/133)
14			30 Jun 1999 (s 17(2))
15	(1)		See Sch 3 below
	(2)		See Sch 4 below
16			23 Dec 1999 (SI 1999/3440)
17			30 Jun 1999 (RA)

Schedule

1			30 Jun 1999 (s 17(2))
2			1 Nov 1999 (S) (SSI 1999/133)
3, Pt	I, para	1–3	1 Apr 2000 (SI 1999/3440)
		4	23 Dec 1999 (SI 1999/3440)
	II		1 Nov 1999 (SSI 1999/133)
4, Pt	I		30 Jun 1999 (repeal of Water Industry Act 1991, s 145 and the heading preceding it) (s 17(2))
			1 Apr 2000 (otherwise) (SI 1999/3440)
	II		1 Nov 1999 (SSI 1999/133)

Welfare Reform and Pensions Act 1999 (c 30)

RA: 11 Nov 1999

Commencement provisions: s 89; Welfare Reform and Pensions Act 1999 (Commencement No 1) Order 1999, SI 1999/3309; Welfare Reform and Pensions Act 1999 (Commencement No 2) Order 1999, SI 1999/3420; Welfare Reform and Pensions Act 1999 (Commencement No 3) Order 2000, SI 2000/629; Welfare Reform and Pensions Act 1999 (Commencement No 4) Order 2000, SI 2000/1047; Welfare Reform and Pensions Act 1999 (Commencement No 5) Order 2000, SI 2000/1116; Welfare Reform and Pensions Act 1999 (Scotland) (Commencement No 6) Order 2000, SSI 2000/111; Welfare Reform and Pensions Act 1999 (Commencement No 7) Order 2000, SI 2000/1382; Welfare Reform and Pensions Act 1999 (Scotland) (Commencement No 8) Order 2000, SSI 2000/238; Welfare Reform and Pensions Act 1999 (Commencement No 9 and Transitional and Savings Provisions)

Welfare Reform and Pensions Act 1999 (c 30)—*contd*

Order 2000, SI 2000/2958; Welfare Reform and Pensions Act 1999 (Commencement No 10, and Transitional Provisions) Order 2001, SI 2001/933; Welfare Reform and Pensions Act 1999 (Commencement No 11) Order 2001, SI 2001/1219; Welfare Reform and Pensions Act 1999 (Commencement No 12) Order 2001, SI 2001/4049, as amended by SI 2002/153; Welfare Reform and Pensions Act 1999 (Commencement No 13) Order 2002, SI 2002/153; Welfare Reform and Pensions Act 1999 (Commencement No 14) Order 2002, SI 2002/381

Section

1, 2		11 Nov 1999 (for the purpose of the exercise of any power to make regulations) (s 89(5)(a))
		1 Oct 2000 (otherwise) (SI 2000/1047)
3	(1)	11 Nov 1999 (for the purpose of the exercise of any power to make regulations) (s 89(5)(a))
		6 Apr 2001 (so far as relates to the provisions of s 3 brought into force on that date) (SI 2001/933)
		8 Oct 2001 (otherwise) (SI 2000/1047)
	(2)	11 Nov 1999 (for the purpose of the exercise of any power to make regulations) (s 89(5)(a))
		6 Apr 2001 (second paragraph only) (SI 2001/933)
		8 Oct 2001 (otherwise) (SI 2000/1047)
	(3)–(5)	11 Nov 1999 (for the purpose of the exercise of any power to make regulations) (s 89(5)(a))
		8 Oct 2001 (otherwise) (SI 2000/1047)
	(6)	11 Nov 1999 (for the purpose of the exercise of any power to make regulations) (s 89(5)(a))
		6 Apr 2001 (otherwise) (SI 2001/933)
	(7)	11 Nov 1999 (for the purpose of the exercise of any power to make regulations) (s 89(5)(a))
		6 Apr 2001 (so far as relates to s 3(6) and the second paragraph of s 3(2)) (SI 2001/933)
		8 Oct 2001 (otherwise) (SI 2001/933)
	(8)	11 Nov 1999 (for the purpose of the exercise of any power to make regulations) (s 89(5)(a))
		6 Apr 2001 (otherwise) (SI 2001/933)
	(9)	11 Nov 1999 (for the purpose of the exercise of any power to make regulations) (s 89(5)(a))
		6 Apr 2001 (so far as relates to definitions "employer" and "relevant employees") (SI 2001/933)

Welfare Reform and Pensions Act 1999 (c 30)—*contd*

Section

3	(9)—*contd*	8 Oct 2001 (otherwise) (SI 2001/933)
4, 5		11 Nov 1999 (for the purpose of the exercise of any power to make regulations) (s 89(5)(a))
		8 Oct 2001 (otherwise) (SI 2000/1047)
6	(1), (2)	11 Nov 1999 (for the purpose of the exercise of any power to make regulations) (s 89(5)(a))
		8 Oct 2001 (otherwise) (SI 2000/1047)
	(3)	See Sch 1 below
	(4)	11 Nov 1999 (for the purpose of the exercise of any power to make regulations) (s 89(5)(a))
		8 Oct 2001 (otherwise) (SI 2000/1047)
7		11 Nov 1999 (for the purpose of the exercise of any power to make regulations) (s 89(5)(a))
		1 Oct 2000 (otherwise) (SI 2000/1047)
8		11 Nov 1999 (for the purpose of the exercise of any power to make regulations) (s 89(5)(a))
		1 Oct 2000 (otherwise, except the definition "designated scheme") (SI 2000/1047)
		8 Oct 2001 (exception noted above) (SI 2000/1047)
9		11 Nov 1999 (for the purpose of the exercise of any power to make regulations) (s 89(5)(a))
		6 Apr 2001 (otherwise) (SI 2000/2958)
10		11 Nov 1999 (for the purpose of the exercise of any power to make regulations) (s 89(5)(a))
		3 Apr 2000 (otherwise) (SI 2000/629)
11	(1)–(3)	11 Nov 1999 (for the purpose of the exercise of any power to make regulations) (s 89(5)(a))
		29 May 2000 (otherwise) (SI 2000/1382)
	(4)–(10)	11 Nov 1999 (for the purpose of the exercise of any power to make regulations) (s 89(5)(a))
		6 Apr 2002 (otherwise) (SI 2002/153)
	(11)	11 Nov 1999 (for the purpose of the exercise of any power to make regulations) (s 89(5)(a))
		29 May 2000 (otherwise) (SI 2000/1382)

Welfare Reform and Pensions Act 1999 (c 30)—*contd*

Section

11	(12)	11 Nov 1999 (for the purpose of the exercise of any power to make regulations) (s 89(5)(a))
		1 Dec 2000 (otherwise) (SI 2000/1382)
12		11 Nov 1999 (for the purpose of the exercise of any power to make regulations) (s 89(5)(a))
		6 Apr 2002 (otherwise) (SI 2002/153)
13	(1), (2)	11 Nov 1999 (for the purpose of the exercise of any power to make regulations) (s 89(5)(a))
		29 May 2000 (so far as relates to s 11(1)–(3), (11) of this Act) (SI 2000/1382)
		6 Apr 2002 (otherwise) (SI 2002/153)
	(3)	11 Nov 1999 (for the purpose of the exercise of any power to make regulations) (s 89(5)(a))
		6 Apr 2002 (otherwise) (SI 2002/153)
14–16		11 Nov 1999 (for the purpose of the exercise of any power to make regulations) (s 89(5)(a))
		6 Apr 2002 (otherwise) (SI 2002/153)
17		11 Nov 1999 (for the purpose of the exercise of any power to make regulations) (s 89(5)(a))
		23 Apr 2001 (otherwise) (SI 2001/1219)
18		See Sch 2 below
19		11 Nov 1999 (for the purpose of the exercise of any power to make regulations) (s 89(5)(a))
		1 Dec 2000 (otherwise) (SI 2000/1116)
20		11 Nov 1999 (for the purpose of the exercise of any power to make regulations) (s 89(5)(a))
		1 Dec 2000 (otherwise) (SI 2000/1047)
21, 22		11 Nov 1999 (for the purpose of the exercise of any power to make regulations) (s 89(5)(a))
		1 Dec 2000 (otherwise) (SI 2000/1116)
23, 24		11 Nov 1999 (for the purpose of the exercise of any power to make regulations) (s 89(5)(a))
		1 Dec 2000 (otherwise) (SI 2000/1047)
25		11 Nov 1999 (for the purpose of the exercise of any power to make regulations) (s 89(5)(a))
		Not in force (otherwise)

Welfare Reform and Pensions Act 1999 (c 30)—*contd*

Section

26–51		11 Nov 1999 (for the purpose of the exercise of any power to make regulations) (s 89(5)(a))
		1 Dec 2000 (otherwise) (SI 2000/1047)
52		11 Nov 1999 (s 89(4)(a))
53		12 Jan 2000 (for the purpose of the exercise of any power to make regulations) (SI 1999/3309)
		2 Apr 2000 (otherwise) (SI 1999/3309)
54–56		24 Apr 2000 (for the purpose of making regulations) (SI 2000/1047)
		9 Apr 2001 (otherwise) (SI 2000/1047)
57, 58		11 Nov 1999 (s 89(4)(a))
59		11 Nov 1999 (for the purpose of the exercise of any power to make regulations) (s 89(5)(b))
		19 Mar 2001 (otherwise) (SI 2000/2958)
60		11 Nov 1999 (s 89(4)(a))
61		11 Nov 1999 (for the purpose of the exercise of any power to make regulations) (s 89(5)(b))
		3 Apr 2000 (otherwise) (SI 1999/3309)
62, 63		3 Nov 2000 (for the purpose of authorising the making of regulations) (SI 2000/2958)
		6 Apr 2001 (otherwise) (subject to transitional provisions) (SI 2000/2958)
64		3 Nov 2000 (for the purpose of authorising the making of regulations) (SI 2000/2958)
		6 Apr 2001 (otherwise) (SI 2000/2958)
65		3 Nov 2000 (for the purpose of authorising the making of regulations) (SI 2000/2958)
		6 Apr 2001 (otherwise) (subject to a saving) (SI 2000/2958)
66		12 Jan 2000 (SI 1999/3309)
67	(1), (2)	12 Jan 2000 (SI 1999/3309)
	(3), (4)	9 Apr 2001 (SI 2000/1382)
68		11 Nov 1999 (s 89(4)(a))
69		17 Apr 2000 (for the purpose of the exercise of powers to make regulations) (SI 2000/1047)
		15 May 2000 (otherwise) (SI 2000/1047)
70		See Sch 8 below
71, 72		11 Nov 1999 (s 89(4)(a), (c))

Welfare Reform and Pensions Act 1999 (c 30)—*contd*

Section

73, 74			22 Dec 1999 (for the purpose of the exercise of any power to make regulations) (SI 1999/3420)
			6 Apr 2000 (otherwise) (SI 1999/3420)
75, 76			22 Dec 1999 (SI 1999/3420)
77, 78			6 Apr 2000 (SI 1999/3420)
79–83			11 Nov 1999 (s 89(4)(d))
84	(1)		See Sch 12 below
	(2)–(4)		11 Nov 1999 (s 89(4)(f))
85	(1), (2)		11 Nov 1999 (s 89(4)(g))
	(3), (4)		1 Dec 2000 (SI 2000/1116)
	(5)		1 Dec 2000 (SI 2000/1047)
	(6), (7)		11 Nov 1999 (s 89(4)(g))
86, 87			11 Nov 1999 (s 89(4)(h))
88			See Sch 13 below
89–91			11 Nov 1999 (s 89(4)(h))

Schedule

1, para	1	(1), (2)	1 Oct 2000 (SI 2000/1047)
		(3)	8 Oct 2001 (SI 2000/1047)
		(4), (5)	1 Oct 2000 (SI 2000/1047)
	2, 3		1 Oct 2000 (SI 2000/1047)
2, para	1, 2		29 May 2000 (SI 2000/1382)
	3, 4		25 Apr 2000 (SI 2000/1047)
	5		11 Nov 1999 (for the purpose of the exercise of any power to make regulations) (s 89(5)(a))
			1 Jan 2002 (otherwise) (SI 2001/4049)
	6		6 Apr 2002 (SI 2002/153)
	7		11 Nov 1999 (for the purpose of the exercise of any power to make regulations) (s 89(5)(a))
			6 Apr 2002 (otherwise) (SI 2001/4049)
	8–13		25 Apr 2000 (SI 2000/1047)
	14		19 Mar 2002 (SI 2002/381)
	15–19		25 Apr 2000 (SI 2000/1047)
3, 4			1 Dec 2000 (SI 2000/1116)
5, 6			1 Dec 2000 (SI 2000/1047)
7			19 Mar 2001 (SI 2000/2958)
8, para	1–19		24 Apr 2000 (for the purpose of making regulations) (SI 2000/1047)
			9 Apr 2001 (otherwise) (SI 2000/1047)
	20		3 Nov 2000 (SI 2000/2958)
	21		3 Nov 2000 (for the purpose of authorising the making of regulations) (SI 2000/2958)
			6 Apr 2001 (otherwise) (SI 2000/2958)
	22		3 Nov 2000 (for the purpose of authorising the making of regulations) (SI 2000/2958)

Welfare Reform and Pensions Act 1999 (c 30)—*contd*

Schedule

8, para	22—*contd*		6 Apr 2001 (otherwise) (subject to transitional provisions) (SI 2000/2958)
	23	(1), (2)	11 Nov 1999 (for the purpose of the exercise of any power to make regulations) (s 89(5)(c))
			13 Dec 1999 (otherwise) (SI 1999/3309)
		(3)	11 Nov 1999 (for the purpose of the exercise of any power to make regulations) (s 89(5)(c))
			3 Apr 2000 (otherwise) (SI 1999/3309)
		(4)	11 Nov 1999 (for the purpose of the exercise of any power to make regulations) (s 89(5)(c))
			13 Dec 1999 (otherwise) (SI 1999/3309)
	24		3 Apr 2000 (SI 1999/3309)
	25		3 Nov 2000 (SI 2000/2958)
	26		3 Nov 2000 (for the purpose of authorising the making of regulations) (SI 2000/2958)
			6 Apr 2001 (otherwise) (subject to a saving) (SI 2000/2958)
	27		6 Apr 2001 (SI 2000/2958)
	28		19 Mar 2001 (SI 2001/933)
	29		11 Nov 1999 (s 89(4)(b))
	30–32		12 Jan 2000 (for the purpose of the exercise of any power to make regulations) (SI 1999/3309)
			2 Apr 2000 (otherwise) (SI 1999/3309)
	33		1 Dec 2000 (SI 2000/1047)
	34		*Not in force*
9, 10			22 Dec 1999 (for the purpose of the exercise of any power to make regulations) (SI 1999/3420)
			6 Apr 2000 (otherwise) (SI 1999/3420)
11			11 Nov 1999 (s 89(4)(d))
12, para	1–4		1 Dec 2000 (SI 2000/1116)
	5–7		1 Dec 2000 (SI 2000/1047)
	8	(1), (2)	1 Dec 2000 (SI 2000/1047)
		(3), (4)	15 Apr 2000 (SI 2000/111)
		(5), (6)	1 Dec 2000 (SI 2000/1047)
	9		1 Dec 2000 (SI 2000/1047)
	10		1 Dec 2000 (SSI 2000/238)
	11, 12		1 Dec 2000 (SI 2000/1047)
	13		11 Nov 1999 (s 89(4)(e))
	14–45		1 Dec 2000 (SI 2000/1047)

Welfare Reform and Pensions Act 1999 (c 30)—*contd*

Schedule

12, para	46	1 Dec 2000 (SI 2000/1047); prospectively repealed by Child Support, Pensions and Social Security Act 2000, s 85, Sch 9, Pt III(1)[1]
	47	1 Dec 2000 (SI 2000/1047)
	48	1 Dec 2000 (SI 2000/1047); prospectively repealed by Child Support, Pensions and Social Security Act 2000, s 85, Sch 9, Pt III(1)[1]
	49–63	1 Dec 2000 (SI 2000/1047)
	64–66	1 Dec 2000 (SI 2000/1116)
	67–72	6 Apr 2002 (SI 2002/153)
	73	25 Apr 2000 (SI 2000/1047)
	74	6 Apr 2000 (SI 1999/3420)
	75	25 Apr 2000 (SI 2000/1047)
	76–78	6 Apr 2000 (SI 1999/3420)
	79–83	11 Nov 1999 (s 89(4)(e))
	84–86	6 Apr 2000 (SI 1999/3420)
	87	11 Nov 1999 (s 89(4)(e))
13, Pt	I	25 Apr 2000 (repeals of or in Pension Schemes Act 1993, ss 73(2)(a)(ii), 96(2)(a), 181(1); Pensions Act 1995, s 8(4); Scotland Act 1998, s 126(1)) (SI 2000/1047)
		23 Apr 2001 (repeal of or in Pensions Act 1995, s 83(3)(a)) (SI 2001/1219)
		1 Jan 2002 (repeal of or in Pension Schemes Act 1993, s 28(1)) (SI 2001/4049)
		19 Mar 2002 (repeals of or in Pensions Act 1995, s 58(6)(a)) (SI 2002/381)
		6 Apr 2002 (repeals of or in Pension Schemes Act 1993, s 55(2A); Pension Schemes (Northern Ireland) Act 1993, s 51(2A)) (SI 2001/4049)
		6 Apr 2002 (repeals of or in Pension Schemes Act 1993, s 159(5); Pensions Act 1995, ss 91(3), 92(2), 94(3), 95) (SI 2002/153)
		Not in force (repeals relating to Pensions Act 1995, s 142, Sch 5)
	II	1 Dec 2000 (repeals of or in Family Law (Scotland) Act 1985) (SI 2000/1047)

Welfare Reform and Pensions Act 1999 (c 30)—*contd*

Schedule

13, Pt	II—*contd*	1 Dec 2000 (repeals of or in Matrimonial Causes Act 1973; Matrimonial and Family Proceedings Act 1984; Family Law Act 1996, ss 9(8), 16) (SI 2000/1116)
		6 Apr 2002 (repeal of or in Family Law Act 1996, s 17) (SI 2001/4049)
	III	1 Dec 2000 (SI 2000/1047)
	IV	3 Nov 2000 (for the purpose of authorising the making of regulations) (SI 2000/2958)
		6 Apr 2001 (otherwise) (subject to a saving) (SI 2000/2958)
	V	2 Apr 2000 (repeals of or in Social Security Contributions and Benefits Act 1992, s 21, Sch 3, Pt I, Sch 4, Pt I; Maternity Allowance and Statutory Maternity Pay Regulations 1994, SI 1994/1230) (SI 1999/3309)
		9 Apr 2001 (repeals of or in Income and Corporation Taxes Act 1988; Social Security Contributions and Benefits Act 1992, s 20(1)(e)(i); Social Security Act 1998, Sch 7, para 78) (SI 2000/1047)
		6 Apr 2002 (repeals of or in Pension Schemes Act 1993, Sch 8, para 24; Jobseekers Act 1995, s 1(4)) (SI 2001/4049)
	VI, VII	6 Apr 2000 (SI 1999/3420)

[1] Orders made under Child Support, Pensions and Social Security Act 2000, s 86, bringing the prospective amendments into force will be noted to that Act

---

Youth Justice and Criminal Evidence Act 1999 (c 23)

RA: 27 Jul 1999

Commencement provisions: s 68(3), (4); Youth Justice and Criminal Evidence Act 1999 (Commencement No 1) Order 1999, SI 1999/3427; Youth Justice and Criminal Evidence Act 1999 (Commencement No 2) Order 2000, SI 2000/1034; Youth Justice and Criminal Evidence Act 1999 (Commencement No 3) Order 2000, SI 2000/1587; Youth Justice and Criminal Evidence Act 1999 (Commencement No 4) Order 2000, SI 2000/2091; Youth Justice and Criminal Evidence Act 1999 (Commencement No 5) Order 2000, SI

Section

1–15	Repealed
16–33	27 Jul 1999 (so far as confers power to make rules of court) (s 68(4))
	Not in force (otherwise)

Youth Justice and Criminal Evidence Act 1999 (c 23)—*contd*
Section

34, 35		4 Sep 2000 (SI 2000/2091)
36, 37		27 Jul 1999 (so far as confers power to make rules of court) (s 68(4))
		Not in force (otherwise)
38, 39		4 Sep 2000 (SI 2000/2091)
40	(1)	27 Jul 1999 (s 68(4))
	(2)	Repealed
41–43		27 Jul 1999 (so far as confers power to make rules of court) (s 68(4))
		4 Dec 2000 (otherwise) (SI 2000/3075)
44–52		27 Jul 1999 (so far as confers power to make rules of court) (s 68(4))
		Not in force (otherwise)
53–57		*Not in force*
58	(1)–(4)	*Not in force*
	(5)	27 Jul 1999 (so far as confers power to make orders) (s 68(4))
		Not in force (otherwise)
59		See Sch 3 below
60		14 Apr 2000 (SI 2000/1034)
61	(1)	27 Jul 1999 (s 68(4))
	(2)	27 Jul 1999 (so far as confers power to make orders) (s 68(4))
		Not in force (otherwise)
	(3)	27 Jul 1999 (s 68(4))
62–66		27 Jul 1999 (s 68(4))
67	(1)	See Sch 4 below
	(2)	Repealed
	(3)	See Sch 6 below
	(4)	See Sch 7 below
68		27 Jul 1999 (s 68(4))
Schedule		
1		Repealed
2		*Not in force*
3		14 Apr 2000 (E, W, NI) (SI 2000/1034)
		Not in force (S)
4, para	1–4	*Not in force*
	5	Repealed
	6, 7	26 Jun 2000 (SI 2000/1587)
	8	Repealed
	9	26 Jun 2000 (SI 2000/1587)
	10	*Not in force*
	11	26 Jun 2000 (SI 2000/1587)
	12–14	*Not in force*
	15–17	14 Apr 2000 (SI 2000/1034)
	18–19	*Not in force*
	20	Repealed

Youth Justice and Criminal Evidence Act 1999 (c 23)—*contd*

Schedule

4, para	21	*Not in force*
	22	14 Apr 2000 (SI 2000/1034)
	23	26 Jun 2000 (SI 2000/1587)
	24	*Not in force*
	25–28	26 Jun 2000 (SI 2000/1587)
	29, 30	Repealed
5		Repealed
6		1 Apr 2000 (repeals of or in Youth Justice and Criminal Evidence Act 1999) (SI 1999/3427)

14 Apr 2000 (E, W) (repeals of or in Registered Designs Act 1949; Children and Young Persons Act 1969; Patents Act 1977; Customs and Excise Management Act 1979; Police and Criminal Evidence Act 1984, ss 69, 70, Sch 3; Companies Act 1985; Criminal Justice Act 1988, ss 23, 24; Finance Act 1994; Value Added Tax Act 1994; Civil Evidence Act 1995[1]; Finance Act 1996; Criminal Procedure and Investigations Act 1996, Sch 1, para 27; Crime and Disorder Act 1998) (SI 2000/1034)

4 Sep 2000 (repeal of or in Criminal Justice Act 1988, s 34A) (subject to a saving) (SI 2000/2091)

4 Dec 2000 (repeals of or in Sexual Offences (Amendment) Act 1976, ss 2, 3 (although commencement of repeal of ss 2, 3(3) does not apply in relation to any trial before a court-martial); Magistrates' Courts Act 1980, Sch 7, para 148; Criminal Justice and Public Order Act 1994, Sch 10, para 35(3) (although the commencement does not apply in relation to any trial before a court-martial); Criminal Procedure and Investigations Act 1996, Sch 1, para 23) (SI 2000/3075)

Not in force (otherwise)

7, para	1	26 Jun 2000 (SI 2000/1587)
	2	Repealed

Youth Justice and Criminal Evidence Act 1999 (c 23)—*contd*

Schedule

7, para	3	*Not in force*
	4	4 Sep 2000 (SI 2000/2091)
	5	4 Dec 2000 (SI 2000/3075)
	6–8	*Not in force*

[1] The Queen's Printer's copy of SI 2000/1034 erroneously purports to bring into force the repeal by Sch 6 to this Act in Criminal Evidence Act 1995; it is assumed that the reference is to Civil Evidence Act 1995

2000

Abolition of Feudal Tenure etc (Scotland) Act 2000 (asp 5)

RA: 9 Jun 2000

Commencement provisions: s 77

Section				
1, 2				*Not in force*
3				9 Jun 2000 (RA)
4–13				*Not in force*
14–16				9 Jun 2000 (RA)
17–51				*Not in force*
52, 53				9 Jun 2000 (RA)
54–57				*Not in force*
58				9 Jun 2000 (RA)
59–61				*Not in force*
62				9 Jun 2000 (RA)
63–66				*Not in force*
67				9 Jun 2000 (RA)
68–70				*Not in force*
71, 72				9 Jun 2000 (RA)
73				*Not in force*
74				9 Jun 2000 (RA)
75				*Not in force*
76	(1)			See Sch 12 below
	(2)			See Sch 13 below
	(3), (4)			9 Jun 2000 (RA)
77				9 Jun 2000 (RA)
Schedule				
1–3				*Not in force*
4				9 Jun 2000 (RA)
5–11				*Not in force*
12, para	1–29			*Not in force*
	30	(1)–(22)		*Not in force*
		(23)	(a)	9 Jun 2000 (RA)
			(b), (c)	*Not in force*
		(24)–(26)		*Not in force*
	31–45			*Not in force*
	46	(1)		*Not in force*
		(2)	(a)	*Not in force*
			(b)	*Not in force*[1]
		(3)–(6)		*Not in force*
	47–63			*Not in force*

Abolition of Feudal Tenure etc (Scotland) Act 2000 (asp 5)—*contd*
Schedule
13   *Not in force*
1   Provided that a day has previously been appointed for the purposes of Sch 12, para 46(2)(b), comes
        into force on the coming into force of the Companies Act 1989, s 92; where such a day has not
        previously been appointed, comes into force on a day to be appointed.

Adults with Incapacity (Scotland) Act 2000 (asp 4)

RA: 9 May 2000

Commencement provisions: s 89(2); Adults with Incapacity (Scotland) Act 2000
     (Commencement No 1) Order 2001, SSI 2001/81

Section

1–5				2 Apr 2001 (SSI 2001/81)
6	(1)			2 Apr 2001 (SSI 2001/81)
	(2)	(a)		1 Apr 2002 (SSI 2001/81)
		(b)	(i)–(iii)	2 Apr 2001 (SSI 2001/81)
			(iv), (v)	1 Apr 2002 (SSI 2001/81)
		(c)	(i), (ii)	2 Apr 2001 (SSI 2001/81)
			(iii)	1 Apr 2002 (SSI 2001/81)
		(d)		2 Apr 2001 (SSI 2001/81)
		(e)		2 Apr 2001 (insofar as relates to continuing attorneys or withdrawers) (SSI 2001/81)
				1 Apr 2002 (otherwise) (SSI 2001/81)
		(f)		2 Apr 2001 (SSI 2001/81)
	(3)	(a)		1 Apr 2002 (SSI 2001/81)
		(b)		2 Apr 2001 (SSI 2001/81)
7, 8				2 Apr 2001 (SSI 2001/81)
9	(1)	(a)–(c)		2 Apr 2001 (SSI 2001/81)
		(d)	(i)	2 Apr 2001 (SSI 2001/81)
			(ii)	1 Apr 2002 (SSI 2001/81)
		(e), (f)		2 Apr 2001 (SSI 2001/81)
		(g)		2 Apr 2001 (insofar as relates to welfare attorneys) (SSI 2001/81)
				1 Apr 2002 (otherwise) (SSI 2001/81)
	(2)			2 Apr 2001 (insofar as relates to welfare attorneys) (SSI 2001/81)
				1 Apr 2002 (otherwise) (SSI 2001/81)
	(3)	(a)		1 Apr 2002 (SSI 2001/81)
		(b)		2 Apr 2001 (SSI 2001/81)
10	(1)	(a)		1 Apr 2002 (SSI 2001/81)
		(b)		2 Apr 2001 (SSI 2001/81)
		(c)	(i)	2 Apr 2001 (SSI 2001/81)
			(ii)	1 Apr 2002 (SSI 2001/81)
		(d)		2 Apr 2001 (SSI 2001/81)
		(e)		2 Apr 2001 (insofar as relates to welfare attorneys) (SSI 2001/81)
				1 Apr 2002 (otherwise) (SSI 2001/81)
	(2)			2 Apr 2001 (SSI 2001/81)
	(3)	(a)		1 Apr 2002 (SSI 2001/81)

Adults with Incapacity (Scotland) Act 2000 (asp 4)—*contd*

Adults with Incapacity (Scotland) Act 2000 (asp 4)—*contd*

Schedule

3, para	7	(1)		2 Apr 2001 (SSI 2001/81)
		(2)	(a)	2 Apr 2001 (SSI 2001/81)
			(b)	*Not in force*
		(3)	(a)–(d)	2 Apr 2001 (SSI 2001/81)
			(e)	*Not in force*
	8–10			2 Apr 2001 (SSI 2001/81)
	11, 12			*Not in force*
	13, 14			2 Apr 2001 (SSI 2001/81)
4, para	1–3			1 Apr 2002 (SSI 2001/81)
	4			2 Apr 2001 (SSI 2001/81)
	5			*Not in force*
	6			1 Apr 2002 (SSI 2001/81)
	7		(a)–(c)	2 Apr 2001 (SSI 2001/81)
			(d)	*Not in force*
	8			2 Apr 2001 (SSI 2001/81)
5, para	1			1 Apr 2002 (SSI 2001/81)
	2, 3			2 Apr 2001 (SSI 2001/81)
	4			*Not in force*
	5, 6			2 Apr 2001 (SSI 2001/81)
	7			2 Apr 2001 (insofar as relates to continuing and welfare attorneys and withdrawers) (SSI 2001/81)
				1 Apr 2002 (otherwise) (SSI 2001/81)
	8			1 Apr 2002 (SSI 2001/81)
	9			2 Apr 2001 (insofar as relates to continuing and welfare attorneys and withdrawers) (SSI 2001/81)
				1 Apr 2002 (otherwise) (SSI 2001/81)
	10, 11			*Not in force*
	12			1 Apr 2002 (SSI 2001/81)
	13, 14			2 Apr 2001 (SSI 2001/81)
	15, 16			1 Apr 2002 (SSI 2001/81)
	17	(1), (2)		1 Apr 2002 (SSI 2001/81)
		(3)–(21)		2 Apr 2001 (insofar as relate to welfare attorneys) (SSI 2001/81)
				1 Apr 2002 (otherwise) (SSI 2001/81)
		(22), (23)		*Not in force*
		(24)	(a)	1 Apr 2002 (SSI 2001/81)
			(b)	2 Apr 2001 (insofar as relates to welfare attorneys) (SSI 2001/81)
				1 Apr 2002 (otherwise) (SSI 2001/81)
	18			1 Apr 2002 (SSI 2001/81)
	19			2 Apr 2001 (SSI 2001/81)
	20, 21			1 Apr 2002 (SSI 2001/81)
	22, 23			2 Apr 2001 (insofar as relate to welfare attorneys) (SSI 2001/81)
				1 Apr 2002 (otherwise) (SSI 2001/81)
	24			1 Apr 2002 (SSI 2001/81)

Adults with Incapacity (Scotland) Act 2000 (asp 4)—*contd*
Schedule

5, para	25	1 Apr 2002 (SSI 2001/81)
	26	2 Apr 2001 (SSI 2001/81)
6		2 Apr 2001 (repeal of Law Reform (Miscellaneous Provisions) (Scotland) Act 1990) (SSI 2001/81)
		1 Apr 2002 (otherwise) (except repeals of or in Improvement of Land Act 1864; Mental Health (Scotland) Act 1984, s 5(2)) (SSI 2001/81)
		Not in force (exceptions noted above)

Appropriation Act 2000 (c 9)

RA: 20 Jul 2000

20 Jul 2000 (RA)

Armed Forces Discipline Act 2000 (c 4)

RA: 25 May 2000

Commencement provisions: s 28(2), (3); Armed Forces Discipline Act 2000 (Commencement and Transitional Provisions) Order 2000, SI 2000/2366
Section

1–25	2 Oct 2000 (subject to transitional provisions and savings) (SI 2000/2366)
26	25 May 2000 (RA)
27	2 Oct 2000 (subject to transitional provisions and savings) (SI 2000/2366)
28	25 May 2000 (RA)
Schedule	
1–4	2 Oct 2000 (subject to transitional provisions and savings) (SI 2000/2366)

Bail, Judicial Appointments etc (Scotland) Act 2000 (asp 9)

RA: 9 Aug 2000

9 Aug 2000 (RA)

Budget (Scotland) Act 2000 (asp 2)

RA: 20 Mar 2000

20 Mar 2000 (RA)

Care Standards Act 2000 (c 14)

RA: 20 Jul 2000

Commencement provisions: s 122; Care Standards Act 2000 (Commencement No 1) Order 2000, SI 2000/2544; Care Standards Act 2000 (Commencement No 1 (England) and Transitional Provisions) Order 2000, SI 2000/2795; Care Standards Act 2000 (Commencement No 1) (Wales) Order 2000, SI 2000/2992; Care Standards Act 2000 (Commencement No 2 and Transitional Provisions) (Wales) Order 2001, SI 2001/139[1]; Care Standards Act 2000 (Commencement No 2 (England) and Transitional Provisions) Order 2001, SI 2001/290[2]; Care Standards Act 2000 (Commencement No 3) (England) Order 2001, SI 2001/731; Care Standards Act 2000 (Commencement No 4) (England) Order 2001, SI 2001/1193; Care Standards Act 2000 (Commencement No 5) (England) Order 2001, SI 2001/1210; Care Standards Act 2000 (Commencement No 6) (England) Order 2001, SI 2001/1536; Care Standards Act 2000 (Commencement No 7 and Transitional, Transitory and Savings (England)) Order 2001, SI 2001/2041[4]; Care Standards Act 2000 (Commencement No 3) (Wales) Order 2001, SI 2001/2190; Care Standards Act 2000 (Commencement No 4) (Wales) Order 2001, SI 2001/2354; Care Standards Act 2000 (Commencement No 5 and Transitional Provisions) (Wales) Order 2001, SI 2001/2504[5]; Care Standards Act 2000 (Commencement No 6) (Wales) Order 2001, SI 2001/2538; Care Standards Act 2000 (Commencement No 7) (Wales) Order 2001, SI 2001/2782; Care Standards Act 2000 (Commencement No 8) (England) Order 2001, SI 2001/3331; Care Standards Act 2000 (Commencement No 9) (England) and Transitional and Savings Provisions) Order 2001, SI 2001/3852[6], as amended by SI 2001/4150; Care Standards Act 2000 (Commencement No 10 (England) and Transitional, Savings and Amendment Provisions) Order 2001, SI 2001/4150[10]

Section		
1–3		1 Jul 2001 (W) (SI 2001/2190)
		20 Nov 2001 (E) (for the purpose only of the exercise of any power to make regulations) (SI 2001/3852)
		1 Jan 2002 (E) (for specified purposes)[7] (SI 2001/3852)
		1 Apr 2002 (E) (otherwise) (SI 2001/3852)
4	(1)	1 Jul 2001 (W) (SI 2001/2190)
		20 Nov 2001 (E) (for the purpose only of the exercise of any power to make regulations) (SI 2001/3852)
		1 Jan 2002 (E) (for specified purposes)[7] (except in so far as it relates to voluntary adoption agencies) (SI 2001/3852)
		1 Apr 2002 (E) (so far as it relates to s 4(4), (6), (8), (9) brought into force by art 3(7) of SI 2001/3852) (SI 2001/3852)

Care Standards Act 2000 (c 14)—*contd*

Section

4	(1)—*contd*	1 Jul 2002 (E) (so far as it relates to s 4(2), (3), (5), (6), (8), (9) brought into force by art 3(8) of SI 2001/3852) (SI 2001/3852)
		Not in force (otherwise)
	(2), (3)	1 Jul 2001 (W) (SI 2001/2190)
		20 Nov 2001 (E) (for the purpose only of the exercise of any power to make regulations) (SI 2001/3852)
		1 Jan 2002 (E) (for specified purposes)[7] (SI 2001/3852)
		1 Jul 2002 (E) (otherwise) (SI 2001/3852)
	(4)	1 Jul 2001 (W) (SI 2001/2190)
		20 Nov 2001 (E) (for the purpose only of the exercise of any power to make regulations) (SI 2001/3852)
		1 Jan 2002 (E) (for specified purposes)[7] (SI 2001/3852)
		1 Apr 2002 (E) (otherwise) (SI 2001/3852)
	(5)	1 Jul 2001 (W) (SI 2001/2190)
		20 Nov 2001 (E) (for the purpose only of the exercise of any power to make regulations) (SI 2001/3852)
		1 Jan 2002 (E) (for specified purposes)[7] (SI 2001/3852)
		1 Jul 2002 (E) (otherwise) (SI 2001/3852)
	(6)	1 Jul 2001 (W) (SI 2001/2190)
		20 Nov 2001 (E) (for the purpose only of the exercise of any power to make regulations) (SI 2001/3852)
		1 Jan 2002 (E) (for specified purposes)[7] (SI 2001/3852)
		1 Apr 2002 (E) (so far as it relates to s 4(4)) (SI 2001/3852)
		1 Jul 2002 (E) (otherwise) (SI 2001/3852)
	(7)	1 Jul 2001 (W) (SI 2001/2190)
		20 Nov 2001 (E) (for the purpose only of the exercise of any power to make regulations) (SI 2001/3852)
		Not in force (otherwise)
	(8)	1 Jul 2001 (W) (SI 2001/2190)
		20 Nov 2001 (E) (for the purpose only of the exercise of any power to make regulations) (SI 2001/3852)

Care Standards Act 2000 (c 14)—*contd*
Section

4	(8)—*contd*	1 Jan 2002 (E) (for specified purposes)[7] (SI 2001/3852)
		1 Apr 2002 (E) (except in so far as it relates to residential family centres) (SI 2001/3852)
		1 Jul 2002 (E) (otherwise) (SI 2001/3852)
	(9)	1 Jul 2001 (W) (SI 2001/2190)
		20 Nov 2001 (E) (for the purpose only of the exercise of any power to make regulations) (SI 2001/3852)
		1 Jan 2002 (E) (for specified purposes)[7] (except in so far as it relates to voluntary adoption agencies) (SI 2001/3852)
		1 Apr 2002 (E) (except in so far as it relates to domiciliary care agencies, nurses agencies and voluntary adoption agencies (SI 2001/3852)
		1 Jul 2002 (E) (in so far as it relates to domiciliary care agencies and nurses agencies) (SI 2001/3852)
		Not in force (otherwise)
5		1 Jul 2001 (W) (SI 2001/2190)
		1 Apr 2002 (E) (in so far as it relates to the Commission) (SI 2001/3852)
		Not in force (otherwise)
6	(1), (2)	9 Apr 2001 (SI 2001/1193)
	(3)	See Sch 1 below
	(4)	9 Apr 2001 (SI 2001/1193)
7	(1)–(6)	1 Apr 2002 (E) (SI 2001/3852)
		Not in force (otherwise)
	(7)	1 Jul 2001 (W) (SI 2001/2190)
		1 Apr 2002 (E) (SI 2001/3852)
8		1 Jul 2001 (W) (for purpose of enabling subordinate legislation to be made) (SI 2001/2190)
		Not in force (otherwise)
9	(1), (2)	*Not in force*
	(3)–(5)	1 Jul 2001 (W) (SI 2001/2190)
		Not in force (otherwise)
10	(1)–(5)	1 Apr 2002 (E) (SI 2001/3852)
		Not in force (otherwise)
	(6)	*Not in force*
	(7)	1 Apr 2002 (E) (SI 2001/3852)
		Not in force (otherwise)

Care Standards Act 2000 (c 14)—*contd*

Section

11	1 Jul 2001 (W) (for purpose of enabling subordinate legislation to be made) (SI 2001/2190)
	20 Nov 2001 (E) (for the purpose only of the exercise of any power to make regulations) (SI 2001/3852)
	1 Apr 2002 (E) (otherwise) (SI 2001/3852)
	Not in force (otherwise)
12	1 Jul 2001 (W) (for purpose of enabling subordinate legislation to be made) (SI 2001/2190)
	20 Nov 2001 (E) (for the purpose only of the exercise of any power to make regulations) (SI 2001/3852)
	1 Jan 2002 (E) (for specified purposes)[7] (SI 2001/3852)
	1 Apr 2002 (E) (otherwise) (SI 2001/3852)
	Not in force (otherwise)
13	1 Jan 2002 (E) (for specified purposes)[7] (SI 2001/3852)
	1 Apr 2002 (otherwise) (E) (SI 2001/3852)
	Not in force (otherwise)
14, 15	1 Jul 2001 (W) (for purpose of enabling subordinate legislation to be made) (SI 2001/2190)
	20 Nov 2001 (E) (for the purpose only of the exercise of any power to make regulations) (SI 2001/3852)
	1 Apr 2002 (E) (otherwise) (SI 2001/3852)
	Not in force (otherwise)
16	1 Jul 2001 (W) (SI 2001/2190)
	20 Nov 2001 (E) (for the purpose only of the exercise of any power to make regulations) (SI 2001/3852)
	1 Apr 2002 (otherwise) (E) (SI 2001/3852)
17–20	1 Apr 2002 (E) (SI 2001/3852)
	Not in force (otherwise)
21	20 Nov 2001 (E) (for the purpose only of enabling a person to bring an appeal against a determination which is treated under Sch 1, para 5(6) to SI 2001/3852, as a decision of the Commission for the purposes of that section (SI 2001/3852)

Care Standards Act 2000 (c 14)—*contd*

Section

21—*contd*		1 Apr 2002 (otherwise) (E) (SI 2001/3852)
		Not in force (otherwise)
22		1 Jul 2001 (W) (SI 2001/2190)
		20 Nov 2001 (E) (SI 2001/3852)
23	(1)–(3)	2 Mar 2001 (E) (SI 2001/731)
		1 Jul 2001 (W) (SI 2001/2190)
	(4)	1 Jul 2001 (W) (SI 2001/2190)
		1 Jan 2002 (E) (in relation to certain applications)[8] (SI 2001/3852)
		1 Apr 2002 (E) (otherwise) (SI 2001/3852)
24		1 Apr 2002 (E) (SI 2001/3852)
		Not in force (otherwise)
25		1 Jul 2001 (W) (SI 2001/2190)
		20 Nov 2001 (E) (for the purpose only of the exercise of any power to make regulations) (SI 2001/3852)
		1 Apr 2002 (E) (otherwise) (SI 2001/3852)
26		1 Apr 2002 (E) (SI 2001/3852)
		Not in force (otherwise)
27		1 Jan 2002 (E) (in relation to certain applications)[8] (SI 2001/3852)
		1 Apr 2002 (E) (otherwise) (SI 2001/3852)
		Not in force (otherwise)
28–30		1 Apr 2002 (E) (SI 2001/3852)
		Not in force (otherwise)
31		20 Nov 2001 (E) (for the purpose only of the exercise of any power to make regulations) (SI 2001/3852)
		1 Jan 2002 (E) (for certain purposes)[9] (SI 2001/3852)
		1 Apr 2002 (E) (otherwise) (SI 2001/3852)
		Not in force (otherwise)
32		1 Jan 2002 (E) (for certain purposes)[9] (SI 2001/3852)
		1 Apr 2002 (E) (so far as not already in force) (SI 2001/3852)
		Not in force (otherwise)
33		1 Jul 2001 (W) (SI 2001/2190)
		20 Nov 2001 (E) (for the purpose only of the exercise of any power to make regulations) (SI 2001/3852)
		1 Apr 2002 (E) (otherwise) (SI 2001/3852)

Care Standards Act 2000 (c 14)—*contd*

Section

34	1 Jul 2001 (W) (SI 2001/2190)
	20 Nov 2001 (E) (for the purpose only of the exercise of any power to make regulations) (SI 2001/3852)
	1 Apr 2002 (E) (otherwise) (SI 2001/3852)
35	1 Jul 2001 (W) (SI 2001/2190)
	20 Nov 2001 (E) (for the purpose only of the exercise of any power to make regulations) (SI 2001/3852)
	1 Apr 2002 (E) (otherwise) (SI 2001/3852)
36	1 Jul 2001 (W) (for purpose of enabling subordinate legislation to be made) (SI 2001/2190)
	20 Nov 2001 (E) (for the purpose only of the exercise of any power to make regulations) (SI 2001/3852)
	1 Apr 2002 (E) (otherwise) (SI 2001/3852)
	Not in force (otherwise)
37	1 Apr 2002 (E) (SI 2001/3852)
	Not in force (otherwise)
38	1 Jul 2001 (W) (SI 2001/2190)
	20 Nov 2001 (E) (SI 2001/3852)
39	19 Feb 2001 (E) (for purposes of enabling an application for registration to be made under Registered Homes Act 1984, s 23(3) (SI 2001/290)
	19 Mar 2001 (E) (otherwise) (SI 2001/290)
	31 Jul 2001 (W) (for purposes of enabling an application for registration to be made under Registered Homes Act 1984, s 23(3) (SI 2001/2504)
	31 Aug 2001 (W) (otherwise) (SI 2001/2504)
40	15 Oct 2000 (E) (for purposes of enabling application for registration to be made under Children Act 1989, Sch 6, para 1(1), (2)) (SI 2000/2795)
	1 Jan 2001 (E) (otherwise) (SI 2000/2795)

Care Standards Act 2000 (c 14)—*contd*

Section

40—*contd*			1 Feb 2001 (W) (for purposes only of enabling application for registration to be made under Children Act 1989, Sch 6, para 1(1), (2)) (SI 2001/139)
			28 Feb 2001 (W) (otherwise) (SI 2001/139)
41			1 Jan 2001 (E) (SI 2000/2795)
			28 Feb 2001 (W) (SI 2001/139)
42			1 Jul 2001 (W) (SI 2001/2190)
			Not in force (otherwise)
43	(1)		1 Jul 2001 (W) (SI 2001/2190)
			20 Nov 2001 (E) (for the purpose only of the exercise of any power to make regulations, in so far as they relate to relevant fostering functions) (SI 2001/3852)
			1 Apr 2002 (E) (in so far as relates to relevant fostering functions) (otherwise) (SI 2001/3852)
			Not in force (otherwise)
	(2)		1 Jul 2001 (W) (SI 2001/2190)
			20 Nov 2001 (E) (for the purpose only of the exercise of any power to make regulations, in so far as they relate to relevant fostering functions) (SI 2001/3852)
			1 Apr 2002 (E) (in so far as relates to relevant fostering functions) (otherwise) (SI 2001/3852)
			Not in force (otherwise)
	(3)	(a)	1 Jul 2001 (W) (SI 2001/2190)
			Not in force (otherwise)
		(b)	1 Jul 2001 (W) (SI 2001/2190)
			20 Nov 2001 (E) (for the purpose only of the exercise of any power to make regulations, in so far as they relate to relevant fostering functions) (SI 2001/3852)
			1 Apr 2002 (E) (in so far as relates to relevant fostering functions) (otherwise) (SI 2001/3852)
			Not in force (otherwise)
44			1 Apr 2002 (E) (in so far as relates to relevant fostering functions) (SI 2001/3852)
			Not in force (otherwise)

Care Standards Act 2000 (c 14)—*contd*

Section

45	(1)-(3)		1 Apr 2002 (E) (in so far as relates to relevant fostering functions) (SI 2001/3852)
			Not in force (otherwise)
	(4)		20 Nov 2001 (E) (for the purpose only of the exercise of any power to make regulations, in so far as they relate to relevant fostering functions) (SI 2001/3852)
			1 Apr 2002 (E) (in so far as relates to relevant fostering functions) (otherwise) (SI 2001/3852)
			Not in force (otherwise)
	(5)		1 Apr 2002 (E) (in so far as relates to relevant fostering functions) (SI 2001/3852)
			Not in force (otherwise)
46	(1)–(6)		1 Apr 2002 (E) (in so far as relates to relevant fostering functions) (SI 2001/3852)
			Not in force (otherwise)
	(7)	(a), (b)	1 Apr 2002 (E) (in so far as relates to relevant fostering functions) (SI 2001/3852)
			Not in force (otherwise)
		(c), (d)	*Not in force*
	(8)		1 Apr 2002 (E) (in so far as relates to relevant fostering functions) (SI 2001/3852)
			Not in force (otherwise)
47			1 Apr 2002 (E) (in so far as relates to relevant fostering functions) (SI 2001/3852)
			Not in force (otherwise)
48			1 Jul 2001 (W) (SI 2001/2190)
			20 Nov 2001 (E) (for the purpose only of the exercise of any power to make regulations) (SI 2001/3852)
			1 Apr 2002 (E) (in so far as relates to relevant fostering functions) (SI 2001/3852)
			Not in force (otherwise)
49			1 Jul 2001 (W) (SI 2001/2190)
			20 Nov 2001 (E) (for the purpose only of issuing statements of national minimum standards so far as they relate to the exercise of relevant fostering functions by local authorities) (SI 2001/3852)

Care Standards Act 2000 (c 14)—*contd*
Section

49—*contd*			1 Apr 2002 (E) (in so far as relates to relevant fostering functions) (otherwise) (SI 2001/3852)
			Not in force (otherwise)
50–52			1 Jul 2001 (W) (SI 2001/2190)
			20 Nov 2001 (E) (for the purpose only of the exercise of any power to make regulations, in so far as they relate to relevant fostering functions) (SI 2001/3852)
			1 Apr 2002 (E) (in so far as relates to relevant fostering functions) (otherwise) (SI 2001/3852)
			Not in force (otherwise)
53			1 Apr 2002 (E) (in so far as relates to relevant fostering functions) (SI 2001/3852)
			Not in force (otherwise)
54	(1)	(a)	7 May 2001 (SI 2001/1536)
		(b)	1 Apr 2001 (SI 2000/2992)
	(2)		*Not in force*
	(3)		1 Apr 2001 (SI 2000/2992)
	(4), (5)		1 Apr 2001 (W) (so far as relates to Care Council for Wales) (SI 2000/2992)
			7 May 2001 (E) (so far as relates to the General Social Care Council) (SI 2001/1536)
	(6)		See Sch 1 below
	(7)	(a)	7 May 2001 (SI 2001/1536)
		(b)	1 Apr 2001 (SI 2000/2992)
55			1 Apr 2001 (W) (SI 2000/2992)
			7 May 2001 (E) (so far as relates to ss 54(1)(a), (4), (5), (6), (7)(a), 59, 60, 62, 63, 65, 66, 71, Sch 1, paras 1–5, 7, 8, 12–14, 16, 18–26) (SI 2001/1536)
			Not in force (otherwise)
56–58			*Not in force*
59, 60			7 May 2001 (E) (so far as relates to the General Social Care Council, for purpose only of t he exercise of any power to make rules and prepare codes of practice) (SI 2001/1536)
			Not in force (otherwise)
61			*Not in force*

Care Standards Act 2000 (c 14)—*contd*
Section

62		7 May 2001 (E) (so far as relates to the General Social Care Council, for purpose only of the exercise of any power to make rules and prepare codes of practice) (SI 2001/1536)
		Not in force (otherwise)
63		7 May 2001 (E) (so far as relates to the General Social Care Council, for purpose only of the exercise of any power to make rules and prepare codes of practice) (SI 2001/1536)
		31 Jul 2001 (W) (SI 2001/2538)
		Not in force (otherwise)
64		*Not in force*
65		7 May 2001 (E) (so far as relates to the General Social Care Council, for purpose only of the exercise of any power to make rules and prepare codes of practice) (SI 2001/1536)
		Not in force (otherwise)
66		7 May 2001 (E) (so far as relates to the General Social Care Council, for purpose only of the exercise of any power to make rules and prepare codes of practice) (SI 2001/1536)
		31 Jul 2001 (W) (SI 2001/2538)
		Not in force (otherwise)
67		1 Oct 2001 (W) (SI 2001/2538)
		Not in force (otherwise)
68–69		*Not in force*
70	(1)	1 Oct 2001 (W) (SI 2001/2538)
		Not in force (otherwise)
	(2)–(5)	20 Jul 2000 (RA)
71		7 May 2001 (E) (so far as relates to the General Social Care Council, for purpose only of the exercise of any power to make rules and prepare codes of practice) (SI 2001/1536)
		31 Jul 2001 (W) (so far as it applies to ss 63, 66 of this Act) (SI 2001/2538)
		Not in force (otherwise)
72		13 Nov 2000 (SI 2000/2992)
72A		Inserted by Children's Commissioner for Wales Act 2001, s 2 (qv)

Care Standards Act 2000 (c 14)—*contd*

Section

72B		Inserted by Children's Commissioner for Wales Act 2001, s 3(1) (qv)
73–75		26 Aug 2001 (SI 2001/2782)
75A		Inserted by Children's Commissioner for Wales Act 2001, s 5(1) (qv)
76–78		26 Aug 2001 (SI 2001/2782)
79	(1)	16 Mar 2001 (E) (for the purpose of enabling the Secretary of State to make regulations under Children Act 1989, ss 79C(1), 79E(2)(a), 79F(1)(b), (2)(b), 79H(1), 79N(5), 79Q(2), (3), 79R(1), (3)(b), 79V, 79W(4)) (SI 2001/1210)
		1 Jul 2001 (W) (for purpose of enabling subordinate legislation to be made under a provision inserted by it into Children Act 1989 and for purposes of inserting Children Act 1989, s 79B(2), (9) (to the extent necessary for the purposes of enabling subordinate legislation to be made under Sch 9A to the 1989 Act)) (SI 2001/2190)
		2 Jul 2001 (E) (otherwise, except for the purposes of Pt XA, ss 79B(8), 79K(5), 79L(6), (7), 79M, 79P(1)–(4), 79Q(2), (3)) (SI 2001/2041)
		2 Sep 2002 (E) (for purpose of giving effect to Pt XA, ss 79P(1), (2), 79Q(2), (3)) (SI 2001/2041)
		Not in force (otherwise)
	(2)	16 Mar 2001 (E) (for the purpose of enabling the Secretary of State to make regulations under Children Act 1989, Sch 9A, paras 1(1), 4(1), (3), 6(2), (4), (7) (SI 2001/1210)
		1 Jul 2001 (W) (for purpose of enabling subordinate legislation to be made under Children Act 1989, Sch 9A) (SI 2001/2190)
		2 Jul 2001 (E) (otherwise) (SI 2001/2041)
		Not in force (otherwise)
	(3), (4)	16 Mar 2001 (E) (SI 2001/1210)
		1 Jul 2001 (W) (SI 2001/2190)
	(5)	2 Jul 2001 (E) (SI 2001/2041)
		Not in force (otherwise)
80	(1)–(7)	*Not in force*

Care Standards Act 2000 (c 14)—*contd*

Section

80	(8)	2 Oct 2000 (for purposes only of Regulations under s 103 of this Act) (SI 2000/2544)
		Not in force (otherwise)
81–93		*Not in force*
94		2 Oct 2000 (SI 2000/2544)
95		*Not in force*
96		15 Sep 2000 (so far as inserts Protection of Children Act 1999, s 2B, for purposes only of definition "relevant enquiry" in s 3(7) of 1999 Act) (SI 2000/2544)
		2 Oct 2000 (otherwise) (SI 2000/2544)
97		*Not in force*
98		1 Apr 2001 (E) (SI 2001/1193)
		1 Jul 2001 (W) (SI 2001/2354)
99		15 Sep 2000 (SI 2000/2544)
100, 101		2 Oct 2000 (SI 2000/2544)
102		*Not in force*
103		2 Oct 2000 (SI 2000/2544)
104		*Not in force*
105	(1)–(4)	20 Nov 2001 (E) (for the purpose only of the exercise of any power to make regulations) (SI 2001/3852)
		1 Apr 2002 (E) (otherwise) (SI 2001/3852)
		Not in force (otherwise)
	(5)	1 Apr 2002 (E) (SI 2001/3852)
		Not in force (otherwise)
106		1 Apr 2002 (E) (SI 2001/3852)
		Not in force (otherwise)
107		1 Jul 2001 (W) (SI 2001/2190)
		20 Nov 2001 (E) (for the purpose only of issuing statements of national minimum standards for safeguarding and promoting the welfare of children for whom accommodation is provided in schools and colleges (SI 2001/3852)
		1 Apr 2002 (E) (otherwise) (SI 2001/3852)
108		1 Jul 2001 (W) (SI 2001/2190)
		20 Nov 2001 (E) (for the purpose only of the exercise of any power to make regulations) (SI 2001/3852)
		1 Apr 2002 (E) (otherwise) (SI 2001/3852)
109, 110		1 Apr 2002 (E) (SI 2001/3852)
		Not in force (otherwise)

Care Standards Act 2000 (c 14)—*contd*

Section

111	(1)	1 Apr 2001 (E) (SI 2001/3852)
		Not in force (otherwise)
	(2)	1 Jul 2002 (E) (in so far as it omits Employment Agencies Act 1973, s 13(7) (b), (c), and the proviso thereto) (SI 2001/3852)
		Not in force (otherwise)
112		1 Jul 2001 (W) (SI 2001/2190)
		4 Oct 2001 (E) (SI 2001/3331)
113	(1)	*Not in force*
	(2)–(4)	1 Apr 2001 (W) (so far as relates to Care Council for Wales) (SI 2000/2992)
		Not in force (otherwise)
114		16 Mar 2001 (E) (SI 2001/1210)
		1 Apr 2001 (W) (so far as relates to Care Council for Wales) (SI 2000/2992)
		1 Jul 2001 (W) (otherwise) (SI 2001/2190)
		Not in force (otherwise)
115		16 Mar 2001 (E) (SI 2001/1210)
		1 Jul 2001 (W) (SI 2001/2190)
		Not in force (otherwise)
116		See Sch 4 below
117	(1)	See Sch 5 below
	(2)	See Sch 6 below
118–123		20 Jul 2000 (RA)

Schedule

1, para	1	16 Mar 2001 (E) (so far as relates to the National Care Standards Commission) (SI 2001/1193)
		1 Apr 2001 (W) (so far as relates to Care Council for Wales) (SI 2000/2992)
		7 May 2001 (E) (so far as relates to the General Social Care Council) (SI 2001/1536)
	2–5	1 Apr 2001 (W) (so far as relates to Care Council for Wales) (SI 2000/2992)
		9 Apr 2001 (E) (so far as relates to the National Care Standards Commission) (SI 2001/1193)
		7 May 2001 (E) (so far as relates to the General Social Care Council) (SI 2001/1536)

Care Standards Act 2000 (c 14)—*contd*
Schedule

1, para	6	16 Mar 2001 (E) (so far as relates to the National Care Standards Commission) (SI 2001/1193)
		1 Apr 2001 (W) (so far as relates to Care Council for Wales) (SI 2000/2992)
		10 Apr 2001 (E) (so far as relates to the General Social Care Council) (SI 2001/1536)
	7, 8	1 Apr 2001 (W) (so far as relates to Care Council for Wales) (SI 2000/2992)
		9 Apr 2001 (E) (so far as relates to the National Care Standards Commission) (SI 2001/1193)
		7 May 2001 (E) (so far as relates to the General Social Care Council) (SI 2001/1536)
	9–11	1 Apr 2001 (SI 2001/1193)
	12–14	1 Apr 2001 (W) (so far as relates to Care Council for Wales) (SI 2000/2992)
		9 Apr 2001 (E) (so far as relates to the National Care Standards Commission) (SI 2001/1193)
		7 May 2001 (E) (so far as relates to the General Social Care Council) (SI 2001/1536)
	15	1 Apr 2001 (SI 2001/1193)
	16	1 Apr 2001 (W) (so far as relates to Care Council for Wales) (SI 2000/2992)
		9 Apr 2001 (E) (so far as relates to the National Care Standards Commission) (SI 2001/1193)
		7 May 2001 (E) (so far as relates to the General Social Care Council) (SI 2001/1536)
	17	1 Apr 2001 (SI 2001/1193)
	18–26	1 Apr 2001 (W) (so far as relates to Care Council for Wales) (SI 2000/2992)
		9 Apr 2001 (E) (so far as relates to the National Care Standards Commission) (SI 2001/1193)
		7 May 2001 (E) (so far as relates to the General Social Care Council) (SI 2001/1536)
	27	1 Apr 2001 (SI 2000/2992)

Care Standards Act 2000 (c 14)—*contd*

Schedule

2			13 Nov 2000 (SI 2000/2992)
2A			Inserted by Children's Commissioner for Wales Act 2001, s 3(2), Sch, Pt 1 (qv)
2B			Inserted by Children's Commissioner for Wales Act 2001, s 4(10), Sch, Pt 2 (qv)
3			1 Jul 2001 (W) (for purpose of enabling subordinate legislation to be made under Children Act 1989, Sch 9A) (SI 2001/2190)
			Not in force (otherwise)
4, paras	1–4		1 Apr 2002 (E) (SI 2001/4150)
			Not in force (otherwise)
	5	(1)	1 Apr 2002 (E) (SI 2001/4150)
			Not in force (otherwise)
		(2)	*Not in force*
		(3)	1 Apr 2002 (E) (SI 2001/4150)
			Not in force (otherwise)
		(4), (5)	*Not in force*
		(6)	1 Jul 2001 (W) (SI 2001/2190)
			Not in force (otherwise)
		(7)	*Not in force*
		(8)	1 Apr 2002 (E) (SI 2001/4150)
			Not in force (otherwise)
		(9)–(11)	*Not in force*
	6		*Not in force*
	7		2 Jul 2001 (E) (SI 2001/2041)
			Not in force (otherwise)
	8–11		1 Apr 2002 (E) (SI 2001/4150)
			Not in force (otherwise)
	12		*Not in force*
	13		2 Jul 2001 (E) (SI 2001/2041)
			Not in force (otherwise)
	14	(1), (2)	2 Jul 2001 (E) (SI 2001/2041)
			Not in force (otherwise)
		(3)	1 Apr 2002 (E) (SI 2001/4150)
			Not in force (otherwise)
		(4)–(6)	*Not in force*
		(7)–(9)	1 Apr 2002 (E) (SI 2001/4150)
			Not in force (otherwise)
		(10)(a)	1 Apr 2002 (E) (SI 2001/4150)
			Not in force (otherwise)
		(10)(b)	*Not in force*
		(11),	1 Apr 2002 (E) (SI 2001/4150)
		(12)	*Not in force* (otherwise)
		(13), (14)	*Not in force*
		(15)	1 Jan 2001 (E) (SI 2000/2795)
			28 Feb 2001 (W) (SI 2001/139)

Care Standards Act 2000 (c 14)—*contd*
Schedule

4, paras	14	(16)	(a)	1 Apr 2002 (E) (SI 2001/4150)
				Not in force (otherwise)
			(b)	2 Jul 2001 (E) (SI 2001/2041)
				Not in force (otherwise)
			(c)	1 Apr 2002 (E) (SI 2001/4150)
				Not in force (otherwise)
			(d)	2 Jul 2001 (E) (SI 2001/2041)
				Not in force (otherwise)
		(17)–(21)		1 Apr 2002 (E) (SI 2001/4150)
				Not in force (otherwise)
		(22)		*Not in force*
		(23)	(a)(i)–(iii)	1 Apr 2002 (E) (SI 2001/4150)
				Not in force (otherwise)
			(iv), (v)	2 Jul 2001 (E) (SI 2001/2041)
				Not in force (otherwise)
			(vi), (vii)	1 Apr 2002 (E) (SI 2001/4150)
				Not in force (otherwise)
			(b)	2 Jul 2001 (E) (SI 2001/2041)
				Not in force (otherwise)
		(24)–(28)		1 Apr 2002 (E) (SI 2001/4150)
				Not in force (otherwise)
		(29)		*Not in force*
	15–18			1 Apr 2002 (E) (SI 2001/4150)
				Not in force (otherwise)
	19			2 Jul 2001 (E) (SI 2001/2041)
				Not in force (otherwise)
	20			1 Apr 2002 (E) (SI 2001/4150)
				Not in force (otherwise)
	21			1 Apr 2002 (E) (except words "and vulnerable adults") (SI 2001/4150)
				Not in force (otherwise)
	22			*Not in force*
	23			1 Apr 2002 (E) (SI 2001/4150)
				Not in force (otherwise)
	24	(1), (2)		1 Apr 2002 (E) (SI 2001/4150)
				Not in force (otherwise)
		(3), (4)		*Not in force*
	25			2 Jul 2001 (E) (SI 2001/2041)
				Not in force (otherwise)
	26	(1), (2) [3]		2 Oct 2000 (SI 2000/2544)
		(3)		1 Apr 2002 (E) (except in so far as it inserts Protection of Children Act 1999, s 9(2)(b) and 9(2)(d) (in so far as s 9(2)(d) relates to ss 68, 87, 88 of the 2000 Act) and s 9(3A)) (SI 2001/3852)
				Not in force (otherwise)
		(4)		2 Oct 2000 (SI 2000/2544)

Care Standards Act 2000 (c 14)—*contd*

Schedule

4, paras	27	*Not in force*
	28	1 Apr 2002 (E) (SI 2001/4150)
		Not in force (otherwise)
	29, 30	1 Apr 2002 (E) (SI 2001/4150)
5, paras	1	1 Jul 2001 (W) (SI 2001/2190)
		Not in force (otherwise)
	2	1 Jul 2001 (W) (for purpose of enabling subordinate legislation to be made) (SI 2001/2190)
		Not in force (otherwise)
	3	26 Aug 2001 (SI 2001/2782)
6		2 Oct 2000 (repeals in or of Protection of Children Act 1999, ss 10, 13(3), (4)) (SI 2000/2544)
		4 Oct 2001 (E) (repeals in or of Chronically Sick and Disabled Persons Act 1970, s 18(1), (3)) (SI 2001/3331)
		1 Apr 2002 (E) (repeals in or of Registered Homes Act 1984 and Children Act 1989, ss 60, 63, Schs 5, 6) (SI 2001/3852)
		1 Apr 2002 (E) (repeals in or of National Assistance Act 1948; London Government Act 1963; Local Authority Social Services Act 1970; Greater London Council (General Powers) Act 1981; Mental Health Act 1983; Public Health (Control of Disease) Act 1984; Greater London Council (General Powers) Act 1984; Children Act 1989 (in so far as not already in force, except definition "child minder" in s 105(1)); National Health Service and Community Care Act 1990; Registered Homes (Amendment) Act 1991; Arbitration Act 1996; Education Act 1996; and Nurses, Midwives and Health Visitors Act 1997) (SI 2001/4150)
		1 Jul 2002 (E) (repeals in or of Employment Agencies Act 1973 and Nurses Agencies Act 1957) (SI 2001/3852)

Care Standards Act 2000 (c 14)—*contd*
Schedule
6—*contd*   1 Jul 2002 (E) (so far as relates to
                                                      Local Government Act 1972; and
                                                      Nurses, Midwives and Health
                                                      Visitors Act 1979) (SI 2001/4150)
                                                      Not in force (otherwise)

1   For transitional provisions, see SI 2001/139, art 3

2   For transitional provisions, see SI 2001/290, art 3

3   The Queen's Printer copy of the Care Standards Act 2000, Sch 4, para 26, contains 2 sub-paras (2)

4   For transitional, transitory and savings provisions, see SI 2001/2041, art 3, Schedule

5   For transitional provisions, see SI 2001/2504, art 3

6   For transitional provisions, see SI 2001/3852, Schs 1, 2

7   The specified purposes are—

     (a) to enable the Commission to consider or obtain information in relation to an application within
         note 8 below;

     (b) to enable the Commission to determine such an application, except for the purpose of enabling
         any effect to be given to the determination of any such application before—

         (i) in the case of an application to which paragraph 13(2) or 14(2) of Sch 1 to SI 2001/3852
             applies, 1 July 2002;

         (ii) in the case of an application for registration under the Care Standards Act 2000, Pt II in
              respect of a residential family centre, a nurses agency or a domiciliary care agency, 1 July 2002;

         (iii) in the case of any other application 1April 2001.

8   The relevant applications are—

     (a) an application which is to be determined by the Commission by virtue of Sch 1, para 1 or 14 to
         SI 2001/3852;

     (b) an application for registration under Part II of the 2000 Act in respect of an establishment or an
         agency referred to in para 15(1) or (2) of Sch 1 to SI 2001/3852 and which is made by a person
         to whom that paragraph applies.

9   The relevant purposes are—

     (a) an application to which note 8 above applies;

     (b) an establishment or agency to which Sch 1, para 5(2) and (3) apply.

10   For transitional provisions, see SI 2001/4150, art 4

Carers and Disabled Children Act 2000 (c 16)

RA: 20 Jul 2000

Commencement provisions: s 12(2)–(4); Carers and Disabled Children Act 2000
    (Commencement No 1) (England) Order 2001, SI 2001/510; Carers and
    Disabled Children Act 2000 (Commencement No 1) (Wales) Order 2001,
    SI 2001/2196

Section
1, 2   1 Apr 2001 (E) (SI 2001/510)
                                                      1 Jul 2001 (W) (SI 2001/2196)
3   *Not in force*
4   1 Apr 2001 (E) (SI 2001/510)
                                                      1 Jul 2001 (W) (SI 2001/2196)

Carers and Disabled Children Act 2000 (c 16)—*contd*
Section

5		1 Apr 2001 (E) (SI 2001/510)
		1 Jul 2001 (W) (SI 2001/2196)
		Prospectively repealed by Health and Social Care Act 2001, s 67, Sch 6, Pt 3[1]
6		1 Apr 2001 (E) (SI 2001/510)
		1 Jul 2001 (W) (SI 2001/2196)
7	(1)	1 Apr 2001 (E) (so far as inserts Children Act 1989, s 17A[2]) (SI 2001/510)
		1 Jul 2001 (W) (so far as inserts Children Act 1989, s 17A[2]) (SI 2001/2196)
		Not in force (otherwise)
	(2), (3)	1 Apr 2001 (E) (SI 2001/510)
		1 Jul 2001 (W) (SI 2001/2196)
8		1 Apr 2001 (E) (SI 2001/510)
		1 Jul 2001 (W) (SI 2001/2196)
9		1 Apr 2001 (E) (except so far as relates to provision of vouchers) (SI 2001/510)
		1 Jul 2001 (W) (except so far as relates to provision of vouchers) (SI 2001/2196)
		Not in force (otherwise)
10		1 Apr 2001 (E) (SI 2001/510)
		1 Jul 2001 (W) (SI 2001/2196)
11	(1)–(3)	1 Apr 2001 (E) (SI 2001/510)
		1 Jul 2001 (W) (SI 2001/2196)
	(4)	1 Apr 2001 (E) (SI 2001/510)
		Not in force (otherwise)
12		20 Jul 2000 (RA)

[1]   Orders made under Health and Social Care Act 2001, s 70(2), bringing the prospective repeal into force are noted to that Act

[2]   Prospectively repealed by Health and Social Care Act 2001, s 67, Sch 6, Pt 3 in so far as inserts s 17A; orders made under Health and Social Care Act 2001, s 70(2), bringing the prospective repeal into force are noted to that Act

Census (Amendment) Act 2000 (c 24)

RA: 28 Jul 2000

28 Jul 2000 (RA)

Census (Amendment) (Scotland) Act 2000 (asp 3)

RA: 10 Apr 2000

10 Apr 2000 (RA)

Child Support, Pensions and Social Security Act 2000 (c 19)

RA: 28 Jul 2000

Commencement provisions: s 86; Child Support, Pensions and Social Security Act 2000 (Commencement No 1) Order 2000, SI 2000/2666; Child Support, Pensions and Social Security Act 2000 (Commencement No 2) Order 2000, SI 2000/2950 (as amended by SI 2000/3166); Child Support, Pensions and Social Security Act 2000 (Commencement No 3) Order 2000, SI 2000/2994, Child Support, Pensions and Social Security Act 2000 (Commencement No 4) Order 2000, SI 2000/3166 (as amended by SI 2001/1252); Child Support, Pensions and Social Security Act 2000 (Commencement No 5) Order 2000, SI 2000/3354; Child Support, Pensions and Social Security Act 2000 (Commencement No 6) Order 2001, SI 2001/153; Child Support, Pensions and Social Security Act 2000 (Commencement No 7) Order 2001, SI 2001/774; Child Support, Pensions and Social Security Act 2000 (Commencement No 8) Order 2001, SI 2001/1252; Child Support, Pensions and Social Security Act 2000 (Commencement No 9) Order 2001, SI 2001/2295, as amended by SI 2002/437; Child Support, Pensions and Social Security Act 2000 (Commencement No 10) Order 2001, SI 2001/2619; Child Support, Pensions and Social Security Act 2000 (Commencement No 11) Order 2002, SI 2002/437

Section		
1	(1), (2)	*Not in force*
	(3)	See Sch 1 below
2		*Not in force*
3–5		10 Nov 2000 (for purpose of making regulations and Acts of Sederunt) (SI 2000/2994)
		Not in force (otherwise)
6		See Sch 2 below
7		10 Nov 2000 (except in so far as it relates to s 28G(2)) (for the purpose of making regulations and Acts of Sederunt) (SI 2000/2994)
		10 Nov 2000 (in so far as it relates to s 28G(2)) (for purpose of making regulations) (SI 2000/2994)
		1 Jan 2001 (in so far as it relates to s 28G(2)) (for all other purposes) (SI 2000/2994)
8		*Not in force*
9, 10		10 Nov 2000 (for purpose of making regulations and Acts of Sederunt) (SI 2000/2994)
		Not in force (otherwise)
11		15 Feb 2001 (SI 2000/3354)
12		*Not in force*
13–15		31 Jan 2001 (SI 2000/3354)
16, 17		10 Nov 2000 (for purpose of making regulations and Acts of Sederunt) (SI 2000/2994)
		2 Apr 2001 (otherwise) (SI 2000/3354)

Child Support, Pensions and Social Security Act 2000 (c 19)—*contd*

Section

18–21		10 Nov 2000 (for purpose of making regulations and Acts of Sederunt) (SI 2000/2994)
		Not in force (otherwise)
22	(1), (2)	31 Jan 2001 (SI 2000/3354)
	(3)	10 Nov 2000 (for purpose of making regulations and Acts of Sederunt) (SI 2000/2994)
		31 Jan 2001 (otherwise) (SI 2000/3354)
	(4)	*Not in force*
23		*Not in force*
24		28 Jul 2000 (RA)
25		10 Nov 2000 (for purpose of making regulations and Acts of Sederunt) (SI 2000/2994)
		Not in force (otherwise)
26		See Sch 3 below
27		10 Nov 2000 (for purpose of making regulations) (SI 2000/2994)
		1 Jan 2001 (for all other purposes) (SI 2000/2994)
28		*Not in force*
29		10 Nov 2000 (for purpose of making regulations and Acts of Sederunt) (SI 2000/2994)
		Not in force (otherwise)
30, 31		8 Jan 2001 (for purposes of making regulations and of making an order appointing the first or second appointed year) (SI 2000/2950, as amended by SI 2000/3166)
		25 Jan 2001 (for purposes of making reports and orders under Pension Schemes Act 1993, ss 42, 42B and 45A) (SI 2001/153)
		6 Apr 2002 (otherwise) (SI 2001/153)
32		8 Jan 2001 (for purposes of making regulations and of making an order appointing the first or second appointed year) (SI 2000/2950, as amended by SI 2000/3166)
		9 Apr 2001 (otherwise) (SI 2001/153)
33	(1), (2)	8 Jan 2001 (for purposes of making regulations and of making an order appointing the first or second appointed year) (SI 2000/2950, as amended by SI 2000/3166)

Child Support, Pensions and Social Security Act 2000 (c 19)—*contd*

Section

33	(1), (2)—*contd*	25 Jan 2001 (for purposes of an order under Social Security Administration Act 1992, s 148A, as inserted by Child Support, Pensions and Social Security Act 2000, s 33(1)) (SI 2001/153)
		6 Apr 2002 (otherwise) (SI 2001/153)
	(3), (4)	8 Jan 2001 (for purposes of making regulations and of making an order appointing the first or second appointed year) (SI 2000/2950, as amended by SI 2000/3166)
		25 Jan 2001 (otherwise) (SI 2001/153)
34, 35		8 Jan 2001 (for purposes of making regulations and of making an order appointing the first or second appointed year) (SI 2000/2950, as amended by SI 2000/3166)
		25 Jan 2001 (for purposes of making reports and orders under Pension Schemes Act 1993, ss 42, 42B and 45A) (SI 2001/153)
		6 Apr 2002 (otherwise) (SI 2001/153)
36		1 Nov 2000 (SI 2000/2950)
37		1 Dec 2000 (SI 2000/3166)
38, 39		28 Jul 2000 (RA)
40		8 Jan 2001 (SI 2000/3166)
41		29 Sep 2000 (SI 2000/2666)
42		1 Dec 2000 (for purposes of authorising the making of regulations) (SI 2000/3166)
		1 Jan 2001 (otherwise) (SI 2000/3166)
43–46		*Not in force*
47, 48		1 Mar 2002 (for the purpose of making regulations and rules) (SI 2002/437)
		1 Apr 2002 (otherwise) (SI 2002/437)
49	(1)	1 Mar 2002 (so far as it inserts Pensions Act 1995, s 72A(1), (2), (3) (except for words "Subject to subsection (4)," and "(apart from any postponement under subsection (4))"), (7), (8)(a), (9) (for the purpose of making regulations and rules)) (SI 2002/437)

Child Support, Pensions and Social Security Act 2000 (c 19)—*contd*

Section

49	(1)—*contd*	1 Apr 2002 (so far as it inserts Pensions Act 1995, s 72A(1), (2), (3) (except for words "Subject to subsection (4)," and "(apart from any postponement under subsection (4))"), (7), (8)(a), (9) (otherwise)) (SI 2002/437)
		Not in force (otherwise)
	(2), (3)	1 Mar 2002 (for the purpose of making regulations and rules) (SI 2002/437)
		1 Apr 2002 (otherwise) (SI 2002/437)
50		1 Mar 2002 (for the purpose of making regulations and rules) (SI 2002/437)
		1 Apr 2002 (otherwise) (SI 2002/437)
51		1 Dec 2000 (SI 2000/3166)
52		1 Jan 2001 (except so far as inserts Pension Schemes Act 1993, s 113(3B) (SI 2000/3166)
		Not in force (exception as noted above)
53		1 Dec 2000 (SI 2000/3166)
54		1 Mar 2002 (for the purpose of making regulations and rules) (SI 2002/437)
		Not in force (otherwise)
55		23 Jul 2001 (SI 2001/2295)
56		See Sch 5 below
57, 58		15 Nov 2000 (for purpose of the exercise of the power to make regulations) (SI 2000/2994)
		9 Apr 2001 (for all other purposes) (SI 2000/2994)
59		1 Jan 2001 (SI 2000/2994)
60		9 Apr 2001 (SI 2000/2994)
61		1 Jan 2001 (SI 2000/2994)
62	(1)–(10)	1 Dec 2000 (for the purposes of making regulations) (SI 2000/2950)
		15 Oct 2001 (in so far as not already in force for the purposes of its application to any person who, as a result of a relevant community order (as defined in s 62(8) of this Act) being made in accordance with s 64(1) of this Act in relation to him, falls to be supervised by an

Child Support, Pensions and Social Security Act 2000 (c 19)—*contd*

Section

62	(1)–(10)—*contd*	officer of the local probation board for any of the probation areas of Derbyshire, Hertfordshire, Teesside and West Midlands) (SI 2001/2619)
		Not in force (otherwise)
	(11)	1 Dec 2000 (for the purposes of making regulations) (SI 2000/2950)
		Not in force (otherwise)
63		1 Dec 2000 (for the purposes of making regulations) (SI 2000/2950)
		15 Oct 2001 (in so far as not already in force for the purposes of its application to any person who, as a result of a relevant community order (as defined in s 62(8) of this Act) being made in accordance with s 64(1) of this Act in relation to him, falls to be supervised by an officer of the local probation board for any of the probation areas of Derbyshire, Hertfordshire, Teesside and West Midlands) (SI 2001/2619)
		Not in force (otherwise)
64	(1)	1 Dec 2000 (for the purposes of making regulations) (SI 2000/2950)
		15 Oct 2001 (for the purposes of its application to any person who, as a result of a relevant community order (as defined in s 62(8) of this Act) being made in accordance with s 64(1) of this Act in relation to him, falls to be supervised by an officer of the local probation board for any of the probation areas of Derbyshire, Hertfordshire, Teesside and West Midlands) (SI 2001/2619)
		Not in force (otherwise)
	(2)	1 Dec 2000 (for the purposes of making regulations) (SI 2000/2950)
		15 Oct 2001 (in so far as not already in force for the purposes of its application to any person who, as a result of a relevant community order (as defined in s 62(8) of this Act) being made in accordance with s 64(1) of this Act in relation to

Child Support, Pensions and Social Security Act 2000 (c 19)—*contd*

Section

64	(2)—*contd*	him, falls to be supervised by an officer of the local probation board for any of the probation areas of Derbyshire, Hertfordshire, Teesside and West Midlands) (SI 2001/2619)
		Not in force (otherwise)
	(3)	1 Dec 2000 (for the purposes of making regulations) (SI 2000/2950)
		Not in force (otherwise)
	(4) (a)	1 Dec 2000 (for the purposes of making regulations) (SI 2000/2950)
		15 Oct 2001 (in so far as not already in force for the purposes of its application to any person who, as a result of a relevant community order (as defined in s 62(8) of this Act) being made in accordance with s 64(1) of this Act in relation to him, falls to be supervised by an officer of the local probation board for any of the probation areas of Derbyshire, Hertfordshire, Teesside and West Midlands) (SI 2001/2619)
		Not in force (otherwise)
	(b)	1 Dec 2000 (for the purposes of making regulations) (SI 2000/2950)
		Not in force (otherwise)
	(5), (6)	1 Dec 2000 (for the purposes of making regulations) (SI 2000/2950)
		15 Oct 2001 (in so far as not already in force for the purposes of its application to any person who, as a result of a relevant community order (as defined in s 62(8) of this Act) being made in accordance with s 64(1) of this Act in relation to him, falls to be supervised by an officer of the local probation board for any of the probation areas of Derbyshire, Hertfordshire, Teesside and West Midlands) (SI 2001/2619)
		Not in force (otherwise)
	(7) (a)–(c)	1 Dec 2000 (for the purposes of making regulations) (SI 2000/2950)
		15 Oct 2001 (in so far as not already in force for the purposes of its application to any person who, as a

Child Support, Pensions and Social Security Act 2000 (c 19)—*contd*

Section

64	(7)	(a)–(c)—*contd*	result of a relevant community order (as defined in s 62(8) of this Act) being made in accordance with s 64(1) of this Act in relation to him, falls to be supervised by an officer of the local probation board for any of the probation areas of Derbyshire, Hertfordshire, Teesside and West Midlands) (SI 2001/2619)
			Not in force (otherwise)
		(d)	1 Dec 2000 (for the purposes of making regulations) (SI 2000/2950)
			Not in force (otherwise)
	(8)		1 Dec 2000 (for the purposes of making regulations) (SI 2000/2950)
			15 Oct 2001 (in so far as not already in force for the purposes of its application to any person who, as a result of a relevant community order (as defined in s 62(8) of this Act) being made in accordance with s 64(1) of this Act in relation to him, falls to be supervised by an officer of the local probation board for any of the probation areas of Derbyshire, Hertfordshire, Teesside and West Midlands) (SI 2001/2619)
			Not in force (otherwise)
	(9)		1 Dec 2000 (for the purposes of making regulations) (SI 2000/2950)
			Not in force (otherwise)
	(10)		1 Dec 2000 (for the purposes of making regulations) (SI 2000/2950)
			15 Oct 2001 (in so far as not already in force for the purposes of its application to any person who, as a result of a relevant community order (as defined in s 62(8) of this Act) being made in accordance with s 64(1) of this Act in relation to him, falls to be supervised by an officer of the local probation board for any of the probation areas of Derbyshire, Hertfordshire, Teesside and West Midlands) (SI 2001/2619)
			Not in force (otherwise)

Child Support, Pensions and Social Security Act 2000 (c 19)—*contd*
Section

64	(11)	1 Dec 2000 (for the purposes of making regulations) (SI 2000/2950) *Not in force* (otherwise)
65	(1)–(6)	1 Dec 2000 (for the purposes of making regulations) (SI 2000/2950) 15 Oct 2001 (in so far as not already in force for the purposes of its application to any person who, as a result of a relevant community order (as defined in s 62(8) of this Act) being made in accordance with s 64(1) of this Act in relation to him, falls to be supervised by an officer of the local probation board for any of the probation areas of Derbyshire, Hertfordshire, Teesside and West Midlands) (SI 2001/2619) *Not in force* (otherwise)
	(7)	1 Dec 2000 (for the purposes of making regulations) (SI 2000/2950) *Not in force* (otherwise)
	(8)	1 Dec 2000 (for the purposes of making regulations) (SI 2000/2950) 15 Oct 2001 (in so far as not already in force for the purposes of its application to any person who, as a result of a relevant community order (as defined in s 62(8) of this Act) being made in accordance with s 64(1) of this Act in relation to him, falls to be supervised by an officer of the local probation board for any of the probation areas of Derbyshire, Hertfordshire, Teesside and West Midlands) (SI 2001/2619) *Not in force* (otherwise)
66		15 Oct 2001 (for the purposes of its application to any person who, as a result of a relevant community order (as defined in s 62(8) of this Act) being made in accordance with s 64(1) of this Act in relation to him, falls to be supervised by an officer of the local probation board for any of the probation areas of Derbyshire, Hertfordshire, Teesside and West Midlands) (SI 2001/2619) *Not in force* (otherwise)

Child Support, Pensions and Social Security Act 2000 (c 19)—*contd*

Section

67	See Sch 6 below
68	See Sch 7 below
69	1 Nov 2000 (SI 2000/2950) (for purposes of making regulations)
	2 Jul 2001 (otherwise) (SI 2001/1252)
70	26 Jun 2001 (for the purpose of making an order) (SI 2001/2295)
	2 Jul 2001 (otherwise) (SI 2001/2295)
71	1 Nov 2000 (SI 2000/2950) (for purposes of making regulations)
	1 Oct 2001 (otherwise) (SI 2001/2295)
72	9 Oct 2000 (SI 2000/2666)
73	1 Nov 2000 (SI 2000/2950) (so far as inserts into Social Security Administration Act 1992, s 170(5), new para (af) into definitions "relevant enactments" and "relevant Northern Ireland enactments", so far as each new para (af) refers to—
	(i) s 69;
	(ii) Sch 7, paras 3, 4, 6, 8–10, 12–16, 19–21, 23 and so far as relating to those paras, para 1 and s 68)
	1 Dec 2000 (for purpose of insertion of Social Security Administration Act 1992, s 170(5), para (af) into definitions "relevant enactments" and "relevant Northern Ireland enactments" so far as each new para (af) refers to ss 62–65) (SI 2000/2950)
	1 Dec 2000 (for purpose of insertion of Social Security Administration Act 1992, s 170(5), para (af) into each definition of "relevant enactments" and "relevant Northern Ireland enactments", so far as each new para (af) refers to s 42) (SI 2000/3166)
	Not in force (otherwise)
74–81	28 Jul 2000 (RA)
82, 83	1 Apr 2001 (SI 2001/774)
84	28 Jul 2000 (RA)
85	See Sch 9 below
86, 87	28 Jul 2000 (RA)

Child Support, Pensions and Social Security Act 2000 (c 19)—*contd*
Schedule

1, 2			10 Nov 2000 (for purpose of making regulations and Acts of Sederunt) (SI 2000/2994)
			Not in force (otherwise)
3, paras	1–10		*Not in force*
	11	(1)	*Not in force*
		(2)	31 Jan 2001 (in so far as affects Child Support Act 1991, s 3(2), for the purposes of ss 15(4A), 44(2A) of the 1991 Act, as inserted respectively by ss 14 and 22(3), and s 44(1) of that Act amended by s 22(2)) (SI 2000/3354)
			Not in force (otherwise)
		(3)–(16)	*Not in force*
		(17)	1 Jan 2001 (SI 2000/2994)
		(18)	10 Nov 2000 (for purpose of making regulations and Acts of Sederunt) (SI 2000/2994)
			Not in force (otherwise)
		(19)–(22)	*Not in force*
	12		*Not in force*
	13	(1)	2 Apr 2001 (SI 2001/1252)
		(2)	*Not in force*
		(3)	2 Apr 2001 (SI 2001/1252)
	14, 15		*Not in force*
4			8 Jan 2001 (for purposes of making regulations and of making an order appointing the first or second appointed year) (SI 2000/2950, as amended by SI 2000/3166)
			Not in force (otherwise)
5, paras	1–3		1 Jan 2001 (SI 2000/3166)
	4–6		28 Jul 2000 (RA)
	7		1 Jan 2001 (SI 2000/3166)
	8	(1)	28 Jul 2000 (RA)
		(2)	1 Jan 2001 (SI 2000/3166)
		(3), (4)	28 Jul 2000 (RA)
	9		1 Jan 2001 (SI 2000/3166)
	10		1 Nov 2000 (SI 2000/2950)
	11		2 Apr 2001 (SI 2001/1252)
	12	(1)	1 Jan 2001 (SI 2000/3166)
		(2)–(4)	*Not in force*
	13		28 Jul 2000 (RA)
	14–17		12 Feb 2001 (for purposes of authorising making of regulations and orders) (SI 2000/3166)
			Not in force (otherwise)

Child Support, Pensions and Social Security Act 2000 (c 19)—*contd*

Schedule

6, paras	1			See paras 2–8 below
	2–6			2 Apr 2001 (SI 2001/1252)
	7			1 Nov 2000 (SI 2000/2950)
	8			1 Nov 2000 (SI 2000/2950) (so far as inserts Social Security Administration Act 1992, s 121DA(1), (7) for purpose of construing s 113 of that Act, as amended by para 7)
				2 Apr 2001 (otherwise) (SI 2001/1252)
	9			2 Apr 2001 (SI 2001/1252)
7, paras	1			1 Nov 2000 (SI 2000/2950) (so far as relates to paras 3, 4, 6, 8–10, 12–16, 19–21, 23 of this Schedule, for purposes of making regulations)
				2 Jul 2001 (otherwise) (SI 2001/1252)
	2			2 Jul 2001 (SI 2001/1252)
	3, 4			1 Nov 2000 (SI 2000/2950) (for purposes of making regulations)
				2 Jul 2001 (otherwise) (SI 2001/1252)
	5			2 Jul 2001 (SI 2001/1252)
	6			1 Nov 2000 (SI 2000/2950) (for purposes of making regulations)
				2 Jul 2001 (otherwise) (SI 2001/1252)
	7			2 Jul 2001 (SI 2001/1252)
	8–10			1 Nov 2000 (SI 2000/2950) (for purposes of making regulations)
				2 Jul 2001 (otherwise) (SI 2001/1252)
	11			2 Jul 2001 (SI 2001/1252)
	12–16			1 Nov 2000 (SI 2000/2950) (for purposes of making regulations)
				2 Jul 2001 (otherwise) (SI 2001/1252)
	17			*Not in force*
	18	(1)		2 Jul 2001 (SI 2001/1252)
		(2)	(a)	2 Jul 2001 (SI 2001/1252)
			(b)	*Not in force*
		(3)–(9)		2 Jul 2001 (SI 2001/1252)
	19–21			1 Nov 2000 (SI 2000/2950) (for purposes of making regulations)
				2 Jul 2001 (otherwise) (SI 2001/1252)
	22	(1)		2 Jul 2001 (except for certain purposes[1]) (SI 2001/1252)
				Not in force (otherwise)
		(2), (3)		2 Jul 2001 (SI 2001/1252)
	23			1 Nov 2000 (SI 2000/2950) (for purposes of making regulations)
				2 Jul 2001 (otherwise) (SI 2001/1252)
8				1 Apr 2001 (SI 2001/774)

Child Support, Pensions and Social Security Act 2000 (c 19)—*contd*

Schedule

9, Pts	I		2 Apr 2001 (repeals of or in Child Support Act 1991, ss 15(10), 40(1), (2); Child Support Act 1995, s 24; Social Security Act 1998, Sch 7, para 28; Social Security Act 1998 (Commencement No 2) Order 1998, SI 1998/2780) (SI 2001/1252)
			Not in force (otherwise)
	II		8 Apr 2001 (SI 2001/153)
	III	(1)	*Not in force*
		(2)	1 Mar 2002 (for the purpose of making regulations and rules) (SI 2002/437)
			1 Apr 2002 (otherwise) (SI 2002/437)
		(3)	1 Dec 2000 (except so far as relates to Pensions Act 1995) (SI 2000/3166)
			Not in force (exception as noted above)
		(4)–(9)	1 Dec 2000 (SI 2000/3166)
		(10)	*Not in force*
		(11)	6 Apr 2002 (SI 2002/437)
	IV		9 Apr 2001 (SI 2000/2994)
	V		*Not in force*
	VI		2 Apr 2001 (SI 2001/1252)
	VII		2 Jul 2001 (except for certain purposes[1]) (SI 2001/1252)
	VIII		28 Jul 2000 (RA)
	IX		1 Apr 2001 (SI 2001/774)

[1] The "certain purposes" are where, pursuant to a request for a further review of a determination under Social Security Act 1998, s 34 relating to housing benefit or council tax benefit (a) an oral hearing by a Review Board constituted under the Housing Benefit (General) Regulations 1987, SI 1987/1971, or the Council Tax Benefit (General) Regulations 1992, SI 1992/1814, has been held and completed before 2 July 2001, the purpose of enabling the Review Board on or after that date to record its decision, or to give or send its decision to persons likely to be affected by it; or (b) a decision on the further review has been given by such a Review Board, whether before, on or after that date, (I) the purpose of enabling the Review Board to correct any accidental error in the record of its decision, (ii) where proceedings are brought by way of judicial review in connection with that decision, the purpose of enabling the Review Board to participate in those proceedings or in any appeal arising out of those proceedings, or (iii) the purpose of giving effect to the Review Board's decision.

Children (Leaving Care) Act 2000 (c 35)

RA: 30 Nov 2000

Commencement provisions: s 8(2)–(5); Children (Leaving Care) Act 2000 (Commencement No 1) (England) Order 2001, SI 2001/2878; Children (Leaving Care) Act 2000 (Commencement No 2 and Consequential Provisions) Order 2001, SI 2001/3070; Children (Leaving Care) Act 2000 (Commencement) (Wales) Order 2001, SI 2001/2191

Section

1–3	1 Oct 2001 (E) (SI 2001/2878)
	1 Oct 2001 (W) (SI 2001/2191)

Children (Leaving Care) Act 2000 (c 35)—*contd*

Section

4		1 Oct 2001 (E) (SI 2001/2878)
		1 Oct 2001 (W) (except so far as Children Act 1989, s 24C(2) relates to Primary Care Trusts) (SI 2001/2191)
		Not in force (otherwise)
5		1 Oct 2001 (E) (SI 2001/2878)
		1 Oct 2001 (W) (SI 2001/2191)
6		10 Sep 2001 (for the purpose of making Regulations) (SI 2001/3070)
		1 Oct 2001 (otherwise) (SI 2001/3070)
7	(1)–(4)	1 Oct 2001 (E) (SI 2001/2878)
		1 Oct 2001 (W) (SI 2001/2191)
	(5)	30 Nov 2000 (RA)
8		30 Nov 2000 (RA)

Church of England (Miscellaneous Provisions) Measure 2000 (No 1)

RA: 28 Jul 2000

Commencement provisions: s 22(2)

The provision of this Measure were brought into force on the following dates by instruments made by the the Archbishops of Canterbury and York, and dated 30 Aug 2000 and 14 Dec 2000 (made under s 22(2))

Section

1–11	1 Jan 2001
12–18	1 Sep 2000
19, 20	1 Jan 2001
21, 22	1 Sep 2000
Schedule	
1	1 Jan 2001
2	1 Jan 2001 (except in so far as relates to para 5(a))
3–8	1 Jan 2001

Consolidated Fund Act 2000 (c 3)

RA: 21 Mar 2000

21 Mar 2000 (RA)

Consolidated Fund (No 2) Act 2000 (c 45)

RA: 21 Dec 2000

21 Dec 2000 (RA)

Countryside and Rights of Way Act 2000 (c 37)

RA: 30 Nov 2000

Commencement provisions: s 103; Countryside and Rights of Way Act 2000 (Commencement No 1) Order 2001, SI 2001/114; Countryside and Rights of Way Act 2000 (Commencement No 1) (Wales) Order 2001, SI 2001/203; Countryside and Rights of Way Act 2000 (Commencement No 2) (Wales) Order 2001, SI 2001/1410

Section			
1			30 Jan 2001 (s 103(2))
2			*Not in force*
3–7			30 Jan 2001 (s 103(2))
8	(1)		30 Jan 2001 (s 103(2))
	(2)		See Sch 3 below
9–11			30 Jan 2001 (s 103(2))
12–14			*Not in force*
15–17			30 Jan 2001 (s 103(2))
18			*Not in force*
19			30 Jan 2001 (s 103(2))
20			*Not in force*
21–45			30 Jan 2001 (s 103(2))
46	(1)	(a)	*Not in force*
		(b)	1 Apr 2001 (E) (SI 2001/114)
			1 May 2001 (W) (SI 2001/1410)
	(2)		*Not in force*
	(3)		See Sch 4 below
47–50			*Not in force*
51			See Sch 5 below
52			30 Jan 2001 (s 103(2))
53–56			*Not in force*
57			See Sch 6 below
58, 59			30 Jan 2001 (s 103(2))
60–63			*Not in force*
64–66			30 Jan 2001 (s 103(2))
67			See Sch 7 below
68			1 Apr 2001 (E) (SI 2001/114)
			1 May 2001 (W) (SI 2001/1410)
69			*Not in force*
70	(1)		*Not in force*
	(2)		1 Apr 2001 (repeal of Highways Act 1980, s 134(5), shall not have effect in relation to any offence under s 134 of the 1980 Act committed before 1 Apr 2001) (E) (SI 2001/114)
			1 May 2001 (repeal of Highways Act 1980, s 134(5), shall not have effect in relation to any offence under s 134 of the 1980 Act committed before 1 May 2001) (W) (SI 2001/1410)

Countryside and Rights of Way Act 2000 (c 37)—*contd*

Section

70	(2)—*contd*		*Not in force (otherwise)*
	(3)		*Not in force*
	(4)		1 Apr 2001 (E) (SI 2001/114)
			1 May 2001 (W) (SI 2001/1410)
71			*Not in force*
72			30 Jan 2001 (E) (SI 2001/114)
			1 May 2001 (W) (SI 2001/1410)
73	(1)–(3)		30 Jan 2001 (s 103(2))
	(4)		See Sch 8 below
74			30 Jan 2001 (s 103(2))
75	(1)		See Sch 9 below
	(2)–(4)		30 Jan 2001 (s 103(2))
76	(1)		See Sch 10 below
	(2)		See Sch 11 below
77–80			30 Jan 2001 (s 103(2))
81	(1)		30 Jan 2001 (s 103(2))
	(2), (3)		30 Nov 2000 (RA)
82–85			1 Apr 2001 (E) (SI 2001/114)
			1 May 2001 (W) (SI 2001/1410)
86	(1)		1 Apr 2001 (E) (SI 2001/114)
			1 May 2001 (W) (SI 2001/1410)
	(2)		See Sch 13 below
	(3)–(10)		1 Apr 2001 (E) (SI 2001/114)
			1 May 2001 (W) (SI 2001/1410)
87	(1)–(5)		1 Apr 2001 (E) (SI 2001/114)
			1 May 2001 (W) (SI 2001/1410)
	(6)		See Sch 14 below
	(7)		1 Apr 2001 (E) (SI 2001/114)
			1 May 2001 (W) (SI 2001/1410)
88–92			1 Apr 2001 (E) (SI 2001/114)
			1 May 2001 (W) (SI 2001/1410)
93			See Sch 15 below
94, 95			30 Jan 2001 (s 103(2))
96			1 Apr 2001 (E) (SI 2001/114)
			1 May 2001 (W) (SI 2001/1410)
97			1 Apr 2001 (E) (SI 2001/114)
			Not in force (otherwise)
98			30 Jan 2001 (s 103(2))
99			30 Jan 2001 (W) (SI 2001/203)
			Not in force (otherwise)
100	(1), (2)		30 Jan 2001 (E) (SI 2001/114)
			Not in force (otherwise)
	(3)		1 Apr 2001 (E) (SI 2001/114)
			Not in force (otherwise)
	(4)		30 Jan 2001 (E) (SI 2001/114)
			Not in force (otherwise)
	(5)	(a)	*Not in force*
		(b)	30 Jan 2001 (E) (SI 2001/114)
			Not in force (otherwise)

Countryside and Rights of Way Act 2000 (c 37)—*contd*

Countryside and Rights of Way Act 2000 (c 37)—*contd*
Schedule

16, Pt	I	1 Apr 2001 (except in so far as repeals Law of Property Act 1925, s 193(2); Local Government Act 1972, Sch 17, para 35A; Local Government (Wales) Act 1994, Sch 6, para 13) (E) (SI 2001/114)
		1 May 2001 (except in so far as repeals Law of Property Act 1925, s 193(2); Local Government Act 1972, Sch 17, para 35A; Local Government (Wales) Act 1994, Sch 6, para 13) (W) (SI 2001/1410)
		Not in force (exceptions noted above)
	II	30 Jan 2001 (repeals of or in Road Traffic Regulation Act 1984, s 22(1)(a)) (E) (SI 2001/114)
		1 Apr 2001 (in so far as repeals Highways Act 1980, s 134(5); note that the repeal of Highways Act 1980, s 134(5), shall not have effect in relation to any offence under s 134 of the 1980 Act committed before 1 Apr 2001) (E) (SI 2001/114)
		1 May 2001 (repeals of or in Road Traffic Regulation Act 1984, s 22(1)(a); Highways Act 1980, s 134(5); note that the repeal of Highways Act 1980, s 134(5), shall not have effect in relation to any offence under s 134 of the 1980 Act committed before 1 May 2001) (W) (SI 2001/1410)
		Not in force (otherwise)
	III, IV	30 Jan 2001 (s 103(2)) (E) (SI 2001/114)
		1 May 2001 (W) (SI 2001/1410)
	V, VI	1 Apr 2001 (E) (SI 2001/114)
		1 May 2001 (W) (SI 2001/1410)

Criminal Justice and Court Services Act 2000 (c 43)

RA: 30 Nov 2000

Commencement provisions: s 80; Criminal Justice and Court Services Act 2000 (Commencement No 1) Order 2000, SI 2000/3302; Criminal Justice and Court Services Act 2000 (Commencement No 2) Order 2001, SI 2001/340; Criminal Justice and Court Services Act 2000 (Commencement No 3) Order 2001, SI 2001/562; Criminal Justice and Court Services Act 2000 (Commencement No 4)

Criminal Justice and Court Services Act 2000 (c 43)—*contd*
   Order 2001, SI 2001/919; Criminal Justice and Court Services Act 2000
   (Commencement No 5) (Scotland) Order 2001, SSI 2001/166; Criminal Justice
   and Court Services Act 2000 (Commencement No 6) Order 2001, SI 2001/1651;
   Criminal Justice and Court Services Act 2000 (Commencement No 7) Order 2001,
   SI 2001/2232; Criminal Justice and Court Services Act 2000 (Commencement
   No 8) Order 2001, SI 2001/3385

Section		
1–3		1 Apr 2001 (SI 2001/919)
4	(1), (2)	1 Apr 2001 (SI 2001/919)
	(3)	See Sch 1 below
	(4), (6)	1 Apr 2001 (SI 2001/919)
5–10		1 Apr 2001 (SI 2001/919)
11	(1)	1 Apr 2001 (SI 2001/919)
	(2)	See Sch 2 below
	(3)	1 Apr 2001 (SI 2001/919)
12–18		1 Apr 2001 (SI 2001/919)
19–22		30 Nov 2000 (s 80(3))
23–25		1 Apr 2001 (SI 2001/919)
26		See Sch 4 below
27–42		11 Jan 2001 (SI 2000/3302)
43–45		1 Apr 2001 (SI 2001/919)
46		*Not in force*
47–50		20 Jun 2001 (for purpose of exercising any power conferred on the Secretary of State to make orders) (SI 2001/2232)
		2 Jul 2001 (otherwise) (SI 2001/2232)
51		*Not in force*
52		20 Jun 2001 (for purpose of exercising any power conferred on the Secretary of State to make orders, except so far as it relates to exclusion orders and exclusion requirements) (SI 2001/2232)
		2 Jul 2001 (otherwise) (except so far as it relates to exclusion orders and exclusion requirements) (SI 2001/2232)
		Not in force (exceptions noted above)
53		*Not in force*
54, 55		1 Apr 2001 (SI 2001/919)
56		1 Feb 2001 (SI 2000/3302)
57		20 Jun 2001 (for purpose of exercising any power conferred on the Secretary of State to make orders, within the following police areas only: Nottinghamshire; Staffordshire; the metropolitan police district) (SI 2001/2232)

Criminal Justice and Court Services Act 2000 (c 43)—*contd*

Section

57—*contd*		2 Jul 2001 (otherwise, within the following police areas only: Nottinghamshire; Staffordshire; the metropolitan police district) (SI 2001/2232) *Not in force* (otherwise)
58		20 Jun 2001 (for purpose of exercising any power conferred on the Secretary of State to make orders) (SI 2001/2232) 2 Jul 2001 (otherwise) (SI 2001/2232)
59		*Not in force*
60		30 Nov 2000 (s 80(3))
61		*Not in force*
62		1 Feb 2001 (SI 2000/3302)
63		1 Feb 2001 (so far as inserts Criminal Justice Act 1991, s 65(5A)(a), (b), s 65(5C) (so far as it applies to sub-s (5A)(a), (b)) (SI 2000/3302) 20 Jun 2001 (so far as inserts Criminal Justice Act 1991, s 65(5A)(c), (5B), (5C) (so far as it applies to sub-s (5A)(c)), s 65(5D), (9), (10)) (for purpose of exercising any power conferred on the Secretary of State to make orders) (SI 2001/2232) 2 Jul 2001 (so far as inserts Criminal Justice Act 1991, s 65(5A)(c), (5B), (5C) (so far as it applies to sub-s (5A)(c)), s 65(5D), (9), (10)) (otherwise) (SI 2001/2232)
64		20 Jun 2001 (for purpose of exercising any power conferred on the Secretary of State to make orders) (SI 2001/2232) 2 Jul 2001 (otherwise) (SI 2001/2232)
65		1 Mar 2001 (SI 2001/340)
66		See Sch 5 below
67–69		1 Apr 2001 (SI 2001/919)
70		20 Jun 2001 (for purpose of exercising any power conferred on the Secretary of State to make orders) (SI 2001/2232) 2 Jul 2001 (otherwise) (SI 2001/2232)
71	(1)–(4)	29 Oct 2001 (SI 2001/3385)
	(5)	*Not in force*
72		1 Mar 2001 (SI 2001/562)
73		1 Apr 2001 (SI 2001/919)
74		See Sch 7 below

Criminal Justice and Court Services Act 2000 (c 43)—*contd*

Criminal Justice and Court Services Act 2000 (c 43)—*contd*

Schedule

7, para					
27					*Not in force*
28					11 Jan 2001 (SI 2000/3302)
29	(1)		(a)–(d)		*Not in force*
			(e)		30 Nov 2000 (s 80(3))
			(f), (g)		*Not in force*
	(2)				30 Nov 2000 (s 80(3))
30, 31					*Not in force*
32	(1), (2)				*Not in force*
	(3)		(c)	(i)	30 Nov 2000 (s 80(3))
				(ii)	*Not in force*
	(4)				30 Nov 2000 (s 80(3))
33–36					*Not in force*
37, 38					1 Apr 2001 (SI 2001/919)
39					*Not in force*
40–53					1 Apr 2001 (SI 2001/919)
54–56					*Not in force*
57, 58					1 Apr 2001 (SI 2001/919)
59, 60					*Not in force*
61					1 Apr 2001 (SI 2001/919)
62–70					*Not in force*
71, 72					1 Apr 2001 (SI 2001/919)
73					*Not in force*
74					See Sch 7 below
75					1 Apr 2001 (SI 2001/919)
76, 77					*Not in force*
78					20 Jun 2001 (for purpose of exercising any power conferred on the Secretary of State to make orders) (SI 2001/2232)
					2 Jul 2001 (otherwise) (SI 2001/2232)
79–82					1 Apr 2001 (SI 2001/919)
83					11 Jan 2001 (SI 2000/3302)
84–97					1 Apr 2001 (SI 2001/919)
98					*Not in force*
99, 100					1 Apr 2001 (SI 2001/919)
101					*Not in force*
102, 103					1 Apr 2001 (SI 2001/919)
104					*Not in force*
105					20 Jun 2001 (for purpose of exercising any power conferred on the Secretary of State to make orders) (SI 2001/2232)
					2 Jul 2001 (otherwise) (SI 2001/2232)
106–109					*Not in force*
110					1 Apr 2001 (SI 2001/919)
111	(a)				1 Apr 2001 (SI 2001/919)
	(b)				*Not in force*
112–115					*Not in force*

Criminal Justice and Court Services Act 2000 (c 43)—*contd*

Schedule

7, para			
116–118			1 Apr 2001 (SI 2001/919)
119			*Not in force*
120–126			1 Apr 2001 (SI 2001/919)
127–130			11 Jan 2001 (SI 2000/3302)
131–133			1 Apr 2001 (SI 2001/919)
134			*Not in force*
135–138			30 Nov 2000 (s 80(3))
139–140			*Not in force*
141			1 Apr 2001 (SI 2001/919)
142			30 Nov 2000 (s 80(3))
143			1 Apr 2001 (SI 2001/919)
144–148			30 Nov 2000 (s 80(3))
149			*Not in force*
150–153			1 Apr 2001 (SI 2001/919)
154–159			11 Jan 2001 (SI 2000/3302)
160			See paras 161–204 below
161	(a)		*Not in force*
	(b)		20 Jun 2001 (for purpose of exercising any power conferred on the Secretary of State to make orders) (SI 2001/2232)
			2 Jul 2001 (otherwise) (SI 2001/2232)
162, 163			20 Jun 2001 (for purpose of exercising any power conferred on the Secretary of State to make orders) (SI 2001/2232)
			2 Jul 2001 (otherwise) (SI 2001/2232)
164			20 Jun 2001 (for purpose of exercising any power conferred on the Secretary of State to make orders, except for the reference in sub-para (b) to Powers of Criminal Courts (Sentencing) Act 2000, Sch 3, paras 2A(4), (5)) (SI 2001/2232)
			2 Jul 2001 (otherwise) (except for the reference in sub-para (b) to Powers of Criminal Courts (Sentencing) Act 2000, Sch 3, paras 2A(4), (5)) (SI 2001/2232)
			Not in force (exception noted above)
165			*Not in force*
166			1 Apr 2001 (SI 2001/919)
167			*Not in force*
168, 169			1 Apr 2001 (SI 2001/919)
170			*Not in force*
171			1 Apr 2001 (SI 2001/919)
172, 173			*Not in force*
174, 175			1 Apr 2001 (SI 2001/919)

Criminal Justice and Court Services Act 2000 (c 43)—*contd*

Schedule

7, para	176–194		Not in force
	195		1 Apr 2001 (SI 2001/919)
	196		20 Jun 2001 (for purpose of exercising any power conferred on the Secretary of State to make orders, except for references to Powers of Criminal Courts (Sentencing) Act 2000, ss 40A(6), 40C(1), (2), Sch 2, para 8, Sch 3 para 1(1A)) (SI 2001/2232)
			2 Jul 2001 (otherwise) (except for references to Powers of Criminal Courts (Sentencing) Act 2000, ss 40A(6), 40C(1), (2), Sch 2, para 8, Sch 3 para 1(1A)) (SI 2001/2232)
			Not in force (exception noted above)
	197	(a)	Not in force
		(b)	1 Apr 2001 (SI 2001/919)
		(c)–(e)	Not in force
		(f)	1 Apr 2001 (so far as relates to definitions "community rehabilitation period", "local probation board") (SI 2001/919)
			20 Jun 2001 (for purpose of exercising any power conferred on the Secretary of State to make orders, so far as relates to drug abstinence orders) (SI 2001/2232)
			2 Jul 2001 (otherwise, so far as relates to drug abstinence orders) (SI 2001/2232)
			Not in force (otherwise)
		(g) (i)	Not in force
		(ii)	20 Jun 2001 (for purpose of exercising any power conferred on the Secretary of State to make orders) (SI 2001/2232)
			2 Jul 2001 (otherwise) (SI 2001/2232)
	198		1 Apr 2001 (SI 2001/919)
	199	(1)	1 Apr 2001 (SI 2001/919)
		(2) (a)	20 Jun 2001 (for purpose of exercising any power conferred on the Secretary of State to make orders, so far as relates to drug abstinence orders) (SI 2001/2232)
			2 Jul 2001 (otherwise, so far as relates to drug abstinence orders) (SI 2001/2232)

Criminal Justice and Court Services Act 2000 (c 43)—*contd*
Schedule

7, para	199	(2)	(a)—*contd*		*Not in force* (otherwise)
			(b)		1 Apr 2001 (save in so far as relates to exclusion and drug abstinence orders) (SI 2001/919)
					20 Jun 2001 (for purpose of exercising any power conferred on the Secretary of State to make orders, so far as relates to drug abstinence) (SI 2001/2232)
					2 Jul 2001 (otherwise, so far as relates to drug abstinence) (SI 2001/2232)
					Not in force (so far as relates to exclusion orders)
			(c)		20 Jun 2001 (for purpose of exercising any power conferred on the Secretary of State to make orders) (SI 2001/2232)
					2 Jul 2001 (otherwise) (SI 2001/2232)
		(3), (4)			1 Apr 2001 (SI 2001/919)
		(5)			1 Apr 2001 (save in so far as relates to exclusion and drug abstinence orders)(SI 2001/919)
					20 Jun 2001 (for purpose of exercising any power conferred on the Secretary of State to make orders, so far as relates to drug abstinence) (SI 2001/2232)
					2 Jul 2001 (otherwise, so far as relates to drug abstinence) (SI 2001/2232)
					Not in force (so far as relates to exclusion orders)
		(6)			20 Jun 2001 (for purpose of exercising any power conferred on the Secretary of State to make orders) (SI 2001/2232)
					2 Jul 2001 (otherwise) (SI 2001/2232)
		(7)–(9)			*Not in force*
		(10)			1 Apr 2001 (so far as it substitutes cross-heading preceding Powers of Criminal Courts (Sentencing) Act 2000, Sch 3, para 7) (SI 2001/919)
					Not in force (otherwise)
		(11)	(a)		*Not in force*
			(b)	(i)	20 Jun 2001 (for purpose of exercising any power conferred on the Secretary of State to make orders) (SI 2001/2232)
					2 Jul 2001 (otherwise) (SI 2001/2232)

Criminal Justice and Court Services Act 2000 (c 43)—*contd*
Schedule

7, para	199	(11)	(b)	(ii)	*Not in force*
			(c)		*Not in force*
		(12)			*Not in force*
		(13)			20 Jun 2001 (for purpose of exercising any power conferred on the Secretary of State to make orders) (SI 2001/2232)
					2 Jul 2001 (otherwise) (SI 2001/2232)
		(14)–(18)			1 Apr 2001 (SI 2001/919)
		(19)			*Not in force*
		(20)			1 Apr 2001 (SI 2001/919)
		(21)	(a)	(i)	*Not in force*
				(ii)	*Not in force*
				(iii)	1 Apr 2001 (save in so far as relates to exclusion orders) (SI 2001/919)
					Not in force (otherwise)
			(b)		20 Jun 2001 (so far as inserts Powers of Criminal Courts (Sentencing) Act 2000, Sch 3, para 19(2)(aa)) (for purpose of exercising any power conferred on the Secretary of State to make orders) (SI 2001/2232)
					2 Jul 2001 (so far as inserts Powers of Criminal Courts (Sentencing) Act 2000, Sch 3, para 19(2)(aa)) (otherwise) (SI 2001/2232)
					Not in force (otherwise)
			(c)		20 Jun 2001 (for purpose of exercising any power conferred on the Secretary of State to make orders) (SI 2001/2232)
					2 Jul 2001 (otherwise) (SI 2001/2232)
			(d)		20 Jun 2001 (so far as inserts Powers of Criminal Courts (Sentencing) Act 2000, Sch 3, para 19(6)) (for purpose of exercising any power conferred on the Secretary of State to make orders) (SI 2001/2232)
					2 Jul 2001 (so far as inserts Powers of Criminal Courts (Sentencing) Act 2000, Sch 3, para 19(6)) (otherwise) (SI 2001/2232)
					Not in force (otherwise)
			(e)		1 Apr 2001 (save in so far as relates to exclusion orders) (SI 2001/919)
					Not in force (otherwise)
		(22), (23)			1 Apr 2001 (SI 2001/919)

Criminal Justice and Court Services Act 2000 (c 43)—*contd*
Schedule

7, para	199	(24)		20 Jun 2001 (for purpose of exercising any power conferred on the Secretary of State to make orders) (SI 2001/2232)
				2 Jul 2001 (otherwise) (SI 2001/2232)
		(25)	(a)	20 Jun 2001 (for purpose of exercising any power conferred on the Secretary of State to make orders) (SI 2001/2232)
				2 Jul 2001 (otherwise) (SI 2001/2232)
			(b), (c)	*Not in force*
		(26)		*Not in force*
		(27)		1 Apr 2001 (SI 2001/919)
	200			1 Apr 2001 (SI 2001/919)
	201	(1)		20 Jun 2001 (for purpose of exercising any power conferred on the Secretary of State to make orders) (SI 2001/2232)
				2 Jul 2001 (otherwise) (SI 2001/2232)
		(2)	(a)	20 Jun 2001 (for purpose of exercising any power conferred on the Secretary of State to make orders) (SI 2001/2232)
				2 Jul 2001 (otherwise) (SI 2001/2232)
			(b)	*Not in force*
		(3)		*Not in force*
	202	(1)		20 Jun 2001 (for purpose of exercising any power conferred on the Secretary of State to make orders) (SI 2001/2232)
				2 Jul 2001 (otherwise) (SI 2001/2232)
		(2)	(a)	20 Jun 2001 (for purpose of exercising any power conferred on the Secretary of State to make orders) (SI 2001/2232)
				2 Jul 2001 (otherwise) (SI 2001/2232)
			(b)	*Not in force*
		(3)		*Not in force*
	203	(1)		1 Apr 2001 (SI 2001/919)
		(2)		1 Apr 2001 (so far as relates to Powers of Criminal Courts (Sentencing) Act 2000, Sch 9, paras 34(a), 153–156) (SI 2001/919)
				Not in force (otherwise)

Criminal Justice and Court Services Act 2000 (c 43)—*contd*
Schedule

7, para	203	(3), (4)	30 Nov 2000 (s 80(3))
		(5)	*Not in force*
	204		*Not in force*
	205–210		1 Apr 2001 (SI 2001/919)
	211		*Not in force*
8			30 Nov 2000 (repeals of or in Crime (Sentences) Act 1997, ss 28, 34, Sch 5, para 5; Powers of Criminal Courts (Sentencing) Act 2000, Sch 9, paras 182, 188) (s 80(3))
			11 Jan 2001 (repeal relating to Protection of Children Act 1999, s 6) (SI 2000/3302)
			1 Apr 2001 (repeals of or in Metropolitan Magistrates' Courts Act 1959; Children and Young Persons Act 1969, s 46(1), Sch 3, para 9(2)(a); Local Government Act 1972; Juries Act 1974; Adoption Act 1976; Magistrates' Courts Act 1980, s 72; Health and Social Services and Social Security Adjudications Act 1983; Children Act 1989; Courts and Legal Services Act 1990; Probation Service Act 1993; Local Government (Wales) Act 1994; Criminal Justice and Public Order Act 1994, Sch 10, paras 72, 73; Crime and Disorder Act 1998; Access to Justice Act 1999; Greater London Authority Act 1999; Powers of Criminal Courts (Sentencing) Act 2000, ss 46(13), 47(5), 64(2), 163, Sch 9, paras 34(a), 153–156; Learning and Skills Act 2000) (SI 2001/919)
			20 Jun 2001 (repeals in or of Powers of Criminal Courts (Sentencing) Act 2000, ss 38, 40(1)(a)) (for purpose of exercising any power conferred on the Secretary of State to make orders) (SI 2001/2232)
			2 Jul 2001 (repeals in or of Powers of Criminal Courts (Sentencing) Act 2000, ss 38, 40(1)(a)) (otherwise) (SI 2001/2232)
			Not in force (otherwise)

Crown Prosecution Service Inspectorate Act 2000 (c 10)

RA: 20 Jul 2000

Commencement provisions: s 3(2) ; Crown Prosecution Service Inspectorate Act 2000
(Commencement) Order 2000, SI 2000/2423

Section

1, 2	1 Oct 2000 (SI 2000/2423)
3	20 Jul 2000 (RA)

Disqualifications Act 2000 (c 42)

RA: 30 Nov 2000

30 Nov 2000 (RA)

Education and Training (Scotland) Act 2000 (asp 8)

RA: 9 Aug 2000

9 Aug 2000 (RA)

Electronic Communications Act 2000 (c 7)

RA: 25 May 2000

Commencement provisions: s 16(2)–(4); Electronic Communications Act 2000
(Commencement No 1) Order 2000, SI 2000/1798

Section

1–6	*Not in force*
7	25 Jul 2000 (SI 2000/1798)
8–10	25 May 2000 (RA)
11, 12	25 Jul 2000 (SI 2000/1798)
13–16	25 May 2000 (RA)

Ethical Standards in Public Life etc (Scotland) Act 2000 (asp 7)

RA: 24 Jul 2000

Commencement provisions: s 37(2), (3); Ethical Standards in Public Life etc (Scotland)
Act 2000 (Commencement No 1) Order 2001, SSI 2001/113; Ethical Standards
in Public Life etc (Scotland) Act 2000 (Commencement No 2 and Transitional
Provisions) Order 2001, SSI 2001/474

Section

1–3	29 Mar 2001 (SSI 2001/113)
4–7	*Not in force*
8, 9	29 Mar 2001 (SSI 2001/113)
10–27	*Not in force*
28	29 Mar 2001 (SSI 2001/113)
29	*Not in force*
30, 31	29 Mar 2001 (SSI 2001/113)
32	*Not in force*

Ethical Standards in Public Life etc (Scotland) Act 2000 (asp 7)—*contd*

Section		
33		1 Jan 2002 (SSI 2001/474)
34, 35		29 Mar 2001 (SSI 2001/113)
36	(1)	See Sch 4 below
	(2)	*Not in force*
37		24 Jul 2000 (RA)
Schedule		*Not in force*
1–3		29 Mar 2001 (SSI 2001/113)
4		29 Mar 2001 (repeal of Local Government Act 1988, s 28) (SSI 2001/113)
		Not in force (otherwise)

Finance Act 2000 (c 17)

RA: 28 Jul 2000

Details of the commencement of Finance Acts are not set out in this work

---

Financial Services and Markets Act 2000 (c 8)

RA: 14 Jun 2000

Commencement provisions: s 431; Financial Services and Markets Act 2000 (Commencement No 1) Order 2001, SI 2001/516; Financial Services and Markets Act 2000 (Commencement No 2) Order 2001, SI 2001/1282; Financial Services and Markets Act 2000 (Commencement No 3) Order 2001, SI 2001/1820; Financial Services and Markets Act 2000 (Commencement No 4 and Transitional Provisions) Order 2001, SI 2001/2364[1]; Financial Services and Markets Act 2000 (Commencement No 5) Order 2001, SI 2001/2632; Financial Services and Markets Act 2000 (Commencement No 6) Order 2001, SI 2001/3436; Financial Services and Markets Act 2000 (Commencement No 7) Order 2001, SI 2001/3538

Section			
1–11			18 Jun 2001 (SI 2001/1820)
12–19			1 Dec 2001 (SI 2001/3538)
20	(1), (2)		1 Dec 2001 (SI 2001/3538)
	(3)		25 Feb 2001 (for the purpose of making orders or regulations) (SI 2001/516)
			1 Dec 2001 (otherwise) (SI 2001/3538)
21			25 Feb 2001 (for the purpose of making orders or regulations) (SI 2001/516)
			1 Dec 2001 (otherwise) (SI 2001/3538)
22			25 Feb 2001 (SI 2001/516)
23–30			1 Dec 2001 (SI 2001/3538)
31	(1)	(a)	1 Dec 2001 (SI 2001/3538)
		(b)	See Sch 3 below
		(c)	See Sch 4 below
		(d)	1 Dec 2001 (SI 2001/3538)

Financial Services and Markets Act 2000 (c 8)—*contd*

Section

31	(2)	1 Dec 2001 (SI 2001/3538)
32–36		1 Dec 2001 (SI 2001/3538)
37		See Sch 3 below
38		25 Feb 2001 (SI 2001/516)
39	(1)	25 Feb 2001 (for the purpose of making orders or regulations) (SI 2001/516) 1 Dec 2001 (otherwise) (SI 2001/3538)
	(2)–(6)	1 Dec 2001 (SI 2001/3538)
40		3 Sep 2001 (SI 2001/2632)
41	(1)	25 Feb 2001 (SI 2001/516)
	(2), (3)	3 Sep 2001 (SI 2001/2632)
42, 43		3 Sep 2001 (for the purposes of permissions coming into force not sooner than the day on which s 19 of this Act comes into force, and applications for such permissions) 1 Dec 2001 (otherwise) (SI 2001/3538)
44–46		3 Sep 2001 (for the purposes of variations or cancellations taking effect not sooner than the day on which s 19 of this Act comes into force, and applications for such variations or cancellations) (SI 2001/2632) 1 Dec 2001 (otherwise) (SI 2001/3538)
47	(1)	25 Feb 2001 (for the purpose of making orders or regulations) (SI 2001/516) 3 Sep 2001 (for the purposes of variations or cancellations taking effect not sooner than the day on which s 19 of this Act comes into force, and applications for such variations or cancellations) (SI 2001/2632) 1 Dec 2001 (otherwise) (SI 2001/3538)
	(2)	3 Sep 2001 (for the purposes of variations or cancellations taking effect not sooner than the day on which s 19 of this Act comes into force, and applications for such variations or cancellations) (SI 2001/2632) 1 Dec 2001 (otherwise) (SI 2001/3538)
	(3)	25 Feb 2001 (for the purpose of making orders or regulations) (SI 2001/516)

Financial Services and Markets Act 2000 (c 8)—*contd*

Section

47	(3)—*contd*	3 Sep 2001 (for the purposes of variations or cancellations taking effect not sooner than the day on which s 19 of this Act comes into force, and applications for such variations or cancellations) (SI 2001/2632)
		1 Dec 2001 (otherwise) (SI 2001/3538)
	(4)–(7)	3 Sep 2001 (for the purposes of variations or cancellations taking effect not sooner than the day on which s 19 of this Act comes into force, and applications for such variations or cancellations) (SI 2001/2632)
		1 Dec 2001 (otherwise) (SI 2001/3538)
48–50		3 Sep 2001 (SI 2001/2632)
51		18 Jun 2001 (for the purpose of giving directions or imposing requirements as mentioned in sub-s (3)) (SI 2001/1820)
		3 Sep 2001 (otherwise) (SI 2001/2632)
52		3 Sep 2001 (SI 2001/2632)
53, 54		3 Sep 2001 (for the purposes of variations and cancellations taking effect not sooner than the day on which s 19 of this Act comes into force) (SI 2001/2632)
		1 Dec 2001 (otherwise) (SI 2001/3538)
55		3 Sep 2001 (SI 2001/2632)
56–58		3 Sep 2001 (for the purposes of prohibition orders coming into force not sooner than the day on which s 19 of this Act comes into force) (SI 2001/2632)
		1 Dec 2001 (otherwise) (SI 2001/3538)
59		18 Jun 2001 (for the purpose of making rules) (SI 2001/1820)
		3 Sep 2001 (for the purposes of approvals coming into force not sooner than the day on which s 19 of this Act comes into force, and applications for such approvals) (SI 2001/2632)
		1 Dec 2001 (otherwise) (SI 2001/3538)
60		18 Jun 2001 (for the purpose of giving directions or imposing requirements as mentioned in sub-s (2) or (4)) (SI 2001/1820)

Financial Services and Markets Act 2000 (c 8)—*contd*

Financial Services and Markets Act 2000 (c 8)—*contd*

Section

81	(1)	18 Jun 2001 (for the purpose of making listing rules) (SI 2001/1820)
		1 Dec 2001 (otherwise) (SI 2001/3538)
	(2)–(4)	1 Dec 2001 (SI 2001/3538)
	(5)	18 Jun 2001 (for the purpose of making listing rules) (SI 2001/1820)
		1 Dec 2001 (otherwise) (SI 2001/3538)
82	(1)	18 Jun 2001 (for the purpose of making listing rules) (SI 2001/1820)
		1 Dec 2001 (otherwise) (SI 2001/3538)
	(2)–(4)	1 Dec 2001 (SI 2001/3538)
	(5)	18 Jun 2001 (for the purpose of making listing rules) (SI 2001/1820)
		1 Dec 2001 (otherwise) (SI 2001/3538)
	(6)	1 Dec 2001 (SI 2001/3538)
	(7)	18 Jun 2001 (for the purpose of making listing rules) (SI 2001/1820)
		1 Dec 2001 (otherwise) (SI 2001/3538)
83		1 Dec 2001 (SI 2001/3538)
84		18 Jun 2001 (SI 2001/1820)
85		1 Dec 2001 (SI 2001/3538)
86		25 Feb 2001 (SI 2001/516)
87	(1)–(3)	18 Jun 2001 (SI 2001/1820)
	(4), (5)	25 Feb 2001 (SI 2001/516)
88	(1)–(3)	18 Jun 2001 (SI 2001/1820)
	(4)–(7)	1 Dec 2001 (SI 2001/3538)
89	(1)	18 Jun 2001 (SI 2001/1820)
	(2)–(4)	1 Dec 2001 (SI 2001/3538)
90–92		1 Dec 2001 (SI 2001/3538)
93, 94		18 Jun 2001 (SI 2001/1820)
95		1 Dec 2001 (SI 2001/3538)
96		18 Jun 2001 (SI 2001/1820)
97		1 Dec 2001 (SI 2001/3538)
98	(1)	18 Jun 2001 (for the purpose of making listing rules) (SI 2001/1820)
		1 Dec 2001 (otherwise) (SI 2001/3538)
	(2)–(5)	1 Dec 2001 (SI 2001/3538)
99–102		18 Jun 2001 (SI 2001/1820)
103		25 Feb 2001 (SI 2001/516)
104		1 Dec 2001 (for the purpose of insurance business transfer schemes only) (SI 2001/3538)
		Not in force (otherwise)
105–107		1 Dec 2001 (SI 2001/3538)
108		25 Feb 2001 (for the purpose of making orders or regulations) (SI 2001/516)
		1 Dec 2001 (otherwise) (SI 2001/3538)
109, 110		1 Dec 2001 (SI 2001/3538)

Financial Services and Markets Act 2000 (c 8)—*contd*

Section

111	(1)	1 Dec 2001 (SI 2001/3538)
	(2)	25 Feb 2001 (for the purpose of introducing Sch 12, Pt I to the extent brought into force by SI 2001/516) (SI 2001/516)
		1 Dec 2001 (otherwise) (SI 2001/3538)
	(3)	1 Dec 2001 (SI 2001/3538)
112–117		1 Dec 2001 (SI 2001/3538)
118	(1), (2)	1 Dec 2001 (SI 2001/3538)
	(3), (4)	25 Feb 2001 (SI 2001/516)
	(5)–(9)	1 Dec 2001 (SI 2001/3538)
	(10)	25 Feb 2001 (SI 2001/516)
119–121		18 Jun 2001 (SI 2001/1820)
122, 123		1 Dec 2001 (SI 2001/3538)
124, 125		18 Jun 2001 (SI 2001/1820)
126–131		1 Dec 2001 (SI 2001/3538)
132	(1)	25 Feb 2001 (for the purpose of the definition "the Tribunal") (SI 2001/516)
		3 Sep 2001 (otherwise) (SI 2001/2632)
	(2)	3 Sep 2001 (SI 2001/2632)
	(3)	25 Feb 2001 (SI 2001/516)
	(4)	See Sch 13 below
133		3 Sep 2001 (SI 2001/2632)
134, 135		25 Feb 2001 (SI 2001/516)
136		18 Jun 2001 (for the purpose of making rules) (SI 2001/1820)
		3 Sep 2001 (otherwise) (SI 2001/2632)
137	(1)–(5)	3 Sep 2001 (SI 2001/2632)
	(6)	25 Feb 2001 (SI 2001/516)
138–141		18 Jun 2001 (SI 2001/1820)
142	(1)–(4)	25 Feb 2001 (SI 2001/516)
	(5)	1 Dec 2001 (SI 2001/3538)
	(6)	25 Feb 2001 (SI 2001/516)
143		18 Jun 2001 (for the purpose of making rules) (SI 2001/1820)
		1 Dec 2001 (otherwise) (SI 2001/3538)
144	(1)–(3)	18 Jun 2001 (SI 2001/1820)
	(4), (5)	25 Feb 2001 (SI 2001/516)
	(6), (7)	18 Jun 2001 (SI 2001/1820)
145	(1)–(4)	18 Jun 2001 (SI 2001/1820)
	(5)	25 Feb 2001 (SI 2001/516)
146, 147		18 Jun 2001 (SI 2001/1820)
148		18 Jun 2001 (for the purpose of giving directions as mentioned in sub-s (3)) (SI 2001/1820)
		3 Sep 2001 (otherwise) (SI 2001/2632)
149		18 Jun 2001 (SI 2001/1820)

Financial Services and Markets Act 2000 (c 8)—*contd*

Section

150	(1), (2)		18 Jun 2001 (for the purpose of making rules) (SI 2001/1820)
			1 Dec 2001 (otherwise) (SI 2001/3538)
	(3)–(5)		25 Feb 2001 (for the purpose of making orders or regulations) (SI 2001/516)
			18 Jun 2001 (for the purpose of making rules) (SI 2001/1820)
			1 Dec 2001 (otherwise) (SI 2001/3538)
151			1 Dec 2001 (SI 2001/3538)
152–164			18 Jun 2001 (SI 2001/1820)
165–167			3 Sep 2001 (SI 2001/2632)
168	(1)–(3)		3 Sep 2001 (SI 2001/2632)
	(4)	(a)	3 Sep 2001 (SI 2001/2632)
		(b)	25 Feb 2001 (for the purpose of making orders or regulations) (SI 2001/516)
			3 Sep 2001 (otherwise) (SI 2001/2632)
		(c)–(i)	3 Sep 2001 (SI 2001/2632)
	(5), (6)		3 Sep 2001 (SI 2001/2632)
169			18 Jun 2001 (for the purpose of preparing a statement of policy as mentioned in sub-s (9)) (SI 2001/1820)
			3 Sep 2001 (otherwise) (SI 2001/2632)
170–177			3 Sep 2001 (SI 2001/2632)
178–181			1 Dec 2001 (SI 2001/3538)
182			18 Jun 2001 (for the purpose of imposing requirements as mentioned in sub-s (1)(b)) (SI 2001/1820)
			1 Dec 2001 (otherwise) (SI 2001/3538)
183	(1)		1 Dec 2001 (SI 2001/3538)
	(2)		25 Feb 2001 (for the purpose of making orders or regulations) (SI 2001/516)
			1 Dec 2001 (otherwise) (SI 2001/3538)
	(3)		1 Dec 2001 (SI 2001/3538)
184–187			1 Dec 2001 (SI 2001/3538)
188	(1)		1 Dec 2001 (SI 2001/3538)
	(2)		25 Feb 2001 (for the purpose of making orders or regulations) (SI 2001/516)
			1 Dec 2001 (otherwise) (SI 2001/3538)
	(3)–(6)		1 Dec 2001 (SI 2001/3538)
189–191			1 Dec 2001 (SI 2001/3538)
192	(a)		25 Feb 2001 (SI 2001/516)
	(b)–(e)		1 Dec 2001 (SI 2001/3538)
193			3 Sep 2001 (SI 2001/2632)

Financial Services and Markets Act 2000 (c 8)—*contd*
Section

194–197		3 Sep 2001 (for the purposes of requirements (as mentioned in s 196) taking effect not sooner than the day on which s 19 of this Act comes into force) (SI 2001/2632)
		1 Dec 2001 (otherwise) (SI 2001/3538)
198		1 Dec 2001 (SI 2001/3538)
199		3 Sep 2001 (for the purposes of requirements (as mentioned in s 196) taking effect not sooner than the day on which s 19 of this Act comes into force) (SI 2001/2632)
		1 Dec 2001 (otherwise) (SI 2001/3538)
200, 201		3 Sep 2001 (SI 2001/2632)
202	(1)	3 Sep 2001 (SI 2001/2632)
	(2)	25 Feb 2001 (for the purpose of making orders or regulations) (SI 2001/516)
		3 Sep 2001 (otherwise) (SI 2001/2632)
203–209		1 Dec 2001 (SI 2001/3538)
210–212		18 Jun 2001 (SI 2001/1820)
213	(1)–(9)	18 Jun 2001 (SI 2001/1820)
	(10)	25 Feb 2001 (for the purpose of making orders or regulations) (SI 2001/516)
		18 Jun 2001 (otherwise) (SI 2001/1820)
214	(1)–(4)	18 Jun 2001 (SI 2001/1820)
	(5)	25 Feb 2001 (for the purpose of making orders or regulations) (SI 2001/516)
		18 Jun 2001 (otherwise) (SI 2001/1820)
	(6)	18 Jun 2001 (SI 2001/1820)
215	(1)–(5)	18 Jun 2001 (SI 2001/1820)
	(6)	25 Feb 2001 (SI 2001/516)
	(7)	18 Jun 2001 (SI 2001/1820)
	(8), (9)	25 Feb 2001 (SI 2001/516)
216–218		18 Jun 2001 (SI 2001/1820)
219–221		1 Dec 2001 (SI 2001/3538)
222		18 Jun 2001 (SI 2001/1820)
223		18 Jun 2001 (for the purpose of fixing an amount by the scheme as mentioned in sub-s (1)) (SI 2001/1820)
		1 Dec 2001 (otherwise) (SI 2001/3538)
224	(1)–(3)	1 Dec 2001 (SI 2001/3538)
	(4)	25 Feb 2001 (for the purpose of making orders or regulations) (SI 2001/516)
		1 Dec 2001 (otherwise) (SI 2001/3538)

Financial Services and Markets Act 2000 (c 8)—*contd*

Section

224	(5)	1 Dec 2001 (SI 2001/3538)
225		18 Jun 2001 (SI 2001/1820)
226, 227		18 Jun 2001 (for the purpose of the making of rules by the Authority and the scheme operator) (SI 2001/1820)
		1 Dec 2001 (otherwise) (SI 2001/3538)
228		1 Dec 2001 (SI 2001/3538)
229		18 Jun 2001 (for the purpose of the making of rules by the Authority and the scheme operator) (SI 2001/1820)
		1 Dec 2001 (otherwise) (SI 2001/3538)
230		18 Jun 2001 (SI 2001/1820)
231–233		1 Dec 2001 (SI 2001/3538)
234		18 Jun 2001 (SI 2001/1820)
235–237		25 Feb 2001 (SI 2001/516)
238		25 Feb 2001 (for the purpose of making orders or regulations) (SI 2001/516)
		18 Jun 2001 (for the purpose of making rules) (SI 2001/1820)
		1 Dec 2001 (otherwise) (SI 2001/3538)
239	(1)–(3)	25 Feb 2001 (SI 2001/516)
	(4), (5)	18 Jun 2001 (SI 2001/1820)
240, 241		1 Dec 2001 (SI 2001/3538)
242		18 Jun 2001 (for the purpose of giving directions or imposing requirements as mentioned in sub-s (3)) (SI 2001/1820)
		3 Sep 2001 (for the purposes of authorisation orders coming into force not sooner than the day on which s 19 of this Act comes into force) (SI 2001/2632)
		1 Dec 2001 (otherwise) (SI 2001/3538)
243–245		3 Sep 2001 (for the purposes of authorisation orders coming into force not sooner than the day on which s 19 of this Act comes into force) (SI 2001/2632)
		1 Dec 2001 (otherwise) (SI 2001/3538)
246		3 Sep 2001 (for the purposes of certificates coming into force not sooner than the day on which s 19 of this Act comes into force) (SI 2001/2632)
		1 Dec 2001 (otherwise) (SI 2001/3538)
247, 248		18 Jun 2001 (SI 2001/1820)

Financial Services and Markets Act 2000 (c 8)—*contd*

Section

249		1 Dec 2001 (SI 2001/3538)
250		3 Sep 2001 (SI 2001/2632)
251	(1)–(3)	3 Sep 2001 (for the purposes of the giving of notice of any proposal to alter a scheme, or to replace its trustee or manager, not sooner than the day on which s 19 of this Act comes into force, and the giving of approval to any such proposal) (SI 2001/2632)
		1 Dec 2001 (otherwise) (SI 2001/3538)
	(4)(a)	3 Sep 2001 (for the purposes of the giving of notice of any proposal to alter a scheme, or to replace its trustee or manager, not sooner than the day on which s 19 of this Act comes into force, and the giving of approval to any such proposal) (SI 2001/2632)
		1 Dec 2001 (otherwise) (SI 2001/3538)
	(4)(b)	1 Dec 2001 (SI 2001/3538)
	(5)	3 Sep 2001 (for the purposes of the giving of notice of any proposal to alter a scheme, or to replace its trustee or manager, not sooner than the day on which s 19 of this Act comes into force, and the giving of approval to any such proposal) (SI 2001/2632)
		1 Dec 2001 (otherwise) (SI 2001/3538)
252		3 Sep 2001 (for the purposes of the giving of notice of any proposal to alter a scheme, or to replace its trustee or manager, not sooner than the day on which s 19 of this Act comes into force, and the giving of approval to any such proposal) (SI 2001/2632)
		1 Dec 2001 (otherwise) (SI 2001/3538)
253		1 Dec 2001 (SI 2001/3538)
254–256		3 Sep 2001 (SI 2001/2632)
257		3 Sep 2001 (for the purposes of directions coming into force not sooner than the day on which s 19 of this Act comes into force) (SI 2001/2632)
		1 Dec 2001 (otherwise) (SI 2001/3538)
258		1 Dec 2001 (SI 2001/3538)

Financial Services and Markets Act 2000 (c 8)—*contd*

Section

259–261			3 Sep 2001 (for the purposes of directions coming into force not sooner than the day on which s 19 of this Act comes into force) (SI 2001/2632)
			1 Dec 2001 (otherwise) (SI 2001/3538)
262			25 Feb 2001 (SI 2001/516)
263			1 Dec 2001 (SI 2001/3538)
264	(1)		25 Feb 2001 (for the purpose of making orders or regulations) (SI 2001/516)
			3 Sep 2001 (for the purposes of—
			(a) the giving of notice under sub-s (1) of intention to make invitations not sooner than the day on which s 19 of this Act comes into force; and
			(b) the giving of notice under sub-ss (2) or (6)) (SI 2001/2632)
			1 Dec 2001 (otherwise) (SI 2001/3538)
	(2)		3 Sep 2001 (for the purposes of—
			(a) the giving of notice under sub-s (1) of intention to make invitations not sooner than the day on which s 19 of this Act comes into force; and
			(b) the giving of notice under sub-ss (2) or (6)) (SI 2001/2632)
			1 Dec 2001 (otherwise) (SI 2001/3538)
	(3)	(a), (b)	3 Sep 2001 (for the purposes of—
			(a) the giving of notice under sub-s (1) of intention to make invitations not sooner than the day on which s 19 of this Act comes into force; and
			(b) the giving of notice under sub-ss (2) or (6)) (SI 2001/2632)
			1 Dec 2001 (otherwise) (SI 2001/3538)
		(c)	25 Feb 2001 (for the purpose of making orders or regulations) (SI 2001/516)
			3 Sep 2001 (for the purposes of—
			(a) the giving of notice under sub-s (1) of intention to make invitations not sooner than the day on which s 19 of this Act comes into force; and
			(b) the giving of notice under sub-ss (2) or (6)) (SI 2001/2632)
			1 Dec 2001 (otherwise) (SI 2001/3538)

Financial Services and Markets Act 2000 (c 8)—*contd*
Section

264	(4)–(7)	3 Sep 2001 (for the purposes of—
		(a) the giving of notice under sub-s (1) of intention to make invitations not sooner than the day on which s 19 of this Act comes into force; and
		(b) the giving of notice under sub-ss (2) or (6)) (SI 2001/2632)
		1 Dec 2001 (otherwise) (SI 2001/3538)
265	(1), (2)	3 Sep 2001 (SI 2001/2632)
	(3)	1 Dec 2001 (SI 2001/3538)
	(4), (5)	3 Sep 2001 (SI 2001/2632)
266		18 Jun 2001 (SI 2001/1820)
267–269		1 Dec 2001 (SI 2001/3538)
270		25 Feb 2001 (for the purpose of making orders or regulations) (SI 2001/516)
		3 Sep 2001 (for the purposes of—
		(a) the giving of notices under sub-s (1)(c); and
		(b) the giving of notice of approval under sub-s (1)(d)(i) coming into force not sooner than the day on which s 19 of this Act comes into force) (SI 2001/2632)
		1 Dec 2001 (otherwise) (SI 2001/3538)
271	(1)	3 Sep 2001 (SI 2001/2632)
	(2)	1 Dec 2001 (SI 2001/3538)
	(3)	3 Sep 2001 (SI 2001/2632)
272, 273		3 Sep 2001 (for the purposes of orders (and applications for orders) coming into force not sooner than the day on which s 19 of this Act comes into force) (SI 2001/2632)
		1 Dec 2001 (otherwise) (SI 2001/3538)
274		18 Jun 2001 (for the purpose of giving directions or imposing requirements as mentioned in sub-s (2)) (SI 2001/1820)
		3 Sep 2001 (for the purposes of orders (and applications for orders) coming into force not sooner than the day on which s 19 of this Act comes into force) (SI 2001/2632)
		1 Dec 2001 (otherwise) (SI 2001/3538)
275, 276		3 Sep 2001 (for the purposes of orders (and applications for orders) coming into force not sooner than the day on which s 19 of this Act comes into force) (SI 2001/2632)

Financial Services and Markets Act 2000 (c 8)—*contd*

Section

275, 276—*contd*			1 Dec 2001 (otherwise) (SI 2001/3538)
277	(1)		3 Sep 2001 (for the purposes of—

(a) the giving of notice under
  sub-s (1) of any proposal to alter a
  scheme not sooner than the day on
  which s 19 of this Act comes into
  force, and the giving of approval to
  any such proposal; and
(b) the giving of notice under sub-s
  (3) of any proposal to replace an
  operator, trustee or depositary not
  sooner than the day on which s 19
  of this Act comes into force)
  (SI 2001/2632)
1 Dec 2001 (otherwise) (SI 2001/3538)

	(2)	(a)	3 Sep 2001 (for the purposes of—

(a) the giving of notice under
  sub-s (1) of any proposal to alter a
  scheme not sooner than the day on
  which s 19 of this Act comes into
  force, and the giving of approval to
  any such proposal; and
(b) the giving of notice under sub-s
  (3) of any proposal to replace an
  operator, trustee or depositary not
  sooner than the day on which s 19
  of this Act comes into force)
  (SI 2001/2632)
1 Dec 2001 (otherwise) (SI 2001/3538)

		(b)	1 Dec 2001 (SI 2001/3538)
	(3)		3 Sep 2001 (for the purposes of—

(a) the giving of notice under sub-s
  (1) of any proposal to alter a
  scheme not sooner than the day on
  which s 19 of this Act comes into
  force, and the giving of approval to
  any such proposal; and
(b) the giving of notice under sub-s
  (3) of any proposal to replace an
  operator, trustee or depositary not
  sooner than the day on which
  s 19 of this Act comes into force)
  (SI 2001/2632)
1 Dec 2001 (otherwise) (SI 2001/3538)

278			18 Jun 2001 (SI 2001/1820)
279–282			3 Sep 2001 (SI 2001/2632)
283	(1)		18 Jun 2001 (SI 2001/1820)
	(2), (3)		1 Dec 2001 (SI 2001/3538)
284	(1)		1 Dec 2001 (SI 2001/3538)

Financial Services and Markets Act 2000 (c 8)—*contd*
Section

284	(2)	25 Feb 2001 (for the purpose of making orders or regulations) (SI 2001/516)
		1 Dec 2001 (otherwise) (SI 2001/3538)
	(3)–(11)	1 Dec 2001 (SI 2001/3538)
285		1 Dec 2001 (SI 2001/3538)
286		25 Feb 2001 (SI 2001/516)
287, 288		18 Jun 2001 (for the purpose of giving directions or imposing requirements as mentioned in sub-s (2)) (SI 2001/1820)
		3 Sep 2001 (otherwise) (SI 2001/2632)
289		3 Sep 2001 (SI 2001/2632)
290		3 Sep 2001 (for the purposes of recognition orders coming into force not sooner than the day on which s 19 of this Act comes into force) (SI 2001/2632)
		1 Dec 2001 (otherwise) (SI 2001/3538)
291		1 Dec 2001 (SI 2001/3538)
292	(1)	3 Sep 2001 (SI 2001/2632)
	(2)–(5)	3 Sep 2001 (for the purposes of recognition orders coming into force not sooner than the day on which s 19 of this Act comes into force) (SI 2001/2632)
		1 Dec 2001 (otherwise) (SI 2001/3538)
293		18 Jun 2001 (for the purpose of making rules) (SI 2001/1820)
		1 Dec 2001 (otherwise) (SI 2001/3538)
294		18 Jun 2001 (for the purpose of giving directions as mentioned in sub-s (2)) (SI 2001/1820)
		3 Sep 2001 (otherwise) (SI 2001/2632)
295		18 Jun 2001 (for the purpose of making rules) (SI 2001/1820)
		1 Dec 2001 (otherwise) (SI 2001/3538)
296		1 Dec 2001 (SI 2001/3538)
297		3 Sep 2001 (SI 2001/2632)
298		3 Sep 2001 (for the purposes of revocation orders under s 297) (SI 2001/2632)
		1 Dec 2001 (otherwise) (SI 2001/3538)
299		18 Jun 2001 (SI 2001/1820)
300, 301		1 Dec 2001 (SI 2001/3538)
302, 303		3 Sep 2001 (SI 2001/2632)
304		1 Dec 2001 (SI 2001/3538)
305		3 Sep 2001 (for the purposes of s 303) (SI 2001/2632)
		1 Dec 2001 (otherwise) (SI 2001/3538)

Financial Services and Markets Act 2000 (c 8)—*contd*
Section

306		3 Sep 2001 (for the purposes of reports issued by the Director under s 303) (SI 2001/2632)
		1 Dec 2001 (otherwise) (SI 2001/3538)
307		3 Sep 2001 (SI 2001/2632)
308, 309		1 Dec 2001 (SI 2001/3538)
310		3 Sep 2001 (for the purposes of s 307) (SI 2001/2632)
		1 Dec 2001 (otherwise) (SI 2001/3538)
311, 312		3 Sep 2001 (SI 2001/2632)
313		25 Feb 2001 (SI 2001/516)
314		3 Sep 2001 (SI 2001/2632)
315	(1), (2)	1 Dec 2001 (SI 2001/3538)
	(3)–(5)	3 Sep 2001 (SI 2001/2632)
316		18 Jun 2001 (for the purpose of giving directions as mentioned in sub-s (1) coming into force not sooner than the day on which s 19 of the Act comes into force) (SI 2001/1820)
		1 Dec 2001 (otherwise) (SI 2001/3538)
317		18 Jun 2001 (SI 2001/1820)
318		18 Jun 2001 (for the purpose of giving directions as mentioned in sub-s (1) coming into force not sooner than the day on which s 19 of the Act comes into force) (SI 2001/1820)
		1 Dec 2001 (otherwise) (SI 2001/3538)
319		18 Jun 2001 (SI 2001/1820)
320	(1), (2)	1 Dec 2001 (SI 2001/3538)
	(3), (4)	3 Sep 2001 (for the purposes of requirements taking effect not sooner than the day on which s 19 of this Act comes into force) (SI 2001/2632)
		1 Dec 2001 (otherwise) (SI 2001/3538)
321		3 Sep 2001 (for the purposes of requirements taking effect not sooner than the day on which s 19 of this Act comes into force) (SI 2001/2632)
		1 Dec 2001 (otherwise) (SI 2001/3538)
322		18 Jun 2001 (for the purpose of making rules coming into force not sooner than the day on which s 19 of the Act comes into force) (SI 2001/1820)
		1 Dec 2001 (otherwise) (SI 2001/3538)

Financial Services and Markets Act 2000 (c 8)—*contd*
Section

323, 324			18 Jun 2001 (SI 2001/1820)
325	(1)–(3)		1 Dec 2001 (SI 2001/3538)
	(4)		3 Sep 2001 (SI 2001/2632)
326			25 Feb 2001 (SI 2001/516)
327	(1)–(5)		1 Dec 2001 (SI 2001/3538)
	(6)		25 Feb 2001 (for the purpose of making orders or regulations) (SI 2001/516)
			1 Dec 2001 (otherwise) (SI 2001/3538)
	(7), (8)		1 Dec 2001 (SI 2001/3538)
328–331			3 Sep 2001 (SI 2001/2632)
332			18 Jun 2001 (SI 2001/1820)
333			1 Dec 2001 (SI 2001/3538)
334	(1), (2)		25 Feb 2001 (SI 2001/516)
	(3), (4)		1 Dec 2001 (SI 2001/3538)
335			25 Feb 2001 (SI 2001/516)
336	(1), (2)		25 Feb 2001 (SI 2001/516)
	(3)		1 Dec 2001 (SI 2001/3538)
337			25 Feb 2001 (SI 2001/516)
338	(1), (2)		25 Feb 2001 (SI 2001/516)
	(3), (4)		1 Dec 2001 (SI 2001/3538)
339			25 Feb 2001 (SI 2001/516)
340			18 Jun 2001 (SI 2001/1820)
341			1 Dec 2001 (SI 2001/3538)
342	(1)–(4)		1 Dec 2001 (SI 2001/3538)
	(5)		25 Feb 2001 (SI 2001/516)
	(6), (7)		1 Dec 2001 (SI 2001/3538)
343	(1)–(4)		1 Dec 2001 (SI 2001/3538)
	(5)		25 Feb 2001 (SI 2001/516)
	(6)–(9)		1 Dec 2001 (SI 2001/3538)
344–346			1 Dec 2001 (SI 2001/3538)
347	(1)	(a)	1 Dec 2001 (for the purpose of enabling the Authority to maintain a record of the approved persons listed below) (SI 2001/3538)
			1 May 2002 (for the purpose of requiring the Authority to maintain a record of persons who appear to the Authority to be authorised persons who are EEA firms or Treaty firms) (SI 2001/3538)
			1 Aug 2002 (for the purpose of requiring the Authority to maintain a record of persons who appear to the Authority to be authorised persons who were immediately before the appointed day, authorised under Financial

Financial Services and Markets Act 2000 (c 8)—*contd*
Section

347	(1)	(a)—*contd*	Services Act 1986 by virtue of holding a certificate issued for the purposes of Part I of that Act by a recognised professional body, within the meaning of that Act) (SI 2001/3538)
		(b)–(g)	1 Dec 2001 (SI 2001/3538)
		(h)	1 Dec 2001 (for the purpose of enabling the Authority to maintain a record of approved persons) (SI 2001/3538)
			1 Dec 2002 (for the purpose of requiring the Authority to maintain a record of approved persons) (SI 2001/3538)
		(i)	1 Dec 2001 (SI 2001/3538)
	(2)	(a)	1 Dec 2001 (for the purpose of enabling the Authority to maintain a record of the approved persons listed below) (SI 2001/3538)
			1 May 2002 (for the purpose of requiring the Authority to maintain a record of persons who appear to the Authority to be authorised persons who are EEA firms or Treaty firms) (SI 2001/3538)
			1 Aug 2002 (for the purpose of requiring the Authority to maintain a record of persons who appear to the Authority to be authorised persons who were immediately before the appointed day, authorised under Financial Services Act 1986 by virtue of holding a certificate issued for the purposes of Part I of that Act by a recognised professional body (within the meaning of that Act) (SI 2001/3538)
		(b)–(f)	1 Dec 2001 (SI 2001/3538)
		(g)	1 Dec 2001 (for the purpose of enabling the Authority to maintain a record of approved persons) (SI 2001/3538)
			1 Dec 2002 (for the purpose of requiring the Authority to maintain a record of approved persons) (SI 2001/3538)

Financial Services and Markets Act 2000 (c 8)—*contd*
Section

347	(3)–(9)		1 Dec 2001 (SI 2001/3538)
348			18 Jun 2001 (SI 2001/1820)
349			25 Feb 2001 (for the purpose of making orders or regulations) (SI 2001/516)
			18 Jun 2001 (otherwise) (SI 2001/1820)
350	(1), (2)		3 Sep 2001 (SI 2001/2632)
	(3)		18 Jun 2001 (SI 2001/1820)
	(4)–(6)		3 Sep 2001 (SI 2001/2632)
	(7)		18 Jun 2001 (SI 2001/1820)
351	(1)–(6)		18 Jun 2001 (SI 2001/1820)
	(7)		25 Feb 2001 (SI 2001/516)
352			18 Jun 2001 (for the purpose of any contravention of s 348) (SI 2001/1820)
			3 Sep 2001 (otherwise) (SI 2001/2632)
353			25 Feb 2001 (SI 2001/516)
354			3 Sep 2001 (SI 2001/2632)
355			20 Jul 2001 (SI 2001/2632)
356–359			1 Dec 2001 (SI 2001/3538)
360			20 Jul 2001 (SI 2001/2632)
361–371			1 Dec 2001 (SI 2001/3538)
372			20 Jul 2001 (for the purpose of making rules[2]) (SI 2001/2632)
			1 Dec 2001 (otherwise) (SI 2001/3538)
373–377			1 Dec 2001 (SI 2001/3538)
378, 379			20 Jul 2001 (SI 2001/2632)
380			18 Jun 2001 (SI 2001/1820)
381			1 Dec 2001 (SI 2001/3538)
382			18 Jun 2001 (SI 2001/1820)
383–386			1 Dec 2001 (SI 2001/3538)
387–394			3 Sep 2001 (SI 2001/2632)
395, 396			18 Jun 2001 (SI 2001/1820)
397	(1)–(8)		1 Dec 2001 (SI 2001/3538)
	(9)–(14)		25 Feb 2001 (SI 2001/516)
398–401			18 Jun 2001 (SI 2001/1820)
402	(1)	(a)	1 Dec 2001 (SI 2001/3538)
		(b)	25 Feb 2001 (for the purpose of making orders or regulations) (SI 2001/516)
			19 Oct 2001 (for the purposes of proceedings for offences under prescribed regulations relating to money laundering) (SI 2001/3436)
	(2), (3)		19 Oct 2001 (for the purposes of proceedings for offences under prescribed regulations relating to money laundering) (SI 2001/3436)
			1 Dec 2001 (otherwise) (SI 2001/3538)

Financial Services and Markets Act 2000 (c 8)—*contd*

Section

403			18 Jun 2001 (SI 2001/1820)
404			1 Dec 2001 (SI 2001/3538)
405	(1)	(a), (b)	3 Sep 2001 (SI 2001/2632)
		(c), (d)	1 Dec 2001 (SI 2001/3538)
	(2)–(5)		3 Sep 2001 (SI 2001/2632)
406			1 Dec 2001 (SI 2001/3538)
407	(1), (2)		3 Sep 2001 (SI 2001/2632)
	(3)		1 Dec 2001 (SI 2001/3538)
408			3 Sep 2001 (for the purposes of determinations coming into force not sooner than the day on which s 19 of this Act comes into force) (SI 2001/2632)
			1 Dec 2001 (otherwise) (SI 2001/3538)
409			25 Feb 2001 (SI 2001/516)
410			18 Jun 2001 (SI 2001/1820)
411			1 Dec 2001 (SI 2001/3538)
412			25 Feb 2001 (for the purpose of making orders or regulations) (SI 2001/516)
			1 Dec 2001 (otherwise) (SI 2001/3538)
413			3 Sep 2001 (SI 2001/2632)
414	(1)–(3)		25 Feb 2001 (SI 2001/516)
	(4)		18 Jun 2001 (SI 2001/1820)
415			18 Jun 2001 (SI 2001/1820)
416	(1)	(a), (b)	1 Dec 2001 (SI 2001/3538)
		(c)	30 Apr 2001 (SI 2001/1282)
	(2)		1 Dec 2001 (SI 2001/3538)
	(3)	(a)	30 Apr 2001 (SI 2001/1282)
		(b), (c)	2 Mar 2002 (SI 2001/3538)
		(d)	1 Dec 2001 (SI 2001/3538)
	(4), (5)		25 Feb 2001 (SI 2001/516)
417			25 Feb 2001 (SI 2001/516)
418			3 Sep 2001 (SI 2001/2632)
419–423			25 Feb 2001 (SI 2001/516)
424	(1), (2)		25 Feb 2001 (SI 2001/516)
	(3)		25 Feb 2001 (for the purpose of making orders or regulations) (SI 2001/516)
			1 Dec 2001 (otherwise) (SI 2001/3538)
425–427			25 Feb 2001 (SI 2001/516)
428			14 Jun 2000 (s 431(1))
429			25 Feb 2001 (SI 2001/516)
430, 431			14 Jun 2000 (s 431(1))
432	(1)		See Sch 20 below
	(2)		See Sch 21 below
	(3)		See Sch 22 below
433			14 Jun 2000 (s 431(1))

Financial Services and Markets Act 2000 (c 8)—*contd*

Schedule

1, para	1–6	18 Jun 2001 (SI 2001/1820)
	7, 8	19 Jul 2001 (for the purpose of enabling the Authority to make the complaints scheme and appoint the investigator) (SI 2001/2364)
		3 Sep 2001 (otherwise) (SI 2001/2632)
	9–21	18 Jun 2001 (SI 2001/1820)
2		25 Feb 2001 (SI 2001/516)
3, para	1–18	25 Feb 2001 (for the purpose of making orders or regulations) (SI 2001/516)
		18 Jun 2001 (for the purpose of making rules) (SI 2001/1820)
		1 Dec 2001 (otherwise) (SI 2001/3538)
	19	25 Feb 2001 (for the purpose of making orders or regulations) (SI 2001/516)
		18 Jun 2001 (for the purpose of making rules) (SI 2001/1820)
		3 Sep 2001 (for the purposes of the giving of notice under sub-para (2) of intention to establish a branch not sooner than the day on which s 19 of this Act comes into force) (SI 2001/2632)
		1 Dec 2001 (otherwise) (SI 2001/3538)
	20	25 Feb 2001 (for the purpose of making orders or regulations) (SI 2001/516)
		18 Jun 2001 (for the purpose of making rules) (SI 2001/1820)
		3 Sep 2001 (for the purposes of the giving of notice under sub-para (1) of intention to provide services not sooner than the day on which s 19 of this Act comes into force) (SI 2001/2632)
		1 Dec 2001 (otherwise) (SI 2001/3538)
	21–24	25 Feb 2001 (for the purpose of making orders or regulations) (SI 2001/516)
		18 Jun 2001 (for the purpose of making rules) (SI 2001/1820)
		1 Dec 2001 (otherwise) (SI 2001/3538)
4, para	1	3 Sep 2001 (SI 2001/2632)
	2	1 Dec 2001 (SI 2001/3538)
	3	3 Sep 2001 (for the purposes of issuing certificates under sub-para (4)) (SI 2001/2632)
		1 Dec 2001 (otherwise) (SI 2001/3538)

Financial Services and Markets Act 2000 (c 8)—*contd*
Schedule

4, para	4			1 Dec 2001 (SI 2001/3538)
	5			3 Sep 2001 (for the purposes of giving notice under sub-para (2) of intention to carry on regulated activities not sooner than the day on which s 19 of this Act comes into force) (SI 2001/2632)
				1 Dec 2001 (otherwise) (SI 2001/3538)
	6			1 Dec 2001 (SI 2001/3538)
5				1 Dec 2001 (SI 2001/3538)
6, para	1–7			3 Sep 2001 (SI 2001/2632)
	8, 9			25 Feb 2001 (for the purpose of making orders or regulations) (SI 2001/516)
				3 Sep 2001 (otherwise) (SI 2001/2632)
7, 8				18 Jun 2001 (SI 2001/1820)
9, para	1–6			25 Feb 2001 (SI 2001/516)
	7			18 Jun 2001 (SI 2001/1820)
10				1 Dec 2001 (SI 2001/3538)
11				25 Feb 2001 (SI 2001/516)
12, para	1–5			1 Dec 2001 (SI 2001/3538)
	6	(1)		1 Dec 2001 (SI 2001/3538)
		(2)		25 Feb 2001 (SI 2001/516)
		(3)		1 Dec 2001 (SI 2001/3538)
	7–10			1 Dec 2001 (SI 2001/3538)
13, para	1–8			3 Sep 2001 (SI 2001/2632)
	9			25 Feb 2001 (SI 2001/516)
	10–13			3 Sep 2001 (SI 2001/2632)
14				18 Jun 2001 (SI 2001/1820)
15				3 Sep 2001 (SI 2001/2632)
16				1 Dec 2001 (SI 2001/3538)
17				18 Jun 2001 (SI 2001/1820)
18, Pt	I–IV			1 Dec 2001 (SI 2001/3538)
	V			2 Jul 2002 (SI 2001/3538)
19, Pt	I			18 Jun 2001 (SI 2001/1820)
	II, para	1–18		18 Jun 2001 (SI 2001/1820)
		19		25 Feb 2001 (for the purpose of making orders or regulations) (SI 2001/516)
				18 Jun 2001 (otherwise) (SI 2001/1820)
20, para	1	(a)		1 Dec 2001 (SI 2001/3538)
		(b)		3 Sep 2001 (SI 2001/2632)
	2	(a)		1 Dec 2001 (SI 2001/3538)
		(b)		3 Sep 2001 (SI 2001/2632)
	3			3 Sep 2001 (SI 2001/2632)
	4, 5			1 Dec 2001 (SI 2001/3538)
	6			3 Jul 2001[1] (SI 2001/2364)
	7	(1), (2)		3 Sep 2001 (SI 2001/2632)
		(3)	(a)	1 Dec 2001 (SI 2001/3538)

Financial Services and Markets Act 2000 (c 8)—*contd*

Schedule

20, para	(b)	3 Sep 2001 (SI 2001/2632)
21		14 Jun 2000 (s 431(1))
22		30 Apr 2001 (repeal of Insurance Brokers (Registration) Act 1977) (SI 2001/1282)
		1 Dec 2001 (otherwise, except repeals in Credit Unions Act 1979) (SI 2001/3538)
		2 Jul 2002 (repeals in Credit Unions Act 1979) (SI 2001/3538)

[1]   For transitional provision, see SI 2001/2364, art 3

[2]   Note that the Queen's Printer copy of SI 2001/2632 purports to bring s 372 into force on 20 July 2001 both for all purposes and for the purpose of making rules only; it is thought that the intention was to bring that section into force for the purpose of making rules only

Football (Disorder) Act 2000 (c 25)

RA: 28 Jul 2000

Commencement provisions: s 5(1); Football (Disorder) Act 2000 (Commencement) Order 2000, SI 2000/2125

Section

1	28 Aug 2000 (SI 2000/2125)
2–7	28 Jul 2000 (s 5(1))

Schedule

1–3	28 Aug 2000 (SI 2000/2125)

Freedom of Information Act 2000 (c 36)

RA: 30 Nov 2000

Commencement provisions: s 87[1]; Freedom of Information Act 2000 (Commencement No 1) Order 2001, SI 2001/1637

Section

1, 2		*Not in force*[1]
3–8		30 Nov 2000 (RA)
9, 10		30 Nov 2000 (so far as confers power to make any order, regulations or code of practice) (RA)
		Not in force (otherwise)[1]
11		*Not in force*[1]
12, 13		30 Nov 2000 (so far as confers power to make any order, regulations or code of practice) (RA)
		Not in force (otherwise)[1]
14–17		*Not in force*[1]
18	(1)	30 Jan 2001 (s 87(2))
	(2), (3)	14 May 2001 (SI 2001/1637)

Freedom of Information Act 2000 (c 36)—*contd*

Section

18	(4)	See Sch 2 below
	(5)–(7)	14 May 2001 (SI 2001/1637)
19		30 Nov 2000 (RA) (so far as relates to approval of publication schemes)
		Not in force (otherwise)[1]
20		30 Nov 2000 (RA) (so far as relates to approval and preparation by the Commissioner of model publication schemes)
		Not in force (otherwise)[1]
21–44		*Not in force*[1]
45, 46		30 Nov 2000 (so far as confers power to make any order, regulations or code of practice) (RA)
		Not in force (otherwise)[1]
47	(1)	30 Nov 2000 (so far as confers power to make any order, regulations or code of practice) (RA)
		Not in force (otherwise)[1]
	(2)–(6)	30 Nov 2000 (RA)
48		30 Nov 2000 (so far as confers power to make any order, regulations or code of practice) (RA)
		Not in force (otherwise)[1]
49		30 Nov 2000 (RA)
50–52		*Not in force*[1]
53		30 Nov 2000 (so far as confers power to make any order, regulations or code of practice) (RA)
		Not in force (otherwise)[1]
54–60		*Not in force*
61		14 May 2001 (so far as relating to Sch 4, paras 1, 4) (SI 2001/1637)
		Not in force (otherwise)[1]
62–66		*Not in force*[1]
67		See Sch 5 below
68		*Not in force*[1]
69		30 Nov 2000 (so far as confers power to make any order, regulations or code of practice) (RA)
		Not in force (otherwise)[1]
70–72		*Not in force*[1]
73		See Sch 6 below
74, 75		30 Nov 2000 (RA)
76		30 Jan 2001 (s 87(2))

Freedom of Information Act 2000 (c 36)—*contd*

Section

77			*Not in force*[1]
78–85			30 Nov 2000 (RA)
86			See Sch 8 below
87			30 Nov 2000 (RA)
88			*Not in force*[1]

Schedule

1			30 Nov 2000 (RA)
2, para	1	(1)	30 Jan 2001 (s 87(2))
		(2)	14 May 2001 (SI 2001/1637)
	2		30 Nov 2000 (RA)
	3	(1)	30 Jan 2001 (s 87(2))
		(2)	14 May 2001 (SI 2001/1637)
2, para	4		30 Jan 2001 (s 87(2))
	5		14 May 2001 (SI 2001/1637)
	6, 7		30 Jan 2001 (s 87(2))
	8	(1)	14 May 2001 (SI 2001/1637)
		(2)	30 Jan 2001 (s 87(2))
	9	(1)	14 May 2001 (SI 2001/1637)
		(2)	30 Jan 2001 (s 87(2))
	10	(a)	30 Jan 2001 (s 87(2))
		(b)	*Not in force*[1]
	11, 12		14 May 2001 (SI 2001/1637)
	13	(1), (2)	30 Jan 2001 (s 87(2))
		(3)	14 May 2001 (SI 2001/1637)
	14	(a)	30 Jan 2001 (s 87(2))
		(b)	14 May 2001 (SI 2001/1637)
	15	(1), (2)	30 Jan 2001 (s 87(2))
		(3)	14 May 2001 (SI 2001/1637)
	16		14 May 2001 (SI 2001/1637)
	17–22		30 Nov 2000 (RA)
3			*Not in force*[1]
4, para	1		14 May 2001 (SI 2001/1637)
	2, 3		*Not in force*[1]
	4		14 May 2001 (SI 2001/1637)
5, para	1–3		*Not in force*[1]
	4		30 Nov 2000 (RA)
	5		*Not in force*[1]
6, para	1		14 May 2001 (SI 2001/1637)
	2–5		*Not in force*[1]
	6, 7		14 May 2001 (SI 2001/1637)
	8		30 Nov 2000 (RA)
7			30 Jan 2001 (s 87(2))
8, Pt	I		30 Nov 2000 (RA)
	II		30 Jan 2001 (s 87(2))
	III		*Not in force*[1]

---

[1]   S 87(3) provides that, except as provided by sub-ss (1), (2) of that section, the Act shall come into force on 30 November 2005 or on such day or days before then as the Secretary of State may by order appoint

Fur Farming (Prohibition) Act 2000 (c 33)

RA: 23 Nov 2000

Commencement provisions: s 7(2), (3); Fur Farming (Prohibition) Act 2000 (Commencement) Order 2001, SI 2001/3854

Section

1–4	1 Jan 2003 (SI 2001/3854)
5	23 Jan 2001 (s 7(3))
6, 7	23 Nov 2000 (RA)

Government Resources and Accounts Act 2000 (c 20)

RA: 28 Jul 2000

Commencement provisions: s 30(1), (2); Government Resources and Accounts Act 2000 (Commencement No 1 and Transitional Provision) Order 2000, SI 2000/3349[1]

Section

1		1 Apr 2001 (SI 2000/3349)
2	(1), (2)	22 Dec 2000 (SI 2000/3349)
	(3)–(6)	1 Apr 2001 (SI 2000/3349)
3		1 Apr 2001 (SI 2000/3349)
4		22 Dec 2000 (SI 2000/3349)
5–9		1 Apr 2001 (SI 2000/3349)
10		22 Dec 2000 (SI 2000/3349)
11		*Not in force*
12, 13		22 Dec 2000 (so far as relate to the specifying of amounts and the giving of directions) (E, S, NI) (SI 2000/3349)
		1 Apr 2001 (otherwise) (E, S, NI) (SI 2000/3349)
		Not in force (W)
14		1 Apr 2001 (SI 2000/3349)
15		22 Dec 2000 (SI 2000/3349)
16–20		28 Jul 2000 (s 5(1))
21		1 Apr 2001 (SI 2000/3349)
22		1 Apr 2001 (SI 2000/3349)
23, 24		22 Dec 2000 (SI 2000/3349)
25, 26		1 Apr 2001 (SI 2000/3349)
27, 28		22 Dec 2000 (SI 2000/3349)
29	(1)	See Sch 1 below
	(2)	See Sch 2 below
30–31		28 Jul 2000 (s 5(1))
Schedule		
1, para	1–16	1 Apr 2001 (SI 2000/3349)
	17	22 Dec 2000 (so far as relates to the preparation and laying of estimates, the giving of directions, and the making of any provision described in House of Commons (Administration) Act 1978, s 3(4)(b), as substituted by Sch 1, para 17 to this Act) (SI 2000/3349)

Government Resources and Accounts Act 2000 (c 20)—*contd*

Schedule

1, para	17—*contd*	1 Apr 2001 (otherwise) (SI 2000/3349)
	18–23	1 Apr 2001 (SI 2000/3349)
	24	22 Dec 2000 (so far as relates to the giving of directions under Government of Wales Act 1998, s 101A(4), as inserted by Sch 1, para 24 to this Act) (SI 2000/3349)
		1 Apr 2001 (otherwise) (except so far as relates to Government of Wales Act 1998, s 101A(7)–(12)) (SI 2000/3349)
		Not in force (exception noted above)
	25–27	1 Apr 2001 (SI 2000/3349)
2		1 Apr 2001 (SI 2000/3349)

[1]   None of the provisions brought into force by this Order shall have effect in relation to the business of any financial year ending with or before 31 Mar 2001, with the exception of s 4, Sch 1, paras 19, 23.

Health Service Commissioners (Amendment) Act 2000 (c 28)

RA: 23 Nov 2000

Commencement provisions: s 4(2)

Section

1–4	23 Feb 2001 (s 4(2))

Insolvency Act 2000 (c 39)

RA: 30 Nov 2000

Commencement provisions: s 16; Insolvency Act 2000 (Commencement No 1 and Transitional Provisions) Order 2001, SI 2001/766; Insolvency Act 2000 (Commencement No 2) Order 2001, SI 2001/1751

Section

1		See Sch 1 below
2–4		*Not in force*
5–13		2 Apr 2001 (SI 2001/766) [1]
14		30 Nov 2000 (s 16(2))
15	(1)	See Sch 5 below
	(2), (3)	*Not in force*
16–18		30 Nov 2000 (RA)
Schedule		
1, para	1–3	*Not in force*
	4	11 May 2001 (only insofar as gives effect to Insolvency Act 1986, Sch A1, paras 5, 45(1)–(3), (5)) (SI 2001/1751)
		Not in force (otherwise)
	5–12	*Not in force*
2, 3		*Not in force*

Insolvency Act 2000 (c 39)—*contd*
Schedule

4	2 Apr 2001 (SI 2001/766)[1]
5	2 Apr 2001 (so far as relates to repeals of or in Insolvency Act 1986, s 218(2), (6)(b); Company Directors Disqualification Act 1986, ss 9(1), 22(4); Companies Act 1989, s 78) (SI 2001/766)
	Not in force (otherwise)

[1]   For transitional provisions, see SI 2001/766, art 3

Learning and Skills Act 2000 (c 21)

RA: 28 Jul 2000

Commencement provisions: s 154; Learning and Skills Act 2000 (Commencement No 1) Order 2000, SI 2000/2114; Learning and Skills Act (Commencement No 1) (Wales) Order 2000, SI 2000/2540; Learning and Skills Act (Commencement No 2 and Savings) Order 2000, SI 2000/2559; Learning and Skills Act 2000 (Commencement No 2) (Wales) Order 2000, SI 2000/3230; Learning and Skills Act 2000 (Commencement No 3 and Savings and Transitional Provisions) Order 2001, SI 2001/654[2]; Learning and Skills Act 2000 (Commencement No 3 and Transitional Provisions) (Wales) Order 2001, SI 2001/1274[3]; Learning and Skills Act 2000 (Commencement No 4) (Wales) Order 2001, SI 2001/2705; Learning and Skills Act 2000 (Commencement No 4) and Transitional Provisions Order 2002, SI 2002/279[5]

Section

1	(1)–(3)		1 Sep 2000 (SI 2000/2114)
	(4)		See Sch 1 below
	(5)		1 Sep 2000 (SI 2000/2114)
2–4			1 Apr 2001 (SI 2001/654)
5	(1)	(a)–(e)	1 Mar 2001 (SI 2001/654)
		(f)	1 Sep 2000 (SI 2000/2114)
		(g)–(i)	1 Mar 2001 (SI 2001/654)
	(2)		1 Sep 2000 (SI 2000/2114)
	(3)		1 Mar 2001 (SI 2001/654)
6	(1), (2)		1 Sep 2000 (SI 2000/2114)
	(3)		1 Mar 2001 (SI 2001/654)
	(4)		1 Mar 2001 (SI 2001/654); prospectively repealed by Special Educational Needs and Disability Act 2001, ss 34(7), 42(6), Sch 9 [4]
	(5)		1 Sep 2000 (SI 2000/2114)
	(6)		1 Mar 2001 (SI 2001/654); prospectively repealed by Special Educational Needs and Disability Act 2001, ss 34(7), 42(6), Sch 9 [4]
7			1 Mar 2002 (SI 2002/279)
8, 9			1 Mar 2001 (SI 2001/654)

Learning and Skills Act 2000 (c 21)—*contd*

Section

10, 11		1 Apr 2001 (SI 2001/654)
12	(1)	1 Sep 2000 (SI 2000/2114)
	(2)	1 Mar 2001 (SI 2001/654)
	(3)–(5)	1 Sep 2000 (SI 2000/2114)
	(6)	1 Mar 2001 (SI 2001/654)
13		1 Apr 2001 (SI 2001/654)
14–18		1 Sep 2000 (SI 2000/2114)
19	(1)–(4)	1 Sep 2000 (SI 2000/2114)
	(5)	See Sch 2 below
20–22		1 Sep 2000 (SI 2000/2114)
23		1 Apr 2001 (SI 2001/654)
24–25		1 Sep 2000 (SI 2000/2114)
26		See Sch 3 below
27		1 Sep 2000 (SI 2000/2114)
28		1 Apr 2001 (SI 2001/654)
29		1 Sep 2000 (SI 2000/2114)
30		19 Sep 2000 (W) (SI 2000/2540)
31–35		1 Apr 2001 (W) (SI 2001/1274)
36		1 Apr 2002 (W) (SI 2001/2705)
37–41		1 Apr 2001 (W) (SI 2001/1274)
42–44		1 Jan 2001 (W) (SI 2000/3230)
45		1 Apr 2001 (W) (SI 2001/1274)
46		1 Jan 2001 (W) (SI 2000/3230)
47		19 Sep 2000 (W) (SI 2000/2540)
48		1 Jan 2001 (W) (SI 2000/3230)
49		19 Sep 2000 (W) (SI 2000/2540)
50		1 Apr 2001 (W) (SI 2001/1274)
51		19 Sep 2000 (W) (SI 2000/2540)
52	(1)–(7)	3 Aug 2000 (SI 2000/2114)
	(8)	See Sch 6 below
53		3 Aug 2000 (SI 2000/2114)
54–59		1 Apr 2001 (SI 2001/654)
60		3 Aug 2000 (SI 2000/2114)
61–68		1 Apr 2001 (SI 2001/654)
69, 70		3 Aug 2000 (SI 2000/2114)
71	(1), (2)	1 Oct 2000 (SI 2000/2559)
	(3)	1 Apr 2001 (SI 2001/654)
72		1 Apr 2001 (SI 2001/654)
73		1 Jan 2001 (W) (SI 2000/3230)
74–80		1 Apr 2001 (W) (SI 2001/1274)
81		1 Apr 2001 (W) (SI 2001/1274)
82–86		1 Apr 2001 (W) (SI 2001/1274)
87		1 Jan 2001 (W) (SI 2000/3230)
88		1 Apr 2001 (W) (SI 2001/1274)
89		1 Apr 2001 (SI 2001/654)
90		1 Oct 2000 (SI 2000/2559)
91		1 Apr 2001 (W) (SI 2001/1274)
92		1 Sep 2000 (SI 2000/2114)
93		1 Jan 2001 (W) (SI 2000/3230)

Learning and Skills Act 2000 (c 21)—*contd*

Section

94		1 Sep 2000 (SI 2000/2114)
95		1 Sep 2000 (E) (SI 2000/2114)
		1 Jan 2001 (W) (SI 2000/3230)
96		1 Sep 2001 (W) (SI 2001/1274)
		1 Sep 2001 (E) (SI 2001/654)
97		1 Aug 2002 (E) (SI 2002/279)
		1 Sep 2002 (W) (SI 2001/2705)
98		1 Apr 2001 (SI 2001/654)
99		1 Apr 2001 (W) (SI 2001/1274)
100	(1)	1 Sep 2001 (SI 2001/654)
	(2)	1 Sep 2001 (W) (SI 2001/1274)
101		1 Sep 2001 (SI 2001/654)
102		1 Sep 2001 (W) (SI 2001/1274)
103	(1)	1 Apr 2001 (W) (so far as necessary for the purposes of s 103(4)(b)) (SI 2001/1274)
		1 Sep 2001 (E) (SI 2001/654)
		Not in force (otherwise)
	(2), (3)	1 Apr 2001 (W) (so far as necessary for the purposes of s 103(4)(b) below) (SI 2001/1274)
		1 Apr 2002 (E) (SI 2002/279)
		Not in force (otherwise)
	(4)	1 Apr 2001 (SI 2001/1274)
	(5)	1 Sep 2001 (W) (SI 2001/1274)
		1 Sep 2001 (E) (SI 2001/654)
104–109		3 Aug 2000 (SI 2000/2114)
110	(1)	1 Sep 2000 (E) (so far as inserts Education Act 1996, s 2(2A) (SI 2000/2114)
		1 Apr 2001 (W) (SI 2001/1274)
		1 Apr 2001 (E) (otherwise) (SI 2001/654)
	(2)	1 Sep 2000 (E) (so far as relates to s 110(3)) (SI 2000/2114)
		1 Apr 2001 (W) (SI 2001/1274)
		1 Aug 2002 (E) (otherwise) (SI 2002/279)
	(3)	1 Sep 2000 (E) (SI 2000/2114)
		1 Apr 2001 (W) (SI 2001/1274)
	(4), (5)	1 Apr 2001 (W) (SI 2001/1274)
		1 Aug 2002 (E) (SI 2002/279)
111, 112		1 Oct 2000 (E) (SI 2000/2559)
		1 Apr 2001 (W) (SI 2001/1274)
113	(1), (2)	See Sch 7 below
	(3)	1 Apr 2001 (E) (SI 2001/654)
		1 Apr 2002 (W) (SI 2001/2705)
114–122		1 Apr 2001 (SI 2001/654)
123–129		1 Apr 2001 (W) (SI 2001/1274)

Learning and Skills Act 2000 (c 21)—*contd*
Section

130, 131			28 Jul 2000 (RA)
132–136			1 Oct 2000 (SI 2000/2559)
137			1 Apr 2001 (W) (SI 2001/1274)
			1 Apr 2001 (otherwise) (SI 2001/654)
138			1 Apr 2001 (W) (SI 2001/1274)
139			3 Aug 2000 (E) (except so far as inserts Teaching and Higher Education Act 1998, s 19(12) (SI 2000/2114)
			1 Oct 2000 (E) (exception as noted above) (SI 2000/2559)
			1 Jan 2001 (W) (SI 2000/3230)
140	(1), (2)		1 Apr 2002 (W) (SI 2001/2705)
			1 Apr 2002 (E) (SI 2002/279)[5]
	(3)		1 Apr 2001 (W) (SI 2001/1274)
			1 Apr 2001 (E) (SI 2001/654)
	(4)		1 Apr 2001 (W) (so far as necessary for the purposes of sub-s (3) above) (SI 2001/1274)
			1 Apr 2001 (E) (SI 2001/654)
			1 Apr 2002 (W) (otherwise) (SI 2001/2705)
	(5)		1 Mar 2001 (E) (SI 2001/654)
			1 Apr 2001 (W) (so far as necessary for the purposes of sub-s (3) above) (SI 2001/1274)
			1 Apr 2002 (W) (otherwise) (SI 2001/2705)
	(6)		1 Apr 2001 (W) (so far as necessary for the purposes of sub-s (3) above) (SI 2001/1274)
			1 Apr 2002 (W) (otherwise) (SI 2001/2705)
141			10 Aug 2000 (E) (SI 2000/2114)
			1 Jan 2001 (W) (SI 2000/3230)
142			1 Apr 2001 (W) (SI 2001/1274)
			1 Apr 2001 (E) (SI 2001/654)
143	(1)	(a)	1 Apr 2001 (W) (SI 2001/1274)
			1 Apr 2001 (E) (SI 2001/654)
		(b), (c)	1 Oct 2000 (E) (SI 2000/2559)
			1 Apr 2001 (W) (SI 2001/1274)
	(2)		1 Oct 2000 (E) (SI 2000/2559)
			1 Apr 2001 (W) (SI 2001/1274)
	(3)		1 Apr 2001 (W) (SI 2001/1274)
			1 Apr 2001 (E) (SI 2001/654)
	(4)		1 Oct 2000 (E) (SI 2000/2559)
			1 Apr 2001 (W) (SI 2001/1274)
	(5)		1 Apr 2001 (W) (SI 2001/1274)
	(6), (7)		1 Oct 2000 (E) (SI 2000/2559)
			1 Apr 2001 (W) (SI 2001/1274)

Learning and Skills Act 2000 (c 21)—*contd*

Learning and Skills Act 2000 (c 21)—*contd*

Schedule

9, para	4—*contd*		1 Sep 2000 (so far as relate to Learning and Skills Council for England) (SI 2000/2114)
			19 Sep 2000 (so far as relates to National Council for Education and Training for Wales) (SI 2000/2540)
	5–9		28 Jul 2000 (RA) (so far as consequential upon ss 130, 131, Sch 8)
			1 Apr 2001 (W) (otherwise) (SI 2001/1274)
			1 Apr 2001 (E) (SI 2001/654)
	10		Repealed
	11		28 Jul 2000 (RA) (so far as consequential upon ss 130, 131, Sch 8)
			1 Apr 2001 (otherwise) (SI 2001/654)
	12, 13		28 Jul 2000 (RA) (so far as consequential upon ss 130, 131, Sch 8)
			1 Apr 2001 (W) (otherwise) (SI 2001/1274)
			1 Apr 2001 (E) (otherwise) (SI 2001/654)
	14		28 Jul 2000 (RA) (so far as consequential upon ss 130, 131, Sch 8)
			1 Oct 2000 (otherwise) (SI 2000/2559)
	15–17		28 Jul 2000 (RA) (so far as consequential upon ss 130, 131, Sch 8)
			1 Apr 2001 (W) (otherwise) (SI 2001/1274)
			1 Apr 2001 (E) (otherwise) (SI 2001/654)
	18, 19		28 Jul 2000 (RA)
	20		28 Jul 2000 (RA) (so far as consequential upon ss 130, 131, Sch 8)
			1 Apr 2001 (W) (otherwise) (SI 2001/1274)
			1 Apr 2001 (E) (otherwise) (SI 2001/654)
	21	(a)	28 Jul 2000 (RA) (so far as consequential upon ss 130, 131, Sch 8)
			1 Apr 2001 (W) (otherwise) (SI 2001/1274)

Learning and Skills Act 2000 (c 21)—*contd*
Schedule

9, para	21	(a)—*contd*	1 Apr 2001 (E) (otherwise) (SI 2001/654)
		(b)	28 Jul 2000 (RA) (so far as consequential upon ss 130, 131, Sch 8)
			1 Jan 2001 (W) (otherwise) (SI 2000/3230)
			1 Apr 2001 (E) (otherwise) (SI 2001/654)
	22		28 Jul 2000 (RA) (so far as consequential upon ss 130, 131, Sch 8)
			1 Apr 2001 (W) (otherwise) (SI 2001/1274)
			1 Apr 2001 (E) (otherwise) (SI 2001/654)
	23		28 Jul 2000 (RA) (so far as consequential upon ss 130, 131, Sch 8)
			1 Oct 2000 (E) (otherwise) (SI 2000/2559)
			1 Apr 2001 (W) (otherwise) (SI 2001/1274)
	24	(1)	28 Jul 2000 (RA) (so far as consequential upon ss 130, 131, Sch 8)
			1 Oct 2000 (E) (otherwise) (SI 2000/2559)
			1 Apr 2001 (W) (otherwise) (SI 2001/1274)
		(2), (3)	28 Jul 2000 (RA) (so far as consequential upon ss 130, 131, Sch 8)
			1 Apr 2001 (W) (otherwise) (SI 2001/1274)
			1 Apr 2001 (E) (otherwise) (SI 2001/654)
		(4)	28 Jul 2000 (RA) (so far as consequential upon ss 130, 131, Sch 8)
			1 Oct 2000 (otherwise) (SI 2000/2559)
			1 Apr 2001 (W) (otherwise) (SI 2001/1274)
	25		28 Jul 2000 (RA) (so far as consequential upon ss 130, 131, Sch 8)
			1 Apr 2001 (W) (otherwise) (SI 2001/1274)
			1 Apr 2001 (E) (otherwise) (SI 2001/654)

Learning and Skills Act 2000 (c 21)—*contd*

Schedule

9, para	26	28 Jul 2000 (RA) (so far as consequential upon ss 130, 131, Sch 8)
		1 Oct 2000 (E) (otherwise) (SI 2000/2559) [1]
		1 Apr 2001 (W) (otherwise) (SI 2001/1274) [2]
	27, 28	28 Jul 2000 (RA) (so far as consequential upon ss 130, 131, Sch 8)
		1 Oct 2000 (E) (for the purposes of application of Further and Higher Education Act 1992, ss 44, 45, to any institution which—
		(a) becomes an institution within the further education sector (within the meaning of s 91(3) of that Act) on or after 1 Oct 2000, or
		(b) was an institution within that sector before 1 Oct 2000 and before that, was a school maintained by a local education authority) (SI 2000/2559)
		Not in force (otherwise)
		1 Apr 2001 (W) (otherwise) (SI 2001/1274)
		Not in force (otherwise)
	29, 30	28 Jul 2000 (RA) (so far as consequential upon ss 130, 131, Sch 8)
		1 Apr 2001 (W) (otherwise) (SI 2001/1274)
		1 Apr 2001 (E) (otherwise) (SI 2001/654)
	31	28 Jul 2000 (RA)
	32, 33	28 Jul 2000 (RA) (so far as consequential upon ss 130, 131, Sch 8)
		1 Apr 2001 (W) (otherwise) (SI 2001/1274)
		1 Apr 2001 (E) (otherwise) (SI 2001/654)
	34	28 Jul 2000 (RA) (so far as consequential upon ss 130, 131, Sch 8)
		1 Jan 2001 (W) (otherwise) (SI 2000/3230)
		1 Apr 2001 (E) (otherwise) (SI 2001/654)

Learning and Skills Act 2000 (c 21)—*contd*

Schedule

9, para	35		28 Jul 2000 (RA) (so far as consequential upon ss 130, 131, Sch 8)
			1 Apr 2001 (otherwise) (SI 2001/654)
	36		28 Jul 2000 (RA) (so far as consequential upon ss 130, 131, Sch 8)
			1 Jan 2001 (W) (otherwise) (SI 2000/3230)
	37–39		28 Jul 2000 (RA) (so far as consequential upon ss 130, 131, Sch 8)
			1 Apr 2001 (otherwise) (SI 2001/654)
	40		28 Jul 2000 (RA) (so far as consequential upon ss 130, 131, Sch 8)
			1 Apr 2001 (W) (otherwise) (SI 2001/1274)
			1 Apr 2001 (E) (otherwise) (SI 2001/654)
	41–43		28 Jul 2000 (RA) (so far as consequential upon ss 130, 131, Sch 8)
			1 Apr 2001 (otherwise) (SI 2001/654)
	44	(1), (2)	28 Jul 2000 (RA) (so far as consequential upon ss 130, 131, Sch 8)
			1 Apr 2001 (W) (otherwise) (SI 2001/1274)
			1 Apr 2001 (E) (otherwise) (SI 2001/654)
		(3), (4)	28 Jul 2000 (RA) (so far as consequential upon ss 130, 131, Sch 8)
			1 Oct 2000 (E) (otherwise) (SI 2000/2559)
			1 Jan 2001 (W) (otherwise) (SI 2000/3230)
	45		28 Jul 2000 (RA) (so far as consequential upon ss 130, 131, Sch 8)
			1 Jan 2001 (W) (otherwise) (SI 2000/3230)
	46		28 Jul 2000 (RA) (so far as consequential upon ss 130, 131, Sch 8)
			1 Apr 2001 (W) (otherwise) (SI 2001/1274)

Learning and Skills Act 2000 (c 21)—*contd*

Schedule

9, para	47, 48	28 Jul 2000 (RA) (so far as consequential upon ss 130, 131, Sch 8)
		1 Apr 2001 (otherwise) (SI 2001/654)
	49	28 Jul 2000 (RA) (so far as consequential upon ss 130, 131, Sch 8)
		1 Apr 2001 (otherwise) (SI 2001/654)
		Prospectively repealed by Special Educational Needs and Disability Act 2001, ss 38(16), 42(6), Sch 9 [4]
	50	28 Jul 2000 (RA) (so far as consequential upon ss 130, 131, Sch 8)
		1 Apr 2001 (otherwise) (SI 2001/654)
	51	28 Jul 2000 (RA) (so far as consequential upon ss 130, 131, Sch 8)
		1 Apr 2001 (W) (otherwise) (SI 2001/1274)
		1 Apr 2001 (E) (otherwise) (SI 2001/654)
	52	(1), (2) 28 Jul 2000 (RA) (so far as consequential upon ss 130, 131, Sch 8)
		1 Apr 2001 (W) (otherwise) (SI 2001/1274)
		1 Apr 2001 (E) (otherwise) (SI 2001/654)
		(3) 28 Jul 2000 (RA) (so far as consequential upon ss 130, 131, Sch 8)
		1 Apr 2001 (otherwise) (SI 2001/654)
	53–56	28 Jul 2000 (RA) (so far as consequential upon ss 130, 131, Sch 8)
		1 Apr 2001 (W) (otherwise) (SI 2001/1274)
		1 Apr 2001 (E) (otherwise) (SI 2001/654)
	57	28 Jul 2000 (RA) (so far as consequential upon ss 130, 131, Sch 8)
		1 Sep 2001 (W) (SI 2001/1274)
		1 Sep 2001 (E) (otherwise) (SI 2001/654)
	58	28 Jul 2000 (RA)

Learning and Skills Act 2000 (c 21)—*contd*
Schedule

9, para	59		28 Jul 2000 (RA) (so far as consequential upon ss 130, 131, Sch 8)
			1 Apr 2001 (W) (otherwise) (SI 2001/1274)
			1 Apr 2001 (E) (otherwise) (SI 2001/654)
	60–63		28 Jul 2000 (RA)
	64		28 Jul 2000 (RA) (so far as consequential upon ss 130, 131, Sch 8)
			1 Oct 2000 (E) (otherwise) (SI 2000/2559)
			1 Jan 2001 (W) (otherwise) (SI 2000/3230)
	65–66		28 Jul 2000 (RA) (so far as consequential upon ss 130, 131, Sch 8)
			1 Apr 2001 (W) (otherwise) (SI 2001/1274)
	67	(1)	See paras (2)–(5) below
		(2)	28 Jul 2000 (RA)
		(3)	28 Jul 2000 (RA) (so far as consequential upon ss 130, 131, Sch 8)
			1 Apr 2001 (E) (otherwise) (SI 2001/654)
			1 Apr 2002 (W) (otherwise) (SI 2001/2705)
		(4)	28 Jul 2000 (RA)
		(5)	28 Jul 2000 (RA) (so far as consequential upon ss 130, 131, Sch 8)
			1 Apr 2001 (W) (otherwise) (SI 2001/1274)
	68		28 Jul 2000 (RA) (so far as consequential upon ss 130, 131, Sch 8)
			1 Apr 2001 (W) (otherwise) (SI 2001/1274)
			1 Apr 2001 (E) (SI 2001/654)
	69		28 Jul 2000 (RA) (so far as consequential upon ss 130, 131, Sch 8)
			10 Sep 2000 (E) (SI 2000/2114)
	70		28 Jul 2000 (RA) (so far as consequential upon ss 130, 131, Sch 8)
			1 Jan 2001 (W) (otherwise) (SI 2000/3230)

Learning and Skills Act 2000 (c 21)—*contd*

Schedule

9, para	71		28 Jul 2000 (RA)
	72–74		28 Jul 2000 (RA) (so far as consequential upon ss 130, 131, Sch 8)
			1 Apr 2001 (W) (otherwise) (SI 2001/1274)
			1 Apr 2001 (E) (otherwise) (SI 2001/654)
	75	(a), (b)	28 Jul 2000 (RA) (so far as consequential upon ss 130, 131, Sch 8)
			1 Apr 2001 (W) (SI 2001/1274)
			1 Apr 2001 (E) (otherwise) (SI 2001/654)
		(c)	28 Jul 2000 (RA) (so far as consequential upon ss 130, 131, Sch 8)
			1 Apr 2001 (W) (so far as relates to s 34 above) (SI 2001/1274)
			1 Apr 2001 (so far as relates to s 5 to this Act) (SI 2001/654)
	76, 77		28 Jul 2000 (RA) (so far as consequential upon ss 130, 131, Sch 8)
			1 Apr 2001 (W) (otherwise) (SI 2001/1274)
	78, 79		28 Jul 2000 (RA) (so far as consequential upon ss 130, 131, Sch 8)
			1 Apr 2001 (W) (otherwise) (SI 2001/1274)
			1 Apr 2001 (E) (otherwise) (SI 2001/654)
	80		28 Jul 2000 (RA) (so far as consequential upon ss 130, 131, Sch 8)
			1 Jan 2001 (E) (otherwise) (SI 2000/2559)
			1 Apr 2001 (W) (otherwise) (SI 2001/1274)
	81		28 Jul 2000 (RA) (so far as consequential upon ss 130, 131, Sch 8)
			1 Jan 2001 (E) (otherwise) (SI 2000/2559)
			1 Jan 2001 (W) (otherwise) (SI 2000/3230)
	82		28 Jul 2000 (RA) (so far as consequential upon ss 130, 131, Sch 8)
			1 Apr 2002 (W) (SI 2001/2705)

Learning and Skills Act 2000 (c 21)—*contd*
Schedule

9, para	83		28 Jul 2000 (RA) (so far as consequential upon ss 130, 131, Sch 8)
			1 Apr 2001 (otherwise) (SI 2001/654)
	84		28 Jul 2000 (RA) (so far as consequential upon ss 130, 131, Sch 8)
			1 Apr 2001 (E) (otherwise) (SI 2001/654)
			1 Apr 2002 (W) (SI 2001/2705)
	85		28 Jul 2000 (RA)
	86		28 Jul 2000 (RA) (so far as consequential upon ss 130, 131, Sch 8)
			1 Jan 2001 (W) (otherwise) (SI 2000/3230)
	87		28 Jul 2000 (RA) (so far as consequential upon ss 130, 131, Sch 8)
			1 Sep 2000 (otherwise) (SI 2000/2114)
	88		28 Jul 2000 (RA) (so far as consequential upon ss 130, 131, Sch 8)
			1 Apr 2001 (otherwise) (SI 2001/654)
	89		28 Jul 2000 (RA) (so far as consequential upon ss 130, 131, Sch 8)
			1 Apr 2001 (E) (otherwise) (SI 2001/654)
	90	(1)–(4)	28 Jul 2000 (RA) (so far as consequential upon ss 130, 131, Sch 8)
			1 Apr 2001 (E) (otherwise) (SI 2001/654)
		(5), (6)	28 Jul 2000 (RA) (so far as consequential upon ss 130, 131, Sch 8)
			1 Apr 2001 (E) (otherwise) (SI 2001/654)
			1 Apr 2002 (W) (otherwise) (SI 2001/2705)
	91		28 Jul 2000 (RA) (so far as consequential upon ss 130, 131, Sch 8)
			1 Apr 2001 (E) (otherwise) (SI 2001/654)
			1 Apr 2002 (W) (otherwise) (SI 2001/2705)

Learning and Skills Act 2000 (c 21)—*contd*

Schedule

9, para	92	28 Jul 2000 (RA) (so far as consequential upon ss 130, 131, Sch 8)
		1 Jan 2001 (W) (otherwise) (SI 2000/3230)
	93	28 Jul 2000 (RA) (so far as consequential upon ss 130, 131, Sch 8)
		19 Sep 2000 (W) (otherwise) (SI 2000/2540)
	94	28 Jul 2000 (RA) (so far as consequential upon ss 130, 131, Sch 8)
		1 Apr 2001 (W) (otherwise) (SI 2001/1274)
10, Pts	I–III	28 Jul 2000 (RA)
	IV	1 Apr 2001 (SI 2001/654)
11		28 Jul 2000 (RA) (so far as consequential upon ss 130, 131, Sch 8)
		3 Aug 2000 (E) (repeals of or in Teaching and Higher Education Act 1998, s 19) (SI 2000/2114)
		1 Oct 2000 (E) (repeal of or in Further and Higher Education Act 1992, ss 28(2)(b), 44(6), 45(6); Teaching and Higher Education Act 1998, s 22(2)(h), (7); School Standards and Framework Act 1998, Sch 30, paras 41, 42) (SI 2000/2559)
		1 Nov 2000 (E) (the repeal in Education Act 1996, s 403(1)) (SI 2000/2559)
		1 Jan 2001 (W) (repeals of or in Further and Higher Education Act 1992, ss 18(4)–(6), 60A, Sch 5A; Education Act 1996, Sch 37, para 113; Teaching and Higher Education Act 1998, ss 19, 22; School Standards and Framework Act 1998, ss 125, 126, Sch 27; Government of Wales Act 1998, s 104(4)) (SI 2000/3230)
		1 Apr 2001 (W) (repeals of or in Superannuation Act 1972, Sch 1, in the list of "Other Bodies" the words "Further Education Funding Council for Wales in receipt of

Learning and Skills Act 2000 (c 21)—*contd*
Schedule
11—*contd*

remuneration."; House of
Commons Disqualification
Act 1975, Sch 1, Pt III the words
"Any member of the Further
Education Funding Council for
Wales in receipt of remuneration.";
Sex Discrimination Act 1975;
Race Relations Act 1976;
Education Reform Act 1988;
Further and Higher Education
Act 1992, ss 1–9, 28(2)(b), 32(2A),
44(6), 45(6), 52(1), 55(1)–(3),
(7)(a), (b), 56, Sch 2; Disability
Discrimination Act 1995, s 19(6)(f),
30(2)–(4); Education Act 1996,
s 15, 509(1)(d) and word "or"
immediately preceding it, Sch 37,
paras 70, 112; Education Act 1997,
s 30(1), (3); Audit Commission
Act 1998, s 36(1), (2); Teaching
and Higher Education Act 1998,
s 26(1), (2), 28(1)(a), 34; School
Standards and Framework Act 1998,
Sch 30, paras 41, 42 (SI 2001/1274)
1 Apr 2001 (repeals of or in
Superannuation Act 1972, Sch 1,
in the list of "Other Bodies" the
words "Further Education Funding
Council for England in receipt of
remuneration"; House of
Commons Disqualification
Act 1975, Sch 1, Pt III, the words
"Any member of the Further
Education Funding Council for
England in receipt of
remuneration"; Sex Discrimination
Act 1975 (so far as relates to
England); Race Relations Act 1976
(so far as relates to England);
Education Reform Act 1988 (so far
as relates to England); Further and
Higher Education Act 1992,
ss 1–9, 32(2A), s 52(1) word
"full-time", ss 55, 56, Sch 1,
para 9, Sch 2 (all so far as they
relate to England), s 91(2);
Disability Discrimination Act 1995,
s 19(6)(e), s 30(2)–(4) (so far as
relates to England); Education

Learning and Skills Act 2000 (c 21)—*contd*
Schedule

11—*contd*	Act 1996, ss 15, 482, 509(1), Sch 37, paras 70, 112, 113 (so far as they relate to England); Audit Commission Act 1998 (so far as relates to England); Teaching and Higher Education Act 1998, s 26(1), (2), 28(1) (so far as relate to England); School Standards and Framework Act 1998, Schs 6, 7, 22 (so far as relate to England), s 142(1)) (SI 2001/654)
	1 Sep 2001 (W) (repeals of or in Education Act 1996, s 403(1); Education Act 1997, s 37(1)–(4), (5)) (SI 2001/1274)
	1 Sep 2001 (E) (repeal of or in Education Act 1997, s 37 (SI 2001/654)
	1 Apr 2002 (W) (repeals of or in School Standards and Framework Act 1998, Sch 7, para 13(4), (7), Sch 22, para 5(1)) (SI 2001/2705)

[1]   For savings provisions, see SI 2000/2559, art 3

[2]   For savings and transitional provisions, see SI 2001/654, art 3

[3]   For savings and transitional provisions, see SI 2001/1274, arts 3, 4

[4]   Orders made under Special Educational Needs and Disability Act 2001, s 43, bringing the prospective repeals into force will be noted to that Act

[5]   For transitional provisions, see SI 2002/279, art 3

Licensing (Young Persons) Act 2000 (c 30)

RA: 23 Nov 2000

Commencement provisions: s 3(2)

Section	
1–3	23 Jan 2001 (s 3(2))
Schedule	23 Jan 2001 (s 3(2))

Limited Liability Partnerships Act 2000 (c 12)

RA: 20 Jul 2000

Commencement provisions: s 19(1), (2); Limited Liability Partnerships Act 2000 (Commencement) Order 2000, SI 2000/3316

Section	
1–18	6 Apr 2001 (SI 2000/3316)
19	20 Jul 2000 (s 19(1))
Schedule	6 Apr 2001 (SI 2000/3316)

Local Government Act 2000 (c 22)

RA: 28 Jul 2000

Commencement provisions: s 108; Local Government Act 2000 (Commencement No 1) Order 2000, SI 2000/2187; Local Government Act 2000 (Commencement No 2) Order 2000, SI 2000/2420; Local Government Act 2000 (Commencement No 3) Order 2000, SI 2000/2836; Local Government Act 2000 (Commencement No 4) Order 2000, SI 2000/2849; Local Government Act 2000 (Commencement) (Wales) Order 2000, SI 2000/2948; Local Government Act 2000 (Commencement No 5) Order 2000, SI 2000/3335; Local Government Act 2000 (Commencement No 6) Order 2001, SI 2001/415; Local Government Act 2000 (Commencement) (No 2) (Wales) Order 2001, SI 2001/1471; Local Government Act 2000 (Commencement No 7) Order 2001, SI 2001/2684

Section			
1, 2			18 Oct 2000 (E) (SI 2000/2836)
			9 Apr 2001 (W) (SI 2001/1471)
3	(1), (2)		18 Oct 2000 (E) (SI 2000/2836)
			9 Apr 2001 (W) (SI 2001/1471)
	(3)–(7)		18 Oct 2000 (E) (SI 2000/2836)
			1 Nov 2000 (W) (SI 2000/2948)
	(8)		18 Oct 2000 (E) (SI 2000/2836)
			9 Apr 2001 (W) (SI 2001/1471)
4	(1), (2)		18 Oct 2000 (E) (SI 2000/2836)
			9 Apr 2001 (W) (SI 2001/1471)
	(3)	(a)	18 Oct 2000 (E) (SI 2000/2836)
			9 Apr 2001 (W) (SI 2001/1471)
		(b)	18 Oct 2000 (E) (SI 2000/2836)
			1 Nov 2000 (W) (SI 2000/2948)
	(4), (5)		18 Oct 2000 (E) (SI 2000/2836)
			1 Nov 2000 (W) (SI 2000/2948)
5	(1)–(4)		18 Oct 2000 (E) (SI 2000/2836)
			9 Apr 2001 (W) (SI 2001/1471)
	(5)		18 Oct 2000 (E) (SI 2000/2836)
			1 Nov 2000 (W) (SI 2000/2948)
	(6)		18 Oct 2000 (E) (SI 2000/2836)
			9 Apr 2001 (W) (SI 2001/1471)
6	(1)–(5)		18 Oct 2000 (E) (SI 2000/2836)
			9 Apr 2001 (W) (SI 2001/1471)
	(6)		18 Oct 2000 (E) (SI 2000/2836)
			1 Nov 2000 (W) (SI 2000/2948)
	(7), (8)		18 Oct 2000 (E) (SI 2000/2836)
			9 Apr 2001 (W) (SI 2001/1471)
7			18 Oct 2000 (E) (SI 2000/2836)
			1 Nov 2000 (W) (SI 2000/2948)
8, 9			18 Oct 2000 (E) (SI 2000/2836)
			9 Apr 2001 (W) (SI 2001/1471)
10			7 Aug 2000 (E) (SI 2000/2187)
			28 Jul 2001 (s 108(4)–(6)) (otherwise)[1]
11	(1)–(4)		7 Aug 2000 (E) (so far as confers power to make Orders or Regulations) (SI 2000/2187)

Local Government Act 2000 (c 22)—*contd*

Section

11	(1)–(4)—*contd*	26 Oct 2000 (E) (otherwise) (SI 2000/2849)
		28 Jul 2001 (s 108(4)–(6)) (otherwise)[1]
	(5), (6)	7 Aug 2000 (E) (so far as confers power to make Orders or Regulations) (SI 2000/2187)
		26 Oct 2000 (E) (otherwise) (SI 2000/2849)
		1 Nov 2000 (W) (SI 2000/2948)
	(7), (8)	7 Aug 2000 (E) (so far as confers power to make Orders or Regulations) (SI 2000/2187)
		26 Oct 2000 (E) (otherwise) (SI 2000/2849)
		28 Jul 2001 (W) (s 108(4)–(6))1
	(9)	7 Aug 2000 (E) (so far as confers power to make Orders or Regulations) (SI 2000/2187)
		26 Oct 2000 (E) (otherwise) (SI 2000/2849)
		1 Nov 2000 (W) (SI 2000/2948)
	(10)	7 Aug 2000 (E) (so far as confers power to make Orders or Regulations) (SI 2000/2187)
		26 Oct 2000 (E) (otherwise) (SI 2000/2849)
		28 Jul 2001 (W) (s 108(4)–(6))1
12	(1)	7 Aug 2000 (E) (SI 2000/2187)
		1 Nov 2000 (W) (SI 2000/2948)
	(2)–(4)	7 Aug 2000 (E) (SI 2000/2187)
		28 Jul 2001 (W) (s 108(4)–(6))[1]
13	(1), (2)	7 Aug 2000 (E) (so far as confers power to make Orders or Regulations) (SI 2000/2187)
		26 Oct 2000 (E) (otherwise) (SI 2000/2849)
		28 Jul 2001 (W) (s 108(4)–(6))[1]
	(3)	7 Aug 2000 (E) (so far as confers power to make Orders or Regulations) (SI 2000/2187)
		26 Oct 2000 (E) (otherwise) (SI 2000/2849)
		1 Nov 2000 (W) (SI 2000/2948)
	(4)	7 Aug 2000 (E) (so far as confers power to make Orders or Regulations) (SI 2000/2187)
		26 Oct 2000 (E) (otherwise) (SI 2000/2849)
		28 Jul 2001 (W) (s 108(4)–(6))1

Local Government Act 2000 (c 22)—*contd*
Section

13	(5), (6)	7 Aug 2000 (E) (so far as confers power to make Orders or Regulations) (SI 2000/2187) 26 Oct 2000 (E) (otherwise) (SI 2000/2849) 1 Nov 2000 (W) (SI 2000/2948)
	(7)–(11)	7 Aug 2000 (E) (so far as confers power to make Orders or Regulations) (SI 2000/2187) 26 Oct 2000 (E) (otherwise) (SI 2000/2849) 28 Jul 2001 (W) (s 108(4)–(6))[1]
	(12)–(14)	7 Aug 2000 (E) (so far as confers power to make Orders or Regulations) (SI 2000/2187) 26 Oct 2000 (E) (otherwise) (SI 2000/2849) 1 Nov 2000 (W) (SI 2000/2948)
14–16		26 Oct 2000 (E) (SI 2000/2849) 28 Jul 2001 (W) (s 108(4)–(6))[1]
17–20		7 Aug 2000 (E) (SI 2000/2187) 1 Nov 2000 (W) (SI 2000/2948)
21		26 Oct 2000 (E) (SI 2000/2849) 28 Jul 2001 (W) (s 108(4)–(6))[1]
22	(1)–(5)	7 Aug 2000 (E) (so far as confers power to make Orders or Regulations) (SI 2000/2187) 26 Oct 2000 (E) (otherwise) (SI 2000/2849) 28 Jul 2001 (W) (s 108(4)–(6))[1]
	(6)–(13)	7 Aug 2000 (E) (so far as confers power to make Orders or Regulations) (SI 2000/2187) 26 Oct 2000 (E) (otherwise) (SI 2000/2849) 1 Nov 2000 (W) (SI 2000/2948)
23		See Sch 1 below
24		26 Oct 2000 (E) (SI 2000/2849) 28 Jul 2001 (W) (s 108(4)–(6))[1]
25	(1)–(4)	7 Aug 2000 (E) (so far as confers power to make Orders or Regulations) (SI 2000/2187) 26 Oct 2000 (E) (otherwise) (SI 2000/2849) 28 Jul 2001 (W) (s 108(4)–(6))[1]
	(5)–(6)	7 Aug 2000 (E) (so far as confers power to make Orders or Regulations) (SI 2000/2187)

Local Government Act 2000 (c 22)—*contd*

Section

25	(5)–(6)—*contd*	26 Oct 2000 (E) (otherwise) (SI 2000/2849)
		1 Nov 2000 (W) (SI 2000/2948)
	(7)	7 Aug 2000 (E) (so far as confers power to make Orders or Regulations) (SI 2000/2187)
		26 Oct 2000 (E) (otherwise) (SI 2000/2849)
		28 Jul 2001 (W) (s 108(4)–(6))[1]
	(8)	7 Aug 2000 (E) (so far as confers power to make Orders or Regulations) (SI 2000/2187)
		26 Oct 2000 (E) (otherwise) (SI 2000/2849)
		1 Nov 2000 (W) (SI 2000/2948)
26		26 Oct 2000 (E) (SI 2000/2849)
		28 Jul 2001 (W) (s 108(4)–(6))[1]
27	(1)–(8)	7 Aug 2000 (E) (so far as confers power to make Orders or Regulations) (SI 2000/2187)
		26 Oct 2000 (E) (otherwise) (SI 2000/2849)
		28 Jul 2001 (W) (s 108(4)–(6))[1]
	(9)–(10)	7 Aug 2000 (E) (so far as confers power to make Orders or Regulations) (SI 2000/2187)
		26 Oct 2000 (E) (otherwise) (SI 2000/2849)
		1 Nov 2000 (W) (SI 2000/2948)
	(11)– (13)	7 Aug 2000 (E) (so far as confers power to make Orders or Regulations) (SI 2000/2187)
		26 Oct 2000 (E) (otherwise) (SI 2000/2849)
		28 Jul 2001 (W) (s 108(4)–(6))[1]
28	(1), (2)	7 Aug 2000 (E) (so far as confers power to make Orders or Regulations) (SI 2000/2187)
		26 Oct 2000 (E) (otherwise) (SI 2000/2849)
		1 Nov 2000 (W) (SI 2000/2948)
	(3)	7 Aug 2000 (E) (so far as confers power to make Orders or Regulations) (SI 2000/2187)
		26 Oct 2000 (E) (otherwise) (SI 2000/2849)
		Not in force (otherwise)
29		26 Oct 2000 (E) (SI 2000/2849)
		28 Jul 2001 (W) (s 108(4)–(6))[1]

Local Government Act 2000 (c 22)—*contd*
Section

30			7 Aug 2000 (E) (SI 2000/2187)
			1 Nov 2000 (W) (SI 2000/2948)
31	(1)	(a)	7 Aug 2000 (E) (so far as confers power to make Orders or Regulations) (SI 2000/2187)
			26 Oct 2000 (E) (otherwise) (SI 2000/2849)
			28 Jul 2001 (W) (s 108(4)–(6))[1]
		(b)	7 Aug 2000 (E) (so far as confers power to make Orders or Regulations) (SI 2000/2187)
			26 Oct 2000 (E) (otherwise) (SI 2000/2849)
			1 Nov 2000 (W) (SI 2000/2948)
	(2)–(9)		7 Aug 2000 (E) (so far as confers power to make Orders or Regulations) (SI 2000/2187)
			26 Oct 2000 (E) (otherwise) (SI 2000/2849)
			28 Jul 2001 (W) (s 108(4)–(6))[1]
32			7 Aug 2000 (E) (SI 2000/2187)
			1 Nov 2000 (W) (SI 2000/2948)
33	(1)–(4)		7 Aug 2000 (E) (so far as confers power to make Orders or Regulations) (SI 2000/2187)
			26 Oct 2000 (E) (otherwise) (SI 2000/2849)
			28 Jul 2001 (W) (s 108(4)–(6))[1]
	(5)–(11)		7 Aug 2000 (E) (so far as confers power to make Orders or Regulations) (SI 2000/2187)
			26 Oct 2000 (E) (otherwise) (SI 2000/2849)
			1 Nov 2000 (W) (SI 2000/2948)
34–36			7 Aug 2000 (E) (SI 2000/2187)
			1 Nov 2000 (W) (SI 2000/2948)
37	(1)	(a)	7 Aug 2000 (E) (so far as confers power to make Orders or Regulations) (SI 2000/2187)
			26 Oct 2000 (E) (otherwise) (SI 2000/2849)
			1 Nov 2000 (W) (SI 2000/2948)
		(b)–(d)	7 Aug 2000 (E) (so far as confers power to make Orders or Regulations) (SI 2000/2187)
			26 Oct 2000 (E) (otherwise) (SI 2000/2849)
			28 Jul 2001 (W) (s 108(4)–(6))[1]

Local Government Act 2000 (c 22)—*contd*

Section

37	(2)–(3)	7 Aug 2000 (E) (so far as confers power to make Orders or Regulations) (SI 2000/2187)
		26 Oct 2000 (E) (otherwise) (SI 2000/2849)
		28 Jul 2001 (W) (s 108(4)–(6))[1]
38		7 Aug 2000 (E) (SI 2000/2187)
		1 Nov 2000 (W) (SI 2000/2948)
39	(1)	7 Aug 2000 (E) (so far as confers power to make Orders or Regulations) (SI 2000/2187)
		26 Oct 2000 (E) (otherwise) (SI 2000/2849)
		1 Nov 2000 (W) (SI 2000/2948)
	(2)	7 Aug 2000 (E) (so far as confers power to make Orders or Regulations) (SI 2000/2187)
		26 Oct 2000 (E) (otherwise) (SI 2000/2849)
		28 Jul 2001 (W) (s 108(4)–(6))[1]
	(3)	7 Aug 2000 (E) (so far as confers power to make Orders or Regulations) (SI 2000/2187)
		1 Nov 2000 (W) (SI 2000/2948)
		Not in force (E) (otherwise)
	(4), (5)	7 Aug 2000 (E) (so far as confers power to make Orders or Regulations) (SI 2000/2187)
		26 Oct 2000 (E) (otherwise) (SI 2000/2849)
		1 Nov 2000 (W) (SI 2000/2948)
	(6)	7 Aug 2000 (E) (so far as confers power to make Orders or Regulations) (SI 2000/2187)
		26 Oct 2000 (E) (otherwise) (SI 2000/2849)
		28 Jul 2001 (W) (s 108(4)–(6))[1]
40		28 Jul 2001 (s 108(4)–(6))[1]
41		7 Aug 2000 (E) (SI 2000/2187)
		1 Nov 2000 (W) (SI 2000/2948)
42, 43		28 Jul 2001 (s 108(4)–(6))[1]
44		7 Aug 2000 (E) (so far as confers power to make Orders or Regulations) (SI 2000/2187)
		1 Nov 2000 (W) (SI 2000/2948)
		Not in force (E) (otherwise)
45	(1)–(4)	7 Aug 2000 (E) (so far as confers power to make Orders or Regulations) (SI 2000/2187)

Local Government Act 2000 (c 22)—*contd*
Section

45	(1)–(4)—*contd*		19 Feb 2001 (E) (otherwise) (SI 2001/415)
			28 Jul 2001 (W) (s 108(4)–(6))[1]
	(5)–(9)		7 Aug 2000 (E) (so far as confers power to make Orders or Regulations) (SI 2000/2187)
			1 Nov 2000 (W) (SI 2000/2948)
			19 Feb 2001 (E) (otherwise) (SI 2001/415)
46			See Sch 3
47, 48			7 Aug 2000 (E) (SI 2000/2187)
			1 Nov 2000 (W) (SI 2000/2948)
49	(1)		19 Dec 2000 (E) (SI 2000/3335)
			19 Dec 2000 (W) (in relation to police authorities) (SI 2000/3335)
			28 Jul 2001 (W) (otherwise) (s 108(4)–(6))[1]
	(2)		1 Nov 2000 (W) (SI 2000/2948)[2]
			19 Dec 2000 (E) (SI 2000/3335)
			19 Dec 2000 (W) (in relation to police authorities) (SI 2000/3335)
	(3), (4)		19 Dec 2000 (E) (SI 2000/3335)
			19 Dec 2000 (W) (in relation to police authorities) (SI 2000/3335)
			28 Jul 2001 (W) (otherwise) (s 108(4)–(6))[1]
	(5)		1 Nov 2000 (W) (SI 2000/2948)[2]
			19 Dec 2000 (E) (SI 2000/3335)
			19 Dec 2000 (W) (in relation to police authorities) (SI 2000/3335)
	(6)	(a), (b)	1 Nov 2000 (W) (SI 2000/2948)[2]
			19 Dec 2000 (E) (SI 2000/3335)
			19 Dec 2000 (W) (in relation to police authorities) (SI 2000/3335)
		(c)–(e)	19 Dec 2000 (E) (SI 2000/3335)
			19 Dec 2000 (W) (in relation to police authorities) (SI 2000/3335)
			28 Jul 2001 (W) (otherwise) (s 108(4)–(6))[1]
		(f)	1 Nov 2000 (W) (SI 2000/2948)[2]
			19 Dec 2000 (E) (SI 2000/3335)
			19 Dec 2000 (W) (in relation to police authorities) (SI 2000/3335)
		(g)–(k)	19 Dec 2000 (E) (SI 2000/3335)
			19 Dec 2000 (W) (in relation to police authorities) (SI 2000/3335)
			28 Jul 2001 (W) (otherwise) (s 108(4)–(6))[1]

Local Government Act 2000 (c 22)—*contd*

Section			
49	(6)	(l), (m)	1 Nov 2000 (W) (SI 2000/2948)[2]
			19 Dec 2000 (E) (SI 2000/3335)
			19 Dec 2000 (W) (in relation to police authorities) (SI 2000/3335)
		(n), (o)	19 Dec 2000 (E) (SI 2000/3335)
			19 Dec 2000 (W) (in relation to police authorities) (SI 2000/3335)
			28 Jul 2001 (W) (otherwise) (s 108(4)–(6))[1]
		(p)	1 Nov 2000 (W) (SI 2000/2948)[2]
			19 Dec 2000 (E) (SI 2000/3335)
			19 Dec 2000 (W) (in relation to police authorities) (SI 2000/3335)
	(7)		1 Nov 2000 (W) (SI 2000/2948)[2]
			19 Dec 2000 (E) (SI 2000/3335)
			19 Dec 2000 (W) (in relation to police authorities) (SI 2000/3335)
50	(1)		19 Dec 2000 (E) (SI 2000/3335)
			19 Dec 2000 (W) (in relation to police authorities) (SI 2000/3335)
			28 Jul 2001 (W) (otherwise) (s 108(4)–(6))[1]
	(2)–(7)		1 Nov 2000 (W) (SI 2000/2948)[2]
			19 Dec 2000 (E) (SI 2000/3335)
			19 Dec 2000 (W) (in relation to police authorities) (SI 2000/3335)
51, 52			19 Dec 2000 (E) (SI 2000/3335)
			19 Dec 2000 (W) (in relation to police authorities) (SI 2000/3335)
			28 Jul 2001 (W) (otherwise) (s 108(4)–(6))[1]
53	(1)–(10)		19 Dec 2000 (E) (SI 2000/3335)
			19 Dec 2000 (W) (in relation to police authorities) (SI 2000/3335)
			28 Jul 2001 (W) (otherwise) (s 108(4)–(6))[1]
	(11), (12)		1 Nov 2000 (W) (SI 2000/2948)[2]
			19 Dec 2000 (E) (SI 2000/3335)
			19 Dec 2000 (W) (in relation to police authorities) (SI 2000/3335)
54	(1)–(4)		19 Dec 2000 (E) (SI 2000/3335)
			19 Dec 2000 (W) (in relation to police authorities) (SI 2000/3335)
			28 Jul 2001 (W) (otherwise) (s 108(4)–(6))[1]
	(5)		1 Nov 2000 (W) (SI 2000/2948)[2]
			19 Dec 2000 (E) (SI 2000/3335)
			19 Dec 2000 (W) (in relation to police authorities) (SI 2000/3335)

Local Government Act 2000 (c 22)—*contd*
Section

54	(6)	19 Dec 2000 (E) (SI 2000/3335)
		19 Dec 2000 (W) (in relation to police authorities) (SI 2000/3335)
		28 Jul 2001 (W) (otherwise) (s 108(4)–(6))[1]
	(7)	1 Nov 2000 (W) (SI 2000/2948)[2]
		19 Dec 2000 (E) (SI 2000/3335)
		19 Dec 2000 (W) (in relation to police authorities) (SI 2000/3335)
55		19 Dec 2000 (E) (SI 2000/3335)
		19 Dec 2000 (W) (in relation to police authorities) (SI 2000/3335)
		28 Jul 2001 (W) (otherwise) (s 108(4)–(6))[1]
56		28 Jul 2001 (s 108(4)–(6))[1]
57–67		19 Dec 2000 (E) (SI 2000/3335)
		19 Dec 2000 (W) (in relation to police authorities) (SI 2000/3335)
		28 Jul 2001 (W) (otherwise) (s 108(4)–(6))[1]
68	(1), (2)	28 Jul 2001 (s 108(4)–(6))[1]
	(3)–(5)	1 Nov 2000 (W) (SI 2000/2948)
		28 Jul 2001 (E) (s 108(4)–(6))[1]
69		28 Jul 2001 (s 108(4)–(6))[1]
70	(1), (2)	1 Nov 2000 (W) (SI 2000/2948)
		28 Jul 2001 (E) (s 108(4)–(6))[1]
	(3)–(5)	28 Jul 2001 (s 108(4)–(6))[1]
71, 72		28 Jul 2001 (s 108(4)–(6))[1]
73	(1)–(6)	1 Nov 2000 (W) (SI 2000/2948)
		28 Jul 2001 (E) (s 108(4)–(6))[1]
	(7)	28 Jul 2001 (s 108(4)–(6))[1]
74		28 Jul 2001 (s 108(4)–(6))[1]
75	(1)	19 Dec 2000 (E) (SI 2000/3335)
		19 Dec 2000 (W) (in relation to police authorities) (SI 2000/3335)
		28 Jul 2001 (W) (otherwise) (s 108(4)–(6))[1]
	(2)	1 Nov 2000 (W) (SI 2000/2948)[2]
		19 Dec 2000 (E) (SI 2000/3335)
		19 Dec 2000 (W) (in relation to police authorities) (SI 2000/3335)
	(3), (4)	19 Dec 2000 (E) (SI 2000/3335)
		19 Dec 2000 (W) (in relation to police authorities) (SI 2000/3335)
		28 Jul 2001 (W) (otherwise) (s 108(4)–(6))[1]
	(5), (6)	1 Nov 2000 (W) (SI 2000/2948)[2]
		19 Dec 2000 (E) (SI 2000/3335)

Local Government Act 2000 (c 22)—*contd*

Local Government Act 2000 (c 22)—*contd*

Section

77	(7), (8)	19 Dec 2000 (E) (SI 2000/3335)
		19 Dec 2000 (W) (in relation to police authorities) (SI 2000/3335)
		28 Jul 2001 (W) (otherwise) (s 108(4)–(6))[1]
78–80		19 Dec 2000 (E) (SI 2000/3335)
		19 Dec 2000 (W) (in relation to police authorities) (SI 2000/3335)
		28 Jul 2001 (W) (otherwise) (s 108(4)–(6))[1]
81	(1)–(4)	19 Dec 2000 (E) (SI 2000/3335)
		19 Dec 2000 (W) (in relation to police authorities) (SI 2000/3335)
		28 Jul 2001 (W) (otherwise) (s 108(4)–(6))[1]
	(5)	1 Nov 2000 (W) (SI 2000/2948)[2]
		19 Dec 2000 (E) (SI 2000/3335)
		19 Dec 2000 (W) (in relation to police authorities) (SI 2000/3335)
	(6), (7)	19 Dec 2000 (E) (SI 2000/3335)
		19 Dec 2000 (W) (in relation to police authorities) (SI 2000/3335)
		28 Jul 2001 (W) (otherwise) (s 108(4)–(6))[1]
	(8)	1 Nov 2000 (W) (SI 2000/2948)[2]
		19 Dec 2000 (E) (SI 2000/3335)
		19 Dec 2000 (W) (in relation to police authorities) (SI 2000/3335)
82	(1)	19 Dec 2000 (E) (SI 2000/3335)
		19 Dec 2000 (W) (in relation to police authorities) (SI 2000/3335)
		28 Jul 2001 (W) (otherwise) (s 108(4)–(6))[1]
	(2), (3)	1 Nov 2000 (W) (SI 2000/2948)[2]
		19 Dec 2000 (E) (SI 2000/3335)
		19 Dec 2000 (W) (in relation to police authorities) (SI 2000/3335)
	(4), (5)	19 Dec 2000 (E) (SI 2000/3335)
		19 Dec 2000 (W) (in relation to police authorities) (SI 2000/3335)
		28 Jul 2001 (W) (otherwise) (s 108(4)–(6))[1]
	(6)	1 Nov 2000 (W) (SI 2000/2948)[2]
		19 Dec 2000 (E) (SI 2000/3335)
		19 Dec 2000 (W) (in relation to police authorities) (SI 2000/3335)
	(7)	19 Dec 2000 (E) (SI 2000/3335)
		19 Dec 2000 (W) (in relation to police authorities) (SI 2000/3335)

Local Government Act 2000 (c 22)—*contd*

Section

82	(7)—*contd*	28 Jul 2001 (W) (otherwise) (s 108(4)–(6))[1]
	(8), (9)	1 Nov 2000 (W) (SI 2000/2948)[2] 19 Dec 2000 (E) (SI 2000/3335) 19 Dec 2000 (W) (in relation to police authorities) (SI 2000/3335)
83	(1)–(3)	1 Nov 2000 (W) (SI 2000/2948)[2] 19 Dec 2000 (E) (SI 2000/3335) 19 Dec 2000 (W) (in relation to police authorities) (SI 2000/3335)
	(4)	19 Dec 2000 (E) (SI 2000/3335) 19 Dec 2000 (W) (in relation to police authorities) (SI 2000/3335) 28 Jul 2001 (W) (otherwise) (s 108(4)–(6))[1]
	(5)–(11)	1 Nov 2000 (W) (SI 2000/2948)[2] 19 Dec 2000 (E) (SI 2000/3335) 19 Dec 2000 (W) (in relation to police authorities) (SI 2000/3335)
	(12)	19 Dec 2000 (E) (SI 2000/3335) 19 Dec 2000 (W) (in relation to police authorities) (SI 2000/3335) 28 Jul 2001 (W) (otherwise) (s 108(4)–(6))[1]
	(13), (14)	1 Nov 2000 (W) (SI 2000/2948)[2] 19 Dec 2000 (E) (SI 2000/3335) 19 Dec 2000 (W) (in relation to police authorities) (SI 2000/3335)
	(15), (16)	19 Dec 2000 (E) (SI 2000/3335) 19 Dec 2000 (W) (in relation to police authorities) (SI 2000/3335) 28 Jul 2001 (W) (otherwise) (s 108(4)–(6))[1]
84–89		28 Sep 2000 (s 108(2))
90		*Not in force*
91		19 Dec 2000 (E) (SI 2000/3335) 19 Dec 2000 (W) (in relation to police authorities) (SI 2000/3335) *Not in force* (W) (otherwise)
92		19 Dec 2000 (E) (SI 2000/3335) 19 Dec 2000 (W) (in relation to police authorities) (SI 2000/3335) 28 Jul 2001 (W) (otherwise) (s 108(4)–(6))[1]
93		19 Dec 2000 (E) (SI 2000/3335) 19 Dec 2000 (W) (in relation to police authorities) (SI 2000/3335) *Not in force* (W) (otherwise)

Local Government Act 2000 (c 22)—*contd*

Section

94, 95			1 Aug 2001 (E) (SI 2001/2684)
			Not in force (otherwise)
96			*Not in force*
97, 98			1 Oct 2000 (E) (SI 2000/2187)
			28 Jul 2001 (W) (s 108(4)–(6))[1]
99	(1), (2)		19 Feb 2001 (E) (SI 2001/415)
			28 Jul 2001 (W) (s 108(4)) [1]
	(3)		19 Feb 2001 (E) (except in so far as relates to s 99(4) as noted below) (SI 2001/415)
			28 Jul 2001 (W) (s 108(4)) [1]
	(4)		28 Jul 2001 (s 108(4))[1]
	(5)–(9)		19 Feb 2001 (E) (SI 2001/415)
			28 Jul 2001 (W) (s 108(4)) [1]
100			1 Nov 2000 (W) (SI 2000/2948)
			19 Feb 2001 (E) (SI 2001/415)
101	(1)		28 Jul 2001 (s 108(4))[1]
	(2)–(5)		1 Nov 2000 (W) (SI 2000/2948)
			28 Jul 2001 (E) (s 108(4)) [1]
102			26 Oct 2000 (E) (SI 2000/2849)
			28 Jul 2001 (W) (s 108(4))
103			25 Aug 2000 (E) (SI 2000/2420)
			28 Jul 2001 (W) (s 108(4)–(6))[1]
104			28 Sep 2000 (s 108(2))
105, 106			28 Jul 2000 (RA)
107	(1)		28 Jul 2001 (s 108(4)–(6))[1]
	(2)		See Sch 6 below
108, 109			28 Jul 2000 (RA)

Schedule

1, para	1–5		26 Oct 2000 (E) (SI 2000/2849)
			28 Jul 2001 (s 108(4)–(6))[1] (otherwise)
	6, 7		7 Aug 2000 (E) (SI 2000/2187)
			28 Jul 2001 (s 108(4)–(6)) (otherwise)[1]
	8	(1)–(3)	28 Jul 2001 (s 108(4)–(6))[1]
		(4), (5)	1 Nov 2000 (W) (SI 2000/2948)
			28 Jul 2001 (E) (s 108(4)–(6))[1]
		(6), (7)	28 Jul 2001 (s 108(4)–(6))[1]
		(8)	1 Nov 2000 (W) (SI 2000/2948)
			28 Jul 2001 (E) (s 108(4)–(6))[1]
	9	(1)–(3)	7 Aug 2000 (E) (SI 2000/2187)
			28 Jul 2001 (s 108(4)–(6)) (otherwise)[1]
		(4)–(6)	7 Aug 2000 (E) (SI 2000/2187)
			1 Nov 2000 (W) (SI 2000/2948)
	10, 11		7 Aug 2000 (E) (SI 2000/2187)
			1 Nov 2000 (W) (SI 2000/2948)
2			28 Jul 2001 (s 108(4)–(6))[1]

Local Government Act 2000 (c 22)—*contd*

Schedule

3		26 Oct 2000 (E) (SI 2000/2849)
		28 Jul 2001 (s 108(4)–(6))[1] (otherwise)
4		19 Dec 2000 (E) (SI 2000/3335)
		19 Dec 2000 (W) (in relation to police authorities) (SI 2000/3335)
		28 Jul 2001 (W) (otherwise) (s 108(4)–(6))[1]
5, para	1–7	26 Oct 2000 (E) (SI 2000/2849)
		28 Jul 2001 (s 108(4)) (otherwise)
	8	*Not in force*
	9–11	19 Dec 2000 (E) (SI 2000/3335)
		19 Dec 2000 (W) (in relation to police authorities) (SI 2000/3335)
		28 Jul 2001 (W) (otherwise) (s 108(4)–(6))[1]
	12, 13	*Not in force*
	14	19 Dec 2000 (E) (SI 2000/3335)
		19 Dec 2000 (W) (in relation to police authorities) (SI 2000/3335)
		28 Jul 2001 (W) (otherwise) (s 108(4)–(6))[1]
	15	*Not in force*
	16–23	26 Oct 2000 (E) (SI 2000/2849)
		28 Jul 2001 (s 108(4)) (otherwise)
	24	28 Jul 2001 (s 108(4))
	25, 26	*Not in force*
	27	28 Jul 2001 (s 108(4)–(6))[1]
	28	19 Dec 2000 (E) (SI 2000/3335)
		19 Dec 2000 (W) (in relation to police authorities) (SI 2000/3335)
		28 Jul 2001 (W) (otherwise) (s 108(4)–(6))[1]
	29	26 Oct 2000 (E) (SI 2000/2849)
		28 Jul 2001 (s 108(4)–(6))[1] (otherwise)
	30–32	19 Dec 2000 (E) (SI 2000/3335)
		19 Dec 2000 (W) (in relation to police authorities) (SI 2000/3335)
		28 Jul 2001 (W) (otherwise) (s 108(4)–(6))[1]
	33	26 Oct 2000 (E) (SI 2000/2849)
		28 Jul 2001 (s 108(4)–(6))[1] (otherwise)
	34	*Not in force*
6		28 Sep 2000 (repeal of Education Act 1996, Sch 37, para 63) (s 108(2))
		1 Oct 2000 (E) (repeal of or in Local Government Act 1972, s 100D(2)) (SI 2000/2187)

Local Government Act 2000 (c 22)—*contd*
Schedule
6—*contd*

18 Oct 2000 (E) (repeals of or in
Local Government (Miscellaneous
Provisions) Act 1976, s 25(8),
Inner Urban Areas Act 1978,
s 13,Housing Act 1985, s 11A(4),
Local Government and Housing
Act 1989, ss 34, 35)
(SI 2000/2836)

26 Oct 2000 (E) (repeals of or in
Local Authority Social Services
Act 1970, ss 2(2), 3(1), 6(5), 107
(to the extent that it relates to
those repeals and to Local
Government Act 2000, Sch 5,
paras 1–7, 16–23, 29, 33)
(SI 2000/2849)

9 Apr 2001 (W) (repeals of or in
Local Government (Miscellaneous
Provisions) Act 1976; Inner Urban
Areas Act 1978; Housing Act 1985;
Local Government and Housing
Act 1989, ss 34, 35)
(SI 2001/1471)

28 Jul 2001 (except repeals of or in
Local Government Act 1972,
ss 80(1)(e), 94–98, 105,
265A(1)(b); Local Government
Act 1974; Local Government
Act 1985; Transport Act 1985;
Financial Services Act 1986; Local
Government and Housing
Act 1989 ss 19, 31, 32(1), Sch 11;
Local Government Finance
Act 1992, Local Government
(Wales) Act 1994, Police and
Magistrates' Courts Act 1994,
Environment Act 1995, Police
Act 1996, Police Act 1997, Audit
Commission Act 1998, Greater
London Authority Act 1999)
(s 108(4)–(6))[1]
Not in force (exceptions noted above)

[1]   The Secretary of State in relation to England, or the National Assembly for Wales in relation to
Wales, may by order provide for any of these provisions to be brought into force in relation to
England or Wales before the time appointed by s 108(4) of this Act (ie, 28 July 2001)

[2]   As to the powers of the Secretary of State and the National Assembly for Wales to bring into force
provisions of this Act in relation to Wales, see s 108(5)(c), (6) of this Act

National Parks (Scotland) Act 2000 (asp 10)

RA: 9 Aug 2000

Commencement provisions: s 37(1); National Parks (Scotland) Act 2000 (Commencement) Order 2000, SSI 2000/312

Section	
1–36	8 Sep 2000 (SSI 2000/312)
37	9 Aug 2000 (RA)
Schedule	
1–5	8 Sep 2000 (SSI 2000/312)

Northern Ireland Act 2000 (c 1)

RA: 10 Feb 2000

Commencement provisions: s 9(2); Northern Ireland Act 2000 (Commencement) Order 2000, SI 2000/396

Section		
1		12 Feb 2000 (SI 2000/396)[1]
2–8		12 Feb 2000 (SI 2000/396)
9	(1), (2)	10 Feb 2000 (s 9(2))
	(3)	12 Feb 2000 (SI 2000/396)
Schedule		12 Feb 2000 (SI 2000/396)

[1]   S 1 ceased to have effect on 30 May 2000 by virtue of SI 2000/1445; it was brought back into force on 11 August 2001 by virtue of the revocation of SI 2000/1445 by SI 2001/2884 but subsequently ceased to have effect again on 12 August 2001 by virtue of SI 2001/2895. It was brought back into force on 22 September 2001 by virtue of the revocation of SI 2001/2895 by SI 2001/3230 but subsequently ceased to have effect again on 23 September 2001 by virtue of SI 2001/3231 (all made under s 2(2) of this Act).

Nuclear Safeguards Act 2000 (c 5)

RA: 25 May 2000

Commencement provisions: s 12(2)

Section	
1–11	*Not in force*
12	25 May 2000 (RA)

Police (Northern Ireland) Act 2000 (c 32)

RA: 23 Nov 2000

Commencement provisions: s 79; Police (Northern Ireland) Act 2000 (Commencement) Order 2000, SR 2000/412; Police (Northern Ireland) Act 2000 (Commencement No 2) Order 2001, SR 2001/132; Police (Northern Ireland) Act 2000 (Commencement No 3 and Transitional Provisions) Order 2001, SR 2001/396

Section		
1		4 Nov 2001 (SR 2001/396)
2	(1)	4 Nov 2001 (SR 2001/396)
	(2)	See Sch 1 below
	(3)	4 Nov 2001 (SR 2001/396)

Police (Northern Ireland) Act 2000 (c 32)—*contd*

Section

	(4)			See Sch 2 below
3	(1), (2)			4 Nov 2001 (SR 2001/396)
	(3)	(a)–(c)		4 Nov 2001 (SR 2001/396)
		(d)	(i), (ii)	4 Nov 2001 (SR 2001/396)
			(iii)	*Not in force*
			(iv)	4 Nov 2001 (SR 2001/396)
		(e)		4 Nov 2001 (SR 2001/396)
	(4)			4 Nov 2001 (SR 2001/396)
4–13				4 Nov 2001 (SR 2001/396)
14–19				*Not in force*
20				30 Mar 2001 (SR 2001/132)
21–23				*Not in force*
24–27				4 Nov 2001 (SR 2001/396)
28–31				*Not in force*
32–38				4 Nov 2001 (SR 2001/396)
39–41				30 Mar 2001 (SR 2001/132)
42				4 Nov 2001 (SR 2001/396)
43, 44				22 Dec 2000 (SR 2000/412)
45				4 Nov 2001 (SR 2001/396)
46, 47				30 Mar 2001 (SR 2001/132)
48				4 Nov 2001 (SR 2001/396)
49				23 Nov 2000 (s 79(2))
50				30 Mar 2001 (SR 2001/132)
51–56				4 Nov 2001 (SR 2001/396)[1]
57	(1)			4 Nov 2001 (SR 2001/396)
	(2)	(a)–(h)		4 Nov 2001 (SR 2001/396)
		(i), (j)		*Not in force*
	(3)–(6)			4 Nov 2001 (SR 2001/396)
58–61				4 Nov 2001 (SR 2001/396)
62				22 Dec 2000 (SR 2000/412)
63, 64				4 Nov 2001 (SR 2001/396)
65				22 Dec 2000 (SR 2000/412)
66				4 Nov 2001 (SR 2001/396)
67, 68				23 Nov 2000 (s 79(2))
69				4 Nov 2001 (SR 2001/396)
70				30 Mar 2001 (SR 2001/132)
71				4 Nov 2001 (SR 2001/396)
72				*Not in force*
73, 74				4 Nov 2001 (SR 2001/396)
75–77				23 Nov 2000 (s 79(2))
78	(1)			See Sch 6 below
	(2)			4 Nov 2001 (SR 2001/396)
	(3)			See Sch 7 below
	(4)			See Sch 8 below
79–81				23 Nov 2000 (RA)
Schedule				
1, Pt	I, II			4 Nov 2001 (SR 2001/396)
	III			23 Nov 2000 (s 79(2))
	IV–VI			4 Nov 2001 (SR 2001/396)

Police (Northern Ireland) Act 2000 (c 32)—*contd*

Schedule

2				4 Nov 2001 (SR 2001/396)
3				*Not in force*
4				23 Nov 2000 (s 79(2))
5				4 Nov 2001 (SR 2001/396)
6, para	1, 2			4 Nov 2001 (SR 2001/396)
	3	(1)–(3)		4 Nov 2001 (SR 2001/396)
		(4)		23 Nov 2000 (s 79(2))
	4	(1), (2)		4 Nov 2001 (SR 2001/396)
		(3)		23 Nov 2000 (s 79(2))
	5–13			4 Nov 2001 (SR 2001/396)
	14			*Not in force*
	15–19			4 Nov 2001 (SR 2001/396)
	20	(1)–(5)		4 Nov 2001 (SR 2001/396)
		(6)		22 Dec 2000 (SR 2000/412)
		(7)		4 Nov 2001 (SR 2001/396)
	21–22			4 Nov 2001 (SR 2001/396)
	23	(1)–(5)		4 Nov 2001 (SR 2001/396)
		(6)	(a)	22 Dec 2000 (SR 2000/412)
			(b)	4 Nov 2001 (SR 2001/396)
		(7), (8)		4 Nov 2001 (SR 2001/396)
	24	(1), (2)		4 Nov 2001 (SR 2001/396)
		(3)		30 Mar 2001 (SR 2001/132)
		(4)		4 Nov 2001 (SR 2001/396)
	25			4 Nov 2001 (SR 2001/396)
7, para	1			23 Nov 2000 (s 79(2))
	2			22 Dec 2000 (SR 2000/412)
	3			*Not in force*
	4			22 Dec 2000 (SR 2000/412)
8				4 Nov 2001 (SR 2001/396)

[1]   Note that the Queen's Printers copy of SR 2001/396 purports to bring s 54 into force twice. However it is thought that this should be a reference to ss 53 and 54.

Political Parties, Elections and Referendums Act 2000 (c 41)

RA: 30 Nov 2000

Commencement provisions: s 163(2)–(6); Political Parties, Elections and Referendums Act 2000 (Commencement No 1 and Transitional Provisions) Order 2001, SI 2001/222; Political Parties, Elections and Referendums Act 2000 (Commencement No 2) Order 2001, SI 2001/3526

Section

1–3			30 Nov 2000 (RA)
4, 5			16 Feb 2001 (SI 2001/222)
6	(1)	(a), (b)	16 Feb 2001 (SI 2001/222)
		(c)	*Not in force*
		(d)	30 Oct 2001 (SI 2001/3526)
		(e)–(g)	16 Feb 2001 (SI 2001/222)
	(2)–(7)		16 Feb 2001 (SI 2001/222)
7, 8			16 Feb 2001 (SI 2001/222)

Political Parties, Elections and Referendums Act 2000 (c 41)—*contd*

Section

9		1 Jul 2001 (SI 2001/222)[2]
10		16 Feb 2001 (SI 2001/222)
11	(1), (2)	16 Feb 2001 (SI 2001/222)[1]
	(3)	16 Feb 2001 (SI 2001/222)
12		30 Nov 2000 (so far as confers power to make an order or regulations) (RA)
		16 Feb 2001 (otherwise) (SI 2001/222)
13		30 Nov 2000 (so far as confers power to make an order or regulations) (RA)
		1 Jul 2001 (otherwise) (SI 2001/222)[2]
14		30 Oct 2001 (so far as relates to Boundary Committee for England) (SI 2001/3526)
		Not in force (otherwise)
15		30 Oct 2001 (SI 2001/3526)
16		30 Nov 2000 (so far as confers power to make an order or regulations) (RA)
		Not in force (otherwise)
17		*Not in force*
18		30 Nov 2000 (so far as confers power to make an order or regulations) (RA)
		30 Oct 2001 (otherwise) (SI 2001/3526)
19, 20		30 Nov 2000 (so far as confers power to make an order or regulations) (RA)
		Not in force (otherwise)
21		16 Feb 2001 (SI 2001/222)
22		14 Dec 2000 (for the purposes of the operation of Sch 23, paras 1–7) (s 163(4))
		16 Feb 2001 (otherwise) (SI 2001/222)
23		30 Nov 2000 (so far as confers power to make an order or regulations) (RA)
		14 Dec 2000 (for the purposes of the operation of Sch 23, paras 1–7) (s 163(4))
		16 Feb 2001 (otherwise) (SI 2001/222)
24, 25		14 Dec 2000 (for the purposes of the operation of Sch 23, paras 1–7) (s 163(4))
		16 Feb 2001 (otherwise) (SI 2001/222)
26		30 Nov 2000 (so far as confers power to make an order or regulations) (RA)
		14 Dec 2000 (for the purposes of the operation of Sch 23, paras 1–7) (s 163(4))
		16 Feb 2001 (otherwise) (SI 2001/222)

Political Parties, Elections and Referendums Act 2000 (c 41)—*contd*
Section

27	14 Dec 2000 (for the purposes of the operation of Sch 23, paras 1–7) (s 163(4))
	16 Feb 2001 (otherwise) (SI 2001/222)
28	30 Nov 2000 (so far as confers power to make an order or regulations) (RA)
	14 Dec 2000 (for the purposes of the operation of Sch 23, paras 1–7) (s 163(4))
	16 Feb 2001 (otherwise) (SI 2001/222)
29–31	14 Dec 2000 (for the purposes of the operation of Sch 23, paras 1–7) (s 163(4))
	16 Feb 2001 (otherwise) (SI 2001/222)
32	30 Nov 2000 (so far as confers power to make an order or regulations) (RA)
	14 Dec 2000 (for the purposes of the operation of Sch 23, paras 1–7) (s 163(4))
	16 Feb 2001 (otherwise) (SI 2001/222)
33	14 Dec 2000 (for the purposes of the operation of Sch 23, paras 1–7) (s 163(4))
	16 Feb 2001 (otherwise) (SI 2001/222)
34	30 Nov 2000 (so far as confers power to make an order or regulations) (RA)
	14 Dec 2000 (for the purposes of the operation of Sch 23, paras 1–7) (s 163(4))
	16 Feb 2001 (otherwise) (SI 2001/222)
35	14 Dec 2000 (for the purposes of the operation of Sch 23, paras 1–7) (s 163(4))
	16 Feb 2001 (otherwise) (SI 2001/222)
36	14 Dec 2000 (s 163(4))
37–40	14 Dec 2000 (for the purposes of the operation of Sch 23, paras 1–7) (s 163(4))
	16 Feb 2001 (otherwise) (SI 2001/222)
41	1 Jan 2002 (SI 2001/3526)
42, 43	30 Nov 2000 (so far as confers power to make an order or regulations) (RA)
	1 Jan 2002 (otherwise) (SI 2001/3526)
44–47	1 Jan 2002 (SI 2001/3526)
48	30 Nov 2000 (so far as confers power to make an order or regulations) (RA)
	1 Jan 2002 (otherwise) (SI 2001/3526)

Political Parties, Elections and Referendums Act 2000 (c 41)—*contd*

Section

49	1 Jan 2002 (SI 2001/3526)
50	16 Feb 2001 (SI 2001/222)[1]
51	30 Nov 2000 (so far as confers power to make an order or regulations) (RA)
	16 Feb 2001 (otherwise) (SI 2001/222)[1]
52–66	16 Feb 2001 (SI 2001/222)[1]
67	30 Nov 2000 (so far as confers power to make an order or regulations) (RA)
	16 Feb 2001 (otherwise) (SI 2001/222)[1]
68, 69	16 Feb 2001 (SI 2001/222)[1]
70	30 Nov 2000 (so far as confers power to make an order or regulations) (RA)
	16 Feb 2001 (otherwise) (SI 2001/222)[1]
71	16 Feb 2001 (SI 2001/222)[1]
72–79	16 Feb 2001 (SI 2001/222)
80	30 Nov 2000 (so far as confers power to make an order or regulations) (RA)
	16 Feb 2001 (otherwise) (SI 2001/222)
81–95	16 Feb 2001 (SI 2001/222)
96	30 Nov 2000 (so far as confers power to make an order or regulations) (RA)
	16 Feb 2001 (otherwise) (SI 2001/222)
97–100	16 Feb 2001 (SI 2001/222)
101	30 Nov 2000 (so far as confers power to make an order or regulations) (RA)
	16 Feb 2001 (otherwise) (SI 2001/222)
102–107	16 Feb 2001 (SI 2001/222)
108, 109	30 Nov 2000 (so far as confers power to make an order or regulations) (RA)
	16 Feb 2001 (otherwise) (SI 2001/222)
110–119	16 Feb 2001 (SI 2001/222)
120	30 Nov 2000 (so far as confers power to make an order or regulations) (RA)
	16 Feb 2001 (otherwise) (SI 2001/222)
121–125	16 Feb 2001 (SI 2001/222)
126	30 Nov 2000 (so far as confers power to make an order or regulations) (RA)
	16 Feb 2001 (otherwise) (SI 2001/222)
127, 128	16 Feb 2001 (SI 2001/222)
129	30 Nov 2000 (so far as confers power to make an order or regulations) (RA)
	16 Feb 2001 (otherwise) (SI 2001/222)

Political Parties, Elections and Referendums Act 2000 (c 41)—*contd*

Section

130		1 Jul 2001 (SI 2001/222)[2]
131		16 Feb 2001 (SI 2001/222)
132	(1)	16 Feb 2001 (SI 2001/222)
	(2)–(4)	1 Jul 2001 (SI 2001/222)[2]
	(5)	16 Feb 2001 (SI 2001/222)
	(6)	1 Jul 2001 (SI 2001/222)[2]
133		30 Nov 2000 (so far as confers power to make an order or regulations) (RA)
		16 Feb 2001 (otherwise) (SI 2001/222)
134, 135		1 Jul 2001 (SI 2001/222)[2]
136		16 Feb 2001 (SI 2001/222)[1]
137–140		16 Feb 2001 (SI 2001/222)
141		1 Apr 2002 (SI 2001/3526)
142		16 Feb 2001 (SI 2001/222)
143		30 Nov 2000 (so far as confers power to make an order or regulations) (RA)
		Not in force (otherwise) [3]
144		16 Feb 2001 (for purposes of drawing up codes referred to in Representation of the People Act 1983, s 93) (SI 2001/222)
		16 Mar 2001 (otherwise) (SI 2001/222)
145		30 Nov 2000 (so far as confers power to make an order or regulations) (RA)
		16 Feb 2001 (otherwise) (SI 2001/222)
146–154		16 Feb 2001 (SI 2001/222)
155		30 Nov 2000 (so far as confers power to make an order or regulations) (RA)
		16 Feb 2001 (otherwise) (SI 2001/222)
156		30 Nov 2000 (RA)
157, 158		16 Feb 2001 (SI 2001/222)
159, 160		30 Nov 2000 (RA)
161, 162		16 Feb 2001 (SI 2001/222)
163		30 Nov 2000 (RA)
Schedule		
1, 2		30 Nov 2000 (RA)
3		*Not in force*
4		30 Nov 2000 (so far as confers power to make an order or regulations) (RA)
		16 Feb 2001 (otherwise) (SI 2001/222)[2]
5		1 Jan 2002 (SI 2001/3526)
6, 7		30 Nov 2000 (so far as confers power to make an order or regulations) (RA)
		16 Feb 2001 (otherwise) (SI 2001/222)[1]

Political Parties, Elections and Referendums Act 2000 (c 41)—*contd*

Schedule

8				30 Nov 2000 (so far as confers power to make an order or regulations) (RA)
				16 Feb 2001 (otherwise) (SI 2001/222)[2]
9, paras	1, 2			16 Feb 2001 (SI 2001/222)
	3	(1)		16 Feb 2001 (SI 2001/222)
		(2)	(a)	16 Feb 2001 (SI 2001/222)[1]
			(b)	16 Feb 2001 (SI 2001/222)
		(3)		16 Feb 2001 (SI 2001/222)
		(4)		16 Feb 2001 (SI 2001/222)[1]
		(5), (6)		16 Feb 2001 (SI 2001/222)
		(7)	(a)	16 Feb 2001 (SI 2001/222)[1]
			(b)	16 Feb 2001 (SI 2001/222)
10	1, 2			16 Feb 2001 (SI 2001/222)
	3	(1)		16 Feb 2001 (SI 2001/222)
		(2)		16 Feb 2001 (SI 2001/222)[1]
		(3)	(a)	16 Feb 2001 (SI 2001/222)[1]
			(b)	16 Feb 2001 (SI 2001/222)
		(4)		16 Feb 2001 (SI 2001/222)
11				30 Nov 2000 (so far as confers power to make an order or regulations) (RA)
				16 Feb 2001 (otherwise) (SI 2001/222)
12				16 Feb 2001 (SI 2001/222)
13				30 Nov 2000 (so far as confers power to make an order or regulations) (RA)
				16 Feb 2001 (otherwise) (SI 2001/222)
14				30 Nov 2000 (so far as confers power to make an order or regulations) (RA)
				16 Feb 2001 (otherwise) (SI 2001/222)
15				30 Nov 2000 (so far as confers power to make an order or regulations) (RA)
				16 Feb 2001 (otherwise) (SI 2001/222)
16				30 Nov 2000 (so far as confers power to make an order or regulations) (RA)
				1 Jul 2001 (otherwise) (SI 2001/222)[2]
17, paras	1–6			16 Feb 2001 (SI 2001/222)
	7–8			16 Feb 2001 (SI 2001/222)[1]
	9, 10			16 Feb 2001 (SI 2001/222)
18, paras	1, 2			16 Feb 2001 (SI 2001/222)
	3–5			1 Jul 2001 (SI 2001/222)[2]
	6			16 Feb 2001 (SI 2001/222)
	7			30 Nov 2000 (so far as confers power to make an order or regulations) (RA)
				1 Jul 2001 (otherwise) (SI 2001/222)[2]

Political Parties, Elections and Referendums Act 2000 (c 41)—*contd*

Schedule

18, paras	8, 9			16 Feb 2001 (SI 2001/222)
	10			1 Jul 2001 (SI 2001/222)²
	11	(a), (b)		1 Jul 2001 (SI 2001/222)²
		(c)		16 Feb 2001 (SI 2001/222)
		(d)		1 Jul 2001 (SI 2001/222)²
	12			16 Feb 2001 (SI 2001/222)
	13			30 Nov 2000 (so far as confers power to make an order or regulations) (RA)
				16 Feb 2001 (otherwise) (SI 2001/222)
	14			30 Nov 2000 (so far as confers power to make an order or regulations) (RA)
				Not in force (otherwise) ³
	15, 16			1 Jul 2001 (SI 2001/222)²
	17–19			16 Feb 2001 (SI 2001/222)
19				30 Nov 2000 (so far as confers power to make an order or regulations) (RA)
				16 Feb 2001 (otherwise) (SI 2001/222)
20				16 Feb 2001 (SI 2001/222)
21, paras	1–5			16 Feb 2001 (SI 2001/222)
	6	(1)		16 Feb 2001 (SI 2001/222)
		(2)		1 Jul 2001 (SI 2001/222)²
		(3)		30 Nov 2000 (so far as confers power to make an order or regulations) (RA)
				Not in force (otherwise)
		(4)		*Not in force*
		(5), (6)		16 Feb 2001 (SI 2001/222)
		(7)	(a)	*Not in force*
			(b)	16 Feb 2001 (SI 2001/222)¹
			(c)	16 Feb 2001 (SI 2001/222)
			(d)	1 Jul 2001 (SI 2001/222)²
		(8), (9)		16 Feb 2001 (SI 2001/222)
	7			*Not in force*
	8–11			16 Feb 2001 (SI 2001/222)
	12	(1)		30 Nov 2000 (RA)
		(2), (3)		16 Feb 2001 (SI 2001/222)
		(4)		30 Nov 2000 (RA)
	13–15			16 Feb 2001 (SI 2001/222)
	16–18			1 Jul 2001 (SI 2001/222)²
22				16 Feb 2001 (so far as relates to Representation of the People Act 1983, ss 72, 75(1B), (1C), 78(6), 79(3), 82(4), 86(9), 101–105, 106(8), 108, 122(8), 138(1), 148–153, 157(5), 159(2), 167(4), 174(6), Sch 1, r 30(5);

Political Parties, Elections and Referendums Act 2000 (c 41)—*contd*

Schedule

22—*contd*	Representation of the People Act 1985, s 14(3)–(5), Sch 3, paras 6, 7; Representation of the People Act 1989, s 6; Local Government Act 1992, s 13; Government of Wales Act 1998, s 11(2); Scotland Act 1998, s 12(2); Registration of Political Parties Act 1998; Greater London Authority Act 1999, Sch 3 (except so far as relates to para 28)) (SI 2001/222)
	16 Mar 2001 (so far as relates to Representation of the People Act 1985, Sch 4, para 35; Broadcasting Act 1996, Sch 10; Greater London Authority Act 1999, Sch 3, para 28) (SI 2001/222)
	1 Jul 2001 (so far as relates to Representation of the People Act 1983, ss 73, 81, Sch 3) (SI 2001/222)[2]
	Not in force (otherwise)
23, paras 1–7	14 Dec 2000 (s 163(4))
8–13	30 Nov 2000 (RA)

[1]   For transitional provisions, see SI 2001/222, Sch 1, Pt II.

[2]   For transitional provisions, see SI 2001/222, Sch 2, Pt II.

[3]   This provision was originally brought into force, for all purposes other than the power to make an order or regulations, on 16 February 2001 by SI 2001/222; however, by virtue of the Election Publications Act 2001, s 1, this provision is deemed not to have come into force on the commencement date, which is thus yet to be appointed.

Postal Services Act 2000 (c 26)

RA: 28 Jul 2000

Commencement provisions: s 130; Postal Services Act 2000 (Commencement No 1 and Transitional Provisions) Order 2000, SI 2000/2957[1], as amended by SI 2001/1148, art 43; Postal Services Act 2000 (Commencement No 2) Order 2001, SI 2001/534; Postal Services Act 2000 (Commencement No 3 and Transitional and Saving Provisions) Order 2001, SI 2001/878[2]; Postal Services Act 2000 (Commencement No 4 and Transitional and Saving Provisions) Order 2001, SI 2001/1148[3]

Section

1		6 Nov 2000 (SI 2000/2957)
2		1 Jan 2001 (SI 2000/2957)
3–5		6 Nov 2000 (SI 2000/2957)
6–10		26 Mar 2001 (SI 2000/2957)
11		6 Nov 2000 (SI 2000/2957)
12	(1), (2)	6 Nov 2000 (SI 2000/2957)

Postal Services Act 2000 (c 26)—*contd*
Section

12	(3)	(a)	6 Nov 2000 (SI 2000/2957)
		(b)	1 Jan 2001 (SI 2000/2957)
		(c)	6 Nov 2000 (SI 2000/2957)
	(4)		6 Nov 2000 (SI 2000/2957)
	(5)		1 Jan 2001 (SI 2000/2957)
13			6 Nov 2000 (SI 2000/2957)
14–29			26 Mar 2001 (SI 2000/2957)
30	(1)		26 Mar 2001 (SI 2000/2957)
	(2)		6 Nov 2000 (SI 2000/2957)
	(3)		26 Mar 2001 (SI 2000/2957)
31			1 Jan 2001 (SI 2000/2957)
32–37			26 Mar 2001 (SI 2000/2957)
38, 39			6 Nov 2000 (SI 2000/2957)
40			26 Mar 2001 (SI 2000/2957)
41			1 Jan 2001 (SI 2000/2957)
42	(1), (2)		1 Jan 2001 (SI 2000/2957)
	(3)		6 Nov 2000 (SI 2000/2957)
43	(1), (2)		6 Nov 2000 (SI 2000/2957)
	(3)	(a)	6 Nov 2000 (SI 2000/2957)
		(b)	1 Jan 2001 (SI 2000/2957)
		(c)–(e)	6 Nov 2000 (SI 2000/2957)
	(4)–(8)		6 Nov 2000 (SI 2000/2957)
44	(1)–(4)		6 Nov 2000 (SI 2000/2957)
	(5)		1 Jan 2001 (SI 2000/2957)
	(6)		6 Nov 2000 (SI 2000/2957)
45, 46			6 Nov 2000 (SI 2000/2957)
47			6 Nov 2000 (in so far as it relates to information required in connection with exercise of Commission's functions under s 44(4) (SI 2000/2957)
			1 Jan 2001 (in so far as it relates to information required in connection with exercise of Commission's functions under ss 42, 44(5)) (SI 2000/2957)
			26 Mar 2001 (otherwise) (SI 2000/2957)
48			6 Nov 2000 (SI 2000/2957)
49			26 Mar 2001 (SI 2000/2957)
50–58			1 Jan 2001 (SI 2000/2957)
59	(1)		1 Jan 2001 (SI 2000/2957)
	(2)		6 Nov 2000 (SI 2000/2957)
	(3)		1 Jan 2001 (SI 2000/2957)
60, 61			1 Jan 2001 (SI 2000/2957)
62–82			6 Nov 2000 (SI 2000/2957)
83–88			26 Mar 2001 (SI 2001/878)
89	(1)–(6)		26 Feb 2001 (SI 2001/534)
89	(7)		26 Mar 2001 (SI 2001/1148) [3]

Postal Services Act 2000 (c 26)—*contd*

Section

89	(8)		26 Feb 2001 (SI 2001/534)
90			26 Mar 2001 (SI 2001/1148) [3]
91, 92			26 Feb 2001 (so far as relate to
			s 89(1)–(6)) (SI 2001/534)
			26 Mar 2001 (otherwise)
			(SI 2001/1148) [3]
93, 94			1 Jan 2001 (SI 2000/2957)
95			26 Mar 2001 (SI 2000/2957)
96			26 Mar 2001 (SI 2001/1148) [3]
97–100			26 Mar 2001 (SI 2000/2957)
101–103			6 Nov 2000 (SI 2000/2957)
104			26 Mar 2001 (SI 2001/1148) [3]
105	(1)		26 Mar 2001 (SI 2001/1148) [3]
	(2)		26 Feb 2001 (SI 2001/534)
	(3)–(5)		26 Mar 2001 (SI 2001/1148) [3]
106–108			26 Mar 2001 (SI 2001/1148) [3]
109			26 Mar 2001 (SI 2001/878)
110, 111			26 Mar 2001 (SI 2001/1148) [3]
112	(1)		26 Mar 2001 (SI 2001/1148) [3]
	(2)–(7)		26 Feb 2001 (SI 2001/534)
	(8)		26 Mar 2001 (SI 2001/1148) [3]
	(9), (10)		26 Feb 2001 (SI 2001/534)
113			26 Mar 2001 (SI 2001/1148) [3]
114	(1), (2)		26 Feb 2001 (so far as relate to
			s 112(2)–(7) (SI 2001/534)
			26 Mar 2001 (otherwise)
			(SI 2001/1148) [3]
	(3)		26 Feb 2001 (SI 2001/534)
115			28 Sep 2000 (s 130(2))
116			25 Mar 2001 (SI 2001/1148)
117, 118			6 Nov 2000 (SI 2000/2957)
119			See Sch 7 below
120–126			28 Jul 2000 (RA)
127	(1)–(3)		28 Jul 2000 (RA)
	(4)		See Sch 8 below
	(5)		28 Jul 2000 (RA)
	(6)		See Sch 9 below
128–131			28 Jul 2000 (RA)

Schedule

1			6 Nov 2000 (SI 2000/2957)
2			1 Jan 2001 (SI 2000/2957)
3, 4			6 Nov 2000 (SI 2000/2957)
5			26 Mar 2001 (SI 2000/2957)
6, para	1		6 Nov 2000 (SI 2000/2957)
	2–10		26 Mar 2001 (SI 2000/2957)
7, para	1, 2		6 Nov 2000 (SI 2000/2957)
	3	(1)(a)	6 Nov 2000 (except in relation to
			Competition Commission and
			Council) (SI 2000/2957)

Postal Services Act 2000 (c 26)—*contd*
Schedule

7, para	3	(1)(a)—*contd*	1 Jan 2001 (in relation to Council) (SI 2000/2957)
			26 Mar 2001 (otherwise) (SI 2000/2957)
		(b)–(n)	6 Nov 2000 (SI 2000/2957)
		(2)	6 Nov 2000 (SI 2000/2957)
		(3)	Substituted (1 Dec 2001) by Postal Services Act 2000 (Disclosure of Information) Order 2001, SI 2001/3617
	4–6		6 Nov 2000 (SI 2000/2957)
8, para	1–5		26 Mar 2001 (SI 2001/1148) [3]
	6, 7		6 Nov 2000 (SI 2000/2957)
	8		6 Nov 2000 (in so far as it relates to Post Office company) (SI 2000/2957)
			1 Jan 2001 (otherwise) (SI 2000/2957)
	9		1 Jan 2001 (SI 2000/2957)
	10		6 Nov 2000 (SI 2000/2957)
	11, 12		26 Mar 2001 (SI 2001/1148) [3]
	13		1 Jan 2001 (SI 2000/2957)
	14	(1)	6 Nov 2000 (SI 2000/2957)
		(2)	1 Jan 2001 (SI 2000/2957)
		(3)	6 Nov 2000 (SI 2000/2957)
	15		6 Nov 2000 (SI 2000/2957)
	16–26		26 Mar 2001 (SI 2001/1148) [3]
	27		6 Nov 2000 (SI 2000/2957)
9			6 Nov 2000 (repeals of or in Post Office (Banking Services) Act 1976; Postal Services Regulations 1999, SI 1999/2107, regs 2, 3) (SI 2000/2957)
			1 Jan 2001 (repeals of or in Post Office Act 1953, ss 29, 44, 45; Parliamentary Commissioner Act 1967, Sch 2; Post Office Act 1969, ss 14, 15; Chronically Sick and Disabled Persons Act 1970, s 14(1), (2); House of Commons Disqualification Act 1975, Sch 1, Pt III; British Telecommunications Act 1981, s 65; Merchant Shipping Act 1995, Sch 13, para 28) (SI 2000/2957)
			26 Mar 2001 (repeals of or in Official Secrets Act 1920; Post Office Act 1969, ss 33, 40, 41, 43, 44, 46–48, 55–63, 66, 67, 72, 73, 84, 119, 129, 135, Schs 2, 3, Sch 4,

Postal Services Act 2000 (c 26)—*contd*
Schedule
9—*contd*

para 21; Northern Ireland
(Modification of Enactments—No 1)
Order 1973, SI 1973/2163; British
Telecommunications Act 1981,
ss 58(1)–(3), 59–61; 63, 64, 66–69,
71–74, 76; Banking Act 1987,
Sch 6, para 10; Scotland Act 1998
(Consequential Modifications)
(No 1) Order 1999, SI 1999/1042;
Postal Services Regulations 1999,
SI 1999/2107, regs 1(3), 4–6)
(SI 2000/2957);

26 Mar 2001 (repeals of or in Post
Office Act 1953, ss 11, 25–28, 32,
52–65, 68–70, 72, 79; Criminal
Justice Act 1967; Forgery and
Counterfeiting Act 1981;
Interception of Communications
Act 1985; Post Office (Abolition
of Import Restrictions)
Regulations 1993, SI 1993/1324)
(SI 2001/878)

26 Mar 2001 (repeals of or in Post
Office Act 1953 (the whole Act,
other than the sections noted
above); Post Office Act 1969, ss 7,
8, 10–12, 28–30, 37–39, 64,
69–71, 75(2), s 80 (except in so far
as it extends to the Bailiwick of
Guernsey), s 81, Sch 9, para 3(2);
Local Government Act 1972,
Sch 29, para 36; British
Telecommunications Act 1981,
s 75, Sch 3, para 51(1), (3); Mental
Health Act 1983, s 134(9);
Miscellaneous Financial Provisions
Act 1983, Sch 2;
Telecommunications Act 1984,
s 99(1), Sch 4, paras 50, 78;
Transport Act 1985, Sch 3, para
22, Sch 7, para 13; Gas Act 1986,
Sch 7, para 10; Water Act 1989,
Sch 25, para 39; Electricity
Act 1989, Sch 16, para 15;
Companies Act 1989, Sch 10,
para 30; Electricity (Northern
Ireland) Order 1992, SI 1992/231
(NI 1), Sch 12, para 7; Police and
Magistrates' Courts Act 1994,

Postal Services Act 2000 (c 26)—*contd*

Schedule

9—*contd*   Sch 4, para 49; Gas Act 1995,
Sch 4, para 9; Police Act 1996;
Gas (Northern Ireland) Order 1996,
SI 1996/275 (NI 2), Sch 6)
(SI 2001/1148) [3]
Not in force (otherwise)

---

[1]   For transitional provisions, see SI 2000/2957, arts 3–8.

[2]   For transitional and saving provisions, see SI 2001/878, arts 3–17.

[3]   For transitional and saving provisions, see SI 2001/1148, arts 3–42.

Powers of Criminal Courts (Sentencing) Act 2000 (c 6)

RA: 25 May 2000

Commencement provisions: s 168

Section

1–15	25 Aug 2000 (s 168(1))
16–32	25 Aug 2000 (s 168(1))
33–36	25 Aug 2000 (s 168(1))
36A	Inserted by Criminal Justice and Court Services Act 2000, s 48 (qv)
36B	Inserted by Criminal Justice and Court Services Act 2000, s 52 (qv)
37	25 Aug 2000 (s 168(1))
38	Repealed
39, 40	25 Aug 2000 (s 168(1))
40A–40C	Prospectively inserted by Criminal Justice and Court Services Act 2000, s 46[1]
41–58	25 Aug 2000 (s 168(1))
58A, 58B	Inserted by Criminal Justice and Court Services Act 2000, s 47 (qv)
58–82	25 Aug 2000 (s 168(1))
82A	Inserted by Criminal Justice and Court Services Act 2000, s 60(1) (qv)
83–86	25 Aug 2000 (s 168(1))
87, 88	*Not in force*
89–92	25 Aug 2000 (s 168(1))
93–98	25 Aug 2000 (s 168(1)); prospectively repealed by Criminal Justice and Court Services Act 2000, ss 74, 75, Sch 7, paras 160, 182, Sch 8[1]
99–107	25 Aug 2000 (s 168(1))
108	25 Aug 2000 (s 168(1)); prospectively repealed by Criminal Justice and Court Services Act 2000, ss 74, 75, Sch 7, paras 160, 188, Sch 8[1]
109–168	25 Aug 2000 (s 168(1))

Powers of Criminal Courts (Sentencing) Act 2000 (c 6)—*contd*

Schedule

Powers of Criminal Courts (Sentencing) Act 2000 (c 6)—*contd*

Schedule

9, paras	66		25 Aug 2000 (s 168(1)); prospectively repealed by Criminal Justice and Court Services Act 2000, ss 74, 75, Sch 7, paras 160, 203(1), (2), Sch 8[1]
	67		25 Aug 2000 (s 168(1))
	68		25 Aug 2000 (s 168(1)); prospectively repealed by Criminal Justice and Court Services Act 2000, ss 74, 75, Sch 7, paras 160, 203(1), (2), Sch 8[1]
	69		25 Aug 2000 (s 168(1))
	70		25 Aug 2000 (s 168(1)); prospectively repealed by Criminal Justice and Court Services Act 2000, ss 74, 75, Sch 7, paras 160, 203(1), (2), Sch 8[1]
	71, 72		25 Aug 2000 (s 168(1))
	73, 74		25 Aug 2000 (s 168(1))
	75, 76		25 Aug 2000 (s 168(1))
	77, 78		25 Aug 2000 (s 168(1)); prospectively repealed by Criminal Justice and Court Services Act 2000, ss 74, 75, Sch 7, paras 160, 203(1), (2), Sch 8[1]
	79–89		25 Aug 2000 (s 168(1))
	90	(1)–(5)	25 Aug 2000 (s 168(1))
		(6)	25 Aug 2000 (s 168(1))
	91–124		25 Aug 2000 (s 168(1))
	125		Repealed
	126–151		25 Aug 2000 (s 168(1))
	152		25 Aug 2000 (s 168(1)); prospectively repealed by Criminal Justice and Court Services Act 2000, ss 74, 75, Sch 7, paras 160, 203(1), (2), Sch 8[1]
	153–156		Repealed
	157–160		25 Aug 2000 (s 168(1))
	161		25 Aug 2000 (s 168(1))
	162–181		25 Aug 2000 (s 168(1))
	182		Repealed, subject to a saving
	183–187		25 Aug 2000 (s 168(1))
	188		Repealed, subject to a saving
	189–193		25 Aug 2000 (s 168(1))
	194, 195		25 Aug 2000 (s 168(1))
	196		25 Aug 2000 (s 168(1))
	197		25 Aug 2000 (s 168(1))
	198–205		25 Aug 2000 (s 168(1))
10–12			25 Aug 2000 (s 168(1))

[1] Orders made under Criminal Justice and Court Services Act 2000, s 80, bringing the prospective amendments into force will be noted to that Act

[2] Orders made under Armed Forces Act 2001, s 39(2), bringing the prospective repeals into force will be noted to that Act

Protection of Animals (Amendment) Act 2000 (c 40)

RA: 30 Nov 2000

Commencement provisions: s 5(3)
Section
1–5   30 Jan 2001 (s 5(3))

Public Finance and Accountability (Scotland) Act 2000 (asp 1)

RA: 17 Jan 2000

Commencement provisions: s 30(1), (2); Public Finance and Accountability (Scotland)
   Act 2000 (Commencement) Order 2000, SSI 2000/10
Section

1–3		1 Apr 2001 (SSI 2000/10)
4	(1)	1 Apr 2000 (SSI 2000/10)
	(2)–(5)	1 Apr 2001 (SSI 2000/10)
5		1 Feb 2000 (for the purpose of enabling credits to be granted to take effect no earlier than 1 Apr 2000) (SSI 2000/10)
		1 Apr 2000 (otherwise) (SSI 2000/10)
6		1 Apr 2000 (SSI 2000/10)
7		1 Apr 2001 (SSI 2000/10)
8, 9		1 Apr 2000 (SSI 2000/10)
10	(1), (2)	1 Feb 2000 (SSI 2000/10)
	(3)	1 Apr 2000 (SSI 2000/10)
	(4)	1 Feb 2000 (for the purpose of enabling directions to be given to take effect no earlier than 1 Apr 2000) (SSI 2000/10)
		1 Apr 2000 (otherwise) (SSI 2000/10)
	(5)	1 Apr 2000 (SSI 2000/10)
	(6)	See Sch 2 below
11	(1)–(6)	1 Apr 2000 (SSI 2000/10)
	(7)	1 Feb 2000 (SSI 2000/10)
	(8)	1 Apr 2000 (SSI 2000/10)
	(9)	1 Feb 2000 (for the purpose of requiring the preparation and examination of proposals under this subsection relating to the financial year beginning with 1 Apr 2000) (SSI 2000/10)
		1 Apr 2000 (otherwise) (SSI 2000/10)
12, 13		1 Feb 2000 (SSI 2000/10)
14	(1)	1 Feb 2000 (SSI 2000/10)
	(2)–(5)	1 Apr 2000 (SSI 2000/10)
15	(1), (2)	1 Feb 2000 (for the purpose of enabling designations of accountable officers and determinations of their functions to be made to take effect no earlier than 1 Apr 2000) (SSI 2000/10)

Public Finance and Accountability (Scotland) Act 2000 (asp 1)—*contd*
Section

15	(1), (2)—*contd*	1 Apr 2000 (otherwise) (SSI 2000/10)
	(3)–(5)	1 Apr 2000 (SSI 2000/10)
	(6), (7)	1 Feb 2000 (for the purpose of enabling designations of accountable officers and determinations of their functions to be made to take effect no earlier than 1 Apr 2000) (SSI 2000/10)
		1 Apr 2000 (otherwise) (SSI 2000/10)
	(8)	1 Apr 2000 (SSI 2000/10)
16–23		1 Apr 2000 (SSI 2000/10)
24	(1)–(4)	1 Apr 2000 (SSI 2000/10)
	(5), (6)	1 Feb 2000 (for the purpose of enabling an order to be made under sub-s (5) to come into force no earlier than 1 Apr 2000) (SSI 2000/10)
		1 Apr 2000 (otherwise) (SSI 2000/10)
	(7)	1 Apr 2000 (SSI 2000/10)
25, 26		1 Apr 2000 (SSI 2000/10)
27–29		19 Jan 2000 (SSI 2000/10)
30		17 Jan 2000 (RA)
Schedule		
1		1 Apr 2000 (SSI 2000/10)
2, para	1–4	1 Apr 2000 (SSI 2000/10)
	5, 6	1 Feb 2000 (for the purpose of enabling Audit Scotland to exercise powers under these paragraphs so as to make provision to take effect no earlier than 1 Apr 2000) (SSI 2000/10)
		1 Apr 2000 (otherwise) (SSI 2000/10)
	7–9	1 Apr 2000 (SSI 2000/10)
3		1 Feb 2000 (SSI 2000/10)
4		1 Apr 2000 (SSI 2000/10)

Race Relations (Amendment) Act 2000 (c 34)

RA: 30 Nov 2000

Commencement provisions: s 10(2)–(4); Race Relations (Amendment) Act 2000
   (Commencement) Order 2001, SI 2001/566
Section

1	26 Mar 2001 (for the purpose of the imposition of a requirement or the giving of an express authorisation by a Minister of the Crown acting personally in accordance with Race Relations Act 1976, s 19D(3)) (SI 2001/566)
	2 Apr 2001 (otherwise) (SI 2001/566)

Race Relations (Amendment) Act 2000 (c 34)—*contd*

Regulation of Investigatory Powers Act 2000 (c 23)

RA: 28 Jul 2000

Commencement provisions: s 83(2); Regulation of Investigatory Powers Act 2000 (Commencement No 1 and Transitional Provisions) Order 2000, SI 2000/2543; Regulation of Investigatory Powers Act 2000 (Commencement No 2) Order 2001, SI 2001/2727

Regulation of Investigatory Powers Act 2000 (c 23)—*contd*
Section

61			25 Sep 2000 (SI 2000/2543)
62	(1)	(a)	25 Sep 2000 (SI 2000/2543)
		(b), (c)	*Not in force*
	(2), (3)		25 Sep 2000 (SI 2000/2543)
63, 64			25 Sep 2000 (SI 2000/2543)
65	(1)		2 Oct 2000 (subject to transitional provisions in SI 2000/2543, art 6) (SI 2000/2543)
	(2)	(a)–(b)	2 Oct 2000 (subject to transitional provisions in SI 2000/2543, art 6) (SI 2000/2543) (SI 2000/2543)
		(c), (d)	*Not in force*
	(3)	(a), (b)	2 Oct 2000 (SI 2000/2543)
		(c)	*Not in force*
		(d)	2 Oct 2000 (SI 2000/2543)
	(4)		2 Oct 2000 (SI 2000/2543)
	(5)	(a), (b)	2 Oct 2000 (SI 2000/2543)
		(c)	*Not in force*
		(d)	2 Oct 2000 (SI 2000/2543)
		(e)	*Not in force*
		(f)	2 Oct 2000 (SI 2000/2543)
	(6), (7)		2 Oct 2000 (SI 2000/2543)
	(8)	(a)	2 Oct 2000 (SI 2000/2543)
		(b)	*Not in force*
		(c)	2 Oct 2000 (SI 2000/2543)
		(d), (e)	*Not in force*
		(f)	2 Oct 2000 (SI 2000/2543)
	(9)		2 Oct 2000 (SI 2000/2543)
	(10)		*Not in force*
	(11)		2 Oct 2000 (SI 2000/2543)
66			*Not in force*
67	(1)		2 Oct 2000 (so far as relates to s 65(2)(a), (b) of this Act) (SI 2000/2543)
			Not in force (otherwise)
	(2)–(8)		2 Oct 2000 (SI 2000/2543)
	(9)		*Not in force*
	(10)–(12)		2 Oct 2000 (SI 2000/2543)
68	(1)–(6)		2 Oct 2000 (SI 2000/2543)
	(7)	(a)–(f)	2 Oct 2000 (SI 2000/2543)
		(g), (h)	*Not in force*
		(i)–(l)	2 Oct 2000 (SI 2000/2543)
		(m)	*Not in force*
		(n)	2 Oct 2000 (except so far as relates to para (m)) (SI 2000/2543)
			Not in force (otherwise) (SI 2000/2543)
	(8)		2 Oct 2000 (SI 2000/2543)

Regulation of Investigatory Powers Act 2000 (c 23)—*contd*

Section

69, 70		2 Oct 2000 (SI 2000/2543)
71, 72		25 Sep 2000 (so far as relate to Pt II (ss 26–48) of this Act, Intelligence Services Act 1994, s 5, or Police Act 1997, Pt III (ss 91–108)) (SI 2000/2543)
		2 Oct 2000 (so far as relate to Pt I, Chapter I (ss 1–20) of this Act)
		13 Aug 2001 (so far as relate to Pt I, Chapter II (ss 21–25) of this Act)
		Not in force (otherwise)
73		2 Oct 2000 (SI 2000/2543)
74–78		25 Sep 2000 (SI 2000/2543)
79		2 Oct 2000 (SI 2000/2543)
80, 81		25 Sep 2000 (SI 2000/2543)
82	(1)	See Sch 4 below
	(2)	See Sch 5 below
	(3)–(6)	2 Oct 2000 (subject to transitional provisions in arts 5,6 in SI 2000/2543) (SI 2000/2543)
83		28 Jul 2000 (RA)

Schedule

1		25 Sep 2000 (SI 2000/2543)
2		*Not in force*
3		2 Oct 2000 (SI 2000/2543)
4, para	1, 2	Repealed
	3	2 Oct 2000 (subject to transitional provisions in SI 2000/2543, art 5) (SI 2000/2543)
	4	25 Sep 2000 (SI 2000/2543)
	5	2 Oct 2000 (subject to transitional provisions in SI 2000/2543, art 5) (SI 2000/2543)
	6	25 Sep 2000 (SI 2000/2543)
	7	2 Oct 2000 (subject to transitional provisions in SI 2000/2543, art 5) (SI 2000/2543)
	8	25 Sep 2000 (SI 2000/2543)
	9–12	2 Oct 2000 (subject to transitional provisions in SI 2000/2543, art 5) (SI 2000/2543)
5		25 Sep 2000 (so far as relates to Intelligence Services Act 1994, ss 6, 7; Police Act 1997[1]; and Crime and Disorder Act 1998) (SI 2000/2543)
		2 Oct 2000 (otherwise and subject to transitional provisions in SI 2000/2543, art 6) (SI 2000/2543)

Regulation of Investigatory Powers Act 2000 (c 23)—*contd*

1   In the Queen Printer's copy of SI 2000/2543, art 2 purports to bring the entry in Sch 5 of this Act relating to Police Act 1997 into force on 25 September 2000, however art 6 of the 2000 SI purports to bring the entry in Sch 5 of this Act relating to s 102 of, Sch 7 to, the 1997 Act into force on 2 October 2000.

Regulation of Investigatory Powers (Scotland) Act 2000 (asp 11)

RA: 28 Sep 2000

Commencement provisions: s 32(2)

Section	
1–31	*Not in force*
32	28 Sep 2000 (RA)

Representation of the People Act 2000 (c 2)

RA: 9 Mar 2000

Commencement provisions: s 17(3); Representation of the People Act 2000 (Commencement) Order 2001, SI 2001/116[1]

Section		
1–7		29 Jan 2001 (so far as confers power to make regulations) (SI 2001/116)
		16 Feb 2001 (otherwise) (SI 2001/116)
8		See Schs 1–3 below
9		16 Feb 2001 (SI 2001/116)
10, 11		9 Mar 2000 (s 17(3))
12	(1)	See Sch 4 below
	(2), (3)	29 Jan 2001 (so far as confers power to make regulations) (SI 2001/116)
		16 Feb 2001 (otherwise) (SI 2001/116)
13		29 Jan 2001 (so far as confers power to make regulations) (SI 2001/116)
		16 Feb 2001 (otherwise) (SI 2001/116)
14	(1)–(3)	9 Mar 2000 (s 17(3))
	(4)	See Sch 5 below
15	(1)	See Sch 6 below
	(2)	See Sch 7 below
16, 17		9 Mar 2000 (s 17(3))
Schedule		
1–4		29 Jan 2001 (so far as confers power to make regulations) (SI 2001/116)
		16 Feb 2001 (otherwise) (SI 2001/116)
5		9 Mar 2000 (s 17(3))
6, para	1–3	29 Jan 2001 (so far as confers power to make regulations) (SI 2001/116)
		16 Feb 2001 (otherwise) (SI 2001/116)
	4	29 Jan 2001 (so far as confers power to make regulations) (SI 2001/116)
		16 Feb 2001 (otherwise) (SI 2001/116)

Representation of the People Act 2000 (c 2)—*contd*
Schedule

6, para	4—*contd*	Para prospectively repealed by Political Parties, Elections and Referendums Act 2000, s 158(2), Sch 22[2]
	5	29 Jan 2001 (so far as confers power to make regulations) (SI 2001/116) 16 Feb 2001 (otherwise) (SI 2001/116)
	6	9 Mar 2000 (s 17(3))
	7–19	29 Jan 2001 (so far as confers power to make regulations) (SI 2001/116) 16 Feb 2001 (otherwise) (SI 2001/116)
7		29 Jan 2001 (so far as confers power to make regulations) (SI 2001/116) 16 Feb 2001 (otherwise) (SI 2001/116)

[1]   For savings, see SI 2001/116, art 2(3)–(5)

[2]   Orders made under Political Parties, Elections and Referendums Act 2000, s 163(2), bringing the prospective repeal into force will be noted to that Act

---

Royal Parks (Trading) Act 2000 (c 13)

RA: 20 Jul 2000

20 Jul 2000 (RA)

Sea Fishing Grants (Charges) Act 2000 (c 18)

RA: 28 Jul 2000

28 Jul 2000 (RA)

Sexual Offences (Amendment) Act 2000 (c 44)

RA: 30 Nov 2000

Commencement provisions: s 7(3); Sexual Offences (Amendment) Act 2000 (Commencement No 1) Order 2000, SI 2000/3303; Sexual Offences (Amendment) Act 2000 (Commencement No 2) (Scotland) Order 2000, SSI 2000/452.

Section

1	(1), (2)	8 Jan 2001 (SI 2000/3303)
	(3)	8 Jan 2001 (SSI 2000/452)
	(4)	8 Jan 2001 (SI 2000/3303)
	(5)	8 Jan 2001 (E, W, NI) (SI 2000/3303) 8 Jan 2001 (S) (SSI 2000/452)
2	(1)–(3)	8 Jan 2001 (SI 2000/3303)
	(4)	8 Jan 2001 (SSI 2000/452)
	(5)	8 Jan 2001 (SI 2000/3303)
3		8 Jan 2001 (E, W, NI) (SI 2000/3303) 8 Jan 2001 (S) (SSI 2000/452)
4	(1), (2)	8 Jan 2001 (E, W, NI) (SI 2000/3303)

Sexual Offences (Amendment) Act 2000 (c 44)—*contd*

Section

4	(1), (2)—*contd*		8 Jan 2001 (S) (SSI 2000/452)
	(3)	(a), (b)	8 Jan 2001 (SI 2000/3303)
		(c)	8 Jan 2001 (SSI 2000/452)
	(4)	(a), (b)	8 Jan 2001 (E, W, NI) (SI 2000/3303)
		(bb)	Prospectively inserted by Regulation of Care (Scotland) Act 2001, s 79, Sch 3, para 25(1), (2)(b)[1]
		(c)	8 Jan 2001 (E, W, NI) (SI 2000/3303) 8 Jan 2001 (S) (SSI 2000/452)
		(d)	8 Jan 2001 (SI 2000/3303)
	(5)–(8)		8 Jan 2001 (E, W, NI) (SI 2000/3303) 8 Jan 2001 (S) (SSI 2000/452)
	(9)		8 Jan 2001 (E, W, NI) (SI 2000/3303) 8 Jan 2001 (S) (SSI 2000/452)
5	(1)		8 Jan 2001 (E, W, NI) (SI 2000/3303) 8 Jan 2001 (S) (SSI 2000/452)
	(2)		8 Jan 2001 (SI 2000/3303)
	(3)		8 Jan 2001 (SSI 2000/452)
	(4)		8 Jan 2001 (SI 2000/3303)
6	(1)		8 Jan 2001 (SI 2000/3303)
	(2)		8 Jan 2001 (SSI 2000/452)
7			30 Nov 2000 (RA)

[1]   Orders made under Regulation of Care (Scotland) Act 2001, s 81(3), bringing the prospective insertion into force will be noted to that Act

---

Standards in Scotland's Schools etc Act 2000 (asp 6)

RA: 14 Jul 2000

Commencement provisions: s 61(2)–(4); Standards in Scotland's Schools etc Act 2000 (Commencement No 1) Order 2000, SSI 2000/258; Standards in Scotland's Schools etc Act 2000 (Commencement No 2 and Transitional Provisions), SSI 2000/298[1]; Standards in Scotland's Schools etc Act 2000 (Commencement No 3 and Transitional Provisions), SSI 2000/361[2], as amended by SSI 2001/400; Standards in Scotland's Schools etc Act 2000 (Commencement No 4) Order 2001, SSI 2001/102; Standards in Scotland's Schools etc Act 2000 (Commencement No 5) Order 2002, SSI 2002/72

Section

1–8	13 Oct 2000 (SSI 2000/361)
9–10	23 Aug 2000 (SSI 2000/298)
11–14	13 Oct 2000 (SSI 2000/361)
15	*Not in force*
16–21	13 Oct 2000 (SSI 2000/361)
22	28 Jul 2000 (SSI 2000/258)
23	14 Jul 2000 (RA)
24–27	13 Oct 2000 (SSI 2000/361)
28	23 Aug 2000 (SSI 2000/298)
29–31	13 Oct 2000 (SSI 2000/361)
32–37	4 Mar 2002 (SSI 2002/72)

Standards in Scotland's Schools etc Act 2000 (asp 6)—*contd*

Section

38		13 Oct 2000 (SSI 2000/361)
39		1 Apr 2002 (SSI 2002/72)
40–43		13 Oct 2000 (SSI 2000/361)
44	(1)–(3)	13 Oct 2000 (SSI 2000/361)
	(4)	13 Oct 2000 (except words "or (vii)" to "numbers") (SSI 2000/361)
		Not in force (otherwise)
	(5)–(7)	13 Oct 2000 (SSI 2000/361)
45		13 Oct 2000 (SSI 2000/361)
46	(1),(2)	13 Oct 2000 (for the purpose of enabling elections to be held and appointments and nominations to be made [amending Teaching Council (Scotland) Act 1965 and bringing those amendments into force to enable elections to be held] prior to 1 Nov 2001 for the Council to be constituted in accordance with the 1965 Act as amended by s 46(1), (2) on that date) (SSI 2000/361)
		1 Nov 2001 (otherwise) (SSI 2000/361)
	(3)	13 Oct 2000 (SSI 2000/361)
	(4)	1 Nov 2001 (SSI 2000/361)
	(5)	13 Oct 2000 (SSI 2000/361)
	(6), (7)	1 Nov 2001 (SSI 2000/361)
47–48		13 Oct 2000 (SSI 2000/361)
49		13 Oct 2000 (so far as inserts Teaching Council (Scotland) Act 1965, ss 9B(a)(i), (b), 9C) (SSI 2000/361)
		Not in force (otherwise)
50		1 Nov 2001 (so far as inserts Teaching Council (Scotland) Act 1965, ss 10, 10A(1), 10B, 10C, 11(1) (except head (ii) and (iii)), 11(8), 11(9) (except the words "or (2) above"), 11(10), 11(11), 11B) (SSI 2000/361)
		Not in force (otherwise)
51		13 Oct 2000 (so far as inserts Teaching Council (Scotland) Act 1965, s 12(1) (except words from "(a) such person" to "or" in the third place it occurs) (SSI 2000/361)
		Not in force (otherwise)
52		13 Oct 2000 (so far as inserts Teaching Council (Scotland) Act 1965, s 17(1), definition "the register") (SSI 2000/361)
		1 Nov 2001 (otherwise) (SSI 2000/361)
53–54		13 Oct 2000 (SSI 2000/361)

Standards in Scotland's Schools etc Act 2000 (asp 6)—*contd*

Section

55				23 Mar 2001 (SSI 2001/102)
56–59				13 Oct 2000 (SSI 2000/361)
60	(1)			See Sch 2 below
	(2)			See Sch 3 below
61				14 Jul 2000 (RA)

Schedule

1					*Not in force*
2, para	1	(1)			13 Oct 2000 (as far as relates to sub-paras (2), (4), (5)(d)(i) below) (SSI 2000/361)
					1 Nov 2001 (otherwise) (SSI 2000/361)
		(2)			13 Oct 2000 (SSI 2000/361)
		(3)			1 Nov 2001 (SSI 2000/361)
		(4)			13 Oct 2000 (SSI 2000/361)
		(5)	(a)–(c)		1 Nov 2001 (SSI 2000/361)
			(d)	(i)	13 Oct 2000 (SSI 2000/361)
				(ii)	1 Nov 2001 (SSI 2000/361)
		(6)			1 Nov 2001 (SSI 2000/361)
	2				*Not in force*
	3	(1), (2)			13 Oct 2000 (SSI 2000/361)
		(3), (4)			*Not in force*
		(5)–(8)			13 Oct 2000 (SSI 2000/361)
		(9)			*Not in force*
3					14 Jul 2000 (so far as relates to Self-Governing Schools etc (Scotland) Act 1989, ss 13–22, 24, Schs 3, 5) (RA)
					13 Oct 2000 (so far as relates to Teaching Council (Scotland) Act 1965; Education (Scotland) Act 1980, s 1(5)(a); School Boards (Scotland) Act 1988) (SSI 2000/361)
					Not in force (otherwise)

[1]   For transitional provisions, see SSI 2000/298, art 4.

[2]   For transitional provisions, see SSI 2000/361, art 4.

Television Licences (Disclosure of Information) Act 2000 (c 15)

RA: 20 Jul 2000

20 Jul 2000 (RA)

Terrorism Act 2000 (c 11)

RA: 20 Jul 2000

Commencement provisions: s 128; Terrorism Act 2000 (Commencement No 1) Order 2000, SI 2000/2800; Terrorism Act 2000 (Commencement No 2) Order 2000, SI 2000/2944; Terrorism Act 2000 (Commencement No 3) Order 2000, SI 2000/421

Terrorism Act 2000 (c 11)—*contd*

Terrorism Act 2000 (c 11)—*contd*

Schedule

4	1–12		19 Feb 2001 (SI 2001/421)
	13	(1)	19 Feb 2001 (SI 2001/421)
		(2) (a)	19 Feb 2001 (SI 2001/421)
		(b)	31 Oct 2000 (SI 2000/2944)
		(3), (4)	31 Oct 2000 (SI 2000/2944)
		(5)–(9)	19 Feb 2001 (SI 2001/421)
	14–26		19 Feb 2001 (SI 2001/421)
	27	(1)	19 Feb 2001 (SI 2001/421)
		(2) (a)	19 Feb 2001 (SI 2001/421)
		(b)	31 Oct 2000 (SI 2000/2944)
		(3), (4)	31 Oct 2000 (SI 2000/2944)
		(5)–(10)	19 Feb 2001 (SI 2001/421)
	28–42		19 Feb 2001 (SI 2001/421)
	43	(1)	19 Feb 2001 (SI 2001/421)
		(2) (a)	19 Feb 2001 (SI 2001/421)
		(b)	31 Oct 2000 (SI 2000/2944)
		(3), (4)	31 Oct 2000 (SI 2000/2944)
		(5)–(9)	19 Feb 2001 (SI 2001/421)
	44–51		19 Feb 2001 (SI 2001/421)
	52		31 Oct 2000 (SI 2000/2944)
	53		19 Feb 2001 (SI 2001/421)
5	1–9		19 Feb 2001 (SI 2001/421)
	10	(1)	19 Feb 2001 (SI 2001/421)
		(2), (3)	31 Oct 2000 (SI 2000/2944)
	11–33		19 Feb 2001 (SI 2001/421)
6	1–3		19 Feb 2001 (SI 2001/421)
	4		31 Oct 2000 (SI 2000/2944)
	5		19 Feb 2001 (SI 2001/421)
	6	(1)	19 Feb 2001 (SI 2001/421)
		(1A), (1B)	Inserted (1 Dec 2001) by Financial Services and Markets Act 2000 (Consequential Amendments and Repeals) Order 2001, SI 2001/3649, art 361
		(2)	31 Oct 2000 (SI 2000/2944)
		(3)	19 Feb 2001 (SI 2001/421)
	7	(1), (2)	19 Feb 2001 (SI 2001/421)
		(3)	31 Oct 2000 (SI 2000/2944)
6A			Inserted by Anti-terrorism, Crime and Security Act 2001, s 3, Sch 2, Pt 1, para 1(1), (3) (qv)
7	1–5		19 Feb 2001 (SI 2001/421)
	6	(1), (2)	19 Feb 2001 (SI 2001/421)
		(3)	See Sch 8 below
		(4)	19 Feb 2001 (SI 2001/421)
	7–15		19 Feb 2001 (SI 2001/421)
	16	(1), (2)	31 Oct 2000 (SI 2000/2944)
		(3)	19 Feb 2001 (SI 2001/421)

Terrorism Act 2000 (c 11)—*contd*

Schedule

7	17	(1)	Substituted by Anti-terrorism, Crime and Security Act 2001, s 119(1), (2) (qv)
		(2), (3)	19 Feb 2001 (SI 2001/421)
		(4)	31 Oct 2000 (SI 2000/2944)
		(5), (6)	19 Feb 2001 (SI 2001/421)
	18		19 Feb 2001 (SI 2001/421)
8, para	1	(1)	31 Oct 2000 (SI 2000/2944)
		(2)–(6)	19 Feb 2001 (SI 2001/421)
	2		19 Feb 2001 (SI 2001/421)
	3		12 Oct 2000 (SI 2000/2800)
	4	(1)–(5)	12 Oct 2000 (SI 2000/2800)
		(6), (7)	19 Feb 2001 (SI 2001/421)
	5–18		19 Feb 2001 (SI 2001/421)
	19		31 Oct 2000 (SI 2000/2944)
	20–37		19 Feb 2001 (SI 2001/421)
9–13			19 Feb 2001 (SI 2001/421)
14, para	1		12 Oct 2000 (SI 2000/2800)
	2–5		19 Feb 2001 (SI 2001/421)
	6	(1)	12 Oct 2000 (SI 2000/2800)
		(2), (3)	19 Feb 2001 (SI 2001/421)
		(4)	12 Oct 2000 (SI 2000/2800)
	7		12 Oct 2000 (SI 2000/2800)
15, 16			19 Feb 2001 (SI 2001/421)

Transport Act 2000 (c 38)

RA: 30 Nov 2000

Commencement provisions: s 275; Transport Act 2000 (Commencement No 1 and Transitional Provisions) Order 2000, SI 2000/3229[1] ; Transport Act 2000 (Commencement No 2) Order 2000, SI 2000/3376; Transport Act 2000 (Commencement No 3) Order 2001, SI 2001/57, as amended by SI 2001/115[2]; Transport Act 2000 (Commencement No 4) Order 2001, SI 2001/242; Transport Act 2000 (Commencement No 5) Order 2001, SI 2001/869; Transport Act 2000 (Commencement No 6) Order 2001, SI 2001/1498; Transport Act 2000 (Commencement No 1) (Wales) Order 2001, SI 2001/2788; Transport Act 2000 (Commencement No 7) Order 2001, SI 2001/3342; Transport Act 2000 (Commencement No 8) Order 2002, SI 2002/658[6]

Section

1, 2		1 Feb 2001 (SI 2001/57)
3		1 May 2001 (SI 2001/1498)
4–29		1 Feb 2001 (SI 2001/57)
30	(1)–(3)	1 Feb 2001 (SI 2001/57)
	(4)	See Schs 1, 2 below
	(5)–(7)	1 Feb 2001 (SI 2001/57)
31, 32		1 Feb 2001 (SI 2001/57)
33		See Sch 3 below
34, 35		1 Feb 2001 (SI 2001/57)

Transport Act 2000 (c 38)—*contd*

Section

36, 37		1 Apr 2001 (SI 2001/869)
38–62		1 Feb 2001 (SI 2001/57)
63		See Sch 6 below
64		See Sch 7 below
65–96		1 Feb 2001 (SI 2001/57)
97		See Sch 8 below
98–101		1 Feb 2001 (SI 2001/57)
102		See Sch 9 below
103–107		1 Feb 2001 (SI 2001/57)
108–113		1 Feb 2001 (E) (SI 2001/57)
		1 Aug 2001 (W) (SI 2001/2788)
114–118		1 Aug 2001 (W) (SI 2001/2788)
		26 Oct 2001 (E) (SI 2001/3342)
119		1 Feb 2001 (E) (SI 2001/57)
		1 Aug 2001 (W) (SI 2001/2788)
120–123		1 Aug 2001 (W) (SI 2001/2788)
		26 Oct 2001 (E) (SI 2001/3342)
124–127		1 Aug 2001 (W) (in relation to powers to make regulations under specified provisions[3]) (SI 2001/2788)
		26 Oct 2001 (E) (SI 2001/3342)
		Not in force (otherwise)
128	(1)–(3)	1 Aug 2001 (W) (in relation to powers to make regulations under specified provisions[3]) (SI 2001/2788)
		26 Oct 2001 (E) (SI 2001/3342)
		Not in force (otherwise)
	(4)	1 Aug 2001 (W) (SI 2001/2788)
		26 Oct 2001 (E) (SI 2001/3342)
	(5)	1 Aug 2001 (W) (in relation to powers to make regulations under specified provisions[3]) (SI 2001/2788)
		26 Oct 2001 (E) (SI 2001/3342)
		Not in force (otherwise)
129		1 Aug 2001 (W) (in relation to powers to make regulations under specified provisions[3]) (SI 2001/2788)
		26 Oct 2001 (E) (SI 2001/3342)
		Not in force (otherwise)
130	(1)–(7)	1 Aug 2001 (W) (in relation to powers to make regulations under specified provisions[3]) (SI 2001/2788)
		26 Oct 2001 (E) (SI 2001/3342)
		Not in force (otherwise)

Transport Act 2000 (c 38)—*contd*

Section

130	(8)	1 Aug 2001 (W) (SI 2001/2788)
		26 Oct 2001 (E) (SI 2001/3342)
131	(1)	1 Aug 2001 (W) (in relation to powers to make regulations under specified provisions[3]) (SI 2001/2788)
		26 Oct 2001 (E) (SI 2001/3342)
		Not in force (otherwise)
	(2)–(4)	1 Aug 2001 (W) (SI 2001/2788)
		26 Oct 2001 (E) (SI 2001/3342)
	(5)	1 Aug 2001 (W) (in relation to powers to make regulations under specified provisions[3]) (SI 2001/2788)
		26 Oct 2001 (E) (SI 2001/3342)
		Not in force (otherwise)
132	(1)–(5)	1 Aug 2001 (W) (in relation to powers to make regulations under specified provisions[3]) (SI 2001/2788)
		26 Oct 2001 (E) (SI 2001/3342)
		Not in force (otherwise)
	(6)	1 Aug 2001 (W) (SI 2001/2788)
		26 Oct 2001 (E) (SI 2001/3342)
133, 134		1 Aug 2001 (W) (SI 2001/2788)
		26 Oct 2001 (E) (SI 2001/3342)
135–143		1 Feb 2001 (E) (SI 2001/57)
		1 Aug 2001 (W) (SI 2001/2788)
144		1 Feb 2001 (E) (except for purpose of enabling regulations to be made as respects civil penalties for bus lane contraventions in relation to roads in Greater London) (SI 2001/57)
		1 Aug 2001 (W) (SI 2001/2788)
		1 Apr 2002 (E) (exception noted above) (SI 2002/658)
145	(1)–(3)	1 Jan 2001 (E) (for purposes of s 150) (SI 2000/3229)
		1 Feb 2001 (E) (for purposes of s 145(4), (5), (7), (8)) (SI 2000/3229)
		1 Jun 2001 (E) (remaining purposes) (SI 2000/3229)
		1 Apr 2002 (W) (SI 2001/2788)
	(4), (5)	1 Feb 2001 (E) (SI 2000/3229)
		1 Aug 2001 (W) (SI 2001/2788)
	(6)	1 Feb 2001 (E) (for purposes of s 145(4), (5), (7), (8)) (SI 2000/3229)
		1 Jun 2001 (E) (remaining purposes) (SI 2000/3229)
		1 Aug 2001 (W) (SI 2001/2788)

Transport Act 2000 (c 38)—*contd*

Section

145	(7), (8)	1 Feb 2001 (E) (SI 2000/3229)
		1 Aug 2001 (W) (SI 2001/2788)
146		1 Jan 2001 (E) (definition "travel concession authority", and the remainder thereof for the purposes of s 150) (SI 2000/3229)
		1 Feb 2001 (E) (definition of "disabled person") (SI 2000/3229)
		1 Jun 2001 (E) (remaining purposes) (SI 2000/3229)
		1 Aug 2001 (W) (SI 2001/2788)
147, 148		1 Jun 2001 (E) (SI 2000/3229)
		1 Aug 2001 (W) (SI 2001/2788)
149	(1), (2)	1 Jan 2001 (E) (for purposes of s 150) (SI 2000/3229)
		1 Jun 2001 (E) (remaining purposes) (SI 2000/3229)
		1 Aug 2001 (W) (SI 2001/2788)
	(3)	1 Jan 2001 (E) (SI 2000/3229)
		1 Aug 2001 (W) (SI 2001/2788)
150		1 Jan 2001 (E) (SI 2000/3229)
		1 Aug 2001 (W) (SI 2001/2788)
151		1 Apr 2001 (SI 2000/3229)
152		1 Feb 2001 (E) (SI 2001/57)
		1 Aug 2001 (W) (SI 2001/2788)
153		See Sch 10 below
154	(1)–(5)	1 Feb 2001 (E) (SI 2000/57)
		1 Aug 2001 (W) (SI 2001/2788)
	(6)	*Not in force*
155		1 Aug 2001 (W) (SI 2001/2788)
		Not in force (otherwise)
156–160		1 Feb 2001 (E) (SI 2001/57)
		1 Aug 2001 (W) (SI 2001/2788)
161		See Sch 11 below
162	(1)	1 Jan 2001 (E) (definition "travel concession authority") (SI 2000/3229)
		1 Feb 2001 (E) (definition "disabled person") (SI 2000/3229)
		1 Jun 2001 (E) (definitions "elderly person", "eligible service", "half-price travel concession", "relevant time") (SI 2000/3229)
		1 Feb 2001 (E) (otherwise) (SI 2001/57)
		1 Aug 2001 (W) (SI 2001/2788)
	(2)	1 Jun 2001 (E) (so far as relates to meaning of "fares") (SI 2000/3229)

Transport Act 2000 (c 38)—*contd*
Section

162	(2)—*contd*		1 Feb 2001 (E) (otherwise) (SI 2001/57)
			1 Aug 2001 (W) (SI 2001/2788)
	(3)		1 Jan 2001 (E) (so far as relates to meaning of "local service") (SI 2000/3229)
			1 Jun 2001 (E) (so far as relates to meaning of "public passenger transport services") (SI 2000/3229)
			1 Feb 2001 (E) (otherwise) (SI 2001/57)
			1 Aug 2001 (W) (SI 2001/2788)
	(4)		1 Feb 2001 (E) (SI 2001/57)
			1 Aug 2001 (W) (SI 2001/2788)
	(5)		1 Jan 2001 (E) (SI 2000/3229)
			1 Aug 2001 (W) (SI 2001/2788)
	(6), (7)		1 Feb 2001 (E) (SI 2001/57)
			1 Aug 2001 (W) (SI 2001/2788)
163	(1)		1 Feb 2001 (E) (SI 2001/57)
			1 Aug 2001 (W) (in relation to powers to make regulations under specified provisions[4]) (SI 2001/2788)
			Not in force (otherwise)
	(2)	(a)	1 Feb 2001 (E) (SI 2001/57)
			1 Aug 2001 (W) (in relation to powers to make regulations under specified provisions[4]) (SI 2001/2788)
			Not in force (otherwise)
		(b)	1 Feb 2001 (E) (SI 2001/57)
			1 Aug 2001 (W) (SI 2001/2788)
	(3)–(6)		1 Feb 2001 (E) (SI 2001/57)
			1 Aug 2001 (W) (in relation to powers to make regulations under specified provisions[4]) (SI 2001/2788)
			Not in force (otherwise)
164, 165			1 Feb 2001 (E) (SI 2001/57)
			1 Aug 2001 (W) (in relation to powers to make regulations under specified provisions[4]) (SI 2001/2788)
			Not in force (otherwise)
166			1 Feb 2001 (E) (SI 2001/57)
			Not in force (otherwise)
167			1 Feb 2001 (E) (SI 2001/57)
			1 Aug 2001 (W) (in relation to powers to make regulations under specified provisions[4]) (SI 2001/2788)
			Not in force (otherwise)

Transport Act 2000 (c 38)—*contd*
Section

168	(1), (2)	1 Feb 2001 (E) (SI 2001/57)
		1 Aug 2001 (W) (in relation to powers to make regulations under specified provisions[4]) (SI 2001/2788)
		Not in force (otherwise)
	(3)	1 Feb 2001 (E) (SI 2001/57)
		1 Aug 2001 (W) (SI 2001/2788)
	(4)	1 Feb 2001 (E) (SI 2001/57)
		1 Aug 2001 (W) (in relation to powers to make regulations under specified provisions[4]) (SI 2001/2788)
		Not in force (otherwise)
169–171		1 Feb 2001 (E) (SI 2001/57)
		1 Aug 2001 (W) (in relation to powers to make regulations under specified provisions[4]) (SI 2001/2788)
		Not in force (otherwise)
172	(1)	1 Feb 2001 (E) (SI 2001/57)
		1 Aug 2001 (W) (SI 2001/2788)
	(2)–(4)	1 Feb 2001 (E) (SI 2001/57)
		1 Aug 2001 (W) (in relation to powers to make regulations under specified provisions[4]) (SI 2001/2788)
		Not in force (otherwise)
173	(1)–(4)	1 Feb 2001 (E) (SI 2001/57)
		1 Aug 2001 (W) (SI 2001/2788)
	(5)–(9)	1 Feb 2001 (E) (SI 2001/57)
		1 Aug 2001 (W) (in relation to powers to make regulations under specified provisions[4]) (SI 2001/2788)
		Not in force (otherwise)
174	(1), (2)	1 Feb 2001 (E) (SI 2001/57)
		1 Aug 2001 (W) (SI 2001/2788)
	(3), (4)	1 Feb 2001 (E) (SI 2001/57)
		1 Aug 2001 (W) (in relation to powers to make regulations under specified provisions[4]) (SI 2001/2788)
		Not in force (otherwise)
	(5)	1 Feb 2001 (E) (SI 2001/57)
		1 Aug 2001 (W) (SI 2001/2788)
	(6)	1 Feb 2001 (E) (SI 2001/57)
		1 Aug 2001 (W) (in relation to powers to make regulations under specified provisions[4]) (SI 2001/2788)
		Not in force (otherwise)
175	(1)	1 Feb 2001 (E) (SI 2001/57)
		1 Aug 2001 (W) (SI 2001/2788)

Transport Act 2000 (c 38)—*contd*
Section

175	(2)–(8)		1 Feb 2001 (E) (SI 2001/57)
			1 Aug 2001 (W) (in relation to powers to make regulations under specified provisions[4]) (SI 2001/2788)
			Not in force (otherwise)
176	(1)		1 Feb 2001 (E) (SI 2001/57)
			1 Aug 2001 (W) (in relation to powers to make regulations under specified provisions[4]) (SI 2001/2788)
			Not in force (otherwise)
	(2)		1 Feb 2001 (E) (SI 2001/57)
			1 Aug 2001 (W) (SI 2001/2788)
	(3)		1 Feb 2001 (E) (SI 2001/57)
			1 Aug 2001 (W) (in relation to powers to make regulations under specified provisions[4]) (SI 2001/2788)
			Not in force (otherwise)
177			1 Feb 2001 (E) (SI 2001/57)
			1 Aug 2001 (W) (in relation to powers to make regulations under specified provisions[4]) (SI 2001/2788)
			Not in force (otherwise)
178	(1)		1 Feb 2001 (E) (SI 2001/57)
			1 Aug 2001 (W) (in relation to powers to make regulations under specified provisions[5]) (SI 2001/2788)
			Not in force (otherwise)
	(2)	(a)	1 Feb 2001 (E) (SI 2001/57)
			1 Aug 2001 (W) (in relation to powers to make regulations under specified provisions[5]) (SI 2001/2788)
			Not in force (otherwise)
		(b)	1 Feb 2001 (E) (SI 2001/57)
			1 Aug 2001 (W) (SI 2001/2788)
	(3)–(7)		1 Feb 2001 (E) (SI 2001/57)
			1 Aug 2001 (W) (in relation to powers to make regulations under specified provisions[5]) (SI 2001/2788)
			Not in force (otherwise)
179, 180			1 Feb 2001 (E) (SI 2001/57)
			1 Aug 2001 (W) (in relation to powers to make regulations under specified provisions[5]) (SI 2001/2788)
			Not in force (otherwise)
181			1 Feb 2001 (E) (SI 2001/57)
			Not in force (otherwise)

Transport Act 2000 (c 38)—*contd*
Section

182	(1)–(4)		1 Feb 2001 (E) (SI 2001/57)
			1 Aug 2001 (W) (in relation to powers to make regulations under specified provisions[5]) (SI 2001/2788)
			Not in force (otherwise)
	(5)		1 Feb 2001 (E) (SI 2001/57)
			1 Aug 2001 (W) (SI 2001/2788)
183	(1), (2)		1 Feb 2001 (E) (SI 2001/57)
			1 Aug 2001 (W) (in relation to powers to make regulations under specified provisions[5]) (SI 2001/2788)
			Not in force (otherwise)
	(3)		1 Feb 2001 (E) (SI 2001/57)
			1 Aug 2001 (W) (SI 2001/2788)
	(4)		1 Feb 2001 (E) (SI 2001/57)
			1 Aug 2001 (W) (in relation to powers to make regulations under specified provisions[5]) (SI 2001/2788)
			Not in force (otherwise)
184–186			1 Feb 2001 (E) (SI 2001/57)
			1 Aug 2001 (W) (in relation to powers to make regulations under specified provisions[5]) (SI 2001/2788)
			Not in force (otherwise)
187	(1)		1 Feb 2001 (E) (SI 2001/57)
			1 Aug 2001 (W) (SI 2001/2788)
	(2)–(4)		1 Feb 2001 (E) (SI 2001/57)
			1 Aug 2001 (W) (in relation to powers to make regulations under specified provisions[5]) (SI 2001/2788)
			Not in force (otherwise)
188			1 Feb 2001 (E) (SI 2001/57)
			1 Aug 2001 (W) (in relation to powers to make regulations under specified provisions[5]) (SI 2001/2788)
			Not in force (otherwise)
189	(1), (2)		1 Feb 2001 (E) (SI 2001/57)
			1 Aug 2001 (W) (SI 2001/2788)
	(3)	(a)	1 Feb 2001 (E) (SI 2001/57)
			1 Aug 2001 (W) (in relation to powers to make regulations under specified provisions[5]) (SI 2001/2788)
			Not in force (otherwise)
		(b)	1 Feb 2001 (E) (SI 2001/57)
			1 Aug 2001 (W) (SI 2001/2788)
	(4)		1 Feb 2001 (E) (SI 2001/57)
			1 Aug 2001 (W) (SI 2001/2788)

Transport Act 2000 (c 38)—*contd*

Transport Act 2000 (c 38)—*contd*

Section

248		Not in force
249		1 Feb 2001 (SI 2001/57)
250		See Sch 26 below
251		1 Feb 2001 (SI 2001/57)
252		See Sch 27 below
253		See Sch 28 below
254		30 Jan 2001 (SI 2001/57)
255, 256		1 Feb 2001 (SI 2001/57)
257		Not in force
258, 259		1 Apr 2002 (SI 2002/658)
260		See Sch 29 below
261		1 Feb 2001 (SI 2001/57)
262	(1)	1 Feb 2001 (SI 2001/57)
	(2)	See Sch 30 below
263		Not in force
264		1 Feb 2001 (SI 2001/57)
265		1 Jul 2001 (SI 2001/1498)
266		1 Feb 2001 (SI 2001/57)
267	(1)	See sub-ss (2)–(8) below
	(2)	1 Apr 2002 (SI 2002/658)
	(3)	1 Feb 2001 (E) (for the purposes of making regulations with regard to appeals under Greater London Authority Act 1999, s 189 made after the date on s 267 is fully in force) (SI 2001/57)
		1 Apr 2002 (otherwise) (SI 2002/658)
	(4)	1 Apr 2002 (SI 2002/658)
	(5)	1 Feb 2001 (E) (for the purposes of making regulations with regard to appeals under Greater London Authority Act 1999, s 189 made after the date on s 267 is fully in force) (SI 2001/57)
		1 Apr 2002 (otherwise) (SI 2002/658)
	(6), (7)	1 Apr 2002 (SI 2002/658)
	(8)	1 Feb 2001 (E) (for the purposes of making regulations with regard to appeals under Greater London Authority Act 1999, s 189 made after the date on s 267 is fully in force) (SI 2001/57)
		1 Apr 2002 (otherwise) (SI 2002/658)
268		1 Feb 2001 (SI 2001/57)
269		30 Nov 2000 (s 275(4))
270		30 Jan 2001 (SI 2001/57)
271–273		1 Feb 2001 (SI 2001/57)
274		See Sch 31 below
275–280		30 Nov 2000 (RA)

Transport Act 2000 (c 38)—*contd*

Schedule

1–3				1 Feb 2001 (SI 2001/57)
4, 5				1 Apr 2001 (SI 2001/869)
6, 7				1 Feb 2001 (SI 2000/57)
8, para	1, 2			1 Feb 2001 (SI 2001/57)
	3–10			1 Apr 2001 (SI 2001/869)
	11–17			1 Feb 2001 (SI 2001/57)
	18			1 Apr 2001 (SI 2001/869)
	19			1 Feb 2001 (SI 2001/57)
9				1 Feb 2001 (SI 2001/57)
10, para	1	(1)	(a)	26 Oct 2001 (E) (SI 2001/3342)
				Not in force (otherwise)
			(b), (c)	1 Feb 2001 (E) (SI 2001/57)
				1 Aug 2001 (W) (SI 2001/2788)
		(2)	(a)	26 Oct 2001 (E) (SI 2001/3342)
				Not in force (otherwise)
			(b), (c)	1 Feb 2001 (E) (SI 2001/57)
				1 Aug 2001 (W) (SI 2001/2788)
	2–11			1 Feb 2001 (E) (SI 2001/57)
				1 Aug 2001 (W) (SI 2001/2788)
	12	(1)		1 Feb 2001 (E) (SI 2001/57)
				1 Aug 2001 (W) (SI 2001/2788)
		(2)		1 Feb 2001 (E) (except words "a quality partnership scheme or") (SI 2001/57)
				1 Aug 2001 (W) (except words "a quality partnership scheme or") (SI 2001/2788)
				26 Oct 2001 (E) (exception noted above) (SI 2001/3342)
				Not in force (otherwise)
		(3)–(5)		1 Feb 2001 (E) (SI 2001/57)
				1 Aug 2001 (W) (SI 2001/2788)
	13–16			1 Feb 2001 (E) (SI 2001/57)
				1 Aug 2001 (W) (SI 2001/2788)
11, para	1			1 Aug 2001 (W) (SI 2001/2788)
				26 Oct 2001 (E) (SI 2001/3342)
				Para prospectively repealed by Transport Act 2000, s 274, Sch 31, Pt II
	2–5			1 Feb 2001 (E) (SI 2001/57)
				1 Aug 2001 (W) (SI 2001/2788)
	6–8			1 Aug 2001 (W) (SI 2001/2788)
				26 Oct 2001 (E) (SI 2001/3342)
	9			1 Feb 2001 (E) (SI 2001/57)
				1 Aug 2001 (W) (SI 2001/2788)
	10	(1)		1 Feb 2001 (E) (SI 2001/57)
				1 Aug 2001 (W) (SI 2001/2788)
		(2)		1 Aug 2001 (W) (SI 2001/2788)
				26 Oct 2001 (E) (SI 2001/3342)

Transport Act 2000 (c 38)—*contd*

Schedule

11, para	10	(3)	1 Feb 2001 (E) (SI 2001/57)
			1 Aug 2001 (W) (SI 2001/2788)
	11–13		1 Feb 2001 (E) (SI 2001/57)
			1 Aug 2001 (W) (SI 2001/2788)
	14		1 Aug 2001 (W) (SI 2001/2788)
			26 Oct 2001 (E) (SI 2001/3342)
	15–19		1 Jun 2001 (E) (SI 2000/3229)
			1 Apr 2002 (W) (SI 2001/2788)
	20		1 Apr 2002 (W) (SI 2001/2788)
			Not in force (otherwise)
	21		1 Aug 2001 (W) (SI 2001/2788)
			26 Oct 2001 (E) (SI 2001/3342)
	22	(1)	1 Feb 2001 (E) (except entry relating to Transport Act 1985, s 111(1)(b)) (SI 2001/57)
			1 Aug 2001 (W) (SI 2001/2788)
			26 Oct 2001 (E) (exception noted above) (SI 2001/3342)
			Sub-para prospectively repealed by Transport Act 2000, s 274, Sch 31, Pt II
		(2)	1 Feb 2001 (E) (except entry relating to Transport Act 1985, s 111(1)(b)) (SI 2001/57)
			20 Feb 2001 (E) (so far as relates to words "operated a local service in contravention of that section" in Transport Act 1985, s 111(1)(b)) (SI 2001/242)
			26 Oct 2001 (E) (so far as relates to words "or section 118(4) or 129(1)(b) of the Transport Act 2000; or" in Transport Act 1985, s 111(1)(b)) (SI 2001/3342)
			1 Aug 2001 (W) (SI 2001/2788)
			Prospectively repealed by Transport Act 2000, s 274, Sch 31, Pt II
	23		1 Apr 2001 (SI 2000/3229)
12, 13			1 Feb 2001 (E) (2001/57)
			Not in force (otherwise)
14			15 Jan 2001 (SI 2000/3376)
15			30 Jan 2001 (SI 2001/57)
16			1 Feb 2001 (SI 2001/57)
17, Pt	I, II		1 Feb 2001 (SI 2001/57)
	III		30 Jan 2001 (SI 2001/57)
18			1 Feb 2001 (SI 2001/57)
19			30 Jan 2001 (SI 2001/57)
20–23			1 Feb 2001 (SI 2001/57)
24			30 Nov 2000 (s 275(4))

Transport Act 2000 (c 38)—*contd*

Schedule

25		1 Feb 2001 (SI 2001/57)
26		15 Jan 2001 (SI 2000/3376)
27, para	1–15	1 Feb 2001 (SI 2001/57)
	16	*Not in force*
	17–49	1 Feb 2001 (SI 2001/57)
	50	15 Jan 2001 (SI 2000/3376)
	51–63	1 Feb 2001 (SI 2001/57)
28		30 Nov 2000 (s 275(4))
29	1–6	*Not in force*
	1–10	1 Apr 2002 (SI 2002/658)
	11	1 Apr 2002 (SI 2002/658)
	12	1 Apr 2002 (SI 2002/658)
30		1 Feb 2001 (SI 2001/57)
31, Pt	I	1 Apr 2001 (SI 2001/869)
	II	1 Apr 2001 (entries relating to Greater London Authority Act 1999) (SI 2000/3229)
		1 Jun 2001 (E) (entries relating to SI 1986/1385, SI 1989/2293) (SI 2000/3229)
		1 Feb 2001 (E) (so far as relates to repeals of or in Transport Act 1968; Transport Act 1983; Local Government Act 1985; Transport Act 1985 (except entries relating to ss 94(4), 104(2), 108(1), 110, 111, 112(2) of that Act)) (SI 2001/57)
		26 Oct 2001 (E) (so far as relates to repeal in Transport Act 1985, s 104(2)) (SI 2001/3342)
		Not in force (otherwise)
	III	1 Feb 2001 (E) (SI 2001/57)
	IV	15 Jan 2001 (so far as relates to repeals of or in Railways Act 1993, ss 7(10), 113) (SI 2000/3376)
		1 Feb 2001 (so far as relates to repeals of or in British Transport Commission Act 1949; Transport Act 1962, s 1(3); British Transport Commission Act 1962; Harbours Act 1964; Docks and Harbours Act 1966; Parliamentary Commissioner Act 1967; Transport (Grants) Act 1972; House of Commons Disqualification Act 1975 (except entry in Sch 1, Pt II, relating to British Railways Board);

Transport Act 2000 (c 38)—*contd*
Schedule

31, Pt	IV—*contd*	Channel Tunnel Act 1987, ss 40, 42; Transport and Works Act 1992; Railways Act 1993 (except entries relating to ss 7(10), 84–116, 129, Schs 7–9, Sch 12, paras 5, 6(2)–(5), 32; Railway Pensions (Protection and Designation of Schemes) Order 1994, SI 1994/1432; Competition Act 1998; Greater London Authority Act 1999; Parliamentary Commissioner Order 1999, SI 1999/277; and Scotland Act 1998 (Transfer of Functions to the Scottish Ministers etc) Order 1999, SI 1999/1750) (SI 2001/57) *Not in force* (otherwise)
	V	1 Apr 2002 (so far as relates to repeals of or in Road Traffic Act 1988, s 131(5), Sch 3; Road Traffic (Driving Licensing and Information Systems) Act 1989) (SI 2002/658) *Not in force* (otherwise)

[1]   For transitional provisions, see SI 2000/3229, arts 3, 4.

[2]   For transitional provisions and savings, see SI 2001/57, Sch 2, Pt II, Sch 3, Pt II.

[3]   The specified provisions are ss 128(4), 130(8), 131(2)–(4), 132(6), 133 and 134 of this Act.

[4]   The specified provisions are ss 163(2)(b), 168(3), 172(1), 173(1)–(4), 174(1), (2), (5), 175(1), and 176(2) of this Act.

[5]   The specified provisions are ss 178(2)(b), 182(5), 183(3), 187(1), 189(1), (2), (3)(b), and (4) of this Act.

[6]   For transitional provisions, see SI 2002/658, art 3.

Trustee Act 2000 (c 29)

RA: 23 Nov 2000

Commencement provisions: s 42(1)–(3); Trustee Act 2000 (Commencement) Order 2001, SI 2001/49.

Section

1–40	1 Feb 2001 (SI 2001/49)
41–43	23 Nov 2000 (RA)
Schedule	
1–4	1 Feb 2001 (SI 2001/49)

Utilities Act 2000 (c 27)

RA: 28 Jul 2000

Commencement provisions: s 110(2); Utilities Act 2000 (Commencement No 1 and Saving) Order 2000, SI 2000/2412; Utilities Act 2000 (Commencement No 2) Order 2000, SI 2000/2917; Utilities Act 2000 (Commencement No 3 and Transitional Provisions) Order 2000, SI 2000/2974[1]; Utilities Act 2000 (Commencement No 4 and Transitional Provisions) Order 2000, SI 2000/3343[2], as amended by SI 2001/1780; Utilities Act 2000 (Commencement No 5 and Transitional Provisions) Order 2001, SI 2001/1781[3]; Utilities Act 2000 (Commencement No 6 and Transitional Provisions) Order 2001, SI 2001/3266[4]

Section			
1	(1), (2)		1 Nov 2000 (SI 2000/2917)
	(3)		1 Oct 2001 (SI 2001/3266)
	(4)		1 Nov 2000 (SI 2000/2917)
2	(1), (2)		1 Nov 2000 (SI 2000/2917)
	(3)		7 Nov 2000 (SI 2000/2974)
	(4)		1 Nov 2000 (SI 2000/2917)
3	(1), (2)		20 Dec 2000 (SI 2000/3343)
	(3)–(5)		1 Nov 2000 (SI 2000/2917)
	(6), (7)		7 Nov 2000 (SI 2000/2974)
	(8)		1 Nov 2000 (SI 2000/2917)
4			7 Nov 2000 (for purpose of requiring the Gas Consumers' Council to prepare and publish its forward work programme) (SI 2000/2974) 20 Dec 2000 (otherwise) (SI 2000/3343)
5	(1)–(9)		20 Dec 2000 (SI 2000/3343)
	(10)		20 Dec 2000 (subject to saving in respect of Sch 7, para 29) (SI 2000/3343) 1 Oct 2001 (otherwise) (SI 2001/3266)
6–16			20 Dec 2000 (SI 2000/3343)
17			7 Nov 2000 (SI 2000/2974)
18	(1)–(4)		7 Nov 2000 (SI 2000/2974)
	(5), (6)		20 Dec 2000 (SI 2000/3343)
	(7)		7 Nov 2000 (SI 2000/2974)
19	(1)–(3)		7 Nov 2000 (SI 2000/2974)
	(4)	(a)	7 Nov 2000 (SI 2000/2974)[1]
		(b)	20 Dec 2000 (SI 2000/3343)
	(5), (6)		7 Nov 2000 (SI 2000/2974)[1]
20	(1)–(4)		7 Nov 2000 (SI 2000/2974)
	(5), (6)		7 Nov 2000 (for purpose of requiring the Gas Consumers' Council to publish statistical information in relation to complaints made by consumers) (SI 2000/2974)[1] 1 Oct 2001 (otherwise) (SI 2001/3266)
	(7)		*Not in force*

Utilities Act 2000 (c 27)—*contd*

Section

21	(1)–(3)		7 Nov 2000 (SI 2000/2974)
	(4)	(a)	7 Nov 2000 (SI 2000/2974)[1]
		(b)	20 Dec 2000 (SI 2000/3343)
	(5)		7 Nov 2000 (SI 2000/2974)[1]
22, 23			7 Nov 2000 (SI 2000/2974)[1]
24	(1)–(3)		7 Nov 2000 (for purpose of enabling the Council to direct gas or electricity licence holder to supply information to it) (SI 2000/2974)
			20 Dec 2000 (otherwise) (SI 2000/3343)
	(4)		20 Dec 2000 (SI 2000/3343)
25, 26			20 Dec 2000 (SI 2000/3343)
27	(1)		29 Sep 2000 (so far as relates to the power to make regulations) (SI 2000/2412)
			7 Nov 2000 (so far as not already in force) (SI 2000/2974)
	(2)		29 Sep 2000 (so far as relates to the power to make regulations) (SI 2000/2412)
			20 Dec 2000 (otherwise) (SI 2000/3343)
	(3)–(7)		29 Sep 2000 (so far as relates to the power to make regulations) (SI 2000/2412)
			7 Nov 2000 (so far as not already in force) (SI 2000/2974)
28	(1), (2)		1 Oct 2001 (SI 2001/3266)
	(3)	(a)	7 Nov 2000 (for purpose of defining "distribution system" wherever it occurs in Pt III (ss 7–27) of this Act) (SI 2000/2974)
			20 Dec 2000 (for purpose of defining a "distribution system" where that term is used in Pts I, II) (SI 2000/3343)
			1 Oct 2001 (otherwise) (SI 2001/3266)
		(b)	1 Oct 2001 (SI 2001/3266)
29			1 Oct 2001 (SI 2001/3266)
30			16 May 2001 (for purpose of enabling the Gas and Electricity Markets Authority to make regulations prescribing— (i) the form and manner in which an application for a generation licence, transmission licence, distribution licence or supply licence, as defined in

Utilities Act 2000 (c 27)—*contd*
Section

30—*contd*		Electricity Act 1989, s 6(1) or an application for the extension or restriction of a distribution or supply licence is to be made; (ii) the information, documents and any fee which should accompany any application; and (iii) the period within which, after the making of the application, the applicant shall publish a notice of the application and the manner of that publication) (SI 2001/1781)[3] 1 Oct 2001 (otherwise) (SI 2001/3266)[4]
31		1 Oct 2001 (SI 2001/3266)
32	(1)	20 Dec 2000 (as far as relates to sub-s (2) of this section) (SI 2000/3343) 16 May 2001 (for the purpose of the determination by the Secretary of State of standard licence conditions pursuant to s 33(1) of this Act) (SI 2001/1781) 1 Oct 2001 (otherwise) (SI 2001/3266)[4]
	(2)	20 Dec 2000 (SI 2000/3343)
	(3)–(8)	16 May 2001 (for the purpose of the determination by the Secretary of State of standard licence conditions pursuant to s 33(1) of this Act) (SI 2001/1781) 1 Oct 2001 (otherwise) (SI 2001/3266)[4]
33	(1), (2)	16 May 2001 (SI 2001/1781)
	(3)	1 Oct 2001 (SI 2001/3266)
34		1 Oct 2001 (SI 2001/3266)
35		16 May 2001 (for the purpose of enabling the Secretary of State to make an order prescribing the percentages and weighting referred to in Electricity Act 1989, s 11A(6), (7) respectively) (SI 2001/1781) 1 Oct 2001 (otherwise) (SI 2001/3266)
36–45		1 Oct 2001 (SI 2001/3266)[4]
46	(1)	16 May 2001 (for purposes of enabling the Secretary of State to consult with the Gas and Electricity Markets Authority and to make regulations relating to the

Utilities Act 2000 (c 27)—*contd*
Section

55		16 May 2001 (for purpose of enabling the Gas and Electricity Markets Authority to determine and arrange for the publication of overall standards of performance in connection with the activities of electricity distributors as provided for in Electricity Act 1989, s 40A(1), (2)) (SI 2001/1781) 1 Oct 2001 (otherwise) (SI 2001/3266)
56		16 May 2001 (for purpose of enabling the Gas and Electricity Markets Authority to comply with the procedures for prescribing or determining standards of performance required by Electricity Act 1989, s 40B) (SI 2001/1781) 1 Oct 2001 (otherwise) (SI 2001/3266)
57		1 Oct 2001 (SI 2001/3266)
58		16 May 2001 (for purpose of enabling the Gas and Electricity Markets Authority to make regulations as provided for in Electricity Act 1989, s 42A) (SI 2001/1781)[3] 1 Oct 2001 (otherwise) (SI 2001/3266)[4]
59	(1)	20 Dec 2000 (for purposes of enabling the Secretary of State to make an order determining turnover and enabling the Authority to consult upon, prepare and publish a statement of policy with respect to the imposition of penalties and the determination of their amount) (SI 2000/3343) 1 Oct 2001 (otherwise) (SI 2001/3266)
	(2), (3)	1 Oct 2001 (SI 2001/3266)
60, 61		1 Oct 2001 (SI 2001/3266)[4]
62		16 May 2001 (for the purpose of enabling the Secretary of State to undertake the consultation required by Electricity Act 1989, s 32(7) before an order may be made by him under s 32(1) of that Act) (SI 2001/1781)[3] 1 Oct 2001 (otherwise) (SI 2001/3266)
63–65		1 Oct 2001 (SI 2001/3266)
66		21 Nov 2000 (subject to a saving) (SI 2000/2412)

Utilities Act 2000 (c 27)—*contd*

Section

67		29 Sep 2000 (SI 2000/2412)
68		28 Jul 2000 (RA)
69–73		1 Oct 2001 (SI 2001/3266)
74	(1)	See sub-ss (2)–(7) below
	(2)	1 Oct 2001 (SI 2001/3266)[4]
	(3)	20 Dec 2000 (SI 2000/3343)
	(4)–(6)	16 May 2001 (for purpose of the determination by the Secretary of State of standard licence conditions pursuant to s 81(2) of the 2000 Act) (SI 2001/1781)
		1 Oct 2001 (otherwise) (SI 2001/3266)[4]
	(7)	16 May 2001 (for purpose of enabling the Gas and Electricity Markets Authority to make regulations prescribing— (i) the form and manner in which an application for the grant, extension or restriction of a licence under Gas Act 1986, s 7 or s 7A is to be made; (ii) the information, documents and fee which accompany any application; and (iii) the period within which, after the making of the application, the applicant should publish a notice of the application and the manner of that publication) (SI 2001/1781)
		1 Oct 2001 (otherwise) (SI 2001/3266)[4]
75		*Not in force*
76–80		1 Oct 2001 (SI 2001/3266)
81	(1), (2)	16 May 2001 (SI 2001/1781)
	(3)	1 Oct 2001 (SI 2001/3266)
82	(1)–(3)	1 Oct 2001 (SI 2001/3266)
	(4)	16 May 2001 (for the purpose of enabling the Secretary of State to make an order prescribing the percentages and weighting referred to in Gas Act 1986, s 23(7), (8) respectively) (SI 2001/1781)[3]
		1 Oct 2001 (otherwise) (SI 2001/3266)
83–89		1 Oct 2001 (SI 2001/3266)
90	(1)	1 Oct 2001 (SI 2001/3266)
	(2)	16 May 2001 (for the purpose of enabling the Gas and Electricity Markets Authority to make and the Secretary of State to consent to the making of regulations prescribing standards of performance in

Utilities Act 2000 (c 27)—*contd*

Section

90	(2)—*contd*	connection with the activities of gas transporters as provided for in Gas Act 1986, s 33AA and the person (where this is not an Authority) by whom a reference shall be determined and the practice and procedure to be followed in connection with any determination of any dispute arising under Gas Act 1986, ss 33A or 33AA or regulations made under either of those sections, as provided for in Gas Act 1986, s 33AB) (SI 2001/1781) 1 Oct 2001 (otherwise) (SI 2001/3266)
91		16 May 2001 (for the purpose of enabling the Gas and Electricity Markets Authority to determine and arrange for the publication of overall standards of performance in connection with the activities of gas transporters as provided for in Gas Act 1986, s 33BA) (SI 2001/1781) 1 Oct 2001 (otherwise) (SI 2001/3266)
92		16 May 2001 (for purpose of enabling the Gas and Electricity Markets Authority to comply with the procedures for prescribing or determining standards of performance required by Gas Act 1986, s 33BAA) (SI 2001/1781) 1 Oct 2001 (otherwise) (SI 2001/3266)
93		1 Oct 2001 (SI 2001/3266)
94		16 May 2001 (for purpose of enabling the Gas and Electricity Markets Authority to make regulations as provided for in Gas Act 1986, s 33D) (SI 2001/1781)[3] 1 Oct 2001 (otherwise) (SI 2001/3266)
95	(1)	20 Dec 2000 (for purposes of enabling the Secretary of State to make an order determining turnover and enabling the Authority to consult upon, prepare and publish a statement of policy with respect to the imposition of penalties and the determination of their amount) (SI 2000/3343) 1 Oct 2001 (otherwise) (SI 2001/3266)

Utilities Act 2000 (c 27)—*contd*

Section

95	(2)–(5)		1 Oct 2001 (SI 2001/3266)
96–99			1 Oct 2001 (SI 2001/3266)[4]
100			20 Dec 2000 (SI 2000/3343)
101–103			1 Oct 2001 (SI 2001/3266)
104			16 May 2001 (SI 2001/1781)
105	(1)–(7)		7 Nov 2000 (SI 2000/2974)
	(8)	(a)	7 Nov 2000 (SI 2000/2974)
		(b)	20 Dec 2000 (SI 2000/3343)
		(c)	7 Nov 2000 (SI 2000/2974)
	(9)–(12)		7 Nov 2000 (SI 2000/2974)
106, 107			29 Sep 2000 (SI 2000/2412)
108			See Schs 6–8 below
109			29 Sep 2000 (SI 2000/2412)
110			28 Jul 2000 (RA)

Schedule

1			1 Nov 2000 (SI 2000/2917)
2, para	1–9		1 Nov 2000 (SI 2000/2917)
	10–14		7 Nov 2000 (SI 2000/2974)
	15–17		1 Nov 2000 (SI 2000/2917)
3			1 Nov 2000 (SI 2000/2917)
4			20 Dec 2000 (for purpose of inserting Electricity Act 1989, Sch 6, para 3(1), (6)–(10)) (SI 2000/3343) 1 Oct 2001 (otherwise) (SI 2001/3266)[4]
5, para	1		16 May 2001 (for purpose of enabling the Gas and Electricity Markets Authority to make and the Secretary of State to consent to the making of regulations under Electricity Act 1989, Sch 7, para 1(1A)) (SI 2001/1781) 1 Oct 2001 (otherwise) (SI 2001/3266)
	2		1 Oct 2001 (SI 2001/3266)
	3	(1), (2)	16 May 2001 (for purpose of enabling the Gas and Electricity Markets Authority to make and the Secretary of State to consent to the making of regulations under Electricity Act 1989, Sch 7, para 1(1A)) (SI 2001/1781) 1 Oct 2001 (otherwise) (SI 2001/3266)
		(3)–(5)	1 Oct 2001 (SI 2001/3266)
	4		16 May 2001 (for purpose of enabling the Gas and Electricity Markets Authority to make and the Secretary of State to consent to the making of regulations under Electricity Act 1989, Sch 7, para 1(1A)) (SI 2001/1781)

Utilities Act 2000 (c 27)—*contd*

Schedule

5, para	4—*contd*		1 Oct 2001 (otherwise) (SI 2001/3266)
	5–8		1 Oct 2001 (SI 2001/3266)⁴
6, para	1		See paras 2–23 below
	2	(1)	16 May 2001 (so far as relates to Gas Act 1986, s 7B and for the purpose of the determination by the Secretary of State of standard licence conditions) (SI 2001/1781)
			1 Oct 2001 (otherwise) (SI 2001/3266)⁴
		(2)	1 Oct 2001 (SI 2001/3266)⁴
	3, 4		1 Oct 2001 (SI 2001/3266)¹
	5		7 Nov 2000 (SI 2000/2974)⁴
	6, 7		1 Oct 2001 (SI 2001/3266)⁴
	8	(1)	20 Dec 2000 (for purpose of entry in sub para (3) below) (SI 2000/3343)
			1 Oct 2001 (otherwise) (SI 2001/3266)
		(2)	1 Oct 2001 (SI 2001/3266)
		(3)	20 Dec 2000 (SI 2000/3343)
		(4)	1 Oct 2001 (SI 2001/3266)
	9, 10		1 Oct 2001 (SI 2001/3266)
	11		20 Dec 2000 (SI 2000/3343)
	12	(a)–(e)	1 Oct 2001 (SI 2001/3266)
		(f)	7 Nov 2000 (SI 2000/2974)
	13		16 May 2001 (for purpose of enabling the Gas and Electricity Markets Authority to make and the Secretary of State to consent to the making of regulations prescribing standards of performance in connection with the activities of gas suppliers as provided for in Gas Act 1986, s 33A) (SI 2001/1781)³
			1 Oct 2001 (otherwise) (SI 2001/3266)
	14		1 Oct 2001 (SI 2001/3266)
	15		7 Nov 2000 (SI 2000/2974)
	16		1 Oct 2001 (SI 2001/3266)
	17		20 Dec 2000 (SI 2000/3343)
	18		1 Oct 2001 (SI 2001/3266)
	19	(a)	7 Nov 2000 (so far as relates to definition "authorised supplier", for purposes of Pt III of this Act) (SI 2000/2974)
			1 Oct 2001 (otherwise) (SI 2001/3266)
		(b)–(d)	1 Oct 2001 (SI 2001/3266)
	20, 21		1 Oct 2001 (SI 2001/3266)
	22	(a)	20 Dec 2000 (SI 2000/3343)
		(b)	7 Nov 2000 (SI 2000/2974)
	23		1 Oct 2001 (SI 2001/3266)
	24		See paras 25–40 below

Utilities Act 2000 (c 27)—*contd*

Schedule

6, para	25		20 Dec 2000 (SI 2000/3343)
	26		1 Oct 2001 (SI 2001/3266)[4]
	27		20 Dec 2000 (SI 2000/3343)
	28		7 Nov 2000 (for the purpose of insertion of "or section 27(4)(b) of the Utilities Act 2000 (order to comply with a direction under section 24 of that Act)" in Electricity Act 1989, s 25(8)) (SI 2000/2974)
			1 Oct 2001 (otherwise) (SI 2001/3266)[4]
	29		20 Dec 2000 (SI 2000/3343)[4]
	30, 31		1 Oct 2001 (SI 2001/3266)[1]
	32		16 May 2001 (for purpose of enabling the Gas and Electricity Markets Authority to make and the Secretary of State to consent to the making of regulations prescribing standards of performance in connection with the activities of electricity suppliers as provided for in Electricity Act 1989, s 39) (SI 2001/1781)[3]
			1 Oct 2001 (otherwise) (SI 2001/3266)[4]
	33		16 May 2001 (for purpose of enabling the Gas and Electricity Markets Authority to determine and arrange for the publication of overall standards of performance in connection with the activities of electricity suppliers as provided for in Electricity Act 1989, s 40) (SI 2001/1781)
			1 Oct 2001 (otherwise) (SI 2001/3266)[4]
	34		1 Oct 2001 (SI 2001/3266)[1]
	35		7 Nov 2000 (SI 2000/2974)
	36, 37		1 Oct 2001 (SI 2001/3266)
	38	(1)	1 Oct 2001 (SI 2001/3266)
		(2)	7 Nov 2000 (so far as relates to definition "authorised supplier", for purposes of Part III of this Act) (SI 2000/2974)
			1 Oct 2001 (otherwise) (SI 2001/3266)
		(3)–(8)	1 Oct 2001 (SI 2001/3266)
	39		1 Oct 2001 (SI 2001/3266)
	40	(a)	20 Dec 2000 (SI 2000/3343)
		(b)	7 Nov 2000 (SI 2000/2974)
	41		1 Oct 2001 (SI 2001/3266)
	42–44		1 Nov 2000 (SI 2000/2917)

Utilities Act 2000 (c 27)—*contd*
Schedule

6, para	45	1 Nov 2000 (so far as inserts in House of Commons Disqualification Act 1975, references to "Gas and Electricity Markets Authority" and "Gas and Electricity Consumer Council") (SI 2000/2917)
		7 Nov 2000 (otherwise) (SI 2000/2974)
	46, 47	1 Oct 2001 (SI 2001/3266)
7, paras	1–23	16 May 2001 (SI 2001/1781)
	24, 25	7 Nov 2000 (SI 2000/2974)
	26	1 Nov 2000 (SI 2000/2917)
	27	20 Dec 2000 (SI 2000/3343)
	28	7 Nov 2000 (SI 2000/2974)
	29	1 Oct 2001 (SI 2001/3266)
	30–32	7 Nov 2000 (SI 2000/2974)
8		7 Nov 2000 (so far as relates to Parliamentary Commissioner Act 1967; Chronically Sick and Disabled Persons Act 1970; House of Commons Disqualification Act 1975 (for purposes of references to Gas Consumers' Council and Chairman of a consumers' committee appointed under Electricity Act 1989, s 2); Northern Ireland Assembly Disqualification Act 1975 (for purposes of references to Gas Consumers' Council and Chairman of a consumers' committee appointed under Electricity Act 1989, s 2); Gas Act 1986, ss 2, 3, 7B(4)(d) and word "and" preceding it, 31, 32A, in s 33A(6)(a) the words "or, with the agreement of either party, by the Council", 33E(2)(a), 40, 42, and in s 48(1) the definition of "the Council" (for all purposes save for its use in Gas Act, s 41 (so long as it remains in force)), Sch 2; Electricity Act 1989, s 2, in s 39(5)(b) the word "either" and words "or, if he thinks fit, by the consumers' committee to which the supplier is allocated or any sub-committee of that committee", ss 42B(2)(a), 45, 47(4), 51–55, 57, Sch 2) (SI 2000/2974)

Utilities Act 2000 (c 27)—*contd*
Schedule

8—*contd*	20 Dec 2000 (so far as relates to Gas Act 1986, s 39 (save in respect of Sch 7, para 29); Electricity Act 1989, s 50 (save in respect of Sch 7, para 29)) (SI 2000/3343)
	16 May 2001 (so far as relates to House of Commons Disqualification Act 1975 (for the purpose of reference to the Chairman of the Gas Consumers' Council only)) (SI 2001/1781)
	1 Oct 2001 (so far as relates to House of Commons Disqualification Act 1975 (for purposes of references to Director General of Gas Supply and Director General of Electricity Supply); Northern Ireland Assembly Disqualification Act 1975 (for purposes of references to Director General of Gas Supply and Director General of Electricity Supply); Gas Act 1986 (in so far as not already in force, except entries relating to ss 5, 7A(12), 8A(1), 36 and Schs 2A, 2B); Insolvency Act 1986; Electricity Act 1989 (in so far as not already in force); Offshore Safety Act 1992; Competition and Service (Utilities) Act 1992; Environment Act 1995; Gas Act 1995 (except entries relating to s 3(2), Schs 1, 3); Fossil Fuel Levy Act 1998; Competition Act 1998) (SI 2001/3266)[4]
	Not in force (otherwise)

1   For transitional provisions see SI 2000/2974, arts 3–12

2   For transitional provisions see SI 2000/3343, arts 3–15, as amended by SI 2001/1780

3   For transitional provisions see SI 2001/1781, arts 3–10

4   For transitional provisions see SI 2001/3266, arts 3–20

Warm Homes and Energy Conservation Act 2000 (c 31)

RA: 23 Nov 2000

Commencement provisions: s 4(3)
Section

1	23 Nov 2000 (RA)
2	23 Nov 2000 (RA) (E)
	Not in force (W)
3, 4	23 Nov 2000 (RA)

2001

Abolition of Poindings and Warrant Sales (Scotland) Act 2001 (asp 1)

RA: 17 Jan 2001

Commencement provisions: s 4(1)
Section

1–3	31 Dec 2002 (s 4(1))[1]
4	17 Jan 2001 (RA)
Schedule	31 Dec 2002 (s 4(1))[1]

---

[1] s 4(1) provides that ss 1–3 of, and the Schedule to, this Act shall come into force on 31 December 2002 or such earlier date as the Scottish Ministers may by order made by Statutory Instrument appoint

---

Anti-terrorism, Crime and Security Act 2001 (c 24)

RA: 14 Dec 2001

Commencement provisions: s 127; Anti-terrorism, Crime and Security Act 2001 (Commencement No 1 and Consequential Provisions) Order 2001, SI 2001/4019[1]; Anti-terrorism, Crime and Security Act 2001 (Commencement No 2) (Scotland) Order 2001, SI 2001/4104; Anti-terrorism, Crime and Security Act 2001 (Commencement No 3) Order 2002, SI 2002/228
Section

1–3	20 Dec 2001 (SI 2001/4019)
4–20	14 Dec 2001 (RA)
21–23	14 Dec 2001 (RA)
	Repealed by Anti-terrorism, Crime and Security Act 2001, s 29(1), (7), (10) as from 14 Mar 2003, subject to sub-ss (2)–(6), and in any event as from 10 November 2006
24–57	14 Dec 2001 (RA)
58–75	*Not in force*
76, 77	14 Dec 2001 (RA)
78	*Not in force*
79–83	14 Dec 2001 (RA)
84	14 Feb 2002 (s 127(3))
85, 86	14 Dec 2001 (RA)
87	14 Feb 2002 (s 127(3))
88–97	14 Dec 2001 (RA)
98, 99	14 Dec 2001 (E, W, NI) (RA)
	7 Jan 2002 (S) (SI 2001/4104)

Anti-terrorism, Crime and Security Act 2001 (c 24)—*contd*
Section

100		14 Dec 2001 (E, W) (RA)
		7 Jan 2002 (S) (SI 2001/4104)
101		See Sch 7 below
102–107		14 Dec 2001 (RA)
108–110		14 Feb 2002 (SI 2002/228)
111–120		14 Dec 2001 (RA)
121		*Not in force*
122–124		14 Dec 2001 (RA)
125		See Sch 8 below
126–129		14 Dec 2001 (RA)

Schedule

1, 2		20 Dec 2001 (SI 2001/4019)
3, 4		14 Dec 2001 (RA)
5, 6		*Not in force*
7, para	1–7	7 Jan 2002 (SI 2001/4104)
	8–33	14 Dec 2001 (RA)
8, Pt	1	20 Dec 2001 (SI 2001/4019)[1]
	2–4	14 Dec 2001 (RA)
	5	14 Dec 2001 (except repeals in or of Nuclear Installations Act 1965) (RA)
		Not in force (exception noted above)
	6	14 Dec 2001 (except repeals in or of British Transport Commission Act 1962, Ministry of Defence Police Act 1987 in relation to Scotland) (RA)
		7 Jan 2002 (S) (in so far as relates to British Transport Commission Act 1962, Ministry of Defence Police Act 1987) (SI 2001/4104)
	7	14 Dec 2001 (except repeals in or of Terrorism Act 2000, Sch 5) (RA)
		Not in force (exception noted above)

[1]   For transitional provisions, see SI 2001/4019, art 2(2)

Appropriation Act 2001 (c 8)

RA: 11 May 2001

11 May 2001 (RA)

Appropriation (No 2) Act 2001 (c 21)

RA: 19 Jul 2001

19 July 2001 (RA)

Armed Forces Act 2001 (c 19)

RA: 11 May 2001

Commencement provisions: s 39(2)–(6); Armed Forces Act 2001 (Commencement No 1)
 Order 2001, SI 2001/3234[1]; Armed Forces Act 2001 (Commencement No 2)
 Order 2002, SI 2002/345

Section				
1				11 May 2001 (RA)
2–16				*Not in force*
17				See Sch 1 below
18				28 Feb 2002 (SI 2002/345)
19				See Sch 2 below
20–22				*Not in force*
23				28 Feb 2002 (SI 2002/345)[2]
24				28 Feb 2002 (SI 2002/345)
25–31				*Not in force*
32	(1)–(8)			*Not in force*
	(9)			See Sch 5 below
33				*Not in force*
34				See Sch 6 below
35–37				11 May 2001 (RA)
38				See Sch 7 below
39				11 May 2001 (RA)
Schedule				
1, 2				28 Feb 2002 (SI 2002/345)
3, 4				*Not in force*
5	1–4			*Not in force*
	5	(1)		*Not in force*
		(2)	(a)	*Not in force*
			(b)	28 Feb 2002 (SI 2002/345)
		(3)		*Not in force*
		(4)		28 Feb 2002 (SI 2002/345)
	6, 7			*Not in force*
6, Pt	1–3			1 Oct 2001 (SI 2001/3234)[1]
	4, 5			11 May 2001 (RA)
	6, para	1–40		1 Oct 2001 (SI 2001/3234)[1]
		41, 42		*Not in force*
		43–49		1 Oct 2001 (SI 2001/3234)
		50	(1)	See sub-paras (2)–(4) below
			(2)	*Not in force*
			(3), (4)	1 Oct 2001 (SI 2001/3234)
		51–54		1 Oct 2001 (SI 2001/3234)
		55, 56		*Not in force*
		57, 58		1 Oct 2001 (SI 2001/3234)
		59		28 Feb 2002 (SI 2002/345)
7, Pt	1			28 Feb 2002 (SI 2002/345)
	2			*Not in force*
	3			1 Oct 2001 (SI 2001/3234)
	4–6			11 May 2001 (RA)
	7			1 Sep 2001 (Repeal of Armed Forces Act 1996, s 1) (s 39(4))

Armed Forces Act 2001 (c 19)—*contd*

Schedule

7, Pt	7—*contd*	1 Oct 2001 (otherwise, except the repeals in or of Naval Discipline Act 1957, s 12A(1) and Courts-Martial (Appeals) Act 1968, s 42) (SI 2001/3234) [1]
		Not in force (exceptions noted above)

[1]   For transitional provisions, see SI 2001/3234, art 3(1), (2)

[2]   For transitional provisions, see SI 2002/345, art 3

Budget (Scotland) Act 2001 (asp 4)

RA: 15 Mar 2001

15 Mar 2001 (RA)

Capital Allowances Act 2001 (c 2)

RA: 22 Mar 2001

Commencement provisions: s 579(1). The Act has effect: (a) for income tax purposes, as respects allowances and charges falling to be made for chargeable periods ending on or after 6 Apr 2001; and (b) for corporation tax purposes, as respects allowances and charges falling to be made for chargeable periods ending on or after 1 Apr 2001.

Children's Commissioner for Wales Act 2001 (c 18)

RA: 11 May 2001

Commencement provisions: s 9(1); Children's Commissioner for Wales Act 2001 (Commencement) Order 2001, SI 2001/2783[1]

Section

1–8	26 Aug 2001 (SI 2001/2783)
9	11 May 2001 (RA)
Schedule	26 Aug 2001 (SI 2001/2783)

[1]   *Erratum* Note that in the Queen's Printer copy of SI 2001/2783, the list of sections brought into force refers to s 5 twice and does not include s 8, however it is thought that the intention was to bring the whole Act into force.

Churchwardens Measure 2001 (No 1)

RA: 10 Apr 2001

Commencement provisions: s 16(2)

The provisions of this Measure were brought into force on 1 Jan 2002 by an instrument made by the Archbishops of Canterbury and York and dated 13 Nov 2001 (made under s 16(2))

Consolidated Fund Act 2001 (c 1)

RA: 22 Mar 2001

22 Mar 2001 (RA)

Consolidated Fund (No 2) Act 2001 (c 25)

RA: 18 Dec 2001

18 Dec 2001 (RA)

Convention Rights (Compliance) (Scotland) Act 2001 (asp 7)

RA: 5 Jul 2001

Commencement provisions: s 15(2), (3); Convention Rights (Compliance) (Scotland) Act 2001 (Commencement) Order 2001, SSI 2001/274

Section			
1, 2			8 Oct 2001 (SSI 2001/274)
3	(1)	(a)	8 Oct 2001 (SSI 2001/274)
		(b)	27 Jul 2001 (insofar as it inserts s 10(2U) of Prisoners and Criminal Proceedings (Scotland) Act 1993) (SSI 2001/274)
			8 Oct 2001 (otherwise) (SSI 2001/274)
		(c)–(e)	8 Oct 2001 (SSI 2001/274)
	(2)–(3)		8 Oct 2001 (SSI 2001/274)
4			See Schedule below
5	(1), (2)		27 Jul 2001 (SSI 2001/274)
	(3)		8 Oct 2001 (SSI 2001/274)
	(4)		27 Jul 2001 (for the purpose of enabling the Scottish Ministers to make regulations under Sch 2, para 3D to Prisoners and Criminal Proceedings (Scotland) Act 1993) (SSI 2001/274)
			8 Oct 2001 (otherwise) (SSI 2001/274)
	(5)		27 Jul 2001 (SSI 2001/274)
	(6)		8 Oct 2001 (SSI 2001/274)
6–10			6 Jul 2001 (s 15(3))
11			5 Sep 2001 (SSI 2001/274)
12–14			6 Jul 2001 (s 15(3))
15			5 Jul 2001 (RA)
Schedule			
para	1–20		8 Oct 2001 (SSI 2001/274)
	21		27 Jul 2001 (SSI 2001/274)
	22–67		8 Oct 2001 (SSI 2001/274)
	68		27 Jul 2001 (SSI 2001/274)
	69–76		8 Oct 2001 (SSI 2001/274)
	77		27 Jul 2001 (for the purpose of applying para 68 of this Schedule) (SSI 2001/274)

Convention Rights (Compliance) (Scotland) Act 2001 (asp 7)—*contd*
Schedule
para   77—*contd*   8 Oct 2001 (otherwise) (SSI 2001/274)
            78–83   8 Oct 2001 (SSI 2001/274)

Criminal Defence Service (Advice and Assistance) Act 2001 (c 4)

RA: 10 Apr 2001

10 Apr 2001 (RA)

Criminal Justice and Police Act 2001 (c 16)

RA: 11 May 2001

Commencement provisions: s 138(2)–(4); Criminal Justice and Police Act 2001
(Commencement No 1) Order 2001, SI 2001/2223; Criminal Justice and Police
Act 2001 (Commencement No 2) Order 2001, SI 2001/3150; Criminal Justice
and Police Act 2001 (Commencement No 3) Order 2001, SI 2001/3736;
Criminal Justice and Police Act 2001 (Commencement No 4 and Transitional
Provisions) Order 2002, SI 2002/344[1]

Section
1   1 Mar 2002 (for the purpose of
                                           making orders) (SI 2002/344)
                                       Not in force (otherwise)
2   *Not in force*
3   1 Mar 2002 (SI 2002/344)
4–11   *Not in force*
12   1 Sep 2001 (SI 2001/2223)
13   19 Jun 2001 (for the purpose of
                                           making orders or regulations)
                                           (SI 2001/2223)
                                       1 Sep 2001 (otherwise) (SI 2001/2223)
14–16   1 Sep 2001 (SI 2001/2223)
17–28   1 Dec 2001 (SI 2001/3736)
29   1 Sep 2001 (SI 2001/2223)
30–32   1 Dec 2001 (SI 2001/3736)
33–36   1 Apr 2002 (SI 2002/344)
37   19 Jun 2001 (for the purpose of
                                           making orders or regulations)
                                           (SI 2001/2223)
                                       1 Apr 2002 (otherwise)
                                           (SI 2002/344)
38   *Not in force*
39–41   1 Aug 2001 (SI 2001/2223)
42, 43   11 May 2001 (RA)
44   1 Aug 2001 (SI 2001/2223)
45   19 Jun 2001 (for the purpose of
                                           making orders or regulations)
                                           (SI 2001/2223)
                                       Not in force (otherwise)

Criminal Justice and Police Act 2001 (c 16)—*contd*

Section			
46, 47			1 Sep 2001 (SI 2001/2223)
48, 49			1 Aug 2001 (SI 2001/2223)
50–70			*Not in force*
71, 72			1 Oct 2001 (SI 2001/3150)
73, 74			*Not in force*
75			1 Aug 2001 (SI 2001/2223)
76, 77			19 Jun 2001 (SI 2001/2223)
78–80			*Not in force*
81–84			11 May 2001 (RA)
85			11 Jul 2001 (s 138(4))
86			1 Aug 2001 (SI 2001/2223)
87–96			*Not in force*
97	(1)–(3)		1 Oct 2001 (SI 2001/3150)
	(4)	(a)	*Not in force*
		(b)–(d)	1 Oct 2001 (SI 2001/3150)
	(5), (6)		1 Oct 2001 (SI 2001/3150)
98, 99			*Not in force*
100			1 Oct 2001 (SI 2001/3150)
101–103			*Not in force*
104	(1), (2)		19 Jun 2001 (SI 2001/2223)
	(3)		1 Apr 2002 (SI 2002/344)
	(4)	(a), (b)	19 Jun 2001 (SI 2001/2223)
		(c)	1 Apr 2002 (SI 2002/344)
	(5)		19 Jun 2001 (except so far as relates to Police Act 1997) (SI 2001/2223)
			1 Apr 2002 (exception noted above) (SI 2002/344)
	(6), (7)		19 Jun 2001 (SI 2001/2223)
	(8)		1 Apr 2002 (SI 2002/344)
	(9)		19 Jun 2001 (SI 2001/2223)
105			19 Jun 2001 (SI 2001/2223)
106	(1)	(a)	19 Jun 2001 (SI 2001/2223)
		(b)	1 Apr 2002 (SI 2002/344)
	(2)		19 Jun 2001 (SI 2001/2223)
107	(1)	(a), (b)	1 Dec 2001 (SI 2001/3736)
		(c)	1 Apr 2002 (SI 2002/344)
	(2), (3)		1 Dec 2001 (SI 2001/3736)
	(4)		1 Apr 2002 (SI 2002/344)
108			1 Apr 2002 (SI 2002/344)
109			11 May 2001 (RA)
110, 111			1 Aug 2001 (SI 2001/2223)
112			1 Apr 2002 (SI 2002/344)
113, 114			1 Aug 2001 (SI 2001/2223)
115			1 Apr 2002 (SI 2002/344)
116	(1)–(6)		1 Apr 2002 (SI 2002/344)
	(7)		11 May 2001 (RA)
117, 118			1 Apr 2002 (SI 2002/344)
119	(1)–(6)		1 Apr 2002 (SI 2002/344)

Criminal Justice and Police Act 2001 (c 16)—*contd*

Section			
119	(7)		11 May 2001 (RA)
120, 121			1 Apr 2002 (SI 2002/344)
122–125			1 Jan 2002 (SI 2001/3736)
126			1 Apr 2002 (SI 2002/344)
127			*Not in force*
128			See Sch 6 below
129			1 Aug 2001 (SI 2001/2223)
130			*Not in force*
131, 132			1 Mar 2002 (SI 2002/344)
133			1 Dec 2001 (SI 2001/3736)
134–136			19 Jun 2001 (SI 2001/2223)
137			See Sch 7 below
138			11 May 2001 (RA)
Schedule			
1			*Not in force*
2, para	1–25		*Not in force*
	26		1 Oct 2001 (SI 2001/3150)
	27		*Not in force*
3–5			*Not in force*
6, para	1, 2		1 Apr 2002 (SI 2002/344)
	3		1 Aug 2001 (SI 2001/2223)
	4–11		1 Apr 2002 (SI 2002/344)
	12		1 Aug 2001 (SI 2001/2223)
	13–20		1 Apr 2002 (SI 2002/344)
	21		1 Apr 2002 (except for insertion of para 4 of Sch 2A to the 1997 Act) (SI 2002/344)
			Not in force (exception noted above)
	22–80		1 Apr 2002 (SI 2002/344)
7, Pt	1		1 Dec 2001 (SI 2001/3736)
	2	(1)	19 Jun 2001 (repeal of Police and Criminal Evidence Act 1984, s 64(4)) (SI 2001/2223)
			Not in force (otherwise)
		(2)	19 Jun 2001 (SI 2001/2223)
	3		*Not in force*
	4		19 Jun 2001 (repeals of or in Police Act 1996, Sch 2, paras 10, 16, Sch 3; Greater London Authority Act 1999) (SI 2001/2223)
			1 Dec 2001 (repeals of or in Police Act 1996, Sch 2, para 25(1), Sch 2A, para 20(1), (2)) (SI 2001/3736)
			1 Jan 2002 (repeals of or in Police Act 1996, ss 12(4)–(6), 13(2) (SI 2001/3736)
			1 Apr 2002 (repeals of or in Police Act 1997) (SI 2002/344)

Criminal Justice and Police Act 2001 (c 16)—*contd*

Schedule

7, Pt	5	(1)	1 Aug 2001 (repeals of or in Local Government Finance Act 1992, ss 32(6A), 43(5A); Police Act 1997, ss 2(6), 18, 48(7), 63, 137(2)(d), Schs 3, 5; Greater London Authority Act 1999, s 86(3), Sch 27, paras 110, 111, 114, 115) (SI 2001/2223)
			1 Apr 2002 (otherwise) (SI 2002/344)
		(2)	1 Apr 2002 (SI 2002/344)
	6		1 Aug 2001 (repeal of or in Bail Act 1976) (SI 2001/2223)
			Not in force (otherwise)

¹   For transitional provisions see SI 2002/344, art 4

Education (Graduate Endowment and Student Support) (Scotland) Act 2001 (asp 6)

RA: 3 May 2001

Commencement provisions: s 5; Education (Graduate Endowment and Student Support) (Scotland) Act 2001 (Commencement) Order 2001, SSI 2001/191

Section

1-3	3 May 2001 (RA)
4	1 Jun 2001 (SSI 2001/191)
5	3 May 2001 (RA)

Election Publications Act 2001 (c 5)

RA: 10 Apr 2001

10 Apr 2001 (RA)

Elections Act 2001 (c 7)

RA: 10 Apr 2001

10 Apr 2001 (RA)

European Communities (Finance) Act 2001 (c 22)

RA: 4 Dec 2001

4 Dec 2001 (RA)

Finance Act 2001 (c 9)

RA: 11 May 2001

Details of the commencement of Finance Acts are not set out in this work

Health and Social Care Act 2001 (c 15)

RA: 11 May 2001

Commencement provisions: s 70(2); Health and Social Care Act 2001 (Commencement No 1) (England) Order 2001, SI 2001/2804; Health and Social Care Act 2001 (Commencement No 2) (England) Order 2001, SI 2001/3167; Health and Social Care Act 2001 (Commencement No 3) (England) Order 2001, SI 2001/3294; Health and Social Care Act 2001 (Commencement No 4) (England) Order 2001, SI 2001/3619; Health and Social Care Act 2001 (Commencement No 5) Order 2001, SI 2001/3752; Health and Social Care Act 2001 (Commencement No 6) (England) Order 2001, SI 2001/3738; Health and Social Care Act 2001 (Commencement No 1) (Wales) Order 2001, SI 2001/3807; Health and Social Care Act 2001 (Commencement No 7) (England) Order 2001, SI 2001/4149; Health and Social Care Act 2001 (Commencement No 9) (Scotland) Order 2002, SSI 2002/75

Section	
1	11 May 2001 (in so far as conferring any power to make an order or regulations which is exercisable by the Secretary of State) (RA)
	22 Oct 2001 (E) (otherwise) (SI 2001/3619) [2]
	Not in force (otherwise)
2	11 May 2001 (in so far as conferring any power to make an order or regulations which is exercisable by the Secretary of State) (RA)
	Not in force (otherwise)
3, 4	11 May 2001 (in so far as conferring any power to make an order or regulations which is exercisable by the Secretary of State) (RA)
	1 Aug 2001 (E) (otherwise) (SI 2001/2804)
	Not in force (otherwise)
5	11 May 2001 (in so far as conferring any power to make an order or regulations which is exercisable by the Secretary of State) (RA)
	Not in force (otherwise)
6	11 May 2001 (in so far as conferring any power to make an order or regulations which is exercisable by the Secretary of State) (RA)
	1 Oct 2001 (E) (otherwise) (SI 2001/3294)
	Not in force (otherwise)
7–12	11 May 2001 (in so far as conferring any power to make an order or regulations which is exercisable by the Secretary of State) (RA)

Health and Social Care Act 2001 (c 15)—*contd*
Section
7–12—*contd*   *Not in force* (otherwise)
13   11 May 2001 (in so far as conferring
                                                        any power to make an order or
                                                        regulations which is exercisable by
                                                        the Secretary of State) (RA)
                                                      1 Aug 2001 (E) (otherwise)
                                                        (SI 2001/2804)
                                                      Not in force (otherwise)
14, 15   11 May 2001 (in so far as conferring
                                                        any power to make an order or
                                                        regulations which is exercisable by
                                                        the Secretary of State) (RA)
                                                      Not in force (otherwise)
16   11 May 2001 (in so far as conferring
                                                        any power to make an order or
                                                        regulations which is exercisable by
                                                        the Secretary of State) (RA)
                                                      14 Dec 2001 (E) (otherwise)
                                                        (SI 2001/3738) [4]
                                                      Not in force (otherwise)
17   11 May 2001 (in so far as conferring
                                                        any power to make an order or
                                                        regulations which is exercisable by
                                                        the Secretary of State) (RA)
                                                      14 Dec 2001 (E) (for all purposes
                                                        except those relating to the
                                                        provision of pharmaceutical
                                                        services) (SI 2001/3738)
                                                      Not in force (otherwise)
18–19   11 May 2001 (in so far as conferring
                                                        any power to make an order
                                                        or regulations which is
                                                        exercisable by the Secretary of
                                                        State) (RA)
                                                      Not in force (otherwise)
20   (1)   See sub-ss (2)–(7) below
                (2)–(5)   11 May 2001 (in so far as conferring
                                                        any power to make an order
                                                        or regulations which is
                                                        exercisable by the Secretary of
                                                        State) (RA)
                                                      22 Nov 2001 (E) (for the purpose
                                                        of making regulations)
                                                        (SI 2001/3738)
                                                      14 Dec 2001 (E) (for all other
                                                        purposes except those relating to
                                                        the provision of pharmaceutical
                                                        services) (SI 2001/3738)
                                                      Not in force (otherwise)

Health and Social Care Act 2001 (c 15)—*contd*
Section

20	(6), (7)	11 May 2001 (in so far as conferring any power to make an order or regulations which is exercisable by the Secretary of State) (RA) *Not in force* (otherwise)
21, 22		11 May 2001 (in so far as conferring any power to make an order or regulations which is exercisable by the Secretary of State) (RA) 22 Nov 2001 (E) (otherwise) (SI 2001/3738) *Not in force* (otherwise)
23		11 May 2001 (in so far as conferring any power to make an order or regulations which is exercisable by the Secretary of State) (RA) *Not in force* (otherwise)
24		11 May 2001 (in so far as conferring any power to make an order or regulations which is exercisable by the Secretary of State) (RA) 22 Nov 2001 (E) (otherwise) (SI 2001/3738) *Not in force* (otherwise)
25		11 May 2001 (in so far as conferring any power to make an order or regulations which is exercisable by the Secretary of State) (RA) 22 Nov 2001 (E) (in so far as inserts ss 49O, 49P, 49Q and 49R) (SI 2001/3738) 22 Nov 2001 (E) (in so far as inserts ss 49F, 49I, 49L, 49M and 49N for the purpose of making regulations) (SI 2001/3738) 14 Dec 2001 (E) (in so far as inserts ss 49F, 49I, 49L, 49M and 49N for all other purposes except those relating to the provision of pharmaceutical services) (SI 2001/3738) 14 Dec 2001 (E) (in so far as inserts ss 49G, 49H, 49J and 49K for all purposes except those relating to the provision of pharmaceutical services) (SI 2001/3738) *Not in force* (otherwise)

Health and Social Care Act 2001 (c 15)—*contd*

Section

26   11 May 2001 (in so far as conferring any power to make an order or regulations which is exercisable by the Secretary of State) (RA)

Not in force (otherwise)

27   11 May 2001 (in so far as conferring any power to make an order or regulations which is exercisable by the Secretary of State) (RA)

1 Oct 2001 (E) (for the purpose of constituting the Family Health Services Appeal Authority and for making rules or regulations in respect of it) (SI 2001/3294)

1 Dec 2001 (E) (otherwise) (SI 2001/3294)

Not in force (otherwise)

28–43   11 May 2001 (in so far as conferring any power to make an order or regulations which is exercisable by the Secretary of State) (RA)

Not in force (otherwise)

44   11 May 2001 (in so far as conferring any power to make an order or regulations which is exercisable by the Secretary of State) (RA)

1 Apr 2002 (S) (otherwise) (SSI 2002/75)

45   11 May 2001 (in so far as conferring any power to make an order or regulations which is exercisable by the Secretary of State) (RA)

19 Dec 2001 (E) (otherwise) (SI 2001/4149)

Not in force (W) (otherwise)

46   11 May 2001 (in so far as conferring any power to make an order or regulations which is exercisable by the Secretary of State) (RA)

1 Aug 2001 (E) (otherwise) (SI 2001/2804)

Not in force (otherwise)

47   (1)–(4)   11 May 2001 (in so far as conferring any power to make an order or regulations which is exercisable by the Secretary of State) (RA)

1 Aug 2001 (E) (otherwise) (SI 2001/2804)

Not in force (otherwise)

Health and Social Care Act 2001 (c 15)—*contd*

Section

47	(5), (6)	11 May 2001 (in so far as conferring any power to make an order or regulations which is exercisable by the Secretary of State) (RA)
		1 Aug 2001 (E) (except in so far as relates to directions given under s 45) (SI 2001/2804)
		19 Dec 2001 (E) (otherwise) (SI 2001/4149)
		Not in force (W) (otherwise)
	(7), (8)	11 May 2001 (in so far as conferring any power to make an order or regulations which is exercisable by the Secretary of State) (RA)
		1 Aug 2001 (E) (otherwise) (SI 2001/2804)
		Not in force (otherwise)
48		11 May 2001 (in so far as conferring any power to make an order or regulations which is exercisable by the Secretary of State) (RA)
		1 Aug 2001 (E) (otherwise) (SI 2001/2804)
		Not in force (otherwise)
49		11 May 2001 (in so far as conferring any power to make an order or regulations which is exercisable by the Secretary of State) (RA)
		1 Oct 2001 (E) (in so far as it relates to certain persons only[1]) (SI 2001/3294)
		3 Dec 2001 (W) (in so far as it relates to certain persons only[3]) (SI 2001/3807)
		Not in force (otherwise)
50	(1)	8 Apr 2002 (SI 2001/3752)
	(2)–(7)	19 Dec 2001 (W) (SI 2001/3807)
		20 Dec 2001 (E) (SI 2001/3752)
		1 Apr 2002 (S) (SSI 2002/75)
	(8)	11 May 2001 (in so far as conferring any power to make an order or regulations which is exercisable by the Secretary of State) (RA)
		19 Dec 2001 (W) (otherwise) (SI 2001/3807)
		20 Dec 2001 (E) (otherwise) (SI 2001/3752)
		1 Apr 2002 (S) (otherwise) (SSI 2002/75)

Health and Social Care Act 2001 (c 15)—*contd*
Section

50	(9)	11 May 2001 (in so far as conferring any power to make an order or regulations which is exercisable by the Secretary of State) (RA) 19 Dec 2001 (W) (otherwise) (SI 2001/3807) 1 Apr 2002 (S) (SSI 2002/75) *Not in force* (otherwise)
	(10)	19 Dec 2001 (W) (SI 2001/3807) 20 Dec 2001 (E) (SI 2001/3752) 1 Apr 2002 (S) (SSI 2002/75)
51		11 May 2001 (in so far as conferring any power to make an order or regulations which is exercisable by the Secretary of State) (RA) 8 Nov 2001(otherwise) (SI 2001/3752)
52		11 May 2001 (in so far as conferring any power to make an order or regulations which is exercisable by the Secretary of State) (RA) 8 Nov 2001(otherwise) (SI 2001/3752)
53		11 May 2001 (in so far as conferring any power to make an order or regulations which is exercisable by the Secretary of State) (RA) 1 Oct 2001 (E) (otherwise) (SI 2001/3167) *Not in force* (W) (S) (otherwise)
54		11 May 2001 (in so far as conferring any power to make an order or regulations which is exercisable by the Secretary of State) (RA) 1 Oct 2001 (E) (otherwise) (SI 2001/3167) *Not in force* (W) (otherwise)
55	(1)–(6)	11 May 2001 (in so far as conferring any power to make an order or regulations which is exercisable by the Secretary of State) (RA) 1 Oct 2001 (E) (for the purpose of enabling a local authority to enter into a deferred payment agreement with a resident who has a beneficial interest in property which he occupies or formerly occupied as his only or main residence) (SI 2001/3167)

Health and Social Care Act 2001 (c 15)—*contd*

Section

55	(1)–(6)—*contd*	*Not in force* (otherwise)
	(7)	11 May 2001 (in so far as conferring any power to make an order or regulations which is exercisable by the Secretary of State) (RA)
		Not in force (otherwise)
	(8)	11 May 2001 (in so far as conferring any power to make an order or regulations which is exercisable by the Secretary of State) (RA)
		1 Oct 2001 (E) (for the purpose of enabling a local authority to enter into a deferred payment agreement with a resident who has a beneficial interest in property which he occupies or formerly occupied as his only or main residence) (SI 2001/3167)
		Not in force (otherwise)
56–58		11 May 2001 (in so far as conferring any power to make an order or regulations which is exercisable by the Secretary of State) (RA)
		Not in force (otherwise)
59–61		11 May 2001 (RA)
62, 63		11 May 2001 (in so far as conferring any power to make an order or regulations which is exercisable by the Secretary of State) (RA)
		Not in force (otherwise)
64–66		11 May 2001 (RA)
67	(1)	See Sch 5 below
	(2)	See Sch 6 below
68–70		11 May 2001 (RA)
Schedule		
1–3		11 May 2001 (in so far as conferring any power to make an order or regulations which is exercisable by the Secretary of State) (RA)
		Not in force (otherwise)
4		11 May 2001 (in so far as conferring any power to make an order or regulations which is exercisable by the Secretary of State) (RA)
		1 Aug 2001 (E) (otherwise) (SI 2001/2804)
		Not in force (otherwise)

Health and Social Care Act 2001 (c 15)—*contd*

Schedule

5, para	1, 2		11 May 2001 (in so far as conferring any power to make an order or regulations which is exercisable by the Secretary of State) (RA) *Not in force* (otherwise)
	3		11 May 2001 (in so far as conferring any power to make an order or regulations which is exercisable by the Secretary of State) (RA) 1 Oct 2001 (E) (for the purpose of constituting the Family Health Services Appeal Authority and for making rules or regulations in respect of it) (SI 2001/3294) 1 Dec 2001 (E) (otherwise) (SI 2001/3294) *Not in force* (otherwise)
	4		11 May 2001 (in so far as conferring any power to make an order or regulations which is exercisable by the Secretary of State) (RA) *Not in force* (otherwise)
	5	(1)	See sub-paras (2)–(17) below
		(2)	11 May 2001 (in so far as conferring any power to make an order or regulations which is exercisable by the Secretary of State) (RA) *Not in force* (otherwise)
		(3)	11 May 2001 (in so far as conferring any power to make an order or regulations which is exercisable by the Secretary of State) (RA) 22 Oct 2001 (E) (otherwise) (SI 2001/3619) *Not in force* (otherwise)
		(4)	11 May 2001 (in so far as conferring any power to make an order or regulations which is exercisable by the Secretary of State) (RA) 22 Nov 2001 (E) (for the purpose of making regulations) (SI 2001/3738) 14 Dec 2001 (E) (for all other purposes except those relating to the provision of pharmaceutical services) (SI 2001/3738) *Not in force* (otherwise)

Health and Social Care Act 2001 (c 15)—*contd*
Schedule

5, para	5	(5)–(7)	11 May 2001 (in so far as conferring any power to make an order or regulations which is exercisable by the Secretary of State) (RA) *Not in force* (otherwise)
		(8)	11 May 2001 (in so far as conferring any power to make an order or regulations which is exercisable by the Secretary of State) (RA) 14 Dec 2001 (E) (otherwise) (SI 2001/3738) [4] *Not in force* (otherwise)
		(9)	11 May 2001 (in so far as conferring any power to make an order or regulations which is exercisable by the Secretary of State) (RA) *Not in force* (otherwise)
		(10)	(a) 11 May 2001 (in so far as conferring any power to make an order or regulations which is exercisable by the Secretary of State) (RA) *Not in force* (otherwise)
			(b) 11 May 2001 (in so far as conferring any power to make an order or regulations which is exercisable by the Secretary of State) (RA) 1 Oct 2001 (E) (for the purpose of constituting the Family Health Services Appeal Authority and for making rules or regulations in respect of it) (SI 2001/3294) 1 Dec 2001 (E) (otherwise) (SI 2001/3294) *Not in force* (otherwise)
		(11), (12)	11 May 2001 (in so far as conferring any power to make an order or regulations which is exercisable by the Secretary of State) (RA) *Not in force* (otherwise)
		13	(a) 11 May 2001 (in so far as conferring any power to make an order or regulations which is exercisable by the Secretary of State) (RA) 1 Oct 2001 (E) (for the purpose of constituting the Family Health Services Appeal Authority and for making rules or regulations in respect of it) (SI 2001/3294)

Health and Social Care Act 2001 (c 15)—*contd*

Schedule

5, para	5	(13)	(a)—*contd*	1 Dec 2001 (E) (otherwise) (SI 2001/3294)
				Not in force (otherwise)
			(b)	11 May 2001 (in so far as conferring any power to make an order or regulations which is exercisable by the Secretary of State) (RA)
				1 Oct 2001 (E) (for the purpose of constituting the Family Health Services Appeal Authority and for making rules or regulations in respect of it) (SI 2001/3294)
				1 Dec 2001 (E) (otherwise) (SI 2001/3294)
				Not in force (otherwise)
			(c)	11 May 2001 (in so far as conferring any power to make an order or regulations which is exercisable by the Secretary of State) (RA)
				Not in force (otherwise)
			(d)	11 May 2001 (in so far as conferring any power to make an order or regulations which is exercisable by the Secretary of State) (RA)
				1 Oct 2001 (E) (for the purpose of constituting the Family Health Services Appeal Authority and for making rules or regulations in respect of it) (SI 2001/3294)
				1 Dec 2001 (E) (otherwise) (SI 2001/3294)
				Not in force (otherwise)
		(14)		11 May 2001 (in so far as conferring any power to make an order or regulations which is exercisable by the Secretary of State) (RA)
				22 Nov 2001 (E) (for the purpose of making regulations) (SI 2001/3738)
				14 Dec 2001 (E) (for all other purposes except those relating to the provision of pharmaceutical services) (SI 2001/3738)
				Not in force (otherwise)
		(15)		11 May 2001 (in so far as conferring any power to make an order or regulations which is exercisable by the Secretary of State) (RA)
				Not in force (otherwise)

Health and Social Care Act 2001 (c 15)—*contd*

Schedule

5, para	5	(16)	11 May 2001 (in so far as conferring any power to make an order or regulations which is exercisable by the Secretary of State) (RA) 14 Dec 2001 (E) (otherwise) (SI 2001/3738) [4] *Not in force* (otherwise)
		(17)	11 May 2001 (in so far as conferring any power to make an order or regulations which is exercisable by the Secretary of State) (RA) *Not in force* (otherwise)
	6–9		11 May 2001 (in so far as conferring any power to make an order or regulations which is exercisable by the Secretary of State) (RA) *Not in force* (otherwise)
	10		11 May 2001 (in so far as conferring any power to make an order or regulations which is exercisable by the Secretary of State) (RA) 1 Oct 2001 (E) (for the purpose of constituting the Family Health Services Appeal Authority and for making rules or regulations in respect of it) (SI 2001/3294) 1 Dec 2001 (E) (otherwise) (SI 2001/3294) *Not in force* (otherwise)
	11		11 May 2001 (in so far as conferring any power to make an order or regulations which is exercisable by the Secretary of State) (RA) *Not in force* (otherwise)
	12	(1), (2)	11 May 2001 (in so far as conferring any power to make an order or regulations which is exercisable by the Secretary of State) (RA) 14 Dec 2001 (E) (for all purposes except those relating to the provision of pharmaceutical services) (SI 2001/3738) *Not in force* (otherwise)
		(3)	11 May 2001 (in so far as conferring any power to make an order or regulations which is exercisable by the Secretary of State) (RA) *Not in force* (otherwise)

Health and Social Care Act 2001 (c 15)—*contd*

Schedule

5, para	13, 14		11 May 2001 (in so far as conferring any power to make an order or regulations which is exercisable by the Secretary of State) (RA)
			Not in force (otherwise)
	15	(1)	See sub-paras (2), (3) below
		(2)	11 May 2001 (in so far as conferring any power to make an order or regulations which is exercisable by the Secretary of State) (RA)
			Not in force (otherwise)
		(3)	11 May 2001 (in so far as conferring any power to make an order or regulations which is exercisable by the Secretary of State) (RA)
			22 Oct 2001 (E) (in so far as relating to functions in relation to the provision of residential accommodation only) (SI 2001/3619)
			Not in force (otherwise)
	16		11 May 2001 (in so far as conferring any power to make an order or regulations which is exercisable by the Secretary of State) (RA)
			Not in force (otherwise)
	17, 18		11 May 2001 (RA)
6			14 Dec 2001 (E) (repeals of or in National Health Service Act 1977, s 29(4), for all purposes except those relating to the provision of pharmaceutical services) (SI 2001/3738)
			14 Dec 2001 (E) (repeals of or in National Health Service Act 1977, ss 46–49E, Sch 9; National Health Service (Amendment) Act 1995) (SI 2001/3738) [4]
			Not in force (otherwise)

---

[1] "Certain persons" means any person: (a) who is provided with accommodation by a local authority under National Assistance Act 1948, s 21(1); and (b) who, if the local authority were also to provide the nursing care in connection with that accommodation, would be liable to make a payment under s 22(3) or 26(3) of that Act either at the standard rate or at a lower rate which is not less than the standard rate minus £110. Notwithstanding that a person ceases to satisfy head (b) above, the Health and Social Care Act 2001, s 49 shall continue to apply to him.

[2] S 1 has effect in England in relation to the determination of allotments and resource limits for the financial year beginning with 1 April 2002 and subsequent financial years; see SI 2001/3619, art 2(2)

Health and Social Care Act 2001 (c 15)—*contd*

3   "Certain persons" means any person: (a) who is provided with accommodation by a local authority
     under National Assistance Act 1948, s 21(1); and (b) who, if the local authority were also to
     provide the nursing care in connection with that accommodation, would be liable to make a
     payment under s 22 or 26 of that Act either at the standard rate or at a lower rate which is not less
     than the standard rate minus £100. Notwithstanding that a person ceases to satisfy head (b) above,
     the Health and Social Care Act 2001, s 49 shall continue to apply to him.

4   For transitional provisions see SI 2001/3738, art 2(5), (6)

House of Commons (Removal of Clergy Disqualification) Act 2001 (c 13)

RA: 11 May 2001

11 May 2001 (RA)

Housing (Scotland) Act 2001 (asp 10)

RA: 18 Jul 2001

Commencement provisions: s 113(1), (2); Housing (Scotland) Act 2001
    (Commencement No 1, Transitional Provisions and Savings) Order 2001,
    SSI 2001/336[1], as amended by SSI 2001/397; Housing (Scotland) Act 2001
    (Commencement No 2, Transitional Provisions, Savings and Variation) Order
    2001, SSI 2001/397[2]; Housing (Scotland) Act 2001 (Commencement No 3,
    Transitional Provisions and Savings) Order 2001, SSI 2001/467[3]

Section	
1, 2	1 Oct 2001 (SSI 2001/336)
3–56	*Not in force*
57–83	1 Nov 2001 (SSI 2001/336)[1]
84	1 Nov 2001 (for the purpose of transferring all of the functions of Scottish Homes to the Scottish Ministers except the functions conferred by Housing (Scotland) Act 1988, s 1(3)(b)) (SSI 2001/397)[2]
	Not in force (otherwise)
85	1 Nov 2001 (SSI 2001/397)
86	*Not in force*
87	1 Nov 2001 (SSI 2001/397)
88	1 Oct 2001 (SSI 2001/336)
89	1 Nov 2001 (SSI 2001/397)
90–94	1 Nov 2001 (SSI 2001/336)
95	1 Oct 2001 (SSI 2001/336)
96–105	*Not in force*
106, 107	1 Nov 2001 (SSI 2001/336)
108	1 Oct 2001 (SSI 2001/336)
109, 110	18 Jul 2001 (RA)
111	1 Oct 2001 (SSI 2001/336)
112	See Sch 10 below
113	18 Jul 2001 (RA)
Schedule	
1–6	*Not in force*

Housing (Scotland) Act 2001 (asp 10)—*contd*

Schedule

7–9				1 Nov 2001 (SSI 2001/336)[1]
10, para	1			1 Nov 2001 (SSI 2001/397)
	2			1 Nov 2001 (SSI 2001/336)
	3–8			*Not in force*
	9	(1)		*Not in force*
		(2)		1 Nov 2001 (SSI 2001/336)
		(3)		*Not in force*
		(4)		1 Nov 2001 (SSI 2001/336)
	10			*Not in force*
	11, 12			1 Nov 2001 (SSI 2001/336)
	13	(1)		*Not in force*
		(2)		19 Dec 2001 (repeal of Housing (Scotland) Act 1987, s 12A) (SSI 2001/467)[3]
				Not in force (otherwise)
		(3)–(16)		*Not in force*
		(17)		19 Dec 2001 (repeal of Housing (Scotland) Act 1987, s 81B) (SSI 2001/467)[3]
				Not in force (otherwise)
		(18) – (23)		*Not in force*
		(24)		1 Nov 2001 (SSI 2001/336)
		(25)–(34)		*Not in force*
		(35)		1 Nov 2001 (SSI 2001/336)
		(36)–(41)		*Not in force*
		(42)		19 Dec 2001 (repeal of Housing (Scotland) Act 1987, Sch 6A) (SSI 2001/467)[3]
				Not in force (otherwise)
	14	(1)		*Not in force*
		(2)–(4)		1 Nov 2001 (SSI 2001/397)
		(5)	(a)	1 Nov 2001 (SSI 2001/336)
			(b), (c)	*Not in force*
		(6)–(8)		1 Nov 2001 (SSI 2001/336)
		(9)		*Not in force*
		(10)		1 Nov 2001 (SSI 2001/397)
		(11)		1 Nov 2001 (so far as relates to para 6) (SSI 2001/336)
				Not in force (otherwise)
		(12)	(a), (b)	*Not in force*
			(c)	1 Nov 2001 (SSI 2001/336)
		(13), (14)		*Not in force*
		(15)		1 Nov 2001 (so far as relates to paras 6, 8, 9) (SSI 2001/336)
				Not in force (otherwise)
	15	(1)		*Not in force*
		(2)		1 Nov 2001 (SSI 2001/336)
		(3), (4)		1 Nov 2001 (SSI 2001/397)
		(5)		*Not in force*

Housing (Scotland) Act 2001 (asp 10)—*contd*

Schedule

10, para	15	(6)	1 Nov 2001 (SSI 2001/397)
		(7)	*Not in force*
		(8)	1 Nov 2001 (SSI 2001/336)
		(9)	*Not in force*
	16–23		*Not in force*
	24		1 Nov 2001 (SSI 2001/397)
	25–27		*Not in force*
	28		1 Nov 2001 (SSI 2001/397)
	29		*Not in force*

[1]   For transitional provisions and savings see SSI 2001/336, art 3

[2]   For transitional provisions and savings see SSI 2001/397, arts 3–6

[3]   For transitional provisions and savings see SSI 2001/467, art 3

Human Reproductive Cloning Act 2001 (c 23)

RA: 4 Dec 2001

4 Dec 2001 (RA)

International Criminal Court Act 2001 (c 17)

RA: 11 May 2001

Commencement provisions: s 82; International Criminal Court Act 2001 (Commencement) Order 2001, SI 2001/2161, as amended by SI 2001/2304

Section

1–6		1 Sep 2001 (SI 2001/2161)
7	(1), (2)	1 Sep 2001 (SI 2001/2161)
	(3)	13 Jun 2001 (for purposes of making any Order in Council, order, rules or regulations) (SI 2001/2161)
		1 Sep 2001 (otherwise) (SI 2001/2161)
	(4)–(6)	1 Sep 2001 (SI 2001/2161)
8–12		1 Sep 2001 (SI 2001/2161)
13	(1), (2)	1 Sep 2001 (SI 2001/2161)
	(3)	13 Jun 2001 (for purposes of making any Order in Council, order, rules or regulations) (SI 2001/2161)
		1 Sep 2001 (otherwise) (SI 2001/2161)
	(4)–(6)	1 Sep 2001 (SI 2001/2161)
14–48		1 Sep 2001 (SI 2001/2161)
49		13 Jun 2001 (for purposes of making any Order in Council, order, rules or regulations) (SI 2001/2161)
		1 Sep 2001 (otherwise) (SI 2001/2161)
50	(1), (2)	1 Sep 2001 (SI 2001/2161)
	(3), (4)	13 Jun 2001 (for purposes of making any Order in Council, order, rules or regulations) (SI 2001/2161)
		1 Sep 2001 (otherwise) (SI 2001/2161)

International Criminal Court Act 2001 (c 17)—*contd*

Section

50	(5), (6)	1 Sep 2001 (SI 2001/2161)
51–78		1 Sep 2001 (SI 2001/2161)
79	(1), (2)	1 Sep 2001 (SI 2001/2161)
	(3)	13 Jun 2001 (for purposes of making any Order in Council, order, rules or regulations) (SI 2001/2161)
		1 Sep 2001 (otherwise) (SI 2001/2161)
	(4), (5)	1 Sep 2001 (SI 2001/2161)
80	(1), (2)	1 Sep 2001 (SI 2001/2161)
	(3)	13 Jun 2001 (for purposes of making any Order in Council, order, rules or regulations) (SI 2001/2161)
		1 Sep 2001 (otherwise) (SI 2001/2161)
81–84		1 Sep 2001 (SI 2001/2161)

Schedule

1, para	1	13 Jun 2001 (for purposes of making any Order in Council, order, rules or regulations) (SI 2001/2161, as amended by SI 2001/2304)
		1 Sep 2001 (otherwise) (SI 2001/2161)
	2–7	1 Sep 2001 (SI 2001/2161)
2–10		1 Sep 2001 (SI 2001/2161)

International Criminal Court (Scotland) Act 2001 (asp 13)

RA: 24 Sep 2001

Commencement provisions: s 30(2); International Criminal Court (Scotland) Act 2001 (Commencement) Order 2001, SSI 2001/456

Section

1–29	17 Dec 2001 (SSI 2001/456)
30	24 Sep 2001 (RA)

Schedule

1–6	17 Dec 2001 (SSI 2001/456)

Leasehold Casualties (Scotland) Act 2001 (asp 5)

RA: 12 Apr 2001

Commencement provisions: ss 1(3), 5(3), 6(2), 7(4)

Section

1	10 May 2000 (s 1(3))
2–4	12 Apr 2001 (RA)
5	10 May 2000 (s 5(3))
6	12 Feb 2001 (s 6(2))
7	10 May 2000 (s 7(4))
8–11	12 Apr 2001 (RA)

Schedule

1, 2	12 Apr 2001 (RA)

Mortgage Rights (Scotland) Act 2001 (asp 11)

RA: 25 Jul 2001

Commencement provisions: s 7(1); Mortgage Rights (Scotland) Act 2001 (Commencement
and Transitional Provision) Order 2001, SSI 2001/418[1]

Section	
1–6	3 Dec 2001 (SSI 2001/418)
7	25 Jul 2001 (RA)
Schedule	3 Dec 2001 (SSI 2001/418)

[1]   For a transitional provision see SSI 2001/418, art 3

Police and Fire Services (Finance) (Scotland) Act 2001 (asp 15)

RA: 5 Dec 2001

Commencement provisions: s 3(2)

Section	
1–2	*Not in force*
3	5 Dec 2001 (RA)

Private Security Industry Act 2001 (c 12)

RA: 11 May 2001

Commencement provisions: s 26(2)

Section	
1–25	*Not in force*
26	11 May 2001 (RA)
Schedule	
1, 2	*Not in force*

Rating (Former Agricultural Premises and Rural Shops) Act 2001 (c 14)

RA: 11 May 2001

Commencement provisions: s 6(2); Rating (Former Agricultural Premises and Rural
Shops) Act 2001 (Commencement No 1) Order 2001, SI 2001/2580

Section		
1	(1), (2)	15 Aug 2001 (SI 2001/2580)
	(3)	17 Jul 2001 (so far as it confers power on the Secretary of State to make an order under Local Government Finance Act 1988, s 43(6F)) (SI 2001/2580)
		15 Aug 2001 (otherwise) (SI 2001/2580)
	(4)	15 Aug 2001 (SI 2001/2580)
2–5		15 Aug 2001 (SI 2001/2580)
6		11 May 2001 (RA)

Regulation of Care (Scotland) Act 2001 (asp 8)

RA: 5 Jul 2001

Commencement provisions: s 81(2), (3); Regulation of Care (Scotland) Act 2001 (Commencement No 1) Order 2001, SSI 2001/304

Section			
1			19 Jul 2001 (s 81(2))
2, 3			*Not in force*
4			19 Jul 2001 (s 81(2))
5	(1), (2)		1 Oct 2001 (SSI 2001/304)
	(3), (4)		*Not in force*
6			1 Oct 2001 (SSI 2001/304)
7–23			*Not in force*
24	(1)		1 Oct 2001 (SSI 2001/304)
	(2), (3)		*Not in force*
25–27			*Not in force*
28			19 Jul 2001 (s 81(2))
29, 30			1 Oct 2001 (SSI 2001/304)
31–42			*Not in force*
43			19 Jul 2001 (s 81(2))
44–52			*Not in force*
53–55			1 Oct 2001 (SSI 2001/304)
56–62			19 Jul 2001 (s 81(2))
63–65			1 Oct 2001 (SSI 2001/304)
66			19 Jul 2001 (s 81(2))
67			1 Oct 2001 (SSI 2001/304)
68, 69			19 Jul 2001 (s 81(2))
70			20 Dec 2001 (SSI 2001/304)
71			1 Oct 2001 (SSI 2001/304)
72, 73			*Not in force*
74–78			19 Jul 2001 (s 81(2))
79			See Sch 3
80	(1)		*Not in force*
	(2)		19 Jul 2001 (s 81(2))
	(3), (4)		1 Oct 2001 (SSI 2001/304)
81			5 Jul 2001 (RA)
Schedule			
1, 2			19 Jul 2001 (s 81(2))
3, para	1–19		*Not in force*
	20		1 Oct 2001 (SSI 2001/304)
	21, 22		*Not in force*
	23	(1)–(6)	*Not in force*
		(7)	1 Oct 2001 (SSI 2001/304)
	24		Repealed *(never in force)*
	25		*Not in force*
4			*Not in force*

Regulatory Reform Act 2001 (c 6)

RA: 10 Apr 2001

10 Apr 2001 (RA)

Salmon Conservation (Scotland) Act 2001 (asp 3)

RA: 14 Feb 2001

Commencement provisions: s 3; Salmon Conservation (Scotland) Act 2001 (Commencement) Order 2001, SSI 2001/116
Section
1, 2   15 Apr 2001 (SSI 2001/116)
3   14 Feb 2001 (RA)

Scottish Local Authorities (Tendering) Act 2001 (asp 9)

RA: 6 Jul 2001

6 Aug 2001 (s 2(2))

Social Security Contributions (Share Options) Act 2001 (c 20)

RA: 11 May 2001

11 May 2001 (RA)

Social Security Fraud Act 2001 (c 11)

RA: 11 May 2001

Commencement provisions: s 20; Social Security Fraud Act 2001 (Commencement No 1) Order 2001, SI 2001/3251; Social Security Fraud Act 2001 (Commencement No 2) Order 2001, SI 2001/3689; Social Security Fraud Act 2001 (Commencement No 3) Order 2002, 2002/117; Social Security Fraud Act 2001 (Commencement No 4) Order 2002, SI 2002/403

Section		
1	(1)–(3)	*Not in force*
	(4)	26 Feb 2002 (SI 2002/403)
	(5)–(8)	*Not in force*
	(9)	26 Feb 2002 (SI 2002/403)
2		*Not in force*
3		28 Jan 2002 (SI 2002/117)
4–6		*Not in force*
7–11		17 Nov 2001 (for the purpose of authorising the making of regulations) (SI 2001/3689)
		1 Apr 2002 (otherwise) (SI 2001/3689)
12		1 Apr 2002 (SI 2001/3689)
13		17 Nov 2001 (for the purpose of authorising the making of regulations) (SI 2001/3689)
		1 Apr 2002 (otherwise) (SI 2001/3689)
14, 15		*Not in force*
16		26 Sep 2001 (for the purpose of authorising the making of regulations) (SI 2001/3251)
		18 Oct 2001 (otherwise) (SI 2001/3251)

Social Security Fraud Act 2001 (c 11)—*contd*

Section

17–19	*Not in force*
20, 21	11 May 2001 (RA)
Schedule	*Not in force*

Special Educational Needs and Disability Act 2001 (c 10)

RA: 11 May 2001

Commencement provisions: s 43; Special Education Needs and Disability Act 2001 (Commencement No 1) Order 2001, SI 2001/2217, as amended by SI 2001/2614[1]; Special Educational Needs and Disability Act 2001 (Commencement No 2) (Wales) Order 2001, SI 2001/3992; Special Educational Needs and Disability Act 2001 (Commencement) (Wales) Order 2002, SI 2002/74

Section

1	15 Jun 2001 (E) (so far as necessary for the purpose of making regulations) (SI 2001/2217) 1 Jan 2002 (E) (otherwise) (SI 2001/2217)[1] 21 Jan 2002 (W) (so far as necessary for the purpose of making regulations) (SI 2002/74) 1 Apr 2002 (W) (otherwise) (SI 2002/74) *Not in force* (otherwise)
2, 3	1 Jan 2002 (E) (SI 2001/2217)[1] 1 Apr 2002 (W) (SI 2002/74) *Not in force* (otherwise)
4, 5	11 May 2001 (so far as necessary for enabling the making of regulations) (RA) 1 Jan 2002 (E) (otherwise) (SI 2001/2217)[1] 1 Apr 2002 (W) (otherwise) (SI 2001/3992) *Not in force* (otherwise)
6	1 Jan 2002 (E) (SI 2001/2217)[1] 1 Apr 2002 (W) (SI 2001/3992) *Not in force* (otherwise)
7	1 Jan 2002 (E) (SI 2001/2217)[1] 1 Apr 2002 (W) (SI 2002/74) *Not in force* (otherwise)
8	15 Jun 2001 (E) (so far as necessary for the purpose of making regulations) (SI 2001/2217)[1] 1 Jan 2002 (E) (otherwise) (SI 2001/2217)[1] 21 Jan 2002 (W) (so far as necessary for the purpose of making regulations) (SI 2002/74)

Special Educational Needs and Disability Act 2001 (c 10)—*contd*
Section

8—*contd*		1 Apr 2002 (W) (otherwise) (SI 2002/74)
		Not in force (otherwise)
9		11 May 2001 (so far as necessary for enabling the making of regulations) (RA)
		1 Jan 2002 (E) (otherwise) (SI 2001/2217)[1]
		1 Apr 2002 (W) (otherwise) (SI 2002/74)
		Not in force (otherwise)
10		See Sch 1 below
11–40		*Not in force*
41		1 Jan 2002 (E) (SI 2001/2217)[1]
		1 Apr 2002 (W) (SI 2001/3992)
42	(1)	See Sch 8 below
	(2)–(4)	11 May 2001 (so far as necessary for enabling the making of regulations) (RA)
		1 Jan 2002 (E) (otherwise) (SI 2001/2217)[1]
		1 Apr 2002 (W) (otherwise) (SI 2001/3992)
	(5)	1 Jan 2002 (E) (SI 2001/2217)[1]
		Not in force (otherwise)
	(6)	1 Jan 2002 (E) (SI 2001/2217)[1]
		See Sch 9 below (W)
43		11 May 2001 (RA)
Schedule		
1, para	1, 2	1 Jan 2002 (E) (SI 2001/2217)[1]
		1 Apr 2002 (W) (SI 2001/3992)
		Not in force (otherwise)
	3	15 Jun 2001 (E) (so far as necessary for the purpose of making regulations) (SI 2001/2217)
		8 Dec 2001 (W) (so far as necessary for the purpose of making regulations) (SI 2001/3992)
		1 Jan 2002 (E) (otherwise) (SI 2001/2217)[1]
		1 Apr 2002 (W) (otherwise) (SI 2001/3992)
		Not in force (otherwise)
	4–13	1 Jan 2002 (E) (SI 2001/2217)[1]
		1 Apr 2002 (W) (SI 2001/3992)
		Not in force (otherwise)
	14	15 Jun 2001 (E) (so far as necessary for the purpose of making regulations) (SI 2001/2217)

Special Educational Needs and Disability Act 2001 (c 10)—*contd*
Schedule

1, para	14—*contd*		8 Dec 2001 (W) (so far as necessary for the purpose of making regulations) (SI 2001/3992)
			1 Jan 2002 (E) (otherwise) (SI 2001/2217)[1]
			1 Apr 2002 (W) (otherwise) (SI 2001/3992)
			Not in force (otherwise)
	15–20		1 Jan 2002 (E) (SI 2001/2217)[1]
			1 Apr 2002 (W) (SI 2001/3992)
			Not in force (otherwise)
2–7			*Not in force*
8, para	1		1 Jan 2002 (E) (SI 2001/2217)[1]
			1 Apr 2002 (W) (SI 2002/74)
	2–4		*Not in force*
	5		1 Jan 2002 (E) (SI 2001/2217)[1]
			1 Apr 2002 (W) (SI 2002/74)
	6–10		11 May 2001 (so far as necessary for enabling the making of regulations) (RA)
			1 Jan 2002 (E) (otherwise) (SI 2001/2217)[1]
			1 Apr 2002 (W) (otherwise) (SI 2002/74)
	11, 12		1 Jan 2002 (E) (SI 2001/2217)[1]
			1 Apr 2002 (W) (SI 2002/74)
	13	(1)–(4)	11 May 2001 (so far as necessary for enabling the making of regulations) (RA)
			1 Jan 2002 (E) (otherwise) (SI 2001/2217)[1]
			1 Apr 2002 (W) (otherwise) (SI 2001/3992)
		(5)	*Not in force*
	14	(1), (2)	1 Jan 2002 (E) (SI 2001/2217)[1]
			1 Apr 2002 (W) (SI 2002/74)
		(3)	11 May 2001 (so far as necessary for enabling the making of regulations) (RA)
			1 Jan 2002 (E) (otherwise) (SI 2001/2217)[1]
			1 Apr 2002 (W) (otherwise) (SI 2002/74)
	15		1 Jan 2002 (E) (SI 2001/2217)[1]
			1 Apr 2002 (W) (SI 2001/3992)
	16		1 Jan 2002 (E) (SI 2001/2217)[1]
			1 Apr 2002 (W) (SI 2002/74)

Special Educational Needs and Disability Act 2001 (c 10)—*contd*

Schedule

8, para	17, 18	15 Jun 2001 (E) (so far as necessary for the purpose of making regulations) (SI 2001/2217)
		1 Jan 2002 (E) (otherwise) (SI 2001/2217)[1]
		21 Jan 2002 (W) (so far as necessary for the purpose of making regulations) (SI 2002/74)
		1 Apr 2002 (W) (otherwise) (SI 2002/74)
	19–23	*Not in force*
9		1 Jan 2002 (E) (repeals of or in Disabled Persons (Services, Consultation and Representation) Act 1986; Education Act 1996, ss 325(1), 336(2), 441(3)(a), Sch 27; School Standards and Framework Act 1998, Sch 30) (SI 2001/2217)[1]
		1 Apr 2002 (W) (repeals of or in Education Act 1996, ss 336(2)(d), 441(3)(a); School Standards and Framework Act 1998, Sch 30, para 186(2)(b)) (SI 2001/3992)
		1 Apr 2002 (W) (repeals of or in Disabled Persons (Services, Consultation and Representation) Act 1986, s 5(1); Education Act 1996, s 325(1), Sch 27, paras 3(4), 8(1)(b)(iii), 9(1), 10) (SI 2002/74)
		Not in force (otherwise)

[1]   SI 2001/2217 is amended by SI 2001/2614 with the effect that 1 Jan 2002 substitutes 1 Sep 2001 as the day appointed for the coming into force of the provisions specified in SI 2001/2217, art 5, Schedule, Pt II

Transport (Scotland) Act 2001 (asp 2)

RA: 25 Jan 2001

Commencement provisions: s 84; Transport (Scotland) Act 2001 (Commencement No 1, Transitional Provisions and Savings) Order 2001, SSI 2001/132; Transport (Scotland) Act 2001 (Commencement No 2) Order 2001, SSI 2001/167

Section

1, 2	1 Apr 2001 (SSI 2001/132)
3	1 Jul 2001 (SSI 2001/132)
4	1 Apr 2001 (SSI 2001/132)
5–10	1 Jul 2001 (SSI 2001/132)
11	1 Apr 2001 (SSI 2001/132)
12–25	1 Jul 2001 (SSI 2001/132)
26	1 Apr 2001 (SSI 2001/132)

Transport (Scotland) Act 2001 (asp 2)—*contd*

Section

27–35			1 Jul 2001 (SSI 2001/132)
36			1 Apr 2001 (SSI 2001/132) [1]
37			1 Jul 2001 (SSI 2001/132)
38	(1)		*Not in force*
	(2)		1 Apr 2001 (SSI 2001/132)
	(3)–(6)		*Not in force*
39			*Not in force*
40	(1)		1 Apr 2001 (SSI 2001/132) [2]
	(2)		1 Jul 2001 (SSI 2001/132)
	(3), (4)		1 Apr 2001 (SSI 2001/132) [2]
41–44			1 Apr 2001 (SSI 2001/132)
45			1 Jul 2001 (SSI 2001/132)
46			1 Apr 2001 (SSI 2001/132)
47			1 Jul 2001 (SSI 2001/132)
48–59			1 Apr 2001 (SSI 2001/132)
60			See Sch 1 below
61–67			1 Apr 2001 (SSI 2001/132)
68			*Not in force*
69–72			1 Apr 2001 (SSI 2001/132)
73	(a), (b)		*Not in force*
	(c), (d)		1 Apr 2001 (SSI 2001/132)
	(e)		*Not in force*
74	(1)–(3)		1 Apr 2002 (SSI 2001/132)
	(4)		1 Apr 2001 (SSI 2001/132)
	(5)		1 Apr 2002 (SSI 2001/132)
75–79			1 Apr 2001 (SSI 2001/132)
80			1 May 2001 (SSI 2001/167)
81, 82			1 Apr 2001 (SSI 2001/132)
83			See Sch 2 below
84			25 Jan 2001 (RA)
Schedule			
1			1 Apr 2001 (SSI 2001/132)
2, para	1–3		1 Jul 2001 (SSI 2001/132)
	4	(1)–(3)	1 Apr 2001 (SSI 2001/132)
		(4)	1 Jul 2001 (SSI 2001/132)
		(5)	1 Apr 2001 (SSI 2001/132)
		(6)–(8)	*Not in force*

[1]   For transitional provisions and savings see SSI 2001/132, art 3
[2]   For transitional provisions and savings see SSI 2001/132, art 4

Vehicles (Crime) Act 2001 (c 3)

RA: 10 Apr 2001

Commencement provisions: s 44; Vehicles (Crime) Act 2001 (Commencement No 1)
Order 2001, SI 2001/3215; Vehicles (Crime) Act 2001 (Commencement No 2)
Order 2001, SI 2001/4059

Section

1–36	*Not in force*
37	1 Oct 2001 (SI 2001/3215)

Vehicles (Crime) Act 2001 (c 3)—*contd*
Section
38			2 Jan 2002 (SI 2001/4059)
39–42			10 Apr 2001 (RA)
43			See Schedule below
44–46			10 Apr 2001 (RA)
Schedule	para	1–6	*Not in force*
		7–10	2 Jan 2002 (SI 2001/4059)

STATUTES NOT YET IN FORCE

The following is a list of provisions of those Statutes, arranged alphabetically, for which no commencement dates have yet been appointed. The list only covers provisions of an Act as it was originally enacted and accordingly does not include provisions which are prospectively inserted or substituted. The list does note where a provision has been repealed without ever having been brought into force; orders made under the relevant amending Act bringing those prospective repeals into force will be noted to that Act in the service to this work.

To establish the commencement date or dates appointed for provisions not listed below, and for details of any commencement orders, please refer to **Is it in Force?**.

Abolition of Feudal Tenure etc (Scotland) Act 2000 (asp 5)

RA: 9 Jun 2000

Section

1, 2				*Not in force*
4–13				*Not in force*
17–51				*Not in force*
54–57				*Not in force*
59–61				*Not in force*
63–66				*Not in force*
68–70				*Not in force*
73				*Not in force*
75				*Not in force*
76	(1)			See Sch 12 below
	(2)			See Sch 13 below

Schedule

1–3				*Not in force*
5–11				*Not in force*
12, para	1–29			*Not in force*
	30	(1)–(22)		*Not in force*
		(23)	(b), (c)	*Not in force*
		(24)–26)		*Not in force*
	31–45			*Not in force*
	46	(1)		*Not in force*
		(2)	(a)	*Not in force*
			(b)[1]	*Not in force*
		(3)–(6)		*Not in force*
	47–63			*Not in force*
13				*Not in force*

[1] Provided that a day has previously been appointed for the purposes of Sch 12, para 46(2)(b), comes into force on the coming into force of the Companies Act 1989, s 92; where such a day has not previously been appointed, comes into force on a day to be appointed.

Abolition of Poindings and Warrant Sales (Scotland) Act 2001 (asp 1)

RA: 17 Jan 2001
Section
1–3   In force 31 Dec 2002 (unless the
                                                 Scottish Ministers by order appoint
                                                 an earlier date)
Schedule   In force 31 Dec 2002 (unless the
                                                 Scottish Ministers by order appoint
                                                 an earlier date)

Access to Justice Act 1999 (c 22)

RA: 27 Jul 1999
Section
24   See Sch 4 below
28   *Not in force*
31   *Not in force*
50–52   *Not in force*
77   *Not in force*
80   *Not in force*
101–103   *Not in force* (S)
106   See Sch 15 below
Schedule
1, 2   *Not in force*
8   *Not in force*
15, Pt   V   (1)   *Not in force* (repeals of or in
                                                 Magistrates' Courts Act 1980,
                                                 s 67(8); Children Act 1989, Sch 11)
                          (2)   *Not in force*

Administration of Justice Act 1982 (c 53)

RA: 28 Oct 1982
Section
23–25   *Not in force*
27, 28   *Not in force*
35   Spent
48   *Not in force*
73   (8)   Spent
75   See Sch 9 below
Schedule
1, Pt   IV   *Not in force*
2   *Not in force*
9, Pt   I   *Not in force* (repeals of or in
                                                 Prevention of Fraud (Investments)
                                                 Act 1958; Administration of Justice
                                                 Act 1977; Supreme Court
                                                 Act 1981, s 126)
              II   *Not in force* (revocation in
                                                 SI 1979/1575)

Administration of Justice Act 1985 (c 61)

RA: 30 Oct 1985
Section

34	(3)		*Not in force*
67	(1)		See Sch 7 below
	(2)		See Sch 8 below

Schedule

7, para	6	*Not in force*
8, Pt	III	*Not in force* (repeals in Legal Aid Act 1974, ss 12(3)–(5), 38(2)–(6)) (now repealed Legal Aid Act 1988, s 45, Sch 6)

Adoption (Intercountry Aspects) Act 1999 (c 18)

RA: 27 Jul 1999
Section

1–8		*Not in force*
10		*Not in force*; prospectively repealed by Care Standards Act 2000, s 117(2), Sch 6
11, 12		*Not in force*
13		*Not in force* (so far as it inserts Adoption Act 1976, s 72(3B); Adoption (Scotland) Act 1978, s 65(3B))
15		*Not in force*
16	(1)	*Not in force*
17		*Not in force*

Schedule

1–3	*Not in force*

Adults with Incapacity (Scotland) Act 2000 (asp 4)

RA: 9 May 2000
Section

35–52				*Not in force*
85				See Sch 3 below
88				See Schs 4–6 below

Schedule

1				*Not in force*
3, para	1	(2)–(4)		*Not in force*
	2	(2)		*Not in force*
	7	(2)	(b)	*Not in force*
		(3)	(e)	*Not in force*
	11, 12			*Not in force*
4, para	5			*Not in force*
	7	(d)		*Not in force*
5, para	4			*Not in force*
	10, 11			*Not in force*

Adults with Incapacity (Scotland) Act 2000 (asp 4)—*contd*
Schedule

5, para	17	(22), (23)	*Not in force*
6			*Not in force* (repeals in the Improvement of Land Act 1864, s 24 and the Mental Health (Scotland) Act 1984, s 5(2))

Agriculture Act 1986 (c 49)

RA: 25 Jul 1986
Section

8	(1)	*Not in force*
	(3)	*Not in force*

Schedule

4	*Not in force* (repeals consequential on s 8)

Ancient Monuments and Archaeological Areas Act 1979 (c 46)

RA: 4 Apr 1979
Section

33–41	*Not in force* (S)

Schedule

2	*Not in force* (S)

Antarctic Act 1994 (c 15)

RA: 5 Jul 1994
Section

33	See Schedule below

Schedule

2	*Not in force* (repeals of Antarctic Treaty Act 1967, ss 6, 7(2)(b), 8–11)

Antarctic Minerals Act 1989 (c 21)

RA:

21 Jul 1989

Whole Act repealed, except ss 14, 20, by Antarctic Act 1994, s 33, Schedule (this Act was never brought into force)

Anti-terrorism, Crime and Security Act 2001 (c 24)

RA: 14 Feb 2001
Section

58–75	*Not in force*
78	*Not in force*

Anti-terrorism, Crime and Security Act 2001 (c 24)—*contd*

Section

101		See Sch 7 below
121		*Not in force*
125		See Sch 8 below

Schedule

5, 6		*Not in force*
8, Pt	5	*Not in force* (repeals of or in Nuclear Installations Act 1965)
	7	*Not in force* (repeals of or in Terrorism Act 2000)

Arbitration Act 1996 (c 23)

RA: 17 Jun 1996

Section

85–87		*Not in force*
107	(1)	See Sch 3 below

Schedule

3, para	1	Spent

Armed Forces Act 1996 (c 46)

RA: 24 Jul 1996

Section

8		*Not in force*
35	(2)	See Sch 7 below
36		*Not in force*

Schedule

2		*Not in force*
7, Pt	III	*Not in force* (repeals of or in Mental Health Act 1983, s 46; Mental Health (Scotland) Act 1984, s 69; Mental Health (Northern Ireland) Order 1986, SI 1986/595 (NI 4), art 52)

Armed Forces Act 2001 (c 19)

RA: 11 May 2001

Section

2–16		*Not in force*
17		See Sch 1 below
19		See Sch 2 below
20–22		*Not in force*
25–31		*Not in force*
32	(1)–(8)	*Not in force*
	(9)	See Sch 5 below
34		See Sch 6 below
38		See Sch 7 below

Armed Forces Act 2001 (c 19)—*contd*

Schedule

3, 4				*Not in force*
5, para	1–4			*Not in force*
	5	(1)		*Not in force*
		(2)	(a)	*Not in force*
		(3)		*Not in force*
	6, 7			*Not in force*
6, Pt	6, paras	41, 42		*Not in force*
		50	(1)	*Not in force* (insofar as it relates to sub-para (2))
			(2)	*Not in force*
		55, 56		*Not in force*
7, Pt	2			*Not in force*
	7			*Not in force* (repeals in or of the Naval Discipline Act 1957, s 12A(1) and the Courts-Martial (Appeals) Act 1968, s 42)

Asylum and Immigration Act 1996 (c 49)

RA: 24 Jul 1996

Section

12	(2)	See Sch 3 below

Schedule

3, para	4	*Not in force*

British Nationality (Hong Kong) Act 1990 (c 34)

RA: 26 Jul 1990

Section

2	(2)	*Not in force*

British Steel Act 1988 (c 35)

RA: 29 Jul 1988

Section

16	(3)	See Sch 2 below

Schedule

2, Pt	II	*Not in force*

British Technology Group Act 1991 (c 66)

RA: 22 Oct 1991

Section

17	(2)	See Sch 2 below

Schedule

2, Pt	II	*Not in force*

Broadcasting Act 1990 (c 42)

RA: 1 Nov 1990

Section

127	(3)	No date (dissolution date for the purposes of s 127(3))
203	(1)	See Sch 20 below
	(3)	See Sch 21 below

Schedule

20, para	36	*Not in force* (so far as replaces the reference to the Independent Broadcasting Authority until that Authority is dissolved by order under s 127(3))
	21	*Not in force* (entries for Cable Authority and Independent Broadcasting Authority in House of Commons Disqualification Act 1975, Sch 1, Pt II; Northern Ireland Assembly Disqualification Act 1975, Sch 1, Pt II)

Broadcasting Act 1996 (c 55)

RA: 24 Jul 1996

Section

82	*Not in force*

Building Act 1984 (c 55)

RA: 31 Oct 1984

Section

12, 13		*Not in force* (other than so far as enable regulations to be made)
20		*Not in force*
31		*Not in force* (other than so far as enables regulations to be made)
33		*Not in force*
38		*Not in force* (other than so far as enables regulations to be made)
42	(1)–(3)	*Not in force*
	(4)–(6)	*Not in force* (other than so far as enable regulations to be made)
	(7)	No date (appointed day for the purposes of s 42(7))
43	(1), (2)	*Not in force*
	(3)	*Not in force* (other than so far as enables regulations to be made)
44, 45		*Not in force*

Building Act 1984 (c 55)—*contd*
Section

133	(2)	*Not in force* (so far as relates to Town and Country Planning Act 1947 (repealed); Atomic Energy Authority Act 1954)

Schedule

7	*Not in force* (repeals of or in Town and Country Planning Act 1947 (repealed); Atomic Energy Authority Act 1954)

Building Societies Act 1986 (c 53)

RA: 25 Jul 1986
Section

35	Repealed (*never in force*)
124	*Not in force* (prospectively repealed by Courts and Legal Services Act 1990, s 125(7), Sch 20)

Schedule

21	*Not in force* (prospectively repealed by virtue of Courts and Legal Services Act 1990, s 125(7), Sch 20)

Care Standards Act 2000 (c 14)

RA: 20 Jul 2000
Section

4	(1)	See sub-ss (2)–(9) below
	(2), (3), (5), (6)	In force fully 1 Jul 2002 (E)
	(7)	*Not in force* (E) (except for the purpose of the exercise of power to make regulations)
	(8)	In force fully 1 Jul 2002 (E)
	(9)	In force 1 Jul 2002 (except in so far as it relates to voluntary adoption agencies)
5		*Not in force* (E) (except in so far as it relates to the Commission)
7	(1)-(6)	*Not in force* (W)
8		*Not in force* (W) (except for purpose of enabling subordinate legislation to be made)
9	(1), (2)	*Not in force*
	(3)–(5)	*Not in force* (E)
10	(1)–(5)	*Not in force* (W)
	(6)	*Not in force*
	(7)	*Not in force* (W)

Care Standards Act 2000 (c 14)—*contd*

Section

11, 12			*Not in force* (W) (except for the purpose of enabling subordinate legislation to be made)
13			*Not in force* (W)
14, 15			*Not in force* (W) (except for purpose of enabling subordinate legislation to be made)
17–21, 24, 26–32			*Not in force* (W)
36			*Not in force* (W) (except for purpose of enabling subordinate legislation to be made)
37			*Not in force* (W)
42			*Not in force* (E)
43	(1), (2)		*Not in force* (E) (except in so far as they relate to relevant fostering functions)
	(3)	(a)	*Not in force* (E)
		(b)	*Not in force* (E) (except in so far as they relate to relevant fostering functions)
44			*Not in force* (E) (except in so far as relates to relevant fostering functions)
			Not in force (W)
45	(1)–(4)		*Not in force* (E) (except in so far as relates to relevant fostering functions)
			Not in force (W)
46	(1)–(6)		*Not in force* (E) (except in so far as relates to relevant fostering functions)
			Not in force (W)
	(7)	(a), (b)	*Not in force* (E) (except in so far as relates to relevant fostering functions)
			Not in force (W)
		(c), (d)	*Not in force*
	(8)		*Not in force* (E) (except in so far as relates to relevant fostering functions)
			Not in force (W)
47			*Not in force* (E) (except in so far as relates to relevant fostering functions)
			Not in force (W)
48			*Not in force* (E) (except for the purpose of the excerise of any power to make regulations and in so far as relates to the relevant fostering functions)
49–52			*Not in force* (E) (except so far as they relate to relevant fostering functions)
53			*Not in force* (E) (except in so far as relates to relevant fostering functions)
			Not in force (W)

Care Standards Act 2000 (c 14)—*contd*

Section

54	(2)	*Not in force*
55		*Not in force* (E) (except so far as relates to ss 54(1)(a), (4), (5), (6), (7)(a), 59, 60, 62, 63, 65, 66, 71, Sch 1, paras 1–5, 7, 8, 12–14, 16, 18–26)
56–58		*Not in force*
59, 60		*Not in force* (E) (except so far as relates to the General Social Care Council, for purpose only of the exercise of any power to make rules and prepare codes of practice)
		Not in force (W)
61		*Not in force*
62		*Not in force* (E) (except so far as relates to the General Social Care Council, for purpose only of the exercise of any power to make rules and prepare codes of practice) (SI 2001/1536)
		Not in force (W)
63		*Not in force* (E) (except so far as relates to the General Social Care Council, for purpose only of the exercise of any power to make rules and prepare codes of practice)
64		*Not in force*
65		*Not in force* (E) (except so far as relates to the General Social Care Council, for purpose only of the exercise of any power to make rules and prepare codes of practice)
		Not in force (W)
66		*Not in force* (E) (except so far as relates to the General Social Care Council, for purpose only of the exercise of any power to make rules and prepare codes of practice)
67		*Not in force* (E)
68–69		*Not in force*
70	(1)	*Not in force* (E), (S), (NI)
71		*Not in force* (E) (except so far as relates to the General Social Care Council, for purpose only of the exercise of any power to make rules and prepare codes of practice)
		Not in force (W) (except so far as it applies to ss 63, 66 of this Act)

Care Standards Act 2000 (c 14)—*contd*

Section

79	(1)	*Not in force* (E) (insofar as relates to Pt XA, ss 79B(8), 79K(5), 79L(6), (7), 79M, 79P(1)–(4), 79Q(2), (3))
		In force 2 Sep 2002 (E) (for purpose of giving effect to Pt XA, ss 79P(1), (2), 79Q(2), (3))
		Not in force (W) (except for purpose of enabling subordinate legislation to be made under a provision inserted by it into Children Act 1989 and for purposes of inserting Children Act 1989, s 79B(2), (9) (to the extent necessary for the purposes of enabling subordinate legislation to be made under Sch 9A to the 1989 Act)
	(2)	*Not in force* (W) (except for purpose of enabling subordinate legislation to be made under Children Act 1989 , Sch 9A)
	(5)	*Not in force* (W)
80	(1)–(7)	*Not in force*
	(8)	*Not in force* (except for purposes of regulations under s 103 of this Act)
81–93		*Not in force*
95		*Not in force*
97		*Not in force*
102		*Not in force*
104		*Not in force*
105, 106, 109, 110		*Not in force* (W)
111	(1)	*Not in force* (W)
	(2)	*Not in force* (E) (except in so far as it omits Employment Agencies Act 1973, s 13(7) (b), (c), and the proviso thereto)
		Not in force (W)
113	(1)	*Not in force*
113	(3), (4)	*Not in force* (so far as relates to the National Care Standards Commission or the General Social Care Council)
114		*Not in force* (S) (NI)
115		*Not in force* (S) (NI)
116		See Sch 4 below
117	(1)	See Sch 5 below
	(2)	See Sch 6 below

Care Standards Act 2000 (c 14)—*contd*

Schedule

3				*Not in force* (W) (except for purpose of enabling subordinate legislation to be made under Children Act 1989, Sch 9A)
				Not in force (E)
4, paras	1			*Not in force* (W), (S)
	2–4			*Not in force* (W)
	5	(1)		*Not in force* (W)
		(2)		*Not in force*
		(3)		*Not in force* (W)
		(4), (5)		*Not in force*
		(6)		*Not in force* (E)
		(7)		*Not in force*
		(8)		*Not in force* (W)
		(9)–(11)		*Not in force*
	6			*Not in force*
	7			*Not in force* (W)
	8			*Not in force* (W)
	9	(1)–(4)		*Not in force* (W)
		(5)		*Not in force* (W), (S)
		(6)–(10)		*Not in force* (W)
	11			*Not in force* (W), (S)
	12			*Not in force*
	13			*Not in force* (W), (S), (NI)
	14	(1), (2)		*Not in force* (W), (S) (application to Scotland repealed as from a day to be appointed)
		(3)		*Not in force* (W)
		(4)–(6)		*Not in force*
		(7)–(9)		*Not in force* (W)
		(10)(a)		*Not in force* (W)
		(10)(b)		*Not in force*
		(11), (12)		*Not in force* (W)
		(13), (14)		*Not in force*
		(16)	(a)	*Not in force* (W)
			(b)	*Not in force* (W), (S)
			(c), (d)	*Not in force* (W)
		(17)–(21)		*Not in force* (W)
		(22)		*Not in force*
4, paras	14	(23)(a)	(i)–(iii)	*Not in force* (W), (S)
			(iv), (v)	*Not in force* (W), (S)
			(vi), (vii)	*Not in force* (W), (S)
		(23)(b)		*Not in force* (W), (S)
		(24)–(28)		*Not in force* (W)
		(29)		*Not in force*
	15–20			*Not in force* (W)
	21			*Not in force* (E) (in so far as it relates to words "and vulnerable adults")
				Not in force (W), (S), (NI)

Care Standards Act 2000 (c 14)—*contd*

Schedule

4, paras	22		Not in force
	23		Not in force (S)
	24	(1), (2)	Not in force (W)
		(3), (4)	Not in force
	25		Not in force (W), (S), (NI)
	26	(3)	Not in force (E) (in so far as it inserts Protection of Children Act 1999, s 9(2)(b) and 9(2)(d) (in so far as s 9(2)(d) relates to ss 68, 87, 88 of the 2000 Act) and s 9(3A))
			Not in force (W)
	27		Not in force
	28		Not in force (W)
5, paras	1		Not in force (E)
	2		Not in force (E)
			Not in force (W) (except for purpose of enabling subordinate legislation to be made)
	6		Not in force (E) (in so far as relates to Public Records Act 1958; Chronically Sick and Disabled Persons Act 1970, s 18 (except sub-ss (1), (3) thereof); Adoption Act 1976; Health and Social Services and Social Security Adjudication Act 1983; Children Act 1989, s 105(1) definition "child minder"; Tribunals and Inquiries Act 1992; Judicial Pensions and Retirement Act 1993; Protection of Children Act 1999, ss 2(9), 7(2), 12(1); and Adoption (Intercountry Aspects) Act 1999
			Not in force (W) (except in so far as relates to Protection of Children Act 1999, ss 10, 13)
			Not in force (S)

Carers and Disabled Children Act 2000 (c 16)

RA: 20 Jul 2000

Section

3		Not in force
7	(1)	Not in force (so far as it inserts Children Act 1989, s 17B)
9		Not in force (so far as it relates to the provision of vouchers)
11	(4)	Not in force (W)

Carriage by Air and Road Act 1979 (c 28)

RA: 4 Apr 1979
Section

1			*Not in force*
3	(4)		*Not in force*
4	(3)		*Not in force*
	(4)		*Not in force* (other than so far as relates to amendment of the Carriage by Air Act 1961 by s 4(1) and amendment of Carriage of Goods by Road Act 1965 by s 4(2))
5			*Not in force* (other than so far as relates to amendment of the Carriage by Air Act 1961 by s 4(1) and amendment of Carriage of Goods by Road Act 1965 by s 4(2))
6	(1)	(c)	*Not in force*
	(2)		*Not in force*
	(4)		*Not in force*

Schedule

1, 2	*Not in force*

Carriage of Passengers by Road Act 1974 (c 35)

RA: 31 Jul 1974
Section

1–6	*Not in force*
Schedule	*Not in force*

Charities Act 1992 (c 41)

RA: 16 Mar 1992
Section

1			'financial year', 'independent examiner' and 'special trust' in sub-s (1), and sub-s (3) (now repealed))
65–74			*Not in force*

Schedule

6, para	9		*Not in force*
	10	(b)	*Not in force*
	13	(2)	Repealed (*never in force*)
7			*Not in force* (repeals of or in Police, Factories &c (Miscellaneous Provisions) Act 1916; House to House Collections Act 1939; Charities Act 1960, s 8(1), (2), (6)(a), (7); Theft Act 1968, Sch 2, Pt III; Local Government Act 1972, Sch 29, paras 22, 23; Charities Act 1985, s 1)

Child Support Act 1991 (c 48)

RA: 25 Jul 1991
Section

30	(2)	*Not in force*
34	(2)	*Not in force*
37	(2), (3)	*Not in force*
58	(12)	*Not in force*

Child Support Act 1995 (c 34)

RA: 19 Jul 1995
Section

2		*Not in force* (in respect of insertion of Child Support Act 1991, s 28B(6) (substituted by Social Security Act 1998, s 86, Sch 7, para 35, Sch 8))
9		*Not in force* (in respect of insertion of Child Support Act 1991, s 28I(1)–(3))
22		*Not in force*
30	(5)	See Sch 3 below
Schedule		
3, para	5	Repealed (*never in force*)
	9	*Not in force*
	13	*Not in force*

Child Support, Pensions and Social Security Act 2000 (c 19)

RA: 28 Jul 2000
Section

1	(1), (2)	*Not in force*
	(3)	See Sch 1 below
2		*Not in force*
3–5		*Not in force* (except for the purpose of making regulations and Acts of Sederunt)
6		See Sch 2 below
8		*Not in force*
9, 10		*Not in force* (except for the purpose of making regulations and Acts of Sederunt)
12		*Not in force*
18–21		*Not in force* (except for the purpose of making regulations and Acts of Sederunt)
22	(4)	*Not in force*
23		*Not in force*
25		*Not in force* (except for the purpose of making regulations and Acts of Sederunt)

Child Support, Pensions and Social Security Act 2000 (c 19)—*contd*

Section

26		See Sch 3 below
28		*Not in force*
29		*Not in force* (except for the purpose of making regulations and Acts of Sederunt)
43–46		*Not in force*
49	(1)	*Not in force* (except so far as it inserts Pensions Act 1995, s 72A(1)–(3) (except for the words "Subject to subsection (4)," and "(apart from any postponement under subsection (4))"), (7), (8)(a), (9))
52		*Not in force* (so far as inserts Pension Schemes Act 1993, s 113(3B))
54		*Not in force* (except for the purpose of making regulations and rules)
56		See Sch 5 below
62	(1)–(10)	*Not in force* (except for the purposes of making regulations and for the purposes of its application to any person who, as a result of a relevant community order (as defined in s 62(8) of this Act) being made in accordance with s 64(1) of this Act in relation to him, falls to be supervised by an officer of the local probation board for any of the probation areas of Derbyshire, Hertfordshire, Teesside and West Midlands)
	(11)	*Not in force* (except for the purposes of making regulations)
63		*Not in force* (except for the purposes of making regulations and for the purposes of its application to any person who, as a result of a relevant community order (as defined in s 62(8) of this Act) being made in accordance with s 64(1) of this Act in relation to him, falls to be supervised by an officer of the local probation board for any of the probation areas of Derbyshire, Hertfordshire, Teesside and West Midlands)
64	(1)	*Not in force* (except for the purposes of making regulations and for the purposes of its application to any person who, as a result of a

Child Support, Pensions and Social Security Act 2000 (c 19)—*contd*
Section

64	(1)—*contd*		relevant community order (as defined in s 62(8) of this Act) being made in relation to him, falls to be supervised by an officer of the local probation board for any of the probation areas of Derbyshire, Hertfordshire, Teesside and West Midlands)
	(2)		*Not in force* (except for the purposes of making regulations and for the purposes of its application to any person who, as a result of a relevant community order (as defined in s 62(8) of this Act) being made in accordance with s 64(1) of this Act in relation to him, falls to be supervised by an officer of the local probation board for any of the probation areas of Derbyshire, Hertfordshire, Teesside and West Midlands)
	(3)		*Not in force* (except for the purposes of making regulations)
	(4)	(a)	*Not in force* (except for the purposes of making regulations and for the purposes of its application to any person who, as a result of a relevant community order (as defined in s 62(8) of this Act) being made in accordance with s 64(1) of this Act in relation to him, falls to be supervised by an officer of the local probation board for any of the probation areas of Derbyshire, Hertfordshire, Teesside and West Midlands)
		(b)	*Not in force* (except for the purposes of making regulations)
	(5), (6)		*Not in force* (except for the purposes of making regulations and for the purposes of its application to any person who, as a result of a relevant community order (as defined in s 62(8) of this Act) being made in accordance with s 64(1) of this Act in relation to him, falls to be

Child Support, Pensions and Social Security Act 2000 (c 19)—*contd*

Section

64	(5), (6)—*contd*	supervised by an officer of the local probation board for any of the probation areas of Derbyshire, Hertfordshire, Teesside and West Midlands)
	(7) (a)–(c)	*Not in force* (except for the purposes of making regulations and for the purposes of its application to any person who, as a result of a relevant community order (as defined in s 62(8) of this Act) being made in accordance with s 64(1) of this Act in relation to him, falls to be supervised by an officer of the local probation board for any of the probation areas of Derbyshire, Hertfordshire, Teesside and West Midlands)
	(d)	*Not in force* (except for the purposes of making regulations)
	(8)	*Not in force* (except for the purposes of making regulations and for the purposes of its application to any person who, as a result of a relevant community order (as defined in s 62(8) of this Act) being made in accordance with s 64(1) of this Act in relation to him, falls to be supervised by an officer of the local probation board for any of the probation areas of Derbyshire, Hertfordshire, Teesside and West Midlands)
	(9)	*Not in force* (except for the purposes of making regulations)
	(10)	*Not in force* (except for the purposes of making regulations and for the purposes of its application to any person who, as a result of a relevant community order (as defined in s 62(8) of this Act) being made in accordance with s 64(1) of this Act in relation to him, falls to be supervised by an officer of the local probation board for any of the probation areas of Derbyshire, Hertfordshire, Teesside and West Midlands)

Child Support, Pensions and Social Security Act 2000 (c 19)—*contd*
Section

64	(11)	*Not in force* (except for the purposes of making regulations)
65	(1)–(6)	*Not in force* (except for the purposes of making regulations and for the purposes of its application to any person who, as a result of a relevant community order (as defined in s 62(8) of this Act) being made in accordance with s 64(1) of this Act in relation to him, falls to be supervised by an officer of the local probation board for any of the probation areas of Derbyshire, Hertfordshire, Teesside and West Midlands)
	(7)	*Not in force* (except for the purposes of making regulations)
	(8)	*Not in force* (except for the purposes of making regulations and for the purposes of its application to any person who, as a result of a relevant community order (as defined in s 62(8) of this Act) being made in accordance with s 64(1) of this Act in relation to him, falls to be supervised by an officer of the local probation board for any of the probation areas of Derbyshire, Hertfordshire, Teesside and West Midlands)
66		*Not in force* (except for the purposes of its application to any person who, as a result of a relevant community order (as defined in s 62(8) of this Act) being made in accordance with s 64(1) of this Act in relation to him, falls to be supervised by an officer of the local probation board for any of the probation areas of Derbyshire, Hertfordshire, Teesside and West Midlands)
68		See Sch 7 below
73		*Not in force* (so far as inserts into Social Security Administration Act 1992, s 170(5), new para (af) into definitions "relevant enactments" and "relevant Northern Ireland enactments", so far as each new para (af) refers to—

Child Support, Pensions and Social Security Act 2000 (c 19)—*contd*

Section

73—*contd*				(i) s 70;
				(ii) Sch 7, paras 2, 5, 7, 11, 17, 18, 22 and so far as relating to those paras, para 1 and s 68)
85				See Sch 9 below

Schedule

1, 2				*Not in force* (except for the purpose of making regulations and Acts of Sederunt)
3, paras	1–10			*Not in force*
	11	(1)		*Not in force*
		(2)		*Not in force* (so far as it changes "absent parent" to "non-resident parent" in the Child Support Act 1991 other than in ss 15(4A) and 44(1), (2A) of that Act)
		(3)–(16)		*Not in force*
		(18)		*Not in force* (except for the purpose of making regulations and Acts of Sederunt)
		(19)–(22)		*Not in force*
	12			*Not in force*
		(2)		*Not in force*
	14, 15			*Not in force*
5, Pt	I, para	12	(2)–(4)	*Not in force*
7, paras	17			*Not in force*
	18	(2)	(b)	*Not in force*
	22	(1)		*Not in force* (for the purposes of reviews relating to housing benefit or council tax benefit held and completed before that date)
	22	(1)		*Not in force* (for the purposes of reviews relating to housing benefit or council tax benefit held and completed before 2 Jul 2001)
9, Pt	I			*Not in force* (except in relation to repeals relating to Child Support Act 1991, ss 15(10), 40(1), (2); Child Support Act 1995, s 24; Social Security Act 1998, Sch 7, para 28; SI 1998/2780)
	III	(1)		*Not in force*
		(3)		*Not in force* (repeal of Pension Act 1995, s 157(7))
		(10)		*Not in force*
	V			*Not in force*

Child Support, Pensions and Social Security Act 2000 (c 19)—*contd*

Schedule

9, Pt	VI	*Not in force* (for the purposes of reviews relating to housing benefit or council tax benefit held and completed before 2 Jul 2001)
	VII	*Not in force* (for the purposes of reviews relating to housing benefit or council tax benefit held and completed before 2 Jul 2001)

Children (Leaving Care) Act 2000 (c 35)

RA: 30 Nov 2000

Section

4	*Not in force* (W) (so far as Children Act 1989, s 24C relates to Primary Care Trusts)

Children Act 1975 (c 72)

RA: 12 Nov 1975

Whole Act repealed (E, W, NI)

Section

70	*Not in force*

Schedule

4, Pt	VII	*Not in force* (in relation to Adoption Act 1958, s 28(2), now spent)

Children and Young Persons Act 1969 (c 54)

RA: 22 Oct 1969

Section

5	(9)	*Not in force* (other than so far as relates to the definition of "the appropriate local authority")

Schedule

4, para	2, 3	Repealed (*never in force*)
	5(1)	*Not in force*
5, para	11	*Not in force*
	55	*Not in force*
6		*Not in force* (repeals in Children and Young Persons Act 1933, ss 55★ (except repeals in sub-ss (2), (4) thereof), 56(1)★, 58, 59(1)★, 77(2), (2A), 79(1)–(3), (5), 80, 81(1), (3), 103, 104, 106(3)–(5), 107(1) (so far as it relates to the definitions of "approved school" and "managers") and Sch 4, paras 1–3, 14;

Children and Young Persons Act 1969 (c 54)—*contd*

Schedule

6—*contd*

Superannuation (Miscellaneous
Provisions) Act 1948, s 14;
Children Act 1948, ss 49(1), 59(2)
(repealed); Criminal Justice
Act 1948, ss 49(1)–(4), (6), 77,
80(1) (so far as it relates to the
definitions of "approved school"
and "remand home"), Sch 9 (so far
as it relates to the Children and
Young Persons Act 1933, ss 58,
77); Magistrates' Courts Act 1952,
s 32 (repealed); Criminal Justice
Act 1961, ss 1, 4, 7(2), 8(1), 10(2)
(repealed), 18, 19; London
Government Act 1963, s 47;
Children and Young Persons
Act 1963, Sch 3, para 15)

★   These entries were repealed by the Crime and Disorder Act 1998, s 120(2), Sch 10; ss 55 and 56 of the
1933 Act were repealed by the Powers of Criminal Courts (Sentencing) Act 2000, s 165, Sch 12, Pt I

Children (Scotland) Act 1995 (c 36)

RA: 19 Jul 1995

Section

98	(1)	See Sch 2 below
105	(4)	See Sch 4 below
	(5)	See Sch 5 below

Schedule

5	*Not in force* (repeal relating to Trusts (Scotland) Act 1921)

Chiropractors Act 1994 (c 17)

RA: 5 Jul 1994

Section

1	(2)	*Not in force* (so far as relates to provisions of this Act not yet in force)
	(3)	*Not in force* (so far as relates to provisions of this Act not yet in force)
	(4)	In force fully 16 Jun 2004
5		*Not in force*
43		*Not in force* (so far as it provides the definition "provisionally registered chiropractor")

Schedule

1, Pt	I, para	3	In force fully 16 Jun 2004
		12	In force fully 16 Jun 2003

Church of England (Miscellaneous Provisions) Measure 1995 (No 2)

RA: 19 Jul 1995

The provisions of this Measure (except s 6) were brought into force on 1 Sep 1995 by an instrument made by the Archbishops of Canterbury and York and dated 26 Jul 1995 (made under s 15(2))

Church of England (Miscellaneous Provisions) Measure 2000 (No 1)

RA: 28 Jul 2000

Not in force

Civil Evidence Act 1968 (c 64)

RA: 25 Oct 1968
Section

1–10	*Not in force* (as regards bankruptcy proceedings)

Civil Evidence Act 1972 (c 30)

RA: 12 Jun 1972
Section

4	(2)–(5)	*Not in force* (as regards bankruptcy proceedings)

Civil Evidence Act 1995 (c 38)

RA: 8 Nov 1995
Section

10		*Not in force*; prospectively repealed (NI) by the Civil Evidence (Northern Ireland) Order 1997, SI 1997/2983 (NI 21), art 13(2), Sch 2, subject to savings
16	(5)	*Not in force*; prospectively repealed (NI) by the Civil Evidence (Northern Ireland) Order 1997, SI 1997/2983 (NI 21), art 13(2), Sch 2, subject to savings

Coal Industry Act 1994 (c 21)

RA: 5 Jul 1994
Section

22	(2)	*Not in force*
67	(1)	See Sch 9 below
	(8)	See Sch 11 below
Schedule		
9, para	7	*Not in force*
	24	*Not in force*
	29, 30	*Not in force*

Coal Industry Act 1994 (c 21)—*contd*
Schedule

9, para	45	*Not in force*
11, Pt	III	*Not in force* (repeals of or in Coal Industry Nationalisation Act 1946, ss 27, 28, 34(1), 35, 37, 41, 55, 56, 59–62, 63(1), (3), (4), 64, 65, Sch 2A; Coal Industry Act 1949, ss 4, 7, 8, 13; Miners' Welfare Act 1952; Coal Industry Act 1962, ss 1, 2, 4; Coal Industry Act 1965, ss 1, 4(1), 5, Sch 1; Coal Industry Act 1967, ss 4, 7, 8; National Loans Act 1968, Sch 1; Coal Industry Act 1971, ss 4, 9, 10; Coal Industry Act 1973, ss 2, 10, Sch 1, paras 2–3; Statutory Corporations (Financial Provisions) Act 1975, Sch 2, Sch 4, para 2; National Coal Board (Finance) Act 1976, ss 2, 4; Coal Industry Act 1977, ss 1, 7, 11(1), 12(1), (2), 13–16, Schs 1, 3, Sch 4, paras 1(1), (7), 2, 3, Sch 5; Coal Industry Act 1980, ss 1, 2, 7, 9–11; Coal Industry Act 1982, ss 3, 5, 6; Miscellaneous Financial Provisions Act 1983, Sch 2; Coal Industry Act 1983, ss 1, 2, 4–6, Schedule; Companies Consolidation (Consequential Provisions) Act 1985, Sch 2; Coal Industry Act 1985, ss 3–5; Coal Industry Act 1987, ss 3, 4, 6–9, 10(2)–(4), Sch 1, paras 1(3), (4), 3, 8, 11(1), (2), 16, 18(1), (2), 21, 27, 30, 34(1)–(3), 36, 41, Schs 2, 3; Companies Act 1989, Sch 18, paras 1, 18; Coal Industry Act 1990, ss 1, 3, 6; Coal Mining Subsidence Act 1991, s 49(4); Coal Industry Act 1992; British Coal and British Rail (Transfer Proposals) Act 1993)
	IV	*Not in force*

Companies Act 1989 (c 40)

RA: 16 Nov 1989
Section

46		*Not in force*
47	(2)–(6)	*Not in force*
48	(3)	*Not in force*

Companies Act 1989 (c 40)—*contd*

Section

65	(2)		*Not in force* (so far as s 65(2)(g) refers to a body established under s 46)
75	(3)	(c)	*Not in force* (so far as s 75(3)(c) refers to a body established under s 46)
92–107			*Not in force*
128			*Not in force*
133			*Not in force*
140	(7), (8)		*Not in force*
145			See Sch 19 below
192			*Not in force* (so far as relates to Financial Services Act 1986, s 47B)
206	(1)		See Sch 23 below
212			See Sch 24 below

Schedule

13		*Not in force*
15, 16		*Not in force*
19, para	13	*Not in force*
23, para	32	*Not in force* (so far as relates to Financial Services Act 1986, Sch 11, para 13B)
24		*Not in force* (repeals of or in Companies Act 1985, ss 160(3), 466(4)–(6), 744 (definitions of "authorised minimum", "expert", "floating charge", "joint stock company", "undistributable reserves"), Sch 24 (the entry relating to s 389(10); Insolvency Act 1985, Sch 6, para 7(3); Insolvency Act 1986, ss 45(5), 53(2), 54(3), 62(5), Sch 10, column 5 (entries relating to ss 45(5), 53(2), 54(3), 62(5)); Financial Services Act 1986, s 13, Sch 11, para 14(3) (but note that Sch 23, Pt I, para 1, Pt II, para 33(1), (4), which also repeal those provisions, have been brought into force); Banking Act 1987, s 90, Sch 6; Criminal Justice (Scotland) Act 1987; Criminal Justice Act 1988; Copyright, Designs and Patents Act 1988)

Note: erroneous repeal of Financial Services Act 1986, s 199(1), by s 212, Sch 24, brought into force on 21 Feb 1990 by SI 1990/142, art 7(d), was revoked by SI 1990/355, art 16, as from 1 Mar 1990

Competition Act 1998 (c 41)

RA: 9 Nov 1998

Section			
1	(a)		*Not in force*
74	(2)		See Sch 13 below
	(3)		See Sch 14 below
Schedule			
5, para	7		*Not in force*
6, para	7		*Not in force*
13, para	11		*Not in force* (except for the purpose of prescribing modifications to the Restrictive Trade Practices Act 1976)
14, Pt	I		*Not in force* (repeal of Restrictive Practices Court Act 1976)

Competition and Service (Utilities) Act 1992 (c 43)

RA: 16 Mar 1992

Section		
6	(1)	*Not in force* (so far as inserts Telecommunications Act 1984, s 27G(8))
7		*Not in force* (so far as inserts Telecommunications Act 1984, s 27H(4))
17		*Not in force*
23		*Not in force*
36		*Not in force*

Contracts (Applicable Law) Act 1990 (c 36)

RA: 26 Jul 1990

Section			
2	(1)		*Not in force* (so far as relates to the Brussels Protocol and the Funchal Convention as defined in s 1)
3	(1), (2)		*Not in force*
	(3)	(b)	*Not in force*

Control of Pollution Act 1974 (c 40)

RA: 31 Jul 1974

Section			
1			Repealed (*never in force*)
24	(1)–(3)		*Not in force*; prospectively repealed by the Litter Act 1983, s 12(3), Sch 2
27	(1)	(b)	Repealed (*never in force*) (S)

Control of Pollution Act 1974 (c 40)—*contd*

Section

28	*Not in force* (S); prospectively repealed by the Environmental Protection Act 1990, s 162, Sch 16, Pt II

Schedule

3, para 7	*Not in force*
4	*Not in force* (repeals of or in Burgh Police (Scotland) Act 1892 (repealed); Public Health (Scotland) Act 1897, s 39 (repealed), Burgh Police (Scotland) Act 1903 (repealed); Salmon and Freshwater Fisheries Act 1923 (repealed); Public Health Act 1936, ss 79, 80; Water (Scotland) Act 1945, s 18 (repealed); Rivers (Prevention of Pollution) Act 1951, s 5(1)(c), (6), (7) and ss 11, 12 (part) (repealed); Local Government (Miscellaneous Provisions) Act 1853, s 8; Radioactive Substances Act 1960, Sch 1, paras 3, 6, 7, 8A, 15 (repealed); London Government Act 1963, s 40(4)(d); Water Resources Act 1963, s 79; Gas Act 1965, s 4(5); Sea Fisheries Regulation Act 1966, s 5(1)(c); Civic Amenities Act 1967, s 23 (repealed); Criminal Justice Act 1967, Sch 3, entries (now spent) relating to Burgh Police (Scotland) Act 1892, s 114 and Public Health Act 1936, s 76(3); Countryside Act 1968, s 22 (repealed); Local Government Act 1972, ss 180, 236. Sch 14, paras 4, 49; Local Government (Scotland) Act 1973, s 136, Sch 16, paras 7–9, Sch 28, para 69 (repealed)

Countryside and Rights of Way Act 2000 (c 37)

RA: 30 Nov 1990

Section

2			*Not in force*
12–14			*Not in force*
18			*Not in force*
20			*Not in force*
46	(1)	(a)	*Not in force*

Countryside and Rights of Way Act 2000 (c 37)—*contd*

Section

46	(2)			*Not in force*
	(3)			See Sch 4 below
47–51				*Not in force*
53–56				*Not in force*
57				See Sch 6 below
60–63				*Not in force*
69				*Not in force*
70	(1)			*Not in force*
	(3)			*Not in force*
71				*Not in force*
97				*Not in force* (W)
99				*Not in force* (E)
100	(1)–(4)			*Not in force* (W)
	(5)	(a)		*Not in force*
		(b)		*Not in force* (W)
101				*Not in force*
102				See Sch 16 below

Schedule

2				*Not in force*
4, para	2, 3			*Not in force*
5				*Not in force*
6, Pt I	para	1–17		*Not in force*
		18	(a)	*Not in force* (E) (to the extent that in the Highways Act 1980, s 325(1)(d) it substitutes for "118, 119" references to ss 118B(4), 119B(4), 119D)
				Not in force (W) (to the extent that in the Highways Act 1980, s 325(1)(d) it substitutes for "118, 119" references to ss 118B(4), 119B(4), 119D)
			(b)	*Not in force*
		19		*Not in force* (E) (to the extent that in the Highways Act 1980, s 326(5) it substitutes for "a public path diversion order" references to a special extinguishment order, a special diversion order or an SSSI diversion order)
				Not in force (W) (to the extent that in the Highways Act 1980, s 326(5) it substitutes for "a public path diversion order" references to a special extinguishment order, a special diversion order or an SSSI diversion order)
		20–24		*Not in force*
Pt II	para	25, 26		*Not in force*

Countryside and Rights of Way Act 2000 (c 37)—*contd*

Schedule

7, para	6, 7	*Not in force*
16, Pt	I	*Not in force* (E) (entries relating to Law of Property Act 1925, s 193(2); Local Government Act 1972, Sch 17, para 35A; Local Government (Wales) Act 1994, Sch 6, para 13)
		Not in force (W) (entries relating to Law of Property Act 1925, s 193(2); Local Government Act 1972, Sch 17, para 35A; Local Government (Wales) Act 1994, Sch 6, para 13)
	II	*Not in force* (E) (entries relating to Wildlife and Countryside Act 1981, ss 54, 56(5), 57(1), Sch 15, para 9; Transport and Works Act 1992, Sch 2, paras 5(2), (4)(a), (d), (e), (6), (7), 6(2)(b), 10(4)(a))
		Not in force (W) (entries relating to Wildlife and Countryside Act 1981, ss 54, 56(5), 57(1), Sch 15, para 9; Transport and Works Act 1992, Sch 2, paras 5(2), (4)(a), (d), (e), (6), (7), 6(2)(b), 10(4)(a))

Courts and Legal Services Act 1990 (c 41)

RA: 1 Nov 1990

Section

12–14		*Not in force*
36–39		*Not in force*
41	(1)–(10)	*Not in force*
	(11)	See Sch 6 below
42		*Not in force*
43	(1)–(3)	*Not in force*
	(4)	See Sch 7 below
	(5)–(12)	*Not in force*
44–52		*Not in force*
53	(1)–(6)	*Not in force* (in relation to exemptions under s 55)
	(7)	See Sch 8 below
	(8), (9)	*Not in force* (in relation to exemptions under s 55)
54		*Not in force*
55	(1)–(3)	*Not in force*
	(4)	See Sch 9 below

Courts and Legal Services Act 1990 (c 41)—*contd*

Section

63	(1)	(b), (c)	*Not in force*
	(3)		*Not in force*
70			*Not in force* (so far as relates to authorised practitioners)
81			See Sch 13 below
89	(8)		See Sch 14 below
104–107			*Not in force*
125	(2)		See Sch 17 below
	(3)		See Sch 18 below
	(7)		See Sch 20 below

Schedule

6, 7		*Not in force*
8		*Not in force* (in relation to exemptions under s 55)
9		*Not in force*
13		*Not in force*
17, para	5	*Not in force*
	19	Repealed (*never in force*)
18, para	1	*Not in force* (so far as relates to the Authorised Conveyancing Practitioners Board and the Conveyancing Ombudsman)
	4	*Not in force*
	6	*Not in force*
	11, 12	*Not in force*
	19	*Not in force*
	22, 23	*Not in force*
	31	*Not in force*
20		*Not in force* (repeals of or in Rent (Agriculture) Act 1976, s 26(3); Rent Act 1977, s 141(4), (5); Housing Act 1980, s 86(3); County Courts Act 1984, ss 63, 75(1), 112(5); Housing Act 1985, ss 110(3), 181(3); Landlord and Tenant Act 1985, s 19(5); Building Societies Act 1986, ss 35, 124; Landlord and Tenant Act 1987, s 52(4), (5), Sch 2, para 2(b); Copyright, Designs and Patents Act 1988, s 290; Housing Act 1988, s 40(4), (5))

Credit Unions Act 1979 (c 34)

RA: 4 Apr 1979

Section

3	(2), (3)	*Not in force*

Crime and Disorder Act 1998 (c 37)

RA: 31 Jul 1998

Section				
51				*Not in force* (except for the purpose of sending any person for trial under s 51 from the petty sessions areas of Bromley, Croydon, and Sutton, the petty sessional divisions of Aberconwy, Arfon, Blackburn, Darwen and Ribble Valley, Burnley and Pendle, Colwyn, Corby, Daventry, Dyffryn Clwyd, Eifionydd and Pwllheli, Gateshead, Kettering, Meirionnydd, Newcastle-under-Lyme and Pirehill North, Newcastle-upon-Tyne, Northampton, Rhuddlan, Staffordshire Moorlands, Stoke-on-Trent, Towcester, Wellingborough, and Ynys Mon/Anglesey)
52	(1)–(5)			*Not in force* (except for the purpose of sending any person for trial under from the petty sessions areas noted to s 51 above)
	(6)			See Sch 3 below
119				See Sch 8 below
	(2)			See Sch 10 below
Schedule				
3				*Not in force* (except for the purpose of making regulations or rules and for sending any person for trial from the petty sessions areas noted s 51 above)
8, para	3			Repealed (*never in force* in part)
	5	(1)	(a)	*Not in force* (except for the purpose of sending any person for trial from the petty sessions areas noted to s 51 above)
		(2)		*Not in force* (except for the purpose of sending any person for trial from the petty sessions areas noted to s 51 above)
	8			*Not in force* (except for the purpose of sending any person for trial from the petty sessions areas noted to s 51 above)
	12			*Not in force* (except for the purpose of sending any person for trial from the petty sessions areas noted to s 51 above)

Crime and Disorder Act 1998 (c 37)—*contd*

Schedule

8, para	28, 29		Repealed (*never in force* in part)
	37		*Not in force* (except for the purpose of sending any person for trial from the petty sessions areas noted to s 51 above)
	40	(2)	*Not in force* (except for the purpose of sending any person for trial from the petty sessions areas noted to s 51 above)
	44, 45		*Not in force* (except for the purpose of sending any person for trial from the petty sessions areas noted to s 51 above)
	48		*Not in force* (except for the purpose of sending any person for trial from the petty sessions areas noted to s 51 above)
	49		Repealed (*never in force* in part)
	52	(2)	Repealed (*never in force* in part)
	63–67		*Not in force* (except for the purpose of sending any person for trial from the petty sessions areas noted to s 51 above)
	86		*Not in force*
	90		*Not in force*
	93		*Not in force* (except for the purpose of sending any person for trial from the petty sessions areas noted to s 51 above)
	125	(a)	*Not in force* (except for the purpose of sending any person for trial from the petty sessions areas noted to s 51 above)
	126		*Not in force* (except for the purpose of sending any person for trial from the petty sessions areas noted to s 51 above)
	127	(a)	Repealed (*never in force* in part)
	128, 129		*Not in force* (except for the purpose of sending any person for trial from the petty sessions areas noted to s 51 above)
10			*Not in force* (repeals of or in Magistrates' Courts Act 1980, ss 125(4)(c), 126 (except for the purpose of sending any person for trial from the petty sessions areas noted to s 51 above); Crime (Sentences) Act 1997, Sch 5)

Crime and Punishment (Scotland) Act 1997 (c 48)

RA: 21 Mar 1997

Section

1				*Not in force*
3				*Not in force* (for purpose of inserting Criminal Procedure (Scotland) Act 1995, s 205C(1) for the purpose of the interpretation of s 205B of that Act)
4				Repealed (*never in force*)
13				*Not in force*
16				*Not in force* (for the purpose of substituting into Prisoners and Criminal Proceedings (Scotland) Act 1993, s 2(1) a reference to sentences imposed under Criminal Procedure (Scotland) Act 1995, s 205A(2))
18				*Not in force* (for purpose of inserting references to ss 205A, 209(1A) into Criminal Procedure (Scotland) Act 1995)
19				*Not in force* (for purposes of inserting Criminal Procedure (Scotland) Act 1995, ss 106A(1), 106A(3) (so far as refers to s 205A(2) of the 1995 Act))
33–41				Repealed (*never in force*)
62	(1)			See Sch 1 below
	(2)			See Sch 3 below
65	(2)–(4)			*Not in force*
	(6)			*Not in force*

Schedule

1, para	1			Repealed (*never in force*)
	3			*Not in force*
	9	(7)		Repealed (*never in force*)
	10	(2)	(a)	Repealed (*never in force*)
	13	(3)		Repealed (*never in force*)
	14	(2)	(a)	Repealed (*never in force*)
		(3)	(e)	Repealed (*never in force*)
		(4)–(7)		Repealed (*never in force*)
		(9)		Repealed (*never in force*)
		(10)	(a)	Repealed (*never in force*)
		(11)	(b)	Repealed (*never in force*)
		(12)–(15)		Repealed (*never in force*)
		(17)		Repealed (*never in force*)
	18	(2)	(a)	*Not in force*
	21	(3)		Repealed (*never in force*)

Crime and Punishment (Scotland) Act 1997 (c 48)—_contd_

Schedule

1, para	21	(23)	_Not in force_ (for purpose of inserting references to s 205A into Criminal Procedure (Scotland) Act 1995)
		(24)	_Not in force_
		(25)	_Not in force_ (for purpose of inserting references to s 205A into Criminal Procedure (Scotland) Act 1995)
		(29)	_Not in force_
		(31)	_Not in force_ (for purpose of inserting references to s 205A into Criminal Procedure (Scotland) Act 1995)
2			Repealed (_never in force_)
3			_Not in force_ (repeals of or in Prisoners and Criminal Proceedings (Scotland) 1993, s 14(2), in s 27(1), in the definition of "supervised release order", the words "(as inserted by section 14 of this Act)")
			Repealed (_never in force_) (repeals of or in Prisons (Scotland) Act 1989, s 39(7); Prisoners and Criminal Proceedings (Scotland) Act 1993, ss 1(1)–(3), (8), 3(2). 5, 6(1), 7, 9, 12(3), 14(4), 16, 17(1), 20(3), 24, in s 27(1), the definitions of "short term prisoner" and "long term prisoner", the words from "but" to the end, and s 27(2), (3), (5), (6) and Sch 1; Criminal Procedure (Scotland) Act 1995, s 44(4), (6)–(10))

Crime (Sentences) Act 1997 (c 43)

_RA:_ 21 Mar 1997

Section

8			Repealed (_never in force_)
9			Repealed (_never in force_
10–27			Repealed (_never in force_)
42			See Sch 2 below
55	(1)		See Sch 4 below
56	(1)		See Sch 5 below
	(2)		See Sch 6 below

Schedule

2, para	4		Repealed (_never in force_)
	8		Repealed (_never in force_)
4, para	1	(1)	_Not in force_ (except so far as relates to offences whose corresponding civil offences are offences to which s 2 would apply)

Crime (Sentences) Act 1997 (c 43)—*contd*

Schedule

4, para	1	(3)		*Not in force*
		(5)		*Not in force*
	2	(1)		*Not in force* (except so far as relates to offences whose corresponding civil offences are offences to which s 2 would apply)
		(3)		*Not in force*
		(5)		*Not in force*
	3	(5)		*Not in force*
	6	(1)	(b)	Repealed (*never in force*)
		(2)		*Not in force*
	7			*Not in force*
	9			Repealed (*never in force*)
	11			Repealed (*never in force*)
	12	(4)		Repealed (*never in force*)
	14			*Not in force*
5, para	1–4			Repealed (*never in force*)
	6			Repealed (*never in force*)
6				*Not in force* (repeals of or in Criminal Justice Act 1967, s 67; Criminal Justice Act 1991, ss 33, 35(1), 36 (except so far as relating to life prisoners), s 37(1), (2), s 37(3) (other than relating to life prisoners), ss 37(6), (7), 38, s 39(1) (so far as relating to long term prisoners), ss 39(2)–(4), (5) (part), (6), 40 (repealed), 41, 42, s 43(1), ss 43(2), (3) (part), 44 (part), 45–47, 49, 50, 51(1) (the definitions of "the Board", "long-term prisoner", "short-term prisoner", "sentence of imprisonment", "sexual offence" and "violent offence"), (2), (2A), (2B) (4), 65, Sch 2, para 14 (repealed))

Criminal Justice Act 1972 (c 71)

RA: 26 Oct 1972

Section

49		*Not in force*
Schedule		
6, Pt	I	*Not in force* (repeal of Aliens Restriction (Amendment) Act 1919, s 8)

Criminal Justice Act 1982 (c 48)

RA: 28 Oct 1982
Section
78   See Sch 16 below
Schedule
16   *Not in force* (repeal of Criminal Justice
                                                            Act 1961, s 38(5)(c), (d))

Criminal Justice Act 1988 (c 33)

RA: 29 Jul 1988
Section
1–21   Repealed (*never in force*)
32   (1)   (a)   *Not in force* (except in relation to
                                                            proceedings for murder,
                                                            manslaughter or any other offence
                                                            of killing any person; proceedings
                                                            being conducted by the Director
                                                            of the Serious Fraud Office under
                                                            Criminal Justice Act 1987, s 1(5);
                                                            and proceedings for serious and
                                                            complex fraud where there has
                                                            been given a notice of transfer
                                                            under s 4 of that Act))
                (3)   *Not in force* (except in relation to
                                                            proceedings noted to sub-s(1)(a)
                                                            above)
150   *Not in force*
151   (1)–(4)   *Not in force*
170   (1)   See Sch 15 below
                (2)   See Sch 16 below
Schedule
1   Repealed (*never in force*)
6, 7   Repealed (*never in force*)
15, para   16   *Not in force*
15, para   16   *Not in force*
                34   Repealed (*never in force*)
                38   Repealed (*never in force* so far as
                                                            relating to para 40)
                40   Repealed (*never in force*)
                54, 55   Repealed (*never in force*)
                57   Repealed (*never in force*)
                81   Repealed (*never in force*)
                83–88   Repealed (*never in force*)
                95, 96   Repealed (*never in force*)
16   *Not in force* (repeals of or in Fugitive
                                                            Offenders Act 1967, ss 8(1), (2),
                                                            11(1), 16(1), Sch 1 (repealed);
                                                            Genocide Act 1969, ss 2(1)(b)
                                                            (repealed), 3(1) (now substituted

Criminal Justice Act 1988 (c 33)—*contd*
Schedule

16—*contd*	by the Extradition Act 1989, s 36(2)); Children and Young Persons Act 1969, s 60(1)(b), (2) (repealed); Costs in Criminal Cases Act 1973, Sch 1, para 3 (repealed); Suppression of Terrorism Act 1978, s 3(2) (repealed); Theft Act 1968, s 5(3) (repealed); Civil Aviation Act 1982, s 93(3) (repealed); Taking of Hostages Act 1982, s 3(1)(b) (repealed), (3), (5); Aviation Security Act 1982, s 9(1)(b), (2), (3) (repealed); Nuclear Material (Offences) Act 1983, s 5(1)(b), (2), (4) (repealed); Prohibition of Female Circumcision Act 1985, s 3(1)(b) (repealed); Insolvency Act 1986, ss 264(1)(d), 266(45), 267(3), 277, 282(2), 293(1), 297(1), 327, 341(4), (5), 327, 341(4), (5), 362(1)(c), 363(1)(a), 385(1), 402; Criminal Justice (Scotland) Act 1987, s 45(7)(c)(ii) (repealed))

Extradition Act 1989, s 38(4) provided for s 136(1) of, and Sch 1, para 4 to, this Act to come into force immediately before 27 Sep 1989 and those provisions were then repealed on that date by s 37(1) of, and Sch 2 to, the 1989 Act

---

Criminal Justice Act 1991 (c 53)

RA: 25 Jul 1991
Section

68			See Sch 8 below
89	(3)		*Not in force* (due to come into force on day appointed by order made by Secretary of State under s 62(1))
101	(1)		See Sch 12 below
Schedule			
8, para	1	(1)	*Not in force*
		(3)	*Not in force* (to the extent that would otherwise apply to Children and Young Persons Act 1933, s 34)
12, para	15	(3)–(5)	*Not in force* (due to come into force on day appointed by order made by Secretary of State under s 62(1))

Criminal Justice Act 1993 (c 36)

RA: 27 Jul 1993
Section

5	(1)	*Not in force*
79	(14)	See Sch 6 below

Schedule

6, Pt	I	*Not in force* (repeals of or in Drug Trafficking Offences Act 1986, ss 1(8), 5(3), 26A(3), 38(2) (repealed))

Criminal Justice and Court Services Act 2000 (c 43)

RA: 30 Nov 2000
Section

46				*Not in force*
51				*Not in force*
52				*Not in force* (in so far as it relates to exclusion orders and exclusion requirements)
53				*Not in force*
57				*Not in force* (except within the following police areas: Nottinghamshire; Staffordshire; the metropolitan police district)
59				*Not in force*
61				*Not in force*
71	(5)			*Not in force*
74				See Sch 7 below
75				See Sch 8 below

Schedule

7, para	5			*Not in force*
	7–11			*Not in force*
	13			*Not in force*
	15	(1)	(a)–(d)	*Not in force*
			(f), (g)	*Not in force*
	16, 17			*Not in force*
	18	(1), (2)		*Not in force*
		(3)	(a), (b)	*Not in force*
			(c) (ii)	*Not in force*
	20			*Not in force*
	22	(1)	(a)–(d)	*Not in force*
			(f), (g)	*Not in force*
	23, 24			*Not in force*
	25	(1), (2)		*Not in force*
		(3)	(a), (b)	*Not in force*
			(c) (ii)	*Not in force*
	27			*Not in force*

Criminal Justice and Court Services Act 2000 (c 43)—*contd*
Schedule

7, para	29	(1)	(a)–(d)		*Not in force*
			(f), (g)		*Not in force*
	30, 31				*Not in force*
	32	(1), (2)			*Not in force*
		(3)	(c)	(ii)	*Not in force*
	33–36				*Not in force*
	39				*Not in force*
	54–56				*Not in force*
	59, 60				*Not in force*
	62–70				*Not in force*
	73				*Not in force*
	76, 77				*Not in force*
	98				*Not in force*
	101				*Not in force*
	104				*Not in force*
	106–109				*Not in force*
	111	(b)			*Not in force*
	112–115				*Not in force*
	119				*Not in force*
	134				*Not in force*
	139, 140				*Not in force*
	149				*Not in force*
	161	(a)			*Not in force*
	164				*Not in force* (reference in sub-para (b) to Powers of Criminal Courts (Sentencing) Act 2000, Sch 3, paras 2A(4), (5))
	165				*Not in force*
	167				*Not in force*
	170				*Not in force*
	172, 173				*Not in force*
	176–194				*Not in force*
	196				*Not in force* (references to Powers of Criminal Courts (Sentencing) Act 2000, ss 40A(6), 40C(1), (2), Sch 2, para 8, Sch 3, para 1(1A))
	197	(a)			*Not in force*
		(c)–(e)			*Not in force*
		(f)			*Not in force* (definitions "affected person" and "exclusion order")
		(g)	(i)		*Not in force*
	199	(2)	(a)		*Not in force* (so far as relates to exclusion orders)
			(b)		*Not in force* (so far as relates to exclusion orders)
		(5)			*Not in force* (so far as relates to exclusion orders)
		(7)–(9)			*Not in force*

Criminal Justice and Court Services Act 2000 (c 43)—*contd*
Schedule

7, para	199	(10)			*Not in force* (except so far as substitutes cross-heading preceding Powers of Criminal Courts (Sentencing) Act 2000, Sch 3, para 7)
		(11)	(a)		*Not in force*
			(b)	(ii)	*Not in force*
			(c)		*Not in force*
		(12)			*Not in force*
		(19)			*Not in force*
		(21)	(a) (i), (ii)		*Not in force*
				(iii)	*Not in force* (so far as relates to exclusion orders)
			(b)		*Not in force* (so far as inserts Powers of Criminal Courts (Sentencing) Act 2000, Sch 3, para 19(2)(ab))
			(d)		*Not in force* (so far as inserts Powers of Criminal Courts (Sentencing) Act 2000, Sch 3, para 19(4), (5))
			(e)		*Not in force* (so far as relates to exclusion orders)
	200	(25)	(b), (c)		*Not in force*
		(26)			*Not in force*
	201	(2)	(b)		*Not in force*
		(3)			*Not in force*
	202	(2)	(b)		*Not in force*
		(3)			*Not in force*
	203	(2)			*Not in force* (except so far as relates to Powers of Criminal Courts (Sentencing) Act 2000, Sch 9, paras 34(a), 153–156)
		(5)			*Not in force*
	204				*Not in force*
	211				*Not in force*
8					*Not in force* (repeals of or in Criminal Justice Act 1948; Prison Act 1953; Army Act 1955; Air Force Act 1955; Naval Discipline Act 1957; Criminal Justice Act 1967; Finance Act 1968; Children and Young Persons Act 1969, s 23; Fire Precautions Act 1971; Magistrates Courts Act 1980, ss 11, 31, 77, 96A, 133, 135, 136, Sch 6A; Imprisonment (Temporary Provisions) Act 1980; Mental Helath Act 1983; Criminal Justice Act 1988; Road Traffic Act 1988; Criminal Procedure (Insanity and Unfitness to Plead) Act 1991;

Criminal Justice and Court Services Act 2000 (c 43)—*contd*

Schedule

8—*contd*	Criminal Justice Act 1991; Local Government Finance Act 1992; Criminal Justice and Public Order Act 1994, ss 117, 125; Drug Trafficking Act 1994; Prisoners' Earnings Act 1996; Powers of Criminal Courts Sentencing Act 2000, ss 76, 78, 87, 93–98, 99, 106, 108, 110, 111, 137, 139, 140, Sch 3, Sch 7, Sch 8, Sch 9, paras 5, 9, 10, 12, 14, 15, 17, 19, 20, 22, 56, 57, 66, 68, 70, 77, 78, 111, 143, 152, 163, 183, 188; Criminal Justice and Court Services Act 2000)

Criminal Justice and Police Act 2001 (c 16)

RA: 11 May 2001

Section

1			*Not in force* (except for the purpose of making orders)
2			*Not in force*
4–11			*Not in force*
38			*Not in force*
45			*Not in force* (except for the purpose of making orders or regulations)
50–70			*Not in force*
73, 74			*Not in force*
78–80			*Not in force*
87–96			*Not in force*
97	(4)	(a)	*Not in force*
98, 99			*Not in force*
101–103			*Not in force*
127			*Not in force*
128			See Sch 6 below
130			*Not in force*
137			See Sch 7 below

Schedule

1			*Not in force*
2, para	1–25		*Not in force*
	27		*Not in force*
3–5			*Not in force*
6, para	21		*Not in force* (so far as relates to insertion of Police Act 1997, Sch 2A, para 4)
7, Pt	2	(1)	*Not in force* (except repeal of Police and Criminal Evidence Act 1984, 64(4))

Enquiry Bureau 020 7400 2518

Criminal Justice and Police Act 2001 (c 16)—*contd*

Schedule

7, Pt	3	*Not in force*
	6	*Not in force* (except repeal in Bail Act 1976)

Criminal Justice and Public Order Act 1994 (c 33)

RA: 3 Nov 1994

Section

21		*Not in force*
44		Repealed (deemed to have been enacted with this repeal)
64	(1)–(3)	*Not in force* (except so far as relating to powers conferred on a constable by s 63)
159	(3)	*Not in force*
165		*Not in force*
168	(1)	See Sch 9 below
	(3)	See Sch 11 below

Schedule

4		Repealed (deemed to have been enacted with this repeal)
9, para	38	*Not in force*

Certain repeals made by Sch 11 were repealed by Criminal Procedure and Investigations Act 1996, s 44, and Sch 11 was deemed to have been enacted as such

Criminal Justice (International Co-operation) Act 1990 (c 5)

RA: 5 Apr 1990

Section

26A, 26B		Repealed (*never in force*)
30	(3)	Repealed (*never in force*)

Criminal Procedure and Investigations Act 1996 (c 25)

RA: 4 Jul 1996

Section

45	Effect (due to come into effect on day appointed by order made by Secretary of State under s 45(8), (9))
62	Effect (due to come into effect on day appointed by order made by Secretary of State under s 62(3), (4))

Crown Agents Act 1995 (c 24)

RA: 19 Jul 1995
Section

8	(4)	No date (dissolution date for the purposes of s 8(4))

Customs and Excise Duties (General Reliefs) Act 1979 (c 3)

RA: 22 Feb 1979
Section

12	No date (appointed day for the purposes of s 12)

Customs and Excise Management Act 1979 (c 2)

RA: 22 Feb 1979
Section

59		*Not in force* (due to come into force on day appointed by order made by Secretary of State under s 59(7))
62	(2)	*Not in force* (due to come into force on day appointed by order made by Secretary of State under s 62(2))

Data Protection Act 1998 (c 29)

RA: 16 Jul 1998
Section

56	(1)–(7)	*Not in force*
	(8)	*Not in force* (except so far as conferring power to make subordinate legislation)
	(9), (10)	*Not in force*

Defamation Act 1996 (c 31)

RA: 4 Jul 1996
Section

2		*Not in force* (NI)
3	(1)–(7)	*Not in force* (NI)
	(8)	*Not in force* (NI)
	(9), (10)	*Not in force* (NI)
4		*Not in force* (NI)
7–10		*Not in force* (NI)
11		*Not in force*
16		See Sch 2 below
17		*Not in force* (NI)

Defamation Act 1996 (c 31)—*contd*
Schedule

2	*Not in force* (repeals of or in Defamation Act (Northern Ireland) 1955; Local Government Act (Northern Ireland) 1972; British Nationality Act 1981, Sch 7 (entry relating to Defamation Act (Northern Ireland) 1955); Local Government (Access to Information) Act 1985, Sch 2, para 3; Education and Libraries (Northern Ireland) Order 1986, SI 1986/594 (NI 3); Broadcasting Act 1990, Sch 20, para 3) (E, W, NI)

Disability Discrimination Act 1995 (c 50)

RA: 8 Nov 1995

In its application to Northern Ireland, this Act is modified; see Sch 8 to this Act
Section

15	(1)	(b)	*Not in force*
16	(5)		See Sch 4, paras 1–4 below
21	(2)	(a)–(c)	In force 1 Oct 2004
	(7)–(9)		*Not in force*
27	(1), (2)		In force 1 Oct 2004
	(4)		In force 1 Oct 2004
	(5)		See Sch 4, paras 5–9 below
29	(1), (2)		Repealed (*never in force*)
30	(7)–(9)		Repealed (*never in force*)
32–36			*Not in force*
39			*Not in force*
49			*Not in force*
62			Repealed (partly *never in force*)
63			*Not in force* (NI)
70	(5)		See Sch 7 below
Schedule			
4, para	5–7		In force 1 Oct 2004
7			*Not in force* (repeals of or in Disabled Persons (Employment) Act 1944, s 22(4); Chronically Sick and Disabled Persons Act 1970, s 16; Employment Protection (Consolidation) Act 1978, Sch 13, para 20(3) (repealed); Local Government and Housing Act 1989, s 7(2); Education Act 1993, s 161(5))

Disability Discrimination Act 1995 (c 50)—*contd*

Schedule	
7—*contd*	*Not in force* (NI) (repeals of or in Disabled Persons (Employment) Act (Northern Ireland) 1945, s 22; Industrial Relations (Northern Ireland) Order 1976, SI 1976/1043 (NI 16), art 68(6) (repealed))

Disability Rights Commission Act 1999 (c 17)

RA: 27 Jul 1999

Section		
14	(2)	See Sch 5 below
Schedule		
5		*Not in force* (repeals of or in Disability Discrimination Act 1995, ss 51(3)–(6), 52(11), 53(4)–(7), 54(8))

Disabled Persons Act 1981 (c 43)

RA: 27 Jul 1981

Section	
6	*Not in force*

Disabled Persons (Northern Ireland) Act 1989 (c 10)

RA: 25 May 1989

Section		
1–3		*Not in force*
4	(b)	*Not in force*
7		*Not in force*
8	(2), (3)	*Not in force*

Disabled Persons (Services, Consultation and Representation) Act 1986 (c 33)

RA: 8 Jul 1986

Section		
1–3		*Not in force*
4	(b)	*Not in force*
7		*Not in force*
8	(2), (3)	*Not in force*
15		Repealed (*never in force*)

Easter Act 1928 (c 35)

RA: 3 Aug 1928

Not in force

Education Act 1997 (c 44)

RA: 21 Mar 1997
Section
52   (5)   Repealed (*never in force*)
57   (1)   See Sch 7 below
            (4)   See Sch 8 below
Schedule
7, para   40   Repealed (*never in force*)
            49   Repealed (partly *never in force*)
8   *Not in force* (repeals of or in Education
                                                 Act 1996, s 423(6),
                                                 Sch 23, para 4(1))

Education Reform Act 1988 (c 40)

RA: 29 Jul 1988
Section
237   (2)   See Sch 13 below
Schedule
13, Pt   *Not in force* (repeal in Education
                                                 Act 1980, s 35(3) (repealed))

Elected Authorities (Northern Ireland) Act 1989 (c 3)

RA: 15 Mar 1989
Section
5   *Not in force*
8   (2)   *Not in force*

Electronic Communications Act 2000 (c 7)

RA: 25 May 2000
Section
1–6   *Not in force*

Employment of Children Act 1973 (c 24)

RA: 23 May 1973

Not in force

Employment Relations Act 1999 (c 26)

RA: 27 Jul 1999
Section
17   *Not in force*
31   See Sch 7 below
44   See Sch 9 below

Employment Relations Act 1999 (c 26)—*contd*
Schedule

7, para	3, 4			*Not in force*
	5			*Not in force* (so far as inserts Employment Agencies Act 1973, s 11B)
	7			*Not in force*
9, Pt	1			*Not in force*
	3			*Not in force* (repeal of Trade Union and Labour Relations (Consolidation) Act 1992, Sch A1, para 163)
	8			*Not in force*
	10			*Not in force* (repeals of or in Employment Rights Act 1996, s 236, Sch 1)

Employment Rights Act 1996 (c 18)

RA: 22 May 1996
Schedule

2, Pt	II, para	16	(1)	*Not in force* (due to come into force on a day appointed by the Secretary of State by order under Sch 2, Pt II, para 16(2) to this Act)
		17	(1)	*Not in force* (due to come into force on a day appointed by the Secretary of State by order under Sch 2, Pt II, para 17(2) to this Act)
		18	(1)	*Not in force* (due to come into force on a day appointed by the Secretary of State by order under Sch 2, Pt II, para 18(2) to this Act)

Employment Rights (Dispute Resolution) Act 1998 (c 8)

RA: 8 Apr 1998
Section

4	*Not in force*

Environment Act 1995 (c 25)

RA: 19 Jul 1995
Section

24		*Not in force*
78		See Sch 10 below
116		See Sch 21 below
118	(4), (5)	*Not in force* (except so far as confers power to make orders or make provision in relation to the exercise of that power)

Environment Act 1995 (c 25)—*contd*

Section

120	(1)			See Sch 22 below
	(2)			See Sch 23 below
	(3)			See Sch 24 below

Schedule

10, para	10	(2)	(a)	*Not in force*
21, para	2	(4)		*Not in force* (for purposes of the application of substituted Water Resources Act 1991, s 222 to Pt II of the Act)
	3			*Not in force*
	5, 6			*Not in force*
22, para	16			Repealed (*never in force*)
	27	(b), (c)		*Not in force*
				Paragraph prospectively repealed by s 120(3) of, and Sch 24 to, this Act
	29	(1)		See sub-paras (21), (22), (26) below
		(21)	(a) (i)	*Not in force*
			(b)–(e)	*Not in force*
		(22)		*Not in force* (except so far as confers power on Secretary of State to make regulations)
	81			*Not in force*
	88			*Not in force*
	95			*Not in force*
	186			*Not in force*
	232	(2)		*Not in force*
23, para	7			*Not in force*
	11			*Not in force*
	15			*Not in force*
24				*Not in force* (repeals of or in Control of Pollution Act 1974, s 30(1); Local Government, Planning and Land Act 1980, s 103(2)(c), Sch 2, para 9(2), (3); Criminal Justice Act 1982, Sch 15, paras 6, 7; Control of Pollution (Amendment) Act 1989, s 2(3)(e); Local Government and Housing Act 1989, s 21(1) (part); Environmental Protection Act 1990, ss 33(1), 54, 75(3); Water Resources Act 1991, s 190(1); Local Government Finance Act 1992, Sch 13, para 95; Local Government (Wales) Act 1994, Sch 9, para 17(12), Sch 16, para 65(5); Environment Act 1995, Sch 22, paras 19–27, 46(11)(a) 182, 231)

Environmental Protection Act 1990 (c 43)

RA: 1 Nov 1990

Section

45	(2)		*Not in force* (E, W) (except so far as enables orders or regulations to be made)
48	(7)		*Not in force*
52	(2)		*Not in force*
	(8)		*Not in force* (except so far as relates to s 52(1), (3))
61			Repealed (*never in force*)
63	(2)		*Not in force*
	(3), (4)		*Not in force*
108	(1)	(a)	*Not in force* (except so far as relates to import or acquisition of genetically modified organisms)
	(2)		*Not in force*
	(3)	(a)	*Not in force*
	(4)		*Not in force*
	(6)		*Not in force*
	(8)		*Not in force*
109			*Not in force*
110			*Not in force* (except so far as relates to import, acquisition, release or marketing of genetically modified organisms)
111	(3)		*Not in force*
112	(3), (4)		*Not in force*
116			*Not in force* (except so far as relates to import, acquisition, release or marketing of genetically modified organisms)
118	(1)	(b)	*Not in force*
		(d)	*Not in force*
		(m)	*Not in force* (except so far as relates to s 111)
122	(1)	(a), (b)	*Not in force* (except so far as empower Secretary of State to make regulations)
143			Repealed (*never in force* in part)
162	(1)		See Sch 15 below
	(2)		See Sch 16 below
	(4)		*Not in force*

Schedule

15, para	17		*Not in force*
	25		*Not in force*
16, Pt	I		*Not in force* (repeals or in Clean Air Act 1956, ss 17(4), 29(1), 31(1), Sch 2; Clean Air Act 1968, s 11; Local Government Act 1972,

Environmental Protection Act 1990 (c 43)—*contd*

Schedule

16, Pt	I—*contd*	s 180(3)(b); Local Government (Scotland) Act 1973, s 142(2)(b); Control of Pollution Act 1974, ss 76(4), 78(1), 79(4), 80(3), 84(1), 103(1)(a), 105(1); Environmental Protection Act 1990, s 79(10) (S))
	II	*Not in force* (repeals of in Control of Pollution Act 1974, ss 11(12), 12–14 (in relation to industrial waste), 16, 17, 19–21, 28–30; Refuse Disposal (Amenity) Act 1978, s 1; Local Government Act 1988, Sch 1, para 1; Water Act 1989, Sch 25, para 48; Electricity Act 1989, Sch 16, para 18; Environmental Protection Act 1990, ss 34(3)(b), 36(8))
	VII	*Not in force* (repeals of Electricity Act 1989, Sch 17, para 37(1)(b); Planning (Consequential Provisions) Act 1990, Sch 2, para 82(2))
	VIII	*Not in force*

Estate Agents Act 1979 (c 38)

RA: 4 Apr 1979

Section

16, 17	*Not in force*
19	*Not in force*
22	*Not in force*

Ethical Standards in Public Life etc (Scotland) Act 2000 (asp 7)

RA: 24 Jul 2000

Section

4–7		*Not in force*
10–27		*Not in force*
29		*Not in force*
32		*Not in force*
36	(1)	See Sch 4 below
	(2)	*Not in force*

Schedule

4	*Not in force* (except repeals of or in Local Government Act 1988)

European Communities Act 1972 (c 68)

RA: 17 Oct 1972
Schedule

3, Pt	II		*Not in force* (repeals of or in Sugar Act 1956, s 17(1) (part), (8), 23(4), 35(2) (definitions of "the Ministers", "molasses", "sugar duty"), (3) (repealed))

Fair Employment (Northern Ireland) Act 1989 (c 32)

RA: 27 Jul 1989
Schedule

2, para	15			*Not in force* (for purposes of any complaint or act to which s 50(2) applies)
	16	(3)	(b)	*Not in force* (for purposes of any complaint or act to which s 50(2) applies)
	17			*Not in force* (for purposes of any complaint or act to which s 50(2) applies)
	21	(c)		*Not in force* (for purposes of any complaint or act to which s 50(2) applies)
	24–26			*Not in force* (for purposes of any complaint or act to which s 50(2) applies)
3				*Not in force* (repeals of or in Fair Employment (Northern Ireland) Act 1976, ss 44–48, 51, 53(4), 57(1) (definitions 'complainant', 'the county court', 'finding' and 'the injured person'), 59(2), Sch 1, para 11, for the purposes of any complaint or act to which s 50(2) of this Act applies)

Family Law Act 1996 (c 27)

RA: 4 Jul 1996
Section

2–15	*Not in force*
16, 17	*Not in force*; s 17 prospectively repealed by Welfare Reform and Pensions Act 1999, s 88, Sch 13, Pt II
18–21	*Not in force*
23–25	*Not in force*
60	*Not in force*

Family Law Act 1996 (c 27)—*contd*

Section

64					Not in force
66	(1)				See Sch 8 below
	(2)				See Sch 9 below
	(3)				See Sch 10 below

Schedule

1–3					Not in force
8, Pt	I, para	1–10			Not in force
		12–15			Not in force
		16	(1)–(3)		Not in force
			(5)	(b)	Not in force[1]
			(6)	(a)	Not in force
		17–25			Not in force
		26–38			Not in force
		39			Repealed (*never in force*)
		40–43			Not in force
9, para	1, 2				Not in force
	5, 6				Not in force
10					Not in force (repeals of or in Domestic and Appellate Proceedings (Restriction of Publicity) Act 1968, s 2(1)(b); Matrimonial Causes Act 1973, ss 1–7, 8(1)(b), 9, 10, 17, 18, 20, 22, 24A(3), 25(2)(h), 28(1), 29(2), 30, 31(2)(a), 41(1), (2), 49, 52(2)(b), Sch 1, para 8; Domicile and Matrimonial Proceedings Act 1973, ss 5(1), (2), 6(3), (4), Sch 1, para 11; Domestic Proceedings and Magistrates' Courts Act 1978, ss 1, 7(1), 63(3), Sch 2, para 38; Magistrates' Courts Act 1980, Sch 7, para 159; Supreme Court Act 1981, s 18(1)(d); Administration of Justice Act 1982, s 16; Matrimonial and Family Proceedings Act 1984, ss 1, 21(f), 27, Sch 1, para 10; Building Societies Act 1986, Sch 21, para 9(f); Family Law Act 1986, Sch 1, para 27; Children Act 1989, Sch 11, para 6(b), Sch 13, paras 33(1), 65(1))

Family Law Reform Act 1987 (c 42)

RA: 15 May 1987

Section

23	Not in force
32	Not in force[1]

Family Law Reform Act 1987 (c 42)—*contd*

Section
33   See Sch 2 below
Schedule
2, para   21–25   *Not in force*

1   Provision not brought into force consequent on errors in Sch 1

Farriers (Registration) Act 1975 (c 35)

RA: 22 May 1975
Section
16   *Not in force* (S, in Highland Region,
                                     Western Isles Islands Area, Orkney
                                     Islands Area, Shetland Islands Area
                                     and all other islands)

Financial Services Act 1986 (c 60)

RA: 7 Nov 1986
Section
53   *Not in force*
58   (1)   (d)   (ii)   *Not in force* (so far as relates to an
                                                     advertisement required or
                                                     permitted to be published by an
                                                     approved exchange under Pt V of
                                                     the Act)
         (2)   Repealed (*never in force*)
134   Repealed (partly *never in force*)
140   See Sch 11 below
158–171   Repealed (*never in force* for more than
                                                     limited purposes)
182   See Sch 13 below
189   See Sch 14 below
208   *Not in force* (except so far as has effect
                                                     in relation to the application of s
                                                     130)
212   (2)   See Sch 16 below
         (3)   See Sch 17 below
Schedule
11, para   17   *Not in force*
14   *Not in force* (for the purposes of
                                                     Rehabilitation of Offenders
                                                     Act 1974 (Exceptions) (Amendment
                                                     No 2) Order 1986, art 1(2)(b), and
                                                     Rehabilitation of Offenders
                                                     (Exceptions) (Amendment) Order
                                                     (Northern Ireland) 1987, art 1(2)(b))
                                     Schedule prospectively repealed by
                                                     Police Act 1997, ss 133(a), 134(2),
                                                     Sch 10

Financial Services Act 1986 (c 60)—*contd*

Schedule

16, para	16		Repealed (*never in force*)
	31		*Not in force*
17			*Not in force* (repeals of Companies Act 1985, ss 58, 59, 60, 62, 82, 83, Sch 3, para 2, and corresponding provisions of Companies (Northern Ireland) Order 1986, SI 1986/1032 (NI 6), in relation to offers by domestic companies of unlisted securities and mutually recognised prospectuses)

Financial Services and Markets Act 2000 (c 8)

RA: 14 Jun 2000

Section

104			*Not in force* (except for the purpose of insurance business transfer schemes)
347	(1)	(a)	*Not in force* (except for the purpose of enabling the Authority to maintain a record of persons –
			(i) who appear to the Authority to be authorised persons who are EEA firms or Treaty firms;
			(ii) who appear to the Authority to be authorised persons who were, immediately before the appointed day, authorised under the Financial Services Act 1986 by virtue of holding a certificate isseued for the purposes of Part I of that Act by a recognised professional body (within the meaning of that Act))
			In force for the purpose listed under head (i) above 1 May 2002
			In force fully 1 Aug 2002
		(h)	*Not in force* (except for the purpose of enabling the Authority to maintain a record of approved persons)
			In force fully 1 Dec 2002
	(2)	(a)	*Not in force* (except for the purpose of enabling the Authority to maintain a record of persons –
			(i) who appear to the Authority to be authorised persons who are EEA firms or Treaty firms;

Financial Services and Markets Act 2000 (c 8)—*contd*
Section

347	(2)	(a)—*contd*	(ii) who appear to the Authority to be authorised persons who were, immediately before the appointed day, authorised under the Financial Services Act 1986 by virtue of holding a certificate isseued for the purposes of Part I of that Act by a recognised professional body (within the meaning of that Act))
			In force for the purpose listed under head (i) above 1 May 2002
			In force fully 1 Aug 2002
		(g)	*Not in force* (except for the purpose of enabling the Authority to maintain a record of approved persons)
432	(3)		See Sch 22 below
Schedule			
22			*Not in force* (repeals in the Credit Unions Act 1979)
			In force fully 2 Jul 2002

Fire Precautions Act 1971 (c 40)

RA: 27 May 1971
Section

3, 4			*Not in force*
12	(2)		*Not in force*
	(9)		*Not in force*
	(11)		*Not in force*
16	(1)	(b)	*Not in force*
	(2)	(b)	*Not in force*
19	(3)	(c)	*Not in force*
34			*Not in force*
36			*Not in force*
40			*Not in force* (so far as relates to ss 3, 4, 12(2), (9))
Schedule			
1, Pt	III		*Not in force*

Fire Safety and Safety of Places of Sport Act 1987 (c 27)

RA: 15 May 1987
Section

10	*Not in force*

Firearms (Amendment) Act 1997 (c 5)

RA: 27 Feb 1997
Section
11–14		Repealed (*never in force*)
19–31		Repealed (*never in force*)
46		Repealed (*never in force*)
52		See Sch 2 below

Schedule
1		Repealed (*never in force*)
2, para	9	*Not in force*
	13	Repealed (*never in force*)

Football Spectators Act 1989 (c 37)

RA: 16 Nov 1989
Section
1	(3)		*Not in force*
	(4)	(b)	*Not in force*
	(5), (6)		*Not in force*
2–7			*Not in force*
10	(6), (7)		*Not in force*
	(8)	(c)	*Not in force*
	(12)	(a), (b)	*Not in force*

Freedom of Information Act 2000 (c 36)

RA: 30 Nov 2000
Section
1, 2		In force 30 Nov 2005 (unless the Secretary of State by order appoints an earlier date)
9, 10		In force 30 Nov 2005 (unless the Secretary of State by order appoints an earlier date) except so far as confer power to make regulations (for which date in force is 30 Nov 2000)
11		In force 30 Nov 2005 (unless the Secretary of State by order appoints an earlier date)
12, 13		In force 30 Nov 2005 (unless the Secretary of State by order appoints an earlier date) except so far as confer power to make regulations (for which date in force is 30 Nov 2000)
14–17		In force 30 Nov 2005 (unless the Secretary of State by order appoints an earlier date)
18	(4)	See Sch 2 below

Freedom of Information Act 2000 (c 36)—*contd*
Section

19		In force 30 Nov 2005 (unless the Secretary of State by order appoints an earlier date) except so far as relating to the approval of publication schemes (for which date in force is 30 Nov 2000)
20		In force 30 Nov 2005 (unless the Secretary of State by order appoints an earlier date) except so far as relating to the approval and preparation by the Commissioner of publication schemes (for which date in force is 30 Nov 2000)
21–44 (Pt II)		In force 30 Nov 2005 (unless the Secretary of State by order appoints an earlier date)
47	(1)	In force 30 Nov 2005 (unless the Secretary of State by order appoints an earlier date)
48		In force 30 Nov 2005 (unless the Secretary of State by order appoints an earlier date)
50–56 (Pt IV)		In force 30 Nov 2005 (unless the Secretary of State by order appoints an earlier date)
57–60 (Pt V)		In force 30 Nov 2005 (unless the Secretary of State by order appoints an earlier date)
61		See Sch 4 below
62–66		In force 30 Nov 2005 (unless the Secretary of State by order appoints an earlier date)
67		See Sch 5 below
68–72		In force 30 Nov 2005 (unless the Secretary of State by order appoints an earlier date)
73		See Sch 6 below
77		In force 30 Nov 2005 (unless the Secretary of State by order appoints an earlier date)
86		See Sch 8 below

Schedule

2, Pt I, para 10	(b)	In force 30 Nov 2005 (unless the Secretary of State by order appoints an earlier date)
3		In force 30 Nov 2005 (unless the Secretary of State by order appoints an earlier date)

Freedom of Information Act 2000 (c 36)—*contd*

Schedule

4, para	2, 3	In force 30 Nov 2005 (unless the Secretary of State by order appoints an earlier date)
5, Pt I, para 1–3		In force 30 Nov 2005 (unless the Secretary of State by order appoints an earlier date)
Pt II, para	5	In force 30 Nov 2005 (unless the Secretary of State by order appoints an earlier date)
6, para	2–5	In force 30 Nov 2005 (unless the Secretary of State by order appoints an earlier date)
8, Pt III		In force 30 Nov 2005 (unless the Secretary of State by order appoints an earlier date)

Friendly Societies Act 1992 (c 40)

RA: 16 Mar 1992

Section

95			See Sch 16 below
97			Repealed (*never in force*)
120	(2)		See Sch 22 below
Schedule			
16, para	1		See para 24 below
	24		*Not in force* (repeal of Friendly Societies Act 1974, s 74)
17			Repealed (*never in force*)
19, Pt	I, para	8	Repealed (*never in force*)
		10	Repealed (*never in force*)
	II, para	26	Repealed (*never in force*)
		28	Repealed (*never in force*)
22, Pt	I		*Not in force* (repeals of or in Industrial Assurance Act 1923, ss 3, 6, 8(1), 19(4); Industrial Assurance and Friendly Societies Act 1948, s 10(1)(a) (part); Friendly Societies Act 1955, s 6; Industrial and Provident Societies Act 1965, s 60(3); Companies Act 1967, Sch 6, Pt II (repealed); Friendly Societies Act 1974, s 74, Sch 6; Financial Services Act 1986, s 189(5)(c))
	II		*Not in force* (repeal of Industrial Assurance (Northern Ireland) Order 1979, SI 1979/1574, arts 5, 9(1)(a) (part))

Fur Farming (Prohibition) Act 2000 (c 33)

RA: 23 Nov 2000
Section
1–4   In force 1 Jan 2003

Further and Higher Education Act 1992 (c 13)

RA: 6 Mar 1992
Section
26   *Not in force* (in respect of persons
                                                            employed by a local authority to
                                                            work solely at the institution the
                                                            corporation is established to
                                                            conduct and who are so employed
                                                            in connection with an arrangement
                                                            for the supply by that local
                                                            authority of goods or services for
                                                            the purposes of that institution in
                                                            pursuance of a bid prepared under
                                                            Local Government Act 1988, s 7)
44, 45   *Not in force* (except in respect of
                                                            institutions which, before they
                                                            became institutions within the
                                                            further education sector, were
                                                            schools maintained by a local
                                                            education authority or grant-
                                                            maintained schools)

Government of Wales Act 1998 (c 38)

RA: 31 Jul 1998
Section
152   See Sch 18 below
Schedule
18, Pt   II   *Not in force* (the reference to the
                                                            General Teaching Council for
                                                            Wales)

Government Resources and Accounts Act 2000 (c 20)

RA: 28 Jul 2000
Section
11   *Not in force*
12, 13   *Not in force* (W)
29   (1)   See Sch 1 below
Schedule
1, para   24   *Not in force* (so far as inserts
                                                            Government of Wales Act 1998,
                                                            s 101A(7) –(12))

Greater London Authority Act 1999 (c 29)

RA: 11 Nov 1999

Section		
63		*Not in force*
199		*Not in force*
217	(1)–(6)	*Not in force*
220–224		*Not in force*[1]
245		See Sch 17 below
287	(2)	*Not in force*[2]
301, 302		*Not in force*
303		*Not in force* (except for the purposes of s 297)
325		See Sch 27 below
326, 327		*Not in force*
405, 406		*Not in force*
408		*Not in force*
411		*Not in force*
413		*Not in force*
423		See Sch 34 below
Schedule		
8		*Not in force*
14, 15		*Not in force*[1]
17, para	11	*Not in force*
27, para	1	*Not in force* (in so far as Metropolitan Police Act 1829, ss 10–12, relate to the Receiver's functions in relation to purposes other than police purposes)
	3	*Not in force* (except so far as Metropolitan Police (Receiver) Act 1861, ss 1, 5, relate to the Receiver's functions in relation to police purposes)
	5	*Not in force* (except so far as Metropolitan Police Act 1886, ss 2, 4, 6, relate to the Receiver's functions in relation to police purposes)
	7	*Not in force* (except so far as Metropolitan Police Act 1887 relates to the Receiver's functions in relation to police purposes)
	8, 9	*Not in force*
	11	*Not in force* (in so far as Metropolitan Police Act 1899, s 1, relates to the Receiver)
	13	*Not in force* (in so far as Crown Lands Act 1936, s 3(2), relates to the Receiver's functions in relation to purposes other than police purposes)

Greater London Authority Act 1999 (c 29)—*contd*

Schedule

27, para	14			*Not in force*
	18			*Not in force*
	39	(2)	(c)	*Not in force*
	40	(2)	(c)	*Not in force*
	64			*Not in force* (in so far as the substitution of Local Government and Housing Act 1989, s 157(6)(f), does not have effect in relation to the Receiver's functions for purposes other than police purposes)
	66	(a)		*Not in force*
	68			*Not in force*
	116			*Not in force*
32				*Not in force*
34, Pt	I			*Not in force* (repeals of or in Trustee Investments Act 1961, Sch 1, Pt II, para 9(d); Local Government Act 1972, s 168(5); Stock Transfer Act 1982, Sch 1, para 7(1)(c); Local Government Finance Act 1988, ss 47(9)(b), 111(3); Local Government and Housing Act 1989, ss 39(3)(e), 155(4)(f), 157(6)(f); Local Government Finance Act 1992, ss 19(3)(e), 53(1), Sch 4, para 5(8)(a); Access to Justice Act 1999, Sch 10, para 40)
	II			*Not in force* (repeals of or in Transport Act 1962, s 67(2A), (15)(b), (16); London Regional Transport Act 1984; Transport Act 1985, Pt II, s 107; Local Government Finance Act 1988, s 88(2)(c), (d); London Regional Transport (Penalty Fares) Act 1992)
	V			*Not in force* (repeal of Private Hire Vehicles (London) Act 1998, s 38)
	VII			*Not in force* (repeals of or in Metropolitan Police Act 1829, ss 1, 4, 5, 10–12, 22; Metropolitan Police (Receiver) Act 1861, ss 1, 5, 9; Metropolitan Police (Receiver) Act 1867, s 1; Metropolitan Police Act 1886, ss 2, 4, 6, 7; Metropolitan Police Act 1887; Metropolitan Police (Receiver) Act 1895; Metropolitan Police Courts Act 1897; Metropolitan

Greater London Authority Act 1999 (c 29)—*contd*
Schedule

34, Pt	VII—*contd*	Police Act 1899, s 1; Crown Lands Act 1936, s 3(2); London Building Acts (Amendment) Act 1939, s 151(1)(bb); Administration of Justice Act 1964, s 38(1); House of Commons Disqualification Act 1975, Sch 1, Pt III (entry relating to the Receiver); Northern Ireland Assembly Disqualification Act 1975, Sch 1, Pt III (entry relating to the Receiver); Town and Country Planning Act 1990, s 336(1)(a); Value Added Tax Act 1994, s 33(3)(f); Local Government (Contracts) Act 1997, s 1(3)(c)
	IX	*Not in force* (repeals of or in Trafalgar Square Act 1844, s 2; Local Government Act 1985, s 88(1), (12(a); Town and Country Planning Act 1990, s 3; Deregulation and Contracting Out Act 1994, s 70(1)(b))

[1]   Ss 220–224 and Schs 14, 15 are not to come into force until London Underground Limited has become a subsidiary of Transport for London; see s 425 (3) of the Act.

[2]   SI 2000/801 purported to bring s 287(2) into force on 3 Jul 2000. However SI 2000/1648, art 3, amends SI 2000/801 so as to provide that s 287(2) has not yet come into force

---

Guard Dogs Act 1975 (c 50)

RA: 1 Aug 1975
Section

2–4	*Not in force*
5	*Not in force* (in relation to ss 2–4, 6)
6	*Not in force*

Health Act 1999 (c 8)

RA: 30 Jun 1999
Section

2	(1)	*Not in force* (W)
	(2)	See Sch 1 below
3–5		*Not in force* (W)
6	(1)	*Not in force* (W)
	(2)	*Not in force*
7		*Not in force* (W)
8		*Not in force* (W)
10		*Not in force*

Health Act 1999 (c 8)—*contd*

Section

11			In force (except that references in National Health Service Act 1977, s 44(3) to arrangements made under s 28C of the 1977 Act are in force for the purposes only of pilot schemes under National Health Service (Primary Care) Act 1997, Pt I)
12	(1)		*Not in force* (W) (so far as substituted National Health Service Act 1977, ss 16D, 17, relate to Primary Care Trusts, and in relation to s 28)
	(3), (4)		*Not in force* (W) (except so far as relates to s 12(1))
18			*Not in force* (W) (so far as relates to Primary Care Trusts)
20			*Not in force* (W) (so far as relates to Primary Care Trusts)
22			*Not in force*
26			*Not in force* (W) (so far as relates to Primary Care Trusts)
27			*Not in force* (W) (so far as substituted National Health Service Act 1977, s 22(1A) relates to Primary Care Trusts)
28			*Not in force* (W) (so far as relates to Primary Care Trusts)
29	(1)		See sub-ss (2)(b), (3) below
	(2)	(b)	*Not in force* (W)
	(3)		*Not in force* (W) (so far as inserted National Health Service Act 1977, s 28BB(2) relates to Primary Care Trusts)
30			*Not in force* (W) (so far as inserted National Health Service Act 1977, s 28A(2B) relates to Primary Care Trusts)
31			*Not in force* (W) (so far as relates to Primary Care Trusts)
33	(1)–(6)		*Not in force* (so far as relate to s 35)
	(7), (8)		*Not in force*
35			*Not in force*
36			*Not in force* (except for the purpose of consulting the industry body and so far as relates to the introduction of a limit under s 34)
37			*Not in force* (except for the purpose of consulting the industry body)

Health Act 1999 (c 8)—*contd*

Section

38	(1)–(4)	*Not in force* (except so far as relates to the exercise of any power conferred by ss 33(6), 34, 37)
	(6)	*Not in force* (except for the purpose of consulting the industry body (other than in relation to ss 33, 35), and except so far as relates to the exercise of any power conferred by ss 33(6), 34, 37)
	(7), (8)	*Not in force* (except so far as relates to the exercise of any power conferred by ss 33(6), 34, 37)
40		*Not in force*
58		*Not in force*
60	(3)	*Not in force* (except so far as relates to repeal of Professions Supplementary to Medicine Act 1960, Sch 1, para 16(2) (so far as it provides that not more than one third of the members of a committee appointed by the Council or a board under para 16(1) may be persons who are not members of the body appointing the committee) and Sch 2, para 1(1) (so far as it provides that, subject to sub-para (2)(b), a person shall not be eligible for membership of the investigating committee or disciplinary committee set up by a board unless he is a member of that board) and Nurses, Midwives and Health Visitors Act 1997, s 10(5), Sch 1, para 7(4))
61		*Not in force*
65	(1)	See Sch 4 below
	(2)	See Sch 5 below

Schedule

1		*Not in force* (W)
2	1–14	*Not in force* (S, NI)
4, para	1	*Not in force* (W)
	2	*Not in force* (E, W)
	3	*Not in force* (W)
	4	See para 7 et seq below
	7	*Not in force* (W)
	8	*Not in force* (except so far as relates to fund-holding practices)

Health Act 1999 (c 8)—*contd*
Schedule

4, para	9			Not in force (W) (so far as substituted National Health Service Act 1977, s 16, relates to Primary Care Trusts)
	10, 11			Not in force (W)
	12	(1)		See sub-paras (2), (3) below
		(2)		Not in force (W)
		(3)	(a)	Not in force (W)
	13			Not in force (W)
	16			Not in force (W)
	17–22			Not in force
	23			Not in force (W)
	25			Not in force (W)
	27	(a)		Not in force (W) (in so far as substituted National Health Service Act 1977, s 91(3)(b)–(d), relate to Primary Care Trusts)
	28, 29			Not in force (W)
	30	(1)		See sub-paras (3), (4) below
		(3), (4)		Not in force (W)
	31	(1)		See sub-paras (2), (4) below
		(2)		Not in force (W)
		(4)		Not in force (W)
	33			Not in force (W)
	34	(a)		Not in force (W)
	35, 36			Not in force (W)
	37	(1)		See sub-paras (2)–(4) below
		(2), (3)		Not in force (W)
		(4)		Not in force (W) (other than so far as relates to the substitution of National Health Service Act 1977, ss 16D, 17)
	38	(1)		See sub-paras (2), (3) below
		(2)	(a)	Not in force (W)
			(c)	Not in force (W)
		(3)		Not in force (W) (so far as inserted National Health Service Act 1977, s 128(1A), relates to s 17A of the 1977 Act and Primary Care Trusts)
	40			Not in force (W)
	41			Not in force
	48–53			Not in force
	64			Not in force
	71	(c)		Not in force (W)
	74			See paras 77–80 below
	77, 78			Not in force (W)
	79	(1)		See sub-paras (2)–(4) below
		(2)	(b)	Not in force (W)
		(3), (4)		Not in force (W)

Health Act 1999 (c 8)—*contd*
Schedule

4, para	80		*Not in force*
	81	(1)	See sub-paras (2), (3) below
		(2) (a)	*Not in force* (W)
		(3)	*Not in force* (W)
	83	(1)	See sub-paras (2), (3), (5), (7) below
		(2), (3)	*Not in force* (W)
		(5)	*Not in force* (W)
		(7)	*Not in force* (W)
	85	(1)	See sub-paras (2), (3) below
		(2) (b)	*Not in force*
		(3)	*Not in force* (W)
	87		*Not in force* (W)
	88	(1)	See sub-paras (2)–(4), (6) below
		(2)–(4)	*Not in force* (W)
		(6)	*Not in force* (W)
	89		*Not in force* (W)

5   *Not in force* (repeals of or in Professions Supplementary to Medicine Act 1960 (other than s 10); National Health Service Act 1966, s 10 (in relation to E, W); National Health Service Act 1977, ss 12(1), 15(1B)–(1D) (other than in relation to fund-holding practices), 49A(5), (6)(a), 49B(4), 97(6), Sch 15, para 37; National Health Service (Scotland) Act 1978, ss 32A(5), (6)(a), 32B(4); National Health Service and Community Care Act 1990, ss 15(4) (in relation to S), 18(1), (3)–(7), 34, 35, Sch 7, para 14(3); Health Service Commissioners Act 1993, s 15(1A), (1B) (other than in E, W); Health Authorities Act 1995, Sch 1, paras 3(a), 6(c), (d) (other than in E, W), 34, 72, 77; National Health Service (Amendment) Act 1995, ss 1, 2(2), 3, 7, 9; Nurses, Midwives and Health Visitors Act 1997; National Health Service (Primary Care) Act 1997, Sch 2, paras 4(3), (4) (other than in relation to fund-holding practices), 53–55, 65(5) (in relation to S), (8)–(10), 69, 71(4), 77, 78)

Health and Safety at Work etc Act 1974 (c 37)

RA: 31 Jul 1974
Section
75			See Sch 7 below
Schedule			
7, para	2	(c)	*Not in force*
	3		*Not in force*
	8, 9		*Not in force*

Health and Social Security Act 1984 (c 48)

RA: 26 Jul 1984
Section
7	(1)–(3)	*Not in force*
21		See Sch 7 below
24		See Sch 8 below
Schedule		
8, Pt	I	*Not in force* (repeals of or in National Health Service Act 1977, ss 19(1)(e), 128(1) (definition of "dispensing optician"), Sch 5, para 6 (part) (repealed and replaced), Sch 9, para 4(e) (now substituted); National Health Service (Scotland) Act 1978, ss 9(1)(e), 108(1) (definition of "dispensing optician"))
	II	*Not in force* (repeal of Social Security Pensions Act 1975, s 38(4) (repealed))

Health and Social Care Act 2001 (c 15)

RA: 11 May 2001
Section
1	*Not in force* (W) (except so far as conferring any power to make an order or regulations which is exercisable by the Secretary of State)
2	*Not in force* (except so far as conferring any power to make an order or regulations which is exercisable by the Secretary of State)
3, 4	*Not in force* (W) (except so far as conferring any power to make an order or regulations which is exercisable by the Secretary of State)
5	*Not in force* (except so far as conferring any power to make an order or regulations which is exercisable by the Secretary of State)

Health and Social Care Act 2001 (c 15)—*contd*
Section

6		*Not in force* (W) (except so far as conferring any power to make an order or regulations which is exercisable by the Secretary of State)
7–12		*Not in force* (except so far as conferring any power to make an order or regulations which is exercisable by the Secretary of State)
13		*Not in force* (W) (except so far as conferring any power to make an order or regulations which is exercisable by the Secretary of State)
14, 15		*Not in force* (except so far as conferring any power to make an order or regulations which is exercisable by the Secretary of State)
16		*Not in force* (W) (except so far as conferring any power to make an order or regulations which is exercisable by the Secretary of State)
17		*Not in force* (E) (in relation to the provision of pharmaceutical services)
		Not in force (W) (except so far as conferring any power to make an order or regulations which is exercisable by the Secretary of State)
18, 19		*Not in force* (except so far as conferring any power to make an order or regulations which is exercisable by the Secretary of State)
20	(1)	See sub-ss (2)–(7) below.
	(2)–(5)	*Not in force* (E) (in relation to the provision of pharmaceutical services)
		Not in force (W) (except so far as conferring any power to make an order or regulations which is exercisable by the Secretary of State)
	(6), (7)	*Not in force* (except so far as conferring any power to make an order or regulations which is exercisable by the Secretary of State)
21, 22		*Not in force* (W) (except so far as conferring any power to make an order or regulations which is exercisable by the Secretary of State)

Health and Social Care Act 2001 (c 15)—*contd*

Section

23		*Not in force* (except so far as conferring any power to make an order or regulations which is exercisable by the Secretary of State)
24		*Not in force* (W) (except so far as conferring any power to make an order or regulations which is exercisable by the Secretary of State)
25		*Not in force* (E) (insertions of ss 49F–49N in so far as they relate to the provision of pharmaceutical services)
		Not in force (W) (except so far as conferring any power to make an order or regulations which is exercisable by the Secretary of State)
26		*Not in force* (except so far as conferring any power to make an order or regulations which is exercisable by the Secretary of State)
27		*Not in force* (W) (except so far as conferring any power to make an order or regulations which is exercisable by the Secretary of State)
28–43		*Not in force* (except so far as conferring any power to make an order or regulations which is exercisable by the Secretary of State)
45		*Not in force* (W) (except so far as conferring any power to make an order or regulations which is exercisable by the Secretary of State)
46		*Not in force* (W) (except so far as conferring any power to make an order or regulations which is exercisable by the Secretary of State)
47	(1)–(4)	*Not in force* (W) (except so far as conferring any power to make an order or regulations which is exercisable by the Secretary of State)
	(5), (6)	*Not in force* (W) (except so far as conferring any power to make an order or regulations which is exercisable by the Secretary of State)
	(7), (8)	*Not in force* (W) (except so far as conferring any power to make an order or regulations which is exercisable by the Secretary of State)

Enquiry Bureau 020 7400 2518

Health and Social Care Act 2001 (c 15)—*contd*

Section

48		*Not in force* (W) (except so far as conferring any power to make an order or regulations which is exercisable by the Secretary of State)
49		*Not in force* (W) (except so far as conferring any power to make an order or regulations which is exercisable by the Secretary of State and except so far as it applies to certain persons[2])
		Not in force (E) (except so far as conferring any power to make an order or regulations which is exercisable by the Seretary of State and except so far as it applies to certain persons[1])
50	(9)	*Not in force* (E) (except so far as conferring any power to make an order or regulations which is exercisable by the Secretary of State)
53		*Not in force* (W), (S) (except so far as conferring any power to make an order or regulations which is exercisable by the Secretary of State)
54		*Not in force* (W) (except so far as conferring any power to make an order or regulations which is exercisable by the Secretary of State)
55	(1)–(6)	*Not in force* (W) (except so far as conferring any power to make an order or regulations which is exercisable by the Secretary of State)
		Not in force (E) (except so far as conferring any power to make an order or regulations which is exercisable by the Secretary of State and except for the purpose of enabling a local authority to enter into a deferred payment agreement with a resident who has a beneficial interest in property which he occupies or formerly occupied as his only or main residence)
	(7)	*Not in force* (except so far as conferring any power to make an order or regulations which is exercisable by the Secretary of State)

Health and Social Care Act 2001 (c 15)—*contd*

Section

55	(8)	*Not in force* (W) (except so far as conferring any power to make an order or regulations which is exercisable by the Secretary of State)
		Not in force (E) (except so far as conferring any power to make an order or regulations which is exercisable by the Secretary of State and except for the purpose of enabling a local authority to enter into a deferred payment agreement with a resident who has a beneficial interest in property which he occupies or formerly occupied as his only or main residence)
56–58		*Not in force* (except so far as conferring any power to make an order or regulations which is exercisable by the Secretary of State)
62, 63		*Not in force* (except so far as conferring any power to make an order or regulations which is exercisable by the Secretary of State)
67	(1)	See Sch 5 below
	(2)	See Sch 6 below

Schedule

1–3			*Not in force* (except so far as conferring any power to make an order or regulations which is exercisable by the Secretary of State)
4			*Not in force* (W) (except so far as conferring any power to make an order or regulations which is exercisable by the Secretary of State)
5, para	1, 2		*Not in force* (except so far as conferring any power to make an order or regulations which is exercisable by the Secretary of State)
	3		*Not in force* (W), (S) (except so far as conferring any power to make an order or regulations which is exercisable by the Secretary of State)
	4		*Not in force* (except so far as conferring any power to make an order or regulations which is exercisable by the Secretary of State)
	5	(1)	See sub-paras (2)–(17) below

Health and Social Care Act 2001 (c 15)—*contd*

Schedule

5, para	5	(2)		*Not in force* (except so far as conferring any power to make an order or regulations which is exercisable by the Secretary of State)
		(3)		*Not in force* (W) (except so far as conferring any power to make an order or regulations which is exercisable by the Secretary of State)
		(4)		*Not in force* (E) (in relation to the provision of pharmaceutical services)
				Not in force (W) (except so far as conferring any power to make an order or regulations which is exercisable by the Secretary of State)
		(5)–(7)		*Not in force* (except so far as conferring any power to make an order or regulations which is exercisable by the Secretary of State)
		(8)		*Not in force* (W) (except so far as conferring any power to make an order or regulations which is exercisable by the Secretary of State)
		(9)		*Not in force* (except so far as conferring any power to make an order or regulations which is exercisable by the Secretary of State)
		(10)	(a)	*Not in force* (except so far as conferring any power to make an order or regulations which is exercisable by the Secretary of State)
			(b)	*Not in force* (W) (except so far as conferring any power to make an order or regulations which is exercisable by the Secretary of State)
		(11), (12)		*Not in force* (except so far as conferring any power to make an order or regulations which is exercisable by the Secretary of State)
		(13)	(a)	*Not in force* (W) (except so far as conferring any power to make an order or regulations which is exercisable by the Secretary of State)
			(b)	*Not in force* (W) (except so far as conferring any power to make an order or regulations which is exercisable by the Secretary of State)

Health and Social Care Act 2001 (c 15)—*contd*

Schedule

5, para	5	(13)	(c)	*Not in force* (except so far as conferring any power to make an order or regulations which is exercisable by the Secretary of State)
			(d)	*Not in force* (W) (except so far as conferring any power to make an order or regulations which is exercisable by the Secretary of State)
		(14)		*Not in force* (E) (in relation to the provision of pharmaceutical services)
				Not in force (W) (except so far as conferring any power to make an order or regulations which is exercisable by the Secretary of State)
		(15)		*Not in force* (except in so far as conferring any power to make an order or regulations which is exercisable by the Secretary of State)
		(16)		*Not in force* (W) (except so far as conferring any power to make an order or regulations which is exercisable by the Secretary of State)
		(17)		*Not in force* (except in so far as conferring any power to make an order or regulations which is exercisable by the Secretary of State)
	6–9			*Not in force* (except so far as conferring any power to make an order or regulations which is exercisable by the Secretary of State)
	10			*Not in force* (W) (except so far as conferring any power to make an order or regulations which is exercisable by the Secretary of State)
	11			*Not in force* (except so far as conferring any power to make an order or regulations which is exercisable by the Secretary of State)
	12	(1), (2)		*Not in force* (E) (in relation to the provision of pharmaceutical services)
				Not in force (W) (except so far as conferring any power to make an order or regulations which is exercisable by the Secretary of State)
		(3)		*Not in force* (except so far as conferring any power to make an order or regulations which is exercisable by the Secretary of State)

Health and Social Care Act 2001 (c 15)—*contd*

Schedule

5, para	13, 14		*Not in force* (except so far as conferring any power to make an order or regulations which is exercisable by the Secretary of State)
	15	(1)	See sub-paras (2), (3) below
		(2)	*Not in force* (except so far as conferring any power to make an order or regulations which is exercisable by the Secretary of State)
		(3)	*Not in force* (E) (except so far as conferring any power to make an order or regulations which is exercisable by the Secretary of State and so far as relating to functions in relation to the provision of residential accomodation only)
			Not in force (W) (except so far as conferring any power to make an order or regulations which is exercisable by the Secretary of State)
	16		*Not in force* (except so far as conferring any power to make an order or regulations which is exercisable by the Secretary of State)
6			*Not in force* (repeals of or in National Assistance Act 1948, s 26A; Parliamentary Commissioner Act 1967, Sch 2; Social Work (Scotland) Act 1968, s 86A; Local Authorities Social Services Act 1970, Sch 1; National Health Service Act 1977, ss 7, 29(4) (so far as it relates to the provision of pharmaceutical services), 33(1B), 34, 42(3), 44(5), 85(1)(d), 100(1)(c), 102(1)(a)(ii), (2)(a), Sch 5A, para 11(2); Health Services Act 1980, s 20(1); National Health Service and Community Care Act 1990, ss 22, 43, 57, Sch 2, para 16(1)(d), Sch 9, para 18(1); Medicinal Products: Prescription by Nurses etc Act 1992, s 2; Social Security Contributions and Benefits Act 1992, s 135(3), (4); Health Authorities Act 1995, Sch 1, paras 23, 29; Community Care (Direct Payments) Act 1996

Health and Social Care Act 2001 (c 15)—*contd*

Schedule

6—*contd*

ss 1–3, 7(4); National Health Service (Primary Care) Act 1997, Sch 2, paras 11, 13, 29, 76; Police Act 1997, s 115(2)(a); Community Care (Residential Accomodation) Act 1998, ss 1, 3(2); Health Act 1999, ss 12(2), 40, 66(5), Sch 4, paras 17–22, 41; Carers and Disabled Children Act 2000, ss 5, 7(1), 9(a); Government Resources and Accounts Act 2000, ss 12(2), 13(2))

1   "Certain persons" means any person: (a) who is provided with accommodation by a local authority under National Assistance Act 1948, s 21(1); and (b) who, if the authority were also to provide the nursing care in connection with that accommodation, would be liable to make a payment under s 22(3) or 26(3) of that Act either at the standard rate or at a lower rate which is not less than the standard rate minus £110. Notwithstanding that a person ceases to satisfy head (b) above, the Health and Social Care Act 2001, s 49 shall continue to apply to him.

2   "Certain persons" means any person: (a) who is provided with accommodation by a local authority under National Assistance Act 1948, s 21(1); and (b) who, if the local authority were also to provide the nursing care in connection with that accommodation, would be liable to make a payment under s 22 or 26 of that Act either at the standard rate or at a lower rate which is not less than the standard rate minus £100. Notwithstanding that a person ceases to satisfy head (b) above, the Health and Social Care Act 2001, s 49 shall continue to apply to him.

Horse Race (Totalisator and Betting Levy Board) Act 1972 (c 69)

RA: 17 Oct 1972

Section

3   *Not in force*

Housing Act 1980 (c 51)

RA: 8 Aug 1980

Whole Act repealed (S)

Section

59	(3)	See Sch 6 below
141		*Not in force* (in relation to Sch 21, para 7)
152	(1)	See Sch 25 below
	(3)	See Sch 26 below

Schedule

6   *Not in force*—it has been stated that amendments made by this Schedule will not be brought into operation (Regulated Tenancies (Procedure) Regulations 1980, SI 1980/1696 (made under Rent Act 1977, s 74))

Enquiry Bureau 020 7400 2518

Housing Act 1980 (c 51)—*contd*
Schedule

21, para	7	*Not in force*
26		*Not in force* (repeals of or in Housing Act 1957, ss 91, 105, 106 (repealed); Housing (Financial Provisions) Act 1958, s 45 (repealed); New Towns Act 1959, s 4 (repealed); Housing Subsidies Act 1967, ss 24(2)–(4), (5A), 24B, 26, 28A (repealed); Town and Country Planning Act 1968, s 39 (repealed); Housing Finance Act 1972, Sch 4, para 14 (repealed); Housing Act 1974, s 79 (repealed), Sch 8, Sch 11 (repealed); Housing Rents and Subsidies Act 1975, ss 1, 2, 4 (repealed); New Towns (Amendment) Act 1976, s 9 (repealed); Supplementary Benefits Act 1976, Sch 7, para 28; Development of Rural Wales Act 1976, ss 18, 22, Sch 5; Rent Act 1977, Sch 12, paras 4, 9 (repealed))

Housing Act 1988 (c 50)

RA: 15 Nov 1988
Section

59	(2), (3)	See Sch 6 below
140	(1)	See Sch 17 below
	(2)	See Sch 18 below
Schedule		
6, para	27	*Not in force*
17, para	79	*Not in force*
18		*Not in force* (repeals of or in Housing Associations Act 1985, ss 55–57, in relation to hostel deficit grant payable before 1 Apr 1991; Housing (Scotland) Act 1987, s 61(4)(b))

Housing Act 1996 (c 52)

RA: 24 Jul 1996
Section

73	*Not in force*
87	*Not in force*

Housing Act 1996 (c 52)—*contd*

Section

119		*Not in force* (except for the purpose of conferring power to make orders, regulations or rules)
227		See Sch 19 below

Schedule

5		*Not in force*
15		*Not in force*
19, Pt	V	*Not in force* (repeal in Leasehold Reform, Housing and Urban Development Act 1993, s 39(3))
	IX	*Not in force* (repeal in Housing Act 1988, s 79(2)(a))
	XIV	*Not in force* (repeals of or in Consumer Credit Act 1974, s 16(1)(f); Building Societies Act 1986, Sch 18, para 18(2))

Housing and Planning Act 1986 (c 63)

RA: 7 Nov 1986

Section

24	(1), (2)		See Sch 5, Pt II below
	(3)		See Sch 12, Pt I below
49	(1)		See Sch 11, Pt I below
	(2)		See Sch 12, Pt III below
53	(1)		See Sch 11, Pt II below
	(2)		See Sch 12, Pt IV below

Schedule

5, Pt	II, para	16	*Not in force*
		27	*Not in force* (so far as relates to definition 'landlord')
12, Pt	I		*Not in force* (repeals of or in Rent Act 1977, s 69(1), Sch 12, para 3; Housing Act 1985, ss 452(2), 453(2))
	III		*Not in force* (repeals of or in Town and Country Planning Act 1971, ss 32(2), 110(1), 287(9) (repealed))
	IV		*Not in force* (repeals of or in Town and Country Planning (Scotland) Act 1972, ss 158(5), (7), 169(4), 273(9) (repealed))

Housing (Scotland) Act 2001 (asp 10)

RA: 18 Jul 2001

Section

3–56	*Not in force*

Housing (Scotland) Act 2001 (asp 10)—*contd*

Section

84				*Not in force* (except for the purpose of transferring all of the functions of Scottish Homes to the Scottish Ministers except the functions conferred by Housing Scotland Act, s 1(3)(b))
86				*Not in force*
96–105				*Not in force*
112				See Sch 10 below

Schedule

1–6				*Not in force*
10, para	3–8			*Not in force*
	9	(1)		*Not in force*
		(3)		*Not in force*
	10			*Not in force*
	13	(1)		*Not in force*
		(2)		*Not in force* (repeal of Housing (Scotland) Act 1987, SS 1, 17C) (SSI 2001/467)
		(3)–(16)		*Not in force*
		(17)		*Not in force* (repeal of Housing (Scotland) Act 1987, s 81A) (SSI 2001/467)
		(18)–(23)		*Not in force*
		(25)–(34)		*Not in force*
		(36)–(41)		*Not in force*
10, para	13	(42)		*Not in force* (repeal of Housing (Scotland) Act 1987, Schs 2–5, 18) (SSI 2001/467)
	14	(1)		*Not in force*
		(5)	(b), (c)	*Not in force*
		(9)		*Not in force*
		(11)		*Not in force* (so far as relates to paras 2, 3(a), 4 and 14)
		(12)	(a), (b)	*Not in force*
		(13), (14)		*Not in force*
		(15)		*Not in force* (so far as relates to paras 10 and 21)
	15	(1)		*Not in force*
		(5)		*Not in force*
		(7)		*Not in force*
		(9)		*Not in force*
	16–23			*Not in force*
	25–27			*Not in force*
	29			*Not in force*

Immigration and Asylum Act 1999 (c 33)

RA: 1 Nov 1999

Section			
5			*Not in force*
16, 17			*Not in force*
25, 26			*Not in force*
32			*Not in force* (for the purpose of clandestine entrants who arrive in the United Kingdom concealed in a ship or aircraft)
34–37			*Not in force* (for the purpose of clandestine entrants who arrive in the United Kingdom concealed in a ship or aircraft)
40	(1)–(8)		*Not in force*
	(11)–(13)		*Not in force*
41			*Not in force*
42	(1)–(7)		*Not in force*
	(8)		See Sch 1 below
44–55			*Not in force*
79			*Not in force*
117	(5)		*Not in force*
146	(2)		*Not in force*
164			*Not in force*
165			*Not in force* (except for the purposes of enabling subordinate legislation to be made under Immigration Act 1971, s 31A, as inserted by this section)
169	(1)		See Sch 14 below
	(2)		See Sch 15 below
	(3)		See Sch 16 below
Schedule			
1, para	1		*Not in force* (for the purposes of s 42 of this Act)
	3, 4		*Not in force* (for the purposes of s 42 of this Act)
10			*Not in force*
14, para	33–36		*Not in force*
	43		See paras 47–49 below
	47, 48		*Not in force*
	49		*Not in force* (in relation to Immigration Act 1971, s 22, so far as that section has effect for the purposes of Sch 2, para 25 to that Act)
	75		*Not in force*
	80	(1)	See sub-para (4) below
		(4)	*Not in force*

Immigration and Asylum Act 1999 (c 33)—*contd*

Schedule

14, para	84		See paras 85, 86 below
	85, 86		*Not in force*
	90	(1)	See sub-para (4) below
		(4)	*Not in force*
	94		See para 97 below
	97		*Not in force*
	99		See paras 100, 107 below
	100		*Not in force*
	107		*Not in force*
	116		*Not in force*
	118		See paras 119, 121 below
	119		Repealed (*never in force*)
	121		*Not in force* (so far as relates to Special Immigration Appeals Commission Act 1997, s 2A(7), (8))
15, para	4	(a)	*Not in force*
	7, 8		*Not in force*
	10		*Not in force*
16			*Not in force* (repeals of or in Family Law Reform Act 1969, s 2(3); Immigration Act 1971, ss 10(1), 22 (so far as that section has effect for the purposes of Sch 2, para 25 to the 1971 Act); Immigration (Carriers' Liability) Act 1987; Immigration Act 1988, ss 8, 9; Asylum and Immigration Appeals Act 1993, ss 6, 12; Asylum and Immigration Act 1996, s 4; Housing Act 1996, ss 183(2), 186)

The Queen's Printer's copy of SI 2000/464 erroneously purports to bring into force the repeal by Sch 16 to this Act of Asylum and Immigration Act 1996, Sch 1. Sch 16 to this Act does not repeal Sch 1 to the 1996 Act; Sch 1 is repealed by Sch 14, para 113 to this Act, which came into force on 3 Apr 2000.

Income and Corporation Taxes Act 1988 (c 1)

RA: 9 Feb 1988

Section

617	(6)	No date (appointed day for the purposes of s 617(6); repealed (9 Apr 2001) Welfare Reform and Pensions Act 1999, ss 70, 88, Sch 8, Pt I, para 1, Sch 13, Pt V)
651A[1]	(2)	*Not in force* (to come into force on a day to be appointed by the Treasury under s 651A(4) of this Act)

Income and Corporation Taxes Act 1988 (c 1)—*contd*
Section

651A[1]	(3)	(b)	*Not in force* (to come into force on a day to be appointed by the Treasury under s 651A(4) of this Act)
812–815			*Not in force* (to come into force on a day to be appointed by the Treasury under s 812(8) of this Act)

[1]   S 651A was inserted by the Finance Act 1998, s 96

Insolvency Act 2000 (c 39)

RA: 30 Nov 2000
Section

1		See Sch 1 below
2–4		*Not in force*
15		See Sch 5 below
Schedule		
1, para	1–3	*Not in force*
	4	*Not in force* (insofar as relates to Insolvency Act 1986, Sch A1, paras 1–4, 6–44, 45(4))
	5–12	*Not in force*
2, 3		*Not in force*
5		*Not in force* (so far as relates to repeals in Insolvency Act 1986, ss 5(2), (3), 27(3)(a), 255(1)(d))

Insurance Companies Act 1982 (c 50)

RA: 28 Oct 1982
Section

36	*Not in force*

Justices of the Peace Act 1997 (c 25)

RA: 19 Mar 1997
Section

50	*Not in force* (to come into force on date to be appointed by the Lord Chancellor under s 74(3)(b) of this Act; section prospectively substituted by Access to Justice Act 1999, s 83(3), Sch 12, paras 9, 13)
Schedule	
3	*Not in force* (to come into force on date to be appointed by the Lord Chancellor under s 74(3)(b) of this Act; substituted by Access to Justice Act 1999, s 106, Sch 15, Pt V(6))

Land Registration (Scotland) Act 1979 (c 33)

RA: 4 Apr 1979

Section

2	(1), (2)	*Not in force* (Banff, Caithness, Moray, Orkeney and Shetland, Ross and Cromarty, Sutherland)[1]
3	(3)	*Not in force* (Banff, Caithness, Moray, Orkeney and Shetland, Ross and Cromarty, Sutherland)[1]

[1]   The Land Register is expected to apply to the remaining counties by 1 Apr 2003, but some transactions will continue to be registrable in the Register of Sasines (Report of the Committee of Public Accounts, Registers of Scotland: Service to Public (Cm 2739))

Late Payment of Commercial Debts (Interest) Act 1998 (c 20)

RA: 11 Jun 1998

Section

1–16	*Not in force* (in relation to all businesses and public sector claims from all business and the public sector)

Law Reform (Miscellaneous Provisions) (Scotland) Act 1990 (c 40)

RA: 1 Nov 1990

Section

19				*Not in force*
22	(1)	(b)		*Not in force*
	(2)	(c)		*Not in force*
25	(1)–(5)			*Not in force*
	(6)			See Sch 2 below
26–29				*Not in force*
32				*Not in force* (except for purpose of provisions relating to making of rules and orders in Solicitors (Scotland) Act 1980, s 60A(2), (3), (5)–(8))
34	(9)	(f)		*Not in force*
		(h)		*Not in force*
36	(4)			*Not in force*
74	(1)			See Sch 8 below
	(2)			See Sch 9 below

Schedule

2				*Not in force*
8, Pt	11, para	22	(1)	*Not in force* (in relation to a recognised financial institution)
		29	(5)(a), (b)	*Not in force* (in relation to a recognised financial institution)
			(d)	*Not in force* (in relation to a recognised financial institution)

Law Reform (Miscellaneous Provisions) (Scotland) Act 1990 (c 40)—*contd*

Schedule

8, Pt	11, para	29	(6)(b)	*Not in force* (in relation to a recognised financial institution)
			(c)	*Not in force*
		36	(1)	*Not in force*
			(7)–(9)	*Not in force*
			(16)	*Not in force*
9				*Not in force* (repeals of or in Sheriff Courts (Scotland) Act 1907, s 40; Divorce Jurisdiction Court Fees and Legal Aid (Scotland) Act 1983, Sch 1, para 7; Law Reform (Miscellaneous Provisions) (Scotland) Act 1985, Sch 1, Pt I, para 4; Legal Aid (Scotland) Act 1986, ss 4(3)(a), (b), 17(3)–(5), 33(3)(c), (d); Legal Aid Act 1988, Sch 4, paras 3(b); Court of Session Act 1988, s 5(g))

Learning and Skills Act 2000 (c 21)

RA: 28 Jul 2000

Section

149			See Sch 9 below

Schedule

9, para	27, 28		*Not in force* (E) (except for the purposes of the application of the Further and Higher Education Act 1992, ss 44, 45 to any institution which: (a) becomes an institution within the higher education sector (within the meaning of s 91(3) of that Act) on or after 1 Oct 2000 or (b) was an institution within that sector before 1 Oct 2000 and before that was a school maintained by a local education authority)
	90	(1)–(4)	*Not in force* (W)

Leasehold Reform, Housing and Urban Development Act 1993 (c 28)

RA: 20 Jul 1993

Section

187	(1)	See Sch 21 below
	(2)	See Sch 22 below

Schedule

21, para	2	*Not in force*

Leasehold Reform, Housing and Urban Development Act 1993 (c 28)—*contd*
Schedule
22   *Not in force* (repeals of or in House of
                                           Commons Disqualification
                                           Act 1975, Sch 1, Pt II; Northern
                                           Ireland Assembly Disqualification
                                           Act 1975, Sch 1, Pt II; Industrial
                                           Development Act 1982, s 15(1),
                                           Sch 2, Pt II, para 17; Miscellaneous
                                           Financial Provisions Act 1983,
                                           Sch 2; Industrial Development
                                           Act 1985, ss 1–4, 6(2); Housing
                                           Act 1985, s 27C; Housing
                                           Act 1988, Sch 9, para 12(2);
                                           Planning (Consequential Provisions)
                                           Act 1990, Sch 2, para 47)

Legal Aid Act 1988 (c 34)

RA: 29 Jul 1988
Section
44   See Sch 4 below
Schedule
4, para   3   *Not in force*
               5   *Not in force*

Litter Act 1983 (c 35)

RA: 13 May 1983
Section
4   *Not in force*
12   (3)   See Sch 2 below
Schedule
2   *Not in force* (repeal of Control of
                                           Pollution Act 1974, s 24(1)–(3))

Local Government Act 1988 (c 9)

RA: 24 Mar 1988
Section
31   See Sch 5 below
Schedule
5, para   2   *Not in force*

Local Government Act 1992 (c 19)

RA: 6 Mar 1992
Section
8   Repealed (*never in force*)
Schedule
4, Pt   I   *Not in force* (repeal in Local
                                           Government Act 1988, s 7(3)(a))

Local Government Act 2000 (c 22)

RA: 28 Jul 2000

Section

39	(3)	*Not in force* (E) (except so far as confers power to make Orders or Regulations)
44		*Not in force* (E) (except so far as confers power to make Orders or Regulations)
90		*Not in force*
91		*Not in force* (W) (except in relation to police authorities in Wales)
93		*Not in force* (W) (except in relation to police authorities in Wales)
94, 95		*Not in force* (W, S)
96		*Not in force*
107	(1)	See Sch 5 below
	(2)	See Sch 6 below

Schedule

5, para	8	*Not in force*
	12, 13	*Not in force*
	15	*Not in force*
	25, 26	*Not in force*
	34	*Not in force*
6		*Not in force* (repeals of or in Local Government Act 1972, ss 80(1)(e), 94–98, 105, 265A(1)(b); Local Government Act 1974, s 30(3), (3A); Local Government Act 1985, Sch 14, para 13; Transport Act 1985, s 74(12); Financial Services Act 1986, Sch 16, para 8(a); Local Government and Housing Act 1989 ss 19, 31, 32(1), Sch 11, paras 22, 23; Local Government Finance Act 1992, Sch 13, para 32; Local Government (Wales) Act 1994, Sch 15, para 25; Police and Magistrates' Courts Act 1994, Sch 4, para 7; Environment Act 1995, Sch 7, paras 9, 10; Police Act 1996, Sch 7, paras 1(2)(h), 21; Police Act 1997, Sch 6, paras 1, 2; Audit Commission Act 1998, ss 16(1)(a), 17(1)–(3), (50(b), (7), (8), 18, 20–23, Sch 3, par 3(1); Greater London Authority Act 1999, s 66, Sch 8, paras 6, 7)

Local Government and Housing Act 1989 (c 42)

RA: 16 Nov 1989

Abbreviation: "orders etc" means "so far as confers on Secretary of State powers to make orders, regulations or determinations, to give or make directions, to specify matters, to require information, to impose conditions or to give guidance or approvals, or make provision with respect to the exercise of any such power"

Section			
9			*Not in force* (S) (except orders etc)
14			*Not in force* (except orders etc)
15			*Not in force* (S) (except orders etc)
16			*Not in force* (S)
17			*Not in force* (S) (except orders etc)
71	(1)		*Not in force* (except orders etc and except for purposes of sub-ss (4)–(6))
	(2), (3)		*Not in force* (except orders etc)
	(5)		*Not in force* (except orders etc and except for purposes of para (a))
	(7)		*Not in force* (except orders etc)
194	(1)		See Sch 11 below
	(2)–(4)		See Sch 12 below
Schedule			
1			*Not in force* (S) (except orders etc)
11, para	3		*Not in force*
	15		Repealed (*never in force*)
	17, 18		*Not in force*
	21		*Not in force*
	24, 25		*Not in force*
	35	(1), (2)	*Not in force*
		(3)	*Not in force* (except orders etc)
	36		*Not in force*
	55–57		*Not in force*
	60		*Not in force*
	92		*Not in force*
	97		*Not in force*
12, Pt	II		*Not in force* (Town Development Act 1952; Town and Country Planning Act 1962, Sch 12 (repealed); Town and Country Planning Act 1968, s 99 (repealed); Town and Country Planning Act 1971, Sch 23 (repealed); Local Government Act 1972, ss 80(1)(a), 137(2A), (2B0, (2C)(a), (8), 185, 265A(1)(g), Sch 18; Water Act 1973, Sch 8, paras 64, 65; Local Government (Scotland) Act 1973, ss 31(1)(a)(ii), 49(1A), 57(3), 111(1)(a), (b), (d), 161(6) (repealed), Sch 10, para 11 (repealed), Sch 20, para 10

Local Government and Housing Act 1989 (c 42)—*contd*

Schedule

12, Pt	II—*contd*	(repealed); Local Government (Scotland) Act 1975, Sch 6, Pt II, para 46; Local Land Charges Act 1975, s 9(2); Justices of the Peace Act 1979, s 59(1)(a) (repealed); New Towns Act 1981, Pt III (ss 42–57) and s 72(1), Sch 9, para 3(2); Acquisition of Land Act 1981, Sch 4, para 1, Table; New Towns and Urban Development Corporations Act 1985, ss 3, 4, Sch 2, para 2, Sch 3, para 7; Local Government Act 1985, Sch 8, paras 8, 9(2); Housing Act 1985, ss 524–526; Housing and Planning Act 1986, ss 15, 20, Sch 3; Abolition of Domestic Rates Etc (Scotland) Act 1987, Sch 1, para 28(a)(ii), (iii) (repealed); Housing Act 1988, ss 103(4) (repealed), 131; Water Act 1989, Sch 25, paras 19, 80(2))

Local Government etc (Scotland) Act 1994 (c 39)

RA: 3 Nov 1994

Section

37			Repealed (*never in force*)
180	(1)		See Sch 13 below
	(2)		See Sch 14 below

Schedule

13, para	7		*Not in force*; prospectively repealed by Merchant Shipping Act 1995, s 314(1), Sch 12
	34		*Not in force*
	62		*Not in force*
	92	(34), (35)	Repealed (*never in force*)
		(48)	*Not in force*
	95	(8), (9)	Repealed (*never in force*)
	100	(3)	*Not in force*
		(9) (j)	*Not in force*
	119	(54) (a)(ii)	Repealed (*never in force*)
		(h)(ii)	Repealed (*never in force*)
	149		Repealed (*never in force*)
	167	(2)	Repealed (*never in force*)
		(4), (5)	Repealed (*never in force*)
		(7)	Repealed (*never in force*)
		(9)	Repealed (*never in force*)

Local Government etc (Scotland) Act 1994 (c 39)—*contd*

Schedule

14   *Not in force* (repeals of or in Local
                                            Government (Scotland) Act 1973,
                                            ss 135(5)(a), (6)(d), (8), 193(2),
                                            200(1)–(6), (8), (9), (11)(b), 225;
                                            Control of Pollution Act 1974,
                                            s 32(6); Local Government
                                            (Scotland) Act 1975, Sch 3, paras
                                            1(1)–(3), (5), 2–21, 26, 29, 30; Local
                                            Government (Miscellaneous
                                            Provisions) (Scotland) Act 1981,
                                            s 27; Stock Transfer Act 1982, s 5(2);
                                            Environmental Protection Act 1990,
                                            ss 36(6), (10), 39(8), 50(5)(a)(iv),
                                            54(4)(c); Local Government Finance
                                            Act 1992, Sch 8, paras 3(2), 4(2),
                                            Sch 13, para 44(a), (b), (d))

Local Government Finance Act 1992 (c 14)

RA: 6 Mar 1992

Section

117   (1)   See Sch 13 below
               (2)   See Sch 14 below

Schedule

13, para   33   *Not in force*

14   *Not in force* (repeals of or in Civil
                                            Jurisdiction and Judgments Act 1982,
                                            Sch 8, para 4(1)(c); Abolition of
                                            Domestic Rates Etc (Scotland)
                                            Act 1987, ss 8, 10 (except sub-s
                                            (7A)), 11, 11A, 12, 13, 15–17, 18
                                            (except sub-s (2A)), 19, 20(1)–(9),
                                            (11), 21–24, 25(2), 26 (except sub-ss
                                            (1), (2)), 29–32, 34, 35, Sch 2, paras
                                            1(1), 2(2)–(4), 3–9, Sch 3, paras 5(2),
                                            (3), 6, Sch 4. Sch 5, paras 7, 8, 11,
                                            Sch 6; Local Government Finance
                                            Act 1988, Sch 12, paras 18–22, 24–
                                            26, 28–36, 38; Local Government
                                            and Housing Act 1989, ss 142–144,
                                            Sch 6, paras 10–15, 22, 24–29))

Local Government (Miscellaneous Provisions) (Scotland) Act 1981 (c 23)

RA: 11 Jun 1981

Section

37   *Not in force*

Local Government (Wales) Act 1994 (c 19)

RA: 5 Jul 1994

Section				
20	(4)			See Sch 6 below
22	(3)–(5)			See Schs 9–11 below
66	(6)			See Sch 16 below
Schedule				
6, para	5–10			Repealed (*never in force*)
	18			Repealed (*never in force*)
	24	(1)	(a)	Repealed (*never in force*)
	28, 29			Repealed (*never in force*)
9, para	17	(4)		*Not in force*
10, para	11	(1)		*Not in force*
11, para	3	(1), (2)		*Not in force*
16, para	11			Repealed (*never in force*)
	40	(2)	(b)	*Not in force*
	57	(6)		Repealed (*never in force*)
	67			Repealed (*never in force*)
	70			Repealed (*never in force*)
	93			Repealed (*never in force*)

Maintenance Orders (Reciprocal Enforcement) Act 1972 (c 18)

RA: 23 Mar 1972

Section		
22	(2)	*Not in force*

Matrimonial and Family Proceedings Act 1984 (c 42)

RA: 12 Jul 1984

Section			
46			See Schs 1, 2 below
Schedule			
1, para	20	(a)	*Not in force*
2, para	3		*Not in force*

Medicines Act 1968 (c 67)

RA: 25 Oct 1968

Section	
135	See Sch 6 below
Schedule	
6	*Not in force* (repeals of Therapeutic Substances Act 1956, ss 1 (part), 3–7, Pt III (repealed))

Merchant Shipping Act 1995 (c 21)

RA: 19 Jul 1995

Section		
60		*Not in force*
80	(2)	*Not in force*

Merchant Shipping Act 1995 (c 21)—*contd*

Section

80	(4)	*Not in force*
111		*Not in force*
115		*Not in force*
118		*Not in force*
119	(2), (3)	*Not in force*
127		*Not in force*
314	(1)	See Sch 12 below

Schedule

12   *Not in force* (repeals in Aliens Restriction
                                             (Amendment) Act 1919, Local
                                             Government etc (Scotland) Act
                                             1994)

Merchant Shipping and Maritime Security Act 1997 (c 28)

RA: 19 Mar 1997

Section

9   See Sch 1 below

Schedule

1, para   6   *Not in force*

Museums and Galleries Act 1992 (c 44)

RA: 16 Mar 1992

Schedule

9   Repealed (*never in force*) (repeal of
                                             Charities Act 1960, Sch 2, paras
                                             (da)–(dd))

National Health Service Act 1966 (c 8)

RA: 10 Mar 1966

Section

10   *Not in force*

National Health Service (Amendment) Act 1986 (c 66)

RA: 7 Nov 1986

Section

5   *Not in force* (insertion of National
                                             Health Service (Scotland)
                                             Act 1978, s 13B)

National Health Service and Community Care Act 1990 (c 19)

RA: 29 Jun 1990

Section

39   (4)   *Not in force* (repeal in second paragraph
                                             of National Health Service
                                             (Scotland) Act 1978, s 23(5))

National Health Service and Community Care Act 1990 (c 19) —*contd*

Section

66	(1)			See Sch 9 below
	(2)			See Sch 10 below

Schedule

9, para	10	(1)		*Not in force*
	30	(1)	(b), (c)	*Not in force*
10				*Not in force* (repeals of or in National Assistance Act 1948, s 41(1) (repealed); Mental Health Act 1959, s 8(1)–(3); Health Services and Public Health Act 1968, s 44(1); Chronically Sick and Disabled Persons Act 1970, s 2(1) (otherwise than in relation to England and Wales); Local Government Act 1972, Sch 23, paras 2(3), (7), 9(1); National Health Service Reorganisation Act 1973, Sch 4, para 45 (repealed); Social Security Act 1975, s 35(6)(a) (repealed); National Health Service Act 1977, s 85(1)(e), (3), (4), Sch 5, Pts I, II, Sch 14, para 13(1)(b), Sch 15, paras 5, 24(1), 63, 67; Health and Social Services and Social Security Adjudications Act 1983, s 30(3); Health and Social Security Act 1984, Sch 3, paras 6(a), 12; Disabled Persons (Services, Consultation and Representation) Act 1986, s 2(5)(b))

National Health Service (Primary Care) Act 1997 (c 46)

RA: 21 Mar 1997

Section

14				Repealed (E, S) (*never in force*)
				Repealed (*never in force* (W))
21, 22				*Not in force*
25, 26				*Not in force*
33				*Not in force*
41	(10)			See Sch 2 below
	(11)			*Not in force*
	(12)			See Sch 3 below

Schedule

2, Pt	I, para	3		See paras 5, 19, 28 below
		19		*Not in force*

National Health Service (Primary Care) Act 1997 (c 46)—*contd*

Schedule

2, Pt	I, para	28		*Not in force* (for the purpose of inserting the definitions "health service body", "personal dental services", "personal medical services")
		32		See paras 33–35, 38, 40–42, 46, 55–57 below
		33, 34		*Not in force*
		40–42		*Not in force*
		46		*Not in force*
		55		*Not in force*; prospectively repealed by Health Act 1999, s 65(2), Sch 5
		56		*Not in force*
		57		*Not in force* (for the purpose of inserting the definitions "health service body", "medical list", "personal dental services", "personal medical services")
		64	(1)	*Not in force* (so far as it relates to para 64(3))
			(3)	*Not in force*
		65	(2)	*Not in force*
	II, para	69		*Not in force*; prospectively repealed by Health Act 1999, s 65(2), Sch 5
		70–76		*Not in force*
		77, 78		*Not in force*; prospectively repealed by Health Act 1999, s 65(2), Sch 5
		79–81		*Not in force*
3, Pt	I			*Not in force* (repeals of or in National Health Service (Scotland) Act 1978, ss 3(1), 20, 23(1), (2)–(6), (8), 24(1)(a))
	II			*Not in force*

National Parks (Scotland) Act 2000 (asp 10)

RA: 9 Aug 2000

Section

1–36	*Not in force*

Schedule

1–5	*Not in force*

National Minimum Wage Act 1998 (c 39)

RA: 31 Jul 1998

Section

2	(1)	*Not in force* (except so far as confers power to make subordinate legislation)

National Minimum Wage Act 1998 (c 39)—*contd*

Section

2	(2)–(8)	*Not in force*
3	(1)	*Not in force*
	(2)	*Not in force* (except so far as confers power to make subordinate legislation)
	(3), (4)	*Not in force*
4	(1)	*Not in force* (except so far as confers power to make subordinate legislation)
	(2)	*Not in force*
9		*Not in force* (except so far as confers power to make subordinate legislation)
26	(5)	Repealed (*never in force*)
41		*Not in force* (except so far as confers power to make subordinate legislation)
42	(1)	*Not in force*
	(2)	*Not in force* (except so far as confers power to make subordinate legislation)
	(3)–(5)	*Not in force*
49	(9), (10)	*Not in force*
51		*Not in force*
53		See Sch 3 below

Schedule

2, para	3	*Not in force* (in relation to the words "(f) any reference to a pay reference period shall be disregarded")
	13	*Not in force* (in relation to the words "(f) any reference to a pay reference period shall be disregarded")
	26	*Not in force* (in relation to the words "(f) any reference to a pay reference period shall be disregarded")
3		*Not in force* (repeal in Employment Rights (Northern Ireland) Order 1996, SI 1996/1919)

New Roads and Street Works Act 1991 (c 22)

RA: 27 Jun 1991

Section

79, 80	*Not in force*
138, 139	*Not in force*

New Roads and Street Works Act 1991 (c 22)—*contd*
Section

167	(1)–(3)	*Not in force* (S) (except so far as relate to Pt II (ss 27–47))
	(6)	*Not in force* (S) (except so far as relates to Pt II (ss 27–47))
169	(3)	*Not in force*

Noise and Statutory Nuisance Act 1993 (c 40)

RA: 5 Nov 1993
Section

9	*Not in force*

Schedule

3	*Not in force*

Northern Ireland Act 1998 (c 47)

RA: 19 Nov 1998
Section

73	(5)	See Sch 8 below
99		See Sch 13 below
100	(2)	See Sch 15 below

Schedule

13, para	1	Repealed (*never in force*)
	10	Repealed (*never in force*)
15		*Not in force* (repeals of or in Fair Employment (Northern Ireland) Act 1976; Fair Employment (Northern Ireland) Act 1989; Northern Ireland (Emergency Provisions) Act 1996; Northern Ireland Act 1998)

Nuclear Explosions (Prohibition and Inspections) Act 1998 (c 7)

RA: 18 Mar 1998

Not in force

Nuclear Safeguards Act 2000 (c 5)

RA: 25 May 2000
Section

1–11	*Not in force*

Offices, Shops and Railway Premises Act 1963 (c 41)

RA: 31 Jul 1963

The following provisions of this Act were not brought into force in relation to premises which are in a covered market place to which s 51 (repealed) of the Act relates: ss 4–22 (repealed); s 23 (repealed (except in so far as the prohibition of heavy work in s 23(1) applies to certain Registrars, etc, in local authority premises and police officers)); ss 24–41 (repealed); ss 42–44; s 45 (repealed); s 46; ss 47, 48, 50 (repealed); s 69; ss 70, 71 (repealed); ss 72–75; ss 76, 77 (repealed); s 78; s 79 (repealed); ss 83, 84; ss 87, 89 (repealed); s 91(4) and Sch 2 (except so far as they relate to the repeal of the Shops Act 1950, s 37)

Offshore Safety Act 1992 (c 15)

RA: 6 Mar 1992

Section		
7	(2)	See Sch 2 below
Schedule		
2		*Not in force* (repeal, for certain purposes, of Gas Act 1986, s 47(5))

Oil and Gas (Enterprise) Act 1982 (c 23)

RA: 28 Jun 1982

Section		
37		See Schs 3, 4 below
Schedule		
3, para	24	Repealed (*never in force*)
	35, 36	Repealed (*never in force*)
	38	Repealed (*never in force*)
4		*Not in force* (repeals of or in Gas Act 1972, s 7(2) (repealed); Employment Protection (Consolidation) Act 1978, s 137(5) (repealed); Employment (Continental Shelf) Act 1978; Wages Councils Act 1979, s 27(5) (repealed))

Patents Act 1977 (c 37)

RA: 29 Jul 1977

Section		
53	(1)	*Not in force*
60	(4)	*Not in force*
86, 87		*Not in force*
88		Repealed (*never in force*)

Pension Schemes Act 1993 (c 48)

RA: 5 Nov 1993
Section
188	(1), (2)	See Sch 5 below
190		See Sch 7 below
Schedule		
5, Pt	II	*Not in force*
7		*Not in force*

Pension Schemes (Northern Ireland) Act 1993 (c 49)

RA: 5 Nov 1993
Section
182	(1), (2)	See Sch 4 below
184		See Sch 6 below
Schedule		
4, Pt	II	*Not in force*
6		*Not in force*

Pensions Act 1995 (c 26)

RA: 19 Jul 1995
Section
42–46		Repealed (*never in force*)
48	(2)	*Not in force*
	(7)–(13)	*Not in force*
91	(3)	*Not in force* (except for purpose of authorising the making of regulations)
		Sub-s (3) prospectively repealed by Welfare Reform and Pensions Act 1999, s 88, Sch 13, Pt I
95		*Not in force* (except or purpose of authorising the making of regulations)
		Section prospectively repealed by Welfare Reform and Pensions Act 1999, s 88, Sch 13, Pt I
122		See Sch 3 below
135		*Not in force*
145		*Not in force*
151		See Sch 5 below
177		See Sch 7 below
180, 181		See ss above
Schedule		
3, para	1–10	Repealed (*never in force*)
5, para	38	*Not in force*
7, Pt	III	*Not in force* (repeals relating to Pension Schemes Act 1993, ss 35, 36, and subject to savings relating to 1993 Act, ss 55–68, 170(1), 171(1))

Pensions Act 1995 (c 26)—*contd*

1   SI 1996/1853 (originally issued as Commencement No 6) was renumbered as Commencement No 7 by the Pensions Act 1995 (Commencement No 6: SI 1996/1853: C 38) (Amendment) Order 1996, SI 1996/2150

Certain provisions of Sch 4 have effect as follows—para 2 has effect on or after 6 Apr 2010 (para 2(2)); para 4 has effect in relation to any person attaining pensionable age on or after 6 Apr 2010 (para 4(2)); para 6(1) comes into force on 6 Apr 2010; and para 6(2)–(4) have effect in relation to incremental periods beginning on or after that date (para 6(5)); paras 18, 19 have effect on or after 6 Apr 2010 (para 20)

Petroleum Act 1998 (c 17)

RA: 11 Jun 1998

Section		
50		See Sch 4 below
51		See Sch 5 below
Schedule		
4, para	8	*Not in force*
	10	*Repealed* (*never in force*)
	11	*Not in force*
	13	*Not in force*
	34	*Not in force*
	40	*Not in force*
5		*Not in force* (repeals of Employment (Continental Shelf) Act 1978, Trade Union and Labour Relations (Consolidation) Act 1992, s 287(5), Employment Rights Act 1996, s 201(5))

Pharmacists (Fitness to Practise) Act 1997 (c 19)

RA: 19 Mar 1997

Section	
1	*Not in force*
Schedule	*Not in force*

Planning and Compensation Act 1991 (c 34)

RA: 25 Jul 1991

Section		
30		*Not in force* (for certain purposes; see SI 1991/2728, arts 3, 4)
61		See Sch 13 below
84	(6)	See Sch 19 below
Schedule		
13, para	44	*Repealed* (*never in force*)
19, Pt	I	*Not in force* (repeal of Town and Country Planning Act 1990, s 221(7)–(9))

Planning and Compensation Act 1991 (c 34)—*contd*
Schedule
19, Pt	IV	*Not in force* (repeals of or in Town and Country Planning (Scotland) Act 1972, ss 41A(6), (7), 101(1), (2), 153A, 159A, 159B, 167B, 167C, 251(1A), 275(1) (definition of "development consisting of the winning and working of minerals") (repealed))

Planning (Consequential Provisions) (Scotland) Act 1997 (c 11)

RA: 27 Feb 1997
Section
3	(1)	See Sch 1 below
Schedule		
1, Pt	I	*Not in force* (repeal relating to Town and Country Planning (Scotland) Act 1997, s 186)

Police Act 1997 (c 50)

RA: 21 Mar 1997
Section
88				See Sch 6 below
109	(2)			See Sch 8 below
112–118				*Not in force*
121				*Not in force*
122	(3)			*Not in force*
123, 124				*Not in force*
126, 127				*Not in force*
129	(a)			*Not in force*
133				*Not in force*
134	(1)			See Sch 9 below
	(2)			See Sch 10 below
Schedule				
6, para	14			*Not in force*
	25, 26			*Not in force*
8, para	1	(3)	(e), (f)	*Not in force*
	2	(6)		*Not in force*
	10			*Not in force* (the reference to para 1(3)(e) in sub-para (1)(a) and the reference to para 1(3)(f) in sub-para (1)(b))
9, para	65			*Not in force*

Police Act 1997 (c 50)—*contd*
Schedule

10	*Not in force* (repeals of or in Financial Services Act 1986, s 189, Sch 14; Banking Act 1987, s 95; Road Traffic Act 1991, s 47; Osteopaths Act 1993, s 39; National Lottery etc Act 1993, s 19; Chiropractors Act 1994, s 40)

Police and Fire Services (Finance) (Scotland) Act 2001 (asp 15)

RA: 5 Dec 2001
Section

1, 2	*Not in force*

Police and Magistrates' Courts Act 1994 (c 29)

RA: 21 Jul 1994
Section

34–38			Repealed (*never in force*)
44			See Sch 5 below
91	(1)		See Sch 8 below
93			See Sch 9 below
Schedule			
5, para	11, 12		Repealed (para 11 (partly), para 12 *never in force*)
	40	(2)	Repealed (*never in force*)
7			Repealed (*never in force*)
8, Pt	I		Repealed (paras 1, 19 (partly), 23 *never in force*)
9, Pt	I		*Not in force* (entries relating to Police Act 1964, ss 53(1), 60; Police and Criminal Evidence Act 1984, ss 67(8), 85(8), 90(3), (4), (6), (8), 91, 92, 94, 97(4), 99(2), 101, 103, 104(1), (2), 105, Sch 4; Courts and Legal Services Act 1990, which have been repealed by Police Act 1996, s 103, Sch 9, Pt I)
	II		*Not in force* (repeals of or in Metropolitan Police Courts Act 1897, ss 3, 4, 7, 11; London Building Acts (Amendment) Act 1939, s 151(1)(bb); Metropolitan Magistrates' Courts Act 1959, ss 3(1), 4(2); Justices of the Peace Act 1979, ss 58, 59(1)(b), 70 (definition of "the Receiver"))

Enquiry Bureau 020 7400 2518

Police and Magistrates' Courts Act 1994 (c 29)—*contd*
Schedule

| 9, Pt | II—*contd* | | | (repealed); Criminal Justice Act 1991, s 79 (part); Social Security (Consequential Provisions) Act 1992, Sch 2, para 58; Pension Schemes Act 1993, Sch 8, para 12)★ |

★ Metropolitan Police Courts Act 1897, London Building Acts (Amendment) Act 1939, s 151(1)(bb), Metropolitan Magistrates' Courts Act 1959, s 4(2) (part), repealed by Greater London Authority Act 1999, ss 325, 423, Sch 27, paras 7, 14, 16, Sch 34, Pt VII

Police (Northern Ireland) Act 1998 (c 32)

RA: 24 Jul 1998
Section

2	(4)	(a)		*Not in force*
25	(4)			*Not in force*
40	(3), (4)			*Not in force*
74	(1)			See Sch 4 below
	(2)			See Sch 5 below
	(3)			See Sch 6 below
76	(2)			*Not in force*

Schedule

4, para	4			*Not in force*
	8, 9			*Not in force*
	20	(3)–(5)		*Not in force*
	21			*Not in force*
	22	(8)		*Not in force*
5, para	4–11			*Not in force*
6				*Not in force* (repeals in Superannuation Act (Northern Ireland) 1972; Superannuation (Northern Ireland) Order 1972; House of Commons Disqualification Act 1975; Northern Ireland Assembly Disqualification Act 1975; Police (Northern Ireland) Order 1987; Police (Amendment) (Northern Ireland) Order 1995, in Art 2(2), the definition "the 1987 Order" and Pt IV)

Police (Northern Ireland) Act 2000 (c 32)

RA: 23 Nov 2000
Section

3	(3)	(d)	(iii)	*Not in force*
14–19				*Not in force*

Police (Northern Ireland) Act 2000 (c 32)—*contd*
Section

21–23			*Not in force*
28–31			*Not in force*
57	(2)	(i), (j)	*Not in force*
72			*Not in force*
78	(1)		See Sch 6 below
	(3)		See Sch 7 below

Schedule

3			*Not in force*
6, para	14		*Not in force*
7, para	3		*Not in force*

Policyholders Protection Act 1997 (c 18)

RA: 19 Mar 1997
Section

1, 2		*Not in force*
6–15		*Not in force*
17–19		*Not in force*
20	(1), (2)	See Sch 4 below
22		See Sch 5 below

Schedule

1–3		*Not in force*
4, Pt	II	*Not in force*
5		*Not in force* (except so far as relates to Friendly Societies Act 1992)

Political Parties, Elections and Referendums Act 2000 (c 41)

RA: 30 No 2000
Section

6	(1)	(c)	*Not in force*
14			*Not in force* (so far as relates to Boundary Commissions for Scotland, Wales and Northern Ireland)
16			*Not in force* (except for the purpose of making orders or regulations)
17			*Not in force*
19–20			*Not in force* (except for the purposes of making orders or regulations)

Schedule

3			*Not in force*
21, para	6	(3)	*Not in force* (except for the purposes of making orders or regulations)
		(4)	*Not in force*
		(7)	(a)	*Not in force*
	7		*Not in force*

Enquiry Bureau 020 7400 2518

Political Parties, Elections and Referendums Act 2000 (c 41)—*contd*
Schedule
22   *Not in force* (entries relating to House of
                                              Commons Disqualification Act
                                              1975, Sch 1, Pt III; Northern
                                              Ireland Assembly Disqualification
                                              Act 1975, Sch 1, Pt III;
                                              Representation of the People
                                              Act 1983, s 201(1); Parliamentary
                                              Constituencies Act 1986, ss 2, 4(2),
                                              Sch 1, Sch 2, para 8;
                                              Representation of the People
                                              Act 1991; Boundary Commissions
                                              Act 1992, ss 1, 2(1)–(3), 3(2), (3);
                                              Representation of the People
                                              Act 2000, Sch 6, para 4)

Pollution Prevention and Control Act 1999 (c 24)

RA: 27 Jul 1999
Section
6   (1)   See Sch 2 below
                 (2)   *Not in force*
Schedule
2, para   2   *Not in force* (otherwise than E, W)
                 4   *Not in force* (otherwise than E, W)
                 7, 8   *Not in force* (otherwise than E, W)
                 13   *Not in force* (otherwise than E, W)
                 15   *Not in force* (otherwise than E, W)
                 19, 20   *Not in force* (otherwise than E, W)
3   *Not in force*

Postal Services Act 2000 (c 26)

RA: 28 Jul 2000
Section
127   (6)   See Sch 9 below
Schedule
9   *Not in force* (repeals of or in Post
                                              Office Act 1969, ss 6, 74, 75(1), 80
                                              (so far as it extends to the Baliwick
                                              of Guernsey), Sch 1; House of
                                              Commons Disqualification
                                              Act 1975, Sch 1, Pt II)

Powers of Criminal Courts (Sentencing) Act 2000 (c 6)

RA: 25 May 2000
Section
87, 88   *Not in force*

Prisoners' Earnings Act 1996 (c 33)

RA: 18 Jul 1996

Not in force

Private Hire Vehicles (London) Act 1998 (c 34)

RA: 28 Jul 1998
Section

4	(2)	*Not in force*
6–14		*Not in force*
15	(4)	*Not in force*
16	(3), (4)	*Not in force*
21	(2)	*Not in force*
22	(2), (3)	*Not in force*
	(7)	*Not in force*
30, 31		*Not in force*
34	(3)	*Not in force*
35		*Not in force*
39		*Not in force*
Schedule		
1, 2		*Not in force*

Private Security Industry Act 2001 (c 12)

RA: 11 May 2001
Section

1–25	*Not in force*
Schedule	
1, 2	*Not in force*

Prosecution of Offences Act 1985 (c 23)

RA: 23 May 1985
Schedule

1, para	11	*Not in force*
2		*Not in force* (repeal in Supreme Court Act 1981, s 77)

Protection of Children Act 1999 (c 14)

RA: 15 Jul 1999
Section

2	(3)–(9)	*Not in force*
	(10)	*Not in force*
8		*Not in force*
10		Repealed (*never in force*)

Enquiry Bureau 020 7400 2518

Railways Act 1993 (c 43)

RA: 5 Nov 1993
Section

132	(8)		See Sch 10 below
152	(1)		See Sch 12 below
	(3)		See Sch 14 below

Schedule

10, para	3	(1)	*Not in force* (so far as repeals Transport Act 1962, s 70)
12, para	32		*Not in force*
14			*Not in force* (repeal of Transport Act 1962, s 70)

Rates Act 1984 (c 33)

RA: 26 Jun 1984
Section

10, 11	*Not in force*

Refuse Disposal (Amenity) Act 1978 (c 3)

RA: 23 Mar 1978
Section

1	(8)	*Not in force* (to come into force on "the relevant date" to be appointed by the Secretary of State by order under s 13(3) of this Act)
		Whole of s 1 prospectively repealed by the Environmental Protection Act 1990, s 162(2), Sch 16, Pt II
4	(2)	*Not in force* (to come into force on "the relevant date" to be appointed by the Secretary of State by order under s 13(3) of this Act)
6	(8)	*Not in force* (to come into force on "the relevant date" to be appointed by the Secretary of State by order under s 13(3) of this Act)

Regulation of Care (Scotland) Act 2001 (asp 8)

RA: 5 Jul 2001
Section

2, 3		*Not in force*
5	(3), (4)	*Not in force*
7–23		*Not in force*
24	(2), (3)	*Not in force*
25–27		*Not in force*
31–42		*Not in force*

Regulation of Care (Scotland) Act 2001 (asp 8)—*contd*
Section

44–52			*Not in force*
67			*Not in force*
72, 73			*Not in force*
79			See Sch 3 below
80	(1)		*Not in force*

Schedule

3, paras	1–19		*Not in force*
	21, 22		*Not in force*
	23	(1)–(6)	*Not in force*
	24		Repealed (*never in force*)
	25		*Not in force*
4			*Not in force*

Regulation of Investigatory Powers Act 2000 (c 23)

RA: 28 Jul 2000
Section

21	(1)–(3)			*Not in force*
	(4)			*Not in force* (except for purpose of giving effect to definition "related communications data" in s 20 of this Act)
	(5)–(7)			*Not in force*
49–56				*Not in force*
57	(2)	(b), (c)		*Not in force*
		(d)	(ii)	*Not in force*
58	(1)	(g)–(i)		*Not in force*
		(j)		*Not in force* (so far as relates to s 58(1)(h), (i) of this Act)
59	(2)	(b)–(e)		*Not in force* (so far as relate to Pt III (ss 49–56) of this Act)
62	(1)	(b), (c)		*Not in force*
65	(2)	(c), (d)		*Not in force*
	(3)	(c)		*Not in force*
	(5)	(c)		*Not in force*
		(e)		*Not in force*
	(8)	(b)		*Not in force*
		(d), (e)		*Not in force*
	(10)			*Not in force*
66				*Not in force*
67	(1)			*Not in force* (so far as relates to s 65(2)(c), (d) of this Act)
	(9)			*Not in force*
68	(7)	(g), (h)		*Not in force*
		(m)		*Not in force*
		(n)		*Not in force* (so far as relates to para (m))
71, 72				*Not in force* (so far as relates to Pt III (ss 49–56) of this Act)

Regulation of Investigatory Powers Act 2000 (c 23)—*contd*
Schedule
2   *Not in force*

Representation of the People Act 1985 (c 50)

RA: 16 Jul 1985
Schedule
1   *Not in force*
5   *Not in force* (repeals of or in
                                                Representation of the People
                                                Act 1993, s 160(1), (2), Sch 1,
                                                rule 5(3))

Reserve Forces Act 1996 (c 14)

RA: 22 May 1996
Section
131   (2)   See Sch 11 below
Schedule
11   *Not in force* (repeals relating to
                                                Reserve Forces Act 1980 ss 10, 11,
                                                13(2)–(4), 16, 17, 18(1), (2), 19,
                                                20(1), 21, 22, 24–26, 28, 29, 30(1),
                                                (2), 31, 32, 34(1)–(3), 35, 36, 38,
                                                39(1)(a), (b), 40–42, 44, 47, 50, 57,
                                                58, 63, 67, 69, 70, 83(1), (2), 87,
                                                93, 100, 101, 120, 139(1), 141–144,
                                                145(1)(b), (2), 146(1)(b), (2),
                                                154(1), 155, Sch 2, Sch 8, paras 1,
                                                4, 5(1), (3), 6–8, 10–15, 16(2), (3),
                                                (5)–(10), 17, 19, 20)

Road Traffic Act 1960 (c 16)

RA: 22 Mar 1960
Section
266   *Not in force*

Road Traffic Act 1974 (c 50)

RA: 31 Jul 1974
Section
24   (3)   See Sch 7 below
Schedule
7   *Not in force* (repeals relating to Road
                                                Traffic Act 1960, ss 130, 131(1)(b),
                                                133(1) (repealed); Road Traffic
                                                Act 1972, s 40(7), Sch 8, para 3
                                                (repealed))

Road Traffic Act 1991 (c 40)

RA: 25 Jul 1991
Section
83 See Sch 8 below
Schedule
8 *Not in force* (repeal in Public Passenger
Vehicles Act 1981, s 66A)

Road Traffic (Consequential Provisions) Act 1988 (c 54)

RA: 15 Nov 1988
Section
4 See Sch 2 below
Schedule
2, para 15–20 *Not in force*

Road Traffic (Driver Licensing and Information Systems) Act 1989 (c 22)

RA: 21 Jul 1989
Section
16 See Sch 6 below
Schedule
6 *Not in force* (repeal of Road Traffic
(Driver Licensing and Information
Systems) Act 1989, Sch 1, para 11)

Road Traffic (NHS Charges) Act 1999 (c 3)

RA: 10 Mar 1999
Section
1–20 *Not in force* (in relation to military
hospitals)

Road Traffic Offenders Act 1988 (c 53)

RA: 15 Nov 1988
Section
27 (4) *Not in force* (S)
30 *Not in force* (S) (except so far as relates
to ss 75–77)
52 (4) *Not in force*
54–58 *Not in force* (S)
59 (1)–(5) *Not in force*
61 *Not in force* (S)

Road Traffic Regulation Act 1984 (c 27)

RA: 26 Jun 1984
Schedule
8, para 3 *Not in force*

Enquiry Bureau 020 7400 2518

Road Traffic (Vehicle Testing) Act 1999 (c 12)

RA: 30 Jun 1999

1	(1), (2)		*Not in force*
	(3)		*Not in force* (so far as relates to insertion of Road Traffic Act 1988, s 45(6A))
2			*Not in force*
4, 5			*Not in force*
7			*Not in force*
Schedule			*Not in force*

Salmon Conservation (Scotland) Act 2001 (asp 3)

RA: 14 Feb 2001
Section

1, 2		*Not in force*

School Standards and Framework Act 1998 (c 31)

RA: 24 Jul 1998
Section

39	(1)			*Not in force* (except so far as relates to the power to make regulations)
112	(3)			*Not in force*
128				*Not in force*
134	(2)			*Not in force*
135				See Sch 28 below
140	(1)			See Sch 30 below
	(3)			See Sch 31 below
Schedule				
28, Pt I, para 5				*Not in force*
30, para	28	(2)	(b)	Repealed (*never in force*)
	64, 65			*Not in force*
	114			*Not in force* (so far as substitutes Education Act 1996, s 438(5)(b))
	116			*Not in force* (so far as substitutes Education Act 1996, s 440(3)(b))
	138			*Not in force*
	185			*Not in force* (so far as relates to the repeal of Education Act 1996, Schs 11–13, 17–19, 22, paras 1–14, 16, Schs 23–25A)
31				*Not in force* (repeals of or in Sex Discrimination Act 1975, Sch 2, para 1; Acquisition of Land Act 1981, s 17(4)(ac); Education Act 1996, ss 16(1)(c), 517,

School Standards and Framework Act 1998 (c 31)—*contd*
Schedule
31—*contd*   Schs 11–13, 17–19, Sch 22,
                             paras 1–14, 16, Schs 23–25A;
                             School Inspections Act 1996,
                             s 9(3)(a); Education Act 1997,
                             s 17(7)(a))

Sea Fish (Conservation) Act 1992 (c 60)

RA: 17 Dec 1992
Section
1   (2)   *Not in force* (n relation to vessels of an
                             overall length of 10 metres or less
                             until such day as may be
                             appointed)

Sea Fisheries Act 1968 (c 77)

RA: 18 Dec 1968
Schedule
2, Pt   II   *Not in force* (so far as it relates to the
                             repeals in Sea Fisheries Act 1883,
                             ss 1–5, 11, 12, 14–22, in s 25, the
                             words "this Act shall apply to the
                             whole of the British Island as
                             defined by this Act and to the seas
                             surrounding the same whether
                             within or without the fishery limit
                             of the British Islands", ss 26, 28,
                             31, Sch 1, Arts XIII–XXIII, XXX,
                             XXXI and XXXIIIl (repealed); Sea
                             Fisheries (Scotland) Amendment
                             Act 1885, s 5; Illegal Trawling
                             (Scotland) Act 1934, s 3; Sea Fish
                             Industry Act 1951, s 25; Sea Fish
                             Industry Act 1962, s 18; Fishery
                             Limits Act 1964, s 3(2) (repealed))

Sexual Offences (Protected Material) Act 1997 (c 39)

RA: 21 Mar 1997

Not in force

Smoke Detectors Act 1991 (c 37)

RA: 25 Jul 1991

Not in force

Social Security Act 1973 (c 38)

RA: 18 Jul 1973

Section

69	(7)		*Not in force*; repealed (NI)
100			See Schs 27, 28 below

Schedule

27, Pt	I, para	24	*Not in force* (the words "or premiums" and "or premium")
		64	*Not in force* (the words "or premiums" and "or premium")
		78	*Not in force* (the words "or premiums" and "or premium")
		80	*Not in force* (the words "or premiums" and "or premium" in sub-paras (a), (b) respectively)
		85	*Not in force*
		88	*Not in force*
28			*Not in force* (entries relating to Superannuation and other Trust Funds (Validation) Act 1927, ss 1–8, 10, 11(2) from "but save as aforesaid" onwards; Superannuation and other Trust Funds (Validation) Act (Northern Ireland) 1928 (repealed))

Social Security Act 1986 (c 50)

RA: 25 Jul 1986

Section

86	(2)	See Sch 11 below

Schedule

11	*Not in force* (repeals of or in Social Security Act 1975, ss 13(5A), 50(5), 91(2), 135(6), Sch 16, para 3 and Social Security Pensions Act 1975, s 6(5), Sch 4, paras 41, 42 and Social Security (Consequential Provisions) Act 1975, Sch 3, para 18, all of which provisions have now been repealed by Social Security (Consequential Provisions) Act 1992, s 3, Sch 1, as from 1 Jul 1992; also repeals of Pensioners' Payments and National Insurance Act 1973, s 7, Schedule; Social Security Act 1985, Sch 5, paras 6(b), 16, as to which see note 1 to that Act ante)

Social Security Act 1989 (c 24)

RA: 21 Jul 1989

Section				
23				See Sch 5 below
31	(2)			See Sch 9 below

Schedule				
5, para	1			*Not in force* (for purpose of giving effect to paras 5(2)(b), (c), 6(3)(b), (c))
	2	(1), (2)		*Not in force* (for purpose of giving effect to paras 5(2)(b), (c), 6(3)(b), (c))
		(3)		*Not in force*
		(4)	(a), (b)	*Not in force*
			(c)	*Not in force* (for purpose of giving effect to paras 5(2)(b), (c), 6(3)(b), (c))
			(d)–(g)	*Not in force*
		(5)		*Not in force* (for purpose of giving effect to paras 5(2)(b), (c), 6(3)(b), (c))
		(6)–(8)		*Not in force*
		(9)		*Not in force* (for purpose of giving effect to paras 5(2)(b), (c), 6(3)(b), (c))
	3	(1)		*Not in force* (for purpose of giving effect to paras 5(2)(b), (c), 6(3)(b), (c))
		(2)		*Not in force*
		(3), (4)		*Not in force* (for purpose of giving effect to paras 5(2)(b), (c), 6(3)(b), (c))
	4			Repealed (*never in force*)
	5	(2)	(b), (c)	*Not in force*
	6	(3)	(b), (c)	*Not in force*
	7	(a)–(c)		*Not in force* (for purpose of giving effect to paras 5(2)(b), (c), 6(3)(b), (c))
		(d)		*Not in force*
		(e)		*Not in force* (for purpose of giving effect to paras 5(2)(b), (c), 6(3)(b), (c))
	8			*Not in force*
	9, 10			*Not in force* (for purpose of giving effect to paras 5(2)(b), (c), 6(3)(b), (c))
	12			*Not in force*
	14			Repealed (*never in force*)
9				*Not in force* (repeals of or in Social Security Act 1975, s 167(1)(b) (repealed); Social Security Pensions

Social Security Act 1989 (c 24)—*contd*
Schedule
9—*contd*

Act 1975, ss 41A(1C), 41B(1A)
(repealed); Social Security
(Miscellaneous Provisions) Act
1977, s 22(2) (repealed);
Social Security Act 1980,
s 14(7) (repealed); Social
Security (Contributions)
Act 1981, s 4(5)(a)
(repealed); Social Security
(Contributions) Act 1982, s 2
(repealed); Social Security
Act 1985, Sch 5, para 32
(repealed); Social
Security Act 1986, s 30(2),
 Sch 3, para 15(b),
Sch 9, Pt III, para 11(b)
(repealed); Social
Security Act 1988, s 2(9)
(repealed); Housing
(Scotland) Act 1988, s 70(4)
(repealed); Housing Act
1988, s 121(5) (repealed))

Social Security Act 1990 (c 27)

RA: 13 Jul 1990
Section
21   (1)   See Sch 6 below
                (2)   See Sch 7 below
Schedule
6, para   29   *Not in force*
7   *Not in force* (repeals of or
                                                in Social Security Act
                                                1975, s 135(5) (repealed);
                                                Social Security Pensions
                                                Act 1975, ss 32(2B)(d)(i),
                                                56L(1)(b), (9), Sch 1A,
                                                 para 7(4)(a), (b) (repealed);
                                                Social Security
                                                (Miscellaneous Provisions)
                                                Act 1977, s 1(7)(b)
                                                (repealed); National Health
                                                Service Act 1977. Sch 15, para
                                                71; National Health
                                                Service (Scotland) Act 1978,
                                                Sch 16, para 44; Social
                                                Security Act 1979, s 4(2)(b)
                                                (repealed);

Social Security Act 1990 (c 27)—*contd*
Schedule
7—*contd*

Social Security Act 1980, Sch 1, para 15 (repealed), Sch 2, Pt I, para 31(b), (c), (h); Social Security Act 1985, Sch 5, paras 12, 22; Social Security Act 1986, s 33(10A) (repealed), Sch 10, paras 68(1), 78, 79; Social Security Act 1989, s 6(2), Sch 3, para 16 (repealed), Sch 6, paras 6, 7, para 8(1)(a) (repealed), Sch 8. para 2(6) (repealed), Sch 9 (entry relating to the Social Security Pensions Act 1975, s 41C(3)(a)(ii))

Social Security Act 1998 (c 14)

RA: 21 May 1998
Section

1	(a), (b)		*Not in force* (for the purposes of housing benefit, council tax benefit and decisions given before 1 Apr 1999 relating to contributions, statutory sick pay, statutory maternity pay and certain pension matters)
2	(2)	(a)	*Not in force* (for the purposes of housing benefit, council tax benefit and decisions given before 1 Apr 1999 relating to contributions, statutory sick pay, statutory maternity pay and certain pension matters)
4	(1)	(a)	*Not in force* (for the purposes of housing benefit, council tax benefit and decisions given before 1 Apr 1999 relating to contributions, statutory sick pay, statutory maternity pay and certain pension matters)
		(c)	*Not in force* (for the purposes of housing benefit, council tax benefit and decisions given before 1 Apr 1999 relating to contributions, statutory sick pay, statutory maternity pay and certain pension matters)

Social Security Act 1998 (c 14)—*contd*
Section

4	(2)	(a)	*Not in force* (for the purposes of housing benefit, council tax benefit and decisions given before 1 Apr 1999 relating to contributions, statutory sick pay, statutory maternity pay and certain pension matters)
		(c), (d)	*Not in force* (for the purposes of housing benefit, council tax benefit and decisions given before 1 Apr 1999 relating to contributions, statutory sick pay, statutory maternity pay and certain pension matters)
8–10			*Not in force* (for the purposes of housing benefit, council tax benefit and decisions given before 1 Apr 1999 relating to contributions, statutory sick pay, statutory maternity pay and certain pension matters)
11			*Not in force* (for the purposes of housing benefit, council tax benefit and decisions given before 1 Apr 1999 relating to contributions, statutory sick pay, statutory maternity pay and certain pension matters)
12	(1)		See Schs 2, 3 below
	(2)–(9)		*Not in force* (for the purposes of housing benefit, council tax benefit and decisions given before 1 Apr 1999 relating to contributions, statutory sick pay, statutory maternity pay and certain pension matters)
13			*Not in force* (for the purposes of housing benefit, council tax benefit and decisions given before 1 Apr 1999 relating to contributions, statutory sick pay, statutory maternity pay and certain pension matters)
14	(1)–(11)		*Not in force* (for the purposes of housing benefit, council tax benefit and decisions given before 1 Apr 1999 relating to contributions, statutory sick pay, statutory maternity pay and certain pension matters)

Social Security Act 1998 (c 14)—*contd*
Section

14	(12)	See Sch 4 below
15		*Not in force* (for the purposes of housing benefit, council tax benefit and decisions given before 1 Apr 1999 relating to contributions, statutory sick pay, statutory maternity pay and certain pension matters)
16	(1)–(3)	*Not in force* (for the purposes of housing benefit, council tax benefit and decisions given before 1 Apr 1999 relating to contributions, statutory sick pay, statutory maternity pay and certain pension matters)
	(6)–(9)	*Not in force* (for the purposes of housing benefit, council tax benefit and decisions given before 1 Apr 1999 relating to contributions, statutory sick pay, statutory maternity pay and certain pension matters)
17		*Not in force* (for the purposes of housing benefit, council tax benefit and decisions given before 1 Apr 1999 relating to contributions, statutory sick pay, statutory maternity pay and certain pension matters)
18	(1)	*Not in force* (for the purposes of housing benefit, council tax benefit and decisions given before 1 Apr 1999 relating to contributions, statutory sick pay, statutory maternity pay and certain pension matters)
19–24		*Not in force* (for the purposes of housing benefit, council tax benefit and decisions given before 1 Apr 1999 relating to contributions, statutory sick pay, statutory maternity pay and certain pension matters)
25		*Not in force* (for the purposes of housing benefit, council tax benefit and decisions given before 1 Apr 1999 relating to contributions, statutory sick pay, statutory maternity pay and certain pension matters)

Social Security Act 1998 (c 14)—*contd*
Section

26	(1)–(7)	*Not in force* (for the purposes of housing benefit, council tax benefit and decisions given before 1 Apr 1999 relating to contributions, statutory sick pay, statutory maternity pay and certain pension matters)
27		*Not in force* (for the purposes of housing benefit, council tax benefit and decisions given before 1 Apr 1999 relating to contributions, statutory sick pay, statutory maternity pay and certain pension matters)
28		*Not in force* (for the purposes of housing benefit, council tax benefit and decisions given before 1 Apr 1999 relating to contributions, statutory sick pay, statutory maternity pay and certain pension matters)
29, 30		*Not in force* (except for the purposes of guardian's allowance, industrial injuries benefit, child benefit and certain pension matters)
33		*Not in force* (for the purposes of housing benefit, council tax benefit and decisions given before 1 Apr 1999 relating to contributions, statutory sick pay, statutory maternity pay and certain pension matters)
35		*Not in force*
36–39		*Not in force* (for the purposes of housing benefit, council tax benefit and decisions given before 1 Apr 1999 relating to contributions, statutory sick pay, statutory maternity pay and certain pension matters)
45		*Not in force* (except (a) so far as authorising the making of regulations; (b) in so far as inserts the Vaccine Damage Payments Act 1979, s 3A(1), (3), (4); and (c) for the purposes of attendance allowance, disability living allowance, invalid care allowance and job seeker's allowance, vaccine

Social Security Act 1998 (c 14)—*contd*

Section		
45—*contd*		damage payments and certain decisions with respect to earnings factors and availability for regular employment)
46		*Not in force* (except (a) so far as authorising the making of regulations; (b) in so far as substitutes the Vaccine Damage Payments Act 1979, s 4(2), (3), and (c) for the purposes of attendance allowance, disability living allowance, invalid care allowance and job seeker's allowance, vaccine damage payments and certain decisions with respect to earnings factors and availability for regular employment)
47		*Not in force* (except (a) so far as authorising the making of regulations; and (b) for the purposes of attendance allowance, disability living allowance, invalid care allowance and job seeker's allowance, vaccine damage payments and certain decisions with respect to earnings factors and availability for regular employment))
58		Repealed (*never in force*)
61		Repealed (*never in force* so far as relates to Social Security Administration Act 1992, s 114A)
67		*Not in force*
74		*Not in force* (for the purposes of housing benefit, council tax benefit and decisions given before 1 Apr 1999 relating to contributions, statutory sick pay, statutory maternity pay and certain pension matters)
83		See Sch 6 below
86	(1)	See Sch 7 below
	(2)	See Sch 8 below
Schedule		
2–5		*Not in force* (for the purposes of housing benefit, council tax benefit and decisions given before 1 Apr 1999 relating to contributions, statutory sick pay, statutory maternity pay and certain pension matters)

Social Security Act 1998 (c 14)—*contd*
Schedule

7, para	3		*Not in force*
	4	(1), (2)	*Not in force* (for the purposes of housing benefit, council tax benefit and decisions given before 1 Apr 1999 relating to contributions, statutory sick pay, statutory maternity pay and certain pension matters)
	5–7		*Not in force* (for the purposes of attendance allowance, disability living allowance, invalid care allowance and job seeker's allowance, vaccine damage payments and certain decisions with respect to earnings factors and availability for regular employment)
	8, 9		*Not in force* (except (a) so far as authorising the making of regulations; and (b) for the purposes of attendance allowance, disability living allowance, invalid care allowance and job seeker's allowance, vaccine damage payments and certain decisions with respect to earnings factors and availability for regular employment)
	10		*Not in force* (except for the purposes of attendance allowance, disability living allowance, invalid care allowance and job seeker's allowance, vaccine damage payments and certain decisions with respect to earnings factors and availability for regular employment)
	11		*Not in force* (for the purposes of housing benefit, council tax benefit and decisions given before 1 Apr 1999 relating to contributions, statutory sick pay, statutory maternity pay and certain pension matters)
	15		*Not in force* (for the purposes of housing benefit, council tax benefit and decisions given before 1 Apr 1999 relating to contributions, statutory sick pay, statutory maternity pay and certain pension matters)

Social Security Act 1998 (c 14)—*contd*
Schedule

7, para	17		*Not in force* (for the purposes of housing benefit, council tax benefit and decisions given before 1 Apr 1999 relating to contributions, statutory sick pay, statutory maternity pay and certain pension matters)
	47	(b)	*Not in force* (for the purposes of housing benefit, council tax benefit and decisions given before 1 Apr 1999 relating to contributions, statutory sick pay, statutory maternity pay and certain pension matters)
	55		*Not in force* (for the purposes of housing benefit, council tax benefit and decisions given before 1 Apr 1999 relating to contributions, statutory sick pay, statutory maternity pay and certain pension matters)
	62		*Not in force* (except for the purposes of contributory benefits (except child's special allowance), severe disablement allowance, benefits for the aged, increases for dependants and graduated retirement benefit)
	64, 65		*Not in force* (except for the purposes of guardian's allowance, industrial injuries benefit, child benefit and certain pension matters)
	66–70		*Not in force* (for the purposes of housing benefit, council tax benefit and decisions given before 1 Apr 1999 relating to contributions, statutory sick pay, statutory maternity pay and certain pension matters)
	71	(a)	*Not in force* (for the purposes of housing benefit, council tax benefit and decisions given before 1 Apr 1999 relating to contributions, statutory sick pay, statutory maternity pay and certain pension matters)
	72	(1), (2)	*Not in force* (for the purposes of housing benefit, council tax benefit and decisions given before 1 Apr 1999 relating to

Social Security Act 1998 (c 14)—*contd*
Schedule

7, para	72	(1), (2)—*contd*	contributions, statutory sick pay, statutory maternity pay and certain pension matters)
		(5)	*Not in force* (for the purposes of housing benefit, council tax benefit and decisions given before 1 Apr 1999 relating to contributions, statutory sick pay, statutory maternity pay and certain pension matters)
	73		*Not in force* (for the purposes of housing benefit, council tax benefit and decisions given before 1 Apr 1999 relating to contributions, statutory sick pay, statutory maternity pay and certain pension matters)
	76		*Not in force* (except for the purposes of contributory benefits (except child's special allowance), severe disablement allowance, benefits for the aged, increases for dependants and graduated retirement benefit)
	77	(10)	Repealed (*never in force*)
		(13)	Repealed (*never in force*)
	78		Repealed (*never in force* in part)
	79	(1)	*Not in force* (for the purposes of housing benefit, council tax benefit and decisions given before 1 Apr 1999 relating to contributions, statutory sick pay, statutory maternity pay and certain pension matters)
	81		*Not in force* (for the purposes of housing benefit, council tax benefit and decisions given before 1 Apr 1999 relating to contributions, statutory sick pay, statutory maternity pay and certain pension matters)
	82		*Not in force* (except for the purposes of attendance allowance, disability living allowance, invalid care allowance and job seeker's allowance, vaccine damage payments and certain decisions with respect to earnings factors and availability for regular employment)

Social Security Act 1998 (c 14)—*contd*
Schedule

7, para	83, 84	*Not in force* (for the purposes of housing benefit, council tax benefit and decisions given before 1 Apr 1999 relating to contributions, statutory sick pay, statutory maternity pay and certain pension matters)
	88, 89	*Not in force* (for the purposes of housing benefit, council tax benefit and decisions given before 1 Apr 1999 relating to contributions, statutory sick pay, statutory maternity pay and certain pension matters)
	95	*Not in force* (for the purposes of housing benefit, council tax benefit and decisions given before 1 Apr 1999 relating to contributions, statutory sick pay, statutory maternity pay and certain pension matters)
	96	*Not in force* (except for the purposes of attendance allowance, disability living allowance, invalid care allowance and job seeker's allowance, vaccine damage payments and certain decisions with respect to earnings factors and availability for regular employment)
	97	*Not in force* (for the purposes of housing benefit, council tax benefit and decisions given before 1 Apr 1999 relating to contributions, statutory sick pay, statutory maternity pay and certain pension matters)
	98	*Not in force* (except for the purposes of attendance allowance, disability living allowance, invalid care allowance and job seeker's allowance, vaccine damage payments and certain decisions with respect to earnings factors and availability for regular employment)
	101–103	*Not in force* (except for the purposes of attendance allowance, disability living allowance, invalid care

Social Security Act 1998 (c 14)—*contd*
Schedule

7, para	101–103—*contd*	allowance and job seeker's allowance, vaccine damage payments and certain decisions with respect to earnings factors and availability for regular employment)
	106–109	*Not in force* (except for the purposes of attendance allowance, disability living allowance, invalid care allowance and job seeker's allowance, vaccine damage payments and certain decisions with respect to earnings factors and availability for regular employment)
	110 (2)	*Not in force* (except for the purposes of attendance allowance, disability living allowance, invalid care allowance and job seeker's allowance, vaccine damage payments and certain decisions with respect to earnings factors and availability for regular employment)
	111–113	*Not in force* (except for the purposes of attendance allowance, disability living allowance, invalid care allowance and job seeker's allowance, vaccine damage payments and certain decisions with respect to earnings factors and availability for regular employment)
	115	*Not in force* (except for the purposes of guardian's allowance, industrial injuries benefit, child benefit and certain pension matters)
	116–118	*Not in force* (for the purposes of housing benefit, council tax benefit and decisions given before 1 Apr 1999 relating to contributions, statutory sick pay, statutory maternity pay and certain pension matters)
	119	*Not in force* (except for the purposes of attendance allowance, disability living allowance, invalid care allowance and job seeker's allowance, vaccine damage payments and certain decisions with respect to earnings factors and availability for regular employment)

Social Security Act 1998 (c 14)—*contd*
Schedule

7, para	120	(a)		*Not in force*
		(b)		*Not in force* (for the purposes of housing benefit, council tax benefit and decisions given before 1 Apr 1999 relating to contributions, statutory sick pay, statutory maternity pay and certain pension matters)
	121	(2)		*Not in force* (for the purposes of housing benefit, council tax benefit and decisions given before 1 Apr 1999 relating to contributions, statutory sick pay, statutory maternity pay and certain pension matters)
	123	(1)	(a)	*Not in force* (for the purposes of housing benefit, council tax benefit and decisions given before 1 Apr 1999 relating to contributions, statutory sick pay, statutory maternity pay and certain pension matters)
		(2)		*Not in force* (for the purposes of housing benefit, council tax benefit and decisions given before 1 Apr 1999 relating to contributions, statutory sick pay, statutory maternity pay and certain pension matters)
	124	(1)	(a)	*Not in force* (for the purposes of housing benefit, council tax benefit and decisions given before 1 Apr 1999 relating to contributions, statutory sick pay, statutory maternity pay and certain pension matters)
		(2)		*Not in force* (for the purposes of housing benefit, council tax benefit and decisions given before 1 Apr 1999 relating to contributions, statutory sick pay, statutory maternity pay and certain pension matters)
	125			*Not in force* (for the purposes of housing benefit, council tax benefit and decisions given before 1 Apr 1999 relating to contributions, statutory sick pay, statutory maternity pay and certain pension matters)

Social Security Act 1998 (c 14)—*contd*

Schedule

7, para	129		*Not in force* (for the purposes of housing benefit, council tax benefit and decisions given before 1 Apr 1999 relating to contributions, statutory sick pay, statutory maternity pay and certain pension matters)
	130	(1)	Repealed (*never in force*)
		(2)	Repealed (*never in force* in part)
	131		*Not in force* (except so far as authorising the making of regulations and for the purposes of guardian's allowance, industrial injuries benefit, child benefit and certain pension matters)
	132		Repealed (*never in force*)
	134–146		*Not in force* (except for the purposes of attendance allowance, disability living allowance, invalid care allowance and job seeker's allowance, vaccine damage payments and certain decisions with respect to earnings factors and availability for regular employment)
	147		*Not in force* (for the purposes of housing benefit, council tax benefit and decisions given before 1 Apr 1999 relating to contributions, statutory sick pay, statutory maternity pay and certain pension matters)
	148		Repealed (*never in force*)
	149–153		*Not in force* (for the purposes of housing benefit, council tax benefit and decisions given before 1 Apr 1999 relating to contributions, statutory sick pay, statutory maternity pay and certain pension matters)
8			*Not in force* (repeals of or in Parliamentary Commissioner Act 1967, Sch 4 (which entries have now been repealed or substituted); Social Security Administration Act 1992, ss 5(1)(n), (o), (4), 6(1)(n), (o); and, except for the purposes of housing benefit, council tax benefit and

Social Security Act 1998 (c 14)—*contd*
Schedule
8—*contd*

decisions given before 1 Apr 1999
relating to contributions, statutory
sick pay, statutory maternity pay
and certain pension matters, repeals
of or in House of Commons
Disqualification Act 1975, Sch 1,
Pt III (except so far as applies to
the entries relating to regional or
other full-time chairmen of child
support appeal tribunals, the Chief
Child Support Officer and
members of a panel appointed
under Tribunals and Inquiries
Act 1992, s 6, of persons to act as
chairmen of child support appeal
tribunals); Health and Social
Services and Social Security
Adjudications Act 1983, s 25,
Sch 8; Social Security
Administration Act 1992, ss 17–61,
62, 64–70, 116(6), 189(1) (the
words "subsection (2) below and
to"), (2), (4) (the words "24 or"),
(5) (the words "(other than the
power conferred by section 24
above)"), (6) (the word "24,"),
(10), 190(4), 191 (the definitions
"commissioner", "the disablement
questions", "5 year general
qualification", "President", "10
year general qualification"), 192(5)
(the words "section 24;"), Sch 2,
paras 1, 2, 4–8, 3, Sch 4, Pt I (the
entry "Adjudication officers", paras
(b)–(d) in the entry "Adjudicating
bodies" and the words "A social
fund officer" in the entry "The
Social Fund"); Social Security
(Consequential Provisions)
Act 1992, Sch 4, para 12; Local
Government Finance Act 1992,
Sch 9, para 14, Sch 13, para 94;
Tribunals and Inquiries Act 1992,
ss 6(4), 13(5)(b), Sch 1, para 41(b),
(c), (e), Sch 3, para 36; Judicial
Pensions and Retirement Act 1993,
Sch 1, Pt II and Sch 5 (other than
entries relating to chairmen of
disability appeal tribunals and to

Social Security Act 1998 (c 14)—*contd*
Schedule
8—*contd*

chairmen of vaccine damage
tribunals), Sch 6, para 21, Sch 7,
para 5(5)(iii), (iv), Sch 8, para 23;
Pension Schemes Act 1993, Sch 8,
paras 25, 33, 34; Social Security
(Incapacity for Work) Act 1994,
s 6(2), Sch 1, paras 11, 46–48;
Deregulation and Contracting Out
Act 1994, Sch 16, para 20;
Pensions Act 1995, Sch 5, para 70;
Industrial Tribunals Act 1996,
s 16(5)(a), Sch 1, para 7;
Arbitration Act 1996, Sch 3,
para 54; Social Security (Recovery
of Benefits) Act 1997, ss 11(6),
12(6)–(8), 13(2), (4); Social
Security Administration (Fraud)
Act 1997, ss 17, 18, Sch 1, para 2;
Social Security Act 1998, s 83,
Sch 6)

Social Security Administration (Fraud) Act 1997 (c 47)

RA: 21 Mar 1997
Section
3

Not in force (so far as it inserts
s 122E(3), (4) into Social Security
Administration Act 1992)

22

See Sch 2 below

Schedule
2

Not in force (repeal of Social Security
Administration Act 1992, s 128A
and the heading preceding that
section)

Social Security and Housing Benefits Act 1982 (c 24)

RA: 28 Jun 1982
Section
48   (5), (6)

See Sch 5 below

Schedule
5

Not in force (repeals in Social Security
Act 1975, s 65(4) (repealed); Social
Security Pensions Act 1975, Sch 4,
para 22) (which amended Housing
Finance Act 1972, Sch 3, which
was repealed (4 Apr 1983) by Sch 5
to this Act))

Social Security Contributions (Transfer of Functions, etc) Act 1999 (c 2)

RA: 25 Feb 1999
Section

1	(1)		See Sch 1 below
	(2)		See Sch 2 below
3	(3)	(c)	*Not in force*; repealed, partly prospectively, by Welfare Reform and Pensions Act 1999, ss 81, 88, Sch 11, para 30, Sch 13, Pt VI
18			See Sch 7 below
26	(3)		See Sch 10 below

Schedule

1, para	17	(c)	*Not in force* (so far as amends Social Security Contributions and Benefits Act 1992, Sch 1, para 6(8))
2			*Not in force* (in relation to functions which are, by virtue of SI 1997/664, art 4, exercisable under SI 1984/380, reg 20(2)(b))
7, para	28		*Not in force*
10			*Not in force* (repeal of Social Security Act 1998, s 16 (4), (5))

Social Security Fraud Act 2001 (c 11)

RA: 11 May 2001
Section

1	(1)–(3), (5)–(8)	*Not in force*
2		*Not in force*
4–6		*Not in force*
14, 15		*Not in force*
17–19		*Not in force*
Schedule		*Not in force*

Special Educational Needs and Disability Act 2001 (c 10)

RA: 11 May 2001
Section

4, 5		*Not in force* (NI) (except so far as necessary for enabling the making of regulations)
6		*Not in force* (NI)
10		See Sch 1 below
11–40		*Not in force*
42	(1)	See Sch 8 below
	(5)	*Not in force* (W)
	(6)	See Sch 9 below

Special Educational Needs and Disability Act 2001 (c 10)—*contd*
Schedule
1			*Not in force* (NI)
2–7			*Not in force*
8, para	2–4		*Not in force*
	13	(5)	*Not in force*
	19–23		*Not in force*
9			*Not in force* (E) (except repeals of or in Disabled Persons (Services, Consultation and Representation) Act 1986; Education Act 1996, ss 325(1), 336(2), 441(3)(a), Sch 27; School Standards and Framework Act 1998, Sch 30)
			Not in force (W) (except repeals of or in Disabled Persons (Services, Consultation and Representation) Act 1986, s 5(1); Education Act 1996, ss 325(1), 336(2)(d), 441(3)(a), Sch 27, paras 3(4), 8(1)(b)(iii), 9(1), 10; School Standards and Framework Act 1998, Sch 30, para 186(2)(b))

Standards in Scotland's Schools etc Act 2000 (asp 6)

RA: 14 Jul 2000
Section
15			*Not in force*
44	(4)		*Not in force* (the words from "or (vii)" to "numbers:")
49			*Not in force* (for the purpose of the inserting and bringing into force s 9B(a)(ii), (c) into the Teaching Council (Scotland) Act 1965)
50			*Not in force* (substituted ss 10A(2)–(5), 11(1)(ii), (iii), (2)–(7), (9) (the words "or (2) above"), 11A of the 1965 Act)
51			*Not in force* (words from "(a) such person" to "or" in the third place where it occurs)
60	(1)		See Sch 2 below
	(2)		See Sch 3 below
Schedule			
2, para	2		*Not in force*
	3	(3), (4)	*Not in force*
		(9)	*Not in force*
3			*Not in force* (so far as relating the Sex Discrimination Act 1975; Race Relations Act 1976; National

Standards in Scotland's Schools etc Act 2000 (asp 6)—*contd*
Schedule
3—*contd*   Health Service (Scotland)
                                             Act 1978; Education (Scotland)
                                             Act 1980, ss 2A, 8, 19, 28A, 48A,
                                             51, 53–58, 123(1), 125A, 135(1);
                                             Education (Scotland) Act 1981;
                                             Representation of the People
                                             Act 1983; Self Governing Schools
                                             etc (Scotland) Act 1989, ss 1–12,
                                             23, 25–53, 69(2), 70(1)(b), 76,
                                             77(2)(a), 80(1), Schs 1, 2, 4,
                                             Schs 7–9, Sch 10, para 3; Children
                                             Act 1989; Environmental
                                             Protection Act 1990; Tribunals and
                                             Inquiries Act 1992; Value Added
                                             Tax Act 1994; Employment
                                             Rights Act 1996; Data Protection
                                             Act 1998)

Statute Law (Repeals) Act 1998 (c 43)

RA: 19 Nov 1998
Section
1   (1)   See Sch 1 below
Schedule
1   *Not in force* (repeal of Public
                                             Notaries Act 1843 as it applies
                                             to the Isle of Man; repeal in
                                             Statute Law (Repeals) Act 1993,
                                             s 3(3))

Teaching and Higher Education Act 1998 (c 30)

RA: 16 Jul 1998
Section
18   *Not in force*
44   (2)   See Sch 4 below
Schedule
4   *Not in force* (repeal of Education
                                             Act 1996, Sch 37, paras 4–7, 98)

Telecommunications Act 1984 (c 12)

RA: 12 Apr 1984
Section
96   *Not in force*

Terrorism Act 2000 (c 11)

RA: 20 Jul 2000
Section
100   *Not in force*

Town and Country Planning Act 1990 (c 8)

RA: 24 May 1990
Section
10–28A   Other than in the following local
                                                         planning authority areas Chapter I
                                                         (ss 10–28A, Sch 2) of Pt II
                                                         (ss 10–54A, Sch 2) of this Act
                                                         comes into force on a day to be
                                                         appointed in relation to that area
                                                         by order made by the Secretary of
                                                         State under s 28(1) of this Act:
                                                         Greater London
                                                         Greater Manchester
                                                         Merseyside
                                                         South Yorkshire
                                                         Tyne and Wear
                                                         West Midlands
                                                         West Yorkshire
322   For transitory provisions, see Planning
                                                         (Consequential Provisions)
                                                         Act 1990, s 6, Sch 4; those transitory
                                                         provisions partially ceased to have
                                                         effect on 2 Jan 1992 (SI 1991/2698),
                                                         so that on that day, s 322 of, and
                                                         Sch 6, para 6(5) to, this Act came
                                                         partially into force
Schedule
2   See ss 10–28A above
6, para   6   (5)   See s 322 above

Trade Union Reform and Employment Rights Act 1993 (c 19)

RA: 1 Jul 1993
Section
31   Repealed (*never in force*)
51   See Sch 10 below
Schedule
10   *Not in force* (repeal of words "subject
                                                         to subsections (3)–(5)" in
                                                         Employment Protection
                                                         (Consolidation) Act 1978, s 138(2),
                                                         so far as they relate to sub-s (3)
                                                         (repealed))

Transport Act 1968 (c 73)

RA: 25 Oct 1968
Section

81		Repealed (*never in force*)
82	(1)–(3)	Repealed (*never in force*)
	(6)	Repealed (*never in force* in part)
83		Repealed (*never in force*)
91, 92		Repealed (*never in force* in part)
99	(1)–(9)	*Not in force* (so far as relate to entry and inspection of any vehicle or to any equipment installed on any vehicle for purposes of original s 97, or any such record as was mentioned in that section as to enacted)
	(10)	*Not in force*

Transport Act 1981 (c 56)

RA: 31 Jul 1981
Schedule

12, Pt	III	*Not in force* (repeals of or in Road Traffic Act 1974, Sch 3; British Railways (No 2) Act 1975, s 21; London Transport Act 1977, s 13(1); British Railways Act 1977, s 14(1); Criminal Justice (Scotland) Act 1980, Sch 7, para 22)

Transport Act 1982 (c 49)

RA: 28 Oct 1982
Section

8–15		*Not in force*
17		*Not in force*
21–26		*Not in force*
66		*Not in force*
72	(a)	*Not in force*
74		See Schs 5, 6 below
Schedule		
5, para	5	*Not in force*
	17	*Not in force*
	20	*Not in force*
	22–24	*Not in force*
6		*Not in force* (repeals or of in Road Traffic Regulation Act 1967, ss 80, 81(4), 87, 107(2) (repealed); Road Traffic Act 1972, ss 45(4), (5), (6)(c) (i), (g), (8), (9), 50(1) (c), 188(4)(b), Sch 7 (repealed); Heavy

Transport Act 1982 (c 49)—*contd*
Schedule
6—*contd*

Commercial Vehicles (Controls
and Regulations) Act 1973, s 1(7)
(repealed); Road Traffic Act 1974,
ss 1, 3(1)(a), (2), (3)(a), (4), (5),
4(1), (4), (5), 5(1), (5), (8), Sch 2,
Pt II, para 16, Sch 5, Pts II, III,
Sch 6, para 8 (repealed); Criminal
Law Act 1977, Sch 12, para 3
(repealed); Transport Act 1968,
Sch 3, paras 3, 5 (repealed); Justices
of the Peace Act 1979, Sch 2,
para 15 (repealed); Transport
Act 1980, s 66(2) (repealed);
Criminal Justice (Scotland)
Act 1980, s 31 (repealed); Public
Passenger Vehicles Act 1981,
s 9(8), Sch 7, paras 13, 14
(repealed))

Transport Act 1985 (c 67)

RA: 30 Oct 1985
Section
1   (3)   See Sch 1 below
139   (1)–(3)   See Sch 8 below
Schedule
8   *Not in force* (repeal of words 'such
                                           number of' and 'as they think fit'
                                           in Town Police Clauses Act 1847,
                                           s 37 (which repeal entry is now
                                           itself repealed))

Transport Act 2000 (c 38)

RA: 30 Nov 2000
Section
124–127   *Not in force* (W, except in relation to
                                           powers to make regulations under
                                           specified provisions[1])
128   (1)–(3)   *Not in force* (W, except in relation to
                                           powers to make regulations under
                                           specified provisions[1])

                (5)   *Not in force* (W, except in relation to
                                           powers to make regulations under
                                           specified provisions[1])
129   *Not in force* (W, except in relation to
                                           powers to make regulations under
                                           specified provisions[1])

Transport Act 2000 (c 38)—*contd*
Section

130	(1)–(7)		*Not in force* (W, except in relation to powers to make regulations under specified provisions[1])
131	(1)		*Not in force* (W, except in relation to powers to make regulations under specified provisions[1])
	(5)		*Not in force* (W, except in relation to powers to make regulations under specified provisions[1])
132	(1)–(5)		*Not in force* (W, except in relation to powers to make regulations under specified provisions[1])
144			*Not in force* (E, for the purposes of enabling regulations to be made as respects civil penalties for bus lane contraventions in relation to roads in Greater London)
153			See Sch 10 below
154	(6)		*Not in force*
161			See Sch 11 below
163	(1)		*Not in force* (W, except in relation to powers to make regulations under specified provisions[2])
	(2)	(a)	*Not in force* (W, except in relation to powers to make regulations under specified provisions[2])
	(3)–(6)		*Not in force* (W, except in relation to powers to make regulations under specified provisions[2])
164, 165			*Not in force* (W, except in relation to powers to make regulations under specified provisions[2])
166			*Not in force* (W)
167			*Not in force* (W, except in relation to powers to make regulations under specified provisions[2])
168	(1), (2)		*Not in force* (W, except in relation to powers to make regulations under specified provisions[2])
	(4)		*Not in force* (W, except in relation to powers to make regulations under specified provisions[2])
169–171			*Not in force* (W, except in relation to powers to make regulations under specified provisions[2])
172	(2)–(4)		*Not in force* (W, except in relation to powers to make regulations under specified provisions[2])

Transport Act 2000 (c 38)—*contd*

Section

173	(5)–(9)		*Not in force* (W, except in relation to powers to make regulations under specified provisions[2])
174	(3), (4)		*Not in force* (W, except in relation to powers to make regulations under specified provisions[2])
	(6)		*Not in force* (W, except in relation to powers to make regulations under specified provisions[2])
175	(2)–(8)		*Not in force* (W, except in relation to powers to make regulations under specified provisions[2])
176	(1)		*Not in force* (W, except in relation to powers to make regulations under specified provisions[2])
	(3)		*Not in force* (W, except in relation to powers to make regulations under specified provisions[2])
177			*Not in force* (W, except in relation to powers to make regulations under specified provisions[2])
178	(1)		*Not in force* (W, except in relation to powers to make regulations under specified provisions[3])
	(2)	(a)	*Not in force* (W, except in relation to powers to make regulations under specified provisions[3])
	(3)–(7)		*Not in force* (W, except in relation to powers to make regulations under specified provisions[3])
179, 180			*Not in force* (W, except in relation to powers to make regulations under specified provisions[3])
181			*Not in force* (W)
182	(1)–(4)		*Not in force* (W, except in relation to powers to make regulations under specified provisions[3])
183	(1), (2)		*Not in force* (W, except in relation to powers to make regulations under specified provisions[3])
	(4)		*Not in force* (W, except in relation to powers to make regulations under specified provisions[3])
184–186			*Not in force* (W, except in relation to powers to make regulations under specified provisions[3])
187	(2)–(4)		*Not in force* (W, except in relation to powers to make regulations under specified provisions[3])

Transport Act 2000 (c 38)—*contd*

Section

188				*Not in force* (W, except in relation to powers to make regulations under specified provisions[3])
189	(3)	(a)		*Not in force* (W, except in relation to powers to make regulations under specified provisions[3])
190				*Not in force* (W, except in relation to powers to make regulations under specified provisions[3])
191				See Sch 12 below
199				See Sch 13 below
223				*Not in force*
228				*Not in force*
248				*Not in force*
252				See Sch 27 below
257–260				*Not in force*
263				*Not in force*
267	(1)			See sub-ss (2)–(8) below
	(2)			*Not in force*
	(3)			*Not in force* (except for the purposes of making regulations with regard to appeals under the Greater London Authority Act 1999, s 189 made after the date on which s 267 of this Act is fully in force)
	(4)			*Not in force*
	(5)			*Not in force* (except for the purposes of making regulations with regard to appeals under the Greater London Authority Act 1999, s 189 made after the date on which s 267 of this Act is fully in force)
	(6), (7)			*Not in force*
	(8)			*Not in force* (except for the purposes of making regulations with regard to appeals under the Greater London Authority Act 1999, s 189 made after the date on which s 267 of this Act is fully in force)
274				See Sch 31 below

Schedule

10, para	1	(1)	(a)	*Not in force* (W)
		(2)	(a)	*Not in force* (W)
	12	(2)		*Not in force* (W, the words "a quality partnership scheme or")
11, para	20			*Not in force* (E)
12, 13				*Not in force* (W)
27, para	16			*Not in force*
29				*Not in force*

Transport Act 2000 (c 38)—*contd*
Schedule
31, Pt   II   *Not in force* (E, entries relating to
                                                        Finance Act 1965, s 92; Finance
                                                        Act 1974, s 54; Excise Duties
                                                        (Surcharges or Rebates) Act 1979,
                                                        Sch 1, para 2; Magistrates' Courts
                                                        Act 1980, Sch 7, para 53; Finance
                                                        Act 1981, s 4(2)(b); Transport
                                                        Act 1985, ss 94(4), 108(1), 110,
                                                        111, 112(2); London Local
                                                        Authorities Act 1996, Pt II;
                                                        Transport Act 2000, ss 146(1), 158,
                                                        Sch 11, paras 1, 22; London Local
                                                        Authorities Act 2000, s 48, Sch 2)
                                                    Not in force (W)
             IV   *Not in force* (entries relating to
                                                        Transport Act 1962, ss 1(1), 3–4A,
                                                        12(1), 13(1A), (9)–(12), 14(4),
                                                        18(6), 19(6), 21A, 22, 27(2), (7),
                                                        (8), 31(2), (6), 32(6), 52(2), 54(1),
                                                        65(1), (4), 67, First Schedule,
                                                        para 3, Sixth Schedule, para 1(5),
                                                        Seventh Schedule, paras 23, 24;
                                                        Transport Act 1968, ss 38, 42,
                                                        44(1)(b)(iv), 49(4), 50(1), 56(2B),
                                                        135(1)(b), 137(8), 159(1); Post
                                                        Office Act 1969, s 20(1)(c);
                                                        Railways Act 1974; House of
                                                        Commons Disqualification
                                                        Act 1975, Sch 1, Pt II; Northern
                                                        Ireland Assembly Disqualification
                                                        Act 1975, Sch 1, Pt II; Transport
                                                        Act 1978, ss 15(6), (7), 21, 24(2);
                                                        Transport Act 1980, Sch 6,
                                                        para 10; Transport Act 1981,
                                                        Sch 3, para 31(4), Sch 4, para 1(3);
                                                        Transport (Finance) Act 1982;
                                                        National Audit Act 1983, Sch 4,
                                                        Pt I; Transport Act 1985,
                                                        ss 118–124, Sch 7, para 6; Channel
                                                        Tunnel Act 1987, ss 22, 39, 41(1),
                                                        (2), (4), Sch 6, para 6; British
                                                        Railways Board (Finance) Act 1991;
                                                        Heathrow Express Railway
                                                        Act 1991, s 41(2); Railways
                                                        Act 1993, ss 84–112, 114–116,
                                                        129, Sch 7, paras 2(7), 7(3), (4),
                                                        Schs 8, 9, Sch 12, paras 5, 6(2)–(5),
                                                        32; Railways Act 1993
                                                        (Consequential Modifications)

Transport Act 2000 (c 38)—*contd*
Schedule

31, Pt	IV—*contd*	(No 2) Order 1994, SI 1994/1649; Employment Rights Act 1996, Sch 1, para 60(2); Railway Heritage Act 1996, s 1(a)–(c); Freedom of Information Act 2000, Sch 1, Pt VI)
	V	*Not in force*

1	The specified provisions are ss 128(4), 130(8), 131(2)–(4), 132(6), 133 and 134 of this Act
2	The specified provisions are ss 163(2)(b), 168(3), 172(1), 173(1)–(4), 174(1), (2), (5), 175(1), and 176(2) of this Act
3	The specified provisions are ss 178(2)(b), 182(5), 183(3), 187(1), 189(1), (2), (3)(b) and (4) of this Act

---

Transport and Works Act 1992 (c 42)

RA: 16 Mar 1992
Section

68	(1)	See Sch 4 below
	(2)	*Not in force*
Schedule		
4, Pt	I	*Not in force* (repeals of or in Railway Employment (Prevention of Accidents) Act 1900, s 13(2); Road Traffic Act 1960, Sch 17)

Transport (Scotland) Act 2001 (asp 2)

RA: 25 Jan 2001
Section

38	(1)	*Not in force*
	(3)–(6)	*Not in force*
39		*Not in force*
68		*Not in force*
73	(a), (b)	*Not in force*
83		See Sch 2 below
Schedule		
2, para	4 (6)–(8)	*Not in force*

Unsolicited Goods and Services (Amendment) Act 1975 (c 13)

RA: 20 Mar 1975
Section

2	(1)	*Not in force*

Note that any regulations made by virtue of s 1 of this Act (inserts Unsolicited Goods and Services Act 1971, s 3A) shall not come into force before the commencement of s 2 of this Act

---

Utilities Act 2000 (c 27)

RA: 28 Jul 2000
Section
20	(7)	*Not in force*
75		*Not in force*
108		See Sch 8 below

Schedule
8   *Not in force* (entries relating to Gas Act 1986, ss 5(1), (2), 7A(12), 8A(1), 36(1), (2)(a), (c), (d), Schs 2A, Sch 2B, paras 7(2), 8(2)(b), 8(4)–6), (8), 9(5); Consumer Protection Act 1987, ss 10(7)(c), 11(7)(c); Gas Act 1995, s 3(2), Sch 1, Sch 3, paras 31–33, 36, 41, 42(1)(a), (2)(a), 48–50)

Vehicle Excise and Registration Act 1994 (c 22)

RA: 5 Jul 1994
Section
20			*Not in force* (to come into force on a day to be appointed by the Secretary of State by order under Sch 4, para 9 to this Act)
45	(1)	(b)	*Not in force* (to come into force on a day to be appointed by the Secretary of State by order under Sch 4, para 9 to this Act)
57	(5)		*Not in force* (so far as refers to 20(4) of this Act; to come into force on a day to be appointed by the Secretary of State by order under Sch 4, para 9 to this Act)

Vehicles (Crime) Act 2001 (c 3)

RA: 10 Apr 2001
Section
1–36		*Not in force*
43		See Schedule below
Schedule	1–6	*Not in force*

Warm Homes and Energy Conservation Act 2000 (c 31)

RA: 23 Nov 2000
Section
2   *Not in force* (W)

Water Act 1983 (c 23)

RA: 9 May 1983
Section
11	(2), (3)	See Sch 5 below
Schedule		
5, Pt	I	*Not in force* (repeal of Local Government (Scotland) Act 1973, Sch 17, para 64)

Water Act 1989 (c 15)

RA: 6 Jul 1989
Section
13		*Not in force* (S) (except so far as relating to the making of subordinate legislation and to schemes under Sch 5)
169		See Sch 23 below
190		See Sch 27 below
Schedule		
17, para	4	*Not in force*
23		*Not in force* (so far as relates to Control of Pollution Act 1984, ss 33 (E, W), 47, 48)
27, Pt	II	*Not in force* (repeals of or in Water Act 1973, ss 34(2), 35(3), 36(1), (2), Sch 6, Pt II; Control of Pollution Act 1974, Sch 2, para 15; House of Commons Disqualification Act 1975, Sch 1, Pt III; Water Act 1983, s 1(2); Public Utility Transfers and Water Charges Act 1988, ss 1, 8(1), (3))

Welfare Reform and Pensions Act 1999 (c 30)

RA: 11 Nov 1999
Section
18		See Sch 2 below
25		*Not in force*
70		See Sch 8 below
84	(1)	See Sch 12 below
85	(5)	*Not in force*
88		See Sch 13 below
Schedule		
8, para	28	*Not in force*
	34	*Not in force*
11		*Not in force*
13, Pt	I	*Not in force* (repeals of or in Pensions Act 1995, ss 142(2), (3), (4)(b), Sch 5, para 80(f))

Enquiry Bureau 020 7400 2518

Youth Justice and Criminal Evidence Act 1999 (c 23)

RA: 27 Jul 1999

Section		
16–33		*Not in force* (except so far as confer power to make rules of court)
36, 37		*Not in force* (except so far as confer power to make rules of court)
44–52		*Not in force* (except so far as confer power to make rules of court)
53–57		*Not in force*
58	(1)–(4)	*Not in force*
	(5)	*Not in force* (except so far as confers power to make orders)
61	(2)	*Not in force* (except so far as confers power to make orders)
67	(1)	See Sch 4 below
	(3)	See Sch 6 below
	(4)	See Sch 7 below
Schedule		
2		*Not in force*
4, para	1–4	*Not in force*
	10	*Not in force*
	12–14	*Not in force*
	18–19	*Not in force*
	21	*Not in force*
	24	*Not in force*
6		*Not in force* (repeals of or in Criminal Evidence Act 1898, s 1; Children and Young Persons Act 1933, s 38; Army Act 1955, s 93(1B), (2); Air Force Act 1955, s 93(1B), (2); Naval Discipline Act 1957, s 60(2), (3); Criminal Appeal Act 1968, s 10(2)(b); Courts-Martial (Appeals) Act 1968, s 36(1); Theft Act 1968, s 30(2); Armed Forces Act 1976, Sch 3, para 3(2); Sexual Offences (Amendment) Act 1976, ss 2, 3 (3) (in relation to any trial before a court-martial), ss 4, 5, 7(4), (5); Sexual Offences (Northern Ireland) Order 1978, SI 1978/460 (NI 5), arts 1(2), 6, 7; Judicature (Northern Ireland) Act 1978, Sch 5, Pt II; Magistrates' Courts Act 1980, ss 125(4)(c)(iii), 126(d); Armed Forces Act 1981, Sch 2, para 9; Police and Criminal Evidence Act 1984, ss 80(1), (5),

Youth Justice and Criminal Evidence Act 1999 (c 23)—*contd*
Schedule

6—*contd*		(8), 82(1); Criminal Justice Act 1988, ss 32(1)(b), (2), (3A)–(3E), (6), 32A, 33A, 158(2)–(4), Sch 13, para 8(2)(b), (3), Sch 15, para 53; Broadcasting Act 1990, Sch 20, paras 26, 27; Criminal Justice Act 1991, ss 52, 54, 55(2)(b), (4), (6), (7), Sch 9, paras 3, 7, Sch 11, paras 1, 37; Sexual Offences (Amendment) Act 1992, ss 5(2), 6(1), 7(2)(b), (e), (3); Criminal Justice and Public Order Act 1994, s 50, Sch 9, paras 11(1)(a), 13, 33, Sch 10, para 32, para 35(3) (in relation to any trial before a court-martial), para 36; Criminal Justice (Northern Ireland) Order 1994, SI 1994/2795 (NI 15), arts 2(3), 18(3), 19–24; Criminal Appeal Act 1995, Sch 2, para 16(2)(b), (3); Criminal Procedure and Investigations Act 1996, s 62, Sch 1, para 33; Armed Forces Act 1996, Sch 1, para 107(a); Criminal Justice (Children) (Northern Ireland) Order 1998, SI 1998/1504 (NI 9), art 22)
7, para	3	*Not in force*
	6–8	*Not in force*